MW00849272

Feature Films, 1950–1959

ALSO BY ALAN G. FETROW:

Feature Films, 1940–1949: A United States Filmography
(McFarland, 1994)

Sound Films, 1927–1939: A United States Filmography
(McFarland, 1992)

Feature Films, 1950–1959

A United States Filmography

by

ALAN G. FETROW

McFarland & Company, Inc., Publishers
Jefferson, North Carolina, and London

LIBRARY OF CONGRESS CATALOGUING-IN-PUBLICATION DATA

Fetrow, Alan G., 1945–
Feature films, 1950–1959 : a United States filmography / by Alan G. Fetrow.
p. cm.
Includes bibliographical references and index.

ISBN 0-7864-0427-2 (cloth binding : 50# alkaline paper) 

1. Motion pictures—United States—Catalogs. I. Title.
PN1993.5.U6F457 1999
016.79143'75'0973—dc21 98-16105

British Library cataloguing data are available

Manufactured in the United States of America

McFarland & Company, Inc., Publishers
Box 611, Jefferson, North Carolina 28640
www.mcfarlandpub.com

Table of Contents

Introduction

The decade of the 1950s saw many changes in the movie industry as it endeavored to compete with television. The small screen was finding its way into more and more homes, where (it was feared) people would stay instead of paying at the box office to see the latest products of Hollywood. Hollywood reacted with various gimmicks to draw patrons into the theaters, among them stereoscopic cinema (better known as 3-D) and wide-screen processes such as CinemaScope, VistaVision and the real curiosity, Cinerama, with its concave split screen. More productions were being presented in color, including many B pictures. This, despite the fact that for most of the decade there was little color programming for television.

Producers (such as Otto Preminger) were beginning to challenge Hollywood's "censorship code" in subtle ways with explicit dialogue heretofore unheard on the American theater screen. Violence and sexuality were also making new inroads, though most of the latter were seen in the form of Brigitte Bardot's bare breasts and buttocks from imported European productions.

Two Guns and a Badge (1954; with Wayne Morris) was the swan song of the B-series western, long a Hollywood staple for program fillers and matinee double bills since the silent era. The 1950s also saw the demise of the chapter play or serial (also from the silent era)—a film which was released in weekly episodes, requiring the viewer to return to the theater each week to see how the hero or heroine fared through the predicament in which they were left by the preceding week's episode. The cheesiness of production values (as well as downright deception on the part of producers) was the major factor in the demise of the serial. Audiences no longer cared whether the hero or heroine survived their peril.

Series films (those with a continuing main character or characters) carried on into the 1950s. *Francis the Talking Mule* and *The Kettle Family* were the most popular, along with the *Bowery Boys* (who evolved originally from the *Dead End Kids* in the 1930s). But this decade brought on the demise of these films also, along with *Bomba the Jungle Boy*, *Jungle Jim*, *Joe Palooka*, *Maggie and Jiggs* and *Blondie* (the latter also having its beginnings in the 1930s).

What some called the "Atomic Age" brought forth many entries in a more or less new genre, namely science fiction and its many subgenres—

like big bugs (*Them*, *The Black Scorpion*, *The Deadly Mantis*, *Tarantula*, *The Beginning of the End*), invaders from outer space (*War of the Worlds*, *The Blob*, *Invasion of the Saucer Men*, *It Conquered the World*, *Invasion of the Body Snatchers*, *The Giant Claw*), and other mutated life-forms (*Attack of the 50-Foot Woman*, *The Amazing Colossal Man*, its sequel *War of the Colossal Beast*, *The Monster That Challenged the World*, *It Came from Beneath the Sea*), just to mention a few.

Teenagers became a major subject of exploitation in the latter part of the decade, with horror flicks such as *Frankenstein's Daughter*, *I Was a Teenage Frankenstein*, *I Was a Teenage Werewolf*, *Daughter of Dr. Jekyll* and *Teenage Zombies*. Further exploitation with teenage delinquents made an appearance via such films as *Hot Rod Girl*, *The Cool and the Crazy*, *Sorority Girl*, *The Motorcycle Gang* and *Dragstrip Riot*. Many of these films were geared to the drive-in movie crowd, another new phenomenon of the 50s. The first drive-in theater opened in the United States in 1949 and the popularity of the open-air theater quickly gained momentum. It offered a new way of movie viewing: instead of in the privacy of your own home, it was in the privacy of your own car. The popularity of the drive-in movie with teenagers soon had theaters cropping up all over America. Alcohol was easy to smuggle into the theater for partying with friends and if you didn't like the movie, you could make out in the backseat. The local drive-in movie theater gained the nickname "passion pit."

The early 1950s saw the hearings conducted by Senator Joseph McCarthy amount to a nationwide witch-hunt for "Communists" in various walks of life, eventually focusing on Hollywood. A number of directors, screenwriters and actors were blacklisted and unable to find work in the industry.

The Basic Format of the Entries

The elements of the entries are as follows: title, studio or production company, year of production and release to the general public (these are most often one and the same). Sometimes two years are listed (e.g., 1951–1952), indicating the film completed production and was copyrighted in the first year, with general release held up until the following year. This will also account for several films listed as 1949–1950 and 1959–1960, which might otherwise appear to stretch beyond the criteria for inclusion.

Cast members follow. Character names are included for any Oscar winners or contenders as well as for top-grossing films of the year. Also included are nonfictional or historical character names. Where applicable, Academy Award winners and nominees are noted.

Additional references are made to various other organizations such as the New York Film Critics and the National Board of Review, in cases where they have given notice to one or more performances. Also noted are film debuts, feature film debuts, and U.S. film debuts; final film appearances of Hollywood stars and supporting actors and actresses are noted, citing retirement ("ret.") or death ("d.") as the reason.

Credits for off-screen personnel such as directors, producers and screenwriters follow, including original authors and source material (unless this is included in the film's synopsis). Other behind-the-scenes credits follow, as merited from film to film, with all-inclusive listings for Oscar wins and nominations in any category. For many musicals, songs and songwriters (new and old) are also listed.

Closing out the credits section are the running time and whether the film has been made available to home video or laserdisc (as of late 1997).

Following the credits is a brief synopsis of the film, as well as notes considered of value to the researcher. When a film has undergone computer coloring (as of late 1997), this is mentioned. Films which made the "10 Best" lists of *Film Daily*, a trade paper, the *New York Times* or the National Board of Review are so noted (with position).

Closing out the synopsis (where applicable) are G.B. titles and other alternate titles ("aka"), all of which have see-references throughout the text.

Many films that were released on a double bill program show their "running mate" in their entry, unless the mate is a British or foreign production. Also listed at the end of the synopsis, if not before, is whether the film is in color, wide-screen, 3-D or stereophonic sound.

Abbreviation Key

A	Actor/Actress (index only)
AA	Academy Award (Oscar winner)
AAN	Academy Award nominee (Oscar contender)
aka	also known as
ASD	Art-Set Decoration
BSA	Best Supporting Actor/Actress (Oscar category)
As.P	Associate Producer
C	Cinematographer (index only)
Ch	Choreographer (index only)
Cos	Costumes (index only)
D	Director
d	film debut (index only)
d.	died (final film)
E	Editor (index only)
Ex.P	Executive Producer
F/X	Special effects
G.B. title	a film title usually used only in Great Britain
ly	lyrics
M	Music (index only)
m	music
MGM	Metro-Goldwyn-Mayer
N	Narrator (index only)
NBR	National Board of Review
P	Producer
q.v.	see also
ret.	retired (final film)
RKO	Radio-Keith-Orpheum
S	Sound recorder (index only)
Sc	Writer or writers of the screenplay
St	Original author (story/novel/stageplay)
unc.	Uncredited (no on-screen credit)
VO	Voice only
W	Writer (index only)

The Filmography

1. Aaron Slick from Punkin Crick (Paramount/Perlberg-Seaton; 1952). *Cast:* Alan Young, Dinah Shore, Robert Merrill, Adele Jergens, Minerva Urecal, Martha Stewart, Fritz Feld, Veda Ann Borg, Chick Chandler. *D:* Claude Binyon; *P:* William Perlberg, George Seaton; *Sc:* Claude Binyon; *Songs:* "I'd Like to Baby You," "Still Water," "Marshmallow Moon," "Why Should I Believe in Love?" Jay Livingston, Ray Evans. (G.B. title: *Marshmallow Moon*) (1:35) Musical-comedy of a rural widow who becomes the target of big city con-artists. Based on the 1919 play by Walter Benjamin Hare. Technicolor.

2. Abbott and Costello Go to Mars (Universal-International; 1953). *Cast:* Bud Abbott, Lou Costello, Robert Paige, Mari Blanchard, Martha Hyer, Horace McMahon, Jack Kruschen, Jean Willes, Joe Kirk, Jack Tesler, Harold Goodwin, Hal Forrest, James Flavin, Russ Conway, Syd Saylor, Paul Newlan, Jackie Loughery, Billy Newell, Anita Ekberg, Grace Lenard, Tim Graham, Ken Christy, Harry Lang, Milt Bronson, Robert Forrest, Dudly Dickerson, Rex Lease, Frank Marlowe, Bobby Barber. *D:* Charles Lamont; *P:* Howard Christie; *St:* Christie, D.D. Beauchamp; *Sc:* Beauchamp, John Grant. (1:17) (video) Considered to be one of the comedy team's lesser efforts, this slapstick comedy has the duo on a spaceship headed for Mars, which actually lands on Venus after making a waylaid stop at the New Orleans Mardi Gras.

3. Abbott and Costello in the Foreign Legion (Universal-International; 1950). *Cast:* Bud Abbott, Lou Costello, Patricia Medina, Walter Slezak, Douglass Dumbrille, Leon Belasco, Marc Lawrence, Tor Johnson, Wee Willie Davis, Fred Nurney, Sam Menacker, Henry Corden, Paul Fierro, Jack Raymond, Dan Seymour, Guy Beach, Alberto Morin, David Gorcey, Charmienne Harker, Jack Shutta, Ernesto Morelli, Chuck Hamilton, Ted Hecht, Buddy Roosevelt, Mahmud Shaikhaly, Bobby Barber. *D:* Charles Lamont; *P:* Robert Arthur; *St:* D.D. Beauchamp; *Sc:* John Grant, Martin Ragaway, Leonard Stern. (1:19) (video) In this slapstick comedy, the duo do a stint in the French Foreign Legion. Their 25th comedy outing.

Abbott and Costello Lost in Alaska *see* **Lost in Alaska**

4. Abbott and Costello Meet Captain Kidd (Warner/Woodley Prods.; 1952). *Cast:* Bud Abbott, Lou Costello, Charles Laughton (Capt. Kidd), Hillary Brooke (Anne Bonney), Bill Shirley, Fran Warren, Leif Erickson (Henry Morgan), Syd Saylor, Rex Lease, Frank Yaconelli, Bobby Barber. *D:* Charles Lamont; *P:* Alex Gottlieb; *Sc:* Howard Dimsdale, John Grant; *Songs:* Bob Russell, Lester Lee. (1:10) (video) Slapstick pirate spoof with songs which finds the duo kidnapped by Captain Kidd who is seeking a treasure. SuperCinecolor.

5. Abbott and Costello Meet Dr. Jekyll and Mr. Hyde (Universal-International; 1953). *Cast:* Bud Abbott, Lou Costello, Boris Karloff (Dr. Henry Jekyll), Craig Stevens, Helen Westcott, Reginald Denny, John Dierkes, Patti McKay, Eddie [Edwin] Parker (a stuntman portraying the active Mr. Hyde), Henry Corden, Marjorie Bennett, Carmen de Lavallade, Arthur Gould-Porter, Herb Deans, Judith Brian, Clyde Cook, John Rogers, Gil Perkins, Hilda Plowright, Keith Hitchcock, Harry Cording, Donald Kerr, Clive Morgan, Tony Marshe, Michael Hadlow. *D:* Charles Lamont; *P:* Howard Christie; *Sc:* Lee Loeb, John Grant. (1:16) (video) Slapstick comedy with the duo locking horns with mild-mannered Dr. Jekyll who it turns out is more than he appears to be. Based on stories by Grant Garrett and Sidney Fields and of course, the characters created by Robert Louis Stevenson in his story, "The Strange Case of Dr. Jekyll and Mr. Hyde."

6. Abbott and Costello Meet the Invisible Man (Universal-International; 1951). *Cast:* Bud Abbott, Lou Costello, Nancy Guild, Adele Jergens, Sheldon Leonard, William Frawley, Gavin Muir, Arthur Franz, John Day, Sam Balter, Syd Saylor, Billy Wayne, Bobby Barber,

Edward Gargan, Paul Maxey, Herbert Vigran, Frankie Van, Carl Sklover, George J. Lewis, Ralph Dunn, Harold Goodwin, Perc Launders, Edith Sheets, Milt Bronson, Richard Bartell, Charles Perry. *D:* Charles Lamont; *P:* Howard Christie; *St:* Hugh Wedlock, Jr., Howard Snyder; *Sc:* Robert Lees, Frederic I. Rinaldo, John Grant. (1:22) (video) Hit comedy of two detectives, helping a boxer, framed for murder, via a formula for invisibility. Suggested by the book *The Invisible Man* by H.G. Wells.

7. **Abbott and Costello Meet the Keystone Kops** (Universal-International; 1955). *Cast:* Bud Abbott, Lou Costello, Fred Clark, Lynn Bari, Mack Sennett (himself), Maxie Rosenbloom, Frank Wilcox, Roscoe Ates, Harold Goodwin (an original Keystone Kop), Hank Mann (an original Keystone Kop), Heinie Conklin (an original Keystone Kop in his final film—d. 1959), Carol Costello, Paul Dubov, Henry Kulky, Jack Daly, William Haade, Joe Devlin, Joe Besser, Harry Tyler, Houseley Stevenson, Byron [Brian] Keith, Marjorie Bennett, Murray Leonard, Donald Kerr, Charles Dorety, Forrest Burns, Don House. *D:* Charles Lamont; *P:* Howard Christie; *St:* Lee Loeb; *Sc:* John Grant. (1:19) (video) Slapstick comedy spoof on the silent era and silent comedy in general as the duo buy Edison's movie studio (in 1912) from a conman and then head to Hollywood to get their money back.

8. **Abbott and Costello Meet the Mummy** (Universal-International; 1955). *Cast:* Bud Abbott, Lou Costello, Marie Windsor, Michael Ansara, Dan Seymour, Kurt Katch, Richard Karlan, Richard Deacon, Peggy King (singing "You Came a Long Way From St. Louis"), Mel Welles, George Khoury, Edwin Parker (Kharis the mummy), Jan Arvan, Michael Vallon, Kem Dibbs, Mitchell Kowal, Ken Alton, Lee Sharon, Hank Mann, Donald Kerr, The Mazzone-Abbott Dancers, The Chandra-Kaly and Hi Dancers. *D:* Charles Lamont; *P:* Howard Christie; *St:* Lee Loeb; *Sc:* John Grant. (1:19) (video) Slapstick comedy with the duo in Egypt looking for a lost tomb and hidden treasure, while there encountering a mobile mummy to boot. Abbott and Costello's final film for Universal.

9. **The Abductors** (20th Century–Fox/Regal Films; 1957). *Cast:* Victor McLaglen (final U.S. film), George Macready, Fay Spain, Gavin Muir, Carl Thayer, John Morley, Carlyle Mitchell, George Cisar, Pat Lawless, James Logan, Jason Johnson. *D:* Andrew V. McLaglen; *P:* Ray Wander; *St: & Sc:* Wander. (1:20) Based on fact melodrama of two men who plot to steal the remains of Abraham Lincoln, with intent of collecting a ransom for their return. Regalscope.

10. **Abilene Trail** (Monogram; 1951). *Cast:* Whip Wilson, Andy Clyde, Tommy Farrell, Steve Clark, Noel Neill, Dennis Moore, Marshall Reed, Lee Roberts, Milburn Morante, Ted Adams, Bill Kennedy, Stanley Price, Lyle Talbot. *D:* Lewis D. Collins; *P:* Vincent M. Fennelly; *Sc:* Harry Fraser. (0:54) Accused horse thieves join a trail drive in this Whip Wilson series western.

11. **About Face** (Warner; 1952). *Cast:* Gordon MacRae, Eddie Bracken, Dick Wesson, Virginia Gibson, Phyllis Kirk, Aileen Stanley, Jr., Joel Grey (film debut), Larry Keating, Cliff Ferre, John Baer. *D:* Roy Del Ruth; *P:* William Jacobs; *Sc:* Peter Milne; *Songs:* "If Someone Had Told Me," "Piano, Bass and Drums," "No Other Girl for Me," "I'm Nobody," "Spring Has Sprung," "Wooden Indian," "Reveille," "Tar Heels," "They Haven't Lost a Father Yet" Charles Tobias–Peter de Rose. (1:34) Technicolor musical-comedy remake of *Brother Rat* (Warner; 1938) involving three military academy cadets, one of which is married and soon to become a father. Popular with movie-goers, but not with the critics, it was based on the successful 1936 play *Brother Rat* by John Monks, Jr. and Fred F. Finklehoffe.

12. **About Mrs. Leslie** (Paramount; 1954). *Cast:* Shirley Booth, Robert Ryan, Marjie Millar, Alex Nicol, Sammy White, James Bell, Eilene Janssen, Philip Ober, Henry [Harry] Morgan, Gale Page (final film—ret.), Virginia Brissac, Ian Wolfe, Isaac Jones, Maidie Norman, Laura Elliot, Nana Bryant, Pierre Watkin, Amanda Blake, Percy Helton, Ric Roman, Mabel Albertson, Edith Evanson, Joan Shawlee, Ellen Corby, Ray Teal, Anne McCrea, Benny Rubin. *D:* Daniel Mann; *P:* Hal B. Wallis; *Sc:* Ketti Frings, Hal Kanter. (1:44) Romantic drama told in flashbacks of the affair between a singer and a business tycoon. Based on the book by Vina Delmar, the film was a box office disappointment.

13. **Above and Beyond** (MGM; 1952). *Cast:* Robert Taylor (Col. Paul Tibbets), Eleanor Parker (Lucey Tibbets), James Whitmore

(Major Uanna), Larry Keating (Maj. Gen. Vernon C. Brent), Larry Gates (Capt. Parsons), Marilyn Erskine (Marge Bratton), Stephen Dunne (Maj. Harry Bratton), Robert Burton (Gen. Samuel E. Roberts), Hayden Rorke (Dr. Ramsey), Larry Dobkin (Dr. Van Dyke), Jack Raine (Dr. Fiske), Jonathan Cott (Dutch Van Kirk), Jeff Richards (Thomas Ferebee), Dick Simmons (Bob Lewis), John McKee (Wyatt Duzenbury), Christie Olsen (Paul Tibbets, Jr.), Barbara Ruick (Mary Malone), Jim Backus (Gen. LeMay), G. Pat Collins (Maj. Gen. Creston), Harlan Warde (Chaplain Downey), Crane Whitley (Gen. Corlane), Don Gibson (Dexter), Ewing Mitchell (Gen. Wolfe), Mack Williams (Gen. Ervine), Dabbs Greer (Haddock), John Hedloe (Lt. Malone), Frank Gerstle (Sgt. Wilson), John Pickard (Miller), Gregory Walcott (Burns), Roger McGee (Johnson), Patrick Conway (radio operator), William Lester, John W. Baer, John Close, Lee MacGregor, Sam McKim, Robert Forrest, Dorothy Kennedy, Robert Fuller. *D: & P:* Melvin Frank, Norman Panama; *St:* (AAN) Beirne Lay, Jr. (1953); *Sc:* Frank, Panama, Lay, Jr.; *Music:* (AAN) Hugo Friedhofer (1953). (2:02) (video) The story of Colonel Paul Tibbets, the man trained to fly the first atomic bomb over Hiroshima, and the effects the mission had on his later personal life. The film placed #9 on the "10 Best" list of the NBR, but did not do well at the box office, probably because the memory of the event was still fresh in the minds of the movie-going public.

14. According to Mrs. Hoyle (Monogram; 1951). *Cast:* Spring Byington, Anthony Caruso, Brett King, Tanis Chandler, Stephen Chase, Robert Karnes, Tristram Coffin, James Flavin, Paul Bryar, Charles Williams, Harry Lauter, Michael Whalen, Leander de Cordova, Frank Jaquet, Wilbur Mack, Marcelle Imhof, Sharon James Lichter, Joey Ray, Ted Stanhope, Don Harvey, Rory Mallinson. *D:* Jean Yarbrough; *P:* Barney Gerard; *Sc:* W. Scott Darling, Gerard. (1:00) Programmer drama of a retired schoolteacher who uses her wiles when hoodlums take over the hotel in which she resides. Taken from the novelette *Mrs. Hoyle and the Hotel Royalston* by Jean Z. Owen.

15. Accused of Murder (Republic; 1956). *Cast:* David Brian, Vera Ralston, Sidney Blackmer, Virginia Grey, Warren Stevens, Lee Van Cleef, Barry Kelley, Richard Karlan, Frank Puglia, Elisha Cook, Jr., Ian MacDonald, Claire Carleton, Greta Thyssen (film debut), Hank Worden, Wally Cassell, Robert Shayne, Simon Scott, John Damler, Gil Rankin, Joseph Corey, Leon Tyler, Harry Lewis, David Bair, Bill Henry, Bob Carney, Victor Sen Yung. *D: & P:* Joseph Kane; *Sc:* Robert Creighton [Bob] Williams; *Song:* "You're in Love" Herb Newman–Buddy Bregman. (1:14) Crime melodrama of a night club singer, suspect in the killing of a crooked lawyer. Based on W.R. Burnett's 1952 novel *Vanity Row.*

16. Ace in the Hole [The Human Interest Story] (Paramount; 1951). *Cast:* Kirk Douglas (Charles Tatum), Jan Sterling ("Best Actress" Award by the NBR/Lorraine), Robert Arthur (Herbie Cook), Richard Benedict (Leo Minosa), Porter Hall (Jacob Q. Boot), Frank Cady (Mr. Federber), Lewis Martin (McCardle), Ray Teal (sheriff), Geraldine Wall (Mrs. Federber), Richard Gaines (Nagel), John Berkes (Papa Minosa), Frances Dominguez (Mama Minosa), Frank Jaquet (Smollett), Harry Harvey (Dr. Hylton), Gene Evans (deputy sheriff), Paul D. Merrill, Stewart Kirk Clawson, Bob Kortman, Ralph Moody, Edith Evanson, William Fawcett, Frank Keith, Bill Sheehan, Basil Chester, Joe J. Merrill, Ken Christy, Bert Moorhouse, Martha Maryman, Larry Hogan, Lester Dorr, Iron Eyes Cody, Jack Roberts. *D: & P:* Billy Wilder; *Sc:* (AAN) Wilder, Lesser Samuels, Walter Newman. (1:52) Tense drama of an out-of-work reporter who stumbles on a situation of a man trapped in an old Indian ruin. To make a name for himself, he turns the situation into a three-ring-circus media event. The film found critical acclaim, receiving the "International Prize" and a music award at the Venice Film Festival, but mass appeal was lacking. Based on a factual incident that occurred in 1925. (retitled: *The Big Carnival*)

17. Across the Badlands (Columbia; 1950). *Cast:* Charles Starrett, Smiley Burnette, Helen Mowery, Stanley Andrews, Bob Wilke (dual role), Dick Elliott, Dick Alexander, Hugh Prosser, Robert W. Cavendish, Charles Evans, Paul Campbell, Harmonica Bill. *D:* Fred F. Sears; *P:* Colbert Clark; *St: & Sc:* Barry Shipman. (0:55) Outlaws are trying to thwart the progress of railroad surveyors in this *Durango Kid* series western. (G.B. title: *The Challenge*)

18. Across the Wide Missouri (MGM; 1951). *Cast:* Clark Gable, Ricardo Montalban, John Hodiak, Adolphe Menjou, Maria Elena Marques, J. Carrol Naish, Jack Holt (final film—d. 1951), Alan Napier, George Chandler, Richard Anderson, Henri Letondal, Douglas

Fowley, Louis Niccolletti Whitmore, Russell Simpson, John Hartman, Frankie Darro, Ben Watson, Howard Keel (narrator). *D:* William A. Wellman; *P:* Robert Sisk; *St:* Frank Cavett, Talbot Jennings; *Sc:* Jennings. (1:18) (video) Technicolor western saga of the westward movement which began in St. Louis in the 19th century. Filmed on location in the Colorado Rockies. Note: Negative preview reports forced major editing of the original product.

19. Act of Love (United Artists/Benagoss; 1953). *Cast:* Kirk Douglas, Dany Robin, Robert Strauss, Barbara Laage, Gabrielle Dorziat, Serge Reggiani, Gregoire Aslan, Marthe Mercadier, Fernand Ledoux, Richard Benedict, Brigitte Bardot, Gilbert Geniat, George Mathews, Leslie Dwyer. *D: & P:* Anatole Litvak; *Sc:* Irwin Shaw. (1:48) Downbeat romantic drama set in wartime Paris in 1944 with a lonely American G.I. falling for a French girl who is on the brink of turning to prostitution for a living. Based on the novel *The Girl on the Via Flaminia* by Alfred Hayes, this U.S.A./French co-production was filmed on location in France.

20. Actors and Sin (United Artists/Sid Kuller; 1952). Two 1945 short stories by Ben Hecht make up this feature film.

A. "Actor's Blood" *Cast:* Edward G. Robinson, Marsha Hunt, Dan O'Herlihy, Rudolph Anders, Alice Key, Ric Roman, Peter Brocco, Elizabeth Root, Joe Mell, Irene Martin, Herb Bernard, Bob Carson. The story of a retired actor who attempts to make the suicide of his daughter look like murder.

B. "Concerning a Woman of Sin" *Cast:* Eddie Albert, Alan Reed, Tracey Roberts, Paul Guilfoyle, Douglas Evans, Jody Gilbert, George Baxter, George Keymas, Toni Carroll, John Crawford, Kathleen Mulqueen, Alan Mendez, Sam Rosen, Jenny Hecht (film debut). Comedy of an agent's dilemma when he receives a screenplay with salacious leanings and finds the author is a nine-year-old girl. *D:-P: & Sc:* Ben Hecht. (1:22) (video)

21. The Actress (MGM; 1953). *Cast:* Spencer Tracy (Clinton Jones), Jean Simmons ("Best Actress" Award from the NBR combined with her work in *Young Bess* [q.v.] and *The Robe* [q.v.]/Ruth Gordon Jones), Teresa Wright (Annie Jones), Anthony Perkins (film debut/Fred Whitmarsh), Mary Wickes (Emma Glavey), Ian Wolfe (Mr. Bagley), Kay Williams (Hazel Dawn), Norma Jean Nilsson (Anna), Dawn Bender (Katherine). *D:* George Cukor; *P:* Lawrence Weingarten; *Sc:* Ruth Gordon; *Costumes:* (AAN) Walter Plunkett. (1:31) Comedy-drama of a young girl's infatuation with becoming a stage actress. A box office disappointment, it was based on Ruth Gordon's autobiographical play *Years Ago.*

22. The Admiral Was a Lady (United Artists/Roxbury; 1950). *Cast:* Edmond O'Brien, Wanda Hendrix, Rudy Vallee, Steve Brodie, Richard Erdman, John(ny) Sands, Hillary Brooke, Richard Lane, Garry Owen, Fred Essler. *D:* Albert S. Rogell (final U.S. film); *P:* Rogell, Jack M. Warner; *St & Sc:* Sidney Salkow, John O'Dea; *Songs:* "Once Over Lightly" and "Everything That's Wonderful" Al Stewart-Earl Rose. (1:27) (video) Romantic comedy of an ex–WAVE who meets up with four men, all of whom hate working for a living.

23. The Adventures of Captain Fabian (Republic; 1951). *Cast:* Errol Flynn, Micheline Presle, Vincent Price, Agnes Moorehead, Victor Francen, Jim Gerald, Helena Manson, Howard Vernon, Roger Blin, Valentine Camax, Georges Flateau, Zanie Campan, Reggie Nalder, Charles Fawcett, Aubrey Bower. *D: & P:* William Marshall (debut); *Sc:* Errol Flynn. (1:40) (video) Swashbuckler of a sea captain charged with murder in old New Orleans. A flop based on the novel *Fadulous Ann Madlock* by Robert Shannon.

24. Adventures of Hajji Baba (20th Century–Fox; 1954). *Cast:* John Derek, Elaine Stewart, Thomas Gomez, Amanda Blake, Paul Picerni, Rosemarie Bowe, Donald Randolph, Melinda Markey, Peter Mamakos, Kurt Katch, Robert Bice, Carl Milletaire. *D:* Don Weis; *P:* Walter Wanger; *Sc:* Richard Collins; *Song:* "Hajji Baba" Dimitri Tiompkin–Ned Washington (sung by Nat "King" Cole). (1:34) Arabian Nights–type adventure of a lonely barber who does in an evil prince and wins the beautiful princess. Based on the 1954 novel by James Morier. Technicolor and CinemaScope.

The Adventures of Quentin Durward (G.B. title) *see* **Quentin Durward**

25. Affair in Havana (Allied Artists; 1957). *Cast:* John Cassavetes, Raymond Burr, Sara Shane, Lilia Lazo, Sergio Pena, Celia Cruz, Jose Antonio Rivero, Miguel Angel Blanco. *D:* Laslo Benedek; *P:* Richard Goldstone; *St:* Janet

Green; *Sc:* Burton Lane, Maurice Zimm. (1:11) Potboiler melodrama of a piano player in Cuba who makes a play for a married woman whose husband is wealthy, but also crippled.

26. Affair in Reno (Republic; 1957). *Cast:* John Lund, Doris Singleton, John Archer, Angela Greene, Alan Hale, Harry Bartell, Howard McNear, Richard Deacon, Thurston Hall (final film—d. 1958), Billy Vincent. *D:* R.G. Springsteen; *P:* Sidney Picker; *St:* Gerald Drayson Adams; *Sc:* John K. Butler. (1:15) Melodrama of a millionaire who hires a PR man to go to Reno and prevent his daughter from marrying a gambler.

27. Affair in Trinidad (Columbia/Beckwith Corp.; 1952). *Cast:* Rita Hayworth (singing voice dubbed by JoAnn Greer/Chris Emery), Glenn Ford (Steve Emery), Alexander Scourby (Max Fabian), Valerie Bettis (who also choreographed/Veronica), Torin Thatcher (Inspector Smythe), Howard Wendell (Anderson), Karel Stepanek (Walters), Steven Geray (Wittol), George Voskovec (Dr. Franz Huebling), Walter Kohler (Peter Bronec), Juanita Moore (Dominique), Gregg Martell (Olaf), Mort Mills (Martin), Robert Boon (pilot), Ralph Moody (coroner), Ross Elliott (Neal Emery), Don Kohler (Mr. Peters), Franz Roehn, John Sherman, Joel Fluellen, Fred Baker, Kathleen O'Malley, Leonidas Ossetynski, Don Blackman, Ivan Browning, Roy Glenn. *D: & P:* Vincent Sherman; *As.P:* Virginia Van Upp; *St:* Van Upp, Berne Giler; *Sc:* Oscar Saul, James Gunn; *Songs:* "I've Been Kissed Before" and "Trinidad Lady" Lester Lee–Bob Russell; *Costumes:* (AAN-b/w) Jean Louis. (1:38) (video) Espionage drama of a night club entertainer whose husband is murdered by an international spy ring. One of the 23 top-grossing films of 1951-52.

28. An Affair to Remember (20th Century–Fox/Jerry Wald Prods., Inc.; 1957). *Cast:* Cary Grant (Nickie Ferrante), Deborah Kerr (Terry McKay/received *Photoplay* Gold Medal Award), Richard Denning (Kenneth), Neva Patterson (Lois), Cathleen Nesbitt (Grandmother), Charles Watts (Hathaway), Fortunio Bonanova (Courbet), Matt Moore (final film—d. 1960/Father McGrath), Louis Mercier (Marius), Geraldine Wall (Miss Webb), Sarah Selby (Miss Lane), Nora Marlowe (Gladys), Genevieve Aumont (Gabrielle), Robert Q. Lewis, Walter Woolf King, Roger Til, Jack Raine, Dino Bolognese, Jack Lomas, Dorothy Adams, Robert Lynn, Patricia Powell, Alena Murray, Minta Durfee, Alberto Morin, Jesslyn Fax, Tommy Nolan, Theresa Emerson, Richard Allan, Tina Thompson, Scotty Morrow, Kathleen Charney, Terry Ross Kelman, Norman Champion III, Mary Carroll, Suzanne Ellers, Juney Ellis, Don Pietro, Paul Bradley, Tony DeMario, Michka Egan, Bert Stevens, Brian Corcoran, Priscilla Garcia, Marc Snow, Anthony Mazzola, Helen Mayon. *D:* Leo McCarey; *P:* Jerry Wald; *St:* McCarey, Mildred Cram; *Sc:* McCarey, Delmer Daves; *Cin:* (AAN) Milton Krasner; *Music:* (AAN) Hugo Friedhofer; *Title Song:* (AAN) Harry Warren (m), Harold Adamson, McCarey (ly), sung by Vic Damone on the soundtrack; *Costumes:* (AAN) Charles LeMaire. (1:55) (video/laserdisc) Romantic comedy-drama of a love affair begun aboard ship that continues on land until a misunderstanding occurs beyond the control of those involved. A remake of McCarey's *Love Affair* (RKO; 1939), it was also remade under that title in 1994. One of the 24 top-grossing films of 1956-57, it also received the *Photoplay* Gold Medal Award. In DeLuxe color, CinemaScope and stereophonic sound.

29. Affair with a Stranger (RKO; 1953). *Cast:* Jean Simmons, Victor Mature, Mary Jo Tarola, Monica Lewis, Jane Darwell, Dabbs Greer, Wally Vernon, Nicholas Joy, Olive Carey, Victoria Horne, Lillian Bronson, George Cleveland, Bill Chapin. *D:* Roy Rowland; *P:* Robert Sparks; *Sc:* Richard Flournoy; *Song:* "Kiss and Run" Sam Coslow (sung by Monica Lewis). (1:29) Marital melodrama concerning the details (via flashback) in the marriage of a Broadway playwright.

30. The Affairs of Dobie Gillis (MGM; 1953). *Cast:* Debbie Reynolds, Bobby Van (title role), Barbara Ruick, Bob Fosse, Hanley Stafford, Lurene Tuttle, Hans Conried, Charles Lane, Kathleen Freeman, Archer MacDonald, Almira Sessions. *D:* Don Weis; *P:* Arthur M. Loew, Jr.; *Sc:* Max Shulman; *Songs:* "I'm Through with Love," "All I Do Is Dream of You," "You Can't Do Wrong Doing Right" and "Those Endearing Young Charms." (1:14) (video) Hit romantic comedy of college kids, based on Max Shulman's book, rounded out with musical numbers. Needless to say, the inspiration for the later TV series with Dwayne Hickman and Tuesday Weld.

The Affairs of Sally (G.B. title) *see* **The Fuller Brush Girl**

31. The African Lion (Buena Vista; 1955). *D:* James Algar; *P:* Walt Disney; *As.P:* Ben Sharpsteen; *Sc:* Algar, Winston Hibler (who also narrates), Ted Sears, Jack Moffitt; *Cin:* Alfred G. & Elma Milotte (who also photographed Disney's Oscar winning short "Beaver Valley" in 1950); *Editor:* Norman Palmer. (1:15) Disney's third "True-Life Adventure" documentary, this one detailing a family of lions in Africa as well as other species of wildlife. A box office hit, it placed #10 on the "10 Best" list of the NBR. Technicolor.

32. African Manhunt (Republic/Trinity Prods.; 1955). *Cast:* Myron Healey, Karin Booth, John Kellogg, Ross Elliott, Ray Bennett, James Edwards. *D:* Seymour Friedman; *P:* Jerry Thomas; *St:* & *Sc:* Arthur Hoerl. (1:10) Low budget adventure of two men and a woman trekking to the African coast with a wanted criminal. Includes much stock footage.

33. The African Queen (United Artists/ Romulus–British Lion–Horizon; 1951). *Cast:* Humphrey Bogart (AA/Charles Allnut), Katharine Hepburn (AAN/Rose Sayer), Robert Morley (the Rev. Samuel Sayer), Peter Bull, Theodore Bikel (film debut), Walter Gotell, Gerald Onn, Peter Swanick, Richard Marner. *D:* (AAN) John Huston; *P:* S.P. Eagle (Sam Spiegel); *Sc:* (AAN) James Agee, Huston. (1:45) (video/ laserdisc) Critically acclaimed drama of the romance between a drunken river steamer captain and a lady missionary. They escape down the Congo River from the Germans in 1914 during the early days of World War I. Based on the novel by C.S. Forester, it became one of the 23 top-grossing films of 1951-52. It took a #4 placement on the "10 Best" list of *Film Daily*, was in nomination for "Best Film" by the New York Film Critics and also received a nomination in the British Academy Awards in 1952. Reworked in 1998 as *Six Days, Seven Nights*. Technicolor.

34. African Treasure (Monogram; 1952). *Cast:* Johnny Sheffield, Laurette Luez, Leonard Mudie, Arthur Space, Lane Bradford, Martin Garralaga, Lyle Talbot, Robert "Smoki" Whitfield, James Adamson, Jack Williams, Wesley Bly, "Sugar Foot" Anderson, Woodrow Wilson [Woody] Strode. *D: & Sc:* Ford Beebe; *P:* Walter Mirisch; *St:* Roy Rockwood. (1:10) "Bomba, the Jungle Boy" is in pursuit of diamond smugglers in the 7th entry in this adventure series. (aka: *Bomba and the African Treasure*)

After Midnight (G.B. title) *see* **Captain Carey, U.S.A.**

35. Against All Flags (Universal-International; 1952). *Cast:* Errol Flynn, Maureen O'Hara, Anthony Quinn, Mildred Natwick, Alice Kelley, Robert Warwick, Harry Cording, John Anderson (film debut), Phil Tully, Lester Matthews, Tudor Owen, Maurice Marsac, James Craven, James Fairfax, Bill Radovich, Michael Ross, Paul Newlan, Lewis Russell, Arthur Gould-Porter, Olaf Hytten. *D:* George Sherman; *P:* Howard Christie; *St:* Aeneas MacKenzie; *Sc:* MacKenzie, Joseph Hoffman. (1:23) (video/laserdisc) Eighteenth century swashbuckler of a British naval officer who infiltrates a pirate stronghold. Remade by this studio in 1967 as *The King's Pirate*. Technicolor.

36. Ain't Misbehavin' (Universal-International; 1955). *Cast:* Rory Calhoun, Piper Laurie, Jack Carson, Mamie Van Doren, Reginald Gardiner, Barbara Britton, Lisa Gaye, Dani Crayne, Carl Post, Roger Etienne, Harris Brown, Isabel Randolph, George Givot, Peter Mamakos. *D:* Edward Buzzell; *P:* Samuel Marx; *St:* "Third Girl From the Right" by Robert Carson; *Sc:* Philip Rapp, Devery Freeman, Buzzell; *Musical Numbers:* "A Little Love Can Go a Long Way" Paul Francis Webster, Sammy Fain, "The Dixie Mambo" Charles Henderson, Sonny Burke, "I Love That Rickey Tickey Tickey" Sammy Cahn, Johnny Scott, "Ain't Misbehavin'" Fats Waller, Andy Razaf. (1:21) Musical of the romance between a wealthy man and an unpolished chorus girl. Technicolor.

37. Air Cadet (Universal-International; 1951). *Cast:* Stephen McNally, Gail Russell, Alex Nicol, Richard Long, Charles Drake, Robert Arthur, Rock Hudson, Peggie Castle, James Best, Parley Baer. *D:* Joseph Pevney; *P:* Aaron Rosenberg; *St:* Robert L. Richards, Robert Soderberg; *Sc:* Richards; *Additional dialogue:* Joseph Hoffman. (1:33) Drama of three men and their training at Randolph Field, Texas to become pilots. (aka: *Jet Men of the Air*)

38. Air Strike (Lippert/Cy Roth; 1955). *Cast:* Richard Denning, Gloria Jean, Don Haggerty, Bill Hudson, Alan Wells, John Kirby, William Halop, James Courtney, Stanley Clements. *D:-P:-St:* & *Sc:* Cy Roth (1:03) Drama of the efforts of a naval commander to create a disciplined crew of jet fighters.

39. Al Capone (Allied Artists/Burrows-Ackerman Prods.; 1959). *Cast:* Rod Steiger (Al

Capone), Fay Spain, James Gregory, Martin Balsam (Mack Kelly/a fictitious name for real life newsman Jake Lingle), Nehemiah Persoff (Johnny Torrio), Murvyn Vye (Bugs Moran), Robert Gist (Dion O'Bannion), Lewis Charles (Hymie Weiss), Joe DeSantis (Big Jim Colosimo), Sandy Kenyon (Bones Corelli), Raymond Bailey, Al Ruscio (Tony Genaro), Louis Quinn (Joe Lorenzo), Peter Dane, Ron Soble (Scalisi), Steve Gravesi, Ben Ari. *D:* Richard Wilson; *P:* John H. Burrows, Leonard Ackerman; *Sc:* Malvin Wald, Henry F. Greenberg. (1:45) (video) A biographical drama of Chicago's infamous crime lord of the 1920s and '30s, which received critical acclaim for authenticity.

40. Al Jennings of Oklahoma (Columbia; 1951). *Cast:* Dan Duryea, Gale Storm, Dick Foran, Gloria Henry, Guinn "Big Boy" Williams, Raymond Greenleaf, Stanley Andrews, John Ridgely, James Millican, Harry Shannon, Helen Brown, Robert Bice, George J. Lewis, Jimmie Dodd, Edwin Parker, James Griffith, William "Bill" Phillips, Robert Phillips, Charles Meredith, William Norton Bailey, Louis Jean Heydt, Harry Cording, Theresa Harris, Myron Healey, George Lloyd, Hank Patterson, George Chesbro, Earle Hodgins, John R. Hamilton, Harry Tyler, Guy Beach, Boyd Stockman, John Dehner. *D:* Ray Nazarro; *P:* Rudolph C. Flothow; *St:* Al Jennings, Will Irwin; *Sc:* George Bricker. (1:17) Fact-based western of a train robber who becomes a respected lawyer. Filmed before in 1915 as *Beating Back* in 6 reels with Al Jennings playing himself. Technicolor.

41. Aladdin and His Lamp (Monogram; 1952). *Cast:* John(ny) Sands, Patricia Medina, Richard Erdman, John Dehner, Billy House, Charles Horvath, Ned Young, Noreen Nash, Rick Vallin, Sujata, Arabella. *D:* Lew Landers; *P:* Walter Wanger; *Sc:* Howard Dimsdale, Millard Kaufman. (1:07) Arabian Nights tale of a pickpocket who falls for Jasmine, the beautiful daughter of the caliph. Cinecolor.

42. Alaska Passage (20th Century–Fox/ Associated Producers; 1959). *Cast:* Bill Williams, Nora Hayden, Lyn Thomas, Leslie Bradley, Nick Dennis, Raymond Hatton, Fred Sherman, Courtland Shepard, Gregg Martell, Jess Kirkpatrick, Jorie Wyler, Tommy Cook, Ralph Sanford. *D: & Sc:* Edward Bernds; *P:* Bernard Glasser. (1:11) Adventure melodrama of an Alaskan trucking company in trouble due to high overhead. Associated Producers' first release through Fox, it was filmed in Regalscope on location in Alaska. Originally ran on a double bill with *The Lone Texan* (q.v.).

43. Alaska Seas (Paramount; 1954). *Cast:* Robert Ryan, Jan Sterling, Brian Keith, Gene Barry, Ross Bagdasarian, Richard Shannon, Ralph Dumke, Fay Roope, Timothy Carey, Peter Coe, Jim Hayward, Aaron Spelling, William Fawcett, Earl Holliman, Richard Kipling, Eugene Roth, Abel Fernandez. *D:* Jerry Hopper; *P:* Mel Epstein; *Sc:* Geoffrey Homes [Daniel Mainwaring], Walter Doniger. (1:18) Action melodrama of feuding partners in an Alaskan salmon cannery. A remake of this studio's 1938 production *Spawn of the North*, it was based on the 1932 novel of that name by (Florence) Barrett Willoughby. Originally ran on a double bill with *Jivaro* (q.v.).

44. Albert Schweitzer (Louis de Rochemont Assoc./Hill and Anderson Prod.; 1957). *D: & P:* Jerome Hill; *Commentary:* Albert Schweitzer; *Additional commentary:* Thomas Bruce Morgan. A documentary feature on the life and work of Albert Schweitzer that garnered a "Best Documentary" Oscar for producer Hill. It also placed #5 on the "10 Best" list of the NBR.

45. Alexander the Great (United Artists/ Robert Rossen; 1956). *Cast:* Richard Burton (Alexander), Fredric March (Philip II of Macedonia), Claire Bloom (Barsine), Danielle Darrieux (Olympias), Harry Andrews (Darius), Barry Jones (Aristotle), Michael Hordern (Demosthenes), Peter Cushing (Memnon), Stanley Baker (Attalus), Niall MacGinnis (Parmenio), Marisa DeLeza, Gustavo Rojo, Ruben Rojo, William Squire, Helmut Dantine, Friedrich Ledebur, Peter Wyngarde, Virgilio Texeira, Teresa Del Rio, Julio Pena, Jose Nieto, Carlos Baena, Larry Taylor, Jose Marco, Ricardo Valle, Carmen Caruilla, Jesus Luque, Ramsay Ames, Mario DeBarros, Ellen Rossen, Carlos Acevedo. *D:-P:* & *Sc:* Robert Rossen. (2:21) (video/laserdisc) Historical epic of the son of Philip II of Macedonia who takes on and conquers the known world of his day. Not the hit Rossen expected, it was filmed on location in Spain and Italy. Technicolor and CinemaScope.

46. Alias Jesse James (United Artists/ Hope Enterprises; 1959). *Cast:* Bob Hope, Rhonda Fleming, Wendell Corey (Jesse James), Jim Davis (Frank James), Mickey Finn, Will Wright, Mike Mazurki, Gloria Talbott, Mary

Young, Sid Melton, George E. Stone, James Burke, Joseph Vitale, Lyle Latell, Harry Tyler, Nestor Paiva, Emory Parnell, I. Stanford Jolley, Richard Alexander, Oliver Blake, Jack Lambert, Ethan Laidlaw, Glenn Strange, J. Anthony Hughes, Iron Eyes Cody + *Cameos:* James Arness (Matt Dillon), James Garner (Bret Maverick), Hugh O'Brian (Wyatt Earp), Gene Autry (himself), Ward Bond (Major Seth Adams), Roy Rogers (himself), Fess Parker (Davy Crockett), Gail Davis (Annie Oakley), Jay Silverheels (Tonto), Bing Crosby (himself), Gary Cooper (himself). *D:* Norman Z. McLeod (final film—ret.); *Ex.P:* Bob Hope; *P:* Jack Hope; *St:* Robert St. Aubrey, Bert Lawrence; *Sc:* William Bowers, Daniel D. Beauchamp; *Songs:* Title song Marilyn & Joe Hooven (m), Dunham (ly); "Ain't A-Hankerin'," "Protection" Arthur Altman–Bud Burtson. (1:32) Comedy of an insurance salesman who heads west and just happens to sell a policy to Jesse James, then doing what he has to, to protect the notorious figure. DeLuxe color.

47. Alice in Wonderland (RKO/Walt Disney; 1951). *Voices:* Kathryn Beaumont (Alice), Ed Wynn (Mad Hatter), Richard Haydn (Caterpillar), Sterling Holloway (Cheshire Cat), Jerry Colonna (March Hare), Verna Felton (Queen of Hearts), Pat O'Malley (Walrus, Carpenter, Tweedledee & Tweedledum), Bill Thompson (White Rabbit, Dodo), Heather Angel (Alice's Sister), Joseph Kearns (Doorknob), Larry Grey (Bill), Queenie Leonard (bird in the tree), Dink Trout (King of Hearts), Doris Lloyd (The Rose), James MacDonald (Dormouse), The Mello Men (Card Painters), Don Barclay. *D:* Clyde Geronimi, Hamilton Luske, Wilfred Jackson; *P:* Walt Disney; *Production Supervisor:* Ben Sharpsteen; *Music:* (AAN) Oliver Wallace; *Songs:* "Very Good Advice," "In a World of My Own," "All in a Golden Afternoon," "Alice in Wonderland," "The Walrus and the Carpenter," "The Caucus Race," "I'm Late," "Painting the Roses Red," "March of the Cards" (Bob Hilliard–Sammy Fain); " 'Twas Brillig" (Don Raye–Gene De-Paul); "A Very Merry Un-Birthday" (Mack David–Al Hoffman–Jerry Livingston); "We'll Smoke the Blighter Out," "Old Father William," and "A E I O U" (Oliver Wallace–Ted Sears). (1:15) (video/laserdisc) Disney's animated tale of young Alice who has a series of strange adventures with some equally strange characters after tumbling down a rabbit hole. Based on the 1865 children's classic by Lewis Carroll [Charles Lutwidge Dodgson], with animated characters inspired by the famous illustrations by John Tenniel. At a cost of $5,000,000, it became one of the 23 top-grossing films of 1950-51, but did not do the business Mr. Disney had anticipated. It may be considered the least popular of all of the Disney animated features, though in the 1960s it found favor with the drug culture. Other versions of the story include a one reel silent in 1903; 1916 (Nonparell Feature Film Co.) in 6 reels; a 1921 silent; Pathe, 1927; Unique Foto Film, 1931; Paramount, 1933; and Bunin-Souvaine, 1950-51, from France with a blend of live action and puppets, *Alice's Adventures in Wonderland* (Great Britain; 1972) a musical and 1986 TV movie with an all-star cast. In Technicolor, the film was in nomination at the Venice Film Festival.

48. All About Eve (20th Century–Fox; 1950). *Cast:* Bette Davis (AAN + "Best Actress" at the 1951 Cannes Film Festival/Margo Channing), Anne Baxter (AAN/Eve Harrington), George Sanders (AA-BSA/Addison DeWitt/who also narrates), Celeste Holm (AAN/Karen Richards), Gary Merrill (Bill Sampson), Hugh Marlowe (Lloyd Richards), Thelma Ritter (AAN/Birdie), Marilyn Monroe (Miss Caswell), Gregory Ratoff (Max Fabian), Barbara Bates (Phoebe), Walter Hampden, Randy Stuart, Craig Hill, Leland Harris, Barbara White, Eddie Fisher (film debut), William Pullen, Claude Stroud, Eugene Borden, Helen Mowery, Steven Geray, Bess Flowers. *D:* (AA) Joseph L. Mankiewicz; *P:* (AA-Best Picture) Darryl F. Zanuck; *Sc:* (AA) Mankiewicz; *Cin:* (AAN-b/w) Milton Krasner; *ASD:* (AAN-b/w) Lyle Wheeler, George Davis (art directors), Thomas Little, Walter M. Scott (sets); *Sound:* (AA) Thomas T. Moulton; *Editor:* (AAN) Barbara McLean; *Music:* (AAN) Alfred Newman; *Costumes:* (AA) Edith Head, Charles LeMaire. (2:18) (video/laserdisc) Critically acclaimed comedy-drama of an aging Broadway actress who takes in a protégé and finds the young actress taking over her life. One of the 23 top-grossing films of 1950-51, it placed #2 on the "10 Best" list of the NBR and #9 on the same list of the *New York Times*. It also won "Best Picture" at the British Academy Awards. In 1951 the Cannes Film Festival voted it the "Special Jury Prize" as well as Bette Davis "Best Actress." This film received 14 Oscar nominations (6 wins) and later emerged as the Broadway musical "Applause." The New York Film Critics also voted it "Best Picture," Ms. Davis "Best Actress" and Mr. Mankiewicz "Best Director."

49. The All-American (Universal-International; 1953). *Cast:* Tony Curtis, Lori Nelson, Richard Long, Mamie Van Doren, Gregg Palmer, Paul Cavanagh, Barney Phillips, Jimmy Hunt, Stuart Whitman, Herman Hickman, Douglas Kennedy, Donald Randolph, Frank Gifford, Tom Harmon (himself), Jim Sears, Elmer Willhoite, Don Moomaw, Fortune Gordein, George Bozanic. *D:* Jesse Hibbs (directorial debut); *P:* Aaron Rosenberg; *St:* Leonard Freeman; *Adapt:* Robert Yale Libott; *Sc:* D.D. Beauchamp. (1:22) Drama of a college football player who goes into a decline after his parents are killed. (G.B. title: *The Winning Way*)

50. All Ashore (Columbia; 1953). *Cast:* Mickey Rooney, Dick Haymes, Peggy Ryan (final film—ret.), Ray McDonald, Barbara Bates, Jody Lawrence, Fay Roope, Jean Willes, Rica Owen, Patricia Walker, Edwin Parker, Dick Crockett, Frank Kreig, Ben Welden, Gloria Pall, Joan Shawlee. *D:* Richard Quine; *P:* Jonie Taps; *St:* Blake Edwards, Robert Wells; *Sc:* Edwards, Quine; *Songs:* Wells, Fred Karger, Lee Scott. (1:20) Technicolor musical-comedy of three sailors on shore leave.

51. All I Desire (Universal-International; 1953). *Cast:* Barbara Stanwyck, Richard Carlson, Lyle Bettger, Marcia Henderson, Lori Nelson, Maureen O'Sullivan, Richard Long, Billy Gray, Lotte Stein, Dayton Lummis, Fred Nurney, Guy Williams, Charles Hand. *D:* Douglas Sirk; *P:* Ross Hunter; *Adapt:* Gina Kaus; *Sc:* James Gunn, Robert Blees. (1:19) (video) Melodrama set at the turn-of-the-century of a woman who returns to the family she deserted years before. Based on the novel *Stopover* by Carol Brink.

52. All Mine to Give (Universal-International/RKO; 1957). *Cast:* Glynis Johns, Cameron Mitchell, Rex Thompson, Patty McCormack, Ernest Truex, Hope Emerson, Alan Hale, Jr., Sylvia Field, Reta Shaw, Stephen Wooten, Butch Bernard, Yolanda White, Terry Ann Ross, Roy Engel, Margaret Brayton, Royal Dano, Rita Johnson (final film—ret.), Ralph Sanford, Ellen Corby, Rosalyn Boulter, Francis DeSales, Jon Provost. *D:* Allen Reisner (feature directorial debut); *P:* Sam Weisenthal; *Sc:* Dale and Katherine Eunson (based on his story "The Day They Gave Babies Away"). (1:42) (video) Nineteenth century frontier family drama of a boy who must find a home for his brother and three sisters on Christmas Eve, following the death of his parents. A production of RKO released by Universal after the former studio closed its doors. (G.B. title: *The Day They Gave Babies Away*) Technicolor.

53. All My Babies (University of California/Center for Mass Communications, Columbia University; 1952). *P:* George Stoney. (0:55) A 16 mm documentary on a midwife delivering black babies in Georgia.

54. All That Heaven Allows (Universal-International; 1955). *Cast:* Jane Wyman, Rock Hudson, Agnes Moorehead, Conrad Nagel, Virginia Grey, Gloria Talbott, William Reynolds, Jacqueline de Wit, Charles Drake, Leigh Snowden, Donald Curtis, Alex Gerry, Gia Scala (film debut). *D:* Douglas Sirk; *P:* Ross Hunter; *Sc:* Peg Fenwick. (1:29) Romantic soaper of a widow who falls for her much younger gardener with following flack from everyone she knows, starting with her children. Based on the novel by Edna L. and Harry Lee, it was photographed in Technicolor.

55. All That I Have (Family Films; 1951). *Cast:* Donald Woods, Houseley Stevenson, Sr., Onslow Stevens, John Eldredge. *D:* William F. Claxton. (1:02) A low budget independent production.

56. All the Brothers Were Valiant (MGM; 1953). *Cast:* Robert Taylor (Joel Shore), Stewart Granger (Mark Shore), Ann Blyth (Priscilla Holt), Keenan Wynn (Silva), James Whitmore (Fetcher), Lewis Stone (Capt. Holt/final film—d. 1953), Betta St. John (native girl), Kurt Kasznar (Quint), Robert Burton (Asa Worthen), Jonathan Cott (Carter), John Lupton (Dick Morrell), Mitchell Lewis (Cook), Peter Whitney (James Finch), James Bell (Aaron Burnham), Leo Gordon (Peter How), Michael Pate (Varde), Clancy Cooper (Smith), Frank DeKova (Stevenson), Henry Rowland (Jones). *D:* Richard Thorpe; *P:* Pandro S. Berman; *Sc:* Harry Brown; *Cin:* (AAN) George Folsey. (1:41) (video) Drama of rivalries and conflict in a New Bedford, Massachusetts whaling family. Based on the novel by Ben Ames Williams, it was previously filmed under the present title in 1922 by Metro and again in 1928 by MGM as *Across to Singapore*. Photographed in Technicolor, it was another moneymaker for the studio.

All the Way *see* **The Joker Is Wild**

57. The Alligator People (20th Century–Fox/Associated Producers; 1959). *Cast:*

Beverly Garland, Bruce Bennett, Lon Chaney, George Macready, Frieda Inescort, Richard Crane, Douglas Kennedy, Vince Townsend, Jr., Ruby Goodwin, Boyd Stockman, John Merrick, Lee Warren, Bill Bradley, Dudley Dickerson, Hal K. Dawson. *D:* Roy Del Ruth; *P:* Jack Leewood; *St:* Orville H. Hampton, Charles O'Neal; *Sc:* Hampton. (1:14) Horror thriller of a woman under the influence of sodium pentathol who relates a tale of her husband disappearing on their wedding night who she tracked to his family home in the southern bayou country, only to find a doctor's experiments partially turned him into an alligator. Photographed in CinemaScope, it ran on a double bill with *The Return of the Fly* (q.v.).

58. Along the Great Divide (Warner; 1951). *Cast:* Kirk Douglas, Virginia Mayo, John Agar, Walter Brennan, Ray Teal, Hugh Sanders, Morris Ankrum, James Anderson (film debut), Charles Meredith. *D:* Raoul Walsh; *P:* Anthony Veiller; *St:* Walter Doniger; *Sc:* Doniger, Lewis Meltzer. (1:28) (video) Western drama of a U.S. marshal out to get the bad guy.

59. The Amazing Colossal Man (American International/Malibu; 1957). *Cast:* Glenn Langan, Cathy Downs, William Hudson, Larry Thor, James Seay, Frank Jenks (final film—ret.), Russ Bender, Hank Patterson, Jimmy Cross, June Jocelyn, Stanley Lachman, Harry Raybould, Jean Moorhead, Scott Peters, Myron Cook, Michael Harris, Bill Cassady, Dick Nelson, Ed Cobb, Paul Hahn, Diana Darwin, Lyn Osborn, Jack Kosslyn, William Hughes, Keith Heatherington. *D: & P:* Bert I. Gordon; *Sc:* Mark Hanna, Gordon. (1:20) (video) In this science fiction, an army colonel survives a plutonium bomb detonation and grows to enormous proportions. Followed by a sequel, *War of the Colossal Beast* (q.v.). *Cat Girl*, a British horror film, filled out the double bill program.

60. The Ambassador's Daughter (United Artists/ Norman Krasna; 1956). *Cast:* Olivia de Havilland, John Forsythe, Adolphe Menjou, Myrna Loy, Edward Arnold, Francis Lederer, Tommy Noonan, Minor Watson. *D:-P:* & *Sc:* Norman Krasna. (1:42) (video) The romance of an ambassador's daughter and an American soldier in Paris is the main story of this comedy. Technicolor and CinemaScope.

61. Ambush at Cimarron Pass (20th Century–Fox/Regal Films; 1958). *Cast:* Scott Brady, Margia Dean, Baynes Barron, William Vaughn, Ken Mayer, John Manier, Keith Richards, Clint Eastwood, John Merrick, Frank Gerstle, Dirk London, Irving Bacon, Desmond Stanley. *D:* Jodie Copelan; *P:* Herbert E. Mendelson; *St:* Robert A. Reeds, Robert W. Woods; *Sc:* Richard G. Taylor, John K. Butler. (1:13) Western of cavalry vs. Indians. Regalscope. Paired on a double bill with *Cattle Empire* (q.v.).

62. Ambush at Tomahawk Gap (Columbia; 1953). *Cast:* John Hodiak, John Derek, David Brian, Maria Elena Marques, Ray Teal, John Qualen, Otto Hulett, Percy Helton, Trevor Bardette, John Doucette. *D:* Fred F. Sears; *P:* Wallace MacDonald; *St:* & *Sc:* David Lang. (1:13) (video) Four ex-cons find themselves besieged by Indians while searching for their spoils in a ghost town. Technicolor.

63. An American Guerrilla in the Philippines (20th Century–Fox; 1950). *Cast:* Tyrone Power, Micheline Presle, Tom Ewell, Bob Patten, Tommy Cook, Juan Torena, Jack Elam, Robert Barrat (Gen. Douglas MacArthur), Carleton Young, Maria Del Val, Eddie Infante, Orlando Martin, Miguel Anzures, Chris de Varga, Eduardo Rivera, Arling Gonzales, Fred Gonzales, Sabu Camacho, Rosa del Rosario, Kathy Ruby, Erlinda Cortez. *D:* Fritz Lang; *P:* & *Sc:* Lamar Trotti. (1:45) World War II drama of an American naval ensign who joins with local partisan fighters in the Philippines following the fall of Bataan. Based on the novel by Ira Wolfert. (G.B. title: *I Shall Return*) Technicolor.

64. An American in Paris (MGM; 1951). *Cast:* Gene Kelly (received a special AA for his choreography/Jerry Mulligan), Leslie Caron (film debut/Lise Bourvier), Oscar Levant (Adam Cook), Georges Guetary (Henri Baurel), Nina Foch (Milo Roberts), Eugene Borden (Georges Mattieu), Martha Bamattre (Mathilde Mattieu), Ann Codee (Therese), George Davis (Francoise), Hayden Rorke (Tommy Baldwin), Paul Maxey (John McDowd), Dick Wessel (Ben Macrow), John Eldredge (Jack Jansen), Anna Q. Nilsson (Kay Jansen), Madge Blake (Edna Mae Bestram), Andre Charisse (dancing partner), Mary Young, Don Quinn, Adele Coray, Lucien Plauzoles, Christian Pasques, Anthony Mazzola, Jeanne Lafayette, Louise Laureau, Alfred Paix, Noel Neill, Nan Boardman, Art Dupuis, Greg McClure, Marie Antoinette Andrews. *D:* (AAN) Vincente Minnelli;

P: (AA=Best Picture + Irving Thalberg Memorial Award) Arthur Freed; *St: & Sc:* (AA) Alan Jay Lerner (with screenplay credited to Lerner pseudonym Alan Lin); *Cin:* (AA-color) Alfred Gilks, John Alton; *ASD:* (AA-color) Cedric Gibbons, Preston Ames (art directors), Edwin B. Willis, Keogh Gleason (sets); *Music:* (AA) Johnny Green, Saul Chaplin; *Costumes:* (AA-color) Orry-Kelly, Walter Plunkett, Irene Sharaff; *Editor:* (AAN) Adrienne Fazan; *Musical Numbers:* "I Got Rhythm," "Embraceable You," "'S Wonderful," "By Strauss," "Tra-La-La-La," "Our Love Is Here to Stay" (George and Ira Gershwin); "Concerto in F" and "An American in Paris" (instrumental music by George Gershwin); "I'll Build a Stairway to Paradise" (music by George Gershwin, lyrics by E. Ray Goetz and B.G. DeSylva). (1:53) (video/laserdisc) Worldwide blockbuster hit musical of the year receiving accolades from all quarters, with the exception of *Show Boat* (q.v.) which grossed more money. One of the 23 top-grossing films of 1951-52, it placed #3 on the "10 Best" lists of both the NBR and *Film Daily*, while placing #7 on the same list of the *New York Times*. The British Academy Awards had it in nomination and the New York Film Critics had it in nomination for "Best Picture" of the year. Technicolor.

65. The Americano (RKO; 1955). *Cast:* Glenn Ford, Frank Lovejoy, Cesar Romero, Ursula Theiss, Abbe Lane, Rodolfo Hoyos, Tom Powers (final film—ret.), Dan White, Frank Marlowe, Salvador Baguez, George Navarro, Nira Monsour. *D:* William Castle; *P:* Robert Stillman; *Sc:* Guy Trosper (based on the magazine serial *Six Weeks South of Texas* [aka: "Trouble in Paradise"] by Leslie T. White. (1:25) (video) South American "western" of an American cowboy delivering Brahma bulls to Brazil. Color.

66. Anastasia (20th Century–Fox; 1956). *Cast:* Ingrid Bergman (AA/Anastasia), Yul Brynner (voted "Best Actor" by the NBR in conjunction with his work in *The Ten Commandments* and *The King and I* [both q.v.] Prince), Helen Hayes (dowager Empress), Akim Tamiroff (Chernov), Martita Hunt (Livenbaum), Felix Alymer (Chamberlain), Sacha Pigeoff (Petrovin), Ivan Desny (Prince Paul), Natalie Schafer (Lissemskaia), Gregoire Gromoff (Stepan), Karel Stepanek (Vlados), Ina De La Hayes (Marusia), Katherine Kath (Maxime), Olaf Pooley (Zhadanov), Olga Valery (Countess Baranova), Eric Pohlman (Von Drivnitz), Alexis Bobrinskoy (Bechmetieff), Peter Sallis (Grischa), Tamara Shayne (Zenia), Henry Vidon (Prince Bolkonoski), Andre Mikhelson, Edward Forsythe, Stanley Zevick, Tutte Lemkow, Anatole Smirnoff, Alan Cuthbertson, Hy Hazell, Mr. Pavlov, Paula Catton, Marguerite Brennan. *D:* Anatole Litvak; *P:* Buddy Adler; *Sc:* Arthur Laurents (based on the play by Marcelle Maurette as adapted by Guy Bolton); *Music:* (AAN) Alfred Newman. (1:45) (video/laserdisc) Critically acclaimed drama of an amnesiac who is passed off as Anastasia, a daughter of Czar Nicholas and Alexandra, who survived the massacre of her family in 1917. On the "10 Best" list of *Film Daily* it placed #5, while the *New York Times* placed it at #10. The NBR gave it a #8 placement. One of the 24 top-grossing films of 1956-57. Ingrid Bergman also received the "Best Actress" Award from the New York Film Critics. The same story was told in the 1986 TV movie *Anastasia: The Mystery of Anna* from different source material. DeLuxe color and CinemaScope.

67. Anatomy of a Murder (Columbia/ Carlyle Prod.; 1959). *Cast:* James Stewart (AAN/ Paul Biegler), Lee Remick (Laura Manion), Ben Gazzara (Lt. Manion), Arthur O'Connell (AAN/Parnell McCarthy), Eve Arden (Maida), Kathryn Grant (Mary Pilant), George C. Scott (AAN/Claude Dancer), Joseph N. Welch (debut/Judge Weaver), Brooks West (Mitch Lodwick), Murray Hamilton (Paquette), Orson Bean (Dr. Smith), Russ Brown (Mr. Lemon), Alexander Campbell (Dr. Harcourt), Joseph Kearns (Mr. Burke), Howard McNear (Dr. Dompierre), Ken Lynch (Sgt. Durgo), John Qualen (Sulo), Duke Ellington (Pie Eye), Royal Beal (Sheriff Battisfore), Ned Wever (Dr. Raschid), Jimmy Conlin (final film—d. 1962/ Madigan), Don Russ (Duane Miller), Lloyd LeVasseur, James Waters, Irv Kupcinet, Mrs. Joseph Welch. *D:* Otto Preminger; *P:* Preminger (AAN=Best Picture); *Sc:* (AAN) Wendell Mayes; *Cin:* (AAN-b/w) Sam Leavitt; *Editor:* (AAN) Louis R. Loeffler. (2:40) (video/laserdisc) Courtroom drama of a soldier accused of murder and the lawyer who defends him. It broke ground with explicit dialogue heretofore unheard on the American movie screen. *Film Daily* voted it "Best Film of the Year," while on the "10 Best" list of the NBR it placed #3 and on the same list of the *New York Times* it placed #5. One of the 26 top-grossing films of 1958-59, the New York Film Critics had it in nomination for "Best Film" while they voted Stewart "Best Actor" and Mayes "Best Writer."

Stewart also received a "Best Actor" award at the Venice Film Festival, while the British Academy Awards also had it in nomination. Filmed on location in the Ishpemming-Marquette area of Michigan, it was based on the book by Robert Traver (a pseudonym of Michigan Supreme Court Justice John D. Voelker).

Anatomy of a Syndicate *see* **The Big Operator**

68. And Now Tomorrow (Westminister Prods.; 1952). *Cast:* Don DeFore, Earle Hodgins, Louise Arthur, Morris Ankrum, Stanley Andrews, Lumsden Hare. *D:* William Watson. (1:10) A low budget independent production.

69. Androcles and the Lion (RKO; 1952). *Cast:* Jean Simmons (U.S. debut), Alan Young, Victor Mature, Robert Newton, Maurice Evans, Elsa Lanchester, Reginald Gardiner, Gene Lockhart, Alan Mowbray, Noel Willman, John Hoyt, Jim Backus, Lowell Gilmore, Jackie (lion who received a #3 PATSY in 1954). *D:* Chester Erskine; *P:* Gabriel Pascal; *Adapt: & Sc:* Erskine, Ken Englund (loosely based on the play by George Bernard Shaw). (1:38) (video) Comedy set in ancient Rome of Christian, Androcles, who pulls a thorn from a lion's paw. The kindness is later repaid in the Roman arena where Christians and lions are to be the day's entertainment.

70. Andy Hardy Comes Home (MGM/Fryman Enterprises; 1958). *Cast:* Mickey Rooney (title role), Patricia Breslin, Fay Holden (final film—ret.), Cecilia Parker (final film—ret.), Sara Haden (final film—ret.), Teddy Rooney, Johnny Weissmuller, Jr., Pat Cawley, Joey Forman, Jerry Colonna, Vaughn Taylor, Frank Ferguson, William Leslie, Tom Dugan, Jeanne Baird, Gina Gillespie, Jimmy Bates, Donald Barry + *via film clip flashbacks:* Judy Garland, Lana Turner, Esther Williams. *D:* Howard W. Koch; *P:* Red Doff; *Sc:* Edward Everett Hutshing, Robert Morris Donley. (1:20) A low budget independently produced Hardy family reunion film (sans Judge Hardy—deceased), as Andy returns to Carvel with his family. Based on characters created by Aurania Rouverol.

71. Angel Face (RKO; 1952). *Cast:* Robert Mitchum, Jean Simmons, Mona Freeman, Herbert Marshall, Leon Ames, Barbara O'Neil, Kenneth Tobey, Raymond Greenleaf, Griff Barnett, Robert Gist, Morgan Farley, Jim Backus, Bess Flowers, Alex Gerry, Gertrude Astor. *D: & P:* Otto Preminger; *St:* Chester Erskine; *Sc:* Frank Nugent, Oscar Millard. (1:31) Melodramatic thriller of a psychotic murderess and her evil deeds.

Angels and the Pirates (G.B. title) *see* **Angels in the Outfield**

72. Angels in the Outfield (MGM; 1951). *Cast:* Paul Douglas, Janet Leigh, Keenan Wynn, Donna Corcoran, Spring Byington, Ellen Corby, Lewis Stone, Bruce Bennett, James Whitmore (voice only), Marvin Kaplan, Jeff Richards John Gallaudet, King Donovan, Don Haggerty, Paul Salata, Fred Graham, John McKee, Patrick J. Molyneaux. *D: & P:* Clarence Brown; *Sc:* George Wells, Dorothy Kingsley (based on a radio play by Richard Conlin). (1:42) (video) Family oriented comedy-fantasy of a little girl's prayers that bring divine intervention to the Pittsburgh Pirates baseball team. Remade in 1994. (G.B. title: *Angels and the Pirates*) Note: President Dwight D. Eisenhower's favorite film, as he acknowledged in an interview.

73. The Angry Red Planet (American International/Sino Prods.; 1959). *Cast:* Gerald Mohr, Nora Hayden, Les Tremayne, Jack Kruschen, Paul Hahn, J. Edward McKinley, Tom Daly, Edward Innes. *D:* Ib Melchior (directorial debut); *P: & St:* Sid Pink; *As.P:* Lou Perloff; *Sc:* Pink, Melchior. (1:23) (video/laserdisc) Science fiction of three men and a woman who make the first trip to Mars and find a hostile environment inhabited by various menacing lifeforms. In Eastmancolor and Cinemagic, the latter, an effect which creates a negative film effect with figures appearing transparent to pinkish red.

74. The Animal World (Warner/Windsor; 1956). *D:-P: & Sc:* Irwin Allen; *Narrators:* Theodore Von Eltz (final film), John Storm; *F/X:* Arthur S. Rhodes. (1:20) Documentary feature in technicolor covering 80,000,000 years of evolution in the animal kingdom, from one-celled sea creatures to the present day species. A 12-minute sequence covering dinosaurs in the prehistoric era was done by Ray Harryhausen.

75. Anna Lucasta (United Artists/Longridge; 1958). *Cast:* Eartha Kitt (title role), Sammy Davis, Jr., Frederick O'Neal, Henry Scott, Rex Ingram, Georgia Burke, James

Edwards, Rosetta Lenoire, Isabelle Cooley, Alvin Childress, Claire Lebya, John Proctor, Charles Swain, Isaac Jones, Wally Earl. *D:* Arnold Laven; *P:* Sidney Harmon; *Sc:* Philip Yordan; *Song:* "That's Anna" Elmer Bernstein–Sammy Cahn (sung by Sammy Davis, Jr.). (1:37) Melodrama of a waterfront prostitute who marries a college boy who is unaware of her profession—and then her past catches up with her. Based on the 1944 Broadway play (originally written by Philip Yordan in 1936) which had an all-black cast. Previously filmed in 1949 by Columbia with an all-white cast. O'Neal, Scott, Burke, Lenoire, Cooley, Childress and Proctor repeat their Broadway roles.

76. An Annapolis Story (Allied Artists; 1955). *Cast:* John Derek, Diana Lynn, Kevin McCarthy, Alvy Moore, Pat Conway, L.Q. Jones, John Kirby, Don Haggerty, Barbara Brown, Betty Lou Gerson, Robert Osterloh, Fran Bennett, John Doucette, Don Kennedy, Tom Harmon. *D:* Don Siegel; *P:* Walter Mirisch; *St:* Dan Ullman; *Sc:* Ullman, Geoffrey Homes [Daniel Mainwaring]. (1:21) (video) Korean conflict drama of two brothers whose relationship becomes strained when they both fall for the same girl. (G.B. title: *The Blue and the Gold*)

77. Annie Get Your Gun (MGM; 1950). *Cast:* Betty Hutton (who received *Photoplay* Gold Medal Award/Annie Oakley—replacing Judy Garland who suffered a complete mental and physical collapse), Howard Keel (an American citizen, making his first U.S. film after making his film debut in a 1948 British film/Frank Butler—a role which propelled him to stardom), Louis Calhern (Buffalo Bill—replacing Frank Morgan who died during production), J. Carrol Naish (Sitting Bull), Edward Arnold (Pawnee Bill), Keenan Wynn (Charlie Davenport), Benay Venuta (Dolly Tate), Clinton Sundberg (Foster Wilson), James H. Harrison (Mac), Bradley Mora (Little Jake), Diana Dick (Nellie), Susan Odin (Jessie), Eleanor Brown (Minnie), Chief Yowlachie (Little Horse), Anne O'Neal (Miss Willoughby), Evelyn Beresford (Queen Victoria), Marjorie Wood (Constance), Elizabeth Flournoy (Helen), Mae Clarke Langdon (Mrs. Adams), Frank Wilcox (Mr. Clay), Andre Charlot (President Loubet of France), Nino Pipitone (King Victor Emmanuel), John Mylong (Kaiser Wilhelm II), Robert Malcolm, Lee Tung Foo, William Tannen, John Hamilton, William "Bill" Hall, Edward Earle, Carl Sepulveda, Carol Henry, Fred Gilman. *D:* George Sidney (replacing Charles Walters, who in turn replaced the original director, Busby Berkeley); *P:* Arthur Freed; *Sc:* Sidney Sheldon; *Cin:* (AAN-color) Charles Rosher; *ASD:* (AAN-color) Cedric Gibbons, Paul Groesse (art directors), Edwin B. Willis, Richard A. Pefferle (sets); *Editor:* (AAN) James E. Newcom; *Music:* (AA-musical) Adolph Deutsch, Roger Edens; *Songs:* "Colonel Buffalo Bill," "Doin' What Comes Naturally," "The Girl That I Marry," "You Can't Get a Man with a Gun," "There's No Business Like Show Business," "My Defenses Are Down," "I'm an Indian Too," "I Got the Sun in the Morning," "Anything You Can Do" and "They Say It's Wonderful." (1:47) (video) The cinematic version (which suffered many production setbacks before getting to the screen) of the hit Broadway production by Dorothy & Herbert Fields with songs by Irving Berlin. Annie Oakley sets her sights on sharpshooter Frank Butler while they travel with Buffalo Bill's Wild West Show. One of the 28 top-grossing films of 1949-50 as well as one of MGM's biggest grossing musicals to date. Technicolor.

78. Another Time, Another Place (Paramount/Lanturn Prods.; 1958). *Cast:* Lana Turner, Barry Sullivan, Glynis Johns, Sean Connery (U.S. debut), Sidney James, Terence Longdon, Doris Hare, Martin Stephens, Robin Bailey, Julian Somers, John LeMesurier, Cameron Hall, Jane Welsh, Bill Frazer. *D:* Lewis Allen; *P:* Joseph Kaufman; *As.P:* Smedley Aston; *Sc:* Stanley Mann; *Title song:* Jay Livingston–Ray Evans. (1:38) (video) World War II drama (set in 1945 London) of an American newspaperwoman who suffers a nervous breakdown following the death of her married lover and establishes a relationship with his widow. Filmed on location in England, this U.S.A./U.K. co-production (in VistaVision) was based on the novel *Weep No More* by Lenore Coffee. Note: It was following her work on this film, that on her return to Hollywood, Turner's boy friend Johnny Stompanato was stabbed to death by her daughter, Cheryl, which made timely headlines for the tabloids.

79. Anything Can Happen (Paramount/Seaton-Perlberg; 1952). *Cast:* Jose Ferrer, Kim Hunter, Kurt Kasznar, Eugenie Leontovich, Oscar Beregei, Nick Dennis, Oscar Karlweiss, Mikhail Rasumny, Gloria Marlowe, Otto Waldis, Alex Danaroff, Natasha Lytess. *D:* George Seaton; *P:* William Perlberg; *Sc:* Seaton, George Oppenheimer. (1:47) Fact-based comedy of the trials and tribulations of a Russian immigrant family trying to get used to the American way of life. Based on the 1945 book by George and Helen Papashvily.

80. Anything Goes (Paramount; 1956). *Cast:* Bing Crosby (in his final film for Paramount), Donald O'Connor, Jeanmaire, Mitzi Gaynor, Phil Harris, Kurt Kasznar, Walter Sande, Richard Erdman, Archer MacDonald, Argentina Brunetti, Alma Macrorie, Dorothy Neumann, James Griffith. *D:* Robert Lewis; *P:* Robert Emmett Dolan; *Sc:* Sidney Sheldon; *Songs:* "All Through the Night," "You're the Top," "I Get a Kick Out of You," "Blow, Gabriel, Blow," "Anything Goes," "It's De-Lovely" (Cole Porter) with three additional songs by Jimmy Van Heusen and Sammy Cahn. (1:46) A musical reworking of the 1936 production by this studio, based on the play by P.G. Wodehouse and Guy Bolton, revised by Russell Crouse and Howard Lindsey with songs by Cole Porter. The plotline concerns two Broadway singers who each hire a leading lady to star in their next show. Technicolor and VistaVision.

81. Apache (United Artists/Hecht-Lancaster/Linden Prods.; 1954). *Cast:* Burt Lancaster (Massai), Jean Peters (Nalinle), John McIntire (Al Sieber), Charles [Bronson] Buchinsky (Hondo), John Dehner (Weddle), Paul Guilfoyle (Santos), Ian MacDonald (Glagg), Walter Sande (Lt. Col. Beck), Morris Ankrum (Dawson), Monte Blue (final film—ret./Geronimo). *D:* Robert Aldrich; *P:* Harold Hecht; *Sc:* James R. Webb. (1:31) (video) Fact-based western in technicolor of one Indian's stand against the encroaching whites. Taken from the 1950 novel *Bronco Apache* by Paul I. Wellman, it became one of the 25 top-grossing films of 1953-54.

82. Apache Ambush (Columbia; 1955). *Cast:* Bill Williams, Richard Jaeckel, Alex Montoya, Movita, Adele August, Tex Ritter, Ray Corrigan, Ray Teal, Don C. Harvey, James Griffith, George Chandler, Harry Lauter, Forrest Lewis, Bill Hale, Robert C. Foulk, James Flavin, George Keymas, Victor Millan, Kermit Maynard. *D:* Fred F. Sears; *P:* Wallace MacDonald; *St:* & *Sc:* David Lang. (1:08) Western of Union and Confederate soldiers in the days of the Civil War who discover a cache of repeating rifles to be used in the overthrow of Texas.

83. Apache Country (Columbia/Gene Autry Prods.; 1952). *Cast:* Gene Autry, Pat Buttram, Carolina Cotton, Harry Lauter, Mary Scott, Sydney Mason, Francis X. Bushman, Gregg Barton, Tom London, Byron Foulger, Mickey Simpson, Iron Eyes Cody, Frank Matts, The Cass County Boys, Tony Whitecloud's Jemez Indians. *D:* George Archainbaud; *P:* Armand Schaefer; *St:* & *Sc:* Norman S. Hall. (1:02) A government man investigates when a gang of outlaws are putting the blame on Indians for their illegal activities. Gene sings "Melt Your Cold, Cold Heart." Photographed in Sepiatone.

84. Apache Drums (Universal-International; 1951). *Cast:* Stephen McNally, Coleen Gray, Willard Parker, Arthur Shields, James Griffith, Armando Silvestre, Georgia Backus, Clarence Muse, James Best, Ray Bennett, Ruthlelma Stevens, Chinto Gusman. *D:* Hugo Fregonese; *P:* Val Lewton; *Sc:* David Chandler. (1:15) Technicolor western of an impending Indian attack on the town of Spanish Boot. Based on the story "Stand at Spanish Boot" by Harry Brown. Note: The final work of producer Val Lewton, who died shortly after completing this film.

85. Apache Territory (Columbia/Rorvic; 1958). *Cast:* Rory Calhoun, Barbara Bates (final film—ret.), John Dehner, Carolyn Craig, Thomas Pittman, Leo Gordon, Myron Healey, Francis DeSales, Frank DeKova, Reg Parton, Bob Woodward, Fred Krone. *D:* Ray Nazarro; *P:* Rory Calhoun, Victor M. Orsatti; *Adapt:* Frank Moss; *Sc:* Charles R. Marion, George W. George. (1:15) White settlers are being attacked by Indians in this western based on the novel *The Last Stand at Papago Wells* by Louis L'Amour. Eastmancolor.

86. Apache War Smoke (MGM; 1952). *Cast:* Gilbert Roland, Robert Horton (film debut), Glenda Farrell, Gene Lockhart, Bobby Blake, Barbara Ruick, Myron Healey, Patricia Tiernan, Henry [Harry] Morgan, Hank Worden, Emmett Lynn, Argentina Brunetti, Douglass Dumbrille. *D:* Harold F. Kress; *P:* Hayes Goetz; *Sc:* Jerry Davis. (1:07) Programmer western involving a stagecoach robbery and an Indian attack on a stagecoach relay station. A remake of *Apache Trail* (MGM; 1942), it was based on *Stage Station* by Ernest Haycox.

87. Apache Warrior (20th Century–Fox/Regal Films; 1957). *Cast:* Keith Larsen (The Apache Kid), Jim Davis, Rudolfo Acosta, John Miljan, Eddie Little Sky, Michael Carr,

George Keymas, Lane Bradford, Eugenia Paul, Damian O'Flynn, Ray Kellogg, Allan Nixon, Karl Davis, Boyd Stockman, Dehl Berti, Nick Thompson, David Carlisle. *D:* Elmo Williams; *P:* Plato Skouras; *St:* Carroll Young, Kurt Neumann; *Sc:* Young, Neumann, Eric Norden. (1:13) Western of a former Apache Indian scout with a personal vendetta. Purported to be based on the exploits of real-life outlaw, The Apache Kid. Reglascope.

88. Apache Woman (American Releasing Corp./Golden State Prods.; 1955). *Cast:* Lloyd Bridges, Joan Taylor, Lance Fuller, Morgan Jones, Paul Birch, Paul Dubov, Jonathan Haze, Dick Miller, Chester Conklin, Lou Place, Gene Marlowe, Jean Howell. *D: & P:* Roger Corman; *Sc:* Lou Rusoff. (1:23) (video) Low budget western involving the investigation into allegations that reservation Indians are responsible for several deaths. Corman's second western. Released theatrically in color.

89. Appointment in Honduras (RKO; 1953). *Cast:* Glenn Ford, Ann Sheridan, Zachary Scott, Rudolfo Acosta, Jack Elam, Ric Roman, Rico Alaniz, Paul Zaramba, Stanley Andrews. *D:* Jacques Tourneur; *P:* Benedict Bogeaus; *St:* Mario Silveira, Jack Cornall; *Sc:* Karen DeWolf. (1:19) (video) An adventurer braves the perils of the jungles of Honduras to deliver money to an exiled political official. Technicolor/Scenic-Scope.

Appointment with a Shadow (1957) (G.B. title) *see* **The Midnight Story**

90. Appointment with a Shadow (Universal-International; 1958). *Cast:* George Nader, Joanna Moore, Brian Keith, Virginia Field, Frank DeKova, Stephen Chase. *D:* Richard Carlson (directorial debut); *P:* Howie Horwitz; *Sc:* Alec Coppel, Norman Jolley. (1:13) Low budget melodrama of one day in the life of an alcoholic news reporter who witnesses a murder. Based on an *Argosy* magazine article titled "If I Should Die" by Hugh Pentecost. CinemaScope.

91. Appointment with Danger (Paramount; 1949-51). *Cast:* Alan Ladd, Phyllis Calvert, Paul Stewart, Jan Sterling, Jack Webb, Stacy Harris, Henry [Harry] Morgan, Fritz Feld, George J. Lewis, David Wolfe, Dan Riss, Harry Antrim, Geraldine Wall, Paul Lees. *D:* Lewis Allen; *P:* Robert Fellows; *Sc:* Richard Breen, Warren Duff. (1:29) Hit melodrama of a nun who is the only witness to the murder of a postal inspector. Produced in 1949 as part of a stockpile of Alan Ladd films for later release, as Ladd had all intentions of leaving the studio when his contract was up.

92. April in Paris (Warner; 1952). *Cast:* Doris Day, Ray Bolger, Claude Dauphin, Eve Miller, George Givot, Paul Harvey, Herbert Farjeon, Wilson Millar, Raymond Largay, John Alvin, Jack Lomas. *D:* David Butler; *P:* William Jacobs; *St: & Sc:* Jack Rose, Melville Shavelson; *Songs include:* "It Must Be Good," "That's What Makes Paris Paree," "The Place You Hold in My Heart" Sammy Cahn–Vernon Duke; "April in Paris" E.Y. Harburg–Duke. (1:41) (video-laserdisc) Technicolor musical-comedy of a diplomat headed for France aboard an ocean liner to better relations between that country and the U.S.A.

93. April Love (20th Century–Fox; 1957). *Cast:* Pat Boone (Nick Conover), Shirley Jones (Liz Templeton), Dolores Michaels (Fran), Arthur O'Connell (Jed), Matt Crowley (Dan Templeton), Jeanette Nolan (Henrietta), Brad Jackson (Al Turner). *D:* Henry Levin; *P:* David Weisbart; *Sc:* Winston Miller; *Title song:* (AAN) Paul Francis Webster, Sammy Fain. (1:39) Teen romance with songs of a city boy's move to Kentucky, the land of horse racing. The title song was a big hit in this remake of *Home in Indiana* (Fox; 1944) which was based on the novel *The Phantom Filly* by George Agnew Chamberlain. DeLuxe color and CinemaScope.

94. Arctic Flight (Monogram; 1952). *Cast:* Wayne Morris, Lola Albright, Alan Hale, Jr., Carol Thurston, Phil Tead, Tom Richards, Anthony "Tony" Garsen, Kenneth MacDonald, Paul Bryar, Dale Van Sickel. *D:* Lew Landers; *P:* Lindsley Parsons; *Sc:* Robert F. Hill, George Bricker (1:18) Adventure melodrama of a bush pilot in Alaska who has his plane chartered by a communist spy posing as a big game hunter. Based on the story "Shadow of the Curtain" by Ewing Scott.

95. Arctic Fury (1954). A feature documentary which is also known under the title *The Living North*, its 1959 re-issue title.

96. Arena (MGM; 1953). *Cast:* Gig Young, Jean Hagen, Polly Bergen, Henry [Harry] Morgan, Barbara Lawrence, Robert Horton, Lee Aaker, Lee Van Cleef, Marilee Phelps, Jim Hayward, George Wallace, Stuart Randall, Morris Ankrum. *D:* Richard Fleischer; *P:* & *St:*

Arthur M. Loew, Jr.; *Sc:* Harold Jack Bloom. (1:23) Western soap opera of an egotistical rodeo star whose marriage is headed for the rocks. Rodeo footage comes from Fiesta de los Vaqueros, an annual event held in Tucson, Arizona. 3-D and Anscocolor.

97. The Arizona Cowboy (Republic; 1950). *Cast:* Rex Allen (film debut), Teala Loring, Gordon Jones, Minerva Urecal, James Cardwell, Roy Barcroft, Stanley Andrews, Harry V. Cheshire, Edmund Cobb, Joseph Crehan, Steve Darrell, Douglas H. Lloyd, Lane Bradford. *D:* R.G. Springsteen; *P:* Franklin Adreon; *As.P:* Melville Tucker; *St:* & *Sc:* Bradford Ropes. (1:07) (video) Western with songs of a World War II veteran who becomes a top rodeo star. Allen's first of 31 series westerns of the early '50s. Note: The title of this film became Rex Allen's nickname.

98. Arizona Manhunt (Republic; 1951). *Cast:* Michael Chapin, Eilene Janssen, James Bell, Lucille Barkley, Roy Barcroft, John Baer, Hazel Shaw, Harry Harvey, Stuart Randall, Ted Cooper. *D:* Fred C. Brannon; *P:* Rudy Ralston; *Sc:* William Lively. (1:00) Entry in the short-lived *Rough Ridin' Kids* series for this studio. A group of kids who help roundup some outlaws and reform an outlaw's daughter. Originally ran on the bottom of a double bill with *The Sea Hornet* (q.v.).

Arizona Mission *see* **Gun the Man Down**

99. Arizona Territory (Monogram; 1950). *Cast:* Whip Wilson, Andy Clyde, Nancy Saunders, Dennis Moore, John Merton, Carl Mathews, Carol Henry, Bud Osborne, Frank Austin, Ted Adams. *D:* Wallace W. Fox; *P:* Vincent M. Fennelly; *St:* & *Sc:* Adele Buffington. (0:56) Whip Wilson series western with a counterfeiting plot.

100. Armored Car Robbery (RKO; 1950). *Cast:* Charles McGraw, Adele Jergens, William Talman, Douglas Fowley, Steve Brodie, Don McGuire; Don Haggerty, James Flavin, Gene Evans. *D:* Richard Fleischer; *P:* Herman Schlom; *St:* Robert Angus, Robert Leeds; *Sc:* Earl Felton, Gerald Drayson Adams. (1:07) B budget crime-melodrama of a cop bent on getting the gang that pulled off an armored car robbery and killed his partner.

101. Army Bound (Monogram; 1951). *Cast:* Stanley Clements, Karen Sharpe, Steve Brodie, John Fontaine, Harry Hayden, Lela Bliss, Gil Stratton, Jr., Danny Welton, Mona Knox, Jean Dean, Louis Tomei, Joey Ray. *D:* Paul Landres; *P:* Ben Schwalb; *St:* & *Sc:* Al Martin. (1:01) Low budget drama of a race car driver, drafted into the army who finds his commanding officer was once his rival.

Army Capers (G.B. title) *see* **The WAC from Walla Walla**

102. Around the World in 80 Days (United Artists/Michael Todd Co., Inc.; 1956). *Cast:* David Niven (Phileas Fogg), Cantinflas (Passepartout), Robert Newton (final film—d. 1956)/Mr. Fix), Shirley MacLaine (Aouda), Charles Boyer (Monsieur Grasse), Joe E. Brown (stationmaster), Martine Carol (tourist), John Carradine (Col. Proctor Stamp), Charles Coburn (clerk), Ronald Colman (railway official), Melville Cooper (steward), Noel Coward (Hesketh-Baggott), Finlay Currie (whist partner), Reginald Denny (police chief), Andy Devine (first mate), Marlene Dietrich (hostess), Luis Miguel Dominguin (bullfighter), Fernandel (coachman), Sir John Gielgud (Foster), Hermione Gingold (sportin' lady), Jose Greco (Spanish dancer), Sir Cedric Hardwicke (Sir Francis Gromarty), Trevor Howard (Fallentin), Glynis Johns (companion), Buster Keaton (conductor), Evelyn Keyes (flirt), Beatrice Lillie (revivalist), Peter Lorre (steward), Edmund Lowe (engineer), Victor McLaglen (helmsman), Col. Tim McCoy (commander), A.E. Mathews (club member), Mike Mazurki (character), John Mills (cabby), Alan Mowbray (consul), Robert Morley (Ralph), Edward R. Murrow (narrator), Jack Oakie (captain), George Raft (bouncer), Gilbert Roland (Achmed Abdullah), Cesar Romero (henchman), Frank Sinatra (piano player), Red Skelton (drunk), Ronald Squire (member), Basil Sydney (member), Harcourt Williams (Hinshaw), Ava Gardner (spectator), Barry Norton (final film—d. 1956). *D:* (AAN) Michael Anderson (U.S. debut); *P:* (AA-Best Picture) Michael Todd; *As.P:* William Cameron Menzies; *Adaptation* & *Sc:* (AA + "Best Writing" by the New York Film Critics) James Poe, John Farrow, S.J. Perelman; *Cin:* (AA-color) Lionel Linden; *ASD:* (AAN-color) James W. Sullivan, Ken Adams (art directors), Ross J. Dowd (sets); *Music:* (AA) Victor Young; *Costumes:* (AAN-color) Miles White; *Editing:* (AA) Gene Ruggiero, Paul Weatherwax. (2:47) (video) Based on Jules Verne's novel, this big-budgeted extravaganza, which utilized almost

70,000 extras, tells of Victorian Phileas Fogg who makes a wager that he can travel around the world and return in 80 days. Notable for the cameo appearances of 44 name stars, it became one of the 24 top-grossing films of 1956-57. Also notable is Georges Méliès' 1902 version of *A Trip to the Moon* (by Verne) in 30 scenes that had a running time of 845 ft. of film. Voted "Best Picture of the Year" by the New York Film Critics, the NBR and *Film Daily* (in 1957), it also placed #8 on the "10 Best" list of the *New York Times*. Filmed on location in London, Southern France, the Mediterranean, India, Hong Kong, Pakistan, Siam (now Thailand), Japan, Spain, Mexico, Egypt and San Francisco and Chatsworth, CA. in the U.S.A. Remade as a TV miniseries. Todd-AO and Eastmancolor.

103. Arrow in the Dust (Allied Artists; 1954). *Cast:* Sterling Hayden, Coleen Gray, Keith Larsen, Tom Tully, Jimmy Wakely (who also sings "The Weary Stranger"), Tudor Owen, Lee Van Cleef, John Pickard, Carleton Young. *D:* Lesley Selander; *P:* Hayes Goetz; *Sc:* Don Martin; *Song:* Jimmy Wakely. (1:20) Technicolor western of a deserting cavalry soldier who assumes the identity of a deceased officer and saves a wagon train from Indians. Based on the story "Platt River Gamble" by L.L. Foreman.

104. Arrowhead (Paramount; 1953). *Cast:* Charlton Heston, Jack Palance, Katy Jurado, Brian Keith, Mary Sinclair, Milburn Stone, Richard Shannon, Lewis Martin, Frank DeKova, Robert Wilke, Peter Coe, John Pickard, Kyle James, Pat Hogan, Mike Ragan [aka: Holly Bane], Chick Hannon, James Burke. *D:* Charles Marquis Warren; *P:* Nat Holt; *Sc:* Warren. (1:45) (video/laserdisc) Hit western of the U.S. Cavalry vs. Apaches in the southwestern United States. Based on W.R. Burnett's *Adobe Walls*, it was photographed in Technicolor.

105. Arson for Hire (Allied Artists/Wm. F. Broidy; 1959). *Cast:* Steve Brodie, Lyn Thomas, Tom Hubbard, Jason Johnson, Frank Scannell, Wendy Wilde, John Merrick, Lari Laine, Antony Carbone, Robert Riordan, Walter Reed, Reed Howes, Lyn Osborn, Frank Richards, Ben Frommer, Lester Dorr, Florence Useem. *D:* Thor Brooks; *P:* William F. Broidy; *As.P:* Erwin Yessin; *St:* & *Sc:* Tom Hubbard. (1:07) Programmer crime melodrama of the unmasking of members of a ruthless arson ring.

106. Artists and Models (Paramount; 1955). *Cast:* Dean Martin, Jerry Lewis, Shirley MacLaine, Dorothy Malone, Eva Gabor, Anita Ekberg, Eddie Mayehoff, Jack Elam, George Winslow, Herbert Rudley, Richard Shannon, Richard Webb, Alan Lee, Kathleen Freeman, Art Baker (himself), Emory Parnell, Carleton Young, Nick Castle. *D:* Frank Tashlin; *P:* Hal B. Wallis; *Play:* Michael Davidson, Norman Lessing; *Adapt:* Don McGuire; *Sc:* Hal Kanter, Herbert Baker, Tashlin; *Songs:* "Inamorata," "Lucky Song," "You Look So Familiar" and "Why You Pretend" Harry Warren–Jack Brooks. (1:49) (video/laserdisc) Comedy with songs of a cartoonist who gets his ideas from his pal's sleep-talking through his dreams. Technicolor and VistaVision.

107. As You Were! (Lippert/Spartan-Rand L Prods.; 1951). *Cast:* William Tracy, Joe Sawyer, Russell Hicks, John Ridgely, Sondra Rodgers, Joan Vohs, Margie Liszt, Rolland Morris, Ed(gar) Dearing, Chris Drake, Maris Wrixon, Roger McGee, John Parrish, Ruth Lee, Frank Faylen, Harold Goodwin. *D:* Fred L. Guiol; *P:* Hal Roach, Jr.; *St:* & *Sc:* Edward E. Seabrook. (0:57) or 1:08) Comedy with the working title of "Present Arms" of an ex–G.I. with a photographic memory who re-enlists. This film utilizes the characters of Sgt. Doubleday (Tracy) and Sgt. Ames (Sawyer), characters created in several streamliners by Hal Roach, Sr. in the 1940s. Followed by a sequel *Mr. Walkie Talkie* (q.v.).

108. As Young as We Are (Paramount/Wm. Alland Prods.; 1958). *Cast:* Robert Harland, Pippa Scott, Linda Watkins, Majel Barrett, Beverly Long, Barry Atwater, Carla Hoffman, Ty [Hardin] Hungerford, Ellen Corby, Harald Dyrenforth, Ross Elliott, Mack Williams. *D:* Bernard Girard; *P:* William Alland; *St:* Meyer Dolinsky; *Sc:* Dolinsky, Alland; *Title song:* Harold Barlow (sung by Andy Russell). (1:16) Low budget drama of a small town high school scandal, perpetrated by an affair between a teacher and one of her teenage students.

109. As Young as You Feel (20th Century–Fox; 1951). *Cast:* Monty Woolley, Thelma Ritter, David Wayne, Jean Peters, Clinton Sundberg, Minor Watson, Ludwig Stossel, Renie Riano, Wally Brown, Rusty [Russ] Tamblyn, Roger Moore. *D:* Harmon Jones (debut); *P:* Lamar Trotti; *St:* Paddy Chayefsky; *Sc:* Trotti. (1:17) (video) Comedy of a man's outrage at being forcibly retired at age 65 by the printing company he works for and his extended efforts to get his job back.

110. Ask Any Girl (MGM/Euterpe; 1959). *Cast:* David Niven, Shirley MacLaine (nominated as "Best Actress" by the British Academy Awards), Gig Young, Rod Taylor, Jim Backus, Claire Kelly, Elisabeth Fraser, Dody Heath, Read Morgan, Mickey Shaughnessy, Carmen Phillips, Helen Wallace, Myrna Hansen, Kasey Rogers, Carrol Byron, Norma French, Kathy Reed. *D:* Charles Walters; *P:* Joe Pasternak; *Sc:* George Wells; *Song:* "I'm in the Mood for Love" Jimmy McHugh–Dorothy Fields. (1:41) (video) Hit comedy of a naïve girl who arrives in New York City seeking a husband, only to find that most of the men she meets are far from her expectations. Based on the 1958 novel by Winifred Wolfe. Metrocolor and CinemaScope.

111. The Asphalt Jungle (MGM; 1950). *Cast:* Sterling Hayden (Dix Handley), Louis Calhern (Alonzo D. Emmerich), Jean Hagen (Doll Donovan), James Whitmore (Gus Minissi), Sam Jaffe (AAN + "Best Actor" at the Venice Film Festival/Doc Erwin Riedenschneider), John McIntire (Police Commissioner Hardy), Marc Lawrence (Cobby), Barry Kelley (Lt. Ditrich), Anthony Caruso (Louis Ciavelli), Teresa Celli (Maria Ciavelli), Marilyn Monroe (Angela Phinlay), William Davis (Timmons), Dorothy Tree (May Emmerich), Brad Dexter (film debut/Bob Brannon), Alex Gerry (Maxwell), Thomas Browne Henry (James X. Connery), James Seay (Janocek), Don Haggerty (Andrews), Henry Rowland (Franz Schurz), Helene Stanley (Jeannie), Raymond Roe (Tallboy), Charles "Chuck" Courtney (Red), Tim Ryan (Jack, the police clerk), Strother Martin (film debut/Karl Anton Smith), Henry Corden (William Doldy), David Hydes (Evans), Eloise Hardt (Vivian), Albert Morin (Eddie Donato), Jean Carter, Ralph Dunn, Pat Flaherty, Frank Cady, Benny Burt, Fred Graham, Saul Gorss, William Washington, Wilson Wood, Jack Warden (film debut). *D:* (AAN + "Best Director" by the NBR) John Huston; *P:* Arthur Hornblow, Jr.; *Sc:* (AAN) Huston, Ben Maddow; *Cin:* (AAN-b/w) Harold Rosson. (1:52) (video/laserdisc) Critically acclaimed "caper" film, involving the planning and execution of a robbery. Based on a story by W.R. Burnett, it was in nomination at the British Academy Awards and was also in nomination for "Best Film" by the New York Film Critics. The NBR and the *New York Times* gave it a #3 and #4 placement, respectively, on their "10 Best" lists. Computer-colored by Turner Entertainment, it has officially been remade three times by MGM studio: *The Badlanders* (q.v.), *Cairo* (1963) and *Cool Breeze* (1972).

Assault of the Rebel Girls *see* **Cuban Rebel Girls**

112. Assignment—Paris (Columbia; 1952). *Cast:* Dana Andrews, Marta Toren, George Sanders, Audrey Totter, Sandro Giglio, Donald Randolph, Herbert Berghof, Ben Astar, Willis Bouchey, Earl Lee, Maurice Doner, Leon Askin (film debut), Paul Hoffman, Jay Adler, Mari Blanchard, Peter Votrian, Georgianna Wulff, Don Gibson, Joe Forte, Don Kohler, Hanne Axman, Paul Javor, Paul Birch (film debut). *D:* Robert Parrish; *P:* Samuel Marx, Jerry Bresler; *Adapt:* Walter Goetz, Jack Palmer White; *Sc:* William Bowers. (1:24) An American newspaperman uncovers a communist conspiracy in Hungary. Based on the 1952 book *Trial by Terror* by Paul and Pauline Gallico, it was filmed on location in Paris.

113. The Astounding She-Monster (American International/Hollywood Intl.; 1958). *Cast:* Robert Clarke, Kenne Duncan, Marilyn Harvey, Jeanne Tatum, Shirley Kilpatrick (title role), Ewing Brown. *D: & P:* Ronnie Ashcroft; *St:* & *Sc:* Frank Hall. (1:00) (video) Ultra low budget sci-fi of a female space visitor who meets up with earthlings at a secluded ski resort. The film which had the working title of "The Astounding She Creature" has a following. (G.B. title: *The Mysterious Invader*)

114. At Gunpoint (Allied Artists; 1955). *Cast:* Fred MacMurray, Dorothy Malone, Walter Brennan, Tommy Rettig, Skip Homeier, John Qualen, Harry Shannon, Whit Bissell, Irving Bacon, Jack Lambert, Frank Ferguson, James Anderson, John Pickard, Charles Morton, Anabel Shaw, Rick Vallin, Kim Charney, Mimi Gibson, James Griffith, Harry Lauter, Byron Foulger, Keith Richards, Lyle Latell, Barbara Woodell, Gertrude Astor, Harry Strang. *D:* Alfred Werker; *P:* Vincent M. Fennelly; *St:* & *Sc:* Daniel B. Ullman. (1:21) (video) Western, in Technicolor, of a storekeeper who kills a holdup man, only to find himself a target of the victim's brother and deserted by everyone in town except his family. (G.B. title: *Gunpoint!*)

115. At Sword's Point (RKO; 1951). *Cast:*

Cornel Wilde, Maureen O'Hara, Robert Douglas, Gladys Cooper, June Clayworth, Dan O'Herlihy, Alan Hale, Jr., Blanche Yurka, Nancy Gates, Edmund Breon (final film—d. 1951), Peter Miles, George Petrie, Moroni Olsen, Boyd Davis, Holmes Herbert, Lucien Littlefield, Claude Dunkin. *D:* Lewis Allen; *P:* Sid Rogell; *St:* Aubrey Wisberg, Jack Pollexfen; *Sc:* Walter Ferris, Joseph Hoffman. (1:21) (video/laserdisc) Technicolor costume swashbuckler involving the offspring of the Three Musketeers who are out to eliminate some royal skullduggery. (G.B. title: *Sons of the Musketeers*)

116. At War with the Army (Paramount/York Picture Corp.–Screen Associates; 1950). *Cast:* Dean Martin (starring debut/Sgt. Vic Puccinelli), Jerry Lewis (starring debut/Pfc. Korwin), Mike Kellin (Sgt. McVey), Jimmy Dundee (Eddie), Polly Bergen (film debut/Helen Palmer), Angela Greene (Mrs. Caldwell, Jean Ruth (Millie), Dick Stabile (Pokey), Tommy Farrell (Corp. Clark), Frank Hyers (Corp. Shaughnessy), Dan Dayton (Sgt. Miller), William Mendrek (Capt. Caldwell), Kenneth Forbes (Lt. Davenport), Paul Livermore (Pvt. Edwards), Ty Perry (Lt. Terray), Douglas Evans, Steven Roberts, Al Negbo, Dewey Robinson, Lee Bennett. *D:* Hal Walker; *Ex.P:* Abner J. Greshler; *P:* Fred W. Finklehoffe; *Sc:* Finklehoffe; *Songs:* "The Navy Gets the Gravy But the Army Gets the Beans," "You and Your Beautiful Eyes" and "Tonda Wanda Hoy" Mack David–Jerry Livingston. (1:33) (video) Service comedy with an army sergeant getting a dumb pfc. to help him out of girl trouble. Based on a play by James B. Allardice, it became one of the 23 top-grossing films of 1950-51.

117. Athena (MGM; 1954). *Cast:* Jane Powell, Debbie Reynolds, Virginia Gibson, Nancy Kilgas, Dolores Starr, Jane Fischer, Cecile Rogers, Edmund Purdom, Vic Damone, Louis Calhern, Evelyn Varden, Linda Christian, Ray Collins, Carl Benton Reid, Howard Wendell, Henry Nakamura, Steve Reeves, Kathleen Freeman, Richard Sabre. *D:* Richard Thorpe; *P:* Joe Pasternak; *Sc:* Leonard Spigelgass, William Ludwig; *Songs:* "Love Can Change the Stars," "Chacun Le Sait," "Venezia," "The Girl Next Door," "Imagine," "I Never Felt Better" and "Vocalize" Hugh Martin–Ralph Blane. (1:35) (video/laserdisc) Romantic musical-comedy centered around a family with seven daughters and a "back to nature" lifestyle. Eastmancolor.

118. The Atomic City (Paramount; 1952). *Cast:* Gene Barry (film debut), Lydia Clarke, Michael Moore, Nancy Gates, Lee Aaker, Milburn Stone, Bert Freed, Frank Cady, Leonard Strong, Houseley Stevenson, Jr., Harry Hausner, John Damler, George M. Lynn, Olan Soule, Anthony Warde. *D:* Jerry Hopper (debut); *P:* Joseph Sistrom; *St:* & *Sc:* (AAN) Sydney Boehm. (1:24) (video) Thriller involving the son of a nuclear scientist, kidnapped by Russians who demand ransom of hydrogen bomb secret papers. Location filming took place at Los Alamos, N.M. atomic energy plant.

119. The Atomic Kid (Republic; 1954). *Cast:* Mickey Rooney, Robert Strauss, Elaine Davis, Bill Goodwin, Whit Bissell, Joey Forman, Hal March, Peter Leeds, Fay Roope, Stanley Adams, Robert E. Keane. *D:* Leslie H. Martinson (debut); *P:* Maurice Duke; *St:* Blake Edwards; *Sc:* Benedict Freeman, John Fenton Murray. (1:26) (video) Comedy of a uranium prospector who survives an atomic detonation because he was eating a peanut butter sandwich.

120. The Atomic Submarine (Allied Artists/Gorham Prods.; 1959). *Cast:* Arthur Franz, Dick Foran, Brett Halsey, Tom Conway, Paul Dubov, Bob Steele, Victor Varconi (final film—ret.), Joi Lansing, Selmer Jackson, Jack Mulhall (final film—ret.), Jean Moorhead, Richard Tyler, Sid Melton, Ken Becker. *D:* Spencer G. Bennet; *P:* Alex Gordon *in association with* Jack Rabin, Irving Block and Jack DeWitt; *Co-P:* Henry Schrage; *Sc:* Orville H. Hampton. (1:12) (video) An atomic submarine, sent to find out what happened to seven other subs and four surface vessels, encounters an underwater flying saucer inhabited by a tentacled alien.

121. Attack! (United Artists/Associates and Aldrich Co., Inc.; 1956). *Cast:* Jack Palance (Lt. Costa), Eddie Albert (Capt. Cooney), Lee Marvin (Col. Bartlett), Robert Strauss (Pvt. Bernstein), Richard Jaeckel (Pvt. Snowden), Buddy Ebsen (Sgt. Tolliver), William Smithers (Lt. Woodruff), Jon Shepodd (Corp. Jackson), Jimmy Goodwin (Pvt. Ricks), Steven Geray (short German), Peter Van Eyck (tall German), Strother Martin (Sgt. Ingersol), Louis Mercier (old Frenchman). *D:* Robert Aldrich; *P:* Aldrich; *Sc:* James Poe. (1:47) "War Is Hell" drama set during World War II's Battle of the Bulge of a company of U.S. soldiers with a cowardly commander. Based on the play *The*

Fragile Fox by Norman Brooks, it was voted "Best Film of the Festival" at the Venice Film Festival, but did not receive "The Golden Lion." One of the 24 top-grossing films of 1956-57.

122. Attack of the Crab Monsters (Allied Artists/Los Altos Prods.; 1957). *Cast:* Richard Garland, Pamela Duncan, Russell Johnson, Leslie Bradley, Mel Welles, Richard Cutting, Beach Dickerson, Tony Miller, Ed Nelson. *D: & P:* Roger Corman; *St:* & *Sc:* Charles Griffith. (1:02) (video) Science fiction of an expedition to a Pacific isle to study the effect of Atomic radiation, who find two giant crabs have eaten and absorbed the knowledge of the previous expedition.

123. Attack of the 50-Ft. Woman (Allied Artists/Woolner Bros.; 1958). *Cast:* Allison Hayes, John Hudson, Roy Gordon, Yvette Vickers, George Douglas, Otto Waldis, Frank Chase, Eileen Stevens, Dale Tate, Tom Jackson, Mike Ross. *D:* Nathan Hertz [Juran]; *P:* Bernard Woolner; *St: & Sc:* Mark Hanna. (1:05) (video/laserdisc) In this cheapo science fiction, a woman with a cheating husband encounters a spherical spaceship and its large inhabitant, the effects of which transform her into a giantess. Originally the top of a double bill with *War of the Satellites* (q.v.). Remade in 1993 by HBO Pictures for cable TV, with a feminist approach. Note: Originally the Woolner brothers had planned a sequel to this "camp classic."

124. Attack of the Giant Leeches (American International; 1959). *Cast:* Ken Clark, Yvette Vickers, Jan Shepard, Michael Emmet, Tyler McVey, Bruno Ve Sota, Gene Roth, Dan White, George Cisar. *D:* Bernard L. Kowalski; *Ex.P:* Roger Corman; *P:* Gene Corman; *Sc:* Leo Gordon. (1:02) (video) Programmer horror melodrama of various locals who fall victim to giant blood-sucking leeches in the Florida Everglades. (aka: *The Giant Leeches*) This little gem from Corman and Co. ran on the bottom of a double bill with *A Bucket of Blood* (q.v.).

125. Attack of the Jungle Women (Barjul International Picts./Sampson; 1959). *Cast:* Uncredited. *D:* Joseph R. Juliano; *P:* A.R. Milton; *St:* John David. Low budget independent adventure of explorers who tangle with headhunters in the jungles of Panama. Filmed on location. Eastmancolor.

126. Attack of the Puppet People (American International; 1958). *Cast:* John Agar, John Hoyt, June Kenney, Michael Mark, Jack Kosslyn, Marlene Willis, Ken Miller, Laurie Mitchell, Scott Peters, Susan Gordon, June Jocelyn, Jean Moorhead, Hank Patterson, Hal Bogart, Troy Patterson, Bill Giorgio, George Diestel, Jaime Forster, Mark Lowell. *D:-P:* & *St:* Bert I. Gordon; *Sc:* George Worthing Yates; *Ex.P:* James H. Nicholson, Samuel Z. Arkoff; *Song:* "You're My Living Doll" Albert Glasser–Don Ferris–Henry Schrage. (1:18) Science fiction of a lonely European dollmaker who discovers a method to shrink people down to doll size which he can animate at will for companionship. Ran as a second feature with *War of the Colossal Beast* (q.v.).

Attack of the Rebel Girls *see* **Cuban Rebel Girls**

127. Auntie Mame (Warner; 1958). *Cast:* Rosalind Russell (AAN/recreating her stage role as Auntie Mame Dennis), Forrest Tucker (Beauregard Burnside), Coral Browne (Vera Charles), Fred Clark (Mr. Babcock), Roger Smith (Patrick Dennis the man/recreating his stage role), Patric Knowles (Lindsay Woolsey), Peggy Cass (AAN/recreating her stage role as Agnes Gooch), Jan Handzlik (film debut/recreating his stage role of Patrick Dennis as a boy), Joanna Barnes (Gloria Upson), Pippa Scott (Pegeen Ryan), Lee Patrick (Mrs. Upson), Willard Waterman (Mr. Upson), Robin Hughes (Brian O'Bannion), Connie Gilchrist (Norah Muldoon), Yuki Shimoda (recreating his stage role as Ito), Brook Byron (Sally Cato), Carol Veazie (Mrs. Burnside), Henry Brandon (Acacius Page), Butch Hengen (Emory), Dub Taylor (veterinarian), Doye O'Dell (Cousin Jeff), Terry Kelman (Michael), Morton DaCosta (Edwin Dennis), Gregory Gay (Vladimir Klinkoff), Gladys Roach (Mrs. Klinkoff), Booth Colman (Perry), Charles Heard (Mr. Feuchtwanger), Robert Gates (Lord Dudley), Mark Dana (Reginald), Dick Reeves (Mr. Krantz), Barbara Pepper (Mrs. Krantz), Chris Alexander (recreating his stage role as Mr. Loomis), Ruth Warren (Mrs. Jennings), Evelyn Ceder, Rand Harper, Paul Davis, Olive Blakeney, Margaret Dumont, Owen McGiveney. *D:* Morton DaCosta; *P:* Uncredited (AAN-Best Picture); *Sc:* Betty Comden, Adolph Green; *Cin:* (AAN-color) Harry Stradling, Jr.; *ASD:* (AAN) Malcolm Bert (art director), George James Hopkins (sets); *Editor:* (AAN) William Zeigler. (2:23) (video/laserdisc) Hit cinematic rendering of the hit Broadway comedy show by Jerome Lawrence and Robert E. Lee from Patrick Dennis' best-seller of memoirs of his eccentric aunt. One of the 26 top-grossing films of 1958-59, it also placed #4 on the "10 Best" list of *Film Daily*. Later musicalized for Broadway as *Mame* which also went to film in 1974. Technicolor and Technirama.

128. Autumn Leaves (Columbia; 1956). *Cast:* Joan Crawford, Cliff Robertson, Vera Miles, Lorne Greene, Ruth Donnelly, Shepperd Strudwick, Selmer Jackson, Maxine Cooper, Marjorie Bennett, Frank Gerstle, Leonard Mudie, Maurice Manson, Bob Hopkins, Frank Arnold, Ralph Volkie, Robert Sherman, Abdullah Abbas, Mary Benoit, Paul Bradley, Bess Flowers. *D:* Robert Aldrich (voted "Best Director" at the Berlin Film Festival); *P:* William Goetz; *St:* & *Sc:* Jack Jenne, Lewis Meltzer, Robert Blees; *Title song:* Joseph Kosma, Jacques Prevert; English lyrics: Johnny Mercer (sung by Nat "King" Cole). (1:47) (video) Drama of an older woman who with marries an unstable younger man with (unbeknownst to her) another wife.

129. The Avengers (Republic; 1950). *Cast:* John Carroll, Adele Mara, Mona Maris (final U.S. film), Fernando Lamas (U.S. film debut), Roberto Airaldi, Jorge Villoldo, Vivian Ray, Vincente Padula, Cecile Lezard, Juan Olaguivel, Eduardo Gardere, Angel M. Gordordo Palacios. *D:* & *P:* John H. Auer; *Sc:* Lawrence Kimble, Aeneas Mackenzie. (1:30) South American "western" of settlers under attack by banditos. Based on the 1930 novel *Don Careless* by Rex Beach.

130. Away All Boats (Universal-International; 1956). *Cast:* Jeff Chandler (Capt. Jeb Hawks), George Nader (Lt. Dave MacDougall), Julia Adams (Nadine MacDougall), Lex Barker (Cdr. Quigley), Charles McGraw (Lt. Mike O'Bannion), William Reynolds (Ensign Kruger), Keith Andes (Dr. Bell), Jock Mahoney (Alvick), John McIntire (Old Man), Frank Faylen (Chief "Pappy" Moran), Grant Williams (Lt. Sherwood), Floyd Simmons (Lt. Robinson), Don Keefer (Ensign Twitchell), Sam Gilman (Lt. Randall), James Westerfield, George Dunn, Kendall Clark, David Janssen, Clint Eastwood. *D:* Joseph Pevney; *P:* Howard Christie; *Sc:* Ted Sherdeman. (1:54) (video) World War II naval drama of a strict captain who must make the best of his inexperienced crew. Based on the 1954 novel by Kenneth M. Dodson, it became one of the 24 top-grossing films of 1955-56. Technicolor and VistaVision.

131. Babes in Bagdad (United Artists/Danziger Bros.; 1952). *Cast:* Paulette Goddard, Gypsy Rose Lee, John Boles (final film—ret.), Richard Ney, Thomas Gallagher, Sebastian Cabot, MacDonald Parke, Natalie Benesh, Hugh Dempster, Peter Bathurst. *D:* Edgar G. Ulmer; *P:* Edward J. & Harry Lee Danziger; *St:* & *Sc:* Felix Feist, Joe Anson; *Additional dialogue:* Reuben Levy, John Roeburt. (1:19) Critically lambasted Arabian Night style satire of shenanigans and intrigue in a caliph's harem. A co-production between the U.S.A., Great Britain and Spain filmed on location in Exotic Color in the latter.

132. Baby Doll (Warner/Newtown Prods., Inc.; 1956). *Cast:* Karl Malden (Archie), Carroll Baker (AAN/Baby Doll), Eli Wallach (film debut/Silva Vacarro), Mildred Dunnock (AAN/Aunt Rose Comfort), Lonny Chapman (Rock), Rip Torn (film debut), Eades Hogue (town marshal), Noah Williamson (deputy) and residents of Benoit, Mississippi. *D:* *&* *P:* Elia Kazan; *Adaptation:* (AAN) Tennessee Williams (of his play "27 Wagons Full of Cotton"); *Cin:* (AAN-b/w) Boris Kaufman. (1:54) (video) Hit controversial drama of a child bride in an unconsummated marriage who is seduced by another man. A condemnation by the Catholic Legion of Decency had movie-goers lined up at the box office. This film was also in nomination at the British Academy Awards.

133. Baby Face Nelson (United Artists/Fryman-Zs Prods.; 1957). *Cast:* Mickey Rooney (title role), Carolyn Jones, Cedric Hardwicke, Ted de Corsia, Jack Elam, Christopher Dark, Emile Meyer, Anthony Caruso, John Hoyt, Dan Terranova, Elisha Cook, Jr., Robert Osterloh. *D:* Don Siegel; *P:* Al Zimbalist; *St:* Robert Adler; *Sc:* Irving Shulman, Daniel Mainwaring. (1:25) The fictionalized rise and fall of 1930s gangster Baby Face Nelson (aka: Lester Gillis).

134. The Bachelor Party (United Artists/Norma Prods.; 1957). *Cast:* Don Murray (Charlie Samson), E.G. Marshall (Walter), Jack Warden (Eddie), Philip Abbott (Arnold), Larry Blyden (Kenneth), Patricia Smith (Helen Samson), Carolyn Jones (AAN/existentialist), Nancy Marchand (Julie), Karen Norris, Barbara Ames, Norma Arden Campbell (stripper). *D:* Delbert Mann; *P:* Harold Hecht; *As.P:* & *Sc:* Paddy Chayefsky. (1:33) Drama of five co-workers out for a night-on-the-town in New York City celebrating the intended nuptials of one of the men. Based on Paddy Chayefsky's television play, it placed #7 on the "10 Best" list of the NBR. It was also in nomination at the Cannes Film Festival and the British Academy Awards.

135. Back at the Front (Universal-International; 1952). *Cast:* Tom Ewell, Harvey Lembeck, Mari Blanchard, Richard Long, Barry Kelley, Vaughn Taylor, Russell Johnson, Palmer Lee [aka: Gregg Palmer], Aram Katcher, George Ramsey, Aen-Ling Chow, Benson Fong. *D:* George Sherman; *P:* Leonard Golstein; *St:* Lou Breslow, Don McGuire; *Sc:* Breslow, McGuire, Oscar Brodney. (1:27) Comedy sequel to *Up Front* (q.v.), this time with Willie (Ewell) and Joe (Lembeck) running wild in post–WW II Japan. Based on cartoon characters created by Bill Mauldin. (aka: *Willie and Joe Back at the Front*).

136. Back from Eternity (RKO; 1956). *Cast:* Robert Ryan, Anita Ekberg, Rod Steiger, Phyllis Kirk, Gene Barry, Keith Andes, Fred Clark, Beulah Bondi, Cameron Prud'Homme, Jesse White, Jon Provost, Adele Mara, Barbara Eden (film debut—bit). *D: & P:* John Farrow; *St:* Richard Carroll; *Sc:* Jonathan Latimer. (1:37) (video) A plane carrying eleven passengers and crew crash lands in the headhunter infested jungles of South America, and when repaired, can take off with only five of their number. A remake of *Five Came Back*, a 1939 production by Farrow for this studio.

137. Back from the Dead (20th Century–Fox/Regal Films; 1957). *Cast:* Peggie Castle, Arthur Franz, Marsha Hunt, Don Haggerty, Marianne Stewart, Evelyn Scott, Helen Wallace, Jeane Wood, James Bell, Ned Glass, Otto Reichow, Jeanne Bates. *D:* Charles Marquis Warren; *P:* Robert Stabler; *Sc:* Catherine Turney (Based on her 1952 novel *The Other One*). (1:18) Low budget horror of a woman tormented by the spirit of her husband's first wife who died as a result of allegiance to a satanic cult. Regalscope. Paired with *The Unknown Terror* (q.v.) on a double bill program.

138. Back to God's Country (Universal-International; 1953). *Cast:* Rock Hudson, Marcia Henderson, Steve Cochran, Hugh O'Brian, Chubby Johnson, Tudor Owen, Arthur Space, John Cliff, Bill Radovich, Pat Hogan, Ivan Triesault, Charles Horvath, Baron (dog—received the PATSY Award of Excellence). *D:* Joseph Pevney; *P:* Howard Christie; *Sc:* Tom Reed. (1:17) Set in the wilderness, a melodrama of a ship's captain and his wife pursued on dogsled by a lecherous villain. Based on the novel by James Oliver Curwood, it is a remake of the 1927 Universal silent by director Irvin Willat and starring Renee Adoree, Robert Frazer and Walter Long. First filmed in 1919 in a U.S./Canadian co-production by director David M. Hartford and starring Nell Shipman, Wheeler Oakman and Wellington Playter with release by First National.

139. Backfire (Warner; 1949–50). *Cast:* Virginia Mayo, Gordon MacRae, Edmond O'Brien, Dane Clark, Viveca Lindfors, Ed Begley, Frances Robinson, Monte Blue, John Ridgely, Sheila Stephens, Richard Rober, David Hoffman, Ida Moore, Leonard Strong. *D:* Vincent Sherman; *P:* Anthony Veiller; *St:* Larry Marcus; *Sc:* Marcus, Ivan Goff, Ben Roberts. (1:31) Melodrama of a man who sets out to prove his best friend innocent of murder.

140. Backlash (Universal-International; 1956). *Cast:* Richard Widmark, Donna Reed, William Campbell, John McIntire, Barton MacLane, Henry [Harry] Morgan, Bob Wilke, Edward C. Platt, Reg Parton, Robert Foulk, Roy Roberts, Phil Chambers, Gregg Barton, Fred Graham, Frank Chase, Jack Lambert. *D:* John Sturges; *P:* Aaron Rosenberg; *Sc:* Borden Chase. (1:23) Technicolor western involving the sole survivor of an Indian massacre and the whereabouts of $60,000 in gold. Taken from a novel by Frank Gruber.

141. The Bad and the Beautiful (MGM; 1952). *Cast:* Lana Turner (Georgia Lorrison), Kirk Douglas (AAN/Jonathan Shields), Walter Pidgeon (Harry Pebbel), Dick Powell (James Lee Bartlow), Barry Sullivan (Fred Amiel), Gloria Grahame (AA/Rosemary Bartlow), Gilbert Roland (Victor "Gaucho" Ribera), Leo G. Carroll (Henry Whitfield), Vanessa Brown (Kay Amiel), Paul Stewart (Syd Murphy), Sammy White (Gus), Elaine Stewart (Lila), Ivan Triesault (Von Ellstein), Kathleen Freeman (Miss March), Marietta Canty (Ida), Robert Burton (McDill), Francis X. Bushman (eulogist), George Lewis (Lionel Donovan), Dee Turnell (Linda Ronley), Barbara Billingsley (Lucien), Madge Blake (Mrs. Rosser), Karen Verne (Rosa), Ben Astar (Joe), Dorothy Patrick (Arlene), Jay Adler (Mr. Z), John Bishop (Ferraday), William E. Green (Hugo Shields), Jonathan Cott, Lucille Knoch, Steve

Forrest (film debut), Perry Sheehan, Ned Glass, Sandy Descher, Bob Carson, Alex Davidoff, Chris Olsen, Bess Flowers, Peggy King, Stanley Andrews, William "Bill" Phillips, Louis Calhern (voice only). *D:* Vincente Minnelli; *P:* John Houseman; *St:* George Bradshaw; *Sc:* (AA) Charles Schnee; *Cin:* (AA-b/w) Robert Surtees; *ASD:* (AA-b/w) Cedric Gibbons, Edward Carfagno (art directors), Edwin B. Willis, Keogh Gleason (sets); *Costumes:* (AA-b/w) Helen Rose. (1:58) (video/laserdisc) Acclaimed hit drama of the rise and fall of a ruthless Hollywood producer/director. The NBR placed it at #7 on their "10 Best" list, with movie audiences making it one of the 26 top-grossing films of 1952-53. It was also in nomination at the British Academy Awards. Computer-colored prints have been produced by Turner Entertainment.

142. Bad Day at Black Rock (MGM; 1954-55). *Cast:* Spencer Tracy (AAN + "Best Actor" at the Cannes Film Festival/John J. MacReedy), Robert Ryan (Reno Smith), Anne Francis (Liz Wirth), Dean Jagger (Tim Horn), Walter Brennan (Doc Velie), John Ericson (Pete Wirth), Ernest Borgnine (Coley Trimble), Lee Marvin (Hector David), Walter Sande (Sam), Russell Collins (Mr. Hastings). *D:* (AAN) John Sturges; *P:* Dore Schary; *As.P:* Herman Hoffman; *Sc:* (AAN) Millard Kaufman. (1:21) (video/laserdisc) Acclaimed drama of a one-armed man who uncovers a dark, dirty secret kept by members of a contemporary small western town. Based on the story "Bad Time at Hondo" by Howard Breslin and Don McGuire, it was in nomination at the British Academy Awards. The *New York Times* placed it at #2 on their "10 Best" list, while the NBR and *Film Daily* placed it at #4 and #5 respectively on theirs. Eastmancolor and CinemaScope. Note: *Platinum High School* (MGM; 1960) was an unconfirmed remake.

143. Bad for Each Other (Columbia; 1954). *Cast:* Charlton Heston, Lizabeth Scott, Dianne Foster (U.S. debut), Mildred Dunnock, Arthur Franz, Ray Collins, Marjorie Rambeau, Lester Matthews, Rhys Williams, Lydia Clarke, Chris Alcaide, Robert Keys, Frank Tully, Ann Robinson, Dorothy Green. *D:* Irving Rapper; *P:* William Fadiman; *Sc:* Irving Wallace, Horace McCoy. (1:23) Drama of a doctor who seeks a career with a society clientele, but settles instead for the poorer residents of a Pennsylvania mining town. Based on "Scalpel" by Mr. McCoy.

The Bad One (G.B. title) *see* **Sorority Girl**

144. The Bad Seed (Warner/Mervyn LeRoy; 1956). *Cast:* Nancy Kelly (final film—ret./AAN/ repeating her stage role as Christine Penmark), Patty McCormack (AAN/repeating her stage role as Rhoda Penmark), Henry Jones (repeating his stage role as LeRoy), Eileen Heckart (AAN/repeating her stage role as Mrs. Daigle), Evelyn Varden (Monica), William Hopper (Kenneth), Paul Fix (Bravo), Jesse White (Emory), Gage Clarke (Tasker), Joan Croydon (Miss Fern), Frank Cady (Mr. Daigle). *D: & P:* Mervyn LeRoy; *Sc:* John Lee Mahin; *Cin:* (AAN-b/w) Hal Rosson. (2:09) (video/laserdisc) Drama of little Rhoda Penmark, evil incarnate, who will stop at nothing, including murder, to get what she wants. Based on the novel by William March and the play by Maxwell Anderson, Hollywood censors required the play's ending be changed for the screen. One of the 24 top-grossing films of 1956-57, it was remade as a TV movie in 1985.

145. The Badge of Marshal Brennan (Allied Artists/Gannaway Prods.; 1957). *Cast:* Jim Davis, Arleen Whelan, Lee Van Cleef, Louis Jean Heydt, Carl Smith, Marty Robbins, Harry Lauter, Douglas Fowley, Lawrence Dobkin. *D: & P:* Albert C. Gannaway; *Sc:* Thomas G. Hubbard; *Song:* "Man on the Run" (Hal Levy–Gannaway) sung by Harve Presnell. (1:14) Western of an outlaw who is mistaken for a deceased marshal. Originally paired on a double bill program with *Death in Small Doses* (q.v.).

146. The Badlanders (MGM/Arcola Prods.; 1958). *Cast:* Alan Ladd, Ernest Borgnine, Katy Jurado, Claire Kelly, Kent Smith, Nehemiah Persoff, Anthony Caruso, Robert Emhardt, Adam Williams, Ford Rainey, John Day, Barbara Baxley. *D:* Delmer Daves; *P:* Aaron Rosenberg; *Sc:* Richard Collins (based on a story by W.R. Burnett). (1:23) (video) Turn-of-the-century western of two men out to heist the yellow metal from a goldmine, each trying to outwit the other for his share. A hit for the studio, the film is actually a remake of *The Asphalt Jungle* (q.v.). Filmed in Arizona in Metrocolor and CinemaScope.

147. Badlands of Montana (20th Century–Fox/Regal Films; 1957). *Cast:* Rex Reason, Margia Dean, Beverly Garland, Keith Larsen, Emile Meyer, Robert Cunningham,

Ralph Peters, Lee Tung Foo, Stanley Farrar, Rankin Mansfield, William Phipps, John Pickard, John Lomma, Paul Newlan, Russ Bender, Jack Kruschen, Elena DaVinci, George Taylor, William Forester, Larry Blake, Ralph Sanford, William Tannen, Roydon Clark, Helen Jay. *D:-P: & Sc:* Daniel B. Ullman; *Song:* "The Man With the Gallant Gun" (Irving Gertz–Hal Levy) sung by Bob Grabeau. (1:15) Two friends on opposite sides of the law are drawn into a gunfight. Regalscope.

148. Badman's Country (Warner/Peerless; 1958). *Cast:* Robert Montgomery (Pat Garrett), Buster Crabbe (Wyatt Earp), Neville Brand (Butch Cassidy), Malcolm Atterbury (Buffalo Bill Cody), Gregory Walcott (Bat Masterson), Russell Johnson (Sundance Kid), Richard Devon (Harvey Logan), Karin Booth, Morris Ankrum, Dan Riss, Lewis Martin, Fred Graham, John Harmon, William Bryant. *D:* Fred F. Sears; *P:* Robert E. Kent; *Sc:* Orville H. Hampton; *Title Song:* Kent (sung by the Mello Men). (1:08) Hollywood once again reshuffles the cards on western historical facts and comes up with Pat Garrett, Wyatt Earp and Buffalo Bill Cody ganging up on badman, Butch Cassidy.

149. Badman's Gold (United Artists/Eagle-Lion Classics; 1951). *Cast:* Johnny Carpenter, Alyn Lockwood, Troy Tarrell, Kenne Duncan, Verne Teters, Jack Daly, Emmett Lynn, Daisy (dog). *D: & P:* Robert Tansey; *Sc:* Robert Emmett (Tansey), Alyn Lockwood. (0:58) Programmer western of a marshal investigating the theft of gold shipments from stagecoaches. Originally half of a double bill with *Skipalong Rosenbloom* (q.v.).

150. Bailout at 43,000 (United Artists/Pine-Thomas-Shane; 1957). *Cast:* John Payne, Karen Steele, Paul Kelly (final film—d. 1956), Richard Eyer, Constance Ford, Eddie Firestone, Gregory Gaye, Adam Kennedy, Steven Ritch, Richard Crane. *D:* Francis D. Lyon; *P:* Howard B. Pine, William Thomas; *Sc:* Paul Monash. (1:18) (video) Programmer drama of a man with second thoughts about testing an ejection seat for jet fighters.

151. Bait (Columbia; 1954). *Cast:* Cleo Moore, John Agar, Hugo Haas, Emmett Lynn, Bruno VeSota, Jan Englund, George Keymas. *D: & P:* Hugo Haas; *Sc:* Samuel W. Taylor; *Song:* Martin Schwab. (1:19) Melodrama of a gold prospector plotting to eliminate his younger partner. Originally ran on a double bill with *Jesse James vs. The Daltons* (q.v.). Note: Prior to the film's credits, Sir Cedric Hardwicke appears as the Devil in a prologue.

The Baited Trap (G.B. title) *see* **The Trap**

152. Bal Tabarin (Republic; 1952). *Cast:* Muriel Lawrence, William Ching, Claire Carleton, Steve Brodie, Steven Geray, Carl Milletaire, Jan Rubini, Tom Powers, Gregory Gaye, Adrienne D'Ambricourt, Herbert Deans. *D:* Philip Ford; *P:* Herbert J. Yates; *St: & Sc:* Houston Branch; *Songs:* Jack Elliott, Tom Mack. (1:24) A chanteuse, in possession of a cache of jewels which belonged to her murdered boss, a jewel fence, hides out at the famous Paris night spot.

153. The Bamboo Prison (Columbia; 1954). *Cast:* Robert Francis, Dianne Foster, Brian Keith, Jerome Courtland, Jack Kelly, E.G. Marshall, Earle Hyman, Murray Matheson, King Donovan, Leo Gordon, Dick Jones, Keye Luke, Richard Loo, George Keymas, Pepe Hern, Weaver Levy, Denis Martin. *D:* Lewis Seiler; *P:* Bryan Foy; *St:* Jack DeWitt; *Sc:* Edwin Blum, DeWitt. (1:19) Korean conflict drama of a P.O.W. who poses as a turncoat to get information from the North Koreans.

154. Band of Angels (Warner; 1957). *Cast:* Clark Gable, Yvonne De Carlo, Sidney Poitier, Efrem Zimbalist, Jr., Rex Reason, Patric Knowles, Andrea King, Torin Thatcher, Ray Teal, Russ Evans, Carolle Drake, Raymond Bailey, Tommie Moore, William Forrest, Noreen Corcoran, Jack Williams, Zelda Cleaver, Juanita Moore, Joe Narcisse, Marshall Bradford, Charles Heard, Roy Barcroft, Curtis Hamilton, Riza Royce, Jim Hayward, Larry Blake, Guy Wilkerson, Bob Steele, Mayo Loizeau, June-Ellen Anthony, Carla Merry, Dan White, Jean G. Harvey, Alfred Meissner, William Fawcett, Ewing Mitchell, Morgan Shaane, Paul McGuire, Martin Smith, Ann Doran, Milas Clark, Jr., Walter Smith, Charles Horvath, William Schallert, Carl Harbaugh, Anthony Ghazlo, Ann Staunton, Robyn Faire. *D:* Raoul Walsh; *P:* Unc.; *Sc:* John Twist, Ivan Goff, Ben Roberts. (2:07) (video) Lavishly produced pre–Civil War costume-melodrama with every cliché associated with the era intact. A woman finds on the death of her white father that she is actually a mulatto and is subsequently sold into slavery to a New Orleans millionaire to be his mistress. Photographed in WarnerColor, it was based on Robert Penn Warren's 1955 novel of the same name.

155. The Band Wagon (MGM; 1953). *Cast:* Fred Astaire (Tony Hunter), Cyd Charisse (Gaby Berard), Jack Buchanan (Jeffrey Cordova), Oscar Levant (Lester Marton), Nanette Fabray (Lily Marton), James Mitchell (Paul Byrd), Robert Gist (Hal Benton), Thurston Hall (Col. Tripp), Ava Gardner (movie star), LeRoy Daniels, Jack Tesler, Dee Turnell, Elynne Ray, Peggy Murray, Judy Landon, Jimmie Thompson, Bert May, John Lupton, Owen McGivney, Sam Hearn, Herbert Vigran, Emory Parnell, Ernest Anderson, Frank Seannon, Stu Wilson, Roy Engel, Al Hill, Paul Bradley, Bobby Watson, Lotte Stein, Robert "Smoki" Whitfield, Dick Alexander, Al Ferguson, Betty Farrington, Bess Flowers. *D:* Vincente Minnelli; *P:* Arthur Freed; *St: & Sc:* (AAN) Betty Comden, Adolph Green; *Music:* (AAN) Adolph Deutsch; *Costumes:* (AAN) Mary Ann Myberg; *Choreography:* Michael Kidd; *Songs:* "Louisiana Hayride," "I Guess I'll Have to Change My Plan," "Dancing in the Dark," "A Shine On Your Shoes," "By Myself," "Something to Remember You By," "I Love Louisa," "You and the Night and the Music," "That's Entertainment" and "Triplets" Arthur Schwartz–Howard Dietz. (1:52) (video/laserdisc) Technicolor musical-comedy of a has-been Hollywood actor who decides to have a go at the Broadway stage. One of the 26 top-grossing films of 1952-53.

156. Bandido (United Artists/Bandido Prods.; 1955–56). *Cast:* Robert Mitchum, Ursula Thiess (final film—ret.), Gilbert Roland, Zachary Scott, Rudolfo Acosta, Jose I. Torvay, Henry Brandon, Douglas Fowley, Victor Junco, Alfonso Sanchez Tello, Arturo Manrique, Margarito Luna, Miguel Inclan, Jose A. Espinosa, Jose Munoz, Manuel Sanchez Novarro, Antonio Sandoval, Alberto Pedret. *D:* Richard Fleischer; *P:* Robert L. Jacks; *St: & Sc:* Earl Felton. (1:32) Action-drama in DeLuxe color and CinemaScope of an American arms dealer who gets mixed up in the 1916 Mexican war.

Bandit General (G.B. title) *see* **The Torch**

157. Bandit Queen (Lippert; 1950). *Cast:* Barbara Britton, Willard Parker (Joaquin Murietta), Philip Reed, Barton MacLane, Martin Garralaga, John Merton, Jack Ingram, Victor Kilian, Thurson Hall, Anna Demetrio, Paul Marion, Pepe Hern, Lalo Rios, Jack Perrin, Cecile Weston, Carl Pitti, Hugh Hooker, Mikel Conrad, Trina Varela, Angie [aka: Angelo Rossito], Nancy Laurents, Minna Phillips, Margia Dean, Felipe Turich, Joe Dominguez, Roy Butler, Elias Gamboa, Chuck Roberson. *D: & P:* William Berke; *St:* Victor West; *Sc:* West, Budd Lesser. (1:09) A female—sort of a Ms. Zorro—heads a gang bent on stopping the theft of Spanish lands in California in the 19th century.

158. The Bandits of Corsica (United Artists/Global; 1953). *Cast:* Richard Greene (dual role), Paula Raymond, Raymond Burr, Lee Van Cleef, Dona Drake, Raymond Greenleaf, Frank Puglia, Nestor Paiva, Paul Cavanagh, Peter Brocco, George J. Lewis, Clayton Moore, Peter Mamakos, William Forrest, John Pickard, Virginia Brissac, Francis J. McDonald, Michael Ansara. *D:* Ray Nazarro; *P:* Edward Small (unc.); *St:* Frank Burt; *Sc:* Richard Schayer. (1:21) Freedom fighters vs. tyrants in this costume swashbuckler set in early 19th century Corsica. As part of the plot involves empathetic twin brothers, there seems to be a story inspiration from Alexandre Dumas. (G.B. title: *Return of the Corsican Brothers*)

159. Bandits of the West (Republic; 1953). *Cast:* Allan Lane, Eddy Waller, Cathy Downs, Roy Barcroft, Trevor Bardette, Ray Montgomery, Byron Foulger, Harry Harvey, Robert Bice, Black Jack (horse). *D:* Harry Keller; *P:* Rudy Ralston (unc.); *St: & Sc:* Gerald Geraghty. (0:54) In this series western, U.S. Marshal "Rocky" Lane investigates the disruption of natural gas lines.

Banner in the Sky *see* **Third Man on the Mountain**

160. Bannerline (MGM; 1951). *Cast:* Keefe Brasselle, Sally Forrest, Lewis Stone, Lionel Barrymore, J. Carrol Naish, Spring Byington, Warner Anderson, Larry Keating, Elisabeth Risdon, Michael Ansara, John Morgan. *D:* Don Weis (directorial debut); *P:* Henry Berman; *Sc:* Charles Schnee. (1:28) Small town melodrama of a young reporter who rallies townspeople against civic corruption. Based on the short story "A Rose is Not a Rose" by Samson Raphaelson.

The Bar Sinister *see* **It's a Dog's Life**

161. The Barbarian and the Geisha (20th Century–Fox; 1958). *Cast:* John Wayne, Eiko

Ando, Sam Jaffe, So Yamamura, Norman Thomson, James Robbins, Morita, Kodaya Ichikawa, Iroshi Yamato, Tokujiro Iketaniuchi, Fuji Kasai, Takeshi Kumagai, Kohichi Umino, Minanogawa, Rintaro Kaga. *D:* John Huston; *P:* Eugene Frenke; *St:* Ellis St. Joseph; *Sc:* Charles Grayson. (1:45) (video) Fictionalized historical drama of U.S. Consul Townsend Harris in Japan, after Commodore Perry forces that country to open its ports to foreign trade. Set in 1856, it was filmed on location. DeLuxe color and CinemaScope.

162. Barbed Wire (Columbia/Gene Autry Prods.; 1952). *Cast:* Gene Autry, Anne James, Pat Buttram, William Fawcett, Leonard Penn, Michael Vallon, Terry Frost, Clayton Moore, Edwin Parker, Sandy Sanders, Pat O'Malley, Stuart Whitman, Alan Bridge, Bud Osborne, Harry Harvey, Zon Murray, Victor Cox, Frankie Marvin, Bobby Clark, Bob Woodward, Duke York, Wesley Hudman. *D:* George Archainbaud; *P:* Armand Schaefer; *St: & Sc:* Gerald Geraghty. (1:01) Cattlemen are illegally attempting to fence off large areas of grazing land. Songs: "Mexicali Rose," "Old Buckaroo." In Sepiatone. (G.B. title: *False News*) Originally ran on a double bill with *The Rough, Tough West* (q.v.).

163. The Barefoot Contessa (United Artists/Figaro, Inc.; 1954). *Cast:* Humphrey Bogart (Harry Dawes), Ava Gardner (Marie Vargas), Edmond O'Brien (AA/Oscar Muldoon), Marius Goring (Alberto Bravano), Valentina Cortesa (Elenora Torlato-Favrini), Rossano Brazzi (Vincenzo Torlato-Favrini), Elizabeth Sellars (Jerry), Warren Stevens (Kirk Edwards), Franco Interlenghi (Pedro), Mari Aldon (Myrna), Bessie Love (Mrs. Eubanks), Bill Fraser (J. Montague Brown), John Parrish (Mr. Black), Jim Gerald (Mr. Blue), Gertrude Flynn (Lulu McGee), John Horne (Hector Eubanks), Robert Christopher (Eddie Blake), Alberto Rabagliati, Tonio Selwart, Margaret Anderson, Enzo Staiola, Maria Zanoli, Renato Chiantoni, Diana Decker, Riccardi Rioli. *D:* Joseph L. Mankiewicz; *As.P*: Forrest E. Johnson; *St:* and *Sc:* (AAN) Mankiewicz. (2:08) (video) Drama of the rise of a Hollywood star, from her humble beginnings in the slums of Madrid to her demise. One of the 27 top-grossing films of 1954-55. Technicolor.

164. The Barefoot Mailman (Columbia; 1951). *Cast:* Robert Cummings, Terry Moore, Jerome Courtland, John Russell, Will Geer, Arthur Shields, Trevor Bardette, Arthur Space, Frank Ferguson, Percy Helton, Ellen Corby, Robert Lynn, Renie Riano, Mary Field. *D:* Earl McEvoy; *P:* Robert Cohn; *Sc:* James Gunn, Francis Swann. (1:23) The adventures of three people, walking from Palm Beach to Miami in 19th century Florida to deliver mail. Photographed in SuperCinecolor, it was based on the novel by Theodore Pratt.

165. The Baron of Arizona (Lippert/Deputy Corp.; 1950). *Cast:* Vincent Price, Ellen Drew, Beulah Bondi, Vladimir Sokoloff, Reed Hadley, Robert Barrat, Robin Short, Barbara Woodell, Tina Rome, Margia Dean, Edward Keane, Gene Roth, Karen Kester, Joseph Green, Fred Kohler, Jr., Tristram Coffin, Angelo Rossito, I. Stanford Jolley, Terry Frost, Zachary Yaconelli, Adolfo Ornelas, Wheaton Chambers, Robert O'Neill, Stephen Harrison, Stuart Holmes, Jonathan Hale, Stanley Price, Sam Flint, Richard Cramer. *D: & Sc:* Samuel Fuller; *P:* Carl K. Hittleman. (1:30) (video) Based on fact costume drama of a woman claiming the Arizona territory through a Spanish land grant. Based on an article in *American Weekly* by Homer Croy.

166. The Barretts of Wimpole Street (MGM; 1957). *Cast:* Jennifer Jones (Elizabeth Barrett), Bill Travers (Robert Browning), John Gielgud (Mr. Barrett), Virginia McKenna (Henrietta Barrett), Susan Stephen, Laurence Naismith, Leslie Phillips, Maxine Audley, Vernon Gray, Jean Anderson, Moultrie Kelsall, Michael Brill, Kenneth Fortescue, Nicholas Hawtrey, Richard Thorpe, Keith Baxter, Brian Smith. *D:* Sidney Franklin (final—ret.); *P:* Sam Zimbalist; *Sc:* John Dighton. (1:45) (video/laserdisc) Lavishly produced U.S.A./U.K. co-production of the romance between Elizabeth Barrett and Robert Browning and her father's attempts to destroy the affair. A remake of the acclaimed 1934 production by this studio (also directed by Franklin), it was based on the 1931 play by Rudolf Besier. Metrocolor and CinemaScope.

167. Barricade (Warner; 1950). *Cast:* Dane Clark, Raymond Massey, Ruth Roman, Robert Douglas, Morgan Farley, George Stern, Walter Coy, Frank Marlowe, Tony Martinez, Robert Griffin. *D:* Peter Godfrey; *P:* Saul Elkins; *St: & Sc:* William Sackheim. (1:15) The eternal battle of good vs. evil shows itself in a western gold mining camp run by a sadist. A reworking of *The Sea Wolf* (1941), by this studio.

168. The Basketball Fix (Realart; 1951). *Cast:* John Ireland, Marshal Thompson, Vanessa Brown, William Bishop, Hazel Brooks, John(ny) Sands, Bobby Hyatt, Walter Sande, Ted Pierson, Johnny Phillips, Lester Sharpe. *D:* Felix Feist; *P:* Edward Leven; *St: & Sc:* Peter R. Brooke, Charles K. Peck, Jr. (1:05) Low budget drama of a basketball player who creates a scandal on the court when he is up to his ears in gambling debts.

169. The Bat (Allied Artists/Liberty Picts.; 1959). *Cast:* Vincent Price, Agnes Moorehead, Gavin Gordon, John Sutton, Lenita Lane, Elaine Edwards, Darla Hood, John Bryant, Harvey Stephens, Mike Steele, Riza Royce, Robert B. Williams. *D: & Sc:* Crane Wilbur; *P:* C.J. Tevlin. (1:20) (video) "Old Dark House" mystery (like they used to make in the 1930s) of a series of murders in a house rented by a mystery writer. Based on the 1920 Broadway play by Mary Roberts Rinehart and Avery Hopwood, which in turn was based on Ms. Rinehart's popular novel *The Circular Staircase* (1908). Filmed twice before as *The Bat*, in 1915 and again in 1926 and again in 1930 as *The Bat Whispers*.

170. The Battle at Apache Pass (Universal-International; 1952). *Cast:* John Lund, Jeff Chandler (Cochise), Beverly Tyler, Bruce Cowling, Susan Cabot, John Hudson, James Best, Regis Toomey, Richard Egan, Hugh O'Brian, Palmer Lee [aka: Gregg Palmer], William Reynolds, Jay Silverheels (Geronimo), Tommy Cook, Jack Elam, Richard Garland, Jack Ingram, John Baer, Paul Smith. *D:* George Sherman; *P:* Leonard Goldstein; *St: & Sc:* Gerald Drayson Adams. (1:25) A western which has Geronimo and a nefarious Indian advisor turning the New Mexico frontier to war, breaking a peace treaty. Followed by a sequel *Taza, Son of Cochise* (q.v.).

171. Battle Circus (MGM; 1953). *Cast:* Humphrey Bogart, June Allyson, Keenan Wynn, Robert Keith, William Campbell, Perry Sheehan, Patricia Tiernan, Adele Longmire, Jonathan Cott, Ann Morrison, Helen Winston, Sarah Selby, Philip Ahn, Steve Forrest, Jeff Richards, Danny Chang, Dick Simmons. *D: & Sc:* Richard Brooks; *P:* Pandro S. Berman; *St:* Allen Rivkin, Laura Kerr. (1:30) (video) Korean conflict melodrama set in a M.A.S.H. unit with romance blossoming between a surgeon and an army nurse.

172. Battle Cry (Warner; 1955). *Cast:* Van Heflin (Col. Huxley), Aldo Ray (Andy), Mona Freeman (Kathy), Nancy Olson (Pat), James Whitmore (Mac), Raymond Massey (Gen. Snipes), Tab Hunter (Danny), Dorothy Malone (Elaine Yarborogh), Anne Francis (Rae), William Campbell (Ski), John Lupton (Marion), Justus McQueen (L.Q.—later: L.Q. Jones/debut), Perry Lopez (Spanish Joe), Fess Parker (Speedy), Jonas Applegarth (Lightower), Tommy Cook (Ziltch), Susan Morrow (Susan), Carleton Young (Major Wellman), Victor Millan (Pedro), Felix Noriego (Indian marine), Glenn Denning (Seabags), Gregory Walcott (Sgt. Beller), Rhys Williams (Enoch Rogers), Chick Chandler (Chaplain Petersen), Willis Bouchey (Mr. Forrester), Sarah Selby (Mrs. Ferguson), Harold Knudsen (Bud Forrester), Frank Ferguson (Mr. Walker), Kay Stewart (Mrs. Walker), Lumsden Hare & Carl Harbaugh (New Zealanders), Hilda Plowright (Mrs. Rogers), Allyn McLerie, George Selk [aka: Budd Buster]. *D:* Raoul Walsh; *P:* Unc.; *Sc:* Leon M. Uris; *Music:* (AAN) Max Steiner. (2:29) (video/laserdisc) World War II drama of U.S. Marines and their training for and action in the Pacific theater. An audience pleaser, it took in $8,000,000 at the box office making it one of the 27 top-grossing films of 1954-55. Based on the best-seller by Leon Uris. WarnerColor and CinemaScope.

173. Battle Flame (Allied Artists; 1959). *Cast:* Scott Brady, Elaine Edwards, Robert Blake, Wayne Heffley, Gordon Jones, Ken Miller, Arthur Walsh, Richard Harrison, Gary Kent, Peggy Moffitt, Jean Robbins, Richard Crane. *D:* R.G. Springsteen; *P:* Lester A. Sansom; *St:* Sansom, Elwood Ullman; *Sc:* Ullman. (1:18) Korean conflict romantic drama of a marine lieutenant recovering from wounds who falls for his nurse and must later, with his company of men, rescue her and other nurses from Chinese communists at Chinyong. Location filming at Mt. Whitney on the eastern edge of Sequoia National Park in California.

174. Battle Hymn (Universal-International; 1956). *Cast:* Rock Hudson (Col. Dean Hess), Anna Kashfi (En Scon Yang), Dan Duryea (Sgt. Herman), Don DeFore (Capt. Skidmore), Martha Hyer (Mary Hess), Jock Mahoney (Major Moore), Alan Hale (mess sergeant), Philip Ahn (old man), Carl Benton Reid (Deacon Edwards), Jung Kyoo Fyo (Korean orphan), James Edwards (Lt. Maples), Richard Loo (Gen. Kim), Bartlett Robinson (Gen. Timberidge), Simon Scott (Lt. Hollis),

Carleton Young (Major Harrison), Art Millan (Capt. Reardon), Teru Shimada, William Hudson, Paul Sorenson. *D:* Douglas Sirk; *P:* Ross Hunter; *Sc:* Charles Grayson, Vincent B. Evans. (1:48) Fact-based Korean war drama of Colonel Dean Hess who airlifts Korean orphans to safety during that conflict, remembering back to World War II when he miscalculated and accidentally bombed a German orphanage. One of the 24 top-grossing films of 1956-57, catering to the family audience. Technicolor and CinemaScope.

The Battle of Powder River (G.B. title) *see* **Tomahawk**

175. Battle of Rogue River (Columbia; 1954). *Cast:* George Montgomery, Richard Denning, Martha Hyer, John Crawford, Emory Parnell, Frank Sully, Willis Bouchey, Michael Granger, Freeman Morse, Bill Bryant, Charles Evans, Lee Roberts, Steven Ritch, Bill Hale, Wesley Hudman, Jimmy Lloyd. *D:* William Castle; *P:* Sam Katzman; *St:* & *Sc:* Douglas Heyes. (1:11) Technicolor western of a renegade white, stirring up Indian hostilities for personal gain.

176. Battle of the Coral Sea (Columbia/Morningside Prods.; 1959). *Cast:* Cliff Robertson, Gia Scala, Teru Shimada, Patricia Cutts, Rian Garrick, Gene Blakely, L.Q. Jones, Robin Hughes, Gordon Jones, Tom Laughlin, Eiji Yamashiro, James T. Goto, K.L. Smith, Carlyle Mitchell, Larry Thor (final film), Patrick Westwood. *D:* Paul Wendkos; *P:* Charles H. Schneer; *St:* Stephen Kandel, *Sc:* Daniel B. Ullman, Kandel. (1:20) World War II drama of a submarine crew captured by the Japanese who, with the help of a Eurasian girl, escape and relay reconnisance leading to victory at the Battle of the Coral Sea.

Battle Shock *see* **A Woman's Devotion**

177. Battle Stations (Columbia; 1956). *Cast:* John Lund, William Bendix, Keefe Brasselle, Richard Boone, William Leslie, James Lydon, George O'Hanlon, Claude Akins, John Craven, Jack Diamond, Eddie Foy III, Dick Cathcart, Chris G. Randall, Robert Forrest, James Lilburn, Gordon Howard, Frank Connor, Eric Bond. *D:* Lewis Seiler; *P:* Bryan Foy; *St:* Ben Finney; *Sc:* Crane Wilbur. (1:21) Wartime drama of life aboard a World War II aircraft carrier.

Battle Stripe *see* **The Men**

178. Battle Taxi (United Artists/Ivan Tors Films, Inc., 1955). *Cast:* Sterling Hayden, Arthur Franz, Marshall Thompson, Leo Needham, Jay Barney, John Goddard, Robert Sherman, Joel Marston, John Dennis, Dale Hutchinson, Andy Andrews, Vance Skarstedt, Michael Colgan, Capt. Vincent McGovern. *D:* Herbert L. Strock; *P:* Ivan Tors, Art Arthur; *St:* Malvin Wald, Arthur; *Sc:* Wald. (1:22) Korean conflict drama of air patrols and the rescue by Helicopter Air Rescue Service of downed pilots.

179. Battle Zone (Allied Artists; 1952). *Cast:* John Hodiak, Linda Christian, Stephen McNally, Martin Milner, Dave Willock, Jack Larson, Richard Emory, Philip Ahn, Carleton Young, John Fontaine, Todd Karns, Gil Stratton, Jr. *D:* Lesley Selander; *P:* Walter Wanger; *St:* & *Sc:* Steve Fisher. (1:21) Korean war drama of two combat photographers in love with the same Red Cross nurse.

180. The Battles of Chief Pontiac (Realart; 1952). *Cast:* Lex Barker, Lon Chaney (title role), Helen Westcott, Berry Kroeger, Roy Roberts, Larry Chance, Kathleen Warren, Ramsey Hill (Gen. Jeffrey Amherst), Guy Teague, James Fairfax, Abner George. *D:* Felix Feist; *P:* Jack Broder; *Sc:* Jack DeWitt. (1:11) Low budget colonial costume actioner involving efforts to establish a peace between the British and Chief Pontiac's Hurons.

181. Battling Marshal (Astor/Yucca Prods.; 1950). *Cast:* Sunset Carson (final starring film), Pat Starling, Forrest Matthews, Lee Roberts, Al Terry, Richard Bartell, A.J. Baxley, Bob Curtis, Pat Gleason, Dale Carson, Don Gray, Stephen Keyes, William Val, Buck Buckley, Joe Hiser. *D:* Oliver Drake; *P:* Walter Mattox; *Sc:* Rose Kreves. (0:55) (video) Several attempts to murder a rancher draw two U.S. marshals to investigate.

182. Bayou (United Artists/American National Films; 1957). *Cast:* Peter Graves, Lita Milan, Douglas Fowley, Tim Carey, Jonathan Haze, Edwin Nelson, Eugene Sondfield, Evelyn Hendrickson, Milton Schneider, Michael R. Romano. *D:* Harold Daniels; *P:* M.A. Ripps; *Sc:* Edward I. Fessler. (1:23) Melodrama of a Cajun girl who falls for a white architect, a new resident of the New Orleans swamp, much to the displeasure of her father. Filmed on location in Louisiana. (Re-release title: *Poor White Trash*)

183. Beachhead (United Artists/Aubrey Schenck; 1954). *Cast:* Tony Curtis, Frank Lovejoy, Mary Murphy, Eduard Franz, Skip Homeier, Alan Wells, Sunshine Akira Fukunaga, John Doucette, Dan Aoki, Steam-boat Mokuahi. *D:* Stuart Heisler; *P:* Howard W. Koch; *Sc:* Richard Alan Simmons. (1:29) World War II drama of four marines sent to an island held by the Japanese to get important information on minefields from a French planter. Photographed in Technicolor on the Solomon and Hawaiian Islands in the Pacific, it was based on Richard G. Hubler's 1946 novel *I've Got Mine.*

184. The Beast from Haunted Cave (Filmgroup; 1959). *Cast:* Michael Forest, Sheila Carol, Frank Wolff, Richard Sinatra (nephew of Frank), Wally Campo. *D:* Monte Hellman; *P:* Gene Corman; *Sc:* Charles Griffith. (1:04) (video) Horror programmer of crooks planning a heist from a goldmine who have their theft ruined by a ski instructor and a monster lurking in a cave. Filmed on location in the Black Hills of South Dakota, the film is a re-working of *Naked Paradise* (q.v.). Re-worked again as *Creature from the Haunted Sea* (1961).

185. The Beast from 20,000 Fathoms (Warner; 1953). *Cast:* Paul Christian, Paula Raymond, Cecil Kellaway, Kenneth Tobey, Donald Woods, Lee Van Cleef, Steve Brodie, Jack Pennick, Ross Elliott, Ray Hyke, Mary Hill, Michael Fox, Alvin Greenman, Frank Ferguson, King Donovan. *D:* Eugene Lourie (directorial debut); *P:* Hal E. Chester, Jack Dietz, Bernard W. Burton; *Sc:* Lou Morheim, Fred Freiberger. (1:20) (video/laserdisc) A prehistoric rhedosaurus thaws out of the Arctic ice following the explosion of an atomic bomb and makes its way to New York City, with a final stop at Coney Island. This monster-on-the-loose hit science fiction was produced for $250,000 and returned $5,000,000 to Warner and its producers. Based on a story by Ray Bradbury titled "The Fog Horn," the special monster effects were by Ray Harryhausen.

186. The Beast of Budapest (Allied Artists/Barlene Corp.; 1958). *Cast:* Gerald Milton, John Hoyt, Greta Thyssen, Michael Mills, Violet Rensing, Joseph Turkel, John Mylong, Booth Colman, Svea Grunfeld, John Banner, Charles Brill, Kurt Katch, Robert Blake, Tommy Ivo, Colette Jackson. *D:* Harmon C. Jones; *P:* Archie Mayo; *St:* Louis Stevens; *Sc:* John McGreevey. (1:12) Drama of communist ruled Hungary and the freedom fighters who revolted in 1956. Originally half of a double bill with *The Bride and the Beast* (q.v.).

187. The Beast of Hollow Mountain (United Artists/Nassour-Peliculas Rodriguez; 1956). *Cast:* Guy Madison, Patricia Medina, Eduardo Noriega, Carlos Rivas, Mario Navarro, Julio Villareal, Pascual Garcia Pena, Margarito Luna, Lupe Carriles, Manuel Arvide, Jose Chavez, Roberto Contreras, Lobo Negro, Jorge Trevino, Armando Gutierrez. *D:* Edward Nassour, Ismael Rodriguez; *P:* Edward and William Nassour; *St:* Willis O'Brien; *Sc:* Robert Hill. (1:20) This U.S.A./Mexican co-production tells the tale of a cattle rancher who finds that some of his cattle, as well as some of the local residents, are disappearing. Filmed on location in Mexico in DeLuxe color, CinemaScope and Regiscope (an animation process).

Beast of Paradise Island *see* **Port Sinister**

Beast of Paradise Isle *see* **Port Sinister**

188. The Beast with a Million Eyes (American Releasing Corp./San Mateo Prods.; 1955). *Cast:* Paul Birch, Lorna Thayer, Dona Cole, Dick Sargent, Leonard Tarver, Chester Conklin. *D: & P:* David Karmansky; *St: & Sc:* Tom Filer. (1:18) (video) Science fiction of desert dwellers who encounter a spaceship and a multifaceted-eye monster that is bent on world control.

189. The Beat Generation (MGM/Albert Zugsmith; 1959). *Cast:* Steve Cochran, Mamie Van Doren, Ray Danton, Fay Spain, Louis Armstrong (himself), Maggie Hayes, Jackie Coogan, Jim Mitchum, Cathy Crosby, Ray Anthony, Dick Contino, Irish McCalla, Vampira [aka: Maila Nurmi], Billy Daniels, Maxie Rosenbloom, Charles Chaplin, Jr., Grabowski, Paul Cavanagh. *D:* Charles Haas; *P:* Albert Zugsmith; *St: & Sc:* Richard Matheson, Lewis Meltzer; *Songs:* "The Real Gone Nothin' Blues," "I'm Off to the Moon," "We're On Our Way," "Speed, Speed, Speed" (Lewis Meltzer–Albert Glasser) all sung by Contino, *Title Song:* Tom Walton–Walter Kent (sung by Armstrong), "Someday You'll Be Sorry" (Louis Armstrong), "Love" (sung by Crosby). (1:35) (laserdisc) Critically panned exploitation-melodrama of a psychotic rapist who, when not assaulting women, hangs out in a waterfront beatnik coffee house. CinemaScope. (aka: *This Rebel Age*)

190. Beat the Devil (United Artists/ Romulus Films–Santana Pictures; 1954). *Cast:* Humphrey Bogart, Gina Lollobrigida, Jennifer Jones, Robert Morley, Peter Lorre, Edward Underdown, Ivor Barnard, Marco Tulli, Marion Perroni, Alex Pochet, Aldo Silvani, Guilio Donnini, Saro Urzi, Juan DeLanda, Manuel Serano, Mimo Peli. *D:* John Huston; *P:* Jack Clayton; *Sc:* Huston, Truman Capote. (1:29) (video/laserdisc) Satirical comedy-drama of a group of people waiting at a small Italian port for a ship's captain to sober up and take them to Africa. Filmed in Italy, the film was considered ahead of its time and has become a cult favorite. Based on the 1951 novel by James Helvick, it placed #10 on the "10 Best" list of the NBR.

Beatsville *see* **The Rebel Set**

191. Beau Brummell (MGM; 1954). *Cast:* Stewart Granger (Beau Brummell/George Bryan), Elizabeth Taylor, Peter Ustinov, Robert Morley (King George III), James Donald, James Hayter, Rosemary Harris, Paul Rogers, Noel Willman, Peter Bull, Charles Carson, Peter Dyneley, Ernest Clark, Mark Dignam, Desmond Roberts (final film), David Horne, Ralph Truman, Elwyn Brook-Jones, George De Warfaz, Henry Oscar, Harold Kasket. *D:* Curtis Bernhardt; *P:* Sam Zimbalist; *Sc:* Karl Tunberg. (1:53) (video) Clyde Fitch's old play was the source material for this lavishly produced costumer of the famous 19th century Casanova, George Bryan (aka: Beau Brummell). A U.S.A./ British co-production, filmed in England, it appeared twice before on the silent screen; (Vitagraph; 1913) with James Young and (Warner; 1924) with John Barrymore. Eastmancolor.

192. Beau James (Paramount; 1957). *Cast:* Bob Hope, Vera Miles, Alexis Smith, Paul Douglas, Darren McGavin, Joe Mantell, Richard Shannon, Walter Catlett (final film—d. 1960/Al Smith), Willis Bouchey, Sid Melton, Horace MacMahon, Jimmy Durante (unbilled cameo—himself), George Jessel (himself), Walter Winchell (narrator). *D:* Melville Shavelson; *P:* Jack Rose; *Sc:* Shavelson, Rose; *Song:* "Will You Love Me in December As You Do in May?" by James J. Walker, Ernest R. Ball. (1:43) Drama with songs of New York City's flamboyant mayor of the 1920s, Jimmy Walker (Hope), including his extra-marital affair and strong allegations of political corruption. Based on the book by Gene Fowler, it was photographed in Technicolor and VistaVision. Note: In British prints of this film, Alastair Cooke replaced Walter Winchell as narrator.

Beautiful But Dangerous (G.B. title) *see* **She Couldn't Say No**

193. Beauty on Parade (Columbia; 1950). *Cast:* Robert Hutton, Ruth Warrick, Lola Albright, John Ridgely, Hillary Brooke, Wally Vernon, Jimmy Lloyd, Donna Gibson, Frank Sully, Robert C. Hasha. *D:* Lew Landers; *P:* Wallace MacDonald; *St:* Arthur E. Orloff; *Sc:* Orloff, George Bricker. (1:06) Programmer drama of the Miss U.S.A. beauty pageant, paired on the bottom of a double bill with *Convicted* (q.v.).

194. Because of You (Universal-International; 1952). *Cast:* Loretta Young, Jeff Chandler, Alex Nicol, Frances Dee, Alexander Scourby, Mae Clarke, Lynne Roberts, Gayle Reed, Billy Wayne, Frances Karath. *D:* Joseph Pevney; *P:* Albert J. Cohen; *St:* Thelma Robison; *Sc:* Ketti Frings. (1:35) Melodrama of a woman jailed on a drug charge who, upon release, meets a decent man, marries him and then takes off with the man who got her jailed in the first place.

195. Because You're Mine (MGM; 1952). *Cast:* Mario Lanza (Renaldo Rossano), James Whitmore (Sgt. Batterson), Doretta Morrow (her only film/Bridget Batterson), Paula Corday (Francesca Landers), Dean Miller (Ben Jones), Eduard Franz (Albert Parkson Foster), Jeff Donnell (Patty Ware), Bobby Van (film debut/Artie Pilcer), Spring Byington (Mrs. Montville), Curtis Cooksey (Gen. Montville), Don Porter (Capt. Loring), Ralph Reed (Horsey), Celia Lovsky (Mrs. Rossano), Alexander Steinert (Maestro Paradori). *D:* Alexander Hall; *P:* Joe Pasternak; *St:* Ruth Brooks Flippen, Sy Gomberg; *Sc:* Karl Tunberg, Leonard Spigelgass. *Title Song:* (AAN) Nicholas Brodszky (m), Sammy Cahn (ly). (1:43) (video) Musical-comedy (tailored for Lanza) of an opera singer who is drafted into the army. Lanza's army of fans made this a big money-maker as well as turning the title song into a major hit. Technicolor.

196. Bedevilled (MGM; 1954-55). *Cast:* Anne Baxter, Steve Forrest, Victor Francen, Simone Renant, Robert Christopher, Joseph Tomelty, Maurice Teynac, Ina De La Hayes, Oliver Hussenot, Jean Ozenne, Jacques Hilling, Raymond Bussieres. *D:* Mitchell Leisen,

Richard Thorpe (unc.); *P:* Henry Berman; *St: & Sc:* Jo Eisinger. (1:25) Melodrama in Eastmancolor and CinemaScope of a chanteuse, a witness to murder, who is protected by a divinity student. Filmed on location in Paris, France.

197. Bedtime for Bonzo (Universal-International; 1951). *Cast:* Ronald Reagan, Diana Lynn, Lucille Barkley, Walter Slezak, Jesse White, Herbert Heyes, Herbert Vigran, Harry Tyler, Ed Clark, Ed Gargan, Joel Friedkin, Brad Browne, Elizabeth Flournoy, Howard Banks, Perc Launders, Brad Johnson, Bill Mauch, Ann Tyrrell. *D:* Frederick de Cordova; *P:* Michel Kraike; *St:* Raphael David Blau, Ted Berkman; *Sc:* Val Burton, Lou Breslow. (1:23) (video) Comedy of a psychology professor who brings a chimpanzee into his home for behavioral study. Somewhat of a cult film, it was followed by the sequel *Bonzo Goes to College* (q.v.).

Beginner's Luck (G.B. title) *see* **Two Dollar Bettor**

198. Beginning of the End (Republic/AB-PT Pictures Corp.; 1957). *Cast:* Peggie Castle, Peter Graves, Morris Ankrum, Richard Benedict, Thomas B. Henry, Than Wyenn, John Close, Don C. Harvey, Steve Warren, Pierre Watkin, Frank Wilcox, Alan Reynolds, Alan Wells, Eilene Janssen, Hylton Socher, Paul Grant, Patricia Dean, James Seay, Larry J. Blake, Douglas Evans, Richard Emory, Hank Patterson, Frank Connor, Don Eltner, Rayford Barnes, Frank Chase. *D:-P: & F/X:* Bert I Gordon; *St: & Sc:* Fred Freiberger, Lester Gorn; *Song:* "Natural, Natural Baby" Lou Bartel, Harriet Kane (sung by Bartel and chorus). (1:13) (video) Low budget science fiction of experiments to increase the size of agricultural produce via radioactive isotopes, which also affect an invading swarm of grasshoppers in the same way. Ran on a double bill with *The Unearthly* (q.v.).

199. Behave Yourself! (RKO/Wald-Krasna Prods.; 1951). *Cast:* Farley Granger, Shelley Winters, Margalo Gillmore, William Demarest, Francis L. Sullivan, Lon Chaney, Jr., Sheldon Leonard, Marvin Kaplan, Henry Corden, Glenn Anders, Allen Jenkins, Elisha Cook, Jr., Hans Conried, Corky (dog—received PATSY Award of Excellence–1952). *D:* George Beck; *P:* Jerry Wald, Norman Krasna, Stanley Rubin; *St:* Beck, Frank Tarloff; *Sc:* Beck; *Song:* Lew Spence, Buddy Ebsen. (1:21) (video) Comedy of a young married couple who come into possession of a lost dog and soon find themselves up to their ears in dead bodies.

200. Behind the High Wall (Universal-International; 1956). *Cast:* Tom Tully, Sylvia Sidney (final film until 1973), John Gavin (film debut), Betty Lynn, Don Beddoe, John Larch, Barney Phillips, Ed Kemmer (film debut), John Beradino, Rayford Barnes, Herbert C. Lytton, Nicky Blair, David Garcia, William Forrest, Frances Osborne, Peter Leeds, Jim Hyland, Bing Russell, Dale Van Sickel, George Barrows, Roy Darmour. *D:* Abner Biberman; *P:* Stanley Rubin; *St:* Wallace Sullivan, Richard K. Polimer; *Sc:* Harold Jack Bloom. (1:25) Melodrama of a prison warden who through a fluke is able to stash a large amount of stolen money. Hiding the fact, he has a man sentenced to death row. A remake of *The Big Guy* (Universal; 1939)

201. Bela Lugosi Meets a Brooklyn Gorilla (Realart/Sunray Picts.–Jack Broder; 1952). *Cast:* Bela Lugosi, Duke Mitchell, Sammy Petrillo, Charlita, Muriel Landers, Al Kikume, Mickey Simpson, Milton Newberger, Martin Garralaga, Ramona (chimpanzee). *D:* William Beaudine; *P:* Maurice Duke; *As.P:* Herman Cohen; *St:* & *Sc:* Tim Ryan; *Additional dialogue:* "Ukie" Sherin, Edmond G. Seward; *Songs:* "Deed I Do" Fred Rose–Walter Hirsch, "Too Soon" Nick Terry. (1:14) (video) Outrageous comedy of two entertainers who get stranded on a desert island with a mad doctor doing experiments with simians. Any similarity between Mitchell and Petrillo and Dean Martin and Jerry Lewis is purely intended. (aka: *The Boys from Brooklyn*)

202. Bell, Book and Candle (Columbia/Phoenix Prods.; 1958). *Cast:* James Stewart (Shepherd Henderson), Kim Novak (Gillian Holroyd), Jack Lemmon (Nicky Holroyd), Ernie Kovacs (Sidney Redlitch), Hermione Gingold (Bianca De Pass), Elsa Lanchester (Queenie), Janice Rule (Merle Kittridge), Howard McNear (Andy White), Pyewacket (cat—received 1st Place PATSY Award in 1959), Philippe Clay, Bek Nelson, The Brothers Candoli, Wolfe Barzell, Joe Barry, Gail Bonney, Monty Ash, Ollie O'Toole, Don Brodie, Dick Crockett, Ted Mapes, James Lamphier. *D:* Richard Quine; *P:* Julian Blaustein; *Sc:* Daniel Taradash; *ASD:* (AAN) Gary Odell (art director), Louis Diage (sets); *Costumes:* (AAN) Jean Louis. (1:43) (video/laserdisc) Technicolor romantic comedy of a man who finds himself under the spell of a beautiful witch. Based on the 1950 Broadway play by John Van Druten, it became one of the 26 top-grossing films of 1958-59.

203. **Belle le Grand** (Republic; 1951). *Cast:* Vera Ralston, John Carroll, William Ching, Muriel Lawrence, Hope Emerson, Grant Withers, Stephen Chase, John Qualen, Henry [Harry] Morgan, Charles Cane, Thurston Hall, Marietta Canty, Glenn Vernon, Don Beddoe, Isabel Randolph, John Holland, Frank Wilcox, Paul Maxey, Pierre Watkin, John Hart, Edward Keane, Sam Flint, Russell Hicks, Ed Cassidy, John Hamilton, Perry Ivins, William Schallert, Maude Eburne, Carl Switzer, Queenie Smith, Peter Brocco, Hal Price, Dick Elliott, Andrew Tombes, Eddie Parks, Fred Hoose, James Kirkwood, John Wengraf, Howard Negley, Ruth Robinson, Gino Corrado, Thomas Browne Henry, James Arness, Eddie Dunn, Emory Parnell, Chester Clute. *D:* Allan Dwan; *P:* Herbert J. Yates; *St:* Peter B. Kyne; *Sc:* D.D. Beauchamp. (1:30) Big budgeted Republic western of a lady gambler who marries a no-account who is more interested in her younger sister. Originally ran on a double bill with co-feature *Missing Women* (q.v.).

204. **The Belle of New York** (MGM; 1952). *Cast:* Fred Astaire, Vera-Ellen, Marjorie Main, Keenan Wynn, Alice Pearce, Clinton Sundberg, Gale Robbins, Lisa Ferraday, Henry Slate, Carol Brewster, Meredith Leeds, Lyn Wilde, Buddy Roosevelt, Roger Davis, Dick Wessel, Percy Helton, Tom Dugan. *D:* Charles Walters; *P:* Arthur Freed; *Sc:* Robert O'Brien, Irving Elinson; *Adaptation:* Chester Erskine; *Songs:* "Oops!," "Bachelor's Dinner Song," "When I'm Out With the Belle of New York," "I Wanna Be a Dancin' Man" Harry Warren-Johnny Mercer; "Let a Little Love Come In" Roger Edens. (1:22) (video/laserdisc) Technicolor musical set in New York City in the Gay 90s and based on an old 19th century musical-comedy play by Hugh Morton and Gustave Kerker.

205. **Belle of Old Mexico** (Republic; 1950). *Cast:* Estelita Rodriguez, Robert Rockwell, Dorothy Patrick, Thurston Hall, Florence Bates, Dave Willock, Gordon Jones, Fritz Feld, Anne O'Neal, Nacho Galindo, Joe Venuti (himself), Edward Gargan, Carlos Molina & Orchestra. *D:* R.G. Springsteen; *P:* Edward J. White; *St: & Sc:* Bradford Ropes, Francis Swann. (1:10) Musical of a college president who agrees to adopt the kid sister of a war buddy, who it turns out is no "kid". Trucolor.

206. **Belles on Their Toes** (20th Century–Fox; 1952). *Cast:* Jeanne Crain, Myrna Loy, Debra Paget, Jeffrey Hunter, Edward Arnold, Hoagy Carmichael, Barbara Bates, Robert Arthur, Verna Felton, Roddy McCaskill, Carol Nugent, Tina Thompson, Teddy Driver, Tommy Ivo, Jimmy Hunt, Anthony Sydes, Martin Milner, Clay Randolph, June Hedin, Robert Easton, Cecile Weston, Syd Saylor. *D:* Henry Levin; *P:* Samuel G. Engel; *Sc:* Phoebe and Henry Ephron. (1:28) A sequel to the hit *Cheaper by the Dozen* (q.v.) which relates how the widow Gilbreth carries on making a living and raising her twelve children. Based on a factual book by Frank B. Gilbreth, Jr. and Ernestine Gilbreth Carey.

207. **Bells of Coronado** (Republic; 1949-50). *Cast:* Roy Rogers, Dale Evans, Pat Brady, Grant Withers, Clifton Young, Robert Bice, Leo Cleary, Stuart Randall, John Hamilton, Edmund Cobb, Foy Willing and Riders of the Purple Sage, Rex Lease, Lane Bradford, Eddie Lee, Trigger (horse). *D:* William Witney; *P:* Edward J. White; *Sc:* Sloan Nibley. (1:07) (video) Trucolor Roy Rogers western, with three songs, of investigations into missing uranium ore and the murder of the mine's owner.

208. **Beloved Infidel** (20th Century-Fox/Jerry Wald; 1959). *Cast:* Gregory Peck (F. Scott Fitzgerald), Deborah Kerr (Sheilah Graham), Eddie Albert, Philip Ober, Herbert Rudley, John Sutton, Karin Booth (final film—ret.), Ken Scott, Buck Class, A. Cameron Grant, Cindy Ames. *D:* Henry King; *P:* Jerry Wald; *Sc:* Sy Bartlett. (2:03) Critically panned drama on the Hollywood affair between married writer F. Scott Fitzgerald and newspaper columnist Sheilah Graham. Based on the book by Ms. Graham and Gerold Frank. DeLuxe color, CinemaScope and stereophonic sound.

209. **Ben-Hur** (MGM; 1959). *Cast:* Charlton Heston (AA/Judah Ben-Hur), Jack Hawkins (Quintus Arrius), Stephen Boyd (Messala), Haya Harareet (Esther), Hugh Griffith (AA + "Best Supporting Actor" Award from the NBR/Sheik Ilderim), Martha Scott (Miriam), Sam Jaffe (Simonides), Cathy O'Donnell (final film—ret./Tirzah), Finlay Currie (Balthasar), Frank Thring (Pontius Pilate), Terence Longden (Drusus), Andre Morrell (Sextus),

Marina Berti (Flavia), George Relph (Tiberius), Adi Berber (Malluch), Stella Vitelleschi (Amrah), Jose Greci (Mary), Laurence Payne (Joseph), John Horsley (Spintho), Richard Coleman (Metellus), Duncan Lamont (Marius), Ralph Truman (aide to Tiberius), Richard Hale (Gaspar), Reginald Lal Singh (Melchior), David Davies (Quaestor), Dervis Ward (jailer), Claude Heater (The Christ), Mino Doro (Gratus), Robert Brown (chief of rowers), Tutte Lemkow (leper), Howard Lang (Hortator), Ferdy Mayne (rescue ship captain), John Le Mesurier (doctor), Stevenson Lang (blind man), Aldo Mozele (Barca), Dino Fazio (Marcello), Michael Cosmo (Raimondo), Remington Olmstead (Decurian), Hugh Billingsley (Mario), Aldo Silvani (man in Nazareth) Cliff Lyons (The Nubian), Joe Yrigoyen (The Egyptian), Joe Canutt (sportsman). *D:* (AA) William Wyler; *P:* (AA-Best Picture) Sam Zimbalist (who died before production was completed); *Sc:* (AAN) Karl Tunberg (with the uncredited participation of Christopher Fry, Maxwell Anderson, S.N. Behrman and Gore Vidal); *Cin:* (AA) Robert L. Surtees; *ASD:* (AA) William A. Horning, Edward Carfagno (art directors), Hugh Hunt (sets); Music (AA) Miklos Rozsa; *Sound:* (AA) Franklin E. Milton and the MGM Sound Dept.; *Editors:* (AA) Ralph E. Winters, John D. Dunning; *Costumes:* (AA) Elizabeth Haffenden; *F/X:* (AA) A. Arnold Gillespie, Robert MacDonald (visual), Milo Lory (audible); *Associate Directors:* Andrew Marton and Yakima Canutt received a "Special Award" from the NBR for the direction and staging of the 15 minute chariot race sequence; *Associate Director:* (sea battle) Mario Soldati; *Assistant Directors:* Gus Agosti, Alberto Cardone; *Additional photography:* Harold E. Wellman, Pietro Portalupi. (3:32) (video/laserdisc) Lew Wallace's *Ben-Hur: A Tale of the Christ* (1880) is brought to the screen with $15,000,000 in grandiose splendor. The story of two friends whose difference of opinion regarding Roman rulership turns them into bitter enemies. Filmed in Italy, with a cast of tens of thousands and 3,000 sets, the film grossed $80,000,000 worldwide on first release, becoming one of the 28 top-grossing films of 1959-60. Receiving twelve nominations, it became an Oscar sweeper with eleven wins. It was voted "Best Film of the Year" at the British Academy Awards and by the New York Film Critics, while the NBR placed it at #2 on their "10 Best" list. The *New York Times* gave it a #9 placement. *Film Daily* placed it at #4 on their "10 Best" list of 1960.

A remake of the equally spectacular 1926 release by this studio with Ramon Novarro and Francis X. Bushman, a silent production which utilized two-color Technicolor sequences for segments depicting The Christ. The present version was photographed in Technicolor and Panavision Camera 65.

Note: The only other version of this story to be filmed was in 1907 by Kalem in one reel (about 10 mins.). It was hyped with "positively the most superb moving picture spectacle ever made in America in sixteen magnificent scenes with illustrated titles." Kalem did not acquire screen rights to the novel and found itself embroiled in a lawsuit brought by the publishers and the author's estate (Wallace died in 1905). It was the first suit ever brought against a film company involving purchase of screen rights. In 1911, Kalem arrived at a settlement of $25,000.

210. Bend of the River (Universal-International; 1952). *Cast:* James Stewart (Glyn McLyntock), J. Arthur Kennedy (Cole Garett), Julia [Julie] Adams (Laura Baile), Rock Hudson (Trey Wilson), Lori Nelson (film debut/ Marjie Baile), Jay C. Flippen (Jeremy Baile), Stepin Fetchit (Adam), Henry [Harry] Morgan (Shorty), Chubby Johnson (Capt. Mello), Howard Petrie (Tom Hendricks), Royal Dano (Long Tom), Jack Lambert (Red), Frank Ferguson (Don Grundy), Frances Bavier (Mrs. Prentiss), Cliff Lyons (Wullie), Jennings Miles (Lock), Frank Chase (Wasco), Lillian Randolph (Aunt Tildy), Hugh Prosser (Johnson), Britt Wood, Gregg Barton, Donald Kerr, Harry Arnie. *D:* Anthony Mann; *P:* Aaron Rosenberg; *Sc:* Borden Chase. (1:31) (video) Acclaimed western drama of the Pacific Northwest in the 1840s, based on the 1950 novel *Bend of the Snake* by Bill Gulick. In Technicolor, it became one of the 23 top-grossing films of 1952-53. (G.B. title: *Where the River Bends*)

211. Beneath the 12-Mile Reef (20th Century–Fox; 1953). *Cast:* Robert Wagner (Tom Petrakis), Terry Moore (Gwyneth Rhys), Gilbert Roland (Mike Petrakis), J. Carrol Naish (Soak), Richard Boone (Thomas Rhys), Angela Clarke (Mama), Peter Graves (Arnold), Jay Novello (Sinan), Jacques Aubuchon (Sofotes), Gloria Gordon (Penny), Harry Carey, Jr. (Griff), James Harakas (Card), Charles Wagenheim (Paul), Marc Krah (Fat George), Rush Williams (David Rhys), Jonathan Jackson, Guy Carleton, Frank Joyner, Jack Pappas, William Llewellyn Johnstone, Jack Burke. *D:* Robert D. Webb; *P:* Robert Bassler; *St: & Sc:* A.I.

Bezzerides; *Cin:* (AAN-color) Edward Cronjager. (1:42) (video/laserdisc) Drama of rival families of sponge divers in the waters of Florida. Technicolor and CinemaScope.

212. Bengal Brigade (Universal-International; 1954). *Cast:* Rock Hudson, Arlene Dahl, Ursula Thiess, Torin Thatcher, Arnold Moss, Daniel O'Herlihy, Harold Gordon, Michael Ansara, Leslie Denison, Shep Menken, John Dodsworth, Ramsey Hill, Sujata and Asoka (specialty dancers). *D:* Laslo Benedek; *P:* Ted Richmond; *Adaptation:* Seton I. Miller; *Sc:* Richard Alan Simmons. (1:26) Action-adventure set in old India of a British officer quelling a native uprising against British rule. Based on Hall Hunter's 1952 novel *Bengal Tiger*. Technicolor. (G.B. title: *Bengal Rifles*)

Bengal Rifles (G.B. title) *see* **Bengal Brigade**

213. Bengazi (RKO/Panamint Pictures; 1955). *Cast:* Richard Conte, Victor McLaglen, Richard Carlson, Mala Powers, Richard Erdman, Hillary Brooke, Maury Hill, Jay Novello, Pedro Gonzales-Gonzales. *D:* John Brahm; *P:* Sam Weisenthal, Eugene Tevlin; *St:* Jeff Bailey; *Sc:* Endre Bohem, Louis Vittes. (1:18) A group of people search for Arab gold that was hidden in a sacred mosque in the Sahara desert during World War II.

214. The Benny Goodman Story (Universal-International; 1956). *Cast:* Steve Allen (Benny Goodman/clarinet dubbed by Goodman, himself), Donna Reed (Alice Hammond), Herbert Anderson (John Hammond), Berta Gersten (Mom Goodman), Robert F. Simon (Pop Goodman), Sammy Davis, Jr. (film debut/ Fletcher Henderson), Dick Winslow (Gil Rodin), Barry Truex (B. Goodman at 16), David Kasday (B. Goodman at 10), Hy Averbach (William Alexander), Wilton Graff (Mr. Hammond), Shep Menken (Harry Goodman), *and as themselves*: Harry James, Gene Krupa, Martha Tilton, Teddy Wilson, Lionel Hampton, Ziggy Elman and Kid Ory. *D:* Valentine Davies (only film as director); *P:* Aaron Rosenberg; *Sc:* Davies; *Songs include:* "Bugle Call Rag" (Elmer Schoebel–Billy Meyers–Jack Pettis); "Goody Goody" (Johnny Mercer–Matty Malneck); "Don't Be That Way" (Goodman-Mitchell Parish–Edgar Sampson); "Stompin' at the Savoy" (Goodman–Sampson–Chick Webb–Andy Razaf); "One O'Clock Jump" (Count Basie); "Moonglow" (Will Hudson-Eddie DeLange–Irving Mills); "Avalon" (Al Jolson–Vincent Rose); "Clarinet Concerto" (Mozart). (1:56) (video) Fact and fiction blend in this Technicolor musical biography of famed big band leader, Benny Goodman. One of the 24 top-grossing films of 1955-56.

215. Bernardine (20th Century–Fox; 1957). *Cast:* Pat Boone (film debut), Terry Moore, Janet Gaynor (only film appearance since 1938), Richard Sargent, Dean Jagger, James Drury, Ronnie Burns, Natalie Schafer, Walter Abel, Isabel Jewell (final film—ret.), Jack Costanzo & orchestra, Edit Angold, Val Benedict, Ernestine Wade, Russ Conway, Tom Pittman, Hooper Dunbar. *D:* Henry Levin; *P:* Samuel G. Engel; *Sc:* Theodore Reeves; *Songs:* Johnny Mercer, Nick Kenny, Charles Kenny, J. Fred Coots. (1:34) Musical romance of several male students who create a mythical dream girl. DeLuxe color and CinemaScope.

216. The Best of Everything (20th Century–Fox/Company of Artists, Inc.; 1959). *Cast:* Hope Lange (Caroline Bender), Stephen Boyd (Mike Rice), Suzy Parker (Gregg Adams), Joan Crawford (Amanda Farrow), Louis Jourdan (David Savage), Diane Baker (April Morrison), Martha Hyer (Barbara Lamont), Brian Aherne (Mr. Shalimar), Robert Evans (Dexter Key), Brett Halsey (Eddie Davis), Donald Harron (Sidney Carter), Sue Carson (Mary Agnes), Linda Hutchings (Jane), Lionel Kane (Paul Landis), Ted Otis (Dr. Ronnie Wood), June Blair (Brenda), Myrna Hansen (Judy Masson), David Hoffman (Joe), Theodora Davitt (Marge Stewart), Nora O'Mahoney, Wally Brown, Alena Murray, Rachel Stephens, Julie Payne. *D:* Jean Negulesco; *P:* Jerry Wald; *Sc:* Edith Sommer, Mann Rubin; *Title song:* (AAN) Alfred Newman (m), Sammy Cahn (ly), sung by Johnny Mathis; *Costumes:* (AAN) Adele Palmer. (2:01) (video) Drama of four women, their individual life problems, all united through a publishing firm. Based on the best-seller by Rona Jaffe, it became one of the 28 top-grossing films of 1959-60. Filmed on locations in New York City in DeLuxe color and CinemaScope.

217. Best of the Badmen (RKO; 1951). *Cast:* Robert Ryan, Claire Trevor, Jack Buetel (Bob Younger), Robert Preston, Walter Brennan, Bruce Cabot (Cole Younger), John Archer, Lawrence Tierney (Jesse James), Barton MacLane, Tom Tyler (Frank James), Robert Wilke (Jim Younger), John Cliff (John Younger), Lee MacGregor, Emmett Lynn, Carleton Young,

Byron Foulger, Larry Johns, Harry Woods, William Tannen, Ed Max, David McMahon, Everett Glass. *D:* William D. Russell (final—to TV); *P:* Herman Schlom; *St:* Robert Hardy Andrews; *Sc:* Andrews, John Twist. (1:23) (video) Technicolor western of a Union army officer who captures several well known outlaws, only to find himself dealing with trumped-up murder charges. Originally ran on a double bill with *Jungle Head-Hunters* (q.v.).

218. The Best Things in Life Are Free (20th Century–Fox; 1956). *Cast:* Gordon MacRae (final film until 1979/B.G. "Buddy" DeSylva), Dan Dailey (Ray Henderson), Ernest Borgnine (Lew Brown), Sherree North (Kitty), Tommy Noonan (Carl), Murvyn Vye (Manny), Phyllis Avery (Maggie Henderson), Larry Keating (Sheehan), Tony Galento (Fingers), Norman Brooks (Al Jolson), Jacques D'Amboise (specialty dancer), Roxanne Arlen (Perky Nicholas), Byron Palmer, Linda Brace, Patty Lou Hudson, Larry Kerr, Julie Van Zandt, Charles Victor, Eugene Borden, Harold Miller, Paul Glass. *D:* Michael Curtiz; *P:* Henry Ephron; *St:* John O'Hara; *Sc:* William Bowers, Phoebe Ephron; *Music:* (AAN) Lionel Newman; *Choreography:* Rod Alexander, Bill Foster; *Songs:* "Birth of the Blues," "Black Bottom," "Good News," "Button Up Your Overcoat," "It All Depends on You," "Keep Your Sunnyside Up," title song and "Sonny Boy." (1:44) Biographical comedy-drama of the famed song writing team of DeSylva, Brown and Henderson. DeLuxe color and CinemaScope.

219. Betrayed (MGM; 1954). *Cast:* Clark Gable, Lana Turner, Victor Mature, Louis Calhern, O.E. Hasse, Wilfrid Hyde-White, Ian Carmichael, Niall MacGinnis, Nora Swinburne, Roland Culver, Leslie Weston, Christopher Rhodes, Lilly Kann, Brian Smith, Anton Diffring. *D: & P:* Gottfried Reinhardt; *Sc:* Ronald Millar, George Froeschel; *Song:* "Johnny Come Home" Walter Goehr (m), Millar (ly). (1:47) (video/laserdisc) World War II drama of an American colonel who falls for a Dutch resistance fighter suspected of being a Nazi collaborator. This film ended Gable's 24-year reign at MGM. Filmed in Eastmancolor on location in Holland and England.

220. Betrayed Women (Allied Artists; 1955). *Cast:* Carole Mathews, Beverly Michaels, Peggy Knudsen, Tom Drake, Sara Haden, John Dierkes, Esther Dale, Paul Savage, Darlene Fields, John Damler, G. Pat Collins, Burt Wenland, Pete Kellett. *D:* Edward L. Cahn; *P:* William F. Broidy; *St:* Paul L. Peil; *Sc:* Steve Fisher. (1:10) Gutsy melodrama of women in prison and their revolt against authority.

221. Between Heaven and Hell (20th Century–Fox; 1956). *Cast:* Robert Wagner (Sam Gifford), Terry Moore (Jenny), Broderick Crawford (Waco), Buddy Ebsen (Willie), Robert Keith (Col. Gozzens), Brad Dexter (Joe Johnson), Mark Damon (Terry), Ken Clark (Morgan), Harvey Lembeck (Bernard Meleski), Skip Homeier (Swanson), L.Q. Jones (Kenny), Tod Andrews (Ray Mosby), Biff Elliot (Tom Thumb), Bart Burns (Raker), Frank Gerstle (Col. Miles), Carl Switzer (Savage), Gregg Martell (Sellers), Frank Gorshin (Millard), Darlene Fields, Ilene Brown, Scotty Morrow, Pixie Parkhurst, Brad Morrow, Scatman Crothers. *D:* Richard Fleischer; *P:* David Weisbart; *Sc:* Harry Brown; *Music:* (AAN) Hugo Friedhofer. (1:34) (video) World War II drama set in the Pacific theater of a wealthy southerner who proves himself in battle. Based on the 1955 novel *The Day the Century Ended* by Francis Gwaltney. DeLuxe color and CinemaScope.

222. Between Midnight and Dawn (Columbia; 1950). *Cast:* Mark Stevens, Gale Storm, Edmond O'Brien, Donald Buka, Gale Robbins, Anthony Ross, Roland Winters, Tito Vuolo, Madge Blake, Philip Van Zandt, Lora Lee Michel, Jack Del Rio, Grazia Narciso, Cliff Bailey, Tony Barr, Peter Mamakos, Earl Breitbard, Wheaton Chambers, Frances Morris. *D:* Gordon Douglas; *P:* Hunt Stromberg; *St:* Gerald Drayson Adams, Leo Katcher; *Sc:* Eugene Ling. (1:29) Crime melodrama of a lawman seeking the killer of his partner. (aka: *Prowl Car*) *Chain Gang* (q.v.) completed the double bill program.

223. Beware My Lovely (RKO; 1952). *Cast:* Ida Lupino, Robert Ryan, Taylor Holmes, Barbara Whiting, James Williams, O.Z. Whitehead, Dee Pollock. *D:* Harry Horner; *P:* Collier Young; *Sc:* Mel Dinelli. (1:17) (video/laserdisc) Melodrama of a widow who hires a handyman and slowly learns that he is psychopathic. Based on *The Man*, a story and play by Mr. Dinelli.

224. Beware of Blondie (Columbia; 1950). *Cast:* Penny Singleton (Blondie), Arthur Lake (final film—to TV and radio/Dagwood Bumstead), Larry Simms (Alexander), Marjorie Kent (Cookie), Danny Mummert (Alvin

(Fuddle), Adele Jergens, Dick Wessel (mailman), Jack Rice, Alyn Lockwood, Emory Parnell (Herbert Woodley), Isabel Withers (Harriet Woodley), Douglas Fowley, William E. Green, Edward Earle (Mr. Dithers). *D:* Edward Bernds; *P:* Milton Feldman; *Sc:* Jack Henley. (1:06) Blondie helps Dagwood out of the clutches of a beautiful swindler, after his boss Mr. Dithers leaves him in charge of the office. Based on the comic strip characters created by Chic Young, this was the 28th and final entry in the long-running series that began in 1938.

225. Beyond a Reasonable Doubt (RKO; 1956). *Cast:* Dana Andrews, Joan Fontaine, Sidney Blackmer, Philip Bourneuf, Shepperd Strudwick, Arthur Franz, Edward Binns, Robin Raymond, Barbara Nichols, William Leicester, Dan Seymour, Rusty Lane, Joyce Taylor, Carleton Young, Trudy Wroe, Joe Kirk, Charles Evans, Wendell Niles. *D:* Fritz Lang; *P:* Bert Friedlob; *St: & Sc:* Douglas Morrow. (1:20) (video) Mystery-melodrama with a twist ending of an attempt to challenge circumstantial evidence as a convicting factor in criminal cases.

226. Beyond Mombasa (Columbia/Tondon Prods.-Hemisphere Films, Ltd.; 1957). *Cast:* Cornel Wilde, Donna Reed, Leo Genn, Ron Randell, Christopher Lee, Dan Jackson, Eddie Calvert, Roy Purcell, Bartholomew Sketch, Clive Morton, Macdonald Parke, Virginia Bedard, Julian Sherrier, Ed Johnson. *D:* George Marshall; *P:* Tony Owen; *Sc:* Richard English, Gene Levitt. (1:30) Action-adventure set in East Africa of a uranium hunter who comes up against a tribe of leopard men. A U.S.A./British co-production based on an unpublished short story by James Eastwood titled "The Mark of the Leopard."

227. Beyond the Purple Hills (Columbia/Gene Autry Prods.; 1950). *Cast:* Gene Autry, Jo Carroll Dennison, Pat Buttram, Don Kay Reynolds, James Millican, Hugh O'Brian, Don Beddoe, Bob Wilke, Roy Gordon, Harry Harvey, Gregg Barton, Pat O'Malley, Merrill McCormack, Frank Ellis, John Cliff, Maudie Prickett, Victor Cox, Jerry Ambler, Lynton Brent, Sandy Sanders, Tex Terry, Ralph Peters, Cliff Barnett, Fenton Jones, Herman Hack, Frank O'Connor, Frankie Marvin, Bobby Clark, Boyd Stockman. *D:* John English; *P:* Armand Schaefer; *St: & Sc:* Norman S. Hall; *Title Song:* Charles and Nick Kenny. (1:09) (video) Western of a young man who is accused of killing his father. Gene proves otherwise. In Sepiatone.

Beyond the River (G.B. title) *see* **The Bottom of the Bottle**

228. Bhowani Junction (MGM; 1956). *Cast:* Ava Gardner (Victoria Jones), Stewart Granger (Col. Rodney Savage), Bill Travers (Patrick Taylor), Francis Matthews (Ranjitt Kasel), Abraham Sofaer (Surabhai), Freda Jackson (The Sadani), Peter Illing (Ghanshyam), Marne Maitland (Govindaswami), Lionel Jeffries (Lt. Graham McDaniel), Edward Chapman (Thomas Jones), Alan Tilvern (Ted Dunphy). *D:* George Cukor; *P:* Pandro S. Berman; *Sc:* Sonya Levien, Ivan Moffatt. (1:50) (video/laserdisc) A lavishly produced historical drama, filmed on location in England and Pakistan (when India refused permission), set during the demise of British rule in India. A U.S.A./British co-production, based on the 1954 best seller by John Masters. Filmed in Eastmancolor and CinemaScope, it became one of the 24 top-grossing films of 1955-56.

229. The Big Beat (Universal-International; 1958). *Cast:* Gogi Grant, William Reynolds, Andra Martin, Jeffrey Stone, Rose Marie, Hans Conried, Bill Goodwin (final film—d. 1958), Howard Miller, Jack Straw, Phil Harvey, Ingrid Goude, Steve Drexel, Charlie Barnet, Buddy Bregman, Alan Copeland, The Dell Vikings, The Diamonds, Fats Domino, The Four Aces, Harry James, The Lancers, Freddy Martin, Russ Morgan, The Mills Brothers, The George Shearing Quintet, Jeri Southern, The Bill Thompson Singers, The Cal Tjader Quintet. *D: & P:* Will Cowan; *St: & Sc:* David P. Harmon; *Songs:* "As I Love You" (Jay Livingston–Ray Evans) by Copeland, Morgan and Shearing; "You're Being Followed" (Arthur Altman–Charles Tobias) by The Mills Brothers; "Can't Wait" (Barry Mirkin–Grace Saxon) by The Dell Vikings; "You've Never Been in Love" (Jack Lloyd–Alan Copeland) by Gogi Grant; "The Big Beat" (Fats Domino–Dave Bartholomew) by Domino; "I'm Walkin'" (Domino–Bartholomew) by Domino; "It's Great When You're Doing a Show" (Eddie Pola/added lyrics by Copeland and Lloyd) by Rose Marie and The Lancers; "Where Mary Go" (Diane Lampert–John Gluck, Jr.) by the Diamonds; "Little Darlin'" (Maurice Williams) by The Diamonds; "Lazy Love" (Bernard Gasso–Irving Fields) by Gogi Grant and Harry James; "I Waited So Long" (Livingston-Evans) by Jeri Southern and Cal Tjader Quintet; "Take My Heart" (Al Alberts–Dave Mahoney) by The Four Aces and "Call Me" (Gasso–Fields) by Grant. (1:22) A bevy of musical numbers and a thin plot make up this feature with a definite eye on the teen market of the day. Eastmancolor. Originally paired on a double bill with *Summer Love* (q.v.).

230. The Big Bluff (United Artists/ Planet Filmplays, Inc.; 1955). *Cast:* John Bromfield, Martha Vickers, Robert Hutton, Rosemarie Bowe, Eve Miller, Max Palmer, Eddie Bee, Robert Bice, Pierre Watkin, Beal Wong, Rusty Wescoatt, Mitchell Kowal, Jack Daly, Paul McGuire, George Conrad, Kay Garrett. *D: & P:* W. Lee Wilder; *St:* Mindret Lord; *Sc:* Fred Freiberger. (1:10) (video) Low budget melodrama of a conman who marries a wealthy woman, knowing she only has a short time to live. When she begins to recover, he then plans her murder.

231. The Big Boodle (United Artists/ Monteflor, Inc.; 1957). *Cast:* Errol Flynn, Pedro Armendariz, Rossana Rory, Jacques Aubuchon, Gia Scala, Sandro Giglio, Carlos Rivas, Charles Todd, Guillermo Alvarez Guedes, Carlos Mas, Rogelio Hernandez, Velia Martinez, Aurora Pita. *D:* Richard Wilson; *P:* Lewis F. Blumberg; *Sc:* Jo Eisinger. (1:23) Melodrama of a casino dealer in pre–Castro Cuba who gets mixed up with counterfeiters. From Robert Sylvester's 1954 novel. (G.B. title: *A Night in Havana*) Originally ran on the top of double bill with *Pharaoh's Curse* (q.v.).

232. The Big Caper (United Artists/ P.T.S. Prods., Inc.; 1957). *Cast:* Rory Calhoun, Mary Costa, James Gregory, Robert Harris, Corey Allen, Paul Picerni, Louise Arthur, Roxanne Arlen, Pat McVey, James Nolan, Florenz Ames, Roscoe Ates, Terry Kelman, Melody Gates. *D:* Robert Stevens (debut); *P:* Howard Pine, William Thomas; *St:* Lionel White; *Sc:* Martin Berkeley. (1:24) Crime-melodrama of a planned bank heist in a small town and how the plans fall apart.

The Big Carnival *see* **Ace in the Hole: The Human Interest Story**

233. The Big Chase (Lippert/Be Be Corp.; 1954). *Cast:* Glenn Langan, Adele Jergens, Lon Chaney, Jr., Jim Davis, Douglas Kennedy, Jay Lawrence, Jack Daly, Joseph Flynn, Lou Roberson, Phil Arnold, Gil Perkins, Tom Walker, Jack Breed, Wheaton Chambers, Iris Menshell. *D:* Arthur D. Hilton; *P:* Robert L. Lippert, Jr.; *St: & Sc:* Fred Freiberger. (1:00) Crime-melodrama of a cop in pursuit of a gang that just heisted an armored car.

234. The Big Circus (Allied Artists/ Saratoga–Vic Mature Pictures; 1959). *Cast:* Victor Mature, Red Buttons, Rhonda Fleming, Kathryn Grant (final film–ret.), Gilbert Roland, Vincent Price, Peter Lorre, David Nelson, Adele Mara, Howard McNear, Charles Watts, Steve Allen (himself) *and circus acts:* Hugo Zacchini (human cannonball), Dick Walker (lion tamer), The Flying Alexanders, Gene Mendez (wirewalker–stunt double for Roland), The Ronnie Lewis Trio, The Jungleland Elephants, Tex Carr and His Chimpanzees, Dick Berg's Movieland Seals. *D:* Joseph M. Newman; *P:* Irwin Allen; *St:* Allen; *Sc:* Allen, Charles Bennett, Irving Wallace; *Title Song:* Sammy Fain–Paul Francis Webster. (1:48) (video) Drama of a circus beset by financial problems and a competitor's saboteur operating secretly in their midst to destroy the circus. Filmed at MGM studios. Technicolor and CinemaScope.

235. The Big Combo (Allied Artists/ Security Picts., Inc.–Theodora Prods., Inc.; 1954–55). *Cast:* Cornel Wilde, Richard Conte, Brian Donlevy, Jean Wallace, Robert Middleton, Lee Van Cleef, Earl Holliman, Helen Walker, Jay Adler, John Hoyt, Ted de Corsia, Helene Stanton, Roy Gordon, Whit Bissell, Philip Van Zandt, Steve Mitchell, Baynes Barron, Rita Gould, Tony Michaels, Bruce Sharpe, Michael Mark, Donna Drew. *D:* Joseph Lewis; *P:* Sidney Harmon; *St: & Sc:* Philip Yordan. (1:26) (video) Film noir of a criminal organization headed by a sadistic boss, his wife who rats on him for his infidelity and the lawmen who bring it all to an end. A gutsy '50s item with a cult following.

236. The Big Country (United Artists/ Anthony-Worldwide; 1958). *Cast:* Gregory Peck (James McKay), Jean Simmons (Julie Maragon), Carroll Baker (Patricia Terrill), Charlton Heston (Steve Leech), Burl Ives (AA/ Rufus Hannassey), Charles Bickford (Major Henry Terrill), Alfonso Bedoya (final film—d. 1957/Ramon), Chuck Connors (Buck Hannassey), Chuck Hayward (Rafe Hannassey), Buff Brady (Dude Hannassey), Jim Burk (Blackie Hannassey), Dorothy Adams, Chuck Roberson, Bob Morgan, John McKee, Jay "Slim" Talbot, Donald Kerr, Ralph Sanford, Harry V. Cheshire, Dick Alexander, Jonathan Peck, Stephen Peck, Carey Paul Peck. *D:* William Wyler; *P:* Wyler, Gregory Peck; *Adaptation:*

Jessamyn West, Wyler; *Sc:* James R. Webb, Sy Bartlett, Robert Wilder; *Music:* (AAN) Jerome Moross. (2:46) (video) Sprawling contemporary western drama of conflicts between various residents of a large western ranch. Based on a *Saturday Evening Post* serial titled *Ambush at Blanco Canyon* by Donald Hamilton, which was released in book form in 1958 as *The Big Country*. Photographed in Technicolor and Technirama on the Drais Ranch near Stockton, CA., the film grossed $5,000,000. The film was in nomination at the British Academy Awards in 1959, and nominated (in '58) by the New York Film Critics as "Best Film."

237. The Big Fisherman (Buena Vista/ Rowland V. Lee Prods.-Centurion; 1959). *Cast:* Howard Keel (Simon Peter), Susan Kohner (Fara), John Saxon (Voldi), Martha Hyer (Herodias), Herbert Lom (Herod-Antipas), Ray Stricklyn (Deran), Marian Seldes (Arnon), Alexander Scourby (David Ben-Sadok), Beulah Bondi (Hannah), Jay Barney (John the Baptist), Charlotte Fletcher (Rennah), Mark Dana (Zendi), Rhodes Reason (Andrew), Michael Branden (aka: Archie Twitchell/Menicus), Brian Hutton (John), Thomas Troupe (James), Marianne Stewart (Ione), Jonathan Harris (Lysias), Leonard Mudie (Ilderan), Peter Adams (Phillip), Jo Gilbert (Deborah), Stuart Randall (Aretas), Herbert Rudley (Tiberius), Phillip Pine (Lucius), James Griffith (beggar), Michael Mark, Joe Di Reda, Francis McDonald (final film—ret.), Perry Ivins, Ralph Moody, Tony Jochim, Don Turner. *D:* Frank Borzage (final film—d. 1962); *P:* Rowland V. Lee; *As.P:* Eric G. Stacey; *Sc:* Howard Estabrook, Lee; *Cin:* (AAN) Lee Garmes; *ASD:* (AAN) John DeCuir (art director), Julia Heron (sets); *Costumes:* (AAN) Renie. (3:00) The story of apostle Simon Peter and the early days of Christianity in the 1st century A.D. Lavishly produced in California in Technicolor, Ultra Panavision 70 and stereophonic sound, it was based on the final published work of author Lloyd C. Douglas. Note: Author Douglas stated shortly before his death in 1951 that he hoped *The Big Fisherman* would remain a book and not become a movie. Some critics agreed.

238. The Big Fun Carnival (Artist-Producers Assoc.; 1957). *Cast:* Marian Stafford, Jared Reed. *D:* Marc Daniels. (1:30) An obscure independent production.

239. The Big Gusher (Columbia; 1951). *Cast:* Wayne Morris, Preston Foster, Dorothy Patrick, Paul E. Burns, Eddie Parker, Emmett Vogan, Fred F. Sears. *D:* Lew Landers; *P:* Wallace MacDonald; *St:* Harold R. Greene; *Sc:* Daniel B. Ullman. (1:08) A low budget action-adventure of the oil fields. Originally ran on the bottom of a double bill with *Never Trust a Gambler* (q.v.).

240. The Big Hangover (MGM; 1950). *Cast:* Van Johnson, Elizabeth Taylor, Percy Waram, Fay Holden, Leon Ames, Edgar Buchanan, Selena Royle, Gene Lockhart, Rosemary DeCamp, Philip Ahn, Matt Moore, Pierre Watkin, Russell Hicks, Gordon Richards. *D:-P:-St: & Sc:* Norman Krasna. (1:22) (video) Dramatic story of a lawyer with an allergy to alcohol and how the affliction affects his personal and professional life.

241. The Big Heat (Columbia; 1953). *Cast:* Glenn Ford, Gloria Grahame, Jocelyn Brando, Alexander Scourby, Lee Marvin, Jeanette Nolan, Peter Whitney, Willis Bouchey, Robert Burton, Adam Williams, Chris Alcaide, Carolyn Jones, John Crawford, John Doucette, Harry Lauter, Dorothy Green, Dan Seymour, Ric Roman, Howard Wendell, Michael Granger, Edith Evanson, Joe Mell, Sid Clute, Norma Randall, Linda Bennett, Herbert Lytton, Ezelle Poule, Byron Kane, Ted Stanhope, Mike Ross, Bill Murphy, Phil Arnold, Mike Mahoney, Pat Miller, Paul Maxey, Charles Cane, Kathryn Eames, Al Eben, Phil Chambers, Robert Forrest. *D:* Fritz Lang; *P:* Robert Arthur; *Sc:* Sydney Boehm. (1:29) (video/laserdisc) Acclaimed *film noir* of a detective who is determined to bust the mob after his wife is killed. Based on a *Saturday Evening Post* serial by William P. McGivern.

242. Big House U.S.A. (United Artists/ Bel-Air–Camden Prods., Inc.; 1955). *Cast:* Broderick Crawford, Ralph Meeker, Reed Hadley, Randy Farr, William Talman, Lon Chaney, Jr., Charles Bronson, Roy Roberts, Peter Votrian, Willis Bouchey. *D:* Howard W. Koch; *P:* Aubrey Schenck; *Sc:* John C. Higgins. (1:22) Melodrama of five cons who break out of Cascabel Island Prison and head to Colorado's Royal George Park where one of the five buried ransom money he collected for a boy he had kidnapped.

243. Big Jim McLain (Warner/Wayne-Fellows; 1952). *Cast:* John Wayne, Nancy Olson, James Arness, Alan Napier, Hans Conried, Veda Ann Borg, Gayne Whitman, Hal Baylor, Robert Keys, John Hubbard, Sarah Padden,

Mme. Soo Yong, Dan Liu, Paul Hurst, Vernon McQueen. *D:* Edward Ludwig; *P:* Robert Fellows; *Story idea:* Richard English; *Sc:* English, James Edward Grant, Eric Taylor. (1:30) (video/laserdisc) Filmed in Hawaii. John Wayne is "Big Jim" in this tale of a man setting out to break up a commie spy ring.

244. The Big Knife (United Artists/Associates and Aldrich Co., Inc.; 1955). *Cast:* Jack Palance, Ida Lupino, Rod Steiger, Shelley Winters, Wendell Corey, Jean Hagen, Ilka Chase, Everett Sloane, Wesley Addy, Paul Langton, Nick Dennis, Bill Walker, Mel Welles, Mike Winkelman. *D: & P:* Robert Aldrich; *Adapt: & Sc:* James Poe. (1:51) A drama which exposes the ruthlessness often associated with the movie industry in Hollywood. Based on Clifford Odet's 1949 play of the same name, it received the "Silver Lion" at the Venice Film Festival.

245. The Big Land (Warner/Jaguar Prods.; 1957). *Cast:* Alan Ladd, Virginia Mayo, Edmond O'Brien, Anthony Caruso, Julie Bishop (final film—ret.), John Qualen, Don Castle, David Ladd (film debut), Jack Wrather, Jr., George J. Lewis, James Anderson, Don Kelly, Charles Watts. *D:* Gordon Douglas; *As. P:* George C. Bertholon; *Adaptation:* David Dortort; *Sc:* Dortort, Martin Rackin; *Song:* "I Leaned on a Man" Wayne Shanklin (m), Leonard Rosenman (ly). (1:32) Western, based on the novel *Buffalo Grass* by Frank Gruber of an alliance between cattlemen and wheat farmers to build a railroad link to bypass unscrupulous buyers. (G.B. title: *Stampeded*) WarnerColor.

246. Big Leaguer (MGM; 1953). *Cast:* Edward G. Robinson, Vera-Ellen, Jeff Richards, Richard Jaeckel, William Campbell, Carl Hubbell, Paul Langton, Al Campanis (himself), Lalo Rios, Bill Crandall, Frank Ferguson, John McKee, Mario Siletti, Bob Trocolor (himself), Tony Ravish (himself). *D:* Robert Aldrich (debut); *P:* Matthew Rapf; *St:* John McNulty, Louis Morheim; *Sc:* Herbert Baker. (1:10) Fact-based programmer sports drama of John B. "Hans" Lobert, a former major league player who runs a camp for baseball players, hopeful of making it in the big time.

247. The Big Lift (20th Century–Fox; 1950). *Cast:* Montgomery Clift, Paul Douglas, Cornell Borchers, O.E. Hasse, Bruni Lobel, Danny Davenport. *D:* George Seaton; *P:* William Perlberg; *St: & Sc:* Seaton. (2:00) (video) Fact-based post-war drama of a massive airlift of supplies into Germany by British and American pilots, following the Russian blockade of Berlin.

248. The Big Night (United Artists/Philip A. Waxman Prods., Inc.; 1951). *Cast:* John Barrymore, Jr., Preston Foster, Joan Lorring, Howard St. John, Dorothy Comingore (final film—ret.), Philip Bourneuf, Howland Chamberlin, Emile Meyer, Myron Healey, Mauri Lynn. *D:* Joseph Losey; *P:* Philip A. Waxman; *Sc:* Losey, Stanley Ellin. (1:15) Drama of a youth who spends a night searching for the man who mercilessly beat his father. Based on the novel *Dreadful Summit* by Mr. Ellin.

The Big North *see* **The Wild North**

249. The Big Operator (MGM/Albert Zugsmith–Fryman Enterprises; 1959). *Cast:* Mickey Rooney, Steve Cochran, Mamie Van Doren, Mel Torme, Ray Danton, Jim Backus, Jackie Coogan, Charles Chaplin, Jr., Vampira [aka: Maila Nurmi], Billy Daniels, Ben Gage, Jay North, Lawrence Dobkin, Leo Gordon, Donald Barry, Ziva Rodann, Joey Forman, Grabowski, Vito Musso. *D:* Charles Haas; *P:* Red Doff; *St:* Paul Gallico; *Sc:* Robert Smith, Allen Rivkin. (1:30) Exploitation melodrama of a ruthless union boss who sets out to eliminate witnesses when called before a Senate Investigating Committee. A remake of *Joe Smith, American* (MGM; 1952), it is based on Mr. Gallico's story "The Adventure of Joe Smith, American." CinemaScope. (aka: *Anatomy of a Syndicate*)

250. The Big Sky (RKO/Winchester Picts. Corp.; 1952). *Cast:* Kirk Douglas (Deakins), Dewey Martin (Boone), Elizabeth Threatt (Teal Eye), Arthur Hunnicutt (AAN/Zeb), Buddy Baer (Romaine), Steven Geray (Jourdonnais), Hank Worden (Poordevil), Jim Davis (Streak), Henri Letondal (Ladadie), Robert Hunter (Chouquette), Booth Colman (Pascal), Paul Frees (MacMasters), Frank DeKova (Moleface), Guy Wilkerson (Longface), Don Beddoe (horse trader), Cliff Clark, Fred Graham, George Wallace, Max Wagner, Charles Regan, Sam Ash, Jim Hayward, Anthony Jochim, Nolan Leary, Frank Lackteen, Ray Hyke, Eugene Borden, Veola Vonn, Cactus Mack, Crane Whitley, Barbara Hawks, Jay Novello, William Self. *D: & P:* Howard Hawks; *Sc:* Dudley Nichols; *Cin:* (AAN-b/w) Russell Harlan. (ort: 2:20) (2:02) (video) Big-budgeted frontier saga of a fur-trapping expedition. Based on A.B. Guthrie,

Jr.'s 1949 novel, computer-colored prints have been produced by Turner Entertainment.

251. Big Timber (Monogram; 1950). *Cast:* Roddy McDowall, Jeff Donnell, Lyn Thomas, Gordon Jones, Tom Greenway, Ted Hecht, Robert Shayne, Lyle Talbot. *D:* Jean Yarbrough; *P:* Lindsley Parsons; *Sc:* Warren Wilson. (1:13) Low budget action-drama set in a lumber camp. (aka: *Tall Timber*)

252. The Big Tip Off (Allied Artists; 1955). *Cast:* Richard Conte, Constance Smith, Bruce Bennett, Cathy Downs, James Millican, Dick Benedict, Sam Flint, Mary Carroll, Murray Alper, Lela Bliss, Harry Guardino, G. Pat Collins, George Sanders, Frank Hanley, Virginia Carroll, Alan Wells, Pete Kellett, Tony Rock, Tony DeMario, Cecil Elliott, Robert Carraher. *D:* Frank McDonald; *P:* William F. Broidy; *St: & Sc:* Steve Fisher. (1:19) Crime-melodrama of a newspaperman and his involvement with a crooked telethon operator.

253. The Big Trees (Warner; 1952). *Cast:* Kirk Douglas, Eve Miller, Patrice Wymore, Edgar Buchanan, John Archer, Alan Hale, Jr., Roy Roberts, Charles Meredith, Harry Cording, Ellen Corby, William Challee, Lester Sharp, Mel Archer, Duke Watson, Lillian Bond, Vici Raaf, Kay Marlow, William Vedder, Sue Casey, Ann Stuart, Art Millan, Iris Adrian. *D:* Felix Feist; *P:* Louis F. Edelman; *St:* Kenneth Earl; *Sc:* John Twist, James R. Webb. (1:29) (video/laserdisc) Set in the redwood forest of California, outdoor adventure of a lumberman at odds with a local religious sect. Author Peter B. Kyne is given no credit, but the film resembles and utilizes stock footage from the 1938 production *Valley of the Giants*. Technicolor.

254. The Bigamist (Filmakers Prods., Inc.; 1953). *Cast:* Edmond O'Brien, Joan Fontaine, Ida Lupino, Edmund Gwenn, Jane Darwell, Kenneth Tobey, John Maxwell, Peggy Maley, Mack Williams, James Todd, James Young, Lillian Fontaine, John Brown, Matt Dennis, Jerry Hausner, Kem Dibbs, Kenneth Drake, Mac Kim, George Lee. *D:* Ida Lupino; *P: & Sc:* Collier Young; *St:* Larry Marcus, Lou Schor. (1:19) (video) Drama of a married traveling salesman who weds another after getting her pregnant, then the first wife finds out about the second wife.

255. Bigger Than Life (20th Century-Fox; 1956). *Cast:* James Mason, Barbara Rush, Walter Matthau, Robert Simon, Christopher Olsen, Roland Winters, Rusty Lane, Rachel Stephens, Kipp Hamilton, Betty Caulfield, Virginia Carroll, Renny McEvoy, Bill Jones, Lee Aaker, Jerry Mathers, Portland Mason, Natalie Masters, Richard Collier, Lewis Charles, William Schallert, John Monoghan, Gus Schilling (final film—d. 1957), Alex Frazer, Mary McAdoo, Gladys Richards, David Bedell, Ann Spencer, Nan Dolan, Eugenia Paul, Mary Carver. *D:* Nicholas Ray; *P:* James Mason; *Sc:* Cyril Hume, Richard Maibaum (based on an article by Berton Roueche). (1:35) Drama of a man who volunteers to be a guinea pig for the experimental drug, cortisone, and the effects it has on him and his family. In nomination at the Venice Film Festival, it was photographed in DeLuxe color and CinemaScope.

256. Bird of Paradise (20th Century-Fox; 1951). *Cast:* Louis Jourdan, Debra Paget, Jeff Chandler, Everett Sloane, Maurice Schwartz, Jack Elam, Prince Lei Lani, Otto Waldis, Alfred Zeisler, Mary Ann Ventura, David K. Bray, Sam Monsarrat, Violet Nathaniel, Solomon Pa. *D:-P: & Sc:* Delmer Daves. (1:40) Romantic adventure-melodrama of a forbidden marriage between a white man and a South Seas native girl. A remake of the 1932 production by RKO which was based on the play by Richard Walton Tully. Technicolor.

257. The Birds and the Bees (Paramount; 1956). *Cast:* George Gobel, Mitzi Gaynor, David Niven, Reginald Gardiner, Fred Clark, Harry Bellaver, Hans Conried, Margery Maude, Clinton Sundberg, Milton Frome, Rex Evans, King Donovan, Mary Treen, Charles Lane, Bartlett Robinson, Douglas Evans, Barry Bernard, Kathryn Card, Vera Burnett, John Benson, Matt Moore, Valerie Allen. *D:* Norman Taurog; *P:* Paul Jones; *Sc:* Sidney Sheldon, Preston Sturges. (1:34) (video) Romantic comedy of the vegetarian son of a meat packer and the ups and downs in his love life. A remake of *The Lady Eve* (Paramount; 1941) which was based on an unpublished story of Monckton Hoffe. Technicolor and VistaVision.

258. Bitter Creek (Allied Artists; 1954). *Cast:* William "Wild Bill" Elliott, Beverly Garland, Veda Ann Borg, Carleton Young, Claude Akins, John Harmon, Dan Mummert, John Pickard, Jim Hayward, Forrest Taylor, Dabbs Greer, Mike Ragan [aka: Holly Bane], Zon Murray, John Larch, Florence Lake, Earle Hodgins, Jane Easton, Joe Devlin. *D:* Thomas

Carr; *P:* Vincent M. Fennelly; *St: & Sc:* George Waggner. (1:14) Western of a man who gets little cooperation from the local townspeople when he seeks to avenge the murder of his brother.

259. The Black Castle (Universal-International; 1952). *Cast:* Richard Greene, Boris Karloff, Stephen McNally, Paula Corday, Lon Chaney, Jr., John Hoyt, Michael Pate, Nancy Valentine, Tudor Owen, Henry Corden, Otto Waldis. *D:* Nathan Juran; *P:* William Alland; *St: & Sc:* Jerry Sackheim. (1:22) (video) Gothic horror-melodrama of a castle presided over by an evil count. Alland's first film as producer.

260. The Black Dakotas (Columbia; 1954). *Cast:* Gary Merrill, Wanda Hendrix, John Bromfield, Noah Beery, Jr., Richard Webb, Fay Roope, James Griffith, Jay Silverheels, Chris Alcaide, Peter Whitney, Howard Wendell, Frank Wilcox, Clayton Moore, Robert F. Simon, John War Eagle, George Keymas, Robert Griffin. *D:* Ray Nazarro; *P:* Wallace MacDonald; *St:* Ray Buffum; *Sc:* Buffum, DeVallon Scott. (1:05) Programmer Technicolor western with greed perpetrating a Sioux uprising during the days of the Civil War.

261. The Black Hand (MGM; 1949–50). *Cast:* Gene Kelly, J. Carrol Naish, Teresa Celli, Marc Lawrence, Frank Puglia, Barry Kelley, Mario Siletti, Carl Milletaire, Peter Brocco, Eleonora Mendelssohn, Grazia Narciso, Maurice Samuels, Burk Symon, Bert Freed, Mimi Aguglia, Maldo Minuti, Carlo Tricoli, Marc Krah, Jimmy Lagano. *D:* Richard Thorpe; *P:* William H. Wright; *St:* Leo Townsend; *Sc:* Luther Davis. (1:33) (video) Turn-of-the-century New York City's "Little Italy" is being terrorized by a secret Sicilian society called "The Black Hand" that intimidates its victims with extortion and murder. This drama deals with the city's law enforcement's efforts to bring it all down.

262. Black Hills Ambush (Republic; 1952). *Cast:* Allan Lane, Eddy Waller, Leslye Banning, Roy Barcroft, Michael Hall, John Vosper, Edward Cassidy, John Cason, Michael Barton, Wesley Hudman, Black Jack (horse). *D: & P:* Harry Keller; *St: & Sc:* M. Coates Webster, Ronald Davidson. (0:53) In this series entry, U.S. Marshall "Rocky" Lane is called in to bring justice to a lawless land.

263. Black Horse Canyon (Universal-International; 1954). *Cast:* Joel McCrea, Mari Blanchard, Race Gentry, Murvyn Vye, Irving Bacon, John Pickard, Ewing Mitchell, Pilar Del Rey, William J. Williams, Henry Wills, Outlaw (horse—received PATSY Award of Excellence in 1955). *D:* Jesse Hibbs; *P:* John W. Rogers; *Adapt:* David Lang; *Sc:* Geoffrey Homes [Daniel Mainwaring] (1:21) Technicolor western with its main focus on a wild black stallion and who owns it. Based on the 1950 novel *The Wild Horse* by Les Savage, Jr. Originally ran on a double bill with *Rails Into Laramie* (q.v.).

264. The Black Knight (Columbia/Warwick; 1954). *Cast:* Alan Ladd, Patricia Medina, Andre Morell, Harry Andrews, Peter Cushing, Anthony Bushell, Laurence Naismith, Patrick Troughton, Bill Brandor, Ronald Adam, Basil Appleby, Jean Lodge, Thomas Moore, Pauline Jameson, John Kelly, Elton Hayes, John Laurie, Olwen Brookes, David Paltenghi. *D:* Tay Garnett; *P:* Irving Allen, Phil C. Samuel, Albert R. Broccoli; *Sc:* Alec Coppel; *Additional dialogue:* Dennis O'Keefe, Bryan Forbes. (1:25) Action-drama set in King Arthur's court tells of a swordsmith's attempts to prove himself worthy of a lady's hand. A U.S.A./British co-production in Technicolor.

265. The Black Lash (Realart; 1952). *Cast:* Lash LaRue, Al "Fuzzy" St. John, Peggy Stewart, Kermit Maynard, Ray Bennett, Byron [Brian] Keith, Jimmy Martin, John [Cason?] Carson, Clarke Stevens, Bud Osborne, Roy Butler, Larry Barton. *D: & P:* Ron Ormond; *Sc:* Kathy McKeel. (0:57) (video) A U.S. marshal is called in to break up a gang of stagecoach robbers.

266. The Black Orchid (Paramount/Ponti-Girosi; 1959). *Cast:* Sophia Loren (voted "Best Actress" at the 1958 Venice Film Festival), Anthony Quinn, Ina Balin (film debut), Mark Richman, Jimmie Baird, Naomi Stevens, Frank Puglia, Virginia Vincent, Whit Bissell, Joe Di Reda, Majel Barrett, Vito Scotti, Zolya Tolma, Jack Washburn, Robert Carricart. *D:* Martin Ritt; *P:* Carlo Ponti, Marcello Girosi; *Sc:* Joseph Stefano. (1:36) (video) Drama of a widower romancing a widow whose ex had a criminal reputation. The widow's offspring object to the new romance. Based on a TV play by Joseph Stefano. VistaVision.

267. Black Patch (Warner/Montgomery Prods., Inc.; 1957). *Cast:* George Montgomery, Diane Brewster, Tom Pittman, Leo Gordon,

House Peters, Jr., Lynn Cartwright [Leo Gordon's real-life wife], George Trevino, Peter Brocco, Sebastian Cabot, Strother Martin, Ted Jacques, Gil Rankin, Stanley Adams, John O'Malley. *D:* *& P:* Allen H. Miner; *St:* *& Sc:* Leo Vincent Gordon. (1:22) Western of a sheriff out to clear his good name.

268. The Black Pirates (Lippert/Salvador Films; 1954). *Cast:* Anthony Dexter, Martha Roth, Lon Chaney, Jr., Robert Clarke, Victor Manuel Mendoza, Alfonso Bedoya, Toni Gerry, Eddy Dutko. *D:* Allen H. Miner; *P:* Robert L. Lippert, Jr.; *St:* *& Sc:* Fred Freiberger, Al C. Ward. (1:12) Swashbuckler of a band of pirates that invade a small Latin American town. A Mexican/U.S.A. co-production that was photographed for the CinemaScope screen in Anscocolor.

269. The Black Rose (20th Century-Fox; 1950). *Cast:* Tyrone Power (Walter of Gurnie), Orson Welles (Bayan), Cecile Aubry (Miriam), Jack Hawkins (Tristram), Michael Rennie (King Edward), Finlay Currie (Alfgar), Herbert Lom (Anemus), Mary Clare (Countess of Lessford), Bobby Blake (Mahmoud), Alfonso Bedoya (Lu Chung), Gibb McLaughlin (Wilderkin), James Robertson Justice (Simeon Beautrie), Henry Oscar (Friar Roger Bacon), Laurence Harvey (Edmond), Torin Thatcher (Harry), Hilary Pritchard (Hal, the miller), Madame Phang (Empress of China), Rufus Cruishank (Dickon), Ley On, Valery Inkijinoff, George Woodbridge, Ben Williams, Peter Drury, Carl Jaffe. *D:* Henry Hathaway; *P:* Louis D. Lighton; *Sc:* Talbot Jennings; *Costumes:* (AAN) Michael Whittaker. (2:00) Lavishly produced Technicolor costumer detailing the adventures of the Saxon, Walter of Gurnie, in the 11th century Orient. Based on the novel by Thomas B. Costain, it was filmed on location in England and North Africa. One of the 28 top-grossing films of 1949-50.

270. The Black Scorpion (Warner/Amex; 1957). *Cast:* Richard Denning, Mara Corday, Carlos Rivas, Mario Navarro, Carlos Musquiz, Pascual Pena, Fanny Schiller, Pedro Galvan, Arturo Martinez. *D:* Edward Ludwig; *P:* Frank Melford, Jack Dietz; *St:* Paul Yawitz; *Sc:* David Duncan, Robert Blees. (1:28) (video) Science fiction of a volcanic eruption which opens a fissure in the earth, unleashing a monstrous stinging arachnid on the population of Mexico. Willis O'Brien was in charge of stop-motion effects.

271. The Black Shield of Falworth (Universal-International; 1954). *Cast:* Tony Curtis, Janet Leigh, David Farrar, Herbert Marshall, Ian Keith, Barbara Rush, Torin Thatcher, Daniel O'Herlihy, Patrick O'Neal, Craig Hill, Doris Lloyd, Rhys Williams, Leonard Mudie, Leo Britt, Gary Montgomery, Robin Camp, Claud Allister. *D:* Rudolph Maté; *P:* Robert Arthur, Melville Tucker; *Sc:* Oscar Brodney. (1:38) Medieval action-drama of a peasant youth who turns out to be a member of the royal family. Based on Howard Pyle's 1954 novel *Men of Iron*, it was this studio's first CinemaScope production. Technicolor.

272. The Black Sleep (United Artists/Bel-Air; 1956). *Cast:* Basil Rathbone, Akim Tamiroff, Lon Chaney, Jr., Bela Lugosi, John Carradine, Herbert Rudley, Patricia Blake, Phyllis Stanley, Tor Johnson, Sally Yarnell, Claire Carleton, George Sawaya, Peter Gordon, Louanna Gardner, Clive Morgan, John Sheffield. *D:* Reginald LeBorg; *P:* Howard W. Koch; *Ex.P:* Aubrey Schenck; *St:* Gerald Drayson Adams; *Sc:* John C. Higgins. (1:21) (video) Reminiscent of horror films of Hollywood's golden age, this entry deals with a brain surgeon in a remote castle conducting experiments on other humans in attempts to cure his wife's brain tumor. (1962 re-release title: *Dr. Cadman's Secret*)

273. Black Tuesday (United Artists/Leonard Goldstein Prods.; 1955). *Cast:* Edward G. Robinson, Peter Graves, Jean Parker, Milburn Stone, Warren Stevens, Jack Kelly, Sylvia Findley, James Bell, Victor Perrin, Hal Baylor, Harry Bartell, Simon Scott, Russell Johnson, Phil Pine, Paul Maxey, William Schallert, Don Blackman, Dick Rich. *D:* Hugo Fregonese; *P:* Robert Goldstein; *St:* *& Sc:* Sydney Boehm; *Title song:* Robert Parrish. (1:20) Reminiscent of 1930s crime films, two convicts arrange the kidnapping of a prison guard's daughter and thus facilitate an escape.

274. The Black Whip (20th Century-Fox/Regal Films; 1956). *Cast:* Hugh Marlowe, Coleen Gray, Angie Dickinson, Richard Gilden, Strother Martin, Paul Richards, Charles Gray, William R. Hamel, Patrick O'Moore, Sheb Wooley, Dorothy Schuyler, Adele Mara, John Pickard, Harry Landers, Howard Culver, Duane Thorsen, Rush Williams, Sid Curtis, Rick Arnold, Robert Garvey, Bill Ward. *D:* Charles Marquis Warren; *P:* Robert Stabler; *St:* *& Sc:* Orville Hampton; *Additional dialogue:*

Sam Peckinpah. (1:17) Low budget western of two brothers who come to the rescue of four dance-hall honeys. Regalscope.

275. Black Widow (20th Century–Fox; 1954). *Cast:* Ginger Rogers, Van Heflin, Gene Tierney, George Raft, Peggy Ann Garner, Reginald Gardiner, Virginia Leith, Otto Kruger, Cathleen Nesbitt, Skip Homeier, Hilda Simms, Harry Carter, Geraldine Wall, Richard Cutting, Mabel Albertson, Aaron Spelling, Wilson Wood, Tony DeMario, Virginia Maples, Frances Driver, Michael Vallon, James F. Stone. *D:-P: & Sc:* Nunnally Johnson. (1:35) A mystery evolves when the body of a young woman is found hanging in the apartment of a Broadway impresario. Based on the 1952 novel by Patrick Quentin. CinemaScope.

276. Blackbeard the Pirate (RKO; 1952). *Cast:* Robert Newton (title role), Linda Darnell, William Bendix, Keith Andes, Torin Thatcher (Sir Henry Morgan), Irene Ryan, Alan Mowbray, Richard Egan, Skelton Knaggs, Dick Wessel, Anthony Caruso, Jack Lambert, Noel Drayton, Pat Flaherty. *D:* Raoul Walsh; *P:* Edmund Grainger; *St:* DeVallon Scott; *Sc:* Alan LeMay. (1:38) (video/laserdisc) Swashbuckling adventure tale in Technicolor of the infamous pirate and his acts of piracy against the Crown.

277. Blackboard Jungle (MGM; 1955). *Cast:* Glenn Ford (Richard Dadier), Anne Francis (Anne Dadier), Louis Calhern (Jim Murdock), Margaret Hayes (Lois Judby Hammond), John Hoyt (Mr. Warnecke), Richard Kiley (Joshua Y. Edwards), Emile Meyer (Mr. Halloran), Warner Anderson (Dr. Bradley), Basil Ruysdael (Prof. A.R. Kraal), Sidney Poitier (Gregory W. Miller), Vic Morrow (film debut/ Artie West), Dan Terranova (Belazi), Rafael Campos (Pete V. Morales), Paul Mazursky (Emmanuel Stoker), Jameel Farah (later: Jamie Farr/ Santini), Danny Dennis (DeLiea), Horace McMahon (detective), David Alpert (Lou Savoldi), Chris Randall (Levy), Yoshi Tomita (Tomita), Gerald Phillips (Carter), Dorothy Neumann (Miss Panucci), Henny Backus (Miss Brady), Paul Hoffman (Mr. Lefkowitz), Tom McKee (Manners), Robert Foulk (Mr. Katz), Manuel Paris, Richard Deacon, Virginia Pherrin. *D:* Richard Brooks; *P:* Pandro S. Berman; *Sc:* (AAN) Brooks; *Cin:* (AAN-b/w) Russell Harlan; *ASD:* (AAN-b/w) Cedric Gibbons, Randall Duell (art directors), Edwin B. Willis, Henry Grace (sets); *Editor:* (AAN) Ferris Webster. (1:41) (video/laserdisc) Juvenile delinquency drama of violence in the New York City school system. This film was one of MGM's biggest for the year, and one of the 27 top-grossing films of 1954-55. Placing #4 on the "10 Best" list of *Film Daily*, the pounding beat of "Rock Around the Clock" on the soundtrack by Bill Haley and the Comets did much to promote the popularity of the new music phenomenon, rock 'n' roll. It was based on the best-seller by Evan Hunter. Computer-colored prints have been produced by Turner Entertainment.

278. Blackjack Ketchum, Desperado (Columbia/Clover Prods.; 1956). *Cast:* Howard Duff, Maggie Mahoney, Victor Jory, David Orrick, Angela Stevens, Pat O'Malley, Don C. Harvey, Kermit Maynard, William Tannen, Ken Christy, Martin Garralaga, Ralph Sanford, Robert Roark, Jack V. Littlefield, Wesley Hudman, George Edward Mather, Sydney Mason, Charles Wagenheim. *D:* Earl Bellamy; *P:* Sam Katzman; *Sc:* Luci Ward, Jack Natteford. (1:16) Western of a reformed gunfighter forced to return to his profession. Based on the novel *Kilkenny* by Louis L'Amour.

279. Blades of the Musketeers (Howco; 1953). *Cast:* Robert Clarke, John Hubbard, Mel Archer, Keith Richards, Paul Cavanagh, Don Beddoe, Kristine Miller, Marjorie Lord, Lyn Thomas, Charles Lang, Peter Mamakos, James Craven, Byron Foulger, Hank Patterson. *D:* Budd Boetticher; *P:* Hal Roach, Jr.; *Sc:* Roy Hamilton. (0:54) The swashbuckling adventures of Alexandre Dumas' four swordsmen. Originally intended as a TV show, but released theatrically instead.

Blaze of Glory (G.B. title) *see* **Boy from Indiana**

280. Blazing Bullets (Monogram; 1951). *Cast:* Johnny Mack Brown, Lois Hall, House Peters, Jr., Stanley Price, Dennis Moore, Edmund Cobb, Milburn Morante (final film—ret.), Forrest Taylor, Edward Cassidy, Carl Mathews, George DeNormand. *D:* Wallace Fox; *P:* Vincent M. Fennelly; *Sc:* George Daniels. (0:51) A series western that involves the kidnapping of a girl's father. This film had the working title of "Gold Bullets."

281. The Blazing Forest (Paramount/ Pine-Thomas; 1952). *Cast:* John Payne, Richard Arlen, Agnes Moorehead, Lynne Roberts, Susan Morrow, William Demarest, Roscoe Ates, Ewing Mitchell, Walter Reed, Jim Davis,

Joey Ray, Joe Garcia, Brett Houston, Max Wagner. *D:* Edward Ludwig; *P:* William H. Pine, William C. Thomas; *St:* & *Sc:* Lewis R. Foster, Winston Miller. (1:30) Technicolor romance of the big timber country, as a logger's affairs of the heart take a back seat to a climactic forest fire.

Blazing Guns (TV title) *see* **Marshall of Heldorado**

282. The Blazing Sun (Columbia/Gene Autry Prods.; 1950). *Cast:* Gene Autry, Lynne Roberts, Pat Buttram, Anne Gwynne, Edward Norris, Gregg Barton, Alan Hale, Jr., Kenne Duncan, Tom London, Pat O'Malley, Nolan Leary, Sam Flint, Steve Darrell, Sandy Sanders, Frankie Marvin, Bob Woodward, Boyd Stockman, Virginia Carroll, Chris Allen, Lewis Martin, Almira Sessions, Charles Coleman. *D:* John English; *P:* Armand Schaefer; *St:* & *Sc:* Jack Townley. (1:10) A contemporary Gene Autry western of sophisticated bank robbers. In Sepiatone.

283. The Blob (Paramount/Tonylyn; 1958). *Cast:* Steven McQueen (starring debut), Aneta Corseaut, Earl Rowe, Olin Howlin, Stephen [Guy] Chase, John Benson, Robert Fields, James Bonnet, Anthony Franke, Molly Ann Bourne, Diane Tabben, George Karas, Lee Patton, Elbert Smith, Hugh Graham, Vince Barbi, Audrey Metcalf, Jasper Deeter, Elinor Hammer, Ralph Roseman, David Metcalf, George Gerberick, Keith Almoney, Tom Ogden, Pamela Curran, Charlie Overdorff, Josh Randolph, Julie Cousins, Eugene Sabel. *D:* Irvin S. Yeaworth, Jr. (debut); *P:* Jack H. Harris; *As.P:* Russell Doughten; *Sc:* Theodore Simonson, Kate Phillips (based on an original idea by Irvin H. Millgate); *Title song:* Burt Bacharach (m), Mack David (ly); *F/X:* Barton Sloane. (1:25) (video/laserdisc) Independently produced at the Valley Forge Film Studios in Pennsylvania, this science fiction catering to the teen audience was brought in at a production cost of $240,000. A meteor crashes to earth containing a protoplasmic blob that grows larger each time it absorbs human flesh it contacts. Photographed in DeLuxe color, it was followed by a sequel *Beware! The Blob* (1972) (aka: *Son of Blob*). Remade in 1988 on a bigger budget with better special effects.

284. The Blonde Bandit (Republic; 1949–50). *Cast:* Dorothy Patrick, Gerald Mohr, Robert Rockwell, Larry J. Blake, Charles Cane, Richard Irving, Argentina Brunetti, Alex Frazer, Nana Bryant, David Clarke, Jody Gilbert, Monte Blue, Eve Whitney, Norman Rudd, Bobby Scott, Bob Wilke, Philip Van Zandt, Ted Jacques, Walter Clinton, Eva Novak, Keith Richards, Lester Dorr, Roy Gordon. *D:* Harry Keller; *As.P:* Sidney Picker; *Sc:* John Butler. (1:00) Programmer crime-melodrama of a young girl who gets mixed up with a thief. Originally ran on a double bill with *Pioneer Marshall*, a 1949 Monte Hale western.

285. Blonde Dynamite (Monogram; 1950). *Cast:* Leo Gorcey, Huntz Hall, Gabriel Dell, Billy Benedict, David Gorcey, Buddy Gorman, Adele Jergens, Harry Lewis, Murray Alper, Bernard Gorcey, Jody Gilbert, John Harmon, Michael Ross, Lynn Davies, Beverlee Crane, Karen Randle, Stanley Andrews, Constance Purdy, Florence Auer, Tom Kennedy, Robert Emmett Keane, Dick Elliott. *D:* William Beaudine; *P:* Jan Grippo; *Sc:* Charles R. Marion. (1:06) In this "Bowery Boys" comedy series entry, our heroes get involved with bank robbers.

286. Blonde Pickup (Globe Roadshows; 1955). *Cast:* Clare Mortensen, Timothy Farrell, Rita Martinez, Peaches Page. *D:* Robert C. Dertano; *P:* George Weiss. (1:21) Indy crime tale of a crooked gym owner who is sought by the law and gangsters for fixing horse races and wrestling matches.

287. Blondie's Hero (Columbia; 1950). *Cast:* Penny Singleton, Arthur Lake, Larry Simms, Danny Mummert, William Frawley, Iris Adrian, Edward Earle, Joe Sawyer, Alyn Lockwood, Teddy Infuhr, Frank Jenks, Dick Wessel, Frank Sully, Jimmy Lloyd, Robert Emmett Keane, Mary Newton, Pat Flaherty, Ted Mapes, Frank Wilcox, Daisy (dog—himself). *D:* Edward Bernds; *P:* Ted Richmond; *St:* & *Sc:* Jack Henley. (1:07) Based on the comic strip characters created by Chic Young, this next-to-last entry in the comedy series has Dagwood joining the Army Reserve.

288. Blood Alley (Warner/Batjac; 1955). *Cast:* John Wayne, Lauren Bacall, Paul Fix, Mike Mazurki, Joy Kim, Berry Kroeger, Anita Ekberg, Henry Nakamura, W.T. Chang, George Chan. *D:* William A. Wellman; *P:* Unc.; *Sc:* A.S. Fleischman (based on his novel). (1:55) (video/laserdisc) Action-adventure of a boatman, ferrying 189 Chinese villagers out of the hands of the communists to freedom in Hong

Kong—with communist forces in hot pursuit. Filmed on location at China Camp in San Raphael near San Francisco, CA. In Warner-Color and CinemaScope.

289. Blood and Steel (20th Century-Fox/Associated Producers; 1959). *Cast:* John Lupton, Ziva Rodann, Brett Halsey, James Edwards, John Brinkley, Allen Jung, James Hong, Bill Saito. *D:* Bernard L. Kowalski; *P:* Gene Corman; *St: & Sc:* Joseph C. Gillette. (1:02) In this low budget World War II drama, a native girl assists four Navy Seabees in scouting out a Japanese-held island for use as a potential U.S. airbase. Originally paired on a double bill with *The Rookie* (q.v.).

290. Blood Arrow (20th Century-Fox/Regal Films/Embassy Prods.; 1958). *Cast:* Scott Brady, Phyllis Coates, Paul Richards, Don Haggerty, Rocky Shahan, Patrick O'Moore, Jeanne Bates, John Dierkes, Diana Darrin, Bill McGraw, Des Slattery, Richard Gilden. *D: & Ex.P:* Charles Marquis Warren; *P:* Robert Stabler; *St: & Sc:* Fred Freiberger. (1:15) Offbeat western of a Mormon girl trekking through hostile Indian territory in search of a life-saving serum for her people who are suffering an outbreak of smallpox. Regalscope.

Blood Creature *see* **Terror Is a Man**

Blood Is My Heritage (G.B. title) *see* **Blood of Dracula**

291. Blood of Dracula (American International/Carmel Prods.; 1957). *Cast:* Sandra Harrison, Louise Lewis, Gail Ganley, Jerry Blaine, Heather Ames, Malcolm Atterbury, Mary Adams, Thomas Browne Henry, Don Devlin, Jeanne Dean, Richard Devon, Paul Maxwell, Carlyle Mitchell, Shirley de Lancey, Michael Hall. *D:* Herbert L. Strock; *P:* Herman Cohen; *St: & Sc:* Ralph Thornton; *Song:* "Puppy Love" Larry Blaine. (1:08) (video) Teen horror of a student at a girls school who comes under the manipulative power of one of her teachers who turns her into a vampire. (G.B. title: *Blood Is My Heritage*) Originally ran on a double bill with *I Was a Teenage Frankenstein* (q.v.).

292. Bloodhounds of Broadway (20th Century-Fox; 1952). *Cast:* Mitzi Gaynor, Scott Brady, Mitzi Green (final film—ret), Marguerite Chapman, Michael O'Shea, Wally Vernon, Henry Slate, George E. Stone, Edwin Max, Richard Allan, Sharon Baird, Paul Wexler, Ralph Volkie, Charles [Bronson] Buchinski, Timothy Carey (film debut), Bill Walker, Alfred Mizner, Emile Meyer. *D:* Harmon Jones; *P:* George Jessel; *St:* Damon Runyon; *Adapt:* Albert Mannheimer; *Sc:* Sy Gomberg; *Songs:* Eliot Daniel, Ben Oakland, Paul Francis Webster; *Choreography:* Bob Sydney. (1:29) A Georgia bayou girl has aspirations to Broadway after meeting a crook on the lam. This Technicolor musical is not a forerunner of the 1989 production of the same name, though both utilize Runyonesque characters.

293. Bloodlust (Crown International; 1959–60). *Cast:* Wilton Graff, June Kenney, Robert Reed, Lilyan Chauvin. *D:-P:-St: & Sc:* Ralph Brooke. (1:29) This low budget horror of a mad doctor preying on teen victims was produced in 1959, but not released theatrically until the early 1960s.

294. Blowing Wild (Warner/United States Pictures; 1953). *Cast:* Gary Cooper, Barbara Stanwyck, Ruth Roman, Anthony Quinn, Ward Bond, Ian MacDonald, Richard Karlan, Juan Garcia. *D:* Hugo Fregonese; *P:* Milton Sperling; *Sc:* Philip Yordan; *Title song:* Dimitri Tiomkin (m), Paul Francis Webster (ly). (1:29) (video/laserdisc) Romantic drama of the Mexican oil fields, where it was filmed on location. A married woman sets her sights on a wildcatter she once had an affair with. Frankie Laine sings the title song.

The Blue and the Gold (G.B. title) *see* **An Annapolis Story**

295. The Blue Angel (20th Century-Fox/Jack Cummings; 1959). *Cast:* Curt Jurgens, May Britt, Theodore Bikel, John Banner, Fabrizio Mioni, Ludwig Stossel (final film—ret.), Wolfe Barzell, Ina Anders, Richard Tyler, Voytek Bolinski, Ken Walker, Del Erickson, Edit Angold, Gene Roth, Stella Stevens, Ilsa Burket, Barbara Luna, Carmen Austin. *D:* Edward Dmytryk; *P:* Jack Cummings; *Sc:* Nigel Balchin (based on the 1930 German screenplay by Karl Zuckmayer, Karl Vollmoeller and Robert Liebmann, which was based on a novel by Heinrich Mann); *Songs* "Falling in Love Again" (Fredrick Hollander), "Lola Lola" (Ray Evans–Jay Livingston), "I Yi Yi" (Mack Gordon–Harry Warren). (1:47) Melodrama of a middle-aged botany professor who becomes thoroughly captivated by a tawdry cabaret singer who he eventually marries. A remake of the 1930 German classic with Marlene Dietrich which most critics felt could not hold a candle to the original. Photographed in DeLuxe color and CinemaScope on locations in Rothenburg, Bavaria.

296. Blue Blood (Monogram; 1951). *Cast:* Bill Williams, Jane Nigh, Arthur Shields, Audrey Long, Lyle Talbot, Harry Shannon, Harry V. Cheshire, William J. Tannen, Milton Kibbee. *D:* Lew Landers; *P:* Ben Schwalb: *Sc:* W. Scott Darling. (1:12) B drama of a horse who is rescued from becoming dogfood. Based on the story "Dog Meat" by Peter B. Kyne, it was photographed in Cinecolor.

297. Blue Canadian Rockies (Columbia/Gene Autry Prods.; 1952). *Cast:* Gene Autry, Gail Davis, Pat Buttram, Carolina Cotton, Ross Ford, Tom London, Mauritz Hugo, Don Beddoe, Gene Roth, John Merton, David Garcia, Bob Woodward, Bill Wilkerson, The Cass County Boys. *D:* George Archainbaud; *P:* Armand Schaefer; *St: & Sc:* Gerald Geraghty. (0:58) (video) Gene steps in when he finds a girl is about to marry a scoundrel. Songs are included in this series western, photographed in Sepiatone. Originally ran on a double bill with *Hangman's Knot* (q.v.).

298. Blue Denim (20th Century–Fox; 1959). *Cast:* Carol Lynley (Janet Willard/repeating her stage role), Brandon de Wilde (Arthur Bartley), Macdonald Carey (Malcolm Bartley), Marsha Hunt (Jessie Bartley), Warren Berlinger (Ernie/repeating his stage role), Buck Class (Axel Sorenson), Nina Shipman (Lillian Bartley), Vaughn Taylor (Prof. Willard), Roberta Shore (Cherie), Mary Young (Aunt Bidda), Michael Caisney (Hobie), Jenny Maxwell (Marion), William Schallert, Juney Ellis, Anthony J. Corso. *D:* Philip Dunne; *P:* Charles Brackett; *Sc:* Edith Sommer, Dunne. (1:29) A night of careless passion due to overactive adolescent hormones leaves a 15-year-old girl and her 16-year-old boyfriend with a dilemma. This melodrama of teens in trouble, with a changed ending from the Broadway play of 1958 by James Leo Herlihy and William Noble, was a phenomenal success among teen audiences of 1959, making it one of the 26 top-grossing films of 1958-59. CinemaScope and stereophonic sound.

299. The Blue Gardenia (Warner/Blue Gardenia Prods.; 1953). *Cast:* Anne Baxter, Richard Conte, Ann Sothern, Raymond Burr, Jeff Donnell, Richard Erdman, George Reeves, Ruth Storey, Ray Walker, Nat "King" Cole (himself). *D:* Fritz Lang; *P:* Alex Gottlieb; *Sc:* Charles Hoffman; *Title song:* Bob Russell, Lester Lee. (1:30) Melodrama of a woman who flees when she believes she has killed a man who attacked her. Based on the story "Gardenia" by Vera Caspary.

300. Blue Grass of Kentucky (Monogram; 1950). *Cast:* Bill Williams, Jane Nigh, Ralph Morgan, Russell Hicks, Robert "Buzzy" Henry, Ted Hecht, Dick Foote, Jack Howard, Bill Terrell, Stephen S. Harrison, Pierre Watkin. *D:* William Beaudine; *P:* Jeffrey Bernerd; *St: & Sc:* W. Scott Darling. (1:11) Romantic drama in cinecolor of rival horse breeding families.

Blue Jeans (G.B. title) *see* **Blue Denim**

301. The Blue Veil (RKO/Wald-Krasna Prod.; 1951). *Cast:* Jane Wyman (AAN/Louise Mason), Charles Laughton (Fred K. Begley), Joan Blondell (AAN/Annie Rawlins), Richard Carlson (Gerald Kean), Agnes Moorehead (Mrs. Palfrey), Don Taylor (Dr. Robert Palfrey), Audrey Totter (Helen Williams), Cyril Cusack (Frank Hutchins), Everett Sloane (D.A.), Natalie Wood (Stephanie Rawlins), Vivian Vance (Alicia), Carlton Young (Mr. Palfrey), Alan Napier (Prof. Carter), Warner Anderson (Bill), Les Tremayne (Joplin), Dan Seymour (Pelt), Dan O'Herlihy (Hugh Williams), Henry [Harry] Morgan (Charles Hall), Gary Jackson (Robert Palfrey, the boy), Gregory Marshall (Harrison Palfrey), Dee Pollack (Tony). *D:* Curtis Bernhardt; *P:* Jerry Wald, Norman Krasna; *St:* Francois Campaux; *Sc:* Norman Corwin. (1:53) Sentimental drama of a woman who loses her husband and child during World War I and spends the rest of her days caring for the children of others. A remake of *Le Voile Bleu*, a 1947 French film.

302. A Blueprint for Murder (20th Century–Fox; 1953). *Cast:* Joseph Cotten, Jean Peters, Gary Merrill, Catherine McLeod, Jack Kruschen, Barney Phillips, Fred Ridgeway, Joyce McCluskey, Mae Marsh, Harry Carter, Jonathan Hale, Walter Sande, Tyler McVey, Teddy Mangean, Aline Towne, Ray Hyke, Charles Collins, Eugene Borden, Carleton Young, Grandon Rhodes, Herbert Butterfield, George Melford. *D: & Sc:* Andrew Stone; *P:* Michael Abel (1:16) A man becomes suspicious of his sister-in-law after the woman's stepdaughter dies and is found to have strychnine in her system. Originally ran on a double bill with *The Kid from Left Field* (q.v.).

303. Blues Busters (Monogram; 1950. *Cast:* Leo Gorcey, Huntz Hall (singing voice dubbed by John Lorenz), Adele Jergens (singing voice dubbed by Gloria Wood), Gabriel Dell, Billy Benedict, David Gorcey, Buddy Gorman, Craig Stevens, Phyllis Coates, Paul Bryar, William Vincent, Matty King, Hank Mann. *D:* William Beaudine; *P:* Jan Grippo; *St: & Sc:* Charles R. Marion; *Additional dialogue:* Bert Lawrence. (1:07) (video) Sach (Hall) has his tonsils removed and as a result gains a beautiful singing voice. A "Bowery Boys" comedy series entry which had the working title of "Bowery Thrush." Originally ran on a double bill with *Hot Rod* (q.v.).

304. The Bob Mathias Story (Allied Artists; 1954). *Cast:* Bob Mathias (himself), Ward Bond, Melba Mathias (herself), Howard Petrie, Ann Doran, Diane Jergens. *D:* Francis D. Lyon; *P:* William E. Selwyn; *St: & Sc:* Richard Collins. (1:19) Sports biography of the first man to win the Olympic decathlon twice, in 1948 and again in 1952. Olympic film footage fills out. (G.B. title: *The Flaming Torch*)

305. Bobby Ware Is Missing (Allied Artists; 1955). *Cast:* Neville Brand, Arthur Franz, Jean Willes, Walter Reed, Paul Picerni, Kim Charney, Thorpe Whitman, Peter Leeds. *D:* Thomas Carr; *P:* Vincent M. Fennelly; *St: & Sc:* Daniel B. Ullman. (1:07) Programmer crime-melodrama, with the law being called in when a young boy is kidnapped.

306. Bodyhold (Columbia; 1949–50). *Cast:* Willard Parker, Lola Albright, Hillary Brooke, Allen Jenkins, Roy Roberts, Gordon Jones, Sammy Menacker, Frank Sully, John Dehner, Billy Varga, Henry Kulky, Wee Willie Davis, Matt McHugh, George H. Lloyd, Ruth Warren, Ray Walker, John R. Hamilton, Ken Ackles, Ed "Strangler" Lewis. *D:* Seymour Friedman; *P:* Rudolph C. Flothow; *St: & Sc:* George W. Bricker. (1:03) Exploitation-melodrama of corruption in the world of professional wrestling.

307. The Bold and the Brave (RKO/Filmakers Releasing Organization; 1956). *Cast:* Wendell Corey (Fairchild), Mickey Rooney (AAN/Dooley), Don Taylor (Preacher), Nicole Maurey (Fiamma), John Smith (Smith), Race Gentry (Hendricks), Ralph Votrian (Wilbur), Bobs Watson (Bob), Tara Summers (Tina), Wright King, Stanley Adams. *D:* Lewis R. Foster; *P:* Hal E. Chester; *Sc:* (AAN) Robert Lewin; *Songs:* Ross Bagdasarian, Mickey Rooney. (1:27) World War II drama of three G.I.s on the Italian front. Superscope.

Bomba and the African Treasure *see* **African Treasure**

Bomba and the Elephant Stampede *see* **Elephant Stampede**

308. Bomba and the Hidden City (Monogram; 1950). *Cast:* Johnny Sheffield, Sue England, Paul Guilfoyle, Robert "Smoki" Whitfield, Damian O'Flynn, Leon Belasco, Charles Latorre. *D:* Ford Beebe; *P:* Walter Mirisch; *Sc:* Carroll Young. (1:11) The 4th entry in this low budget series (which started in 1949) with the jungle boy helping a girl who has been sold into slavery. Based on a character created by Roy Rockwood. (aka: *The Hidden City*)

309. Bomba and the Jungle Girl (Monogram; 1952). *Cast:* Johnny Sheffield, Karen Sharpe, Walter Sande, Suzette Harbin, Martin Wilkins, Morris Buchanan, Leonard Mudie, Don Blackman, Bruce Carruthers, Jack Clisby, Amanda Randolph, Roy Glenn, Bill Walker. *D: & Sc:* Ford Beebe; *P:* Walter Mirisch. (1:10) Jungle adventure with "Bomba the Jungle Boy" trying to find out what happened to his parents. The 7th entry in the series, as well as the final one to be released by Monogram. Several other entries in the series were released under the Allied Artists banner. Based on the character created in the 1920s series of adventure books by Roy Rockwood. (aka: *Jungle Girl*)

Bomba and the Lion Hunters (G.B. title) *see* **The Lion Hunters**

Bomba and the Safari Drums (G.B. title) *see* **Safari Drums**

310. Bombers B-52 (Warner; 1957). *Cast:* Natalie Wood, Karl Malden, Marsha Hunt, Efrem Zimbalist, Jr., Dean Jagger, Don Kelly, Nelson Leigh, Stuart Whitman. *D:* Gordon Douglas; *P:* Richard Whorf; *St:* Sam Rolfe; *Sc:* Irving Wallace. (1:46) U.S. Air Force drama of a veteran pilot's dilemma with keeping his old job or taking a higher paying civilian job, as well as his disapproval of his daughter's choice of boy friends. WarnerColor and CinemaScope. (G.B. title: *No Sleep Till Dawn*)

Bombs Over China *see* **Hong Kong**

311. Bonanza Town (Columbia; 1951). *Cast:* Charles Starrett, Fred F. Sears, Smiley Burnette, Myron Healey, Luther Crockett, Paul McGuire, Charles Horvath, Vernon Dent, Ted Jordan, Al Wyatt, Slim Duncan. *D:* Fred F. Sears; *P:* Colbert Clark; *Sc:* Barry Shipman, Bert Horswell. (0:56) A man thought to be dead is still alive. An entry in the "Durango Kid" western series. (G.B. title: *Two Fisted Agent*)

Bonaventure (G.B. title) *see* **Thunder on the Hill**

312. Bonjour Tristesse (Columbia/Wheel Prods., Ltd.; 1958). *Cast:* Deborah Kerr, David Niven, Jean Seberg, Mylene Demengeot, Geoffrey Horne, Juliette Greco, Walter Chiari, Martita Hunt, Roland Culver, Jean Kent, David Oxley, Tutte Lemkow, Elga Andersen, Jeremy Burnham, Eveline Eyfel. *D:* Otto Preminger, John Palmer (unc.); *P:* Preminger; *Sc:* Arthur Laurents. (1:34) (video) Drama of a young girl's interference in her father's romance with his mistress. Critically panned for the most part, it is set on the French Riviera and is based on the 1955 book by Francois Sagan. Technicolor and Videoscope.

313. The Bonnie Parker Story (American International/Albany Prods.; 1958). *Cast:* Dorothy Provine (title role), Jack Hogan, Richard Bakalyan, Joseph Turkel, William Stevens, Ken Lynch, Douglas Kennedy, Patt Huston, Joel Colin, Jeff Morris, Jim Beck, Stanley Livingston, Carolyn Hughes, John Halloran, Madeline Foy, Sid Lassick, Howard Wright, Karl Davis, Raymond Guth, Frank Evans (voice only). *D:* William Witney; *Ex.P:* James H. Nicholson, Samuel Z. Arkoff; *P:-St:* & *Sc:* Stanley Shpetner; *Narrator:* Vince Williams. (1:21) Exploitation crime-melodrama of how circumstances force a girl into a life of robbery and murder, dying in a hail of Texas Rangers' bullets. Note: For some reason, Clyde Barrow becomes Guy Darrow in this one.

314. Bonzo Goes to College (Universal-International; 1952). *Cast:* Maureen O'Hara, Charles Drake, Gigi Perreau, Edmund Gwenn, Irene Ryan, Gene Lockhart, Guy Williams, John Miljan, Jerry Paris, Bonzo (chimp—received #2 PATSY Award in 1953). *D:* Frederick de Cordova; *P:* Ted Richmond; *St:* Leo Lieberman; *Sc:* Lieberman, Jack Henley (based on a character created by Raphael David Blau and Ted Berkman). (1:19) This comedy sequel to *Bedtime for Bonzo* (q.v.) has the title simian passing his college entrance exam and joining the college football team to win the big game.

315. Boots Malone (Columbia; 1951–52). *Cast:* William Holden (title role), Johnny Stewart, Stanley Clements, Basil Ruysdael, Carl Benton Reid, Ralph Dumke, Ed Begley, Hugh Sanders. *D:* William Dieterle; *P:* & *Sc:* Milton Holmes. (1:42) (video) Drama of the racetrack and the training of a young jockey.

Bop Girl *see* **Bop Girl Goes Calypso**

316. Bop Girl Goes Calypso (United Artists/Bel-Air; 1957). *Cast:* Judy Tyler (film debut), Bobby Troup, Margo Woode, Lucien Littlefield, Mary Kaye Trio, Nino Tempo, George O'Hanlon, Jerry Barclay, Judy Harriet, Gene O'Donnell, Edward Kafafian, George Sawaya, Jerry Frank, Dick Standish, The Goofers, Lord Flea Calypsonians, The Titans, The Cubanos. *D:* Howard W. Koch; *P:* Aubrey Schenck; *St:* Hendrik Vollaerts; *Sc:* Arnold Belgard. (1:19) Programmer musical of someone with the naïve notion that calypso music will replace rock 'n' roll! (aka: *Bop Girl*) Note: Judy Tyler received only one other film credit, *Jailhouse Rock* (q.v.), before being killed in an auto crash in 1957.

317. Border Fence (Astor; 1951). *Cast:* Walt Wayne, Lee Morgan, Mary Nord, Steve Raines, Harry Garcia. *D:* Norman Sheldon, H.W. Kier. (1:29) A low budget independently produced western.

318. Border Outlaws (Eagle-Lion/United International; 1950). *Cast:* Spade Cooley (himself), Maria Hart, Bill Edwards, Bill Kennedy, George Slocum, John Laurenz, Douglas Wood, Bud Osborne, John Carpenter, The Six Metzetti Brothers (includes Richard Talmadge). *D:* Richard Talmadge; *P:* Talmadge, Jack Seaman; *Sc:* Arthur Hoerl. (0:57) (video) Low budget western affair of attempts to capture a drug smuggler, complete with Cooley's trademark western swing music. A Jack Schwarz production for United International. (G.B. title: *The Phantom Horseman*)

319. Border Rangers (Lippert/Don Barry Prods.; 1950). *Cast:* Don Barry, Robert Lowery, Wally Vernon, Pamela Blake, Lyle Talbot, Bill Kennedy, Paul Jordan, Alyn Lockwood, John Merton, Tom Monroe, George Keymas, Tom Kennedy, Eric Norden, Bud Osborne, Claude Stroud, Ezelle Poule. *D: & P:* William Berke; *St: & Sc:* Berke, Victor West. (0:57) A Texas Ranger joins a gang in order to get the killers of his brother and sister-in-law.

320. Border River (Universal-International; 1954). *Cast:* Joel McCrea, Yvonne De Carlo, Pedro Armendariz, Ivan Triesault, Alfonso Bedoya, Erika Nordin, Howard Petrie, George J. Lewis, Nacho Galindo, George Wallace, Martin Garralaga, Lane Chandler, Charles Horvath, Britt Wood, Fred Beir, Monte Montague, Pilar Del Rey. *D:* George Sherman; *P:* Albert J. Cohen; *St:* Louis Stevens; *Sc:* Stevens, William Sackheim. (1:20) Technicolor Civil War-era western of a Confederate major attempting to get funds in a last ditch effort to buy guns and ammunition for the failing cause.

321. Border Saddlemates (Republic; 1952). *Cast:* Rex Allen, Ko-Ko (horse), Mary Ellen Kay, Slim Pickens, Forrest Taylor, Roy Barcroft, Jimmy Moss, Zon Murray, Keith McConnell, Bud Osborne, The Republic Rhythm Riders. *D:* William Witney; *P:* Edward J. White; *Sc:* Albert DeMond; *Song:* "Roll On Border Moon" (Jack Elliott). (1:07) (video) A government agent uncovers a counterfeiting operation on the Canadian border.

322. Border Treasure (RKO; 1950). *Cast:* Tim Holt, Richard Martin, Jane Nigh, John Doucette, House Peters, Jr., Inez Cooper, Julian Rivero, Kenneth MacDonald, Vince Barnett, David Leonard, Robert Peyton, Tom Monroe. *D:* George Archainbaud; *P:* Herman Schlom; *Sc:* Norman Houston. (1:00) Outlaws steal donations collected for Mexican earthquake victims. Tim and his pal Chito set out to retrieve it. Originally the second feature on a double bill with *Outrage* (q.v.).

323. Borderline (Universal-International; 1950). *Cast:* Fred MacMurray, Claire Trevor, Raymond Burr, Roy Roberts, Jose Torvay, Lita Baron, Morris Ankrum, Nacho Galindo, Charles Lane, Don Diamond, Pepe Hern, Richard Irving. *D:* William Seiter; *P:* Seiter, Milton H. Bren, *Sc:* Devery Freeman. (1:28) (video) Romantic comedy blends with melodrama as two undercover agents for the law fall for each other, neither knowing the true identity of the other.

324. Born Reckless (Warner; 1959). *Cast:* Mamie Van Doren, Jeff Richards, Arthur Hunnicutt, Carol Ohmart, Tom Duggan, Tex Williams (himself), Donald Barry, Nacho Galindo, Orlando Rodriguez, Johnny Olenn and his Group, Jeanne Carmen. *D:* Howard W. Koch; *P:* Aubrey Schenck; *St:* Schenck, Richard Landau; *Sc:* Landau; *Songs:* Title song, "A Little Longer," "Home Type Girl," "Separate the Men From the Boys" (Buddy Bregman) all sung by Van Doren, "Something to Dream About" (Charles Singleton–Larry Coleman) sung by Van Doren, "Song of the Rodeo" (Bregman-Stanley Styne) sung by Williams, "You're Lovable You" sung by Olenn and Group. (1:19) Contemporary western romance with songs and a rodeo setting. Originally ran on a double bill with *Island of Lost Women* (q.v.).

325. Born to Be Bad (RKO; 1950). *Cast:* Joan Fontaine, Robert Ryan, Zachary Scott, Joan Leslie, Mel Ferrer, Harold Vermilyea, Virginia Farmer, Kathleen Howard (final film—ret.), Dick Ryan, Bess Flowers, Joy Aallward, Hazel Boyne, Irving Bacon, Gordon Oliver. *D:* Nicholas Ray; *P:* Robert Sparks; *Sc:* Edith Sommer, Robert Soderberg, George Oppenheimer. (1:33) (video) Melodrama of a woman who breaks up a man's marriage and keeps him on a string while seeing her other boyfriend regularly. Based on the 1928 novel *All Kneeling* by Anne Parrish.

326. Born to Be Loved (Universal-International/H.H. Prods., Inc.; 1959). *Cast:* Carol Morris, Vera Vague [aka: Barbara Jo Allen/final film—ret.], Hugo Haas, Dick Kallman, Jacqueline Fontaine, Billie Bird, Pat Goldin, Robert C. Foulk, Mary Esther Denver, Margot Baker, Tony Jochim. *D:-P: & Sc:* Hugo Haas; *As. P:* Robert Erlick; *Songs:* Title song (Franz Steininger–Walter Bullock), "One Good Kiss Deserves Another" (Steininger–Eddie Pola), "Fata Morgana" (a piano concerto by Haas). (1:22) Romantic drama involving an elderly voice teacher, a singing student, a wealthy widow and a young dressmaker.

327. Born to the Saddle (Astor; 1953). *Cast:* Chuck Courtney, Donald Woods, Leif Erickson, Karen Morley, Rand Brooks, Glenn Strange, Dolores Priest, Fred Kohler, Jr., Dan White, Milton Kibbee, Boyd Davis, Bob Anderson, Lucille Thompson. *D:* William Beaudine;

P: Hall Shelton; *Sc:* Adele Buffington. (1:13) Low budget western outing of a man with ulterior motives who hires a young boy to train a horse for a race. Based on the story "Quarter Horse" by Gordon Young. In color.

328. Born Yesterday (Columbia; 1950). *Cast:* Judy Holliday (AA/Billie Dawn), Broderick Crawford (Harry Brook), William Holden (Paul Verrall), Howard St. John (Jim Devery), Frank Otto (Eddie), Larry Oliver (Norval Hodges), Barbara Brown (Mrs. Hodges), Grandon Rhodes (Sanborn), Claire Carleton (Helen), Robert "Smoki" Whitfield (bootblack), Helen Eby-Rock (manicurist), William Mays (bellboy), David Pardoll (barber), Mike Mahoney (elevator operator), John L. Morley (native), Charles Cane (policeman), Paul Marion, Ram Singh. *D:* (AAN) George Cukor; *P:* (AAN-Best Picture) S. Sylvan Simon; *Sc:* (AAN) Albert Mannheimer; *Costumes:* (AAN-b/w) Jean Louis. (1:43) (video/laserdisc) Acclaimed comedy of a gruff tycoon who hires a tutor for his dumb blonde girl friend. *Film Daily* placed it at #5 on their "10 Best" list, while the *New York Times* placed it at #10 on theirs. One of the 23 top-grossing films of 1950-51, it was also in nomination at the Venice Film Festival. Based on the play by Garson Kanin, it was remade in 1993.

329. The Boss (United Artists/Boss Prods.; 1956). *Cast:* John Payne, William Bishop, Gloria McGhee, Doe Avedon, Robin Morse, Joe Flynn (film debut), Gil Lamb, Roy Roberts, Rhys Williams, Bill Phipps, Bob Morgan, Alex Frazer, John Mansfield, George Lynn, Harry Cheshire. *D:* Byron Haskin; *P:* Frank N. Seltzer, John Payne (unc.); *Sc:* Ben Perry, Payne (unc.). (1:28) The rise of a ruthless crime boss in a midwestern American city following World War I.

330. Botany Bay (Paramount; 1953). *Cast:* Alan Ladd, James Mason, Patricia Medina, Cedric Hardwicke, Murray Matheson, John Hardy, Dorothy Patten, Anita Bolster, Hugh Pryse, Malcolm Lee Beggs, Jonathan Harris, Alec Harford, Noel Drayton, Brendan Toomey, Ben Wright. *D:* John Farrow; *P:* Joseph Sistrom; *Sc:* Jonathan Latimer. (1:33) (video) Popular action-adventure of a British prison ship transporting its cargo in late 18th century to Australia, the ship being helmed by a sadistic captain. Based on the 1944 novel by Charles Nordhoff and James Norman Hall, the film was produced in 1951 as part of Paramount's backlog of Ladd's films.

Both Ends of the Candle (G.B. title) *see* **The Helen Morgan Story**

331. The Bottom of the Bottle (20th Century–Fox; 1956). *Cast:* Van Johnson, Joseph Cotten, Ruth Roman, Jack Carson, Margaret Hayes, Bruce Bennett, Brad Dexter, Peggy Knudsen, Jim Davis, Margaret Lindsay, Nancy Gates, [Pedro] Gonzales-Gonzales, John Lee, Shawn Smith, Ted Griffin, Ernestine Barrier, Walter Woolf King. Sandy Descher, Kim Charney. *D:* Henry Hathaway; *P:* Buddy Adler; *Sc:* Sydney Boehm. (1:28) Drama of an alcoholic ex-con who seeks acceptance by his brother. Based on the 1949 book *Le Fond de la Bouteille* by Georges Simenon. DeLuxe color and CinemaScope. (G.B. title: *Beyond the River*)

332. The Bounty Hunter (Warner/Transcona; 1954). *Cast:* Randolph Scott, Dolores Dorn, Marie Windsor, Howard Petrie, Dub Taylor, Tyler MacDuff, Archie Twitchell [aka: Michael Branden], Mary Lou Holloway, Charles Delaney, Fess Parker, Billy Vincent, Ernest Borgnine, Harry Antrim, Robert Keys, Paul Picerni, Phil Chambers. *D:* Andre De Toth; *P:* Sam Bischoff; *St:* Winston Miller, Finlay McDermid; *Sc:* Miller. (1:19) Western of a bounty hunter on the trail of his quarry, three murderous train robbers. WarnerColor.

Bourbon St. Shadows *see* **Invisible Avenger**

333. Bowery Battalion (Monogram; 1951). *Cast:* Leo Gorcey, Huntz Hall, Virginia Hewitt, Donald MacBride, Russell Hicks, Billy Benedict, David Gorcey, Buddy Gorman, Bernard Gorcey, Selmer Jackson, John Bleifer, Al Eben, Frank Jenks, Michael Ross, Emil Sitka, Harry Lauter, William R. Ruhl. *D:* William Beaudine; *P:* Jan Grippo; *St: & Sc:* Charles R. Marion; *Additional dialogue:* Bert Lawrence. (1:09) In this comedy series entry, the "Bowery Boys" are in uniform and on the trail of spies.

334. The Bowery Boys Meet the Monsters (Allied Artists; 1954). *Cast:* Leo Gorcey, Huntz Hall, Bernard Gorcey, David Gorcey, Bennie Bartlett, John Dehner, Lloyd Corrigan, Paul Wexler, Ellen Corby, Laura Mason, Norman Bishop, Steve Calvert, Rudy Lee, Paul Bryar, Pat Flaherty, Jack Diamond. *D:* Edward

Bernds; *P:* Ben Schwalb; *St: & Sc:* Elwood Ullman, Bernds. (1:01) Title implies all in this low budget comedy series entry.

335. Bowery to Bagdad (Allied Artists; 1955). *Cast:* Leo Gorcey, Huntz Hall, David Gorcey, Bennie Bartlett, Bernard Gorcey, Joan Shawlee, Robert Bice, Dick Wessel, Rayford Barnes, Michael Ross, Eric Blore (final film—ret.), Rick Vallin, Paul Marion, Jean Willes, Charlie Lung, Leon Burbank. *D:* Edward Bernds; *P:* Ben Schwalb; *St: & Sc:* Elwood Ullman, Bernds. (1:04) Comedy series entry, with the "Bowery Boys" finding an old lamp. When they polish it, out pops a genie (played by Blore).

335A. Boy from Indiana (Eagle-Lion/Ventura Pictures; 1950). *Cast:* Lon McCallister, Lois Butler, Billie Burke, George Cleveland, Rol Laughner, Victor Cox, Jerry Ambler, Allen Church, Jeanne Patterson, Texas Dandy (horse). *D:* John Rawlins; *P:* Frank Melford; *Sc: & St:* Otto Englander. (1:06) Low budget racetrack drama of a young jockey caring for an injured horse while preparing him for the big race. (G.B. title: *Blaze of Glory*)

336. The Boy from Oklahoma (Warner; 1954). *Cast:* Will Rogers, Jr., Nancy Olson, Anthony Caruso, Lon Chaney, Jr., Wallace Ford, Clem Bevans, Merv Griffin, Louis Jean Heydt, Slim Pickens, Sheb Wooley, Harry Lauter, James Griffith, Charles Watts, John Cason, Guy Teague, Tom Monroe, George Chesebro, George Lloyd, John Weldon, Forrest Taylor, Jack Daly, Guy Wilkerson, Britt Wood, Frank Marlowe, Emile Avery, Bud Osborne, Charles Wagenheim, Tyler MacDuff, Denver Pyle, Ted Mapes. *D:* Michael Curtiz; *P:* David Weisbart; *St:* Michael Fessier; *Sc:* Frank Davis, Winston Miller. (1:28) An easy-going law student finds himself sheriff of a rowdy town. Mr. Fessier's story appeared in *Saturday Evening Post.* Photographed in WarnerColor, this film was the basis for the Warner Brothers TV series *Sugarfoot* which starred Will Hutchins.

337. Boy on a Dolphin (20th Century-Fox; 1957). *Cast:* Alan Ladd (Dr. James Calder), Sophia Loren (Phaedra), Clifton Webb (Victor Parmalee), Jorge Mistral (Rhif), Laurence Naismith (Dr. Hawkins), Alexis Minotis (government man), Piero Giagnoni (Niko), Charles Fawcett (Bill B. Baldwin), Gertrude Flynn (Miss Dill), Charlotte Terrabust (Mrs. Baldwin), Margaret Stahl (Miss Baldwin), Orestes Rallis, The Penegrysis Greek Folk Dance and Songs Society. *D:* Jean Negulesco; *P:* Samuel G. Engel; *Sc:* Ivan Moffat, Dwight Taylor; *Music:* (AAN) Hugo Friedhofer; *Title song:* Takes Morakis, J. Fermanglou (m), Paul Francis Webster (Eng.ly). (1:43) (video) The search for a sunken treasure in the waters of the Grecian isles. Based on the 1955 novel by David Divine. Note: This film was Loren's starring debut in an American film, though she first appeared on screen as an unbilled extra in *Quo Vadis* (q.v.). DeLuxe color and CinemaScope.

The Boys from Brooklyn *see* **Bela Lugosi Meets a Brooklyn Gorilla**

338. The Brain Eaters (American International; 1958). *Cast:* Edwin Nelson, Alan Frost, Jack Hill, Joanna Lee, Jody Fair, David Hughes, Robert Ball, Greigh Phillips, Orville Sherman, Leonard Nimoy, Doug Banks, Henry Randolph. *D:* Bruno VeSota; *P:* Edwin Nelson; *As. P:* Stanley Bickman; *St: & Sc:* Gordon Urquhart (loosely based on Robert Heinlein's "Puppet Masters") (1:00) (video) Science fiction cult item of parasites that bore their way to the earth's surface in a metal cone and begin attaching themselves to people and taking control of their brains. Ran on a double bill with *The Spider* (q.v.).

339. The Brain from Planet Arous (Howco International; 1958). *Cast:* John Agar, Joyce Meadows, Robert Fuller, Thomas Browne Henry, Ken Terrell, Henry Travis, Tim Graham, E. Leslie Thomas, Bill Giorgio. *D:* Nathan Hertz [Juran]; *P:* Jacques Marquette; *St: & Sc:* Ray Buffum. (1:10) (video) Science fiction of an evil alien intelligence named Gor who inhabits the brain of a nuclear physicist with a plan to conquer the world. Bent on stopping Gor, another alien named Vol inhabits the brain of the physicist's dog.

340. Branded (Paramount; 1950). *Cast:* Alan Ladd (Choya), Mona Freeman (Ruth Lavery), Charles Bickford (Mr. Lavery), Robert Keith (Leffingwell), Joseph Calleia (Rubriz), Peter Hansen (Tonio), Selena Royle (Mrs. Lavery), Tom Tully (Ransome), George Lewis (Andy), Robert Kortman (Hank), John Berkes (Tatto), Pat Lane (Jake), Martin Garralaga (Hernandez), Edward Clark (Dad Travis), Natividad Vacio (peon), Julia Montoya (Joe's wife), John Butler (Spig), Jimmie Dundee (Link), Salvador Baguez (Roberto), Milburn Stone (Dawson), Ed Piel (Tully), Frank McCarroll, Len Hendry, Olan Soule. *D:* Rudolph Maté; *P:* Mel

Epstein; *Sc:* Sydney Boehm, Cyril Hume. (1:35) (video/laserdisc) A cowpoke poses as a man's long-missing son in this hit western based on the novel *Montana Rides* by Evan Evans. One of the 23 top-grossing films of 1950-51. Technicolor.

341. The Brass Legend (United Artists/Bob Goldstein Prods.; 1956). *Cast:* Hugh O'Brian, Nancy Gates, Donald MacDonald, Raymond Burr, Reba Tassell, Robert Burton, Eddie Firestone, Willard Sage, Stacy Harris, Norman Leavitt, Russell Simpson, Robert Griffin, Dennis Cross, Michael Garrett, Jack Farmer. *D:* Gerd Oswald; *P:* Herman Cohen; *St:* George Zuckerman, Jess Arnold; *Sc:* Don Martin. (1:19) Western of a sheriff who arrests a wanted man and the unusual circumstances that follow.

The Brat (G.B. title) *see* **Sons of New Mexico**

342. The Bravados (20th Century–Fox; 1958). *Cast:* Gregory Peck (Jim Douglas), Joan Collins (Josepha Velarde), Stephen Boyd (Bill Zachary), Albert Salmi (BSA from the NBR combined with his work on *The Brothers Karamazov*—q.v./Ed Taylor), Henry Silva (Lujan), Kathleen Gallant (Emma), Barry Coe (Tom), George Voskovec (Gus Steinmetz), Herbert Rudley (Sheriff Eloy Sanchez), Lee Van Cleef (Alfonso Parral), Andrew Duggan (padre), Ken Scott (Primo), Gene Evans (Butler), Jack Mather (Quinn), Joe DeRita (Simms), Robert Adler (Tony Mirabel), Jason Wingreen (Nicholas), Robert Griffin (Loomis), Ada Carrasco (Mrs. Parral), Juan Garcia (Pepe Martinez), Jacqueline Evans (Mrs. Barnes), Alicia del Lago (Angela Lujan), The Ninos Cantores De Morelia Choral Group. *D:* Henry King; *P:* Herbert B. Swope, Jr.; *Sc:* Philip Yordan. (1:38) (video) Popular "adult" western character study of a man tracking down the four men he believes raped and murdered his wife. Filmed in Mexico in Technicolor and CinemaScope, it was based on the novel by Frank O'Rourke.

The Brave and the Beautiful (G.B. title) *see* **The Magnificent Matador**

343. The Brave Bulls (Columbia; 1951). *Cast:* Mel Ferrer (Luis Bello), Miroslava (Linda de Calderon), Anthony Quinn (Raul Fuentes), Eugene Iglesias (Pepe Bello), Jose Torvay (Eladio Gomez), Charlita (Raquelita), Jose-Luis Lopez Vasquez (Yank Delgado), Alfonso Alvirez (Loco Ruiz), Alfredo Aguilar (Pancho Perez), Francisco Balderas (Monkey Garcia), Felipe Mota (Jackdaw), Pepe Lopez (Enrique), Jose Meza (Little White), Vincent Cardenas (Coyo Salinas), Manuel Orozco, Estevan Dominquez, Silviana Sanchez, Francisco Reiguera, Enita Arozamena, Luis Corona, Esther Laquin, Fanny Schiller, Juan Assaei, M. du P. Castillo, Delfino Morales, Rita Conde, Ramon D. Mesa, Fernando Del Valle. *D: & P:* Robert Rossen; *Sc:* John Bright. (1:47) Based on the book by Tom Lea, this drama of a matador who loses his courage placed #2 on the "10 Best" list of the *New York Times.* Note: Prints of this film that were shown outside of the U.S. were available with added explicit bullfight footage.

344. The Brave One (Universal-International/RKO/King Bros. Prods., Inc.; 1956). *Cast:* Michel Ray (Leonardo), Rodolfo Hoyos (Rafael Rosillo), Elsa Cardenas (film debut/Maria), Carlos Navarro (Don Alejandro), Joi Lansing (Marion Randall), Fermin Rivera (himself), George Trevino (Salvador), Carlos Fernandez (Manuel). *D:* Irving Rapper; *P:* Maurice and Frank King; *St:* (AA) Robert Rich (pseudonym of Dalton Trumbo—a blacklisted writer who received his Oscar in 1975); *Sc:* Harold Franklin, Merrill G. White; *Sound:* (AAN) John Myers; *Editor:* (AAN) Merrill G. White. (1:40) (video) Family drama of a young Mexican boy who saves his pet bull from the bullring. In color and CinemaScope.

345. Brave Warrior (Columbia; 1952). *Cast:* Jon Hall, Christine Larson, Michael Ansara (The Prophet), Jay Silverheels (Tecumseh), Harry Cording, George Eldredge, James Seay, Leslie Denison, Rory Mallinson, Rusty Wescoatt, Bert Davidson, William P. [Bill] Wilkerson, Gilbert V. Perkins. *D:* Spencer G. Bennet; *P:* Sam Katzman; *St: & Sc:* Robert E. Kent. (1:13) Loosely based on fact, this action-adventure in Technicolor relates Indian hostilities during the Shawnee uprising in the early 19th century.

346. Breakdown (Realart; 1952–53). *Cast:* Ann Richards (final film—ret.), William Bishop, Anne Gwynne (final film—ret.), Sheldon Leonard, Wally Cassell, Richard Benedict, John Vosper, Roy Engel, Joe McTurk, Norman Rainey, Hall Bartlett, Elena Strangelo, Michelle King, Gene Covelli, Al Cantor. *D: & P:* Edmond Angelo; *Sc:* Robert Abel (based on his play "The Samson Slasher"). (1:16) A heavyweight boxer framed for murder and imprisoned finds the guilty party.

347. The Breaking Point (Warner; 1950). *Cast:* John Garfield, Patricia Neal, Phyllis Thaxter, Juano Hernandez, Ralph Dumke, William Campbell (film debut), Sherry Jackson, Wallace Ford, Edmon Ryan, Guy Thomajan, Donna Jo Boyce, Victor Sen Yung, Peter Brocco, John Doucette, James Griffith. *D:* Michael Curtiz; *P:* Jerry Wald; *Sc:* Ranald MacDougall. (1:37) Critically acclaimed remake of *To Have and Have Not* (Warner; 1944), based on Ernest Hemingway's work of a skipper who will charter his boat to anyone with the right price. Remade as *The Gun Runners* (q.v.).

348. Breakthrough (Warner; 1950). *Cast:* David Brian, John Agar, Frank Lovejoy, William Campbell, Greg McClure, Paul Picerni (film debut), Dick Wesson, Richard Monahan, Eddie Norris, Matt Willis, Suzanne Dalbert, William Self, Danny Arnold, Dani Sue Nolan, Howard Negley. *D:* Lewis Seiler; *P:* Bryan Foy; *St:* Joseph I. Breen, Jr.; *Sc:* Bernard Girard, Ted Sherdeman. (1:31) (video) World War II drama of the training of an infantry platoon who eventually get their "trial by fire" at the invasion of Normandy.

349. A Breath of Scandal (Paramount/Titanus-Ponti; 1959). *Cast:* Sophia Loren, John Gavin, Maurice Chevalier, Isabel Jeans, Angela Lansbury, Tullio Carminati, Roberto Risso, Carlo Intermann, Milly Vitale, Adrienne Gessner, Frederick Von Ledebur. *D:* Michael Curtiz; *P:* Carlo Ponti, Marcello Girosi; *As.P:* Eugene Allen; *Sc:* Walter Bernstein. (1:38) (video) A U.S.A./Italian co-produced costumer of a princess romanced by an American. Filmed on location in Rome and Vienna, it was based on Ferenc Molnar's play *Olympia* as adapted by Sidney Howard. In Technicolor and VistaVision, it was released in the U.S. in 1960.

350. The Bride and the Beast (Allied Artists/Adrian Weiss; 1958). *Cast:* Charlotte Austin (final film—ret.), Lance Fuller, Johnny Roth, Steve Calvert (gorilla), William Justine, Jeanne Gerson, Gil Frye, Slick Slavin, Bhogwan Singh, Jean Ann Lewis. *D:-P: & St:* Adrian Weiss; *Sc:* Edward D. Wood, Jr. (1:18) (video) Strange melodrama of a woman who finds she was a gorilla in a former life, winding up in residence with a band of African gorillas. (aka: *Queen of the Gorillas*) Originally ran on a double bill with *The Beast of Budapest* (q.v.).

Bride of the Atom *see* **Bride of the Monster**

351. Bride of the Gorilla (Realart; 1951). *Cast:* Barbara Payton, Lon Chaney, Jr., Raymond Burr, Tom Conway, Paul Cavanagh, Carol Varga, Paul Maxey, Woodrow Strode, Martin Garralaga, Moyna MaGill, Felippa Rock. *D:* Curt Siodmak (debut); *P:* Jack Broder; *Sc:* Siodmak. (1:05) (video) In the jungle, a woman flirts with the foreman of her husband's plantation. When he dies from a snakebite, she marries the foreman, only to find he is cursed and turns into a gorilla by night. Note: *Leonard Maltin's 1996 Movie & Video Guide* lists the running time of this film as 1:16.

352. Bride of the Monster (Banner Prods., Inc.; 1955). *Cast:* Bela Lugosi, Tor Johnson, Tony McCoy, Loretta King, Harvey B. Dunne, George Becwar, Paul Marco, Don Nagel, Bud Osborne, John Warren, Ann Wilner, Dolores Fuller, William Benedict, Ben Frommer, Conrad Brooks, Eddie Parker (stunt double for Lugosi). *D: & P:* Edward D. Wood, Jr.; *Ex.P:* Donald McCoy; *As.P:* Tony McCoy; *St: & Sc:* Wood, Jr., Alex Gordon. (1:08) (video) Science fiction of a mad scientist attempting to create a race of supermen via his atomic ray machine. Ed Wood, Jr. strikes (out) again! (aka: *Bride of the Atom*) (Sequel: *Night of the Ghouls*—q.v.)

353. The Bridges at Toko-Ri (Paramount; 1954). *Cast:* William Holden (Lt. Harry Brubaker, USNR). Grace Kelly (Nancy Brubaker), Fredric March (Rear Adm. George Tarrant), Mickey Rooney (Mike Forney), Robert Strauss (Beer Barrell), Charles McGraw (Comm. Wayne Lee), Keiko Awaji (Kimiko), Earl Holliman (Nestor Gamidge), Richard Shannon (Lt. [S.G.] Olds), Willis B. Bouchey (Capt. Evans), Nadene Ashdown (Kathy Brubaker), Cheryl Lynn Callaway (Susie), Paul Kruger (Capt. Parker), James Jenkins, Marshall V. Beebe, Charles Tannen, Teru Shimada, Dennis Weaver, Gene Reynolds, James Hyland, Robert A. Sherry, Gene Hardy, Jack Roberts, Rollin Moriyama, Robert Kino, Corey Allen (film debut). *D:* Mark Robson; *P:* George Seaton, William Perlberg; *Sc:* Valentine Davies; *F/X:* (AA) (unc.); *Editor:* (AAN) Alma Macrorie (1955). (1:43) (video/laserdisc) Critically acclaimed Korean war drama of a navy flyer called out of retirement for a mission to bomb a series of bridges in North Korea. Based on the best-seller by James Michener, it became one of the 27 top-grossing films of 1954-55 and was voted "Best Film of the Year" by the *New York Times*. Technicolor and VistaVision.

354. Brigadoon (MGM; 1954). *Cast:* Gene Kelly (Tommy Albright), Van Johnson (Jeff Douglas), Cyd Charisse (singing voice of Carole Richards/Fiona Campbell), Elaine Stewart (Jane Ashton), Barry Jones (Mr. Lundie), Hugh Laing (Harry Beaton), Albert Sharpe (Andrew Campbell), Virginia Bosler (Jean Campbell), Jimmy Thompson (Charlie Chisholm Dalrymple), Tudor Owen (Archie Beaton), Owen McGivney (Angus), Dee Turnell (Ann), Dody Heath (Meg Brockie), Eddie Quillan (Sandy), Madge Blake (Mrs. McIntosh), Hugh Boswell (Mr. McIntosh), George Chakiris (dancer), Warren Macgregor (tinker), Hank Mann, Oliver Blake, Paul Bryar, Dick Simmons, Stuart Whitman. *D:* Vincente Minnelli; *P:* Arthur Freed; *Sc:* Alan Jay Lerner; *Choreography:* Gene Kelly; *ASD:* (AAN) Cedric Gibbons, Preston Ames (art directors), Edwin B. Willis, Keogh Gleason (sets); *Sound:* (AAN) Wesley C. Miller; *Costumes:* (AAN) Irene Sharaff; *Songs:* "The Heather on the Hill," "From This Day On," "The Gathering of the Clans," "The Wedding Dance," "I'll Go Home With Bonnie Jean," "It's Almost Like Being in Love," "Brigadoon," "The Chase," "Prologue" and "Waiting For My Dearie" Alan Jay Lerner–Frederick Loewe. (1:48) (video/laserdisc) Lerner & Loewe's smash Broadway musical-fantasy of a magical town in Scotland that appears for only one day, every one hundred years. In CinemaScope and Anscocolor, it became one of the 27 top-grossing films of 1954-55.

355. The Brigand (Columbia; 1952). *Cast:* Anthony Dexter, Jody Lawrence, Anthony Quinn, Gale Robbins, Ron Randell, Carl Benton Reid, Fay Roope, Carleton Young, Ian MacDonald, Holmes Herbert (final film—ret.), Lester Matthews, Barbara Brown, Walter Kingsford, Donald Randolph, Mari Blanchard. *D:* Phil Karlson; *P:* Edward Small; *St:* George Bruce; *Sc:* Jesse L. Lasky, Jr. (1:33) Technicolor costume adventure, based on *Brigand, A Romance of the Reign of Don Carlos* by Alexandre Dumas.

356. Bright Leaf (Warner; 1950). *Cast:* Gary Cooper, Patricia Neal, Lauren Bacall, Donald Crisp, Jack Carson, Gladys George, Elizabeth Patterson, Jeff Corey, Thurston Hall, Taylor Holmes, Jimmy [James] Griffith, Marietta Canty, William Walker. *D:* Michael Curtiz; *P:* Henry Blanke; *Sc:* Ranald MacDougall. (1:49) A tobacco farmer creates a cigarette empire and gets back at those who did him dirty. Based on the 1948 novel by Foster Fitz-Simons.

357. Bright Road (MGM; 1953). *Cast:* Dorothy Dandridge, Harry Belafonte (film debut), Robert Horton, Philip Herburn, Barbara Ann Sanders, Maidie Norman, Renee Beard, Howard McNeely, Robert McNeely, Patti Marie Ellis, Joy Jackson, Fred Moultrie, James Moultrie, Carolyn Ann Jackson. *D:* Gerald Mayer; *P:* Sol Baer Fielding; *Sc:* Emmett Lavery. (1:09) Low budget drama of a southern school teacher dealing with a troublesome student at an all-black school. Based on the short story "See How They Run" by Mary Elizabeth Vroman.

358. Bright Victory (Universal-International; 1951). *Cast:* Arthur Kennedy (AAN + "Best Actor" by the NYFC/Larry Nevins), Peggy Dow (Judy Greene), Julia [Julie] Adams (Chris Paterson), James Edwards (Joe Morgan), Jim Backus (Bill Grayson), Nana Bryant (Mrs. Nevins), Will Geer (Mr. Nevins), Minor Watson (Mr. Paterson), Murray Hamilton (Pete Hamilton), Rock Hudson (Cpl. John Flagg), Joan Banks (Janet Grayson), Marjorie Crossland (Mrs. Paterson), Richard Egan (Sgt. John Masterson), Russell Dennis (Pvt. Fred Tyler), Donald Miele (Moose Garvey), Larry Keating (Jess Coe), Hugh Reilly (Capt. Phelan), Mary Cooper (Nurse Bailey), Ken Harvey (Scanlon), Phil Faversham (Lt. Atkins), Jerry Paris (Reynolds), Robert F. Simon, Ruth Esherick, Bernard Hamilton, Robert Anderson, June Whitley, Sydney Mason, Richard Karlan, Billy Newell, Virginia Mullen, Glen Charles Gordon, Alice Richey, Sara Taft, Thaddeus Jones, John M. Robinson. *D:* Mark Robson; *P:* Robert Buckner; *Sc:* Buckner; *Sound:* (AAN) Leslie I. Carey. (1:36) An acclaimed drama of a blinded veteran of World War II and his attempts to readjust to civilian life with his handicap. Based on the novel *Lights Out* by Baynard H. Kendrick, it placed #9 on the "10 Best" list of *Film Daily*, was in nomination at the Cannes Film Festival and placed #5 at the Berlin Film Festival. (G.B. title: *Lights Out*)

359. Bring Your Smile Along (Columbia; 1955). *Cast:* Frankie Laine, Keefe Brasselle, Constance Towers, Lucy Marlow, William Leslie, Mario Siletti, Ruth Warren, Jack Albertson, Bobby Clark, Murray Leonard, Ida Smeraldo. *D:* Blake Edwards (debut); *P:* Jonie Taps; *St:* Edwards, Richard Quine; *Sc:* Edwards. (1:23) Technicolor musical-comedy of a song writing team.

Brink of Hell (G.B. title) *see* **Toward the Unknown**

360. Broken Arrow (20th Century–Fox; 1950). *Cast:* James Stewart (Tom Jeffords), Jeff Chandler (AAN/Cochise), Debra Paget (Sonseeahray), Basil Ruysdael (Gen. Howard), Will Geer (Ben Slade), Joyce MacKenzie (Terry), Arthur Hunnicutt (Duffield), Raymond Bramley (Col. Bernall), Jay Silverheels (Goklia), Argentina Brunetti (Nalikadeya), Jack Lee (Boucher), Robert Adler (Lonergan), Robert Griffin (Lowrie), Billy Wilkerson (Juan), Mickey Kuhn (Chip Slade), Chris Willow Bird (Nochalo), J.W. Cody (Pionsenay), John War Eagle (Nahilzay), Charles Soldani (Skinyea), Iron Eyes Cody (Teese), Robert Foster Dover (Machogee), John Marston (Maury), Harry Carter, Edward Rand, John Doucette, Richard Van Opel, Nacho Galindo, Trevor Bardette. *D:* Delmer Daves; *P:* Julian Blaustein (first film); *Sc:* (AAN) Michael Blankfort (fronting for blacklisted Albert Maltz); *Cin:* (AAN) Ernest Palmer. (1:33) (video) Fact-based historical western of the efforts of Tom Jeffords and Cochise to sooth hostilities between whites and Indians in the 19th century Southwest. Based on the novel *Blood Brother* by Elliott Arnold, it became one of the 28 top-grossing films of 1949-50. The premiere episode of the popular TV series which began in 1956 was adapted from this film. Technicolor.

361. Broken Lance (20th Century–Fox; 1954). *Cast:* Spencer Tracy (Matt Devereaux), Jean Peters (Barbara), Robert Wagner (Joe Devereaux), Richard Widmark (Ben), Katy Jurado (AAN/Senora Devereaux), Hugh O'Brian (Mike Devereaux), Carl Benton Reid (Clem Lawton), Eduard Franz (Two Moons), Earl Holliman (Denny Devereaux), E.G. Marshall (The Governor), Philip Ober (Van Cleve), Robert Burton (Mac Andrews), Robert Adler (O'Reilly), Robert Grandlin, Harry Carter, Nacho Galindo, Julian Rivero, Edmund Cobb, Russell Simpson, King Donovan, George E. Stone, Paul Kruger, John Epper, Jack Mather, James F. Stone. *D:* Edward Dmytryk; *P:* Sol C. Siegel; *St:* (AA) Philip Yordan; *Sc:* Richard Murphy. (1:36) (video/laserdisc) The wealthy patriarch of a western family sees his relationships with his sons deteriorating following his re-marriage. A western remake of this studio's 1949 production *House of Strangers* which was based on a novel by Joe Weidman. In CinemaScope with color by DeLuxe.

362. The Broken Star (United Artists/ Bel-Air–Northridge Prods.; 1956). *Cast:* Howard Duff, Bill Williams, Lita Baron, Henry Calvin, Douglas Fowley, Addison Richards, Joel Ashley, John Pickard, William Phillips, Dorothy Adams, Joe Dominguez. *D:* Lesley Selander; *P:* Howard W. Koch; *St: & Sc:* John C. Higgins. (1:22) A deputy sheriff finds that one of his fellow deputies is responsible for a robbery and murder.

363. Bronco Buster (Universal-International; 1952). *Cast:* John Lund, Scott Brady, Joyce Holden, Chill Wills, Don Haggerty, Casey Tibbs, Dan Poore, Pete Crump, Bill Williams, Jerry Ambler. *D:* Budd Boetticher; *P:* Ted Richmond; *St:* Peter B. Kyne; *Sc:* Horace McCoy, Lillie Hayward. (1:20) Drama of the rodeo and two buddies who part ways over the same girl. Technicolor.

364. The Brothers Karamazov (MGM/ Avon Prods.; 1958). *Cast:* Yul Brynner (Dmitri Karamazov), Maria Schell (Grushenka), Claire Bloom (Katya), Lee J. Cobb (AAN/Fyodor Karamazov), Richard Basehart (Ivan Karamazov), Albert Salmi (film debut + voted "Best Supporting Actor" by the NBR combined with his work on *The Bravados*—q.v./Smerdyakov), William Shatner (film debut/Alesey Karamazov), Judith Evelyn (Mme. Anna Hohlakov), Edgar Stehli (Grigory), Harry Townes (Ippolit Kirillov), Miko Oscard (Illusha Snegiryov), David Opatashu (Capt. Snegiryov), Simon Oakland (film debut/Mavrayek), Jay Adler (pawnbroker), Frank DeKova (Capt. Vrublevski), Ann Morrison (Marya), Gage Clarke (defense counsel), Mel Welles (Trifon Borrissovitch), Shepard Menken (Peter), William Vedder (Father Zossima), Steven Roberts (Michael), Charles Horvath, Sam Buffington, Frederick Ledebur, Giselle D'Arc, Gloria Pall, Than Wyenn, Jerry Riggio, Leonard Graves, Stafford Repp, George Barrows, Hal Norman, Michael Mark, Ziva Rodann, Guy Prescott, John W. Zweers, John Warren Leland, Dorothy Neumann, Molly Glessing, Mary Ann Bernard, Len Lesser, Harry Hines, Gregg Martell. *D:* Richard Brooks; *P:* Pandro S. Berman; *As.P:* Kathryn Hereford; *Adaptation:* Julius J. & Philip G. Epstein; *Sc:* Brooks. (2:26) (video) Drama of four brothers and their varied reactions to the death of their domineering father. Based on the English translation by Constance Garnett of Feodor Dostoyevsky's acclaimed novel. Despite critical acclaim, the film suffered at the box office. It was in nomination at the Cannes Film Festival and placed #8 on the "10 Best" list of the NBR. Filmed before in Germany in 1931 as *Karamazov.* MetroColor. Note: The role of Grushenka was coveted by Marilyn Monroe who expressed major disappointment when she was not cast.

365. The Brothers Rico (Columbia; 1957). *Cast:* Richard Conte, Dianne Foster, Kathryn Grant, Larry Gates, James Darren, Argentina Brunetti, Lamont Johnson, Paul Picerni, Harry Bellaver, Paul Dubov, Rudy Bond, William Phipps, Richard Bakalyan, Mimi Aguglia, Maggie O'Byrne, George Cisar, Peggy Maley, Jane Easton. *D:* Phil Karlson; *P:* Lewis J. Rachmil; *Sc:* Lewis Meltzer, Ben Perry. (1:32) The two brothers of an accountant are targeted by the mob in this crime drama based on *Les Frères Rico*, a novelette by Georges Simenon. Remade in 1972 as *The Family Rico*, a TV movie.

366. The Buccaneer (Paramount; 1958). *Cast:* Yul Brynner (Jean Lafitte), Claire Bloom (Bonnie Brown), Charles Boyer (Dominique You), Inger Stevens (Annette Claiborne), Henry Hull (Ezra Pevney), E.G. Marshall (Gov. Claiborne), Charlton Heston (Andrew Jackson), Lorne Greene (Mercier), Ted de Corsia (Capt. Rumbo), Douglass Dumbrille (collector), Robert F. Simon (Capt. Brown), Sir Lancelot (Scipio), Fran Jeffries (Cariba), George Mathews (Pyke), Leslie E. Bradley (Capt. McWilliams), Bruce Gordon (Gramby), Barry Kelley (Comm. Patterson), Robert Warwick (Lockyer), Steven Marlo (Beluche), James Todd (Mr. Whipple), Jerry Hartleben (Miggs), Theodora Davitt (Marie Claiborne), Wally Richard (Lt. Shreve), Reginald Sheffield (final film—d. 1957/Tripes), Stephen Chase (Col. Butler), Woodrow Strode (Toro), Paul Newlan (Capt. Flint), Norma Varden (Mme. Hilaire), Ashley Cowan (Mouse), Julio DeDiego (Miquel), Manuel Rojas (Orlando Corona), Syl Lamont (Lobo), Paul Wexler (Horse Face), Kathleen Freeman (Tina), Mimi Gibson (Marjorie), Leonard Graves (Chighizola), Friedrich Ledebur, Jr. (Capt. Bart), Judd Holdren (Maj. Reed), Robin Hughes (Lt. Rogers), Jack Kruschen (Hans), Mike Mazurki (Tarsus), Chester Jones (Coto), Alberto Morin (Maj. Latour), John Dierkes, Ken Miller, Onslow Stevens, Iris Adrian, James Seay, Julia Faye (final film—ret.), John Hubbard, Brad Johnson, Harry Shannon, Henry Brandon, Billie Lee Hart, Raymond Greenleaf, Harlan Warde, Sr., Charles Meredith, Mickey Finn, Eric Alden, Jack Pennick, Frank Hagney. *D:* Anthony Quinn; *Ex.P:* Cecil B. DeMille; *P:* Henry Wilcoxon; *Adaptation:* Jeannie Macpherson (of Lyle Saxon's *Lafitte the Pirate*); *Sc*: Jesse Lasky, Jr., Bernice Mosk (based on the 1938 screenplay by Harold Lamb, C. Gardiner Sullivan and Edwin Justus Mayer; *Costumes:* (AAN) Ralph Jester, Edith Head, John Jensen. (2:01) (video/laserdisc) Produced "under the personal supervision of Cecil B. DeMille," this epic adventure—a remake of the 1938 production by DeMille—of the War of 1812 about Jean Lafitte and Andrew Jackson was a lavishly produced box office bomb. Technicolor and VistaVision.

367. Buccaneer's Girl (Universal-International; 1950). *Cast:* Yvonne DeCarlo, Phillip Friend, Elsa Lanchester, Andrea King, Robert Douglas, Norman Lloyd, Jay C. Flippen, Douglass Dumbrille, Verna Felton, Henry Daniell, John Qualen, Connie Gilchrist, Ben Welden, Dewey Robinson, Peggie Castle (film debut). *D:* Frederick de Cordova; *P:* Robert Arthur; *St:* Joe May, Samuel R. Golding; *Sc:* Harold Shumate, Joseph Hoffman. (1:17) Technicolor romantic adventure of a singer's involvement with a notorious pirate who turns out to be not so notorious, once all is revealed.

368. Buchanan Rides Alone (Columbia/Scott-Brown; 1958). *Cast:* Randolph Scott, Craig Stevens, Barry Kelley, Tol Avery, Peter Whitney, Manuel Rojas, Robert Anderson, L.Q. Jones, Joe De Santis, William Leslie, Jennifer Holden, Nacho Galindo, Roy Jenson, Don C. Harvey, Terry Frost, Barbara James, Jim B. Leon, Leo Ogletree, Frank Scannell, Al Wyatt, Riley Hill. *D:* Budd Boetticher; *P:* Harry Joe Brown; *As.P:* Randolph Scott; *Sc:* Charles Lang, Jr. (1:18) Western drama of a drifter who unwillingly gets mixed up in a local feud, perpetrated by a corrupt family. Based on the novel *The Name's Buchanan* by Jonas Ward, it was photographed in ColumbiaColor (Technicolor).

369. Buckaroo Sheriff of Texas (Republic; 1951). *Cast:* Michael Chapin, Eilene Janssen, James Bell, Hugh O'Brian, Steve Pendleton, Tristram Coffin, William Haade, Selmer Jackson, Ed Cassidy, Eddie Dunn, Alice Kelley. *D:* Philip Ford; *As.P:* Rudy Ralston; *St:* & *Sc:* Arthur Orloff. (1:00) A gang of kids round up the bad guys in the premiere entry of the *Rough Ridin' Kids* series of four films. A Republic experiment that proved unpopular, it originally was paired on a double bill with *California Passage* (q.v.).

370. A Bucket of Blood (American International/James H. Nicholson & Samuel Z. Arkoff; 1959). *Cast:* Dick Miller, Barboura Morris, Anthony Carbone, Julian Burton, Ed Nelson,

John Brinkley, John Shaner, Judy Bamber, Myrtle Domerel, Burt Convy, Jhean Burton. *D: & P:* Roger Corman; *Sc:* Charles B. Griffith. (1:06) (video) Black comedy of a beatnik coffee-house busboy with aspirations to become a famous sculptor who "cheats" and creates critically acclaimed works of art by covering the corpses of his murder victims with clay. This low budget endeavor was Mr. Corman's prelude to his cult classic of 1960 *The Little Shop of Horrors*. The second feature on this double bill was *Attack of the Giant Leeches* (q.v.).

371. The Buckskin Lady (United Artists/Bishop-Hittleman Pictures, Inc.; 1957). *Cast:* Patricia Medina, Richard Denning, Gerald Mohr, Henry Hull, Hank Worden, Robin Short, Richard Reeves, Dorothy Adams, Frank Sully, George Cisar, Louis Lettiere, Byron Foulger, John Dierkes. *D: & P:* Carl K. Hittleman; *St:* Francis S. Chase, Jr.; *Sc:* David Lang, Hittleman. (1:06) The girl friend of a bank robber is attracted to the town's new doctor in this low budget western.

372. Buffalo Bill in Tomahawk Territory (United Artists/Jack Schwarz Prods., Inc.; 1952). *Cast:* Clayton Moore (title role), Slim Andrews, Rodd Redwing, Sharon Dexter, Eddie Phillips, Tom Hubbard, Chief Yowlachie, Chief Thundercloud (final film—d. 1955), Charlie Hughes, Helena Dare, Charles Harvey. *D:* Bernard B. Ray; *P:* Ray, Edward Finney; *St: & Sc:* Sam Newman, Nat Tanchuck. (1:06) (video) Low budget western with Buffalo Bill Cody coming to the rescue of Indians whose land is lusted after by whites because of its gold deposits.

373. Bugles in the Afternoon (Warner/Cagney Prods., Inc; 1951–52). *Cast:* Ray Milland, Helena Carter, Hugh Marlowe, Forrest Tucker, Barton MacLane, George Reeves, James Millican, Harry Lauter, Mary Adams, Lucille Shamburger, Gertrude Michael, Stuart Randall, William "Bill" Phillips, Hugh Beaumont, Dick Rich, John Pickard, John War Eagle, Sheb Wooley, Charles Evans, Nelson Leigh, Ray Montgomery, Virginia Brissac, John Doucette, Bud Osborne, Bob Steele. *D:* Roy Rowland; *P:* William Cagney; *Sc:* Harry Brown, Geoffrey Homes [Daniel Mainwaring]. (1:25) (video) Conflicts between cavalrymen, who in turn are in conflict with warring Sioux Indians, form the plot of this western which is based on a 1949 novel by Ernest Haycox.

374. A Bullet for Joey (United Artists/Bischoff-Diamond Corp.; 1955). *Cast:* Edward G. Robinson, George Raft, Audrey Totter, Peter Van Eyck, George Dolenz, Peter Hanson, Karen Verne, Henri Letondal, Ralph Smiley, John Cliff, Joseph Vitale, Bill Bryant, Stan Malotte, Toni Gerry, Sally Blane (final film appearance and the only one since 1939), Steven Geray, John Alvin, Bill Henry. *D:* Lewis Allen; *P:* Samuel Bischoff, David Diamond; *St:* James Benson Nablo; *Sc:* A.I. Bezzerides, Geoffrey Homes [Daniel Mainwaring]. (1:25) Espionage melodrama of a communist organization that kidnaps a nuclear scientist. Filmed in Canada.

375. A Bullet Is Waiting (Columbia/Welsch Prods., Inc.; 1954). *Cast:* Jean Simmons, Rory Calhoun, Stephen McNally, Brian Aherne, Shep (dog—won PATSY Award of Excellence in 1955). *D:* John Farrow; *P:* Howard Welsch; *St:* Thames Williamson; *Sc:* Williamson, Casey Robinson. (1:22) (video) A sheriff, transporting a prisoner, finds his charge is innocent after their plane is forced down in the desert. Technicolor.

376. The Bullfighter and the Lady (Republic/John Wayne Prods.; 1951). *Cast:* Robert Stack (Chuck Regan), Joy Page (Anita de la Vega), Gilbert Roland (Manolo Estrada), Virginia Grey (Elizabeth Flood), John Hubbard (Barney Flood), Katy Jurado (film debut/Chelo Estrada), Antonio Gomez (himself), Ismael Perez (Panchito), Rudolfo Acosta (Juan), Ruben Padilla (Dr. Siena), Dario Ramirez (Pepe Mora). *D:* Budd Boetticher; *P:* John Wayne; *St:* (AAN) Boetticher, Ray Nazarro; *Sc:* James Edward Grant; *Song:* Victor Young–Jack Elliott. (1:27) + (restored Director's Print which runs 2:04) (video/laserdisc) Acclaimed drama of an American learning the bullfighting game in Mexico. Through recklessness, he causes the death of his mentor, a famed matador beloved by the people.

377. Bullwhip! (Allied Artists/Romson-Broidy Prod.; 1956). *Cast:* Guy Madison, Rhonda Fleming, James Griffith, Don Beddoe, Peter Adams, Dan Sheridan, Burt Nelson, Al Terry, Hank Worden, Barbara Woodell, Rhys Williams, Jay Reynolds, Tim Graham, Rick Vallin, Wayne Mallory, Don Shelton, Jack Reynolds, Frank Griffin, J.W. Cody, Jack Carr, Saul Gorss. *D:* Harmon Jones; *Ex.P:* William F. Broidy; *P:* Helen Ainsworth; *Sc:* Adele Buffington; *Title song:* Hal Cooper–James Griffith (sung by Frankie Laine). (1:20) (video) Western drama of a man facing a dilemma: hang on a bogus murder rap or marry the girl. In DeLuxe color and CinemaScope, it was remade in 1978 as *Goin' South.*

378. Bunco Squad (RKO; 1950). *Cast:* Robert Sterling, Joan Dixon, Ricardo Cortez, Douglas Fowley, Elisabeth Risdon, Marguerite Churchill (final film appearance and only film since 1936), John Kellogg, Bernadene Hayes, Robert Bice, Dante (himself), Vivian Oakland (final film—ret.). *D:* Herbert I. Leeds; *P:* Lewis J. Rachmil; *St:* Reginald Tanner; *Sc:* George E. Callahan. (1:07) Programmer crime-melodrama of a bunco cop out to put a phony séance operation out of business.

379. Bundle of Joy (RKO; 1956). *Cast:* Eddie Fisher, Debbie Reynolds, Adolphe Menjou, Tommy Noonan, Nita Talbot, Una Merkel, Melville Cooper, Bill Goodwin, Howard McNear, Robert H. Harris, Mary Treen, Edward S. Brophy, Gil Stratton, Scott Douglas. *D:* Norman Taurog; *P:* Edmund Grainger; *St:* Felix Jackson; *Sc:* Norman Krasna, Robert Carson, Arthur Sheekman; *Songs:* "I Never Felt This Way Before," "Bundle of Joy," "Lullaby in Blue," "Worry About Tomorrow," "All About Love," "Someday Soon," "What's So Good About Morning" and "You're Perfect in Every Department" Josef Myrow–Mack Gordon. (1:40) (video) A department store salesgirl finds an infant, decides to keep it and causes various romantic and other complications and misunderstandings. A Technicolor musical remake of *Bachelor Mother* (RKO; 1939).

380. The Burglar (Columbia; 1957). *Cast:* Dan Duryea, Jayne Mansfield, Martha Vickers, Peter Capell, Mickey Shaughnessy, Wendell Phillips, Phoebe Mackay, Stewart Bradley, John Facenda, Frank Hall, Bob Wilson, Steve Allison, Richard Emory, Andrea McLaughlin. *D:* Paul Wendkos (directorial debut); *P:* Louis W. Kellman; *Sc:* David Goodis (based on his book). (1:30) Film noir of three crooks who come up against a crooked cop after they steal a valuable necklace. Loosely remade as *The Burglars*, a French/Italian co-production of 1972.

Burning Arrows *see* **Captain John Smith and Pocahontas**

381. The Burning Hills (Warner; 1956). *Cast:* Tab Hunter, Natalie Wood, Skip Homeier, Eduard Franz, Earl Holliman, Claude Akins, Ray Teal, Frank Puglia, Hal Baylor, Tyler MacDuff, Rayford Barnes, Tony Terry. *D:* Stuart Heisler; *P:* Richard Whorf; *Sc:* Irving Wallace. (1:33) (video) A young rancher clashes with the son of a ruthless cattle baron. Based on the novel by Louis L'Amour, it was photographed in WarnerColor and CinemaScope.

382. Bus Stop (20th Century–Fox; 1956). *Cast:* Marilyn Monroe (Cherie), Don Murray (AAN-BSA/film debut/Bo), Arthur O'Connell (Virgil), Betty Field (Grace), Eileen Heckart (Vera), Robert Bray (Carl), Hope Lange (film debut/Elma), Terry Kelman (Gerald), J.M. Dunlap (Orville), Hans Conried, Casey Adams [aka: Max Showalter], Henry Slate, Helen Mayon, Lucille Knox, Kate MacKenna, George Selk [aka: Budd Buster], Mary Carroll, Phil J. Munch, Fay L. Ivor, G.E. "Pete" Logan, Jim Katugi Noda. *D:* Joshua Logan; *P:* Buddy Adler; *Sc:* George Axelrod; *Songs:* "Theme from Bus Stop" (A Paper of Pins) by Ken Darby, "(That Old) Black Magic" (written in 1943 by Johnny Mercer and Harold Arlen). (1:36) (video/laserdisc) Acclaimed comedy-drama of a brash but naïve rodeo cowboy who sets his sights on a saloon singer, determined to marry her without even asking. Based on the 1955 play by William Inge, it placed #4 on the "10 Best" list of the *New York Times*, while on the same list of the NBR it placed #10. One of the 24 top-grossing films of 1955-56, it was also an unsuccessful TV series. DeLuxe color and CinemaScope. (aka: *The Wrong Kind of Girl*) Note: In reviews of this film, the critics finally acknowledged Monroe's acting ability.

383. The Bushwhackers (Realart; 1952). *Cast:* John Ireland, Wayne Morris, Lawrence Tierney, Dorothy Malone, Lon Chaney, Myrna Dell, Frank Marlowe, Bill Holmes, Jack Elam, Bob Wood, Charles Trowbridge, Stuart Randall, George Lynn, Norman Leavitt, Eddie Parks, Ted Jordan, Kit Guard, Venise Grove, Gordon Wynne, Evelyn Bispham, Jack Harden, Gabriel Conrad. *D:* Rod Amateau (directorial debut); *P:* Jack Broder, Larry Finley; *Sc:* Amateau, Thomas Gries. (1:10) (video) Western drama of a man returning from the Civil War in search of a peaceful life but finds that things are not as they were when he left. (G.B. title: *The Rebel*)

384. The Buster Keaton Story (Paramount/Forum Prods., Inc.–Robert Smith; 1956-57). *Cast:* Donald O'Connor (title role), Ann Blyth, Rhonda Fleming, Peter Lorre, Larry

Keating, Richard Anderson, Dave Willock (Joe Keaton), Jackie Coogan, Claire Carleton (Myrna Keaton), Larry White (Buster at age 7), Dan Seymour, Mike Ross, Nan Martin, Robert Christopher, Richard Aherne, Tim Ryan, Joe Forte, Ralph Dumke, Larry Rio, Constance Cavendish, Ivan Triesault, Pamela Jason, Keith Richards, Dick Ryan, Guy Wilkerson, Liz Slifer, Cecil B. DeMille. *D:* Sidney Sheldon; *P: & Sc:* Sheldon, Robert Smith. (1:31) Critically panned fictionalized biography of the great comedian of Hollywood silents. Keaton himself restaged the movie recreations. VistaVision.

385. But Not for Me (Paramount/Seaton-Perlberg; 1959). *Cast:* Clark Gable, Carroll Baker, Lilli Palmer, Lee J. Cobb, Barry Coe, Thomas Gomez, Wendell Holmes, Charles Lane, Tom Duggan. *D:* Walter Lang; *P:* George Seaton, William Perlberg; *Sc:* John Michael Hayes; *Title song:* George and Ira Gershwin (sung by Ella Fitzgerald); *Song:* "The Typewriter" (music by Leroy Anderson). (1:45) (video) A young secretary with theatrical aspirations falls for her aging theatrical producer/boss who has to deal with his own feelings in the situation. Based on Samson Raphaelson's play *Accent on Youth* which was filmed in 1935 under that title, followed by a remake in 1950 titled *Mr. Music* (q.v.). Location filming in New York City. VistaVision.

386. Bwana Devil (United Artists/Gulu Pictures Co.; 1952). *Cast:* Robert Stack, Barbara Britton, Nigel Bruce, Ramsey Hill, Paul McVey, Hope Miller, Pat O'Moore, Pat Aherne, John Dodsworth, Bhogwan Singh, Bhupesh Guha, Bal Seirgakar, Kalu K. Sonkur, Milas Clark, Jr. *D:-P: & Sc:* Arch Oboler; *Cin:* Joseph Biroc. (1:19) Notable as the first commercial 3-D film, which had to be viewed through Polaroid glasses to achieve the desired effect. Publicity hype of "A Lion in Your Lap" made this ultra low budget tale. Shot entirely in California, a story of railroad workers in Africa being devoured by lions until done in by a great white hunter. One of the 26 top-grossing films of 1952-53, it was photographed in Anscocolor and set the stage (or screen) for the gimmicky 3-D craze of the early 1950s.

387. By the Light of the Silvery Moon (Warner; 1953). *Cast:* Doris Day, Gordon MacRae, Leon Ames, Rosemary DeCamp, Billy Gray, Mary Wickes, Russell Arms, Maria Palmer, Walter Flannery, Geraldine Wall, John Maxwell, Carol Forman, Merv Griffin. *D:* David Butler; *P:* William Jacobs; *Sc:* Robert O'Brien, Irving Elinson (based on the "Penrod Stories" of Booth Tarkington); *Songs include:* "By the Light of the Silvery Moon" (Gus Edwards-Edward Madden); "I'll Forget You" (Ernest R. Ball–Annelu Burns); "Your Eyes Have Told Me So" (Gus Kahn–Egbert Van Alstyne); "Be My Little Baby Bumble Bee" (Stanley Murphy-Henry I. Marshall); "If You Were the Only Girl in the World" (Clifford Grey–Nat D. Ayer); "Ain't We Got Fun" (Kahn–Richard Whiting); "King Chanticleer" (Ayer). (1:41) (video/laserdisc) Post–World War I romantic musical of young lovers trying to adjust. A bevy of old standards made this sequel to *On Moonlight Bay* (q.v.) popular at the box office.

388. The Caddy (Paramount/York Pictures; 1953). *Cast:* Dean Martin (Joe Anthony), Jerry Lewis (Harvey), Donna Reed (Kathy Taylor), Barbara Bates (Lisa Anthony), Joseph Calleia (Papa Anthony), Fred Clark (Mr. Baxter), Clinton Sundberg (Charles), Marshall Thompson (Bruce Reeber), Marjorie Gateson (final film—ret./Mrs. Taylor), Frank Puglia (Mr. Spezzato), Lewis Martin (Mr. Taylor), Howard Smith (golf official), Romo Vincent (Eddie Lear), Argentina Brunetti (Mama Anthony), John Gallaudet (Mr. Bell), Sam Snead (himself), Ben Hogan (himself), Byron Nelson (himself), Julius Boros (himself), Jimmy Thomson (himself), Harry E. Cooper (himself), Charles Irwin, Houseley Stevenson, Jr., Freeman Lusk, Keith McConnell, Henry Brandon, Maurice Marsac, Donald Randolph, Stephen Chase, Tom Harmon. *D:* Norman Taurog; *P:* Paul Jones; *St:* Danny Arnold; *Sc:* Edmund Hartmann, Arnold; *Additional dialogue:* Ken Englund; *Songs:* "That's Amore" (AAN), "What Wouldcha Do Without Me?," "One Big Love," "You're the Right One" and "It's a Whistle-in Kind of Mornin'" (Harry Warren–Jack Brooks). (1:35) (video) The comedy team hit the pro-golf circuit, with Martin as the golfer and Lewis his agoraphobic caddy and golf advisor. The film is more notable for the hit song "That's Amore" that it produced.

Cage of Doom (G.B. title) *see* **Terror from the Year 5,000**

389. Caged (Warner; 1950). *Cast:* Eleanor Parker (AAN/Marie Allen), Agnes Moorehead (Ruth Benton), Hope Emerson (AAN/Evelyn Harper), Ellen Corby (Emma), Betty Garde (Kitty Stark), Jan Sterling (Smoochie), Lee Patrick (Elvira Powell), Olive Deering (June),

Jane Darwell (isolation matron), Gertrude Michael (Georgia), Sheila Stevens (Helen), Joan Miller (Claire), Marjorie Crossland (Cassie), Gertrude Hoffman (Millie), Lynn Sherman (Ann), Queenie Smith (Mrs. Warren), Naomi Robison (Hattie), Esther Howard (Grace), Marlo Dwyer (Julie), Wanda Tynan (Meta), Peggy Wynne (Lottie), Frances Morris (Mrs. Foley), Edith Evanson (Miss Barker), Yvonne Rob (Elaine), Ann Tyrrell (Edra), June Whipple (Ada), Sandra Gould (Skip), Taylor Holmes (Sen. Donnolly), Eileen Stevens, Grace Hayes, Don Beddoe, Charles Meredith, George Baxter, Guy Beach, Harlan Warde, Bill Hunter, Barbara Esback, Marjorie Wood, Evelyn Dockson, Hazel Keener, Jane Crowley, Gail Bonney, Doris Kemper, Lovyss Bradley, Ezelle Poule, Margaret Lambert, Eva Nelson, Rosemary O'Neil, Jean Calhoun, Nita Talbot, Marie Melish, Pauline Creasman, Joyce Newhard, Helen Eby-Rock, Sheila Stuart, Claudia Cauldwell, Tina Menard, Carole Shannon, Gladys Roach, Virginia Engels, Bill Haade, Ruth Warren, Davison Clark, Pauline Drake, Gracille LaVinder, Bill Wayne, Doris Whitney, Grace Hampton, Helen Mowery, Helen Spring, Frances Henderson. *D:* John Cromwell; *P:* Jerry Wald; *Sc:* (AAN) Virginia Kellogg, Bernard C. Schoenfeld. (1:36) A starkly brutal drama of women behind bars and one innocent girl, who becomes an embittered inmate while doing a stretch for a crime committed by her husband. At the Venice Film Festival, Eleanor Parker was voted "Best Actress" for her portrayal of Marie Allen. Remade in 1962 as *House of Women.*

390. The Caine Mutiny (Columbia; 1954). *Cast:* Humphrey Bogart (AAN/Capt. Queeg), Jose Ferrer (Lt. Barney Greenwald), Van Johnson (Lt. Steve Maryk), Fred MacMurray (Lt. Tom Keefer), Robert Francis (film debut/Ensign Willie Keith), May Wynn (May Wynn), Tom Tully (AAN/Capt. DeVriess), E.G. Marshall (Lt. Cdr. Challee), Arthur Franz (Lt. Paynter), Lee Marvin (Meatball), Warner Anderson (Capt. Blakely), Claude Akins (Horrible), Katharine Warren (Mrs. Keith), Jerry Paris (Ensign Harding), Steve Brodie (Chief Budge), Todd Karns (Stillwell), Whit Bissell (Lt. Cdr. Dickson), James Best (Lt. Jorgenson), Joe Haworth (Ensign Carmody), Guy Anderson (Ensign Rabbitt), James Edwards (Whittaker), Don Dubbins (Urban), David Alpert (Engstrand), Dayton Lummis (Uncle Lloyd), James Todd (Commodore Kelvey), Eddie Laguna (Winston), Don Keefer, Patrick Miller, Ted Cooper, Don Dillaway. *D:* Edward Dmytryk; *P:* (AAN-Best Picture) Stanley Kramer; *Sc:* (AAN) Stanley Roberts; *Music:* (AAN) Max Steiner; *Editors:* (AAN) William A Lyon, Henry Batista; *Sound:* (AAN) John P. Livadary. (2:05) (video/laserdisc) Critically acclaimed drama of a mutiny aboard a U.S. naval vessel, followed by a court martial of the mutineers. Based on the 1951 Pulitzer Prize–winning novel by Herman Wouk, it was voted "Best Film of the Year" by *Film Daily* and was in nomination at the British Academy Awards. In Technicolor, it became one of the 25 top-grossing films of 1953-54. In 1988, *The Caine Mutiny Court Martial* was made for TV and was based on Mr. Wouk's 1953 play.

391. Calamity Jane (Warner; 1953). *Cast:* Doris Day (Calamity Jane), Howard Keel (Wild Bill Hickok), Allyn Ann McLerie (Katie Brown), Philip Carey (Lt. Gilmartin), Dick Wesson (Francis Fryer), Paul Harvey (Henry Miller), Chubby Johnson (Rattlesnake), Gale Robbins (Adelaide Adams). *D:* David Butler; *P:* William Jacobs; *Sc:* James O'Hanlon; *Music:* (AAN) Ray Heindorf; *Sound:* (AAN) William A. Mueller; *Songs include:* "Secret Love" (AA-Best Song), "The Deadwood Stage," "Higher Than a Hawk," "Tis Harry I'm Plannin' To Marry," "The Black Hills of Dakota," "A Woman's Touch" + 4 others (Sammy Fain–Paul Francis Webster). (1:40) (video/laserdisc) Hit musical-western-romance of rowdy Calamity Jane who gets it in her mind she might attract a man if she acts more like a lady. The song "Secret Love," which won the Oscar, also became one of Doris Day's biggest selling hits. Technicolor.

392. California Conquest (Columbia/ Esskay Pictures; 1952). *Cast:* Cornel Wilde, Teresa Wright, Alfonso Bedoya, Lisa Ferraday, Eugene Iglesias, John Dehner, Ivan Lebedeff, Tito Renaldo, Renzo Cesana, Baynes Barron, Rico Alaniz, William P. [Bill] Wilkerson, Edward Colmans, George Eldredge, Hank Patterson, Alex Montoya. *D:* Lew Landers; *P:* Sam Katzman; *Sc:* Robert E. Kent. (1:19) Western of an attempted Russian takeover of California in the early 1800s. Based on *Don Peon* by Johnston McCulley. Technicolor.

393. California Passage (Republic; 1950). *Cast:* Forrest Tucker, Adele Mara, Estelita Rodriguez, Jim Davis, Peter Miles, Charles Kemper, Bill Williams, Rhys Williams, Paul Fix, Francis McDonald, Eddy Waller, Iron Eyes Cody, Charles Stevens, Alan Bridge, Ruth Brennan. *D:* & *As.P:* Joseph Kane; *St:* & *Sc:* James Edward Grant; *Songs:* "Second-Hand Romance,"

"I'm Goin' 'Round in Circles" (Harold Spina-Jack Elliott). (1:30) Big budgeted Republic western of a saloon owner who falls for the sister of a man he accidentally killed. Originally ran on a double bill program with co-feature *Buckaroo Sheriff of Texas* (q.v.).

394. Call Me Madam (20th Century-Fox; 1953). *Cast:* Ethel Merman (Mrs. Sally Adams, repeating her Broadway role), Donald O'Connor (Kenneth), Vera-Ellen (Princess Maria), George Sanders (Cosmo Constantine), Billy DeWolfe (Pemberton Maxwell), Helmut Dantine (Prince Hugo), Walter Slezak (Tantinnin), Steven Geray (Sebastian), Ludwig Stossel (Grand Duke), Lilia Skala (Grand Duchess), Charles Dingle (Sen. Brockway), Emory Parnell (Sen. Gallagher), Percy Helton (Sen. Wilkins), Oscar Beregi (Chamberlain), Nestor Paiva (Miccoli), Torben Meyer (Rudolph), John Wengraf (Ronchin), Leon Belasco, Sidney Marion, Richard Garrick, Walter Woolf King, Olan Soule, Fritz Feld, Erno Verebes, Hannelore Axman, Lal Chand Mehra. *D:* Walter Lang; *P:* Sol C. Siegel; *Sc:* Arthur Sheekman; *Music:* (AA) Alfred Newman; *Costumes:* (AAN-color) Irene Sharaff; *Songs include:* "It's a Lovely Day Today" (by O'Connor and Vera-Ellen/voice dubbed by Carole Richards); "You're Just in Love" (by Merman & O'Connor); "Marrying for Love" (by Sanders); "The Ocarina" (by Vera-Ellen & Chorus). (1:57) Musical-comedy of a Washington hostess who is named ambassador to a small European nation called Lichtenburg. Loosely based on the real-life Perle Mesta and the Broadway success by Howard Lindsey and Russell Crouse with songs by Irving Berlin. One of the 26 top-grossing films of 1952-53.

395. Call Me Mister (20th Century–Fox; 1951). *Cast:* Betty Grable, Dan Dailey, Danny Thomas, Dale Robertson, Benay Venuta, Richard Boone, Jeffrey Hunter, Frank Fontaine, Harry Von Zell, Dave Willock, Robert Ellis, Jerry Paris, Lou Spencer, Art Stanley, Bob Roberts, Tommy Bond (final film—ret.), Frank Clark, Bobby Short, Fred Libby, Ken Christy, Russ Conway, Robert Scott, Dabbs Greer, Mack Williams, Maylia, Steven Clark, Robert Easton, John McKee, Robert Rockwell, John McGuire, Paul Burke (film debut). *D:* Lloyd Bacon; *P:* Fred Kohlmar; *Sc:* Albert E. Lewin, Burt Styler; *Choreography:* Busby Berkeley; *Songs:* "Going Home Train," "Military Life" (Harold J. Rome–Jerry Seelen); "I Just Can't Do Enough For You Baby," "Japanese Girl Like American Boy," "Love is Back in Business" (Mack Gordon–Sammy Fain); "Lament to the Pots and Pans" (Seelen–Earl K. Brent) and "I'm Gonna Love That Guy" (Frances Ash). (1:36) Technicolor musical set during the Korean War of a man seeking to get reunited with his wife, an entertainer in camp shows. Based on the Broadway musical revue by Harold J. Rome and Arnold M. Auerbach.

396. Call of the Klondike (Monogram; 1950). *Cast:* Kirby Grant, Chinook the Wonder Dog, Anne Gwynne, Lynne Roberts, Tom Neal, Russell Simpson, Paul Bryar, Pat Gleason, Duke York, Marc Krah. *D:* Frank McDonald; *P:* Lindsley Parsons, William F. Broidy; *St:* James Oliver Curwood; *Sc:* Charles Long. (1:06) Northwoods adventure of a Mountie, his dog and a young woman who find a gold mine and uncover a pair of killers while searching for the lady's father. Part of a series.

397. Callaway Went Thataway (MGM; 1951). *Cast:* Fred MacMurray, Dorothy McGuire, Howard Keel (dual role), Jesse White, Fay Roope, Natalie Schafer, Stan Freberg, Elizabeth Taylor (cameo), Clark Gable (cameo), Esther Williams (cameo), Douglas Kennedy, Elisabeth Fraser, Johnny Indrisano, Don Haggerty, Dorothy Andre, James Harrison, Carl Sepulveda, Hank Weaver, Ned Glass, Glen Gallagher, Wayne Treadway, Harold Cornsweet, Kay Scott, Margie Liszt, Emmett Lynn, Billy Dix, Lynn Farr, Rocky Camron, Glenn Strange, John Banner, Ann Robin, B.G. Norman, Mickey Little, Ben Strobach, Paul Fierro, Burnu Acquanetta, Carlos Conde, Paul "Tiny" Newlan, Paul Bryar, Douglas Fowley, Helen Eby-Rock, Mae Clarke, Hugh Beaumont, Sam Herrera, Roque Ybarra. *D:-P: & Sc:* Norman Panama, Melvin Frank. (1:21) In this popular Hollywood comedy spoof, a real cowboy subs for a wayward former movie cowboy star, now an alcoholic recluse. (G.B. title: *The Star Said No*)

398. Calling Homicide (Allied Artists; 1956). *Cast:* Bill Elliott, Don Haggerty, Kathleen Case, Myron Healey, Jeanne Cooper, Thomas Browne Henry, Lyle Talbot, Almira Sessions, Herb Vigran, James Best, John Dennis. *D: & Sc:* Edward Bernds; *P:* Ben Schwalb. (1:00) In this low budget crime-melodrama, the murders of a young cop and a modeling school operator are clues in breaking up a phony adoption racket.

Calypso (G.B. title) *see* **Manfish**

399. Calypso Heat Wave (Columbia/Clover Prods.; 1957). *Cast:* Johnny Desmond (film debut), Merry Anders, Meg Myles, Paul Langton, Joel Grey, Michael Granger, George E. Stone, Pierce Lyden, Darla Hood, Gil Perkins, William Challee, The Tarriers, The Hi-Los, Maya Angelou (herself), Dick Whittinghill (himself), The Treniers, Mac Niles & the Calypsonians. *D:* Fred F. Sears; *P:* Sam Katzman; *St:* Orville H. Hampton; *Sc:* David Chandler; *Songs:* "Swing Low, Sweet Chariot" (traditional); "My Sugar is So Refined" (written in 1946 by Sidney Lippman [m], Sylvia Dee, Josephine Proffitt [ly], both performed by the Hi-Los); "Banana Boat Song" (Day-O) (Written and performed by the Tarriers, e.g. Alan Arkin, Bob Carey, Erik Darling); "Day Old Bread and Canned Beans" and "Rock Joe" (performed by the Treniers); "Run Joe" (Sung by Angelou). (1:26) "Fad" musical attempt to capitalize on the calypso craze of the late 1950s.

400. Calypso Joe (Allied Artists; 1957). *Cast:* Herb Jeffries, Angie Dickinson, Edward Kemmer, Stephen Bekassy, Laurie Mitchell, Claudia Drake, Murray Alper, Linda Terrace, Charles R. Keane, Genie Stone, Robert Sherman, Lord Flea and His Calypsonians, The Lester Horton Dancers, Duke of Iron, Herb Jeffries Calypsomaniacs, The Easy Riders. *D:* Edward Dein; *P:* William F. Broidy; *Sc:* Edward and Mildred Dein; *Songs include:* "There's Only One Love (Between a Man and a Woman)" + six others (by Herb Jeffries and Richard Hazard); "Marianne" (written by Terry Gilkyson, Frank Miller and Richard Dehr) and "Sweet Sugar Cane" (both performed by the Easy Riders). (1:16) Programmer musical with romantic interludes set during the calypso fad of the late 1950s. Ran on a double bill with *Hot Rod Rumble* (q.v.).

Camels West (G.B. title) *see* **Southwest Passage**

401. Cannibal Attack (Columbia; 1954). *Cast:* Johnny Weissmuller (himself), Judy Walsh, David Bruce, Bruce Cowling, Charles Evans, Steve Darrell, Joseph A. Allen, Jr. *D:* Lee Sholem; *P:* Sam Katzman; *Sc:* Carroll Young. (1:09) (video) Thieves are dressed up like crocodiles intent on stealing cobalt. A low budget jungle adventure which is an extension of the "Jungle Jim" series minus the name, the rights of which were transferred to Screen Gems, Inc.

402. Canyon Ambush (Monogram/Silvermine Prods.; 1952). *Cast:* Johnny Mack Brown, Phyllis Coates, Lee Roberts, Dennis Moore, Hugh Prosser, Marshall Reed, Denver Pyle, Pierce Lyden, Stanley Price, Bill Koontz, Frank Ellis, Russ Whiteman, Carol Henry, George DeNormand. *D:* Lewis D. Collins; *P:* Vincent M. Fennelly; *Sc:* Joseph Poland. (0:53) A masked rider is suspected to be behind several robberies in this J.M. Brown series western which had a pre-release title "Guns Along the Border."

403. Canyon Crossroads (United Artists/M.P.T. Prods.; 1955). *Cast:* Richard Basehart, Phyllis Kirk, Stephen Elliott, Russell Collins, Charles Wagenheim, Richard Hale, Alan Wells, Tommy Cook, William Pullen. *D:* Alfred Werker; *P:* William Joyce; *St: & Sc:* Emmett Murphy, Leonard M. Heideman. (1:23) Contemporary western, filmed on location in Colorado, of various people in search of uranium, all for different reasons.

Canyon Pass (G.B. title) *see* **Raton Pass**

404. Canyon Raiders (Monogram; 1951). *Cast:* Whip Wilson, Fuzzy Knight, Jim Bannon, Riley Hill, Phyllis Coates, I. Stanford Jolley, Barbara Woodell, Marshall Reed, Bill Kennedy. *D:* Lewis D. Collins; *P:* Vincent M. Fennelly; *St: & Sc:* Jay Kilgore. (0:54) (video) Thieves are trying to sell stolen horses to the U.S. Army in this Whip Wilson series western.

405. Canyon River (Allied Artists; 1956). *Cast:* George Montgomery, Marcia Henderson, Peter Graves, Richard Eyer, Walter Sande, Robert Wilke, Alan Hale, Jr., John Harmon, Jack Lambert, William Fawcett. *D:* Harmon Jones; *P:* Richard Heermance; *Sc:* Daniel B. Ullman. (1:20) A trail drive from Oregon to Wyoming is attacked by Indians as well as a gang of outlaws, bent on getting the beef for themselves. DeLuxe color and CinemaScope.

406. Captain Black Jack (Classic Pictures; 1952). *Cast:* George Sanders, Patricia Roc, Agnes Moorehead, Herbert Marshall, Marcel Dalio, Jose Neito. *D: & P:* Julien Duvivier; *Sc:* Duvivier, Charles Spaak. (1:30) (video) On the French Riviera, a doctor exposes a gang of drug runners headed by a wealthy socialite. A French-American co-production. (aka: *Captain Blackjack*)

Captain Blood, Fugitive (G.B. title) *see* **Captain Pirate**

407. Captain Carey, U.S.A. (Paramount; 1950). *Cast:* Alan Ladd (Webster Carey), Wanda Hendrix (Giula DeCresci), Francis Lederer (Barone Rocco DeGreffi), Joseph Calleia (Dr. Lunati), Celia Lovsky (Countess Francesca DeCresci), Angela Clarke (Serafina), Roland Winters (Acuto), Luis Alberni (Sandro), Rusty [Russ] Tamblyn (Pietro), Richard Avonde (Count Carlo DeCresci), Frank Puglia (Luigi), Jane Nigh (Nancy), George Lewis (Giovanni), David Leonard (blind musician), Virginia Farmer (Angelina), Paul Lees (Frank), Henry Escalante (Brutus). *D:* Mitchell Leisen; *P:* Richard Maibaum; *Sc:* Robert Thoeren; *Song:* (AA) "Mona Lisa" (Jay Livingston–Ray Evans) sung by Nat "King" Cole. (1:22) Post-war melodrama of an ex-military man who returns to an Italian town to find the Nazi collaborators responsible for the deaths of many of the town's residents during World War II. Based on the novel by Martha Albrand, the film is more notable for its Oscar winning theme song that sold a million copies for Nat "King" Cole. (G.B. title: *After Midnight*)

408. Captain Horatio Hornblower (Warner; 1951). *Cast:* Gregory Peck (title role), Virginia Mayo (Lady Barbara Wellesley), Robert Beatty (Lt. William Bush), James Robertson Justice (Quist), Denis O'Dea (Admiral Leighton), Terence Morgan (Lt. Gerard), Richard Hearne (Polwheal), James Kenney (Midshipman Longley), Moultrie R. Kelsall (Lt. Crystal), Michael Dolan (Gundarson), Stanley Baker (Mr. Harrison), John Witty (Capt. Etenza), Christopher Lee (Captain), Kynaston Reeves (Lord Hood), Ingeborg Wells (Hebe), Ronald Adam (Adm. Macartney), Michael Goodliffe (Caillard), Amy Veness (Mrs. McPhee), Alec Mango (El Supremo). *D:* Raoul Walsh; *P:* Gerry Mitchell; *Adapt:* C.S. Forester; *Sc:* Ben Roberts, Aeneas Mackenzie. (1:56) (video/laserdisc) Seafaring adventure of the British hero during the Napoleonic Wars. Based on three novels of the 1940s by C.S. Forester, this U.S.A./British coproduction became one of the 23 top-grossing films of 1950-51. Filmed on location in England in Technicolor. (G.B. title: *Captain Horatio Hornblower R.N.*)

409. Captain John Smith and Pocahontas (United Artists/Eclipse Films, Inc.; 1953). *Cast:* Anthony Dexter (Capt. John Smith), Jody Lawrence (Pocahontas), Robert Clarke (John Rolfe), Douglass Dumbrille (Powhatan), James Seay, Alan Hale, Jr., Stuart Randall, Philip Van Zandt, Shepard Menken, Henry Rowland, Anthony Eustrel (King James), Joan Nixon, Franchesca de Scaffa, Eric Colmar, William Cottrell. *D:* Lew Landers; *P:-St: & Sc:* Aubrey Wisberg, Jack Pollexfen. (1:15) Adventure tale of pre–Colonial America which plays with the facts of the historical characters involved. (G.B. title: *Burning Arrows*) Pathécolor. Originally ran on a double bill with *Song of the Land* (q.v.).

410. Captain Kidd and the Slave Girl (United Artists/Reliance-Superior Pictures, Inc.; 1954). *Cast:* Anthony Dexter (Capt. Kidd), Eva Gabor, Alan Hale, Jr., James Seay, Sonia Sorell, Richard Karlan, Noel Cravat, Lyle Talbot, Mike Ross, Jack Reitzen, Robert Long, Bill Cottrell, William Tannen, John Crawford. *D:* Lew Landers; *P:-St. & Sc:* Aubrey Wisberg, Jack Pollexfen. (1:22) Costume swashbuckling adventure of the titled pirate off to find some buried treasure. So what else is new? CFI color. Originally on a double bill with *The Yellow Tomahawk* (q.v.).

411. Captain Lightfoot (Universal-International; 1955). *Cast:* Rock Hudson, Barbara Rush, Jeff Morrow, Kathleen Ryan, Finlay Currie, Denis O'Dea, Geoffrey Toone, Milton Edwards, Harold Goldblatt, Charles Fitzsimmons, Louis Studley, Christopher Casson, Philip O'Flynn, Shay Gorman, Edward Aylward, James Devlin, Mike Nolan, Kenneth MacDonald, Oliver McGauley, Robert Bernal, Nigel Fitzgerald, Paul Farrell, Austin Meldon, Sheila Brenna, Alden Grennell, George Blankley, Lord Mount Charles, Lady Mount Charles, Edward Lexy, Peter Dix, Sean Mooney. *D:* Douglas Sirk; *P:* Ross Hunter; *St:* W.R. Burnett; *Sc:* Burnett, Oscar Brodney. (1:31) Costume drama filmed on location in Ireland of the 19th century Irish rebellion against the English. Technicolor and CinemaScope.

412. Captain Pirate (Columbia; 1952). *Cast:* Louis Hayward, Patricia Medina, John Sutton, Charles Irwin, George Givot, Ted de Corsia, Rex Evans, Malu Gatica, Sven-Hugo Borg, Robert McNeely, Lester Matthews, Ian Wolfe, Jay Novello, Robert Bice, Genevieve Aumont, Mario Siletti, Nina Koshetz, Sandro Giglio, Maurice Marsac. *D:* Ralph Murphy; *P:* Harry Joe Brown; *Sc:* Robert Yale Libott, Frank Burt, John Meredyth Lucas. (1:25) Pirate adventure of Captain Peter Blood, seeking the man who framed him. Based on Rafael Sabatini's *Captain Blood Returns*. (G.B. title: *Captain Blood, Fugitive*) Technicolor.

413. Captain Scarlett (United Artists/ Craftsman Prods., Inc.; 1953). *Cast:* Richard Greene, Leonora Amar, Manolo Fabregas, Eduardo Noriega, Nedrick Young, Isobel del Puerto, Carlos Musquiz, George Trevino. *D:* Thomas H. Carr; *P:-St: & Sc:* Howard Dimsdale. (1:15) (video) Costume swashbuckler of a Robin Hood–type set in 19th century southern France. Filmed in Mexico. Technicolor.

414. The Captive City (United Artists/ Aspen Prods., Inc.; 1952). *Cast:* John Forsythe, Joan Camden, Harold J. Kennedy, Marjorie Crossland, Ray Teal, Victor Sutherland, Martin Milner, Geraldine Hall, Hal K. Dawson, Ian Wolfe, Gladys Hurlbut, Jess Kirkpatrick, Paul Newlan, Frances Morris, Charles Wagenheim, Paul Brinegar, Vic Romito, Charles Regan, Senator Estes Kefauver (prologue & denouement). *D:* Robert Wise; *P:* Theron Warth; *St:* Alvin Josephy, Jr.; *Sc:* Karl Kamb, Josephy, Jr. (1:30) Melodrama, with a basis in fact, of a reporter who exposes a story of small town corruption. Originally on a double bill program with *Without Warning* (q.v.).

415. Captive Girl (Columbia; 1950). *Cast:* Johnny Weissmuller, Anita Lhoest, Buster Crabbe, John Dehner, Rick Vallin, Rusty Wescoatt, Nelson Leigh. *D:* William Berke; *P:* Sam Katzman; *Sc:* Carroll Young. (1:13) A girl who grew up in the jungle is the focus of this entry in the "Jungle Jim" series, which was based on the comic strip character created by Alex Raymond.

416. Captive of Billy the Kid (Republic; 1952). *Cast:* Allan Lane, Penny Edwards, Grant Withers, Clem Bevans, Roy Barcroft, Mauritz Hugo, Frank McCarroll, Clayton Moore, Gary Goodwin, Richard Emory, Black Jack (horse). *D:* Fred C. Brannon; *P:* Harry Keller; *Sc:* M. Coates Webster, Richard Wormser. (1:04) Series entry with U.S. Marshal "Rocky" Lane setting his sights on a gang that is after some loot stashed by Billy the Kid.

417. Captive Women (RKO; 1952). *Cast:* Robert Clarke, Margaret Field, Gloria Saunders, Ron Randell, Stuart Randall, Paula Dorety, Robert Bice, Chili Williams, William Schallert, Eric Colmar, Douglas Evans. *D:* Stuart Gilmore; *P:-St: & Sc:* Aubrey Wisberg, Jack Pollexfen. (1:07) Three diverse groups of individuals who survived the nuclear destruction of New York City are in conflict with each other. Science fiction on a low budget. (re-release title: *1000 Years from Now*/aka: *3000 A.D.*)

418. The Capture (RKO; 1950). *Cast:* Lew Ayres, Teresa Wright, Victor Jory, Duncan Renaldo, Jacqueline White, Jimmy Hunt, Barry Kelley, William Bakewell, Milton Parsons, Frank Matte, Edwin Rand, Felipe Turich. *D:* John Sturges; *P: & Sc:* Niven Busch. (1:31) (video) Melodrama set in rural Mexico of a detective who believes he may have killed an innocent man.

419. Carbine Williams (MGM; 1952). *Cast:* James Stewart, Jean Hagen, Wendell Corey, Carl Benton Reid, Paul Stewart, Otto Hulett, Herbert Heyes, Rhys Williams, James Arness, Porter Hall, Leif Erickson, Ralph Dumke, Fay Roope, Henry Corden, Howard Petrie, Frank Richards, Stuart Randall, Dan Riss, Bert LeBaron, Emile Meyer, Willis Bouchey, Bobby Hyatt, Duke York, Richard Reeves, Robert Foulk, Harry Cheshire, Lillian Culver, Marlene Lyden, Norma Jean Cramer, Robert Van Orden, Jordan Corenweth, Harry Mackin, Bob Alden, Jon Gardner, Erik Nielsen, Sam Flint, Nolan Leary, Marshall Bradford, Fiona O'Shiel, George Pembroke, James Harrison. *D:* Richard Thorpe; *P:* Armand Deutsch; *Sc:* Art Cohn. (1:30) (video) Biographical drama of the man who invented the carbine rifle, his domestic life and his inability to keep out of trouble with the law. Computer-colored prints have been produced by Turner Entertainment.

420. Career (Paramount/Hal B. Wallis; 1959). *Cast:* Anthony Franciosa (Sam Lawson), Dean Martin (Maury Novak), Shirley MacLaine (Sharon Kensington), Carolyn Jones (Shirley Drake), Joan Blackman (Barbara), Robert Middleton (Mr. Kensington), Donna Douglas (Marjorie Burke), Frank McHugh (Charlie), Jerry Paris (Allan Burke), Chuck Wassil (Eric Peters), Alan Hewitt (Matt Helmsley), Mary Treen, Marjorie Bennett. *D:* Joseph Anthony; *P:* Hal B. Wallis; *Sc:* James Lee; *Cin:* (AAN-b/w) Joseph LaShelle; *ASD:* (AAN-b/w) Hal Pereira, Walter Tyler (art directors), Sam Comer, Arthur Krams (sets); *Costumes:* (AAN-b/w) Edith Head. (1:45) (video) Drama with some acclaim of a young actor with an alcoholic wife, who attempts to make a name for himself on Broadway. Based on the original Broadway play by Bill Lee, it was in nomination by the New York Film Critics for "Best Picture" of the year.

421. The Careless Years (United Artists/ Bryna; 1957). *Cast:* Dean Stockwell, Natalie Trundy, John Larch, Barbara Billingsley, James Stephenson, Maureen Cassidy, Alan Dinehart III,

Virginia Christine, Bobby Hyatt, Hugh Sanders, Claire Carleton, Liz Slifer. *D:* Arthur Hiller (feature debut); *P: & Sc:* Edward Lewis; *Songs:* title song, "Butterfingers Baby" (Joe Lubin). (1:10) Adolescent oriented drama of high school teens who want to marry, but meet opposition from their parents.

422. Cargo to Capetown (Columbia; 1950). *Cast:* Broderick Crawford, John Ireland, Ellen Drew, Edgar Buchanan, King Donovan, Ted de Corsia, Frank Reicher, Gregory Gaye, Leonard Strong, Robert Espinoza, Peter Mamakos, Tom Stevenson. *D:* Earl McEvoy; *P: & Sc:* Lionel Houser. (1:20) A shipboard drama of romantic rivalry.

423. Caribbean (Paramount/Pine-Thomas; 1952). *Cast:* John Payne, Arlene Dahl, Sir Cedric Hardwicke, Francis L. Sullivan, Woody Strode, Willard Parker, Dennis Hoey (final film—ret.), Clarence Muse, William Pullen, Walter Reed, Ramsey Hill, John Hart, Zora Donahoo, Ezeret Anderson, Kermit Pruitt, Dan Ferniel, Rosalind Hayes. *D:* Edward Ludwig; *P:* William H. Pine, William C. Thomas; *Sc:* Frank L. Moss, Ludwig. (1:37) Lots of swash & buckle in this Technicolor 18th century romantic costumer of a fight against invading pirates. Based on the 1926 novel *Carib Gold* by Ellery H. Clark.

Caribbean Gold (G.B. title) *see* **Carribbean**

424. The Cariboo Trail (20th Century-Fox; 1950). *Cast:* Randolph Scott, George "Gabby" Hayes (final film—ret.), Bill Williams, Karin Booth, Victor Jory, Douglas Kennedy, Jim Davis, Dale Robertson, Mary Stuart, James Griffith, Lee Tung Foo, Anthony Hughes, Ray Hyke, Mary Kent, Jerry Root, Cliff Clark, Dorothy Adams, Fred Libby, Michael Barret, Smith Ballew, "Kansas" Moehring, Tom Monroe. *D:* Edwin L. Marin; *P:* Nat Holt; *St:* John Rhodes Sturdy; *Sc:* Frank Gruber. (1:21) (video/laserdisc) Cattlemen oppose the influx of homesteaders who are destroying their grazing lands. Filmed in Colorado in Cinecolor.

425. Carmen Jones (20th Century–Fox; 1954). *Cast:* Dorothy Dandridge (AAN-singing voice dubbed by Marilyn Horne/Carmen), Harry Belafonte (singing voice dubbed by LaVern Hutcherson/Joe), Olga James (Cindy Lou), Pearl Bailey (Frankie), Diahann Carroll (film debut/Myrt), Roy Glenn (Rum), Nick Stewart (Dink), Joe Adams (singing voice dubbed by Marvin Hayes/Husky), Broc[k] Peters (film debut/Sgt. Brown), Sandy Lewis (T-Bone), Mauri Lynn (Sally), DeForest Covan. *D: & P:* Otto Preminger; *Book & Lyric:* Oscar Hammerstein II; *Sc:* Harry Kleiner; *Music:* (AAN) Herschel Burke Gilbert; *Songs:* "Stand Up and Fight," "Beat Out the Rhythm on a Drum," "Dere's a Café on de Corner," "Lift 'em Up and Put 'em Down," "Dat's Love (I Go For You, But You're Taboo)," "You Talk Just Like My Maw," "Dis Flower," "De Cards Don't Lie," "My Joe," "Dat's Our Man" and "Whizzin' Away Along de Track" (1:45) (video/laserdisc) Romantic musical-drama with an all-black cast, set in a World War II Southern town. Based on the opera "Carmen" by Georges Bizet. One of the 27 top-grossing films of 1954-55, it was in nomination for "Best Picture" by the New York Film Critics and the British Academy Awards in 1955. It also placed #3 at the Berlin Film Festival. DeLuxe color, CinemaScope and stereophonic sound.

426. Carnival Rock (Howco; 1957). *Cast:* Susan Cabot, Brian Hutton, David J. Stewart, Dick Miller, Iris Adrian, Jonathan Haze, Ed Nelson, Chris Alcaide, Horace Logan, Yvonne Peattie, Gary Hunley, Frankie Ray, Dorothy Neumann, Clara Andressa, Terry Blake, The Platters, David Houston, Bob Luman, The Shadows, The Blockbusters. *D: & P:* Roger Corman; *Sc:* Leo Lieberman. (1:15) (video) Musical with guest shots, involving a romantic triangle between a night club owner, a singer and a gambler.

427. Carnival Story (RKO; 1954). *Cast:* Anne Baxter, Steve Cochran, Lyle Bettger, George Nader, Jay C. Flippen, Helene Stanley, Adi Berber. *D:* Kurt Neumann; *P:* Maurice and Frank King; *St:* Marcel Klauber, C.B. Williams; *Sc:* Hans Jacoby, Neumann. (1:34) (video) Romantic drama of a man, romantically obsessed with a female high diver, who will stop at nothing, including murder to possess her. Filmed on location in Munich, Germany. Technicolor.

428. Carolina Cannonball (Republic; 1955). *Cast:* Judy Canova, Andy Clyde, Ross Elliott, Sig Rumann, Leon Askin, Jack Kruschen, Frank Wilcox, Roy Barcroft. *D:* Charles Lamont; *P:* Herbert J. Yates; *St:* Frank Gill, Jr.; *Sc:* Barry Shipman. (1:14) Rural comedy of an atomic missile that lands in a ghost town inhabited only by a girl and her grandfather. Inept foreign agents are not far behind.

429. Carousel (20th Century–Fox; 1956). *Cast:* Gordon MacRae (Billy Bigelow), Shirley Jones (Julie Jordan), Cameron Mitchell (Jigger Craigin), Barbara Ruick (Miss Carrie Pipperidge), Claramae Turner (Cousin Nettie Fowler), Robert Rounseville (Mr. Enoch Snow), Gene Lockhart (Starkeeper), Audrey Christie (Mrs. Mullen), Susan Lucket (Louise), John Dehner (Mr. Bascombe), Jacques D'Amboise (Louise's dance partner), Fred Tweddell (Capt. Watson), Dee Pollock (Enoch Snow, Jr.), Richard Deacon (policeman), William Le Massena (Heavenly Friend), Sylvia Stanton, Tor Johnson, Mary Orozco, Harry "Duke" Johnson, Angelo Rossito, Marion Dempsey, Ed Mundy. *D:* Henry King; *P:* Henry Ephron; *Sc:* Henry & Phoebe Ephron; *Choreography:* Rod Alexander; *Louise's ballet:* staged by Agnes de Mille; *Songs & Musical numbers:* "The Carousel Waltz," "You're a Queer One, Julie Jordan!", "Mr. Snow," "If I Loved You," "June is Bustin' Out All Over," "Soliloquy," "Blow High, Blow Low," "When the Children Are Asleep," "A Real Nice Clambake," "Stonecutters Cut It On Stone," "What's the Use of Wonderin'?", "You'll Never Walk Alone." (2:08) (video/laserdisc) Musical-fantasy set in a small Maine coastal town in 1873. A former carnival barker, now deceased, seeks permission to return to earth for one day and help the teenage daughter he never knew. Based on the huge 1945 Broadway success by Richard Rodgers and Oscar Hammerstein II as adapted by Benjamin F. Glazer from Ferenc Molnar's *Liliom.* Filmed twice before as *Liliom,* in 1930 and 1934, and in 1921 as *A Trip to Paradise.* Lavishly produced, it became one of the 24 top-grossing films of 1955-56, but wound up $2,000,000 in the red. DeLuxe color and CinemaScope 55.

430. Carrie (Paramount; 1952). *Cast:* Laurence Olivier (George Hurstwood), Jennifer Jones (Carrie Meeber), Miriam Hopkins (Julie Hurstwood), Eddie Albert (Charles Drouet), Basil Ruysdael (Mr. Fitzgerald), Ray Teal (Allan), Barry Kelley (Slawson), Sara Berner (Mrs. Oransky), William Reynolds (George Hurstwood, Jr.), Harry Hayden (O'Brien), Walter Baldwin (Mr. Meeber), Dorothy Adams (Mrs. Meeber), Jacqueline de Wit (Minnie), Lester Sharpe (Blum), Don Beddoe (Goodman), Harlan Briggs (final film—d. 1952/Joe Brant), Len Hendry (Frank), Irene Winston (Anna), Melinda Plowman, Royal Dano, Albert Astar, William N. Bailey, James Flavin, Harry Denny, Martin Doric, Jack Gargan, Eric Alden, Donald Kerr, Jerry James, Jean DeBriac, Margaret Field, Nolan Leary, F. Patrick Henry, Jasper D. Weldon, Mike P. Donovan, Roy Butler, Anitra Sparrow, Charles Halton, Bob Foulk, Raymond Russell Roe, Leon Tyler, Ralph Sanford, G. Raymond Nye, Bruce Carruthers, James Davies, Ethan Laidlaw, George Melford, Al Ferguson, John Alvin, Gail Bonney, Lois Hall, Bill Meader, Allen Ray, Bill Sheehan, Sherry Hall, Richard Kipling, Howard Mitchell, Herman Nowlin, Charles B. Smith, Jim Hayward, Dulce Daye, Jay K. Eaton, Kenneth Patterson, Mike Mahoney, Judith Adams, Harry Hines, Ralph Moody, Slim Gault, Kit Guard, Daria Massey, Edward Clark, Gerry Ganzer, Julius Tannen, Oliver A. Cross, Jack Roberts, Harper Goff, Snub Pollard, Jack Low, Charley McAvoy, Cliff Clark, Frank Wilcox, Allen D. Sewall, Paul E. Burns, Edward J. Marr, Douglas Carter, Frances Morris, Stuart Holmes, Franklin Farnum, James Cornell, Elmo Lincoln (final film—d. 1952). *D: & P:* William Wyler; *Sc:* Ruth Goetz, Augustus Goetz; *ASD:* (AAN) Hal Pereira, Roland Anderson (art directors), Emile Kuri (sets); *Costumes:* (AAN) Edith Head. (1:58) (video/laserdisc) Drama of a farm girl who goes to Chicago at the turn-of-the-century, studies for a career as an actress and becomes the object of affection of a married man. Filmed in 1950 and shelved by the studio for two years, it was based on Theodore Dreiser's *Sister Carrie,* printed in 1900 and held up by the publisher for twelve years because they felt it was too controversial. The film was in nomination at the British Academy Awards and the Venice Film Festival.

431. Carson City (Warner; 1952). *Cast:* Randolph Scott, Raymond Massey, Lucille Norman, Richard Webb, James Millican, Larry Keating, George Cleveland, William Haade, Don Beddoe, Thurston Hall, Vince Barnett, Jack Woody, James Smith, Guy Tongue, Billy Vincent, Ida Moore, Sarah Edwards, Edgar Dearing, Russ Clark, Iris Adrian, Nick Thompson, Frank McCarroll, Post Park, Jack Daley, Mickey Simpson, Edmund Cobb, John Halloran, Mikel Conrad, Zon Murray, House Peters, Jr., Rory Mallinson, Ray Bennett, Karen Hale, Stanley Blystone, Stanley Andrews, Richard Reeves, George Eldredge, Charles Evans, Kenneth MacDonald, George Sherwood, Pierce Lyden, Les O'Pace. *D:* Andre De Toth; *P:* David Weisbart; *St:* Sloan Nibley; *Sc:* Nibley, Winston Miller. (1:26) Western of the difficulties encountered in laying railroad tracks from Virginia City, Montana, to Carson City, Nevada. The first production of this studio to utilize WarnerColor, another name for Eastmancolor.

432. Casa Manana (Monogram; 1951). *Cast:* Robert Clarke, Virginia Welles, Robert Karnes, Tony Roux, Carol Brewster, Paul Maxey, Jean Richey, The Rios Brothers [Frank, Larry & Jim], Eddie LeBaron and Orchestra, Spade Cooley (final film), Yadira Jimenez, Zarco and D'Lores, The Mercer Brothers, Armando and Lita, Betty and Beverly, Olga Perez, Davis and Johnson. *D:* Jean Yarbrough; *P:* Lindsley Parsons; *Sc:* Bill Raynor; *Songs include:* "Bounce," "People Like You," "I Hear a Rhapsody," "Madame Will Drop Her Shawl," "Cielito Lindo," "Pancho Grande" and "Fifty Games of Solitaire on Saturday Night" by Davis and Johnson, Ray Evans, Jay Livingston, Otis Bigelow, Harold Cooke, Jack Baker, George Fragos and Dick Gasparre. Musical romance of a man who purchases a nightclub so that his girlfriend can be the star singing-attraction.

433. Casanova's Big Night (Paramount; 1954). *Cast:* Bob Hope, Joan Fontaine, Vincent Price (title role), Audrey Dalton, Basil Rathbone, Raymond Burr, Frieda Inescort, Hope Emerson, Hugh Marlowe, Primo Carnera, Robert Hutton, John Carradine, John Hoyt, Lon Chaney, Jr., Arnold Moss, Frank Puglia, Paul Cavanagh, Romo Vincent, Henry Brandon, Natalie Schafer, Joan Shawlee, Lucien Littlefield, Douglas Fowley, Nestor Paiva, Barbara Freking, Oliver Blake. *D:* Norman Z. McLeod; *P:* Paul Jones; *St:* Aubrey Wisberg; *Sc:* Hal Kanter, Edmund Hartmann; *Songs:* Jay Livingston, Ray Evans. (1:25) (video) A tailor's assistant, hired by a nobleman to test the faithfulness of his wife-to-be, manages to get involved in the court intrigues of old Venice. A box office comedy hit. Technicolor.

434. The Case Against Brooklyn (Columbia/Morningside Prods.; 1958). *Cast:* Darren McGavin, Margaret Hayes, Warren Stevens, Peggy McCay, Tol Avery, Emile Meyer, Nestor Paiva, Robert Osterloh, Brian G. Hutton, Joseph Turkel, Bobby Helms (himself), Herb Vigran, Thomas B. Henry, Cheerio Meredith, Booth Colman, Michael Garth. *D:* Paul Wendkos; *P:* Charles H. Schneer; *St:* Daniel B. Ullman; *Sc:* Raymond T. Marcus; *Song:* "Jacqueline" (Mort Garson–Bob Hilliard) sung by Helms. (1:22) A rookie cop uncovers corruption in the police department. Based on a *True Magazine* article by Ed Reid.

435. Cash McCall (Warner; 1959). *Cast:* James Garner, Natalie Wood, Nina Foch, Dean Jagger, E.G. Marshall, Henry Jones, Otto Kruger, Roland Winters, Edward C. Platt, Edgar Stehli, Linda Watkins, Parley Baer, Chet Stratton, Dabbs Greer, Olan Soule, Walter Coy, Robert Clarke. *D:* Joseph Pevney; *P:* Henry Blanke; *Sc:* Lenore Coffee, Marion Hargrove. (1:42) (video) A business tycoon sets out to romance the daughter of his failing competitor. Based on the novel by Cameron Hawley, the film was a box office flop.

436. Cassino To Korea (Paramount; 1950). *D:* Edward Genock; *P:* A.J. Richards; *Narrator:* Quentin Reynolds. Korean war documentary.

437. Cast a Long Shadow (United Artists/ Mirisch; 1959). *Cast:* Audie Murphy, Terry Moore, James Best, John Dehner, Rita Lynn, Denver Pyle, Ann Doran, Stacy B. Harris, Robert Foulk, Wright King, Alan Dinehart III, Joe Partridge. *D:* Thomas Carr; *P:* Walter M. Mirisch: *St:* Martin G. Goldsmith; *Sc:* John McGreevey, Goldsmith. (1:22) A bastard drifter suddenly finds himself heir to a large ranch. Based on the novel by Wayne D. Overholser.

438. Cat on a Hot Tin Roof (MGM/ Avon; 1958). *Cast:* Elizabeth Taylor (AAN/ Maggie "the Cat"), Paul Newman (AAN/ Brick), Burl Ives (Big Daddy Pollitt/repeating his stage role), Jack Carson (Gooper), Judith Anderson (Big Mama), Madeleine Sherwood (Mae/ repeating her stage role), Larry Gates (Dr. Baugh), Vaughn Taylor (Deacon Davis), Vince Townsend, Jr. (Lacy), Zelda Cleaver (Sookey), Brian Corcoran (Boy), Hugh Corcoran (Buster), Rusty Stevens (Sonny), Patty Ann Gerrity (Dixie), Deborah Miller (Trixie), Tony Merrill, Jeane Wood, Bobby Johnson. *D:* (AAN + "Best Director" by the *New York Times*) Richard Brooks; *P:* (AAN-"Best Picture") Lawrence Weingarten; *Sc:* (AAN) Brooks, James Poe; *Cin:* (AAN) William Daniels. (1:48) (video/laserdisc) Screen adaptation of Tennessee Williams Pulitzer Prize–winning 1955 play. The Pollitts, a Southern family faced with the fact that their patriarch is at death's door, spend the film kissing up to him; all except his married son Brick, who refuses to sleep with his sexually starved wife (leaving another film open to the implied subject of homosexuality—still taboo on the screen in 1958). One of the 26 top-grossing films of 1957-58 as well as MGM's top grosser of the year and the 10th biggest in the studio's history. It placed #2 on the "10 Best" list of *Film Daily,* with the *New York Times* and the NBR giving it a #5 and #6 placement on their same lists, respectively. The film was also in nomination at the British Academy Awards. Remade in 1985 as a TV movie. Note: Williams' play also received the New York Drama Critic's Circle Award. MetroColor.

439. Cat-Women of the Moon (Astor; 1953–54). *Cast:* Sonny Tufts, Victor Jory, Marie Windsor, Bill Phipps, Douglas Fowley, Carol Brewster, Suzanne Alexander, Susan Morrow, Judy Walsh, Bette Arlen, Ellye Marshall, Roxann Delman. *D:* Arthur Hilton; *P: & St:* Al Zimbalist, Jack Rabin; *Sc:* Roy Hamilton (1:04) (video) Science fiction of a rocketship which lands on the dark side of the moon, an area inhabited by a race of telepathic cat-women who plot to steal the ship and head for earth. Remade as *Missile to the Moon* (q.v.). (aka: *Rocket to the Moon*) 3-D.

440. The Catered Affair (MGM; 1956). *Cast:* Bette Davis (Mrs. Tom Hurley), Ernest Borgnine (Tom Hurley), Debbie Reynolds ("Best Supporting Actress" Award from the NBR/Jane Hurley), Barry Fitzgerald (final U.S. film/Uncle Jack Conlon), Rod Taylor (Ralph Halloran), Robert Simon (Mr. Halloran), Madge Kennedy (Mrs. Halloran), Dorothy Stickney (Mrs. Rafferty), Carol Veazie (Mrs. Casey), Ray Stricklyn (Eddie Hurley), Joan Camden (Alice), Jay Adler (Sam Leiter), Dan Tobin (caterer), Paul Denton (Bill), Augusta Merighi (Mrs. Musso), Howard Graham (Joe), Thomas Dillon (Father Murphy), Janice Carroll, Joan Bradshaw, Harry Hines, Mae Clarke, Jimmie Fox, John Costello, Don Devlin, Sammy Shack. *D:* Richard Brooks; *P:* Sam Zimbalist; *Sc:* Gore Vidal. (1:33) (video) The wife of a Brooklyn cab driver is determined that her daughter will have an expensive wedding. Based on the TV play by Paddy Chayefsky, it placed #7 on the "10 Best" list of the NBR. Computer-colored prints have been produced by Turner Entertainment. (G.B. title: *Wedding Breakfast*)

441. Catskill Honeymoon (Martin Cohen Prods.; 1950). *Cast:* Michal Michalesko, Jan Bart, Bas Sheva, Bobby Colt, Henrietta Jacobson, Julius Adler, Mary LaRoche, David and Dorothy Paige, Irving Grossman, Diana Goldberg, The Feder Sisters, Gita Stein, Abe Lax, Al Murray, Max & Rose Bozhky, Cookie Bowers, Mike Hammer. *D:* Joe Berne; *P:* Martin Cohen; *Sc:* Joel Jacobson; *Songs:* "Scattered Toys," "My Mistake" (Hy Jacobson, Nick Kenny & Charles Kenny). (1:35) Basically an independently filmed variety show at Ma Holder Young's Gap Hotel in Parksville, New York, centered around a couple who are celebrating their 50th wedding anniversary.

442. Cattle Drive (Universal-International; 1951). *Cast:* Joel McCrea, Dean Stockwell, Chill Wills, Leon Ames, Henry Brandon, Howard Petrie, Bob Steele, Griff Barnett, Chuck Roberson, Frances Dee (photo only). *D:* Kurt Neumann; *P:* Aaron Rosenberg; *Sc:* Jack Natteford, Lillie Hayward. (1:17) Family oriented western drama of a spoiled brat who has his attitude adjusted on a rough trail drive. Filmed on location in Death Valley, California, in Technicolor.

443. Cattle Empire (20th Century–Fox; 1958). *Cast:* Joel McCrea, Gloria Talbott, Phyllis Coates, Don Haggerty, Bing Russell, Paul Brinegar, Hal K. Dawson, Richard Shannon, Charles Gray, Duane Grey, Patrick O'Moore, Steve Raines, Jack Lomas, Rocky Shahan, Ronald Foster, Ted Smile, Edward Jauregui, Nesdon Booth, Bill Hale, Howard B. Culver, Bill McGraw. *D:* Charles Marquis Warren; *P:* Robert Stabler; *St:* Daniel B. Ullman; *Sc:* Endre Bohem, Eric Norden. (1:23) A group of wealthy ranchers ask a man they once sent to jail to drive their cattle to market. DeLuxe color, CinemaScope and stereophonic sound. Originally ran on a double bill with *Ambush at Cimarron Pass* (q.v.).

444. Cattle Queen (United International; 1951). *Cast:* Maria Hart, Drake Smith, William Fawcett, Robert Gardette, John Carpenter, Edward Clark, Emile Meyer, Jim Pierce, Joe Bailey, Douglas Wood, Alyn Lockwood, I. Stanford Jolley, Lane Chandler, William N. Bailey, Frank Marlowe, Roger Anderson, Verne Teters, Steve Conte, Robert H. Robinson. *D:* Robert Tansey; *P:* Jack Schwarz [Jack Seeman]; *St:* Robert Emmett [Tansey]; *Sc:* Frances Kavanaugh. (1:12) Programmer western of a lady rancher who sets out to eliminate an outlaw gang. (aka: *Queen of the West*)

445. Cattle Queen of Montana (RKO; 1954). *Cast:* Barbara Stanwyck, Ronald Reagan, Gene Evans, Lance Fuller, Anthony Caruso, Jack Elam, Yvette Dugay, Morris Ankrum, Chubby Johnson, Myron Healey, Rodd Redwing, Paul Birch, Byron Foulger, Burt Mustin, Roy Gordon, Tom Steele, Dorothy Andre, Danny Fisher, Bob Burrows, Wayne Bursam, John Cason, Bob Woodward, Betty Hanna, Riza Royce, Ralph Sanford. *D:* Allan Dwan; *P:* Benedict Bogeaus;

St: Thomas Blackburn; *Sc:* Robert Blees, Howard Estabrook. (1:28) (video) Western drama in Technicolor and Super-Scope of an undercover agent aiding a lady rancher whose father has just been killed by Indians. Filmed on location near Glacier National Park, Montana.

446. Cattle Town (Warner; 1952). *Cast:* Dennis Morgan, Philip Carey, Amanda Blake, Rita Moreno, Ray Teal, Paul Picerni, Jay Novello, Sheb Wooley, George O'Hanlon, Bob Wilke, Charles Meredith, Merv Griffin, Boyd "Red" Morgan, A. Guy Teague, Jack Kenney. *D:* Noel Smith (final film—ret.); *P:* Bryan Foy; *Sc:* Thomas W. Blackburn. (1:11) Following the Civil War, a feud erupts between western ranchers and newly arrived squatters seeking homes.

447. Cause for Alarm (MGM; 1951). *Cast:* Loretta Young, Barry Sullivan, Margalo Gillmore, Bruce Cowling, Irving Bacon, Richard Anderson, Art Baker, Bradley Mora, Georgia Backus, Don Haggerty, Kathleen Freeman, Robert Easton, Carl Switzer, Earle Hodgins. *D:* Tay Garnett; *P:* Tom Lewis [husband of Loretta Young]; *Sc:* Lewis, Mel Dinelli. (1:13) (video) Suspense thriller of a suburban housewife dealing with the antics of her psychotic husband. Based on a story and radio play by Larry Marcus.

Cavalry Charge *see* **The Last Outpost**

448. Cavalry Scout (Monogram; 1951). *Cast:* Rod Cameron, Audrey Long, Jim Davis, James Millican, James Arness, John Doucette, William Phillips, Stephen Chase, Rory Mallinson, Eddy Waller, Paul Bryar, Frank Wilcox, Cliff Clark. *D:* Lesley Selander; *P:* Walter Mirisch; *Sc:* Daniel B. Ullman, Thomas Blackburn. (1:18) (video) A civilian scout is assigned to find items stolen from a military arsenal, including two Gatling guns. Cinecolor.

449. Cave of Outlaws (Universal-International; 1951). *Cast:* Macdonald Carey, Alexis Smith, Victor Jory, Edgar Buchanan, Hugh O'Brian, Houseley Stevenson, Charles Horvath, Jimmy Van Horn, Tim Graham, Clem Fuller. *D:* William Castle; *P:* Leonard Goldstein; *St: & Sc:* Elizabeth Wilson. (1:16) An ex-con returns to Carlsbad Caverns (in New Mexico) to find loot he buried there prior to his incarceration for a train robbery. Technicolor.

450. Cease Fire (Paramount; 1953). *D:* Owen Crump; *P:* Hal B. Wallis. Feature length Korean war semi-documentary, filmed on location, of a U.S. infantry company playing their real-life roles.

451. Cell 2455, Death Row (Columbia; 1955). *Cast:* William Campbell, Robert Campbell, Marian Carr, Kathryn Grant, Paul Dubov, Harvey Stephens, Vince Edwards, Allen Nourse, Diane De Laire, Tyler MacDuff, Eleanor Audley, Howard Wright, Bart Bradley, Buck Kartalian, Thom Carney, Joe Forte, Glenn Gordon, Jimmy Murphy, Jerry Mikelson, Bruce Sharpe, Wayne Taylor. *D:* Fred F. Sears; *P:* Wallace MacDonald; *Sc:* Jack DeWitt. (1:17) Autobiography of "red light bandit" Caryl Chessman, a convicted rapist-murderer, detailing his early life up to his years on death row. Note: Chessman was finally executed in 1960 after spending 12 years on death row.

452. A Certain Smile (20th Century-Fox; 1958). *Cast:* Rossano Brazzi (Lue Ferrand), Joan Fontaine (Francoise Ferrand), Christine Carere (Dominique Vallon), Bradford Dillman (film debut/Bertrand Griot), Eduard Franz (M. Vallon), Kathryn Givney (Mme. Griot), Steven Geray (Denis), Trude Wyler (Mme. Denis), Sandy Livingston (Catherine), Renate Hoy (Mlle. Minot), Muzaffer Tema (Pierre), Katherine Locke (Mme. Vallon), Johnny Mathis (himself). *D:* Jean Negulesco; *P:* Henry Ephron; *Sc:* Frances Goodrich, Albert Hackett; *ASD:* (AAN) Lyle Wheeler, John DeCuir (art directors), Walter M. Scott, Paul S. Fox (sets); *Costumes:* (AAN) Charles LeMaire, Mary Wills; *Title song:* (AAN) Sammy Fain–Paul Francis Webster (sung by J. Mathis). (1:46) A young French student becomes enamoured of her fiancé's married uncle. Based on the novella by Francoise Sagan, it was filmed on location in France in DeLuxe color and CinemaScope.

453. Cha-Cha-Cha Boom! (Columbia; 1956). *Cast:* Prez Prado (himself), The Mary Kaye Trio (themselves), Helen Grayco (herself), Luis Arcaraz (himself), Manny Lopez (himself), Stephen Dunne, Alix Talton, Jose Gonzales-Gonzales, Sylvia Lewis, Charles Evans, Howard Wright, Dante DePaulo. *D:* Fred F. Sears; *P:* Sam Katzman; *Sc:* James B. Gordon, Benjamin H. Kline; *Songs:* "Get Happy" (Ted Koehler–Harold Arlen); "Lonesome Road" (Gene Austin–Nathaniel Shilkret); "Save Your Sorrow" (Buddy DeSylva–Al Sherman) + new songs: "Lily's Lament," "Year Round Love," "Cuban Rock and Roll," "Voodoo Suite," "Crazy, Crazy" and "Mambo No. 8." (1:18) Low budget musical of a talent scout in search of new talent in Cuba. Originally paired on a double bill with *Reprisal!* (q.v.).

454. Chain Gang (Columbia; 1950). *Cast:* Douglas Kennedy, Marjorie Lord, Emory Parnell, William "Bill" Phillips, Thurston Hall, Harry Cheshire, Don C. Harvey, George Eldredge, Rusty Wescoatt, Frank Wilcox, William G. Lechner, William Tannen, Dorothy Vaughan, William Fawcett, George Robotham. *D:* Lew Landers; *P:* Sam Katzman; *Sc:* Howard J. Green. (1:10) Melodrama of brutality among men incarcerated on a chain gang and an undercover reporter attempting to expose same. Originally ran as a co-feature on a double bill with *Between Midnight and Dawn* (q.v.).

455. Chain Lightning (Warner; 1950). *Cast:* Humphrey Bogart, Eleanor Parker, Raymond Massey, Richard Whorf (final film as an actor), James Brown, Roy Roberts, Morris Ankrum, Fay Baker, Fred Sherman. *D:* Stuart Heisler; *P:* Anthony Veiller; *St:* J. Redmond Prior; *Sc:* Liam O'Brien, Vincent Evans; *Song:* "Bless Them All" (J. Hughes, Frank Lake, Al Stillman). (1:34) (video) An ex–World War II flyer agrees to test a new jet plane.

456. Chain of Circumstance (Columbia; 1951). *Cast:* Richard Grayson, Margaret Field, Marta Mitrovich, Harold J. Kennedy, Helen Wallace, Connie Gilchrist, Lawrence Dobkin, Sumner Getchell, James Griffith, Oliver Blake, Percy Helton, Douglas Fowley, Carleton Young. *D:* Will Jason; *P:* Wallace MacDonald; *Sc:* David Lang. (1:08) Melodrama of a young couple who are implicated in a theft. Based on an article in *True Story* magazine, it ran on a double bill with *Criminal Lawyer* (q.v.).

457. Chain of Evidence (Allied Artists; 1957). *Cast:* Bill Elliott, James Lydon, Don Haggerty, Claudia Barrett, Tina Carver, Ross Elliott, Meg Randall, Timothy Carey, John Bleifer, Dabbs Greer, John Close, Hugh Sanders. *D:* Paul Landres; *P:* Ben Schwalb; *Sc:* Elwood Ullman. (1:04) Programmer melodrama of an amnesiac who takes the rap for a woman who killed her spouse.

458. Chained for Life (Classic Films; 1950). *Cast:* Violet and Daisy Hilton, Allen Jenkins. *D:* Harry L. Fraser; *P:* George Moscov; *Sc:* Nat Tanchuck. (1:21) (video) Exploitation melodrama starring the [Siamese] Hilton twins, with one sister being accused of murder. The Hilton twins are better known for their appearance in Tod Browning's *Freaks*, a 1932 production for MGM.

The Challenge (G.B. title) *see* **Across the Badlands**

459. Challenge the Wild (United Artists/ Graham; 1954). *Cast:* George and Sheila Graham, Zimmie-the-Black-Tail-Fawn, Pat McGeehan (narrator). *D:-P:-Sc: & Cin:* Frank Graham. (1:09) Documentation in Anscocolor about the expedition of a family of four into the North American wilderness, complete with much wildlife footage.

460. Champ for a Day (Republic; 1953). *Cast:* Alex Nicol, Audrey Totter, Charles Winninger, Hope Emerson, Joseph Wiseman, Barry Kelley, Henry [Harry] Morgan, Jesse White, Horace McMahon, Grant Withers, Eddy Waller, Richard Wessel, Hal Baylor. *D: & P:* William A. Seiter; *Sc:* Irving Shulman. (1:30) Melodrama of a boxer dealing with crooked fight promoters and the murder of his manager. Based on the story "The Disappearance of Dolan" by William Fay.

461. Champagne for Caesar (United Artists/Harry H. Popkin; 1950). *Cast:* Ronald Colman, Celeste Holm, Vincent Price, Barbara Britton, Art Linkletter, Byron Foulger, Ellye Marshall, Vici Raaf, Douglas Evans, Lyle Talbot, Gabriel Heatter, George Fisher, Peter Brocco, Brian O'Hara, John Eldredge, George Leigh, John Hart, Jack Daly, Gordon Nelson, Herbert Lytton, George Meader, Caesar (the champagne-loving parrot, with voice supplied by Mel Blanc). *D:* Richard Whorf; *P:* George Moskov, Harry M. Popkin; *St: & Sc:* Hans Jacoby, Fred Brady. (1:39) (video/laserdisc) Acclaimed comedy spoof of radio game shows, with a genius possessing a photographic memory (Colman) for reading material going for the big money and the show's sponsor (Price) doing everything he can to prevent same.

462. Charade (Portland/Monarch; 1953). *Cast:* James Mason (triple role), Pamela Mason (triple role), Scott Forbes, Paul Cavanagh, Bruce Lester, John Dodsworth, Judy Osborne, Sean McClory, Vince Barnett. *D:* Roy Kellino; *P:* James Mason; *Sc:* James & Pamela Mason. (1:23) A feature made up of three separate stories: "Portrait of a Murderer," "Duel at Dawn" and "The Midas Touch," three dramas, each starring the Masons.

463. The Charge at Feather River (Warner; 1953). *Cast:* Guy Madison (Miles Archer), Frank Lovejoy (Sgt. Baker), Helen Westcott (Anne McKeever), Vera Miles (Jennie McKeever), Dick Wesson (Cullen), Onslow Stevens (Grover Johnson), Ron Hagerthy (Johnny McKeever), Steve Brodie (Ryan), Neville Brand (Morgan), Henry Kulky (Smiley), Fay Roope (Lt. Col. Kilrain), Lane Chandler (Poinsett), James Brown (Connor), Rand Brooks (Adams), Ben Corbett (Carver), John Damler (Dabney), Louis Tomei (Curry), Carl Andre (Hudkins), Fred Kennedy (Leech), Dub Taylor (Darowicz), Ralph Brooke (Wilhelm), David Alpert (Griffin), Fred Carson (Chief Thunder Hawk), Vivian Mason (Mamie), Wayne Taylor, Richard Bartlett, Joe Bassett, Dennis Dengate, John Pickard. *D:* Gordon Douglas; *P:* David Weisbart; *St: & Sc:* James R. Webb. (1:36) A U.S. cavalry detachment rescues two white sisters who had been held by the Cheyenne for five years. Lots of "in your face" 3-D effects made this one of the 26 top grossing films of 1952-53. WarnerColor.

464. Charge of the Lancers (Columbia; 1954). *Cast:* Paulette Goddard, Jean Pierre Aumont, Richard Stapley, Karin Booth, Charles Irwin, Ben Astar, Lester Matthews, Gregory Gaye, Ivan Triesault, Lou Merrill, Charles Horvath, Tony Roux, Fernanda Eliscu. *D:* William Castle; *P:* Sam Katzman; *Sc:* Robert E. Kent. (1:13) Espionage and romance during the Crimean War, as a gypsy girl and a British officer find love. Technicolor.

465. Cheaper by the Dozen (20th Century–Fox; 1950). *Cast:* Clifton Webb (Frank B. Gilbreth), Jeanne Crain (Ann Gilbreth), Myrna Loy (Lillian Gilbreth), Betty Lynn (Libby Lancaster), Edgar Buchanan (Dr. Burton), Barbara Bates (Ernestine Gilbreth), Mildred Natwick (Mrs. Mebane), Sara Allgood (final film—d. 1950/Mrs. Monahan), Anthony Sydes (Fred Gilbreth), Roddy McCaskill (Jack Gilbreth), Norman Ollestad (Frank Gilbreth, Jr.), Carole Nugent (Lillie Gilbreth), Jimmy Hunt (William Gilbreth), Teddy Driver (Dan Gilbreth), Betty Barker (Mary Gilbreth), Frank Orth (Higgins), Craig Hill (Tom Black), Evelyn Varden (school principal), Virginia Brissac (Mrs. Benson), Walter Baldwin (Jim Bracken), Bennie Bartlett (Joe Scales), Syd Saylor (plumber), Ken Christy (mailman), Mary Field (music teacher). *D:* Walter Lang; *P: & Sc:* Lamar Trotti. (1:25) Family oriented comedy set in the early part of the century about a couple with a family of twelve children. Photographed in Technicolor, it was based on the book by Frank Gilbreth, Jr. and Ernestine Gilbreth Carey and became one of the 28 top-grossing films of 1949-50. Followed by the sequel *Belles on Their Toes* (q.v.).

466. Cherokee Uprising (Monogram; 1950). *Cast:* Whip Wilson, Andy Clyde, Lois Hall, Iron Eyes Cody, Sam Flint, Forrest Taylor, Marshall Reed, Chief Yowlachie, Lee Roberts, Stanley Price, Lyle Talbot, Edith Mills. *D:* Lewis D. Collins; *P:* Vincent M. Fennelly; *Sc:* Daniel B. Ullman. (0:57) Two U.S. marshals investigate the cause of Indian hostilities in this Whip Wilson series western.

467. Chicago Calling (United Artists/Arrowhead-Joseph Justman; 1951). *Cast:* Dan Duryea, Mary Anderson, Gordon Gebert, Marsha Jones, Judy Brubaker, Ross Elliott, Roy Engel, Melinda Plowman, Bob Fallon, Jean Harvey, Grace Loman, Carl Vernell, Chuck Flynn, Bud Stark, Dick Curtis, Mel Plough, Eleanor Radcliff, Bill Lechner, Steve Pendleton, Roy Glenn, Rudy McKool, Gene Roth, Norman Field, Lorin Raker, Smitty (dog). *D:* John Reinhardt; *P:* Peter Berneis; *Sc:* Reinhardt, Berneis. (1:14) Drama of a man in a fit of despair trying to find out if his daughter, who was in an accident in Chicago, will be okay. At the same time he tries to get money to pay his back phone bill so his service will not be shut off.

468. Chicago Confidential (United Artists/Peerless; 1957). *Cast:* Brian Keith, Beverly Garland, Dick Foran, Beverly Tyler, Elisha Cook, Jr., Paul Langton, Anthony George, Douglas Kennedy, Gavin Gordon, Buddy Lewis, Jack Lambert, John Morley, Benny Burt, Mark Scott, Henry Rowland, George Cisar, John Indrisano, John Pelletti, Joe McGuinn, Asa Maynor, Jean Dean, Sharon Lee, Phyllis Coates, Lynne Storey, Nancy Marlowe, Harlan Warde, John Hamilton, Jack Kenney, Joey Ray, Tom Wade, Ralph Volkie, Jack Carr, Carl Princi, Helen Jay, Charles Meredith, Keith Byron, Jim Bannon, Myron Cook, Dennis Moore, Thomas B. Henry, Frank Marlowe, Linda Brent. *D:* Sidney Salkow; *P:* Robert E. Kent; *Sc:* Raymond T. Marcus. (1:13) Filmed on location and based on the bestseller by Jack Lait and Lee Mortimer, this programmer melodrama deals with labor union corruption in the Windy City.

Chicago Masquerade (G.B. title) *see* **Little Egypt**

469. Chicago Syndicate (Columbia/Clover; 1955). *Cast:* Dennis O'Keefe, Abbe Lane, Paul Stewart, Xavier Cugat, Allison Hayes, Dick Cutting, Chris Alcaide, William Challee, John Zaremba, George Brand, Mark Hanna, Carroll McComas, Hugh Sanders. *D:* Fred F. Sears; *P:* Sam Katzman; *St:* William B. Sackheim; *Sc:* Joseph Hoffman. (1:24) (video) Crime-melodrama of an accountant who works undercover to expose mob activities.

470. Chief Crazy Horse (Universal-International; 1955). *Cast:* Victor Mature (title role), Suzan Ball (final film—d. 1955), John Lund, Ray Danton (film debut), Keith Larsen, James Millican, David Janssen, Robert Warwick, Paul Guilfoyle, Dennis Weaver, Morris Ankrum, Donald Randolph, Robert F. Simon, Stuart Randall, Pat Hogan, John Peters, Henry Wills, Charles Horvath, David Miller. *D:* George Sherman; *P:* William Alland; *St:* Gerald Drayson Adams: *Sc:* Adams, Franklin Coen. (1:26) Western drama of the famous Sioux warchief who in real life was never photographed. Technicolor and CinemaScope. (G.B. title: *Valley of Fury*)

471. China Corsair (Columbia; 1951). *Cast:* Jon Hall, Lisa Ferraday, Ron Randell, Douglas Kennedy, Ernest Borgnine (film debut), John Dehner, Marya Marco, Philip Ahn, Peter Mamakos, Weaver Levy. *D:* Ray Nazarro; *P:* Rudolph C. Flothow; *Sc:* Harold R. Greene. (1:16) Romantic adventure-melodrama with a shipboard setting and skullduggery involving some antique jade. Originally ran on a double bill with *Sirocco* (q.v.).

472. China Doll (United Artists/Romina-Batjac; 1958). *Cast:* Victor Mature, Li Li Hua, Ward Bond, Bob Mathias, Johnny Desmond, Elaine Curtis, Stuart Whitman, Ann McCrea, Danny Chang, Ken Perry, Tiger Andrews, Steve Mitchell, Donald Barry, Ann Paige, Denver Pyle, Tita Aragon. *D: & P:* Frank Borzage; *Ex. P:* Robert E. Morrison; *St:* James Benson Nablo, Thomas F. Kelly; *Sc:* Kitty Buhler; *Song:* "Suppose" sung by Desmond. (1:28) Offbeat World War II story of an American officer who marries his Chinese housekeeper and fathers a daughter. She comes to the United States years later, as both her parents had been killed in the war. Note: This film marked Borzage's return to directing, since being blacklisted in 1948.

473. China Gate (20th Century–Fox; 1957). *Cast:* Gene Barry, Angie Dickinson, Nat "King" Cole, Paul Dubov, Lee Van Cleef, George Givot, Gerald Milton, Neyle Morrow, Marcel Dalio, Maurice Marsac, Warren Hsieh, Paul Busch, Sasha Harden, James Hong, William Soo Hoo, Walter Soo Hoo, Weaver Levy. *D:-P: & Sc:* Samuel Fuller. (1:36) (video) An American soldier of fortune joins his ex-wife on a mission in French Indo-China helping French Legionnaires destroy a Chinese ammunition dump. CinemaScope. Originally paired on a double bill with *The Storm Rider* (q.v.).

474. China Venture (Columbia; 1953). *Cast:* Edmond O'Brien, Barry Sullivan, Jocelyn Brando, Leo Gordon, Richard Loo, Dayton Lummis, Leon Askin, Alvy Moore, Dabbs Greer, Philip Ahn, Frank Wilcox, James Anderson, Rex Reason, Todd Karns. *D:* Don Siegel; *P: & St:* Anson Bond; *Sc:* George Worthing Yates, Richard Collins. (1:23) World War II drama involving attempts to capture a Japanese general.

475. The Cimarron Kid (Universal-International; 1952). *Cast:* Audie Murphy, Beverly Tyler, Roy Roberts, Yvette Dugay, Hugh O'Brian, John Hudson, James Best, Noah Beery, Jr. (Bob Dalton), Palmer Lee [aka: Gregg Palmer/film debut/Grat Dalton], Rand Brooks (Emmett Dalton), William Reynolds (Will Dalton), Leif Erickson, David Wolfe, John Hubbard, John Bromfield, Frank Silvera, Richard Garland, Eugene Baxter. *D:* Budd Boetticher; *P:* Ted Richmond; *St:* Louis Stevens, Kay Leonard; *Sc:* Stevens. (1:24) The Dalton gang hits the outlaw trail with the Cimarron Kid in this Technicolor western.

476. Cinderella (RKO/Walt Disney Prods.; 1950). *Voices:* Ilene Woods (Cinderella), William Phipps (Prince Charming), Eleanor Audley (stepmother), Rhoda Williams, Lucille Bliss (stepsisters), Verna Felton (Fairy Godmother), Luis Van Rooten (King-Grand Duke), James MacDonald (Jacques & Gus/mice), Don Barclay, Claire DuBrey. *D:* Wilfred Jackson, Hamilton Luske, Clyde Geronimi; *P:* Walt Disney; *Prod. Supervisor:* Ben Sharpsteen; *Original St:* Charles Perrault; *Film St: & Sc:* Kenneth Anderson, Ted Sears, Homer Brightman, Joe Rinaldi, William Peet, Harry Reeves, Winston Hibler, Erdman Penner; *Sound:* (AAN) C.O. Slyfield (director), Harold J. Steck, Robert O. Cook (recorders); *Music:* (AAN) Oliver Wallace, Paul J. Smith; *Songs:* "A Dream is a Wish Your Heart Makes," "Cinderella," "Bibbidi Bobbidi Boo" (AAN-Best Song), "So This Is Love," "The Work Song" and "Sing, Sweet Nightingale"

(Mack David–Jerry Livingston–Al Hoffman). (1:14) (video/laserdisc) A variation on the story originated by the Brothers Grimm which tells of a poor girl who overcomes various obstacles and marries Prince Charming. Audiences "ate it up" and made it one of the 28 top-grossing films of 1949-50. In 1951 at the Berlin Film Festival it was voted "Best of the Festival" and "Best Musical." At the Venice Film Festival it was nominated for a "Special Award" along with the Disney nature short *Beaver Valley*. Technicolor.

477. Cinerama Holiday (Stanley Warner Cinerama Corp.; 1955). *Cast:* John & Betty Marsh, Fred & Beatrice Troller, Martin Weldon (narrator). *D:* Robert Bendick, Philippe de Lacy; *P: & Sc:* Louis de Rochemont; *As.P:* Otis Carney, Borden Mace, Thomas Orchard; *Adaptation:* Carney, Louis de Rochemont III (derived in part from "America Through a French Looking Glass" by Renee and Pierre Gosset-1953); *Narration:* John Stuart Martin. (2:00) Basically a staged travelogue which follows the Marshs, a young couple from Kansas City, as they tour Europe and the Trollers, a couple from Zurich, Switzerland, as they tour the United States. This was the 2nd Cinerama feature which followed in the footsteps of the popular *This Is Cinerama* (q.v.), presented only in theaters with specially equipped Cinerama screens, comprised of a picture made up of three separate projected images on a curved screen, which gives the viewer a feeling of participating in the action. Technicolor-Cinerama.

Cinerama South Seas Adventure *see* **South Seas Adventure**

Circle of Fear (G.B. title) *see* **Raiders of Tomahawk Creek**

478. City Beneath the Sea (Universal-International; 1953). *Cast:* Robert Ryan, Anthony Quinn, Mala Powers, Suzan Ball, George Mathews, Karel Stepanek, Lalo Rios, Hilo Hattie, Woody Strode, John Warburton, Peter Mamakos, Barbara Morrison, LeRol Antoine, Leon Lontoc, Marya Marco, Bernie Gozier. *D:* Budd Boetticher; *P:* Albert J. Cohen; *Sc:* Jack Harvey, Ramon Romero. (1:27) Technicolor adventure of deep-sea divers in search of a fortune in gold in the sunken city of Port Royal, Jamaica, a pirate stronghold which sank beneath the waves during an earthquake in an age gone by. Based on *Port Royal—Ghost City Beneath the Sea* by Harry E. Rieseberg. (G.B. title: *One Hour to Doom's Day*)

The City Is Dark (G.B. title) *see* **Crime Wave**

The City Jungle (G.B. title) *see* **The Young Philadelphians**

479. City of Bad Men (20th Century-Fox; 1953). *Cast:* Jeanne Crain, Dale Robertson, Richard Boone, Lloyd Bridges, Carole Mathews, Carl Betz, Whitfield Connor, Hugh Sanders, Rudolfo Acosta, Pasqual Garcia Pena, Harry Carter, Robert Adler, John Doucette, Alan Dexter, Don Haggerty, Barbara Fuller, Leo V. Gordon, Anthony Jochim, Gil Perkins, George Melford, John Day, James Best, Richard Cutting, George Selk [aka: Budd Buster], Charles Tannen, Kit Carson, Douglas Evans, Charles B. Smith, Tom McDonough, Harry Hines, Jane Easton, Leo Curley, Gordon Nelson, Harry Brown. *D:* Harmon Jones; *P:* Leonard Goldstein; *St: & Sc:* George W. George, George F. Slavin. (1:21) Western of outlaws who plan to steal the receipts from the James J. Corbett–Bob Fitzsimmons fight in 1897 Carson City, Nevada. Technicolor.

480. City of Fear (Columbia/Orbit Prods.; 1959). *Cast:* Vince Edwards, Lyle Talbot, John Archer, Steven Ritch, Patricia Blair, Joseph Mell, Sherwood Price, Cathy Browne, Kelly Thorsden, Jean G. Harvey, Tony Lawrence. *D:* Irving Lerner; *P:* Leon Chooluck; *St: & Sc:* Steven Ritch, Robert Dillon. (1:21) A city-wide manhunt ensues after an ex-convict mistakenly steals a container of radioactive material.

481. City of Shadows (Republic; 1955). *Cast:* Victor McLaglen, John Baer, Kathleen Crowley, Anthony Caruso, June Vincent, Richard Reeves, Paul Maxey, Frank Ferguson, Richard Travis, Kay Kuter, Nicolas Koster, Gloria Pall, Fern Hall. *D:* William Witney; *As.P:* William J. O'Sullivan; *Sc:* Houston Branch. (1:10) Melodrama of the rise of a crime boss, via help from a young law student.

City on a Hunt *see* **No Escape**

482. City Story (Davis; 1954). *Cast:* Ann Doran, June Kenney, Warner Anderson, Herbert Lytton. *D:* William Beaudine; *P:* Paul F. Heard; *Sc:* Margaret Fitts. (1:18) Independent religious drama of a minister who is concerned about the declining attendance in his church and seeks the advice of an incarcerated woman.

483. City That Never Sleeps (Republic; 1953). *Cast:* Gig Young, Mala Powers, William Talman, Edward Arnold, Chill Wills, Marie Windsor, Paula Raymond, Otto Hulett, John Kelly, Wally Cassell, Ron Hagerthy, James Andelin, Thomas Poston, Leonard Diebold, Emmett Vogan, Bunny Kacher, Philip L. Boddy, Thomas Jones, Tom Irish, Walter Woolf King, Helen Gibson, Gil Herman, Clark Howat. *D: & As.P:* John H. Auer; *St: & Sc:* Steve Fisher. (1:30) (video) Crime melodrama of a married cop and his infatuation with a café singer.

484. Clash by Night (RKO/Wald-Krasna Prod.; 1952). *Cast:* Barbara Stanwyck (Mae), Paul Douglas (Jerry), Robert Ryan (Earl), Marilyn Monroe (Peggy), J. Carrol Naish (Uncle Vince), Keith Andes (Joe Doyle), Silvio Minciotti (Papa), Diane & Deborah Stewart (twin infants), Julius Tannen, Bert Stevens, William Bailey, Mario Siletti, Bill Slack, Art Dupuis, Frank Kreig, Tony Dante. *D:* Fritz Lang; *P:* Harriet Parsons; *Sc:* Alfred Hayes; *Song:* "I Hear a Rhapsody" (Dick Gasparre–Jack Baker–George Fragos). (1:45) (video/laserdisc) Drama of love, marriage and marital infidelity, based on the play by Clifford Odets. One of the 23 top-grossing films of 1951-52.

485. Clipped Wings (Allied Artists; 1953). *Cast:* Leo Gorcey, Huntz Hall, Bernard Gorcey, David Condon [aka: David Gorcey], Bennie Bartlett, Renie Riano, Todd Karns, June Vincent, Mary Treen, Philip Van Zandt. Frank Richards, Michael Ross, Elaine Riley, Jean Dean, Anne Kimbell, Fay Roope, Henry Kulky, Lyle Talbot, Ray Walker, Arthur Space, Conrad Brooks, Lou Nova. *D:* Edward Bernds; *P:* Ben Schwalb; *St:* Charles R. Marion; *Sc:* Marion, Elwood Ullman. (1:05) (video) Slip (L. Gorcey) and Sach (Hall) enlist in the U.S. Air Force by mistake and then wind up capturing an enemy spy ring. A popular entry in the long-running "Bowery Boys" comedy series.

486. Close to My Heart (Warner; 1951). *Cast:* Ray Milland, Gene Tierney, Fay Bainter, Howard St. John, Mary Beth Hughes, Ann Morrison, James Seay, Eddie Marr, Baby John Winslow (himself), Nan Boardman, Elizabeth Flournoy, John Alvin, Louis Jean Heydt, Ralph Byrd, Kathleen Stendal, Lois Hall, Rodney Bell, George LaMond, Fred Graham, Lee Prather. *D: William Keighley; P:* William Jacobs; *Sc:* James R. Webb. (1:30) A woman wants to adopt a baby, but meets opposition from her husband when it is revealed the boy's father was a convicted murderer. Based on *A Baby for Midge* by Mr. Webb.

487. The Clown (MGM; 1952–53). *Cast:* Red Skelton, Tim Considine, Jane Greer, Loring Smith, Philip Ober, Lou Lubin, Jonathan Cott, Fay Roope, Don Beddoe, Steve Forrest, Walter Reed, Edward Marr, Ned Glass, Steve Carruthers, Billy Barty, Lucille Knoch, David Saber, Sandra Gould, Gil Perkins, Danny Richards, Jr., Mickey Little, Charles Calvert, Karen Steele, Jack and Bob Heasley (twins), Helene Millard, Forrest Lewis, Charles [Bronson] Buchinsky, Robert Ford, John McKee, Jan Wayne, Vici Raaf, Jesse Kirkpatrick, Martha Wentworth, Inge Jolles, Harry Stanton, Linda Bennett, Wilson Wood, Frank Nelson, Thomas Dillon, Paula Raymond, James Horan, Al Freeman, Tom Urray, Mary Foran, Sharon Saunders, David Blair, Brick Sullivan, Cy Stevens, G. Pat Collins, Shirley Mitchell, Robert R. Stephenson, Jimmie Thompson, Allen O'Locklin, Tony Merrill, Al Hill, Jerry Schumacher, Barry Reagan, Lennie Bremen, Lee Phelps, Joe Evans, Walter Ridge, George Boyce, Donald Kerr, Mickey Golden, Roger Moore, Jules Brock, Eva Martell, Neva Martell. *D:* Robert Z. Leonard; *P:* William H. Wright; *St:* Frances Marion; *Adapt:* Leonard Praskins; *Sc:* Martin Rackin. (1:31) (video) Sentimental drama of a washed-up alcoholic comic, his ex-wife and his devoted son. A remake of *The Champ* (MGM; 1931).

The Clue (G.B. title) *see* **Outcast of Black Mesa**

488. The Cobweb (MGM; 1955). *Cast:* Richard Widmark, Lauren Bacall, Gloria Grahame, Charles Boyer, Lillian Gish, John Kerr (film debut), Susan Strasberg (film debut), Oscar Levant (final film—ret.), Tommy Rettig, Paul Stewart, Adele Jergens, Jarma Lewis, Fay Wray, Edgar Stehli, Sandra Descher, Bert Freed, Mabel Albertson, Oliver Blake, Olive Carey, Eve McVeagh, Virginia Christine, Jan Arvan, Ruth Clifford, Myra Marsh, James Westerfield, Marjorie Bennett, Stuart Holmes. *D:* Vincente Minnelli; *P:* John Houseman; *Sc:* John Paxton, William Gibson. (2:04) (laserdisc) An all-star cast in a flop Hollywood adaptation of William Gibson's acclaimed novel of staff and patients at a plush psychiatric hospital. Eastmancolor and CinemaScope.

489. Code of the Silver Sage (Republic; 1950). *Cast:* Allan Lane, Eddy Waller, Kay Christopher, Roy Barcroft, Rex Lease, Lane Bradford,

William Ruhl, Richard Emory, Forrest Taylor, Kenne Duncan, Hank Patterson, John Butler, Black Jack (horse). *D:* Fred C. Brannon; *As.P:* Gordon Kay; *St: & Sc:* Arthur E. Orloff. (1:00) U.S. marshal "Rocky" Lane intervenes when he learns a dictator plans on setting up shop in the U.S. An entry in Lane's western series.

490. Code Two (MGM; 1953). *Cast:* Ralph Meeker, Sally Forrest, Keenan Wynn, Robert Horton, James Craig, Elaine Stewart, Jeff Richards, Jonathan Cott, Robert Burton, William Campbell, Fred Graham. *D:* Fred M. Wilcox; *P:* William Grady, Jr.; *St: & Sc:* Marcel Klauber. (1:09) Programmer of Los Angeles motorcycle patrolmen in training.

491. Cole Younger, Gunfighter (Allied Artists; 1958). *Cast:* Frank Lovejoy (final film—to TV/d. 1962), Abby Dalton, James Best, Jan Merlin, George Keymas, John Maxwell, Frank Ferguson, Myron Healey, Dan Sheridan, Douglas Spencer, Ainsley Pryor, Joseph H. Hamilton. *D:* R.G. Springsteen; *P:* Ben Schwalb; *Sc:* Daniel Mainwaring. (1:18) This western, based on Clifton Adams' *The Desperado*, set in 1870s Texas, spins the tale of a gunfighter and how he gained his notorious reputation. DeLuxe color and CinemaScope. Originally ran on a double bill with *Hell's Five Hours* (q.v.).

492. Colorado Ambush (Monogram; 1951). *Cast:* Johnny Mack Brown, Myron Healey, Lois Hall, Tommy Farrell, Christine McIntyre, Lyle Talbot, Lee Roberts, Marshall Bradford, Joe McGuinn, John Hart, Roy Butler, George DeNormand. *D:* Lewis D. Collins; *P:* Vincent M. Fennelly; *St: & Sc:* Myron Healey. (0:52) The murders of Wells Fargo messengers brings about an investigation in this western series entry.

493. Colorado Ranger (Lippert; 1949-50). *Cast:* Jimmie Ellison, Russ Hayden, Raymond Hatton, Fuzzy Knight, Betty [Julie] Adams, Tom Tyler, George J. Lewis, George Chesebro, John Cason, Stanley Price, Stephen Carr, Dennis Moore, Jimmie Martin, Gene Roth, Bud Osborne, I. Stanford Jolley, Joseph Richards. *D:* Thomas Carr; *P:* Ron Ormond; *St: & Sc:* Ormond, Maurice Tombragel. (0:55) (video) Kidnappers form the plot line in this "Four Star" series western, the fourth in a series of six. (TV title: *Guns of Justice*). Note: This series is also knows as the "Shamrock & Lucky" series.

494. Colorado Sundown (Republic; 1952). *Cast:* Rex Allen, Mary Ellen Kay, Slim Pickens, Ko-Ko (horse), June Vincent, Fred Graham, John Daheim, Louise Beavers, Chester Clute (final film—d. 1956), Clarence Straight, The Republic Rhythm Riders. *D:* William Witney; *P:* Edward J. White; *St:* Eric Taylor; *Sc:* Taylor, William Lively. (1:07) (video) A cowboy helps a friend retain possession of his inherited ranch in this western series entry.

495. The Colossus of New York (Paramount/Wm. Alland Prods., Inc.; 1958). *Cast:* John Baragrey, Mala Powers, Ross Martin, Otto Kruger, Robert Hutton, Charles Herbert, Ed Wolff (title role). *D:* Eugene Lourie; *P:* William Alland; *St:* Willis Goldbeck; *Sc:* Thelma Schnee. (1:10) Science fiction of a man who implants the brain of his deceased scientist son into the body of a gargantuan robot which at the climax of the film goes on a murderous rampage at the United Nations. Top-of-the-bill feature which ran with *The Space Children* (q.v.).

496. Colt .45 (Warner; 1949–50). *Cast:* Randolph Scott (Steve Farrell), Ruth Roman (Beth Donovan), Zachary Scott (Jason Brett), Lloyd Bridges (Paul Donovan), Alan Hale (Sheriff Harris), Ian MacDonald (Miller), Chief Thundercloud (Walking Bear), Luther "Lute" Crockett (Judge Tucker), Walter Coy (Carl), Charles Evans (sheriff of Red Rock), Buddy Roosevelt, Stanley Andrews, Hal Taliaferro, Art Miles, Barry Reagan, Aurora Navarro, Paul Newlan, Franklyn Farnum, Ed Peil, Sr., Jack Watt, Ben Corbett, Kansas Moehring. *D:* Edwin L. Marin; *P:* Saul Elkins; *St: & Sc:* Thomas Blackburn. (1:14) Hit western, which became one of the 28 top-grossing films of 1949-50, of what happens when a pair of Colt .45s fall into the wrong hands. This sleeper was also the basis for a later TV series by the studio. Technicolor. (aka: *Thundercloud*)

497. Column South (Universal-International; 1953). *Cast:* Audie Murphy, Joan Evans, Robert Sterling, Ray Collins, Dennis Weaver, Russell Johnson, Palmer Lee [aka: Gregg Palmer], Jack Kelly, Johnny Downs, Ralph Moody, Bob Steele, Ray Montgomery, Richard Garland, James Best, Ed Rand. *D:* Frederick de Cordova; *P:* Ted Richmond; *St: & Sc:* William Sackheim. (1:24) Pre–Civil War western of U.S. Cavalry vs. Navajo Indians. Technicolor.

498. Comanche (United Artists/Carl Krueger; 1956). *Cast:* Dana Andrews, Kent

Smith, Linda Cristal (a Mexican actress in her U.S. debut), John Litel, Henry Brandon, Nestor Paiva, Reed Sherman, Stacy Harris, Mike Mazurki, Lowell Gilmore. *D:* George Sherman; *P:-St: & Sc:* Carl Krueger. (1:27) Whites vs. Indians in a 19th century western tale of hostilities, purported to be based on fact. DeLuxe color and CinemaScope.

499. Comanche Territory (Universal-International; 1950). *Cast:* Maureen O'Hara, Macdonald Carey, Charles Drake, Will Geer, James Best (film debut), Pedro de Cordoba, Edmund Cobb, Rick Vallin, Ian MacDonald, Iron Eyes Cody, Parley Baer, Glenn Strange. *D:* George Sherman; *P:* Leonard Goldstein; *St:* Lewis Meltzer; *Sc:* Meltzer, Oscar Brodney. (1:16) (video) Early 19th century western with Jim Bowie championing the rights of Indians at the prey of greedy whites. Technicolor.

500. Combat Squad (Columbia/Jack Broder Prod.; 1953). *Cast:* John Ireland, Lon McCallister (final film—ret.), Hal March, George E. Stone, Norman Leavitt, Myron Healey, Don Haggerty, Tristram Coffin, David Holt, Robert Easton, Dick Fortune, Jill Hollingsworth, Linda Danson, Neva Gilbert. Eileen Howe, Paul Keast, Dirk Evans, Bob Peoples. *D:* Cy Roth; *P:* Jerry Thomas; *St: & Sc:* Wyott Ordung. (1:12) Programmer Korean conflict drama.

501. Come Back, Africa (Lionel Rogosin; 1959). *D: & P:* Lionel Rogosin; *Sc:* Rogosin, Lewis N'Kosi, Blake Modisane, Dube-Dube. (1:23) (video) Critically acclaimed docudrama of native black Africans living in South Africa under Apartheid and the specific story of one man's problems. An all non-professional cast—with the exception of Miriam Makeba—more or less improvised the story and dialogue. Filmed secretly in Johannesburg and Sophiatown, South Africa, without the cooperation or knowledge of the white South African government. Released in the U.S. in 1960.

502. Come Back, Little Sheba (Paramount/Wallis-Hazen, Inc.; 1952). *Cast:* Burt Lancaster (Doc Delaney), Shirley Booth (film debut/AA + "Best Actress" honors from the NBR, the New York Film Critics and the Cannes Film Festival-1953, repeating her stage role as Lola Delaney), Terry Moore (AAN/Marie Loring), Richard Jaeckel (Turk Fisher), Philip Ober (Ed Anderson), Edwin Max (Elmo Huston), Lisa Golm (Mrs. Coffman), Walter Kelley (Bruce), Paul McVey (postman), Peter Leeds (milkman), Anthony Jochim (Mr. Cruthers), Kitty McHugh (Pearl Stinson), Beverly Mook (Judy Coffman), Virginia Mullen (Henrietta), Virginia Hall (blonde), William Haade (intern). *D:* Daniel Mann (the stage director, making his directorial film debut); *P:* Hal B. Wallis; *Sc:* Ketti Frings; *Ed:* (AAN) Warren Low. (1:39) (video/laserdisc) Drama of an overly emotional and sentimental housewife coping with her drunken husband and the antics of her young female tenant. Based on the hit Broadway play by William Inge which also garnered Miss Booth a "Tony" Award for her performance. One of the 26 top-grossing films of 1952-53, it placed #6 and #10 respectively on the "10 Best" lists of *Film Daily* and the *New York Times*. The 1953 Cannes Film Festival voted it "Best Dramatic Film," while the New York Film Critics had it in nomination for "Best Film." It was also placed in nomination at the British Academy Awards.

503. Come Fill the Cup (Warner; 1951). *Cast:* James Cagney (Lew Marsh), Phyllis Thaxter (Paula Copeland), Raymond Massey (John Ives), James Gleason (Charley Dolan), Gig Young (AAN/Boyd Copeland), Selena Royle (Dolly Copeland), Larry Keating (Julian Cuscaden), Charlita (Maria Diego), Sheldon Leonard (Lennie Garr), Douglas Spencer (Ike Bashaw), John Kellogg (Don Bell), William Bakewell (Hal Ortman), John Alvin (Travis Ashbourne III), King Donovan (Kip Zunches), Norma Jean Macias (Ora), Henry Blair (Bobby), Elizabeth Flournoy (Lila), Torben Meyer, James Flavin. *D:* Gordon Douglas; *P:* Henry Blanke; *Sc:* Ivan Goff, Ben Roberts. (1:53) Drama of an ex-newspaperman and his battle with alcohol, the reason he initially lost his job. Based on the novel by Harlan Ware.

504. Come Next Spring (Republic; 1956). *Cast:* Steve Cochran, Ann Sheridan, Walter Brennan, Sherry Jackson, Richard Eyer, Edgar Buchanan, Sonny Tufts, Harry Shannon, Rad Fulton, Mae Clarke, Roscoe Ates, Wade Ruby, James Best. *D:* R.G. "Bud" Springsteen; *P:* Herbert J. Yates; *St: & Sc:* Montgomery Pittman; *Title song:* Max Steiner (m). Lenny Adelson (ly), sung by Tony Bennett. (1:38) Rural Americana of a man who returns to his Arkansas farm and the family he abandoned years before and tries to make things right. Trucolor.

505. The Come On (Allied Artists; 1956). *Cast:* Anne Baxter, Sterling Hayden, John Hoyt, Jesse White, Walter "Wally" Cassell, Lee

Turnbull, Alex Gerry, Paul Picerni, Karolee Kelly, Theodore Newton, Tyler McVey. *D:* Russell Birdwell; *P:* Lindsley Parsons; *Sc:* Warren Douglas, Whitman Chambers. (1:22) A vagabond falls for a married woman who wants him to help her kill her husband. Based on the novel by Mr. Chambers, it was photographed in SuperScope.

506. Comin' 'Round the Mountain (Universal-International; 1951). *Cast:* Bud Abbott, Lou Costello, Dorothy Shay, Kirby Grant, Joe Sawyer, Guy Wilkerson, Glenn Strange, Ida Moore, Shaye Cogan, Bob Easton, Margaret Hamilton, Russell Simpson, Virgil "Slats" Taylor, O.Z. Whitehead, Norman Leavitt, Jack Kruschen, Peter Mamakos, Barry Brooks, Joe Kirk, William Fawcett, Harold Goodwin. *D:* Charles Lamont; *P:* Howard Christie; *St: & Sc:* Robert Lees, Frederic I. Rinaldo; *Additional dialogue:* John Grant; *Songs:* "You Broke Your Promise" (George Wyle–Irving Taylor–Eddie Pola); "Agnes Clung" (Hessie Smith–Dorothy Shay); "Why Don't Someone Marry Mary Ann?" (Wilbur Beatty–Britt Wood); "Sagebrush Sadie" (Wood). (1:16) (video) Abbott and Costello comedy with songs of a rural treasure hunt, complete with hillbilly feuds and bushels of corn.

507. The Command (Warner; 1954). *Cast:* Guy Madison, Joan Weldon, James Whitmore, Carl Benton Reid, Ray Teal, Bob Nichols, Harvey Lembeck, Don Shelton, Gregg Barton, Boyd "Red" Morgan, Zachary Yaconelli, Renata Vanni, Tom Monroe. *D:* David Butler; *P:* David Weisbart; *Adaptation:* Samuel Fuller; *Sc:* Russell Hughes. (1:28) A wagon train in Wyoming must contend with Indians as well as a smallpox epidemic. Based on a serialized *Saturday Evening Post* novel titled *The White Invader* by James Warner Bellah, it was photographed originally in 3-D but not released in that process. Warner Brothers first film in CinemaScope, it was also in WarnerColor.

508. The Company She Keeps (RKO; 1950). *Cast:* Lizabeth Scott, Jane Greer, Dennis O'Keefe, Fay Baker, John Hoyt, James Bell, Don Beddoe, Bert Freed, Irene Tedrow, Marjorie Wood, Marjorie Crossland, Virginia Farmer, Jeff Bridges (film debut/the infant). *D:* John Cromwell; *P:* John Houseman; *St: & Sc:* Ketti Frings. (1:22) Romantic melodrama of a female parolee who falls for the boyfriend of her parole officer.

509. Compulsion (20th Century–Fox; 1959). *Cast:* Orson Welles (Jonathan Wilk), Dean Stockwell (Judd Steiner), Bradford Dillman (Artie Straus), Diane Varsi (Ruth Evans), E.G. Marshall (Horn), Martin Milner (Sid Brooks), Richard Anderson (Max Steiner), Robert Simon (Lt. Johnson), Edward Binns (Tom Daly), Robert Burton (Mr. Straus), Wilton Graff (Mr. Steiner), Louise Lorimer (Mrs. Straus), Gavin McLeod (Padua), Terry Becker (Benson), Russ Bender (Edgar Llewellyn), Gerry Lock (Emma), Harry Carter (Detective Davis), Simon Scott (Detective Brown), Voltaire Perkins (judge). *D:* Richard Fleischer; *P:* Richard D. Zanuck; *Sc:* Richard Murphy. (1:43) (video) Critically acclaimed drama based on the 1956 novel and the 1957 Broadway play adaptation by Meyer Levin. The story of Nathan Leopold, Jr. and Richard Loeb (with fictional names), two young men who murdered a 14-year-old boy in 1924 to create the perfect crime and the nationwide sensation created by the subsequent trial when they were caught. At the Cannes Film Festival, the three male leads (Welles, Stockwell and Dillman) all received "Best Actor" awards. It placed #8 on the "10 Best" list of *Film Daily* and was also in nomination at the British Academy Awards. CinemaScope and high fidelity stereophonic sound.

Confessions of a Sorority Girl *see* **Sorority Girl**

510. Confidence Girl (United Artists/ Fanwill Prods., Inc.; 1952). *Cast:* Tom Conway, Hillary Brooke, Eddie Marr, Dan Riss, Jack Kruschen, John Gallaudet, Paul Livermore, Aline Towne, Hellen Van Tuyl, Walter Kingsford, Charlie Collins, Bruce Edwards, Tyler McVey, Paul Guilfoyle, Edmund Cobb, Pamela Duncan, Barbara Woodell, Madge Crane, Roy Engel, Margo Karen, Yvonne Peattie, Joel Allen, John Phillips, Helen Chapman, Leo Cleary, Carmen Clothier, Gilbert Frye, Duke York, Michael Vallon. *D:-P:-St: & Sc:* Andrew L. Stone. (1:21) Crime melodrama of two con artists, one posing as a clairvoyant, the other as a detective.

511. Confidentially Connie (MGM; 1953). *Cast:* Van Johnson, Janet Leigh, Louis Calhern, Walter Slezak, Gene Lockhart, Kathleen Lockhart, Marilyn Erskine, Hayden Rorke, Barbara Ruick, Robert Burton, Arthur Space, June Whitley, Dick Sands, Phil Tead, Byron Foulger. *D:* Edward Buzzell; *P:* Stephen Ames; *St:* Herman Wouk, Max Shulman; *Sc:* Shulman.

(1:13) MGM programmer comedy of a pregnant wife whose concerns with her financial household budget force her to plot to get her professor husband ousted from his underpaying job.

512. Congo Crossing (Universal-International; 1956). *Cast:* Virginia Mayo, George Nader, Peter Lorre, Tonio Selwart, Michael Pate, Rex Ingram, Kathryn Givney, Tudor Owen, Raymond Bailey, George Ramsey, Bernard Hamilton, Harold Dyrenforth, Maurice Doner. *D:* Joseph Pevney; *P:* Howard Christie; *St:* Houston Branch; *Sc:* Richard Alan Simmons. (1:25) Melodrama of a playgirl, suspected of murder, fleeing to an area of Africa that has no extradition laws. Technicolor.

513. The Conqueror (RKO/A Howard Hughes Presentation; 1955–56). *Cast:* John Wayne, Susan Hayward, Pedro Armendariz, Agnes Moorehead, Thomas Gomez, John Hoyt, William Conrad, Ted de Corsia, Leslie Bradley, Lee Van Cleef, Peter Mamakos, Leo Gordon, Richard Loo, Ray Spiker, Sylvia Lewis, Jarma Lewis, Pat McMahon, George E. Stone, Phil Arnold, Torben Meyer, Pat Lawler, Pat Tiernan, John George, Weaver Levy, Michael Granger, Fred Aldrich, Paul Hoffman, Lane Bradford, Carl Vernell, Fred Graham, Gregg Barton, Ken Terrell, Jeanne Gerson, Chivwit Indian tribe. *D: & P:* Dick Powell; *As.P:* Richard Sokolove; *St: & Sc:* Oscar Millard. (1:51) (video) Critically panned, lavishly produced historical costume adventure about conflict between Mongols and Tartar tribesmen. Filmed on location at a former atomic test site in Utah, it was adapted from the 1954 book *A Caravan to Camul* by John Clou. Technicolor and CinemaScope.

514. Conquest of Cochise (Columbia; 1953). *Cast:* John Hodiak (title role), Joy Page, Robert Stack, Fortunio Bonanova, Rico Alaniz, Edward Colmans, Alex Montoya, Steven Ritch, Carol Thurston, Rodd Redwing, Robert E. Griffith, John Crawford, Joseph Waring, Poppy del Vando, Guy Edward Hearn. *D:* William Castle; *P:* Sam Katzman; *St:* DeVallon Scott; *Sc:* Scott, Arthur Lewis. (1:10) (video) The U.S. Army's attempts to bring Cochise and his band of Apaches to peaceful terms. Technicolor.

515. Conquest of Space (Paramount/George Pal; 1955). *Cast:* Walter Brooke, Eric Fleming, Mickey Shaugnessy, Phil Foster, William Redfield, William Hopper, Ross Martin (film debut), Benson Fong, Vito Scotti, John Dennis, Michael Fox, Iphigenie Castiglioni. *D:* Byron Haskin; *P:* George Pal; *Adaptation:* Philip Yordan, Barre Lyndon, George Worthing Yates; *Sc:* James O'Hanlon. (1:20) (video) Science fiction of the first manned spaceship to Mars. Based on *The Mars Project*, a 1949 book by Chesley Bonestell and Willy Ley. Technicolor.

516. Convicted (Columbia; 1950). *Cast:* Glenn Ford, Broderick Crawford, Millard Mitchell, Dorothy Malone, Carl Benton Reid, Frank Faylen, Will Geer, Martha Stewart, Henry O'Neill, Douglas Kennedy, Ed Begley, John Doucette, Ilka Gruning, Whit Bissell, Fred F. Sears, Fred Graham, Eddie Parker, James Millican, Ray Teal, Clancy Cooper, Harry Cording, Griff Barnett, John A. Butler, Peter Virgo, Robert Malcolm, James Bush, William Tannen, William E. Green, Charles Cane, Wilton Graff, Vincent Renno, Richard Hale, William Vedder, Alphonse Martell, Harry Harvey, Marshall Bradford, Jimmie Dodd, Bradford Hatton, Benny Burt, Thomas Kingston, Jay Barney, Chuck Hamilton, Charles Sherlock. *D:* Henry Levin; *P:* Jerry Bresler; *Sc:* William Bowers, Fred Niblo, Jr., Seton I. Miller. (1:31) The efforts of a D.A. to free an innocent man from prison. Based on the play *The Criminal Code* by Martin Flavin which was previously filmed by this studio in 1931 under the original title and again in 1938 as *Penitentiary.* (aka: *One Way Out*) The top of a double bill with *Beauty on Parade* (q.v.).

517. The Cool and the Crazy (American International/Imperial Prods.; 1958). *Cast:* Scott Marlowe, Gigi Perreau, Richard Bakalyan, Dick Jones, Shelby Storck, Marvin J. Rosen, Carolin von Mayrhouse, Robert Hadden, Anthony Pawley, James Newman, Joe Adelman, Kenneth Plumb, Jackie Storck, Leonard Belove, Jim Bysol, John Hannahan, John Quilhas, Paul Culp, Bob Hall, Frank Tebeck, Bill Stevens, Jeanne Gallagher, Dona Baldwin, Ruth Marquez, Gaul Greenwell, Dorothy Haefling. *D:* William Witney; *P:* E.C. Rhoden, Jr.; *St: & Sc:* Richard C. Sarafian; *Songs:* Bill Nolan, Ronnie Norman. (1:18) Newly released from reform school, a youth supplies marijuana to some teens who smoke the weed and go ballistic. Filmed on location in Kansas City. Originally paired on a double bill with *Dragstrip Riot* (q.v.).

518. Cop Hater (United Artists/Barbizon Prods., Inc.; 1957–58). *Cast:* Robert Loggia, Gerald O'Loughlin, Ellen Parker, Shirley Ballard, Russell Hardie, Hal Riddle, William Neff,

Gene Miller, Miriam Goldina, Lincoln Kilpatrick, Ralph Stanley, Ted Gunther, John Seven, Glenn Cannon, Jerry Orbach, Vince[nt] Gardenia (film debut), Thomas Nello, Kate Harkin, Alan Manson, Sandra Stevens, Alan Gergnan, Joan Kalionzes, Lulu King, John Gerstad. *D:* & *P:* William Berke; *Sc:* Harry Kane. (1:15) A man kills two cops as a smokescreen to confuse the investigation when he kills a third, the real target he is after. Based on the novel by Ed McBain, it was filmed on location in New York City.

519. Copper Canyon (Paramount; 1950). *Cast:* Ray Milland, Hedy Lamarr, Macdonald Carey, Mona Freeman, Harry Carey, Jr., Frank Faylen, Hope Emerson, James Burke, Francis Pierlot, Taylor Holmes, Peggy Knudsen, Percy Helton, Philip Van Zandt, Erno Verebes, Paul Lees, Robert Watson, Georgia Backus, Ian Wolfe, Robert Kortman, Nina Mae McKinney, Len Hendry, Earl Hodgins, Robert Stephenson, Buddy Roosevelt, Julia Faye, Hank Bell, Joe Whitehead, Ethan Laidlaw, Russell Kaplan, Alan Dinehart III, Rex Lease, Stanley Andrews, Kit Guard, Stuart Holmes. *D:* John Farrow; *P:* Mel Epstein; *Sc:* Jonathan Latimer; *Song:* Jay Livingston. (1:23) (video/laserdisc) Post–Civil War western of a Confederate veteran who is helping displaced Southerners find homesteads and mine copper. Based on a story by Richard English, the film only had moderate success at the box office. Technicolor.

520. Copper Sky (20th Century–Fox/Regal Films–Emirau Prods.; 1957). *Cast:* Jeff Morrow, Coleen Gray, Strother Martin, Paul Brinegar, John Pickard, Patrick O'Moore, Rocky Shahan, Rush Williams, Rodd Redwing, William R. Hamel, Jack Lomas, Bill McGraw, Jerry Oddo. *D:* Charles Marquis Warren; *P:* & *St:* Robert Stabler; *Sc:* Eric Norden. (1:16) Following the massacre of the residents of a small western town by Indians, the town drunk and the newly arrived school marm trek across the desert to safety. A programmer western in Regalscope.

Corky (G.B. title) *see* **Corky of Gasoline Alley**

521. Corky of Gasoline Alley (Columbia; 1951). *Cast:* Scotty Beckett, James Lydon, Don Beddoe, Gordon Jones, Patti Brady, Susan Morrow, Kay Christopher, Madelon Mitchel, Dick Wessel, Harry Tyler, Ralph Votrian, John Doucette, Charles Williams, Lester Matthews, Jack Rice, Ludwig Stossel, John Dehner, Lewis Russell. *D:* Edward Bernds; *P:* Wallace MacDonald; *St:* & *Sc:* Bernds. (1:20) A man has to deal with a mooching relative of his wife in this comedy, based on Frank O. King's comic strip creation *Gasoline Alley*. The final entry in a short series of two films. (G.B. title: *Corky*) Originally ran on a double bill with *Hills of Utah* (q.v.).

522. The Cosmic Man (Allied Artists/Tutura Pictures; 1959). *Cast:* Bruce Bennett, John Carradine, Angela Greene, Paul Langton, Scotty Morrow, Lyn Osborn, Walter Maslow, Robert Lytton. *D:* Herbert Greene; *P:* Robert A. Terry; *As.P:* Harry Marsh; *St:* & *Sc:* Arthur C. Pierce. (1:12) (video) B budget science fiction of a spherical object which lands near an air base and a mysterious visitor (Carradine) from the sphere, claiming he has come to earth on a mission of peace.

The Cost of Living *see* **The Prowler**

523. Count the Hours (RKO/Ben-Bo Prods.; 1953). *Cast:* Teresa Wright, Macdonald Carey, Dolores Moran, Adele Mara, Edgar Barrier, John Craven, Jack Elam, Ralph Sanford, Ralph Dumke. *D:* Don Siegel; *P:* Benedict Bogeaus; *St:* Doane R. Hoag; *Sc:* Hoag, Karen DeWolf. (1:15) Drama of a man falsely accused of murdering his employers, while his wife and the local D.A. try to set the record straight. (G.B. title: *Every Minute Counts*)

524. Count Three and Pray (Columbia/Copa Prods., Inc.; 1955). *Cast:* Van Heflin, Joanne Woodward (film debut), Phil Carey, Raymond Burr, Allison Hayes, Myron Healey, Nancy Kulp, James Griffith, Richard Webb, John Cason, Jean Willes, Robert Burton, Steve Raines, Kathryn Givney, Vince Townsend, Adrienne Marden, Jimmy Hawkins, Juney Ellis. *D:* George Sherman; *P:* Ted Richmond, Tyrone Power (unc.); *Sc:* Herb Meadow. (1:42) Post-Civil War Americana of the effects created by a new preacher in a small Southern town. Based on *Calico Pony* by Mr. Meadow.

525. Count Your Blessings (MGM; 1959). *Cast:* Deborah Kerr, Rossano Brazzi, Maurice Chevalier, Martin Stephens, Tom Helmore, Patricia Medina, Steve Geray, Ronald Squire, Mona Washbourne, Lumsden Hare, Kim Parker, Frank Kreig. *D:* Jean Negulesco; *P:* & *Sc:* Karl Tunberg. (1:42) Critically panned comedy, based on Nancy Mitford's 1956 novel

The Blessing, tells the tale of a wife, her philandering husband and their son. Filmed on locations in London and Paris. CinemaScope and MetroColor.

526. Counterplot (United Artists/A.J. Howard Odell Prods.; 1959). *Cast:* Forrest Tucker, Allison Hayes, Gerald Milton, Edmundo Rivera Alvarez, Jackie Wayne, Miguel Angel Alvarez, Richard Vernie, Charles Gibbs, Rita Tanno, Art Bedard, Ulises Brenes, Guardo Albani, Paul Davila, Ted Smith, Yvonne Peck. *D: & P:* Kurt Neumann (final film—d. 1958); *St: & Sc:* Richard Blake. (1:16) Programmer melodrama of a man hiding out in Puerto Rico after being accused of a murder he didn't commit.

527. Counterspy Meets Scotland Yard (Columbia; 1950). *Cast:* Howard St. John, Amanda Blake, Ron Randell, June Vincent, Fred F. Sears, John Dehner, Lewis Martin, Rick Vallin, Ted Jordan, Jimmy Lloyd, Paul Marton, Gregory Gaye, Robert Bice, John Doucette, Douglas Evans. *D:* Seymour Friedman; *P:* Wallace MacDonald; *St: & Sc:* Harold R. Greene. (1:07) Based on *Counterspy*, a radio program created by Phillips H. Lord, this espionage programmer was the second and final entry in a short-lived series on the exploits of *David Harding, Counterspy*. (St John).

528. The Country Girl (Paramount; 1954). *Cast:* Bing Crosby (AAN + "Best Actor" by the NBR/Frank Elgin), Grace Kelly (AA + "Best Actress" by the NBR and the New York Film Critics, combined with her work on *Rear Window* and *Dial M for Murder* [both q.v.]/ Georgie Elgin), William Holden (Bernie Dodd), Anthony Ross (Phil Cook), Gene Reynolds (Larry), Eddie Ryder (Ed), Robert Kent (final film—d. 1954/Paul Unger), Jacqueline Fontaine (singer-actress), John W. Reynolds (Henry Johnson), Jonathan Provost (Jimmie), Chester Jones (Ralph), Ida Moore, Frank Scannell, Ruth Rickaby, Hal K. Dawson, Howard Joslin, Charles Tannen, Bob Alden. *D:* (AAN) George Seaton; *P:* (AAN) Seaton, William Perlberg; *Sc:* (AA) Seaton (based on Clifford Odets' play—aka: *Winter Journey*); *Songs:* "Live and Learn," "The Pitchman" and "The Search is Through" Harold Arlen, Ira Gershwin; *Cin:* (AAN) John F. Warren; *ASD:* (AAN) Hal Pereira, Roland Anderson (art directors), Sam Comer, Grace Gregory (sets); *Choreography:* Robert Alton (final film—d. 1957). (1:44) (video) Critically acclaimed drama of a weak-willed alcoholic singer, emotionally dependent on his wife, who tries for a comeback via the help of a willing producer. On the "10 Best" lists of the NBR, *Film Daily* and the *New York Times*, it placed #3, #4 and #9 respectively. It was also in nomination at the Cannes Film Festival in 1955 and with the New York Film Critics it was in nomination for "Best Film."

529. Country Music Holiday (Paramount/Aurora Prods.; 1958). *Cast:* Ferlin Husky, Zsa Zsa Gabor, Rocky Graziano, Faron Young, June Carter, Jesse White, Cliff Norton, Rod Brasfield, Hope Sansberry, Patty Duke, Art Ford, Lew Parker, Al Fisher, Lou Marks, The Jordanaires, Lonzo and Oscar, The LaDell Sisters, Drifting Johnny Miller, Bernie Nee, Cliff Norton, Clyde Woods. *D:* Alvin Ganzer; *P:* Ralph Serpe, Howard B. Kreitsek; *St: & Sc:* H.B. Cross; *Songs:* "Country Music Holiday" (Hal David–Burt Bacharach) sung by Nee; "The Face of Love" (Johnny Lehmann–Stan Lebowsky) sung by Young; "Somewhere There's Sunshine" (Pat Ballard) sung by Husky; "Terrific Together" (Augustus Stevenson–David Hill–Jimmy Williams) sung by Husky; "Don't Walk Away From Me" (Brook Benton–Clyde Otis) sung by Husky; "Wang Dang Doo" (Jean Norris–Bill Beasley–T.J. Adams) sung by the LaDell sisters; "Goodbye My Darling" (Benton–Otis) sung by Lonzo and Oscar; "Wide Wide World" (Dave Dreyer) sung by Husky; "My Home Town" (Smiley Burnette) sung by Husky; "Little Miss Ruby" (Neal Matthews, Jr.) sung by the Jordanaires; "Albuquerque" (Johnny Miller) sung by Miller; "When It Rains It Pours" (Slick Slavin) sung by Young; "Nine Percent" (Belford Hendricks–Benton–Otis) sung by Young; and "Just One More Chance" (Sam Coslow–Arthur Johnston) sung by Husky. (1:21) Low budget musical with fourteen songs of a small town Tennessee boy who makes it big as a country music star on TV.

530. County Fair (Monogram/Jeffrey Bernerd Prods.; 1950). *Cast:* Rory Calhoun, Jane Nigh, Florence Bates, Warren Douglas, Raymond Hatton, Emory Parnell, Rory Mallinson, Harry Cheshire, Milton Kibbee, Joan Vohs, Clarence Muse, George L. Spaulding, Nolan Leary, Sam Flint, Bob Carson, Heinie Conklin, Benny Corbett, Jasper Weldon, Jack Mower, Frank O'Connor, Stanley Blystone, Joe Forte, Renny McEvoy. *D:* William Beaudine; *P:* Walter Mirisch: *Sc:* W. Scott Darling. (1:16) A girl falls for the wealthy owner of a racehorse. Cinecolor. Note: No relation to either *The County*

Fair (Monogram; 1932) or *County Fair* (Monogram; 1937).

531. The Courage of Black Beauty (20th Century–Fox; 1957). *Cast:* John Crawford, Mimi Gibson, John Bryant, Diane Brewster, J. Pat O'Malley, Russell Johnson, Ziva Rodann. *D:* Harold Shuster; *P:* Edward L. Alperson; *Sc:* Steve Fisher (using Anne Sewell's *Black Beauty* as source material); *Songs:* "Black Beauty" (Alperson–Paul Herrick); "The Donkey Game Song" (Alperson–Dick Hughes–Richard Stapley). (1:18) Drama of a motherless boy who raises his beloved horse and almost loses it because of an act of carelessness by his estranged father. In Pathécolor.

532. The Court Jester (Paramount/Dena Enterprises; 1956). *Cast:* Danny Kaye (Hawkins), Glynis Johns (Maid Jean), Basil Rathbone (Sir Ravenhurst), Angela Lansbury (Princess Gwendolyn), Cecil Parker (King Roderick), Mildred Natwick (Griselda), John Carradine (Giacomo), Robert Middleton (Sir Griswold), Michael Pate (Sir Locksley), Alan Napier (Sir Brockhurst), Edward Ashley (Black Fox), Herbert Rudley (Captain of the Guard), Noel Drayton (Fergus), Lewis Martin (Sir Finsdale), Patrick Aherne (Sir Pertwee), Richard Kean (archbishop), Larry Pennell (novice knight), Hermine's Midgets, The American Legion Zouaves, Tudor Owen, Charles Irwin, Leo Britt, Russell Gaige, Ray Kellogg, Eric Alden, William Pullen, Joel Smith, Robin Hughes, Robert E. Smith, Nels Nelson, Edward Gibbons, Thomas J. Cotton, Billy Curtis, A.J. "Buster" Resmondo, Irving Fulton, Little Billy Rhodes, Frank Delfino, Henry Lewis Stone, George Louis Spotts, Irving Douglas, Harry Monty, Floyd Hugh Dixon, James B. Jordan, Robert Smith, Robert Hart, Burnell Dietch, Chad Dee Block, Leo Wheeler, John P. O'Malley, Leslie Denison, Paul "Tiny" Newlan, Trevor Ward, Michael Mahoney, Phyllis Coughlan, William Cartledge, Len Hendry, Claud Wuhrman, Harry Lloyd Nelson, John O'Malley. *D:-P:-St: & Sc:* Norman Panama, Melvin Frank; *Songs:* "Life Could Not Better Be," "Outfox the Fox," "I'll Take You Dreaming," "My Heart Knows a Love Song" (Sylvia Fine–Sammy Cahn); "Maladjusted Jester" (Fine). (1:41) (video/laserdisc) A satirical spoof of medieval costume adventure films as a Robin Hood wanna-be becomes the court jester to an evil usurping king. He also encounters court intrigue involving the true infant-king targeted for assassination and of course, romance. Woefully, no nominations, merits or awards were bestowed on this hilarious outing, but the proof was in the paybox, as appreciable audiences made it one of the 24 top-grossing films of 1955-56. Technicolor and VistaVision.

533. The Court-Martial of Billy Mitchell (Warner/United States Pictures; 1955). *Cast:* Gary Cooper (General Billy Mitchell), Charles Bickford (Gen. Gurthrie), Ralph Bellamy (Cong. Frank Feid), Rod Steiger (Maj. Allan Guillion), Elizabeth Montgomery (film debut/Margaret Lansdowne), Fred Clark (Col. Moreland), James Daly (Col. Herbert White), Jack Lord (Comdr. Zachary Lansdowne), Peter Graves (Capt. Elliott), Darren McGavin (Russ Peters), Charles Dingle (Sen. Fullerton), Robert Simon (Admiral Gage), Dayton Lummis (Gen. Douglas MacArthur), Tom McKee (Capt. Eddie Rickenbacker), Steve Roberts (Maj. Carl Spaatz), Herbert Heyes (Gen. John J. Pershing), Robert Brubaker (Maj. H.H. Arnold), Ian Wolfe (Pres. Calvin Coolidge), Phil Arnold (Fiorella LaGuardia), Will Wright (Adm. William S. Sims), Steve Holland (Stu Stewart), Adam Kennedy (Yip Ryan), Manning Ross (Ted Adams), Carleton Young (Gen. Pershing's aide), Griff Barnett, Edward Keane, Anthony Hughes, John Maxwell, Ewing Mitchell, Max Wagner, Jack Perrin, Gregory Walcott, Robert Williams, Edna Holland, William Forrest, Frank Wilcox, William Henry, Peter Adams, Charles Chaplin, Jr., Joel Smith, Jordan Shelley, Fred Perce, Al Page, George Mayon, Michael Lally. Cy Malis, Kirby Grant (final film—to TV as "Sky King"). *D:* Otto Preminger; *P:* Milton Sperling; *St: & Sc:* (AAN) Sperling, Emmett Lavery. (1:40) (video/laserdisc) Courtroom drama of General Billy Mitchell, who went to trial in 1925 after going public with statements that the U.S. military was incompetent and negligent in not building up their air power following World War I. One of the 24 top-grossing films of 1955-56. It is notable to mention that the bombing of Pearl Harbor in 1941 proved Mitchell right and the military wrong. WarnerColor and CinemaScope. (G. B. title: *One Man Mutiny*)

534. Covered Wagon Raid (Republic; 1950). *Cast:* Allan Lane, Eddy Waller, Lyn Thomas, Alex Gerry, Byron Barr, Dick Curtis, Marshall Reed, Pierce Lyden, Sherry Jackson, Rex Lease, Lester Dorr, Lee Roberts, Wee Willie Keeler. *D:* R.G. Springsteen; *As.P:* Gordon Kay; *St: & Sc:* M. Coates Webster. (1:00) A gang of outlaws are robbing and murdering local settlers in this "Rocky Lane" series western.

535. Cow Country (Allied Artists: 1953). *Cast:* Edmond O'Brien, Helen Westcott, Bob Lowry, Barton MacLane, Peggie Castle, Robert H. Barrat, James Millican, Don Beddoe, Robert Wilke, Raymond Hatton, Chuck Courtney, Steve Clark, Rory Mallinson, Marshall Reed, Tom Tyler (final film—d. 1954), Sam Flint, Jack Ingram, George J. Lewis, Brett Houston. *D:* Lesley Selander; *P:* Scott R. Dunlap; *Adaptation:* Tom Blackburn; *Sc:* Adele Buffington. (1:22) The Texas Panhandle in the 1880s is the setting for this western, detailing the plight of ranchers against drought and depression. Based on the 1947 novel *Shadow Range* by Curtis Bishop.

536. Cow Town (Columbia/Gene Autry Prods.; 1950). *Cast:* Gene Autry, Gail Davis, Harry Shannon, Jock [Mahoney] O'Mahoney, Clark "Buddy" Burroughs, Harry Harvey, Blackie Whiteford, Steve Darrell, Bud Osborne, Pat O'Malley, Ralph Sanford, Sandy Sanders, Chuck Roberson, House Peters, Jr., Ted Mapes, Robert Hilton, Herman Hack, Victor Cox, Frank McCarroll, Felice Raymond, Holly Bane [aka: Mike Ragan], Frankie Marvin, Champion, Jr. (horse). *D:* John English; *P:* Armand Schaefer; *St: & Sc:* Gerald Geraghty. (1:10) (video) A range war breaks out over barbed wire in this entry of Autry's western series. In Sepiatone. Originally paired on a double bill with *David Harding, Counterspy* (q.v.).

537. Cowboy (Columbia/Phoenix Pictures; 1958). *Cast:* Glenn Ford (Tom Reece), Jack Lemmon (Frank Harris), Anna Kashfi (Maria Vidal), Brian Donlevy (Doc Bender), Dick York (Charlie), Victor Manuel Mendoza (Mendoza), Richard Jaeckel (Paul Curtis), King Donovan (Joe Capper), Vaughn Taylor (Mr. Fowler), Eugene Iglesias (Manuel Arriega), James Westerfield (Mike Adams), Robert "Buzz" Henry (Slim Barrett), Frank DeKova (Alcaide), Donald Randolph (Senor Vidal), William Leslie (Tucker), Guy Wilkerson (Peggy), Amapola Del Vando (aunt), Bek Nelson (Charlie's girl). *D:* Delmer Daves; *P:* Julian Blaustein; *Sc:* Edmund H. North; *Editor:* (AAN) William A. Lyon, Al Clark. (1:32) A tenderfoot learns the ropes after joining a tough trail drive. Based on *My Reminiscences as a Cowboy* by Frank Harris. Technicolor.

538. The Cowboy (Lippert/Elmo Williams; 1954). *D:* Elmo Williams; *P:* Williams, Larry Dobkin; *Sc:* Lorraine Williams; *Narrators:* Tex Ritter, William Conrad, John Dehner, Lawrence [Larry] Dobkin; *Song:* "Dodge City Trail" sung by Ritter on the sound track. (1:09) A documentary on the American cowboy, past and present. Eastmancolor.

539. The Cowboy and the Prizefighter (Eagle-Lion/Equity; 1949–50). *Cast:* Jim Bannon, "Little Brown Jug" [Don Kay Reynolds], Emmett Lynn, Lou Nova, Don Haggerty, Karen Randle, John Hart, Marshall Reed, Forrest Taylor. *D:* Lewis D. Collins; *P:-St: & Sc:* Jerry Thomas. (1:00) Red Ryder (Bannon) puts the crimps to a crooked fight promoter and a pugilist bully (Nova) in this, the 4th (and final) entry in the latter-day "Red Ryder" series, based on a character created by Fred Harman. Cinecolor. Originally ran on a double bill with *The Gay Lady*, a 1949 British production.

540. Crash Landing (Columbia/Clover Prods.; 1958). *Cast:* Gary Merrill, Nancy Davis, Irene Hervey, Roger Smith, Bek Nelson, Jewell Lain, Sheridan Comerate, Richard Keith, Celia Lovsky, Lewis Martin, Hal Torey, John McNamara, Dayle Rodney, Rodolfo Hoyos, Kim Charney, Robin Warga, Robert Whiteside, Ronald Green, Richard Newton. *D:* Fred F. Sears; *P:* Sam Katzman (unc.); *St: & Sc:* Fred Frieberger. (1:16) Programmer drama of passengers' reactions when they learn the plane they are on is going to be forced down in the ocean.

541. Crashing Las Vegas (Allied Artists; 1956). *Cast:* Leo Gorcey (final "Bowery Boys" feature), Huntz Hall, David Condon [aka: David Gorcey], Jimmy Murphy, Mary Castle, Nicky Blair, Mort Mills, Don Haggerty, Doris Kemper, Jack Rice, Bob Hopkins, John Bleifer, Dick Foote, Emil Sitka, Don Marlowe, Jack Grinnage, Terry Frost, Minerva Urecal, Frank Scannell, Joey Ray, Jack Chefe, Frank Hagney, Speer Martin, Jimmy Brandt, Cosmo Sardo, Alfred Tonkel. *D:* Jean Yarbrough; *P:* Ben Schwalb; *St: & Sc:* Jack Townley. (1:02) In this "Bowery Boys" comedy, Sach (Hall) is electrically shocked into becoming a whiz-kid with consistent numbers and wins at roulette in Las Vegas, drawing the attention of some local hoods.

542. Crashout (Filmakers; 1955). *Cast:* William Bendix, Arthur Kennedy, Luther Adler, William Talman, Gene Evans, Marshall Thompson, Beverly Michaels, Gloria Talbott, Adam Williams, Percy Helton, Melinda Markey, Chris Olsen, Adele St. Maur, Edward Clark, Tom Dugan, Morris Ankrum. *D:* Lewis R. Foster; *P:* Hal E. Chester; *St: & Sc:* Foster,

Chester. (1:28) (video) Six convicts break out of prison and head for a stash of gold coins, hidden by one of the six.

543. Crazy Over Horses (Monogram; 1951). *Cast:* Leo Gorcey, Huntz Hall, Billy Benedict, Bennie Bartlett, Ted de Corsia, Allen Jenkins, Bernard Gorcey, Gloria Saunders, Tim Ryan, David Condon [aka: David Gorcey], Russell Hicks, Peggy Wynne, Bob Peoples, Michael Ross, Perc Launders, Leo "Ukie" Sherin, Robert "Smoki" Whitfield, Sam Balter, Ray Page, Darr Smith, Wilbur Mack, Gertrude Astor, Bill Cartledge, Whitey Hughes, Delmar Thomas, Bernard Pludow, Ben Frommer. *D:* William Beaudine; *P:* Jan Grippo; *St: & Sc:* Tim Ryan, Max Adams (unc.?). (1:05) The "Bowery Boys" become involved with crooks who are fixing horse races in this comedy series entry. (G.B. title: *Win, Place and Show*)

544. Crazylegs, All-American (Republic/Hall Bartlett Prods.; 1953). *Cast:* Elroy "Crazylegs" Hirsch (himself), Lloyd Nolan (Win Brockmeyer), Joan Vohs (Ruth), James Millican (Ram's coach), Bob Waterfield (himself), Bob Kelley (himself), James Brown (Bill), John Brown (Keller), Norman Field (Mr. Hirsch), Louise Lorimer (Mrs. Hirsch), Joseph Crehan (Hank Hatch), Joel Marston (Joey), Bill Brundige (himself), Win Hirsch (himself), Melvyn Arnold (himself), The Los Angeles Rams (themselves). *D:* Francis D. Lyon (directorial debut); *P:-St: & Sc:* Hall Bartlett; *Editor:* (AAN) Irvine [Cotton] Warburton. (1:27) Biographical sports drama with authentic film footage of the titled football player, from his high school days to his days with the Los Angeles Rams.

545. Creature from the Black Lagoon (Universal-International; 1954). *Cast:* Richard Carlson, Julia [Julie] Adams, Richard Denning, Antonio Moreno, Nestor Paiva, Whit Bissell, Bernie Gozier, Henry Escalante, Ricou Browning (title role). *D:* Jack Arnold; *P:* William Alland; *St:* Maurice Zimm; *Sc:* Harry Essex, Arthur A. Ross; *Make-up:* Bud Westmore, Jack Kevan. (1:19) (video/laserdisc) Action-adventure of an expedition down the Amazon River that discovers a humanoid denizen of that South American waterway. A big hit for the studio, it was followed by the sequel *Revenge of the Creature* (q.v.). 3-D.

546. The Creature Walks Among Us (Universal-International; 1956). *Cast:* Jeff Morrow, Rex Reason, Gregg Palmer, Leigh Snowden, Maurice Manson, James Rawley, David McMahon, Paul Fierro, Lillian Molieri, Larry Hudson, Frank Chase, Don Megowan, Ricou Browning (title role). *D:* John Sherwood; *P:* William Alland; *St: & Sc:* Arthur A. Ross. (1:18) (video/laserdisc) Sequel to *Revenge of the Creature* (q.v.) in which the gillman undergoes an operation to make him more human, emphasized by the fact that he even wears human clothing in this one.

547. Creature with the Atom Brain (Columbia/Clover Prods.; 1955). *Cast:* Richard Denning, Angela Stevens, S. John Launer, Michael Granger, Gregory Gaye, Linda Bennett, Tristram Coffin, Harry Lauter, Larry Blake, Charles Evans, Pierre Watkin, Lane Chandler, Nelson Leigh, Don C. Harvey, Paul Hoffman, Edward Coch, Karl Davis. *D:* Edward L. Cahn; *P:* Sam Katzman; *St: & Sc:* Curt Siodmak. (1:09) Bottom-of-the-bill science fiction-horror of a mad scientist (an ex-Nazi, no less) who creates zombies from dead men by implanting atomic brains in their heads. Originally ran as the lower half of a double bill with *It Came From Beneath the Sea* (q.v.).

548. Crime Against Joe (United Artists/Bel-Air Prods.–Sunrise Pictures; 1955-56). *Cast:* John Bromfield, Julie London, Henry Calvin, Patricia Blake, Joel Ashley, John Pickard, Robert Keys, Alika Louis, Frances Morris, Rhodes Reason, Mauritz Hugo, Joyce Jameson, Morgan Jones, James Parnell. *D:* Lee Sholem; *P:* Howard W. Koch; *St:* Decla Dunning; *Sc:* Robert C. Dennis. (1:09) When a man awakens from a drunken binge, he finds that he is being accused of murdering a girl.

549. Crime and Punishment, U.S.A. (Allied Artists/Sanders Associates; 1959). *Cast:* George Hamilton (film debut), Mary Murphy, Frank Silvera, Marian Seldes, John Harding, Wayne Heffley, Eve McVeagh, Tony Merrill, Lew Brown, Sid Clute, Ken Drake, Jim Hyland, Len Lesser. *D:* Denis Sanders (directorial debut); *P:* Terry Sanders; *As.P:* Jacqueline Donnet; *Sc:* Walter Newman. (1:36) Feodor Dostoyevsky's famous novel *Crime and Punishment* has been updated and transposed to an American setting, relating the story of a law student who commits robbery and murder and then begins to suffer pangs of guilt. Critics were reasonably impressed. Note: In Leonard Maltin's *1996 Movie and Video Guide*, the running time of this film is listed as 78 minutes.

550. Crime in the Streets (Allied Artists/ Lindbrook Prods.; 1956). *Cast:* James Whitmore, John Cassavetes (repeating his TV role), Mark Rydell (repeating his TV role), Sal Mineo (repeating his TV role), Denise Alexander, Malcolm Atterbury, Peter Votrian, Virginia Gregg, Ray Stricklyn, Daniel Terranova, Will Kuluva (repeating his TV role), Peter Miller, Steve Rowland, James Ogg, Robert Alexander, Duke Mitchell, Richard Curtis, Doyle Baker. *D:* Don Siegel; *P:* Vincent M. Fennelly; *Sc:* Reginald Rose (adapted from his TV play). (1:31) (video) Drama of a gang of juvenile delinquents and their leader who has murder on his mind. Adapted from a TV play that appeared on the "Elgin Playhouse."

551. Crime of Passion (United Artists; Bob Goldstein Prods.; 1957). *Cast:* Barbara Stanwyck, Sterling Hayden, Raymond Burr, Fay Wray, Virginia Grey, Royal Dano, Robert Griffin, Malcolm Atterbury, Dennis Cross, S. John Launer, Jay Adler, Brad Trumbull, Skipper McNally, Robert Quarry, Jean Howell, Peg LaCentra, Nancy Reynolds, Marjorie Owens, John Conley, Stuart Whitman, Eddie Kafafian, Geraldine Wall, Helen Jay, Sally Yarnell, Madelon Erin, Nan Dolan, *D:* Gerd Oswald; *P:* Herman Cohen; *St: & Sc:* Jo Eisinger. (1:24) (video) Suspense drama of a cop whose wife, an ambitious newspaper woman, beds her husband's boss, with the intent of getting her husband a promotion. He isn't promoted, then the boss is murdered.

The Crime of the Century (G.B. title) *see* **Walk East on Beacon**

552. Crime Wave (Warner; 1954). *Cast:* Sterling Hayden, Gene Nelson, Phyllis Kirk, Ted de Corsia, Charles [Bronson] Buchinsky, Jay Novello, James Bell, Dub Taylor, Gayle Kellogg, Mack Chandler, Timothy Carey, Richard Benjamin, Sandy Sanders, Harry Lauter, Joe Bassett, Dennis Dengate, Fred Coby, Mary Alan Hokanson, Diane Fortier, Ruth Lee, Eileen Elliott, Fritz Feld, Bill Schroff, Shirley O'Hara, Shirley Whitney, Charles Cane, Don Gibson, Bert Moorhouse, Jack Kenney, Harry Wilson, Faith Kruger, Tome Clarke, Guy Wilkerson, Lyle Latell. *D:* Andre De Toth; *P:* Bryan Foy; *Adaptation:* Bernard Gordon, Richard Wormser; *Sc:* Crane Wilbur. (1:13) Crime melodrama of an ex-con's attempts to go straight and the difficulties he encounters. Based on the story "Criminal's Mark" by John and Ward Hawkins, which appeared in *Saturday Evening Post.* (G.B. title: *The City Is Dark*)

553. Criminal Lawyer (Columbia; 1951). *Cast:* Pat O'Brien, Jane Wyatt, Carl Benton Reid, Mary Castle, Robert Shayne, Mike Mazurki, Jerome Cowan, Marvin Kaplan, Douglas Fowley, Mickey Knox, Louis Jean Heydt, Wallis Clark, Grandon Rhodes, Darryl Hickman. *D:* Seymour Friedman; *P:* Rudolph C. Flothow; *St: & Sc:* Harold R. Greene. (1:13) The trials and tribulations of a lawyer are the subject of this melodrama which ran on a double bill program with *Chain of Circumstance* (q.v.).

554. The Crimson Kimono (Columbia/ Globe Enterprises; 1959). *Cast:* Victoria Shaw, Glenn Corbett, James Shigeta (film debut), Anna Lee, Paul Dubov, Neyle Morrow, Jaclynne Greene, Gloria Pall, Barbara Hayden, George Yoshinaga, Kaye Elhardt, Aya Oyama, George Okamura, Rev. Ryosho S. Sogabe, Robert Okazaki, Fuji, Robert Kino, Rollin Moriyama, Jack Carol, Brian O'Hara, Carol Nugent, David McMahon, Harrison Lewis, Walter Burke, Torau Mori, Edo Mita, Chiyo Toto, Katie Sweet, Stafford Repp, Nina Roman, Allen Pincen (stunt double), Stacey Morgan (stunt double). *D:-P:-St: & Sc:* Samuel Fuller. (1:21) Offbeat crime melodrama of two detectives who investigate when a stripper by the name of Sugar Torch is gunned down on the streets of Los Angeles. A minor cult item for Fuller followers.

555. The Crimson Pirate (Warner/Norma Prods.; 1952). *Cast:* Burt Lancaster, Nick Cravat, Eva Bartok, Torin Thatcher, Noel Purcell, Margot Grahame, James Hayter, Leslie Bradley, Frederick Leicester, Eliot Makeham, Frank Pettingill, Dagmar Winter, Christopher Lee. *D:* Robert Siodmak; *P:* Harold Hecht; *St: & Sc:* Roland Kibbee. (1:44) (video/laserdisc) Full of action and comic overtones, this hit swashbuckler has gained a cult following over the years. Photographed in Technicolor on locations in England and Spain.

556. Cripple Creek (Columbia/Resolute Prods.; 1952). *Cast:* George Montgomery, Karin Booth, Jerome Courtland, William Bishop, Richard Egan, Don Porter, John Dehner, Roy Roberts, George Cleveland, Byron Foulger, Zon Murray, Harry Cording, Chris Alcaide, Robert Bice, Robert Armstrong, Grandon Rhodes, Peter Brocco, Cliff Clark. *D:* Ray Nazarro; *P:* Edward Small; *St: & Sc:* Richard

Schayer. (1:18) Technicolor western of government agents on the trail of gold smugglers. Originally ran on the top of a double bill with *Junction City* (q.v.).

557. Crisis (MGM; 1950). *Cast:* Cary Grant, Jose Ferrer, Paula Raymond, Signe Hasso, Ramon Novarro, Antonio Moreno, Gilbert Roland, Leon Ames, Teresa Celli, Pedro de Cordoba (final film—d. 1950), Vincente Gomez, Martin Garralaga, Soledad Jimenez, Jose [Joe] Dominguez, Robert Tafur, Maurice Jara, Rodolfo Hoyos, Jr., Rita Conde, Roque Ybarra, Felipe Turich, Charles Rivero, Mickey Contreras, Captain Garcia, Carlos Conde, George Lewis, Carlo Tricoli, Kenneth Garcia, Harry Vejar, Trina Varela, Bridget Carr, Audrey Betz, Robert Lugo, Myron Marks, Alex Montoya, Margaret Martin, Juan Duval, Al Haskell, Rafael Gomez, Zachary Yaconelli, Fernando Del Valle, A. Carillo, Robert Polo, Jerry Riggio, Melba Meredith, Lillian Israel, Carlotta Monti, Connie Montoya, George Navarro, Orlando Beltran, Eddie Gomez, Neyle Morrow, Pepe Hern, David Cota, George Brady, Joaquin Garay, Larry Crane, Danilo Valenti, Sam Herrera, William M. MacCormack, Carlos Figueroa, Robert Cabal, Manuel Paris, Carlos Barbee, Amapola Del Vando. *D:* Richard Brooks (directorial debut); *P:* Arthur Freed; *Sc:* Brooks. (1:35) An American doctor and his wife are held in a South American country, to care for the country's ailing dictator. Based on *The Doubters* by George Tabori. Computer-colored by Turner Entertainment.

558. The Crooked Circle (Republic/Ventura Prods.; 1958). *Cast:* John Smith, Fay Spain, Steve Brodie, Don Kelly, Robert Armstrong, John Doucette, Philip Van Zandt, Richard Karlan, Bob Swan, Don Haggerty, Peter Mamakos. *D:* Joe Kane; *P:* Rudy Ralston; *St: & Sc:* Jack Townley. (1:12) Melodrama of a young boxer who gets mixed up with crooked fight promoters and eventually goes against them at the peril of his own life.

559. Crooked River (Lippert; 1949-50). *Cast:* Jimmie Ellison, Russell Hayden, Raymond Hatton, Fuzzy Knight, Betty [Julie] Adams, Tom Tyler, George J. Lewis, John Cason, Stephen Carr, Stanley Price, George Chesebro, Dennis Moore, Bud Osborne, Jimmie Martin, Cliff Taylor, Carl Mathews, Helen Gibson, George Sowards, Scoop Martin, Joe Phillips. *D:* Thomas Carr; *P:* Ron Ormond; *Sc:* Ormond, Maurice Tombragel. (0:55) Shamrock (Ellison) sets out to avenge the murders of his parents. The 3rd entry (of 6) in the "Four Star" series of westerns which has also been referred to as the "Shamrock and Lucky" series. (TV title: *The Last Bullet*)

560. The Crooked Web (Columbia/Clover Prods.; 1955). *Cast:* Frank Lovejoy, Mari Blanchard, Richard Denning, John Mylong, Harry Lauter, Steven Ritch, Louis Merrill, Roy Gordon, John Hart, Richard Emory, Van Des Autels, George Cisar, Harry Dyrenforth, Judy Clark. *D:* Nathan Hertz [Juran]; *P:* Sam Katzman; *St: & Sc:* Lou Breslow. (1:17) Melodrama of government agents out to bring a wanted fugitive back to Germany to face murder charges.

561. Crosswinds (Paramount/Pine-Thomas; 1951). *Cast:* John Payne, Rhonda Fleming, Forrest Tucker, Robert Lowery, Alan Mowbray, John Abbott, Frank Kumagai. *D:* Lewis R. Foster; *P:* William H. Pine, William C. Thomas; *Sc:* Foster. (1:33) Actioner of an adventurer out to retrieve gold from a plane that crashed in New Guinea, who encounters local headhunters and thieves in the process. Based on the novel *New Guinea Gold* by Thomson Burtis, who also adapted his novel for the screen. (aka: *Jungle Attack*) Technicolor.

562. Crowded Paradise (Tudor Pictures, Inc./Imps, Inc.; 1956). *Cast:* Hume Cronyn, Nancy Kelly, Frank Silvera, Enid Rudd, Mario Alcaide, Stefan Schnable, David Opatashu, Ralph Dunn, Carlos Montalban, Santos Oretega, Miriam Colon, Marita Reid, Henry Silva. *D:* Fred Pressburger; *P:* Ben Gradus; *Sc:* Arthur Forrest; *Additional scenes:* Marc Connelly. (1:34) (video) Drama of an idealistic Puerto Rican youth who arrives in New York City and runs afoul of his bigoted landlord.

The Cruel Swamp *see* **Swamp Women**

563. The Cruel Tower (Allied Artists/Lindsley Parsons Prods.; 1956). *Cast:* John Ericson, Mari Blanchard, Charles McGraw, Steve Brodie, Peter Whitney, Alan Hale, Jr., Diana Darrin, Carol Kelly, Barbara Bel Wright. *D:* Lew Landers; *P:* Lindsley Parsons; *Sc:* Warren Douglas. (1:19) Two men, one with acrophobia, work as steeplejacks while both have affections for the same woman. Based on the 1955 novel by William B. Hartley.

564. Cruisin' Down the River (Columbia; 1953). *Cast:* Dick Haymes (final film—ret.),

Audrey Totter, Billy Daniels, Cecil Kellaway, Connie Russell, Douglas Fowley, Johnny Downs (final film—ret.), Larry Blake, Benny Payne, The Bell Sisters, Byron Foulger, Dick Crockett, Ezre Ivan (specialty dancer). *D:* Richard Quine; *P:* Jonie Taps; *St:* & *Sc:* Blake Edwards, Quine; *Songs:* "Cruisin' Down the River" (Eily Beadell–Nell Tollerton); "There Goes That Song Again" (Jule Styne–Sammy Cahn); "Pennies From Heaven" (Arthur Johnston–Sonny Burke); "Sing You Sinners" (W. Frank Harling–Sam Coslow); "Swing Low, Sweet Chariot" (traditional); "Father Dear" (Emmet G. Coleman). (1:19) Technicolor musical of a singer from New York who inherits a riverboat—much in need of repair. Originally ran on a double bill with *Mission Over Korea* (q.v.).

Cruising Casanovas (G.B. title) *see* **Gobs and Gals**

565. The Cry Baby Killer (Allied Artists; 1958). *Cast:* Harry Lauter, Jack Nicholson (film debut), Carolyn Mitchell, Brett Halsey, Lynn Cartwright, Ralph Reed, John Shay, Barbara Knudson, Jordan Whitfield, Claude Stroud, Ruth Swanson, William A. Forester, John Weed, Frank Richards, Bill Erwin, James Fillmore, Ed Nelson, Mitzi McCall, Leo Gordon (bit), Roger Corman (bit). *D:* Jus Addiss; *P:* Roger Corman; *Co-P:* David Kramarsky, David March; *St:* Leo Gordon; *Sc:* Gordon, Melvin Levy; *Song:* "Cry Baby Cry" (Dick Kallman). (1:02) Juvenile delinquency melodrama of a youth who shoots two others in a fight and believing he has killed them, takes refuge in a storeroom with three hostages. Notable as Nicholson's first film, it ran on a double bill with *Hot Car Girl* (q.v.).

566. Cry Danger (RKO/Olympic Prods.; 1950–51). *Cast:* Dick Powell, Rhonda Fleming, Richard Erdman, William Conrad, Regis Toomey, Jean Porter, Jay Adler, Joan Banks, Gloria Saunders, Hy Averbach, Renny McEvoy, Lou Lubin, Benny Burt. *D:* Robert Parrish (directorial debut); *P:* Sam Wiesenthal, W.R. Frank; *St:* Jerome Cady; *Sc:* William Bowers. (1:19) (video) A man who is released from prison gets more than he bargained for when he begins investigating who actually stole the money he was sent to prison for.

567. A Cry in the Night (Warner/Jaguar Prods.; 1956). *Cast:* Edmond O'Brien, Brian Donlevy, Natalie Wood, Raymond Burr, Richard Anderson, Irene Hervey, Carol Veazie, Herb Vigran, Anthony Caruso, Mary Lawrence, George J. Lewis, Peter Hanson, Tina Carver. *D:* Frank Tuttle; *As.P:* George C. Bertholon; *Sc:* David Dortort. (1:15) Crime melodrama of police investigating the kidnapping of a young girl (Wood) by a sexual psychopath (Burr). Based on the 1955 novel *All Through the Night* by Whit Masterson.

568. Cry Murder (Film Classics; 1950). *Cast:* Jack Lord (film debut), Carole Mathews, Howard Smith, Hope Miller, Tom Pedi, Eugene Smith, Harry Clark, Tom Ahearne, William Gibberson, Bill Dwyer, Lionel Maclyn. *D:* Jack Glenn; *P:* Edward Leven; *Sc:* James Carhardt. (1:03) Mystery-melodrama of a woman's plight when a disreputable New York artist uncovers some old letters. Based on the play by A.B. Shiffrin. Originally paired on a double bill with *Guilty Bystander* (q.v.).

569. Cry of the Hunted (MGM; 1953). *Cast:* Vittorio Gassman, Barry Sullivan, Polly Bergen, William Conrad, Mary Zavian, Robert Burton, Harry Shannon, Jonathan Cott. *D:* Joseph H. Lewis; *P:* William Grady, Jr.; *St:* Jack Leonard, Marion Wolfe; *Sc:* Leonard. (1:20) Chase-melodrama of a lawman on the trail of an escaped convict in the swamps of Louisiana. Filmed on location.

570. Cry Terror! (MGM/Virginia & Andrew L. Stone Prods.; 1958). *Cast:* James Mason, Rod Steiger, Inger Stevens, Neville Brand, Angie Dickinson, Kenneth Tobey, Jack Klugman Jack Kruschen, Carleton Young, Barney Phillips, Terry Ann Ross, Portland Mason, Harlan Warde, Ed Hinton, Chet Huntley (himself), Roy Neal (himself), Jonathan Hole, William Schallert, Marjorie Bennett, Mae Marsh. *D:* & *Sc:* Andrew L. Stone; *P:* Andrew & Virginia Stone. (1:36) Critically acclaimed suspense thriller of a madman who forces a family to become part of a half-million dollar extortion plot, involving a bomb planted on an airplane. Computer-colored by Turner Entertainment.

571. Cry Tough (United Artists/Canon/Hecht–Hill–Lancaster; 1959). *Cast:* John Saxon, Linda Cristal, Joseph Calleia, Harry Townes, Don Gordon, Perry Lopez, Frank Puglia, Penny Santon, Joe De Santis, Arthur Batanides, Barbara Luna, Paul Clarke, John Sebastian, Nira Monsour. *D:* Paul Stanley; *P:* & *Sc:* Harry Kleiner. (1:23) A Puerto Rican youth gets out of prison after a year's incarceration, only to find himself drawn back into trouble with his former gang. Based on the 1949 novel by Irving Shulman.

572. Cry Vengeance (Allied Artists; 1954). *Cast:* Mark Stevens, Martha Hyer, Skip Homeier, Joan Vohs, Douglas Kennedy, Don Haggerty, Cheryl Callaway, Warren Douglas, Mort Mills, John Doucette, Lewis Martin, Dorothy Kennedy. *D: & As.P:* Mark Stevens; *P:* Lindsley Parsons; *St: & Sc:* Warren Douglas, George Bricker. (1:23) (video) Suspense drama of a man seeking the party responsible for killing his family and sending him to prison for three years.

573. Cuban Fireball (Republic; 1950-51). *Cast:* Estelita Rodriguez (herself), Warren Douglas, Mimi Aguglia, Leon Belasco, Donald MacBride, Rosa Turich, John Litel, Tim Ryan, Russ Vincent, Edward Gargan, Victoria Horne, Jack Kruschen, Pedro de Cordoba, Olan Soule, Tony Barr, Luther Crockett. *D:* William Beaudine; *P:* Sidney Picker; *St:* Charles E. Roberts; *Sc:* Roberts, Jack Townley; *Songs include:* "A Slave," "Lost and Found" (Aaron Gonzales-Jack Elliott), "Un Poquito De Tu Amor" (Julian Gutierres). (1:18) Musical-comedy of a woman's adventures on her way to collect a huge inheritance. Originally ran on a double bill with *Night Riders of Montana* (q.v.).

574. Cuban Rebel Girls (Joseph Brenner Assoc./An Exploit Film–An Errol Flynn Presentation; 1959). *Cast:* Errol Flynn (final film—d. 1959), Beverly Aadland, John McKay, Marie Edmund, Jackie Jackler, Ben Ostrovsky, Regnier Sanchez, Esther Oliva, Todd Brody, Al Brown, Clelle Manon. *D: & P:* Barry Mahon; *Sc: & Narrator:* Errol Flynn. (1:08) (video) While vacationing in Cuba, Errol Flynn becomes sympathetic to Castro's cause for overthrowing Batista, becoming involved with a band of female rebels fighting in the mountains. A low budget independent exploitation item if ever there was one. Filmed in Cuba with the co-operation of Fidel Castro's army. This film ran on a double bill with *Violent Women* (q.v.). (aka: *Assault of the Rebel Girls* and *Attack of the Rebel Girls*)

575. Cult of the Cobra (Universal-International; 1955). *Cast:* Faith Domergue, Richard Long, Marshall Thompson, Jack Kelly, Kathleen Hughes, David Janssen, Myrna Hansen, William Reynolds, Leonard Strong, James Dobson, Walter Coy, The Carlsons (dance team), Olan Soule, Helen Wallace, Mary Alan Hokanson, John Halloran, Alan Reynolds. *D:* Francis D. Lyon; *P:* Howard Pine; *St:* Jerry Davis; *Sc:* Davis, Cecil Maiden, Richard Collins. (1:22) (video) Horror tale of six servicemen who accidentally interrupt a secret ceremony of cobra worshippers and find themselves under a death curse. Originally ran on a double bill with *Ma and Pa Kettle at Waikiki* (q.v.).

576. Curfew Breakers (Screen Guild; 1957). *Cast:* Regis Toomey, Paul Kelly, Cathy Downs, Marilyn Madison, Sheila Urban. *D:* Alex Wells; *P:* Charles E. King. (1:18) Independent exploitation-melodrama with songs of an investigation into the murder of a gas station attendant, with the culprits finally being exposed as juveniles.

The Curse of Dracula *see* **The Return of Dracula**

577. Curse of the Faceless Man (United Artists/Vogue; 1958). *Cast:* Richard Anderson, Elaine Edwards, Adele Mara, Luis Van Rooten, Gar Moore, Jan Arvan, Felix Locher, Bob Bryant (title role). *D:* Edward L. Cahn; *P:* Robert E. Kent; *St: & Sc:* Jerome Bixby. (1:06) Archeologists excavating the ruins of Pompeii uncover a gladiator "alive" and encased in lava who seeks to save his reincarnated long-lost-love from the Vesuvius eruption. This horror film ran as a second feature with *It! The Terror from Beyond Space* (q.v.).

578. Curse of the Undead (Universal-International; 1959). *Cast:* Eric Fleming, Kathleen Crowley, Michael Pate, John Hoyt, Bruce Gordon, Jimmy Murphy, Edward Binns, Helen Kleeb, Jay Adler, Edwin Parker, John Truax, Frankie Van, Rush Williams, Alan Reynolds, Amzie Strickland. *D:* Edward Dein; *P:* Joseph Gershenson; *St: & Sc:* Edward and Mildred Dein. (1:19) Offbeat horror-western, in the fact that the bad guy (Pate) is actually a vampire-gunfighter. Low budget, but at least a tad novel.

579. Curtain Call at Cactus Creek (Universal-International; 1950). *Cast:* Donald O'Connor, Gale Storm, Vincent Price, Walter Brennan, Eve Arden, Chick Chandler, Joe Sawyer, Harry Shannon, Rex Lease, Paul Maxey, I. Stanford Jolley, Eddy Waller. *D:* Charles Lamont; *P:* Robert Arthur; *St:* Howard Dimsdale, Stanley Roberts; *Sc:* Dimsdale; *Songs include:* "Be My Little Baby Bumble Bee" (Stanley Murphy–Henry I. Marshall); "Waiting at the Church" (Henry Pether–F.W. Leigh); "Are You from Dixie?" (Jack Yellen–George Cobb–Fred Arndt). (1:26) Western comedy of the misadventures of a theatrical troupe on the Arizona frontier. (G.B. title: *Take the Stage*) Technicolor.

580. Curucu, Beast of the Amazon (Universal-International/Jewel Enterprises, Inc.; 1956). *Cast:* John Bromfield (final film—ret.), Beverly Garland, Tom Payne, Harvey Chalk, Sergio De Oliviera, Wilson Viana, Larry Thomas. *D:-St: & Sc:* Curt Siodmak; *P:* Richard Kay, Harry Rybnick. (1:16) B budget jungle adventure in Eastmancolor, of a "monster" reported to be killing local natives. Originally ran on a double bill with *The Mole People* (q.v.).

581. Customs Agent (Columbia; 1950). *Cast:* William Eythe (final film—ret.), Marjorie Reynolds, Griff Barnett, Howard St. John, Jim Backus, Robert Shayne, Denver Pyle, John Doucette, Harlan Warde, James Fairfax, Clark Howat, Marya Marco, Guy Kingsford, William "Bill" Phillips. *D:* Seymour Friedman; *P:* Rudolph C. Flothow; *St:* Hal [Harold J.] Smith; *Sc:* Russell S. Hughes, Malcolm Stuart Boylan. (1:11) Programmer crime melodrama of drugs being smuggled into the U.S. from China.

582. Cyclone Fury (Columbia; 1951). *Cast:* Charles Starrett, Fred F. Sears, Smiley Burnette, Clayton Moore, Louis Lettieri, Bob Wilke, George Chesebro, Frank O'Connor, Merle Travis & His Bronco Busters. *D:* Ray Nazarro; *P:* Colbert Clark; *St: & Sc:* Barry Shipman, Ed Earl Repp. (0:54) "Durango Kid" western series entry with the Kid [aka: Steve Reynolds] coming to the aid of an Indian youth. Originally ran as the lower half of a double bill with *The Lady and the Bandit* (q.v.).

583. The Cyclops (Allied Artists/B & H Prods., Inc.; 1957). *Cast:* James Craig, Gloria Talbott, Lon Chaney, Jr., Tom Drake, Duncan Parkin (title role). *D:-P:-Sc: & F/X:* Bert I. Gordon. (1:15) (video) Low budget science fiction of a missing man who is found, but is now a mutant giant via his exposure to radioactivity. This one ran as the top attraction on a double bill with *Daughter of Dr. Jekyll* (q.v.).

584. Cyrano de Bergerac (United Artists/Stanley Kramer; 1950). *Cast:* Jose Ferrer (AA/Cyrano), Mala Powers (Roxanne Robin), William Prince (Baron Christian de Neuvillette), Morris Carnovsky (Capt. Le Bret), Ralph Clanton (Count Antoine de Guiche), Lloyd Corrigan (Ragueneau), Virginia Farmer (Duenna), Edgar Barrier (Cardinal), Albert Cavens (Viscount Valvert), Arthur Blake (Montfleury), Don Beddoe (the meddler), Percy Helton (Bellerose), Virginia Christine (Sister Marthe), Elena Verdugo, Gil Warren, Philip Van Zandt, Eric Sinclair, Richard Avonde, Paul Dubov, John Crawford, Jerry Paris, Robin Hughes, Francis Pierlot, John Harmon. *D:* Michael Gordon; *P:* Stanley Kramer; *Adaptation & Sc:* Carl Foreman (based on the English translation by Brian Hooker of Edmond Rosten's 1897 verse play). (1:52) (video/laserdisc) Costume romance of a man, ashamed of his long nose, who loves the fair Roxanne and can only relate his love through verse, read to her by a friend. The NBR's "10 Best" list gave it a #8 placement, while the same list of *Film Daily* placed it at #6. Previously filmed in 1925 by Atlas, with a French remake in 1990. The story was given a contemporary treatment in 1987 as *Roxanne.* Computer-colored prints have been produced.

585. D-Day: The Sixth of June (20th Century–Fox; 1956). *Cast:* Robert Taylor, Dana Wynter, Richard Todd, Edmond O'Brien, John Williams, Jerry Paris, Robert Gist, Richard Stapley, Ross Elliott, Alex Finlayson, Marie Brown, Rama Bai, Dabbs Greer, Boyd "Red" Morgan, Queenie Leonard, Geoffrey Steel, George Pelling, Cyril Delevanti, Conrad Feia, Richard Aherne, Victoria Ward, Patricia McMahon, John Damler, Thomas B. Henry, Damian O'Flynn, Ben Wright, Howard Price, Reggie Dvorak, Chet Marshall, Parley Baer, Ashley Cowan, June Mitchell. *D:* Henry Koster; *P:* Charles Brackett; *Sc:* Ivan Moffat, Harry Brown. (1:46) (video) Triangular romantic drama, partially told in flashbacks and set prior to and during the Normandy invasion of 1944. Photographed in DeLuxe color and CinemaScope, this box office hit was based on the 1955 novel *The Sixth of June* by Lionel Shapiro. (aka: *The Sixth of June*)

586. The D.I. (Warner/Mark VII Ltd.; 1957). *Cast:* Jack Webb, Don Dubbins, Jackie Loughery, Lin McCarthy, Monica Lewis, Virginia Gregg, Jeannie Beacham, Lu Tobin, Earle Hodgins, Jeanne Baird, Barbara Pepper, Melody Gale and Men of the U.S. Marine Corps. *D: & P:* Jack Webb; *St: & Sc:* James Lee Barrett (from his TV play). (1:46) (video) Drama and comedy set in the U.S. Marine Corps' Parris Island bootcamp, and one drill instructor's attempts to make "one good man" out of a misfit. Remade and updated in 1970 as the TV movie *Tribes.*

587. Daddy Long Legs (20th Century-Fox; 1955). *Cast:* Fred Astaire (Jervis Pendleton), Leslie Caron (Julie), Terry Moore (Linda), Thelma Ritter (Miss Pritchard), Fred Clark (Griggs), Charlotte Austin (Sally), Larry Keating (Alexander Williamson), Kathryn Givney (Gertrude), Sara Shane (Pat), Kelly Brown (Jimmy McBride), Numa Lapeyre (Jean), Ann Codee (Mme. Sevanne), Steven Geray (Emile), Percival Vivian (Professor), Ralph Dumke (Mr. Bronson), Damian O'Flynn (Larry Hamilton), Hellen Van Tuyl (college dean), Kathryn Card (Mrs. Carrington), Joseph Kearns, Larry Kent, Charles Anthony Hughes, Tim Johnson, Harry Seymour, Olan Soule, J. Anthony Hughes, George Dunn, Ray Anthony & Orchestra. *D:* Jean Negulesco; *P:* Samuel G. Engel; *Sc:* Phoebe & Henry Ephron (based on the novel and play by Jean Webster); *Music:* (AAN) Alfred Newman; *ASD:* (AAN-color) Lyle Wheeler, John DeCuir (art directors), Walter M. Scott, Paul S. Fox (sets); *Songs:* "Something's Gotta Give" (AAN), "History of the Beat," "C-A-T Spells Cat," "Daddy Long Legs," "Welcome Egghead," "Dream," "Sluefoot;" *Dances:* "Hong Kong," "Texas Millionaire," "International Playboy," "Guardian Angel," "The Daydream," "Dancing Through Life," "Something's Gotta Give" and "Sluefoot" (Johnny Mercer). (2:06) (video/laserdisc) Musical of a wealthy international playboy who finances the education of a French waif who later, not knowing him to be her benefactor, falls in love with him. One of the 27 top-grossing films of 1954-55, it was previously filmed in 1919, 1931 and in 1935 as *Curly Top* with Shirley Temple. Technicolor and CinemaScope.

588. Daddy-O (American International/Imperial; 1959). *Cast:* Dick Contino, Sandra Giles, Bruno Ve Sota, Gloria Victor, Ron McNeil, Jack McClure, Sonia Torgeson, Kelly Gordon, Joseph Donte, Bob Banas, Hank Mann (final film—ret.), Joseph Martin. *D:* Lou Place; *P:* Elmer C. Rhoden, Jr.; *St: & Sc:* David Moessinger. (1:14) (video) A truck driver who is also a race car driver and a rock singer is accused of the murder of his best friend. He finds himself involved in a Mexican smuggling operation when he tries to clear himself. Paired with *Road Racers* (q.v.) on a double bill. (aka: *Out on Probation*)

589. Dakota Incident (Republic; 1956). *Cast:* Linda Darnell, Dale Robertson, John Lund, Ward Bond, Skip Homeier, Regis Toomey, Irving Bacon, John Doucette, Whit Bissell, William Fawcett, Malcolm Atterbury, Charles Horvath, Diane DuBois. *D:* Lewis R. Foster; *As.P:* Michael Baird; *Sc:* Frederick Louis Fox. (1:28) (video) Western character study of passengers who survive a stagecoach attack by Indians. Trucolor.

590. The Dakota Kid (Republic; 1951). *Cast:* Michael Chapin, Eilene Janssen, James Bell, Margaret Field, Robert Shayne, Roy Barcroft, Dean Morton (title role), Mauritz Hugo, House Peters, Jr., Lee Bennett, Mike Ragan [aka: Holly Bane]. *D:* Philip Ford; *P:* Rudy Ralston; *St: & Sc:* William Lively; *Song:* "What Are Cowboys Made Of?" Jule Styne, Eddie Cherkose. (1:10) A group of kids help lawmen roundup an outlaw gang. The second entry in the "Rough Ridin' Kids" series.

591. Dakota Lil (20th Century-Fox/Alson Prods., Inc.; 1950). *Cast:* George Montgomery, Rod Cameron, Marie Windsor, John Emery, Wallace Ford, Jack Lambert, Larry Johns, Marion Martin, James Flavin, J. Farrell MacDonald, Walter Sande, Bill Perrott, Lillian Bronson, Kenneth MacDonald, Clancy Cooper, Albert Morin, Frank Lackteen, Joel Friedkin, Saul Gorss, Bob Morgan, Leo McMahon, Jamesson Shade, Ben Harris, Alvin Hammer, John Dako, Tom Greenway, Nacho Galindo, Soledad Jimenez, Daniel Estrada, Rosa Turich, Bryan Hightower, Arne Hjorth. *D:* Lesley Selander; *P:* Edward L. Alperson; *St:* Frank Gruber; *Sc:* Maurice Geraghty. (1:28) Western drama of counterfeiters who draw the attention of U.S. Treasury agents. Cinecolor.

592. Dallas (Warner; 1950). *Cast:* Gary Cooper, Ruth Roman, Steve Cochran, Raymond Massey, Barbara Payton, Leif Erickson, Antonio Moreno, Reed Hadley (Wild Bill Hickok), Jerome Cowan, Will Wright, Monte Blue, Byron [Brian] Keith, Gil Donaldson, Zon Murray, Steve Dunhill, Charles Watts, Jose Dominguez, Gene Evans, Jay "Slim" Talbot, Billie Bird, Frank Kreig, Tom Fadden, Hal K. Dawson, Buddy Roosevelt, Dolores Corvall, Alex Montoya, Fred Graham, Charles Horvath, Carl Andre, Ann Lawrence, O.Z. Whitehead, Mike Donovan, Glenn Thompson, Frank McCarroll, Larry McGrath, Dewey Robinson, Al Ferguson, Buddy Shaw, Roy Bucko, Dave Dunbar, Oscar Williams, Fred Kelsey, Benny Corbett. *D:* Stuart Heisler; *P:* Anthony Veiller; *St: & Sc:* John Twist. (1:34) Following the days of the Civil War, an ex-Confederate guerrilla heads to Dallas, Texas, posing as a Yankee marshal to rid the town of its two-legged vermin. Technicolor. Note: B. Reeves "Breezy" Eason was second unit director on this film and it was his final production prior to his retirement—d. 1956.

593. The Dalton Girls (United Artists/ Bel-Air–Clark Prods., Inc.; 1957). *Cast:* Merry Anders, Penny Edwards, Lisa Davis, Sue George, John Russell, Ed Hinton, Glenn Dixon, Johnny Western, Malcolm Atterbury, Douglas Henderson, Boyd "Red" Morgan, Kevin Enright, Al Wyatt, H.E. Willmering, K.C. MacGregor, David Swapp. *D:* Reginald LeBorg; *Ex.P:* Aubrey Schenck; *P:* Howard W. Koch; *St:* Herbert Purdum; *Sc:* Maurice Tombragel. (1:11) Another Hollywood re-write of western historical facts, as the sisters of the Dalton brothers hit the outlaw trail after their male siblings fall victim to lawmen.

594. The Daltons' Women (Realart/ Howco-Western Adventures; 1950). *Cast:* Tom Neal, Pamela Blake, Jack Holt, Lash LaRue, Al St. John, Jacqueline Fontaine, Raymond Hatton, Lyle Talbot, Tom Tyler, J. Farrell MacDonald, Terry Frost, Stanley Price, Bud Osborne, Lee Bennett, Cliff Taylor, Buff Brown, Clarke Stevens, Jimmie Martin, Archie Twitchell [aka: Michael Branden]. *D:* Thomas Carr; *P:* Ron Ormond; *Sc:* Ormond, Maurice Tombragel. (1:20) A western town is besieged by a gang of outlaws, headed by the local saloonkeeper.

595. Damn Citizen! (Universal-International; 1957–58). *Cast:* Keith Andes, Maggie Hayes, Gene Evans, Lynn Bari, Jeffrey Stone, Clegg Hoyt, Ann Robinson, Edward C. Platt, Sam Buffington, Kendall Clark, Rusty Lane, Charles Horvath, Carolyn Kearney, Aaron M. Kohn (himself), Rev. J.D. Grey (himself), Richard R. Foster (himself), Pershing Gervais, Aaron A. Edgecombe, Rev. Robert H. Jamieson, Paul S. Hostetler, Nathaniel F. Oddo, Dudley C. Foley, Jr., Charles A. Murphy, George M. Trussell, Jack Dempsey, Frank Hay, Tiger Flowers, John Schowest. *D:* Robert Gordon; *P:* Herman Webber; *St: & Sc:* Stirling Silliphant. (1:28) Based on fact melodrama of World War II veteran Colonel Francis C. Grevemberg's (Andes), cleaning up corruption in the Louisiana State Police.

596. Damn Yankees (Warner/George Abbott-Stanley Donen; 1958). *Cast:* Tab Hunter (Joe Hardy), Gwen Verdon (Lola/final film—ret.), Ray Walston (Applegate), Russ Brown (Van Buren), Shannon Bolin (Meg Boyd), Nathaniel Frey (Smokey), Jimmy Komack (Rocky), Rae Allen (Gloria), Robert Shafer (Joe Boyd), Jean Stapleton (film debut/Sister), Albert Linville (Vernon), Bob Fosse (mambo dancer/who also choreographed with Pat Ferrier), Elizabeth Howell (Doris). *D: & P:* George Abbott (final film), Stanley Donen; *As.P:* Frederick Brisson, Robert Griffith, Harold Prince; *Sc:* Abbott; *Music:* (AAN) Ray Heindorf; *Songs:* "Six Months Out of Every Year," "Goodbye, Old Girl," "(You Gotta Have) Heart," "Shoeless Joe From Hannibal, Mo.," "Whatever Lola Wants," "A Little Brains, A Little Talent," "Those Were the Good Old Days," "Who's Got the Pain?" "Two Lost Souls," "The Game" and "There's Something About an Empty Chair" (written especially for the film) by Richard Adler and Jerry Ross. (1:50) (video/laserdisc) George Abbott's hit 1955 Broadway musical is successfully brought to the screen, utilizing the entire Broadway cast, with the exception of Hunter and Fosse. An aging ballplayer makes a deal with the devil (here called Mr. Applegate) to play for the Washington Senators, but gets more than he bargained for when Applegate also conjures up a seductress to lure him away from his wife. Based on the play by Abbott and Douglass Wallop and Wallop's novel *The Year the Yankees Lost the Pennant*, it took a #7 placement on the "10 Best" list of the *New York Times*. Technicolor. (G.B. title: *What Lola Wants*) Note: "A Man Doesn't Know" and "Near to You," two original songs from the show, were dropped from the film.

597. The Damned Don't Cry (Warner; 1950). *Cast:* Joan Crawford, David Brian, Steve Cochran, Kent Smith, Hugh Sanders, Selena Royle, Jacqueline de Wit, Morris Ankrum, Eddie Marr, Allan Smith, Tristram Coffin, Ned Glass, Dabbs Greer, Paul McGuire, Rory Mallinson, John Maxwell, Lyle Latell, Edith Evanson, Richard Egan (film debut), Sara Perry, Jimmy Moss. *D:* Vincent Sherman; *P:* Jerry Wald; *St:* Gertrude Walker; *Sc:* Harold Medford, Jerome Weidman. (1:43) Melodrama of a woman who thinks she can better her position in life by leaving her husband and taking up with a local hood.

597-A. Dance Hall Racket (Astor; 1953). *Cast:* Lenny Bruce, Honey Harlowe, Timothy Farrell, Sally Marr. *D:* Phil Tucker; *Sc:* Bruce. (1:00) (video) Independent crime melodrama of a tough hood and his crime lord boss. Definitely a '50s curio if for no other reason than the appearance of Bruce, his wife Honey Harlowe, a professional stripper, and his mother, Marr.

598. Dance with Me Henry (United Artists/Kiddyland; 1956). *Cast:* Bud Abbott (final film—ret.), Lou Costello, Ted de Corsia, Gigi Perreau, Rusty Hamer, Mary Wickes, Ron Hargrave, Sherry Alberoni, Frank Wilcox, Richard Reeves, Paul Sorenson, John Cliff, Robert Shayne, Phil Garris, Walter Reed, Eddie Marr, David McMahon, Gil Rankin, Rod Williams. *D:* Charles Barton; *P:* Bob Goldstein; *St:* William Kozlenko, Leslie Kardos; *Sc:* Devery Freeman. (1:19) (video) Two guys own an amusement park and adopt two kids, as well as getting involved with gangsters who have loot hidden somewhere in the park. Abbott and Costello's final film as a comedy team.

599. Danger Zone (Lippert/Spartan; 1951). *Cast:* Hugh Beaumont, Edward Brophy, Richard Travis, Tom Neal, Pamela Blake, Virginia Dale (final film—ret.), Ralph Sanford, Paula Drew, Jack Reitzen, Edward Clark, Richard Monahan, Don Garner. *D: & P:* William Berke; *Sc:* Julian Harmon (based on a radio play by Louis Morheim and Herbert Margolis). (0:56) Two separate stories featuring amateur detective Denny O'Brien (Beaumont) make up this mystery programmer.

600. Dangerous Crossing (20th Century-Fox; 1953). *Cast:* Jeanne Crain, Michael Rennie, Casey Adams [aka: Max Showalter], Carl Betz (film debut), Mary Anderson, Marjorie Hoshelle, Willis Bouchey, Yvonne Peattie, Karl Ludwig Lindt, Gayne Whitman, Anthony Jochim, Charles Tannen, Adrienne Marden, Harry Carter, Harry Seymour, Madge Blake. *D:* Joseph M. Newman; *P:* Robert Bassler; *Sc:* Leo Townsend (based on John Dickson Carr's radio play "Cabin B-16"). (1:15) In this mystery melodrama, Mr. and Mrs. Bowman set sail together on their honeymoon cruise. Shortly thereafter Mr. Bowman disappears and when Mrs. Bowman investigates, she finds that no one remembers seeing him. Remade in 1992 as the cable TV movie *Treacherous Crossing.*

Dangerous Inheritance (G.B. title) *see* **Girls' School**

601. Dangerous Mission (RKO; 1954). *Cast:* Victor Mature, Piper Laurie, Vincent Price, William Bendix, Betta St. John, Steve Darrell, Marlo Dwyer, Walter Reed, Dennis Weaver, Harry Cheshire, George Sherwood, Maureen Stephenson, Fritz Apking, Kem Dibbs, John Carlyle, Frank Griffin, Trevor Bardette, Roy Engel, Grace Hayle, Jim Potter, Mike Lally, Sam Shack, Craig Moreland, Ralph Volkie, Bert Moorhouse, Virginia Linden, Chet Marshall, Helen Brown, Chester Jones, Richard Newton, Bill White, Jr., Charles Cane, Jack Chefe, Steve Rowland, Russ Thorson, Robert Carraher. *D:* Louis King; *P:* Irwin Allen; *St:* Horace McCoy, James Edmiston; *Sc:* McCoy, W.R. Burnett, Charles Bennett. (1:15) (video) Mystery-melodrama of a girl who, after witnessing a gangland murder, flees to Glacier National Park with a cop and a killer in hot pursuit. In 3-D and Technicolor, Allen sets the stage for his later disaster flicks by including a forest fire and an avalanche on a hotel. Note: This viewer thinks the editing lacks continuity.

602. Dangerous When Wet (MGM; 1953). *Cast:* Esther Williams, Fernando Lamas, Jack Carson, Charlotte Greenwood, Denise Darcel, William Demarest, Donna Corcoran, Tom and Jerry (animated), Barbara Whiting, Bunny Waters, Henri Letondal, Paul Bryar, Jack Raine, Richard Alexander, Tudor Owen, Ann Codee, Michael Dugan, Roger Moore, Reginald Simpson, John McKee, Arthur Gould-Porter, Eugene Borden, James Fairfax, Aminta Dyne, Molly Glessing, Pat O'Moore, Jimmy Aubrey. *D:* Charles Walters; *P:* George Wells; *St: & Sc:* Dorothy Kingsley; *Songs:* "I Get Out Of Bed On the Right Side," "Ain't Nature Grand?", "I Like Men," "Fifi" and "In My Wildest Dreams" Arthur Schwartz, Johnny Mercer. (1:35) (video/laserdisc) Technicolor musical romance of a woman and her attempts to swim the English Channel.

603. Daniel Boone, Trail Blazer (Republic; 1956). *Cast:* Bruce Bennett (title role), Lon Chaney, Faron Young, Damian O'Flynn, Kem Dibbs, Jacqueline Evans (Rebecca Boone), Freddy Fernandez (Israel Boone), Nancy Rodman (Susannah Boone), Carol Kelly (Jemima Boone), Eduardo Noriega (Squire Boone), Claude Brooke, Fred Kohler, Jr., Lee Morgan, Gordon Mills, John Ainley. *D:* Albert C. Gannaway, Ismael Rodriguez; *P:* Gannaway; *Sc:* Tom Hubbard, John Patrick; *Songs:* Gannaway, Hal Levy. (1:16) (video) Historical frontier saga of Daniel Boone and party, leaving North Carolina to settle in Kentucky. Partially filmed in Mexico. Trucolor.

604. Darby O'Gill and the Little People (Buena Vista/Walt Disney Prods.; 1959). *Cast:* Albert Sharpe, Jane Munro (U.S. debut), Sean Connery (U.S. debut/ if one ignores *Another Time, Another Place* [q.v.], a British/U.S. co-production filmed in England), Jimmy O'Dea, Kieron Moore, Estelle Winwood, Walter Fitzgerald, Denis O'Dea, J.G. Devlin, Jack MacGowran, Farrell Pelly, Nora O'Mahoney. *D:* Robert Stevenson; *P:* Walt Disney; *Sc:* Lawrence E. Watkin; *Songs:* "The Wishing Song" and "Pretty Irish Girl" Oliver Wallace, Lawrence E. Watkin; *Animation:* Joshua Meador. (1:30) (video/laserdisc) Technicolor Disney fantasy (which had its earliest groundwork laid in the mid-1940s), suggested by the "Darby O'Gill" stories by H.T. Kavanagh. An elderly storyteller/caretaker to the governor's estate captures the wily leprechaun king and insists the little man grant him three wishes. In spite of a lot of pre-publicity and excellent special effects by Peter Ellenshaw and Eustace Lycett, this film became a major box office disappointment for Disney.

605. Darby's Rangers (Warner; 1958). *Cast:* James Garner, Etchika Choureau, Jack Warden, Edward [Edd] Byrnes, Venetia Stevenson, Torin Thatcher, Peter Brown, Corey Allen, Murray Hamilton, Stuart Whitman, David Janssen, Joan Elan, Andrea King, Bill Wellman, Jr., Adam Williams, Frieda Inescort, Reginald Owen, Philip Tonge, Edward Ashley, Raymond Bailey, Willis Bouchey. *D:* William A. Wellman; *P:* Martin Rackin; *Sc:* Guy Trosper. (2:01) (video) Popular World War II drama of an American commando unit in training in England, prior to seeing service in Europe and Africa. Romantic relief is also included, being based on the 1945 book by Major James Altieri. (G.B. title: *The Young Invaders*)

606. Dark City (Paramount; 1950). *Cast:* Charlton Heston (professional film debut), Lizabeth Scott, Viveca Lindfors, Dean Jagger, Jack Webb, Don DeFore, Henry [Harry] Morgan, Ed Begley, Mike Mazurki, Walter Sande, Mark Keuning, Stanley Prager, Walter Burke, Byron Foulger, Ralph Peters, Greta Granstedt, Stan Johnson, Otto Waldis, John Bishop, Sally Corner, Mike Mahoney, James Dundee, Dewey Robinson, Jeffrey Sayre, Bill Sheehan, Robin Camp, Jack Carroll, William J. Cartledge, Edward Rose, Fred Aldrich, Owen Tyree, Franz J. Roehn, Jay Morley, Mike P. Donovan. *D:* William Dieterle; *P:* Hal B. Wallis; *Adaptation:* Ketti Frings; *Sc:* Larry Marcus, John Meredyth Lucas; *Songs:* "If I Didn't Have You" (Harold Spina-Jack Elliott); "That Old Black Magic" (Harold Arlen–Johnny Mercer); "I Wish I Didn't Love You So" (Frank Loesser); "I'm in the Mood for Love" (Jimmy McHugh–Dorothy Fields) and "Letter from a Lady in Love." (1:28) (video) Melodrama of a bookie on the run from a psychotic gangster, out to do him in. Notable for being Heston's first Hollywood film. Based on the novel *No Escape* by Lawrence B. (Larry) Marcus.

The Dark Page (G.B. title) *see* **Scandal Sheet**

607. Dark Venture (First National Releasing; 1955–56). *Cast:* John [Calvert] Trevlac, John Carradine, Ann Cornell. *D: & Sc:* John Calvert. (1:21) Low budget independent African adventure of a man seeking a madman who is guarding an elephant's graveyard.

The Darkest Hour *see* **Hell on Frisco Bay**

608. Darling, How Could You? (Paramount; 1951). *Cast:* Joan Fontaine, John Lund, Mona Freeman, Peter Hanson, David Stollery, Gertrude Michael, Lowell Gilmore, Robert Barrat, Angela Clarke, Virginia Farmer, Mary Murphy, Allan Douglas, Frank Elliott, Billie Burke, Willard Waterman, John Bryant, Gordon Arnold, Dave Willock, Gloria Winters, Robin Hughes, Maureen Lynn Reimer, Patsy O'Byrne, Maria J. Tavares, Fred Zendar, Houseley Stevenson, William Meader, Jimmie Dundee, Charles Sherlock, Rudy Lee, Mickey Little, Kathryn Towne, Dolores Hall, Percy Helton, Robert E. Burns. *D:* Mitchell Leisen; *P:* Harry Tugend; *Sc:* Dodie Smith, Lesser Samuels. (1:36) This 19th century domestic comedy about a couple and their three children was a box office fizzle, being based on Sir James M. Barrie's play *Alice-Sit-by-the-Fire* (1919). (G.B. title: *Rendezvous*)

609. A Date with Death (Favorite Films/Pacific Intl.; 1959). *Cast:* Gerald Mohr, Liz Renay, Harry Lauter, Stephanie Farnay, Ed Erwin, Robert Clarke, Boyd "Red" Morgan, Lew Markman, Tony Redman, Frank Bellew, William Purdy, Ray Dearholt, Melford Lehrman, Ken[ne] Duncan. *D:* Harold Daniels; *P:* William S. Edwards; *Ex.P:* John Miller; *St: & Sc:* Robert C. Dennis. (1:21) Low budget crime-melodrama of a vagrant who assumes the identity of a murdered New York detective and becomes involved in cleaning up a crime syndicate. PsychoRama.

610. Daughter of Dr. Jekyll (Allied Artists/Film Venturers; 1957). *Cast:* John Agar, Gloria Talbott, Arthur Shields, John Dierkes, Martha Wentworth, Mollie McCart. *D:* Edgar

G. Ulmer; *P:-St: & Sc:* Jack Pollexfen. (1:07) (video) Low budget horror film of a girl who learns that her father was the infamous Dr. Jekyll. When a series of murders occur around town, guess who is suspect? It ran on the bottom of a double bill with *The Cyclops* (q.v.).

Daughter of Horror *see* **Dementia**

611. The Daughter of Rosie O'Grady (Warner; 1949–50). *Cast:* June Haver, Gordon MacRae (Tony Pastor), James Barton, Debbie Reynolds, S.Z. "Cuddles" Sakall, Gene Nelson, Jane Darwell, Sean McClory, Marsha Jones, Irene Seidman, Oscar O'Shea, Jack Lomas, Kendall Kopps, Virginia Lee. *D:* David Butler; *P:* William Jacobs; *St:* Jack Rose, Melville Shavelson; *Sc:* Rose, Shavelson, Peter Milne; *Songs include:* Title song (M.C. Bride–Walter Donaldson); "As We Are Today" (Charles Tobias-Ernesto Lecuona); "My Own True Love and I" (M.K. Jerome–Jack Scholl); "Ma Blushin' Rosie" (Edgar Smith–James Stromberg); "The Rose of Tralee" (Charles Glover); "A Farm Off Old Broadway," "A Picture Turned to the Wall," "Winter, Winter" (A. Bryan–Gumble) and "Winter Serenade" (Tobias–Lecuona). (1:44) Turn-of-the-century romantic musical-comedy which was a nice moneymaker for the brothers Warner. Technicolor.

612. David and Bathsheba (20th Century–Fox; 1951). *Cast:* Gregory Peck (David, the man), Susan Hayward (Bathsheba), Raymond Massey (Nathan), Kieron Moore (Uriah), James Robertson Justice (Abishai), Jayne Meadows (Michal), John Sutton (Ira), Dennis Hoey (Joab), Walter Talun (Goliath), Paula Morgan (adulteress), Francis X. Bushman (King Saul), Teddy Infuhr (Jonathan), Leo Pessin (David, the boy), Gwyneth [Gwen] Verdon (specialty dancer), Gilbert Barnett (Absalom), John Burton (priest), Lumsden Hare (old shepherd), George Zucco (final film—ret./Egyptian ambassador), Allan Stone (Amnon), Paul Newlan (Samuel), Holmes Herbert (Jesse), Robert Stephenson, Harry Carter, Richard Michelson, Dick Winters, John Duncan, James Craven. *D:* Henry King; *P:* Darryl F. Zanuck; *St: & Sc:* (AAN) Philip Dunne; *Cin:* (AAN-color) Leon Shamroy; *ASD:* (AAN-color) Lyle Wheeler, George Davis (art directors), Thomas Little, Paul S. Fox (sets); *Music:* (AAN) Alfred Newman; *Costumes:* (AAN-color) Charles LeMaire, Edward Stevenson. (1:56) (video/laserdisc) A lavishly produced Technicolor biblical epic which became one of the 23 top-grossing films of 1950-51.

613. David Harding, Counterspy (Columbia; 1950). *Cast:* Willard Parker, Howard St. John (title role), Audrey Long, Raymond Greenleaf, Harlan Warde, Alex Gerry, Fred F. Sears, John Dehner, Anthony Jochim, Jock Mahoney, John Pickard, Steve Darrell, Jimmy Lloyd, Charles Quigley, Allen Matthews. *D:* Ray Nazarro; *P:* Milton Feldman; *St: & Sc:* Clint Johnson, Tom Reed. (1:10) Espionage programmer of murder at a plant that produces torpedoes. Based on the *Counterspy* radio series created by Phillips H. Lord. The premiere entry in a short series of two films, it was originally paired on a double bill program with *Cow Town* (q.v.).

614. Davy Crockett and the River Pirates (Buena Vista; 1956). *Cast:* Fess Parker, Buddy Ebsen, Jeff York, Kenneth Tobey, Clem Bevans (final film—ret.), Irvin Ashkenazy, Mort Mills, Paul Newlan, Frank Richards, Walter Catlett, Douglass Dumbrille. *D:* Norman Foster; *Ex.P:* Walt Disney; *P:* Bill Walsh; *St: & Sc:* Thomas Blackburn, Foster; *Songs:* "Ballad of Davy Crockett" (revised lyrics), "King of the River" and "Yaller Yaller Gold" (George Bruns–Blackburn). (1:21) (video/laserdisc) A feature film for theatrical release which was fashioned from two episodes of *The Adventures of Davy Crockett*, the Disney TV show. Both being set around 1810, the first part tells of a keelboat race down the Mississippi River, blending into the second tale of whites pirating on the Ohio River disguised as Indians. Technicolor.

615. Davy Crockett, Indian Scout (United Artists/Edward Small Prods. Inc.; 1950). *Cast:* George Montgomery (title role), Ellen Drew, Philip Reed, Noah Beery, Jr., Robert Barrat, Paul Guilfoyle, Addison Richards, Erik Rolfe, William Wilkerson, John Hamilton, Vera Marshe, Chief Thundercloud, Ray Teal, Kenne Duncan, Jimmy Moss. *D:* Lew Landers; *P:* Edward Small; *St:* Ford Beebe; *Sc:* Richard Schayer. (1:11) A frontiersman, who is actually a nephew of the legendary frontiersman, and his Indian friend lead a wagon train to safety. The film has been retitled *Indian Scout.*

616. Davy Crockett, King of the Wild Frontier (Buena Vista; 1955). *Cast:* Fess Parker (title role), Buddy Ebsen, Basil Ruysdael (Andrew Jackson), Hans Conried, William Bakewell (final film appearance until 1975), Kenneth Tobey (Col. Jim Bowie), Pat Hogan, Helene Stanley (Polly Crockett), Nick Cravat, Don Megowan (Col. Bill Travis), Mike Mazurki, Jeff

Thompson, Henry Joyner, Benjamin Hornbuckle, Eugene Brindel, Ray Whitetree, Hal Youngblood, Jim Maddux, Robert Booth, Campbell Brown. *D:* Norman Foster; *Ex.P:* Walt Disney; *P:* Bill Walsh; *St: & Sc:* Tom Blackburn; *Songs:* "The Ballad of Davy Crockett" (Blackburn–George Bruns); "Farewell" (Bruns). (1:33) (video) Originally a three-part story on Walt Disney's Sunday night TV show, this theatrical feature was edited from them and released accordingly. The adventure story concerns Crockett's days as an Indian fighter, his dealings with the U.S. Government in Congress and his final days at the Alamo. Technicolor.

617. Dawn at Socorro (Universal-International; 1954). *Cast:* Rory Calhoun, Piper Laurie, David Brian, Kathleen Hughes, Alex Nicol, Edgar Buchanan, Skip Homeier, Mara Corday, Roy Roberts, Lee Van Cleef, James Millican, Stanley Andrews, Richard Garland, Paul Brinegar, Philo McCullough, Forrest Taylor. *D:* George Sherman; *P:* William Alland; *St: & Sc:* George Zuckerman. (1:20) Western of a gunfighter with a desire to reform. Technicolor.

Dawn Comes Late (G.B. title) *see* **Guerrilla Girl**

618. A Day of Fury (Universal-International; 1956). *Cast:* Dale Robertson, Mara Corday, Jock Mahoney, Carl Benton Reid, Jan Merlin, John Dehner, Dee Carroll, Sheila Bromley, James Bell, Dani Crayne, Dayton Lummis, Howard Wendell, Charles Cane, Phil Chambers, Sydney Mason, Helen Kleeb, Harry Tyler. *D:* Harmon Jones; *P:* Robert Arthur; *St:* James Edmiston; *Sc:* Edmiston, Oscar Brodney. (1:18) Offbeat western drama of a man unable to come to grips with changes taking place in his town. Technicolor.

619. Day of the Bad Man (Universal-International; 1957–58). *Cast:* Fred MacMurray, Joan Weldon, John Ericson, Marie Windsor, Edgar Buchanan, Robert Middleton, Skip Homeier, Eduard Franz, Peggy Converse, Robert Foulk, Ann Doran, Lee Van Cleef, Eddy Waller, Christopher Dark, Don Haggerty, Chris Alcaide. *D:* Harry Keller; *P:* Gordon Kay; *Sc:* Lawrence Roman. (1:21) A small western town is turned upside down with its citizens terrorized by four men bent on seeing that a jailed relative isn't hanged. Based on *Raiders Die Hard* by John M. Cunningham. Eastmancolor and CinemaScope.

620. Day of the Outlaw (United Artists/Security Pictures, Inc.; 1959). *Cast:* Robert Ryan, Burl Ives, Tina Louise, Alan Marshal (final film—d. 1961), Nehemiah Persoff, David Nelson, Venetia Stevenson, Donald Elson, Helen Westcott, Robert Cornthwaite, Jack Lambert, Frank DeKova, Lance Fuller, Paul Wexler, Jack Woody, DeForest Kelley, Elisha Cook, Jr., William Schallert, Michael McGreevey, Dan Sheridan, Arthur Space, Betsy Jones Moreland, George Ross. *D:* Andre De Toth; *P:* Sidney Harmon; *Sc:* Philip Yordan. (1:31) An isolated town in the hills of Wyoming suddenly finds itself taken over by a band of six outlaws. Based on the 1955 novel by Lee Wells.

621. Day of Triumph (Century Films, Inc.; 1954). *Cast:* Lee J. Cobb (Zadok), Robert Wilson (Jesus Christ), Ralph Freud (Caiaphas), Tyler McVey (Peter), Touch [Mike] Connors (Andrew), Toni Gerry (Cloas), Joanne Dru (Mary Magdalene), James Griffith (Judas), Everett Glass (Annas), Lowell Gilmore (Pilate), Anthony Warde (Barabbas), Peter Whitney (Nikator), John Stevenson. *D:* Irving Pichel (final film—d. 1954), John T. Coyle; *P:* James K. Friedrich; *As.P:* Spencer H. Lees; *St:* & Sc: Arthur T. Horman. (1:50) (video) The biblical story of the Crucifixion and Resurrection of Jesus Christ, told in a straightforward style. Eastmancolor.

622. The Day the Earth Stood Still (20th Century–Fox; 1951). *Cast:* Michael Rennie, Patricia Neal, Hugh Marlowe, Sam Jaffe, Billy Gray, Frances Bavier, Lock Martin, Drew Pearson (himself), Frank Conroy, Carleton Young, Fay Roope, Edith Evanson, Robert Osterloh, Tyler McVey, James Seay, John Brown, Marjorie Crossland, Glenn Hardy, House Peters, Jr., H.V. Kaltenborn (himself), Elmer Davis (himself), Rush Williams, Olan Soule, Gil Herman, James Craven, Harry Lauter, Wheaton Chambers, Dorothy Neumann, George Lynn, Freeman Lusk, John Burton, George Reeves, Harry Harvey, Stuart Whitman. *D:* Robert Wise; *P:* Julian Blaustein; *Sc:* Edmund H. North. (1:32) (video/laserdisc) Acclaimed classic science fiction of an alien (Rennie) who arrives on earth with his guardian robot, Gort (Martin), and a warning from other civilizations in the universe that continued use of atomic power will endanger the earth's very existence. Based on *Farewell to the Master* by Harry Bates. Note: "Klaatu barada nikto" has become a classic catch phrase among aficionados of this film.

623. The Day The World Ended (American Releasing/Golden State Prods.; 1956). *Cast:* Richard Denning, Lori Nelson, Adele Jergens, Paul Birch, Touch [Mike] Connors, Raymond Hatton, Paul Dubov, Jonathan Haze, Paul Blaisdell (mutant + makeup). *D: & P:* Roger Corman; *St: & Sc:* Lou Rusoff. (1:22) (video) Notable as Roger Corman's first science fiction film as director, it relates the conflicting personalities of the seven survivors of a nuclear catastrophe which has obliterated the rest of the world's population, as well as their attempts at survival against cannibalistic mutants. Remade as *In the Year 2889* (1966). SuperScope. Originally ran on a double bill with *The Phantom From 10,000 Leagues* (q.v.).

The Day They Gave Babies Away (G.B. title) *see* **All Mine to Give**

624. Dead Man's Trail (Monogram/Frontier Pictures; 1952). *Cast:* Johnny Mack Brown, James Ellison (final film—ret.), Barbara Allen, I. Stanford Jolley, Terry Frost, Lane Bradford, Gregg Barton, Richard Avonde, Dale Van Sickel, Stanley Price. *D:* Lewis Collins; *P:* Vincent M. Fennelly; *Sc:* Joseph Poland, Melville Shyer. (0:59) Series western involving the murder of an escaped convict.

The Dead That Walk (G.B. title) *see* **Zombies of Mora Tau**

Deadline (G.B. title) *see* **Deadline—U.S.A.**

Deadline Midnight (G.B. title) *see* **-30-**

625. Deadline—U.S.A. (20th Century-Fox; 1952). *Cast:* Humphrey Bogart, Ethel Barrymore, Kim Hunter, Ed Begley, Warren Stevens, Paul Stewart, Martin Gabel, Joseph De Santis, Joyce MacKenzie, Audrey Christie, Fay Baker, Jim Backus, Carleton Young, Selmer Jackson, Fay Roope, Parley Baer, Bette Francine, John Doucette, June Eisner, Richard Monohan, Harry Tyler, Joseph Sawyer, Florence Shirley, Kasia Orzazewski, Raymond Greenleaf, Irene Vernon, Alex Gerry, William Forrest, Edward Keane, Clancy Cooper, Tom Powers, Thomas B. Henry, Ashley Cowan, Howard Negley, Phil Terry, Joe Mell, Luther Crockett, Joseph Crehan, Ann McCrea, Larry Dobkin, Everett Glass, Willis Bouchey, Tudor Owen, Paul Dubov, Harris Brown. *D:-St: & Sc:* Richard Brooks; *P:* Sol C. Siegel. (1:27) (video) Acclaimed drama of a newspaper and the efforts of the editor and others to keep the paper solvent despite financial difficulties.

626. The Deadly Mantis (Universal-International; 1957). *Cast:* Craig Stevens, William Hopper, Alix Talton, Donald Randolph, Pat Conway, Florenz Ames, Paul Smith, Phil Harvey, Paul Campbell, Jack Mather, George Lynn, Skipper McNally, Harold Lee, Floyd Simmons, Helen Jay. *D:* Nathan Juran; *P: & St:* William Alland; *Sc:* Martin Berkeley; *F/X:* Fred Knoth. (1:18) (video) A giant praying mantis, frozen in a polar icecap, is released on civilization following an earthquake to wreak havoc on Washington, D.C., and New York City. (aka: *The Incredible Praying Mantis* and *Third Party Risk*)

627. Dear Brat (Paramount; 1951). *Cast:* Mona Freeman, Edward Arnold, Billy DeWolfe, Lyle Bettger, Mary Phillips, Natalie Wood, William Reynolds, Frank Cady, Lillian Randolph, Irene Winston, Patty Lou Arden. *D:* William A. Seiter; *P:* Mel Epstein; *St: & Sc:* Devery Freeman (based on characters created by Norman Krasna). (1:22) Comedy of a girl causing upset in her family when she befriends a criminal trying to reform. The third film in a short series, following *Dear Ruth* (1947) and *Dear Wife* (1949).

628. Death in Small Doses (Allied Artists; 1957). *Cast:* Peter Graves, Mala Powers, Chuck Connors, Merry Anders, Roy Engel, Robert B. Williams, Harry Lauter, Pete Kooy, Robert Christopher. *D:* Joseph Newman; *P:* Richard Heermance; *Sc:* John McGreevey. (1:18) Truckers are wrecking their rigs while hopped-up on bennies (benzedrine) and a government man investigates to nail the suppliers. A low budget melodrama based on a factual magazine article by Arthur L. Davis which appeared in *Saturday Evening Post*. Originally the bottom of a double bill with *The Badge of Marshal Brennan* (q.v.).

629. Death of a Salesman (Columbia/Stanley Kramer Co.; 1951). *Cast:* Frederic March (AAN/Willy Loman), Mildred Dunnock (AAN-BSA/repeating her Broadway role as Linda Loman), Kevin McCarthy (AAN-film debut/repeating his London stage role as Biff), Cameron Mitchell (repeating his Broadway role as Happy), Howard Smith (repeating his Broadway role as Charley), Royal Beal (Ben), Don Keefer (Bernard), Jesse White (Stanley), Claire Carleton (Miss Francis), David Alpert (Howard Wagner), Elisabeth Fraser (Miss Forsythe), Patricia Walker (Letta), Gail Bonney, Roger Broaddus, Beverly Aadland, Wanda Perry,

Christa Gail Walker, Jeanne Bates, Paul Bryar. *D:* Laslo Benedek; *P:* Stanley Kramer; *Sc:* Stanley Roberts; *Cin:* (AAN) Frank Planer; *Music:* (AAN) Alex North. (1:55) Critically acclaimed drama based on the 1949 Arthur Miller play of a salesman, pondering his life, which he considers a failure. The NBR, *Film Daily* and the *New York Times* placed it at #4, #7, and #9 respectively on their "10 Best" lists. The Berlin Film Festival gave it a #7 placement while the Venice Film Festival awarded Mr. March "Best Actor" honors. The British Academy Awards had it in nomination and the New York Film Critics had it in nomination for "Best Film." Remade in 1985 as a TV movie.

630. Death of a Scoundrel (RKO/Charles Martin Prods.; 1956). *Cast:* George Sanders, Yvonne De Carlo, Zsa Zsa Gabor, Victor Jory, Nancy Gates, Coleen Gray, John Hoyt, Lisa Ferraday, Tom Conway, Celia Lovsky, Werner Klemperer, Justice Watson, John Sutton, Curtis Cooksey, Gabriel Curtiz, Morris Ankrum, George Brent (in his final film appearance until 1978), Robert Morgan, Jewel Lane. *D:-P:-St: & Sc:* Charles Smith. (1:59) (video/laserdisc) Drama, telling in flashback, the events and incidents in the life of the "ultimate" low-life, which led to his final comeuppance. Purported to be based on real-life con artist Serge Rubenstein, who was found murdered in his New York apartment in 1955.

631. Decision at Sundown (Columbia/Producers Actors Prod.; 1957). *Cast:* Randolph Scott, Karen Steele, John Carroll, Valerie French, John Archer, Noah Beery, Jr., Andrew Duggan, Ray Teal, John Litel, Vaughn Taylor, Richard Deacon, H.M. Wynant, Guy Wilkerson, James Westerfield, Bob Steele, Abel Fernandez, Reed Howes, Jim Hayward. *D:* Budd Boetticher; *P:* Randolph Scott, Harry Joe Brown; *Sc:* Charles Lang, Jr. (1:17) (video) When his wife commits suicide, a gunman goes after the man he considers responsible. A Technicolor western based on the book by Vernon I. Fluharty (a pseudonym of Michael Carder).

632. Decision Before Dawn (20th Century–Fox; 1951). *Cast:* Richard Basehart (Lt. Rennick), Gary Merrill (Col. Devlin), Oskar Werner (Happy), Hildegarde Neff (Hilde), Dominique Blanchar (Monique), O.E. Hasse (Oberst Von Ecker), Wilfried Seyfert (Scholtz-S.S. man), Hans Christian Blech (Tiger), Helene Thimig (Fraulein Schnider), Robert Freytag (Paul), George Tyne (Sgt. Watkins), Adolph Lodel (Kurt), Arno Assman (Ernst), Loni Heuser (Fritzi), Walter Janssen (Fiedl), Erich Ebert (Freddy), Ruth Brandt, Liselotte Kirschbaum, Eva Marie Andres, Aguste Hansen-Kleinmichel, Martin Urtel, Otto Friebel, Paul Schwed, Meta Weber, Henriett Speidel, Ingeborg Luther, Almut Bachmann, Ruth Trumpp, Egon Lippert, Gerhard Kittler, Rainier Geldern, Klaus Kinski, Von Schmidel, Arnulf Schroder, Bert Brandt, Erich Jelde, Max Herbst, Klaus Krause, Alex Hohenlohe, Clemens Wildemrod, Jasper Gertzen, Ulrich Volkmar, Hans Mohrhard, Kurt Marquardt, Jochen Diestelmann, Luitpold Kummer, Heinrich Berg, Dieter Wilsing, Elfe Gearhart, Rudolph Heimann, Werner Fuetterer, Liesolotte Steinwig, Elizabeth Millberg, Ulla Best, Katja Jobs, Eva Maria Hoppe, Maria Landrock, Sonja Kosta, Ernst Hoechstaetter, Harold Wolff, Wolfgang Kuhnemann, Walter Ladengast, Gerhard Steinberg, Peter Luhr, Maria Wimmer, Ursula Voss. *D:* Anatole Litvak; *P:* (AAN-Best Picture) Litvak, Frank McCarthy; *Sc:* Peter Viertel; *Editor:* (AAN) Dorothy Spencer. (1:59) World War II espionage story of a German P.O.W. who agrees to become a spy for his American captors. Based on *Call It Treason* (1949) by George Locke Howe, it placed #7 on the "10 Best" list of the NBR, while on the same list of the *New York Times* it took a #10 placement. One of the 23 top-grossing films of 1951-52.

633. The Decks Ran Red (MGM/Virginia & Andrew Stone Prod.; 1958). *Cast:* James Mason, Dorothy Dandridge, Broderick Crawford, Stuart Whitman, Katharine Bard, Jack Kruschen, David R. Cross, Joel Fluellen, John Gallaudet, Hank Patterson, Harry Bartell, Guy Kingsford, Jonathan Hole, Harlan Warde, Joel Marston, Ed Hinton, Marshall Kent, Robert Christopher, Art Lewis. *D: & Sc:* Andrew L. Stone; *P:* Andrew L. and Virginia Stone (the latter who also edited and wrote the music score). (1:24) Drama of two crewmen on a freighter who mutiny in an attempt to sell their ship for half a million dollars in salvage. This film had the working title of "Terror at Sea."

634. Deep in My Heart (MGM; 1954). *Cast:* Jose Ferrer (Sigmund Romberg), Merle Oberon, Helen Traubel, Doe Avedon, Tamara Toumanova, Paul Stewart, Douglas Fowley, Jim Backus, Walter Pidgeon, Paul Henreid (Florenz Ziegfeld), Isobel Elsom, James Mitchell, Rosemary Clooney (final film), Gene Kelly, Fred Kelly [brother to Gene/for those of you who never knew he had a brother—their only appearance on film together], Jane Powell, Vic Damone, Ann Miller, Cyd Charisse, Howard Keel, Tony Martin, William Olvis, David Burns, Russ Tamblyn, Joan Weldon, Robert Easton, Suzanne Luckey, Ludwig Stossel, Else Neft, Norbert Schiller, Torben Meyer, Reuben Wendorff, Franz Roehn, Laiola Wendorff, Henri Letondal, Lane Nakano, John Alvin, Jean Vander Pyl, Mary Alan Hokanson, Maudie Prickett, Henry Sylvester, Bob Carson, Robert Watson, Marjorie Liszt, Gail Bonney, Jean Dante, Dulce Daye, Margaret Bacon, Gloria Moore, Lulumae Bohrman, Tailor Boswell, Richard Beavers, Gordon Wynne, Mitchell Kowal (Oscar Hammerstein), Joe Roach, Dee Turnell. *D:* Stanley Donen; *P:* Roger Edens; *Sc:* Leonard Spigelgass; *Songs:* "One Alone," "The Desert Song," "Lover Come Back to Me," "Softly, as in a Morning Sunrise," "When I Grow Too Old to Dream," "Goodbye Girls," "Mr. and Mrs.," "Fat, Fat Fatima," "Jazza, Jazza, Doo, Do," "Serenade," "Will You Remember," "Miss U.S.A.," "Leg of Mutton," "Stout-hearted Men," "Road to Paradise," "One Kiss," "Auf Wiedersehen," "Your Land and My Land" and "It." (2:12) (video/laserdisc) Sigmund Romberg, songwriter of many of Broadway's famous operettas, is the focus of this filmed bio-pic with production numbers of his famous works stealing the show. Based on the 1949 book by Elliott Arnold, it showed good returns at the box office. Eastmancolor.

635. The Deep Six (Warner/Jaguar-Alan Ladd Enterprises; 1958). *Cast:* Alan Ladd, Dianne Foster, William Bendix, Keenan Wynn, James Whitmore, Efrem Zimbalist, Jr., Joey Bishop (film debut), Barbara Eiler, Ross Bagdasarian, Walter Reed, Jeanette Nolan, Peter Hansen, Richard Crane, Morris Miller, Perry Lopez, Warren Douglas, Nestor Paiva, Robert Whiteside, Robert Clarke, Carol Lee Ladd, Ann Doran, Jerry Mathers, Franz Roehn and officers and men of the *U.S.S. Stephen Potter*. *D:* Rudolph Maté; *P:* Martin Rackin; *Sc:* John Twist, Rackin, Harry Brown. (1:45) (video) World War II drama of a Quaker gunnery officer whose pacifist beliefs conflict with his present life situation. Based on the 1953 novel by Martin Dibner. WarnerColor.

636. The Deerslayer (20th Century–Fox/Regal Films; 1957). *Cast:* Lex Barker, Forrest Tucker, Cathy O'Donnell, Rita Moreno, Jay C. Flippen, Carlos Rivas, John Halloran, Joseph Vitale, Rocky Shahan, Carol Henry, Phil Schumacker, George Robotham. *D: & P:* Kurt Neumann; *Sc:* Carroll Young, Neumann. (1:17) Frontier adventure, close to James Fenimore Cooper's 1841 novel *Deerslayer*, of a scalp hunter living at an isolated island fort with his two daughters, who has the local Indians in an uproar. A white frontiersman and his Indian blood brother try to smooth things out. Previous versions of the story: Vitagraph, 1913; (Germany, 1920; Selznick, 1923; and a 1943 independent production released through Republic. Another version appeared in 1978 as a TV movie. DeLuxe color and Regalscope.

637. The Defiant Ones (United Artists/Lomitas Prod., Inc.–Curtleigh Prod., Inc.; 1958). *Cast:* Tony Curtis (AAN/John "Joker" Jackson), Sidney Poitier (AAN + a nomination for "Best Actor" at the British Academy Awards + "Best Actor" at the Berlin Film Festival/Noah Cullen), Theodore Bikel (AAN/Sheriff Max Muller), Charles McGraw (Capt. Frank Gibbons), Lon Chaney (Big Sam), King Donovan (Solly), Claude Akins (Mac), Lawrence Dobkin (editor), Whit Bissell (Lou Gans), Carl Switzer (final film—d. 1959/Angus), Kevin Coughlin (the kid), Cara Williams (AAN/the woman), Boyd "Red" Morgan (Joe), Robert Hoy (Wilson), Don Brodie (state trooper). *D:* (AAN + "Best Director" by the New York Film Critics) Stanley Kramer; *P:* (AAN-Best Picture) Kramer; *Sc:* (AA + "Best Screenplay" by the New York Film Critics) to Harold Jacob Smith & Nathan E. Douglas [the latter a pseudonym of black-listed screenwriter-actor Nedrick Young]; *Cin:* (AA-b/w) Sam Leavitt; *Editor:* (AAN) Frederic Knudtson. (1:37) (video/laserdisc) Critically acclaimed drama of two convicts—one black, the other white—escaping through a Southern swamp while shackled together. Voted "Best Film of the Year" by the New York Film Critics, it also placed #5 and #6 respectively on the "10 Best" lists of *Film Daily* and the *New York Times*. It was also in nomination at the British Academy Awards and Tony Curtis received the *Photoplay* Gold Medal Award. One of the 26 top-grossing films of 1958-59, it was remade in 1986 as a TV movie. Filmed on location in Georgia. Note: Carl "Alfalfa" Switzer was shot to death at the age of 32 years in January 1959, over an argument about a $50 bet. His death was ruled "justifiable homicide."

638. The Delicate Delinquent (Paramount/York Pictures; 1957). *Cast:* Jerry Lewis (Sidney Pythias), Martha Hyer (Martha), Darren McGavin (Mike Damon), Horace McMahon (Capt. Riley), Milton Frome (Mr. Herman), Robert Ivers (Monk), Richard Bakalyan (Artie),

Joseph Corey (Harry), Mary Webster (Patricia), Jefferson Searles (Mr. Crow), Rocky Marciano (himself), Emory Parnell (Sgt. Levitch), Emile Meyer (Kelly), Dave Willock (Cadet Goerner), Mike Ross (police sergeant), Don Megowan, Irene Winston, Teru Shimada, Kazuo Togo, Don McGuire, Taggart Casey. *D: & Sc:* Don McGuire; *P:* Jerry Lewis. (1:40) (video/laserdisc) Slapstick and drama in the first solo effort for Jerry Lewis after splitting with former partner, Dean Martin. With help from a seasoned officer, a youth becomes a rookie cop after being dragged in with a bunch of delinquent hoodlums. One of the 24 top-grossing films of 1956-57, it was based on Mr. McGuire's original, *Damon and Pythias*. VistaVision.

639. The Delinquents (United Artists/Imperial Prod., Inc.; 1957). *Cast:* Tom Laughlin, Peter Miller, Richard Bakalyan, Rosemary Howard, Helene Hawley, Leonard Belove, Lotus Corelli, James Lantz, Christine Altman, George Kuhn, Pat Stedman, Norman Zands, James Leria, Jet Pinkston, Kermit Echols, Joe Adelman. *D:-P: & Sc:* Robert Altman (feature debut). (1:14) Teen exploitation-melodrama directed at the double bill drive-in movie crowd. A youth is drawn into a gang of delinquents because his girl's father won't let her go steady! Filmed on location in Kansas City.

640. Dementia (API/Rizzoli Film-van Wolfe; 1955). *Cast:* Adrienne Barrett, Bruno VeSota, Ben Roseman, Richard Barron, Ed Hinkle, Lucille Howland, Jebbie VeSota, Faith Parker, Gayne Sullivan, Ed McMahon (narrator). *D:-P:-St: & Sc:* John Parker. (0:55) (video) Offbeat horror-melodrama of a woman who pushes a man from a balcony to his death when he attempts to sexually assault her. Afterward she attempts to deal with what happened, sorting out whether it was real or just a dream. Banned by the New York censors in 1955. (aka: *Daughter of Horror*)

641. Demetrius and the Gladiators (20th Century–Fox; 1954). *Cast:* Victor Mature (Demetrius), Susan Hayward (Messalina), Michael Rennie (Peter), Debra Paget (Lucia), Anne Bancroft (Paula), Jay Robinson (Caligula), Barry Jones (Claudius), William Marshall (black actor/Glycon), Richard Egan (Dardanius), Ernest Borgnine (Strabo), Charles Evans (Cassius Chaerea), Everett Glass (Kaeso), Karl Davis (Macro), Jeff York (Albus), John Cliff (Varus), Barbara James & Willetta Smith (specialty dancers), Fred Graham (Decurion), Selmer Jackson, Carmen de Lavallade, Douglas Brooks, Dayton Lummis, George Eldredge, Paul Richards, Ray Spiker, Gilbert Perkins, Woody Strode, Paul Stader, Jim Winkler, Lyle Fox, Dick Sands, Paul "Tiny" Newlan, Allan Kramer, Paul Kruger, George Bruggeman, William Forrest, Jack Finlay, Peter Mamakos, Shepard Menken, Harry Cording, Satin (tiger/won PATSY 1955 Award of Excellence), Richard Burton & Jean Simmons (flashback clip from *The Robe*). *D:* Delmer Daves; *P:* Frank Ross; *Sc:* Philip Dunne (based on characters created by Lloyd C. Douglas in *The Robe*). (1:41) (video/laserdisc) Drama set in the early days of Christianity with the trials and tribulations of the slave, Demetrius, who came into possession of the robe worn by Jesus prior to his crucifixion. A sequel to *The Robe* (q.v.), it became one of the 25 top-grossing films of 1953-54. Technicolor and CinemaScope.

642. The Denver and the Rio Grande (Paramount; 1952). *Cast:* Edmond O'Brien, Sterling Hayden, Dean Jagger, Laura Elliot, Lyle Bettger, J. Carrol Naish, ZaSu Pitts, Tom Powers, Robert Barrat, Paul Fix, Don Haggerty, James Burke. *D:* Byron Haskin; *P:* Nat Holt; *St: & Sc:* Frank Gruber. (1:29) (video) Western, with a climactic train wreck, of railroad builders rivaling each other while they battle the elements in an effort to link up the west. Technicolor.

643. Deported (Universal-International; 1950). *Cast:* Jeff Chandler, Marta Toren, Claude Dauphin, Marina Berti, Silvio Minciotti, Carlo Rizzo, Mimi Aguglia, Adriano Ambrogi, Richard Rober, Michael Tor, Erminio Spalia, Dino Nardi, Guido Celano, Tito Vuolo. *D:* Robert Siodmak; *P:* Robert H. Buckner; *St:* Lionel Shapiro; *Sc:* Buckner. (1:20) Drama of an Italian-born American gangster who is deported to his homeland. Filmed in Italy.

644. Desert Desperadoes (RKO/Venturini–Express–Nasht; 1959). *Cast:* Ruth Roman, Akim Tamiroff, Othelo Toso, Gianni Glori, Arnoldo Foa, Alan Furlan, Nino Marchetti. *D:* Steve Sekely; *P:* John Nasht; *St: & Sc:* Victor Stoloff, Robert Hill. (1:21) Low budget costume-drama of a rich merchant and a Roman soldier who fall for a woman they find stranded in the desert. Filmed on locations in Italy and Egypt. (retitled: *The Sinner*)

645. The Desert Fox (20th Century–Fox; 1951). *Cast:* James Mason (Erwin Rommel),

Cedric Hardwicke (Dr. Karl Strolin), Jessica Tandy (Frau Rommel), Luther Adler (Hitler), Everett Sloane (Gen. Burgdorf), Leo G. Carroll (Field Marshal Von Rundstedt), George Macready (Gen. Fritz Bayerlein), Eduard Franz (Col. Von Stauffenberg), Desmond Young (himself/voice supplied by Michael Rennie), William Reynolds (Manfred Rommel), Charles Evans (Gen. Schultz), Richard Boone (Aldinger), Walter Kingsford (Admiral Ruge), John Hoyt (Keitel), Don De Leo (Gen. Maisel), Richard Elmore, John Vosper, Dan O'Herlihy, Scott Forbes, Victor Wood, Lester Matthews, Mary Carroll, Paul Cavanagh, Jack Baston, Carleton Young, Freeman Lusk, Robert Coote, Sean McClory, Lumsden Hare, John Goldsworthy, Ivan Triesault, Trevor Ward, Philip Van Zandt. *D:* Henry Hathaway; *P: & Sc:* Nunnally Johnson. (1:28) (video/laserdisc) Critically acclaimed war drama of Hitler's Field Marshal Erwin Rommel, his personal life and the Nazi campaign in North Africa. Based on *Rommel—The Desert Fox*, a 1950 biography by Desmond Young. (G.B. title: *Rommel—Desert Fox*)

646. The Desert Hawk (Universal-International; 1950). *Cast:* Yvonne De Carlo, Richard Greene, Jackie Gleason, George Macready, Rock Hudson, Joe Besser, Carl Esmond, Ann Pearce, Lois Andrews, Marc Lawrence, Frank Puglia, Lucille Barkley, Donald Randolph, Ian MacDonald, Nestor Paiva, Richard Hale, Mahmud Shaikhaly, Buddy Roosevelt, Terry Frost, Jack Raymond, Virginia Hunter, Lester Sharpe, Ben Welden, Michael Ross, George Bruggeman, Fred Libby, Michael Ansara, Jan Arvan, Milton Kibbee, Frank Lackteen, Dale Van Sickel, Chet Brandenberg, Vic Romito, Eileen Howe, Hazel Shaw, Norma De Landa, Marian Dennish, Barbara Kelly, Vonne Lester, Lane Bradford, Shirley Ballard, Bob Anderson, Robert Filmer, Bob Wilke, Bruce Riley, Louis A. Nicoletti, Wally Walker, Mike Portanova, Wilson Millar, Phil Barnes, Frank Malet, Wendy Waldron, Harold Cornsweet, Lucille Barnes. *D:* Frederick de Cordova; *P:* Leonard Goldstein; *St:* Aubrey Wisberg, Jack Pollexfen; *Sc:* Gerald Drayson Adams. (1:17) Technicolor Arabian Nights style action-adventure of a blacksmith who butts heads with a nefarious ruler.

647. Desert Hell (20th Century–Fox/Regal Films–Emirau Prods.; 1958). *Cast:* Brian Keith, Barbara Hale, Richard Denning, Johnny Desmond, Philip Pine, Richard Shannon, Duane Grey, Charles Gray, Lud Veigel, Richard Gilden, Ronald Foster, Patrick O'Moore, John Verros, Bill Hamel, Roger Etienne, Felix Locher, Michael Pate, Ben Wright, Albert Carrier, Bhogwan Singh. *D:-Ex.P: & St:* Charles Marquis Warren; *P:* Robert Stabler; *Sc:* Endre Bohem. (1:22) Action-adventure with the French Foreign Legion trying to quell an uprising by an Arab tribe of Tauregs. Regalscope.

648. Desert Legion (Universal-International; 1953). *Cast:* Alan Ladd, Arlene Dahl, Richard Conte, Akim Tamiroff, Leon Askin, Oscar Beregi, Anthony Caruso, George J. Lewis, Sujata and Asoka (specialty dancers), Henri Letondal, Peter Coe, Ivan Triesault, Don Blackman, Dave Sharpe, Ted Hecht, Pat Lane, Elsa Edsman. *D:* Joseph Pevney; *P:* Ted Richmond; *Sc:* Irving Wallace, Lewis Meltzer. (1:25) Technicolor adventure of a French Foreign Legionnaire, the sole survivor of his company's massacre, who finds himself in a lost city where life is utopian. Based on the 1927 novel *The Demon Caravan* by Georges Arthur Surdez.

649. Desert of Lost Men (Republic; 1951). *Cast:* Allan Lane, Mary Ellen Kay, Irving Bacon, Roy Barcroft, Ross Elliott, Cliff Clark, Boyd "Red" Morgan, Kenneth MacDonald, Leo Cleary, Steve Pendleton, Herman Hack, Black Jack (horse). *D: & P:* Harry Keller; *St: & Sc:* M. Coates Webster. (0:54) Deputy marshal Rocky Lane is on the trail of an outlaw gang made up of well known wanted men from different areas of the west.

650. Desert Passage (RKO; 1952). *Cast:* Tim Holt, Richard Martin, Joan Dixon, Walter Reed, Clayton Moore, Dorothy Patrick, John Dehner, Lane Bradford, Denver Pyle, Francis McDonald, Michael Mark. *D:* Lesley Selander; *P:* Herman Schlom; *St: & Sc:* Norman Houston. (1:02) (video) A prison parolee goes in search of stolen bank loot. The final series western done by Holt for RKO.

Desert Patrol (G.B. title) *see* **El Alamein**

651. Desert Pursuit (Monogram; 1952). *Cast:* Wayne Morris, Virginia Grey, Anthony Caruso, George Tobias, Emmett Lynn, Gloria Talbott, John Doucette, Frank Lackteen, Robert Bice, Billy Wilkerson. *D:* George Blair; *P:* Lindsley Parsons; *Sc:* W. Scott Darling. (1:11) Offbeat western of a man and woman fleeing across Death Valley from three camel mounted Arabs intent on getting the gold they are carrying. Based on the 1937 novel *Desert Voices* by Kenneth Perkins.

652. The Desert Rats (20th Century-Fox/Panoramic; 1953). *Cast:* Richard Burton (Capt. MacRoberts), Robert Newton (Bartlett), Robert Douglas (General), Torin Thatcher (Barney), Chips Rafferty (Smith), Charles Tingwell (Lt. Carstairs), James Mason (voted "Best Actor" by the NBR combined with his performances in *Face to Face* [q.v.], *A Man Between* [British] and *Julius Caesar* [q.v.], repeating his role of Erwin Rommel in *The Desert Fox*-[q.v.], Charles Davis (Pete), Ben Wright (Mick), James Lilburn (Communications), Ray Harden (Hugh), John O'Malley (Riley), Richard Peel (Rusty), John Alderson (Corporal), Michael Pate (Capt. Currie), Frank Pulaski (Maj. O'Rourke), Charles Keane (Sgt. Donaldson), Pat O'Moore (Jim), Trevor Constable (Ginger), Albert Taylor (Jensen), Arno Frey (Kramm), Alfred Zeisler (Von Helmholtz), John Wengraff, Charles Fitzsimmons. *D:* Robert Wise; *P:* Robert L. Jacks; *St: & Sc:* (AAN) Richard Murphy. (1:28) (video) Acclaimed war drama of a British captain who takes over the 9th Australian Division at Tobruk in 1941, holding out against the insurmountable Nazi force of Erwin Rommel.

653. Desert Sands (United Artists/Bel-Air; 1955). *Cast:* Ralph Meeker, Marla English, J. Carrol Naish, John Smith, Ron Randell, John Carradine, Keith Larsen, Lita Milan, Otto Waldis, Terence de Marney, Nico Minardos, Jarl Victor, Mort Mills, Peter Mamakos, Albert Carrier, Philip Tonge, Peter Bourne, Peter Norman, Joseph Waring, Aaron Saxon, Bela Kovacs. *D:* Lesley Selander; *P:* Howard W. Koch; *Sc:* George W. George, George F. Slavin, Danny Arnold. (1:27) Melodramatic actioner of the French Foreign Legion, which was based on the 1954 novel *Punitive Action* by John Robb. Technicolor and SuperScope.

654. The Desert Song (Warner; 1953). *Cast:* Gordon MacRae, Kathryn Grayson, Raymond Massey, Steve Cochran, Allyn McLerie, Dick Wesson, Ray Collins. *D:* H. Bruce Humberstone; *P:* Rudi Fehr; *Sc:* Roland Kibbee; *Songs include:* "The Desert Song," "Long Live the Night," "The Riff Song," "Romance," "Gay Parisienne" and "One Alone." (1:50) (video) Romance, action and songs highlight this 4th go-round of the 1926 operetta by Lawrence Schwab, Otto Harbach, Frank Mandel, Sigmund Romberg and Oscar Hammerstein II. Previously filmed by this studio in 1929, as an early musical, and 1943. Germany also produced a version in 1939. Technicolor.

655. Designing Woman (MGM; 1957). *Cast:* Gregory Peck (Mike Hagen), Lauren Bacall (Marilla Hagen), Dolores Gray (Lori Shannon), Sam Levene (Ned Hammerstein), Tom Helmore (Zachary Wilde), Mickey Shaughnessy (Maxie Stultz), Jesse White (Charlie Arneg), Chuck Connors (Johnnie "O"), Ed Platt (Marin J. Daylor), Jack Cole (Randy Owen), Alvy Moore (Luke Coslow), Carol Veazie (Gwen). *D:* Vincente Minnelli; *P:* Dore Schary, George Wells; *St: & Sc:* (AA) Wells (based on a suggestion by Helen Rose). (1:57) (video/laserdisc) Glossy comic escapism of the marital discord that erupts when a fashion designer and a sportswriter tie the knot. Metrocolor and CinemaScope.

656. Desire Under the Elms (Paramount/Don Hartman Prods.; 1958). *Cast:* Sophia Loren (U.S. debut, if you ignore her appearance as an extra in *Quo Vadis*-q.v./Anna Cabot), Anthony Perkins (Eben Cabot), Burl Ives (Ephraim Cabot), Frank Overton (Simeon Cabot), Pernell Roberts (Peter Cabot), Rebecca Wells (Lucinda), Jean Willes (Florence), Anne Seymour (Eben's mother), Roy Fant (Fiddler), Greta Granstedt (Min), Butch Bernard (young Eben). *D:* Delbert Mann; *P:* Don Hartman; *Sc:* Irwin Shaw; *Cin:* (AAN-b/w) Daniel L. Fapp. (1:54) (video/laserdisc) Drama of greed for land, and a married woman who falls for her stepson. Set in the rural area of New England in the 1840s, it was in nomination at the Cannes Film Festival and based on the 1924 stage hit by Eugene O'Neill. VistaVision.

657. Desiree (20th Century–Fox; 1954). *Cast:* Marlon Brando (Napoleon Bonaparte), Jean Simmons (Desiree Clary), Merle Oberon (Josephine), Michael Rennie (Bernadotte), Cameron Mitchell (Joseph Bonaparte), Elizabeth Sellars (Julie), Charlotte Austin (Paulette), Cathleen Nesbitt (Mme. Bonaparte), Evelyn Varden (Marie), Isobel Elsom (Madame Clary), John Hoyt (Talleyrand), Alan Napier (Despereaux), Nicolas Koster (Oscar), Richard Deacon (Etienne), Edith Evanson (Queen Hedwig), Carolyn Jones (Mme. Tallien), Sam Gilman (Fouche), Larry Crane (Louis Bonaparte), Judy Lester (Caroline Bonaparte), Richard Van Cleemput (Lucien Bonaparte), Florence Dublin (Eliza Bonaparte), Louis Borell (Baron Morner), Peter Bourne (Count Brahe), Dorothy Neumann (Queen Sofia), David Leonard (Barras), Siw Paulsson (Princess Sofia), Lester Matthews (Caulaincourt), Gene Roth (Von Essen), Leonard George (Pope Pius VII), Colin Kenny (Gen.

Becker), Richard Garrick (Count Reynaud), Violet Rensing (Marie Louise), Bert Stevens, George Brand, Kay Kuter, Sven-Hugo Borg, Jack George, Jack Mather, Juney Ellis, Harry Carter, Marina Koshetz, A. Cameron Grant. *D:* Henry Koster; *P:* Julian Blaustein; *Sc:* Daniel Taradash; *ASD:* (AAN-color) Lyle Wheeler, Leland Fuller (art directors), Walter M. Scott, Paul S. Fox (sets); *Costumes:* (AAN-color) Charles LeMaire, Rene Hubert. (1:50) (video) Fictional romantic drama, which best can be described as an anti-historical costume soap opera, of a woman's infatuation with the French conqueror, though she spurned him before his claim to fame. DeLuxe color and CinemaScope.

658. The Desk Set (20th Century–Fox; 1957). *Cast:* Spencer Tracy, Katharine Hepburn, Gig Young, Joan Blondell, Dina Merrill (film debut), Sue Randall, Neva Patterson, Harry Ellerbee, Nicholas Joy, Diane Jergens, Merry Anders, Ida Moore, Rachel Stephens, Sammy Ogg, King Mojave, Charles Heard, Harry Evans, Hal Taggart, Jack M. Lee, Bill Duray, Dick Gardner, Renny McEvoy, Jesslyn Fax, Shirley Mitchell. *D:* Walter Lang; *P:* Henry Ephron; *Sc:* Henry and Phoebe Ephron. (1:43) (video/laserdisc) Romantic comedy of an efficiency expert, hired to make the research department of a TV network operate more smoothly. Of course, he bangs heads with the manager of the department, who feels her job is in jeopardy because of a memory machine he invented. A box office hit, it was based on the 1956 Broadway play by William Marchant. (G.B. title: *His Other Woman*) DeLuxe color and CinemaScope.

659. The Desperado (Allied Artists/Silvermine Prods.; 1954). *Cast:* Wayne Morris, Beverly Garland, James J. Lydon, Dabbs Greer, Rayford Barnes, Lee Van Cleef (dual role), Nestor Paiva, Roy Barcroft, John Dierkes, I. Stanford Jolley, Florence Lake, Richard Shackleton, Charles Garland. *D:* Thomas Carr; *P:* Vincent M. Fennelly; *Sc:* Geoffrey Homes [Daniel Mainwaring]. (1:19) An outlaw and a lawman team up against carpetbaggers in 19th century Texas. One of a series of six westerns starring Morris, it was based on the novel by Clifton Adams.

660. The Desperadoes Are in Town (20th Century–Fox/Regal Films; 1956). *Cast:* Robert Arthur, Kathy Nolan, Rhys Williams, Rhodes Reason, Dave O'Brien (final film—ret.), Kelly Thordsen, Mae Clarke, Robert Osterloh, William Challee, Carol Kelly, Frank Sully, Morris Ankrum, Richard Wessel, Dorothy Granger, Tod Griffin, Nancy Evans, Ann Stepins, Byron Foulger. *D: & P:* Kurt Neumann; *Sc:* Earle Snell, Neumann. (1:12) Western of a man who befriends an ex-outlaw, only to seek retribution when the latter is killed by two of his former partners. Based on the story "The Outlaws Are in Town" by Bennett Foster (*Saturday Evening Post* May 28, 1949). Regalscope.

661. Desperadoes' Outpost (Republic; 1952). *Cast:* Allan Lane, Eddy Waller, Roy Barcroft, Myron Healey, Lyle Talbot, Claudia Barrett, Lee Roberts, Lane Bradford, Ed Cassidy, Charles Evans, Zon Murray, Slim Duncan, Black Jack (horse). *D:* Philip Ford; *P:* Rudy Ralston; *St: & Sc:* Albert DeMond, Arthur Orloff. (0:54) Government agent "Rocky" Lane is on the trail of those responsible for stagecoach sabotage. An entry in his western series, it originally ran as a co-feature with *Tropical Heat Wave* (q.v.).

662. The Desperate Hours (Paramount; 1955). *Cast:* Humphrey Bogart, Frederic March, Arthur Kennedy, Martha Scott, Dewey Martin, Mary Murphy, Richard Eyer, Robert Middleton, Gig Young, Ray Collins, Alan Reed, Bert Freed, Whit Bissell, Ray Teal, Ric Roman, Michael Moore, Don Haggerty, Pat Flaherty, Beverly Garland, Louis Lettieri, Ann Doran, Walter Baldwin. *D:* William Wyler (voted "Best Director" by the NBR); *P:* Wyler; *Sc:* Joseph Hayes. (1:52) (video/laserdisc) Nailbiting suspense predominates this acclaimed hit thriller of a family of four being held hostage by three escaped convicts. Based on the novel and Broadway play by Mr. Hayes which had its roots in a real-life incident. Remade in 1990. VistaVision.

663. Desperate Search (MGM; 1952). *Cast:* Howard Keel, Jane Greer, Patricia Medina, Keenan Wynn, Dick Simmons, Robert Burton, Lee Aaker, Linda Lowell, Michael Dugan, Elaine Stewart, Jonathan Cott, Jeff Richards, Robert Whitney, Gil Dennis. *D:* Joseph Lewis; *P:* Matthew Rapf; *Sc:* Walter Doniger. (1:12) Programmer drama of a father's search for his two children after the plane they were on crashes in the Canadian wilderness. Based on the novel *The Desperate Search* by Arthur Mayse.

Desperate Siege *see* **Rawhide**

664. Destination Big House (Republic; 1950). *Cast:* Dorothy Patrick, Robert Rockwell,

James Lydon, Robert Armstrong, Larry J. Blake, John Harmon, Claire DuBrey, Richard Benedict, Mickey Knox, Danny Morton, Mack Williams, Olan E. Soule, Peter Prouse, Norman Field. *D:* George Blair; *P:* William Lackey; *St:* Mortimer Braus; *Sc:* Eric Taylor. (1:00) Melodrama of a school teacher on vacation at a mountain cabin dealing with an invasion of crooks in search of $80,000 in hidden loot. Originally ran on a double bill program with *Woman From Headquarters* (q.v.).

Destination Danger (G.B. title) *see* **Eyes of the Jungle**

665. Destination Gobi (20th Century-Fox; 1953). *Cast:* Richard Widmark, Don Taylor, Casey Adams [aka: Max Showalter], Murvyn Vye, Darryl Hickman, Martin Milner, Ross Bagdasarian, Judy Dann, Rudolfo Acosta, Russell Collins, Leonard Strong, Anthony Earl Numkena [aka: Earl Holliman], Edgar Barrier, Alvy Moore, Stuart Randall, William Forrest, Bert Moorhouse, Jack Raine. *D:* Robert Wise; *P:* Stanley Rubin; *St:* Edmund G. Love; *Sc:* Everett Freeman. (1:29) Fact-based World War II drama about a contingent of men in the Gobi desert. After their commanding officer is killed, they must make an 800 mile trip across the desert to the coast. Technicolor.

666. Destination Moon (Eagle-Lion Classics/George Pal Prods.; 1950). *Cast:* John Archer (Jim Barnes), Warner Anderson (Dr. Charles Cargraves), Tom Powers (General Thayer), Dick Wesson (Joe Sweeney), Erin O'Brien-Moore (Emily Cargraves), Ted Warde (Brown), Woody Woodpecker (guest). *D:* Irving Pichel; *P:* George Pal; *Sc:* Robert A. Heinlein, Rip Van Ronkel, James O'Hanlon; *F/X:* (AA) George Pal; *ASD:* (AAN) Ernst Fegte (art director), George Sawley (sets); *Cartoon sequence:* Walter Lantz. (1:31) (video/laserdisc) A rocketship lands on the moon and the four men on board discover they don't have enough fuel to return to earth. Based on the 1947 novel *Rocketship Galileo* by Robert A Heinlein. The *New York Times* placed it at #5 on their "10 Best" list. Popular in 1950, but slow pacing may put present-day viewers to sleep. Technicolor.

667. Destination Murder (RKO; 1950). *Cast:* Joyce MacKenzie, Stanley Clements, Hurd Hatfield, Albert Dekker, Myrna Dell, James Flavin, John Dehner, Richard Emory, Norma Vance, Suzette Harbin, Buddy Swan, Burt Wenland, Franklyn Farnum, Steve Gibson's Redcaps. *D:* Edward L. Cahn; *P:* Cahn, Maurie M. Suess; *St: & Sc:* Don Martin; *Songs:* "Let's Go to a Party" (James Springs–Steve Gibson); "Palace of Stone" (Springs). (1:12) Film noir with many plot twists of a woman's investigation into a murder of her father. Originally ran on the top of a double bill with Tim Holt's *Rider From Tucson* (q.v.).

668. Destination 60,000 (Allied Artists; 1957). *Cast:* Preston Foster, Pat Conway, Jeff Donnell, Coleen Gray, Bobby Clark, Denver Pyle, Russ Thorsen, Anne Barton. *D:-St: & Sc:* George W. Waggner; *P:* Jack J. Gross, Philip N. Krasne. (1:06) Programmer drama, with much stock footage, of an aircraft manufacturer who is testing a new jet plane.

669. Destry (Universal-International; 1955). *Cast:* Audie Murphy, Mari Blanchard, Lyle Bettger, Edgar Buchanan, Thomas Mitchell, Lori Nelson, Mary Wickes, Wallace Ford, Alan Hale, Jr., George Wallace, Lee Aaker, Trevor Bardette, Walter Baldwin, Richard Reeves, Frank Richards, Mitchell Lawrence, Ralph Peters, John Doucette. *D:* George Marshall; *P:* Stanley Rubin; *St:* Felix Jackson; *Sc:* D.D. Beauchamp, Edmund H. North. (1:35) Technicolor western of a shy sheriff who cleans up a western town. Based on the book by Max Brand [a pseudonym of Frederick Faust], it was first filmed in 1932 by this studio with Tom Mix as *Destry Rides Again* and remade under that title in 1939 with James Stewart and Marlene Dietrich (a classic). Rehashed in 1950 as *Frenchie* (q.v.). Later a TV series.

670. Detective Story (Paramount; 1951). *Cast:* Kirk Douglas (Jim McLeod), Eleanor Parker (AAN/Mary McLeod), William Bendix (Lou Brody), Cathy O'Donnell (Susan), George Macready (Karl Schneider), Horace McMahon (repeating his stage role/Lt. Monahan), Gladys George (Miss Hatch), Joseph Wiseman (repeating his stage role/first burglar), Lee Grant (AAN + "Best Actress" at the Cannes Film Festival/ film debut—repeating her stage role as the shoplifter), Gerald Mohr (Tami Giacoppetti), Frank Faylen (Gallagher), Craig Hill (Arthur), Michael Strong (Lewis Abbott), Luis Van Rooten (Joe Feinson), Bert Freed (Dakis), Warner Anderson (Sims), Grandon Rhodes (O'Brien), William "Bill" Phillips (Callahan), Russell Evans (Barnes), Edmund F. Cobb (Detective Ed), Bert Mustin (Willie the janitor), James Maloney (Mr. Prickett), Howard Joslin (Gus Keogh), Mike Mahoney (Coleman), Catherine Doucet

(Mrs. Farragut), Ann Codee (Frenchwoman), Ralph Montgomery (Finney), Pat Flaherty (desk sergeant), Bob Scott (Mulvey), Harper Goff (Gallants), Donald Kerr (taxi driver). *D:* (AAN) William Wyler; *P:* Wyler; *Sc:* (AAN) Philip Yordan, Robert Wyler. (1:43) Drama of a police detective and his wife at home and various people who pass through his life on the job at a New York City precinct. Based on the hit 1949 Broadway play by Sidney Kingsley, it placed #4, #5 and #8 respectively on the "10 Best" lists of *Film Daily*, the NBR and the *New York Times*. One of the 23 top-grossing films of 1951-52, it was also in nomination at the British Academy Awards.

671. **Devil Goddess** (Columbia; 1955). *Cast:* Johnny Weissmuller (himself), Angela Stevens, Selmer Jackson, William Tannen, Ed Hinton, William H. Griffith, Frank Lackteen, Abel Fernandez, Vera M. Francis, George Berkeley. *D:* Spencer G. Bennet; *P:* Sam Katzman; *St:* Dwight V. Babcock; *Sc:* George H. Plympton. (1:10) B budget jungle adventure with Weissmuller (in his final film appearance until 1970) leading a professor and his daughter on a trek into the jungle. The final entry in the series which began as *Jungle Jim* in 1948, and closed with Weissmuller using his own name in the final three entries due to a loss of copyright.

672. **The Devil Makes Three** (MGM; 1952). *Cast:* Gene Kelly, Pier Angeli, Richard Egan, Richard Rober, Claus Clausen, Wilfred Seyfert, Margot Rielscher, Annie Rosar, Harold Benedict, Otto Gebuhr, Gertrud Wolle, Heinrich Gretler, Charlotte Flemming, Charles Gordon Howard, Burn Kruger, Claus Benton Lombard, Ivan Petrovich, Sepp Rist, Michael Tellering. *D:* Andrew Marton; *P:* Richard Goldstone; *St:* Lawrence Bachmann; *Sc:* Jerry Davis. (1:36) Drama of a U.S. military man returning to Germany to thank the family who helped him during World War II. He falls for their daughter and gets involved in black market intrigue. Filmed on locations in Munich, Salzburg and Berchtesgaden.

673. **Devil's Canyon** (RKO; 1953). *Cast:* Virginia Mayo, Dale Robertson, Stephen McNally, Arthur Hunnicutt, Robert Keith, Jay C. Flippen, George J. Lewis, Whit Bissell, Morris Ankrum, James Bell, William Phillips, Earl Holliman, Irving Bacon, Jim Hayward, Fred Coby, John Cliff, Glenn Strange, Murray Alper, Harold "Stubby" Kruger, Paul Fix, Gregg Martell, Larry Blake. *D:* Alfred Werker; *P:* Edmund Grainger; *St:* Bennett R. Cohen, Norton S. Parker; *Adapt:* Harry Essex; *Sc:* Fredrick Hazlitt Brennan. (1:32) (video) Offbeat western of a marshal sent to the Arizona Territorial Prison at the turn-of-the-century, on a trumped up charge, after killing two men in self defense. In Natural Vision 3-D and Technicolor.

674. **The Devil's Disciple** (United Artists/ Hecht-Hill-Lancaster/Bryna Prod.; 1959). *Cast:* Kirk Douglas, Burt Lancaster, Janette Scott, Laurence Olivier (Gen. Burgoyne), Eva Le Gallienne, Harry Andrews, Basil Sydney, George Rose, Neil McCallum, David Horne, Mervyn Johns, Erik Chitty, Jenny Jones. *D:* Guy Hamilton; *P:* Harold Hecht; *Sc:* John Dighton, Roland Kibbee. (1:22) (video) Based on the satirical play by George Bernard Shaw, this U.S.A./British co-production lends itself to why the British lost the colonies during the American Revolution. Filmed in England.

675. **Devil's Doorway** (MGM; 1949-50). *Cast:* Robert Taylor, Louis Calhern, Paula Raymond, Marshall Thompson, Edgar Buchanan, Rhys Williams, Fritz Leiber (final film—d. 1949), Bruce Cowling, Spring Byington, James Millican, Chief Big Tree, Harry Antrim. *D:* Anthony Mann; *P:* Nicholas Nayfack; *St: & Sc:* Guy Trosper. (1:24) Offbeat western, which found critical acclaim, of an American Indian Civil War veteran who returns to his people to fight injustice from the white man. It was in nomination for "Best Film" with the New York Film Critics.

676. **The Devil's Hairpin** (Paramount/ Theodore Prods.; 1957). *Cast:* Cornel Wilde, Jean Wallace, Mary Astor, Arthur Franz, Paul Fix, Larry Pennell, Gerald Milton, Ross Bagdasarian, Jack Kosslyn, Morgan Jones, Louis Wilde, Jack Latham, Mabel Lillian Rea, Dorene Porter, Sue England, John Indrisano, Mike Mahoney, Les Clark, Henry Blair, Gil Stuart, George Gilbreth, Gordon Mills, John Benson. *D: & P:* Cornel Wilde; *Sc:* Wilde, James Edmiston; *Songs:* Ross Bagdasarian, Van Cleave. (1:22) A race car driver makes a comeback after becoming involved in some dirty track shenanigans. Based on *The Fastest Man on Earth* by Mr. Edmiston. Technicolor and VistaVision.

677. **The Devil's Partner** (Filmgroup/ Huron; 1958-61). *Cast:* Ed Nelson (dual role), Jean Allison, Edgar Buchanan, Richard Crane, Spencer Carlisle, Byron Foulger, Claire Carleton. *D:* Charles R. Rondeau; *P:* Hugh M. Hooker; *St:*

& *Sc:* Stanley Clements, Laura J. Mathews, Dorrell McGowan. (original running time 1:15, cut to 1:01) Low budget horror film of an old man possessed by the devil, who dies and returns as his younger self, spreading his evil among the local residents of a remote Texas town. Produced in 1958, but not released theatrically until 1961.

678. The Devil's Sleep (Screen Art; 1949–51). *Cast:* Lita Grey Chaplin, John Mitchum, William Thomason, Tracy Lynn. *D:* W. Merle Connell; *St:* Danny Arnold, Richard McMahon; *Sc:* Arnold, Connell, McMahon. (1:21) Low budget independent melodrama of members of a drug ring who react when a lady judge of the juvenile court investigates their activities.

679. Dial M for Murder (Warner; 1954). *Cast:* Ray Milland (Tony Wendice), Grace Kelly (voted "Best Actress" by the NBR and the New York Film Critics combined with her performances in *The Country Girl* and *Rear Window*—both q.v./Margot Wendice), Robert Cummings (Mark Halliday), John Williams (voted "Best Supporting Actor" by the NBR combined with his performance in *Sabrina*—q.v./Inspector Hubbard), Anthony Dawson (Capt. Lesgate), Leo Britt (narrator), Patrick Allen (film debut/ Pearson), George Leigh (William), Alfred Hitchcock (man in photo), George Alderson, Robin Hughes, Guy Doleman, Thayer Roberts, Sanders Clark, Robert Dobson, Major Sam Harris, Jack Cunningham. *D:* & *P:* Alfred Hitchcock; *Sc:* Frederick Knott (based on his hit play). (1:45) (video/laserdisc) A man's plot to murder his wife for her money goes awry, with the following investigation providing enough mystery and suspense to make this one of the 25 top-grossing films of 1953-54. Remade in 1981 as a TV movie and in 1998 as *A Perfect Murder*. 3-D and WarnerColor.

680. Dial 1119 (MGM; 1950). *Cast:* Marshall Thompson, Virginia Field, Andrea King, Sam Levene, Leon Ames, Keefe Brasselle, Richard Rober, James Bell, William Conrad, Dick Simmons, Hal Fieberling, Ralph Roberts. *D:* Gerald Mayer (feature directorial debut); *P:* Richard Goldstone; *St:* Hugh King, Don McGuire; *Sc:* John Monks, Jr. (1:15) Programmer suspense drama of a psychotic gunman holding a group of barroom patrons hostage. (G.B. title: *The Violent Hour*)

681. Dial Red O (Allied Artists; 1955). *Cast:* Bill Elliott, Keith Larsen, Helene Stanley, Paul Picerni, Jack Kruschen, Elaine Riley, Robert Bice, Rick Vallin, George Eldredge, John Phillips, Regina Gleason, Rankin Mansfield, William J. Tannen, Mort Mills. *D:* & *Sc:* Daniel B. Ullman; *P:* Vincent M. Fennelly. (1:03) Modestly budgeted crime-melodrama of an escaped mental patient who is suspected when his ex-wife is murdered.

682. The Diamond Queen (Warner; 1953). *Cast:* Fernando Lamas, Arlene Dahl, Gilbert Roland, Sheldon Leonard, Michael Ansara, Jay Novello, Richard Hale, Sujata and Asoka (specialty dancers), Evelyn Finley. *D:* John Brahm; *P:* Frank Melford; *As.P:* Edward L. Alperson, Jr.; *St:* & *Sc:* Otto Englander. (1:20) Costume adventure, set in 17th century India, involving a French adventurer's search for a blue diamond for the crown of King Louis XIV. Eastmancolor.

683. Diamond Safari (20th Century-Fox/Regal Films; 1958). *Cast:* Kevin McCarthy, Andre Morell, Betty McDowall, Robert Bice, Gert Van Den Bergh, Patrick Simpson, John Clifford, Michael McNeile, Joel Herholdt, Joanna Douglas, Geoffrey Tsobe, Harry Mekels, Thomas Buson, Frances Driver. *D:* & *P:* Gerald Mayer (final before moving to TV); *Ex.P:* Edward Dukoff; *St:* & *Sc:* Larry [Lawrence B.] Marcus. (1:07) Low budget independent production involving a crackdown on diamond smugglers. Filmed primarily on location in Johannesburg, South Africa. Regalscope.

684. Diane (MGM; 1956). *Cast:* Lana Turner (title role), Pedro Armendariz (Francis I), Roger Moore (King Henry II), Cedric Hardwicke, Marisa Pavan (Catherine de Medici), Torin Thatcher, Henry Daniell, Taina Elg, John Lupton, Geoffrey Toone, Paul Cavanagh, Melville Cooper, Sean McClory, Ian Wolfe, Gene Reynolds, Ronald Green, Michael Ansara, Basil Ruysdael, Christopher Dark, Marc Cavell, John O'Malley, Peter Gray, Mickey Maga, Ronald Anton, Percy Helton, James Drury, Bob Dix, Stuart Whitman, Alicia Ibanez, Ann Brendon, Fay Morley, Barbara Darrow, Ann Staunton, Bunny Cooper. *D:* David Miller; *P:* Edwin H. Knopf; *Sc:* Christopher Isherwood. (1:50) (video) There were disappointing box office returns on this lavishly produced 16th century historical costumer set in the France of King Henry II and his ladylove Diane de Poitiers. Based on the book *Diane de Poitiers* by John Erskine, it was photographed in Eastmancolor and CinemaScope.

685. Diary of a High School Bride (American International/James H. Nicholson and Samuel Z. Arkoff—Alta Vista Prods.; 1959). *Cast:* Anita Sands (film debut), Ronald Foster, Chris Robinson, Wendy Wilde, Louise Arthur, Barney Biro, Richard Gering, Peggy Miller, Elvira Corona, Clark Alan, Joan Connors, Al Laurie, Glenn Hughes, Dodie Drake, Lili Rosson, Luree Nicholson, Loretta Nicholson, John Hart, John Garrett, Don Hicks, Larry Shuttleworth, Gloria Victor. *D: & P:* Burt Topper; *St:* Mark and Jan Lowell; *Sc:* Topper, Jan Lowell; *Songs:* title song, "When I Say Bye Bye" Tony Casanova. (1:12) Teen oriented melodrama of a 17-year-old high school senior who marries a 24-year-old law student, thus meeting opposition from her parents and her former boy friend, the son of a Hollywood studio owner. Ran on a double bill with *The Ghost of Dragstrip Hollow* (q.v.).

686. The Diary of Anne Frank (20th Century–Fox; 1959). *Cast:* Millie Perkins (film debut—received *Photoplay* Gold Medal Award as "Best Female Newcomer"/Anne Frank), Joseph Schildkraut (repeating his stage role as Otto Frank), Shelley Winters (AA/Mrs. Van Daan), Ed Wynn (AAN/Mr. Dussell), Richard Beymer (Peter Van Daan), Gusti Huber (repeating her stage role/Mrs. Frank), Lou Jacobi (repeating his stage role/Mr. Van Dann), Diane Baker (film debut/Margot Frank), Douglas Spencer (Kraler), Dody Heath (Miep Gies). *D:* (AAN) George Stevens; *P:* (AAN-Best Picture) Stevens; *As.P:* George Stevens, Jr.; *Sc:* Frances Goodrich, Albert Hackett; *Cin:* (AA-b/w) William C. Mellor (co-cinematographer: Jack Cardiff); *ASD:* (AA-b/w) Lyle Wheeler, George Davis (art directors), Walter M. Scott, Stuart A. Reiss (sets); *Music:* (AAN) Alfred Newman; *Costumes:* (AAN-b/w) Charles LeMaire, Mary Wills. (2:50) (video/laserdisc) Drama, detailing the lives of eight Dutch Jews who spent two years hiding from the Nazis in the attic of an Amsterdam factory. Based on *Anne Frank: The Diary of a Young Girl* by Anne Frank as translated from the Dutch by B.M. Mooyart and the 1955 play adapted from it by Frances Goodrich and Albert Hackett. The *New York Times* voted it "Best Film of the Year" while the "10 Best" lists of *Film Daily* and the NBR placed it #2 and #4 respectively. In nomination with the New York Film Critics, it also became one of the 26 top-grossing films of 1958-59. Location filming in Amsterdam. Remade in 1980 as a TV movie. CinemaScope. Note 1: The play by Goodrich and Hackett received the Pulitzer Prize, the New York Drama Critics Award and the Antionette Perry Award. Note 2: *The Attic: The Hiding of Anne Frank*, a 1988 TV movie based on the book *Anne Frank Remembered* by Miep Gies told the story from the perspective of the woman (an employee of Otto Frank) who chose to provide the hiding place.

Dick Turpin's Ride (G.B. title) *see* **The Lady and the Bandit**

687. Dig That Uranium (Allied Artists; 1955–56). *Cast:* Leo Gorcey, Huntz Hall, Bernard Gorcey, Mary Beth Hughes, Raymond Hatton, Myron Healey, Richard Powers [aka: Tom Keene], Harry Lauter, Francie McDonald, David [Gorcey] Condon, Bennie Bartlett, Paul Fierro, Frank Jenks, Don C. Harvey, Carl Switzer. *D:* Edward Bernds; *P:* Ben Schwalb; *St: & Sc:* Elwood Ullman, Bert Lawrence. (1:01) In this comedy series entry, the "Bowery Boys" buy a mine out west. When they go to claim it, they find others are also after the mine.

688. Dino (Allied Artists/Block-Kramarsky; 1957). *Cast:* Sal Mineo (title role), Brian Keith, Susan Kohner, Frank Faylen, Joe DeSantis, Penny Santon, Pat DeSimone, Richard Bakalyan, Mollie McCart, Cindy Robbins, Rafael Campos, Don C. Harvey, Michael Mineo, Ken Miller, Joel Collins, Kip King, Byron Foulger. *D:* Thomas Carr; *P:* Bernice Block; *Sc:* Reginald Rose (based on his TV play). (1:33) (video) Drama based on the acclaimed TV play (which also starred Mineo) of a juvenile felon. Newly released from prison, he comes under the wing of a social worker who helps him straighten out his life.

689. Diplomatic Courier (20th Century-Fox; 1952). *Cast:* Tyrone Power, Patricia Neal, Stephen McNally, Hildegarde Neff, Karl Malden, James Millican, Stefan Schnabel, Herbert Berghof, Arthur Blake, Helene Stanley, Michael Ansara, Sig Arno, Alfred Linder, Lee Marvin, Peter Coe, Tyler McVey, Dabbs Greer, Carleton Young, Charles LaTorre, Tom Powers, Monique Chantal, Lumsden Hare, Russ Conway, Stuart Randall, Charles [Bronson] Buchinski, Mario Siletti, Hugh Marlowe, E.G. Marshall. *D:* Henry Hathaway; *P:* Casey Robinson; *Sc:* Robinson, Liam O'Brien. (1:37) (video) Espionage melodrama which was based on the 1945 novel *Sinister Errand* by Peter Cheyney.

690. Disc Jockey (Allied Artists; 1951). *Cast:* Ginny Simms, Tom Drake, Jane Nigh,

Michael O'Shea, Lenny Kent, Jerome Cowan, *and as themselves*: Tommy Dorsey, George Shearing, Sarah Vaughan, Herbert Jeffries, Nick Lucas, The Weavers, Jack Fina, Vito Musso, Red Nichols, Red Norvo, Ben Pollack, Joe Venuti, Foy Willing and Riders of the Purple Sage, Russ Morgan, Martin Block, Joe Adams, Joe Allison, Bill Anson, Doug Arthur, Don Bell, Paul Brenner, Bob Clayton, Paul Dixon, Ed Gallaher, Dick Gilbert, Bill Gordon, Maurice Hart, Bruce Hayes, Eddie Hubbard, Bea Kalmus, Les Malloy, Paul Masterson, Ed McKenzie, Tom Mercein, Gil Newsome, Gene Norman, Art Pallans, Bob Poole, Norman Prescott, Fred Robbins, Ernie Simon, Larry Wilson. *D:* Will Jason; *P:* Maurice Duke; *St: & Sc:* Clark E. Reynolds; *Songs:* "Let's Meander Through the Meadow," "Show Me You Love Me" (S. Steuben-Roz Gordon); "Nobody Wants Me," "After Hours" (Gordon), "Disc Jockey," "In My Heart" (Herb Jeffries-Dick Hazard); "Peaceful Country," "Riders of the Purple Sage" (Foy Willing), "Brain Wave" (George Shearing); "Oh Look at Me Now" (John DeVries–Joe Bushkin); "The Roving Kind" (Jessie Cavanaugh–Arnold Stanton). (1:17) Musical of a DJ-promoter who claims he can make an overnight sensation of an unknown singer with only massive radio exposure.

Disc Jockey Jamboree (G.B. title) *see* **Jamboree**

691. The Disembodied (Allied Artists; 1957). *Cast:* Paul Burke, Allison Hayes, John E. Wengraf, Eugenia Paul, Joel Marston, Robert Christopher, Norman Fredric, A.E. Ukonu, Paul Thompson, Otis Greene. *D:* Walter Grauman (directorial debut); *P:* Ben Schwalb; *St: & Sc:* Jack Townley. (1:05) Horror thriller about voodoo in the jungle. It filled out a double bill program with *From Hell It Came* (q.v.).

692. Distant Drums (Warner/United States Pictures, Inc.; 1951). *Cast:* Gary Cooper, Mari Aldon (film debut), Richard Webb, Ray Teal, Arthur Hunnicutt, Robert Barrat (Gen. Zachary Taylor), Clancy Cooper, Dan White, Lee Roberts, Larry Carper, Gregg Barton, Sheb Wooley, Mel Archer, Angelita McCall, Warren MacGregor, George Scanlan, Carl Harbaugh, Beverly Brandon, Sidney Capo. *D:* Raoul Walsh; *P:* Milton Sperling; *St:* Niven Busch; *Sc:* Busch, Martin Rackin. (1:41) (video/laserdisc) Acclaimed Technicolor adventure saga of early 19th century Florida with Seminole Indians on the warpath, after being supplied with arms by gun smugglers. A re-working of the director's 1945 production *Objective, Burma!*

The Dividing Line (G.B. title) *see* **The Lawless**

Dr. Cadman's Secret *see* **The Black Sleep**

693. A Dog of Flanders (20th Century-Fox; 1959). *Cast:* David Ladd, Donald Crisp, Theodore Bikel, Max Croiset, Monique Ahrens, Siohban Taylor, John Soer, Gisport Terserteeg, Catherine Holland, Lo Van Hensberger, Spike (dog—received #2 PATSY Award in 1961). *D:* James B. Clark; *P:* Robert B. Radnitz; *Sc:* Ted Sherdeman. (1:36) (video) Family drama, which received minor acclaim, of a Dutch boy yearning to be a famous painter who befriends an injured dog. Based on the 1872 novel by Ouida [a pseudonym of Louise De La Ramee], it was first filmed by Metro-Goldwyn in 1924 as *A Boy of Flanders*. Remade in 1935 by RKO as *A Dog of Flanders*. In DeLuxe color, CinemaScope and stereophonic sound.

694. A Dog's Best Friend (United Artists/Premium Pictures; 1959–60). *Cast:* Bill Williams, Marcia Henderson, Roger Mobley, Charles Cooper, [Harry] Dean Stanton, Roy Engel, Jimmy Baird, Terry Ann Ross. *D:* Edward L. Cahn; *P:* Robert E. Kent; *Sc:* Orville H. Hampton. (1:10) Melodrama of an adopted boy who treats a wounded dog that was trained by a man who committed a murder.

695. The Domino Kid (Columbia/Rorvic; 1957). *Cast:* Rory Calhoun, Kristine Miller, Andrew Duggan, Yvette Dugay, Peter Whitney, Eugene Iglesias, James Griffith, Roy Barcroft, Denver Pyle, Robert Burton, Ray Corrigan, Wes Christensen, Don Orlando, Bart Bradley. *D:* Ray Nazarro; *P:* Rory Calhoun, Victor M. Orsatti; *Sc:* Kenneth Gamet, Hal Biller. (1:14) A Confederate soldier seeks revenge after the war when he returns to Texas and finds his father and brother have been killed. This was Calhoun's first independent production. Note: *Motion Picture Guide* credits Calhoun with the original story, while *Who Wrote the Movie* credits its screenwriters, Gamet and Biller.

696. Donovan's Brain (United Artists/Dowling; 1953). *Cast:* Lew Ayres, Gene Evans, Nancy Davis, Steve Brodie, Lisa K. Howard, Tom Powers, Peter Adams, Victor Sutherland, Michael Colgan, Kyle James, Stapleton Kent, John Hamilton, Harlan Warde, Paul Hoffman,

William Cottrell, Tony Merrill, Faith Langley, Mark Lowell, Shimen Ruskin. *D: & Sc:* Felix Feist; *P:* Tom Gries; *Adaptation:* Hugh Brooke. (1:23) (video/laserdisc) A scientist keeps the brain of a wealthy industrialist alive after the latter is killed in a plane crash, with the brain soon gaining control over the scientist's life. Based on the 1943 novel by Curt Siodmak, it was first filmed in 1944 by Republic as *The Lady and the Monster*. Remade in Germany in 1965 as *The Brain*.

697. Don't Bother to Knock (20th Century–Fox; 1952). *Cast:* Richard Widmark, Marilyn Monroe, Anne Bancroft (film debut), Donna Corcoran, Jeanne Cagney, Lurene Tuttle, Elisha Cook, Jr., Jim Backus, Verna Felton, Willis Bouchey, Don Beddoe, Gloria Blondell, Grace Hayle, Michael Ross, Eda Reis Merin, Victor Perrin, Dick Cogan, Robert Foulk, Olan Soule, Emmett Vogan. *D:* Roy Baker; *P:* Julian Blaustein; *Sc:* Daniel Taradash. (1:16) (video) Drama of a couple who hire a woman (Monroe) to babysit with their daughter (Corcoran), not knowing the woman is under emotional strain over the loss of her fiance in the war and had been in a mental institution. Based on the 1950 novel *Mischief* by Charlotte Armstrong, it was remade as the TV movie *The Sitter*.

698. Don't Give Up the Ship (Paramount/Hal B. Wallis-Joseph Hazen; 1959). *Cast:* Jerry Lewis, Dina Merrill, Diana Spencer, Mickey Shaughnessy, Robert Middleton, Gale Gordon, Claude Akins, Mabel Albertson, Hugh Sanders, Richard Shannon, Chuck Wassil. *D:* Norman Taurog; *P:* Hal B. Wallis; *As.P:* Paul Nathan; *St:* Ellis Kadison; *Sc:* Herbert Baker, Edmund Beloin, Henry Garson. (1:29) (video) Hit comedy of a navy ensign who lost a battleship during World War II and has no memory of what became of it. A novel idea that is considered one of Lewis' better comedies. VistaVision.

699. Don't Go Near the Water (MGM/Avon Prod.; 1957). *Cast:* Glenn Ford (Lt. Max Siegel), Gia Scala (Melora), Earl Holliman (Adam Garrett), Anne Francis (Lt. Alice Tomlen), Keenan Wynn (Gordon Ripwell), Fred Clark (Lt. Comdr. Clinton Nash), Eva Gabor (Deborah Aldrich), Russ Tamblyn (Ensign Tyson), Jeff Richards (Lt. Ross Pendleton), Mickey Shaughnessy (Farragut Jones), Howard Smith (Adm. Boatwright), Romney Brent (Mr. Alba), Mary Wickes (Janie), Jack Straw (Lt. Comdr. Gladstone), Robert Nichols (Lt. Comdr. Hereford), John Alderson (Lt. Comdr. Diplock), Jack Albertson (Rep. George Jansen), Charles Watts (Rep. Arthur Smithfield), Julian Rivero (Mr. Seguro), Ike Gibson (Lt. Comdr. Pratt), Don Burnett (Lt. Hepburn), Hugh Boswell (Jerry Wakely), John Dennis (Corp. Donohue), Steve Warren (Seaman Flaherty), William Ogden Joyce (Lt. Boone), John L. Cason (Seabee Metkoff), Paul Bryar (Lt. Comdr. Flaherty), Wilson Wood, Gregg Martell. *D:* Charles Walters; *P:* Lawrence Weingarten; *Sc:* Dorothy Kingsley, George Wells; *Title Song:* Bronislau Kaper (m), Sammy Cahn (ly), sung by The Lancers. (1:42) (video) This wartime comedy was one of the 26 top-grossing films of 1957-58. Set on an obscure Pacific island, this film is about efforts to build a recreation hall for military personnel. Based on the 1956 novel by William Brinkley, it also took a #9 placement on the "10 Best" list of *Film Daily*. Metrocolor and CinemaScope.

700. Don't Knock the Rock (Columbia/Clover; 1956). *Cast:* Alan Dale, Patricia Hardy, Fay Baker, Jana Lund, Gail Ganley, Pierre Watkin, George Cisar, Dick Elliott, Jovada & Jimmy Ballard, Bill Haley and the Comets (themselves), Alan Freed (himself), Little Richard (himself/singing "Long Tall Sally" and "Tutti Frutti"). The Treniers (themselves), Dave Appell & His Applejacks (themselves). *D:* Fred F. Sears; *P:* Sam Katzman; *St: & Sc:* Robert E. Kent, James B. Gordon. (1:25) Adult opposition to rock 'n' roll in its early days is the focus of this musical with a teen orientation. A follow-up to the popular *Rock Around the Clock* (q.v.), it ran on a double bill with *Rumble on the Docks* (q.v.).

701. Double Crossbones (Universal-International; 1949–51). *Cast:* Donald O'Connor, Helena Carter, Will Geer, John Emery, Stanley Logan, Hope Emerson (Ann Bonney), Alan Napier (Capt. Kidd), Robert Barrat (Henry Morgan), Louis Bacigalupi (Blackbeard), Kathryn Givney, Hayden Rorke, Morgan Farley, Charles McGraw, Glenn Strange, Gregg Martell, Jeff Chandler (narrator). *D:* Charles T. Barton; *P:* Leonard Goldstein; *St: & Sc:* Oscar Brodney; *Additional dialogue:* John Grant; *Songs:* "Percy Had a Heart," "Song of Adventure" Dan Shapiro–Lester Lee. (1:15) Comedy of an apprentice shopkeeper who is mistaken for a notorious pirate. Technicolor.

702. Double Deal (RKO/Bel-Air; 1950). *Cast:* Marie Windsor, Richard Denning, Taylor Holmes, Fay Baker, James Griffith, Carleton

Young, Tom Browne Henry, Jim Hayward, Richard Reeves, Paul E. Burns. *D:* Abby Berlin; *P:* James T. Vaughn; *St:* Don McGuire; *Sc:* Lee Herman, Charles S. Belden. (1:23) (video) Melodrama of a wildcatter who gets mixed up in murder on the oil fields. Note: A major discrepancy exists between two sources for running times on this film. *Video Movie Guide 1997* lists it at 83 minutes, while *Motion Picture Guide* lists it at 64 minutes.

703. Double Dynamite (RKO; 1948–51). *Cast:* Frank Sinatra, Jane Russell, Groucho Marx, Don McGuire, Howard Freeman, Harry Hayden, Nestor Paiva, Lou Nova, Joe Devlin, Frank Orth, William Edmunds, Russ Thorsen, Charles Coleman, Ida Moore, Hal K. Dawson, George Chandler, Jean De Briac, Benny Burt, Billy Snyder, Bill Erwin, Charles Regan, Dick Gordon, Mike Lally, Jack Jahries, Gil Perkins, Jack Gargan, Claire DuBrey, Harry Kingston, Kermit Kegley, Virgil Johansen, William Norton Bailey, Jack Chefe, Al Murphy, Jim Nolan, Lee Phelps, Lillian West, Dickie Derril, Charles Sullivan, Harold Goodwin. *D:* Irving Cummings, Sr. (final film—ret.); *P:* Irving Cummings, Jr.; *Sc:* Melville Shavelson; *Additional dialogue:* Harry Crane; *Songs:* "It's Only Money," "Kisses and Tears" Jule Styne–Sammy Cahn. (1:20) (video) Romantic comedy of a bank clerk who wins $60,000 on the ponies. A situation arises where the bank funds are short and he is suspect, though bank officials know nothing of his racetrack earnings. Based on a story by Lee Rosten and a character created by Mannie Manheim, the film was produced in 1948, with theatrical release held up until 1951. Originally ran on a double bill with *Jungle of Chang*, a 1940 Swedish re-release. (aka: *It's Only Money*, which was also the original working title)

704. Double Jeopardy (Republic; 1955). *Cast:* Rod Cameron, Gale Robbins, Allison Hayes, Jack Kelly. *D:* R.G. Springsteen; *St: & Sc:* Don Martin. (1:10) Melodrama of a real estate agent who must prove his innocence when accused of killing a blackmailer. A remake of *The Crooked Road* (Republic; 1940).

705. Down Among the Sheltering Palms (20th Century–Fox; 1953). *Cast:* William Lundigan, Jane Greer, Mitzi Gaynor, David Wayne, Gloria DeHaven, Gene Lockhart, Jack Paar, Alvin Greenman, Billy Gilbert, Henry Kulky, Lyle Talbot, Ray Montgomery, George Nader, Fay Roope, David Ahdar, Sialofi Jerry Talo, Clinton Bagwell, Charles Tannen, Claud Allister, Edith Evanson, Steve Wayne, Richard Grayson, John Baer, Jean Charney, Barney Phillips, Lee Marvin, Henry Slate, Joe Turkel, David Wolfson, James Ogg, Ray Hyke, Roger McGee, Richard Monohan. *D:* Edmund Goulding; *P:* Fred Kohlmar; *Sc:* Claude Binyon, Albert Lewin, Burt Styler (based on a magazine serial by Edward Hope); *Songs:* "I'm a Ruler of a South Sea Island," "Who Will It Be When the Time Comes?", "What Makes a Difference," "All of Me," Title song, and "When You're in Love" Ralph Blane–Harold Arlen. (1:26) Technicolor musical romance set at an island army base in the South Pacific.

706. Down Laredo Way (Republic; 1953). *Cast:* Rex Allen, Ko-Ko (horse), Slim Pickens, Dona Drake, Marjorie Lord, Roy Barcroft, Clayton Moore, Judy Nugent, Percy Helton, Zon Murray. *D:* William Witney; *P:* Rudy Ralston; *St: & Sc:* Gerald Geraghty. (0:54) In this series western, Allen is a rodeo performer who breaks the case on a series of diamond robberies that resulted in murder and left an 8-year-old girl orphaned.

707. Down Three Dark Streets (United Artists/Edward Small-Challenge Pictures; 1954). *Cast:* Broderick Crawford, Martha Hyer, Ruth Roman, Marisa Pavan, Casey Adams [aka: Max Showalter], Kenneth Tobey, Gene Reynolds, William Johnstone, Harlan Warde, Jay Adler, Claude Akins, Suzanne Alexander, Myra Marsh, Joe Bassett, Dede Gainor, Alan Dexter, Alexander Campbell, Larry Hudson. *D:* Arnold Laven; *P:* Arthur Gardner, Jules V. Levey; *Sc:* Gordon and Mildred N. Gordon, Bernard C. Schoenfeld. (1:25) Crime thriller of an FBI agent who takes on three intertwining cases that his deceased colleague had been working on. Based on the 1953 novel *Case File FBI* by the Gordons.

708. Dragnet (Warner/Mark VII Prods., Ltd.; 1954). *Cast:* Jack Webb (Sgt. Joe Friday), Ben Alexander (Sgt. Frank Smith), Richard Boone (Capt. Hamilton), Stacy Harris (Max Troy), Ann Robinson (Grace Downey), Virginia Gregg (Mrs. Starkie), Dub Taylor (Miller Starkie), Georgia Ellis (Belle Davitt), Willard Sage (Chester Davitt), Jim Griffith (Jesse Quinn), Vic Perrin (Adolph Alexander), Malcolm Atterbury (Lee Reinhard), Cliff Arquette (Charlie Weaver), Dennis Weaver (Capt. Lohrman), James Anderson (Fred Kemp), Monte Masters (Fabian Gerard), Olan Soule (Ray Pinker), Dick Cathcart (Roy Cleaver), Meg

Myles (Cuban singer), Virginia Christine (Mrs. Caldwell), Herb Vigran (Mr. Archer), Fred Dale (Officer Tilden), Roy Whaley (Sgt. McCreadie), Charles Hibbs (Ken, stenotypist), Guy Hamilton (Walker Scott), George Sawaya (McQueen), Eddy King (himself), Jean Dean (Pat, script secretary), Harry Bartell (Lt. Stevens), Bill Brundige (Hank Wild), Ramsay Williams (Wesley Cannon), Gayle Kellogg (Officer Keeler), Ken Peters (Officer Gene James), Harry Lauter (Officer Greely), Herb Ellis, Mauritz Hugo, Art Gilmore, Dick Paxton, Ross Elliott, Harlan Warde. *D:* Jack Webb; *P:* Stanley Meyer; *Sc:* Richard L. Breen (based on an actual case from the Los Angeles police files). (1:29) (video) The first theatrical release to be taken from a popular TV series has L.A.'s finest, Sgts. Joe Friday and Frank Smith, investigating the murder of an ex-con. As one might expect, one of the 27 top-grossing films of 1954-55. Two other films with the same title were based on the show, one produced in 1969 as a TV movie and the other, a 1987 spoof of the show. WarnerColor.

709. Dragonfly Squadron (Allied Artists; 1953). *Cast:* John Hodiak, Barbara Britton, Bruce Bennett, Jess Barker, Gerald Mohr, Chuck Connors, Harry Lauter, Pamela Duncan, Adam Williams, John Lupton, Benson Fong, John Hedloe, Fess Parker, Gene Wesson. *D:* Lesley Selander; *P:-St: & Sc:* John Champion. (1:22) (video) A tough U.S. Air Force major, who is training South Korean troops, runs into an old flame who believes her husband to be dead. This war melodrama climaxes with a tank assault by the North Koreans. Originally part of a double bill program with *The World for Ransom* (q.v.).

710. Dragon's Gold (United Artists/Cavalcade; 1953). *Cast:* John Archer, Hillary Brooke, Noel Cravat, Dayton Lummis, Merritt Stone, Marvin Press, Eric Colmar, Frank Yaconelli, Wyott Ordung, Reginald Singh. Roy Engel, Gilbert Frye, Leemei Chu, Wong Artarne, Juney Ellis, Bruce Payne, Keith Hitchcock, Ernestine Barrier, Philip Van Zandt, Anthony Jochim, Mauritz Hugo, Charles Victor, Esther Lee, Joseph Kim, Harvey Dunn, Audrey Lau, David Chow. *D:-P:-St: & Sc:* Aubrey Wisberg, Jack Pollexfen. (1:10) Melodrama of oriental intrigue, as a bonding investigator looks into the claimed theft of $7,000,000.

711. Dragoon Wells Massacre (Allied Artists; 1957). *Cast:* Barry Sullivan, Dennis O'Keefe, Mona Freeman, Katy Jurado, Sebastian Cabot, Casey Adams [aka: Max Showalter], Jack Elam, Trevor Bardette, Hank Worden, Warren Douglas, John War Eagle, Jon Shepodd, Judy Stranges, Alma Beltram. *D:* Harold Schuster; *P:* Lindsley Parsons; *St:* Oliver Drake; *Sc:* Warren Douglas. (1:28) Western drama, in DeLuxe color and CinemaScope, of various people trapped at a relay station targeted for an Indian attack.

712. Dragstrip Girl (American International/Golden State Prods.; 1957). *Cast:* Fay Spain, Steve Terrell, John Ashley, Frank Gorshin, Russ Bender, Tommy Ivo, Grazia Narciso, Tito Vuolo, Dorothy Bruce, Don Shelton, Carla Mercy, Leon Tyler, George Dockstader, Bill Welsh, Edmund Cobb, Woody Lee, Judy Bamber. *D:* Edward L. Cahn; *P:* Alex Gordon; *St: & Sc:* Lou Rusoff. (1:09) (video) Hot rods and drag racing are the stuff of this programmer teen exploitation-melodrama geared to the drive-in crowd.

713. Dragstrip Riot (American International/Trans World Prods.; 1958). *Cast:* Yvonne Lime, Gary Clarke, Fay Wray (final film—ret.), Bob Turnbull, Connie Stevens, Gabe DeLutri, Marcus Dyrector, Ted Wedderspoon, Barry Truex, Marilyn Carroll, Marla Ryan, Steve Ihnat, Tony Butula, Carolyn Mitchell, Joan Chandler, Marc Thompson, Allan Carter. *D:* David Bradley; *P:* O. Dale Ireland; *Ex.P:* Jonathan Daniels, Victor Purcell; *As.P:* Basil Bradbury; *St:* Ireland, George Hodgins; *Sc:* Hodgins; *Additional St: and dialogue:* V.J. Rheims. (1:08) Teen oriented melodrama of a youth newly arrived in Los Angeles who becomes involved with local drag racers and trouble. (aka: *The Reckless Age*) *The Cool and the Crazy* (q.v.) completed the drive-in double bill program.

714. Drango (United Artists/Earlmar; 1957). *Cast:* Jeff Chandler, John Lupton, Joanne Dru, Morris Ankrum, Ronald Howard (U.S. debut), Julie London, Donald Crisp, Helen Wallace, Walter Sande, Milburn Stone (final film—moved to TV as a regular on the *Gunsmoke* series), Parley Baer, Amzie Strickland, Charles Horvath, Barney Phillips, David Stollery, Phil Chambers, Chubby Johnson, Edith Evanson, Anthony Jochim, Mimi Gibson, Paul Lukather, Damian O'Flynn, Katherine Warren, David Saber, Chuck Webster, Maura Murphy. *D:* Hall Bartlett, Jules Bricken; *P:-St: & Sc:* Bartlett. (1:32) Drama of a Union Army officer assigned to rebuild a small town in Georgia that his men sacked during the Civil War, and the hostility he meets from the local citizenry.

715. Dream Wife (MGM; 1953). *Cast:* Cary Grant (Clemson Reade), Deborah Kerr (Effie), Walter Pidgeon (Walter McBride), Betta St. John (film debut/Tarji), Eduard Franz (Khan), Buddy Baer (Vizier), Les Tremayne (Ken Landwell), Donald Randolph (Ali), Bruce Bennett (Charlie Elkwood), Richard Anderson (Henry Malvine), Dan Tobin (Mr. Brown), Movita Casteneda (Rima), Gloria Holden (Mrs. Landwell), Jill Clayworth (Mrs. Elkwood), Dean Miller (George), Steve Forrest (Louis), Patricia Tiernan (Pat), Mary Lawrence (Mrs. Malvine), Faire Binney (Mrs. Parker), Jonathan Cott, Dan Barton, Kay Riehl, Edward Cassidy, Jean Andre, Perry Sheehan, Harry Stanton, Steve Carruthers, James Farrar, Virginia Mullen, Marie Brown, Dick Rich, Bert Moorhouse, Jimmy Moss, Gail Bonney, Lillian Culver, Forbes Murray, Donald Dillaway, Gayne Whitman, John Alvin, Dorothy Kennedy, William Hamel, Allen O'Locklin, Andre d'Arcy, William McCormick, Bernie Gozier, Mohamed Ilbagi, Jim Cronin, Paul F. Smith, Alphonse Martel, Jack Chefe, Margie Liszt, Charles Sullivan, William Vedder, Vernon Rich, Robert E. Nichols, Kathleen Freeman, Aram Katcher, Rudy Rama, Bob Lugo, Dabbs Greer, Hassan Khayyam, Gordon Richards, Jack George, Beryl McCutcheon, Margaret Hedin, Inez Gorman. *D:* Sidney Sheldon; *P:* Dore Schary; *St:* Alfred Lewis Levitt; *Sc:* Sheldon, Herbert Baker, Levitt; *Costumes:* (AAN) Helen Rose, Herschel McCoy; *Songs:* Jamshid Sheibani, Charles Wolcott. (1:40) Hit comedy of a marriage entered into to promote "good will." Computer-colored prints have been produced by Turner Entertainment.

716. Dreamboat (20th Century–Fox; 1952). *Cast:* Clifton Webb, Ginger Rogers, Anne Francis, Jeffrey Hunter, Elsa Lanchester, Fred Clark, Paul Harvey, Ray Collins, Helene Stanley, Richard Garrick, George Barrows, Jay Adler, Marietta Canty, Laura Brooks, Emory Parnell, Helen Hatch, Harry Cheshire, Everett Glass, Paul Maxey, Sandor Szabo, Leo Cleary, Lee Turnbull, Helen Brown, Al Herman, Howard Banks, Jack Mather, Matt Mattox, Frank Radcliffe, Gwen Verdon, Bob Easton, Marjorie Halliday, Donna Lee Hickey [later: May Wynn], Richard Allan, Clive Morgan, Crystal Reeves, Vici Raaf, Barbara Woodell, Don Kohler, Robert B. Williams, Tony DeMario, Joe Recht, Steve Carruthers, Warren Mace, Victoria Horne, Bob Nichols, Paul Kruger, Alphonse Martell, Fred Graham, Jean Corbett, Mary Treen, Richard Karlan. *D: & Sc:* Claude Binyon; *P:* Sol C. Siegel. (1:23) Comedy which involves the showing of old silent movies on TV hosted by an actress who appeared in them, only now she is hawking cosmetics during commercial breaks. Her former co-star, now a respected college professor, sees what is being done to his old films and sues. Based on *The Love Man*, a serialized novel by John D. Weaver which appeared in *Collier's Magazine* in 1950.

717. Drive a Crooked Road (Columbia; 1954). *Cast:* Mickey Rooney, Dianne Foster, Kevin McCarthy, Jack Kelly, Harry Landers, Jerry Paris, Paul Picerni, Dick Crockett, Mort Mills, Peggy Maley, Mike Mahoney, George Paul, John Damler, John Close, Patrick Miller, Diana Dawson, Irene Bolton, Linda Danson, Mel Roberts, John Fontaine, Howard Wright, Jean Engstrom, Richard Cutting. *D:* Richard Quine; *P:* Jonie Taps; *St:* James Benson Nablo; *Adaptation:* Quine; *Sc:* Blake Edwards. (1:23) A crime-melodrama in which a race car driver is forced to drive a getaway car for two crooks.

718. Drum Beat (Warner/Jaguar; 1954). *Cast:* Alan Ladd, Audrey Dalton, Charles Bronson, Marisa Pavan, Robert Keith, Rudolfo Acosta, Warner Anderson, Anthony Caruso, Elisha Cook, Jr., Richard Gaines, Hayden Rorke (Gen. U.S. Grant), Edgar Stehli, Frank DeKova, Isabel Jewell, Perry Lopez, Willis Bouchey, George J. Lewis, Frank Ferguson, Richard Cutting, Paul Wexler, Pat Lawless, Peggy Converse, Peter Hansen, Strother Martin. *D:-St: & Sc:* Delmer Daves; *P:* Alan Ladd (unc.), Daves. (1:51) (video) Fact-based western of an Indian fighter who attempts to bring peace to the California/Oregon border by a like confrontation with Modoc chief Captain Jack (Bronson). In CinemaScope and WarnerColor, this was Ladd's first production under his own "Jaguar" banner. Filmed on location in Coconino National Forest in northern Arizona.

Drum Crazy (G.B. title) *see* **The Gene Krupa Story**

719. Drums Across the River (Universal-International; 1954). *Cast:* Audie Murphy, Lisa Gaye, Lyle Bettger, Walter Brennan, Hugh O'Brian, Mara Corday, Jay Silverheels, Morris Ankrum, Regis Toomey, James Anderson, George Wallace, Bob Steele, Lane Bradford, Emile Meyer, Gregg Barton, Howard McNear,

Kenneth Terrell. *D:* Nathan Juran; *P:* Melville Tucker; *St:* John K. Butler; *Sc:* Butler, Lawrence Roman. (1:18) A treacherous white man uses underhanded methods to get gold from Indian land which by treaty is off limits to whites. Technicolor.

720. Drums in the Deep South (RKO/King Bros. Prods.; 1951). *Cast:* James Craig, Barbara Payton, Guy Madison, Barton MacLane, Craig Stevens, Tom Fadden, Robert Osterloh, Taylor Holmes, Lewis Martin, Peter Brocco, Dan White, Robert Easton, Louis Jean Heydt, Myron Healey. *D:* William Cameron Menzies; *P:* Maurice and Frank King; *Sc:* Philip Yordan, Sidney Harmon. (1:27) (video) Civil War drama set during Sherman's march through Georgia to the sea. Based on the 1948 book *Woman With a Sword* by Hollister Noble. Super-Cinecolor.

721. Drums of Tahiti (Columbia; 1954). *Cast:* Dennis O'Keefe, Patricia Medina, Francis L. Sullivan, George Keymas, Sylvia Lewis, Cicely Browne, Raymond Lawrence, Frances Brandt. *D:* William Castle; *P:* Sam Katzman; *St:* Robert E. Kent; *Sc:* Kent, Douglas Heyes. (1:13) Action-adventure of an American gunrunner who comes to the aid of Tahitian natives in their fight against French rule. 3-D and Technicolor.

722. Duchess of Idaho (MGM; 1950). *Cast:* Esther Williams, Van Johnson, John Lund, Paula Raymond, Clinton Sundberg, Amanda Blake, Eleanor Powell (final film—ret.), Red Skelton, Dick Simmons, Lena Horne, Mel Torme, Connie Haines, Tommy Farrell, Sig Arno, The Jubalaires (themselves), Charles Smith, John Louis Johnson, Roger Moore, Bunny Waters, Dorothy Douglas, Mae Clarke, Johnny Trebach, Suzanne Ridgeway, Larry Steers, Allen Ray, Harold Miller. *D:* Robert Z. Leonard; *P:* Joe Pasternak; *St: & Sc:* Dorothy Cooper, Jerry [Jerome L.] Davis. (1:38) (video) Technicolor triangular romantic musical set in Sun Valley, Idaho. A hit for MGM.

723. Duel at Apache Wells (Republic; 1957). *Cast:* Anna Maria Alberghetti, Ben Cooper, Jim Davis, Harry Shannon, Francis McDonald, Bob Steele, Frank Puglia, Argentina Brunetti, Ian MacDonald, John Dierkes, Ric Roman, Dick Elliott. *D: & P:* Joseph Kane; *St: & Sc:* Bob [Robert Creighton] Williams. (1:10) In this Republic oater, a man returns to set the record straight on the murder of his father and the theft of his land. In Naturama.

724. The Duel at Silver Creek (Universal-International; 1952). *Cast:* Audie Murphy, Faith Domergue, Stephen McNally, Susan Cabot, Gerald Mohr, Eugene Iglesias, Kyle James, Walter Sande, George Eldredge, Lee Marvin, James Anderson. *D:* Don Siegel; *P:* Leonard Goldstein; *St:* Gerald Drayson Adams; *Sc:* Adams, Joseph Hoffman. (1:17) Technicolor western of lawmen vs. murderous claim jumpers.

Duel in Durango *see* **Gun Duel in Durango**

725. Duel on the Mississippi (Columbia/Clover Prods.; 1955). *Cast:* Patricia Medina, Lex Barker, Warren Stevens, Craig Stevens, John Dehner, Ian Keith, Chris Alcaide, John Mansfield, Celia Lovsky, Lou Merrill, Mel Welles, Jean Del Val, Baynes Barron, Vincent M. Townsend, Jr. *D:* William Castle; *P:* Sam Katzman; *St: & Sc:* Gerald Drayson Adams. (1:12) Early 19th century costumer of the female owner of a gambling ship and her difficulties with local plantation owners. Technicolor.

726. Duffy of San Quentin (Warner; 1954). *Cast:* Louis Hayward, Joanne Dru, Paul Kelly, Maureen O'Sullivan, George Macready, Horace McMahon, Irving Bacon, Joel Fluellen, Joseph Turkel, Jonathan Hale, Michael McHale, Peter Brocco. *D: & Sc:* Walter Doniger; *P: & St:* Doniger, Berman Swartz. (1:18) Prison melodrama of Warden Clinton T. Duffy (Kelly) and his attempted reforms at San Quentin Prison in California. Based on his 1950 book *The San Quentin Story* which he co-wrote with Dean Jennings. Followed by a sequel, *The Steel Cage* (q.v.). (G.B. title: *Men Behind Bars*)

Dynamite Anchorage *see* **Murder Is My Beat**

727. Dynamite Pass (RKO; 1950). *Cast:* Tim Holt, Richard Martin, Lynne Roberts, Regis Toomey, Robert Shayne, Don C. Harvey, Cleo Moore, John Dehner, Don Haggerty, Ross Elliott, Denver Pyle. *D:* Lew Landers; *P:* Herman Schlom; *St: & Sc:* Norman Houston. (1:01) (video) A toll-road owner attempts to block the building of a new road that would bypass his bread-and-butter. A Tim Holt series western.

728. The Eagle and the Hawk (Paramount/Pine-Thomas; 1950). *Cast:* John Payne,

Rhonda Fleming, Dennis O'Keefe, Thomas Gomez, Fred Clark, Frank Faylen, Eduardo Noriega, Grandon Rhodes, Walter Reed, Margaret Martin. *D:* Lewis R. Foster; *P:* William H. Pine, William C. Thomas; *Sc:* Foster, Geoffrey Homes [Daniel Mainwaring]. (1:43) Action-adventure played against the backdrop of the 1863 Mexican revolution. Based on the unpublished story "A Mission for General Houston" by Jess Arnold. Technicolor. (aka: *Spread Eagle*)

729. Earth vs. the Flying Saucers (Columbia; 1955). *Cast:* Hugh Marlowe, Joan Taylor, Donald Curtis, Morris Ankrum, John Zaremba, Thomas B. Henry, Grandon Rhodes, Larry Blake, Harry Lauter, Charles Evans, Clark Howat, Frank Wilcox, Alan Reynolds. *D:* Fred F. Sears; *P:* Charles H. Schneer; *St:* Curt Siodmak; *Sc:* George Worthing Yates, Raymond T. Marcus; *F/X:* Ray Harryhausen, Russ Kelly. (1:22) (video/laserdisc) Earth is under attack by an alien invasion force from outer space, until an American scientist comes to the rescue. Suggested by "Flying Saucers from Outer Space," a 1953 writing by Major Donald E. Keyhoe. (aka: *Invasion of the Flying Saucers*) Originally the top of a double bill with *The Werewolf* (q.v.).

Earth vs. the Spider *see* **The Spider**

730. East of Eden (Warner; 1955). *Cast:* James Dean (AAN-starring debut/Cal), Julie Harris (Abra), Raymond Massey (Adam), Burl Ives (Sam), Jo Van Fleet (AA-film debut/Kate), Richard Davalos (Aron), Albert Dekker (Will), Lois Smith (Anne), Harold Gordon (Mr. Albrecht), Richard Garrick (Dr. Edwards), Timothy Carey (Joe), Nick Dennis (Rantini), Lonny Chapman (Roy), Mario Siletti (Piscora), Jonathan Haze (Piscora's son), Barbara Baxley, Bette Treadville, Tex Mooney, Harry Cording, Loretta Rush, Bill Phillips, Jack Carr, Roger Creed, Effie Laird, Wheaton Chambers, Ed Clark, Al Ferguson, Franklyn Farnum, Rose Plummer, John George, Earle Hodgins, C. Ramsay Hill, Edward McNally. *D:* (AAN) Elia Kazan; *P:* Kazan; *Sc:* (AAN) Paul Osborn. (1:55) (video/laserdisc) Critically acclaimed drama of two brothers vying for the love of their father. Based on the 1952 novel by John Steinbeck, it placed #2 and #3 respectively on the "10 Best" lists of the NBR and *Film Daily.* At the Cannes Film Festival it was voted "Best Domestic Film" while the British Academy Awards also had it in nomination. Remade in 1982 as a TV mini-series. WarnerColor and CinemaScope.

731. East of Sumatra (Universal-International; 1952–53). *Cast:* Jeff Chandler, Marilyn Maxwell, Anthony Quinn, Suzan Ball, Jay C. Flippen, John Sutton, Scatman Crothers, Aram Katcher, Eugene Iglesias, Anthony Eustrel, Peter Graves, James Craven, John Warburton, Michael Dale, Gilchrist Stuart, Charles Horvath, Earl Holliman. *D:* Budd Boetticher; *P:* Albert J. Cohen; *St:* Louis L'Amour, Jack Natteford; *Adaptation:* Natteford; *Sc:* Frank J. Gill, Jr. (1:21) Technicolor action-adventure of a tin miner trying to prevent an uprising on a South Pacific island. Note: Suzan Ball received a knee injury during production, which developed into cancer, resulting in her death in 1955 at age 22.

732. Easy to Love (MGM; 1953). *Cast:* Esther Williams, Van Johnson, Tony Martin, John Bromfield, Carroll Baker (film debut), Edna Skinner, King Donovan, Paul Bryar, Eddie Oliver, Benny Rubin, Edward Clark, June Whitley, Emory Parnell, David Newell, Sondra Gould, Lillian Culver, Fenton Hamilton, Harriett Brest, Helen Dickson, Ann Luther, Maude Erickson, Peggy Remington, Violet Seton, Dorothy Vernon, Richard Downing Pope, Bud Gaines, Byron Kane, Reginald Simpson, Joe Mell, Hal Berns, Margaret Bert. *D:* Charles Walters; *P:* Joe Pasternak; *St:* Laslo Vadnay; *Sc:* Vadnay, William Roberts; *Songs:* Title song (Cole Porter); "Coquette" (Carmen Lombardo–Johnny Green–Gus Kahn); "Beautiful Spring" (Paul Lincke); "That's What a Rainy Day is For," "Look Out! I'm Romantic," "Didja Ever?" (Vic Mizzy–Mann Curtis). (1:36) (video) Lavishly produced Technicolor musical romance of two men vying for the affections of an aquatic star at Cypress Gardens, Florida. This box office hit had aquatic choreography by Busby Berkeley.

The Easy Way *see* **Room For One More**

733. The Eddie Cantor Story (Warner; 1953). *Cast:* Keefe Brasselle (Eddie Cantor), Marilyn Erskine (Ida Cantor), Aline MacMahon (Grandma Esther), Arthur Franz, Alex Gerry, Greta Granstedt, Gerald Mohr, William Forrest (Florenz Ziegfeld), Jackie Barnett (Jimmy Durante), Will Rogers, Jr. (Will Rogers), Tristram Coffin, Hal March (Gus Edwards), Ann Doran, Susan Odin, Owen Pritchard, Douglas Evans, Richard Monda. *D:* Alfred E. Green; *P: & St:* Sidney Skolsky; *Sc:* Jerome Weidman, Ted Sherdeman, Skolsky; *Songs include:* "If You Knew Susie" (Joseph Meyer–B.G. DeSylva);

"Making Whoopee," "Yes Sir, That's My Baby" (Gus Kahn–Walter Donaldson); "How Ya Gonna Keep 'Em Down on the Farm" (Donaldson–Sam M. Lewis–Joe Young); "Now's the Time to Fall in Love" (Al Lewis–Al Sherman); "Ida, Sweet as Apple Cider" (Eddie Leonard–Eddie Munson); "Ma (He's Makin' Eyes at Me)" (Sidney Clare–Con Conrad); "Margie" (Benny Davis-Conrad–J. Russell Robinson); "You Must Have Been a Beautiful Baby" (Johnny Mercer–Harry Warren); "Yes, We Have No Bananas" (Frank Silver–Irving Cohn); "Will You Love Me in December As You Do in May?" (James J. Walker-Ernest R. Ball); "Be My Little Baby Bumble Bee" (Stanley Murphy–Henry I. Marchall); "Oh, You Beautiful Doll" (A. Seymour Brown-Nat D. Ayer); "Bye Bye Blackbird" (Mort Dixon-Ray Henderson); "If I Were a Millionaire" (Will Cobb–Gus Edwards). (1:55) Hollywood's Technicolor biographical salute to entertainer Eddie Cantor. Lambasted by the critics, box office receipts came up short.

734. The Eddy Duchin Story (Columbia, 1956). *Cast:* Tyrone Power (ghosted by Carmen Cavallaro on the piano/Eddy Duchin), Kim Novak (Marjorie Delrichs), Victoria Shaw (Chiquita), James Whitmore (Lou Sherwood), Shepperd Strudwick (Mr. Wadsworth), Rex Thompson (Peter Duchin—age 12), Frieda Inescort (Mrs. Wadsworth), Gloria Holden (Mrs. Duchin), Larry Keating (Leo Reisman), Mickey Maga (Peter Duchin—age 5), John Mylong (Mr. Duchin), Gregory Gaye (Philip), Richard Crane, Xavier Cugat (himself), Warren Hsieh, Jack Albertson, Carlyle Mitchell, Lois Kimbrell, Ralph Gamble (Mayor Jimmy Walker), Richard Cutting, Brad Trumbull, Gloria Ann Simpson, Rick Person, Michael Legend, Betsy Jones Moreland, Kirk Alyn. *D:* George Sidney; *P:* Jerry Wald; *As.P:* Jonie Taps; *St:* (AAN) Leo Katcher; *Sc:* Samuel Taylor; *Cin:* (AAN-color) Harry Stradling; *Music:* (AAN) Morris Stoloff, George Duning; *Sound:* (AAN) John Livadary; *Songs include:* "What is This Thing Called Love" (Cole Porter); "Till We Meet Again" (Ray Egan–Richard A. Whiting); "Blue Moon," "Manhattan" (Richard Rodgers–Lorenz Hart); "The Man I Love" (George & Ira Gershwin); "Brazil" (Ary Baroso–Bob Russell); "You're My Everything" (Harry Warren–Mort Dixon–Joe Young); "La Vie En Rose" (Edith Piaf–R.S. Louiguy); "Let's Fall in Love" (Harold Arlen–Ted Koehler); "Shine On Harvest Moon" (Jack Norworth–Nora Bayes); "It Must Be True" (Gus Arnheim–Gordon Clifford–Harry Barris); "Exactly Like You" (Dorothy Fields–Jimmy McHugh); "Dizzy Fingers" (Zez Confrey); "I'll Take Romance" (Oscar Hammerstein II–Ben Oakland); "Smiles" (J. Will Callahan–Lee S. Roberts), "Shine" (Cecil Mack–Lew Brown-Ford Dabney); "Sweet Sue" (Will J. Harris–Victor Young); "Ain't She Sweet" (Jack Yellen–Milton Ager); "April Showers" (Buddy "B.G." DeSylva–Louis Silvers); "Three O'Clock in the Morning" (Dorothy Terriss–Julian Robledo); "Nocturne in E-flat Major" (Frederic Chopin). (2:03) (video/laserdisc) This musical biography of the popular pianist-bandleader of the 1930s and '40s became one of the 24 top-grossing films of 1955-56. Technicolor and CinemaScope.

735. Edge of Doom (RKO/Sam Goldwyn; 1950). *Cast:* Dana Andrews, Farley Granger, Joan Evans, Robert Keith, Paul Stewart, Mala Powers, Adele Jergens, Harold Vermilyea, John Ridgely, Douglas Fowley, Mabel Paige, Howland Chamberlain, Houseley Stevenson, Sr., Jean Innes, Ellen Corby, Ray Teal, Mary Field, Virginia Brissac, Frances Morris. *D:* Mark Robson, Charles Vidor (unc.); *P:* Samuel Goldwyn; *Sc:* Philip Yordan, Ben Hecht (unc.) (1:39) Downbeat drama involving the murder of a Catholic priest by a troubled youth and the subsequent investigation by another priest. Based on the 1949 novel by Leo Brady, it placed #5 on the "10 Best" list of the NBR. (G.B. title: *Stronger Than Fear*)

736. Edge of Eternity (Columbia/Thunderbird; 1959). *Cast:* Cornel Wilde, Victoria Shaw, Mickey Shaughnessy, Edgar Buchanan, Rian Garrick, Jack Elam, Dabbs Greer, Alexander Lockwood, Tom Fadden, John Roy, Wendell Holmes, George Cisar, Buzz Westcott, Ted Jacques, Paul Bailey, George "Smokey" Ross, Hope Summers, John Ayres, Don Siegel (bit). *D: & As.P:* Don Siegel; *P:* Kendrick Sweet; *St:* Knut Swenson [Marion Hargrove], Ben Markson; *Sc:* Richard Collins. (1:20) Low budget mystery-melodrama of a sheriff investigating a murder at a local mining operation. Location filming at the Grand Canyon in Arizona. Eastmancolor and CinemaScope.

737. Edge of Fury (United Artists/Wisteria; 1958). *Cast:* Michael Higgins, Lois Holmes, Jean Allison, Doris Fesette, Malcolm Lee Beggs, Beatrice Furdeaux, John Harvey, Craig Kelly, Mary Elizabeth Boylan. *D:* Robert Gurney, Jr., Irving Lerner; *P: & Sc:* Gurney, Jr.; *Adapt:* Ted Berkman, Raphael Blau. (1:17) A woman and her two daughters unknowingly befriend a psychopathic young man while staying at a beach cottage. Based on the 1948 novel *Wisteria Cottage* by Robert M. Coates.

738. Edge of Hell (Universal-International/Hugo Haas; 1956). *Cast:* Hugo Haas, Francesca de Scaffa, Ken Carlton, June Hammerstein, Jeffrey Stone, Syra Marti, Tracey Roberts, John Vosper, Tony Jochim, Julie Mitchum, Pat Goldin, Michael Mark, Tom Wilson, Sid Melton, Walter Kahn, Peter Besbas, Flip (dog). *D:-P:-St: & Sc:* Hugo Haas. (1:16) Strange sentimental melodrama of a poor old man and his beloved performing dog, Flip. (aka: *Tender Hearts*) Originally ran on a double bill with *I've Lived Before* (q.v.).

739. Edge of the City (MGM; 1957). *Cast:* John Cassavetes, Sidney Poitier (reprising his TV role), Jack Warden, Ruby Dee, Kathleen Maguire, Ruth White (film debut), Robert Simon, Val Avery, William A. Lee, John Kellogg, David Clarke, Estelle Hemsley, Charles Jordan, Ralph Bell. *D:* Martin Ritt (directorial debut); *P:* David Susskind; *Sc:* Robert Alan Aurther (based on his 1955 TV play *A Man is Ten Feet Tall*). (1:25) Acclaimed drama of the relationship between a black dock worker and a white army deserter. The film was in nomination at the British Academy Awards and has been computer-colored by Turner Entertainment. (G.B. title: *A Man Is Ten Feet Tall*)

740. Egypt by Three (Filmakers; 1953). *Cast:* Ann Stanville, Jackie Craven, Paul Campbell, Abbas Fares, Charles Fawcett, Mahmoud el Milgul, Hassan el Baroudi, Charles Mendick, Eddie Constantine, Nabila Nouhy, The Coptic Priests of the Church of Abu Sefen, Joseph Cotten (narrator). *D: & P:* Victor Stoloff; *St:* Joseph Morheim; *Sc:* Joseph Morheim, Fred Frieberger, Lou Morheim. (1:16) This feature film is made up of three separate dramatic stories, set in exotic Egypt, joined by narration by Joseph Cotten. The first tells the tale of an adulterous knife thrower, the second of a caravan beset by cholera and the third of smuggled diamonds inside baked loaves of holy bread.

741. The Egyptian (20th Century–Fox; 1954). *Cast:* Jean Simmons (Merit), Victor Mature (Horemheb), Gene Tierney (Baketamon), Michael Wilding (Akhnaton), Bella Darvi (Nefer), Peter Ustinov (Kaptah), Edmond Purdom (Sinuhe), Judith Evelyn (Taia), Henry Daniell (Mekere), John Carradine (grave robber), Carl Benton Reid (Senmut), Tommy Rettig (Thoth), Anitra Stevens (Nefertiti), Donna Martell, Mimi Gibson, Carmen de Lavallade, Harry Thompson, George Melford, Lawrence Ryle, Ian MacDonald, Michael Granger, Don Blackman, Mike Mazurki, Peter Reynolds, Tyler McDuff, Angela Clarke, Edmund Cobb, George Chester, Michael Ansara, Harry [Henry] Corden, Geraldine Bogdonovich, Eghiche Harout, Tiger Joe Marsh, Karl Davis, Paul Salata, Joan Winfield. *D:* Michael Curtiz; *P:* Darryl F. Zanuck; *Sc:* Philip Dunne, Casey Robinson; *Cin:* (AAN-color) Leon Shamroy. (2:20) (video/laserdisc) A lowly physician becomes involved in the court of Pharaoh Akhnaton, who espouses monotheistic beliefs in the old Egypt of many gods. Lavishly produced in DeLuxe color and CinemaScope, it was loosely based on the 1949 novel by Mike Waltari. A box office dud.

742. Eight Iron Men (Columbia/Stanley Kramer Co.; 1952). *Cast:* Bonar Colleano, Arthur Franz, Lee Marvin, Richard Kiley, Nick Dennis, James Griffith, Dick Moore, George Cooper, Barney Phillips, Robert Nichols, Richard Grayson, Douglas Henderson, Mary Castle, David McMahon. *D:* Edward Dmytryk; *P:* Stanley Kramer; *Sc:* Harry Brown (based on his 1946 play *A Sound of Hunting*). (1:20) World War II drama of eight soldiers, trapped in a bombed out house and forced to repel relentless attacks by the enemy.

743. Eighteen and Anxious (Republic/AB-PT; 1957). *Cast:* Mary Webster, William Campbell, Martha Scott, Jackie Loughery, Jim Backus, Ron Hagerthy, Jackie Coogan, Damian O'Flynn, Katherine Barrett, Charlotte Wynters, Yvonne Craig, Joyce Andre, Slick Slavin, Benny Rubin. *D:* Joe Parker; *P:* Edmond Chevie; *St: & Sc:* Dale and Katherine Eunson. (1:33) In this melodrama, a teenage girl is faced with a dilemma when she finds she is pregnant. Though secretly married, she has no proof of the nuptials after her husband is killed. Originally ran on a double bill with *Panama Sal* (q.v.).

744. El Alamein (Columbia; 1953). *Cast:* Scott Brady, Edward Ashley, Robin Hughes, Rita Moreno, Michael Pate, Peter Brocco, Peter Mamakos, Ray Page, Benny Rubin, Henry Rowland. *D:* Fred F. Sears; *P:* Wallace MacDonald; *St:* Herbert Purdum; *Sc:* Purdum, George Worthing Yates, Horace McCoy (unc.). (1:06) In this World War II drama, a group of men are trapped by the Nazis at a desert oasis that is being used by the Afrika Korps as a gasoline dump. (G.B. title: *Desert Patrol*)

745. El Paso Stampede (Republic; 1953). *Cast:* Allan Lane, Phyllis Coates, Eddy Waller, Stephen Chase, Roy Barcroft, Edward Clark, Tom Monroe, Stanley Andrews, William Tannen, John Hamilton, Grant Withers (photo only), Black Jack (horse). *D:* Harry Keller; *P:* Rudy Ralston; *St: & Sc:* Arthur E. Orloff. (0:53) Special investigator "Rocky" Lane is sent to find out what became of cattle that were destined for the U.S. army fighting in the Spanish-American War. This was Lane's final series western for Republic.

746. Elephant Stampede (Monogram; 1951). *Cast:* Johnny Sheffield, Donna Martell, Edith Evanson, Martin Wilkins, John Kellogg, Myron Healey, Leonard Mudie, Guy Kingsford, James Adamson, Max Thrower, James Payne. *D: & Sc:* Ford Beebe; *P:* Walter Mirisch. (1:10) "Bomba the Jungle Boy" goes up against men who are illegally killing elephants for ivory. The 6th entry in this programmer adventure series based on a character created by Roy Rockwood. (aka: *Bomba and the Elephant Stampede*)

747. Elephant Walk (Paramount; 1954). *Cast:* Elizabeth Taylor (replacing Vivien Leigh-still visible in some long shots—who had a breakdown during production), Dana Andrews, Peter Finch, Abraham Sofaer, Abner Biberman, Noel Drayton, Rosalind Ivan (final film—ret.), Philip Tonge, Edward Ashley, Barry Bernard, Leo Britt, Mylee Havlani, Jack Raine, Victor Millan, Norma Varden, Carlos Rivero, Delmar Costello, Satini Pualioa, The Madhyma Lanka Mandala Dancers (themselves), Henry Carr, William Bengal Alwiss, Reginald Lal Singh, Charles Heard, Rodd Redwing, Adolfo Ornelas, Leslie Sketchley. *D:* William Dieterle; *P:* Irving Asher; *Sc:* John Lee Mahin. (1:43) (video) Triangular romantic-melodrama, set on an exotic Ceylonese tea plantation, of a young wife who must cope with a negligent husband haunted by his late domineering father, the elements, plague and finally a rampaging herd of elephants demolishing her home. Photographed in Technicolor, it was based on the 1949 novel by Robert Standish [pseudonym of Digby George Gerahty] and proved a winner at the box office.

Ellen (G.B. title) *see* **The Second Woman**

748. Elopement (20th Century–Fox; 1951). *Cast:* Clifton Webb, Anne Francis, Charles Bickford, William Lundigan, Reginald Gardiner, Evelyn Varden, Margalo Gillmore, Tommy Rettig, J. Farrell MacDonald (final film—d. 1952), Julia Dean, Howard Price, Willis Bouchey (film debut), Maude Wallace, Selmer Jackson, Norman Leavitt, Doris Kemper, Frank Ferguson, Michael Ross, Parley Baer, Robert Foulk. *D:* Henry Koster; *P:* Fred Kohlmar; *St: & Sc:* Bess Taffel. (1:22) Romantic/domestic comedy of an eloping couple who are pursued by their irate parents.

749. Emergency Hospital (United Artists/ Bel-Air–Sunrise Pictures, Inc.; 1956). *Cast:* Margaret Lindsay, Walter Reed, Byron Palmer, Rita Johnson, John Archer, Jim Stapleton, Peg La Centra, Frank Fenton, George Cisar, Tito Vuolo, Mary Carver, Joy Lee, Vera Francis, Maxine Gates, Robert Keys, Jan Englund, Mark Lowell, William "Red" Murphy, George Sawaya, Gary Gray, Rhodes Reason, William Boyett, Saul Martell, John Merrick. *D:* Lee Sholem; *P:* Howard W. Koch; *St: & Sc:* Don Martin. (1:02) Programmer melodrama of activities in a hospital during one 12-hour shift.

750. Emergency Wedding (Columbia; 1950). *Cast:* Larry Parks, Barbara Hale, Willard Parker, Una Merkel, Alan Reed, Eduard Franz, Irving Bacon, Don Beddoe, Jim Backus, Ian Wolfe, Teru Shimada, Myron Welton, Helen Spring, Greg McClure, Boyd Davis, Pierre Watkin, Myron Healey, Harry Harvey, Jean Willes, William Forrest, Queenie Smith, Jerry Mickelsen, George Meader, Dorothy Vaughan, Sydney Mason, Lucille Shamburger, Arthur Howard, Virginia Cruzon, Grace Burns, Elsa Peterson, Cosmo Sardo, Joe Palma, Frank Arnold, Wilson Benge, Mike Lally, Warren Mace, Shirley Ballard, Stephen Chase, Mary Emery, Thomas F. Martin, Thomas Patrick McCormick, Billy Nelson, James O'Gatty, Ted Jordan, William E. Green, James Conaty, James Carlisle, Bobby Johnson, Vivian Mason, Kathleen O'Malley, Louise Kane, Frank Cady, Ann Tyrrell, Simon "Stuffy" Singer, Paul Bradley, John Kascier, Richard LaMarr, Elizabeth Flournoy, Mary Newton, Ruth Warren, Muriel Maddox, Marjorie Stapp, Beverly Crane, Ted Stanhope, Henry Sylvester. *D:* Edward Buzzell; *P:* Nat Perrin; *St:* Dalton Trumbo; *Sc:* Perrin, Claude Binyon. (1:18) Marital comedy of a man who is jealous of his wife's male patients in her medical practice. A remake of *You Belong to Me* (Columbia; 1941). (G.B. title: *Jealousy*)

751. Enchanted Island (Warner/RKO-Waverly; 1958). *Cast:* Dana Andrews, Jane Powell (final film—ret.), Don Dubbins, Arthur Shields, Ted de Corsia, Friedrich Ledebur, Augustin Fernandez, Francisco Reiguera, Les Hellman, Eddie Saenz, Dale Van Sickel, Paul Stader.

D: Allan Dwan; *P:* Benedict Bogeaus; *Sc:* James Leicester, Harold Jacob Smith; *Title song:* Robert Allen. (1:34) (video) 19th century South Sea island romantic adventure of Americans who desert their whaling ship and come ashore on an island inhabited by cannibals. Based on Herman Melville's 1846 novel *Typee*. This was an RKO production in Technicolor that was released by Warner Brothers after the former studio closed down operations.

End as a Man (G.B. title) *see* **The Strange One**

752. The Enemy Below (20th Century–Fox; 1957). *Cast:* Robert Mitchum (Capt. Murrell), Curt Jurgens (U.S. debut/Von Stolberg), Al [David] Hedison (Lt. Ware), Theodore Bikel (Schwaffer), Russell Collins (doctor), Kurt Kreuger (Von Holem), Frank Albertson (C.P.O. Crain), Biff Elliot (quartermaster), Alan Dexter (Mackeson), Doug McClure (film debut/ Ensign Merry), Jeff Daley (Corky), David Blair (Ellis), Joe Di Reda (Robbins), Ralph Manza (Lt. Bonelli), Ted Perritt (messenger), Jimmy Bayes (Quiroga), Arthur La Ral (Kunz), Frank Obershall (Braun), Robert Boon (chief engineer), Werner Reichow (Mueller), Peter Dane (Andrews, the radio operator), Lee J. Winters (Striker), David Post (Lewis), Ronnie Rondell, Ralph Reed, Maurice Doner, Jack Kramer, Robert Whiteside, Dan Tann, Dale Cummings, Sasha Harden, Michael McHale, Joe Brooks, Thomas Beyl, Richard Elmore, Vincent Deadrick, Dan Nelson, Roger Cornwell. *D: & P:* Dick Powell; *Sc:* Wendell Mayes; *F/X:* (AA) Walter Rossi. (1:38) (video) Acclaimed World War II drama of the American captain of a destroyer escort, and the game of cat and mouse he plays with a German U-boat commander. Based on the 1956 novel by D.A. [Denys Arthur] Rayner, it took a #8 placement on the "10 Best" list of the NBR. DeLuxe color and CinemaScope.

753. The Enforcer (Warner/United States Pictures; 1951). *Cast:* Humphrey Bogart, Zero Mostel, Ted de Corsia, Everett Sloane, Roy Roberts, King Donovan, Lawrence Tolan, Bob Steele, Don Beddoe, Adelaide Klein, Tito Vuolo, John Kellogg, Jack Lambert, Patricia Joiner, Susan Cabot, Mario Siletti, Alan Foster, Harry Wilson, Pete Kellett, Barry Reagan, Dan Riss, Art Dupuis, Bud [Bill] Wolfe, Creighton Hale, Patricia Hayes, Robert Strong, Mike Lally, George Meader, Ralph Dunn, Perc Launders, John Maxwell, Tom Dillon, Brick Sullivan, Howard Mitchell, Monte Pittman, Louis Lettieri, Greta Granstedt, Chuck Hamilton, Jay Morley, Richard Bartell, Karen Kester, Eula Guy. *D:* Bretaigne Windust, Raoul Walsh (unc.); *P:* Milton Sperling; *St: & Sc:* Martin Rackin. (1:27) (video/laserdisc) Acclaimed dramatic thriller of a D.A. out to break up a syndicate of hired killers operating nationwide. (G.B. title: *Murder, Inc.*)

754. Escapade in Japan (Universal-International/RKO; 1957). *Cast:* Teresa Wright, Cameron Mitchell, Jon Provost, Roger Nakagawa, Philip Ober, Kuniko Miyake, Fujita, Katsuhiko Haida, Tatsuo Saito, Hideko Koshikawa, Ureo Egawa, Frank Tokunaga, Ayako Hidaka, Clint Eastwood. *D: & P:* Arthur Lubin; *St: & Sc:* Winston Miller. (1:30) (video) Family oriented adventure of a Japanese boy helping an American boy reunite with his parents. Filmed on location in Japan, the film was produced by RKO, but released by Universal when RKO closed its doors. Technirama and color.

755. Escape from Fort Bravo (MGM; 1953). *Cast:* William Holden, Eleanor Parker, John Forsythe, William Demarest, William Campbell, Polly Bergen, Richard Anderson, Carl Benton Reid, John Lupton, Howard McNear, Alex Montoya, Forrest Lewis, Fred Graham, William Newell, Frank Matts, Charles Stevens, Michael Dugan, Valerie Vernon, Phil Rich, Glenn Strange, Harry Cheshire, Eloise Hardt, Richard P. Beele. *D:* John Sturges; *P:* Nicholas Nayfack; *St:* Philip Rock, Michael Pate; *Sc:* Frank Fenton; *Songs:* "Yellow Stripes" Stan Jones, "Soothe My Lonely Heart" Jeff Alexander. (1:38) (video) Hit western set in 1863's Arizona territory, the conflict that exists between Confederate and Union soldiers, as well as their conflict with the local Indians. Anscocolor.

756. Escape from Red Rock (20th Century–Fox/Regal Films; 1958). *Cast:* Brian Donlevy, Eileen Janssen, Gary Murray, Jay C. Flippen, William Phipps, Myron Healey, Nesdon Booth, Rick Vallin, Dan White, Andre Adoree, Courtland Shepard, Tina Menard, Natividad Vacio, Linda Dangell, Joe Becker, Roydon Clark, Zon Murray, Ed Hinton, Frosty Royce, Frank Richards, Eumenia Blanco, Hank Patterson, Eileen Stevens, Frank Marlowe, Elena Da Vinci, Dick Crockett, Bud Osborne (final film—ret.), Sailor Vincent, The Adamson Twins, Al Baffert, Vincent Padula. *D: & Sc:* Edward Bernds; *P:* Bernard Glasser. (1:15) Western of a man who flees into the Mexican desert, after being forced into participating in a bank robbery in which a woman was killed. Regalscope.

757. Escape from San Quentin (Columbia; 1957). *Cast:* Johnny Desmond, Merry Anders, Richard Devon, Roy Engel, William Bryant, Ken Christy, Larry Blake, Don Devlin, Victor Millan, John Merrick, Norman Frederic, Barry Brooks, Lennie Smith. *D:* Fred F. Sears; *P:* Sam Katzman; *St:* *&* *Sc:* Raymond T. Marcus; *Song:* "Lonely Lament" by Johnny Desmond. (1:21) In this programmer melodrama, three men escape from California's San Quentin prison.

Escape Me If You Can (G.B. title) *see* **St. Benny the Dip**

758. Escape to Burma (RKO/Filmcrest; 1955). *Cast:* Robert Ryan, Barbara Stanwyck, David Farrar, Murvyn Vye, Robert Warwick, Reginald Denny, Lisa Montell, Peter Coe, Anthony Numkena [aka: Earl Holliman], Alex Montoya, Lal Chand Mehra, Robert Cabal, William Benegal Raw, John Mansfield, Gavin Muir, Pete Kooy, Bob Corby, Polly Burson, Bill Cartledge, Neyle Morrow, Henry Van Horn, Henry Escalante, Sharon Lee, Jackie Loughery, Gloria Marshall, Paul Fierro, Artie Ortego, John Dodsworth, Billy Wilkerson, Tom Humphrey, Carl Mathews, Riley Sunrise, George Deere, Art Felix, Joe Milan, Leo McMahon, Manuel Ybarra, Jose Saenz, Kuka Tuitama, Rocky Barry, Joe Ferrante, Wag Bessing, Jimmy Van Horn, Tim Nelson, Roger (leopard), Neil (chimpanzee), Emma, Tessie, Little Babe, Marge, Judy & Mary (elephants). *D:* Allan Dwan; *P:* Benedict Bogeaus; *Sc:* Talbot Jennings, Hobart Donavan. (1:26) (video) Adventure melodrama of a man on the run from a murder charge, who meets and falls for the female owner of a tea plantation. Based on the story "Bow Tamely to Me" by Kenneth Perkins, it was filmed on location at a California animal compound in Technicolor and SuperScope.

759. Escort West (United Artists/Romina-Batjac; 1959). *Cast:* Victor Mature, Elaine Edwards, Faith Domergue, Reba Waters, Noah Beery, Jr., Rex Ingram, Leo Gordon, John Hubbard, Harry Carey, Jr., William Ching, Slim Pickens, Roy Barcroft, Ken Curtis, X Brands, Chuck Hayward, Charles Soldani, Claire DuBrey, Syd Saylor (final film—d. 1962). *D:* Francis D. Lyon; *P:* Robert E. Morrison, Nate H. Edwards; *St:* Steven Hayes; *Sc:* Leo Gordon, Fred Hartsook. (1:15) A widowed Confederate veteran of the Civil War, traveling with his 10-year-old daughter, comes upon two sisters and a black soldier, the sole survivors of a Modoc Indian attack, who are in possession of a U.S. army payroll. Filmed in California's San Fernando Valley.

760. The Eternal Sea (Republic; 1955). *Cast:* Sterling Hayden, Alexis Smith, Dean Jagger, Ben Cooper, Hayden Rorke, Virginia Grey, Douglas Kennedy, Louis Jean Heydt, Richard Crane, Morris Ankrum, Frank Ferguson, John Maxwell. *D:* *&* *As.P:* John H. Auer; *Ex.P:* Herbert J. Yates; *St:* William Wister Haines; *Sc:* Allen Rivkin. (1:43) Biographical drama of Rear Admiral John H. Hoskins, who maintained his position as commander of an aircraft carrier, despite his loss of a leg in a Japanese attack.

Every Minute Counts (G.B. title) *see* **Count the Hours**

761. Everybody's Dancin' (Lippert/Nunes-Cooley Prods.; 1950). *Cast:* Spade Cooley, Dick Lane, Barbara Woodell, Ginny Jackson, Hal Derwin, James Millican, Lyle Talbot, Michael Whalen, Sid Melton, Tex Cromer, Les Anderson, Fred Kelsey, Dorothy Lloyd, Bobby Hyatt, George Meader, Eddie Borden, Sons of the Pioneers, Dan Rense, Chuy Reyes & Orchestra, The Flying Taylors, The Great Velardi, Roddy McDowall, Adele Jergens, Jimmy Ellison, Russell Hayden, Virginia MacPherson. *D:* Will Jason; *P:* Bob Nunes; *As.P:* Spade Cooley; *St:* Nunes, Cooley; *Sc:* Dorothy Raison; *Songs include:* "Foolish Tears" by Jackson; "Oblivious" by Derwin; "Deep Freeze Dinah" by Cromer; "I Shook" by Anderson; and "Rhumba Boogie" by Reyes & Orchestra. (1:05) Programmer musical of a phony promoter's attempts to save a dance palace.

762. Everything But the Truth (Universal-International; 1956). *Cast:* Maureen O'Hara, John Forsythe, Tim Hovey, Frank Faylen, Les Tremayne, Addison Richards, Paul Birch, Jeanette Nolan, Bert Atwater, Roxanne Arlen, Ray Walker, Donald Dillaway, Ken Osmond, Bill Anders, Dorothy Abbott, Arnold Ishii, Gertrude Astor. *D:* Jerry Hopper; *P:* Howard Christie; *St:* Stanley Roberts, Sheridan Gibney (based on an idea by Roberts and Val Burton); *Sc:* Herb Meadow. (1:23) Family comedy of what happens when it is instilled in a young boy to always tell the truth. Eastmancolor.

763. Everything I Have Is Yours (MGM; 1952). *Cast:* Marge and Gower Champion,

Dennis O'Keefe, Eduard Franz, Monica Lewis, Dean Miller, John Gallaudet, Jonathan Cott, Diane Cassidy, Elaine Stewart, Robert Burton, Jean Fenwick, Mimi Gibson, Wilson Wood. *D:* Robert Z. Leonard; *P:-St: & Sc:* George Wells; *Additional dialogue:* Ruth Brooks Flippen; *Choreography:* G. Champion, Nick Castle. *Songs include:* "Derry Down Dilly" (Johnny Green–Johnny Mercer); "Like Monday Follows Sunday" (Green–Clifford Grey–Rex Newman-Douglas Furber); "17,000 Telephone Poles" (Saul Chaplin); "Serenade For a New Baby" (Green), "My Heart Skips a Beat" (Bob Wright–Chet Forrest–Walter Donaldson); Title song (Harold Adamson–Burton Lane). (1:31) Musical of a married dance team (the Champions) who find that a night of love has produced unexpected results, just when they are about to get their big break on Broadway. Technicolor.

The Evil Force (G.B. title) *see* **4D Man**

764. Excuse My Dust (MGM; 1951). *Cast:* Red Skelton, Sally Forrest (singing voice dubbed by Gloria Grey), Macdonald Carey, William Demarest, Raymond Walburn, Monica Lewis, Jane Darwell, Lillian Bronson, Guy Anderson, Paul Harvey, Marjorie Wood, Lee Scott, Alex Gerry, Jim Hayward, Will Wright, Ed Peil, Sr., Sheree North (film debut/unbilled bit). *D:* Roy Rowland; *P:* Jack Cummings; *St: & Sc:* George Wells; *Choreography:* Hermes Pan; *Songs:* "Spring is Sprung," "Lorelei Brown," "That's for the Children," "Get a Horse," "Going Steady" and "I'd Like to Take You Out Dreaming" Arthur Schwartz–Dorothy Fields. (1:22) Technicolor musical-comedy of an eccentric inventor (ca. 1895) whose latest invention of the horseless carriage causes problems with his girl's father, who happens to own the local livery stable.

765. Executive Suite (MGM; 1954). *Cast:* William Holden (McDonald Walling), June Allyson (Mary Blemond Walling), Barbara Stanwyck (Julie O. Tredway), Frederic March (Loren Phineas Shaw), Walter Pidgeon (Frederick Alderson), Shelley Winters (Eva Bardeman), Paul Douglas (Josiah Dudley), Louis Calhern (George Nyle Caswell), Dean Jagger (Jesse Grimm), Nina Foch (AAN + "Best Supporting Actress" Award from the NBR/Erica Martin), Tim Considine (Mike Walling), William Phipps (Bill Lundeen), Lucille Knoch (Mrs. Caswell), Mary Adams (Sarah Grimm), Virginia Brissac (Edith Alderson), Edgar Stehli (Julius Steigel), Harry Shannon (Ed Benedeck), Charles Wagenheim (Luigi Cassoni), Roy Engel (Jimmy Farrell), Raoul Freeman (Avery Bullard), Bob Carson (Lee Ormond), Kasia Orzazewski (Liz), Burt Mustin (Sam Teal), Helen Brown (Miss Clark), May McAvoy (Grimm's secretary), Ann Tyrrell (Shaw's secretary), Ray Mansfield (Alderson's secretary), Jonathan Cott, Willis Bouchey, John Doucette, Esther Michelson, Gus Schilling, Paul Bryar, John Banner, Maidie Norman, Dan Riss, Wilson Wood, Matt Moore. *D:* Robert Wise; *P:* John Houseman; *Sc:* Ernest Lehman; *Cin:* (AAN-b/w) George Folsey; *ASD:* (AAN-b/w) Cedric Gibbons, Edward Carfagno (art directors), Edwin B. Willis, Emile Kuri (sets); *Costumes:* (AAN-b/w) Helen Rose. (1:44) (video) Acclaimed drama of corporate board members in a power struggle. Based on the 1952 novel by Cameron Hawley, it placed #5 on the "10 Best" list of the NBR and #8 on the same list of *Film Daily*. It received the "Special Jury Prize" at the Venice Film Festival and was in nomination at the British Academy Awards. One of the 25 top-grossing films of 1953-54, it was also the basis for a later TV series.

Expedition Moon *see* **Rocketship X-M**

766. Experiment Alcatraz (RKO/Crystal; 1950). *Cast:* John Howard, Joan Dixon, Walter Kingsford, Lynne Carter, Robert Shayne, Kim Spalding, Sam Scar, Kenneth MacDonald, Dick Cogan, Frank Cady, Byron Foulger, Ralph Peters, Lewis Martin, Harry Lauter, Raymond Largay. *D: & P:* Edward L. Cahn; *St: & Sc:* Orville H. Hampton (based on a screenplay by George W. George and George F. Slavin). (0:58) A doctor is experimenting with a radioactive drug on prison inmates, with the premise that if they survive, they will be granted a pardon.

767. Eyes of the Jungle (Lippert/Arrow Prods.; 1953). *Cast:* Jon Hall, Ray Montgomery, Edgar Barrier, Victor Millan, Frank Fenton, Robert Shayne, Leonard Penn, M'Liss McClure, Merrill McCormack, James Fairfax, William Tannen, Charles Stevens, Alyce Lewis. *D:* Paul Landres; *P:* Rudolph Flothow; *Sc:* Barry Shipman, Sherman L. Lowe. (1:19) A feature-length jungle adventure pieced together from episodes of the TV series *Ramar of the Jungle* and released theatrically. (G.B. title: *Destination Danger*)

Eyes of the Skies (G.B. title) *see* **Mission Over Korea**

768. F.B.I. Girl (Lippert/JEDGAR Prods.; 1951). *Cast:* Cesar Romero, George Brent, Audrey Totter, Tom Drake, Raymond Burr, Raymond Greenleaf, Margia Dean, Don Garner, Alexander Pope, Richard Monohan, Tom Noonan and Pete Marshall, Jan Kayne, Joy [Joi] Lansing, Byron Foulger, Walter Coy, Joel Marston, Marie Blake [aka: Blossom Rock], Fenton Earnshaw, O.Z. Whitehead. *D: & P:* William Berke; *St:* Rupert Hughes; *Sc:* Richard Landau, Dwight V. Babcock. (1:14) A crooked politician and his dirty dealings are uncovered by a female F.B.I. employee.

769. The FBI Story (Warner/Mervyn LeRoy; 1959). *Cast:* James Stewart (Chip Hardesty/narrator), Vera Miles (Lucy Hardesty), Murray Hamilton (Sam Crandall), Larry Pennell (George Crandall), Nick Adams (Jack Graham), Diane Jergens (Jennie, the adult), Joyce Taylor (Anne, the adult), Victor Millan (Mario), Jean Willes (Anna Sage "The Lady in Red"), Parley Baer (Harry Dakins), Fay Roope (Dwight MacCutcheon), Buzz Martin (Mike, the adult), Ed Prentiss (U.S. Marshal/radio announcer), Paul George (Whitey), Scott Peters (John Dillinger), Ann Doran (Mrs. Ballard), William Phipps ("Baby Face" Nelson), Paul Smith (Taylor), Eleanor Audley (Mrs. Graham), Bert Mustin (Schneider), Guy Wilkerson (Cliff), Nesdon Booth (Sandy), J. Edgar Hoover (himself), Robert Gist, Kenneth Mayer, Forrest Taylor, John Damler, Harry Harvey, Sam Flint, Grandon Rhodes, Ray Montgomery, Lori Martin. *D: & P:* Mervyn LeRoy; *Sc:* Richard L. Breen, John Twist. (2:29) (video/laserdisc) Technicolor drama of America's Federal Bureau of Investigation from its beginnings, as seen through the eyes of one agent, with added details on his family life and episodic exploits involving his work. Based on the 1956 best-seller by Don Whitehead, it became one of the 28 top-grossing films of 1959-60. Location filming took place in Washington, D.C., and New York City.

770. The Fabulous Senorita (Republic; 1952). *Cast:* Estelita (Rodriguez), Robert Clarke, Nestor Paiva, Marvin Kaplan, Rita Moreno, Leon Belasco, Tito Renaldo, Tom Powers, Emory Parnell, Olin Howlin, Vito Scotti, Martin Garralaga, Nita Del Rey. *D:* R.G. Springsteen; *As.P:* Sidney Picker; *St:* Jack Townley, Charles R. Marion; *Sc:* Townley, Charles E. Roberts. (1:20) Romantic comedy of a senorita who falls for a college professor, though she is set to marry the son of a wealthy banker.

771. A Face in the Crowd (Warner/Newton Prod.; 1957). *Cast:* Andy Griffith (film debut), Patricia Neal, Anthony Franciosa, Walter Matthau, Lee Remick (film debut), Percy Waram, Rod Brosfield, Charles Irving, Howard Smith, Paul McGrath, Kay Medford, Alexander Kirkland (final film—ret.), Marshall Neilan (final film—d. 1958), Big Jeff Bess, Henry Sharp, Bennett Cerf (himself), Faye Emerson (herself), Betty Furness (herself), Virginia Graham (herself), Burl Ives (himself), Sam Levenson (himself), John Cameron Swayze (himself), Mike Wallace (himself), Earl Wilson (himself), Walter Winchell (himself), Rip Torn, Lois Nettleton (film debut). *D: & P:* Elia Kazan; *Sc:* Budd Schulberg; *Songs:* "Mama Git-tar," "Free Man in the Morning" Tom Glazer–Schulberg. (2:05) (video) Drama of a country boy who is turned into a popular TV personality by a promoter and the media. The film opened to critical acclaim and placed #7 on the "10 Best" list of *Film Daily*, but showed poor returns at the box office. Based on the short story "Your Arkansas Traveler" by Budd Schulberg.

772. Face of a Fugitive (Columbia/Morningside; 1959). *Cast:* Fred MacMurray, Lin McCarthy, Dorothy Green, Alan Baxter, Myrna Fahey, James Coburn, Francis DeSales, Gina Gillespie, Ron Hayes, Paul E. Burns, Robert "Buzz" Henry, John Milford, James Gavin, Hal K. Dawson, Stanley Farrar, Rankin Mansfield, Harrison Lewis. *D:* Paul Wendkos; *Ex.P:* Charles H. Schneer; *P:* David Hailweil; *Sc:* Daniel B. Ullman, David T. Chantler. (1:21) A former outlaw's past catches up with him while trying to live under another identity in another town. In Eastmancolor, it was based on the 1956 short story "Long Gone" by Peter Dawson.

773. Face of Fire (Allied Artists/Mardi Gras; 1959). *Cast:* Cameron Mitchell, James Whitmore, Bettye Ackerman, Miko Oscard, Royal Dano, Robert Simon, Richard Erdman, Howard Smith, Lois Maxwell, Jill Donahue. *D:* Albert Band; *P:* Band, Louis Garfinkle; *As.P:* Gustav Unger; *Sc:* Garfinkle. (1:23) Drama of a simple handyman, horribly disfigured in a fire while saving his employer's young son, and the rejection he receives from local townspeople. Based on Stephen Crane's 1899 short story "The Monster," it was filmed in Sweden.

774. Face to Face (RKO/Theasquare Prods., Inc.; 1952). A feature film made up of two separate stories: 1. "The Secret Sharer" *Cast:* James Mason (who won the "Best Actor" Award from the NBR combined with his work in *The Desert Rats* [q.v.], *Julius Caesar* [q.v.] and *The Man Between*, a British production), Gene Lockhart, Michael Pate, Albert Sharpe, Sean McClory, Alec Harford. *D:* John Brahm; *P:* Huntington Hartford; *Sc:* Aeneas Mackenzie. Drama of a novice sea captain who finds a wanted fugitive aboard his ship. Based on the 1928 story by Joseph Conrad. 2. "The Bride Comes to Yellow Sky" *Cast:* Robert Preston, Marjorie Steele, Minor Watson, Dan Seymour, Olive Carey, James Agee. *D:* Bretaigne Windust; *P:* Hartford; *Sc:* James Agee. Western drama of a sheriff who has to deal with an old man who believes in and lives by the "law of the gun." Based on the story by Stephen Crane. (1:32) (video)

775. **Fair Wind to Java** (Republic; 1953). *Cast:* Fred MacMurray, Vera Ralston, Robert Douglas, Victor McLaglen, John Russell, Buddy Baer, Claude Jarman, Jr., Grant Withers, Howard Petrie, Paul Fix, William Murphy, Sujata (specialty dancer), Philip Ahn, Stephan Bekassy, Keye Luke, John Halloran, Howard Chuman, Mailoa Kalili, Al Kikume, Blackie Whiteford, Chuck Hayward, Richard Reeves, Virginia Brissac. *D: & P:* Joseph Kane; *Sc:* Richard Tregaskis. (1:32) South Seas adventure of a trader making his fortune with diamonds, and another bent on getting the diamonds for himself. Based on the 1948 novel by Garland Roark, the film climaxes with a volcanic eruption, done by the brothers Lydecker, Howard and Theodore. Trucolor.

False News (G.B. title) *see* **Barbed Wire**

776. **The Family Secret** (Columbia/Santana Prods.; 1951). *Cast:* John Derek, Lee J. Cobb, Jody Lawrence, Erin O'Brien-Moore, Henry O'Neill, Santos Ortega, Carl Benton Reid, Peggy Converse, Jean Alexander, Dorothy Tree, Onslow Stevens, Whit Bissell, Bill Walker, Frances E. Williams, Mary Alan Hokanson. *D:* Henry Levin; *P:* Robert Lord; *St:* Marie Baumer, James Cavanaugh; *Sc:* Francis Cockrell, Andrew Solt. (1:25) (video) Drama of a man who defends another on a murder charge, knowing his own son is guilty of the killing. Originally ran on a double bill with *Harlem Globetrotters* (q.v.).

777. **Fancy Pants** (Paramount; 1950). *Cast:* Bob Hope (Humphrey), Lucille Ball (Aggie Floud), Bruce Cabot (Carl Belknap), Jack Kirkwood (Mike Floud), Lea Penman (Effie Floud), Hugh French (George Van Bassingwell), Eric Blore (Sir Wimbley), John Alexander (Teddy Roosevelt), Joseph Vitale (Wampum), Norma Varden (Lady Maude), Colin Keith-Johnston (Twombley), Virginia Kelley (Rosalind), Joe Wong (Wong), Robin Hughes (Cyril), Percy Helton (Mayor Fogarty), Hope Sansberry (Millie), Grace Gillern Albertson (Dolly), Oliver Blake (Mr. Andrews), Edgar Dearing (Mr. Jones), Alva Marie Lacy (Daisy), Ida Moore (dual role/Betsy & Bessie), Ethel Wales (Mrs. Wilkins), Jean Ruth (Miss Wilkins), Almira Sessions (Belle), Chester Conklin, Jimmie Dundee, Bob Kortman, Major Sam Harris, Gilchrist Stuart, Charley Cooley, Olaf Hytten, Alex Frazer, Howard Petrie, Ray Bennett. *D:* George Marshall; *P:* Robert Welch; *Sc:* Edmund Hartmann, Robert O'Brien; *Songs:* "Fancy Pants," "Home Cookin'," "Yes, M'Lord" Jay Livingston–Ray Evans. (1:32) (video/laserdisc) Comedy of a newly rich American girl who acquires an English butler. Based on the novel by Harry Leon Wilson, it is a Technicolor remake of *Ruggles of Red Gap*, filmed thrice under that title, in 1918 by Essanay, in 1923 by Paramount and the better known 1935 version by Paramount. One of the 28 top-grossing films of 1949-50.

778. **Fangs of the Arctic** (Monogram/Allied Artists; 1953). *Cast:* Kirby Grant, Chinook the Wonder Dog, Lorna Hansen, Warren Douglas, Leonard Penn, Richard Avonde, Robert Sherman, John Close, Roy Gordon, Kit Carson. *D:* Rex Bailey; *P:* Lindsley Parsons; *Sc:* Bill Raynor; *Additional dialogue:* Warren Douglas. (1:03) Low budget adventure of a Mountie and his dog, investigating illegal fur trapping. Based on a story by James Oliver Curwood, it was part of a series begun in 1949.

779. **Fangs of the Wild** (Lippert/Jesse James Corp.; 1954). *Cast:* Charles Chaplin, Jr., Onslow Stevens, Margia Dean, Freddy Ridgeway, Phil Tead, Robert Stevenson, Buck (dog). *D: & Story idea:* William F. Claxton; *P:* Robert L. Lippert, Jr.; *Sc:* Orville Hampton. (1:12) A small boy, witness to a murder believed by others to have been a hunting accident, finds himself targeted by the killer. (aka: *Follow the Hunter*).

The Fantastic Disappearing Man (G.B. title) *see* **The Return of Dracula**

780. **The Far Country** (Universal-International; 1955). *Cast:* James Stewart (Jeff Webster),

Ruth Roman (Ronda Castle), Corinne Calvet (Renee Vallon), John McIntire (Mr. Gannon), Walter Brennan (Ben Tatem), Jay C. Flippen (Rube), Henry [Harry] Morgan (Ketchum), Steve Brodie (Ives), Connie Gilchrist (Hominy), Chubby Johnson (Dusty), Royal Dano (Luke), Bob Wilke (Madden), Jack Elam (Newberry), Kathleen Freeman (Grits), Eddy Waller (Yukon Sam), Robert Foulk (Kingman), Eugene Borden (Doc Vallon), Allan Ray (Bosun), Gregg Barton (Rounds), Connie Van (Molasses), Guy Wilkerson (Tanana Pete), Stuart Randall (Capt. Benson), Chuck Roberson (Latigo), Jack Williams (Shep), William J. Williams (Gant), Paul Bryar (sheriff), Terry Frost (Joe Merin), Edwin Parker (Carson), Don C. Harvey (Tom Kane), Angeline Engler (Mrs. Kingman), Charles Sweetlove (Porcupine Smith), John Doucette, Damian O'Flynn, John Halloran, Robert Bice, Marjorie Stapp, Gina Holland, Andy Brennan, Carl Harbaugh, Paul Savage, James W. Horan, Gerard Baril, Ted Kemp, John Mackin, Dick Taylor, Dick Dickinson, Ted Mapes, Len McDonald, Jack Dixon. *D:* Anthony Mann; *P:* Aaron Rosenberg; *St: & Sc:* Borden Chase. (1:36) (video) A critically acclaimed 19th century drama of the Alaskan gold fields and a cattleman delivering a herd of beef, with the intent of selling them at a high price. One of the 27 top-grossing films of 1954-55. Technicolor.

781. The Far Horizons (Paramount/Pine-Thomas; 1955). *Cast:* Charlton Heston (Meriwether Lewis), Fred MacMurray (William Clark), Donna Reed (Sacajawea), William Demarest, Barbara Hale, Herbert Heyes (President Thomas Jefferson), Ralph Moody, Argentina Brunetti, Alan Reed, Eduardo Noriega, Larry Pennell, Lester Matthews, Helen Wallace, Walter Reed, Voltaire Perkins, Joe Canutt, Julia Montoya, Bill Phipps, Tom Monroe, LeRoy Johnson, Bob Herron, Herman Scharff, Al Wyatt, Vernon Rich, Bill Walker, Margarita Martin, Frank Fowler, Fran Bennett. *D:* Rudolph Maté; *P:* William H. Pine, William C. Thomas; *Sc:* Winston Miller, Edmund H. North. (1:48) A partially fabricated version of the Lewis and Clark expedition into the Pacific Northwest in 1803 to 1806, including romance with their Indian guide. Based on the novel *Sacajawea of the Shoshones* by Della Gould Emmons, it was in VistaVision and Technicolor. (aka: *The Untamed West*)

782. A Farewell to Arms (20th Century-Fox/Selznick Co., Inc.; 1957). *Cast:* Rock Hudson (received *Photoplay* Gold Medal Award/Lt. Frederick Henry), Jennifer Jones (Nurse Catherine Barkley), Vittorio De Sica (AAN/Major Allessandro Rinaldi), Alberto Sordi (Father Galli), Mercedes McCambridge (Miss Van Campen), Oscar Homolka (Dr. Emerich), Elaine Stritch (Helen Ferguson), Leopoldo Trieste (Pussini), Franco Interlenghi (Aymo), Georges Brehat (Capt. Bassi), Memmo Carotenuto (Nino), Victor Francen (Col. Valentini), Joan Shawlee, Guido Martufi, Umberto Spadaro, Umberto Sacripanti, Albert D'Amerio, Giacomo Rossi-Stuart, Carlo Pedersoli, Alex Revides, France Mancinelli, Patrick Crean, Guidarino Guidi, Luigi Barzini, Diana King, Clelia Matania, Edward Linkers, Johanna Hofer, Carlo Licari, Angelo Galassi, Carlo Hintermann, Tiberio Mitri, Peter Illing, Sam Levene, Eva Kotthaus, Gisella Mathews, Vittorio Jannitti. *D:* Charles Vidor (final completed film—d. 1959/replacing John Huston); *P:* David O. Selznick (final film as producer); *Sc:* Ben Hecht. (2:32) (video) World War I drama of an ambulance driver who falls for a nurse. Based on Ernest Hemingway's 1929 novel, it was previously filmed by Paramount in 1932 (a version considered superior to this remake). It took a #10 placement on the "10 Best" list of the NBR and went on to become one of the 26 top-grossing films of 1957-58. DeLuxe color and CinemaScope.

783. Fargo (Monogram/Silvermine Prods.; 1952). *Cast:* William "Wild Bill" Elliott, Phyllis Coates, Myron Healey, Fuzzy Knight, Jack Ingram, Arthur Space, Robert Wilke, Terry Frost, Robert Bray, Tim Ryan, Florence Lake, Stanley Andrews, Richard Reeves, Eugene [Gene] Roth, Denver Pyle, I. Stanford Jolley, Stanley Price, House Peters, Jr. *D:* Lewis D. Collins; *P:* Vincent M. Fennelly; *St: & Sc:* Joseph Poland, Jack DeWitt. (1:09) Western melodrama of a range war incited by the introduction of barbed wire to the prairie. Sepiatone.

784. The Farmer Takes a Wife (20th Century–Fox; 1953). *Cast:* Betty Grable, Dale Robertson, Thelma Ritter, John Carroll, Eddie Foy, Jr., Charlotte Austin (film debut), Kathleen Crowley, Mary [Merry] Anders, Donna Lee Hickey [May Wynn], Noreen Michaels, Ruth Hall, William Pullen, Mort Mills, Juanita Evers, Lee Turnbull, Gwen Verdon, Howard Negley, Joanne Jordan, Gene Roth, Mel Pogue, Gordon Nelson, Ralph Sanford, Don Garrett, Ted Jordan, Kermit Maynard, Jack Harris, Lee Phelps, Donald Kerr, Martin Deane, Bobby Hyatt, Brad Mora, Ed Hinton, Max Wagner, John Close, Paul Kruger, Fred Aldrich, Ralph Montgomery, Fred Graham, Jack Stoney, John

Butler, Emile Meyer, Wesley Hudman. *D:* Henry Levin; *P:* Frank P. Rosenberg; *Sc:* Walter Bullock, Sally Benson, Joseph Fields; *Songs:* "We're in Business," "On the Erie Canal," "We're Doing It for the Natives in Jamaica," "When I Close My Door," "Today, I Love Everybody," "Somethin' Real Special," "With the Sun Warm Upon Me" and "Can You Spell Schenectady?" Harold Arlen–Dorothy Fields. (1:20) (video) A musical remake of the 1935 dramatic film with the same name, about life and love along the Erie Canal in the 1850s. Adapted from the 1935 play *Low Bridge* by Frank B. Elser and Marc Connelly, which in turn was taken from the novel *Rome Haul* by Walter D. Edmonds.

785. The Fast and the Furious (American Releasing Corp./Palo Alto; 1954). *Cast:* John Ireland, Dorothy Malone, Bruce Carlisle, Marshall Bradford, Jean Howell, Larry Thor, Robin Morse, Bruno VeSota, Iris Adrian. *D:* John Ireland, Edwards Sampson; *P: & St:* Roger Corman; *Sc:* Jerome Odlum, Jean Howell. (1:13) (video) A man flees after being framed for murder. In an attempt to get into Mexico, steals a Jaguar (and the lady owner), joins a race, finds love, and returns to clear his name. Note: The first film of American Releasing Corporation that later became American International Pictures.

786. Fast Company (MGM; 1953). *Cast:* Howard Keel, Polly Bergen, Marjorie Main, Nina Foch, Robert Burton, Horace McMahon, Iron Eyes Cody, Carol Nugent, Joaquin Garay, Sig Arno, Perry Sheehan, Pat Goldin, Jonathan Cott, Benny Burt, Jack Kruschen, Paul Brinegar, Jess Kirkpatrick, Lou Smith. *D:* John Sturges; *P:* Henry Berman; *Sc:* William Roberts, Don Mankiewicz. (1:07) Programmer comedy of an inherited racehorse that prances to music, and the romance which develops between the owner and the trainer of the horse. Based on the story "Rocky's Rose" by Eustace Cockrell.

787. Fast on the Draw (Lippert; 1950). *Cast:* Jimmie Ellison, Russell Hayden, Raymond Hatton, Fuzzy Knight, Betty [Julie] Adams, Tom Tyler, George J. Lewis, John Cason, Stanley Price, Stephen Carr, Dennis Moore, George Chesebro, Judith Webster, Jimmie Martin, Bud Osborne, Helen Gibson, Cliff Taylor, James Van Horn, Bud Hooker, I. Stanford Jolley, Gene Roth, Ray Jones, Roy Butler, Eugene Lay, Fraser McMinn. *D:* Thomas Carr; *P:* Ron Ormond; *St: & Sc:* Ormond, Maurice Tombragel. (0:57) The 6th and final entry in the "Four Star" (Shamrock & Lucky) series, this one of a ranger with a hangup about guns. (aka: *Sudden Death*)

788. The Fastest Gun Alive (MGM; 1956). *Cast:* Glenn Ford, Jeanne Crain, Broderick Crawford, Russ Tamblyn, Allyn Joslyn, Leif Erickson, John Dehner, Noah Beery, Jr., J.M. Kerrigan (final film—ret.), Rhys Williams, Virginia Gregg, Chubby Johnson, John Doucette, William "Bill" Phillips, Paul Birch, Christopher Olsen, Florenz Ames, Joseph Sweeney, Addison Richards, Michael Dugan, Glenn Strange, Earle Hodgins, Bud Osborne, Dub Taylor. *D:* Russell Rouse; *P:* Clarence Greene; *Sc:* Frank D. Gilroy, Rouse. (1:32) (video) Hit western drama of a married storekeeper who has trouble shaking his past reputation as a fast gun. Based on the TV play *The Last Notch* by Mr. Gilroy, computer-colored prints have been produced by Turner Entertainment.

789. The Fat Man (Universal-International; 1951). *Cast:* J. Scott Smart, Julie London, Rock Hudson, Emmett Kelly (film debut), Clinton Sundberg, Jayne Meadows, John Russell, Jerome Cowan, Lucille Barkley, Teddy Hart, Robert Osterloh, Harry Lewis, Marvin Kaplan, Ken Niles, Ed Max, Bob Roark, Mary Young, Tristram Coffin, Peter Brocco, Tom Keene, Shimen Ruskin, Harry Tyler, Robert Jordan, Gertrude Graner, Guy Wilkerson, George Wallace, Cheerio Meredith, Art Lind, Everett Hart, Abe Goldstein, Jack Chefe, Eric Alden. *D:* William Castle; *P:* Aubrey Schenck; *St:* Leonard Lee; *Sc:* Lee, Harry Essex. (1:17) A corpulent detective/gourmet named Brad Runyan investigates the murders of a doctor and his nurse. Based on a popular radio show of the day and a character created by Dashiell Hammett.

790. Father Is a Bachelor (Columbia; 1950). *Cast:* William Holden, Coleen Gray, Mary Jane Saunders, Charles Winninger, Stuart Erwin, Clinton Sundberg, Gary Gray, Billy Gray, Sig Rumann, Tommy Ivo, Lloyd Corrigan, Peggy Converse, Arthur Space, Hank Worden, Dooley Wilson, William Tannen, Ruby Dandridge, Eddy Waller. *D:* Norman Foster, Abby Berlin; *P:* S. Sylvan Simon; *St:* James Edward Grant; *Sc:* Aleen Leslie, Grant. (1:23) Comedy of a transient and his five "adopted" orphans, who decide he needs a wife.

791. Father Makes Good (Monogram; 1950). *Cast:* Raymond Walburn, Walter Catlett, Gary Gray, Mary Stuart, Barbara Brown,

Olin Howlin, Jack Kirkwood, Betty King, George Nokes, Robert Emmett Keane, Mary Field. *D:* Jean Yarbrough; *P:* Peter Scully; *Sc:* D.D. Beauchamp. (1:01) The 3rd entry in the "Henry Latham" comedy series (begun in 1949), with our hometown hero (Walburn) buying his own cow to spite the town's mayor (Catlett), when the latter imposes a milk tax. Based on the story "Journey at Sunrise" by Mr. Beauchamp which appeared in *Good Housekeeping*.

792. Father of the Bride (MGM; 1950). *Cast:* Spencer Tracy (AAN/Stanley T. Banks), Joan Bennett (Ellie Banks), Elizabeth Taylor (Kay Banks), Don Taylor (Buckley Dunston), Billie Burke (Mrs. Doris Dunston), Leo G. Carroll (Mr. Massoula), Moroni Olsen (Herbert Dunston), Melville Cooper (Mr. Tringle), Taylor Holmes (Warner), Paul Harvey (Rev. A.I. Galsworthy), Frank Orth (Joe), Tom Irish (Ben Banks), Rusty [Russ] Tamblyn (Tommy Banks), Marietta Canty (Delilah), Willard Waterman, (Dixon), Nancy Valentine (Fliss), Mary Jane Smith (Effie), Jacqueline Duval (Peg), Fay Baker (Miss Bellamy), Frank Hyers (Duffy), Chris Drake, Douglas Spencer, Paul Maxey, Peter Thompson, Carleton Carpenter, Frank Cady, Lillian Bronson, Thomas Browne Henry, Dewey Robinson, Ed Gargan, Ralph Peters, Dick Wessel, Dick Alexander, Joe Brown, Jr., Jim Hayward, Gil Perkins, William "Bill" Phillips. *D:* Vincente Minnelli; *P:* (AAN-Best Picture) Pandro S. Berman; *Sc:* (AAN) Frances Goodrich, Albert Hackett. (1:33) (video/laserdisc) Hit comedy of a father's frustrations with the up-and-coming marriage of his daughter. Based on the 1949 novel by Edward Streeter, it placed #3 on the "10 Best" list of the *New York Times*. One of the 28 top-grossing films of 1949-50, computer-colored prints have been produced by Turner Entertainment. Remade successfully in 1991. Followed by the sequel *Father's Little Dividend* (q.v.).

793. Father Takes the Air (Monogram/Mayfair; 1951). *Cast:* Raymond Walburn, Walter Catlett, Gary Gray, Florence Bates, M'Liss McClure, Barbara Brown, James Brown, George Nokes, Tom Dugan, Billy Bletcher, Maxine Semon, Don Hicks, Joan Valerie, Sam Flint. *D:* Frank McDonald; *P:* Peter Scully; *St: & Sc:* D.D. Beauchamp. (1:01) The 5th and final entry in the "Henry Latham" (Walburn) comedy series, with Henry's daughter (McClure) operating a flying school, which eventually gets our hometown hero into another pickle.

794. Father's Little Dividend (MGM; 1951). *Cast:* Spencer Tracy (Stanley Banks), Joan Bennett (Ellie Banks), Elizabeth Taylor (Kay Dunston), Don Taylor (Buckley Dunston), Billie Burke (Doris Dunston), Moroni Olsen (Herbert Dunston), Marietta Canty (Delilah), Frank Faylen (policeman), Rusty [Russ] Tamblyn (Tommy Banks), Tom Irish (Ben Banks), Hayden Rorke (Dr. Andrew Nordell), Paul Harvey (Rev. Galsworthy), James Menzies (Mike), Thomas Menzies (Red), Donald Clark (baby/the dividend), Betty Thompson, Dabbs Greer, Robert B. Williams, Frank Sully, Harry Hines, Nancy Valentine, Wendy Waldron, Lon Poff, George Bruggeman. *D:* Vincente Minnelli; *P:* Pandro S. Berman; *Sc:* Albert Hackett, Frances Goodrich. (1:22) (video/laserdisc) Comedy of a man who does not look forward to the birth of his first grandchild. A sequel to *Father of the Bride* (q.v.) and based on characters created by Edward Streeter in his book of that name. One of the 23 top-grossing films of 1950-51, computer-colored prints have been produced by Turner Entertainment. Remade in 1995 as *Father of the Bride, Part II*.

795. Father's Wild Game (Monogram; 1950). *Cast:* Raymond Walburn, Walter Catlett, Jane Darwell, Gary Gray, Barbara Brown, M'Liss McClure, Fred Libby, George Nokes, Roscoe Ates, Ralph Sanford, Emmett Vogan, Maxine Semon, Doris Kemper, Ann Tyrrell. *D:* Herbert I. Leeds (final film—ret.); *P:* Peter Scully; *Sc:* D.D. Beauchamp. (1:01) The 4th entry in the "Henry Latham" comedy series. Our hometown hero (Walburn) takes to the woods to supply his family with meat after feeling the local butcher's prices are too high. Based on the story "A Hunting We Will Go" by Mr. Beauchamp.

796. Fear and Desire (Joseph Burstyn/Kubrick; 1953). *Cast:* Frank Silvera, Kenneth Harp, Paul Mazursky, Steve Coit, Virginia Leith, David Allen (narrator). *D: & P:* Stanley Kubrick (debut); *St: & Sc:* Howard O. Sackler, Kubrick (unc.). (1:08) War drama, produced on a $40,000 budget, of four soldiers trapped behind enemy lines attempting to rejoin their unit. Note: Kubrick also did the cinematography and editing of this, his first feature film.

797. Fear Strikes Out (Paramount; 1957). *Cast:* Anthony Perkins, Karl Malden, Norma Moore, Perry Wilson, Adam Williams, Peter J. Votrian, Dennis McMullen, Bail Land, Brian Hutton, Bart Burns, Rand Harper, Howard Price, George Pembroke, Morgan Jones, Bing Russell,

James McNally, Edward [Edd] Byrnes, Ralph Montgomery, Robert Victor Stern, June Jocelyn, Wade Cagle, Courtland Shepard, Heather Hopper, Mary Benoit, Don Brodie, Richard Bull, Gere Craft, John Benson, Eric Alden, Don McGuire, Marilyn Malloy. *D:* Robert Mulligan (feature directorial debut); *P:* Alan Pakula (first film); *Sc:* Ted Berkman, Raphael Blau. (1:40) (video/laserdisc) Critically acclaimed hit drama of baseball star Jimmy Piersall (Perkins) and his mental breakdown under pressure from his domineering father (Malden). In wide screen VistaVision, it was based on Piersall's autobiography, written with Albert S. Hirschberg.

798. Fearless Fagan (MGM; 1952). *Cast:* Janet Leigh, Carleton Carpenter, Keenan Wynn, Richard Anderson, Ellen Corby, Barbara Ruick, John Call, Robert Burton, Wilton Graff, Parley Baer, Jonathan Cott, Jackie (lion/received 1st Place PATSY Award in 1953). *D:* Stanley Donen; *P:* Edwin H. Knopf; *As.P:* Sidney Franklin, Jr.; *St:* Franklin, Jr., Eldon Griffiths; *Adaptation:* Frederick Hazlitt Brennan; *Sc:* Charles Lederer. (1:19) Family oriented novelty-comedy of a dimwit recruit (Carpenter) drafted into the army who reports for duty with his pet lion, Fearless Fagan.

799. The Fearmakers (United Artists/ Pacemaker; 1958). *Cast:* Dana Andrews, Dick Foran, Mel Torme, Marilee Earle, Veda Ann Borg, Kelly Thorsden, Robert Fortier, Roy Gordon, Joel Marston. *D:* Jacques Tourneur; *P:* Martin H. Lancer; *As.P:* Leon Chooluck; *Sc:* Elliot West, Chris Apley. (1:23) Cold War melodrama of a Korean POW who returns to his Washington, D.C., advertising agency and finds communists have infiltrated and are manipulating public opinion polls to suit their own ends. Based on the 1945 novel by Darwin L. Teilhet.

800. Federal Agent at Large (Republic; 1950). *Cast:* Dorothy Patrick, Robert Rockwell, Kent Taylor, Estelita Rodriguez, Thurston Hall, Frank Puglia, Roy Barcroft, Denver Pyle, Jonathan Hale, Robert Kent, Kenneth MacDonald, Sonia Darrin, Frank McFarland, John McGuire. *D:* George Blair; *As.P:* Stephen Auer; *St: & Sc:* Albert DeMond. (1:00) A U.S. Treasury agent infiltrates a gang of gold smugglers operating on the Mexican border and falls for the female leader.

801. Federal Man (Eagle-Lion; 1950). *Cast:* William Henry, Pamela Blake, Robert Shayne, Lyle Talbot, George Eldredge, Movita Castaneda, John Laurenz, William Edwards, Lori Irving, Ben Moselle, Dennis Moore, Noel Cravat, Paul Hoffman, Joseph Turkel, Bill Lester, Carlos Schipa. *D:* Robert Tansey; *P:* Jack Schwarz; *St: & Sc:* Sam Neuman, Nat Tanchuck. (1:07) Semi-documentary style crime-melodrama of an agent sent by the federal narcotics agency to investigate several agents killed in the line of duty, while investigating a drug smuggling ring on the Mexican border.

Female *see* **The Violent Years**

802. The Female Animal (Universal-International; 1958). *Cast:* Hedy Lamarr (final film—ret.), Jane Powell, Jan Sterling, George Nader, Jerry Paris, James Gleason, Gregg Palmer, Ann Doran, Mabel Albertson, Richard H. Cutting, Yvonne Peattie, Casey Adams [aka: Max Showalter], Douglas Evans, Aram Katcher, Almira Sessions, Isabel Dawn, Richard Avonde, Laurie Mitchell, Walter Kelly, Bob Wegner. *D:* Harry Keller; *P:* Albert Zugsmith; *St:* Zugsmith; *Sc:* Robert Hill. (1:24) Soap-styled melodrama of a Hollywood actress, her adopted daughter and another actress, all out to snag the same man.

803. Female Jungle (American Releasing Corp./Burt Kaiser Prods.; 1956). *Cast:* Lawrence Tierney, John Carradine, Jayne Mansfield, Burt Kaiser, Kathleen Crowley, James Kodl, Tex Thorsen, Jack Hill, Bruce Carlisle, Connie Cezon, Robert Davis, Gordon Urquhart, Bill Layne, Bruno VeSota, Jean Lewis. *D:* Bruno VeSota; *P:* Burt Kaiser; *St: & Sc:* Kaiser, VeSota. (0:56) (video) Crime melodrama of a murdered film actress and the police sergeant who investigates, sorting out the red herrings. (aka: *The Hangover*)

804. Female on the Beach (Universal-International; 1955). *Cast:* Joan Crawford, Jeff Chandler, Jan Sterling, Cecil Kellaway, Natalie Schafer, Judith Evelyn, Charles Drake, Stuart Randall, Marjorie Bennett, Romo Vincent, Nan Boardman, Jack Reitzen, Jim Ryland, Helene Heigh, Judy Pine, Ed Fury. *D:* Joseph Pevney; *P:* Albert Zugsmith; *Sc:* Robert Hill, Richard Alan Simmons. (1:37) Melodrama of the wealthy widow of a Las Vegas gambler who takes up residence at a beach house, where it is rumored that the former tenant may have been murdered, but if so, who? Based on the play "The Besieged Heart" by Robert Hill.

805. Fence Riders (Monogram; 1950). *Cast:* Whip Wilson, Andy Clyde, Reno Browne, Myron Healey, Riley Hill, Ed Cassidy, Terry Frost, Frank McCarroll, George DeNormand, Holly Bane [aka: Mike Ragan], John Merton, Buck Bailey, Carl Mathews, Johnny Mack Brown (extra). *D: & P:* Wallace Fox; *St: & Sc:* Eliot Gibbons. (0:57) Whip Wilson series western of a lady rancher beset by cattle rustlers.

806. Feudin' Fools (Monogram; 1952). *Cast:* Leo Gorcey, Huntz Hall, Anne Kimbell, Dorothy Ford, Paul Wexler, Bennie Bartlett, David Gorcey [aka: David Condon], Bernard Gorcey, Oliver Blake, Bob Easton, O.Z. Whitehead, Lyle Talbot, Leo 'Ukie' Sherin, Benny Baker, Russell Simpson, Fuzzy Knight, Arthur Space, Robert Bray, Bob Keys, Stanley Blystone. *D:* William Beaudine; *P:* Jerry Thomas; *St: & Sc:* Bert Lawrence, Tim Ryan. (1:03) Comedy series entry which has "The Bowery Boys" journeying to the Kentucky hills where they manage to get involved in a hillbilly feud.

807. The Fiend Who Walked the West (20th Century–Fox; 1958). *Cast:* Hugh O'Brian, Robert Evans, Dolores Michaels, Linda Christian, Stephen McNally, June Blair, Edward Andrews, Ron Ely, Ken Scott, Emile Meyer, Gregory Morton, Georgia Simmons, Shari Lee Bernath. *D:* Gordon Douglas; *P:* Herbert B. Swope, Jr.; *Sc:* Harry Brown, Philip Yordan (adapted from the novel by Eleazar Lipsky which formed the material for the screenplay by Ben Hecht and Charles Lederer for *Kiss of Death*). (1:41) (video) Offbeat western-melodrama of a maniacal killer (Evans) who escapes from prison to wreak murder and mayhem on a rural area. A remake of *Kiss of Death*, a 1947 production from this studio.

808. Fifty Years Before Your Eyes (Warner; 1950). *Narrators:* Quentin Reynolds, H.V. Kaltenborn, Dwight Weist, Milton Cross, Norman Brokenshire, Andre Baruch, Clem McCarthy, Don Donaldson. *D:* Robert G. Youngson; *P: & St:* Alfred Butterfield; *Sc:* Butterfield, Thomas H. Wolf; *Editors:* Albert Heimes, Leonard C. Hein. (1:10) Documentary of newsreel film clips, from the funeral of England's Queen Victoria to the Cold War and the threat of World War III. A prologue also uses clips from movies to highlight the country's progress from the landing of the Pilgrims to the winning of the west.

809. The Fighter (United Artists/GH Prods.; 1952). *Cast:* Richard Conte, Lee J. Cobb, Vanessa Brown, Frank Silvera, Martin Garralaga, Roberta Haynes, Hugh Sanders, Claire Carleton, Argentina Brunetti, Rodolfo Hoyos, Jr., Margaret Padilla, Paul Fierro, Rico Alaniz, Paul Marion, Robert Wells. *D:* Herbert Kline; *P:* Alex Gottlieb; *Sc:* Aben Kandel, Kline. (1:18) (video) Melodrama of a Mexican boxer who takes on a major contender in hopes of using prize money to buy guns for the 1910 Mexican revolution and avenge his family's murder. Based on Jack London's story "The Mexican." (aka: *The First Time*)

810. Fighter Attack (Monogram/Allied Artists; 1953). *Cast:* Sterling Hayden, J. Carroll Naish, Joy Page, Kenneth Tobey, Anthony Caruso, Frank DeKova, Paul Fierro, Maurice Jara, Tony Dante, David Leonard, James Flavin, Harry Lauter, John Fontaine, David Bond, Louis Lettiere, Joel Marston. *D:* Lesley Selander; *P:* William A. Calihan, Jr.; *St: & Sc:* Simon Wincelberg; *Song:* "Nina" Marlin Skiles, Sol Meyer. (1:20) (video) World War II drama of an American fighter squadron leader who joins some members of the Italian underground to destroy a Nazi supply dump. Cinecolor.

811. The Fighting Chance (Republic; 1955). *Cast:* Rod Cameron, Julie London, Ben Cooper, Taylor Holmes, Howard Wendell, Mel Welles, Bob Steele, Paul Birch, Carl Milletaire, Rodolfo Hoyos, Jr., John Damler, Sam Scar. *D:* William Witney; *As.P:* William J. O'Sullivan; *St:* Robert Blees; *Sc:* Houston Branch. (1:10) A jockey and a horse trainer both vie for the affections of the same girl.

812. Fighting Coast Guard (Republic; 1951). *Cast:* Brian Donlevy, Forrest Tucker, Ella Raines, John Russell, Richard Jaeckel, William Murphy, Martin Milner, Steve Brodie, Hugh O'Brian, Tom Powers, Jack Pennick, Olin Howlin, Damian O'Flynn, Morris Ankrum, James Flavin, Roy Roberts, Sandra Spence, Eric Pedersen, The Sons of the Pioneers. *D: & P:* Joseph Kane; *St:* Charles Marquis Warren; *Sc:* Kenneth Gamet. (1:26) World War II action drama—with stock footage—of Coast Guard training for the Pacific theatre.

813. The Fighting Lawman (Allied Artists/Westwood; 1953). *Cast:* Wayne Morris, Virginia Grey, John Kellogg, Harry Lauter, Myron Healey, John Pickard, Rick Vallin, Dick Rich. *D:* Thomas Carr; *P:* Vincent M. Fennelly; *St: & Sc:* Dan Ullman. (1:11) One in a series of six westerns starring Morris. This one has a lawman on the trail of a woman who is following four bank robbers, intent on stealing their loot.

The Fighting 7th (G.B. title) *see* **Little Big Horn**

814. The Fighting Stallion (Eagle-Lion/Jack Schwarz Prods.; 1950). *Cast:* Bill Edwards, Doris Merrick, Forrest Taylor, Rocky Camron, John Carpenter, Maria Hart, Don C. Harvey, [William] Merrill McCormack, Concha Ybarra, Robert Carson. *D:* Robert Tansey; *P:* Jack Schwarz; *St:* George F. Slavin; *Sc:* Frances Kavanaugh. (1:02) A war veteran, who is losing his sight, trains a wild stallion which later saves his life. This feature originally ran on a double bill with *Forbidden Jungle* (q.v.).

815. Fighting Trouble (Allied Artists; 1956). *Cast:* Huntz Hall, Stanley Clements, Adele Jergens, Joseph Downing, Queenie Smith, John Bleifer, Thomas Browne Henry, David Gorcey, Laurie Mitchell, Danny Welton, Charles Williams, Clegg Hoyt, William Boyett, Tim Ryan, Michael Ross, Benny Burt, Ann Griffith, Ric Vallin. *D:* George Blair; *P:* Ben Schwalb; *St: & Sc:* Elwood Ullman. (1:01) Latter-day "Bowery Boys" series entry, with Sach (Hall) and Duke (Clements—replacing Leo Gorcey) becoming newspaper photographers bent on getting the goods on a local crime syndicate boss.

816. Finders Keepers (Universal-International; 1951). *Cast:* Tom Ewell, Julia [Julie] Adams, Evelyn Varden, Dusty Henley, Harold Vermilyea, Douglas Fowley, Richard Reeves, Jack Elam, Herbert Anderson, Harvey Lembeck, Madge Blake. *D:* Frederick de Cordova; *P:* Leonard Goldstein; *St: & Sc:* Richard Morris. (1:15) The basis of this low budget comedy is what happens when a young boy comes home with a bundle of stolen bank notes.

Fine and Dandy (G.B. title) *see* **West Point Story**

817. Finger Man (Allied Artists; 1955). *Cast:* Frank Lovejoy, Forrest Tucker, Peggie Castle, Timothy Carey, John Cliff, William Leicester, Glenn Gordon, John Close, Hugh Sanders, Evelynne Eaton, Charles Maxwell, Lewis Charles. *D:* Harold Schuster; *P:* Lindsley Parsons; *St:* Morris Lipsius, John Lardner; *Sc:* Warren Douglas. (1:22) (video) Crime melodrama of an ex-con, caught by the feds in continued criminal activity, who agrees to help bring down a local crime figure in lieu of spending more time in jail.

818. Fingerprints Don't Lie (Lippert/Spartan Prods.; 1951). *Cast:* Richard Travis, Sheila Ryan, Sid Melton, Tom Neal, Margia Dean, Lyle Talbot, Michael Whalen, Richard Emory, Rory Mallinson, George Eldredge, Dee Tatum, Karl Davis, Syra Marty, Forbes Murray, Zon Murray, Roy Butler. *D:* Sam Newfield; *P:* Sigmund Neufeld; *St:* Rupert Hughes; *Sc:* Orville Hampton. (1:07) Programmer mystery-melodrama of a fingerprint expert out to nab the killer of the town mayor.

819. The Fireball (20th Century–Fox/Thor Prods.; 1950). *Cast:* Mickey Rooney, Pat O'Brien, Beverly Tyler, James Brown, Marilyn Monroe, Ralph Dumke, Bert Begley, Milburn Stone, Sam Flint, John Hedloe, Glenn Corbett (film debut). *D:* Tay Garnett; *P:* Bert Friedlob; *St: & Sc:* Garnett, Horace McCoy. (1:23) Drama of a youth who runs away from an orphanage and aspires to become a star of the roller derby. He succeeds, but fame goes to his head, alienating those around him.

820. Fireman, Save My Child (Universal-International; 1954). *Cast:* Spike Jones and the City Slickers, Buddy Hackett [replacing Lou Costello], Hugh O'Brian [replacing Bud Abbott], Tom Brown, Adele Jergens, George Cleveland, Willis Bouchey, Henry Kulky, Harry Cheshire, Madge Blake, Tristram Coffin, John Cliff + Bud Abbott & Lou Costello (still visible in some long shots). *D:* Leslie Goodwins; *P:* Howard Christie; *St:* Lee Loeb; *Sc:* Loeb, John Grant; *Musical numbers:* "Poet and Peasant Overture" by Franz von Suppe; "Dance of the Hours" by Amilcare Ponchielli; "In a Persian Market" by Ketelby (as rendered in the unique style of Spike Jones and the City Slickers). (1:19) Slapstick comedy centered around the modernization of a San Francisco firehouse in 1910. Originally intended as a starring vehicle for Abbott and Costello, but revamped when the latter became ill. Note: No relation to the 1932 Joe E. Brown comedy for Warners with the same title.

821. The First Legion (United Artists/Sedif; 1951). *Cast:* Charles Boyer, William Demarest, Lyle Bettger, Barbara Rush, Leo G. Carroll, Walter Hampden, Clifford Brooke, H.B. Warner, Dorothy Adams, Wesley Addy (film debut), Taylor Holmes, Molly Lamont, Queenie Smith, George Zucco, John McGuire,

Jacqueline DeWit, Bill Edwards. *D: & P:* Douglas Sirk; *Sc:* Emmett Lavery. (1:26) (video) Drama of what happens when a miracle is believed to have occurred in a Jesuit seminary in a small American town. Based on the 1934 Broadway play "La Premiere Legion" by Mr. Lavery.

First Marines *see* **Tripoli**

822. The First Texan (Allied Artists; 1956). *Cast:* Joel McCrea (Sam Houston), Felecia Farr, Jeff Morrow (Jim Bowie), Wallace Ford, Abraham Sofaer, Jody McCrea, Chubby Johnson, Dayton Lummis (Stephen Austin), Rodolfo Hoyos, William Hopper (William Travis), Roy Roberts, Frank Puglia, James Griffith (Davy Crockett), Nelson Leigh, David Silva (Santa Ana), Slavador Baguez, Carl Benton Reid (Andrew Jackson), Scott Douglas, William Phipps. *D:* Byron Haskin; *P:* Walter Mirisch: *St: & Sc:* Daniel B. Ullman. (1:22) Western biographical drama of Sam Houston and the liberation of Texas from Mexico. Technicolor and CinemaScope.

The First Time (U.A./1952) *see* **The Fighter**

823. The First Time (Columbia/Norma Prods.-Halburt Prods., Inc.; 1952). *Cast:* Robert Cummings, Barbara Hale, Bill Goodwin, Jeff Donnell, Carl Benton Reid, Mona Barrie, Kathleen Comegys, Cora Witherspoon, Virginia Christine, Paul Harvey, Bea Benaderet. *D:* Frank Tashlin; *P:* Harold Hecht; *St:* Jean Rouverol, Hugo Butler; *Sc:* Tashlin, Dane Lussier. (1:29) Comedy of first time parents dealing with their newborn.

824. The First Traveling Saleslady (RKO; 1956). *Cast:* Ginger Rogers, Barry Nelson, Carol Channing, David Brian, James Arness, Clint Eastwood, Robert Simon, Frank Wilcox, Daniel M. White, Harry Cheshire, John Eldredge, Robert Hinkle, Jack Rice, Kate Drain Lawson, Edward Cassidy (Theodore Roosevelt), Fred Essler, Bill Hale, Lovyss Bradley, Nora Bush, Ann Kunde, Jeanette Miller, Kathy Marlowe, Lynn Noe, Joan Tyler, Hans Herbert, Robert Easton, Belle Mitchell, Ian Murray, Roy Darmour, Peter Croydon, Al Cavens, Paul Bradley, Hal Taggart, Gilmore Bush, John Connors, Lester Dorr, Frank Scannell, Paul Keast, Mauritz Hugo, Julius Evans, Stanley Farrar, Charles Tannen, Hank Patterson, Britt Wood, James Stone, Cactus Mack, Deacon Moor, Lane Chandler, Chalky Williams, George Barrows, George Baxter, George Brand, Tristram Coffin, Theron Jackson, Herbert Deans, William Fawcett, Casey MacGregor, William Forrest, Jim Hayward, Earle Hodgins, Johnny Lee, Pierce Lyden, Tony Roux, Clarence Muse. *D: & P:* Arthur Lubin; *St: & Sc:* Stephen Longstreet, Devery Freeman; *Songs:* "A Corset Can Do a Lot For a Lady" + Title song: Irving Gertz, Hal Levy. (1:32) In this Technicolor western comedy, set in the last decade of the 19th century, an Eastern corset designer (Rogers) heads west with her secretary (Channing) to sell barbed wire. Note: This screenplay was purportedly written with Mae West in mind.

825. Five (Columbia/Lobo Prods.; 1951). *Cast:* William Phipps, Susan Douglas, James Anderson, Charles Lampkin, Earl Lee. *D:-P:-St: & Sc:* Arch Oboler. (1:33) Drama of four men and a woman who survive nuclear devastation. Paired on a double bill with Gene Autry's *Whirlwind* (q.v.).

826. Five Against the House (Columbia/Doyle Prods.; 1955). *Cast:* Guy Madison, Kim Novak, Brian Keith, Alvy Moore, William Conrad, Kerwin Mathews, Jack Diamond, Jean Willes, John Zaremba, George Brand, Mark Hanna, Hugh Sanders, Carroll McComas. *D:* Phil Karlson; *P:* Stirling Silliphant; *Sc:* Silliphant, William Bowers, John Barnwell. (1:24) Crime drama of five college students who plot the robbery of a casino in Reno, Nevada. Based on a story by Jack Finney which appeared in *Good Housekeeping*.

827. 5 Fingers (20th Century–Fox; 1952). *Cast:* James Mason (Cicero), Danielle Darrieux (Anna), Michael Rennie (George Travers), Walter Hampden (Sir Frederic), Oscar Karlweiss (Moyzisch), Herbert Berghof (Col. von Richter), John Wengraf (Von Papen), A. Ben Astar (Siebert), Roger Plowden (McFadden), Michael Pate (Morrison), Ivan Triesault (Steuben), Hannelore Axman (Von Papen's secretary), David Wolfe (Da Costa), Larry Dobkin (Santos), Keith McConnell (Johnson), Nestor Paiva, Antonio Filauri, Richard Loo, Jeroma Moshan, Alberto Morin, Stuart Hall, Otto Waldis, Frank Hemingway (narrator), Leo Mostovoy, Sadik Tarian, Eghiche Harout, Konstantin Shayne, Marc Snow, Martin Garralaga, Lumsden Hare, Stanley Logan, Lester Matthews, Salvador Baguez, Faith Kruger, John Sutton (narrator). *D:* (AAN) Joseph L. Mankiewicz; *P:* Otto Lang; *Sc:* (AAN) Michael Wilson,

Mankiewicz (unc.). (1:48) (video) Espionage drama, set during World War II, of a valet to the British ambassador in Ankara, Turkey, who sells secret British documents to the Nazis. Based on the 1950 novel *Operation Cicero* by L. C. Moyzisch which had a factual source. It placed #4 on the "10 Best" lists of both the NBR and the *New York Times*, while placing #10 on the same list of *Film Daily*. (aka: *Operation Cicero*)

828. Five Gates to Hell (20th Century-Fox/Associated Producers; 1959). *Cast:* Neville Brand, Dolores Michaels, Patricia Owens, Ken Scott, Nobu McCarthy, Benson Fong, John Morley, Gerry Gaylor, Greta Chi, Nancy Kulp, Linda Wong, Irish McCalla, Shirley Knight. *D:-P:-St: & Sc:* James Clavell; *As.P:* Byron Roberts. (1:38) Offbeat and brutal melodramatic war film, set during the French Indo-China conflict, of seven nurses and two doctors captured from a Red Cross field hospital to perform surgery on a critically ill warlord. Filmed on location in Malibu, CA. CinemaScope.

829. Five Guns West (American Releasing Corp.; 1955). *Cast:* John Lund, Dorothy Malone, Touch [Michael] Connors, Jonathan Haze, Paul Birch, John Ingram, Larry Thor (film debut), Bob Campbell, James Stone. *D:* Roger Corman (directorial debut); *P:* Corman; *St: & Sc:* Robert Wright Campbell. (1:18) Civil War–era western of five murderers released from prison to join the Confederate army, with the assignment to rob a Union stagecoach of its gold. Pathécolor.

830. The Five Pennies (Paramount/Dena Prods.; 1959). *Cast:* Danny Kaye (Ernest Loring/"Red Nichols"), Barbara Bel Geddes (Willa Stutzmeyer/"Bobbie Meredith"), Louis Armstrong (himself), Harry Guardino (Tony Valani), Bob Crosby (Wil Paradise), Bobby Troup (Artie Shutt), Susan Gordon (Dorothy Nichols—ages 6 to 8), Tuesday Weld (Dorothy Nichols—ages 12 to 14), Ray Anthony (Jimmy Dorsey), Shelly Manne (Dave Tough), Ray Daly (Glenn Miller), Valerie Allen (Tommye Eden), Ned Glass (Murray), Paul Sullivan (Richard), Frank C. Radcliffe (specialty dancer), Bob Hope (himself), Earl Barton (choreographer + the film's choreographer), Peter Potter, Blanche Sweet (a silent screen actress in her final and only film appearance since 1930), Tito Vuolo, Joe McTurk, Carol Sydes [aka: Cindy Carol], Susan Seaforth, Richard Shavelson, Charles Herbert, Babette Bain. *D:* Melville Shavelson; *P:* Jack Rose; *As.P:* Sylvia Fine; *St:* Robert Smith; *Sc:* Shavelson, Rose; *Cin:* (AAN-color) Daniel L. Fapp; *Music:* (AAN) Leith Stevens; *Costumes:* (AAN-color) Edith Head; *Songs:* Title song (AAN), "Lullaby in Ragtime," "Follow the Leader," "Good Night—Sleep Tight," "Five Pennies Saints" ("When the Saints Go Marching In" with special lyrics), "Schnitzelbank" (all by Sylvia Fine) + "Steven's Blues," "My Blue Heaven," "Ja Da," "After You've Gone," "Bill Bailey Won't You Please Come Home," "Battle Hymn of the Republic," "Carnival of Venice," "Paradise," "Back Home Again in Indiana," "Wail of the Wind," "Washington and Lee Swing," "Runnin' Wild," "The Music Goes 'Round and 'Round," "Mary Had a Little Lamb," "Out of Nowhere," "That's A-Plenty," "Jingle Bells," "Back Bay Shuffle" and "Largo Al Factotum (The Barber of Seville)." (1:57) (video) Hit sentimental biography of coronetist Red Nichols (who plays on the soundtrack), complete with twenty-five musical interludes. In Technicolor and VistaVision, it became one of the 26 top-grossing films of 1958-59.

831. Five Steps to Danger (United Artists/Grand Prods., Inc.; 1957). *Cast:* Sterling Hayden, Ruth Roman, Werner Klemperer, Richard Gaines, Charles Davis, Jeanne Cooper, Peter Hansen, Karl Lindt, John Merrick, John Mitchum. *D:-P: & Sc:* Henry S. Kesler; *St:* Donald Hamilton, Turnley Walker. (1:20) Cold war spy melodrama, with its source material, a *Saturday Evening Post* serial by Mr. Hamilton.

832. The 5000 Fingers of Dr. T (Columbia/Stanley Kramer; 1953). *Cast:* Peter Lind Hayes (Zabladowski), Mary Healey (Mrs. Collins), Hans Conried (Dr. Terwilliker), Tommy Rettig (Bart), John "Jack" Heasley (Uncle Whitney), Robert "Bob" Heasley (Uncle Judson), Noel Cravat (Sgt. Lunk), Henry Kulky (Stroogo). *D:* Roy Rowland; *P:* Stanley Kramer; *St:* Theodor Geisel [aka: Dr. Seuss]; *Sc:* Geisel, Allan Scott; *Music:* (AAN) Frederick Hollander, Morris Stoloff. (1:29) (video/laserdisc) Technicolor fantasy with musical numbers of a young boy and his nightmare involving his piano teacher. A film which created very little interest at the box office.

833. Fixed Bayonets (20th Century–Fox; 1951). *Cast:* Richard Basehart, Gene Evans, Michael O'Shea, Richard Hylton, Craig Hill, Skip Homeier, Henry Kulky, Richard Monohan, Paul Richards, Tony Kent, Don Orlando, Patrick Fitzgibbon, Neyle Morrow, George Wesley, Mel Pogue, David Wolfson, George

Conrad, Buddy Thorpe, Al Negbo, Wyott Ordung, Pat Hogan, James Dean, John Doucette, Bill Hickman, Kayne Shew. *D: & Sc:* Samuel Fuller; *P:* Jules Buck. (1:32) During the Korean conflict, a platoon of soldiers is cut off from the rest of the company and one by one the officers are killed off, leaving a corporal, the highest ranking man, to be responsible for the safety of the rest of the men. Based on the novel by John Brophy.

834. The Flame and the Arrow (Warner/ Norma-F.R. Prods.; 1950). *Cast:* Burt Lancaster (Dardo), Virginia Mayo (Anne), Robert Douglas (Allessandro), Aline MacMahon (Nonna Bartoli), Frank Allenby (Ulrich), Nick Cravat (Piccolo), Lynn Baggett (Francesca), Gordon Gebert (Rudi), Francis Pierlot (Papa Pietro), Norman Lloyd, Victor Kilian, Robin Hughes. *D:* Jacques Tourneur; *P:* Harold Hecht, Frank Ross; *Sc:* Waldo Salt; *Cin:* (AAN) Ernest Haller; *Music:* (AAN) Max Steiner. (1:28) (video/ laserdisc) Technicolor swashbuckling actioner of an Italian peasant who sets out to do away with a tyrannical land grabber. One of the 28 top-grossing films of 1949-50.

835. Flame and the Flesh (MGM; 1954). *Cast:* Lana Turner, Pier Angeli, Carlos Thompson, Bonar Colleano, Charles Goldner, Peter Illing, Rosalie Crutchley, Marne Maitland, Eric Pohlman, Catherina Ferraz, Alex de Gallier. *D:* Richard Brooks; *P:* Joe Pasternak; *St:* Auguste Bailly; *Sc:* Helen Deutsch; *Songs:* "Languida," "By Candlelight" and "Then I Loved" Nicholas Brodszky, Jack Lawrence. (1:44) This box office disappointment is a triangular romantic-drama that was filmed on location in Italy and Great Britain. Technicolor.

836. The Flame Barrier (United Artists/ Gramercy Pictures, Inc.; 1958). *Cast:* Arthur Franz, Kathleen Crowley, Robert Brown, Vincent Padula, Rodd Redwing, Kaz Oran, Grace Mathews, Pilar Del Rey, Larry Duran, Bernie Gozier, Roberto Contreras. *D:* Paul Landres; *P:* Arthur Gardner, Jules V. Levey; *St:* George Worthing Yates; *Sc:* Yates, Pat Fielder. (1:10) An earth satellite, down in the jungle, has returned to earth with a gelatinous, alien life form that doubles in size everyday and is capable of consuming human flesh. (aka: *It Fell from the Flame Barrier*) Originally paired on a double bill with *The Return of Dracula* (q.v.).

837. Flame of Araby (Universal-International; 1951). *Cast:* Maureen O'Hara, Jeff Chandler, Maxwell Reed, Lon Chaney, Jr., Buddy Baer, Susan Cabot, Richard Egan, Royal Dano, Dewey Martin, Neville Brand, Henry Brandon, Judith Braun, Tony Barr, Frederic Berest, Cindy Garner, Noreen Michaels, Richard Hale, Virginia Brissac, Dorothy Ford, William Tannen, Andre Charlot, Joe Kamaryt, Lillian Ten Eyck, Leon Charles, Chuck Hamilton, Barry Brooks, Diamond (horse—received PATSY Award of Excellence in 1952). *D:* Charles Lamont; *P:* Leonard Goldstein; *As.P:* Ross Hunter; *St: & Sc:* Gerald Drayson Adams. (1:17) A Technicolor costumer set in far east Tunisia involving a prize horse.

838. Flame of Calcutta (Columbia/Esskay Pictures; 1953). *Cast:* Denise Darcel, Patric Knowles, Paul Cavanagh, George Keymas, Joseph Mell, Ted Thorpe, Leonard Penn, Gregory Gaye, Edward Clark, Robin Hughes, Sujata and Asoka (specialty dancers). *D:* Seymour Friedman; *P:* Sam Katzman; *St:* Sol Shor; *Sc:* Robert E. Kent. (1:10) A good vs. evil Technicolor costume adventure, set in 18th century India.

839. Flame of Stamboul (Columbia; 1951). *Cast:* Richard Denning, Lisa Ferraday, Norman Lloyd, George Zucco, Nestor Paiva, Donald Randolph, Peter Brocco, Peter Mamakos, Paul Marion. *D:* Ray Nazarro; *P:* Wallace MacDonald; *St: & Sc:* Daniel B. Ullman. (1:08) Espionage programmer centered around a cunning spy known as "The Voice."

840. Flame of the Islands (Republic; 1955). *Cast:* Yvonne De Carlo, Howard Duff, Zachary Scott, Kurt Kasznar, Barbara O'Neil, James Arness (final theatrical film before moving to TV and the long-running series "Gunsmoke" as Sheriff Matt Dillon), Frieda Inescort, Lester Matthews, Donald Curtis, Nick Stewart, John Pickard, Leslie Denison, Peter Adams. *D: & P:* Edward Ludwig; *Sc:* Bruce Manning; *Songs:* "Bahama Mama," "Take It or Leave It" Sonny Burke, Jack Elliott. (1:30) (video) Melodrama of a woman who runs a gambling casino in the Bahamas and the gangsters who try to muscle in on her operation. Based on the unpublished story "Rebel Island" by Adele Comandini. Trucolor.

841. Flaming Feather (Paramount; 1951). *Cast:* Sterling Hayden, Forrest Tucker, Barbara Rush, Arleen Whelan, Carol Thurston, Edgar Buchanan, Victor Jory, Richard Arlen, Ian MacDonald, Robert Kortman, George Cleveland, Ethan Laidlaw, Paul Burns, Don Dunning, Ray

Teal, Nacho Galindo, Frank Lackteen, Donald Kerr, Gene Lewis, Larry McGrath, Herman Nowlin, Brian Hightower. *D:* Ray Enright; *P:* Nat Holt; *St: & Sc:* Gerald Drayson Adams; *Additional dialogue:* Frank Gruber. (1:17) Technicolor western of a gang of vigilantes, out to retrieve a white woman, taken by renegade Indians.

842. The Flaming Teen-Age (Truman; 1956). *Cast:* Noel Reyburn, Ethel Barrett, Jerry Frank, Shirley Holmes. *D: & P:* Irvin S. Yeaworth, Charles Edwards; *St: & Sc:* Jean Yeaworth, Ethel Barrett. (1:07) A low budget independent exploitation item—evidenced by the title—styled like a documentary, involving the evils of drink and drugs.

The Flaming Torch (G.B. title) *see* **The Bob Mathias Story**

843. The Flaming Urge (1953). *Cast:* Harold Lloyd, Jr., Cathy Downs. (1:07) Obscure production of an arsonist.

844. Flat Top (Allied Artists; 1952). *Cast:* Sterling Hayden (Dan Collier), Richard Carlson (Joe Rodgers), William Phipps (Red Kelley), John Bromfield ("Snakehips" McKay), Keith Larsen (Barney Smith), William Schallert (Longfellow), Tod Karns (Judge), Phyllis Coates (Dorothy), Dave Willock (Willie), Walter Coy. *D:* Lesley Selander; *P:* Walter Mirisch; *St: & Sc:* Steve Fisher; *Editor:* (AAN) William Austin. (1:23) (video) Original World War II combat footage enhances this drama of fighter pilots in training on an aircraft carrier. Cinecolor.

Flesh and Flame *see* **Night of the Quarter Moon**

845. Flesh and Fury (Universal-International; 1952). *Cast:* Tony Curtis, Mona Freeman, Jan Sterling, Wallace Ford, Connie Gilchrist, Katherine Locke, Harry Guardino, Harry Shannon, Joe Gray, Ron Hargrave, Harry Raven, Ted Stanhope, Louis Jean Heydt, Nella Walker, Ken Patterson, Virginia Gregg, Grace Hayle, Frank Wilcox, Harry Cheshire, Tommy Farrell, George Eldredge, Bruce Richardson, Beatrice Gray, Edwin Parker, Sam Pierce, Karl "Killer" Davis, Ed Hinton, Sally Yarnell, Ed Hinkle, Bryan Forbes, Lucille Curtis. *D:* Joseph Pevney; *P:* Leonard Goldstein; *St:* William Alland; *Sc:* Bernard Gordon. (1:22) Successful drama of a young deaf-mute boxer who finds himself torn between two women, one who loves him, the other who uses him. (working title: "Hear No Evil")

846. Flesh and the Spur (American International/Hy Prods.; 1956). *Cast:* John Agar, Marla English, Touch [Michael] Connors, Raymond Hatton, Joyce Meadows, Kenne Duncan, Maria Monay, Frank Lackteen, Richard Alexander, Kermit Maynard, Bud Osborne, Buddy Roosevelt, Michael Harris, Mel Gaines, Eddie Kafafian. *D:* Edward L. Cahn; *P:* Alex Gordon; *Sc:* Charles B. Griffith, Jr., Mark Hanna; *Additional dialogue:* Cahn, Lou Rusoff; *Title song:* Rose Bagdasarian. (1:20) A cowboy searches for the killer of his twin brother. Eastmancolor.

847. The Flesh Merchant (Joseph Brenner Associates; 1956). *Cast:* Joy Reynolds, Mariko Perri, Lisa Rack, Guy Manford. *D: & P:* W. Merle Connell; *Sc:* Peter Perry, Jr., Jay M. Kude. (1:30) Prostitution is the focal point of this independent low budget "study" of the world's oldest profession.

848. Flight Nurse (Republic; 1953). *Cast:* Joan Leslie, Forrest Tucker, Arthur Franz, Jeff Donnell, Ben Cooper, James Holden, Kristine Miller, Maria Palmer, Richard Simmons, James Brown, Hal Baylor. *D:* Allan Dwan; *Ex.P:* Herbert J. Yates; *St: & Sc:* Alan LeMay; "The Nurse's Prayer" Edith A. Aynes. (1:30) Anti-communist propaganda and a romantic triangle highlight this melodrama of nurses during the Korean conflict.

849. Flight to Hong Kong (United Artists/Sabre Prods.; 1956). *Cast:* Rory Calhoun, Barbara Rush, Dolores Donlon, Soo Yong, Pat Conway, Mel Welles, Werner Klemperer, Paul Picerni, Rhodes Reason, Aram Katcher, Bob Hopkins, Timothy Carey, Carleton Young, Aaron Saxon, Noel Cravat, Guy Prescott, Barry Brooks, George Barrows, Booth Colman, Ralph Smiley, Paul Brinegar. *D: & P:* Joseph M. Newman; *St:* Newman, Edward G. O'Callaghan, Gustave Field; *Sc:* O'Callaghan, Leo Townsend. (1:28) Melodrama of a pilot who works for an overseas crime syndicate, based in Hong Kong.

850. Flight to Mars (Monogram; 1951). *Cast:* Marguerite Chapman, Cameron Mitchell, Arthur Franz, Virginia Houston, John Litel, Morris Ankrum, Richard Gaines, Lucille Barkley, Robert H. Barrat, Edward Earle, William Forrest, Bob Peoples, Tony Marsh, Tristram

Coffin, Bill Neff, Trevor Bardette, Russ Conway, Raymond Bond, Everett Glass, David Bond, Wilbur Mack, Stanley Blystone, William Bailey, Frank O'Connor. *D:* Lesley Selander; *P:* Walter Mirisch; *St:* & *Sc:* Arthur Strawn. (1:12) (video) Science fiction of a trip to the red planet which uncovers a proposed invasion of earth by Martians. This Cinecolor production was Monogram's first venture into this genre.

851. Flight to Tangier (Paramount/Nat Holt & Co.; 1953). *Cast:* Joan Fontaine, Jack Palance, Corinne Calvet, Robert Douglas, Marcel Dalio, Jeff Morrow, Richard Shannon, Murray Matheson, John Doucette, John Pickard, James Anderson, Don Dunning, Eric Alden, Bob Templeton, Peter Coe, Madeleine Holmes, John Wengraf, Otto Waldis, Jerry Paris, Rene Chatenay, Albert D'Arno, Anthony DeMario, Karin Vengay, Pilar Del Rey, Josette Deegan, Mark Hanna, Rodd Redwing. *D:-St:* & *Sc:* Charles Marquis Warren; *P:* Nat Holt. (1:30) Adventure melodrama of spies and treasure hunters searching the North African desert for the wreckage of a plane that crashed with a cargo of gold on board. Technicolor and 3-D.

852. Flood Tide (Universal-International; 1958). *Cast:* George Nader, Cornell Borchers, Michel Ray, Judson Pratt, Joanna Moore, Charles E. Arnt, Russ Conway, John Morley, John Maxwell, Carl Benson, Della Malzarn, Hugh Lawrence. *D:* Abner Biberman (final theatrical film before becoming a TV director); *P:* Robert Arthur; *St:* Barry Trivers; *Sc:* Dorothy Cooper. (1:22) Low budget drama of a crippled boy with a jealous obsession for his mother that all but destroys those around him. CinemaScope.

853. The Fly (20th Century–Fox; 1958). *Cast:* Al [David] Hedison (Andre), Patricia Owens (Helene), Vincent Price (Francois), Herbert Marshall (Inspector Charas), Kathleen Freeman (Emma), Charles Herbert (Philippe), Betty Lou Gerson (Nurse Andersone), Eugene Borden (Dr. Ejoute), Torben Meyer (Gaston). *D:* & *P:* Kurt Neumann; *Sc:* James Clavell. (1:34) (video/laserdisc) Near classic sci-fi/horror of a man who invents a machine to teleport matter from one place to another, experimenting on himself with disastrous results. One of the 26 top-grossing films of 1957-58, it was followed by the sequel *Return of the Fly* (q.v.). Based on a short story by George Langelaan, it was remade in 1986. DeLuxe color and CinemaScope.

854. The Flying Fontaines (Columbia/Clover Prods.; 1959). *Cast:* Michael Callan, Evy Norlund, Joan Evans, Rian Garrick, Roger Perry, Joe DeSantis, John Van Dreelan, Jeanne Manet, Barbara Kelley, Dorothy Johnson, Pierre Watkin, Murray Parker, William Quinn. *D:* George Sherman; *P:* Sam Katzman; *St:* & *Sc:* Lee Erwin, Donn Mullally. (1:24) The romantic intentions of a high-wire artist lead to tragedy in this big-top drama. Eastmancolor.

855. Flying Leathernecks (RKO/Howard Hughes; 1951). *Cast:* John Wayne, Robert Ryan, Don Taylor, William Harrigan, Janis Carter, Jay C. Flippen, Carleton Young, Brett King, Maurice Jara, Steve Flagg [aka: Michael St. Angel], Britt Norton, Adam Williams, Lynn Stalmaster, Barry Kelley, Sam Edwards, James Flavin, Harlan Warde, Harry Lauter, John Mallory, James Dobson, Michael Devery, Douglas Henderson, Ralph Cook, Adam York, Gail Davis, Gordon Gebert, Melville Robert, Elaine Robert. *D:* Nicholas Ray; *P:* Edmund Grainger (for Hughes); *St:* Kenneth Gamet; *Sc:* James Edward Grant. (1:42) (video/laserdisc) Hit drama of World War II and a flight commander at Guadalcanal who alienates his men and brings criticism from his second-in-command for being a hard-nosed disciplinarian, a trait he espouses because it gets his job done. Technicolor.

856. The Flying Missile (Columbia; 1950). *Cast:* Glenn Ford, Viveca Lindfors, Henry O'Neill, Carl Benton Reid, John Qualen, Joseph Sawyer, Anthony Ross, Harry Shannon, Ross Ford, Paul Harvey, Kenneth Tobey, Jerry Paris, Grandon Rhodes, James Seay, Richard Quine (final film as an actor), Charles Evans, Zachary A. Charles. *D:* Henry Levin; *P:* Jerry Bresler; *St:* N. Richard Nash, Harvey S. Haislip; *Sc:* Richard English, James Gunn. (1:33) World War II drama of a submarine commander who attempts to prove that guided missiles can be successfully launched from his sub.

Follow the Hunter *see* **Fangs of the Wild**

857. Follow the Sun (20th Century–Fox; 1951). *Cast:* Glenn Ford, Anne Baxter, Dennis O'Keefe, June Havoc, Larry Keating, Roland Winters, Nana Bryant, Sam Snead (himself), James Demarest (himself), Dr. Cary Middlecoff (himself), Harold Blake, Ann Burr, Harmon Stevens, Louise Lorimer, Harry Antrim, Jeffrey Sayre, Homer Welborne, D. Scotty Chisholm, William Janssen, William Forrest, Eugene

Gericke, Gil Herman, Jewel Rose, Jim Pierce, Beverlee White, Emmett Vogan, Grantland Rice, James Flavin, Myrtle Anderson, Esther Somers, Al Demarest, Lester Dorr, John Trebach, Warren Stevens, William Walker. *D:* Sidney Lanfield; *P:* Samuel G. Engel; *Sc:* Frederick Hazlitt Brennan. (1:33) Golfer Ben Hogan (Ford) is the subject of this biography, detailing his comeback to the sport following a crippling auto accident. Based on an article titled "He Follows the Sun Again" by Mr. Brennan which appeared in *Reader's Digest.*

858. Footlight Varieties (RKO; 1951). *Cast:* Jack Paar, Liberace, The Sportsmen, Frankie Carle and Orch., Jerry Murad and His Harmonicats, Leon Errol (final film—d. 1951). *D:* Hal Yates. (1:07) Paar is the host of a group of variety acts in this program filler.

859. Footsteps in the Night (Allied Artists; 1957). *Cast:* Bill Elliott (final film—ret.), Don Haggerty, Eleanore Tanin, Douglas Dick, Robert Shayne, James Flavin, Gregg Palmer, Harry Tyler, Ann Griffith, Zena Marshall. *D:* Jean Yarbrough; *P:* Ben Schwalb; *St:* Albert Band; *Sc:* Band, Elwood Ullman. (1:02) Crime melodrama of the investigation into the murder of a gambler.

860. For Heaven's Sake (20th Century-Fox; 1950). *Cast:* Clifton Webb, Joan Bennett, Robert Cummings, Edmund Gwenn, Joan Blondell, Gigi Perreau, Jack LaRue, Harry Von Zell, Tommy Rettig, Dick Ryan, Charles Lane, Robert Kent, Whit Bissell, Ashmead Scott, Dorothy Neumann, Esther Somers, Jack Daly, Bob Harlow, Perc Launders, Richard Thorne, Albert Pollet, Sid Fields, Gordon Nelson, Arno Frey, Albert Frey, Betty [Julie] Adams, William O'Leary, Gilbert Fallman, Sue Casey. *D: & Sc:* George Seaton; *P:* William Perlberg. (1:32) Comedy-fantasy of an angel (Webb) sent from heaven to assist a married couple in having a baby. He finds himself a whiz at gambling and goes astray, needing assistance himself from another angel (Gwenn). Based on a play called "May We Come In?" by Harry Segall.

861. For Men Only (Lippert/H-N Prods.; 1952). *Cast:* Paul Henreid, Margaret Field, James Dobson, Kathleen Hughes, Russell Johnson, Vera Miles, Robert Sherman, Douglas Kennedy, Robert Carson, Virginia Mullen, O.Z. Whitehead, Arthur Marshall, Frank Mathias. *D: & P:* Paul Henreid; *St:* Lou Morheim, Herbert Margolis; *Sc:* Morheim. (1:33) Drama of cruel fraternity hazing on a college campus and efforts to stop it. (aka: *The Tall Lie*)

862. For the First Time (MGM/Corona; 1959). *Cast:* Mario Lanza (final film—d. 1959), Zsa Zsa Gabor, Johanna von Koczian, Kurt Kasznar, Hans Sohnker, Peter Capell, Renzo Cesana, Sandro Giglio. *D:* Rudolph Maté; *P:* Alexander Gruter; *St: & Sc:* Andrew Solt; *Songs:* "Ave Maria" (Giuseppe Verdi); "Oh Mon Amour," "Bavarian Drinking Song," "Vesti La Giubba" from "Pagliacci" (Ruggiero Leoncavallo); "La Donna de Mobile" from "Rigoletto," "Niun Mi Tema," "Grand March" (Verdi); "O Sole Mio" (Eduardo de Capuz); "Ich Liebe Dich" (Edvard Grieg); "Come Prima" (M. Panzeri–S. Paola Tacani–Mary Bond); "Capri, Capri," "Pineapple Picker" (George Stoll). (1:37) (video) Romantic drama of an opera singer who travels Europe, performing concerts to earn money for an operation for his deaf girlfriend. In Technicolor and Technirama, this film was a co-production of the U.S.A., Germany and Italy.

863. Forbidden (Universal-International; 1953). *Cast:* Tony Curtis, Joanne Dru, Lyle Bettger, Marvin Miller, Victor Sen Yung, Peter J. Mamakos, Mae Tai Sing, Howard Chuman, Weaver Levy, Alan Dexter, David Sharpe, Harold Fong, Mamie Van Doren, Aen-Ling Chow, Leemoi Chu, Barry Bernard, Harry Lauter, Reginald Sheffield, Alphonse Martell, Al Ferguson, Jimmy Gray, Spencer Chan. *D:* Rudolph Maté; *P:* Ted Richmond; *St:* William Sackheim; *Sc:* Gil Doud, Sackheim. (1:24) A hood (Bettger) sends a henchman (Curtis) to Macao to retrieve the widow (Dru) of another hood before she spills the beans.

864. Forbidden Island (Columbia; 1959). *Cast:* Jon Hall, Nan Adams, John Farrow, Jonathan Haze, Greigh Phillips, Dave "Howdy" Peters, Tookie Evans, Martin Denny, Bob LaVarre, Bill Anderson, Abraham Kaluna. *D:-P:-St: & Sc:* Charles B. Griffith; *Title song:* Martin Denny. (1:06) Adventure programmer of a hunt for sunken treasure. Location filming in Hawaii and Florida. Columbia color.

865. Forbidden Jungle (Eagle-Lion/Jack Schwarz Prods.; 1950). *Cast:* Don Harvey, Forrest Taylor, Alyce Louis, Robert Cabal, Tamba (chimp). *D:* Robert Tansey; *P:* Jack Schwarz; *St: & Sc:* Frances Kavanaugh. (1:07) A white hunter suspects a young boy living wild in the jungle is actually his grandson. A low budget adventure padded with much stock footage that ran on a double bill with *The Fighting Stallion* (q.v.).

866. Forbidden Planet (MGM; 1956). *Cast:* Walter Pidgeon (Dr. Morbius), Anne Francis (Altaira), Leslie Nielsen (Comdr. Adams), Warren Stevens (Lt. "Doc" Ostrow), Jack Kelly (Lt. Farman), Earl Holliman (Cook), George Wallace (Bosun), James Drury (Strong), Robert Dix (Grey), Richard Anderson (Chief Quinn), Jimmy Thompson (Youngerford), Harry Harvey, Jr. (Randall), Roger McGee (Lindstrom), Peter Miller (Moran), Morgan Jones (Nichols), Richard Grant (Silvers), Robby the Robot (himself). *D:* Fred McLeod Wilcox; *P:* Nicholas Nayfack; *St:* Irving Block, Allen Adler; *Sc:* Cyril Hume; *F/X:* (AAN) A. Arnold Gillespie, Irving Ries, Wesley C. Miller. (1:38) (video/laserdisc) Acclaimed science fiction of space travelers who set down on a planet where a scientist has created his own empire with only his daughter and a versatile robot. The storyline follows William Shakespeare's *The Tempest*, but the bard receives no screen credit. Eastmancolor and CinemaScope.

867. Force of Arms (Warner; 1951). *Cast:* William Holden, Nancy Olson, Frank Lovejoy, Gene Evans, Paul Picerni, Dick Wesson, Katharine Warren, Ross Ford, [Virgil] "Slats" Taylor, Ron Hagerthy, Amelia Kova, Robert Roark, Donald Gordon, Ron Hargrave, Mario Siletti, Argentina Brunetti, Anna Demetrio, Jay Richards, Henry Kulky, Andy Mariani, Francesco Cantania, Lea Lamedico, Adriana Page, Phillip Carey, Bob Ohlen, Joan Winfield, John McGuire. *D:* Michael Curtiz; *P:* Anthony Veiller; *Sc:* Orin Jannings. (1:40) (video) World War II romantic drama, reminiscent of Hemingway's *A Farewell to Arms* (Paramount; 1932), of the tormented affair between a G.I. and a WAC. Based on *Italian Story* by Richard N. Tregaskis.

868. Foreign Intrigue (United Artists/Mandeville Films; 1956). *Cast:* Robert Mitchum, Ingrid [Thulin] Tulean (U.S. debut), Genevieve Page (U.S. debut), Frederick O'Brady, Eugene Deckers, Inga Tidblad, John Padovano, Frederick Schrecker, Lauritz Falk, Peter Copley, Nil Sperber, Ralph Brown, George Hubert, Jean Galland, Jim Gerald, John Stark, Gilbert Robin, Valentine Camax, Robert Le Beal, Albert Simmons. *D:-P: & Sc:* Sheldon Reynolds; *St:* Reynolds, Harold Jack Bloom, Gene Levitt; *Song:* "Foreign Intrigue Concerto" Charles Norman. (1:40) A man investigates the death of a millionaire who was a client of the firm he works for. Filmed in Sweden, Vienna and on the Riviera in Eastmancolor, it is based on the TV series of the same name.

869. Forever Darling (MGM/Zandra Prods.; 1956). *Cast:* Lucille Ball, Desi Arnaz (final film), James Mason, Louis Calhern, John Emery, Mabel Albertson, Natalie Schafer, John Hoyt, Ralph Dumke, Nancy Kulp, Willis B. Bouchey, Ruth Brady. *D:* Alexander Hall (final film—ret.); *P:* Desi Arnaz; *St:* Marya Mannes; *Sc:* Helen Deutsch; *Title song:* Sammy Cahn (sung by the Ames Brothers). (1:36) (video/laserdisc) Marital fantasy-comedy of a husband (Arnaz) driven to the brink of divorce by his wife's (Ball) behavior, until her guardian angel (Mason) materializes to save the day.

870. Forever Female (Paramount; 1953). *Cast:* Ginger Rogers, William Holden, Paul Douglas, Pat Crowley (film debut), James Gleason, Marjorie Rambeau, Jesse White, King Donovan, Marion Ross, George Reeves, Richard Shannon, Vic Perrin, Russell Gaige, Sally Mansfield, Kathryn Grant, Rand Harper, Henry Dar Boggia, Victor Romito, Hyacinte Railla, Alfred Paix, Walter Reed, Josephine Whittell, Almira Sessions, Joel Marston, Grayce Hampton, David Leonard, Maidie Norman, Vince M. Townsend, Jr., Michael Darrin, Richard Garland, William Leslie, Dulce Daye. *D:* Irving Rapper; *P:* Pat Duggan; *St: & Sc:* Philip and Julius Epstein. (1:33) (video) Backstage comedy of an actress who refuses to accept the fact that she is too old to play an ingenue role, which is also sought by a much younger actress. Suggested by the play *Rosalind* by Sir James M. Barrie. A box office dud.

Forgery (G.B. title) *see* **Southside 1-1000**

871. Fort Algiers (United Artists/Erco Pictures; 1953). *Cast:* Yvonne De Carlo, Carlos Thompson (U.S. debut), Raymond Burr, Leif Erickson, Anthony Caruso, John Dehner, Robert Boon, Henry Corden, Joe Kirk, Bill Phipps, Sandra Gale, Charles Evans. *D:* Lesley Selander; *P:* Joseph N. Ermolieff; *St:* Frederick Stephani; *Sc:* Theodore St. John; *Song:* "I'll Follow You" Michel Michelet, Yvonne De Carlo. (1:18) Low budget adventure tale of the French Foreign Legion, revolting Arabs, desert oil fields and a female French agent posing as a cabaret singer.

872. Fort Bowie (United Artists/Bel-Air-Oak Pictures; 1958). *Cast:* Ben Johnson, Jan Harrison, Kent Taylor, Jane Davi, Larry Chance, J. Ian Douglas, Peter Mamakos, Jerry Frank, Johnny Western, Ed Hinton, Barbara Parry. *D:* Howard W. Koch; *P:* Aubrey Schenck; *St: &*

Sc: Maurice Tombragel. (1:20) Programmer western of U.S. Cavalry vs. Indians.

873. Fort Defiance (United Artists/Ventura Pictures; 1951). *Cast:* Dane Clark, Ben Johnson, Peter Graves, Tracey Roberts, George Cleveland, Dennis Moore, Iron Eyes Cody, Ralph Sanford, Craig Woods, Dick Elliott, Kit Guard, Duke York, Phil Rawlins, Jerry Ambler, Slim Hightower, Wesley Hudman. *D:* John Rawlins; *P:* Frank Melford; *St: & Sc:* Louis Lantz. (1:21) Western of a Civil War deserter and his blind brother, involved with others preparing for an impending attack by Navajo Indians. Cinecolor.

874. Fort Dobbs (Warner; 1958). *Cast:* Clint Walker (starring debut), Virginia Mayo, Brian Keith, Richard Eyer, Russ Conway, Michael Dante. *D:* Gordon Douglas; *P:* Martin Rackin; *Sc:* George W. George, Burt Kennedy (based on their story "Backtrack"). (1:30) A fugitive from a murder charge comes to the aid of a woman and her son besieged by Comanche Indians.

875. Fort Dodge Stampede (Republic; 1951). *Cast:* Allan Lane, Mary Ellen Kay, Roy Barcroft, Chubby Johnson, Trevor Bardette, Bruce Edwards, Wesley Hudman, William Forrest, Chuck Roberson, Rory Mallinson, Jack Ingram, Kermit Maynard, Black Jack (horse). *D: & P:* Harry Keller; *St: & Sc:* Richard Wormser. (1:00) In this series entry, deputy sheriff "Rocky Lane" relinquishes his badge to pursue an outlaw gang that is after concealed loot.

876. Fort Massacre (United Artists/Mirisch; 1958). *Cast:* Joel McCrea, Forrest Tucker, Susan Cabot, John Russell, Anthony Caruso, Robert Osterloh, Denver Pyle, George Neise, Rayford Barnes, Guy Prescott, Larry Chance, Irving Bacon (final film—ret.), Claire Carleton, Francis J. McDonald, Walter Kray. *D:* Joseph M. Newman; *P:* Walter M. Mirisch; *St: & Sc:* Martin M. Goldsmith. (1:20) Offbeat western of a cavalry sergeant who jeopardizes the safety of his men due to his obsessive hatred of Indians, as they were responsible for the deaths of his wife and children. DeLuxe color and CinemaScope.

877. Fort Osage (Monogram; 1952). *Cast:* Rod Cameron, Jane Nigh, Morris Ankrum, Douglas Kennedy, John Ridgely, William Phipps, I. Stanford Jolley, Lane Bradford, Iron Eyes Cody, Barbara Woodell, Russ Conway, Anne Kimbell, Hal Baylor, Barbara Allen. *D:* Lesley Selander; *P:* Walter Mirisch; *St: & Sc:* Daniel B. Ullman. (1:12) (video) Western of a wagon train attacked by Indians on the way to California.

878. Fort Savage Raiders (Columbia; 1951). *Cast:* Charles Starrett, John Dehner, Smiley Burnette, Trevor Bardette, Fred F. Sears, Sam Flint, John Cason, Dusty Walker, Peter Thompson, Frank Griffin. *D:* Ray Nazarro; *P:* Colbert Clark; *St: & Sc:* Barry Shipman. (0:54) "The Durango Kid" tangles with an outlaw gang made up of escaped convicts that is headed by an army deserter.

879. Fort Ti (Columbia/Esskay Pictures; 1953). *Cast:* George Montgomery (Capt. Pedediah Horn), Joan Vohs (Fortune Mallory), Irving Bacon (Sgt. Monday Wash), James Seay (Mark Chesney), Howard Petrie (Major Rogers), Lester Matthews (Lord Jeffrey Amherst), Louis D. Merrill (Raoul de Moreau), Cicely Browne (Bess Chesney), Ben Astar (Francois Leroy), Phyllis Fowler (Running Otter), George Lee (Capt. Delecroix). *D:* William Castle; *P:* Sam Katzman; *St: & Sc:* Robert E. Kent. (1:13) Historical costumer set during the French and Indian war of an attempt by Roger's Rangers to get Fort Ticonderoga away from the French. This action-adventure in Naturalvision 3-D and Technicolor became one of the 26 top-grossing films of 1952-53.

880. Fort Vengeance (Monogram/Allied Artists; 1953). *Cast:* James Craig, Rita Moreno, Keith Larsen, Reginald Denny, Charles Irwin, Morris Ankrum, Guy Kingsford, Michael Granger, Patrick Whyte, Paul Marion, Emory Parnell. *D:* Lesley Selander; *P:* Walter Wanger; *As.P:* William Calihan, Jr.; *St: & Sc:* Dan Ullman. (1:15) Northwoods action-adventure of Mounties who quell an Indian uprising while in the pursuit of fur thieves. Cinecolor.

881. Fort Worth (Warner; 1951). *Cast:* Randolph Scott, David Brian, Phyllis Thaxter, Helena Carter, Dick Jones, Emerson Treacy, Paul Picerni, Lawrence Tolan, Ray Teal, Bob Steele, Walter Sande, Chubby Johnson. *D:* Edwin L. Marin (final film—d. 1951); *P:* Anthony Veiller; *Sc:* John Twist (based on his story "Across the Panhandle"). (1:20) Western of a newspaper editor in Fort Worth, Texas, who tries the printed word, but finds the gun is what is needed to clean out the town. Technicolor.

882. Fort Yuma (United Artists/Bel-Air-Camden Prods.; 1955). *Cast:* Peter Graves, Joan Vohs, John Hudson, Joan Taylor, Addison Richards, Abel Fernandez, Stanley Clements, John Pickard, James Lilburn, William "Bill" Phillips, Lee Roberts, Edmund Penney. *D:* Lesley Selander; *P:* Howard W. Koch; *St: & Sc:* Danny Arnold. (1:18) (video) Western drama of an Indian-hating cavalry officer who is in conflict with the opposing views of his scout. Originally ran on the top of a double bill with *Killer's Kiss* (q.v.). Technicolor.

The Fortune Hunter (G.B. title) *see* **The Outcast**

883. Fortunes of Captain Blood (Columbia; 1950). *Cast:* Louis Hayward, Patricia Medina, George Macready, Alfonso Bedoya, Dona Drake, Lowell Gilmore, Wilton Graff, Curt Bois, Lumsden Hare, Billy Bevan (final film—ret.), Harry Cording, Sven-Hugo Borg, Duke York, Terry Kilburn, Charles Irwin, Martin Garralaga, James Fairfax, Alberto Morin, Nick Volpe, Georges Renavent. *D:* Gordon Douglas; *P:* Harry Joe Brown; *Sc:* Michael Hogan, Frank Burt, Robert Libott. (1:30) Costume adventure of physician Peter Blood taking to the high seas as a notorious pirate to right some wrongs. Based on Rafael Sabatini's 1936 novel *The Fortunes of Captain Blood.*

884. Forty Guns (20th Century–Fox/ Globe Enterprises; 1957). *Cast:* Barbara Stanwyck, Barry Sullivan, Dean Jagger, John Ericson, Gene Barry, Robert Dix, Jack "Jidge" Carroll, Gerald Milton, Paul Dubov, Ziva Rodann, Hank Worden, Neyle Morrow, Chuck Roberson, Chuck Hayward, Eve Brent, Sandra Wirth, Eddie Parks. *D:-P: & Sc:* Samuel Fuller; *Songs:* "High Ridin' Woman" Harold Adamson; Harry Sukman, "God Has His Arms Around Me" Adamson, Victor Young (sung by "Jidge" Carroll). (1:20) In this western, a powerful woman by the name of Jessica Drummond has set herself up as the ruler of Tombstone, Arizona, and has forty mounted guns to back her up. A film with cult appeal and a Fuller following. CinemaScope. (aka: *Woman with a Whip*)

885. The Forty-Niners (Monogram/Allied Artists; 1954). *Cast:* William "Wild Bill" Elliott, Virginia Grey, Henry [Harry] Morgan, John Doucette, Lane Bradford, I. Stanford Jolley, Denver Pyle, Ralph Sanford, Gregg Barton, Harry Lauter, Earle Hodgins, Dean Cromer. *D:* Thomas Carr; *P:* Vincent M. Fennelly; *St: & Sc:* Dan Ullman. (1:11) Western melodrama of a man who takes on the guise of a wanted murderer in order to catch three others wanted in a killing.

886. The 49th Man (Columbia; 1953). *Cast:* John Ireland, Richard Denning, Suzanne Dalbert, Robert C. Foulk, Touch [Michael] Connors, Richard Avonde, William R. Klein, Cicely Browne, Tommy Farrell, Peter Marshall, Genevieve Aumont, Chris Alcaide, George Milan, Joseph Mell, Robert Hunter, Michael Colgan, Jean Del Val, George Dee. *D:* Fred F. Sears; *P:* Sam Katzman; *St:* Ivan Tors: *Sc:* Harry J. Essex. (1:13) Espionage melodrama of foreign agents attempting to smuggle parts of an atomic bomb into the U.S., with later intent on the bomb's detonation. Originally ran on a double bill with *The Juggler* (q.v.).

887. Four Boys and a Gun (United Artists/Security Pictures; 1957). *Cast:* Frank Sutton, Larry Green, James Franciscus (film debut), William Hinant, Otto Hulett, Robert Dryden, J. Pat O'Malley, Diana Herbert, Patricia Sloan, Nancy Devlin, Patricia Bosworth, David Burns, Anne Seymour, Frank Gero, Karl Swenson, Noel Glass, Lisa Osten, Sid Raymond, George McIver, Frank Campanella. *D: & P:* William Berke; *Sc:* Philip Yordan, Leo Townsend. (1:14) Teen exploitation melodrama of four youths who plan a robbery and find themselves wrongly implicated in a cop killing. Based on the 1944 novel by Willard Wiener.

888. 4D Man (Universal-International/ Fairview; 1959). *Cast:* Robert Lansing (film debut), Lee Meriwether, James Congdon, Robert Strauss, Edgar Stehli, Patty Duke, Guy Raymond, Chick James, Jasper Deeter, Dean Newman, George Kayara, Elbert Smulyh. *D:* Irvin Shortess Yeaworth, Jr.; *P:* Yeaworth, Jr., Jack H. Harris; *Story idea:* Harris; *Sc:* Theodore Simonson, Cy Chermak. (1:25) (video) Science fiction of a man experimenting with electrical currents that enable matter to pass through matter. Filmed at Valley Forge, PA. DeLuxe color. (G.B. title: *The Evil Force*) (aka: *The Master of Terror*)

889. Four Fast Guns (Universal-International/Phoenix Film Studio; 1959). *Cast:* James Craig, Martha Vickers, Edgar Buchanan, Brett Halsey, Paul Richards, Blue Wright, Richard Martin, John Swift, Paul Raymond. *D: & P:* William Hole, Jr.; *Ex.P:* Kenneth Altose; *Sc:* James Edmiston, Dallas Gaultois. (1:12) Low budget western of a "town tamer" who sets out to do his thing in a small Arizona town, only to meet opposition from the town's crippled overlord. The first production from Arizona's Phoenix Film Studio, it was filmed in that state.

890. Four Girls in Town (Universal-International; 1956). *Cast:* George Nader, Julie Adams, Gia Scala, Elsa Martinelli, Marianne Cook, Helene Stanton, Sydney Chaplin, John Gavin, Rock Hudson, Grant Williams, Herbert Anderson, Ainslee Pryor, Judson Pratt, Hy Averback, James Bell, Mabel Albertson, Dave Barry, Maurice Marsac, Irene Corlett, Eugene Mazzola, Phil Harvey, Cynthia Patrick, Charles Tannen, Renata Vanni, Robert Boon, Jack Mather, Franco Corsaro, John Bryant, Helen Andrews, Rodney Bell, Stephen Ellis, Frank Chase, Voltaire Perkins, Clarence Straight, Robert Hoy, Rex May, Shirley de Burgh, Giselle D'Arc, Marie Kassova, Gisele Verlaine, Hubie Kerns, George Calliga, Evelyn Ford, Kitty Muldoon, George Nardelli. *D:* Jack Sher; *P:* Aaron Rosenberg; *St: & Sc:* Sher; *Theme song:* "Rhapsody for Four Girls" Alex North. (1:25) Drama, set in Hollywood, of four hopeful actresses auditioning for a part in a movie vacated by another actress. Technicolor and CinemaScope.

891. Four Guns to the Border (Universal-International; 1954). *Cast:* Rory Calhoun, Colleen Miller, George Nader, Walter Brennan, Nina Foch, John McIntire, Charles Drake, Jay Silverheels, Nestor Paiva, Mary Field, Robert Hoy, Robert Herron, Reg Parton, Donald Kerr. *D:* Richard Carlson; *P:* William Alland; *St:* Louis L'Amour; *Sc:* George Van Marter, Franklin Coen. (1:22) Four outlaws rob a bank and head for the Mexican border, but meet their waterloo after coming to the aid of a girl and her father besieged by Apaches.

892. The Four-Poster (Columbia/Stanley Kramer Co.; 1952). *Cast:* Rex Harrison (John), Lilli Palmer (voted "Best Actress" at the Venice Film Festival/Abby). *D:* Irving Reis (final film—d. 1953); *P:* Stanley Kramer; *Sc:* Allan Scott; *Cin:* (AAN) Hal Mohr (in 1953). (1:43) Acclaimed comedy-drama of a man and woman who play out scenes of their life, from marriage to death, around their four-poster bed. Based on the play by Jan de Hartog, it became the basis for the Broadway musical *I Do, I Do.*

893. The Four Skulls of Jonathan Drake (United Artists/Vogue Pictures; 1959). *Cast:* Eduard Franz, Valerie French, Henry Daniell, Grant Richards, Paul Cavanagh (final film—d. 1959), Howard Wendell, Paul Wexler, Lumsden Hare, Frank Gerstle. *D:* Edward L. Cahn; *P:* Robert E. Kent; *St: & Sc:* Orville H. Hampton. (1:10) B budget horror of an anthropologist, the victim of a family curse, who has his head grafted onto the body of a deceased Ecuadorian medicine man. This feature originally ran on the top of a double bill with *Invisible Invaders* (q.v.).

894. Fourteen Hours (20th Century-Fox; 1951). *Cast:* Richard Basehart (voted "Best Actor" by the NBR/Robert Cosick), Paul Douglas (Dunnigan), Barbara Bel Geddes (Virginia), Debra Paget (Ruth), Agnes Moorehead (Mrs. Cosick), Robert Keith (Mr. Cosick), Howard Da Silva (Lt. Moksar), Jeffrey Hunter (Danny), Martin Gabel (film debut/Dr. Strauss), Grace Kelly (film debut/Mrs. Fuller), Jeff Corey, (Sgt. Farley), James Millican (Sgt. Boyle), Donald Randolph (Dr. Benson), Willard Waterman (Mr. Harris), Ann Morrison (Mrs. Dunnigan), Russell Hicks (Regan), Frank Faylen, Kenneth Harvey, George MacQuarrie, Forbes Murray, George Putnam, Ossie Davis, David Burns, Henry Slate, Harvey Lembeck, Lou Polan, Brad Dexter, Shep Menken, Joyce Van Patten, George Baxter, Bernard Burks, Michael Fitzmaurice, John Cassavetes (film debut/extra). *D:* Henry Hathaway; *P:* Sol C. Siegel; *Sc:* John Paxton; *ASD:* (AAN-b/w) Lyle Wheeler, Leland Fuller (art directors), Thomas Little, Fred J. Rode (sets). (1:32) Drama of a man perched on the ledge of a skyscraper, threatening to leap to his death, while several separate stories emerge from the people on or near the scene. Based on the story "The Man on the Ledge" by Joel Sayre which was based on a factual incident occurring in 1938. It was voted "Best Film of the Year" by the *New York Times*, placed #10 on the "10 Best" list of the NBR and was in nomination at the Venice Film Festival and the British Academy Awards.

895. Foxfire (Universal-International; 1955). *Cast:* Jane Russell, Jeff Chandler, Dan Duryea, Mara Corday, Barton MacLane, Frieda Inescort, Celia Lovsky, Charlotte Wynters, Eddy Waller, Arthur Space, Phil Chambers, Robert Bice, Vici Raaf, Grace Lenard, Guy Wilkerson, Lillian Bronson, Mary Carroll, Lisabeth Fielding, Dabbs Greer, Hal K. Dawson, Charmienne Harker, Grace Hayle, Beulah Archuletta, Billy Wilkerson, Chebon Jadi, Leon Charles, Jimmy Casino, Charles Soldani, Martin Cichy, Manley Suathojame, R.H. Baldwin. *D:* Joseph Pevney; *P:* Aaron Rosenberg, Anya Seton; *Sc:* Ketti Frings; *Title song:* Henry Mancini, Jeff Chandler (sung by Chandler). (1:31)

Marital drama of an Eastern socialite who marries a half-breed Apache mining engineer, followed by a series of cultural clashes. Based on the 1951 novel by Robert Simon, it was photographed in Technicolor.

896. Francis Covers the Big Town (Universal-International; 1953). *Cast:* Donald O' Connor, Yvette Dugay, Gene Lockhart, Nancy Guild, William Harrigan, Larry Gates, Silvio Minciotti, Lowell Gilmore, Gale Gordon, Hanley Stafford, Forrest Lewis, Michael Ross, Louis Mason, Charles J. Flynn, Francis (mule—received #2 PATSY Award in 1954), Chill Wills (voice only). *D:* Arthur Lubin; *P:* Leonard Goldstein; *St: & Sc:* Oscar Brodney. (1:26) (video) The fourth entry in the hit comedy series, with the talking mule and pal Peter Stirling going to work for a newspaper and getting involved in a murder trial. Based on characters created by author David Stern.

897. Francis Goes to the Races (Universal-International; 1951). *Cast:* Donald O'Connor (Peter Stirling), Piper Laurie (Frances Travers), Cecil Kellaway (Col. Travers), Jesse White (Frank Damer), Barry Kelley (Mallory), Hayden Rorke (Rogers), Vaughn Taylor (Harrington), Peter Brocco (Dr. Marberry), Don Beddoe (Dr. Quimby), Bill Walker (Sam), Francis (mule—received #2 PATSY Award in 1952), Chill Wills (voice only), Larry Keating, Jack Wilson, Ed Max, George Webster. *D:* Arthur Lubin; *P:* Leonard Goldstein; *St:* Robert Arthur; *Sc:* Oscar Brodney, David Stern (based on characters he created). (1:28) (video/laserdisc) The second entry in the hit money-making "Francis" series. In this one, the talking mule relays up-and-coming winners of horse races, as well as psychoanalyzing a filly who is a potential winner at the racetrack. One of the 23 top-grossing films of 1950-51.

898. Francis Goes to West Point (Universal-International; 1952). *Cast:* Donald O'Connor, Lori Nelson, Alice Kelley, William Reynolds, Palmer Lee [aka: Gregg Palmer], Les Tremayne, Otto Hulett, David Janssen, James Best, Paul Burke, Cliff Clark, Leonard Nimoy, Francis (mule—received PATSY "Craven Award" in 1953), Chill Wills (voice only). *D:* Arthur Lubin; *P:* Leonard Goldstein; *St: & Sc:* Oscar Brodney; *Additional dialogue:* Dorothy Reid. (1:21) (video) The third entry in the popular series with the talking mule getting involved with pal Peter Stirling at the U.S. Military Academy. Based on characters created by David Stern. Originally paired on a double bill with *Sally and Saint Anne* (q.v.).

899. Francis in the Haunted House (Universal-International; 1956). *Cast:* Mickey Rooney, Virginia Welles, James Flavin, Paul Cavanagh, Mary Ellen Kay, David Janssen, Ralph Dumke, Richard Gaines, Richard Deacon, Dick Winslow, Charles Horvath, Timothy Carey, Helen Wallace, Edward Earle, John Maxwell, Glen Kramer, Francis (mule—received #3 PATSY Award in 1957), Paul Frees (voice only). *D:* Charles Lamont (final film—ret.); *P:* Robert Arthur; *St: & Sc:* Herbert Margolis, William Raynor. (1:20) (video) The loquacious quadruped helps rid a supposed haunted house of a gang creating reproductions of famous artworks. The seventh and final entry in the "Francis, the Talking Mule" comedy series which was based on a character created by David Stern.

900. Francis in the Navy (Universal-International; 1955). *Cast:* Donald O'Connor (dual role), Martha Hyer, Richard Erdman, Jim Backus, David Janssen, Clint Eastwood (his 2nd film), Martin Milner, Leigh Snowden, Paul Burke, Phil Garris, Myrna Hansen, Jane Howard, William Forrest, Virginia O'Brien (final film—ret.), Francis (mule—received #2 PATSY Award in 1956), Chill Wills (voice only). *D:* Arthur Lubin (final film); *P:* Stanley Rubin; *St: & Sc:* Devery Freeman. (1:20) (video) The sixth entry in the popular "Francis" series has the talking mule drafted into the U.S. Navy. Based on characters created by David Stern. Note: Arthur Lubin, who directed the first six "Francis" films, was also the inspiration behind "Mr. Ed," TV's talking horse.

901. Francis Joins the WACS (Universal-International; 1954). *Cast:* Donald O'Connor, Julia [Julie] Adams, Chill Wills (who also supplies the voice of Francis), Lynn Bari, ZaSu Pitts, Mamie Van Doren, Allison Hayes, Joan Shawlee, Mara Corday, Karen Kadler, Elsie Holmes, Olan Soule, Anthony Rodecki, Richard Deems, Sam Woody, Francis (mule—received #2 PATSY Award in 1955). *D:* Arthur Lubin; *P:* Ted Richmond; *St:* Herbert Baker; *Sc:* Devery Freeman, James B. Allardice. (1:34) (video) The fifth entry in the hit money-making comedy series has Peter Stirling (O'Connor) being drawn back into the military (by clerical error, of course) into a WAC unit. One of the more amusing gimmicks in this entry is that Chill Wills appears as an army general whose voice just happens to sound like that of Francis, the talking mule. Based on characters by David Stern.

902. Frankenstein—1970 (Allied Artists/A–Z Prods., Inc.; 1958). *Cast:* Boris Karloff, Tom Duggan, Jana Lund, Donald Barry, Charlotte Austin, Irwin Berke, Rudolph Anders, John Dennis, Norbert Schiller, Mike Lane. *D:* Howard W. Koch; *P:* Aubrey Schenck; *St:* Schenck, Charles A. Moses; *Sc:* George Worthing Yates, Richard Landau. (1:23) (video) Dr. Frankenstein's grandson is working on his forbear's experiment with money he acquired from a television production company that is using his castle. CinemaScope.

903. Frankenstein's Daughter (Astor/Layton; 1958). *Cast:* John Ashley, Sandra Knight, Donald Murphy, Sally Todd, Harold Lloyd, Jr., Felix Locher, Wolfe Barzell, John Zaremba, Robert Dix, Harry Wilson, Voltaire Perkins, Charlotte Fortney, Bill Coontz, George Barrows, The Page Cavanaugh Trio. *D:* Richard Cunha; *P:* Marc Frederic; *St: & Sc:* H.E. Barrie; *Songs:* "Daddy-Bird," "Special Date" Page Cavanaugh. (1:25) (video) Low budget horror exploitation with a descendant of Dr. Frankenstein (now known as Dr. Frank) who continues his ancestor's work. Geared to the teen-trade, it ran on a double bill with *Missile to the Moon* (q.v.). (aka: *She Monster of the Night*)

904. Fraulein (20th Century–Fox; 1958). *Cast:* Dana Wynter, Mel Ferrer, Dolores Michaels, Maggie Hayes, Theodore Bikel, Helmut Dantine, Herbert Berghof, James Edwards, Ivan Triesault, Blandine Ebinger, Luis Van Rooten, Jack Kruschen. *D:* Henry Koster; *P:* Walter Reisch; *Sc:* Leo Townsend. (1:38) In postwar Berlin, a German girl helps an American soldier and eventually finds herself captured by the communists. Based on the 1956 novel *Erika* by James McGovern.

905. The French Line (RKO/Howard Hughes; 1953–54). *Cast:* Jane Russell, Gilbert Roland, Arthur Hunnicutt, Mary McCarty, Joyce MacKenzie, Paula Corday (final film—ret.), Scott Elliott, Craig Stevens, Laura Elliot, Steven Geray, John Wengraf, Michael St. Angel [aka: Steven Flagg], Barbara Darrow, Barbara Dobbins, Ray Bennett, Al Cavens, Jo Gilbert, Frank Marlowe, Nick Stuart, Charles Smith, Allen Ray, Jeffrey Sayre, Ralph Volkie, Carlos Albert, Robert Dayo, Donald Moray, Joseph Rubino, Renald Dupont, Bess Flowers, Theresa Harris, Peggy Leon, Leoda Richards, Ramona Magrill, John Mooney, George Wallace, Lane Bradford, Edward Short, Edward Coch, Wayne Taylor, Pierre Chandler, Frederick Stevens, Arthur Dulac, Jack Chefe, William Forrest, Louis Mercier, Buck Young, Sue Casey, Mary Ellen Gleason, Mary Langan, Bobette Bentley, Gloria Watson, Dede Moore, Helen Chapman, Gloria Pall, Dawn Oney, Joi Lansing, Joyce Johnson, Lonnie Pierce, Mary Jane Carey, Toni Carroll, Sandy Descher, Wanda Ottoni, Shirley Patterson, Lucien Plauzoles, Lomax Study, Billy Daniels, Jack Boyle, Joel Friend, Suzanne Ames, Babs Cox, Anne Ford, Virginia Bates, Katherine Cassidy, Liz Slifer, Stanley Farrar, Marina Cisternas, Dan Bernaducci, Fritz Feld, Marie Rabasse, Bert LeBaron *and models:* Jean Moorhead, Mary Rodman, Charmienne Harker, Dolores Michaels, Suzanne Alexander, Eileen Coghlan, Rosemary Colligan, Millie Doff, Jane Easton, Jarma Lewis, Helene Hayden, Ellye Marshall, Marilyn [Kim] Novak (film debut), Pat Sheehan, Maureen Stephenson, Shirley Tegge, Beverly Thompson, Doreen Woodbury, Devvy Davenport, Barbara Lohrman, Dolly Summers, Phyllis St. Pierre, Shirley Buchanan. *D:* Lloyd Bacon; *P:* Edmund Grainger (for Howard Hughes); *St:* Matty Kemp, Isabel Dawn; *Sc:* Mary Loos, Richard Sale; *Songs:* "Comment Allez-Vous?," "Well, I'll Be Switched," "Any Gal from Texas," "What Is This That I Feel?," "With a Kiss," "By Madame Fuelle," "Wait Till You See Paris," "Poor Andre," "The French Line" (cut from the final release print), and "Lookin' For Trouble" Andre Josef Myrow, Ralph Blane, Robert Wells. (1:42) (video) Critically panned musical-comedy of a Texas millionairess who goes on a spree in gay Paree. Condemnation by the Catholic Legion of Decency helped fill movie theatre seats. The whole inspiration for this Technicolor production seems to be centered around Russell's bosom in 3-D.

906. Frenchie (Universal-International; 1950). *Cast:* Shelley Winters, Joel McCrea, Paul Kelly, John Emery, Marie Windsor, Elsa Lanchester, John Russell, George Cleveland, Regis Toomey, Paul E. Burns, Frank Ferguson, Lawrence Dobkin, Lucille Barkley. *D:* Louis King; *P:* Michel Kraike; *St: & Sc:* Oscar Brodney. (1:20) A Technicolor reworking of the 1939 Universal western classic *Destry Rides Again* of a girl who returns to the town of Bottleneck to find out who killed her father.

Fresh from Paris *see* **Paris Follies of 1956**

907. Friendly Persuasion (Allied Artists/B-M Prod.; 1956). *Cast:* Gary Cooper (Jess Birdwell), Dorothy McGuire (voted "Best Actress" by the NBR/Eliza Birdwell), Anthony Perkins (AAN/Josh Birdwell), Richard Eyer (Little Jess), Phyllis Love (Mattie Birdwell), Marjorie Main (widow Hudspeth), Robert Middleton (Sam Jordan), Mark Richman (Gard Jordan), Walter Catlett (Prof. Quigley), Richard Hale (Elder Purdy), Joel Fluellen (Enoch), John Smith (Caleb), Edna Skinner (Opal Hudspeth), Marjorie Durant (Pearl Hudspeth), Frances Farwell (Ruby Hudspeth), Theodore Newton (army major), Samantha the goose (received #1 PATSY Award in 1957), Frank Jenks (shell game operator), Jean Inness (Mrs. Purdy), Diane Jergens (Elizabeth—Quaker girl), Mary Carr (final film and her only film appearance since 1945/Emma—Quaker woman), Henry Rowland (O'Hara), Ivan Rasputin (Billy Goat), Steve Warren (Haskell), Norman Leavitt (Clem), Don Kennedy (Buster), Earle Hodgins (shooting gallery operator), Richard Garland (bushwhacker), Nelson Leigh (minister), Joe Turkel, James Anderson, Helen Kleeb, John Craven, Harry Hines, Donald Kerr, Tom London, John Pickard, Charles Halton (final film—d. 1959). *D:* (AAN) William Wyler; *P:* (AAN-Best Picture) Wyler; *As.P:* Robert Wyler; *Sc:* (uncredited/Oscar nomination withdrawn due to blacklisting) Michael Wilson; *Songs:* (AAN) "Friendly Persuasion" (Thee I Love) sung by Pat Boone over credits; "Mocking Bird in a Willow Tree," "Marry Me, Marry Me," "Indiana Holiday" and "Coax Me a Little" Dimitri Tiomkin, Paul Francis Webster; *Sound recording:* (AAN) Westrex Sound Services, Inc. (Gordon R. Glennan) and Samuel Goldwyn Sound Dept. (Gordon Sawyer). (2:20) (video/laserdisc) Critically acclaimed 19th century Americana of the Birdwells, a Quaker family living in Ohio, at the time the Civil War threatens to disrupt their lives and their pacifist beliefs. Set in 1862, it was based on the 1945 novel *The Friendly Persuasion* by Jessamyn West. The recipient of the "Golden Palm" (Best Film) at the 1957 Cannes Film Festival, it also placed #4, #5 and #9 respectively on the "10 Best" lists of *Film Daily*, the NBR and the *New York Times*. One of the 24 top-grossing films of 1956-57, it was photographed in DeLuxe color. Reworked in 1975 as a TV movie that was retitled *Except for Me and Thee*.

Fright *see* **The Spell of the Hypnotist**

Frightened City (G.B. title) *see* **The Killer That Stalked New York**

Frigid Wife *see* **A Modern Marriage**

908. Frisco Tornado (Republic; 1950). *Cast:* Allan Lane, Eddy Waller, Martha Hyer, Stephen Chase, Ross Ford, Mauritz Hugo, Lane Bradford, Hal Price, Rex Lease, George Chesebro, Edmund Cobb, Bud Geary, Black Jack (horse). *D:* R.G. Springsteen; *As.P:* Gordon Kay; *St: & Sc:* M. Coates Webster. (1:00) In this western series entry, U.S. marshal "Rocky Lane" is sent into an area to break up an illegal protection racket.

909. The Frogmen (20th Century-Fox; 1951). *Cast:* Richard Widmark (Lt. Comdr. John Lawrence), Dana Andrews (Flannigan), Gary Merrill (Lt. Comdr. Pete Vincent), Jeffrey Hunter (Creighton), Warren Stevens (Hodges), Robert Wagner (Lt. [J.G.] Franklin), Harvey Lembeck (Camarsie), Robert Rockwell (Lt. Doyle), Henry Slate (Sleepy), Robert Adler (Chief Ryan), Bob Patten (Lt. Klinger), Harry Flowers (Kinselia), William Bishop (Ferriso), Fay Roope (Admiral Dakers), William N. Neil (Comdr. Miles), James Gregory (C.P.O. Lane), Robert Hardie (Capt. Radford), Parley Baer (Dr. Ullman), Norman McKay (Capt. Phillips), Sydney Smith (Gen. Coleson), Peter Leeds, Richard Allan, Frank Donahue, Jack Warden, Ray Hyke, George Yoshinaga, Harry Hamada, Rush Williams. *D:* Lloyd Bacon; *P:* Samuel G. Engel; *St:* (AAN) Oscar Millard; *Sc:* John Tucker Battle; *Cin:* (AAN-b/w) Norbert Brodine. (1:36) Acclaimed World War II drama, set in the Pacific theatre, of an underwater demolition team and their new hard-nosed commanding officer, whom all soon come to despise.

910. From Hell It Came (Allied Artists/Milner Bros. Prod.; 1957). *Cast:* Tod Andrews, Tina Carver, Linda Watkins, John McNamara, Gregg Palmer, Robert Swan, Baynes Barron, Suzanne Ridgeway, Mark Sheeler, Lee Rhodes, Grace Matthews, Tani Marsh, Chester Hayes, Lenmana Guerin. *D:* Dan Milner; *P:* Jack Milner; *St:* J. Milner, Richard Bernstein; *Sc:* Bernstein; *Makeup:* Paul Blaisdell. (1:11) Low budget horror film set on a remote Pacific island involving the murder of a chief's son, who returns in the form of a walking tree—called "Tobonga" by the natives—to mete justice to those responsible for his death. This one was originally paired on a double bill program with *The Disembodied* (q.v.). Note: When released to TV in the 1960s, this film carried at least three alternate titles, one of which was *Up From the Depths*, each one avoiding the use of the word "Hell" in the title.

911. From Hell to Texas (20th Century-Fox; 1958). *Cast:* Don Murray, Diane Varsi, Chill Wills, Dennis Hopper, R.G. Armstrong, Jay C. Flippen, Margo, John Larch, Ken Scott, Rudolfo Acosta, Harry Carey, Jr., Jose Torvay, Malcolm Atterbury, Salvador Baguez, Jerry Oddo. *D:* Henry Hathaway; *P:* Robert Buckner; *Sc:* Buckner, Wendell Mayes. (1:40) Western of a man pursued into the desert by the father and two brothers of the young man he just killed. Based on the 1957 book *The Hell-Bent Kid*—which was also the working title of this film—by Charles O. Locke. In DeLuxe color and CinemaScope, the critics were impressed. (G.B. title: *Manhunt*)

912. From Here to Eternity (Columbia; 1953). *Cast:* Burt Lancaster (AAN/Sgt. Milton Warden), Deborah Kerr (AAN/Karen Holmes), Montgomery Clift (AAN/Robert E. Lee Prewitt), Frank Sinatra (AA-BSA/Angelo Maggio), Donna Reed (AA-BSA/Lorene), Ernest Borgnine (Sgt. "Fatso" Judson), Philip Ober (Capt. Dana Holmes), Jack Warden (Corp. Buckley), Mickey Shaughnessy (Sgt. Leva), Harry Bellaver (Mazzioli), George Reeves (Sgt. Maylon Stark), John Dennis (Sgt. Ike Galovitch), Tim Ryan (Sgt. Pete Karelson), Barbara Morrison (Mrs. Kipfer), Kristine Miller (Georgette), Jean Willes (Annette), Merle Travis (Sal Anderson), Claude Akins (film debut/Sgt. Baldy Dhom), Robert Wilke (Sgt. Henderson), Don Dubbins (Friday Clark), John Cason (Corp. Paluso), Joan Shawlee (Sandra), Angela Stevens (Jean), Arthur Keegan (Treadwell), Robert Karnes (Sgt. Turp Thornhill), Douglas Henderson (Corp. Champ Wilson), John Bryant (Capt. Ross), Mary Carver (Nancy), Vicki Bakken (Suzanne), Margaret Barstow (Roxanne), Delia Salvi (Billie), Al Sargent (Nair), William Lundmark (Bill), Tyler McVey (Major Stern), Willis Bouchey, Weaver Levy. *D:* (AA) Fred Zinneman; *P:* (AA-Best Picture) Buddy Adler; *Sc:* (AA) Daniel Taradash; *Cinematography:* (AA-b/w) Burnett Guffey; *Music:* (AAN) Morris Stoloff, George Duning; *Costumes:* (AAN-b/w) Jean Louis; *Sound Recording:* (AA) John P. Livadary; *Editor:* (AA) William A. Lyon. (1:58) (video/laserdisc) James Jones' 1951 best-seller comes to the screen (less profanity and expletives), telling the dramatic story of various military and civilian personnel in pre–Pearl Harbor Hawaii, culminating in the Japanese attack on that U.S. naval base. Voted "Best Film" by *Film Daily* and the New York Film Critics, with the latter also bestowing accolades on Burt Lancaster as "Best Actor" and Fred Zinneman as "Best Director." "Eternity" also received the *Photoplay* Gold Medal and the "Special Recognition Prize" at the 1954 Cannes Film Festival. Voted #3 and #7 respectively on the "10 Best" lists of the NBR and the *New York Times*, it was also in nomination at the British Academy Awards. One of the 26 top-grossing films of 1952-53, it was remade in 1979 as a TV miniseries, which also sparked a brief TV series.

913. From the Earth to the Moon (Warner/RKO; 1958). *Cast:* Joseph Cotten, George Sanders, Debra Paget, Don Dubbins, Patric Knowles, Melville Cooper (final film—ret.), Carl Esmond, Henry Daniell, Ludwig Stossel, Morris Ankrum (President U.S. Grant). *D:* Byron Haskin; *P:* Benedict Bogeaus; *Sc:* James Leicester, Robert Blees. (1:40) (video/laserdisc) Nineteenth century science fiction of a scientist who believes man can make it to the moon and sets out to prove it. Based on Jules Verne's 1865 book of the same name, it was produced by RKO, but released by Warner Brothers when the former studio closed its doors. Filmed in Mexico. Technicolor.

914. Frontier Gambler (American Releasing Corp.; 1956). *Cast:* John Bromfield, Coleen Gray, Jim Davis, Kent Taylor, Margia Dean, Veda Ann Borg, Tracey Roberts, Stanley Andrews, Roy Engel, Frank Sully, Pierce Lyden, Rick Vallin, John Merton, Nadene Ashdown, Ewing Brown, Helen Jay. *D:* Sam Newfield; *P:* Sigmund Neufeld; *Sc:* Orville Hampton. (1:16) Programmer western of a deputy marshal who is sent to investigate the murder of a powerful woman in a small western town.

915. Frontier Gun (20th Century–Fox/Regal Films; 1958). *Cast:* John Agar, Joyce Meadows, Barton MacLane, Robert Strauss, Morris Ankrum, James Griffith, Lyn Thomas, Leslie Bradley, Doodles Weaver, Mike Ragan [aka: Holly Bane], Claire DuBrey, Tom Daly, Sammy Ogg, George Brand, Dan Simmons, Daniel White, Sydney Mason, Boyd Stockman. *D:* Paul Landres; *P:* Richard E. Lyons; *As.P:* Maury Dexter; *St: & Sc:* Stephen Kandel. (1:10) Though slow on the draw, a man is pressured into becoming sheriff of a western town full of troublemakers. Regalscope.

916. The Frontier Phantom (Realart/Western Adventure; 1952). *Cast:* Lash LaRue (in his final starring series western), Al St. John, Virginia Herrick, Archie Twitchell [aka: Michael Branden], Clarke Stevens, Bud Osborne,

Cliff Taylor, Kenne Duncan, George Chesebro, Sandy Sanders, Buck Garrett, Jack O'Shea, Frank Ellis, Roy Butler, Larry Barton. *D: & P:* Ron Ormond; *St: & Sc:* Maurice Tombragel, June Carr. (0:56) Two U.S. marshals set out to break up a counterfeiting ring.

Frontier Scout (G.B. title) *see* **Quincannon, Frontier Scout**

917. Frontier Woman (1956). *Cast:* Cindy Carson, Lance Fuller, Ann Kelly, James Clayton, Rance Howard, Curtis Dorsett, Mario Galento. *D: & P:* Ron Ormond. (1:20) An obscure low budget western.

918. The Fugitive Kind (United Artists/Jurow–Shepherd–Pennebaker; 1959). *Cast:* Marlon Brando, Anna Magnani, Joanne Woodward, Maureen Stapleton, Victor Jory, R.G. Armstrong, Emory Richardson, Spivy, Sally Gracie, Lucille Benson, John Baragrey (final film—ret.), Ben Yaffee, Joe Brown, Jr., Virgilia Chew, Frank Borgman, Janice Mars, Debbie Lynch. *D:* Sidney Lumet; *P:* Martin Jurow, Richard A. Shepherd; *As.P:* George Justin; *St:* Tennessee Williams, Meade Roberts. (2:15) (video) Based on Mr. Williams play, *Orpheus Descending*, this drama relates the tale of a drifter who comes to a small town and romances two different women. Filmed on location in New York City and Milton, N.Y., it was remade in 1990 for cable TV under the play's original title.

919. Fugitive Lady (Republic/Venus Prods.; 1951). *Cast:* Janis Paige, Binnie Barnes, Massimo Serato, Eduardo Ciannelli, Tony Centa, Alba Arnova, Dino Galvani, Rosina Galli, John Fostini, Luciana Danieli, Michael Tor, Alex Sergeroli, Joop Van Hulsen, Giulio Marchetti. *D:* Sidney Salkow; *P:* M.J. Frankovich; *Sc:* John O'Dea; *Song:* "My Guy" Alberto Barberis, Suzanne MacPherson (sung by Paige). (1:18) A melodrama, related in flashback, of events leading up to a man's fall from a cliff to his death. The question being: was it a murder or a suicide? Filmed on location in Italy, it was based on the novel by Doris Miles Disney.

Full House (G.B. title) *see* **O'Henry's Full House**

920. Full of Life (Columbia; 1956). *Cast:* Judy Holliday, Richard Conte, Salvatore Baccaloni (a Metropolitan Opera star making his film debut), Esther Minciotti, Silvio Minciotti, Joe DeSantis, Penny Santon, Arthur Lovejoy, Eleanor Audley, Trudy Marshall (final film—ret.), Walter Conrad, Sam Gilman. *D:* Richard Quine; *P:* Fred Kohlmar; *Sc:* John Fante. (1:31) (video) Comedy-drama of a pregnant wife's attempts to deal with her old-fashioned Italian father-in-law, who has just become a resident in her home. Based on Mr. Fante's 1952 book of the same name.

921. The Fuller Brush Girl (Columbia; 1950). *Cast:* Lucille Ball, Eddie Albert, Carl Benton Reid, Gale Robbins, Jeff Donnell, Lee Patrick, Jerome Cowan, John Litel, Fred Graham, Jack Perrin, Sid Tomack, Arthur Space, Billy Vincent, Lorin Raker, Lelah Tyler, Sarah Edwards, Lois Austin, Isabel Randolph, Isabel Withers, Donna Boswell (dual role), Gregory Marshall (dual role), Red Skelton (Fuller Brush man), Jay Barney, Shirley Whitney, Joel Robinson, Gail Bonney, John Doucette, Charles Hamilton, Jack Little, Joseph Palma, Cy Malis, James L. Kelly, Barbara Pepper, Myron Healey, Bud Osborne, Paul Bryar, Paul E. Burns, Joseph Crehan, Jean Willes, George Lloyd, Cliff Clark, Val Avery, Syd Saylor, Frank Wilcox. *D:* Lloyd Bacon; *P:* uncredited; *St: & Sc:* Frank Tashlin. (1:25) (video/laserdisc) Hit slapstick comedy of a door-to-door Fuller Brush salesgirl who gets involved in murder. A follow-up to Columbia's 1948 top-grossing hit *The Fuller Brush Man* with Red Skelton (who reprises his role in a bit in this film). (G.B. title: *The Affairs of Sally*)

922. Funny Face (Paramount; 1957). *Cast:* Audrey Hepburn (Jo Stockton), Fred Astaire (Dick Avery), Kay Thompson (Maggie Prescott), Michel Auclair (U.S. debut/Prof. Emile Flostre), Robert Flemyng (Paul Duval), Dovima (Marion), Virginia Gibson (Baba), Sue England (Laura), Ruta Lee (Lettie), Suzy Parker & Sunny Harnett (specialty dancers/"Pink number"), Alex Gerry (Dovitch), Iphigenie Castiglioni (Armande), Nancy Kilgas (Melissa), Paul Smith (Steve), Diane Du Bois (Mimi), Karen Scott (Gigi), Elizabeth "Lizz" Slifer (Madame La Farge), Don Powell & Carole Eastman (specialty dancers), Jean Del Val, Albert D'Arno, Nina Borget, Marilyn White, Louise Glenn, Heather Hopper, Cecile Rogers, Emilie Stevens, Bruce Hoy, Nesdon Booth. *D:* Stanley Donen; *P:* Roger Edens; *St: & Sc:* (AAN) Leonard Gershe; *Cin:* (AAN) Ray June; *ASD:* (AAN) Hal Pereira, George Davis (art directors), Sam Comer, Ray Moyer (sets); *Costumes:* (AAN) Edith Head, Hubert De Givenchy; *Choreography:* Eugene Loring, Fred Astaire; *Songs:* "Funny Face," " 'S Wonderful," "How Long Has This

Been Going On?," "Let's Kiss and Make Up," "He Loves and She Loves," "Clap Yo' Hands," (George and Ira Gershwin), "Think Pink," "Bonjour Paris," "Basal Metabolism," "Oh How to Be Lovely," and "Marche Funebre" (Roger Edens-Leonard Gershe). (1:43) (video/laserdisc) Critically acclaimed hit musical-romance of a photographer who turns a plain girl into a chic Paris fashion model. Astaire's character was based on famous fashion photographer Richard Avedon. Filmed on location in Paris, New York and Hollywood. The *New York Times* placed it at #2 on their "10 Best" list, while the NBR gave it a #6 placement. In Technicolor and VistaVision, it was also in nomination at the Cannes Film Festival. Note: The NBR gave a special award to this film for photographic innovations by John P. Fulton and Farciot Edouart.

923. **The Furies** (Paramount/Wallis-Hazen, Inc.; 1950). *Cast:* Barbara Stanwyck (Vance Jeffords), Walter Huston (final film—d. 1950/ T.C. Jeffords), Wendell Corey (Rip Darrow), Gilbert Roland (Juan Herrera), Judith Anderson (Florence Burnette), Thomas Gomez (El Tigre), Beulah Bondi (Mrs. Anaheim), John Bromfield (Clay Jeffords), Albert Dekker (Reynolds), Blanche Yurka (Herrera's mother), Louis Jean Heydt (Bailey), Wallace Ford (Scotty Hyslip, Frank Ferguson (Dr. Grieve), Movita Castaneda (Chiquita), Myrna Dell (Dallas Hart), Lou Steele (Aguirre Herrera), Pepe Hern (Felix Herrera), Rosemary Pettit (Carol Ann), Craig Kelly (young Anaheim), Charles Evans (old Anaheim), Jane Novak, Arthur Hunnicutt, James Davies, Douglas Grange, Baron Lichter, Joe Dominquez, Artie Del Rey, Eddy C. Waller, Georgia Clancy, Nolan Leary, Sam Finn, Richard Kipling. *D:* Anthony Mann; *P:* Hal B. Wallis; *Sc:* Charles Schnee; *Cin:* (AAN-b/w) Victor Milner; *Song:* "T.C. Round-up Time" Jay Livingston, Ray Evans. (1:49) Western drama, with a psychological bent, of the intense relationship between a wealthy cattle rancher and his rebellious daughter. Based on the 1948 novel by Niven Busch.

924. **Fury at Gunsight Pass** (Columbia; 1956). *Cast:* David Brian, Neville Brand, Richard Long, Lisa Davis, Katherine Warren, Percy Helton, Morris Ankrum, Addison Richards, Wally Vernon, Paul E. Burns, James Anderson, Joe Forte, Frank Fenton, George Keymas, Robert Anderson, Frank Coby, John Lehmann, Guy Teague. *D:* Fred F. Sears; *P:* Wallace MacDonald; *St:* & *Sc:* David Lang. (1:08) Programmer western of two bank robbers who hold a town for ransom in order to retrieve their loot, stolen by one of the town's residents.

925. **Fury at Showdown** (United Artists/ B.G. Prods., Inc.; 1957). *Cast:* John Derek, John Smith, Carolyn Craig, Nick Adams, Gage Clarke, Robert E. Griffin, Malcolm Atterbury, Rusty Lane, Sydney Smith, Frances Morris, Tyler MacDuff, Robert Adler, Norman Leavitt, Ken Christy, Tom McKee. *D:* Gerd Oswald; *P:* John Beck (for Bob Goldstein); *Sc:* Jason James. (1:15) A gunfighter is trying to go straight as a cattle rancher with his brother, until his brother is killed and he must again take up his guns. Based on the 1955 novel *Showdown Creek* by Lucas Todd.

926. **Fury in Paradise** (Filmakers; 1955). *Cast:* Peter Thompson, Rea Iturbi, Edwards [Eduardo] Noriega, Felipe Nolan, Jose Espinosa, Fran [Fanny] Schiller, Carlos Rivas, Claud Brooks. *D:-St:* & *Sc:* George Bruce; *P:* Alfonso Sanchez-Tello. (1:17) In this low budget U.S.A./Mexican co-production, a gringo gets involved in a Mexican revolution. Eastmancolor.

927. **Fury of the Congo** (Columbia; 1951). *Cast:* Johnny Weissmuller, Sherry Moreland, Lyle Talbot, Bill Henry, Joel Friedkin, Paul Marion, George Eldredge, Rusty Wescoatt, Pierce Lyden, Blanca Vischer, John Hart. *D:* William Berke; *P:* Sam Katzman; *St:* & *Sc:* Carroll Young. (1:09) (video) Series entry with "Jungle Jim" searching for a lost professor. He also gets mixed up with a gang in search of a new narcotic drug, secreted by large spiders, called Okongos. Based on the comic strip character created by Alex Raymond.

Fury Unleashed *see* **Hot Rod Gang**

928. **The Fuzzy Pink Nightgown** (United Artists/Russ-Field Corp.; 1957). *Cast:* Jane Russell, Keenan Wynn, Ralph Meeker, Fred Clark, Una Merkel, Adolphe Menjou, Benay Venuta, Robert H. Harris, Bob Kelley, John Truax, Milton Frome, Dick Haynes. *D:* Norman Taurog; *P:* Robert Waterfield; *Sc:* Richard Alan Simmons. (1:27) Comedy of a Hollywood star, kidnapped on the night of the opening of her latest feature *The Kidnapped Bride*, making the kidnapping sound like a publicity stunt. Based on the 1956 novel by Sylvia Tate.

929. **G.I. Jane** (Lippert/Murray Prods., Inc.; 1951). *Cast:* Jean Porter, Tom Neal, Iris

Adrian, Jimmie Dodd, Jean Mahoney, Jimmie Lloyd, Mara Lynn, Michael Whalen, Robert [Bobby] Watson, Phil Arnold, Jim Cross, Alan Ray, Richard Monohan, Jean Coleman, Amie Bates, Jeri Strong, Olive Krushat, Jack Reitzen, Mark Lowell, Loren Welch, Garrett Marks, Jimmie Parnell, Diane Mumby, Monte Pittman, Vic Massey. *D:* Reginald LeBorg; *P:* Murray Lerner; *St:* Lerner; *Sc:* Jan Jeffries; *Songs:* "Gee, I Love My G.I. Jane," "I Love Girls" (Jimmie Dodd); "Baby I Can't Wait" (Dian Manners-Johnny Clark), and "What's To Be Is Gonna Be" (Teepee Mitchell–Johnny Anz). (1:02) Programmer musical-comedy of an army sergeant attempting to get female army officers transferred to his base.

930. Gaby (MGM; 1956). *Cast:* Leslie Caron, John Kerr, Sir Cedric Hardwicke, Taina Elg, Margalo Gillmore, Scott Marlowe, Joe Di Reda, Joseph Corey, Ian Wolfe, James Best, Gloria Wood, Marda Onyx, Ruta Lee, Lisa Montell. *D:* Curtis Bernhardt; *P:* Edwin H. Knopf; *Sc:* Albert Hackett, Frances Goodrich, Charles Lederer; *Song:* "Where or When" Richard Rodgers–Lorenz Hart. (1:37) World War II romance, set in England, of a ballerina and a soldier. Based on Robert E. Sherwood's play *Waterloo Bridge* and the 1940 screenplay for the film of that name by S.N. Behrman, Paul H. Rameau and George Froeschel. Previously filmed as *Waterloo Bridge* by Universal in 1931. Eastmancolor and CinemaScope.

931. The Gambler from Natchez (20th Century–Fox/Panoramic; 1954). *Cast:* Dale Robertson, Debra Paget, Thomas Gomez, Lisa Daniels, Kevin McCarthy, Douglas Dick, John Wengraf, Jay Novello, Woody Strode, Peter Mamakos, Donald Randolph, Henri Letondal, Ivan Triesault. *D:* Henry Levin; *P:* Leonard Goldstein; *St:* Gerald Drayson Adams; *Sc:* Adams, Irving Wallace. (1:28) The son of a man who was shot by three others, when he was accused of cheating at cards, seeks revenge for the killing. Set in the 1840s, it was photographed in Technicolor.

932. Gambling House (RKO; 1950). *Cast:* Victor Mature, Terry Moore, William Bendix, Zachary A. Charles, Basil Ruysdael, Donald Randolph, Cleo Moore, Damian O'Flynn, Ann Doran, Eleanor Audley, Gloria Winters, Don Haggerty, William E. Green, Jack Kruschen, Eddy Fields, Victor Paul, Joseph Rogato, Guy Zanette, Kirk Alyn, Jack Stoney, Sherry Hall, Vera Stokes, Leonidas Ossetynski, Loda Halama, Homer Dickinson, Forrest Burns, Karl Davis, Chester Jones, Bert Moorhouse, Art Dupuis, Stanley Price. *D:* Ted Tetzlaff; *P:* Warren Duff; *St:* Erwin Gelsey; *Sc:* Marvin Borowsky, Allen Rivkin. (1:20) A gambler faces deportation after beating a murder rap when it is discovered that he does not have naturalization papers.

933. Gang Busters (Film Division of General Teleradio/Visual Drama, Inc.–Terry Turner; 1955). *Cast:* Myron Healey, Don C. Harvey, Sam Edwards, Frank Gerstle, Frank Richards, Kate MacKenna, Rusty Wescoatt, William Justine, Allan Ray, William Fawcett, Ed Colbrook, Charles Victor, Bob Carson, Joyce Jameson, Mike Ragan [aka: Holly Bane], Ed Hinton, Robert Bice. *D:* Bill Karan; *P:* William J. Faris (who also edited), William H. Clotheir (who also photographed); *Sc:* Phillips H. Lord (with revisions by Karan). (1:18) (video) Crime melodrama of notorious criminals and their repeated escape attempts from prison. Adapted from the popular radio series.

934. Gang War (20th Century–Fox/Regal Films; 1958). *Cast:* Charles Bronson, Kent Taylor, Jennifer Holden, John Doucette, Gloria Henry, Gloria Grey, Barney Phillips, Ralph Manza, George Eldredge, Billy Snyder, Jack Reynolds, Dan Simmons, Larry Gelbmann, Jack Littlefield, Ed Wright, Shirle Haven, Arthur D. Gilmore, Don Giovanni, Jack Finch, Stephen Masino, Stacey Marshall, Lyn Guild, Lennie Geer, Helen Jay, Marion Sherman, Whit Bissell. *D:* Gene Fowler, Jr.; *P:* Harold E. Knox; *Sc:* Louis Vittes. (1:15) Gangsters target a high school teacher after he witnesses a gangland murder and identifies the killers. Based on the novel *The Hoods Take Over* by Ovid Demaris. Regalscope.

The Gangster We Made *see* **The Vicious Years**

935. Garden of Eden (Excelsior Pictures; 1954–57). *Cast:* Mickey Knox, Jamie O'Hara, Karen Sue Trent, John Gude, R.G. Armstrong (film debut), Jane Rose, Paula Morris, Stephen Gray, Arch W. Johnson, Norval E. Packwood, Jane Sterling, John Royal. *D:* Max Nosseck (final U.S. film); *P:* Walter Bibo; *Sc:* Nosseck, Nat Tanchuck. (1:10) An obscure independent exploitation piece which espouses the fact that nudism is a respectable way of life, for those who choose it. Tri-Art color.

936. Garden of Evil (20th Century–Fox; 1954). *Cast:* Gary Cooper, Susan Hayward, Richard Widmark, Hugh Marlowe, Cameron Mitchell, Rita Moreno, Victor Manuel Mendoza, Fernando Wagner, Arturo Soto Bangel, Manuel Donde, Antonio Bribiesca, Salvador Terroba. *D:* Henry Hathaway; *P:* Charles Brackett; *St:* Fred Frieberger, William Tunberg; *Sc:* Frank Fenton; *Songs:* "La Negra Noche" (Emilio D. Uranga); "Aqui" Ken Darby–Lionel Newman. (1:40) Western of a woman who hires three men to escort her into 1850s Mexico to search for her husband. Technicolor and CinemaScope.

The Gargon Terror (G.B. title) *see* **Teenagers from Outer Space**

937. The Garment Jungle (Columbia; 1957). *Cast:* Lee J. Cobb, Kerwin Mathews, Gia Scala, Richard Boone, Valerie French, Robert Loggia, Joseph Wiseman, Harold J. Stone, Adam Williams, Willis Bouchey, Wesley Addy, Dick Crockett, Robert Ellenstein, Celia Lovsky, Jon Shepodd, Betsy Jones Moreland, Dale Van Sickel, George Robotham, Judson Taylor, Suzanne Alexander, Ellie Kent, Gloria Pall, Millicent Deming, Shirley Buchanan, Anne Carroll, Laurie Mitchell, Kathy Marlowe, Peggy O'Connor, Bonnie Bolding, Marilyn Hanold, June Tolley, Madeline Darrow, Jan Darlyn, June Kirby, Jean Lewis, Joan Granville, Irene Seidner, Irene King, Hal Taggart, Paul Knight, Paul Weber, Paul Power, Donald Kirke, Archie Savage, Dorothe Kellogg, Lillian Culver, Kenneth Gibson, Sid Melton, Bob Hopkins, Betty Koch, F. Marlowe, Diane DeLaire. *D:* Vincent Sherman, Robert Aldrich (unc.); *P:-St: & Sc:* Harry Kleiner. (1:28) Crime drama of corruption and murder in the garment industry. Based on the articles "Gangsters in the Dress Business" by Lester Velie that appeared in *Reader's Digest* in 1955.

938. Gasoline Alley (Columbia; 1951). *Cast:* Scotty Beckett (Corky Wallet), Jimmy Lydon (Skeezix), Susan Morrow (Hope Wallet), Don Beddoe, Patti Brady, Madelon Mitchel, Dick Wessel, Gus Schilling, Kay Christopher, Byron Foulger, Virginia Toland, Jimmy Lloyd, Ralph Peters, William Forrest, Charles Halton, Charles Williams, Christine McIntyre. *D:* Edward Bernds; *P:* Milton Feldman; *Sc:* Bernds. (1:16) Comedy of a young married couple who go into business with their own diner. Based on the characters created in the comic strip by Frank O. King. Followed by *Corky of Gasoline Alley* (q.v.). Paired on a double bill with *Gene Autry and the Mounties* (q.v.).

939. The Gazebo (MGM/Avon Prods.; 1959). *Cast:* Glenn Ford (Elliott Nash), Debbie Reynolds (Nell Nash), Carl Reiner (Harlow Edison), Doro Merande (Matilda), John McGiver (Sam Thorpe), Mabel Albertson (Mrs. Chandler), Bert Freed (Lt. Joe Jenkins), Martin Landau (The Duke), Robert Ellenstein (Ben), Richard Wessel (Louis the Louse), Herman (pigeon/received #2 PATSY Award in 1960). *D:* George Marshall; *P:* Lawrence Weingarten; *Sc:* George Wells; *Song:* "Something Called Love" Walter Kent, Walton Farrar; *Costumes:* (AAN) Helen Rose. (1:40) (video) Off-the-wall comic moneymaker for MGM involving a pigeon, a backyard gazebo and a murder victim buried under said structure. Based on the 1958 Broadway play by Alec Coppel, it was photographed in CinemaScope. Computer-colored prints have been produced by Turner Entertainment.

940. The Geisha Boy (Paramount/York Pictures; 1958). *Cast:* Jerry Lewis, Marie McDonald, Sessue Hayakawa, Barton MacLane, Suzanne Pleshette (film debut), Nobu Atsumi McCarthy, Robert Kazuyoshi Hirano, Ryuzo Demura, Alex Gerry, Gil Hodges, The Los Angeles Dodgers, Harry the Hare (rabbit—received #3 PATSY Award in 1959), Alec Guinness (appearing in a clip from *Bridge on the River Kwai*). *D:* Frank Tashlin; *P:* Jerry Lewis; *As.P:* Ernest D. Glucksman; *St:* Rudy Makool; *Sc:* Tashlin. (1:36) (video) Comedy of an incompetent magician, up to his ears in trouble in Japan. Technicolor and VistaVision.

941. Geisha Girl (Realart; 1952). *Cast:* Martha Hyer, William Andrews, Archer MacDonald, Kekao Yokoo, Teddy Nakamura, Harry Okawa, Tatsuo Saito, Michyo Naoki, Ikio Suwamura, Ralph Nagara, Shinzo Takada, Pearl Hamada. *D: & P:* George Breakston, C. Ray Stahl; *Sc:* Stahl. (1:07) Melodrama of two soldiers, heading home after having served a tour of duty in Korea, who get involved with an American stewardess on the trail of potential saboteurs. Filmed on location in Japan.

942. Gene Autry and the Mounties (Columbia/Gene Autry Prods., 1951). *Cast:* Gene Autry, Elena Verdugo, Pat Buttram, Carleton Young, Gregg Barton, House Peters, Jr., Trevor Bardette, Francis McDonald, Nolan Leary, Boyd Stockman, Richard Emory, Herbert Rawlinson, Jim Frasher, Jody Gilbert, Teddy Infuhr, Bruce Carruthers, Billy Gray, Robert Hilton, John R. McKee, Roy Butler, Steven Elliott,

Chris Allen, Champion, Jr. (horse). *D:* John English; *P:* Armand Schaefer; *St:* & *Sc:* Norman S. Hall; *Songs:* "Blue Canadian Rockies" (Cindy Walker); "Anetora" (Doris Anderson–Gene Andrea); "Love's Riorneall" (sung by Verdugo). (1:10) Gene heads to Canada to capture a gang of bank robbers. Sepiatone. *Gasoline Alley* (q.v.) completed the double bill.

943. The Gene Krupa Story (Columbia/ Philip A. Waxman; 1959). *Cast:* Sal Mineo (title role/drum solos dubbed by Gene Krupa), Susan Kohner, James Darren, Susan Oliver, Yvonne Craig, Lawrence Dobkin, Celia Lovsky, Gavin McLeod, John Bleifer, Shelly Manne (Davey Tough), Buddy Lester (himself), Red Nichols (himself), Bobby Troup (Tommy Dorsey), Anita O'Day (herself). *D:* Don Weis; *P:* Philip A. Waxman; *As.P:-St:* & *Sc:* Orin Jannings; *Songs:* "Battle of the Sexes" (Leith Stevens); "Cherokee" (Ray Noble); "Exactly Like You" (Dorothy Fields–Jimmy McHugh); "I Love My Baby" (Bud Green–Harry Warren); "In the Mood" (Andy Razaf–Joe Garland); "Indiana" (Ballard MacDonald–James Hanley); "Memories of You" (Razaf–Eubie Blake); "On the Sunny Side of the Street" (Fields–McHugh); "Royal Garden Blues" (Clarence Williams–Spencer Williams); "Oahu Dance" (Stevens–Noble) and "Let There Be Love" (Ian Grant–Lionel Rand). (1:42) (video/ laserdisc) Biography of jazz drummer Gene Krupa, detailing his rise to fame followed by his downfall through involvement with drugs. (G.B. title: *Drum Crazy*)

The Gentle Sergeant (G.B. title) *see* **Three Stripes in the Sun**

944. Gentlemen Marry Brunettes (United Artists/Russ-Field Corp.–Voyager; 1955). *Cast:* Jane Russell (dual role), Jeanne Crain (dual role/singing voice dubbed by Anita Ellis), Scott Brady (singing voice dubbed by Robert Farnom), Alan Young (triple role), Rudy Vallee (himself), Guy Middleton, Eric Pohlman, Ferdy Mayne, Leonard Sachs, Guido Lorraine, Derck Sydney, Boyd Caheen, Robert Favart, Duncan Elliott, Gini Young, Carmen Nesbitt, Juliet Prowse, (film debut), Maurice Lane, Penny Dane, Michael Balfour, Edward Tracy. *D:* Richard Sale; *P:* Robert Waterfield, Sale; *Sc:* Sale, Mary Loos; *Songs:* Title song (Herbert Spencer-Earle Hagen); "You're Driving Me Crazy" (Walter Donaldson), "Have You Met Miss Jones?," "My Funny Valentine" (Richard Rodgers–Lorenz Hart); "Miss Annabelle Lee" (Sidney Clare-Lew Pollack); "I Wanna Be Loved By You" (Bert Kalmar–Harry Ruby) and "Ain't Misbehavin'" (Andy Razaf–Fats Waller). (1:37) Musical follow-up to *Gentlemen Prefer Blondes* (see below) of two sisters who find romance in Paris. In Technicolor and CinemaScope, it was based on Anita Loos' 1928 book *But Gentlemen Marry Brunettes*.

945. Gentlemen Prefer Blondes (20th Century–Fox; 1953). *Cast:* Marilyn Monroe (received *Photoplay* Gold Medal/Lorelei), Jane Russell (Dorothy), Charles Coburn (Sir Francis Beekman), Elliott Reid (Malone), Tommy Noonan (Gus Esmond), George Winslow (Henry Spofford III), Taylor Holmes (Gus Esmond, Sr.), Norma Varden (Lady Beekman), Howard Wendell (Watson), Henri Letondal (Grotier), Leo Mostovoy (Phillipe), Alex Frazer (Pritchard), Harry Carey, Jr. (Winslow), Ray Montgomery (Peters), Alvy Moore (Anderson), Robert Nichols (Evans), Charles Tannen (Ed), Jimmy Young (Stevens), William Cabanne (Sims), Alfred Paix (Pierre), Marcel Dalio (magistrate), Steven Geray, George Davis, Alphonse Martell, Jimmie & Freddie Moultrie, Jean DeBriac, George Dee, Peter Camlin, George Chakiris, Jean Del Val, Charles De Ravenne, John Close, Philip Sylvestre, Jack Chefe, Max Willenz, Rolfe Sedan, Robert Foulk, Ralph Peters, Harry Seymour. *D:* Howard Hawks; *P:* Sol C. Siegel; *Sc:* Charles Lederer; *Songs:* "Diamonds Are a Girl's Best Friend" (Jule Styne–Leo Robin); "Ain't There Anyone Here for Love?" (Hoagy Carmichael–Harold Adamson); "A (Two) Little Girl(s) from Little Rock," "Bye, Bye, Baby" (Styne–Robin); "When Love Goes Wrong" (Carmichael–Adamson). (1:31) (video/laserdisc) Technicolor musical-comedy-romance of two American showgirls who head for Paris in search of rich husbands. Based on the 1927 play by Anita Loos and Joseph Fields, it was previously filmed as a silent in 1928, with many other variations of the story appearing on film since. One of the 26 top-grossing films of 1952-53. Note: Russell's singing voice dubbed by Eileen Wilson.

946. Geraldine (Republic; 1953). *Cast:* John Carroll, Mala Powers, Jim Backus, Stan Freberg, Kristine Miller, Leon Belasco, Ludwig Stossel, Earl Lee, Alan Reed, Nana Bryant, Carolyn Jones. *D:* R.G. Springsteen; *As.P:* Sidney Picker; *St:* Peter Milne, Doris Gilbert; *Sc:* Milne, Frank Gill, Jr.; *Songs:* "Wintertime of Love" (Edward Heyman–Victor Young); "Geraldine" (Sidney Clare–Young); "Flaming Lips" (Stan Freberg); "Rat Now" (Fuzzy Knight); "Black is the Color," "Along the Colorado Trail" and "The Foggy Dew" (all traditional with lyrics of Irwin Coster). (1:30) Musical-comedy involving a dispute as to who has the legal rights to a song.

947. Ghost Chasers (Monogram; 1951). *Cast:* Leo Gorcey, Huntz Hall, Billy Benedict, David Gorcey, Buddy Gorman, Jan Kayne, Lela Bliss, Phil Van Zandt, Bernard Gorcey, Robert Coogan, Michael Ross, Donald Lawton, Hal Gerard, Marshall Bradford, Paul Bryar, Argentina Brunetti, Doris Kemper, Belle Mitchell, Pat Gleason, Bob Peoples, Lloyd Corrigan, Marjorie Eaton, Bess Flowers. *D:* William Beaudine; *P:* Jan Grippo; *Sc:* Charles R. Marion; *Additional dialogue:* Bert Lawrence. (1:09) (video) The "Bowery Boys" get unexpected help when they set out to expose some phony spiritualists.

948. Ghost Diver (20th Century–Fox/Regal Films; 1957). *Cast:* James Craig, Audrey Totter, Pira Louis, Nico Minardos, Lowell Brown, Rodolfo Hoyos, Jr., George Trevino, Elena DaVinci, *and stunt people*: Paul Stader, Diane Webber, Robert Lorenz, Richard Geary, Tom Garland, Michael Dugan. *D: & Sc:* Richard Einfeld, Merrill G. White; *P:* Einfeld. (1:16) Adventure-melodrama of men in search of a sunken city and hidden treasure. Regalscope.

949. The Ghost of Dragstrip Hollow (American International/Alta Vista Prods.; 1959). *Cast:* Jody Fair, Martin Braddock, Russ Bender, Leon Tyler, Elaine Dupont, Henry McCann, Sanita Pelkey, Dorothy Neumann, Kirby Smith, Jean Tatum, Jack Ging, Nancy Anderson, Beverly Scott, Bill St. John, Judy Howard, Tommy Ivo, Paul Blaisdell (a Hollywood monster makeup artist), George Dockstader, Marvin Almars. *D:* William Hole, Jr.; *P: & Sc:* Lou Rusoff; *As.P:* Bart Carre; *Songs:* "Charge Geronimo!," "Ghost Train" (Nick Venet); "Tongue Tied" (Jimmy Maddin); "He's My Guy" (Charlotte Basser); "I Promise You" (Bruce Johnston–Judy Harriet). (1:05) Horror-comedy with rock 'n' roll songs of a hot rod club ousted from their headquarters, who find new quarters in a "haunted house." This feature ran on a double bill with *Diary of a High School Bride* (q.v.).

950. Ghost of the China Sea (Columbia/Polynesian Prods., Ltd.; 1958). *Cast:* David Brian, Lynn Bernay, Jonathan Haze, Harry Chang, Gene Bergman, Kam Fong Chun, Mel Prestige, Jaime Del Rosario, Dan Taba, Bud Pente. *D:* Fred F. Sears (final film—d. 1957); *P:* Charles B. Griffith; *St: & Sc:* Griffith. (1:19) Four people flee through the Philippine jungle during the World War II Japanese invasion. Filmed in Hawaii.

951. Ghost of Zorro (Republic; 1959). *Cast:* Clayton Moore, Pamela Blake, Roy Barcroft, George J. Lewis, Gene Roth, John Crawford, I. Stanford Jolley, Steve Clark, Steve Darrell, Dale Van Sickel, Tom Steele, Marshall Reed, Jack O'Shea, Holly Bane [aka: Mike Ragan], Bob Reeves, Eddie Parker, Stanley Blystone, Joe Yrigoyen, George Chesebro, Charles King, Kenneth Terrell, Robert Wilke, Art Dillard, Frank Ellis. *D:* Fred C. Brannon; *P:* Uncredited; *Sc:* Royal Cole, William Lively, Sol Shor. (1:09) A descendant of Don Diego (aka: Zorro) uses his disguise to oust outlaws bent on sabotaging construction of telegraph lines. A condensed feature version of the 1949 serial of the same name.

952. Ghost Town (United Artists/Bel-Air–Sunrise Pictures; 1956). *Cast:* Kent Taylor, John Smith, Marian Carr, John Doucette, Serena Sands, William "Bill" Phillips, Gary Murray, Joel Ashley, Gilman H. Rankin, Ed Hashim. *D:* Allen Miner; *P:* Howard W. Koch; *St: & Sc:* Jameson Brewer. (1:16) Programmer western of stagecoach passengers forced into a ghost town after being attacked by Indians.

953. Giant (Warner/Giant Prods.; 1956). *Cast:* Elizabeth Taylor (Leslie Lynnton Benedict), Rock Hudson (AAN + *Photoplay* Gold Medal/Bick Benedict), James Dean (AAN-final film—d. 1955 in auto crash/Jett Rink), Mercedes McCambridge (AAN/Luz Benedict), Chill Wills (Uncle Bawley), Jane Withers (Vashti Snythe), Robert Nichols (Pinky Snythe), Dennis Hopper (Jordan Benedict III), Elsa Cardenas (Juana), Fran Bennett (Judy Benedict), Carroll Baker (Luz Benedict II), Earl Holliman (Bob Dace), Paul Fix (Dr. Horace Lynnton), Judith Evelyn (Mrs. Horace Lynnton), Carolyn Craig (Lacey Lynnton), Rod(ney) Taylor (Sir David Karfrey), Alexander Scourby (Old Polo), Sal Mineo (Angel Obregon II), Monte Hale (final film—ret./Bale Clinch), Mary Ann Edwards (Adarene Clinch), Napoleon Whiting (Swazey), Charles Watts (Whiteside), Maurice Jara (Dr. Guerra), Victor Millan (Angel Obregon), Pilar Del Rey (Mrs. Obregon), Felipe Turich (Gomez), Sheb Wooley (Gabe Target), Ray Whitley (Watts), Tina Menard (Lupe), Ana Maria Majalca (Petra), Mickey Simpson (Sarge), Noreen Nash (Lona Lane), Guy Teague

(Harper), Natividad Vacio (Eusubio), Max Terhune (final film—ret./Dr. Walker), Ray Bennett (Dr. Borneholm), Barbara Barrie (Mary Lou Decker), George Dunne (Vern Decker), Slim Talbot (Clay Hodgins), Tex Driscoll (Clay Hodgins, Sr.), Juney Ellis (Essie Lou Hodgins), Francisco Villalobos (Mexican priest), War Winds (horse—received #2 PATSY Award in 1957). *D:* (AA) George Stevens; *P:* (AAN + *Photoplay* Gold Medal for "Best Picture") George Stevens, Henry Ginsberg; *Sc:* (AAN) Fred Guiol, Ivan Moffat; *ASD:* (AAN-color) Boris Leven (art director), Ralph S. Hurst (sets); *Music:* (AAN-non musical) Dimitri Tiomkin; *Costumes:* (AAN-color) Moss Mabry, Marjorie Best; *Editors:* (AAN) William Hornbeck, Philip W. Anderson, Fred Bohanan. (3:21) (video/laserdisc) Generational drama of a wealthy Texas oil family. Based on Edna Ferber's sprawling 1952 novel, it produced $12,000,000 in box office receipts making it one of the 24 top-grossing films of 1956-57. It placed #2 on the "10 Best" list of *Film Daily* and #7 on the same list of the *New York Times*. The New York Film Critics also had it in nomination for "Best Film." WarnerColor.

954. The Giant Claw (Columbia/Clover Prods.; 1957). *Cast:* Jeff Morrow, Mara Corday, Morris Ankrum, Louis D. Merrill, Edgar Barrier, Robert Shayne, Morgan Jones, Clark Howat, Ruell Shayne. *D:* Fred F. Sears; *P:* Sam Katzman; *Sc:* Samuel Newman, Paul Gangelin. (1:16) (video) Earth is threatened by a giant bird-like creature from outer space. Top-of-the-bill B budget sci-fi which falls into the "so bad it's good" category.

955. Giant from the Unknown (Astor/Screencraft Enterprises; 1958). *Cast:* Edward Kemmer, Sally Fraser, Buddy Baer (title role), Morris Ankrum, Bob Steele, Jolene Brand. *D:* Richard E. Cunha; *P:* Arthur A. Jacobs; *As.P:* Marc Frederic; *St: & Sc:* Frank Hart Taussig, Ralph Brooke. (1:17) (video) Low budget horror flick of a giant Spanish conquistador with a bent for mayhem, who is revived by a bolt of lightning, after hundreds of years in suspended animation. Originally ran on the top-of-the-bill with *She Demons* (q.v.).

956. The Giant Gila Monster (Hollywood Pictures Corp./McLendon Radio Pictures; 1959). *Cast:* Don Sullivan, Lisa Simone, Shug Fisher, Jerry Cortwright, Beverly Thurman, Don Flourney, Clarke Browne, Pat Simmons, Pat Reaves, Fred Graham, Ann Sonka, Bob Thompson, Cecil Hunt, Grady Vaughn, Ken Knox, Janice Stone, Tommie Russel, Yolanda Salas, Howard Ware, Stormy Meadows, Desmond Dhooge. *D: & St:* Ray Kellogg (directorial debut); *P:* Ken Curtis; *Ex.P:* Gordon McLendon; *Sc:* Jay Simms; *Songs:* "My Baby She Rocks," "I Ain't Made That Way," "The Mushroom Song" Don Sullivan. (1:14) (video) Independent low budget science fiction, with rock 'n' roll songs, of teens in a southwestern desert community who combat the titled terrible lizard. Originally ran on a double bill with *The Killer Shrews* (q.v.).

The Giant Leeches *see* **Attack of the Giant Leeches**

957. Gidget (Columbia; 1959). *Cast:* Sandra Dee (title role), Cliff Robertson, James Darren, Arthur O'Connell, Mary La Roche, Joby Baker, Tom Laughlin, Sue George, The Four Preps (themselves), Robert Ellis, Jo Morrow, Doug McClure, Yvonne Craig, Burt Metcalfe, Patti Kane, Richard Newton, Ed Hinton. *D:* Paul Wendkos; *P:* Lewis J. Rachmil; *Sc:* Gabrielle Upton; *Songs:* "Gidget," Fred Karger, Patti Washington (sung by Darren & Four Preps); "The Next Best Thing to Love" Karger, Stanley Styne (sung by Darren) and "Cinderella" Glen Larson, Bruce Bellard (sung by Four Preps). (1:35) (video/laserdisc) Teen oriented romantic-comedy of love blossoming between sweet young Gidget and surfer "Moon Doggie." Based on the 1957 book by Frederick Kohner, this box office winner was followed by *Gidget Goes Hawaiian* (1961) as well as two TV series. Eastmancolor and CinemaScope.

958. A Gift for Heidi (RKO; 1958). *Cast:* Douglas Fowley, Sandy Descher, Van Dyke Parks. *D:* George Templeton. (1:11) Low budget kiddie oriented story of a little girl who learns some things about life. Photographed in color, it was based on the character created by Johanna Spyri.

959. The Gift of Love (20th Century-Fox; 1958). *Cast:* Lauren Bacall, Robert Stack, Evelyn Rudie, Lorne Greene, Anne Seymour, Edward Platt, Joseph Kearns. *D:* Jean Negulesco; *P:* Charles Brackett; *Sc:* Luther Davis; *Title song:* Sammy Fain, Paul Francis Webster (sung by Vic Damone). (1:45) Sentimental drama of a childless couple who adopt a little girl. When the mother dies, the father cannot cope with the loss and the child, and returns her to the orphanage. Based on the short story "The Little Horse" by Nelia Gardner White, it is a remake of *Sentimental Journey* (Fox; 1946) with another remake under that title appearing in TV movie format in 1984. DeLuxe color and CinemaScope.

960. Gigi (MGM/Arthur Freed Prods., Inc.; 1958). *Cast:* Leslie Caron (Gigi/singing voice dubbed by Betty Wand), Maurice Chevalier (Honoré Lachaille/received honorary AA for career achievement), Louis Jourdan (Gaston Lachaille), Hermione Gingold (Mme. Alvarez), Eva Gabor (Liane d'Exelmans), Jacques Bergerac (Sandomir), Isabel Jeans (Aunt Alicia), John Abbott (Manuel), Edwin Jerome (Charles, the butler), Lydia Stevens (Simone), Maurice Marsac (Prince Berensky), Monique Van Vooren, Dorothy Neumann, Maruja Plose, Marilyn Sims, Richard Bean, Pat Sheahan. *D:* (AA + "Best Directed Movie" by Screen Director's Guild/Vincente Minnelli); *P:* (AA-Best Picture + "Best Produced Picture" by Screen Producer's Guild/Arthur Freed); *Sc:* (AA + "Best American Musical" by Screenwriter's Guild/Arthur Freed); *Sc:* (AA + "Best American Musical" by Screenwriter's Guild/Alan Jay Lerner); *Cinematography:* (AA) Joseph Ruttenberg; *ASD:* (AA) William A. Horning, Preston Ames (art directors), Harry Grace, Keogh Gleason (sets); *Music:* (AA) André Previn; *Costumes:* (AA) Cecil Beaton; Editor: (AA) Adrienne Fazan; *Songs:* "It's a Bore," "Gigi" (AA-Best Song), "The Parisians," "The Night They Invented Champagne," "Say a Prayer for Me Tonight," "Thank Heaven For Little Girls" (a big hit), "I Remember It Well," "I'm Glad I'm Not Young Anymore," "Gossip" and "Waltz at Maxim's (She's Not Thinking of Me)" Frederick Loewe, Alan Jay Lerner. (1:56) (video/laserdisc) Critically acclaimed turn-of-the-century musical of a young waif being groomed as a courtesan. Based on the story by Colette [pseudonym of Sidonie Gabrielle], it previously had a non-musical incarnation by Spalter International in 1950, as well as a stage version with Audrey Hepburn. One of the 26 top-grossing films of 1957-58 ($15,000,000 gross worldwide!) it also received the *Photoplay* Gold Medal. The *New York Times* placed it at #2 on their "10 Best" list, while *Film Daily* placed it as #3 on theirs. The NBR gave it a #10 placement, while the British Academy Awards had it in nomination in 1959 and the New York Film Critics had it in nomination for "Best Film." In Technicolor and CinemaScope, location exteriors were filmed in Paris.

961. The Girl Can't Help It (20th Century–Fox; 1956). *Cast:* Tom Ewell, Jayne Mansfield (starring debut), Edmond O'Brien, Henry Jones, Julie London (herself), John Emery, Juanita Moore, Barry Gordon, Ray Anthony, Little Richard, Fats Domino, Gene Vincent and His Blue Caps, The Platters, The Treniers, Eddie Fontaine, Abbey Lincoln, The Chuckles, Johnny Olenn, Nino Tempo, Eddie Cochran. *D: & P:* Frank Tashlin; *Sc:* Tashlin, Herbert Baker. (1:39) (video) Popular musical—of time capsule quality—of a gangster who seeks to have his moll promoted into a rock 'n' roll star. Musical numbers include "Blue Monday" by Fats Domino; "Twenty Flight Rock" by Eddie Cochran; "Be Bop a Lula" by Gene Vincent and His Blue Caps; "She's Got It," the title song; "Ready Teddy" by Little Richard; "Cry Me a River" by Julie London and "You'll Never Know" by The Platters. DeLuxe color and CinemaScope.

A Girl for Joe *see* **Force of Arms**

The Girl from 5000 A.D. *see* **Terror from the Year 5000**

962. The Girl from San Lorenzo (United Artists/Inter-America Prods., Inc.; 1950). *Cast:* Duncan Renaldo, Leo Carrillo (final film—to TV), Jane Adams, Bill Lester, Byron Foulger, Don Harvey, Lee Phelps, Edmund Cobb, Leonard Penn, David Sharpe, Wesley Hudman. *D:* Derwin Abrahams; *P:* Philip N. Krasne; *As.P:* Renaldo; *St: & Sc:* Ford Beebe. (0:59) The Cisco Kid (Renaldo), and Pancho (Carrillo) bring some stagecoach robbers to justice, in this, the final feature film to portray O. Henry's character. The duo then moved to their long-running TV series, portraying the same characters.

963. The Girl He Left Behind (Warner; 1956). *Cast:* Tab Hunter, Natalie Wood, Jessie Royce Landis, Jim Backus, Henry Jones, Murray Hamilton, Alan King, James Garner, David Janssen, Vinton Haworth, Wilfrid Knapp, Les Johnson, Raymond Bailey, Florenz Ames, Fredd Wayne, Ernestine Wade. *D:* David Butler; *P:* Frank P. Rosenberg; *Sc:* Guy Trosper. (1:42) Comedy of a spoiled young man who is drafted into the peacetime army. Based on the novel *Girl He Left Behind; or All Quiet in the Third Platoon* by Marion Hargrove.

964. The Girl in Black Stockings (United Artists/Bel-Air–Palm Prods., Inc.; 1957). *Cast:* Lex Barker, Anne Bancroft, Ron Randell, Mamie Van Doren, Marie Windsor, John Holland, John Dehner, Richard Cutting, Diana Vandervlis, Gene O'Donnell, Larry Chance, Stuart

Whitman, Gerald Frank, Karl MacDonald, Norman Leavitt, David Dwight, Mark Bennett, Mickey Whiting. *D:* Howard W. Koch; *P:* Aubrey Schenck; *Sc:* Richard H. Landau. (1:13) (video) Programmer whodunit set at a posh Utah resort where several girls have been murdered. Based on the novel *Wanton Murder* by Peter Godfrey.

965. A Girl in Every Port (RKO; 1952). *Cast:* Groucho Marx, Marie Wilson, William Bendix, Don DeFore, Gene Lockhart, Dee Hartford, Hanley Stafford, Teddy Hart, Percy Helton, George E. Stone, Rodney Wooten. *D: & Sc:* Chester Franklin; *P:* Irwin Allen, Irving Cummings, Jr. (1:26) (video/laserdisc) Comedy of two sailors who lay out a scheme to win a horse race. Based on the story "They Sell Sailors Elephants" by Frederick Hazlitt Brennan.

The Girl in Room 17 (G.B. title) *see* **Vice Squad**

966. The Girl in the Kremlin (Universal-International; 1957). *Cast:* Lex Barker, Zsa Zsa Gabor (dual role), Jeffrey Stone, Maurice Manson (Stalin), William Schallert, Natalia Daryll, Aram Katcher, Norbert Schiller, Elena Da Vinci, Kurt Katch, Michael Fox, Phillipa Fallon, Charles Horvath, Vanda Depre, Alfred Linder, Gabor Curtiz, Delia Maltzahn, Wanda Ottoni, Richard Richonne, Carl Sklover, Peter Besbas, Franz Roehn, Albert Szabo, Henry Rowland, Dale Van Sickel. *D:* Russell Birdwell; *P:* Albert Zugsmith; *St:* Harry Ruskin, DeWitt Bodeen; *Sc:* Gene L. Coon, Robert Hill. (1:21) Programmer melodrama which presents itself on the premise that Joseph Stalin did not die in 1953, but is alive and well in Greece, after undergoing plastic surgery.

967. The Girl in the Red Velvet Swing (20th Century–Fox; 1955). *Cast:* Ray Milland (Stanford White), Joan Collins (Evelyn Nesbit Thaw), Farley Granger (Harry K. Thaw), Luther Adler, Cornelia Otis Skinner, Glenda Farrell, Frances Fuller, Philip Reed, Gale Robbins, James Lorimer, John Hoyt, Harvey Stephens, Emile Meyer, Richard Travis, Harry Seymour, Ainslie Pryor, Kay Hammond, Betty Caulfield, Karolee Kelly, Jack Raine, Hellen Van Tuyl, Robert Simon, Paul Glass, Paul Power, Fred Essler, Ivan Triesault, Raymond Bailey, Charles Tannen, Edmund Cobb, James Conaty, Marjorie Hellen, Diane DuBois, Suzanne Alexander, Peggy Connelly, Rosemary Ace, Jean McCallen, Leslie Parrish, Oliver Cross, Max Wagner, Steve Darrell, Henry Kulky, Edith Evanson, William Forrest, Stuart Holmes, Major Sam Harris. *D:* Richard Fleischer; *P:* Charles Brackett; *Sc:* Walter Reisch, Brackett. (1:49) Lavishly produced costume-period piece involving the murder of architect Stanford White by looney millionaire Harry K. Thaw at New York City's Winter Garden in 1906. Hard facts are twisted or changed altogether. Note: Evelyn Nesbit's notoriety in the case won her several movie roles in the silent era.

968. Girl in the Woods (Republic/AB-PT Pictures; 1958). *Cast:* Forrest Tucker, Maggie Hayes, Barton MacLane, Diana Francis, Murvyn Vye, Paul Langton, Joyce Compton (final film—ret.), Kim Charney, Mickey Finn, Bartlett Robinson, George Lynn, Harry Raybould, Joey Ray. *D:* Tom Gries; *P:* Harry L. Mandell; *Sc:* Oliver Crawford, Marcel Klauber. (1:11) B budget northwoods melodrama of rival lumber companies and a lumberjack accused of robbery. Based on the novel *Blood on the Branches* by Mr. Crawford.

969. The Girl in White (MGM; 1952). *Cast:* June Allyson, Arthur Kennedy, Gary Merrill, Mildred Dunnock, Jesse White, Marilyn Erskine, Gar Moore, Don Keefer, James Arness, Guy Anderson, Ann Tyrrell, Curtis Cooksey, Carol Brannon, Ann Morrison, Jo Gilbert, Erwin Kalser, Kathryn Card, Jonathan Cott, Joan Valerie, Coleman Francis, A. Cameron Grant, David Fresco. *D:* John Sturges; *P:* Armand Deutsch; *Sc:* Irmgard von Cube, Allen Vincent, Philip Stevenson. (1:32) Biographical drama of Emily Dunning in 1902, the first woman doctor to work in a New York City public hospital. Based on the 1950 autobiographical work *Bowery to Bellevue* by Emily (Dunning) Barringer. (G.B. title: *So Bright the Flame*)

970. The Girl Most Likely (Universal-International/RKO; 1957). *Cast:* Jane Powell, Cliff Robertson, Keith Andes, Kaye Ballard (film debut), Tommy Noonan, Una Merkel, Kelly Brown, Judy Nugent, Frank Cady, Nacho Galindo, Chris Essay, Valentin de Vargas, Joseph Kearns, Julia Montoya, Paul Garay, Gloria De Ward, Gail Ganley, Harvey Hohneckey, Bob Banas, Joyce Blunt, Tex Brodus, Buddy Bryant, Maurice Kelly, Tommy Ladd, Todd Miller, Dean Myles, Howard Parker, Donna Poyet, Paul Rees, Bruce Stowell, Lida Thomas. *D:* Mitchell Leisen; *P:* Stanley Rubin; *Sc:* Devery Freeman; *Musical Numbers:* "The Girl Most Likely" (Bob Russell–Nelson Riddle); "All the Colors of the Rainbow," "I Don't Know What

I Want," "Balboa," "We Gotta Keep Up With the Jones" and "Crazy Horse" (Hugh Martin–Ralph Blane); *Choreography:* Gower Champion. (1:38) (video/laserdisc) A musical remake of *Tom, Dick and Harry* (RKO; 1941) about a small town girl who can't decide which of the three men in her life she wants to marry. Based on the Oscar nominated screenplay by Paul Jarrico (who goes uncredited on this remake). Produced by RKO but released by Universal after the former studio folded. Technicolor.

971. The Girl Next Door (20th Century-Fox; 1953). *Cast:* Dan Dailey, June Haver (final film—ret.), Dennis Day, Billy Gray, Cara Williams, Natalie Schafer, Clinton Sundberg, Hayden Rorke, Mary Jane Saunders, Donna Lee Hickey [May Wynn], Lyn Wilde, Mona Knox, June Wurster, Beverly Thompson, Gregg Sherwood, Michael Ross, Herbert Vigran, Charles Wagenheim, Don Kohler, Robert Carraher. *D:* Richard Sale; *P:* Robert Bassler; *St:* Ladislaus Bus-Fekete, Mary Helen Fay; *Sc:* Isobel Lennart; *Songs:* "If I Love You a Mountain," "I'd Rather Have a Pal Than a Gal—Anytime," "Nowhere Gal" (Mack Gordon–Josef Myrow). (1:32) Technicolor musical-comedy of a Broadway star who takes up residence away from the big city and becomes romantically involved with a cartoonist who resides next door.

Girl of the Year (G.B. title) *see* **The Petty Girl**

972. The Girl on the Bridge (20th Century-Fox/Hugo Haas; 1951). *Cast:* Hugo Haas, Beverly Michaels, Robert Dane, Tony Jochim, John Close, Darr Smith, Judy Clark, Maria Bibikoff, Al Hill, Richard Pinner, Joe Duval, Rose Marie Valenzuea, Alan Ray, William Kahn, Jimmy Moss. *D: & P:* Hugo Haas; *St: & Sc:* Haas, Arnold Phillips. (1:16) Melodrama which had the working title of "The Bridge" about an old watchmaker who falls for his young female employee and soon gets in over his head in blackmail and murder.

973. The Girl Rush (Paramount/Independent Artists Pictures; 1955). *Cast:* Rosalind Russell, Fernando Lamas, Gloria DeHaven, Eddie Albert, Marion Lorne, James Gleason, Douglas Fowley, Jesse White, Larry Gates, George Chandler, Shelley Fabares, Matt Mattox, Don Crichton, George Chakiris, Dorothy Gordon, Frances Lansing, Marjorie Bennett, Karolee Kelly, Hal K. Dawson, Hickey Kamm, Orlando Sicilia, Sherlock Feldman, Alexander Rhein, Vincent Padula, Arthur Gould-Porter, Sid Tomack, Eddie Ryder, Lyle Latell, Freeman Lusk, George Pembroke, Frank Mills, Len Hendry, Darlene Fields, Marcoreta Hellman, Mike Mahoney, Kathy Johnson, Richard Kipling, Ralph Montgomery, Deborah Sydes, Lorna Simans. *D:* Robert Pirosh; *P:* Robert Alton, Frederick Brisson; *St:* Phoebe and Henry Ephron; *Sc:* Pirosh, Jerome Davis; *Songs:* "An Occasional Man," "Take a Chance," "We're Alone," Title song, "Champagne," "Birmingham," "Out of Doors," "Choose Your Partner," "My Hillbilly Heart" Hugh Martin, Ralph Blane. (1:24) The lights of Las Vegas are the backdrop of this musical-comedy of a woman who inherits half-interest in a gambling casino, finds the place is a dump and decides to make it a top attraction. Technicolor and VistaVision.

974. The Girl Who Had Everything (MGM; 1953). *Cast:* Elizabeth Taylor, Fernando Lamas, William Powell, Gig Young, James Whitmore, Robert Burton, William Walker, Harry Bartell, Elmer Peterson (himself), Dan Riss, Paul Harvey, Dean Miller, Wilson Wood, Doug Carter, Emory Parnell, Earle Hodgins, Frank Dae, Roy Butler, John McKee, Bobby Johnson, Anthony Warde, Philip Van Zandt, Jonathan Cott, John Maxwell, Stu Wilson, James Horne, Perry Sheehan, Dee Turnell, Sally Musick, George Brand, A. Cameron Grant, George Sherwood, Pat O'Malley, Jack Sterling. *D:* Richard Thorpe; *P:* Armand Deutsch; *Sc:* Art Cohn. (1:09) (video) Melodrama of a girl who falls for her attorney father's criminal client. A remake of *A Free Soul* (MGM; 1931), it was based on the 1927 novel by Adela Rogers St. Johns.

Girls in Action (G.B. title) *see* **Operation Dames**

975. Girls in Prison (American International/Golden State Prods.; 1956). *Cast:* Richard Denning, Joan Taylor, Adele Jergens (final film—ret.), Helen Gilbert, Lance Fuller, Jane Darwell, Raymond Hatton, Phyllis Coates, Diana Darrin, Mae Marsh, Laurie Mitchell, Diane Richards, Luana Walters, Riza Royce. *D:* Edward L. Cahn; *P:* Alex Gordon; *St: & Sc:* Lou Rusoff; *Song:* "Tom's Beat" Ronald Stein (sung by Richards). (1:26) (video) Title tells all in this melodrama with several inmates planning a breakout to search for stolen bank loot.

976. Girls in the Night (Universal-International; 1953). *Cast:* Joyce Holden, Glenda

Farrell, Harvey Lembeck, Patricia Hardy, Anthony Ross, Glen Roberts, Jaclynne Greene, Susan Odin, Don Gordon, Billy Wayne. *D:* Jack Arnold; *P:* Albert J. Cohen; *Sc:* Ray Buffum. (1:23) Melodrama of juvenile delinquency and a family's move from the tenements of New York City to a better neighborhood. Not a tale of prostitution as the title tends to suggest. (aka: *Life After Dark*)

Girls Never Tell (G.B. title) *see* **Her First Romance**

977. The Girls of Pleasure Island (Paramount; 1953). *Cast:* Don Taylor, Leo Genn, Elsa Lanchester, Philip Ober, Joan Elan, Audrey Dalton, Dorothy Bromley, Gene Barry, Peter Baldwin, Richard Shannon, Arthur E. Gould-Porter, Barry Bernard, Leon Lontoc, Michael Ross, Johnny Downs. *D:* F. Hugh Herbert, Alvin Ganzer; *P:* Paul Jones; *Sc:* Herbert. (1:35) In 1945, 1,500 U.S. marines land on an island to establish an air strip, but find resentment from an English couple residing there with their three lovely daughters. Based on the 1949 novel *Pleasure Island* by William Maier, this comedy was a box office flop. Technicolor.

978. Girls on the Loose (Universal-International/Jewell Enterprises, Inc.; 1958). *Cast:* Mara Corday, Lita Milan, Barbara Bostock, Mark Richman, Joyce Barker, Abby Dalton, Jon Lormer, Ronald Green, Fred Kruger, Paul Lambert, Monica Henreid. *D:* Paul Henreid; *P:* Harry Rybnick, Richard Kay; *As.P:* Edward E. Barison; *Sc:* Alan Friedman, Dorothy Raison, Allen Rivkin; *Songs:* "I Was a Little Too Lonely" Jay Livingston, Ray Evans; "How Do You Learn to Love?" Dixie Philpott, Ray Whitaker, Dolores Hampton. (1:17) Low budget melodrama of five girls who pull off a robbery, then hide the loot, hoping to retrieve it later. Based on the unpublished story "Take Five from Five" by Friedman, Raison and Julian Harmon, it originally ran on a double bill with *Live Fast, Die Young* (q.v.).

979. Girls' School (Columbia; 1950). *Cast:* Joyce Reynolds (final film—ret.), Ross Ford, Laura Elliot, Julia Dean, Thurston Hall, Leslye Banning, Joyce Otis, Louise Beavers, Sam McDaniel, Wilton Graff, Grant Calhoun, Mary Ellen Kay, Boyd Davis, Harry Cheshire, Joan Vohs, Diantha Pattison, Toni Newman. *D:* Lew Landers; *P:* Wallace MacDonald; *St:* Jack Henley; *Sc:* Brenda Weisberg. (1:01) Programmer of a girl's dilemma when she learns her inheritance was stolen. No relation to the 1938 production of the same name by this studio. (G.B. title: *Dangerous Inheritance*)

980. Girls Town (MGM/Albert Zugsmith; 1959). *Cast:* Mamie Van Doren, Mel Torme, Paul Anka, Ray Anthony, Maggie Hayes, Cathy Crosby, Gigi Perreau, Elinor Donahue, Gloria Talbott, Sheilah Graham, Jim Mitchum, Dick Contino, Harold Lloyd, Jr., Charles Chaplin, Jr. (final film—ret.), Peggy Moffitt, The Platters (themselves), Jody Fair, Peter Leeds, Nan Peterson, Grabowski, Karen Von Unge, Susanne Sydney, Nancy Root, Wendy Wilde, Bobi Byrnes, Gloria Rhoads, Phyllis Douglas. *D:* Charles Haas; *P:* Albert Zugsmith; *St:* Robert Hardy Andrews; *Sc:* Robert Smith; *Songs:* Title song, "Time to Cry," "I'm Just a Lonely Boy," "Hey Mama," "I Love You" (Paul Anka); "Wish It Were Me" (Buck Ram) and "Ave Maria" (Charles Gounod). (1:32) (video) Teen market exploitation-melodrama of a girl wrongly incarcerated at a reform school run by Catholic nuns. (aka: *Innocent and the Damned*)

981. Give a Girl a Break (MGM; 1953). *Cast:* Marge and Gower Champion, Debbie Reynolds, Helen Wood, Bob Fosse, Kurt Kasznar, Richard Anderson, William Ching, Larry Keating, Lurene Tuttle, Donna Martell. *D:* Stanley Donen; *P:* Jack Cummings; *Sc:* Frances Goodrich, Albert Hackett; *Songs:* Title song, "In Our United States," "It Happens Every Time," "Nothing Is Impossible," "Applause, Applause" (Burton Lane–Ira Gershwin); "Challenge Dance" (Andre Previn–Saul Chaplin); *Choreography:* Gower Champion, Donen. (1:21) (video) Technicolor musical of three hopefuls vying for a starring role in a Broadway show. Based on a story idea by Vera Caspary.

982. The Glass Menagerie (Warner/ Charles K. Feldman Group; 1950). *Cast:* Jane Wyman, Kirk Douglas, Gertrude Lawrence (final film—d. 1952), Arthur Kennedy, Ralph Sanford, Ann Tyrrell, John Compton, Gertrude Graner, Sarah Edwards, Louise Lorimer, Chris Alcaide, Perdita Chandler, Sean McClory, James Horne, Marshall Romer. *D:* Irving Rapper; *P:* Jerry Wald, Charles K. Feldman; *Sc:* Tennessee Williams, Peter Berneis. (1:46) Drama of a family of three, each living in their own fragile private world. Based on the 1945 play by Tennessee Williams, it was remade as a TV movie in 1973 and again as a theatrical release in 1987.

983. The Glass Slipper (MGM; 1955). *Cast:* Leslie Caron, Michael Wilding, Keenan

Wynn, Estelle Winwood, Elsa Lanchester, Amanda Blake, Barry Jones, Lisa Daniels, Lurene Tuttle, Liliane Montevecchi, Roland Petit's Ballet de Paris, Walter Pidgeon (narrator). *D:* Charles Walters; *P:* Edwin H. Knopf; *Sc:* Helen Deutsch; *Theme song:* Deutsch, Bronislau Kaper. (1:33) (video) The "Cinderella" story with fantasy ballet sequences. Photographed in Eastmancolor and based on the 1697 fairy tale by Charles Perrault, it was a major box office disappointment.

984. The Glass Wall (Columbia/Shane-Tors; 1953). *Cast:* Vittorio Gassman (U.S. debut), Gloria Grahame, Ann Robinson, Douglas Spencer, Jerry Paris, Robin Raymond, Elizabeth Slifer, Richard Reeves, Joseph Turkel, Else Neft, Michael Fox, Ned Booth, Kathleen Freeman, Juney Ellis, Jack Teagarden, Shorty Rogers and band. *D:* Maxwell Shane; *P:* Ivan Tors; *St: & Sc:* Tors, Shane. (1:19) Drama of a European refugee in America who goes into hiding when facing deportation.

985. The Glass Web (Universal-International; 1953). *Cast:* Edward G. Robinson, John Forsythe, Kathleen Hughes, Marcia Henderson, Richard Denning, Hugh Sanders, Harry O. Tyler, Jean Willes, Beverly Garland, Kathleen Freeman, Clark Howat, Paul Dubov, John Heistand, Bob Nelson, Dick Stewart, Jeri Lou James, Duncan Richardson, Jack Kelly, Alice Kelley, Lance Fuller, Brett Halsey, Eve McVeagh, Jack Lomas, Helen Wallace, Howard Wright, Herbert C. Lytton, James Stone, John Verros, Benny Rubin, Eddie Parker, Tom Greenway, Donald Kerr. *D:* Jack Arnold; *P:* Albert J. Cohen; *Sc:* Robert Blees, Leonard Lee. (1:21) Melodramatic thriller set in a TV studio involving a writer who is mixed up in murder and blackmail. Based on the 1952 novel *Spin the Glass Web* by Max Simon Ehrlich, it was photographed in 3-D.

986. Glen or Glenda (Paramount/Screen Classics; 1953). *Cast:* Bela Lugosi, Lyle Talbot, Daniel Davis (aka: Edward D. Wood, Jr./title role[s]), Dolores Fuller (the real life Mrs. Wood), "Tommy" Haynes, Timothy Farrell, Charles Crofts, Conrad Brooks, Henry Bedereski, George Weiss. *D: & Sc:* Edward D. Wood, Jr. (directorial debut); *P:* George E. Weiss. (1:07) (video/laserdisc) The quality of any film known under five separate titles is immediately suspect, as is this melodrama of a man who yearns to wear his girl friend's angora sweater when he goes out on the town in drag. The banner "Screen Classics" which accompanies this film aptly describes it, as this is the film which started Edward D. Wood, Jr. on his way to becoming a "Hollywood legend." (aka: *He or She, I Led Two Lives, I Changed My Sex* and *The Transvestite*)

987. The Glenn Miller Story (Universal-International; 1954). *Cast:* James Stewart (Glen Miller), June Allyson (received *Photoplay* Gold Medal/Helen Burger), Charles Drake (Don Haynes), Henry [Harry] Morgan (Chummy), George Tobias (Si Schribman), Frances Langford (final film—ret./herself), Louis Armstrong (himself), Gene Krupa (himself), Ben Pollack (himself), Barton MacLane (General Arnold), Sig Rumann (Kranz), Irving Bacon (Mr. Miller), Kathleen Lockhart (Mrs. Miller), James Bell (Mr. Burger), Katherine Warren (Mrs. Burger), Dayton Lummis (Colonel Spalding), Marion Ross (Polly Haynes), Phil Garris (Joe Becker), Deborah Sydes (Jonnie Dee), The Modernaires (themselves), Ruth Hampton (girl singer), Damian O'Flynn (Colonel Baker), Carleton Young (adjutant general), William Challee (sergeant), Steve Pendleton (Lt. Col. Baessell), Harry Harvey, Sr. (doctor), Leo Mostovoy (Dr. Schillinger), Nino Tempo (Wilbur Schwartz), Babe Russin (himself), Bonnie Eddy (Irene), Anthony Sydes (Herbert), Dick Ryan, Hal K. Dawson, The Mello-Men, The Rolling Robinsons, Lisa Gaye, Robert A. Davis, Carl Vernell. *D:* Anthony Mann; *P:* Aaron Rosenberg; *St: & Sc:* (AAN) Valentine Davies, Oscar Brodney; *Music:* (AAN) Joseph Gershenson, Henry Mancini; *Sound Recording:* (AA) Leslie I. Carey; *Songs include:* "Moonlight Serenade" (Miller-Mitchell Parish); "In the Mood" (Andy Razaf-Joe Garland); "String of Pearls" (Eddie DeLange-Jerry Gray); "I Know Why" and "Chattanooga Choo Choo" (Mack Gordon–Harry Warren). (1:56) (video/laserdisc) Hollywood's Technicolor biographical salute to one of America's best-loved big band leaders who died in 1944 when his military plane disappeared. It was voted "Best Film of the Year" by the *New York Times* and placed #9 on the "10 Best" list of *Film Daily*. One of the 25 top-grossing films of 1953-54.

988. Glory (RKO/David Butler Prods.; 1955). *Cast:* Margaret O'Brien (singing voice dubbed by Norma Zimmer), Walter Brennan, Charlotte Greenwood, John Lupton, Byron Palmer, Lisa Davis, Gus Schilling, Theron Jackson, Hugh Sanders, Walter Baldwin, Harry Tyler, Paul Burns, Leonid Kinskey (final film—ret.), Madge Blake. *D: & P:* David Butler; *St:* Gene Markey; *Sc:* Peter Milne; *Songs:* Title song, "Getting Nowhere Road" and "Kentucky (Means Paradise)" M.K. Jerome, Ted Koehler. (1:39) (video) Family oriented tale of Kentucky horse racing and a woman who owns a champion horse. Technicolor and SuperScope.

989. Glory Alley (MGM; 1952). *Cast:* Ralph Meeker, Leslie Caron, Kurt Kasznar, Gilbert Roland, John McIntire, Louis Armstrong, Jack Teagarden (himself), Dick Simmons, Dan Seymour, Larry Gates, Pat Goldin, John Indrisano, Mickey Little, Pat Valentino, David McMahon, George Garver. *D:* Raoul Walsh; *P:* Nicholas Nayfack; *St: & Sc:* Art Cohn; *Songs:* "St. Louis Blues" (W.C. Handy); Title song and "That's What the Man Said" (George Stoll). (1:19) Drama, with jazz interludes, of a boxer, a New Orleans honky-tonk dancer, and the former's decision to quit the fight game. Theatre attendance was lacking for this one.

990. The Glory Brigade (20th Century-Fox; 1953). *Cast:* Victor Mature, Alexander Scourby, Lee Marvin, Richard Egan, Nick Dennis, Roy Roberts, Alvy Moore, Russell Evans, Henry Kulky, Gregg Martell, Lamont Johnson, Carleton Young, Frank Gerstle, Stuart Nedd, George Michaelides, John Verros, Alberto Morin, Archer MacDonald, Peter Mamakos, Father Patrinakos, John Haretakis, Costas Morfis, David Gabbal, Nico Minardos, George Saris, Jonathan Hale. *D:* Robert D. Webb; *P:* William Bloom; *St: & Sc:* Franklin Coen. (1:21) Korean War drama of the conflict that erupts between American G.I.s and Greek soldiers while on a mission to gather information regarding the enemy's strength.

991. Go for Broke! (MGM; 1951). *Cast:* Van Johnson (Lt. Michael Grayson), Lane Nakano (Sam), George Miki ("Chick"), Akira Fukunaga (Frank), Ken K. Okamoto ("Kaz"), Henry Oyasato (Ohhara), Harry Hamada (Masami), Henry Nakamura (Tommy), Warner Anderson (Col. Charles W. Pence), Don Haggerty (Sgt. Wilson I. Culley), Gianna [Maria] Canale (Rosina/U.S. debut), Dan Riss (Capt. Solari), George Tanaguchi (Ohhara's brother), Frank Okada (platoon leader), Walter Reed, Hugh Beaumont, Frank Wilcox, Tsutomu Paul Nakamura, Edward Earle, Freeman Lusk, Richard Anderson, Henry Guttman, Mario Siletti, John Banner, Ann Codee, Jack Reilly, Louis Mercier, Tony Christian, Toru Iura. *D:* Robert Pirosh; *P:* Dore Schary; *St: & Sc:* (AAN) Pirosh; *Song:* "The Meaning of Love" Pirosh, Alberto Columbo, Ken Okamoto. (1:32) (video) Hit World War II drama of a bigoted Texaan, on orders to train and lead the Nisei (American-born Japanese soldiers) during that conflict. The exploits of the 442nd Regimental Combat Team made this one of the 23 top-grossing films of 1950-51.

992. Go, Johnny, Go! (Hal Roach/Valiant Films; 1958). *Cast:* Alan Freed (himself), Jimmy Clanton (film debut), Sandy Stewart, Chuck Berry (himself), Herbert Vigran, Frank Wilcox, Barbara Woodell, Milton Frome, Joe Crantons, Inga Boling, Eddie Cochran, The Flamingos, The Cadillacs, Jackie Wilson, Jo-Ann Campbell, Harvey [Fuqua], Ritchie Valens (only film appearance—d. 1959 in a plane crash). *D:* Paul Landres; *P:* Alan Freed; *Ex.P:* Hal Roach, Jr.; *St: & Sc:* Gary Alexander; *Songs:* "My Love is Strong" (sung by Clanton), "Once Again" (sung by Clanton and Stewart), "Angel Face" (Clanton), "You'd Better Know It" (Wilson), "Go, Johnny, Go" (Berry), "Jay Walker" (Cadillacs), "Jump, Children" (Flamingos), "Heavenly Father" (Stewart), "Memphis, Tennessee" (Berry), "Ship on a Stormy Sea" (Clanton), "Teenage Heaven" (Cochran), "Oh, My Head" (Valens), "Playmates" (Stewart), "Don't Be Afraid to Love" (Harvey), "Little Queenie" (Berry), "Please, Mr. Johnson" (Cadillacs), "Mama, Can I Go Out" (Campbell), "It Takes a Long, Long Time" (Clanton) and "Now the Day is Over" (Clanton). (1:15) (video/laserdisc) D.J. Alan Freed turns a runaway orphan boy into a popular singing sensation. Nineteen songs by the cast and popular guest stars fill out the rest of the film.

993. Go, Man, Go (United Artists/Sirod Prods., Inc.; 1954). *Cast:* Dane Clark, Pat Breslin, Sidney Poitier, Edmon Ryan, Harlem Globetrotters (themselves), Bram Nossen, Anatol Winogradoff, Carol Sinclair, Ellsworth Wright, Ruby Dee, Celia Boodkin, Slim Gaillard, Frieda Altman, Mort Marshall, Jean Shore, Jule Benedic, Jerry Hauer, Marty Glickman, Bill Stern, Lew Hearn. *D:* James Wong Howe (a cinematographer in his directorial debut); *P:* Anton M. Leader; *St: & Sc:* Arnold Becker. (1:22) Basketball drama of Harlem Globetrotters' manager, Abe Saperstein, and how he turned the team into a renowned institution.

994. Gobs and Gals (Republic; 1952). *Cast:* George Bernard, Bert Bernard, Robert Hutton, Cathy Downs, Gordon Jones, Florence Marley, Leon Belasco, Emory Parnell, Leonid Kinskey,

Tommy Rettig, Minerva Urecal, Donald MacBride, Henry Kulky. *D:* R.G. Springsteen; *As.P:* Sidney Picker; *St: & Sc:* Arthur T. Horman. (1:26) Comic complications arise when two south sea island sailors send love letters to various females, including a picture of their commanding officer with each letter. *Wild Horse Ambush* (q.v.) completed the double bill program.

995. God Is My Partner (20th Century-Fox/Regal Films; 1957). *Cast:* Walter Brennan, John Hoyt, Marion Ross, Jesse White, Nelson Leigh, Charles Lane, Ellen Corby, Paul Cavanagh, Nancy Kulp, John Harmon, Charles Gray. *D:* William F. Claxton; *P:* Sam Hersh; *St: & Sc:* Charles Francis Royal. (1:20) Drama of an elderly surgeon who wishes to donate $50,000 to religious causes, but family members take him to court and declare him incompetent to handle his finances. Regalscope.

996. The Goddess (Columbia/Carnegie Prods.; 1958). *Cast:* Kim Stanley (film debut/ Emily Ann Faulkner), Betty Lou Holland (the mother), Joan Copeland (the aunt), Gerald Hiken (the uncle), Steven Hill (John Tower), Joyce Van Patten (Hillary), Lloyd Bridges (Dutch Seymour), Bert Freed (Lester Brackman), Donald McKee (R.M. Lucas), Louise Beavers (the cook), Elizabeth Wilson (secretary), Werner Klemperer (Mr. Woolsey), Joan Linville (Joanna), Patty Duke (film debut/ Emily age 8), Bert Brinckerhoff (the boy), Gerald Petrarca (the minister), Linda Soma (bridesmaid), Curt Conway (the writer), David White (Burt Harris), Chris Flanagan (Emily age 4), Margaret Brayton (Mrs. Woolsey), Fred Herrick (the elder), Gail Haworth (Emily's daughter), Roy Shuman, John Lawrence, Mike O'Dowd, Sid Raymond. *D:* John Cromwell; *P:* Milton Perlman; *St: & Sc:* (AAN + "Best Screenplay" by the *New York Times*) Paddy Chayefsky. (1:45) (video) Drama of the rise of a Hollywood star, somewhat inspired by the career of Marilyn Monroe. This film received a "Special Award" at the Brussel's Film Festival. It also placed #3 and #7 respectively on the "10 Best" lists of the *New York Times* and the NBR.

997. God's Little Acre (United Artists/ Security Pictures; 1958). *Cast:* Robert Ryan (Ty Ty Walden), Aldo Ray (Bill Thompson), Tina Louise (film debut/Griselda), Buddy Hackett (Pluto), Jack Lord (Buck Walden), Fay Spain (Darlin' Jill), Vic Morrow (Shaw Walden), Helen Westcott (Rosamund), Lance Fuller (Jim Leslie), Rex Ingram (Uncle Felix), Michael Landon (Dave Dawson), Russell Collins. *D:* Anthony Mann; *P:* Sidney Harmon; *Sc:* Philip Yordan; *Title song:* Elmer Bernstein. (1:50) (video) "Adult" drama, with touches of comedy, of a family of farmers in depression-era Georgia. Critics were divided on this box office bonanza based on Erskine Caldwell's 1933 book which turned a nice profit, becoming one of the 26 top-grossing films of 1957-58. The *New York Times* placed it at #4 on their "10 Best" list and the Venice Film Festival also had it in nomination.

998. Gog (United Artists/Ivan Tors Prods.; 1954). *Cast:* Richard Egan, Constance Dowling, Herbert Marshall, John Wengraf, Philip Van Zandt, Byron Kane, Michael Fox, Valerie Vernon, Steve Roberts, David Alpert, William Schallert, Marian Richman, Jeanne Dean, Tom Daly, Alex Jackson, Patti Taylor, Beverly Jocher, Aline Towne, Al Bayer, Andy Andrews, Julian Ludwig. *D:* Herbert L. Strock; *P: & St:* Ivan Tors; *Sc:* Tom Taggart, Richard G. Taylor. (1:25) Science fiction of an underground installation in New Mexico working on robots that are controlled by a thinking machine called NOVAC (Nuclear Operative Variable Automatic Confuser), then control is taken over by alien craft. Photographed in 3-D with color by Color Corporation of America.

999. Going Steady (Columbia/Clover Prods.; 1958). *Cast:* Molly Bee, Alan Reed, Jr., Irene Hervey, Bill Goodwin, Ken Miller, Susan Easter, Linda Watkins, Byron Foulger, Hugh Sanders, Florence Ravenel, Ralph Moody, Carlyle Mitchell. *D:* Fred F. Sears; *P:* Sam Katzman; *St:* Budd Grossman, Sumner A. Long; *Sc:* Grossman; *Song:* "Going Steady (With a Dream)" Fred Karger, Richard Quine. (1:19) (video) Teen oriented romantic-comedy of young love and marriage. Critically acclaimed by *Variety*.

Going to Town (G.B. title) *see* **Ma and Pa Kettle Go to Town**

1000. Gold Fever (Monogram; 1952). *Cast:* John Calvert, Ralph Morgan (final film—d. 1956), Ann Cornell, Gene Roth, Tom Kennedy, Judd Holdren, George Morrell, Danny Rense, Bobby Graham. *D:* Leslie Goodwins; *P:* John Calvert; *St:* Calvert; *Sc:* Edgar C. Anderson, Jr., Cliff Lancaster. (1:03) Low budget western of crooks bent on getting an old prospector's gold mine.

1001. Gold Raiders (United Artists/Bernard Glasser, Inc.; 1951). *Cast:* George O'Brien (final film until 1964), The Three Stooges (Moe Howard, Shemp Howard, Larry Fine), Sheila Ryan, Clem Bevans, Monte Blue, Lyle Talbot, John Merton, Al Baffert, Hugh Hooker, Bill Ward, Fuzzy Knight, Dick Crockett, Roy Canada. *D:* Edward Bernds; *P:* Bernard Glasser; *St:* *&* *Sc:* Elwood Ullman, William Lively. (0:56) (video) Slapstick comedy-western which has the Three Stooges saving the west from ore hijackers. (G.B. title: *Stooges Go West*)

1002. The Goldbergs (Paramount; 1950). *Cast:* Gertrude Berg (Molly Goldberg), Philip Loeb (Jake Goldberg), Larry Robinson (Sammy Goldberg), Arlene McQuade (Rosalie Goldberg), Eduard Franz, Eli Mintz, Betty Walker, David Opatashu, Barbara Rush, Peter Hansen, Edit Angold, Sara Krohner, Helen Brown, Josephine Whittell, Shari Robinson, Erno Verebes. *D:* Walter Hart; *P:* Mel Epstein; *St:* *&* *Sc:* Gertrude Berg, N. Richard Nash. (1:23) Radio and TV's popular show, created by Gertrude Berg, of a Jewish family living in the Bronx (N.Y.), emerges as a theatrical feature with Molly enduring various headaches when an old flame (Franz)—now wealthy—comes to visit her family. (retitled: *Molly*)

1003. The Golden Age of Comedy (Distributors Corp. of America/Ro-Co Prods., Inc.; 1957). A compilation of silent comedy clips from Mack Sennet and Hal Roach, featuring Laurel and Hardy, Carole Lombard, Ben Turpin, Will Rogers, Harry Langdon, Snub Pollard, Jean Harlow, The Keystone Kops, and others. *D:-P:* *&* *Sc:* Robert Youngson. (1:18) (video/laserdisc).

1004. The Golden Blade (Universal-International; 1953). *Cast:* Rock Hudson, Piper Laurie, George Macready, Gene Evans, Kathleen Hughes, Steven Geray, Edgar Barrier, Anita Ekberg (film debut), Alice Kelley, Erika Norden, Valerie Jackson, Renate Hoy, Vic Romito, Jack Baston, Harry Wilson, Olga Lunick, Dorinda Clifton, Dennis Weaver, Guy Williams, Dayton Lummis, Bill Radovich, Harry Mendoza, Harry Lang, Fred Graham, Zachary Yaconelli, George "Shorty" Chirello, Martin Cichy. *D:* Nathan Juran; *P:* Richard Wilson; *St:* *&* *Sc:* John Rich. (1:20) A Technicolor costume fantasy-swashbuckler set in old Baghdad.

1005. Golden Girl (20th Century–Fox; 1951). *Cast:* Mitzi Gaynor (Lotta Crabtree), Dale Robertson (Tom Richmond), Dennis Day (Mart), James Barton (Mr. Crabtree), Una Merkel (Mrs. Crabtree), Raymond Walburn (Cornelius), Gene Sheldon (Sam Jordan), Carmen D'Antonio (Lola Montez), Michael Ross, Harry Carter, Lovyss Bradley, Emory Parnell, Luther Crockett, Harris Brown, Kermit Maynard, Robert Nash, Jessie Arnold. *D:* Lloyd Bacon; *P:* George Jessel; *St:* Albert Lewis, Arthur Lewis; *Sc:* Walter Bullock, Charles O'Neal, Gladys Lehman; *Songs:* "Dixie" (Daniel Decatur Emmett); "Carry Me Back to Old Virginny," "Oh, Dem Golden Slippers" (James A. Bland); "California Moon" (George Jessel–Sam Lerner–Joe Cooper); "Sunday Morning" (Eliot Daniel–Ken Darby); "Kiss Me Quick and Go My Honey" (Daniel); "Never" (AAN-Best Song/Daniel-Lionel Newman); "When Johnny Comes Marching Home" (Patrick S. Gilmore); "Believe Me If All Those Endearing Young Charms" (Thomas Moore–Matthew Locke); "La Donna E. Mobile" (from "Rigoletto" by Giuseppe Verdi). (1:47) Costume musical set in California in the days of the Civil War, and of singer Lotta Crabtree who finds herself being attracted to a Confederate spy. Technicolor. Note: The real Lotta Crabtree, a very beautiful young woman in her day, was lorded over by a protective stage mother throughout her career.

1006. The Golden Gloves Story (Eagle-Lion/Central National Picture–Pathé Industries; 1950). *Cast:* James Dunn, Dewey Martin, Gregg Sherwood, Devin O'Morrison, Kay Westfall, Arch Ward (himself), Johnny Behr (himself), Dickie Conon, Fern Persons, John "Red" Kullers, Tony Zale (himself), Issy Kline (himself), Black Brickhouse, Dick Mastro, Michael McGuire, Art van Harvey. *D:* Felix Feist; *P:* Carl Krueger; *St:* D.D. Beauchamp, William F. Seller; *Sc:* Joe Anson, Feist. (1:16) Pugilism drama of two young fighters out to win the same girl and the same championship, utilizing real boxing footage.

1007. The Golden Hawk (Columbia; 1952). *Cast:* Rhonda Fleming, Sterling Hayden, Helena Carter, John Sutton, Paul Cavanagh, Michael Ansara, Raymond Hatton, Alex Montoya, Albert Pollet, David Bond, Donna Martell, Mary Munday, Poppy A. del Vando. *D:* Sidney Salkow; *P:* Sam Katzman; *Sc:* Robert E. Kent. (1:23) Technicolor action-adventure of a pirate seeking revenge for the death of his mother. Based on the 1946 book by Frank Yerby.

1008. The Golden Horde (Universal-International; 1951). *Cast:* Ann Blyth, David

Farrar (U.S. debut), George Macready, Henry Brandon, Richard Egan, Howard Petrie, Marvin Miller (Genghis Khan), Peggie Castle, Donald Randolph, Poodles Hanneford, Leon Belasco, Lucille Barkley, Karen Varga, Robert Hunter. *D:* George Sherman; *P:* Howard Christie, Robert Arthur; *St:* Harold Lamb; *Sc:* Gerald Drayson Adams. (1:16) Technicolor romantic costume-adventure set around the siege of Samarkan by Genghis Khan in 1220 A.D. (aka: *Golden Horde of Genghis Khan*)

1009. The Golden Idol (Monogram/Allied Artists; 1954). *Cast:* Johnny Sheffield, Anne Kimbell, Lane Bradford, Paul Guilfoyle, Leonard Mudie, Robert "Smoki" Whitfield, Roy Glenn, Rick Vallin, James Adamson, William Tannen, Don Harvey. *D:-P: & Sc:* Ford Beebe. (1:11) In this low budget series entry, "Bomba, the Jungle Boy" steps in to help Watusi tribesmen retrieve a valuable golden idol, stolen from them by nasty Arabs. Based on the character created by Roy Rockwood.

1010. The Golden Mistress (United Artists/R.K.; 1954). *Cast:* John Agar, Rosemarie Bowe, Abner Biberman (final film as actor), Andre Narcisse, Jacques Molant, Kiki, Pierre Blain, André Contant, National Folklore Theatre of Haiti, Shibley Talamus, Napoleon Bernard, André Germain. *D:* Joel Judge (pseudonym for Biberman); *P:* Richard Kay, Harry Rybnick; *St:* Lew Hewitt; *Sc:* Judge (Biberman), Hewitt. (1:22) Technicolor action-adventure of a boat skipper and a New York model who discover sunken treasure in a Caribbean lake. Filmed on location in Haiti.

1011. The Golden Twenties (RKO/Times Film Corp.; 1950). A compilation of film clips presented by the "March of Time," documenting the 1920s. *P:* Richard de Rochemont; *St: & Sc:* Frederick Lewis Allen, Samuel W. Bryant. (1:08)

1012. Goldtown Ghost Raiders (Columbia/Gene Autry Productions; 1953). *Cast:* Gene Autry, Gail Davis, Smiley Burnette, Kirk Riley, Carleton Young, John Doucette, Denver Pyle, Neyle Morrow, Steve Conte, Champion (horse). *D:* George Archainbaud; *P:* Armand Schaefer; *St: & Sc:* Gerald Geraghty. (0:57) Offbeat Gene Autry western. Gene plays a circuit judge involved with the unusual case of a man accused of murdering a man that he already spent time in jail for killing years before. Sepiatone.

1013. Good Day for a Hanging (Columbia/Morningside; 1958). *Cast:* Fred MacMurray, Maggie Hayes, Robert Vaughn, Joan Blackman, James Drury, Wendell Holmes, Stacy Harris, Edmon Ryan, Kathryn Card, Emile Meyer, Bing Russell, Russell Thorsen, Denver Pyle, Phil Chambers, Howard McNear, Rusty Swope, Harry Lauter, Gregg Barton, Michael Garth, Tom London, William Fawcett, William Baskin, Robert Bice. *D:* Nathan Juran; *P:* Charles H. Schneer; *Sc:* Daniel B. Ullman, Maurice Zimm. (1:25) Western of a sheriff's attempts to prove guilt in his predecessor's murder. Based on the story "The Reluctant Hangman" by Jo Carpenter. Eastmancolor.

1014. The Good Humor Man (Columbia; 1950). *Cast:* Jack Carson, Lola Albright, George Reeves, Jean Wallace, Peter Miles, Frank Ferguson, David Sharpe, Chick Collins, Eddie Parker, Pat Flaherty, Arthur Space, Richard Egan, Jack Overman, Victoria Horne. *D:* Lloyd Bacon; *P:* S. Sylvan Simon; *Sc:* Frank Tashlin. (1:19) Slapstick comedy of an ice cream vendor who gets himself involved in a payroll robbery. Based on the story "Appointment With Fear" by Roy Huggins.

1015. Good Morning, Miss Dove (20th Century–Fox; 1955). *Cast:* Jennifer Jones (title role), Robert Stack, Kipp Hamilton, Robert Douglas, Peggy Knudsen, Marshall Thompson, Chuck Connors, Biff Elliot, Jerry Paris, Mary Wickes, Ted Marc, Dick Stewart, Vivian Marshall, Richard Deacon, Bill Walker, Than Wyenn, Leslie Bradley, Robert Lynn, Edward Firestone, Cheryl Callaway, Mark Engel, Tim Cagney, Linda Bennett, Kenneth Osmond, Paul Engel, Tiger Fafara, Martha Wentworth, Virginia Christine, Junius Matthews, Reba Tassell, Gary Diamond, Myna Cunard. A. Cameron Grant, Janet Brandt, Linda Brace, Ann Tyrrell, Nan Dolan, Betty Caulfield, Elmore Vincent, Vincent Perry, Steve Darrell, Milas Clark, Leonard Ingoldsby, Carol Savage, Tim Haldeman, Michael Gainey, Ernest Dotson, Mary Carroll, Sarah Selby, Jo Gilbert, Pamela Beaird, Carol Sydes, Lydia Reed, Jean Innes, Maudie Prickett, Catherine Howard, John Heistand, Edward Mundy, Tim Johnson, Jean Andren, Jane Crowley, Eleanore Vogel, Mae Marsh, Virginia Carroll, Elizabeth Flournoy, George Dunn, Herb Vigran, Charles Webster, Richard Cutting, Sam McDaniel, William Hughes. *D:* Henry Koster; *P:* Samuel G. Engel; *Sc:* Eleanore Griffin. (1:47) Sentimental Americana, told in flashbacks, of how one teacher had an effect on the lives of so many residents of a small New England town. Based on the 1954 novel by Frances Gray Patton, the film did not show the returns that the studio expected. DeLuxe color and CinemaScope.

1016. Goodbye My Fancy (Warner; 1951). *Cast:* Joan Crawford, Frank Lovejoy, Robert Young, Eve Arden, Lurene Tuttle, Howard St. John, Janice Rule (film debut), Viola Roache, Ellen Corby, Morgan Farley, Virginia Gibson, John Qualen, Ann Robin, Mary Carver, Creighton Hale, Frank Hyers, John Alvin, John Hedloe, Phil Tead, Larry Williams, Frederick Howard, Lucius Cook. *D:* Vincent Sherman; *P:* Henry Blanke; *Sc:* Ivan Goff, Ben Roberts. (1:46) Comedy-drama based on Fay Kanin's 1949 Broadway success (aka: *Most Likely to Succeed*) of a congresswoman who returns to her college alma mater to receive an honorary degree and finds romance.

1017. Good-Bye, My Lady (Warner/Batjac Prods.; 1956). *Cast:* Walter Brennan, Brandon de Wilde, Phil Harris, Sidney Poitier, William Hopper, Louise Beavers, Lady (dog—received PATSY Award of Excellence—1957). *P:* (uncredited) *& D:* William A. Wellman; *Sc:* Sid Fleischman; *Song:* "When Your Boy Becomes a Man" (Don Powell–Moris Erby). (1:34) (video/laserdisc) Sentimental family drama of a 14-year-old boy, living in the swampland of Mississippi. He finds a basenji dog he names Lady and becomes attached to, only to learn the dog is lost, with a hefty reward for her return. Based on the 1954 novel by James Street. (aka: *The Boy and the Laughing Dog*).

1018. Gorilla at Large (20th Century-Fox/Panoramic; 1954). *Cast:* Cameron Mitchell, Anne Bancroft, Raymond Burr, Lee J. Cobb, Charlotte Austin, Peter Whitney, Lee Marvin, Warren Stevens, Jack G. Kellogg, Charles Tannen. *D:* Harmon Jones; *Ex.P:* Robert L. Jacks; *P:* Leonard Goldstein (unc.); *St: & Sc:* Leonard Praskin, Barney Slater. (1:24) (video) Several people (including a resident gorilla) are suspect when a series of murders occur at an amusement park. A mystery-thriller which was photographed in Technicolor and 3-D.

The Grace Moore Story (G.B. title) *see* **So This Is Love**

Grave Robbers from Outer Space *see* **Plan 9 from Outer Space**

1019. The Great American Pastime (MGM; 1956). *Cast:* Tom Ewell, Anne Francis, Ann Miller (final film—ret.), Dean Jones, Rudy Lee, Ann Morriss, Judson Pratt, Raymond Bailey, Wilfrid Knapp, Bob Jellison, Raymond Winston, Tod Ferrell, Paul Engel, Gene O'Donnell, Nathaniel Benchley, Smidgeon (dog). *D:* Herman Hoffman; *P:* Henry Berman; *St: & Sc:* Nathaniel Benchley. (1:29) Comedy of a father's problems when he agrees to manage his son's little league team.

1020. The Great Caruso (MGM; 1951). *Cast:* Mario Lanza (Enrico Caruso), Ann Blyth (Dorothy Benjamin), Dorothy Kirsten (Louise Heggar), Jarmila Novotna (Maria Selka), Richard Hagerman (Carlo Santi), Carl Benton Reid (Park Benjamin), Eduard Franz (Giulio Gatti-Casazza), Ludwig Donath (Alfredo Brazzi), Alan Napier (Jean de Reszke), Paul Javor (Antonio Scotti), Carl Milletaire (Gino), Shepard Menken (Fucito), Vincent Renno (Tullio), Nestor Paiva (Egisto Barretto), Peter Edward Price (Caruso as a boy), Mario Siletti (Papa Caruso), Angela Clarke (Mrs. Caruso), Ian Wolfe (Hutchins), Yvette Dugay (Musetta), Argentina Brunetti (Mrs. Barretto), Maurice Samuels (Papa Gino), Lucine Amara (Blanche Thebom), Robert E. Bright (Nicolo Moscona), Marina Koshetz (Teresa Celli), Gilbert Russell (Guiseppe Valdengo), Edit Angold (Hilda), Antonio Filauri (Papa Riccardo), Peter Brocco (Father Bronzetti), David Bond (Father Angelico), Charles Evans (Finch), Matt Moore (Max), Sherry Jackson (Musetta as a child), Mario DeLaval (Ottello Carmini), Anthony Mazzola (Fucito—age 8), Mae Clarke. *D:* Richard Thorpe; *P:* Joe Pasternak; *Sc:* Sonya Levien, William Ludwig; *Music:* (AAN) Peter Herman Adler, Johnny Green; *Costumes:* (AAN) Helen Rose, Gile Steele; *Sound recording:* (AA) Douglas Shearer; *Song:* "The Loveliest Night of the Year" (which became a hit, based on the melody of the Viennese waltz "Over the Waves" with lyrics by Paul Francis Webster). (1:49) (video/laserdisc) Fictionalized Technicolor biographical musical of the renowned Italian operatic tenor of the late 19th and early 20th century. A runaway surprise smash hit and one of the 23 top-grossing films of 1950-51. Twenty-seven vocal offerings, which included nine operatic sequences, fostered the film and the star's popularity, resulting in Lanza receiving the *Photoplay* Gold Medal. Based on the 1945 biography *Enrico Caruso, His Life and Death* by Dorothy Caruso, it also took a #10 placement on the "10 Best" list of *Film Daily*.

1021. Great Day in the Morning (RKO/Edmund Grainger Prods.; 1956). *Cast:* Virginia Mayo, Robert Stack, Ruth Roman, Alex Nicol, Raymond Burr, Leo Gordon, Regis Toomey, Peter Whitney, Dan White, Donald MacDonald, Carleton Young. *D:* Jacques Tourneur; *P:* Edmund Grainger; *Sc:* Lesser Samuels. (1:32) (video) Pre–Civil War drama of Colorado's gold rush and opposing sentiments about separating from the Union. Based on the 1950 novel by Robert Hardy Andrews. Technicolor and SuperScope.

1022. The Great Diamond Robbery (MGM; 1953). *Cast:* Red Skelton, Cara Williams, James Whitmore, Dorothy Stickney, Kurt Kasznar, Harry Bellaver, Reginald Owen, George Mathews, Connie Gilchrist, Sig Arno (final film—ret.), Steven Geray. *D:* Robert Z. Leonard; *P:* Edwin H. Knopf; *St:* Laslo Vadnay; *Sc:* Vadnay, Martin Rackin. (1:09) Programmer comedy of a diamond cutter who is duped by a jewel thief.

1023. The Great Jesse James Raid (Lippert/Zezebel Prods.; 1953). *Cast:* Willard Parker (Jesse James), Barbara Payton, Tom Neal (final film—retired due to press notoriety), Wallace Ford, James Anderson, Jim Bannon (Bob Ford), Richard Cutting, Barbara Woodell, Marin Sais, Earle Hodgins, Tom Walker, Joan Arnold, Helene Hayden, Steve Pendleton, Bob Griffin, Robin Moore, Ed Russell, Rory Mallinson. *D:* Reginald LeBorg; *P:* Robert L. Lippert, Jr.; *St: & Sc:* Richard Landau. (1:13) Legendary outlaw, Jesse James, plans on going for one last robbery. Anscocolor.

1024. The Great Jewel Robber (Warner; 1950). *Cast:* David Brian, Marjorie Reynolds, Jacqueline de Wit, Alix Talton, John Archer, Perdita Chandler, Warren Douglas, Robert B. Williams, John Morgan, Bigelow Sayre, Claudia Barrett, Fred Coby, Mayor Stanley Church (of New Rochelle, N.Y.). *D:* Peter Godfrey; *P:* Bryan Foy; *St: & Sc:* Borden Chase. (1:31) The film recounts the exploits of real life jewel robber, Gerard Graham Dennis (with his permission). Based on the story "Life Gerard Graham Dennis" by Chase and Mr. Dennis.

1025. The Great Locomotive Chase (Buena Vista/Walt Disney Prods.; 1956). *Cast:* Fess Parker, Jeffrey Hunter, Jeff York, John Lupton, Eddie Firestone, Kenneth Tobey, Don Megowan, Claude Jarman, Jr. (final film—ret. at age 22), Harry Carey, Jr., Lennie Geer, George Robotham, Stan Jones, Marc Hamilton, John Wiley, Slim Pickens, Morgan Woodward, W.S. Bearden, Harvey Hester, Douglas Blackley [aka: Robert Kent]. *D:* Francis D. Lyon; *Ex.P:* Walt Disney; *P: & Sc:* Lawrence E. Watkin; *Song:* "Sons of Old Aunt Dinah" Stan Jones, Watkin. (1:25) (video) Fact-based Civil War story of Andrew's Raiders, headed by James J. Andrews (Parker), a Union spy, who pose as Confederates and abscond with a train, with the train's conductor William A. Fuller (Hunter) in hot pursuit. A box office winner, the story was also the basis for Buster Keaton's 1927 silent classic *The General.* (retitled: *Andrew's Raiders*)

1026. The Great Man (Universal-International; 1956). *Cast:* Jose Ferrer, Dean Jagger, Keenan Wynn, Julie London, Joanne Gilbert, Ed Wynn, Jim Backus, Russ Morgan, Edward C. Platt, Robert Foulk, Lyle Talbot, Vinton Haworth, Henny Backus, Janie Alexander, Vicki Dugan, Robert Schwartz, Hallene Hill. *D:* Jose Ferrer; *P:* Aaron Rosenberg; *Sc:* Al Morgan, Ferrer; *Song:* "The Meaning of the Blues" Leah Worth, Bobby Troup (sung by Julie London). (1:32) Drama of a beloved TV personality who dies, with the truth of what he was really like coming to the surface when a man attempts to put together a memorial. Based on the 1955 novel by Mr. Morgan, it was voted "Best Film of the Year" by the *New York Times.*

1027. The Great Missouri Raid (Paramount; 1950). *Cast:* Macdonald Carey (Jesse James), Ellen Drew, Wendell Corey (Frank James), Ward Bond, Bruce Bennett (Cole Younger), Bill Williams (Jim Younger), Anne Revere (Mrs. Samuels), Edgar Buchanan, Louis Chastland, Louis Jean Heydt (Charley Ford), Barry Kelley, James Millican, Guy Wilkerson, Ethan Laidlaw, Tom Tyler, Paul Fix, James Griffith, Steve Pendleton, Paul Lees (Bob Younger), Robert Bray, Bob Osterloh, Alan Wells, Whit Bissell (Bob Ford). *D:* Gordon Douglas; *P:* Nat Holt; *As.P: & Sc:* Frank Gruber (based on his novel *Broken Lance*). (1:23) (video) Another western of Frank and Jesse James, with the Younger brothers, and their exploits as outlaws following the Civil War. Technicolor.

1028. The Great Plane Robbery (United Artists/Belsam Prods.; 1950). *Cast:* Tom Conway, Margaret Hamilton, Lynne Roberts, Steve Brodie, David Bruce, Marcel Journet, Gilbert Frye, Ralph Dunn, Lucille Barkley, Paul Campbell, Beverly Jons. *D:* Edward L. Cahn; *P:* Sam Baerwitz; *Sc:* Richard G. Hubler, Baerwitz. (1:01)

Robbery, murder and intrigue are the plot ingredients of this melodrama set aboard a transcontinental airliner in flight.

1029. The Great Rupert (Eagle-Lion/George Pal Prods.; 1950). *Cast:* Jimmy Durante, Terry Moore, Tom Drake, Frank Orth, Sara Haden, Queenie Smith, Chick Chandler, Jimmy Conlin, Hugh Sanders, Donald T. Beddoe, Candy Candido, Clancy Cooper, Harold Goodwin, Frank Cady, Irving Pichel (bit). *D:* Irving Pichel; *P:* George Pal; *St:* Ted Allen; *Sc:* Laslo Vadnay. (1:26) (video) Family oriented comedy about a poor family of acrobats who suddenly begin to find loads of money in the walls of their home, put there by a squirrel who is removing it from a miserly neighbor's house. The squirrel is a puppet created by George Pal. Originally ran on a double bill with *The Hidden Room* (aka: *Obsession*), a British production.

1030. The Great St. Louis Bank Robbery (United Artists/Guggenheim and Assoc.–Columbia Broadcasting System, Inc.; 1959). *Cast:* Steve McQueen, David Clarke, Graham Denton, Molly McCarthy, James Dukas, The St. Louis Police Department. *D:* Charles Guggenheim, John Stix, *P:* Guggenheim; *As.P:* & *Sc:* Richard T. Heffron; *Song:* "Night Train" Bernardo Segall, Peter Udell; *Guitar ballads:* composed and sung by Jim Symington. (1:26) Low budget crime-melodrama of a bank heist that goes awry. Filmed on location, it is based on a factual incident.

1031. The Great Sioux Uprising (Universal-International; 1953). *Cast:* Jeff Chandler, Faith Domergue, Lyle Bettger, Stacy Harris, Peter Whitney, Stephen Chase, John War Eagle, Walter Sande, Clem Fuller, Glenn Strange, Ray Bennett, Julia Montoya, Charles Arnt, Rosa Rey, John Ingram, Lane Bradford, Boyd "Red" Morgan, Dewey Drapeau. *D:* Lloyd Bacon; *P:* Albert J. Cohen; *St:* J. Robert Bren, Gladys Atwater; *Sc:* Bren, Atwater, Melvin Levy; *Additional dialogue:* Frank Gill, Jr. (1:20) Western of a crooked rancher who is contracted to supply horses to the U.S. cavalry.

1032. The Greatest Show on Earth (Paramount; 1952). *Cast:* Betty Hutton (Holly), Cornel Wilde (Sebastian), Charlton Heston (Brad), Dorothy Lamour (Phyllis), Gloria Grahame (Angel), James Stewart (Buttons), Henry Wilcoxon (detective), Emmett Kelly (himself), Lyle Bettger (Klaus), Lawrence Tierney (Henderson), John Kellogg (Harry), John Ridgely (Jack Steelman), Frank Wilcox (circus doctor), Robert Carson (ringmaster), Lillian Albertson (Button's mother), Julia Faye (Birdie), John Ringling North (himself), Tuffy Genders (Tuffy), John Parrish (Jack Lawson), Keith Richards (Keith), Brad Johnson (reporter), Adele Cook Johnson (Mabel), Lydia Clarke (circus girl), John Merton (Chuck), Lane Chandler (Dave), Bradford Hatton (Osborne), Herbert Lytton (foreman), Norman Field (Truesdale), Everett Glass (board member), Lee Aaker (boy), Ethan Laidlaw (Hank), Edmond O'Brien (midway barker), William Boyd (final film/Hopalong Cassidy), Bing Crosby (cameo), Bob Hope (cameo), Mona Freeman (cameo), Nancy Gates (cameo), Clarence Nash, Bess Flowers, Lou Jacobs, Felix Adler, The Liberty Horses, The Flying Concellos, Paul Jung, The Maxellos. *D:* (AAN) Cecil B. DeMille; *P:* (AA-Best Picture) DeMille; *As.P:* Henry Wilcoxon; *St:* (AA) Frederick M. Frank, Theodore St. John, Frank Cavett; *Sc:* Frank, St. John, Barre Lyndon; *Costumes:* (AAN) Edith Head, Dorothy Jeakins, Miles White; *Editor:* (AAN) Anne Bauchens; *Songs:* "Be a Jumping Jack," "The Greatest Show on Earth" (Ned Washington–Victor Young); "Popcorn and Lemonade," "Sing a Happy Song," "Picnic in the Park" (John Murray Anderson–Henry Sullivan); "Lovely Luawana Lady" (E. Ray Goetz–John Ringling North). (2:33) (video/laserdisc) DeMille's Technicolor salute to the Big Top with various personal stories of performers. Includes a plethora of circus acts from the Ringling Bros. Barnum and Bailey Circus, with whose cooperation this production was filmed in Sarasota, Florida. It was voted "Best Film of the Year" by the *New York Times* and placed #3 on the "10 Best" list of *Film Daily*. The New York Film Critics had it in nomination for "Best Film." A bonanza of paying moviegoers made it one of the 23 top-grossing films of 1951-52; in fact it became the studio's top-grossing film to date.

1033. The Green-Eyed Blonde (Warner/Arwin Prods.; 1957). *Cast:* Susan Oliver, Melinda Plowman, Beverly Long, Norma Jean Nilsson, Tommie Moore, Carla Merey, Sallie Brophy, Jean Inness, Olive Blakeney, Anne Barton, Tom Greenway, Margaret Brayton, Raymond Foster, Betty Lou Gerson, Roy Glenn, Stafford Repp, Evelyn Scott. *D:* Bernard Girard; *P:* Martin Melcher; *As.P:-St:-Sc:* Sally Stubblefield. (1:16) Bottom-of-the-bill programmer of a rebellious teen sentenced to a girls' reformatory where the inmates hide an infant belonging to one of the girls.

1034. Green Fire (MGM; 1954). *Cast:* Stewart Granger, Grace Kelly, Paul Douglas, John Ericson, Murvyn Vye, Jose Torvay, Robert Tafur, Jose Dominguez, Nacho Galindo, Charlita, Natividad Vacio, Rico Alaniz, Paul Marion, Bobby Dominguez, Joe Herrera, Charles Stevens, Martin Garralaga, Alberto Morin, Rodolfo Hoyos, Jr., Lillian Molieri, Marie Delgado, Juli Loffredo, Frances Dominguez, Tina Menard. *D:* Andrew Marton; *P:* Armand Deutsch; *Sc:* Ivan Goff, Ben Roberts; *Songs:* Miklos Rozsa, Jack Brooks. (1:40) (video) Hit romantic adventure set in Colombia, South America, of the steamy affair between a green fire (emeralds) prospector and the female owner of a coffee plantation. Based on the 1942 novel by Peter W. Rainier. Eastmancolor and CinemaScope.

1035. The Green Glove(United Artists/Benagoss Prods.; 1952). *Cast:* Glenn Ford, Geraldine Brooks, Cedric Hardwicke, George Macready, Gaby André, Jany Holt, Roger Treville, Juliette Greco, Georges Tabet, Mel Lemmonier, Paul Bonifas, Jean Bretonniers. *D:* Rudolph Maté; *P:* George Maurer; *St: & Sc:* Charles Bennett. (1:28) (video) Melodrama of a bejeweled gauntlet, stolen from a church during World War II, and the man seeking to return it after getting involved in murder. A co-production between the U.S. and France.

1036. Green Mansions (MGM; 1959). *Cast:* Audrey Hepburn, Anthony Perkins, Lee J. Cobb, Sessue Hayakawa, Henry Silva, Nehemiah Persoff, Michael Pate, Estelle Hemsley. *D:* Mel Ferrer; *P:* Edmund Grainger; *Sc:* Dorothy Kingsley; *Title song:* Bronislau Kaper, Paul Francis Webster (sung by Perkins). (1:44) (video) Amazon jungle romance of an adventurer and his idealistic affair with Rima the Bird Girl, fated to remain in her jungle habitat. Based on W.H. (Wm. Henry) Hudson's 1904 classic best-seller. Despite location filming in Venezuela, Colombia and British Guiana, the critics were not kind. Metrocolor and CinemaScope.

1037. The Groom Wore Spurs (Universal-International/Fidelity Picts.; 1951). *Cast:* Ginger Rogers, Jack Carson, Joan Davis, Stanley Ridges (final film—d. 1951), James Brown, John Litel, Victor Sen Yung, Mira McKinney, Gordon Nelson, George Meader, Kemp Niver, Franklyn Farnum, Kate Drain Lawson, Robert B. Williams, Richard Whorf (himself). *D:* Richard Whorf (final as director before becoming a producer); *P:* Howard Welsch; *St:* Robert Carson; *Sc:* Carson, Robert Libott, Frank Burt. (1:20) (video) Comedy of a lady attorney who marries a cowboy actor and winds up defending him on murder charges. Based on "Legal Bride," a story that appeared in *Collier's* in 1949.

1038. Grounds for Marriage (MGM; 1950). *Cast:* Van Johnson, Kathryn Grayson, Paula Raymond, Barry Sullivan, Lewis Stone, Reginald Owen, Richard Hagerman, Theresa Harris, Guy Rennie, Richard Atchison, Firehouse Five Plus Two (themselves), Milton Cross (narrator). *D:* Robert Z. Leonard; *P: & St:* Samuel Marx; *Sc:* Allen Rivkin, Laura Kerr. (1:31) Romantic comedy—with selected arias from *Carmen* and *La Bohème*—of an opera singer and her ex-husband, a doctor. Box office response was tepid.

1039. Guerrilla Girl (United Artists/Liberty Bell Motion Pictures; 1953). *Cast:* Helmut Dantine, Marianna, Irene Champlin, Ray Julian, Michael Vale, Gerald Lee, Charlotte Paul, Dora Weissman. *D: & P:* John Christian; *St: & Sc:* John Byrne, Ben Parker. (1:20) Programmer of a Greek government official who, following World War II, finds that the girl he once loved is now a member of the Communist Party. (G.B. title: *Dawn Comes Late*)

1040. Guilty Bystander (Film Classics/Laurel Films; 1950). *Cast:* Zachary Scott, Faye Emerson, Mary Boland (final film—ret.), Sam Levene, J. Edward Bromberg (final film—d. 1951), Kay Medford, Jed Prouty (final film—ret.), Harry Landers, Dennis Harrison, Elliot Sullivan, Garney Wilson, Ray Julian. *D:* Joseph Lerner; *P:* Rex Carlton; *Sc:* Don Ettlinger. (1:31) Melodrama of a cop on the skids, who hits the bottle, until informed by his ex-wife that their son has been kidnapped. Based on the 1947 novel of the same name by Wade Miller, it originally ran on a double bill with *Cry Murder* (q.v.).

1041. Gun Battle at Monterey (Allied Artists/C-B Pictures Corp.; 1957). *Cast:* Sterling Hayden, Pamela Duncan, Ted de Corsia, Mary Beth Hughes, Lee Van Cleef, Charles Cane, Pat Comiskey, Byron Foulger, Mauritz Hugo, I. Stanford Jolley, Michael Vallon, Fred Sherman, George Baxter, John Damler. *D:* Carl K. Hittleman, Sidney A. Franklin, Jr.; *P:* Hittleman; *St:* Frank Fenton, Leonard Resner; *Sc:* Jack Leonard, Lawrence Resner. (1:07) Western revenge tale of a man out to get his former friend who bushwhacked him and left him for dead.

1042. Gun Belt (United Artists/Global Prods.; 1953). *Cast:* George Montgomery, Tab Hunter, Helen Westcott, John Dehner, William Bishop, Douglas Kennedy, Jack Elam, Joe Haworth, Hugh Sanders, Willis Bouchey, James Millican (Wyatt Earp), Bruce Cowling (Virgil Earp), Boyd Stockman, Boyd "Red" Morgan, Chuck Roberson, William Phillips, Jack Carry. *D:* Ray Nazarro; *P:* Edward Small; *St:* Arthur Orloff; *Sc:* Richard Schayer, Jack DeWitt. (1:17) Technicolor western tale of an ex-outlaw attempting to go straight and finds himself framed by his own brother in a bank robbery.

1043. Gun Brothers (United Artists/Grand Prods.; 1956). *Cast:* Buster Crabbe, Neville Brand, Ann Robinson, Lita Milan, James Seay, Michael Ansara, Walter Sande, Roy Barcroft, Slim Pickens, Dorothy Ford. *D:* Sidney Salkow; *P:* uncredited; *St:* Gerald Drayson Adams; *Sc:* Richard Schayer, Adams. (1:19) Western of two brothers—one a rancher, the other an outlaw—who find their relationship tested by the lie of a jealous Indian girl.

1044. Gun Duel in Durango (United Artists/Peerless Prods.; 1957). *Cast:* George Montgomery, Ann Robinson, Steve Brodie, Bobby Clark, Frank Ferguson, Donald Barry, Henry Rowland, Denver Pyle, Mary Treen, Boyd "Red" Morgan, Al Wyatt, Joe Yrigoyen. *D:* Sidney Salkow; *P:* Robert E. Kent; *St: & Sc:* Louis Stevens. (1:13) An outlaw finds his efforts to go straight hampered by several obstacles put in his path. (retitled: *Duel in Durango*)

1045. Gun Fever (United Artists/Jackson-Weston Prods.; 1958). *Cast:* Mark Stevens, John Lupton, Larry Storch, Jana Davi, Aaron Saxon, Jerry Barclay, Norman Frederic, Clegg Hoyt, Jean Innes, Russell Thorsen, Michael Himm, Iron Eyes Cody, Eddie Little, John Goddard, Vic Smith, Robert Stevenson, William Erwin, David Bond, Cyril Delevanti, George Selk [aka: Budd Buster]. *D:* Mark Stevens; *P:* Harry Jackson, Sam Weston; *Co-Producer:* Edward L. Rissien; *St:* Harry S. Franklin, Julius Evans; *Sc:* Stanley H. Silverman, Stevens. (1:21) When their parents are killed by a band of Indians led by a white renegade, two brothers set out on a trail of vengeance.

1046. Gun for a Coward (Universal-International; 1957). *Cast:* Fred MacMurray, Jeffrey Hunter, Dean Stockwell, Janice Rule, Josephine Hutchinson, Chill Wills, Betty Lynn, Iron Eyes Cody, Robert Hoy, Jane Howard, John Larch, Paul Birch, Bob Steele, Frances Morris, Marjorie Stapp. *D:* Abner Biberman; *P:* William Alland; *St: & Sc:* R. Wright Campbell. (1:28) Western drama of three brothers, their relationships with each other and those around them. Eastmancolor and CinemaScope.

1047. Gun Fury (Columbia; 1953). *Cast:* Rock Hudson, Donna Reed, Phil Carey, Roberta Haynes, Lee Marvin, Leo Gordon, Neville Brand, John Cason, Ray Thomas, Forrest Lewis, Robert Herron, Pat Hogan, Phil Rawlins, Mel Welles, Post Park, Don Carlos. *D:* Raoul Walsh; *P:* Lewis J. Rachmil; *Sc:* Irving Wallace, Roy Huggins. (1:23) (video/laserdisc) Hit Technicolor western of a man seeking to retrieve his wife who was kidnapped in a stagecoach holdup. Based on the 1952 writing "Ten Against Caesar" by Kathleen G. George and Robert A. Granger. Originally in 3-D.

1048. Gun Glory (MGM; 1957). *Cast:* Stewart Granger, Rhonda Fleming, Chill Wills, Steve Rowland, James Gregory, Jacques Aubuchon, Arch Johnson, William Fawcett, Carl Pitti, Lane Bradford, Rayford Barnes, Ed Mundy, Gene Coogan, Michael Dugan, Jack Montgomery, Bud Osborne, May McAvoy, Charles Herbert, Steve Widders. *D:* Roy Rowland; *P:* Nicholas Nayfack; *Sc:* William Ludwig. (1:29) (video) A reformed gunman returns to his town, only to get the cold-shoulder from the local residents. When a gun-toting menace begins to terrorize the local citizenry, attitudes toward him begin to change. Based on the 1955 novel *Man of the West* by Philip Yordan, it was photographed in Metrocolor and CinemaScope.

The Gun Runner (G.B. title) *see* **Santiago**

1049. The Gun Runners (United Artists/Seven Arts; 1958). *Cast:* Audie Murphy, Eddie Albert, Patricia Owens, Everett Sloane, Gita Hall, Richard Jaeckel, Paul Birch, Jack Elam, John Harding, Peggy Maley, Carlos Romero, Lita Leon, Edward Colmans, Steven Peck, Ted Jacques, John Qualen, Freddie Roberto. *D:* Don Siegel; *P:* Clarence Green; *Sc:* Paul Monash, Daniel Mainwaring; *Songs:* Joe Lubin. (1:23) Melodrama of arms dealers hiring a fishing boat to take weapons to Cuban rebels. Based on Ernest Hemingway's *To Have and Have Not*, filmed first in 1944 (Warner) and remade as *The Breaking Point* (q.v.). Note: Hemingway's novel was expanded from one of his previously written short stories titled "One Trip Across."

1050. The Gun That Won the West (Columbia/Clover Prods.; 1955). *Cast:* Dennis Morgan, Paula Raymond, Richard Denning, Chris O'Brien, Kenneth MacDonald, Robert Bice, Michael Morgan, Roy Gordon, Howard Wright, Richard H. Cutting, Howard Negley. *D:* William Castle; *P:* Sam Katzman; *St: & Sc:* James B. Gordon. (1:11) Western which revolves around the use of the Springfield rifle against Indians who are disrupting the laying of railroad tracks.

1051. Gun the Man Down (United Artists/Batjac Prods.; 1956). *Cast:* James Arness, Angie Dickinson, Robert Wilke, Emile Meyer, Don Megowan, Michael Emmett, Harry Carey, Jr., Frank Fenton. *D:* Andrew V. McLaglen (directorial debut); *P:* Robert E. Morrison; *St:* Sam C. Freedle; *Sc:* Burt Kennedy. (1:18) Western of a man seeking revenge on his girl and former gang members who abandoned him when he was wounded during a holdup. (retitled: *Arizona Mission*) Originally ran on a double bill with *The Peacemaker* (q.v.).

1052. Gunfight at Dodge City (United Artists/Mirisch Co.; 1959). *Cast:* Joel McCrea (Bat Masterson), Julie Adams, Nancy Gates, John McIntire, Richard Anderson, James Westerfield, Harry Lauter, Don Haggerty, Wright King, Walter Coy, Myron Healey, Mauritz Hugo, Henry Kulky. *D:* Joseph M. Newman; *P:* Walter M. Mirisch; *St:* Daniel B. Ullman; *Sc:* Ullman, Martin M. Goldsmith. (1:21) Bat Masterson gets more than he bargained for when he buys half-interest in a saloon and becomes sheriff of one of the Old West's most infamous cow towns. DeLuxe color and CinemaScope.

1053. Gunfight at the O.K. Corral (Paramount/Wallis-Hazen; 1957). *Cast:* Burt Lancaster (Wyatt Earp), Kirk Douglas (John H. "Doc" Holliday), Rhonda Fleming (Laura Denbow), Jo Van Fleet (["Big Nose"] Kate Fisher), John Ireland (Johnny Ringo), Lyle Bettger (Ike Clanton), Frank Faylen (Cotton Wilson), Earl Holliman (Charles Bassett), Ted de Corsia (Shanghai Pierce), Dennis Hopper (Billy Clanton), Whit Bissell (John P. Clum), George Mathews (John Shanssey), John Hudson (Virgil Earp), DeForest Kelley (Morgan Earp), Martin Milner (James Earp), Kenneth Tobey (Bat Masterson), Harry B. Mendoza (Cockeyed Frank Loving), Charles Herbert (Tommy Earp), Lee Van Cleef (Ed Bailey), Joan Camden (Betty Earp), Olive Carey (Mrs. Clanton), Brian Hutton (Rick), Nelson Leigh (Mayor Kelley), Jack Elam (Tom McLowery), Lee Roberts (Finn Clanton), Mickey Simpson (Frank McLowery), Henry Wills (Alby), William S. Meigs (Wayne), Tony Merrill, Roger Creed, Anthony "Tony" Jochim, James Davies, Joe Forte, Gregg Martell, Dennis Moore, Max Power, Courtland Shepard, Morgan Lane, Paul Gary, Don Castle, Bill Williams, Frank Carter, Edward Ingram, Bing Russell, Dorothy Abbott, Ethan Laidlaw, John Benson, Richard J. Reeves, Frank Hagney, Robert C. Swan, Len Hendry, Trude Wyler, John Maxwell. *D:* John Sturges; *P:* Hal B. Wallis; *As.P:* Paul Nathan; *Sc:* Leon Uris; *Editor:* (AAN) Warren Low; *Sound:* (AAN) George Dutton and the Paramount Sound Dept.; *Title song:* Dimitri Tiomkin, Ned Washington (sung by Frankie Laine). (2:02) (video/laserdisc) Dramatic interpretation about the famous western historical event of lawmen vs. the Clanton gang. A worldwide hit, it became one of the 24 top-grossing films of 1956-57. Suggested by the 1954 article "The Killer" by George Scullin. Technicolor and VistaVision.

1054. The Gunfighter (20th Century-Fox; 1950). *Cast:* Gregory Peck (Jimmy Ringo), Helen Westcott (Peggy Walsh), Millard Mitchell (Sheriff Mark Street), Jean Parker (Molly), Karl Malden (Mac), Skip Homeier (Hunt Bromley), Anthony Ross (Charlie), Verna Felton (Mrs. Pennyfeather), Ellen Corby (Mrs. Devlin), Richard Jaeckel (Eddie), Alan Hale, Jr. (1st brother), John Pickard (3rd brother), David Clarke (2nd brother), B.G. Norman (Jimmie), Angela Clarke (Mac's wife), Cliff Clark (Jerry Marlowe), Alberto Morin (Pablo), Kenneth Tobey (Swede), Michael Branden [aka: Archie Twitchell] (Johnny), Eddie Parks (barber), Ferris Taylor (grocer), Hank Patterson (Jake), Mae Marsh (Mrs. O'Brien), Jean Innes (Alice Marlowe), Eddie Ehrhart (Archie), Kim Spalding (clerk), Credda Zajac (Mrs. Cooper), Anne Whitfield (Carrie Lou), Harry Shannon (bartender), Houseley Stevenson (Barlow), James Millican (Pete), William Vedder (minister), Ed Mundy (loafer). *D:* Henry King; *P:* Nunnally Johnson; *St:* (AAN) William Bowers, Andre De Toth; *Sc:* Bowers, William Sellers, Johnson (unc.). (1:24) (video/laserdisc) Critically acclaimed psychological western-drama of a gunfighter who is trying to live down his notorious past. Remade for TV in 1957 as "End of a Gun" for *The 20th Century-Fox Hour.*

1055. Gunfire (Lippert; 1950). *Cast:* Donald Barry (dual role), Robert Lowery, Wally Vernon, Pamela Blake, Claude Stroud, Leonard

Penn, Gaylord [Steve] Pendleton, Tommy Farrell, Dean Reisner, Paul Jordan, Steve Conte, Robert Anderson, Gil Fallman, Kathleen Maggnetti, Bill [Wm. Norton] Bailey. *D: & P:* William Berke; *St: & Sc:* Victor West, Berke. (0:59) Programmer western of an ex-outlaw accused of a series of robberies.

1056. Gunfire at Indian Gap (Republic/ Ventura Prods.; 1957). *Cast:* Vera Ralston, Anthony George, George Macready, Barry Kelley, John Doucette, George Keymas, Chubby Johnson, Glenn Strange, Dan White, Steve Warren, Chuck Hicks, Sarah Selby. *D:* Joe Kane; *P:* Rudy Ralston; *St: & Sc:* Barry Shipman. (1:10) Western of three outlaws, after gold, at a stagecoach relay station. Naturama.

1057. The Gunman (Monogram/Silvermine Prods.; 1952). *Cast:* Whip Wilson, Fuzzy Knight, Phyllis Coates, Rand Brooks, Terry Frost, Lane Bradford, I. Stanford Jolley, Richard Avonde, Gregg Barton, Russ Whiteman, Robert Bray. *D:* Lewis Collins; *P:* Ben Schwalb; *Sc:* Charles R. Marion. (0:52) Whip Wilson series-western of lawmen vs. lawless men. (aka: *Mr. Hobo*)

1058. Gunman's Walk (Columbia; 1958). *Cast:* Van Heflin, Tab Hunter, Kathryn Grant, James Darren, Mickey Shaughnessy, Robert F. Simon, Edward Platt, Ray Teal, Paul Birch, Michael Granger, Will Wright, Chief Blue Eagle, Bert Convy, Paul E. Burns, Paul Bryar, Everett Glass, Dorothy Adams, Bek Nelson, Willis Bouchey, Ewing Mitchell, Sam Flint. *D:* Phil Karlson; *P:* Fred Kohlmar; *St:* Ric Hardman; *Sc:* Frank Nugent; *Song:* "I'm a Runaway" Fred Karger, Richard Quine (sung by Tab Hunter). (1:37) Western drama of a man raising two sons who have opposing outlooks on life. One is a law-abiding citizen, the other lives by the gun. Technicolor and CinemaScope.

1059. Gunmen from Laredo (Columbia; 1959). *Cast:* Robert Knapp, Jana Davi, Walter Coy, Paul Birch, Don C. Harvey, Clarence Straight, Jerry Barclay, Ron Hayes, X. Brands, Charles Horvath, Jean Moorhead, Harry Antrim. *D: & P:* Wallace MacDonald; *St: & Sc:* Clarke E. Reynolds. (1:07) Programmer western of a man who escapes from jail to find the man who committed the murder he was doing time for. Columbia color.

1060. Gunmen of Abilene (Republic; 1950). *Cast:* Allan Lane, Eddy Waller, Donna Hamilton, Roy Barcroft, Peter Brocco, Selmer Jackson, Duncan Richardson, Arthur Walsh, Don C. Harvey, Don Dillaway, George Chesebro, Steve Clark, Black Jack (horse). *D:* Fred C. Brannon; *As.P:* Gordon Kay; *St: & Sc:* M. Coates Webster. (1:00) "Rocky Lane" series western of an undercover deputy marshal out to thwart gold thieves.

1061. Gunplay (RKO; 1951). *Cast:* Tim Holt, Richard Martin, Joan Dixon, Harper Carter, Robert Bice, Marshall Reed, Jack Hill, Leo McMahon, Robert Wilke, Cornelius O'Keefe. *D:* Lesley Selander; *P:* Herman Schlom; *St: & Sc:* Ed Earl Repp. (1:00) (video) Tim Holt series-western of two cowpokes out to find the men who killed a small boy's father.

Gunpoint (G.B. title) *see* **At Gunpoint**

1062. Guns Don't Argue! (Visual Drama, Inc., in association with Terry Turner; 1957). *Cast:* Myron Healey (John Dillinger), Jean Harvey (Ma Barker), Paul Dubov (Alvin Karpis), Sam Edwards (Fred Barker), Tamar Cooper (Bonnie Parker), Baynes Barron (Clyde Barrow), Richard Crane (Homer Van Meter), Douglas Wilson (Pretty Boy Floyd), Jim Davis, Lyle Talbot, Sydney Mason, Lash LaRue, Jeanne Carmen, Ann Morriss, Aline Towne, Regina Gleason, Ralph Moody, Jeanne Bates, Hellen Van Tuyl, Knobby Schaeffer, Russell Whitney, Robert Kendall, Coulter Irwin, Sam Flint, Bill Baldwin. *D:* Bill Karn, Richard C. Kahn; *P:* William J. Faris; *Sc:* unc. (1:29) Unintentionally hilarious dialogue prevails in this obscure rendering of the F.B.I.'s attempts to bring to justice the likes of John Dillinger, Ma Barker, Alvin Karpis, Bonnie and Clyde, Baby Face Nelson, Homer Van Meter and Pretty Boy Floyd. A historically inaccurate melodrama with abundant anachronisms places this in the "so bad it's good" category.

1063. Guns, Girls and Gangsters (United Artists/Imperial Pictures; 1958). *Cast:* Mamie Van Doren, Gerald Mohr, Lee Van Cleef, Grant Richards, Elaine Edwards, John Baer, Carlo Fiore, Paul Fix, W. Beal Wong. *D:* Edward L. Cahn; *P: & Sc:* Robert E. Kent; *St:* Paul Gangelin, Jerry Sackheim. (1:10) Heist melodrama of a Las Vegas nightclub singer and two hoods who plan to rob an armored truck transporting casino loot from Vegas to Los Angeles.

1064. The Guns of Fort Petticoat (Columbia/Brown-Murphy Pictures, Inc.; 1957).

Cast: Audie Murphy, Kathryn Grant, Hope Emerson, Sean McClory, James Griffith, Jeff Donnell, Jeanette Nolan, Madge Meredith, Ernestine Wade, Ray Teal, Nestor Paiva, Charles Horvath, Peggy Maley, Isobel Elsom, Patricia Livingston, Kim Charney, Dorothy Crider, Ainslie Pryor. *D:* George Marshall; *P:* Harry Joe Brown; *Sc:* Walter Doniger. (1:22) (video) Offbeat western of a deserting cavalry officer who rallies a group of Texas frontier women to defend themselves against marauding Indians. Based on the short story "Petticoat Brigade" by C. William Harrison. Technicolor.

Guns of Justice (TV title) *see* **Colorado Ranger**

1065. Gunsight Ridge (United Artists/ Libra Prods.; 1957). *Cast:* Joel McCrea, Mark Stevens, Joan Weldon, Darlene Fields, Addison Richards, Carolyn Craig, Robert Griffin, Slim Pickens, I. Stanford Jolley, George Chandler, Herbert Vigran, Jody McCrea, Martin Garralaga, Cindy Robbins. *D:* Francis D. Lyon; *P:* Robert Bassler; *Sc:* Talbot & Elizabeth Jennings; *Song:* "The Ballad of Gunsight Ridge" David Raksin. (1:25) Western of a Wells Fargo agent sent to investigate a series of stagecoach holdups. Originally ran on a double bill with *Enemy from Space*, a British production.

1066. Gunslinger (American Releasing Corp./Santa Clara Prods.; 1956). *Cast:* John Ireland, Beverly Garland, Allison Hayes, Martin Kingsley, Jonathan Haze, Chris Alcaide, Dick Miller, Bruno Ve Sota, William Schallert, Margaret Campbell, Aaron Saxon, Chris Miller. *D: & P:* Roger Corman; *St: & Sc:* Mark Hanna, Charles B. Griffith. (1:23) (video) Offbeat western of a woman who takes over the job as town marshal when her husband is killed in the line of duty, and soon finds herself the target of a crooked saloon keeper. Note: For Roger Corman aficionados, this one was filmed in six days.

1067. Gunslingers (Monogram; 1950). *Cast:* Whip Wilson, Andy Clyde, Reno Browne [aka: Reno Blair], Dennis Moore, Riley Hill, Sarah Padden, Hank Bell, Bill Kennedy, Steve Clark, George Chesebro, Carl Mathews, Frank McCarroll, Reed Howes, Carol Henry, George DeNormand, Frank Ellis, Ray Jones. *D: & P:* Wallace Fox; *St: & Sc:* Adele Buffington. (0:55) Whip Wilson programmer western of a man wrongfully accused of cattle rustling.

1068. Gunsmoke (Universal-International; 1953). *Cast:* Audie Murphy, Susan Cabot, Paul Kelly, Charles Drake, Mary Castle, Donald Randolph, Jack Kelly, Jesse White, William Reynolds, Chubby Johnson, Edmund Cobb, Clem Fuller. *D:* Nathan Juran; *P:* Aaron Rosenberg; *Sc:* D.D. Beauchamp; *Songs:* "See What the Boys in the Backroom Will Have" Frederick Hollander, Frank Loesser; "True Love" Frederic Herbert, Arnold Hughes. (1:18) Western of a hired gun looking for a job in Montana. Based on the novel *Roughshod* by Norman A. Fox.

1069. Gunsmoke In Tucson (Allied Artists; 1958). *Cast:* Mark Stevens, Forrest Tucker, Gale Robbins (final film until 1972), Vaughn Taylor, John Ward, Kevin Hagen, Bill Henry, Richard Reeves, John Cliff, Gail Kobe, George Keymas, Zon Murray, Paul Engel, Anthony Sydes. *D:* Thomas Carr; *Ex.P:* Herbert Kaufman; *P:* William D. Coates; *As.P:* Robert Joseph, Herbert Rolsten; *St: & Sc:* Paul Leslie Peil, Joseph; *Song:* "I Need A Man" Bebe Blake, Jack Hoffman, Emil Cadkin (sung by Robbins). (1:20) Western melodrama of a range feud which sparks a confrontation between a lawman and his outlaw brother. Based on the novel *Tucson* by Mr. Peil, it was filmed on location in Arizona. DeLuxe color and CinemaScope.

Gunsmoke Range *see* **Montana Incident**

1070. The Guy Who Came Back (20th Century–Fox; 1951). *Cast:* Paul Douglas, Joan Bennett, Linda Darnell, Don DeFore, Billy Gray, Zero Mostel, Edmon Ryan, Ruth McDevitt, Walter Burke, Henry Kulky, Dick Ryan, Robert B. Williams, Ted Pearson, Mack Williams, Garnett Marks, Shirley Tegge, Charles Conrad, Grandon Rhodes, John H. Hamilton, John Close, Tom Hanlon, Harry Seymour, Lillian West, Jack Davis, J. Anthony Hughes, Rodney Bell, John Smith, Warren Farlow, Wayne Farlow, Donald Gordon, Whitey Haupt, Tommie Menzies, Pat Mitchell, Thomas Browne Henry, Emile Meyer, Harry Harvey, Hal Baylor, Mike Marienthal, Gale Pace, Stanley Pinto, Robert Foulk. *D:* Joseph Newman; *P:* Julian Blaustein; *Sc:* Allan Scott; *Song:* "Keep Your Eye on the Ball" Ken Darby. (1:31) Drama of a pro football player trying to deal with the fact that he is past his prime for the sport, and how this affects his marriage. Based on the *Saturday Evening Post* story "The Man Who Sank the Navy" by William Fay.

1071. Guys and Dolls (MGM/Samuel Goldwyn Prods., Inc.; 1955). *Cast:* Marlon Brando

(Sky Masterson), Jean Simmons (Sarah Brown), Frank Sinatra (Nathan Detroit), Vivian Blaine (repeating her stage role/Miss Adelaide), Robert Keith (Lt. Brannigan), Stubby Kaye (repeating his stage role/Nicely Nicely Johnson), B.S. Pully (repeating his stage role/Big Jule), Johnny Silver (repeating his stage role/Benny Southstreet), Sheldon Leonard (Harry the Horse), Danny Dayton (Rusty Charlie), George E. Stone (Society Max), Regis Toomey (Arvid Abernathy), Kathryn Givney (General Cartwright), Veda Ann Borg (Laverne), Mary Alan Hokanson (Agatha), Joe McTurk (Angie the Ox), Kay Kuter (Calvin), Johnny Indrisano (Liverlips Louie), Stapleton Kent, Renee Renor, Matt Murphy, Harry Wilson, Earle Hodgins, Harry Tyler, Major Sam Harris, Franklyn Farnum, Frank Richards, Julian Rivero, *and Goldwyn Girls*: Larri Thomas, Jann Darlyn, June Kirby, Madelyn Darrow, Barbara Brent. *D: & Sc:* Joseph L. Mankiewicz; *P:* Samuel Goldwyn; *Cin:* (AAN) Harry Stradling; *ASD:* (AAN) Oliver Smith, Joseph C. Wright (art directors), Howard Bristol (sets); *Music:* (AAN) Jay Blackton, Cyril Mockridge; *Costumes:* (AAN) Irene Sharaff; *Choreography:* Michael Kidd; *Songs:* "Fugue for Tinhorns," "Follow the Fold," "The Oldest Established (Permanent Floating Crap Game in New York)," "I'll Know," "Adelaide's Lament," Title song, "If I Were a Bell," "Take Back Your Mink," "Luck Be a Lady," "Sit Down, You're Rockin' the Boat," "Sue Me" (film only), "Pet Me, Papa" (film only), and "A Woman in Love" (film only) Frank Loesser. (2:30) (video/laserdisc) Hit filming of the Broadway musical smash of 1950 by Jo Swerling and Abe Burrows, based on a story by Damon Runyon. One of the 24 top-grossing films of 1955-56, it was also in nomination at the British Academy Awards.

1072. Gypsy Colt (MGM; 1954). *Cast:* Donna Corcoran, Ward Bond, Frances Dee (final film—ret.), Larry Keating, Lee Van Cleef, Bobby Hyatt, Nacho Galindo, Rodolfo Hoyos, Jr., Bobby Dominguez, Joe Dominguez, Jester Hairston, Peggy Maley, Gypsy (horse—received 1st Place PATSY Award in 1955). *D:* Andrew Marton; *P:* William Grady, Jr., Sid Franklin; *Sc:* Martin Berkeley. (1:12) (video) Horse replaced dog in this remake of *Lassie Come Home*, based on the 1940 book by Eric Knight. A family in dire financial straits sells their daughter's horse to a racing stable. Anscocolor.

1073. H.M.S. Pinafore (Hoffberg; 1950). An independent filmed record of Gilbert and Sullivan's 1878 satirical operetta as performed by the California Opera Co. (1:10)

1074. Half a Hero (MGM; 1953). *Cast:* Red Skelton, Jean Hagen, Charles Dingle, Hugh Corcoran, Willard Waterman, Mary Wickes, Dorothy Patrick, Polly Bergen, Frank Cady, King Donovan, Billie Bird, Dabbs Greer, Kathleen Freeman. *D:* Don Weis; *P:* Matthew Rapf; *St: & Sc:* Max Shulman. (1:11) Programmer comedy of a New York writer who moves his family to the suburbs to get firsthand data, finding he is married to a "keep up with Joneses" type.

1075. Half Angel (20th Century–Fox; 1951). *Cast:* Loretta Young, Joseph Cotten, Cecil Kellaway, Basil Ruysdael, Jim Backus, Irene Ryan, John Ridgely, Therese Lyon, Mary George, Mary Tarosi, Gale Pace, Steve Pritko, Edwin Max, Art Smith, Jack Davidson, Roger Laswell, William Johnstone, Harris Brown, Herbert Vigran, Freeman Lusk, Lou Nova, Luther Crockett, Junius Matthews. *D:* Richard Sale; *P:* Julian Blaustein; *St:* George Carleton Brown; *Sc:* Robert Riskin; *Song:* "My Castle in the Sand" Alfred Newman, Ralph Blane. (1:17) Comedy of a woman with a split personality, neither aware of the other and each personality getting involved with a different man. Technicolor.

1076. The Half-Breed (RKO; 1952). *Cast:* Robert Young, Janis Carter (final film—ret.), Jack Beutel, Barton MacLane, Reed Hadley, Porter Hall, Connie Gilchrist, Sammy White, Damian O'Flynn, Frank Wilcox, Charles Delaney, Tom Monroe, Judy Walsh, Lee MacGregor, Coleen Calder, Marietta Elliott, Jeane Cochran, Betty Leonard, Shirley Whitney, Mary Menzies, Shelah Hackett. *D:* Stuart Gilmore; *P:* Herman Schlom; *St:* Robert Hardy, Andrews; *Sc:* Harold Shumate, Richard Wormser; *Additional dialogue:* Charles Hoffman. (1:21) (video) Western of profiteers who take advantage of a half-breed and incite him into leading his Indian tribe against whites. Technicolor.

1077. The Halliday Brand (United Artists/Collier Young Assoc.; 1957). *Cast:* Joseph Cotten, Viveca Lindfors, Betsy Blair, Ward Bond, Bill Williams, Jay C. Flippen, Christopher Dark, Jeanette Nolan, John Dierkes, Glenn Strange, I. Stanford Jolley, John Ayres, Robin Short, Jay Lawrence, George Lynn, John Halloran, Michael Hinn. *D:* Joseph H. Lewis; *P:* Collier Young; *St: & Sc:* George W. George, George F. Slavin. (1:17) Western drama of a wealthy rancher (also the town sheriff) who has a falling-out with family members, after allowing the lynching of a half-breed who had been courting his daughter.

1078. Halls of Montezuma (20th Century–Fox; 1950). *Cast:* Richard Widmark (Lt. Anderson), Walter [Jack] Palance (Pigeon Lane), Reginald Gardiner (Sgt. Johnson), Robert Wagner (Coffman), Karl Malden (Doc), Richard Hylton (Cpl. Conroy), Richard Boone (film debut/Lt. Col. Gilfilan), Skip Homeier (Pretty Boy), Don Hicks (Lt. Butterfield), Jack Webb (Correspondent Dickerman), Bert Freed (Slattery), Neville Brand (Sgt. Zelenko), Martin Milner (Pvt. Whitney), Philip Ahn (Nomura), Howard Chuman (Capt. Makino), Frank Kumagai (Romeo), Fred Coby (Capt. McCreavy), Paul Lees (Capt. Seaman), Chris Drake (Frank), William Hawes (Paskowicz), Roger McGee (Davis), Helen Hatch (Aunt Emma), Rollin Moriyama (Fukado), Ralph Nagai (Willie), Richard Allan (Pvt. Stewart), Jack Lee, Fred Dale, George Conrad, Harry McKim, Mob McLean, Clarke Stevens, Michael Road, Marion Marshall, Harry Carter. *D:* Lewis Milestone; *P:* Robert Bassler; *St: & Sc:* Michael Blankfort. (1:53) (video) World War II drama about a company of marines in the Pacific who are assigned the task of destroying Japanese rockets and taking prisoners, only they encounter a crafty enemy who begins to decimate their number. One of the 23 top-grossing films of 1950-51. Technicolor.

1079. Handle with Care (MGM; 1958). *Cast:* Dean Jones (starring debut), Joan O'Brien, Thomas Mitchell, John Smith, Burt Douglas, Walter Abel, Royal Dano, Anne Seymour, Ted de Corsia, Peter Miller. *D:* David Friedkin; *P:* Morton Fine; *St:* Samuel and Edith Grafton; *Sc:* Friedkin, Fine. (1:22) Low budget melodrama of a law student investigating suspected government corruption in a small town. This one originally ran as a second feature on a double bill with *High School Confidential* (q.v.).

1080. The Hanging Tree (Warner/Baroda Prods., Inc.; 1959). *Cast:* Gary Cooper (Doc Joe Trail), Maria Schell (Elizabeth Mahler), Karl Malden (Frenchy Plante), George C. Scott (film debut/Grubb), Karl Swenson (Mr. Flaunce), Virginia Gregg (Mrs. Flaunce), John Dierkes (Society Red), King Donovan (Wonder), Ben Piazza (Rune), Slim Talbot, Bud Osborne, Guy Wilkerson, Annette Claudier, Clarence Straight. *D:* Delmer Daves; *P:* Martin Jurow, Richard Shepherd; *Sc:* Wendell Mayes, Halsted Welles; *Title song:* (AAN) Jerry Livingston, Mack David (sung by Marty Robbins). (1:46) (video) Offbeat western set during the gold rush of a Swiss immigrant who has her sight restored by a frontier doctor with a troubled past. Based on the 1957 novel by Dorothy B. Johnson. Technicolor.

1081. The Hangman (Paramount; 1959). *Cast:* Robert Taylor, Tina Louise, Fess Parker, Jack Lord, Mickey Shaugnessy, Shirley Harmer, Gene Evans, Mabel Albertson, James Westerfield, Lucille Curtis. *D:* Michael Curtiz; *P:* Frank Freeman, Jr.; *St:* Luke Short; *Sc:* Dudley Nichols. (1:26) Offbeat western of a deputy sheriff who tracks a wanted fugitive to a town, only to find the entire town is protecting the man.

1082. Hangman's Knot (Columbia/Producers Actors Corp.; 1952). *Cast:* Randolph Scott, Donna Reed, Claude Jarman, Jr., Frank Faylen, Glenn Langan, Richard Denning, Lee Marvin, Jeanette Nolan, Ray Teal, Monte Blue, Guinn Williams, Reed Howes, Clem Bevans, John Call, Edward Earle, Post Park, Frank Hagney, Frank Yaconelli. *D:* Roy Huggins (only film as director); *P:* Harry Joe Brown; *St: & Sc:* Huggins. (1:21) (video) Western drama of Confederate soldiers who rob a Union gold shipment and later learn the Civil War had ended prior to the theft. Originally ran on a double bill with *Blue Canadian Rockies* (q.v.). Technicolor.

The Hangover *see* **Female Jungle**

1083. Hannah Lee (Realart; 1953). *Cast:* Macdonald Carey, Joanne Dru, John Ireland, Don Haggerty, Peter Ireland, Stuart Randall, Frank Ferguson, Ralph Dumke, Tom Powers, Tristram Coffin, Norman Leavitt, Alex Pope, Harold Kennedy, Kay Riehl, Ruth Whitney, Dean Cromer, Paul Keast, Robin Morse, Joe McGuinn, Bill Hale, Dick Fortune, Alex Frazer, Mort Mills, Ferris Taylor, Helen Servis, Ann Loos, Crane Whitley, Charles Keane. *D:* John Ireland, Lee Garmes; *P:* Jack Broder; *Sc:* MacKinlay Kantor, Rip Van Ronkle. (1:18) Low budget western of ruthless cattlemen who hire an equally ruthless gunman to clear the land of homesteaders, but meet opposition from the local sheriff and a lady saloon keeper. Based on Mr. Kantor's novel *Wicked Waster*, it was photographed in 3-D and Pathécolor. (retitled: *Outlaw Territory*)

1084. Hans Christian Andersen (RKO/Sam Goldwyn Prods.; 1952). *Cast:* Danny Kaye (title role), Farley Granger (Niels), Jeanmaire (Doro), Joey Walsh (Peter), Philip Tonge (Otto), Jeanne Lafayette (Celine), Peter Votrian (Lars), Erik Bruhn, Roland Petit (who also choreographed), John Brown, John Qualen, Robert Malcolm, George Chandler, Fred Kelsey, Gil Perkins. *D:* Charles Vidor; *P:* Samuel Goldwyn; *St:* Myles Connolly; *Sc:* Moss Hart; *Cin:* (AAN-color) Harry Stradling; *ASD:* (AAN-color) Richard Day, Clave (art directors), Howard Bristol (sets); *Music:* (AAN) Walter Scharf; *Costumes:* (AAN-color) Clave, Mary Wills, Madame Karinska; *Sound:* (AAN) Gordon Sawyer; *Songs:* "Thumbelina" (AAN-Best song), "Ugly Duckling," "Inch Worm," "I'm Hans Christian Andersen," "No Two People," "Wonderful, Wonderful Copenhagen," "Anywhere I Wander" and "The King's New Clothes" all by Frank Loesser. (2:00) (video/laserdisc) Fictionalized musical biography of the vagabond teller of childrens' stories. Lavishly produced, it was in nomination by the New York Film Critics as "Best Picture," as well as becoming one of the 26 top-grossing films of 1952-53. Technicolor.

1085. Hansel and Gretel (RKO/Michael Meyerberg-Hansel and Gretel Co.; 1954). Voices: Anna Russell, Mildred Dunnock, Frank Rogier, Delbert Anderson, Helen Boatwright, Constance Brigham, Apollo Boys Choir. *D:* John Paul; *P:* Michael Meyerberg; *Sc:* Padraic Colum. (1:12) (video/laserdisc) The Brothers Grimm (Jacob and Wilhelm K.) early–19th century fairy tale of two children who outwit a wicked witch bent on having them for supper. Based on the play by Adelheid Wette and scored with the opera music of Engelbert Humperdinck, the story is told with electronically controlled puppets called Kinemins, which received a special award from the NBR for "development of a new method for moving puppets." In Technicolor, it also received other minor awards and nominations.

1086. Happy Anniversary (United Artists/Fields; 1959). *Cast:* David Niven, Mitzi Gaynor, Carl Reiner (film debut), Loring Smith, Monique Van Vooren, Phyllis Povah (reprising her stage role), Elizabeth Wilson, Patty Duke, Kevin Coughlin. *D:* David Miller; *P:* Ralph Fields; *Sc:* Joseph Fields, Jerome Chodorov; *Songs:* Title song, "I Don't Regret a Thing" Robert Allen, Al Stillman. (1:21) Domestic comedy of a married couple, celebrating their 13th anniversary, who find their daughter on a TV show spilling the beans about her father's pre-marital indiscretions. Based on the hit 1954 Broadway play *Anniversary Waltz* by screenwriters Fields and Chodorov.

1087. The Happy Road (MGM/Kerry Prods.; 1957). *Cast:* Gene Kelly, Barbara Laage, Michael Redgrave, Bobby Clark, Brigitte Fossey (U.S. debut), Roger Treville, Colette Dereal, Jess Hahn, Maryse Martin, Roger Saget, Van Doude, Claire Gerard, Colin Mann, Alexandre Rignault, T. Bartlett, J. Dufilo. *D: & P:* Gene Kelly; *St:* Arthur Julien, Harry Kurnitz; *Sc:* Joseph Morheim, Julien, Kurnitz; *Title song:* George Van Parys (sung by Maurice Chevalier). (1:20) Family style comedy-drama of an American father and a French mother joining forces to find their offspring who have run away from school. Filmed on location in France.

1088. The Happy Time (Columbia/Stanley Kramer Co.; 1952). *Cast:* Charles Boyer, Louis Jourdan, Marsha Hunt, Kurt Kasznar, Linda Christian, Bobby Driscoll, Marcel Dalio, Jeanette Nolan, Jack Raine, Richard Erdman, Marlene Cameron, Will Wright, Eugene Borden, Gene Collins, Ann Faber, Kathryn Sheldon, Maurice Marsac. *D:* Richard Fleischer; *P:* Stanley Kramer; *Sc:* Earl Felton. (1:34) Comedy of everyday life in a family of French-Canadians. Set in the 1920s, it was based on the play *Happy Time* by Samuel Taylor and the book by Robert L. Fontaine.

1089. The Happy Years (MGM; 1950). *Cast:* Dean Stockwell, Darryl Hickman, Scotty Beckett, Leon Ames, Margalo Gillmore, Leo G. Carroll, Robert Wagner (film debut), Donn Gift, Peter Thompson, Jerry Mikelsen, Alan Dinehart III, David Bair, Danny Mummert, Eddie LeRoy, George Chandler, Claudia Barrett. *D:* William A. Wellman; *P:* Carey Wilson; *Sc:* Harry Ruskin. (1:50) Comedy of life at a turn-of-the-century prep school and one juvenile's difficulty adapting to the program. Based on the "Lawrenceville School Stories" by Owen Johnson that appeared in *Saturday Evening Post*. Moderately successful nostalgia for the box office. Technicolor.

1090. Harbor of Missing Men (Republic; 1950). *Cast:* Richard Denning, Barbara Fuller, Steven Geray, Aline Towne, Percy Helton, George Zucco, Paul Marion, Ray Teal, Robert Osterloh, Fernanda Eliscu, Gregory Gay, Jimmie Kelly, Barbara Stanley, Neyle Morrow, Charles LaTorre. *D:* R.G. Springsteen; *As.P:* Sidney Picker; *St: & Sc:* John K. Butler. (1:00)

Crime melodrama of a fishing boat owner who smuggles on the side. When some money is stolen from him, he is targeted for death by his crime boss.

1091. Hard, Fast and Beautiful (RKO/ Filmakers; 1951). *Cast:* Claire Trevor, Sally Forrest, Carleton G. Young, Robert Clarke, Kenneth Patterson, Marcella Cisney, Joseph Kearns, William Hudson, George Fisher, Arthur Little, Jr., Bert Whitley, Edwin Reimers, Don Kent, William Irving, Barbara Brier, Marilyn Mercer, Robert Ryan (cameo), Ida Lupino (cameo). *D:* Ida Lupino; *P:* Collier Young; *Sc:* Martha Wilkerson. (1:19) Drama of a tennis player who slowly becomes aware that her mother has been manipulating every facet of her life. Based on the 1930 novel *American Girl* by John R. Tunis.

1092. The Hard Man (Columbia/Romson Prods.; 1957). *Cast:* Guy Madison, Valerie French, Lorne Greene, Barry Atwater, Trevor Bardette, Myron Healey, Robert Burton, Rudy Bond, Renata Vanni, Rickie Sorenson, Frank Richards, Robert B. Williams. *D:* George Sherman; *P:* Helen Ainsworth; *Sc:* Leo Katcher (based on his 1957 book). (1:20) In this Technicolor western, the new deputy sheriff falls for the wife of a rancher who is involved in a range war.

1093. The Harder They Fall (Columbia; 1956). *Cast:* Humphrey Bogart (final film—d. 1957/Eddie Willis), Rod Steiger (Nick Benko), Jan Sterling (Beth Willis), Mike Lane (Toro Moreno), Max Baer (Buddy Brannen), Jersey Joe Walcott (George), Edward Andrews (Jim Weyerhause), Harold J. Stone (Art Leavitt), Carlos Montalban (Luis Agrandi), Felice Orlandi (Vince Fawcett), Nehemiah Persoff (Leo), Herbie Faye (Max), Rusty Lane (Danny McKeogh), Jack Albertson (Pop), Abel Fernandez (Chief Firebird), Tommy Herman (Tommy), Vinnie De Carlo (Joey), Pat Comiskey (Gus Dundee), Marian Carr (Alice), Matt Murphy (Sailor Rigazzo), Tina Carver (Mrs. Banks), Val Avery (film debut/ Frank), Lillian Carver (Mrs. Hardin), Richard Norris, Don Kohler, Ralph Gamble, Charles Tannen, Mark Scott, Russ Whiteman, J. Lewis Smith, Everett Glass, William Roerick, Jack Daly, Mort Mills, Stafford Repp, Sandy Sanders, Emily Belser, Joe Herrera, Diane Mumby, Elaine Edwards, Anthony Blankley, Penny Carpenter, Pan Dane, Joe Greb. *D:* Mark Robson; *P: & Sc:* Philip Yordan; *Cin:* (AAN-b/w) Burnett Guffey. (1:49) (video) Acclaimed drama of a sportswriter who exposes corruption in the fight game. Based on the 1947 book by Budd Schulberg, it was in nomination at the Cannes Film Festival.

1094. Harem Girl (Columbia; 1952). *Cast:* Joan Davis (final film before moving to TV in her series *I Married Joan*), Peggie Castle, Arthur Blake, Paul Marion, Henry Brandon, Donald Randolph, Minerva Urecal, Peter Mamakos, John Dehner, Peter Brocco, Wilson Miller, Russ Conklin, Guy Teague, Alan Foster, Ric Roman, Nick Thompson, Robert Tafur, Peter Virgo, Shepard Menken, George Khoury, Pat Walter, Vivian Mason, Helen Reichmann. *D: & St:* Edward Bernds; *P:* Wallace MacDonald; *Sc:* Bernds, Elwood Ullman. (1:10) Slapstick comedy of a secretary who poses as her boss, a princess, when a murder plot is discovered. The 2nd feature on a double bill with *Storm Over Tibet* (q.v.).

1095. Harlem Follies (Classic Pictures-Herald Pictures; 1950). *Cast:* Savannah Churchill, Sheila Guyse, John Kirby and Band, Laveda Carter, Anna Cornell, Deek Watson & the Brown Dots, Sid Catlett's Band, Juanita Hall, Stepin Fetchit, Slam Stewart Trio, Paterson and Jackson, Rubel Blakey, Basil Spears, Leonard and Zolo, Apus and Estallita, Al Young and Norma Shepard. A musical-comedy revue designed for all-black audiences.

1096. Harlem Globetrotters (Columbia/ Sidney Buchman Enterprises; 1951). *Cast:* Thomas Gomez, Dorothy Dandridge, Bill Walker, Angela Clarke, Peter Thompson, Steve Roberts, Peter Virgo, Ray Walker, Angela Clarke, Peter Thompson, Steve Roberts, Peter Virgo, Ray Walker, Al Eben, Ann E. Allen, William Forrest, Tom Greenway *and Harlem Globetrotters*: Billy Brown, Roscoe Cumberland, William "Pop" Gates, Marques Haynes, Louis "Babe" Pressley, Ermer Robinson, Ted Strong, Reese "Goose" Tatum, Frank Washington, Clarence Wilson, Inman Jackson. *D:* Phil Brown, Will Jason (basketball sequences only); *P:* Buddy Adler, Alfred Palca; *Sc:* Palca. (1:15) Low budget drama centered around the famous comedic basketball wizards and their manager, Abe Saperstein. Originally ran on a double bill with *The Family Secret* (q.v.).

1097. Harlem Hotshots (1953). *Cast:* Lionel Hampton, Dizzy Gillespie, Ruth Brown, Big Joe Turner, Bill Bailey. (0:50) (video) A concert of various rhythm & blues and jazz performers.

1098. Harlem Jazz Festival (1955). *Cast:* Lionel Hampton & Orchestra, Quincy Jones, Sarah Vaughan, The Count Basie Septet (performing "I Cried For You"), Dinah Washington (singing "My Lean Baby"), and Nat "King" Cole (singing "For Sentimental Reasons"). *D:* Joseph Kohn. (0:51) A musical revue in 16 mm; designed for the all black audience.

Harlem Rock 'n' Roll (G.B. title) *see* **Rock 'n' Roll Revue**

1099. Harriet Craig (Columbia; 1950). *Cast:* Joan Crawford (title role), Wendell Corey, Lucile Watson, Allyn Joslyn, William Bishop, K.T. Stevens, Raymond Greenleaf, Ellen Corby, Virginia Brissac, Douglas Wood, Mira McKinney, Fiona O'Shiel, Patric Mitchell, Kathryn Card, Al Murphy, Susanne Rosser. *D:* Vincent Sherman; *P:* William Dozier; *Sc:* Anne Froelick, James Gunn. (1:34) Drama, based on the 1925 Pulitzer Prize–winning play by George Edward Kelly, of a woman who is more concerned with her possessions than her family. A remake of *Craig's Wife*, the original title of the play, first filmed by Pathé as a 1928 silent and again by Columbia in 1936.

1100. Harvey (Universal-International; 1950). *Cast:* James Stewart (AAN/Elwood P. Dowd), Josephine Hull (AA-BSA/repeating her stage role—Veta Louise Simmons), Peggy Dow (Miss Kelly), Charles Drake (Dr. Sanderson), Cecil Kellaway (Dr. Chumley), Victoria Horne (repeating her stage role/Myrtle Mae), Jesse White (film debut—repeating his stage role/Wilson), William Lynn (Judge Gaffney), Wallace Ford (Lofgren), Nana Bryant (Mrs. Chumley), Grace Mills (Mrs. Chauvenet), Clem Bevans (Herman), Ida Moore (Mrs. McGiff), Richard [Dick] Wessel (Cracker), Maudie Prickett (Elvira), Grayce Hampton (Mrs. Strickleberger), Minerva Urecal (Nurse Dunphy), Ruthelma Stevens (Miss LaFay), Almira Sessions (Mrs. Halsey), Eula Guy (Mrs. Johnson), Sam Wolfe (Minninger), Polly Bailey (Mrs. Krausmeyer), Harry Hines (Meegles), Aileen Carlyle (Mrs. Tewksbury), Sally Corner (Mrs. Cummings), Pat Flaherty, Norman Leavitt, Ed Max, Anne O'Neal, William Val, Gino Corrado, Don Brodie. *D:* Henry Koster; *P:* John Beck; *Adaptation & Sc:* Mary C. Chase, Oscar Brodney. (1:44) (video/laserdisc) Critically acclaimed classic-comedy of an inebriate and his constant companion, a 6' 3" invisible white rabbit (Lepus Pooka) named Harvey. Based on the 1949 Pulitzer Prize–winning Broadway success by Ms. Chase, this laugh riot became one of the 23 top-grossing films of 1950-51. Remade in 1997 as a TV movie.

1101. Has Anybody Seen My Gal? (Universal-International; 1952). *Cast:* Piper Laurie, Rock Hudson, Charles Coburn, Lynn Bari, Gigi Perreau, William Reynolds, Larry Gates, Skip Homeier, Paul Harvey, Gloria Holden, James Dean, Frank Ferguson, Forrest Lewis, Fred Nurney, Sally Creighton, Helen Wallace, Willard Waterman, Fritz Feld, Emory Parnell, Charles Flynn, Barney Phillips, William Fawcett, Edna Holland, Leon Tyler, Charles Williams, Paul Bryar, Joey Ray, Sam Pierce, Harmon Stevens, Lyn Wilde, Donna Leary, Spec O'Donnell, Larry Carr, Earl Spainard, Eric Alden. *D:* Douglas Sirk; *P:* Ted Richmond; *St:* Eleanor H. Porter; *Sc:* Joseph Hoffman; *Songs:* "Gimme a Little Kiss, Will Ya Huh?" (Roy Smith–Roy Turk–Maceo Pinkard); "It Ain't Gonna Rain No More" (Wendell Hall); "Tiger Rag" (Jelly Roll Morton), "When the Red, Red Robin (Comes Bob-Bob-Bobbin' Along)" (Harry Woods) and "Five Foot Two, Eyes of Blue." (1:28) Nostalgic 1920s comedy—with musical interludes—of a man who wishes to leave an inheritance to the surviving family of the girl he loved many years before, but who rejected his proposal of marriage. Technicolor.

1102. A Hatful of Rain (20th Century-Fox; 1957). *Cast:* Anthony Franciosa (AAN + "Best Actor" at the Venice Film Festival, repeating his stage role/Polo), Eva Marie Saint (Celia Pope), Don Murray (Johnny Pope), Lloyd Nolan (John Pope, Sr.), Henry Silva (Mother), Gerald O'Loughlin (Chuck), William Hickey (Apples). *D:* Fred Zinneman; *P:* Buddy Adler; *Sc:* Michael V. Gazzo, Alfred Hayes. (1:49) Drama in wide-screen CinemaScope of a married father-to-be and his drug addiction. Based on the 1955 play by Mr. Gazzo, it received the "Italian Critic's Prize" at the Venice Film Festival and was in nomination for "Best Picture" with the New York Film Critics. The *New York Times* and *Film Daily* both placed it at #5 on their "10 Best" lists, while the NBR placed it at #9 on theirs.

1103. Havana Rose (Republic; 1951). *Cast:* Estelita Rodriguez, Bill Williams, Hugh Herbert (final film—d. 1952), Florence Bates, Fortunio Bonanova, Leon Belasco, Nacho Galindo, Martin Garralaga, Rosa Turich, Tom Kennedy, Manuel Paris, Bob Easton, Felix and His Martiniques. *D:* William Beaudine; *As.P:* Sidney

Picker; *Sc:* Charles E. Roberts, Jack Townley. (1:17) Romantic comedy with songs (including "Babalu") of an ambassador's daughter and the problems she causes for her father.

1104. Have Rocket, Will Travel (Columbia; 1959). *Cast:* Moe Howard, Larry Fine, Joe DeRita (his first as Curley Joe, replacing Joe Besser), Jerome Cowan, Anna-Lisa, Robert Colbert, Don Lamond (narrator). *D:* David Lowell Rich; *P:* Harry Romm; *Sc:* Raphael Hayes; *Title song:* George Duning, Stanley Styne. (1:16) (video) The Three Stooges starring in their first feature film, a science fiction–comedy about an accidental trip to Venus where the trio find assorted lifeforms, including a talking unicorn. Note: The Stooges previously appeared in feature films, but only in supporting roles, their starring vehicles being only their long series of comedy shorts.

1105. The Hawk of Wild River (Columbia; 1952). *Cast:* Charles Starrett, Smiley Burnette, Jack [Jock] Mahoney, Donna Hall, Clayton Moore (title role), Edwin Parker, Jim Diehl, Lane Chandler, Syd Saylor, John Cason, LeRoy Johnson, Jack Carry, Sam Flint. *D:* Fred F. Sears; *P:* Colbert Clark; *Sc:* Howard J. Green. (0:53) Series western which pits the "Durango Kid" against an outlaw whose choice of weapons is bow and arrow.

1106. He Laughed Last (Columbia; 1956). *Cast:* Frankie Laine, Lucy Marlow, Anthony Dexter, Richard Long, Alan Reed, Jesse White, Florenz Ames, Peter Brocco, Paul Dubov, Henry Slate, Joe Forte, Robin Morse, Dale Van Sickel, Mara McAfee, John Cason, Richard Benedict, David Tomack, John Truax. *D:* & *Sc:* Blake Edwards; *P:* Jonie Taps; *St:* Richard Quine, Edwards; *Songs:* "Strike Me Pink," "Save Your Sorrows" Arthur Morton. (1:16) A 1920s Technicolor gangster spoof which tells in flashback the story of a flapper who inherits a night club formerly owned by a gangland figure.

He or She *see* **Glen or Glenda**

1107. He Ran All the Way (United Artists/Roberts Pictures; 1951). *Cast:* John Garfield (final film—blacklisted in 1951 and died in 1952), Shelley Winters, Wallace Ford, Selena Royle, Gladys George, Bobby Hyatt, Norman Lloyd, Clancy Cooper, Keith Hetherington, Renny McEvoy, Dale Van Sickel, (A.) Cameron Grant, James Magill, Robert Davis, Vici Raaf, John Morgan, Ralph Brooks, Jimmy Ames, Robert Karnes, Mark Lowell, Lucille Sewall. *D:* John Berry; *P:* Bob Roberts; *Sc:* Guy Endore, Hugo Butler. (1:17) Acclaimed melodrama of a cop killer who holes up in the home of a family until the coast is clear. Based on the 1947 novel by Sam Ross.

1108. Headline Hunters (Republic; 1955). *Cast:* Rod Cameron, Julie Bishop, Ben Cooper, Raymond Greenleaf, Chubby Johnson, John Warburton, Nacho Galindo, Virginia Carroll, Howard Wright, Stuart Randall, Edward Colmans, Joe Besser. *D:* William Witney; *P:* William J. O'Sullivan; *Sc:* Fredric Louis Fox, John K. Butler. (1:10) Low budget melodrama of a newspaper's cub reporter whose passion for his job gets him in hot water with some local crime figures. A remake of this studio's 1940 production *Behind the News.*

1109. Hear Me Good (Paramount/Mackaren Co.; 1957). *Cast:* Hal March, Merry Anders, Joe E. Ross, Jean Willes, Milton Frome, Joey Faye, Richard Bakalyan, Tom Duggan. *D:-P:* & *Sc:* Don McGuire. (1:20) Low budget comedy effort of a con man who fixes a beauty contest, only to have the disgruntled mobster boyfriend of one of the girls on his tail. VistaVision.

1110. Heart of the Rockies (Republic; 1951). *Cast:* Roy Rogers, Penny Edwards, Gordon Jones, Foy Willing and Riders of the Purple Sage, Ralph Morgan, Fred Graham, Mira McKinney, Robert "Buzz" Henry, William Gould, Pepe Hern, Rand Brooks, Trigger (horse), Bullet (dog). *D:* William Witney; *As.P:* Edward J. "Eddy" White; *St:* & *Sc:* Eric Taylor; *Songs:* Foy Willing, Geri Gallian, Jack Elliott. (1:07) (video 0:54) Western of a highway construction crew made up of juvenile offenders who run afoul of a local ranch foreman. No relation to the 1937 production of the same name by this studio.

1111. Heaven Knows Mr. Allison (20th Century–Fox; 1957). *Cast:* Robert Mitchum (Mr. Allison), Deborah Kerr (AAN + "Best Actress" by the New York Film Critics/Sister Angela). *D:* John Huston; *P:* Buddy Adler, Eugene Frenke; *Sc:* (AAN) John Lee Mahin, Huston. (1:47) Critically acclaimed World War II drama of a marine and a Roman Catholic nun, stranded and trying to survive against insurmountable odds on a Japanese held Pacific island. It placed #8 on the "10 Best" list of *Film Daily,* was in nomination for "Best Picture" with the New York Film Critics, as well as in nomination at the British Academy Awards. Based on the 1952 novel by Charles Shaw, it became one of the 24 top-grossing films of 1956-57. Filmed on location on Tobago, British West Indies, in DeLuxe color and CinemaScope.

Helen Keller in Her Own Words *see* **Helen Keller in Her Story**

1112. Helen Keller in Her Story (A Nancy Hamilton Presentation; 1955). *P:* (AA-Best Documentary) Nancy Hamilton; *Narration:* James Shute; *Narrator:* Katherine Cornell. (0:45) (video) Feature documentary, in 16 mm, with Helen Keller evoking her own personal drama and giving hope to others who are blind and deaf. Number nine on the "10 Best" list of the NBR. (aka: *The Unconquered* and *Helen Keller in Her Own Words*)

1113. The Helen Morgan Story (Warner; 1957). *Cast:* Ann Blyth (final film—ret./ singing voice dubbed by Gogi Grant), Paul Newman, Richard Carlson, Gene Evans, Walter Woolf King, Cara Williams, Virginia Vincent, Alan King. *D:* Michael Curtiz; *P:* Martin Rackin; *St: & Sc:* Oscar Saul, Dean Reisner, Stephen Longstreet, Nelson Gidding; *Choreography:* LeRoy Prinz; *Songs:* "Bill" (Jerome Kern–P.G. Wodehouse); "Don't Ever Leave Me" (Kern-Oscar Hammerstein II); "Can't Help Lovin' Dat Man" (Kern–Hammerstein II); "Why Was I Born?" (Kern–Hammerstein II); "I Can't Give You Anything but Love" (Dorothy Fields-Jimmy McHugh); "If You Were the Only Girl in the World" (Clifford Grey–Nat D. Ayer); "The Love Nest" (Otto Harbach–Louis A. Hirsch); "I'll Get By" (Fred Ahlert–Roy Turk); "Body and Soul" (Edward Heyman–Robert Sour–Frank Eyton–John Green); "Avalon" (Vincent Rose–Al Jolson); "Breezin' Along with the Breeze" (Haven Gillespie–Seymour Simons-Richard Whiting); "Someone to Watch Over Me" (George and Ira Gershwin); "Do Do Do" and "I've Got a Crush on You" (The Gershwins). (1:58) (video) Fictionalized Hollywood biopic of the original "torch singer" of the 1920s and '30s, whose career faded when an unhappy love life led to alcoholism, followed by death at the age of 41 from cirrhosis of the liver. CinemaScope. (G.B. title: *Both Ends of the Candle*)

1114. Helen of Troy (Warner; 1955). *Cast:* Rossana Podesta (Helen), Jacques Sernas (Paris), Stanley Baker (Achilles), Cedric Hardwicke (Priam), Harry Andrews (Hector), Niall MacGinnis (Menelaus), Nora Swinburne (Hecuba), Robert Douglas (Agamemnon), Torin Thatcher (Ulysses), Brigitte Bardot (Andraste), Janette Scott (Cassandra), Ronald Lewis (Aeneas), Eduardo Ciannelli (Andros), Marc Lawrence (Diomedes), Maxwell Reed (Ajax), Robert Brown (Polydorus), Barbara Cavan (Cora), Terence Longdon (Patroclus), Patricia Marmount (Andromache), Guido Notare (Nestor), Tonio Selwart (Adelphous), George Zoritch, Edmond Knight. *D:* Robert Wise; *P:* uncredited; *Adaptation:* Hugh Gray, N. Richard Nash; *Sc:* John Twist, Gray. (1:58) Lavishly produced, but critically panned, spectacle (filmed in Rome) of the Greek woman whose face launched a thousand ships and brought on the Trojan War. A remake of *The Private Life of Helen of Troy* (aka: *Helen of Troy*), the second production of Alexander Korda in the U.S.A. (First National; 1927). Based on Homeric legend, it was one of the 24 top-grossing films of 1955-56, but wound up $4,000,000 in the red for Warner Brothers. WarnerColor and CinemaScope.

1115. Hell and High Water (20th Century–Fox; 1954). *Cast:* Richard Widmark (Adam Jones), Bella Darvi (film debut/Denise), Victor Francen (Prof. Martell), Cameron Mitchell ("Ski" Brodski), Gene Evans (Chief Holter), David Wayne (Dugboat Walker), Stephen Bekassy (Neuman), Richard Loo (Fujimori), Peter Scott (Happy), Henry Kulky (McCrossin), Wong Artarne (Chin Lee), Robert Adler (Welles), Don Orlando (Carpino), Rollin Moriyama (Joto), John Gifford (Torpedo), William Yip (Ho-Sin), Leslie Bradley (Mr. Aylesworth), John Wengraf (Col. Schuman), Harry Denny (McAuliff), Harry Carter (quartermaster), Tommy Walker, Edo Mita, Ramsey Williams, Robert B. Williams, Harlan Warde, Neyle Morrow. *D:* Samuel Fuller; *P:* Raymond A. Klune; *Sc:* Fuller, Jesse L. Lasky, Jr.; *St:* David Hempstead; *F/X:* (AAN) Ray Kellogg. (1:43) Drama, romance and action highlight this tale of a submarine on a demolition mission in the arctic. Technicolor and CinemaScope.

Hell Bent for Glory (G.B. title) *see* **Lafayette Escadrille**

1116. Hell Bound (United Artists/Bel-Air–Clark Prods.; 1957). *Cast:* John Russell, June Blair, Stuart Whitman, Margo Woode, George Mather, Stanley Adams, Gene O'Donnell, Frank Fenton, Virginia De Lee, Dehl Berti, Samee Tong, Charles Webster, Edward DeRoo, Marge Evans, Ann Daro, Frank McGrath, Kay Garrett, Bob Strong, George Mayon, Boyd "Red" Morgan, Richard Martin, Jerry Frank, Larry Thor,

Scott Peters, *and in 16 mm film within the film*: Dick Standish, William Flaherty, George H. Whiteman. *D:* Edward J. Hole, Jr. (directorial debut); *P:* Howard W. Koch; *St:* Richard Landau, Arthur Orloff; *Sc:* Landau. (1:09) Crime melodrama of attempts by a crime figure to steal $2,000,000 worth of wartime surplus narcotics.

1117. Hell Canyon Outlaws (Republic/Jerold Zukor Prods.; 1957). *Cast:* Dale Robertson, Brian Keith, Rossana Rory, Dick Kallman, Don Megowan, Mike Lane, Buddy Baer, Charles Fredericks, Alexander Lockwood, James Nusser, James Maloney, William Pullen, George Ross, Vincent Padula, George Pembroke, Tom Hubbard. *D:* Paul Landres; *P:* T. Frank Woods; *St: & Sc:* Allan Kaufman, Max Glandbard; *Song:* Dick Kallman (sung by him). (1:12) Western of a sheriff who stands up against an outlaw gang that has taken over his town. (aka: *The Tall Trouble*)

The Hell Creatures *see* **Invasion of the Saucer Men**

1118. Hell on Devil's Island (20th Century–Fox/Regal Films; 1957). *Cast:* Helmut Dantine, William Talman, Donna Martell, Jean Willes, Rex Ingram, Robert Cornthwaite, Jay Adler, Peter Adams, Edward Colmans, Mel Welles, Charles Bohbot, Alan Lee, Henry Rowland, Edward Coch, Paul Brinegar, Allen Pinson, Roy Jensen, Elena Da Vinci, Edwin "Ed" Nelson, Paul MacWilliams. *D:* Christian Nyby; *P:* Leon Chooluck, Laurence Stewart; *St:* Arndt Giusti, Ethel Giusti; *Sc:* Steven Ritch. (1:13) Melodrama of a French journalist sentenced to the island prison following World War II. When released, he helps the island governor put an end to an operation using ex-cons to mine for gold. Regalscope.

1119. Hell on Frisco Bay (Warner/Jaguar; 1955). *Cast:* Alan Ladd, Edward G. Robinson, Joanne Dru, William Demarest, Paul Stewart, Perry Lopez, Fay Wray, Renata Vanni, Nestor Paiva, Stanley Adams, Willis Bouchey, Peter Hansen, Anthony Caruso, George J. Lewis, Tina Carver, Rod[ney] Taylor, Peter Votrian, Jayne Mansfield, Mae Marsh. *D:* Frank Tuttle; *As.P:* George C. Bertholon; *Sc:* Sydney Boehm, Martin Rackin. (1:38) (video) Melodrama of a ruthless crime syndicate operating on the docks of San Francisco. Based on the serialized story *The Darkest Hour* by William P. McGivern which appeared in *Collier's*. WarnerColor and CinemaScope. (aka: *The Darkest Hour*)

1120. Hell Ship Mutiny (Republic/Lovina; 1957). *Cast:* Jon Hall, John Carradine, Peter Lorre, Roberta Haynes, Mike Mazurki, Charles Mauu, Stanley Adams, Danny Richards, Jr., Felix Locher (the father of Jon Hall, making his film debut at age 75), Peter Coe, Michael Barrett, Salvador Baguez, Salty (chimpanzee). *D:* Lee Sholem, Elmo Williams; *P:* George Bilson; *As.P:* Jon Hall; *St: & Sc:* DeVallon Scott, Wells Root. (1:06) (video) Adventure melodrama of island natives being forced to dive for pearls, until a ship's captain puts an end to the misdeeds of the greedy pair at the helm of the operation.

1121. Hell Squad (American International; 1958). *Cast:* Wally Campo, Brandon Carroll, Fred Gavlin, Greg Stuart, Cecil Addis, Leon Schrier, Don Chambers, Jack Sowards, Larry Shuttleworth, Jerry Bob Weston, Gordon Edwards, Jim Hamilton, Ben Bigelow, Jow Hearn, Jack N. Krammer, Dick Walsh, Curtis Lozer, Bob Williams, John Amos. *D:-P:-St: & Sc:* Burt Topper (debut); *Ex.P:* James H. Nicholson, Samuel Z. Arkoff. (1:04) (video) Low budget World War II drama of an American patrol lost in the Tunisian desert during the North African campaign. Originally ran on a double bill with *Tank Battalion* (q.v.).

1122. Hellcats of the Navy (Columbia/Morningside; 1957). *Cast:* Ronald Reagan, Nancy Davis, Arthur Franz, Robert Arthur, William Leslie, William "Bill" Phillips, Harry Lauter, Joseph Turkel, Michael Garth, Don Keefer, Selmer Jackson, Maurice Manson. *D:* Nathan Juran; *P:* Charles H. Schneer; *Sc:* David Lang, Raymond T. Marcus. (1:21) (video) World War II drama of a submarine commander who faces criticism from his crew. Based on *Hellcats of the Sea*, a 1955 book by Charles A. Lockwood and Hans Christian Adamson, an introduction to the film is delivered by Fleet Admiral Chester A. Nimitz.

1123. Hellgate (Lippert/Commando Films; 1952). *Cast:* Sterling Hayden, Joan Leslie, Ward Bond, James Arness, Peter Coe, John Pickard, Robert Wilke, Kyle James, Richard Emory, Richard Paxton, William R. Hamel, Marshall Bradford, Sheb Wooley, Rory Mallinson, Pat Coleman, Timothy Carey, Ed Hinton, Kyle Anderson, Stanley Price, Rodd Redwing. *D: & Sc:* Charles Marquis Warren; *P: & Screen story:*

John C. Champion. (1:27) Nineteenth century drama of an innocent doctor sent to prison who saves the day when an epidemic strikes. A rehash of *The Prisoner of Shark Island* (Fox; 1936), with the same fact-based story the subject of *The Ordeal of Dr. Mudd*, a 1980 TV movie.

1124. Hello God (William Marshall; 1951). *Cast:* Errol Flynn, Sherry Jackson, Joe Muzzuca, Armando Formica, William Marshall (narrator). *D:-P: & Sc:* William Marshall. (1:04) A U.S.A./Italian co-production of an unnamed soldier who relates the stories of four separate soldiers who died on the beach at Anzio during World War II. Flynn originally got involved in this production in an attempt to get out of his Warner Brothers contract. A film which has had few showings, all of which have been in Europe.

1125. Hell's Crossroads (Republic; 1957). *Cast:* Stephen McNally, Peggie Castle, Robert Vaughn (Bob Ford), Barton MacLane, Harry Shannon, Henry Brandon (Jesse James), Douglas Kennedy (Frank James), Grant Withers, Myron Healey (Cole Younger), Frank Wilcox, Jean Howell, Morris Ankrum. *D:* Franklin Adreon; *P:* Rudy Ralston; *St:* John K. Butler; *Sc:* Butler, Barry Shipman. (1:13) In this western, a member of the James gang meets opposition when he endeavors to go straight. Widescreen Naturama.

1126. Hell's Five Hours (Allied Artists/ Muriel Corp.; 1958). *Cast:* Stephen McNally, Coleen Gray, Vic Morrow, Robert Foulk, Dan Sheridan, Maurice Manson, Will J. White, Ray Ferrell, Charles J. Conrad, Robert Christopher. *D:-P:-St: & Sc:* Jack L. Copeland; *As.P:* Walter A. Hanneman. (1:13) Melodrama about a disgruntled former employee of a rocket fuel plant who plans to blow the place to smithereens. The 2nd feature on a double bill with *Cole Younger, Gunfighter* (q.v.).

1127. Hell's Half Acre (Republic; 1954). *Cast:* Wendell Corey, Evelyn Keyes, Elsa Lanchester, Marie Windsor, Nancy Gates, Leonard Strong, Jesse White, Keye Luke, Philip Ahn, Robert Sheild, Clair Widenaar, Robert Costa. *D: & P:* John H. Auer; *St: & Sc:* Steve Fisher; *Songs:* "Polynesian Rhapsody" (Fisher–Jack Pitman); "Lani" (Pitman). (1:30) A combination of murder-mystery and crime-melodrama, set in the Hawaiian Islands, of a gangster who winds up in trouble when he assumes a new identity and attempts to go straight.

Hell's Highway *see* **Violent Road**

1128. Hell's Horizon (Columbia/Gravis Prods.; 1955). *Cast:* John Ireland, Marla English, Bill Williams, Hugh Beaumont, Larry Pennell, Chet Baker, William Schallert, Jerry Paris, Paul Levitt, John Murphy, Wray Davis, Mark Scott, Kenne Duncan, Don Burnett, Stanley Adams. *D:-St: & Sc:* Tom Gries; *P:* Wray Davis. (1:19) A bridge is the target of an American bomber crew in this Korean conflict drama.

1129. Hell's Island (Paramount/Pine-Thomas; 1955). *Cast:* John Payne, Mary Murphy, Francis L. Sullivan, Eduardo Noriega, Paul Picerni, Arnold Ross, Walter Reed, Pepe Hern, Robert Cabal, Sandor Szabo, Mario Siletti, Matty Fain, Ralph Dumke, Paul Marion, Lillian Molieri, Guillermo Barreto, Victor Bartell, Edward Coch, Marguerita Martin, Don Orlando, Julia Montoya, Paul Regas, Carlos Rivero, Argentina Brunetti, David Garcia, Nacho Galindo, Jose G. Gonzales, Ben Frommer, Romiro Jaloma, Delmar Costello, Alex Montoya, Henry Escalante, Manuel Lopez, Jose Oliviera, Joseph Heredia, Tom Bernard. *D:* Phil Karlson; *P:* William H. Pine, William C. Thomas; *St:* Jack Leonard, Martin M. Goldsmith; *Sc:* Maxwell Shane. (1:23) Treachery and deceit raise their ugly heads in this tale of adventurers searching the Caribbean for a priceless ruby lost in a plane crash. Technicolor and VistaVision. (aka: *Love Is a Weapon*)

1130. Hell's Outpost (Republic; 1954). *Cast:* Rod Cameron, Joan Leslie, John Russell, Chill Wills, Jim Davis, Kristine Miller, Ben Cooper, Taylor Holmes, Barton MacLane, Ruth Lee, Oliver Blake, Arthur Q. Bryan, Harry Woods, Robert "Buzz" Henry, John Dierkes, Sue England, Almira Sessions, Lizz Slifer, Don Kennedy, Paul Stader, George Dockstader, Alan Bridge, Don Brodie, Edward Clark, Gil Harmon, James Lilburn, Ruth Brennan. *D:* Joseph Kane; *P:* Mark Hellings, Bryan Foy; *Sc:* Kenneth Gamet. (1:29) Following the Civil War, a man returns to his mining claim, but meets opposition from a corrupt local banker. Based on the 1953 novel *Silver Rock* by Luke Short [pseudonym of Frederick Dilley Glidden].

1131. Her First Romance (Columbia; 1951). *Cast:* Margaret O'Brien, Allen Martin, Jr., Jimmy Hunt, Sharyn Moffett, Ann Doran, Lloyd Corrigan, Eleanor [Elinor] Donahue, Susan Stevens, Marissa O'Brien, Arthur Space, Otto Hulett, Lois Pace, Harlan Warde, Maudie

Prickett. *D:* Seymour Friedman; *P:* uncredited; *Sc:* Albert Mannheimer. (1:12) Low budget romantic-drama, set in a summer camp, of a girl who gets in trouble when she falls for a boy much older than herself. Based on *City Boy* by Herman Wouk.

1132. Her 12 Men (MGM; 1954). *Cast:* Greer Garson, Robert Ryan, Barry Sullivan, Richard Haydn, Barbara Lawrence, James Arness, Rex Thompson, Tim Considine, David Stollery, Ian Wolfe, Frances Bergen (mother of Candace), Ronald MacDonald, Dale Hartleben, Ivan Triesault, Stuffy Singer, Peter Votrian. *D:* Robert Z. Leonard; *P:* John Houseman; *Sc:* William Roberts, Laura Z. Hobson. (1:30) Drama of a lady schoolteacher at an all-boys school. Based on *Snips and Snails* by Louise Baker, this was Garson's final film for MGM. Anscocolor.

1133. Here Come the Girls (Paramount/ Hope Enterprises; 1953). *Cast:* Bob Hope, Tony Martin, Arlene Dahl, Rosemary Clooney, Millard Mitchell, William Demarest, Fred Clark, Robert Strauss, Zamah Cunningham, Frank Orth, Johnny Downs, Virginia Leith, Sherree North, Phyllis Coates, Dale Van Sickel, Lois Hall, Nancy Kulp, Hugh Sanders, Inesita, Pepito Perez, Vivian Mason, Alex Jackson, Russ Saunders, Everett Coreill, Loren B. Brown and the Four Step Brothers: Alfred T. Williams, Maceo Edward Anderson, Prince C. Spencer, Rufus L. McDonald. *D:* Claude Binyon; *P:* Paul Jones; *St:* Edmund Hartmann; *Sc:* Hartmann, Hal Kanter; *Songs:* "Girls Are Here to Stay," "Never So Beautiful," "You Got Class," "Desire," "When You Love Someone," "Ali Baba Be My Baby," "Heavenly Days," "See the Circus" and "Peace" Jay Livingston, Ray Evans. (1:17) (video) Set in 1900, this hit comedy relates the story of chorus boy, Stanley Snodgrass (Hope), who finds himself the target of a relentless, mad killer. Technicolor.

1134. Here Come the Jets (20th Century-Fox/Associated Producers; 1959). *Cast:* Steve Brodie, John Doucette, Lyn Thomas, Mark Dana, Jean Carson, Carleton Young, Joseph Turkel, Gloria Moreland, Vikki Duggan, I. Stanford Jolley, B.B. Hughes, Walter Maslow, Tiger Marsh. *D:* Gene Fowler, *P:* Richard Einfeld; *St: & Sc:* Louis Vittes; *Title song:* Fowler, Paul Dunlap. (1:12) A traumatized Korean War jet pilot attempts to regain his self respect after hitting the alcoholic skids.

1135. Here Come the Marines (Monogram; 1952). *Cast:* Leo Gorcey, Huntz Hall, David [Gorcey] Condon, Bennie Bartlett, Gil Stratton, Jr., Hanley Stafford, Myrna Dell, Arthur Space, Bernard Gorcey, Paul Maxey, Tim Ryan, Murray Alper, William Newell, Riley Hill, Lisa Wilson, James Flavin, Robert Coogan, Leo "Ukie" Sherin, Sammy Finn, Buck Russell, Stanley Blystone, Chad Mallory, Perc Launders, Alan Jeffory, Bob Cudlip, Bob Peoples, William Vincent, Jack Wilson, Dick Paxton, Barbara Grey, Courtland Shepard, William Bailey, Paul Bradley. *D:* William Beaudine; *P:* Jerry Thomas; *St: & Sc:* Tim Ryan, Charles R. Marion, Jack Crutcher. (1:06) "Bowery Boys" series entry which had the working title of "Bowery Leathernecks," with the gang being drafted into the marine corps where they wind up solving a murder. (G.B. title: *Tell It To the Marines*)

1136. Here Come the Nelsons (Universal-International; 1952). *Cast:* Ozzie Nelson, Harriet Nelson (final theatrical film before moving to TV), David Nelson (film debut), Ricky Nelson (film debut), Rock Hudson, Barbara Lawrence, Sheldon Leonard, Jim Backus, Paul Harvey, Gale Gordon, Ann Doran, Chubby Johnson, Lillian Bronson, Ed Max, Paul Brinegar, Maynard Holmes, Frank Nelson, Arthur Q. Bryan, Ed Clark, William Haade, Harry Cheshire, Milton Kibbee, Lorin Raker, Harold Goodwin, Stuart Wilson, Irwin Jay Berniker, Edna Smith, Forrest Burns. *D:* Frederick de Cordova; *P:* Aaron Rosenberg; *St: & Sc:* Ozzie Nelson, Donald R. Nelson, William Davenport. (1:15) Situation comedy which is another motion picture version of a popular radio show, *The Adventures of Ozzie and Harriet*, which is also a prelude to the later popular TV series. (aka: *Meet the Nelsons*)

1137. Here Comes the Groom (Paramount; 1951). *Cast:* Bing Crosby (Pete), Jane Wyman (Emmadel Jones), Alexis Smith (Winifred Stanley), Franchot Tone (Wilbur Stanley), James Barton (Pa Jones), Robert Keith (George Dregnan), Jacky Gencel (Bobby), Beverly Washburn (Suzi), Connie Gilchrist (Ma Jones), Walter Catlett (McGonigle), Alan Reed (Mr. Godfrey), Minna Gombell (Mrs. Godfrey), Howard Freeman (Governor), Maidel Turner (Aunt Abby), H.B. Warner (Uncle Elihu), Nicholas Joy (Uncle Prentiss), Ian Wolfe (Uncle Adam), Ellen Corby (Mrs. McGonigle), Irving Bacon (Baines), Ted Thorpe (Paul Pippett), Art Baker (radio announcer), Anna Maria Alberghetti

(Therese), Dorothy Lamour (herself), Louis Armstrong (himself), Frank Fontaine (himself), Phil Harris (himself), Cass Daley (herself), Chris Appel (Marcel), Charles Halton (Cusick), Charles Lane (Burchard: FBI), Adeline de Walt Reynolds (Aunt Amy), Charles Evans (mayor), James Burke, Laura Elliot, Odette Myrtil, Rev. Neal Dodd, J. Farrell MacDonald, Carl Switzer, Walter McGrail, Howard Joslin. *D: & P:* Frank Capra; *As.P:* Irving Asher; *St:* (AAN) Robert Riskin, Liam O'Brien; *Sc:* Virginia Van Upp, O'Brien, Myles Connolly; *Songs:* "In the Cool, Cool, Cool of the Evening" (AA-Best Song) Johnny Mercer, Hoagy Carmichael; "Misto Christofo Columbo," "Caro Nome," "Bonne Nuit," "Your Own Little House," Ray Evans, Jay Livingston. (1:53) (video/laserdisc) Comedy of what a man will do to win his ladylove. One of the 23 top-grossing films of 1950-51.

Here Lies Love *see* **The Second Woman**

1138. He's a Cockeyed Wonder (Columbia; 1950). *Cast:* Mickey Rooney, Terry Moore, William Demarest, Charles Arnt, Ross Ford, Ned Glass, Mike Mazurki, Douglas Fowley, William "Bill" Phillips, Ruth Warren, Eddy Waller, Frank Ferguson. *D:* Peter Godfrey; *P:* Rudolph C. Flothow; *St: & Sc:* John Henley. (1:16) Comedy of a young man who captures the bad guys and marries the girl.

1139. Hey Boy! Hey Girl! (Columbia; 1959). *Cast:* Louis Prima, Keely Smith, James Gregory, Henry Slate, Kim Charney, Barbara Heller, Asa Maynor, Sam Butera & the Witnesses. *D:* David Lowell Rich; *P:* Harry Romm; *As.P:* Barbara Belle; *St: & Sc:* Raphael Hayes, James West; *Songs:* Title song (J. Thomas–O. McLollie); "Autumn Leaves" (Johnny Mercer–Joseph Kosma); "A Banana Split for My Baby" (Louis Prima–Stan Irwin); "Nitey-Nite" (Prima–Keely Smith–Barbara Belle); "Oh, Marie" (E. Dicapua); "Lazy River" (Hoagy Carmichael–Sidney Arodin); "You Are My Love" (Joe Seuter); "Fever" (Johnny Davenport-Eddie Cooley); "When the Saints Go Marching In" (traditional). (1:21) "Let's put on a show" musical involving a church benefit.

1140. Hiawatha (Allied Artists; 1952). *Cast:* Vincent Edwards, Yvette Dugay, Keith Larsen, Eugene Iglesias, Armando Silvestre, Michael Tolan, Ian MacDonald, Katherine Emery, Morris Ankrum, Stephen Chase, Stuart Randall, Richard Bartlett, Michael Granger, Robert Bice, Gene Peterson, Henry Corden. *D:* Kurt Neumann; *P:* Walter Mirisch; *Sc:* Arthur Strawn, Dan Ullman. (1:19) A tale of the American red man and inter-tribal conflict. Based on Henry Wadsworth Longfellow's classic 1898 poem. First filmed by IMP in 1909 on 1 reel. Cinecolor.

The Hidden City *see* **Bomba and the Hidden City**

Hidden Face *see* **Jail Bait**

1141. Hidden Fear (United Artists/St. Aubrey-Kohn; 1957). *Cast:* John Payne, Alexander Knox, Conrad Nagel, Natalie Norwick, Anne Neyland, Elsie Albin, Paul Erling, Mogens Brandt, Buster Larsen, Knud Rex, Marianne Schleiss, Kjeld Jacobsen, Preben Mahrt, Kjeld Petersen. *D:* Andre De Toth; *P:* Robert St. Aubrey, Howard E. Kohn II: *St: & Sc:* De Toth, John and Ward Hawkins. (1:23) Crime melodrama of an American cop traveling to Denmark to help his sister, who is being held for murder and winds up uncovering a counterfeiting ring. A co-production of the U.S.A. and Denmark, filmed on location in Copenhagen.

1142. Hidden Guns (Republic; 1956). *Cast:* Richard Arlen, Bruce Bennett, John Carradine, Faron Young, Angie Dickinson, Lloyd Corrigan, Damian O'Flynn, Irving Bacon, Tom Hubbard, Guinn "Big Boy" Williams, Edmund Cobb, Ben Welden, Gordon Terry, Bill Coontz, Ron Kennedy, Bill Ward, Raymond L. Morgan, Charles Heard, Michael Darrin. *D:* Albert C. Gannaway; *P:* Gannaway, C.J. VerHalen; *Sc:* Sam Roeca, Gannaway; *Songs:* Gannaway, Hal Levy. (1:06) The local sheriff and his son oppose the outlaw gang that has overrun their town.

Hidden Secret (G.B. title) *see* **A Yank in Indo-China**

1143. The Hidden World (Small World Co.; 1958). *P:* (AAN-Best Documentary) Robert Snyder; *St: & Sc:* Snyder, M.C. Sonnabend. A documentary feature film.

1144. The Hideous Sun Demon (Pacific International/Clarke-King; 1959). *Cast:* Robert Clarke, Patricia Manning, Nan Peterson, Patrick Whyte, Fred La Porta, Bill Hampton, Donna Conkling, Xandra Conkling, Del Courtney. *D: & P:* Robert Clarke; *Co-Directors:* Thomas Boutross, Gianbatista Cassarino; *Sc:* E.S. Seeley, Jr., Doane Hoag; *Song:* "Strange Pursuit" Marilyn King. (1:14) (video) Ultra low budget science fiction of a young scientist who turns into a lizard-like creature when exposed to the sun, prompted by previous over-exposure to radioactivity. (aka: *The Sun Demon* and *Terror from the Sun*)

1145. The High and the Mighty (Warner/Wayne-Fellows Prods.; 1954). *Cast:* John Wayne (Dan Roman), Claire Trevor (AAN-BSA/May Hoist), Laraine Day (Lydia Rice), Robert Stack (Sullivan), Jan Sterling (AAN-BSA/Sally McKee), Phil Harris (Ed Joseph), David Brian (Ken Childs), Robert Newton (Gustave Pardee), Paul Kelly (Flaherty), Sidney Blackmer (Humphrey Agnew), Doe Avedon (Stewardess Spalding), Karen Sharpe (Nell Buck), John Smith (Milo Buck), Julie Bishop (Lillian Pardee), [Pedro] Gonzales-Gonzales (Gonzalez), John Howard (Howard Rice), Wally Brown (Wilby), William Campbell (Hobie Wheeler), Ann Doran (Mrs. Joseph), John Qualen (Jose Locota), Paul Fix (Frank Briscoe), George Chandler (Ben Sneed), Joy Kim (Dorothy Chen), Michael Wellman (Toby Field), Douglas Fowley (Alsop), Regis Toomey (Garfield), Carl Switzer (Ensign Keim), Robert Keys (Lt. Mowbray), William DeWolf Hopper (Roy), William Schallert (dispatcher), Julie Mitchum (Susie), Robert Easton, Philip Van Zandt. *D:* (AAN) William A. Wellman; *P:* uncredited; *Sc:* Ernest K. Gann; *Music:* (AA) Dimitri Tiomkin; *Theme song:* (AAN) Tiomkin; *Editor:* (AAN) Ralph Dawson. (2:27) An airliner enroute from Honolulu to San Francisco loses an engine, setting the stage for dramatic interaction between passengers and crew on board. Based on the 1953 best seller by Mr. Gann, it placed #5 on the "10 Best" list of *Film Daily* and went on to become one of the 25 top-grossing films of 1953-54. WarnerColor and CinemaScope.

1146. The High Cost of Loving (MGM; 1958). *Cast:* Jose Ferrer, Gena Rowlands (film debut), Joanne Gilbert, Jim Backus, Bobby Troup, Philip Ober, Edward Platt, Werner Klemperer, Charles Watts. *D:* Jose Ferrer; *P:* Milo O. Frank, Jr.; *St:* Frank, Jr., Rip Van Ronkle; *Sc:* Van Ronkle. (1:27) Domestic comedy of a married couple and their numerous problems. CinemaScope.

1147. High Lonesome (Eagle-Lion/Arfan Prods.; 1950). *Cast:* John Barrymore, Jr., Chill Wills, John Archer, Lois Butler, Kristine Miller, Basil Ruysdael, Jack Elam, Dave Kashner, Frank Cordell, Clem Fuller, Hugh Aiken, Howard Joslin. *D:-St: & Sc:* Alan LeMay; *P:* George Templeton; *Song:* "Twenty Miles from Carson" Chill Wills. (1:20) Psychological melodrama, set in the West, of a youth who becomes involved with a pair of escaped convicts bent on revenge. Technicolor.

1148. High Noon (United Artists/Stanley Kramer Prods.; 1952). *Cast:* Gary Cooper (AA + "Best Actor" Award from the New York Film Critics + *Photoplay* Gold Medal/Will Kane), Thomas Mitchell (Jonas Henderson), Lloyd Bridges (Harvey Pell), Katy Jurado (Helen Ramirez), Grace Kelly (Amy Kane), Otto Kruger (Percy Mettrick), Lon Chaney (Martin Howe), Henry [Harry] Morgan (William Fuller), Ian MacDonald (Frank Fuller), Eve McVeagh (Mildred Fuller), Harry Shannon (Cooper), Lee Van Cleef (film debut/Jack Colby), Bob Wilke (James Pierce), Sheb Wooley (Ben Miller), Tom London (Sam), Ted Stanhope, Larry Blake, William Phillips, Jeanne Blackford, William Newell, Lucien Prival, Guy Beach, Howland Chamberlain, Morgan Farley, Virginia Christine, Virginia Farmer, Jack Elam, Paul Dubov, Harry Harvey, Tim Graham, Nolan Leary, Tom Greenway, Dick Elliott, John Doucette. *D:* (AAN + "Best Director" from the New York Film Critics) Fred Zinneman; *P:* (AAN-Best Picture + "Best Picture" from the New York Film Critics) Stanley Kramer; *Sc:* (AAN) Carl Foreman; *Music Score:* (AA) Dimitri Tiomkin; *Song:* (AA-Best Song) "Do Not Forsake Me Oh My Darlin'" (aka: "Theme from *High Noon*") Tiomkin, Ned Washington (sung by Tex Ritter); *Editing:* (AA) Elmo Williams, Harry Gerstad. (1:24) (video/laserdisc) Classic western of a lawman forced to face a gang of gunmen bent on killing him on his wedding day. The film is unique in that every minute of its running time unfolds as actual time in the scenario. Voted "Best Film of the Year" by *Film Daily*, it placed #2 and #5 respectively on the "10 Best" lists of the NBR and the *New York Times*. Based on the short story "The Tin Star" by John W. Cunningham, it became one of the 23 top-grossing films of 1951-52. Computer-colored prints have been produced. *High Noon—Part II: The Return of Will Kane*, an unnecessary and dull sequel, showed up on TV in 1980.

1149. High School Big Shot (Filmgroup/Sparta; 1959). *Cast:* Tom Pittman, Virginia Aldridge, Howard Viet, Malcolm Atterbury, Stanley Adams. *D:-St: & Sc:* Joel Rapp (debut); *P:* Stan Bickman. (1:05) A high school youth is played for a sucker when he helps a female classmate write her term paper and they get caught. To further appease her, he attempts a robbery at his place of employment. Originally ran on a drive-in double bill with *T-Bird Gang* (q.v.).

1150. High School Confidential! (MGM/Albert Zugsmith; 1958). *Cast:* Russ Tamblyn, Jan Sterling, John Drew Barrymore, Mamie Van Doren, Diane Jergens, Ray Anthony, Jerry Lee Lewis, Jackie Coogan, Charles Chaplin, Jr., Lyle Talbot, William Wellman, Jr., Burt Douglas, Phillipa Fallon, Robin Raymond, James Todd, Texas Joe Foster, Diana Darrin, Carl Thayler, Irwin Berke, Michael Landon. *D:* Jack Arnold; *P:* Albert Zugsmith; *Screen story:* Robert Blees; *Sc:* Blees, Lewis Meltzer; *Special material:* Mel Welles; *Title song:* Jerry Lee Lewis, Ron Hargrave (sung by Lewis). (1:25) (video/laserdisc) Critically panned melodrama of a young narcotics agent who infiltrates a high school with the intent of ferreting out marijuana pushers. Based on the personal experiences of Texas Joe Foster. CinemaScope (aka: *Young Hellions*) Originally ran on the top of a double bill with *Handle with Care* (q.v.).

1151. High School Hellcats (American International/Indio Prods.; 1958). *Cast:* Yvonne Lime, Brett Halsey, Jana Lund, Suzanne Sydney, Heather Ames, Nancy Kilgas, Rhoda Williams, Don Shelton, Viola Harris, Robert Anderson, Martin Braddock, Arthur Marshall. *D:* Edward Bernds; *P:* Charles "Buddy" Rogers; *Ex.P:* James H. Nicholson, Samuel Z. Arkoff; *St: & Sc:* Mark and Jan Lowell. (1:10) Teen exploitation melodrama of a girl who gets involved with a private high school sorority called the "Hellcats," eventually suspecting one of the girls of murder and setting herself up to be the next victim. (aka: *School for Violence*) Originally ran as the 2nd feature on a drive-in double bill with *Hot Rod Gang* (q.v.).

1152. High Society (Allied Artists; 1955). *Cast:* Leo Gorcey, Huntz Hall, David [Gorcey] Condon, Bennie Bartlett, Bernard Gorcey, Ronald Keith, Dayton Lummis, Amanda Blake (final theatrical film before moving to TV and her long-running role as "Miss Kitty" on *Gunsmoke*), Gavin Gordon, Addison Richards, Kem Dibbs, Paul Harvey, Dave Barry. *D:* William Beaudine; *P:* Ben Schwalb; *St:* Elwood Ullman, Edward Bernds; *Sc:* Bert Lawrence, Jerome S. Gottler. (1:01) "Bowery Boys" comedy which has them introduced into society when they get involved with a wealthy confidence man who convinces them that Sach (Hall) is heir to a fortune. Note: Through an oversight in balloting, Ullman and Bernds found themselves erroneously nominated for an Oscar for their "original story."

1153. High Society (MGM/Sol C. Siegel Prods.; 1956). *Cast:* Bing Crosby (C.K. Dexter-Haven), Grace Kelly (Tracy Lord), Frank Sinatra (Mike Connor), Celeste Holm (Liz Imbrie), John Lund (George Kittredge), Louis Calhern (final film—d. 1956/Uncle Willie), Sidney Blackmer (Seth Lord), Louis Armstrong (himself), Margalo Gillmore (Mrs. Seth Lord), Lydia Reed (Caroline Lord), Richard Keene (Mac), Gordon Richards, Richard Garrick, Reginald Simpson, Ruth Lee, Helen Spring, Paul Keast, Hugh Boswell. *D:* Charles Walters; *P:* Sol C. Siegel; *Sc:* John Patrick; *Music:* (AAN) Johnny Green, Saul Chaplin; *Songs:* "True Love" (AAN-Best Song), "High Society," "Well, Did You Evah?," (from the 1939 Broadway production "DuBarry Was a Lady"), "You're Sensational," "Who Wants to Be a Millionaire?," "Little One," "Now You Has Jazz," "Mind If I Make Love to You?" and "I Love You, Samantha" all by Cole Porter. (1:47) (video/laserdisc) Based on Philip Barry's play *The Philadelphia Story*, this remake of that 1940 production by this studio has nine songs added, of which "True Love" sung by Crosby and Kelly became a fantastic hit. One of the 24 top-grossing films of 1955-56 and the studio's biggest money-maker for the year.

High Venture (G.B. title) *see* **Passage West**

High Vermillion (G.B. title) *see* **Silver City**

1154. Highway Dragnet (Allied Artists; 1954). *Cast:* Richard Conte, Joan Bennett, Wanda Hendrix, Reed Hadley, Mary Beth Hughes, Iris Adrian, Harry Harvey, Tom Hubbard, Frank Jenks, Murray Alper, Zon Murray, House Peters, Jr., Joseph Crehan (final film—ret.), Tony Hughes, Bill Hale, Fred Gabourie. *D:* Nathan Juran; *P:* William F. Broidy, Jack Jungmeyer; *As.P:* Roger Corman; *St:* U.S. Anderson, Corman; *Sc:* Herb Meadow, Jerome Odlum, Tom Hubbard, Fred Eggers. (1:10) An ex-marine takes to the road when he becomes the main suspect in the murder of an ex–Las Vegas model, hooking up along the way with a fashion photographer and her model.

1155. Highway 301 (Warner; 1950). *Cast:* Steve Cochran, Virginia Grey, Gaby Andre, Edmon Ryan, Robert Webber, Wally Cassell, Aline Towne, Richard Egan, Edward Norris. *D:-St: & Sc:* Andrew L. Stone; *P:* Bryan Foy. (1:23) Stark crime-melodrama, factually based on the exploits of the Tri-State Gang that operated in Maryland, Virginia and North Carolina.

1156. The Highwayman (Allied Artists/ Jack Dietz Prods.; 1951). *Cast:* Charles Coburn, Wanda Hendrix, Philip Friend, Cecil Kellaway, Victor Jory, Scott Forbes, Virginia Huston, Dan O'Herlihy, Henry [Harry] Morgan, Albert Sharpe, Lowell Gilmore, Alan Napier. *D:* Lesley Selander; *P:* Hal E. Chester; *Sc:* Jan Jeffries. (1:22) Costume adventure set in 18th century England of the exploits of a gang of Robin Hood wanna-bes. Based on the poem by Alfred Noyes and a story by Jack DeWitt and Renault Duncan (Duncan Renaldo). Cinecolor.

1157. Hi-Jacked (Lippert; 1950). *Cast:* Jim Davis, Marcia [Mae] Jones, Sid Melton, David Bruce, Paul Cavanagh, House Peters, Jr., Ralph Sanford, Iris Adrian, George Eldredge, William E. Green, Margia Dean, Kit Guard, Lee Phelps, Myron Healey, Lee Bennett. *D:* Sam Newfield; *P:* Sigmund Neufeld; *St:* Raymond L. Schrock, Fred Myton; *Sc:* Myton, Orville H. Hampton. (1:06) A trucker is accused of hijacking his own rig.

1158. Hilda Crane (20th Century–Fox; 1956). *Cast:* Jean Simmons, Guy Madison, Jean Pierre Aumont, Evelyn Varden, Judith Evelyn, Peggy Knudsen, Gregg Palmer, Richard Garrick, Jim Hayward, Sandee Marriot, Don Shelton, Helen Mayon, Blossom Rock [nee: Marie Blake], Jay Jostyn. *D: & Sc:* Philip Dunne; *P:* Herbert B. Swope, Jr. (1:27) Romantic melodrama of a woman who returns to her home town and an old boy friend after two failed marriages and a major career slump. Based on a 1951 play by Samson Raphaelson. DeLuxe color and CinemaScope.

1159. Hills of Oklahoma (Republic; 1950). *Cast:* Rex Allen, Fuzzy Knight, Elisabeth Fraser, Elisabeth Risdon, Roscoe Ates, Rex Lease, Robert Karnes, Robert Emmett Keane, Trevor Bardette, Lee Phelps, Edmund Cobb, Ted Adams, Lane Bradford, Johnny Downs, Michael Carr, Ko-Ko (horse). *D:* R.G. Springsteen; *As.P:* Franklin Adreon; *St:* Olive Cooper; *Sc:* Cooper, Victor Arthur; *Song:* "Curtains of Night" Will S. Hayes. (1:07) (video) Cattleman Allen, driving his herd to a meat packing plant, is beset by cattle rustlers intent on preventing same.

Hills of the Brave (G.B. title) *see* **The Palomino**

1160. Hills of Utah (Columbia/Gene Autry Productions; 1951). *Cast:* Gene Autry, Elaine Riley, Pat Buttram, Onslow Stevens, Denver Pyle, Harry Lauter, William Fawcett, Tom London, Tommy Ivo, Stanley Price, Boyd Stockman, Kenne Duncan, Donna Martell, Sandy Sanders, Teddy Infuhr, Lee Morgan, Billy Griffith, Bob Woodward, Champion (horse). *D:* John English; *P:* Armand Schaefer; *Sc:* Gerald Geraghty; *Songs:* "Back to Utah," "Easter Day." (1:10) (video) Autry oater involving a feud between cattlemen and copper miners. Photographed in Sepiatone, it was based on the novel *The Doctor at Coffin Gap* by Les Savage, Jr. Originally ran on a double bill with *Corky of Gasoline Alley* (q.v.).

The Hindu *see* **Sabaka**

1161. The Hired Gun (MGM/Rorvic Prods.; 1957). *Cast:* Rory Calhoun, Anne Francis, Vince Edwards, John Litel, Chuck Connors, Robert Burton, Guinn "Big Boy" Williams, Reg[is] Parton, Salvador Baguez. *D:* Ray Nazarro; *P:* Rory Calhoun, Victor M. Orsatti; *Sc:* David Lang, Buckley Angell. (1:03) A lawman bringing in a female prisoner for hanging begins to suspect she is innocent of the crime for which she was condemned. CinemaScope.

1162. His Kind of Woman (RKO/Howard Hughes Presentation; 1950-51). *Cast:* Robert Mitchum, Jane Russell, Vincent Price, Tim Holt, Charles McGraw, Marjorie Reynolds, Raymond Burr, Leslye Banning, Jim Backus, Philip Van Zandt, John Mylong, Carleton G. Young, Erno Verebes, Dan White, Richard Berggren, Stacy Harris, Robert Cornthwaite, Jim Burke, Paul Frees, Joe Granby, Daniel DeLaurentis, John Sheehan, Sally Yarnell, Anthony Caruso, Robert Rose, Tol Avery, Paul Fierro, Mickey Simpson, Ed Rand, Jerry James, Joel Fluellen, Len Hendry, Joey Ray, Barry Brooks, Stuart Holmes, Jim Davis, Marie Sen Yung, Mary Brewer, Mamie Van Doren, Barbara Freking, Jerri Jordan, Joy Windsor, Marietta Elliott, William Justine, Bill Nelson, Bud [Bill] Wolfe, Ralph Gomez, Mike Lally, Saul Gorss, Gerry Ganzer. *D:* John Farrow; *P:* Robert Sparks; *Sc:* Frank Fenton, Jack Leonard; *Songs:* Jimmy McHugh, Harold Adamson. (2:00) (video) Melodrama of a man who goes to Mexico to pick up $50,000, but finds there is a lot more involved than he counted on. A film with a cult following, it was based on the story "Star Sapphire" by Gerald Drayson Adams.

1163. His Majesty O'Keefe (Warner/ Hecht-Lancaster; 1953). *Cast:* Burt Lancaster, Joan Rice, Andre Morell, Abraham Sofaer,

Archie Savage, Benson Fong, Teresa Prendergast, Lloyd Berrell, Charles Horvath, Philip Ahn, Guy Doleman, Grant Taylor, Alexander Archdale, Harvey Adams, Warwick Ray, Paddy Mulelly, Jim Crawford, Mr. McLardy, Niranjan Singh. *D:* Byron Haskin; *P:* Harold Hecht; *Sc:* Borden Chase, James Hill; *Songs:* "Emerald Isle" Dimitri Tiomkin, Paul Francis Webster. (1:32) (video) Action, adventure and romance in the South Seas as a freebooter plans on trading gunpowder for copra with the local natives. Loosely based on a real-life character, from the 1950 novel by Lawrence Klingman and Gerald Green. Filmed on location on Viti Levu, one of the Fijian Islands. Technicolor.

His Other Woman (G.B. title) *see* **The Desk Set**

1164. Hit and Run (United Artists/Hugo Haas Prods.; 1957). *Cast:* Cleo Moore (final film—ret.), Hugo Haas (dual role), Vince Edwards, Dolores Reed, Mari Lea, Pat Goldin, Carl Milletaire, Julie Mitchum, Robert Cassidy, John Zaremba, Steve Mitchell, Jan Englund, Dick Paxton. *D:-P: & Sc:* Hugo Haas; *St:* Herbert Q. Phillips; *Song:* "What Good'll It Do Me" Frank Steininger (sung by Ella Mae Morse). (1:24) Melodrama of a man who assumes the identity of his twin brother after seeing the latter killed. Originally ran on a double bill with *Spring Reunion* (q.v.).

1165. Hit Parade of 1951 (Republic 1950). *Cast:* John Carroll (dual role), Marie McDonald, Estelita Rodriguez, Frank Fontaine, Grant Withers, Mikhail Rasumny, Steve Flagg [aka: Michael St. Angel], Paul Cavanagh, Ed Gargan, Gus Schilling, Rose Rosett, Wade Crosby, Duke York, Al Murphy, Firehouse Five Plus Two, The Bobby Ramos Band. *D: & P:* John H. Auer; *St:* Aubrey Wisberg; *Sc:* Elizabeth Reinhardt, Wisberg, Lawrence Kimble; *Songs:* "Square Dance Samba," "You're So Nice," "How Would I Know," "Wishes Come True," "You Don't Know the Other Side of Me" (Al Rinker–Floyd Huddleston), "Boca Chico" (Sy Miller–Betty Garrett). (1:25) Musical of a gambler, deeply in debt, who switches identities with a look-alike singer and each begin to enjoy their new identity. (aka: *The Song Parade*)

1166. Hit the Deck (MGM; 1955). *Cast:* Jane Powell, Tony Martin, Debbie Reynolds, Vic Damone, Ann Miller, Russ Tamblyn, Walter Pidgeon, Kay Armen, Gene Raymond, Jane Darwell, Richard Anderson, J. Carrol Naish, Alan King (film debut), Henry Slate, The Jubalaires (themselves), Frank Reynolds. *D:* Roy Rowland; *P:* Joe Pasternak; *Sc:* Sonya Levien, William Ludwig; *Songs:* "Hallelujah," "Lucky Bird," "Leo-Leo," "Join the Navy," "Why Oh Why" (Leo Robin–Clifford Grey–Vincent Youmans), "A Kiss or Two," "The Lady from the Bayou" (Robin–Youmans), "Sometimes I'm Happy" (Grey–Youmans–Irving Caesar), "I Know That You Know" (Youmans–Anne Caldwell), "More Than You Know" (Youmans–Billy Rose–Edward Eliscu), "Keepin' Myself for You" (Youmans-Sidney Clare), "Ciribiribee" (A. Pestalozza). (1:52) (video/laserdisc) A musical of sailors on leave in search of romance. The 1922 play *Shore Leave* by Hubert Osborne was first filmed in 1925 by First National. It was then adapted by Herbert Fields and Vincent Youmans to the 1927 Broadway musical *Hit the Deck* and filmed under that title for 1930 release by RKO, followed by a 1936 remake titled *Follow the Fleet* also by RKO. The property was then sold to MGM. Eastmancolor and CinemaScope.

1167. The Hitchhiker (RKO/Filmakers; 1953). *Cast:* Edmond O'Brien, Frank Lovejoy, William Talman (title role), Jose Torvay, Sam Hayes, Wendell Niles, Jean Del Val, Clark Howat, Natividad Vacio, Rodney Bell, Nacho Galindo, Martin Garralaga, Tony Roux, Jerry Lawrence, Felipe Turich, Joe Dominguez, Rosa Turich, Orlando Veltran, George Navarro, June Dinneen, Al Ferrara, Henry Escalante, Taylor Flaniken, Wade Crosby, Kathy Riggins, Gordon Barnes, Ed Hinton, Larry Hudson. *D:* Ida Lupino; *P:* Collier Young; *St:* Daniel Mainwaring (unc.); *Adaptation:* Robert Joseph; *Sc:* Lupino, Young. (1:11) Offbeat film noir which packed a wallop in its day. Two men on a fishing trip pick up a hitchhiker, learning in a very short time that their passenger is a psychotic killer, holding them hostage on his way to Baja, CA.

1168. Hoedown (Columbia; 1950). *Cast:* Eddy Arnold (himself), Jeff Donnell, Jock [Mahoney] O'Mahoney, Guinn "Big Boy" Williams, Carolina Cotton (herself), Fred F. Sears, Don C. Harvey, Charles Sullivan, Ray Walker, Douglas Fowley, Harry Harvey, The Pied Pipers (themselves), The Oklahoma Wranglers [the Willis brothers/themselves]. *D:* Ray Nazarro; *P:* Colbert Clark; *Sc:* Barry Shipman. (1:04) Bank robbers use a dude ranch as a hideout in this musical with a country-western flavoring.

1169. Hold Back the Night (Allied Artists/Hayes Goetz Prods.; 1956). *Cast:* John Payne,

Mona Freeman, Peter Graves, Chuck Connors, Abby Dalton, Bob Nichols, John Wilder, Bob Easton, Stanley Cha, Nicky Blair, John Craven, Nelson Leigh. *D:* Allan Dwan; *P:* Hayes Goetz; *Sc:* John C. Higgins, Walter Doniger. (1:20) Korean conflict drama of U.S. marines in action, with flashbacks to the company leader's personal life. Based on the 1952 novel by Pat Frank.

1170. Hold Back Tomorrow (Universal-International/Hugo Haas; 1955). *Cast:* Cleo Moore, John Agar, Frank DeKova, Dallas Boyd, Steffi Sidney, Mel Welles, Harry Guardino, Mona Knox, Arlene Harris, Kay Riehl, Jan Englund, Pat Goldin. *D:-P: & Sc:* Hugo Haas; *Title song:* Franz [Frank Steininger] Steinger. (1:15) Offbeat melodrama of a man sentenced to hang and what develops between him and a down-and-out hooker, delivered to him in his cell as his last request.

1171. Hold That Hypnotist (Allied Artists; 1957). *Cast:* Huntz Hall, Stanley Clements, Jane Nigh, Robert Foulk, James Flavin, Queenie Smith, David [Gorcey] Condon, Jimmy Murphy, Murray Alper, Dick Elliott, Mel Welles (Blackbeard the pirate). *D:* Austen Jewell; *P:* Ben Schwalb; *St: & Sc:* Dan Pepper. (1:01) "Bowery Boys" comedy with Sach (Hall) put under the spell of an evil hypnotist. He regresses Sach back to a past life in the days of Blackbeard the pirate in an attempt to find the location of a buried treasure.

1172. Hold That Line (Monogram; 1952). *Cast:* Leo Gorcey, Huntz Hall, John Bromfield, Bennie Bartlett, David [Gorcey] Condon, Mona Knox, Veda Ann Borg, Gil Stratton, Jr., Taylor Holmes, Bernard Gorcey, Bob Nichols, Gloria Winters, Francis Pierlot, Pierre Watkin, Byron Foulger, Paul Bryar, Bob Peoples, Tom Hanlon, George Lewis, Al Eben, Ted Stanhope, Percival Vivian, Tom Kennedy, Bert Davidson, Marjorie Eaton, Jean Dean, Ted Jordan, Steve Wayne, George Sanders (not the), Marvelle Andre. *D:* William Beaudine; *P:* Jerry Thomas; *St: & Sc:* Charles R. Marion, Tim Ryan; *Additional dialogue:* Bert Lawrence. (1:04) The "Bowery Boys" go to an Ivy League college in this comedy series entry, climaxed by the proverbial "big game."

1173. A Hole in the Head (United Artists/SinCap; 1959). *Cast:* Frank Sinatra (Tony Manetta/narrator), Edward G. Robinson (Mario Manetta), Eleanor Parker (Eloise Rogers), Eddie Hodges (film debut/Ally Manetta), Carolyn Jones (Shirl), Thelma Ritter (Sophie Manetta), Keenan Wynn (Jerry Marks), Joi Lansing (Dorine), George DeWitt (Mendy), Jimmy Komack (Julius Manetta), Dub Taylor (Fred), Connie Sawyer (repeating her stage role/Miss Wexler), Benny Rubin (Abe Diamond), Ruby Dandridge (Sally), Joyce Nizzari (Alice), Bill Walker (Andy), B.S. Pully, Pupi Campo, Robert B. Williams, Emory Parnell. *D: & P:* Frank Capra; *Sc:* Arnold Shulman; *Songs:* "High Hopes" (AA-Best Song), "All My Tomorrows" James Van Heusen, Sammy Cahn. (2:00) (video/laserdisc) Comedy of a widower with an 11-year-old son, facing foreclosure on his Florida hotel due to his inability to manage money. Originally a 1955 TV play titled *The Heart's a Forgotten Hotel* by Mr. Shulman, which also became a stageplay in 1957. The film changed the ethnicity of the main characters from Jewish to Italian. Filmed on location in Cypress Gardens, Florida, in DeLuxe color and CinemaScope. The *New York Times* placed it at #6 on their "10 Best" list and it went on to become one of the 26 top-grossing films of 1958-59.

1174. Holiday for Lovers (20th Century-Fox; 1959). *Cast:* Clifton Webb, Jane Wyman, Jill St. John, Carol Lynley, Paul Henreid, Gary Crosby, Nico Minardos, Wally Brown, Henny Backus, Nora O'Mahoney, Buck Class, Al Austin, Gardner McKay, Jose Greco, Nestor Amaral and Orchestra. *D:* Henry Levin; *P:* David Weisbart; *Sc:* Luther Davis; *Title song:* James Van Heusen, Sammy Cahn. (1:43) Comedy of a father with two adolescent daughters, who constantly interferes in the girls' romantic pursuits while on holiday in South America. Based on the 1957 Broadway play by Ronald Alexander. DeLuxe color and CinemaScope.

1175. Holiday for Sinners (MGM; 1952). *Cast:* Gig Young, Keenan Wynn, Janice Rule, Richard Anderson, William Campbell, Edith Barrett, Michael Chekhov, Porter Hall, Sandro Giglio, Ralph Dumke, Frank DeKova, Will Wright, Jack Raine. *D:* Gerald Mayer; *P:* John Houseman; *Sc:* A.I. Bezzerides. (1:12) New Orleans Mardi Gras is the backdrop for this programmer drama of four people with problems. Based on the 1939 novel *Days Before Lent* by Hamilton Basso, it flopped at the box office.

1176. Holiday Rhythm (Lippert; 1950). *Cast:* Mary Beth Hughes, David Street, Wally Vernon, Tex Ritter, Donald MacBride, Chuy Reyes and His Mambo Orchestra, Ike Carpenter & Orchestra, Nappy LaMare & His Dixieland Band, George Arnold and His "Rhythm on Ice" Show, The Cass County Boys, Sid Melton, Tom Noonan & Pete Marshall, Bobby Chang, Glenn Turnbull, Regina Day, Vera Lee, Tom Laddy, Bill Burns & His Birds, Bertil Unger, Gustav Unger, Eva Martell, Neva Martell, Gloria Grey, Alan Harris, Moana, Freddie Letuli, Lynn Davis, Richard Farmer, Jack Reitzen, Manuel Serrano, Ricci Mari, Neila Mavi, The Four Moroccans. *D:* Jack Scholl; *P:* Jack Leewood; *St: & Sc:* Lee Wainer; *Songs:* Title song (Wainer), "Lost in a Dream" (Paul Herrick–Bert Shefter), "I'll Think It Over" (M.K. Jerome-Jack Scholl), all performed by Hughes and Street, "Old Chisholm Trail" by Ritter, "Pass the Biscuits, Mirandy" by Cass County Boys, and "Concussion Mambo" by Reyes and Orchestra. (1:10—some prints run 1:00) Programmer musical-comedy with many variety acts.

1177. Hollywood or Bust (Paramount; 1956). *Cast:* Dean Martin, Jerry Lewis, Pat Crowley, Anita Ekberg (herself), Maxie Rosenbloom, Willard Waterman, Mike Ross, Frank Wilcox, Kathryn Card, Wendell Niles, Richard Karlan, Jack McElroy, Tracey Roberts, Ben Welden, Ross Westlake, Gretchen Houser, Sandra White, Adele August, Mr. Bascom (great dane—received PATSY Award of Excellence in 1957). *D:* Frank Tashlin; *P:* Hal B. Wallis; *St: & Sc:* Erna Lazarus; *Songs:* "A Day in the Country," Title song, "Let's Be Friendly," "It Looks Like Love" and "The Wild and Woolly West" Charles O'Curran, Sammy Fain, Paul Francis Webster. (1:34) (video) In this, the final pairing of Martin and Lewis as a comedy team, Jerry is a starstruck movie fan on his way to Hollywood who picks up gambler Dean and they in turn pick up Pat and all head for tinsel town. Technicolor and VistaVision.

1178. Hollywood Story (Universal-International; 1951). *Cast:* Richard Conte, Julia [Julie] Adams, Richard Egan, Henry Hull, Fred Clark, Jim Backus, Houseley Stevenson, Joel McCrea (cameo), Frances X. Bushman. Betty Blythe, William Farnum, Helen Gibson (final film), Paul Cavanagh, Elmo Lincoln (cameo), Katherine Meskill, Louis Lettieri. *D:* William Castle; *P:* Leonard Goldstein; *Sc:* Frederick Kohner, Fred Brady. (1:17) Crime drama with a basis in fact involving the murder of a famous Hollywood director of the silent screen. Note: The inspiration for this film was the unsolved 1922 murder of silent film director William Desmond Taylor. The reverberations of which destroyed the careers of actresses Mabel Normand and Mary Miles Minter due to their known association with the deceased. In 1986 the book *Cast of Killers* labeled Charlotte Shelby (the mother of Ms. Minter) as the killer of Mr. Taylor, based on notes found in the papers of director King Vidor following his death.

Hollywood Stunt Man *see* **Hollywood Thrill-Makers**

1179. The Hollywood Ten (1951). *D: & P:* John Berry. A feature length independent documentary in 16 mm helmed by Mr. Berry to raise defense funds for Herbert Biberman, Edward Dmytryk, Adrian Scott, Alvah Bessie, Lester Cole, Ring Lardner, Jr., John Howard Lawson, Albert Maltz, Samuel Ornitz and Dalton Trumbo. All were subpoenaed in 1947 to appear before the House Committee on Un-American Activities investigating communist infiltration of the film industry. A second McCarthy-era witch hunt in 1951 named more than 300 others associated with the film industry, who were purported to have had past or present affiliations with the Communist Party, including Mr. Berry.

1180. Hollywood Thrill-Makers (Lippert/B.B. Ray Prods.; 1954). *Cast:* James Gleason, Bill Henry, Theila [Diana] Darrin, Jean Holcombe, James Macklin, George Wilhelm, Robert Paquin, Janet Clark. *D:* Bernard B. Ray; *P:* Maurice Kosloff; *St:* Ray; *Sc:* Janet Clark. (0:56) Melodrama of a Hollywood stunt man. (aka: *Movie Stunt Men* and *Hollywood Stunt Man*)

1181. Hollywood Varieties (Lippert/Spartan Prods.; 1948–50). *Cast:* The Hoosier Hot Shots, Shaw and Lee, 3 Rio Brothers, Glenn Vernon and Eddie Ryan, Britt Wood, Peggy Stewart, Twirl, Whirl and a Girl, DePina Troupe, Lois Ray, The Four Dandies, Hector and His Pals (a dog act), Paul Gordon, Johnson Brothers, Sandy and His Seals, Dolores Parker, Shavd Sherman, Sammy Wolfe, Charles Cirillo, Aurora Roche, Cliff Taylor, Russell Trent, The Carlyle Dancers [Evilyn Hetzer, Toby Ford, Kay Whyne, Virginia Nolan, Aileen Marlowe, Devvy Davenport and Barbara Mohr]. *D:* Paul Landres; *P:* June Carr, Paul Schreibman. (1:00) A revue of various musical-comedy vaudeville acts, hosted by Robert Alda. Produced in 1948 and released in January 1950.

1182. Home Before Dark (Warner/Mervyn LeRoy; 1958). *Cast:* Jean Simmons, Dan O'Herlihy, Rhonda Fleming, Efrem Zimbalist, Jr., Mabel Albertson, Stephen Dunne, Joan Weldon, Joanna Barnes, Kathryn Card, Marjorie

Bennett, Johnstone White, Eleanor Audley. *D: & P:* Mervyn LeRoy; Sc: Eileen and Robert Bassing; *Title song:* Jimmy McHugh, Sammy Cahn (sung by Mary Kaye). (2:16) Drama of a woman returning to her home and trying to readjust her life after having been committed to a mental institution for a nervous breakdown caused by "delusions." Based on the 1957 novel by Eileen Bassing, location filming took place at Marblehead and Boston, Massachusetts.

1183. Home Town Story (MGM; 1951). *Cast:* Jeffrey Lynn, Donald Crisp, Marjorie Reynolds, Alan Hale, Jr., Marilyn Monroe, Barbara Brown, Melinda Plowman, Glenn Tryon, Nelson Leigh, Renny McEvoy, Griff Barnett, Virginia Campbell, Harry Harvey, Speck Noblitt, Byron Foulger. *D: & Sc:* Arthur Pierson; *P:* Pierson, John K. Ford. (1:01) (video) Melodramatic propaganda, commissioned by General Motors, of a disgruntled young man who sees the error of his thinking when faced with a personal crisis.

1184. The Homesteaders (Allied Artists/ Silvermine Prods.; 1953). *Cast:* William Elliott, Bob Lowry, Barbara Allen, George Wallace, Emmett Lynn, Robert "Buzz" Henry, Rick Vallin, Stanley Price, William Fawcett, James Seay, Tom Monroe, Ray Walker, Barbara Woodell. *D:* Lewis D. Collins; *P:* Vincent M. Fennelly; *St: & Sc:* Sid Theil, Milton Raison. (1:02) (video) Western of outlaws going after dynamite being transported to the U.S. army on a settlers' wagon train.

1185. Hondo (Warner/Wayne-Fellows; 1953). *Cast:* John Wayne (Hondo), Geraldine Page (AAN-BSA/Angie Lowe), Ward Bond (Buffalo), Michael Pate (Vittorio), Lee Aaker (Johnny), James Arness (Lennie), Rudolfo Acosta (Silva), Leo Gordon (Ed Lowe), Tom Irish (Lt. McKay), Paul Fix (Major Sherry), Rayford Barnes (Pete), Sam (dog—received 1st Place PATSY in 1954). *D:* John Farrow; *P:* Robert Fellows; *Sc:* James Edward Grant. (1:24) (video) Acclaimed western of a U.S. cavalry dispatcher who comes across an isolated ranch run by an abandoned wife and her young son who have no fear of pending Apache hostilities. Based on "The Gift of Cochise" a story by Louis L'Amour which appeared in *Collier's*, it became one of the 25 top-grossing films of 1953-54. Warnercolor and 3-D.

1186. Honeychile (Republic; 1951). *Cast:* Judy Canova, Eddie Foy, Jr., Alan Hale, Jr., Walter Catlett, Roy Barcroft, Claire Carleton, Karolyn Grimes, Brad Morrow, Leonid Kinsky, Fuzzy Knight, Gus Schilling, Irving Bacon, Roscoe Ates, Ida Moore, Sarah Edwards, Emory Parnell, Dick Elliott, Dick Wessel, William Fawcett, Robin Winans, Stanley Blystone, Donia Bussey, John Crawford, Cecil Elliott, Cecile Weston. *D:* R.G. Springsteen; *As.P:* Sidney Picker; *St: & Sc:* Jack Townley, Charles E. Roberts; *Songs:* Title song (Jack Elliott–Harold Spina), "Ragmop" (Johnny Lee Wills–Deacon Anderson, arranged by Elliott), "Tutti Frutti" (Elliott–Ann Canova), "More Than I Care to Remember" (Ted Johnson–Matt Terry). (1:29) Comedy of a hillbilly girl who writes a song, thought by a music publisher to have been written by a more famous songwriter. Trucolor.

1187. Hong Kong (Paramount/Pine-Thomas; 1951). *Cast:* Ronald Reagan, Rhonda Fleming, Nigel Bruce, Marvin Miller, Danny Chang, Lady May Lawford, Claud Allister, Lowell Gilmore. *D:* Lewis Foster; *P:* William H. Pine, William C. Thomas; *Sc:* Winston Miller; *St:* Foster. (1:32) A thief attempts to steal a priceless jeweled artifact from an orphan boy, but is reformed by love. Technicolor. (aka: *Bombs Over China*)

1188. Hong Kong Affair (Allied Artists/ Claremont Pictures; 1958). *Cast:* Jack Kelly, May Wynn, Richard Loo, Lo Lita Shek, Gerald Young, James Hudson, Michael Bulmer. *D:* Paul F. Heard; *P:* Heard, J. Raymond Friedgen; *Ex.P:* Herbert R. Ebenstein; *Sc:* Herbert G. Luft, Heard, Friedgen, Helene Turner; *Title song:* Louis Forbes (m), Paul Herrick (ly), sung by Ronnie Deauville. (1:19) Filmed on location melodrama of an ex–GI who ventures to Hong Kong to find out why his half interest in a tea business hasn't been paying off and gets involved with a front for opium smuggling.

1189. Hong Kong Confidential (United Artists/Vogue Pictures; 1958). *Cast:* Gene Barry, Beverly Tyler, Allison Hayes, Noel Drayton, Ed Kemmer, Michael Pate, Rico Alaniz, W. Beal Wong, Mel Prestige, King Calder, Bryan Roper, Philip Ahn, Walter Woolf King, Joe Vitale, Asa Maynor, Lou Krugman, Owen McGivney, Bill Saito, Jack Kenney. *D:* Edward L. Cahn. *P:* Robert E. Kent; *St: & Sc:* Orville H. Hampton. (1:07) Programmer melodrama of the kidnapping of a wealthy Arab's son by Russians.

1190. The Hoodlum (United Artists/ Jack Schwarz Prods.; 1951). *Cast:* Lawrence Tierney, Allene Roberts, Edward Tierney, Lisa Golm,

Marjorie Riordan, Stuart Randall, Ann Zika, John DeSimone, Tom Hubbard, Eddie Foster, O.Z. Whitehead, Richard Barron, Rudy Rama. *D:* Max Nosseck; *P:* Maurice Kosloff; *St: & Sc:* Sam Neuman, Nat Tanchuck. (1:01) (video) Programmer melodrama of a career criminal and how he affects the lives of those around him.

1191. Hoodlum Empire (Republic; 1952). *Cast:* Brian Donlevy, Claire Trevor, Forrest Tucker, Vera Ralston, Luther Adler, John Russell, Gene Lockhart, Grant Withers, Taylor Holmes, Roy Barcroft, William Murphy, Richard Jaeckel, Don Beddoe, Roy Roberts, Richard Benedict, Phillip Pine, Damian O'Flynn, Pat Flaherty, Ric Roman, Douglas Kennedy, Don Haggerty, Francis Pierlot, Sarah Spencer, Thomas Browne Henry, Jack Pennick, Dick Wessel, Paul Livermore, Fred Kohler, Jr., Tony Dante, Tom Monroe, Leah Waggner, Betty Ball, William Schallert, John Phillips, Joe Bailey, Lee Shumway, Charles Trowbridge, Elizabeth Flournoy, John Halloran, John Pickard, Gil Herman, Mervin Williams, Mikel Conrad, Richard Reeves, Matty Fain, Stanley Waxman, Sid Tomack, Eddie Foster, Sydney Mason, Whit Bissell, Dick Paxton, Sam Scar, George Volk, Don Michael Dysdale, Andy Brennan. *D: & As.P:* Joseph Kane; *Ex.P:* Herbert J. Yates; *St:* Bob Considine; *Sc:* Bruce Manning, Considine. (1:38) (video) Crime melodrama of a former mobster who after serving time in the military, wishes to start a new life operating a gas station, but finds himself inadvertently drawn back into the crime syndicate. This film found its inspiration from Senator Estes Kefauver's 1950-51 investigation into organized crime.

1192. Horizons West (Universal-International; 1952). *Cast:* Robert Ryan, Julia [Julie] Adams, Rock Hudson, John McIntire, Judith Braun, Raymond Burr, James Arness, Frances Bavier, Dennis Weaver (film debut), Mae Clarke, Tom Powers, Rudolfo Acosta, John Hubbard, Douglas Fowley, Walter Reed, Raymond Greenleaf, Tom Monroe, Dan White, John Harmon, Robert Bice, Dan Moore, Alberto Morin, Peter Mamakos, Eddie Parker, Monte Montague, Forbes Murray, Buddy Roosevelt. *D:* Budd Boetticher; *P:* Albert J. Cohen; *St: & Sc:* Louis Stevens. (1:21) (video) Western of three ex-soldiers returning home to Texas following the Civil War. Technicolor.

A Horse Named Comanche *see* **Tonka**

1193. The Horse Soldiers (United Artists/Mirisch Co./Mahin-Rackin Prods.; 1959). *Cast:* John Wayne (Col. John Marlowe), William Holden (Major Henry Kendall), Constance Towers (Hannah Hunter), Althea Gibson (film debut/Lukey), Hoot Gibson (final film—d. 1962/Brown), Anna Lee (Mrs. Buford), Russell Simpson (sheriff), Stan Jones (Gen. Ulysses S. Grant), Carleton Young (Col. Jonathan Miles), Basil Ruysdael (commandant), Judson Pratt (Sgt. Kirby), Willis Bouchey (Col. Phil Seacord), William Leslie (Maj. Richard Gray), Ken Curtis (Wilkie), Bing Russell (Dunker), Hank Worden (Deacon), Ron Hagerthy (bugler), Donald Foster (Dr. Marvin), Jack Pennick (Sgt.-Major Mitchell), Richard Cutting (General Sherman), O.Z. Whitehead (Hopkins), William Forrest (Gen. Steve Hurlburt), Chuck Hayward (Woodward), Strother Martin (Virgil), Denver Pyle (Joe), Walter Reed, Charles Seel, Bill Henry, Fred Graham, Major Sam Harris, Cliff Lyons, William Wellman, Jr., Jan Stine, Fred Kennedy (a stunt man who was killed during production when he fell from a horse). *D:* John Ford; *P: & Sc:* John Lee Mahin, Martin Rackin; *Song:* "I Left My Love" Stan Jones. (1:59) (video/laserdisc) Civil War epic which was based on the novel by Harold Sinclair, detailing the exploits of real life Union Colonel Benjamin Grierson who sabotaged Confederate supply lines in Tennessee in 1863. Filmed in DeLuxe color on location in Louisiana and Mississippi, it became one of the 26 top-grossing films of 1958-59.

Horsie *see* **Queen for a Day**

1194. Hostile Country (Lippert; 1950). *Cast:* Jimmie Ellison, Russ Hayden, Raymond Hatton, Fuzzy Knight, Betty [Julie] Adams, Tom Tyler, George J. Lewis, John Cason, Stanley Price, Stephen Carr, Dennis Moore, George Chesebro, Bud Osborne, Jimmie Martin, Judith Webster, Jimmy Van Horn, Cliff Taylor, Ray Jones, I. Stanford Jolley, George Sowards, J. Farrell MacDonald. *D:* Thomas Carr; *P:* Ron Ormond; *As.P:* Ira Webb; *St: & Sc:* Ormond, Maurice Tombragel. (1:01) (video) The premiere entry in the "Shamrock and Lucky" [Four Star] series of six films with the saddle pals coming to the aid of a lady rancher. (TV title: *Outlaw Fury*)

1195. The Hot Angel (Paramount/Paragon Prods.; 1958). *Cast:* Edward Kemmer, Jackie Loughery, Lyle Talbot, Mason Alan Dinehart, Zon Teller, Heather Ames, Steffi Sidney, John Nolan, Richard Stauffer, Kathi Thornton., Harold Mallet. *D:* Joseph Parker; *P:-St: & Sc:*

Stanley Kallis; *As.P:* Kenny Kessler. (1:13) Programmer melodrama of a flying surveyor forced down over an area containing uranium deposits. Filmed on location at the Grand Canyon in Arizona.

1196. Hot Blood (Columbia; 1956). *Cast:* Jane Russell, Cornel Wilde, Luther Adler, Joseph Calleia, Mikhail Rasumny (final film—d. 1956), Nina Koshetz, Helen Westcott, Wally Russell, Nick Dennis, Richard Deacon, Robert C. Foulk, John Raven, Joe Merritt, Ethan Laidlaw, Peter Brocco, Ross Bagdasarian, Manuel Paris. *D:* Nicholas Ray; *P:* Howard Welsch, Harry Tatelman; *St:* Jean Evans; *Sc:* Jesse L. Lasky, Jr.; *Songs:* "Tsara Tsara," "I Could Learn to Love You" Les Baxter, Ross Bagdasarian. (1:25) Romantic drama set in the world of gypsies. Technicolor and CinemaScope.

Hot Car Girl (1956) *see* **Hot Rod Girl**

1197. Hot Car Girl (Allied Artists/Santa Cruz Prods.; 1958). *Cast:* Richard Bakalyan, June Kenney, John Brinkley, Robert Knapp, Jana Lund, Sheila McKay, Bruno VeSoto, Grace Albertson, Hal Smith, Tyler McVey. *D:* Bernard Kowalski (directorial debut); *Ex.P:* Roger Corman; *P:* Gene Corman; *St: & Sc:* Leo Gordon. (1:11) Teen exploitation of two youths who run afoul of the law selling stolen auto parts to pay for beer parties, with one eventually committing murder and dragging his girlfriend into the whole mess. Originally ran on a double bill with *The Cry Baby Killer* (q.v.), another Corman quickie.

1198. Hot Cars (United Artists/Bel-Air-Sunrise Pictures; 1956). *Cast:* John Bromfield, Joi Lansing, Mark Dana, Carol Shannon, Ralph Clanton, Robert Osterloh, Dabbs Greer, Charles Keane, Kurt Katch, George Sawaya, John Merrick, Maurice Marks, Joan Sinclair, Marilee Earle, Vic Cutrier, Paula Hill. *D:* Donald McDougall; *P:* Howard W. Koch; *Sc:* Don Martin, Richard Landau. (1:00) As the title implies, a programmer involving a gang with a stolen car operation who deceive a car salesman into getting involved in the racket. Based on the novel *Sellout* by M. Haile Chace.

Hot Horse *see* **Once Upon a Horse**

1199. Hot Lead (RKO; 1951). *Cast:* Tim Holt, Richard Martin, Joan Dixon, Ross Elliott, John Dehner, Stanley Andrews, Robert Wilke, Kenneth MacDonald, Paul Marion, Lee MacGregor, Paul E. Burns. *D:* Stuart Gilmore; *P:* Herman Schlom; *St: & Sc:* William Lively. (1:00) (video) In this Holt series western, a gang of outlaws plant one of their own at a telegraph office to get information on gold shipments. (aka: *A Taste of Hot Lead*)

Hot Lead (1957) *see* **Run of the Arrow**

1200. Hot News (Allied Artists; 1953). *Cast:* Stanley Clements, Gloria Henry, Ted de Corsia, Veda Ann Borg, Scotty Beckett, Mario Siletti, Carl Milletaire, James Flavin, Hal Baylor, Paul Bryar, Myron Healey. *D:* Edward Bernds; *P:* Ben Schwalb; *Sc:* Charles R. Marion, Elwood Ullman. (1:01) A former boxer becomes a sports columnist and exposes the ruthless head of a sport-gambling operation. This melodrama ran as the 2nd feature on a double bill with *Jack Slade* (q.v.).

1201. Hot Rod (Monogram; 1950). *Cast:* James Lydon, Art Baker, Gil Stratton, Jr., Gloria Winters, Myron Healey, Tommy Bond, Jean Dean, Bret Hamilton, Marshall Reed, Dennis Moore, William Vincent. *D:* Lewis D. Collins; *P:* Jerry Thomas; *St: & Sc:* Daniel B. Ullman. (1:01) Juvenile melodrama of a youth who converts his car to a hot rod, creating difficulties with his father, a judge. To make matters worse, it is found that the car was involved in a fatal hit-and-run accident. Originally the co-feature on a double bill with *Blues Busters* (q.v.).

1202. Hot Rod Gang (American International/Indio Prods.; 1958). *Cast:* John Ashley, Jody Fair, Gene Vincent and the Bluecaps, Steve Drexel, Henry McCann, Maureen Arthur, Gloria Grant, Dorothy Newman, Helen Spring, Doodles Weaver, Lester Dorr, Russ Bender, Claire DuBrey, Dub Taylor, Scott Peters, Robert Whiteside, Simmy Bow, Earl McDaniels, Kay Wheeler, Eddie Cochran. *D:* Lew Landers; *Ex.P:* Charles "Buddy" Rogers; *P:* Lou Rusoff; *St: & Sc:* Rusoff; *Songs:* "Dance in the Street," "Baby Blue," "Lovely Loretta," "Dance to the Bop" (performed by Vincent & the Bluecaps), "Annie Laurie" (sung by Ashley). (1:12) Another exploitation item from the studio of James H. Nicholson and Samuel Z. Arkoff as a teen gets a job singing with Gene Vincent's band to earn money for the entrance fee in a big hot rod race. (aka: *Fury Unleashed*) Designed for the teen drive-in movie trade, this was part of a double bill with *High School Hellcats* (q.v.).

1203. Hot Rod Girl (American International/Nacirema Prods.; 1956). *Cast:* Lori Nelson,

John Smith, Chuck Connors, Frank J. Gorshin, Roxanne Arlen, Mark Andrews, Carolyn Kearney, Ed Reider, Del Erickson, Fred Essler, Russ Thorsen, Charles Keane, Dabbs Greer. *D:* Leslie H. Martinson; *P:* Norman T. Herman; *St: & Sc:* John W. McGreevey. (1:19) (video) Teen oriented melodrama of a cop who takes steps to halt the rising tide of illegal drag racing in the community, but his sustained efforts backfire. (aka: *Hot Car Girl*)

1204. Hot Rod Rumble (Allied Artists/ Nacirema Prods.; 1957). *Cast:* Leigh Snowden, Richard Hartunian, Brett Halsey, Wright King, Joey Forman, Larry Dolgin, John Brinkley, Chuck Webster, Ned Glass, Phil Adams, Joe Mell. *D:* Leslie H. Martinson; *P:* Norman T. Herman; *St: & Sc:* Meyer Dolinsky. (1:19) Teen crime melodrama of a youthful hot rod enthusiast who is accused of running his girlfriend's car off the road, the accident killing the girl that was riding with her. Originally ran on a double bill with *Calypso Joe* (q.v.).

1205. Hot Shots (Allied Artists; 1956). *Cast:* Huntz Hall, Stanley Clements, Joi Lansing, Jimmy Murphy, David Gorcey, Queenie Smith, Philip Phillips, Mark Dana, Robert Shayne, Henry Rowland, Dennis Moore, Isabel Randolph, Frank Marlowe, Joe Kirk, Ray Walker. *D:* Jean Yarbrough; *P:* Ben Schwalb; *St:* Jack Townley, *Sc:* Townley, Elwood Ullman. (1:01) A latterday entry in the "Bowery Boys" series which finds Sach (Hall) and Duke (Clements) in the TV industry, finding themselves involved with an 8-year-old TV brat who is eventually kidnapped for ransom.

1206. Hot Spell (Paramount/Hal Wallis-Joseph Hazen; 1958). *Cast:* Shirley Booth (final film—ret.), Anthony Quinn, Shirley MacLaine, Earl Holliman, Eileen Heckart, Warren Stevens, Clint Kimbrough, Jody Lawrence, Harlan Warde, Valerie Allen, Irene Tedrow, Stafford Repp, Bill Walker, Louise Franklin, Anthony Jochim, Johnny Lee, Elsie Waller, Len Hendry, John Indrisano, Watson H. Downs, William Duray, Tony Merrill, Fred Zendar. *D:* Daniel Mann; *P:* Hal B. Wallis; *Sc:* James Poe. (1:26) (video) Drama of a marriage which hits the rocks when the husband starts seeing a younger woman, with the couple's offspring's reactions to the whole situation. In nomination for "Best Film" with the New York Film Critics, it was based on the play *Next of Kin* by Lonnie Coleman [pseudonym of William Laurence Coleman]. Set in New Orleans, it bombed at the box office.

1207. Hot Summer Night (MGM; 1957). *Cast:* Leslie Nielsen, Colleen Miller, Edward Andrews, Jay C. Flippen, James Best, Paul Richards, Robert Wilke, Claude Akins, Marjorie Hellen, Marianne Stewart. *D:* David Friedkin; *P:* Morton S. Fine; *Sc:* Friedkin, Fine. (1:25) Melodrama of a reporter in search of an interview with the leader of an outfit specializing in bank robberies. Based on the story "Capital Offense" by Edwin P. Hicks.

1208. Houdini (Paramount; 1953). *Cast:* Tony Curtis, Janet Leigh, Torin Thatcher, Angela Clarke, Sig Rumann, Stefan Schnable, Connie Gilchrist, Ian Wolfe, Michael Pate, Mabel Paige (final film—d. 1954), Mary Murphy, Joanne Gilbert, Malcolm Lee Beggs, Frank Orth, Barry Bernard, Douglas Spencer, Peter Baldwin, Richard Shannon, Elsie Ames, Nick Arno, Esther Garber, Norma Jean Eckart, Lewis Martin, Lawrence Ryle, Jody Gilbert, Edward Clark, Grace Hayle, Fred Essler, Arthur Gould-Porter, Alec Harford, Tudor Owen, Harry Hines, Oliver Blake, Cliff Clark, Harold Neiman, Erno Verebes, Anthony Warde, Frank Jacquet, Billy Bletcher, Lyle Latell, Torben Meyer, Tor Johnson. *D:* George Marshall; *P:* George Pal; *Sc:* Philip Yordan. (1:45) (video) Technicolor Hollywood biopic of famed magician/escape artist Harry Houdini (Curtis), blending much fiction with fact. Based on the 1928 book by Harold Kellock, the publicity hype and the star made the film a box office success. Note: Harry Houdini made two silent films for Paramount, *The Grim Game* (1919) and *Terror Island* (1920), but he never clicked as a movie star.

1209. Hound Dog Man (20th Century-Fox/Jerry Wald; 1959). *Cast:* Fabian (film debut), Carol Lynley, Stuart Whitman, Arthur O'Connell, Dodie Stevens, Betty Field, Dennis Holmes, Royal Dano, Margo Moore, Claude Akins, Edgar Buchanan, Jane Darwell, L.Q. Jones, Virginia Gregg, Rachel Stephens, Jim Beck, Hope Summers, Harry Carter. *D:* Don Siegel; *P:* Jerry Wald; *As.P:* Curtis Harrington; *Sc:* Fred Gipson (based on his 1949 book), Winston Miller; *Songs:* Title song, "What Big Boy?," "This Friendly World," "Pretty Little Girl," "Single," "I'm Growing Up," "Hill-Top Song" and "Hay-Foot, Straw-Foot" by Ken Darby, Frankie Avalon, Sol Ponti, Robert Marcucci, Peter de Angelis, Doc Pomus and Mort Shuman. (1:27) Hit lightweight family-fare with eight songs, of two brothers who come to idolize a shiftless, free spirited man who would rather do nothing more than spend his days hunting, fishing and avoiding any responsibility. Filmed on location at Big Bear, California, in DeLuxe color, CinemaScope and stereophonic sound.

1210. The Hour of 13 (MGM; 1952). *Cast:* Peter Lawford, Dawn Addams, Roland Culver, Colin Gordon, Derek Bond, Leslie Dwyer, Michael Hordern, Heather Thatcher, Jack McNaughton, Fabia Drake, Michael Goodliffe. *D:* Harold French; *P:* Hayes Goetz; *Sc:* Leon Gordon, Howard Emmett Rogers. (1:19) A reformed jewel thief seeks the killer of several bobbies in late 19th century London. Based on the 1933 novel *Mystery of the Dead Police* by Philip MacDonald, the film is a remake of *The Mystery of Mr. X* (1934).

1211. The House by the River (Republic/ Fidelity Pictures; 1950). *Cast:* Louis Hayward, Lee Bowman, Jane Wyatt, Dorothy Patrick, Ann Shoemaker, Jody Gilbert, Peter Brocco, Howland Chamberlain, Margaret Seddon, Sarah Padden, Kathleen Freeman, Will Wright, Leslie Kimmell, Effie Laird. *D:* Fritz Lang; *P:* Howard Welsch; *Sc:* Mel Dinelli. (1:28) (video) A man accidentally kills his housemaid while trying to seduce her, then attempts to get his brother to help him cover up the crime, with the brother eventually becoming the main suspect. Based on the 1921 novel by A.P. Herbert.

1212. House of Bamboo (20th Century-Fox; 1955). *Cast:* Robert Ryan, Robert Stack, Shirley Yamaguchi, Cameron Mitchell, Brad Dexter, Sessue Hayakawa, Biff Elliott, Sandro Giglio, Eiko Hanabusa, Harry Carey, Jr., Peter Gray, Robert Quarry, DeForest Kelley, John Doucette, Teru Shimada, Robert Hosai, Jack Maeshiro, May Takasugi, Robert Okazaki, Neyle Morrow, Kazue Ikeda, Clifford Arashiro, Robert Kino, Frank Kwanaga, Rollin Moriyama, Reiko Sato, Sandy "Chikaye" Azeka, Fuji, Frank Jumagai, Harris Matsushige, Kinuko Ann Ito, Barbara Uchiyamada, Fred Dale, Barry Coe, Reiko Hayakawa, A. Sandy Ozeka, Samuel Fuller, The Shochiku Troupe from Kokusai Theater. *D:* Samuel Fuller; *P:* Buddy Adler; *St: & Sc:* Harry Kleiner; *Additional dialogue:* Fuller; *Title song:* Leigh Harline, Jack Brooks. (1:42) Stark drama, set in post-war Japan, of a group of ex-servicemen who form a criminal organization with pachinko parlors as their lucrative source of income, and the ruthless boss (Ryan) who runs the operation. A remake of *The Street with No Name*, a 1948 production from this studio. DeLuxe color and CinemaScope.

1213. House of Numbers (MGM, 1957). *Cast:* Jack Palance (dual role), Barbara Lang, Harold J. Stone, Edward Platt, Burt Douglas. *D:* Russell Rouse; *P:* Charles Schnee; *Sc:* Rouse, Don Mankiewicz. (1:31) Partially filmed on location at California's San Quentin prison, this drama tells of twin brothers, one attempting to spring the other from prison and take his place. Taken from a 1956 novel by Jack Finney, which appeared in *Cosmopolitan*. CinemaScope.

1214. House of Wax (Warner; 1953). *Cast:* Vincent Price (Henry Jarrod), Phyllis Kirk (Sue Allen), Frank Lovejoy (Lt. Tom Brennan), Carolyn Jones (Cathy Gray), Paul Picerni (Scott Andrews), Roy Roberts (Matthew Burke), Charles [Bronson] Buchinsky (Igor), Paul Cavanagh (Sidney Wallace), Angela Clarke (Mrs. Andrews), Dabbs Greer (Sgt. Jim Shane), Ned Young (Leon Averill), Philip Tonge (Bruce Alison), Riza Royce (Ma Flanagan), Mary Lou Holloway (Millie), Reggie Rymal, Ruth Warren, Richard Benjamin, Jack Mower, Grandon Rhodes, Frank Ferguson, Oliver Blake, Leo Curley, Merry Townsend, Lyle Latell. *D:* Andre De Toth; *P:* Bryan Foy; *St:* Charles Belden; *Sc:* Crane Wilbur. (1:28) (video/laserdisc) Horror-thriller of a demented and disfigured sculptor who recreates his burned out wax museum by using human corpses as a foundation for his "life-like" exhibits. The best known and most popular of the 3-D movies of the early 1950s, it became one of the 26 top-grossing films of 1952-53. A remake of this studio's 1933 2-color Technicolor production *Mystery of the Wax Museum*. WarnerColor, WarnerPhonic sound and of course, 3-D.

1215. House on Haunted Hill (Allied Artists/Susian Associates Prod.; 1958). *Cast:* Vincent Price, Carol Ohmart, Richard Long, Alan Marshal, Carolyn Craig, Elisha Cook, Jr., Julie Mitchum, Leona Anderson, Howard Hoffman. *D: & P:* William Castle; *As.P: & Sc:* Robb White. (1:15) (video/laserdisc) Mystery-thriller of five people invited to a "haunted" house by the eccentric, wealthy owners, each guest receiving $10,000 if they spend the night. On arriving, each guest also receives a loaded gun. Shown theatrically with the silly Castle gimmick "Emergo" which had a skeleton slide over the audience on a wire at a designated point during the film.

1216. The House on Telegraph Hill (20th Century–Fox; 1951). *Cast:* Richard Basehart (Alan Spender), Valentina Cortesa (Victoria Kowelska), William Lundigan (Major Marc

Anders), Fay Baker (Margaret), Gordon Gebert (Chris), Kei Thing Chung (houseboy), Steve Geray (Dr. Burkhardt), Herbert Butterfield (Callahan), John Burton (Mr. Whitmore), Katherine Meskill (Mrs. Whitmore), Mario Siletti (Tony), Natasha Lytess (Karin), Tamara Schee (Maria), Ashmead Scott (Inspector Hardy), Tom McDonough (Farrell), Harry Carter (Detective Ellis), Charles Wagenheim, David Clarke, Mary Young, Henry Rowland, Les O'Pace, Don Kohler. *D:* Robert Wise; *P:* Robert Bassler; *Sc:* Elick Moll; *ASD:* (AAN-b/w) Lyle Wheeler, John DeCuir (art directors), Thomas Little, Paul S. Fox (sets). (1:33) Successful mystery-thriller about a survivor of a World War II Nazi concentration camp who assumes the identity of a dead prisoner, goes to San Francisco to meet the son of the dead woman, and finds herself and the boy are targeted for death. Based on the 1948 novel *The Frightened Child* by Dana Lyon.

The House on the Square (G.B. title) *see* **I'll Never Forget You**

1217. Houseboat (Paramount/Scribe Prods.; 1958). *Cast:* Cary Grant (Tom Winters), Sophia Loren (Cinzia Zaccardi), Martha Hyer (Carolyn Gibson), Harry Guardino (Angelo Donatello), Eduardo Ciannelli (Arturo Zaccardi), Murray Hamilton (Alan Wilson), Mimi Gibson (Elizabeth Winters), Paul Petersen (David Winters), Charles Herbert (Robert Winters), Madge Kennedy (Mrs. Farnsworth), John Litel (Mr. Farnsworth), Werner Klemperer (Harold Messner), Peggy Connelly (Elizabeth Wilson), Marc Wilder (specialty dancer), Pat Moran (clown), Kathleen Freeman, Helen Brown, Florence MacAfee, Julian Rivero, Ernst Brengk, Mary Forbes, William R. Remick, Wally Walker, Brooks Benedict, Joe McTurk, Gilda Oliva. *D:* Mel(ville) Shavelson; *P:* Jack Rose; *As.P:* Hal C. Kern; *St: & Sc:* (AAN) Shavelson, Rose; *Songs:* "Almost in Your Arms" (love song from *Houseboat*) (AAN-Best Song) sung by Sam Cooke, "Bing! Bang! Bong!" (sung by Loren) Jay Livingston, Ray Evans. (1:50) (video/laserdisc) Acclaimed domestic-romantic comedy of a widower with three children who hires a housekeeper for their houseboat residence. Filmed on location in Washington, D.C., in Technicolor and VistaVision, it became one of the 26 top-grossing films of 1958-59. Note: The final film of cinematographer Ray June who died in 1958.

1218. The Houston Story (Columbia/ Clover Prods; 1956). *Cast:* Gene Barry, Barbara Hale, Edward Arnold, Paul Richards, Jeanne Cooper, Frank Jenks, John Zaremba, Chris Alcaide, Jack V. Littlefield, Paul Levitt, Fred Krone, Pete Kellett, Leslie Hunt, Claudia Bryar, Larry W. Fultz, Charles Gray. *D:* William Castle; *P:* Sam Katzman; *St: & Sc:* James B. Gordon. (1:19) A low budget crime-melodrama of pilferage in the oilfields.

1219. How to Be Very, Very Popular (20th Century–Fox; 1955). *Cast:* Betty Grable (final film—ret.), Sheree North, Robert Cummings, Charles Coburn, Tommy Noonan, Orson Bean, Fred Clark, Charlotte Austin, Alice Pearce, Rhys Williams, Andrew Tombes (final film—ret.), Emory Parnell, Harry Carter, Noel Toy, Jesslyn Fax, Jack Mather, Mike Lally, Milton Parsons, Harry Seymour, Hank Mann, Leslie Parrish, Janice Carroll, Jean Holcombe, Iona McKenzie, Howard Petrie, Jean Walters, Stanley Farrar, Willard Waterman, Anthony Redondo. *D:-P: & Sc:* Nunnally Johnson (based on a play by Howard Lindsay from a novel by Edward Hope and another play by Lyford Moore and Harlan Thompson); *Title song:* Jule Styne, Sammy Cahn, "Bristol Bell" Ken Darby, Lionel Newman. (1:29) Romantic comedy with musical numbers of two strippers who are hidden by a group of college students after they witness the murder of another stripper. A remake of *True to the Army* (Paramount; 1942) which was a remake of *She Loves Me Not* (Paramount; 1934). DeLuxe color and CinemaScope. Note: If you miss North's gyrational dance to "Shake, Rattle and Roll" you're missing the highpoint of the film!

1220. How to Make a Monster (American International/Sunset Prods.; 1958). *Cast:* Robert H. Harris, Paul Brinegar, Gary Conway, Gary Clarke, Malcolm Atterbury, Dennis Cross, Morris Ankrum, Walter Reed, Paul Maxwell, Eddie Marr, Heather Ames, Robert Shayne, Rod Dana, Jacqueline Ebeier, Joan Chandler, Thomas B. Henry, John Phillips, Pauline Myers, John Ashley. *D:* Herbert L. Strock; *P:* Herman Cohen; *Ex.P:* James H. Nicholson, Samuel Z. Arkoff; *St: & Sc:* Kenneth Langtry, Cohen; *Song:* "You've Got to Have Ee-ooo" Paul Dunlap, Skip Redwine. (1:14) (video) Low budget thriller of a movie studio makeup artist who snaps when he learns the studio is going to make musical-comedies instead of horror films, thus putting him out of a job. The film's final sequence is in color. This one was matched on a double bill with *Teenage Caveman* (q.v.).

1221. How to Marry a Millionaire (20th Century–Fox; 1953). *Cast:* Betty Grable (Loco),

Marilyn Monroe (Pola), Lauren Becall (Schatze Page), David Wayne (Freddie Denmark), Rory Calhoun (Eben), Cameron Mitchell (Tom Brockman), Alex D'Arcy (J. Stewart Merrill), Fred Clark (Waldo Brewster), William Powell (J.D. Hanley), George Dunn (Mike, the elevator man), Tudor Owen (Mr. Otis), Percy Helton (Benton), Maurice Marsac (Antoine), Rankin Mansfield (Bennett), Jan Arvan (Tony), Herbert Deans (Stewart), Hope Landin (Mrs. Salem), Merry Anders, Charlotte Austin, Ruth Hall, Lida Thomas, Beryl McCutcheon (models), Harry Carter, Robert Adler, Emmett Vogan, Hermione Sterler, Ivis Goulding, Ralph Reed, Abney Mott, Dayton Lummis, Van Des Autels, Eric Wilton, Ivan Triesault, Georges Saurel, Tom Greenway, James Stone, Tom Martin, Eve Finnell, Benny Burt, Richard Shackleton. *D:* Jean Negulesco; *P: & Sc:* Nunnally Johnson (based on the play *The Greeks Had a Word for It* by Zoe Akins and the play *Loco* by Dale Eunson and Katherine Albert); *Costumes:* (AAN-color) Charles LeMaire, Travilla. (1:35) (video/laserdisc) Hit romantic-comedy, which was in nomination at the British Academy Awards, of three single girls who go to New York in search of millionaire husbands. A remake of *Three Little Girls in Blue* (Fox; 1946) which was a remake of *Moon Over Miami* (Fox; 1941), which was a remake of *Three Blind Mice* (Fox; 1938) which was a remake of *The Greeks Had a Word for It* (retitled: *Three Broadway Girls*—U.A./Goldwyn; 1934). Technicolor and CinemaScope.

How to Rob a Bank (G.B. title) *see* **A Nice Little Bank That Should be Robbed**

1222. Huk (United Artists/Pan Pacific Pictures; 1956). *Cast:* George Montgomery, Mona Freeman, John Baer, James Bell, Ramio Barri, Teddy Benavedes, Ben Perez, Mario Barri. *D:* John Barnwell; *P:* Collier Young; *Sc:* Stirling Silliphant. (1:24) Graphic post–World War II action-drama filmed on location in the Philippines, of a man attempting to save his plantation from a band of marauding Huks, a band of guerrilla fighters with a bent for blood. In Eastmancolor, it was based on the novel by Mr. Silliphant.

1223. Human Desire (Columbia; 1954). *Cast:* Glenn Ford, Gloria Grahame, Broderick Crawford, Edgar Buchanan, Kathleen Case, Peggy Maley, Diane DeLaire, Grandon Rhodes, Dan Seymour, John Pickard, Paul Brinegar, Dan Riss, Victor Hugo Greene, John Zaremba, Carl Lee, Olan Soule. *D:* Fritz Lang; *P:* Lewis J. Rachmil; *Sc:* Alfred Hayes. (1:30) (video) Romantic drama of a man who finds himself enmeshed in a murder plot schemed by a beautiful woman. A remake of the 1938 French film *La Bête Humaine* (U.S. title: *The Human Beast*) which was based on the 1933 work of that name by Emile Zola.

1224. The Human Jungle (Allied Artists; 1954). *Cast:* Gary Merrill, Jan Sterling, Paula Raymond, Emile Meyer, Regis Toomey, Chuck Connors, Pat Waltz, George Wallace, Chubby Johnson, Don Keefer, Rankin Mansfield, Lamont Johnson, Leo Cleary, Florenz Ames, Claude Akins, Hugh Boswell, James Westerfield. *D:* Joseph M. Newman; *P:* Hayes Goetz; *St:* William Sackheim; *Sc:* Sackheim, Daniel Fuchs; *Song:* Max Rich. (1:22) A police captain accepts a new job in a crime ridden district and in his attempts to clean it up, finds he is not only dealing with the local criminal element, but with police corruption as well.

1225. Humphrey Takes a Chance (Monogram; 1950). *Cast:* Joe Kirkwood, Jr., Leon Errol, Robert Coogan, Lois Collier, Jack Kirkwood, Andrew Tombes, Stanley Prager, Tim Ryan, Almira Sessions, Joel Friedkin, Tom Neal, Gil Lamb, Chester Conklin, Hank Mann, Clarence Hennecke, Chester Clute, Victoria Horne, Mary Happy, Frank Sully, Eddie Gribbon, Jim Drum, Paul Gardini, Iris Adrian. *D:* Jean Yarbrough; *P:* Hal E. Chester; *St: & Sc:* Henry Blankfort. (1:14) The 9th entry in the "Joe Palooka" series with Knobby Walsh (Errol) running Humphrey (Coogan) for mayor of a small town. Based on characters created in Ham Fisher's comic strip. (aka: *Joe Palooka in Humphrey Takes a Chance*).

1226. Hunt the Man Down (RKO; 1950). *Cast:* Gig Young, Lynne Roberts, Mary Anderson, Willard Parker, Carla Balenda, Gerald Mohr, James Anderson, John Kellogg, Harry Shannon, Cleo Moore, Christy Palmer, Paul Frees, James Seay. *D:* George Archainbaud; *P:* Lewis J. Rachmil; *St: & Sc:* DeVallon Scott. (1:08) (video) Melodrama of a defense attorney who takes on the case of a fugitive, originally convicted of a murder he didn't commit 12 years before. Part of a double bill with *Law of the Badlands* (q.v.), a Tim Holt western.

1227. The Hunters (20th Century–Fox; 1958). *Cast:* Robert Mitchum, Robert Wagner, Richard Egan, May Britt, Lee Phillips, John Gabriel, Stacy Harris, Victor Sen Yung, Candace Lee, Joy Jostyn, Leon Lontoc, John Doucette,

Vinnie DeCarlo, Larry Thor, Ralph Manza, Nobu McCarthy, Nina Shipman, Alena Murray, Robert Reed, Jimmy Baya, John Caler, Bob Olen, Mae Maeshire, Frank Kumagai, Chiyoko Tota Baker, Kam Tong, Rachel Stephens, Mary Song, James Yabi, Whamok Kim, Mabel Lim, Frank Tang. *D: & P:* Dick Powell (final as director); *Sc:* Wendell Mayes. (1:48) (video) Korean war drama of an air force major who falls for the wife of a pilot who is shot down behind enemy lines and sets out to rescue him. Based on the 1957 novel by James Salter, it was photographed in DeLuxe color and CinemaScope.

1228. Hunters of the Deep (Distributors Corp. of America; 1955). *P:* Tom Gries; *Sc:* Gries, Allan Dowling. (1:04) A feature-length documentary on undersea life.

1229. Hurricane Island (Columbia; 1951). *Cast:* Jon Hall, Marie Windsor, Marc Lawrence, Romo Vincent, Karen Randle, Jo Gilbert, Edgar Barrier, Nelson Leigh, Marshall Reed, Don C. Harvey, Rick Vallin, Russ Conklin, Lyle Talbot, Alex Montoya, Zon Murray, Rusty Wescoatt. *D:* Lew Landers; *P:* Sam Katzman; *St: & Sc:* David Mathews. (1:11) Costume adventure of explorer Ponce de Leon (Barrier) and the search for the Fountain of Youth. A hurricane climaxes as expected. Super CineColor.

1230. Hurricane Smith (Paramount; 1952). *Cast:* Yvonne De Carlo, John Ireland (title role), James Craig, Forrest Tucker, Lyle Bettger, Richard Arlen, Mike Kellin, Murray Matheson, Henry Brandon, Emile Meyer, Stuart Randall, Ralph Dumke, Kim Spalding, Don Dunning, Ethan Laidlaw, Eric Alden, Al Kikume, George Barton, Loren D. Brown, James A. Cornell, Clint Dorrington, Leo J. McMahon, King Mojave, Fred N. Revelala, Jack Trent, Leon Lontoc, Leon C. "Buck" Young, Cliff Clark, Anthony Warde, Ted Ryan, Eddie Magill, Harvey Parry, Maiola Kalili. *D:* Jerry Hopper; *P:* Nat Holt; *As.P:* Harry Templeton; *Sc:* Frank Gruber. (1:30) South Seas romantic action-adventure involving a search for gold. In Technicolor, it was based on *Hurricane Williams* by Gordon Ray Young.

1231. I Bury the Living (United Artists/ Maxim; 1958). *Cast:* Richard Boone, Theodore Bikel, Peggy Maurer, Herbert Anderson, Howard Smith, Robert Osterloh, Russ Bender, Glenn Vernon, Lynn Bernay, Cyril Delevanti, Ken Drake, Matt Moore. *D:* Albert Band; *P:* Louis Garfinkle, Band; *St: & Sc:* Garfinkle. (1:16) (video) Offbeat low budget thriller of a cemetery manager who believes he may have the power over life and death by placing either white or black pins in the gravesites on the cemetery map.

1232. I Can Get It for You Wholesale (20th Century–Fox; 1951). *Cast:* Susan Hayward, Dan Dailey, George Sanders, Sam Jaffe, Randy Stuart, Marvin Kaplan, Harry Von Zell, Barbara Whiting, Vicki Cummings, Ross Elliott, Richard Lane, Mary Phillips, Benna Bard, Steven Geray, Charles Lane, Jan Kane, Marion Marshall, Jayne Hazard, Aline Towne, Eda Reis Merin, Marjorie Hoshelle, Doris Kemper, Elizabeth Flournoy, Jack P. Carr, Tamara Shayne, Ed Max, David Wolfe, Harry Hines, Diane Mumby, Shirlee Allard, Beverly Thompson, Michael Hogan, Bess Flowers. *D:* Michael Gordon; *P:* Sol C. Siegel; *Sc:* Abraham Polonsky, Vera Caspary. (1:30) Drama of a New York model who aspires to and opens her own business—manufacturing clothing designed by her. Based on the novel by Jerome Weidman, which was later adapted to a Broadway musical with Barbra Streisand. (retitled: *Only the Best*)

I Changed My Sex *see* **Glen or Glenda**

1233. I Confess (Warner/Alfred Hitchcock Prods.; 1953). *Cast:* Montgomery Clift, Anne Baxter, Karl Malden, Brian Aherne, O.E. Hasse, Dolly Haas, Roger Dann, Charles Andre, J. Pratt, Ovila Legare, Gilles Pelletier, Nan Boardman, Henry Corden, Carmen Gingras, Renee Hudson, Albert Godderis. *D: & P:* Alfred Hitchcock; *Sc:* George Tabori, William Archibald. (1:35) (video/laserdisc) A Catholic priest hears the confession of a murderer, subsequently finding himself accused of the murder when it is learned the murdered man was blackmailing him. Based on the 1902 play *Nos Deux Conscience* [Our Two Consciences] by Paul Anthelme, it was filmed on location in Quebec, Canada, and was in nomination at the Cannes Film Festival.

1234. I Cover the Underworld (Republic; 1955). *Cast:* Sean McClory (dual role), Joanne Jordan, Robert Middleton, Jaclynne Greene, Lee Van Cleef, James Griffith, Hugh Sanders, Roy Roberts, Peter Mamakos, Robert Crosson, Frank Gerstle, Willis Bouchey, Philip Van Zandt. *D:* R.G. Springsteen; *P:* Herbert J. Yates; *Sc:* John K. Butler. (1:10) Crime melodrama of a divinity student who helps lawmen break up a criminal organization, but problems arise when his twin brother breaks out of prison and almost defeats the plan.

1235. I Died a Thousand Times (Warner; 1955). *Cast:* Jack Palance, Shelley Winters, Lori Nelson, Lee Marvin, Earl Holliman, Perry Lopez, [Pedro] Gonzales-Gonzales, Lon Chaney, Howard St. John, Ralph Moody, James Millican, Olive Carey, Richard [Dick] Davalos, Bill Kennedy, Dennis Hopper, Mae Clarke, Peggy Maley, Dub Taylor, Dick Reeves, Chris Alcaide, Larry Hudson, John Pickard, Karolee Kelly, John Stephenson, Hugh Sanders, Howard Hoffman, Nick Adams, Darren Dublin, Myrna Fahey, Herbert Vigran, David McMahon, Paul Brinegar, Wendell Niles, John Daheim, Dennis Moore, Mickey Simpson, Steve Darrell, Gil Perkins, Larry Blake, Nesdon Booth, Ed Fury, Larve Farlow, Hubie Kerns, Tony Hughes, Mary Benoit, Paul Power, Charles Watts, Donald Dillaway, Fay Baker, James Seay. *D:* Stuart Heisler; *P:* Willis Goldbeck; *Sc:* W.R. Burnett. (1:48) (video) Melodrama of the hunt for a maniacal killer in the Sierra mountains. A remake of this studio's *High Sierra* (1941) and based on the novel by Mr. Burnett. WarnerColor and CinemaScope.

1236. The I Don't Care Girl (20th Century–Fox; 1952). *Cast:* Mitzi Gaynor, David Wayne, Oscar Levant, Bob Graham, Craig Hill, Warren Stevens, Hazel Brooks, Marietta Canty, Sam Hearn, Wilton Graff (Flo Ziegfeld), Dwayne Ratliff, Bill Foster, Gwyneth [Gwen] Verdon, Betty Onge, Ruth Hall, Barbara Carroll, George Jessel (himself). *D:* Lloyd Bacon; *P:* George Jessel; *Sc:* Walter Bullock; *Songs:* "I Don't Care" (Jean Lenox–Harry O. Sutton); "The Beale Street Blues" (W.C. Handy); "The Johnson Rag" (Jack Lawrence–Guy H. Hall, Harry Kleinkauf); "This Is My Favorite City" (Mack Gordon–Josef Myrow); "Here Comes Love Again" (Jessel–Eliot Daniel); "On the Mississippi" (Ballard MacDonald–Harry Carroll-Arthur Fields); "Hello, Frisco, Hello" (Louis A. Hirsch–Gene Bucks); "Pretty Baby" (Gus Kahn–Tony Jackson–Egbert Van Alstyne); "Oh, You Beautiful Doll" (Nat D. Ayer–Seymour Brown); "Liebestraum" (Franz Liszt), "Piano Concerto No. 1" (Liszt); "Little G Minor Fugue" (Johann Sebastian Bach); "Largo Al Factotum" (Giacchino Rossini). (1:18) In this musical-biography, a producer (Jessel) seeks details on the life of turn-of-the-century vaudevillian entertainer, Eva Tanquay (Gaynor). Technicolor.

1237. I Dream of Jeanie (Republic; 1952). *Cast:* Ray Middleton (Edwin P. Christy), Bill Shirley (Stephen Foster), Muriel Lawrence, Eileen Christy, Lynn Bari, Richard Simmons, Robert Neil, Andrew Tombes, James Dobson, Percy Helton, Glenn Turnbull, Louise Beavers, James Kirkwood, Carl Dean Switzer, Freddie Moultrie, Rex Allen (narrator & Mr. Tambo). *D:* Allan Dwan; *P:* Herbert J. Yates; *Sc:* Alan LeMay; *Songs include:* "I Dream of Jeanie with the Light Brown Hair," "My Old Kentucky Home," "The Old Folks at Home," "Ring, Ring de Banjo," "Swanee River," "Old Dog Tray," "Oh, Susanna," "Camptown Races," "On Wings of Song," "Lo! Hear the Gentle Lark," "A Ribbon in Your Hair," "I See Her Still in My Dreams," "Come Where My Love Lies Dreaming" + 8 more by Stephen Foster; "Head Over Heels" (Laura Lee–Allan Dwan). (1:30) The third fictionalized biography of famed songwriter Stephen Foster is brought to the screen as a romantic musical-drama. The two previous bios were *Harmony Lane* (Mascot—a forerunner of Republic; 1935) and *Swanee River* (Fox; 1939). Trucolor. Note: E.P. Christy was the founder of the musical group The Christy Minstrels who were famous for making many of Foster's songs famous (in blackface). The New Christy Minstrels, a 1960s folk group derived their name from Mr. Christy's troupe.

1238. I Killed Geronimo (Eagle-Lion; 1950). *Cast:* James Ellison, Chief Thundercloud (Geronimo), Virginia Herrick, Smith Ballew, Dennis Moore, Ted Adams, Myron Healey, Luther Crockett, Jean Andren, Wesley Hudman, Harte Wayne. *D:* John Hoffman; *P:* Jack Schwarz; *St: & Sc:* Sam Neuman, Nat Tanchuck. (1:03) Low budget western of an army officer who comes face-to-face with the Apache leader, Geronimo, while pursuing gunrunners supplying rifles to the Apaches.

1239. I Killed Wild Bill Hickok (Associated Artists/Wheeler Co.; 1956). *Cast:* John (Carpenter) Forbes, Helen Westcott, Tom Brown (Hickok), Virginia Gibson, Denver Pyle, I. Stanford Jolley, Frank "Red" Carpenter, R.J. Thomas, Roy Canada, Harvey Dunne, Bill Chaney, Bron Delar, Phil Barton, Bill Mims, Billy Dean, Lee Sheldon. *D:* Richard Talmadge; *P: & Sc:* John Carpenter. (1:03) B budget independent western in color. Film is padded with much stock footage of a horse rancher who goes after Wild Bill Hickok when his young daughter becomes the innocent victim in a shootout.

I Led Two Lives *see* **Glen or Glenda**

1240. I Love Melvin (MGM; 1953). *Cast:* Donald O'Connor, Debbie Reynolds, Una Merkel, Allyn Joslyn, Noreen Corcoran, Jim Backus, Richard Anderson, Barbara Ruick, Les Tremayne, Robert Taylor (cameo), Howard Keel (cameo). *D:* Don Weis; *P:* George Wells; *St:* Laslo Vadnay; *Sc:* Wells, Ruth Brooks Flippen; *Songs:* "A Lady Loves," "Saturday Afternoon Before the Game," "I Wanna Wander," "We Have Never Met as of Yet," "Life Has Its Funny Little Ups and Downs," "Where Did You Learn to Dance?," and "And There You Are," Mack Gordon, Josef Myrow. (1:16) (video) Hit Technicolor musical-comedy of a guy who tries to get to first base with a girl by leading her to believe he can get her on a cover of *Look* magazine.

1241. I Married a Monster from Outer Space (Paramount; 1958). *Cast:* Tom Tryon, Gloria Talbott, Peter Baldwin, Robert Ivers, Chuck Wassil, Valerie Allen, Ty [Hardin] Hungerford, Ken Lynch, John Eldredge, James Anderson, Alan Dexter, Jean Carson, Jack Orrison, Maxie Rosenbloom, Steve London, Mary Treen. *D: & P:* Gene Fowler, Jr.; *St: & Sc:* Louis Vittes; *Makeup:* Charles Gemora; *F/X:* John P. Fulton. (1:18) (video) Science fiction with a cult following of aliens from outer space attempting to conquer the earth via inhabiting bodies of humans.

1242. I Married a Woman (Universal-International/RKO-Gomalco; 1956–58). *Cast:* George Gobel, Diana Dors, Adolphe Menjou, Jessie Royce Landis, Nita Talbot, William Redfield, Steve Dunne, John McGiver, Steve Pendleton, Cheerio Meredith, Kay Buckley, Angie Dickinson, Stanley Adams, John Wayne (cameo). *D:* Hal Kanter; *P:* William Bloom; *Sc:* Goodman Ace. (1:20) (video/laserdisc) Domestic comedy of a Madison Avenue ad man, his problems with his business, his neglected wife and his mother-in-law. Filmed in 1956, this sat on the shelf at RKO until after they closed their doors, and was finally released by Universal. The fantasy sequence is in color.

1243. I, Mobster (20th Century–Fox/Alco-Edward L. Alperson; 1958). *Cast:* Steve Cochran, Lita Milan, Robert Strauss, Celia Lovsky, Lili St. Cyr (herself), John Brinkley, Yvette Vickers, Jeri Southern (herself), Grant Withers (final film—d. 1959), John Mylong, Wally Cassell, Robert Shayne, Frank Gerstle. *D:* Roger Corman; *P:* Edward L. Alperson, R. Corman, Gene Corman; *St:* Joseph Hylton Smith; *Sc:* Steve Fisher; *Songs:* "Give Me Love," "Lost, Lonely and Looking For Love" (Edward L. Alperson, Jr.–Jerry Winn). (1:20) (video) A gangster relates how he became a crime kingpin, while testifying before the Senate Rackets Investigating Committee. CinemaScope.

I Shall Return (G.B. title) *see* **An American Guerrilla in the Philippines**

1244. I Shot Billy the Kid (Lippert; 1950). *Cast:* Don Barry (Billy the Kid), Robert Lowery (Pat Garrett), Wally Vernon, Tom Neal (Charlie Bowdrie), Wendy Lee, Archie Twitchell [aka: Michael Branden], Claude Stroud (Lew Wallace), John Merton, Bill Kennedy, Jack Perrin, Richard Farmer, Felice Richmond, Judith Allen, Barbara Woodell, Dick Lane, Sid Melton, Harry Marud, Tommy Monroe. *D: & P:* William Berke; *St: & Sc:* Ford Beebe, Orville H. Hampton. (0:59) (video) Programmer western with Pat Garrett relating the tale of Billy the Kid, a good guy gone bad.

1245. I, the Jury (United Artists/Parklane; 1953). *Cast:* Biff Elliot, Preston Foster, Peggie Castle, Alan Reed, Margaret Sheridan, Elisha Cook, Jr., Frances Osborne, Robert Cunningham, Paul Dubov, John Qualen, Mary Anderson, Tani & Dran Seitz (twins), Robert Swanger. *D:* Harry Essex; *P:* Victor Saville; *Sc:* Essex. (1:27) Hollywood's first attempt to bring tough detective Mike Hammer (Elliot) to the screen. Hammer investigates several suspects who may have murdered his friend. Based on Mickey Spillane's pulp fiction novel of the same name, it was remade in 1982. Originally in 3-D.

1246. I Want to Live! (United Artists/Figaro, Inc.; 1958). *Cast:* Susan Hayward (AA + voted "Best Actress" by the New York Film Critics and the *New York Times*/Barbara Graham), Simon Oakland (Ed Montgomery), Virginia Vincent (Peg), Theodore Bikel (Carl Palmberg), Wesley Lau (Henry Graham), Philip Coolidge (Emmett Perkins), Lou Krugman (Jack Santo), James Philbrook (Bruce King), Bartlett Robinson (district attorney), Gage Clark (Richard Tibrow), Joe De Santis (Al Matthews), John Marley (Father Devers), Peter Breck (Ben Miranda), Marion Marshall (Rita), Dabbs Greer, Raymond Bailey, Alice Backes, Gertrude Flynn, Russell Thorsen, Stafford Repp, Gavin McLeod, Olive Blakeney, Lorna Thayer, Evelyn Scott, Jack Weston, Leonard Bell, George Putnam, Bill Stout, Jason Johnson, Rusty Lane, S. John Launer, Dan Sheridan, Wendell Holmes. *D:*

(AAN) Robert Wise; *P:* Walter Wanger; *Sc:* (AAN) Nelson Gidding, Don Mankiewicz; *Cin:* (AAN-b/w) Lionel Linden; *Editor:* (AAN) William Hornbeck; *Sound:* (AAN) Gordon E. Sawyer/Goldwyn Studio Sound Dept.; *Jazz music performed by:* Gerry Mulligan, Shelly Manne, Art Farmer, Bud Shank, Red Mitchell, Frank Rosolino, Pete Jolly. (2:00) (video/laserdisc) Dramatic rendering of the story of Barbara Graham, a woman convicted on murder charges and sentenced to die in the gas chamber. Based on newspaper articles by reporter Ed Montgomery and letters of Barbara Graham, who was executed in 1953. It placed #9 on the "10 Best" list of the *New York Times* in 1958 and on the same list of *Film Daily* in 1959. A box office take of $3,000,000 made it one of the 26 top-grossing films of 1958-59. Remade in 1983 as a TV movie.

1247. I Want You (RKO/Sam Goldwyn; 1951). *Cast:* Dana Andrews (Martin Greer), Dorothy McGuire (Nancy Greer), Farley Granger (Jack Greer), Peggy Dow (final film—ret./Carrie Turner), Robert Keith (Thomas Greer), Mildred Dunnock (Sarah Greer), Russell Collins (Judge Jonathan Turner), Martin Milner (George Kress, Jr.), Jim Backus (Harvey Landrum), Marjorie Crossland (Mrs. Celia Turner), Walter Baldwin (George Kress, Sr.), Walter Sande (Ned Iversen), Peggy Maley (Gladys), Jerrilyn Flannery (Anne Greer), Erick Nielsen (Tony Greer), Ann Robin (Gloria), Carol Savage (Caroline Kuptka), Harry Lauter (Art Stacey), Charles Marsh (Mr. Jones), Ralph Brooks (Albert), James Adamson, Frank Sully, Robert Johnson, David McMahon, Melodi Lowell, Jimmy Ogg, Jean Andren, Don Hayden, Dee Carroll, Lee Turnbull, Rolland Morris, Al Murphy, Paul Smith. *D:* Mark Robson; *P:* Samuel Goldwyn; *Sc:* Irwin Shaw (based on stories by Edward Newhouse); *Sound:* (AAN) Gordon Sawyer. (1:42) Successful Americana of the effects of the Korean conflict on various people, depicted from the perspective of the homefront in 1951.

1248. I Was a Communist for the F.B.I. (Warner; 1951). *Cast:* Frank Lovejoy (Matt Cvetic), Dorothy Hart (Eve Merrick), Philip Carey (Mason), James Millican (Jim Blandon), Richard Webb (Crowley), Ron Hagerthy (Dick Cvetic), Russ Conway (Frank Cvetic), Hope Kramer (Ruth Cvetic), Kasia Orzazewski (Mrs. Cvetic), Eddie Norris (Harmon), Ann Morrison (Miss Nova), Konstantin Shayne (Gerhardt Eisler), Roy Roberts (Father Novac), Paul McGuire (McIntyre), Eric Nielsen (Jackie), Bill Lester (Brown), John Crawford (McGowan), Johnny Bradford (Dobbs), Jimmy Gonzales (Brennan), David McMahon (Masonvitch), Hugh Sanders (Garson), Lyle Latell (Cahill), William Forrest (Senator Wood), Bert Moorhouse (Senator Gray), Douglas Evans, Janet Barrett, Karen Hale, Jim O'Gatty, Joseph Smith, Frank Marlowe, Barry Sullivan, Mike Ross, Lenita Lane, Alma Mansfield, Anne Kimbell, Paula Sowl, Charles Sherlock, George Magrill, Grace Lenard, Roy Engel, Ernest Anderson, "Sugarfoot" Anderson, Charles Horvath, Phil Tully, Howard Negley, Bobby Gilbert, James Adamson, Mary Alan Hokanson, Mildred Boyd, Barry Reagan, Chuck Colean, Dick Gordon, William N. Bailey, Paul Bradley, Buddy Shaw. *D:* Gordon Douglas; *P:* (AAN-Best Documentary) Bryan Foy; *Sc:* Crane Wilbur. (1:23) Based on fact, this melodrama tells of one man's infiltration of various communist organizations in the U.S. Based on *I Posed as a Communist for the F.B.I.* by Matt Cvetic as told to Pete Martin, it is relayed in a documentary style. A definite curio of the McCarthy era, playing heavily on the communist paranoia of the period.

1249. I Was a Shoplifter (Universal-International; 1950). *Cast:* Scott Brady, Mona Freeman, Andrea King, Charles Drake, Anthony [Tony] Curtis, Gregg Martell, Robert Gist, Larry Keating, Rock Hudson, Michael Raffetto, Nana Bryant, Harold Goodwin, Nestor Paiva, Charles Watts, Marshall Reed, Mickey O'Ryan, Conrad Binyon, Steve Darrell, Paul Fierro, Peggie Castle, Charles McGraw. *D:* Charles Lamont; *P:* Leonard Goldstein; *St: & Sc:* Irwin Gielgud. (1:22) Melodrama of a girl's involvement with a shoplifting ring and the undercover cop who comes to her aid. Note: Alexis Smith was suspended from Universal for refusing to appear in this film.

1250. I Was a Teenage Frankenstein (American International/Santa Rosa Prods.; 1957). *Cast:* Whit Bissell, Phyllis Coates, Robert Burton, Gary Conway (title role), George Lynn, John Cliff, Marshall Bradford, Claudia Bryar, Angela Blake, Russ Whiteman, Charles Seel, Paul Keast, Gretchen Thomas, Joy Stoner, Larry Carr, Pat Miller. *D:* Herbert L. Strock; *P:* Herman Cohen; *St: & Sc:* Kenneth Langtry. (1:12) (video) A car full of teenagers crashes outside Professor Frankenstein's laboratory with all inside the car killed, giving the scientist the idea to follow in his ancestor's footsteps. The final electrocution sequence is in color. (G.B. title:

Teenage Frankenstein). Originally the top half of a horror double bill with *Blood of Dracula* (q.v.).

1251. I Was a Teenage Werewolf (American International; 1957). *Cast:* Michael Landon, Yvonne Lime, Whit Bissell, Tony Marshall, Dawn Richard, Barney Phillips, Ken Miller, Cindy Robbins, Michael Rougas, Robert Griffin, Joseph Mell, Malcolm Atterbury, Eddie Marr, Vladimir Sokoloff, Louise Lewis, S. John Launer, Guy Williams, Dorothy Crehan. *D:* Gene Fowler, Jr. (directorial debut); *P:* Herman Cohen; *Sc:* Ralph Thornton; *Songs:* Jerry Blaine. (1:10) (video) A troubled teenager (Landon) with a hair-trigger temper falls under the spell of a psychiatrist (Bissell) who reverts him to a primal state through hypnosis. Of the teen oriented horror flicks of the 1950s, this one borders on classic for its genre. Originally ran on the top half of a double bill with *Invasion of the Saucer Men* (q.v.).

1252. I Was an American Spy (Allied Artists; 1951). *Cast:* Ann Dvorak, Gene Evans, Douglas Kennedy, Richard Loo, Leon Lontok, Chabing, Philip Ahn, Marya Marco, Nadene Ashdown, Lisa Ferraday, Howard Chuman, Freddie Revelala, James Leong, Leo Abbey, Escolastico Baucin, Toshi Nakaki, Jerry Fujikawa, Weaver Levy, Celeste Madamba, Andres Lucas, Frank Jenks, Gil Herman, George Fields, Dennis Moore, Kei Thing Chung, Richard Bartlett, Riley Hill, Lane Nakano, Bret Hamilton, Ed Sojin, Jr., Li Sun, Wong Artarne, Eddie Lee, Remedos Jacobe, William Yip, William Yakota, Frank Iwanaga, Harold Fong, Harry Hamada, Lane Bradford, John Damler, Jack Reynolds, Angel Cruz, William Tannen. *D:* Lesley Selander; *P:* David Diamond; *Sc:* Sam Roeca. (1:24) Fact-based war drama of female spy, Claire Phillips, operating in Manila during World War II, first fighting as a guerrilla and then opening a nightclub designed to get information from Japanese soldiers. A prologue to the film is delivered by General Mark W. Clark. Based on the book *Manila Espionage* by Claire Phillips and Myron G. Goldsmith.

1253. I'd Climb the Highest Mountain (20th Century–Fox; 1951). *Cast:* Susan Hayward, William Lundigan, Rory Calhoun, Barbara Bates, Gene Lockhart, Lynn Bari, Ruth Donnelly, Kathleen Lockhart, Alexander Knox, Jean Innes, Frank Tweddell, Jerry Vandiver, Richard Wilson, Dorothea Carolyn Sims, Thomas Syfan, Grady Starnes, Kay & Fay Fogg (twins), Claude Stowers, Dr. Wallace Roger, Myrtle Stovall, Bobby C. Canup, Nina G. Brown, Arispah Palmer, Caroline White. *D:* Henry King; *P: & Sc:* Lamar Trotti. (1:27) (video) Rural Americana set in the Blue Ridge Mountains of Georgia. A country preacher and his city-bred wife try to make a difference in the lives of the people in their charge, facing many challenges in the process. Based on the novel by Corra Harris, it was filmed on location in Technicolor.

Idols in the Dust (G.B. title) *see* **Saturday's Hero**

If You Feel Like Singing (G.B. title) *see* **Summer Stock**

1254. I'll Cry Tomorrow (MGM; 1955). *Cast:* Susan Hayward (AAN + voted "Best Actress" at the 1956 Cannes Film Festival/Lillian Roth), Richard Conte (Tony Hardeman), Eddie Albert (Burt McGuire), Jo Van Fleet (Katie), Don Taylor (Wallie), Ray Danton (David Tredman), Margo (Selma), Virginia Gregg (Ellen), Don Barry (Jerry), David Kasday (David as a child), Carole Ann Campbell (Lillian as a child), Peter Leeds (Richard), Voltaire Perkins (Mr. Byrd), Bob Dix (Henry), Anthony Jochim (Paul the butler), Eve McVeagh (Ethel), Gail Ganley (Lillian—age 15), Tol Avery, Guy Wilkerson, Tim Carey, Henry Kulky, Charles Tannen, Ken Patterson, George Lloyd, Nora Marlowe, Stanley Farrar, Harlan Warde, Peter Brocco, Kay English, Veda Ann Borg, Robert B. Williams, Bob Hopkins, Vernon Rich, Herbert C. Lytton, George Selk [aka: Budd Buster], Cheerio Meredith. *D:* Daniel Mann; *P:* Lawrence Weingarten; *Sc:* Helen Deutsch, Jay Richard Kennedy; *Cin:* (AAN-b/w) Arthur S. Arling; *ASD:* (AAN-b/w) Cedric Gibbons, Malcolm Brown (art directors), Edwin B. Willis, Hugh B. Hunt (sets); *Costumes:* (AA-b/w) Helen Rose; *Songs:* "Sing You Sinners" (Sam Coslow-W. Franke Harling); "When the Red, Red Robin Comes Bob-Bob-Bobbin' Along," "Happiness Is Just A Thing Called Joe" (E.Y. Harburg-Harold Arlen). (1:57) (video/laserdisc) Biographical drama of singer Lillian Roth, star of stage and screen (in the early 1930s), her failed marriages and her bout with alcoholism. One of the 24 top-grossing films of 1955-56, it was based on the international best-seller by Roth, Mike Connolly and Gerold Frank. Computer-colored by Turner Entertainment.

1255. I'll Get By (20th Century–Fox; 1950). *Cast:* June Haver (Liza Martin), William

Lundigan (William Spencer), Gloria DeHaven (Terry Martin), Dennis Day (Freddy Lee), Harry James (himself), Thelma Ritter (Miss Murphy), Steve Allen (Peter Pepper), Danny Davenport (Chester Dooley), Dick Winslow (Cooky Myers), Tom Hanlon, Peggy O'Connor, Harry Lauter, Harry Seymour, Don Hicks, Charles Tannen, Kathleen Hughes, Vincent Renno, Bob McCord, Paul Picerni, John Butler, Stanley Prager, Frank Mills, Reginald Gardiner (cameo), Jeanne Crain (cameo), Dan Dailey (cameo), Victor Mature (cameo). *D:* Richard Sale; *P:* William Perlberg; *St:* Robert Ellis, Helen Logan, Pamela Harris; *Sc:* Sale, Mary Loos; *Songs:* "Deep in the Heart of Texas" (June Hershey–Don Swander); "You Make Me Feel So Young" (Mack Gordon–Josef Myrow); "I've Got the World on a String" (Ted Koehler-Harold Arlen), "Once in a While" (Bud Green-Michael Edwards); "Yankee Doodle Blues" (B.G. DeSylva–Irving Caesar–George Gershwin); "Fifth Avenue," "There Will Never Be Another You" (Gordon–Harry Warren); "McNamara's Band" (Shamus O'Connor–J.J. Stanford), "It's Been a Long, Long Time" (Sammy Cahn–Jule Styne); "No Love, No Nothin'" (Leo Robin-Warren); "Auld Lang Syne" (lyrics: Robert Burns); "Taking a Chance on Love" (John Latouche-Ted Fetter–Vernon Duke); "I'll Get By" (Roy Turk–Fred Ahlert); *Music:* (AAN) Lionel Newman. (1:22) Technicolor musical-romance of two songwriters who hook up with two sisters who sing for Harry James. A remake of *Tin Pan Alley* (Fox; 1940).

I'll Get You for This (G.B. title) *see* **Lucky Nick Cain**

1256. I'll Give My Life (Howco/Concordia; 1959). *Cast:* John Bryant, Angie Dickinson, Russell Collins, Katherine Warren, Jon Shepodd, Donald Woods, Stuart Randall, Richard Benedict, Milton Woods, Sam Flint, Mimi Gibson. *D:* William F. Claxton; *P:* Sam Hersh; *Sc:* Herbert Moulton. (1:19) Drama of a young man who meets opposition from his father after earning an engineering degree and then making a decision to become a missionary.

1257. I'll Never Forget You (20th Century–Fox; 1951). *Cast:* Tyrone Power, Ann Blyth, Michael Rennie, Dennis Price, Beatrice Campbell, Kathleen Byron, Raymond Huntley, Irene Browne, Robert Atkins, Ronald Adam, Gibb McLaughlin, Hamlyn Benson, Ronald Simpson, Felix Alymer, Diane Hart, Tom Gill, Alexander McCrindle, Jill Clifford, Peter Drury, Victor Maddern, Alec Finter, Anthony Pelly, Catherine Carlton, Richard Carrickford, Rose Howlett, Arthur Denton. *D:* Roy (Ward) Baker; *P:* Sol C. Siegel; *Sc:* Ranald MacDougall. (1:29) Romantic fantasy-drama of a contemporary man who is transported via an electrical storm to 18th century England where he begins to live the life of one of his ancestors. A remake of *Berkeley Square* (Fox Film; 1933) with Leslie Howard and Heather Angel, based on the play of that name by John Balderston which was adapted from the story "The Sense of the Past" by Henry James. Later adapted to the Broadway musical *On A Clear Day You Can See Forever* which was also filmed in 1970. The film switches to Technicolor after opening in black and white. (G.B. title: *The House on the Square*)

1258. I'll See You in My Dreams (Warner; 1951). *Cast:* Doris Day (Grace LeBoy Kahn), Danny Thomas (Gus Kahn), Frank Lovejoy (Walter Donaldson), Patrice Wymore, James Gleason, Mary Wickes, Else Neft, Minna Gombell (final film—ret.), Jim Backus, Julie Oshins, Harry Antrim, William Forrest (Florenz Ziegfeld), Bunny Lewbel, Robert Lyden, Mimi Gibson, Christy Olson, Dick Simmons, Jack Williams, Clarence Landry, Ray Kellogg, George Neise (Isham Jones), Vince Barnett, Dan Barton. *D:* Michael Curtiz; *P:* Louis F. Edelman; *St:* Grace Kahn, Edelman; *Sc:* Jack Rose, Melville Shavelson; *Songs by Kahn include:* "Ain't We Got Fun" and "Ukulele Lady" (with Richard Whiting and Ray Egan); "The One I Love Belongs to Somebody Else," "I'll See You in My Dreams," "It Had to Be You" and "Swingin' Down the Lane" (with Isham Jones); "My Buddy," "Makin' Whoopee!," "Yes, Sir, That's My Baby," "Carolina in the Morning" and "Love Me or Leave Me" (with Walter Donaldson); "I Wish I Had a Girl" (with wife Grace LeBoy Kahn); "Nobody's Sweetheart" (with Billy Meyers-Elmer Schoebel & Ernie Erdman); "Pretty Baby" (with Egbert Van Alstyne & Tony Jackson); "Memories" (with Van Alstyne); "I Never Knew" (with Ted Fio Rito); "Toot Toot Tootsie, Goodbye" (with Al Jolson–Erdman & Dan Russo); "No No Nora" (with Fio Rito & Erdman); "Your Eyes Have Told Me So" (with Van Alstyne & Walter Blausfuss); "San Francisco" (with Bronislau Kaper and Walter Jurmann); "The Carioca" (with Edward Eliscu & Vincent Youmans); "I'm Through With Love" (with Fud Livingston & Matty Malneck); "Liza" (George and Ira Gershwin) and "Shine on Harvest Moon" (Jack Norworth–Nora Bayes, without the participation of Kahn). (1:49) (video/laserdisc) Popular Hollywood biopic of song lyricist Gus Kahn with choreographed numbers by LeRoy Prinz.

1259. Illegal (Warner; 1955). *Cast:* Edward G. Robinson, Nina Foch, Hugh Marlowe, Robert Ellenstein, DeForest Kelley, Jay Adler, James McCallion, Albert Dekker, Howard St. John, Jayne Mansfield (her 2nd film), Ellen Corby, Edward Platt, Jan Merlin, Clark Howat, Henry Kulky, Addison Richards, Lawrence Dobkin, George Ross, John McKee, Barry Hudson, Kathy Marlowe, Charles Evans, Ted Stanhope, Jonathan Hale, Marjorie Stapp, Fred Coby, Max Wagner, John Cliff, Henry Rowland, Julie Bennett, Pauline Drake, Roxanne Arlen, Archie Twitchell [aka: Michael Branden], Stewart Nedd, Herb Vigran, Chris Alcaide. *D:* Lewis Allen; *P:* Frank P. Rosenberg; *Sc:* W.R. Burnett, James R. Webb. (1:28) (video) A district attorney becomes a defense lawyer when his secretary is accused of murder. Based on the play by Frank J. Collins, this drama is a remake of this studio's 1932 production *The Mouthpiece.*

1260. Imitation General (MGM; 1958). *Cast:* Glenn Ford, Red Buttons, Taina Elg, Dean Jones, Kent Smith, Tige Andrews, John Wilder, Ralph Votrian. *D:* George Marshall; *P:* William Hawks; *St:* William Chamberlain; *Sc:* William Bowers. (1:28) World War II comedy of an army sergeant posing as a deceased general. Photographed in CinemaScope in Ventura County, CA.

1261. Imitation of Life (Universal-International; 1959). *Cast:* Lana Turner (Lora Meredith), John Gavin (Steve Archer), Sandra Dee (Susie—age 16), Dan O'Herlihy (David Edwards), Susan Kohner (AAN/Sarah Jane—age 18), Robert Alda (Allen Loomis), Juanita Moore (AAN/Annie Johnson), Mahalia Jackson (singing "Trouble of the World"), Terry Burnham (Susie—age 6), Karen Dicker (Sarah Jane—age 8), Troy Donahue (Frankie), Than Wyenn (Romano), Peg Shirley (Fay), Joel Fluellen (minister), John Vivyan, Lee Goodman, Ann Robinson, Sandra Gould, David Tomack, Jack Weston, Billy House, Maida Severn. *D:* Douglas Sirk (final film—ret.); *P:* Ross Hunter; *Sc:* Eleanore Griffin, Allan Scott; *Songs:* Title song (Sammy Fain–Paul Francis Webster) sung by Earl Grant, "Empty Arms" (Arnold Hughes–Frederick Herbert) sung by Kohner. (2:04) (video) Drama of two women whose lives cross—the one a successful actress with a neglected daughter, the other, her employee, a black woman with a light-skinned daughter who is determined to pass for white. Based on the novel by Fannie Hurst, it was a remake of this studio's 1934 Oscar nominated production of the same name. One of the 26 top-grossing films of 1958-59, it was photographed in Eastmancolor and CinemaScope.

1262. The Immoral Mr. Teas (Pad-Ram Enterprises; 1959). *Cast:* W. Ellis Teas. *D:-P: & Sc:* Russ Meyer. (1:03) (video) Comedy of a man who gains the ability to see through women's clothing. This was Meyer's debut film and the first soft-core "Adults Only" porn-flick to receive commercial theatrical release, returning over $1,000,000 on a $24,000 investment.

1263. In a Lonely Place (Columbia/Santana Pictures; 1950). *Cast:* Humphrey Bogart, Gloria Grahame, Frank Lovejoy, Carl Benton Reid, Jeff Donnell, Art Smith, Robert Warwick, Martha Stewart, Morris Ankrum, William Ching, Steven Geray, Hadda Brooks, Alice Talton, Jack Reynolds, Ruth Warren, Ruth Gillette, Prince Michael Romanoff (himself), Arno Frey, Billy Gray, Myron Healey, Guy Beach, Lewis Howard, Pat Barton, Cosmo Sardo, Don Hanin, George Davis, Melinda Erickson, Jack Jahries, David Bond, Robert Lowell, Tony Layng, Robert Davis, Laura K. Brooks, Jack Santoro, Frank Marlowe, Evelyn Underwood, Hazel Boyne, Mike Lally, John Mitchum, Joy Hallward, Allen Pinson, Oliver Cross, June Vincent, Charles Cane. *D:* Nicholas Ray; *P:* Robert Lord, Henry S. Kesler; *St:* Edmund H. North; *Sc:* Andrew Solt. (1:31) (video) Acclaimed film noir of a Hollywood screenwriter who finds himself implicated in murder. Based on the book by Dorothy B. Hughes.

1264. In Love and War (20th Century–Fox/Jerry Wald; 1958). *Cast:* Robert Wagner, Dana Wynter, Jeffrey Hunter, Hope Lange, Bradford Dillman, Sheree North, France Nuyen, Mort Sahl (film debut), Steven Gant, Harvey Stephens, Paul Comi, Joe Di Reda, Buck Class, Lili Valenti, James Bell, Frank Murphy, Mary Patton, Murvyn Vye, Edward "Tap" Canutt, Veronica Cartwright, Brian Corcoran, Nelson Leigh. *D:* Philip Dunne; *P:* Jerry Wald; *Sc:* Edward Anhalt. (1:51) World War II soap opera style drama of three marines, their private lives and their first taste of action during an invasion of a Japanese-held island. Based on the novel *The Big War* by Anton Myrer. Filmed on locations at Stanford University in San Francisco and the Monterey Peninsula in DeLuxe color and CinemaScope.

1265. In Old Amarillo (Republic; 1951). *Cast:* Roy Rogers, Estelita Rodriguez, Penny Edwards, Pinky Lee, Roy Barcroft, Pierre Watkin, Ken Howell, Elisabeth Risdon, William Holmes, Alan Bridge, Kermit Maynard, The Roy Rogers Riders, Trigger (horse). *D:* William Witney; *P:* Edward J. "Eddy" White: *Sc:* Sloan Nibley; *Songs:* "Under the Lone Star Moon," "Wasteland," "If I Ever Fall in Love" Foy Willing, Jack Elliott. (1:07) (video) Roy Rogers series western of cattle ranchers who have to contend with a devastating drought, as well as a crook who is out to take advantage of their situation. Originally the top half of a western double bill with *Wells Fargo Gunmaster* (q.v.).

1266. In the Money (Allied Artists; 1958). *Cast:* Huntz Hall, Stanley Clements, Leonard Penn, John Dodsworth, Patricia Donahue, Eddie LeRoy, David Gorcey, Paul Cavanagh, Leslie Denison, Ashley Cowan, Dick Elliott, Ralph Gamble, Patrick O'Moore, Owen McGiveney. *D:* William Beaudine; *P:* Richard Heermance; *St:* Al Martin; *Sc:* Jack Townley, Martin, Elwood Ullman, Bert Lawrence. (1:01) The final entry in the "Bowery Boys" series finds Sach (Hall) unknowingly getting involved with diamond smugglers when he is hired to accompany a French poodle to England.

1267. The Incredible Petrified World (Governor Films/C.B.M. Prods.; 1958). *Cast:* John Carradine, Robert Clarke, Allen Windsor, Phyllis Coates, Lloyd Nelson, George Skaff, Sheila Noonan, Maurice Bernard, Joe Maierhouser, Harry Raven, Jack Haffner. *D: & P:* Jerry Warren; *St: & Sc:* John W. Sterner. (1:18) (video) Low budget science fiction of four people descending into the ocean in a diving bell, discovering a strange and unusual world within the depths. Originally ran on a double bill with *Teenage Zombies.*

The Incredible Praying Mantis *see* **The Deadly Mantis**

1268. The Incredible Shrinking Man (Universal-International; 1957). *Cast:* Grant Williams, Randy Stuart, April Kent, Paul Langton, Raymond Bailey, William Schallert, Frank Scannell, Helen Marshall, Diana Darrin, Billy Curtis. *D:* Jack Arnold; *P:* Albert Zugsmith; *Sc:* Richard Matheson; *F/X:* Clifford Stine, Roswell A. Hoffman, Everett H. Broussard. (1:21) (video/laserdisc) Critically acclaimed science fiction of a man exposed to a radioactive fog, who gradually begins to diminish in size, being forced to adapt to the changing world around him as he gets smaller and smaller. Based on the novel *The Shrinking Man* by Mr. Matheson. Note: *The Incredible Shrinking Woman* (Universal; 1981) is considered a credited remake of this film since it credits Matheson's book as source material.

1269. The Indestructible Man (Allied Artists; 1956). *Cast:* Lon Chaney, Marian Carr, Robert Shayne, Ross Elliott, Kenneth Terrell, Marvin Ellis, Stuart Randall, Casey Adams [aka: Max Showalter]. *D: & P:* Jack Pollexfen; *St: & Sc:* Sue Bradford, Vy Russell. (1:10) (video) Minimally budgeted science fiction film of an executed murderer, brought back to life, who seeks revenge on those who sentenced him to death.

1270. The Indian Fighter (United Artists/Bryna; 1955). *Cast:* Kirk Douglas, Elsa Martinelli (film debut), Walter Matthau, Walter Abel, Lon Chaney, Eduard Franz, Diana Douglas, Alan Hale, Jr., Elisha Cook, Jr., Michael Winkelman, Harry Landers, William Phipps, Robert "Buzz" Henry, Ray Teal, Frank Cady, Hank Worden, Lane Chandler. *D:* Andre De Toth; *P:* William Schorr; *St:* Ben Kadish; *Sc:* Frank Davis, Ben Hecht. (1:28) (video) Frontier saga of an Indian scout leading a wagon train through hostile Indian territory. Filmed on location in Oregon. DeLuxe color and CinemaScope.

Indian Killer (G.B. title) *see* **Okefenokee**

Indian Scout *see* **Davy Crockett, Indian Scout**

1271. Indian Territory (Columbia/Gene Autry Productions; 1950). *Cast:* Gene Autry, Gail Davis, Pat Buttram, Kirby Grant, James Griffith, Philip Van Zandt, Chief Yowlachie, Chief Thundercloud, Pat Collins, Frank Lackteen, Kenne Duncan, Charles Stevens, Frank Ellis, Roy Gordon, Robert Carson, Boyd Stockman, Frankie Marvin, Sandy Sanders, Bert Dodson, John R. McKee, Nick Rodman, Wesley Hudman, Robert Hilton, Roy Butler, Chief Thundersky, Champion, Jr. (horse). *D:* John English; *P:* Armand Schaefer; *St: & Sc:* Norman S. Hall. (1:10) Gene Autry series western of an undercover man, working with the Union army, who uncovers a plot by some whites to stir up trouble on the frontier with the Indians. The film utilizes footage from *Arizona* (Columbia; 1940). In Sepiatone, it originally ran on the top of a double bill with *Rookie Fireman* (q.v.).

1272. Indian Uprising (Columbia/Edward Small; 1952). *Cast:* George Montgomery, Audrey Long (final film—ret.), Carl Benton Reid, Eugene Iglesias, Joseph Sawyer, John Baer, Miguel Inclan (Geronimo), Eddy Waller, Douglas Kennedy, Robert Shayne, Robert Dover, Hugh Sanders, Fay Roope, Robert Griffin, Hank Patterson, John Call, Peter Thompson. *D:* Ray Nazarro; *P:* Edward Small; *St: & Sc:* Kenneth Gamet, Richard Schayer. (1:15) (video) Geronimo leads his Apaches on the warpath when he finds that whites are stealing Indian gold. In Super CineColor, it ran on a double bill with *Scandal Sheet* (q.v.).

1273. Indiscreet (Warner/Grandon Prods.; 1958). *Cast:* Cary Grant (Philip Adams), Ingrid Bergman (Ann Kalman), Cecil Parker (Alfred Munson), Phyllis Calvert (Margaret Munson), David Kossoff (Carl Banks), Megs Jenkins (Doris Banks), Oliver Johnston (Finleigh), Middleton Woods, Michael Anthony, Frank Hawkins, Richard Vernon, Eric Francis, Diane Clare. *D: & P:* Stanley Donen; *As.P:* Sidney Streeter; *Sc:* Norman Krasna; *Title song:* Sammy Cahn, James Van Heusen. (1:40) (video) Hit Technicolor romantic-comedy of a playboy who falls for a worldly actress. Filmed on location in London and in nomination at the British Academy Awards, it was based on Mr. Krasna's unsuccessful 1953 Broadway play *Kind Sir.* One of the 26 top-grossing films of 1957-58. Remade in 1988 as a TV movie.

Indiscretion (G.B. title) *see* **Indiscretion of an American Wife**

1274. Indiscretion of an American Wife (Columbia; 1953). *Cast:* Jennifer Jones, Montgomery Clift, Gino Cervi, Richard Beymer (film debut), Paolo Stoppa, Mando Bruno. *D: & P:* Vittorio De Sica; *Sc:* Caesare Zavattini, Luigi Chiarini, Giorgio Prosperi, Truman Capote; Costumes: (AAN-b/w) Christian Dior. (U.S. version—1:03/Italian version—1:27) (video) Romantic drama of an adulterous affair at an Italian railway station. Based on Mr. Zavattini's *Terminal Station.* A U.S.A./Italian co-production. (original title: *Terminal Station*)—(G.B. title: *Indiscretion*)—(Italian title: *Stazione Termini*)

1275. Inferno (20th Century–Fox; 1953). *Cast:* Robert Ryan, Rhonda Fleming, William Lundigan, Larry Keating, Henry Hull, Carl Betz, Robert Burton, Everett Glass, Adrienne Marden, Barbara Pepper, Henry Carter, Robert Adler, Dan White. *D:* Roy Baker; *P:* William Bloom; *St: & Sc:* Francis Cockrell. (1:23) After suffering a broken leg in the desert, a wealthy playboy is left to die by his cheating wife and his business partner, with the bulk of the plot dealing with his efforts to survive the elements. In Technicolor and 3-D (Fox's 1st), it was remade in 1973 as the TV movie *Ordeal.*

1276. The Inn of the Sixth Happiness (20th Century–Fox; 1958). *Cast:* Ingrid Bergman (voted "Best Actress" by the NBR/Gladys Aylward), Curt Jurgens (Capt. Lin Nan), Robert Donat (received a special citation for valor from the NBR in his final film—d. 1958/The Mandarin), Athene Seyler (Mrs. Sarah Lawson), Ronald Squire (Sir Francis), Moultrie Kelsall (Dr. Robinson), Richard Wattis (Mr. Murfin), Peter Chong (Yang), Tsai Chin (Sui-Lan), Edith Sharpe (secretary), Noel Hood (Miss Thompson), Burt Kwouk (Li), Ronald Kyaing (Young Lin), Louise Lin (Mai-Da), Ye Min (Bai Boa), Judith Lai (Sixpense), Frank Goh (Timothy), Joan Young, Lian-Shin Yang, Zed Zakari, Frank Blaine, Michael Wee, Andre Mikhelson, Stanislaw Mikula, Lin Chen, Ronald Lee, Christopher Chen, Aung Min. *D:* (AAN) Mark Robson; *P:* Buddy Adler (final film—d. 1960); *Sc:* Isobel Lennart. (2:38) (video) Factual story of an English servant woman who realizes her dream to become a missionary. She is sent to China where she encounters prejudice, later leading over a hundred orphan children to safety when Japan invades China. Based on the novel *The Small Woman* by Alan Burgess, it became one of the 26 top-grossing films of 1958-59. Filmed in Wales and England. DeLuxe color and CinemaScope.

Innocent and the Damned *see* **Girls Town**

1277. Inside Detroit (Columbia/Clover Prods.; 1955). *Cast:* Dennis O'Keefe, Pat O'Brien, Tina Carver, Margaret Field, Mark Damon, Larry Blake, Joseph Turkel, Ken Christy, Paul Bryar, Guy Kingsford, Robert E. Griffin, Dick Rich, Norman Leavitt, Katherine Warren. *D:* Fred F. Sears; *P:* Sam Katzman; *Sc:* Robert E. Kent, James B. Gordon. (1:20) Drama of the U.A.W. labor union and an unscrupulous individual who tries to gain control. The film is relayed in a semi-documentary style.

1278. Inside Straight (MGM; 1951). *Cast:* David Brian, Arlene Dahl, Barry Sullivan, Mercedes McCambridge, Lon Chaney, Jr., Claude Jarman, Jr., Paula Raymond, John Hoyt, Monica Lewis, Roland Winters, Barbara Billingsley, Richard Hale, Hayden Rorke, Jerry Hartleben, Dale Hartleben, Lou Nova. *D:* Gerald Mayer; *P:* Richard Goldstone; *Sc:* Guy Trosper. (1:29) During a card game in 19th century San Francisco, an ambitious gambler who has accumulated a fortune looks back on his life and questions whether it was all worth it.

1279. Inside the Mafia (United Artists/ Premium; 1959). *Cast:* Cameron Mitchell, Elaine Edwards, Robert Strauss, Jim L. Brown, Ted de Corsia, Grant Richards, Richard Karlan, Frank Gerstle, Sid Clute, Louis Jean Heydt, Steve Roberts, Hal Torey, Carl Milletaire, Carol Nugent, Edward Platt, Michael Monroe, Jack Daley, Jim Bannon, Anthony Carbone, Raymond Guth, Jack Kenney, House Peters, Jr., Sheldon Allman, Tony Warde, Donna Dale, John Hart. *D:* Edward L. Cahn; *P:* Robert E. Kent; *Sc:* Orville H. Hampton. (1:12) Exploitable crime-melodrama with lots of bang-bang about a crime figure holding hostages at an airport in an attempt to take over a crime syndicate. Originally ran on a double bill with *Subway in the Sky,* a German production.

1280. Inside the Walls of Folsom Prison (Warner; 1951). *Cast:* Steve Cochran, David Brian, Ted de Corsia, Philip Carey, Scott Forbes, Dick Wesson, Lawrence Tolan, Ed Norris, Dorothy Hart, Paul Picerni, William Campbell, Matt Willis, *and Folsom Prison convicts:* 07321 (murder), 08438 (arson), 04327 (forgery), 06752 (kidnapping). *D: & Sc:* Crane Wilbur; *P:* Bryan Foy. (1:27) Melodrama of a prison guard captain (Brian) who attempts to provide more humane conditions in his prison. Set in the 1920s and based on *Folsom Story* by Crane Wilbur, it was filmed on location.

1281. Insurance Investigator (Republic; 1951). *Cast:* Richard Denning, Audrey Long, John Eldredge, Hillary Brooke, Reed Hadley, Jonathan Hale, Roy Barcroft, Wilson Wood, William Tannen, Philip Pine, Crane Whitley, Ruth Lee, Patricia Knox, M'Liss McClure, Maurice Samuels. *D:* George Blair; *P:* William Lackey; *St:* Gertrude Walker, Beth Brown; *Sc:* Walker. (1:00) Crime melodrama of an insurance investigator who suspects an accidental death was actually murder. Originally ran on a double bill with *Silver City Bonanza* (q.v.), a Rex Allen western.

1282. Interlude (Universal-International; 1957). *Cast:* June Allyson, Rossano Brazzi, Marianne Cook, Francoise Rosay, Keith Andes, Frances Bergen, Jane Wyatt, Lisa Helwig, Herman Schwedt, Anthony Tripoli, John Stein. *D:* Douglas Sirk; *P:* Ross Hunter; *Adaptation:* Inez Cook; *Sc:* Daniel Fuchs, Franklin Coen; *Title song:* Frank Skinner, Paul Francis Webster (sung by the McGuire Sisters). (1:30) The romance of an American woman and a married conductor in Europe forms the basis of this drama. Based on the novel *Serenade* by James M. Cain, and the 1939 screenplay by Dwight Taylor of its predecessor *When Tomorrow Comes.* In Technicolor and CinemaScope, it was remade in Great Britain in 1968 as *Interlude.*

1283. International Counterfeiters (Republic/CCC Prods.; 1958). *Cast:* Gordon Howard, Irina Garden, Kurt Meisel, Hans Nielsen, Paul Bildt, Barbara Ruetting. *D:* Franz Cap; *P: & Story idea:* Arthur Brauner; *Sc:* Paul H. Rameau. (1:10) Low budget melodrama of an American lawyer who gets involved with Interpol and its pursuit of counterfeiters in Berlin. Filmed on location in Germany.

1284. Interrupted Melody (MGM; 1955). *Cast:* Glenn Ford (Dr. Thomas King), Eleanor Parker (AAN/Marjorie Lawrence—singing voice dubbed by Eileen Farrell), Roger Moore (Cyril Lawrence), Cecil Kellaway (Bill Lawrence), Peter Leeds (Dr. Ed Ryson), Evelyn Ellis (Clara), Walter Baldwin (Jim Owens), Ann Codee (Madame Gilly), Leopold Sachse (himself), Stephen Bekassy (Comte Claude des Vigneux), Charles R. Keane (Ted Lawrence), Fiona Hale (Eileen Lawrence), Phyllis Altivo (Louise), Sandra Descher (Suzie), Andre Charlot (Monsieur Bertrand), Jack Raine (Mr. Norson), Gloria Rhods (Mrs. Schultz), Rudolf Petrak, William Olvis, Doris Lloyd, Alex Frazer, Penny Santon, Gabor Curtiz, Claude Stroud, Paul McGuire, Doris Merrick, Frieda Stoll, Stuart Whitman, Eileen Farrell. *D:* Curtis Bernhardt; *P:* Jack Cummings; *St: & Sc:* (AA) William Ludwig, Sonya Levien; *Costumes:* (AAN-color) Helen Rose; *Songs and operatic numbers:* "Musetta's Waltz" from Giacomo Puccini's *La Bohème*; "Habanera" from Georges Bizet's *Carmen*; "Over the Rainbow" Harold Arlen, E.Y. Harburg; "Brunnhilde's Immolation" from Richard Wagner's *Götterdämmerung*; "Seguidilla" from *Carmen*; "Finale to Act One" from Giuseppe Verdi's *Il*

Trovatore; "One Fine Day" from Puccini's *Madama Butterfly*; and "Waltzing Matilda" A.B. Paterson, Marie Cowan. (1:46) (video) Acclaimed drama, in a sentimental vein, of Australian opera star Marjorie Lawrence who was confined to a wheelchair after being stricken with polio at the height of her career. Based on her autobiography, it became one of the 27 top-grossing films of 1954-55. Eastmancolor and CinemaScope.

1285. Invaders from Mars (20th Century-Fox; 1953). *Cast:* Jimmy Hunt, Helena Carter (final film—ret.), Arthur Franz, Morris Ankrum, Leif Erickson, Hillary Brooke, Max Wagner, Milburn Stone, Walter Sande, Janine Perreau, John Eldredge, Robert Shayne, Luce Potter, Lock Martin, Max Palmer, Bill Phipps. *D:* William Cameron Menzies (final film—ret.); *P:* Edward L. Alperson; *St:* John Tucker Battle; *Sc:* Richard Blake, Battle, Menzies. (1:18) (video/laserdisc) Acclaimed science fiction of a small boy who awakens one night to a sound. On looking out his window, he sees a spaceship burrowing into the ground behind his house, setting the stage for alien control of his family and neighbors. In Cinecolor, it was remade in 1986.

1286. Invasion of the Body Snatchers (Allied Artists; 1956). *Cast:* Kevin McCarthy, Dana Wynter, Larry Gates, King Donovan, Carolyn Jones, Jean Willes, Ralph Dumke, Virginia Christine, Tom Fadden, Kenneth Patterson, Guy Way, Eileen Stevens, Beatrice Maude, Jean Andren, Bobby Clark, Everett Glass, Dabbs Greer, Pat O'Malley (final film—ret.), Guy Rennie, Marie Selland, Whit Bissell, Sam Peckinpah (film debut), Richard Deacon, Harry Vejar. *D:* Don Siegel; *P:* Walter Wanger; *Sc:* Daniel Mainwaring, Sam Peckinpah (unc.). (1:20) (video/laserdisc) A genuine science fiction cult classic. Tale of a small California town being taken over by alien life forces, which emerge from pods, in forms which duplicate and replace the town's residents. Based on Jack Finney's book *The Body Snatchers* (aka: *Sleep No More*), it was remade in 1978 and again in 1994 as *Body Snatchers*. Computer-colored prints by Turner Entertainment are available on home video.

Invasion of the Flying Saucers *see* **Earth vs. the Flying Saucers**

Invasion of the Hell Creatures *see* **Invasion of the Saucer Men**

1287. Invasion of the Saucer Men (American International; 1957). *Cast:* Steve Terrell, Gloria Castillo, Frank Gorshin, Raymond Hatton, Lyn Osborn, Russ Bender, Douglas Henderson, Sam Buffington, Jason Johnson, Don Shelton, Scott Peters, Jan Englund, Kelly Thorsden, Bob Einer, Patti Lawler, Calvin Booth, Ed Nelson, Jim Bridges, Roy Darmour, Audrey Conti, Joan Dupuis, Jimmy Pickford, Orv Mohler, Buddy Mason, Angelo Rossito, Floyd Dixon, Dean Neville, Edward Peter Gibbons. *D:* Edward L. Cahn; *P:* James H. Nicholson, Robert J. Gurney, Jr.; *St:* Paul Fairman; *Sc:* Gurney, Jr., Al Martin. (1:09) (video) Science fiction comedy of pint-sized aliens with oversized heads who immobolize their victims by making them drunk via alcohol injected through needles from aliens' fingertips. Originally the lower half of a double bill with *I Was a Teenage Werewolf* (q.v.).

1288. Invasion U.S.A. (Columbia/American Prods.; 1952). *Cast:* Gerald Mohr, Peggie Castle, Dan O'Herlihy, Robert Bice, Tom Kennedy, Wade Crosby, Erik Blythe, Phyllis Coates, Noel Neill, Aram Katcher, Edward G. Robinson, Jr. *D:* Alfred E. Green; *P:* Albert Zugsmith, Robert Smith; *St:* Smith, Franz Spencer; *Sc:* Smith. (1:13) (video) Ultra low budget "cold war" programmer of a hoax perpetrated on a group of barroom patrons. Much stock footage and inserted film clips.

1289. Invisible Avenger (Republic; 1958). *Cast:* Richard Derr, Mark Daniels, Helen Westcott, Jeanne Neher, Dan Mullin (dual role), Lee Edwards, Jack Doner, Steve Dano, Leo Bruno, Sam Page. *D:* James Wong Howe, John Sledge, Ben Parker; *P:* Eric Sayers, Emanuel Demby; *Sc:* George Bellak, Betty Jeffries. (1:00) Programmer melodrama of Lamont Cranston [aka: "The Shadow"] (Derr), a man with the ability to make himself invisible, who saves the exiled president of Santa Cruz and his daughter from the president's twin brother, now dictator of the island. Filmed on location in New Orleans and based on the old radio show character "The Shadow" created by Maxwell Grant [pseudonym of Walter B. Gibson]. (re-release title: *Bourbon St. Shadows*)

1290. The Invisible Boy (MGM/Pan Prods.; 1957). *Cast:* Richard Eyer, Philip Abbott, Diane Brewster, Harold J. Stone, Robert H. Harris, Dennis McCarthy, Alexander Lockwood, John O'Malley, Gage Clark, Than Wyenn, Jefferson Dudley Searles, Alfred Linder, Ralph Votrian, Michael Miller, Robby the

Robot. *D:* Herman Hoffman; *P:* Nicholas Nayfack; *St:* Edmund Cooper; *Sc:* Cyril Hume. (1:25) (video) Science fictioner of attempts to destroy a power-crazed computer which has gone berserk and the young boy who finally succeeds where everyone else fails.

1291. **Invisible Invaders** (United Artists/Premium; 1959). *Cast:* John Agar, Jean Byron, Robert Hutton, John Carradine, Philip Tonge, Hal Torey, Eden Hartford, Jack Kenney, Paul Langton, Don Kennedy, Chuck Niles. *D:* Edward L. Cahn; *P:* Robert E. Kent; *Sc:* Samuel Newman. (1:07) Ultra low budget science fiction about invisible aliens from the moon who possess human corpses. Film uses much stock footage from newsreels. Originally ran on the lower half of a double bill with *The Four Skulls of Jonathan Drake* (q.v.).

1292. **Invitation** (MGM; 1951). *Cast:* Dorothy McGuire, Van Johnson, Louis Calhern, Ruth Roman, Ray Collins, Michael Chekhov, Lisa Golm, Barbara Ruick, Matt Moore, Diane Cassidy, Stapleton Kent, Norman Field, Patrick Conway, Alex Gerry, Lucille Curtis. *D:* Gottfried Reinhardt; *P:* Lawrence Weingarten; *St:* Jerome Weidman; *Sc:* Paul Osborn. (1:24) Popular hanky-soaker of a woman with only a year to live whose father pays a man to marry her. After love blossoms, she finds out the truth. The notable theme music by Bronislau Kaper was first used in *A Life of Her Own* (q.v.).

1293. **Invitation to the Dance** (MGM; 1952–56). *Cast:* Gene Kelly, Igor Youskevitch, Claire Sombert, David Kasday, Carol Haney, David Paltenghi, Daphne Dale, Claude Bessy, Tommy Rall, Tamara Toumanova, Belita, Irving Davies, Diana Adams. *D: & Sc:* Gene Kelly; *P:* Arthur Freed. (1:33) (video) An experimental musical which relates three different stories, in dance, without dialogue. The Hanna-Barbera cartoon world is used in the final story, combined with live action. A major box office disappointment. Filmed in 1952 with release delayed until 1956. It did receive the "Golden Bear" at the 1956 Berlin Film Festival. Techniolor.

1294. **The Iron Glove** (Columbia; 1954). *Cast:* Robert Stack, Ursula Theiss, Richard Stapley, Charles Irwin, Leslie Bradley, Alan Hale, Jr., Paul Cavanagh, Otto Waldis, Eric Feldary, Rica Owen, David Bruce, Shirley Whitney, Ingard Dawson, Louis D. Merrill. *D:* William Castle; *P:* Sam Katzman; *St:* Samuel J. Jacoby, Robert E. Kent; *Sc:* Jesse L. Lasky, Jr., DeVallon Scott, Douglas Heyes. (1:17) Action, adventure and romance are the main ingredients of this Technicolor costume swashbuckler.

1295. **Iron Man** (Universal-International; 1951). *Cast:* Jeff Chandler, Evelyn Keyes, Stephen McNally, Rock Hudson, Joyce Holden, Jim Backus, James Arness, Steve Martin, George Baxter, Paul Javor, Eddie Simms, Raymond Gray, Walter "Whitey" Ekwart, John Maxwell, Larry J. Blake, Ken Patterson, Herbert Vigran, Peter Scott, Gene Wesson, Johnny Call, Steve Roberts, Bob Evans, Frank Marlowe, Charles Sullivan, Stu Wilson, James Lennon, Barbara Ann Knudson, Gregg Sherwood, Cy Ring, Ethan Laidlaw, John Indrisano, Mushy Callahan, Frank Moran, John Carpenter, Jack Nikovich. *D:* Joseph Pevney; *P:* Aaron Rosenberg; *St:* William R. Burnett; *Sc:* George Zuckerman, Borden Chase. (1:21) A coal miner becomes a fighter in this pugilistic drama, previously filmed in 1931 and again in 1937 as *Some Blondes Are Dangerous.*

1296. **The Iron Mistress** (Warner; 1952). *Cast:* Alan Ladd, Virginia Mayo, Phyllis Kirk, Joseph Calleia, Alf Kjellin, Douglas Dick, Anthony Caruso, Richard Carlyle, Ned Young, Don Beddoe, George Voskovec, Robert Emhardt, Jay Novello, George J. Lewis, Harold Gordon, Daria Massey, Gordon Nelson, Nick Dennis, Sarah Selby, Dick Paxton, Edward Colmans, Ramsey Hill, Eugene Borden, Jean Del Val, Amanda Randolph, Reed Howes, Dick Cogan, Salvador Baguez, Madge Blake, David Wolfe, Richard Crane. *D:* Gordon Douglas; *P:* Henry Blanke; *Sc:* James R. Webb. (1:50) Hollywood story of the exploits of James Bowie, inventor of the Bowie knife, who died with the heroes who fought at the Alamo. Based on the novel by Paul I. Wellman. Technicolor.

1297. **Iron Mountain Trail** (Republic; 1953). *Cast:* Rex Allen, Slim Pickens, Nan Leslie, Grant Withers, Roy Barcroft, Alan Bridge, Forrest Taylor, George H. Lloyd, John Hamilton, Ko-Ko (horse). *D:* William Witney; *P:* Edward J. "Eddy" White; *St:* William Lively; *Sc:* Gerald Geraghty. (0:54) Rex Allen series western of a postal inspector investigating lost mail shipments.

1298. **The Iron Sheriff** (United Artists/Grand Prods.; 1957). *Cast:* Sterling Hayden, Constance Ford, John Dehner, Darryl Hickman, Kent Taylor, Walter Sande, Frank Ferguson,

King Donovan, Mort Mills, Peter Miller, Kathy Nolan, I. Stanford Jolley, Will Wright, Ray Walker, Bob Williams. *D:* Sidney Salkow; *P:* Jerome C. Robinson; *Sc:* Seeleg Lester. (1:13) Programmer western of a sheriff attempting to prove the innocence of his son who has been implicated in robbery and murder during a stagecoach holdup.

1299. The Iroquois Trail (United Artists/Edward Small; 1950). *Cast:* George Montgomery, Brenda Marshall (final film—ret.), Monte Blue, Sheldon Leonard, Glenn Langan, Paul Cavanagh, Reginald Denny, Dan O'Herlihy, Holmes Herbert, John Doucette. *D:* Phil Karlson; *P:* Bernard Small; *Sc:* Richard Schayer. (1:25) James Fenimore Cooper's *Leather Stocking Tales* was the basis of this costume actioner, set during the French and Indian War of the 18th century. (G.B. title: *The Tomahawk Trail*)

1300. Island in the Sky (Warner/Wayne-Fellows; 1953). *Cast:* John Wayne, Lloyd Nolan, Walter Abel, James Arness, Andy Devine, Allyn Joslyn, James Lydon, Harry Carey, Jr., Sean McClory, Hal Baylor, Wally Cassell, Regis Toomey, Gordon Jones, Frank Fenton, Robert Keys, Sumner Getchell, Paul Fix, Jim Dugan, George Chandler, Louis Jean Heydt, Bob Steele, Darryl Hickman, Touch [Mike] Connors, Carl Switzer, Cass Gidley, Guy Anderson, Tony DeMario, Ann Doran, Dawn Bender, Phyllis Winger, Tim Wellman, Mike Wellman, Tom Irish, Richard Walsh, Gene Coogan, John Indrisano. *D:* William A. Wellman; *P:* John Wayne, Robert Fellows; *Sc:* Ernest K. Gann (based on his novel). (1:48) (video) Drama of a transport plane downed in Greenland during World War II, the battle with the elements by the survivors and the search party sent to rescue them.

1301. Island in the Sun (20th Century-Fox/Darryl F. Zanuck; 1957). *Cast:* James Mason (Maxwell Fleury), Joan Fontaine (Mavis Norman), Dorothy Dandridge (Margot Seaton), Joan Collins (Jocelyn Fleury), Michael Rennie (Hilary Carson), Diana Wynyard (Mrs. Fleury), John Williams (Col. Whittingham), Stephen Boyd (Euan Templeton), Patricia Owens (Sylvia Fleury), Basil Sydney (Julian Fleury), John Justin (Denis Archer), Ronald Squire (the governor), Hartley Power (Bradshaw), Harry Belafonte (David Boyeur). *D:* Robert Rossen; *P:* Darryl F. Zanuck; *Sc:* Alfred Hayes; *Songs:* Title song, "Lead Man Holler" H. Belamonte, Irving "Lord" Burgess. (1:59) Soap-style drama of various members of the Fleury family and their assorted problems, all set against the luscious backdrop of the Carribbean islands. One of the 24 top-grossing films of 1956-57. Based on Alec Waugh's novel, it was photographed in DeLuxe color and CinemaScope.

1302. Island of Allah (Joseph Brenner/Studio Alliance; 1956). *Cast:* Isa Sabbagh, Nasir Ibn Mubarek, Fatima Bint Ali, James C. Stewart, Albert Clements, Ira Constad, John R. Jones, Said Shawa, Zafir Hussaini, Princess Yasmina, Fredric March (narrator). *D: & P:* Richard Lyford. (1:18) A low budget independent production which amounts to a travelogue in color and a look at historical events in Arabia.

1303. Island of Lost Women (Warner/Jaguar; 1959). *Cast:* Jeff Richards, Venetia Stevenson, John Smith, Diane Jergens, June Blair, Alan Napier, Gavin Muir, George Brand. *D:* Frank Tuttle (final film—d. 1963); *P:* Albert J. Cohen; *As.P:* George C. Bertholon; *St:* Prescott Chaplin; *Sc:* Ray Buffum. (1:11) A plane is forced down on a remote island with the pilot and his passenger, a reporter, coming into conflict with the island's residents, a mad scientist and his three virginal daughters. Originally ran on a double bill with *Born Reckless* (q.v.).

Island of Monte Cristo (G.B. title) *see* **Sword of Venus**

Island Woman *see* **Island Women**

1304. Island Women (United Artists/Security; 1958). *Cast:* Marie Windsor, Vince Edwards, Marilee Earle, Leslie Scott, Irene Williams, Kay Barnes, Paul White, Maurine Duvalier, George Symonette, "Blind Blake" Higgs, "Peanuts" Taylor, Vincent Martin, "Chippie" Chipman, Becky Chipman, Johnny Kemp, Harold McNair, Naomi, Sweet Richard, David Kemp. *D: & P:* William Berke; *As.P:* Eugene Gutowski; *St:* Andrew Alexander; *Sc:* Philip Yordan; *Songs:* "Calypso Island," "Island Woman," "Basket on Head," "Wanna Do Nothin', All Day," "All Suit, No Man," "Digby, Digby," "For You I'm Crazy Like Mad," "Calypso King," "Scratch My Back," "Never Mind the Noise in the Market," "Hold 'Em Joe," "Cocoanut Water, Gin and Rum" and "Goombay" Alice D. Simms, Charles Lofthouse. (1:12) A calypso-craze musical-romance of a charter boat captain who finds he has his hands full when a woman and her niece both set their sights on him. (aka: *Island Woman*)

1305. Istanbul (Universal-International; 1957). *Cast:* Errol Flynn, Cornell Borchers, Torin Thatcher, Leif Erickson, John Bentley, Peggy Knudsen, Martin Benson, Werner Klemperer, Nat "King" Cole, Jan Arvan, Nico Minardos, Ted Hecht, David Bond, Roland Varno, Hillevi Rombin, Frederic Melchior, Vladimir Sokoloff, Didi Ramati, Otto Reichow, Michael Dale, Peri Hatman, Michael Raffetto, Albert Carrier, Edward Colmans, Paul Thierry, Franco Corsaro, Peter Norman, Bobker Ben Ali, Manuel Paris, George Calliga. *D:* Joseph Pevney; *P:* Albert J. Cohen; *St:* Seton I. Miller; *Sc:* Miller, Barbara Gray, Richard Alan Simmons; *Songs:* "When I Fall in Love" (Victor Young–Edward Heymann) and "I Was a Little Too Lonely" (Jay Livingston-Ray Evans), both sung by Cole. (1:24) Melodrama of an American pilot who buys a diamond bracelet in Istanbul and finds himself pursued by smugglers and customs agents. In Technicolor and CinemaScope, the film is a remake of this studio's *Singapore* (1947).

1306. It Came from Beneath the Sea (Columbia/Clover Prods.; 1955). *Cast:* Kenneth Tobey, Faith Domergue, Donald Curtis, Ian Keith, Del Courtney, Lt. C. Griffiths, Harry Lauter, Capt. R. Peterson, Dean Maddox, Jr., Tol Avery, Ed Fisher, Ray Storey, Jack V. Littlefield, Jules Irving, Rudy Puteska. *D:* Robert Gordon; *P:* Charles H. Schneer; *St:* George Worthing Yates; *Sc:* Yates, Hal Smith; *F/X:* Ray Harryhausen, Jack Erickson. (1:19) (video/laserdisc) Science fiction of a giant mutant octopus that rises from the depths of the ocean to wreak havoc on seagoing vessels and eventually the city of San Francisco. For the most part, critics gave their approval to this premiere Schneer/Harryhausen collaboration, which ran on the top of a double bill with *Creature With the Atom Brain* (q.v.).

1307. It Came from Outer Space (Universal-International; 1953). *Cast:* Richard Carlson, Barbara Rush, Charles Drake, Kathleen Hughes, Russell Johnson, Joseph Sawyer, Dave Willock, Alan Dexter, George Eldredge, Brad Jackson, Warren MacGregor, George Selk [aka: Budd Buster], Edgar Dearing, Morey Amsterdam. *D:* Jack Arnold; *P:* William Alland; *Sc:* Harry Essex. (1:20) (video) Acclaimed science fiction of a spaceship that crashes in the Arizona desert with alien visitors assuming identities of the local citizenry until they can repair their ship. Based on Ray Bradbury's story "The Meteor," it was photographed in 3-D.

1308. It Conquered the World (American International/Sunset Pictures; 1956). *Cast:* Peter Graves, Beverly Garland, Lee Van Cleef, Sally Fraser, Charles B. Griffith, Russ Bender, Jonathan Haze, Richard "Dick" Miller, Karen Kadler, Paul Blaisdell (alien). *D:* & *P:* Roger Corman; *St:* & *Sc:* Lou Rusoff. (1:08) (video) Science fiction on a minimal budget of a Venusian who makes contact with an earth scientist. He believes the alien has friendly intentions, but events which occur when the Venusian lands prove otherwise. Remade in 1968 as *Zontar, the Thing from Venus.*

It Fell from the Flame Barrier *see* **The Flame Barrier**

1309. It Grows on Trees (Universal-International; 1952). *Cast:* Irene Dunne (final film—ret.), Dean Jagger, Joan Evans, Richard Crenna, Edith Meiser, Les Tremayne, Forrest Lewis, Sandy Descher, Dee Pollock, Malcolm Lee Beggs, Frank Ferguson, Bob Sweeney, Emile Avery, John Damler, Clark Howat, Elmer Peterson, Dee J. Thompson, Thurston Hall, Cliff Clark, Marie Blake, Hal K. Dawson, Jimmie Dodd, Anthony Radecki, Charles Gibb, Perc Launders, Charles McAvoy, Mary Benoit, Vera Burnett, William O'Leary, Bob Carney, Burman Bodil, Ralph Montgomery, Jack Reynolds, Bob Edgecomb, Jeanne Blackford, Frank Howard, Robert Strong, Walter Clinton, Chuck Courtney. *D:* Arthur Lubin; *P:* Leonard Goldstein; *Sc:* Leonard Praskins, Barney Slater. (1:24) Comedy-fantasy of a woman who plants two trees in her backyard, only to find they begin sprouting U.S. currency in lieu of leaves.

1310. It Happened to Jane (Columbia/Arwin; 1959). *Cast:* Doris Day, Jack Lemmon, Ernie Kovacs, Steve Forrest, Teddy Rooney, Russ Brown, Parker Fennelly, Mary Wickes, Walter Greaza, Philip Coolidge, Casey Adams [aka: Max Showalter], John Cecil Holm, Dick Crockett, Gina Gillespie, Dave Garroway, Robert Paige, Garry Moore, Bill Cullen, Jayne Meadows, Henry Morgan, Betsy Palmer, Gene Rayburn, Bess Myerson, Steve McCormick. *D:* & *P:* Richard Quine; *Ex.P:* Martin Melcher; *St:* Norman Katkov, Max Wilk; *Sc:* Katkov; *Songs:* "Be Prepared" Fred Karger, Quine; Title song Joe Lubin, I.J. Roth. (1:38) Romantic-comedy of a lady with a lobster business who, along with her lawyer, tangles with an unscrupulous railroad tycoon who cheated her. Filmed on locations in New England. (aka: *Twinkle and Shine*) Eastmancolor and CinemaScope.

1311. It Happens Every Thursday (Universal-International/Anton M. Leader Prods.; 1953). *Cast:* Loretta Young (final theatrical film before moving to TV), John Forsythe, Frank McHugh, Edgar Buchanan, Jimmy Conlin, Jane Darwell, Palmer Lee [aka: Gregg Palmer], Gladys George (final film—d. 1954), Regis Toomey, Dennis Weaver, Harvey Grant, Willard Waterman, Edith Evanson, Edward Clark, Kathryn Card, Eddy Waller, Laureen Perreau. Francis Pierlot, Edward Earle, Marie Blake, Sylvia Sims, Francis Ford, Richard Eyer, Walter Lawrence, Rudee [Rudy] Lee, George Ramsey. *D:* Joseph Pevney; *P:* Leonard Goldstein; *Adaptation:* Barney Slater, Leonard Praskins; *Sc:* Dane Lussier. (1:20) Comedy-drama of a married couple from New York who buy a failing small town newspaper and attempt to revive it.

1312. It Should Happen to You (Columbia; 1954). *Cast:* Judy Holliday (Gladys Glover), Jack Lemmon (film debut/Pete Sheppard), Peter Lawford (Evan Adams III), Michael O'Shea (final film—to TV/Brod Clinton), Connie Gilchrist (Mrs. Riker), Vaughn Taylor (Entrikin), Heywood Hale Broun (sour man), Whit Bissell (Robert Grau), Rex Evans (Con Cooley), Art Gilmore (Don Toddman), Wendy Barrie (final film—ret.), Constance Bennett, Melville Cooper, Ilka Chase (TV panel show guests), Walter Klavun (Bert Piazza), Lennie Bremen (Allie), Ralph Dumke (Beckhard), Chick Chandler, Cora Witherspoon, Jack Kruschen, John Saxon (film debut), Frank Nelson, Mary Young, James Nusser, Edwin Chandler, Stan Malotte, Robert Berger, Earl Keen, George Becwar, Tom Hennesy, Leo Curley, Ted Thorpe, Tom Cound, Stephany Hampson, Sandra Lee, Harold J. Kennedy, Don Richards, James Hyland, Margaret McWade, George Kitchel, Stanley Orr, Herbert Lytton. *D:* George Cukor; *P:* Fred Kohlmar; *Sc:* Garson Kanin; *Costumes:* (AAN-b/w) Jean Louis. (1:26) (video/laserdisc) Acclaimed comedy of New York actress Gladys Glover who, in an effort to gain publicity, rents billboards to advertise herself all over the city.

It Stalked the Ocean Floor *see* **The Monster from the Ocean Floor**

1313. It Started with a Kiss (MGM/Arcola; 1959). *Cast:* Glenn Ford (Sgt. Joe Fitzpatrick), Debbie Reynolds (Maggie Apflebar), Eva Gabor (Marquessa de la Rey), Gustavo Rojo (Antonio Soriano), Fred Clark (Gen. O'Connell), Edgar Buchanan (Congressman Tappe), Henry [Harry] Morgan (Charles Meridan), Robert Warwick (final film—ret./Congressman Muir), Frances Bavier (Mrs. Tappe), Netta Packer (Mrs. Muir), Alice Backes (Sally Meridan), Carmen Phillips (Belvah), Robert Cunningham, Robert Hutton, Members of the Society of Songs and Dances of Spain. *D:* George Marshall; *P:* Aaron Rosenberg; *St:* Valentine Davies; *Sc:* Charles Lederer; *Title song:* Rudy Render, Lederer (sung by Reynolds). (1:44) (video) Hit comedy, the title implying what led an American army officer into marriage with his free-spirited wife. Filmed on location in Spain, it became one of the 28 top-grossing films of 1959-60. MetroColor and CinemaScope.

1314. It! The Terror from Beyond Space (United Artists/Vogue; 1958). *Cast:* Marshall Thompson, Shawn Smith, Kim Spalding, Ann Doran, Dabbs Greer, Ray Corrigan (the title "It"/final film—ret.), Paul Langton, Robert Bice, Richard Benedict, Richard Hervey, Thom Carney. *D:* Edward L. Cahn; *P:* Robert E. Kent; *Sc:* Jerome Bixby. (1:09) (video) A spaceship returns to earth from Mars in 1972, with the sole surviving crew member accused of doing away with the rest of the crew on a 1968 expedition. This science fiction ran on a double bill with *Curse of the Faceless Man* (q.v.) and seems to have been the inspiration for *Alien* (Fox; 1979). (aka: *It! The Vampire from Beyond Space*)

1315. It's a Big Country (MGM; 1951). *Cast:* Marjorie Main. Keefe Brasselle, Bobby Hyatt, Nancy Davis, Fredric March, Angela Clarke, S.Z. Sakall, Janet Leigh, Gene Kelly, Gary Cooper, Keenan Wynn, Ethel Barrymore, George Murphy, William Powell, James Whitmore, Van Johnson, Lewis Stone, Leon Ames, Sharon McManus, Elisabeth Risdon, Bill Baldwin, Mickey Martin, Ned Glass, William H. Welsh, Sherry Hall, Fred Santley, Henry Sylvester, Roger Moore, Harry Stanton, Roger Cole, June Hedin, Luana Mehlberg, Jeralyn Alton, Jacqueline Kenley, Tony Taylor, Benny Burt, George Economides, Hal Hatfield, George Conrad, Richard Grindle, Anthony Lappas, Tom Nickols, David Alpert, Costas Morfis, A. Cameron Grant, Don Fields, Jerry Hunter, Donald Gordon, Lucille Curtis, Dolly Arriaga, Elena Savanarola, Carol Nugent, George McDonald, Charles Myers, David Wyatt, Mickey Little, Tiny Francone, Rhea Mitchell. *D:* Don Weis, Don Hartman, Charles Vidor, Clarence Brown, John Sturges, Richard Thorpe, William Wellman; *P:* Robert Sisk; *Sc:* Dore Schary, William Ludwig, Helen Deutsch, George Wells,

Allen Rivkin, Dorothy Kingsley, Isobel Lennart (based on stories by: Edgar Brooke, Ray Chordes, Joseph Petracca, Lucille Schlossberg, Claudia Cranston and John McNulty—based on an idea by Schary). (1:28) (video) Seven separate stories relay various aspects of life in the United States, each by a different director. Originally nine episodes, with two being eliminated before release. In England, only six of the seven stories were shown. A box office bomb.

1316. It's a Dog's Life (MGM; 1955). *Cast:* Jeff Richards, Jarma Lewis, Edmund Gwenn, Dean Jagger, Richard Anderson, Sally Fraser, J.M. Kerrigan, Wildfire (the canine star of this film who deservedly won the 1st Place PATSY Award in 1956). *D:* Herman Hoffman; *P:* Henry Berman; *Sc:* John Michael Hayes. (1:28) (video) Offbeat doggie tale of a bull terrier's rise from life in the slums to a life of luxury, told from his perspective. Based on the novel *The Bar Sinister* by Richard Harding Davis, it was previously filmed by Pathé in 1927 as *Almost Human*. Eastmancolor and CinemaScope. (aka: *The Bar Sinister*)

1317. It's a Small World (Eagle-Lion; 1950). *Cast:* Paul Dale, Lorraine Miller, Will Geer, Nina Koshetz, Steve Brodie, Anne Sholter, Todd Karns, Margaret Field, Shirley Mills, Thomas Browne Henry, Harry Harvey, Paul E. Burns, Jacqui Snyder, Lora Lee Michel. *D:* William Castle; *P:* Peter Scully; *St: & Sc:* Otto Schreiber, Castle; *Title song:* Karl Hajos, Charles Newman. (1:14) Obscure exploitation-melodrama of a midget and how he deals with the problems in his life.

1318. It's Always Fair Weather (MGM; 1955). *Cast:* Gene Kelly (Ted Riley), Cyd Charisse (Jackie Leighton), Dan Dailey (Doug Hallerton), Michael Kidd (film debut/Angie Valentine), Dolores Gray (Madeline Bradville), David Burns (Tim), Jay C. Flippen (Charles Z. Culloran), Steve Mitchell (Kid Mariacchi), Hal March (Rocky Lazar), Paul Maxey (Mr. Fielding), Peter Leeds (Mr. Trasker), Alex Gerry (Mr. Stamper), Madge Blake (Mrs. Stamper), Wilson Wood (Roy), Richard Simmons (Mr. Grigman), Almira Sessions, Eugene Borden. *D:* Gene Kelly, Stanley Donen; *P:* Arthur Freed; *St: & Sc:* (AAN) Betty Comden, Adolph Green; *Music:* (AAN) Andre Previn; *Songs:* "Baby, You Knock Me Out," "Thanks a Lot, but No Thanks," "Stillman's Gym," "March, March," "Why Are We Here (Blue Danube)?," "Music Is Better Than Words," "Once Upon a Time," "The Time For Parting," "I Like Myself" (Andre Previn, Adolph Green, Betty Comden); "Situation Wise," "Sleeper Phones," "The Binge" and "Ten Year Montage" (Previn). (1:42) (video/laserdisc) Critically acclaimed musical of three ex-servicemen who get together for a reunion ten years after the end of World War II, only to find they have nothing in common. The *New York Times* placed it at #8 on their "10 Best" list. In Eastmancolor and CinemaScope, box office returns were disappointing.

It's Only Money *see* **Double Dynamite**

1319. Ivanhoe (MGM; 1952). *Cast:* Robert Taylor (Ivanhoe), Elizabeth Taylor (Rebecca), Joan Fontaine (Rowena), George Sanders (De Bois-Guilbert), Emlyn Williams (Wamba), Robert Douglas (Sir Hugh de Bracy), Finlay Currie (Cedric), Felix Alymer (Isaac), Francis DeWolff (Font De Boeuf), Guy Rolfe (Prince John), Norman Wooland (King Richard), Basil Sydney (Waldemar Fitzurse), Harold Warrender (Robin of Locksley), Patrick Holt. *D:* Richard Thorpe; *P:* (AAN-Best Picture) Pandro S. Berman; *Adaptation:* Aeneas Mackenzie; *Sc:* Noel Langley; *Cin:* (AAN-color) F.A. Young; *Music:* (AAN) Miklos Rozsa. (1:46) (video/laserdisc) Lavishly produced in England, this medieval costumer is based on Sir Walter Scott's 1820 romance novel. On the "10 Best" lists of *Film Daily* and the *New York Times*, it placed #5 and #6 respectively. One of the 26 top-grossing films of 1952-53. First filmed by director Herbert Brenon in England in 1913 in four reels. Remade in 1982. Also a TV series. Technicolor.

1320. I've Lived Before (Universal-International; 1956). *Cast:* Jock Mahoney, Leigh Snowden, John McIntire, Ann Harding, Jerry Paris, Raymond Bailey, Simon Scott, Vernon Rich, Phil Harvey, April Kent, Brad Morrow, Jane Howard, Lorna Thayer, James Seay, Madelon Mitchel, Mike Dale, Ray Quinn, Bill Anders, Marjorie Stapp, Mike Portanova, Charles Conrad, Beatrice Gray, Earl Hansen, Palmer Wray Sherill, Jimmy Casino, Blanche Taylor. *D:* Richard Bartlett; *P:* Howard Christie; *Sc:* Norman Jolley, William Talman. (1:22) Melodrama (in an offbeat vein) of a pilot who encounters a widow; she believes he is the reincarnation of her husband who was killed in World War I. Originally ran on a double bill with *Edge of Hell* (q.v.).

1321. Jack and the Beanstalk (Warner; 1952). *Cast:* Bud Abbott, Lou Costello, Dorothy

Ford, Buddy Baer (dual role), James Alexander (dual role), Shaye Cogan (dual role), Barbara Brown, David Stollery, William Farnum (final film—d. 1953), Joe Kirk, Johnny Conrad & Dancers, Patrick the Harp. *D:* Jean Yarbrough; *P:* Alex Gottlieb; *Treatment:* Pat Costello; *Sc:* Nat Curtis; *Songs:* "I Fear Nothing," "He Never Looked Better in His Life," "Darlene" and "Dreamer's Cloth" Lester Lee, Bob Russell. (1:18) (video) Abbott and Costello do their thing with the famous fairy tale. The film opens in Sepiatone and changes to SuperCinecolor. First filmed in 1902 (Edison).

1322. Jack McCall, Desperado (Columbia; 1953). *Cast:* George Montgomery (title role), Angela Stevens, Douglas Kennedy (Wild Bill Hickok), James Seay, Eugene Iglesias, Jay Silverheels, Gene Roth, Joe McGuinn, John Hamilton, Stanley Blystone, William Tannen, Selmer Jackson, Alva Lacy. *D:* Sidney Salkow; *P:* Sam Katzman; *St:* David Chandler; *Sc:* John O'Dea. (1:16) (video) Civil War–era western drama of a wronged man seeking revenge. Technicolor.

1323. Jack Slade (Allied Artists; 1953). *Cast:* Mark Stevens, Dorothy Malone, Barton MacLane, John Litel, Paul Langton, Harry Shannon, John Harmon, Jim Bannon, Lee Van Cleef, Ron Hargrave, Sammy Ogg, Nelson Leigh, David May, John Halloran, Richard Reeves, Dorothy Kennedy, Duane Thorsen, Harry Landers, Ann Navarro. *D:* Harold Schuster; *P:* Lindsley Parsons; *Sc:* Warren Douglas. (1:29) Biographically styled fictional western drama of outlaw Jack Slade (Stevens) and the circumstances that led him to his eventual end. (G.B. title: *Slade*) Originally ran on the top of a double bill with *Hot News* (q.v.).

1324. The Jackie Robinson Story (Eagle-Lion; 1950). *Cast:* Jackie Robinson (himself), Ruby Dee (Rae Robinson), Minor Watson (Branch Rickey), Louise Beavers, Richard Lane, Harry Shannon, Ben Lessy, Bill Spaulding (himself), Joel Fluellen, Billy Wayne, Bernie Hamilton, Kenny Washington, Pat Flaherty, L. McGrath, Emmett Smith, Howard Louis MacNeely (J. Robinson as a boy), George Dockstader. *D:* Alfred E. Green; *P:* Mort Briskin; *St:* Louis Pollock; *Sc:* Lawrence Taylor, Arthur Mann. (1:16) (video) Biographical sports-drama of baseball's Jackie Robinson, the first black player to break the color barrier in the major leagues when he joined the Brooklyn Dodgers. Originally ran on a double bill with *The Torch* (q.v.).

1325. The Jackpot (20th Century–Fox; 1950). *Cast:* James Stewart, Barbara Hale, James Gleason, Fred Clark, Alan Mowbray, Patricia Medina, Natalie Wood, Tommy Rettig, Robert Gist, Lyle Talbot, Charles Tannen, Bigelow Sayre, Dick Cogan, Jewel Rose, Eddie Firestone, Estelle Etterre, Claude Stroud, Joan Miller, Caryl Lincoln, Walter Baldwin, Valerie Mark, Syd Saylor, John Qualen, Fritz Feld, Kathryn Sheldon, Robert Dudley, Billy Wayne, Minerva Urecal, Milton Parsons, Kim Spalding, Dulce Daye, Andrew Tombes, Marjorie Holliday, Carol Savage, June Evans, Harry Hines, Ann Doran, Jerry Hausner, Billy Lechner, Sam Edwards, George Conrad, Joe Barney, Jack Mather, Harry Carter, Colin Ward, Ken Christy, Peggy O'Connor, Jack Roper, Dick Curtis, Guy Way, Elizabeth Flournoy, Franklin "Pinky" Parker, Robert Bice, Tudor Owen, John Roy, John Bleifer, Bill Nelson, Philip Van Zandt, Frances Budd. *D:* Walter Lang; *P:* Samuel G. Engel; *Sc:* Phoebe and Henry Ephron. (1:26) (video) Comedy of an average married man with two children who lives in a small town. Via the telephone, he answers the jackpot question on a radio quiz show. Chaos reigns when truckloads of prizes (that he is unable to pay the taxes on) are delivered to his residence.

1326. Jaguar (Republic; 1956). *Cast:* Sabu, Chiquita, Barton MacLane, Jonathan Hale (final film—ret.), Touch [Michael] Connors, Jay Novello, Fortunio Bonanova, Nacho Galindo, Rodd Redwing, Pepe Hern, Raymond Rosas. *D:* George Blair; *As.P:* Mickey Rooney, Maurice Duke; *Sc:* John Fenton Murray, Benedict Freeman. (1:06) B budget melodrama of murder at an oil field, with the chief suspect a South American Indian boy thought to have been under the influence of drugs.

1327. Jail Bait (Howco; 1954). *Cast:* Dolores Fuller, Lyle Talbot, Herbert Rawlinson (final film—d. 1954), Steve Reeves, Clancy Malone, Tim Farrell, Theodora Thurman, Cotton Watts, Chick, Conrad Brooks. *D: & P:* Edward D. Wood, Jr.; *St: & Sc:* Wood, Jr., Alex Gordon. (1:10) (video/laserdisc) Low budget crime-melodrama involving a holdup that results in murder, and a plastic surgeon who alters the face of the killer.

1328. Jail Busters (Allied Artists; 1955). *Cast:* Leo Gorcey, Huntz Hall, Bennie Bartlett, David [Gorcey] Condon, Bernard Gorcey, Percy Helton, Barton MacLane, Anthony Caruso, Murray Alper, Michael Ross, Fritz Feld, Lyle

Talbot, Henry Kulky, Emil Sitka, John Harmon, Henry Tyler. *D:* William Beaudine; *P:* Ben Schwalb; *St: & Sc:* Edward Bernds, Elwood Ullman. (1:01) "Bowery Boys" series entry with the boys getting thrown in jail to get a news story, finding themselves stuck there when the editor who helped them stage a robbery absconds with the loot.

1329. Jailhouse Rock (MGM/Avon Prods.; 1957). *Cast:* Elvis Presley, Judy Tyler (final film—killed in a 1957 car crash), Mickey Shaughnessy, Vaughn Taylor (who also narrates), Jennifer Holden, Dean Jones, Anne Neyland, Grandon Rhodes, Katherine Warren, Don Burnett, The Jordanaires, George Cisar, Glenn Strange, John Indrisano, Dorothy Abbott, Robert Bice, Hugh Sanders, Percy Helton, Peter Adams, William Forrest, Dan White, Robin Raymond, John Day, S. John Launer, Dick Rich, Elizabeth Slifer, Gloria Pall, Fred Coby, Walter Johnson, Frank Kreig, William Tannen, Wilson Wood, Tom McKee, Donald Kerr, Carl Milletaire, Francis DeSales, Harry Hines. *D:* Richard Thorpe; *P:* Pandro S. Berman; *As.P:* Kathryn Hereford; *St:* Ned Young; *Sc:* Guy Trosper; *Songs:* "Jailhouse Rock," "One More Day," "Young and Beautiful," "I Wanna Be Free," "Don't Leave Me Now," "Treat Me Nice" and "Baby, I Don't Care" Jerry Leiber, Mike Stoller. (1:36) (video/laserdisc) Hit musical-drama of a young man sent to prison on a manslaughter charge after killing another in a barroom fight. In prison he learns to play the guitar and becomes a rock 'n' roll singer on release. Presley's third film is considered by many—except his harshest critics—to be his best film. The title song became a big hit and the film grossed $4,000,000 for MGM. Computer-colored prints have been produced by Turner Entertainment. CinemaScope.

1330. Jalopy (Allied Artists; 1953). *Cast:* Leo Gorcey, Huntz Hall, David [Gorcey] Condon, Bennie Bartlett, Bernard Gorcey, Robert Lowery, Jane Easton, Leon Belasco, Richard Benedict, Murray Alper, Tom Hanlon, Mona Knox, Conrad Brooks, Robert Rose, George Dockstader, George Barrows, Fred Lamont, Teddy Mangean, Bud [Bill] Wolfe, Carey Loftin, Louis Tomei, Dude Criswell, Pete Kellett, Carl Saxe, Dick Crockett. *D:* William Beaudine; *P:* Ben Schwalb; *St:* Tim Ryan, Jack Crutcher; *Sc:* Ryan, Crutcher, Edmond Seward, Jr., Bert Lawrence. (1:02) Hit "Bowery Boys" series entry with Sach (Hall) inventing a super-fuel to help Slip (L. Gorcey) win the cash prize in a jalopy race and save Louis Dombroski's (B. Gorcey) store. Note: This entry marked a revamping of the series to get the boys out of their juvenile image that existed since 1937.

1331. Jamaica Run (Paramount/Pine-Thomas; 1953). *Cast:* Ray Milland, Arlene Dahl, Wendell Corey, Patric Knowles, Laura Elliot, Carroll McComas, William Walker, Murray Matheson, Clarence Muse, Michael Moore, Rex Evans, Robert Warwick, Lester Matthews, Robert A. Davis. *D:* Lewis R. Foster; *P:* William H. Pine, William C. Thomas; *Sc:* Foster. (1:32) In the Caribbean, a salvage diver gets involved with greedy family members seeking an estate. Based on the novel *The Neat Little Corpse* by Max Murray. Technicolor.

1332. Jamboree (Warner; 1957). *Cast:* Kay Medford, Robert Patine, Freda Holloway, Paul Carr, Dave King-Wood, Aaron Schroeder. *Guest Stars:* Fats Domino, Buddy Knox, Jimmy Bowen, Jodi Sands, Charlie Gracie, Slim Whitman, Jerry Lee Lewis (film debut), The Four Coins, Lewis Lymon and the Teenchords, Connie Francis (film debut), Rocco and His Saints, Frankie Avalon (film debut), Count Basie & Orchestra, Carl Perkins, Joe Williams, Sandy Singer, Andy Martin, Rob Coby. *DJs:* Joe Smith, Joe Finan, Keith Sandy, Zenas Sears, Milt Grant, Dick Clark (film debut), Barry Kaye, Ray Perkins, Gerry Myers, Jocko Henderson, Ed Bonner, Robin Seymour, Dick Whittinghill, Howard Miller, Werner Goetz, Chris Howland, Jack Payne, Jack Jackson, Tony Travis, Leonard Schneider, Jean Martin. *D:* Roy Lockwood; *P:* Max J. Rosenberg, Milton Subotsky; *Sc:* Leonard Kantor; *Songs:* "Jamboree," "Great Balls of Fire," "Record Hop Tonight," "For Children of All Ages," "Glad All Over," "Who Are We to Say?," "Teacher's Pet," "Siempre," "Cool Baby," "Sayonara," "Toreador," "Your Last Chance," "If Not for You," "Unchain My Heart," "A Broken Promise," "One O'Clock Jump," "I Don't Like You No More," "Cross Over," "Hula Love," "Wait and See" and "Twenty-Four Hours a Day." (1:11) A time capsule of musical stars and groups of the day, featuring 21 rock 'n' roll, rockabilly and jazz numbers and 21 radio disc jockeys, overshadowing a feeble romance/business plot. (G.B. title: *Disc Jockey Jamboree*) Note: The *Motion Picture Guide* lists the running time of this film as 1:25.

The James Brothers (G.B. title) *see* **The True Story of Jesse James**

1333. The James Dean Story (Warner; 1957). *D: & P:* George W. George, Robert

Altman; *Narrator:* Martin Gabel; *Song:* "Let Me Be Loved" Jay Livingston, Ray Evans. (1:22) (video/laserdisc) Documentary feature on the life of movie/TV/stage actor James Byron Dean, whose promising career was cut short on September 30, 1955. At the age of 24 years, he was killed when his Porsche was involved in a highway accident on the way to a sports car race. The film utilizes stills, film clips and interviews with the people who knew and worked with him.

1334. Japanese War Bride (20th Century-Fox; 1952). *Cast:* Don Taylor, Shirley Yamaguchi, Cameron Mitchell, Marie Windsor, James Bell, Louise Lorimer, Philip Ahn, Sybil Merritt, Lane Nakano, Kathleen Mulqueen, Orley Lindgren, George Wallace, May Takasugi, William Yokota, Susie Matsumoto, Weaver Levy, Jerry Fujikawa, Chieko Sato, Tetsu Komai, Hisa Chiba, David March. *D:* King Vidor; *P:* Joseph Bernhard; *St:* Anson Bond; *Sc:* Catherine Turney. (1:31) Drama of a Korean War veteran who marries his Japanese nurse and brings her home to his California farm, where they face lingering resentment against the Japanese from World War II.

1335. The Jayhawkers (Paramount/Panama-Frank; 1959). *Cast:* Jeff Chandler, Fess Parker, Nicole Maurey, Henry Silva, Herbert Rudley, Jimmy Carter, Shari Lee Bernath, Leo Gordon, Frank DeKova, Don Megowan. *D:* Melvin Frank; *P:* Frank, Norman Panama; *Sc:* Frank, A.I. Bezzerides, Joseph Petracca, Frank Fenton. (1:40) (video) Hit adult western drama of a band of guerrillas trying to get control of Kansas prior to the days of the American Civil War. Technicolor and VistaVision.

1336. Jazz Festival (Studio Films, Inc.; 1955). *Cast:* Lionel Hampton, Ruth Brown, Larry Darnell, Cab Calloway, The Clovers, Herb Jeffries, Bill Bailey, Dinah Washington, Nipsey Russell, Mantan Moreland, Duke Ellington, The Larks, Count Basie, Sarah Vaughan. *D:* Joseph Kohn; *P:* Ben Frye. (1:10) A musical-comedy revue designed for the all-black audience.

1337. The Jazz Singer (Warner; 1953). *Cast:* Danny Thomas (Jerry Golding), Peggy Lee (Judy Lane), Mildred Dunnock (Mrs. Golding), Eduard Franz (Cantor Golding), Tom Tully (McGurney), Alex Gerry (Uncle Louie), Allyn Joslyn (George Miller), Harold Gordon (Rabbi Roth), Hal Ross (Joseph), Justin Smith (Phil Stevens), Anitra Stevens (Yvonne). *D:* Michael Curtiz; *P:* Louis F. Edelman; *Sc:* Frank Davis, Leonard Stern, Lewis Meltzer; *Music:* (AAN) Ray Heindorf, Max Steiner; *Songs include:* "I Hear the Music Now" (Sammy Fain–Jerry Seelen); "This is a Very Special Day" (Peggy Lee); "Living the Life I Love" (Fain–Seelen); "Just One of Those Things" (Cole Porter); "I'm Looking Over a Four Leaf Clover" (Mort Dixon–Harry Woods); "Birth of the Blues" (B.G. DeSylva–Lew Brown–Ray Henderson); "Lover" (Richard Rodgers–Lorenz Hart); "If I Could Be With You" (Henry Creamer–Jimmy Johnson); "Breezin' Along with the Breeze" (Richard A. Whiting–Seymour Simons–Haven Gillespie); "I'll String Along with You" (Al Dubin–Harry Warren); "What Are New Yorkers Made Of?," "Hush-A-Bye" and "Oh Moon" (Fain–Seelen). (1:47) (video) An updated Technicolor remake of Warner's 1927 legendary "first talkie" with a Korean veteran choosing show business over a religious career in the synagogue where his father is a cantor. Based on the play by Samson Raphaelson, it was remade again in 1980 in another updated format.

1338. Jeanne Eagels (Columbia; 1957). *Cast:* Kim Novak (title role/singing voice dubbed by Eileen Wilson), Jeff Chandler (Sal Satori), Agnes Moorehead (Mme. Neilson), Charles Drake (John Donahue), Larry Gates (Al Brooks), Virginia Grey (Elsie Esmond), Gene Lockhart (final film—d. 1957/Equity Board president), Joe DeSantis (Frank Satori), Murray Hamilton (Chick O'Hara), Will Wright (Marshal), Lowell Gilmore (Rev. Dr. Davidson), Juney Ellis (Mrs. Davidson), Beulah Archuletta (Mrs. Horn), Jules Davis (Mr. Horn), Florence MacAfee (Mrs. McPhail), Snub Pollard (Bates), Johnny Tarangelo (Pvt. Griggs), Bert Spencer (Dr. McPhail), Richard Harrison (Cpl. Hodgson), Michael Dante (Sgt. O'Hara), Joseph Turkel (Eddie), George Neise (Jerry), Doris Lloyd (Mrs. Corliss), Joe Mell (Kevin), Alyn Lockwood (Rosalie Satori), Ted Marcuse (Dr. Richards), William "Tex" Carr (specialty fire eater), Joseph Novack, Ward Wood, Myrtle Anderson, Charles Couch, William Couch, Sammy Finn, Wallace Ross, Walter Ridge, Richard Gaines, Patricia Mowry, Junius Matthews, George DeNormand, Tom McAfee, Eleanor Audley, Bill Suiter, Myna Cunard, Bob Hopkins, Judd Holdren, John Celentano, Tommy Nolan, Raymond Greenleaf, Carlyle Mitchell, James Gonzales, Jennie Lea, Helen Marr Van Tuyl, Bradford Jackson, Lillian Culver, Deon Robb, Rebecca Godinez, Irving Mitchell, George

J. Lewis, Frances Driver, Joan Harding, Reita Green, Myrna Fahey, Joy Stoner, Hal LeSuer, Leon Tyler, Giselle D'Arc, Lee Trent, Kenneth Gibson, Jean Vachon, Whitey Haupt, Paul De Rolf, Larry Larson, Gary Pagett, Nanette [Fabray] Fabares, Brenda Lomas, Eugene Jackson, Jimmy Murphy, Cosmo Sardo, Larry Blake, Walter Conrad, Eugene Sherman, Frank Borzage, Lou Borzage, Jack Arno. *D:* & *P:* George Sidney; *St:* Daniel Fuchs; *Sc:* Fuchs, Sonya Levien, John Fante. (1:49) Fact blends with fiction in this biographical drama of ill-fated 1920s stage and screen actress Jeanne Eagels, her rise to fame and her fall through drugs and alcohol. One of the 24 top-grossing films of 1956-57.

1339. Jennifer (Allied Artists; 1953). *Cast:* Ida Lupino, Howard Duff, Robert Nichols, Mary Shipp, Matt Dennis (himself), Ned Glass, Kitty McHugh, Russ Conway, Lorna Thayer. *D:* Joel Newton; *P:* Berman Schwartz; *Sc:* Virginia Myers. (1:13) Melodrama of a woman who encounters problems after becoming the new caretaker to a large estate, particularly after she discovers a murder.

1340. Jeopardy (MGM; 1953). *Cast:* Barbara Stanwyck, Ralph Meeker, Barry Sullivan, Lee Aaker, Bud [Bill] Wolfe, Saul Gorss, Bob Castro, Paul Fierro, Juan Torena, Felipe Turich, Natividad Vacio, George Derrick, Rico Alaniz, Salvador Baguez, Charles Stevens, Margarita Martin, Alex Montoya, Louis Tomei, Ken Terrell, George Navarro, Carlos Conde. *D:* John Sturges; *P:* Sol Fielding; *Sc:* Mel Dinelli, Maurice Zimm. (1:08) Programmer thriller of a family in Mexico who run afoul of a crazed killer. Based on the radio play "A Question of Time" by Mr. Zimm.

Jerrico, the Wonder Clown *see* **Three-Ring Circus**

1341. Jesse James vs. the Daltons (Columbia; 1954). *Cast:* Brett King, Barbara Lawrence, James Griffith (Bob Dalton), William Phipps (Bill Dalton), Rory Mallinson (Bob Ford), John Cliff (Grat Dalton), William Tannen (Emmett Dalton), Richard Garland, Nelson Leigh, Raymond Largay. (1:05) The supposed son of the famous outlaw joins the Dalton gang to find out the truth about his father. Originally in 3-D and Technicolor, it ran on a double bill with *Bait* (q.v.).

1342. Jesse James' Women (United Artists/Panorama; 1954). *Cast:* Don Barry (Jesse James), Peggie Castle, Jack Beutel (Frank James), Lita Baron, Joyce Rhed, Betty Brueck, Laura Lee, Sam Keller (Cole Younger). *D:* Donald Barry (only film as director); *P:* Lloyd Royal, T.V. Garroway; *Sc:* D.D. Beauchamp; *Songs:* "Careless Lover" George Antheil; "In the Shadows of My Heart" Stan Jones. (1:23) Low budget offbeat western of the legendary outlaw and some of his romantic escapades. Eastmancolor.

1343. Jet Attack (American International; 1958). *Cast:* John Agar, Audrey Totter, Gregory Walcott, James Dobson, Leonard Strong, Nicky Blair, Victor Sen Yung, Joe Hamilton, Guy Prescott, George Cisar, Stella Lynn, Robert Carricart, Weaver Levy, Paul Power, Hal Bogart, Madeline Foy, Bob Gilbreath. *D:* Edward L. Cahn; *Ex.P:* James H. Nicholson; *P:* Alex Gordon; *Co-Producer:* Israel M. Berman; *As.P:* Mark Hanna; *St:* Hanna; *Sc:* Orville H. Hampton. (1:08) (video) This Korean War drama tells of American efforts to locate a missing radar scientist, trapped behind communist lines. It originally ran on a double bill with *Suicide Battalion* (q.v.). (aka: *Jet Squad* and *Through Hell to Glory*)

1344. Jet Job (Monogram; 1952). *Cast:* Stanley Clements, Elena Verdugo, John Litel, Bob Nichols, Tom Powers, Dorothy Adams, Todd Karns, Paul Stanton, Dave Willock, John Kellogg, Russ Conway, Steve Roberts, Arthur Space, William Forrest, William Tannen. *D:* William Beaudine; *P:* Ben Schwalb; *Sc:* & *St:* Charles R. Marion. (1:03) Programmer melodrama of rival airplane manufacturers, both after the same U.S. Army contract.

Jet Men of the Air *see* **Air Cadet**

1345. Jet Pilot (Universal-International/RKO-Howard Hughes; 1950–57). *Cast:* John Wayne, Janet Leigh, Jay C. Flippen, Paul Fix, Richard Rober (final film—d. 1952), Roland Winters, Hans Conried, Ivan Triesault, John Bishop, Perdita Chandler, Joyce Compton, Ernie Pyle, Elizabeth Flournoy, Jack Overman, Kenneth Tobey, Harry Lauter, Vince Gironda, Armand Tanny, Ruthelma Stevens, Lois Austin, Ruth Lee, Alan Dinehart III, Phil Arnold, Tom Daly, Keith McConnell, Herbert Lytton, Nelson Leigh, Al Murphy, Mike Lally, Theodore Rand, Joey Ray, Robert "Smoki" Whitfield, Jane Easton, Dorothy Abbott, Janice Hood, Allen Matthews, Darrell Huntley, Billy Vernon, Gene Roth, Jimmy Dime, Paul Bakanas, Michael Mark, Gregg Barton, Jack Shea, Gene

Evans, Bill Erwin, Richard Norris, Dave Ormond, Mamie Van Doren (film debut?), Barbara Freking, Wendell Niles, Bill "Chuck" Yeager, John Morgan, Joan Jordan, Joan Whitney, Sylvia Lewis, Paul Frees, Don Haggerty, Carleton Young. *D:* Josef von Sternberg, Nicholas Ray (unc.); *Ex.P:* Howard Hughes; *P: & Sc:* Jules Furthman. (1:52) (video/laserdisc) An aviation drama of a pilot who marries a Russian defector. Production for this film began in 1949, was completed in 1950, but due to perfectionist tampering by executive producer Howard Hughes, release of the film was held up until 1957—after RKO closed its doors. Note: Another prime example of how multi-millionaire Howard Hughes lost millions *trying to make movies*!

Jet Squad *see* **Jet Attack**

1346. Jiggs and Maggie Out West (Monogram; 1950). *Cast:* Joe Yule (Jiggs), Renie Riano (Maggie), George McManus (himself), Tim Ryan (Dinty Moore), Jim Bannon, Riley Hill, Pat Goldin, June Harrison, Terry McGinnis, Henry "Bomber" Kulkovich [aka: Henry Kulky], Billy Griffith, Kenne Duncan, Tom Kennedy, William Vincent. *D:* William Beaudine; *P:* Barney Gerard; *St:* Gerard, Eddie Cline; *Sc:* Gerard, Adele Buffington. (1:06) The fifth and final entry in the "Jiggs and Maggie" comedy series started in the late 1940s. In this one they head to a western ghost town in search of gold. Based on the characters created in the comic strip *Bringing Up Father* by George McManus.

1347. Jim Thorpe—All American (Warner; 1951). *Cast:* Burt Lancaster (title role), Charles Bickford (Glen S. "Pop" Warner), Steve Cochran, Phyllis Thaxter, Dick Wesson, Jack Big Head, Suni Warcloud, Al Mejia, Nestor Paiva, Hubie Kerns (Tom Ashenbrunner), Ed Max, Jimmy Morse (Jim Thorpe, Jr.), Billy Gray (Jim Thorpe as a young man). *D:* Michael Curtiz; *P:* Everett Freeman; *Sc:* Freeman, Douglas Morrow; *Additional dialogue:* Frank Davis. (1:47) (video/laserdisc) Biopic of famed American Indian athlete—of Sac and Fox heritage—who won the Pentathlon and Decathlon at the 1912 Olympics; subsequently stripped of his medals for playing pro-baseball in college. Based on the biography by Russell G. Birdwell and Jim Thorpe and the story "Bright Path" by Mr. Morrow and Vincent X. Flaherty. (G.B. title: *Man of Bronze*) Note: Thorpe's medals and records were later reinstated posthumously.

The Jim Vaus Story *see* **Wiretappers**

1348. Jivaro (Paramount/Pine-Thomas; 1954). *Cast:* Fernando Lamas, Rhonda Fleming, Brian Keith, Lon Chaney, Jr., Richard Denning, Rita Moreno, Marvin Miller, Morgan Farley, Pascual Pena, Nestor Paiva, Charles Lung, Gregg Barton, Kay Johnson, Rosa Turich, Marian Mosick, Richard Bartell, Eugenia Paul. *D:* Edward Ludwig; *P:* William H. Pine, William C. Thomas; *Sc:* Winston Miller. (1:31) South American jungle adventure of three men and a beautiful woman searching the Amazon for gold, who run headlong into a tribe of headhunters. Based on *Lost Treasure of the Andes* by David Duncan. (G.B. title: *Lost Treasure of the Amazon*) Originally ran on a double bill with *Alaska Seas* (q.v.). Technicolor.

1349. Joe Butterfly (Universal-International; 1957). *Cast:* Audie Murphy, George Nader, Burgess Meredith (title role), Kieko Shima, Keenan Wynn, Fred Clark, Shinpei Shimazaki, Charles McGraw, Reiko Higa, Tatsuo Saito, Chizu Shimazaki, Herbert Anderson, Eddie Firestone, Harold Goodwin, Willard Willingham, John Agar. *D:* Jesse Hibbs; *P:* Aaron Rosenberg; *Sc:* Sy Gomberg, Jack Sher, Marion Hargrove. (1:30) Military comedy set in American-occupied Japan following the World War II surrender. Based on a play by Evan Wylie and Jack Ruge. Technicolor and CinemaScope.

1350. Joe Dakota (Universal-International; 1957). *Cast:* Jock Mahoney, Luana Patten, Charles McGraw, Barbara Lawrence, Claude Akins, Lee Van Cleef, Anthony Caruso, George Dunn, Paul Birch, Steve Darrell, Rita Lynn, Gregg Barton, Jeanne Wood, Juney Ellis, Anthony Jochim. *D:* Richard Bartlett; *P:* Howard Christie; *St: & Sc:* William Talman, Norman Jolley; *Song:* "The Flower of San Antone" Mack David, Ray Joseph. (1:19) Western of a stranger in town who uncovers skullduggery in the oil drilling business, as well as in the suspicious death years before of his Indian friend. Originally ran on a double bill with *Run of the Arrow* (q.v.). Eastmancolor.

1351. The Joe Louis Story (United Artists/Walter P. Chrysler, Jr.; 1953). *Cast:* Coley Wallace, Paul Stewart, Hilda Simms, James Edwards, John Marley, Dotts Johnson, Carl "Rocky" Latimer, Ossie Davis, Royal Beal, Ruby Goldstein (himself), Anita Ellis, Evelyn Ellis, John Marriott, P. Jay Sidney, Isaac Jones, Buddy Thorpe (Max Schmeling), Ralph Santley, Ellis Larkins Trio, Herb Ratner, David Kurlan, Norman Rose, Jose F. Draper. *D:* Robert Gordon;

P: Stirling Silliphant (first film); *Sc:* Robert Sylvester. (1:28) (video) Sincere dramatic biopic of the "Brown Bomber's" (Wallace) life, from his boyhood in Chicago to his marriage to Marva (Simms) and his final defeat as heavyweight champ in 1951 by Rocky Marciano. Actual fight footage fills in non-recreated events.

Joe Palooka in Humphrey Takes a Chance *see* **Humphrey Takes a Chance**

1352. Joe Palooka in the Squared Circle (Monogram; 1950). *Cast:* Joe Kirkwood, Jr., James Gleason, Lois Hall, Edgar Barrier, Myrna Dell, Robert Coogan, Dan Seymour, Charles Halton, Frank Jenks, Greg McClure, Eddie Gribbon, Robert Griffin, John Harmon, Jack Roper, Sue Carlton, William Haade, Stanley Prager, Marvin Williams, Hal Fieberling, John Merrick, Paul Bryar. *D:* Reginald LeBorg; *P:* Hal E. Chester; *St:* B.F. Melzer; *Sc:* Jan Jeffries. (1:03) In the tenth entry in this series begun in the 1940s, the young boxer (Kirkwood, Jr.) witnesses a gangland murder. Based on the comic strip created by Ham Fisher. (G.B. title: *The Squared Circle*)

Joe Palooka in Triple Cross *see* **Triple Cross**

1353. Joe Palooka Meets Humphrey (Monogram; 1950). *Cast:* Joe Kirkwood, Jr., Leon Errol (dual role), Pamela Blake, Robert Coogan, Jerome Cowan, Joe Besser, Don McGuire, Donald MacBride, Curt Bois, Clem Bevans, Frank Sully, Eddie Gribbon, Meyer Grace, Lillian Bronson, Sam Balter, Frosty Royce, Russ Kaplan, Sandra Gould, Bert Conway, Ray Walker, Knox Manning. *D:* Jean Yarbrough; *P:* Hal E. Chester; *Sc: & St:* Henry Blankfort. (1:05) The 8th entry in the boxing series, designed to introduce a new regular character, hulking Humphrey (Coogan). Based on the comic strip characters created by Ham Fisher, it had the pre-release title of "Honeymoon for Five."

1354. John Paul Jones (Warner/Samuel Bronston: 1959). *Cast:* Robert Stack, Marisa Pavan, Charles Coburn (Benjamin Franklin), Erin O'Brien, Macdonald Carey (Patrick Henry), Jean-Pierre Aumont (King Louis XVI), Peter Cushing, Bruce Cabot, Bette Davis (Catherine the Great), Tom Brannum, Basil Sydney, Archie Duncan, David Farrar, Susana Canales (Marie Antoinette), Jorge Riviere, Mia Farrow (film debut/bit), Thomas Gomez, Judson Laure, Bob Cunningham, John Charles Farrow, Eric Pohlman (King George III), Pepe Nieto, John Crawford (George Washington), Patrick Villiers, Frank Latimore, Ford Rainey, Bruce Seton, Paul Curran, George Rigaud, Rupert Davies, Nicholas Brady, Robert Ayres (John Adams), Christopher Rhodes, MacDonald Parke, John Phillips (John Hancock), David Phethean, Mitchell Kowal, Reed DeRouen, Charles Wise, Archie Lyall, Al Brown, Randolph McKenzie, Phil Brown, Felix DePomes. *D:* John Farrow (final film—d. 1963); *P:* Samuel Bronston; *Sc:* Farrow, Jesse Lasky, Jr. (2:06) (video) At a cost of $4,000,000, this lavishly produced historical costume-drama of the 18th century naval hero (Stack) made little impression on the critics or the movie-going public. Based on the story "Nor'wester" by Clements Ripley, it was in Technicolor and Technirama.

1355. Johnny Concho (United Artists/Kent; 1956). *Cast:* Frank Sinatra, Keenan Wynn, William Conrad, Phyllis Kirk, Wallace Ford, Christopher Dark, Howard Petrie, Harry Bartell, Dan Riss, Robert Osterloh, Dorothy Adams, John Qualen, Willis Bouchey, Jean Byron, Leo Gordon, Wilfred Knapp, Claude Akins, Ben Wright, Joe Bassett. *D:* Don McGuire; *P:* Frank Sinatra, Frank Sanicola; *Sc:* David P. Harmon, McGuire. (1:24) Western drama adapted from "The Man Who Owned the Town" by Mr. Harmon (from a TV production on *Studio One*). A coward (Sinatra) lives in the shadowed protection of his older brother, until the brother is killed by gunmen and the coward must face reality or run.

1356. Johnny Dark (Universal-International; 1954). *Cast:* Tony Curtis, Piper Laurie, Don Taylor, Paul Kelly, Ilka Chase, Sidney Blackmer, Russell Johnson, Ruth Hampton, Joseph Sawyer, Robert Nichols, Pierre Watkin, Ralph Montgomery, William Leslie, Brett Halsey, Scatman Crothers (himself), Vernon Rich, Robert Bice, Byron Kane, Emily Belser, Don Mitchell, Rick Burgess, John McKee. *D:* George Sherman; *P:* William Alland; *Sc:* Franklin Coen. (1:25) Technicolor drama with romance and race cars, culminating in the big auto race finale. Remade by this studio in 1964 as *The Lively Set*.

1357. Johnny Guitar (Republic; 1954). *Cast:* Joan Crawford (Vienna), Sterling Hayden (title role), Mercedes McCambridge (Emma Small), Scott Brady (Dancin' Kid), Ward Bond (John McIvers), Ben Cooper (Turkey Ralston), Ernest Borgnine (Bart Lonergan), John Carradine (Old Tom), Royal Dano (Corey), Frank Ferguson (Marshall Williams), Paul Fix (Eddie), Rhys Williams (Mr. Andrews), Ian MacDonald (Pete), Will Wright (Ned), John Maxwell (Jake), Robert Osterloh (Sam), Frank Marlowe (Frank), Trevor Bardette (Jenks), Sumner Williams, Sheb Wooley, Denver Pyle, Clem Harvey. *D:* Nicholas Ray; *P:* uncredited; *Sc: & St:* Philip Yordan. (1:50) (video/laserdisc) Hit offbeat western with a psychological bent of a self-righteous malicious woman (McCambridge) who wants a female saloon owner (Crawford), out of the town and her life, one way or the other. In Trucolor, it became one of the 25 top-grossing films of 1953-54 and has a cult following.

1358. Johnny One-Eye (United Artists/ Benedict Bogeaus; 1950). *Cast:* Pat O'Brien, Wayne Morris, Dolores Moran, Gayle Reed, Lawrence Cregar, Jack Overman, Raymond Largay, Donald Woods, Harry Bronson. *D:* Robert Florey (final film—ret.); *P:* Benedict Bogeaus; *Sc:* Richard H. Landau. (1:17) The story of a hood on the lam from the law who gets tied up with a little girl and her dog, Johnny One-Eye. Based on the story by Damon Runyon.

1359. Johnny Rocco (Allied Artists/Scott R. Dunlap; 1958). *Cast:* Richard Eyer, Stephen McNally, Coleen Gray, James Flavin, Russ Conway, Leslie Bradley, Frank Wilcox, M.G. [Matty] Fain, Harry Loftin, John Mitchum, Bob Mitchell, The Mitchell Boys Choir. *D:* Paul Landres; *P:* Scott R. Dunlap; *St:* Richard Carlson; *Sc:* James O'Hanlon, Samuel E. Roeca. (1:24) Crime melodrama of a son (Eyer) whose hood father (McNally) is mixed up with drug smuggling and the son witnesses the murder of a motorcycle cop.

1360. Johnny Tremain (Buena Vista; 1957). *Cast:* Hal Stalmaster (debut and only film/title role), Luana Patten, Jeff York, Sebastian Cabot, Richard Beymer, Walter Sande (Paul Revere), Rusty Lane (Samuel Adams), Whit Bissell (Josiah Quincy), Will Wright, Virginia Christine, Walter Coy, Geoffrey Toone, Ralph Clanton (General Gage), Gavin Gordon, Lumsden Hare, Anthony Ghazlo, Jr., Charles Smith. *D:* Robert Stevenson; *P:* Walt Disney; *Sc:* Tom Blackburn; *Songs:* "Johnny Tremain," "The Liberty Tree" (George Bruns–Blackburn). (1:20) (video) Only Walt Disney would tackle the American Revolution as film subject matter, something the rest of Hollywood considered "poison" following the dismal failure of D.W. Griffith's *America* in 1924. Based on the novel by Esther Forbes (which blends fiction with historical fact) of a young Boston silversmith who joins the Sons of Liberty and participates in the Boston Tea Party. In 1775 he joins the confrontation at Lexington Green, where the "shot heard 'round the world" was fired, marking the beginning of America's fight for independence from England. In Technicolor, it was originally filmed to be shown in two parts on the Disney TV show, but was released theatrically instead.

1361. Johnny Trouble (Warner/Clarion; 1957). *Cast:* Ethel Barrymore (final film—d. 1959), Cecil Kellaway, Carolyn Jones, Rand Harper, Jesse White, Paul Wallace, Edward [Edd] Byrnes, Edward Castagna, Nino Tempo, Jim Bridges, Paul Lukather, James Bell, Samuel Colt, Kip King, Gavin Muir, Stuart Whitman, Jack Larson. *D:* John H. Auer (final film—ret.); *Ex.P:* John Carroll; *P:* Auer; *St:* Ben Ames Williams; *Sc:* Charles O'Neal, David Lord. (1:20) Drama of an elderly woman who awaits the return of the son who walked out on her years before. She believes the young man she meets to be her grandson. A remake of *Someone to Remember* (Republic; 1943).

1362. The Joker Is Wild (Paramount/ A.M.B.L. Prod.; 1957). *Cast:* Frank Sinatra (Joe E. Lewis), Jeanne Crain (Letty Page), Mitzi Gaynor (Martha Stewart), Eddie Albert (Austin Mack), Beverly Garland (Cassie Mack), Jackie Coogan (Swifty Morgan), Barry Kelley (Capt. Hugh McCarthy), Ted de Corsia (Georgie Parker), Leonard Graves (Tim Coogan), Valerie Allen (Flora), Harold Huber (Harry Bliss), Ned Glass (Johnson), Ned [Ed H.] Wever (Dr. Pierson), Walter Woolf King (Mr. Page), John Harding (Allen), James Cross (Jack), Hank Henry (burlesque comedian), Dennis McMullen, Wally Brown, Don Beddoe, Mary Treen, Paul Bryar, Sid Melton, Dick Elliott, Lucy Knoch, William Pullen, F. Oliver McGowan, James J. Cavanaugh, Harriette Tarler, Paul Hill, George Offerman, Eric Wilton, Kit Guard, Paul T. Salata, Bill Hickman, John D. Benson. *D:* Charles Vidor; *P:* Samuel J. Briskin; *Sc:* Oscar Saul; *Song:* "All the Way" (AA-Best Song) James Van Heusen, Sammy Cahn. (2:06) Successful biographical drama based on *The Life of Joe E. Lewis* by Art Cohn. In VistaVision, it became one of the 26 top-grossing films of 1957-58. (1966 re-release title: *All the Way*)

1363. The Journey (MGM/Alby; 1959). *Cast:* Deborah Kerr, Yul Brynner, Jason Robards, Jr. (film debut), Robert Morley, E.G.

Marshall, Ann Jackson, Kurt Kasznar, David Kossoff, Ronny Howard (film debut), Anouk Aimee (U.S. debut), Gerard Oury, Marie Daems, Flip Mark, Barbara Von Nady, Maurice Sarfati, Siegfried Schurenberg, Maria Urban, Jerry Fujikawa, Erica Vaal, Dimitry Fedotoff, Leonid Pylajew, Wolf Neuber, Michael Szekely, Charles Regnier, Ivan Petrovich, Ernst Konstantin. *D: & P:* Anatole Litvak; *Sc:* George Tabori. (2:03) Drama of various people seeking escape from Budapest, Hungary, in 1956 following the revolt against communist rule. A U.S.A./Austrian co-production, filmed in Austria in MetroColor.

1364. Journey Into Light (20th Century-Fox; 1951). *Cast:* Sterling Hayden, Viveca Lindfors, Thomas Mitchell, Ludwig Donath, H.B. Warner, Jane Darwell, John Berkes, Peggy Webber, Paul Guilfoyle, Charles Evans, Marion Martin, Everett Glass, Raymond Bond, Billie Bird, O.Z. Whitehead, Myron Healey, Byron [Brian] Keith, Kathleen Mulqueen, Leslie Turner, Fritz Feld, Lorin Raker, Emmett Lynn, Paul Brinegar, David Marsh, Bernard Gorcey, Lynn Whitney, Helene Huntington, Kate Drain Lawson, Fred Aldrich, Ed Hinton, Robert "Smoki" Whitfield. *D:* Stuart Heisler; *P: & St:* Anson Bond, Joseph Bernhard; *Sc:* Stephen Nordi, Irving Shulman. (1:27) A New England minister loses his faith when his alcoholic wife commits suicide. He heads west and winds up at a skid row mission, where several incidents and people help restore his faith in the calling.

1365. Journey to Freedom (Republic; 1957). *Cast:* Jacques Scott, Genevieve Aumont, George Graham, Morgan Lane, Jean Ann Lewis, Peter E. Besbas, Don McArt, Dan O'Dowd, Barry O'Hara, Fred Kohler, Jr., Tor Johnson, Don Marlowe, Miles Shepard. *D:* Robert C. Dertano; *P:* Stephen C. Apostolof; *St:* Apostolof, Herbert F. Niccolls; *Sc:* Niccolls. (1:00) Melodrama of a man involved with "Voice of Freedom" radio broadcasts who is pursued by Russian agents from Bulgaria to the United States.

1366. Journey to the Center of the Earth (20th Century–Fox/Joseph M. Schenck—Cooga Mooga Film Prods., Inc.; 1959). *Cast:* James Mason (Prof. Oliver Lindenbrook), Pat Boone (Alec McEwen), Arlene Dahl (Carla), Diane Baker (Jenny), Thayer David (Count Saknussem), Peter Ronson (Hans), Alex Finlayson (Prof. Bayle), Ben Wright (Paisley), Mary Brady (Kirsty), Robert Adler, Alan Napier, Frederick Halliday, Alan Caillou, Gertrude (duck). *D:* Henry Levin; *P:* Charles Brackett; *Sc:* Walter Reisch, Brackett; *ASD:* (AAN) Lyle R. Wheeler, Franz Bachelin, Henry Blumenthal (art directors), Walter M. Scott, Joseph Kish (sets); *F/X:* (AAN) L.B. Abbott, James B. Gordon, Emil Kosa, Jr. (visual), Carl Faulkner (audible); *Sound:* (AAN) Carl Faulkner (20th Century–Fox Sound Dept.); *Songs:* "Twice as Tall," "The Faithful Heart" James Van Heusen, Sammy Cahn and "My Love is Like a Red, Red Rose" Robert Burns—set to music by Van Heusen. (2:12) (video/laserdisc) Hit fantasy-adventure of an expedition into the bowels of the earth. Based on the 1864 novel by Jules Verne, it became one of the 28 top-grossing films of 1959-60. Location filming at Carlsbad Caverns, New Mexico, in DeLuxe color and CinemaScope. *Where Time Began*, a 1978 Spanish production, was also based on Verne's book.

1367. Joy Ride (Allied Artists; 1958). *Cast:* Rad Fulton, Ann Doran, Regis Toomey, Nicholas King, Robert Levin, Jim Bridges, Roy Engel, Robert Colbert, Robert Anderson. *D:* Edward Bernds; *P:* Ben Schwalb; *St:* C.B. Gilford; *Sc:* Christopher Knopf. (1:05) Four teens yearn to take a man's new sports car for a ride, only he has other ideas after they terrorize his wife.

1368. Jubal (Columbia; 1956). *Cast:* Glenn Ford, Felicia Farr, Ernest Borgnine, Valerie French, Rod Steigler, Basil Ruysdael, Noah Beery, Jr., Charles Bronson, Jack Elam, John Dierkes, Robert "Buzz" Henry, Robert Burton, Robert Knapp, Juney Ellis, Don C. Harvey, Guy Wilkerson, Larry Hudson, Mike Lawrence. *D:* Delmer Daves; *P:* William Fadiman; *Sc:* Russell S. Hughes, Daves. (1:41) (video/laserdisc) Shakespeare's *Othello* seems to be the story inspiration for this western drama of marital jealousy on the range. In Technicolor and CinemaScope, it was based on the book *Jubal Troop* by Paul I. Wellman.

1369. Jubilee Trail (Republic; 1954). *Cast:* Vera Ralston, Joan Leslie, Forrest Tucker, John Russell, Ray Middleton, Pat O'Brien, Buddy Baer, Jim Davis, Barton MacLane, Richard Webb, James Millican, Nina Varela, Martin Garralaga, Charles Stevens, Nacho Galindo, Don Beddoe, John Holland, William Haade, Alan Bridge, John Halloran, Stephen Chase, Dan M. White, Sayre Dearing, Eugene Borden, Rodolfo Hoyos, Jr., Bud [Bill] Wolfe, Paul Stader, Morris Buchanan, Maurice Jara, Rosa Turich, Manuel Lopez, Perry Lopez, Claire Carleton,

Victor Sen Yung, Edward Colmans, George Navarro, Grant Withers, Glenn Strange, Frank Puglia, Pepe Hern, Felipe Turich, Joe Dominguez, Emil Sitka, Emmett Lynn, Tex Terry, Rocky Shahan, Chuck Hayward, Jack O'Shea, Jack Elam, Tina Menard, Robert "Buzz" Henry, Rico Alaniz, Don Haggerty, Peter Ortiz, John Mooney, Alma Beltran, Anna Navarro, Gloria Varela, Linda Danceil, Brett Houston, Bill Chandler, Norman Kent, Joe Ploski, Bob Burrows, Pilar Del Rey, James Lilburn, Raymond Johnson, Manuel Paris, Charles Sullivan, Ralph Brooks, Ted Smile. *D:* Joseph Inman Kane; *P:* Herbert J. Yates; *Sc:* Bruce Manning; *Songs:* "Clap Your Hands," "A Man Is a Man," "Saying No" and "Jubilee Trail" Victor Young, Sidney Clare. (1:43) (video) A big budget melodramatic western soap opera of a married man who meets a former flame and their illegitimate child on a wagon train to California. He winds up dead when he refuses to take responsibility for his pre-marital dalliance. Based on the best seller by Gwen Bristow, it was photographed in Trucolor and ran on the top of a double bill with Rex Allen's *Red River Shore* (q.v.).

1370. The Juggler (Columbia/Stanley Kramer Prods.; 1953). *Cast:* Kirk Douglas, Milly Vitale, Paul Stewart, Joey Walsh, Alf Kjellin, Beverly Washburn, Charles Lane, John Banner, Richard Benedict, Jay Adler, Oscar Karlweis, John Bleifer, Greta Granstedt, Shep Menken, Gabriel Curtiz. *D:* Edward Dmytryk; *P:* Stanley Kramer; *Sc:* Michael Blankfort. (1:25) Drama of post-war Israel and a Jewish refugee who is forced to come to terms with his former incarceration in a concentration camp. Based on the novel by Mr. Blankfort, it was filmed on location in Israel. It originally ran on the top of a double bill with *The 49th Man* (q.v.).

1371. Juke Box Rhythm (Columbia/Clover Prods.; 1959). *Cast:* Jo Morrow, Jack Jones, Brian Donlevy, George Jessel (himself/final film), Hans Conried, Karin Booth, Marjorie Reynolds, Frieda Inescort, Edgar Barrier, Fritz Feld, Hortense Petra, The Earl Grant Trio, The Nitwits, Johnny Otis, The Treniers. *D:* Arthur Dreifuss; *P:* Sam Katzman; *St:* Lou Morheim; *Sc:* Mary C. McCall, Jr., Earl Baldwin; *Songs:* "Juke Box Jamboree" (Richard Quine–Fred Karger–Stanley Styne); "I Feel It Right Here" by Earl Grant; "The Freeze" by Jack Jones and Grant; "Coming and Going" (instrumental); "Make Room for the Joy" by Jones; "Let's Fall in Love" by George Jessel and Jo Morrow; "Get Out of the Car" by the Treniers; "Willie and the Hand Jive" by Johnny Otis; "Last Night" by Grant; "12th Street Rag" by the Nitwits; "Spring Is the Season for Remembering" by Jessel, and excerpts from Offenbach's "La Gaiete Parisienne" by the Nitwits. (1:22) Musical-romance of a European princess who encounters a schemer when she visits New York City.

1372. Julie (MGM/Arwin Prods.; 1956). *Cast:* Doris Day (Julie Benton), Louis Jourdan (Lyle Benton), Barry Sullivan (Cliff Henderson), Frank Lovejoy (Det. Capt. Pringle), Jack Kelly (co-pilot), Ann Robinson (Valerie), Jack Kruschen (Det. Mace), Mae Marsh (hysterical passenger), John Gallaudet (Det. Cole), Harlan Warde (Det. Pope), Aline Towne (Denice Martin), Pamela Duncan (Peggy), Hank Patterson (Ellis), Ed Hinton (pilot), Barney Phillips (doctor), Carleton Young, Edward Marsh. *D:* Andrew L. Stone; *P:* Martin Melcher; *Sc:* (AAN) Stone; *Title song:* (AAN) Leith Stevens, Tom Adair. (1:39) Overly melodramatic thriller of an airline hostess who finds she is married to a psychotic killer. A moneymaker for the studio, it has been computer-colored by Turner Entertainment.

1373. Julius Caesar (Brandon/Avon Prods.; 1949–52). *Cast:* Charlton Heston (Marcus Antonius), David Bradley (Brutus), Helen Ross (Calpurnia), Molly Darr (Portia), Grosvenor Glenn (Cassius), Harold Tasker (Julius Caesar), William Russell (Casca), Robert Holt (Octavius Caesar), Theodore Cloak (Emil Lepidus), Frederick Roscoe (Decius Brutus), Arthur Sus (Cinna), Cornelius Peeples (Popilius), Alfred Edyvean (Flavius), John O'Leary (Marullus), Homer Dietmeier (Artemidorus), Don Walker (soothsayer), Russell Bruebner (Cinna the Poet), George Gilbert (Strato), George Hinners (Lucius), Sam Needham (Pindarus) and Jeffrey Hunter (in his non-professional film debut). *D: & P:* David Bradley. (1:30) A non-commercial feature length production shot in 16 mm in 1949 at Northwestern University on a budget of $15,000. Based on William Shakespeare's Elizabethan play, it was released theatrically in 1952 to critical acclaim. Previously filmed in Great Britain (1911), in 1908 by Vitagraph in one reel, and again in Italy in 1914 as a six reel feature.

1374. Julius Caesar (MGM; 1953). *Cast:* Marlon Brando (AAN + "Best Actor" nomination at the British Academy Awards/Mark Antony), James Mason (voted "Best Actor" by the NBR combined with his performances in *Face to Face* and *The Desert Rats* [both q.v.] and *The Man Between*, a British production/Brutus), John Gielgud (a "Best British Actor" nomination at the British Academy Awards/Cassius), Louis Calhern (Julius Caesar), Edmond O'Brien (Casca), Greer Garson (Calpurnia), Deborah Kerr (Portia), George Macready (Marullus), Michael Pate (Flavius), Richard Hale (soothsayer), Alan Napier (Cicero), John Hoyt (Decius Brutus), Tom Powers (Metellus Cimber), William Cottrell (Cinna), Jack Raine (Trebonius), Ian Wolfe (Casius Ligarius), John Hardy (Lucius), Morgan Farley (Artemidorus), Bill Phipps (Antony's servant), Douglas Watson (Octavius Caesar), Douglass Dumbrille (Lepidus), Rhys Williams (Lucillus), Michael Ansara (Pindarus), Dayton Lummis (Messala), Thomas Browne Henry (Volumnius), Edmund Purdom (Strato), Lumsden Hare (Publius), Victor Perry (Popilius Lena), John Lupton (Varro), Preston Hanson (Claudius), John Parrish (Titinius), Joe Waring (Clitus), Steven Roberts (Dardanius), O.Z. Whitehead (Cinna the Poet), Ned Glass (cobbler), Chester Stratton (Caesar's servant), Michael Tolan (officer), Paul Guilfoyle, John Doucette, Lawrence Dobkin (citizens of Rome). *D:* Joseph Mankiewicz; *P:* (AAN-Best Picture) John Houseman; *Cin:* (AAN-b/w) Joseph Ruttenberg; *ASD:* (AA-b/w) Cedric Gibbons, Edward Carfagno (art directors), Edwin B. Willis, Hugh Hunt (sets); *Music:* (AAN) Miklos Rozsa. (2:00) (video/laserdisc) Critically acclaimed drama of a political power struggle in ancient Rome, based on the play by William Shakespeare. A profit-maker at the box office, it was voted "Best Film of the Year" by the NBR and took a #4 placement on the "10 Best" list of the *New York Times*. Remade in 1970.

1375. Jump Into Hell (Warner; 1955). *Cast:* Jacques Sernas (U.S. debut), Kurt Kasznar, Arnold Moss, Peter Van Eyck, Marcel Dalio, Norman Dupont, Lawrence Dobkin, Pat Blake, Irene Montwill, Alberto Morin, Joseph Waring, Maurice Marsac, Louis Mercier, Peter Bourne, Roger Valmy, Lisa Montell, George Chan, Jack Scott, Harold Dyrenforth, Leon Lontoc. *D:* David Butler; *P:* David Weisbart; *Sc:* Irving Wallace. (1:32) War drama utilizing newsreel footage of France's Indo-China battle at Dien Bien Phu.

1376. Jumping Jacks (Paramount; 1952). *Cast:* Dean Martin, Jerry Lewis, Mona Freeman, Don DeFore, Robert Strauss, Marcy McGuire, Richard Erdman, Ray Teal, Danny Arnold, Edwin Max, Alex Gerry, Charles Evans. *D:* Norman Taurog; *P:* Hal B. Wallis; *Sc:* Robert Lees, Fred Rinaldo, Herbert Baker; *Songs:* "Keep a Little Dream Handy," "Do the Parachute Jump," "I Can't Resist a Boy in Uniform," "What Have You Done for Me Lately?," "I Know a Dream When I See One" and "Big Blue Sky" Jerry Livingston, Mack David. (1:36) (video/laserdisc) Comedy of an entertainer who goes to Ft. Benning, Georgia, to put on a show, becoming a paratrooper through a mix-up.

1377. Junction City (Columbia; 1952). *Cast:* Charles Starrett, Kathleen Case, Smiley Burnette, Jack [Jock] Mahoney, John Dehner, Hal Taliaferro (final film—ret.), Steve Darrell, George Chesebro, Chris Alcaide, Frank Ellis, Anita Castle, Mary Newton, Robert Bice, Hal Price, Bob Woodward, Joel Friedkin, Harry Tyler, The Sunshine Boys. *D:* Ray Nazarro; *P:* Colbert Clark; *Sc:* Barry Shipman. (0:54) "Durango Kid" series western about a girl who becomes the target of a killer after inheriting a gold mine. Originally ran on the lower half of a double bill with *Cripple Creek* (q.v.).

1378. The Jungle (Lippert/Voltaire-Modern Theatres Ltd.; 1952). *Cast:* Rod Cameron, Cesar Romero, Marie Windsor, Sulochana, M.N. Nambiar, David Abraham, Rama Krishna, Chitra Devi. *D:* & *P:* William Berke; *St:* & *Sc:* Carroll Young, Orville H. Hampton. (1:14) (video) Adventure-drama of prehistoric mammoths causing trouble among the local Indian elephants. A U.S.A./India co-production, filmed in India in Sepiatone.

Jungle Attack *see* **Crosswinds**

1379. Jungle Gents (Allied Artists; 1954). *Cast:* Leo Gorcey, Huntz Hall, David [Gorcey] Condon, Bennie Bartlett, Bernard Gorcey, Patrick O'Moore, Rudolph Anders, Harry Cording, Woody Strode, Laurette Luez, Jett Norman [later: Clint Walker/Tarzan), Joel Fluellen, Eric Snowden, Murray Alper, Emory Parnell, Emil Sitka, Roy Glenn, Sr., John Harmon, Pat Flaherty. *D:* Edward Bernds; *P:* Ben Schwalb; *Sc:* Elwood Ullman, Bernds. (1:04) While visiting in Africa the "Bowery Boys" find that Sach (Hall) has the ability to smell diamonds and therein lies the plot of this comedy series entry.

Jungle Girl *see* **Bomba and the Jungle Girl**

1380. Jungle Head-Hunters (RKO; 1951). *P:* Julian Lesser; *Narration:* Joseph Anson, Larry

Lansburgh. (1:06) A feature documentary-travelogue in color. Ran on the lower half of a double bill with *Best of the Badmen* (q.v.).

1381. Jungle Heat (United Artists/Bel-Air; 1957). *Cast:* Lex Barker, Mari Blanchard, Glenn Langan, James Westerfield, Rhodes Reason, Miyoko Sasaki, Glenn Dixon, Bob Okazaki, Jerry Frank, Daniel Wong, Andrew Gross, Yun Kui Chang, Kunio Fudimura, Leo Ezell. *D:* Howard W. Koch; *P:* Aubrey Schenck; *Sc:* Jameson Brewer. (1:15) Melodrama of five columnists out to destroy the plantations and industries of Hawaii in the days preceding the Pearl Harbor attack.

1382. Jungle Jim in the Forbidden Land (Columbia; 1952). *Cast:* Johnny Weissmuller, Angela Greene, Lester Matthews, Jean Willes, William Tannen, George Eldredge, Frederic Berest, Clem Erickson, William Fawcett, Frank Jaquet, Tamba (chimpanzee). *D:* Lew Landers; *P:* Sam Katzman; *Sc:* Samuel Newman. (1:04) A safari goes in search of the "missing link" in this B budget entry in the "Jungle Jim" adventure series, based on the comic strip by Alex Raymond. Originally ran on a double bill with *Night Stage to Galveston* (q.v.). Some sequences in Sepiatone.

1383. Jungle Man-Eaters (Columbia; 1954). *Cast:* Johnny Weissmuller, Karin Booth, Richard Stapley, Bernie Hamilton, Lester Matthews, Paul Thompson, Louise Franklin, Gregory Gaye, Vince M. Townsend, Jr., Tamba (chimpanzee). *D:* Lee Sholem; *P:* Sam Katzman; *Sc:* Samuel Newman. (1:07) "Jungle Jim" tangles with cannibals while on the trail of diamond smugglers in this low budget series entry. Based on the comic strip character created by Alex Raymond.

1384. Jungle Manhunt (Columbia; 1951). *Cast:* Johnny Weissmuller, Sheila Ryan, Bob Waterfield, Rick Vallin, Lyle Talbot, William P. [Billy] Wilkerson, Tamba (chimpanzee). *D:* Lew Landers; *P:* Sam Katzman; *Sc:* Samuel Newman. (1:06) In this series entry, "Jungle Jim" leads a search for a missing football player. Based on the comic strip character created by Alex Raymond.

1385. Jungle Moon Men (Columbia; 1955). *Cast:* Johnny Weissmuller, Jean Byron, Bill Henry, Helene Stanton, Myron Healey, Billy Curtis, Frank Sully, Michael Granger, Benjamin F. Chapman, Jr., Kenneth L. Smith, Ed Hinton. *D:* Charles S. Gould; *P:* Sam Katzman; *St:* Jo Pagano; *Sc:* Dwight V. Babcock, Pagano. (1:10) Johnny tangles with a jungle priestess who has discovered the secret of eternal life. An extension of the "Jungle Jim" series without the name.

1386. Jungle Stampede (Republic; 1950). *Cast:* George Breakston. *D: & P:* George Breakston; *Narration:* Ronald Davidson. (1:00) A documentary-travelogue.

1387. Jupiter's Darling (MGM; 1954). *Cast:* Esther Williams, Howard Keel (Hannibal), George Sanders, Marge and Gower Champion, Norma Varden, Richard Haydn, William Demarest, Douglass Dumbrille, Henry Corden, Michael Ansara, Martha Wentworth, John Olszewski, Chris Alcaide, Tom Monroe, Bruno VeSota, Paul Maxey, William Tannen, Alberto Morin, Richard Hale, Frank Jaquet, Paul Newlan, Jack Shea, Mitchell Kowal, Frank Radcliffe, Mort Mills, Gene Roth, Michael Dugan, The Swimming Cherubs. *D:* George Sidney; *P:* George Wells; *Sc:* Dorothy Kingsley; *Songs:* "I Have a Dream," "If This Be Slav'ry," "I Never Trust a Woman," "Hannibal's Victory March," "Don't Let This Night Get Away," "The Life of an Elephant" (Burton Lane–Harold Adamson), "Horatio's Narration" (Saul Chaplin–George Wells–Adamson). (1:36) (video/laserdisc) A lavish musical of Hannibal crossing the Alps on his way to destroy Rome and the woman who attempts to seduce him. Based on the 1920s Broadway success *The Road to Rome* by Robert E. Sherwood. Technicolor and CinemaScope. Note: Director Sidney, Williams and the Champions were cut from the MGM payroll after this box office belly-flopper.

1388. Just Across the Street (Universal-International; 1952). *Cast:* Ann Sheridan, John Lund, Robert Keith, Cecil Kellaway, Natalie Schafer, Harvey Lembeck, Alan Mowbray, George Eldredge, Burt Mustin, Billie Bird, Jack Kruschen, Lou Lubin, Herbert Vigran, Steve Roberts, Fritzi Dugan, George "Shorty" Chirello, Miles Shepard, Wally Walker. *D:* Joseph Pevney; *P:* Leonard Goldstein; *Sc: & St:* Roswell Rogers, Joel Malone. (1:18) A romantic comedy of mistaken identity which leads to situations that are not what they appear to be. Originally ran on a double bill with *The Scarlet Angel* (q.v.).

1389. Just for You (Paramount; 1952). *Cast:* Bing Crosby (Jordan Blake), Jane Wyman (Caroline Hill), Ethel Barrymore (Allida de

Bronkhart), Robert Arthur (Jerry Blake), Natalie Wood (Barbara Blake), Cora Witherspoon (final film—d. 1957/Mrs. Angeline), Regis Toomey (Hodges), Ben Lessy (Georgie Polansky), Art Smith (Leo), Leon Tyler (David McKenzie), Willis Bouchey (Hank Ross), Herbert Vigran (George), Nancy Hale, Franklyn Farnum, Brick Sullivan, Buck Harrington, Jack Mulhall, Max Keith, Robert S. Scott, Irene Martin, Daniel Nagrin, Mariam Pandork, Florence Lessing, Bess Flowers, Mary Bayless. *D:* Elliott Nugent (final film—ret.); *P:* Pat Duggan; *Sc:* Robert Carson; *Songs:* "I'll Si-Si Ya in Bahia," "Zing a Little Zong" (AAN-Best Song), "He's Just Crazy for Me," "The Live Oak Tree," "A Flight of Fancy," "On the 10:10 (from Ten-Ten Tennessee)" and "Just for You" Harry Warren, Leo Robin. (1:44) (video) Musical romance of a busy Broadway producer who neglects his two teenage children. Based on Stephen Vincent Benet's "Famous," it went on to become one of the 23 top-grossing films of 1951-52. Technicolor.

1390. Just This Once (MGM; 1952). *Cast:* Janet Leigh, Peter Lawford, Richard Anderson, Lewis Stone, Marilyn Erskine, Douglas Fowley, Benny Rubin, Hanley Stafford, Henry Slate, Jerry Hausner, Charles Watts. *D:* Don Weis; *P:* Henry Berman; *St:* Max Trell; *Sc:* Sidney Sheldon. (1:30) Romantic comedy of a girl hired to supervise the spending habits of a millionaire (who is rapidly depleting his fortune).

1391. Juvenile Jungle (Republic/Coronado; 1958). *Cast:* Corey Allen, Rebecca Welles, Richard Bakalyan, Anne Whitfield, Joe Di Reda, Joe Conley, Walter Coy, Taggart Casey, Hugh Lawrence, Leon Tyler, Harvey Grant, Louise Arthur. *D:* William Witney; *P:* Sidney Picker; *Sc:* Arthur T. Horman. (1:09) Delinquency tale of a teen gang set on kidnapping the daughter of a liquor store owner and holding her for $40,000 ransom. It originally ran on a double bill with *Young and Wild* (q.v.). Naturama.

1392. Kangaroo (20th Century–Fox; 1951). *Cast:* Maureen O'Hara, Peter Lawford, Richard Boone, Finlay Currie, Chips Rafferty, Letty Craydon, Charles Tingwell, Ron Whelan, John Fegan, Guy Doleman, Reg Collins, Clyde Combo, Henry Murdock, Sid Chambers, Joe Tomal, Archie Hull, James Doogue, Bill Bray, Ossie Wenban, Alex Cann, Kleber Claux, Larry Crowhurst, Dennis Glenny, Stan Tolhurst, John Clark, Frank Catchlove, Eve Abdullah, Frank Ransom, Douglas Ramsey, Alan Bardsley. *D:* Lewis Milestone; *P:* Robert Bassler; *St:* Martin Berkeley; *Sc:* Harry Kleiner. (1:24) Australia's outback provides the setting for this Technicolor romantic adventure which was filmed on location.

1393. The Kangaroo Kid (Allied Australian; 1950). *Cast:* Jock [Mahoney] O'Mahoney, Veda Ann Borg, Douglass Dumbrille, Martha Hyer, Alec Kellaway, Guy Doleman, Alan Gifford, Grant Taylor, Haydee Seldon, Frank Ransome, Clarrie Woodlands. *D:* Lesley Selander; *P:* Howard C. Brown; *St:* Anthony Scott Veitch; *Sc:* Sherman Lowe. (1:12) This Australian/U.S.A co-production is an action-adventure of a man sent down under to bring a crook back to the States. More precisely, it could be called an Australian "western."

1394. Kansas City Confidential (United Artists/Edward Small; 1952). *Cast:* John Payne, Coleen Gray, Preston Foster, Dona Drake, Jack Elam, Neville Brand, Lee Van Cleef, Mario Siletti, Howard Negley, Helen Kleeb, Red Ryan, Vivi Janiss, George Wallace, Archie Twitchell [aka: Michael Branden], House Peters, Jr., George Dockstader, Don House, Brick Sullivan, Jack Shea, Tom Dillon, Tom Greenway, Paul Fierro, Kay Wiley, Harry Hines, Don Orlando, Al Hill, Mike Lally, Charles Sherlock, Frank Scannell, Charles Sullivan, Carlos Rivas, Sam Scar, Barry Brooks, Eddie Foster, Joey Ray, Paul Hogan, Paul Dubov, Ric Roman, Sam Pierce, Eduardo Coch, William Haade, Charles Cane, Ray Bennett, Orlando Beltran, Carleton Young, Phil Tead, Lee Phelps. *D:* Phil Karlson; *P:* Edward Small; *St:* Harold R. Green, Rowland Brown; *Sc:* George Bruce, Harry Essex. (1:38) (video) Graphic action-drama of an ex-con, nailed as a prime suspect in an armored truck robbery, who has to hunt down the guilty parties.

1395. Kansas Pacific (Allied Artists; 1953). *Cast:* Sterling Hayden, Eve Miller, Barton MacLane, Harry Shannon, Reed Hadley (Quantrill), Tom Fadden, Douglas Fowley, Irving Bacon, Myron Healey, James Griffith, Clayton Moore, Jonathan Hale, Bob Keys. *D:* Ray Nazarro; *P:* Walter Wanger; *Sc:* Dan Ullman. (1:13) (video) Efforts to complete the Kansas-Pacific railroad in the 1860s are constantly being undermined by Confederate soldiers. Cinecolor.

1396. Kansas Raiders (Universal-International; 1950). *Cast:* Audie Murphy (Jesse James), Brian Donlevy (Quantrill), Marguerite Chapman, Scott Brady, John Kellogg, Tony Curtis (Kit Dalton), James Best (Cole Younger), Dewey

Martin (James Younger), Richard Arlen, Richard Long (Frank James), George Chandler, Charles Delaney, Richard Egan, David Wolfe, Mira McKinney, Sam Flint, Buddy Roosevelt, Larry McGrath, Ed Peil, Sr. *D:* Ray Enright; *P:* Ted Richmond; *St: & Sc:* Robert L. Richards. (1:20) Fact-based Western of William Quantrill's infamous band of guerrilla raiders and a youth named Jesse James who joins the gang. Originally ran on a double bill with *Prelude to Fame*, a British release. Technicolor.

1397. Kansas Territory (Monogram; 1952). *Cast:* William Elliott, Peggy Stewart, House Peters, Jr., Fuzzy Knight, Lane Bradford, I. Stanford Jolley, Lyle Talbot, Stanley Andrews, Marshall Reed, Terry Frost, John Hart, William Fawcett, Lee Roberts, Ted Adams, Pierce Lyden. *D:* Lewis D. Collins; *P:* Vincent M. Fennelly; *St: & Sc:* Daniel B. Ullman. (1:04) "Wild" Bill Elliott western of a former outlaw, seeking revenge for the death of his brother—until he learns the truth about the man. Sepiatone.

1398. Kathy O (Universal-International; 1958). *Cast:* Dan Duryea, Jan Sterling, Patty McCormack (title role), Mary Fickett, Sam Levene, Mary Jane Croft, Ricky Kelman, Ainslie Pryor, Barney Phillips, Mel Leonard, Casey Walters, Terry Kelman, Walter Wolf King, Alexander Campbell, Joseph Sargent, Mary Carver. *D:* Jack Sher; *P:* Sy Gomberg; *Sc:* Sher, Gomberg; *Song:* Charles Tobias, Ray Joseph, Sher. (1:39) Drama of a temperamental female child movie star who drives her studio publicist up the wall. Based on the story "Memo on Kathy O'Rourke" by Mr. Sher that appeared in *Saturday Evening Post*. Eastmancolor and CinemaScope.

1399. Katie Did It (Universal-International; 1951). *Cast:* Ann Blyth, Mark Stevens, Cecil Kellaway, Craig Stevens, Jesse White, Harold Vermilyea, William Lynn, Elizabeth Patterson, Jimmy Hunt, Irving Bacon, Raymond Largay, Ethyl May Halls, Peter Leeds. *D:* Frederick de Cordova; *P:* Leonard Goldstein; *Sc:* Jack Henley; *Additional dialogue:* Oscar Brodney. (1:21) The romance of a small town girl and a suave New York City artist.

Keep It Cool (G.B. title) *see* **Let's Rock**

1400. Kelly and Me (Universal-International; 1957). *Cast:* Van Johnson, Piper Laurie, Martha Hyer, Onslow Stevens, Herbert Anderson, Gregory Gay, Dan Riss, Maurice Manson, Douglas Fowley, Frank Wilcox, Yvonne Peattie, Elizabeth Flournoy, Lyle Latell, Kelly (dog—received #3 PATSY Award in 1958). *D:* Robert Z. Leonard (final film—ret.); *P:* Robert Arthur; *Sc: & St:* Everett Freeman. (1:26) Family fare of a song-and-dance man who becomes a big hit with a white German shepherd dog named Kelly in the early days of talking pictures in Hollywood. Technicolor and CinemaScope.

1401. The Kentuckian (United Artists/Hecht-Lancaster; 1955). *Cast:* Burt Lancaster, Dianne Foster, Diana Lynn, John McIntire, Donald MacDonald, Una Merkel, Walter Matthau (film debut), John Carradine, John Litel, Clem Bevans, Rhys Williams, Edward Norris (final film—ret.), Douglas Spencer, Paul Wexler, Lee Erickson, Lisa Ferraday, Whip Wilson, Faro (dog—received #3 PATSY Award in 1956). *D:* Burt Lancaster; *P:* Harold Hecht; *Sc:* A.B. Guthrie, Jr. (1:43) (video/laserdisc) A frontier epic set in the 1820s of a backwoods widower and his son on their way to Texas. Based on the novel *The Gabriel Horn* by Felix Holt. Technicolor and CinemaScope.

1402. Kentucky Jubilee (Lippert; 1951). *Cast:* Jerry Colonna, Jean Porter, James Ellison, Fritz Feld, Raymond Hatton, Vince Barnett, Michael Whalen, Chester Clute, Archie Twitchell [aka: Michael Branden], Russell Hicks, Si Jenks, Margia Dean, Ralph Sanford, Tom Plank, Jack Reitzen, Jack O'Shea, Cliff Taylor, Bob Carney, Charley Williams, Marvelle Andre, Phil Arnold, Johnny Howard, George Sanders (not the), George Chesebro, Mickey Simpson, The McQuaig Twins, Leo "Carrot Top" Anderson, Claude Casey, Fred Kirby, Slim Andrews, The Broome Brothers, Edna and Gracia Dreon, Donna Kaye, Frankie Randall, Chris Randall, Buck and Chickie Eddy, Y-Knot Twirlers, Bobby Clark (not the noted comedian), Glen Story, John Braislin, Peggy McGuiggan. *D: & P:* Ron Ormond; *Sc:* Maurice Tombragel, Ormond. (1:12) A programmer musical-comedy with many specialty acts.

1403. Kentucky Rifle (Howco-International; 1955-56). *Cast:* Chill Wills, Lance Fuller, Cathy Downs, Henry Hull, Jess Barker, Jeanne Cagney, Sterling Holloway, John Pickard, John Alvin, I. Stanford Jolley, Rory Mallinson, George Keymas, Clyde Houck, Alice Ralph. *D:* Carl K. Hittleman; *Ex.P:* Ira S. Webb; *Sc: & St:* Hittleman, Lee J. Hewitt. (1:20) (video) A low budget independent western of a wagon and its occupants who are banned from a wagon train, when it is found Comanches are after the load of Kentucky rifles the wagon is carrying. In color.

1404. The Kettles in the Ozarks (Universal-International; 1956). *Cast:* Marjorie Main, Arthur Hunnicutt, Una Merkel, Ted de Corsia, Richard Eyer, David O'Brien, Joe Sawyer, Richard Deacon, Sid Tomack, Pat Goldin, Harry Hines, Jim Hayward, Olive Sturges, George Arglen, Eddie Pagett, Cheryl Callaway, Pat Morrow, Bonnie Franklin, Louis DaPron, Sarah Padden, Roscoe Ates, Kathryn Sheldon, Stuart Holmes, Elvia Allman, Paul Wexler, Robert Easton. *D:* Charles Lamont; *P:* Richard Wilson; *Sc: & St:* Kay Lenard. (1:21) (video) The eighth entry in the hit rustic comedy series—sans Pa—has the Kettle family going for a visit to Uncle Sedge in the Ozark mountains.

1405. The Kettles on Old MacDonald's Farm (Universal-International; 1957). *Cast:* Marjorie Main (final film—ret.), Parker Fennelly, Gloria Talbott, John Smith, George Dunn, Claude Akins, Roy Barcroft, Pat Morrow, Ricky Kelman, Donald Baker, George Arglen, Polly Burson, Hallene Hill, Sara Taft, Harvey B. Dunne, Don Clark, Boyd "Red" Morgan, Glenn Thompson, Edna Smith, Verna Korman, Roger Creed, Frank Hagney, Henry Wills, Clem Fuller, Carl Saxe, George Barrows, Eva Novak, Chuck Hamilton, George Hickman, Three Toes (bear). *D:* Virgil Vogel; *P:* Howard Christie; *St: & Sc:* William Raynor, Herbert Margolis. (1:19) The ninth and final entry in the "Kettle" series, with Ma finding herself a new husband as well as doing a little matchmaking herself.

1406. Key to the City (MGM; 1950). *Cast:* Clark Gable, Loretta Young, Frank Morgan (final film—d. 1949), Marilyn Maxwell, James Gleason, Raymond Burr, Lewis Stone, Raymond Walburn, Pamela Britton, Clinton Sundberg, Marion Martin, Bert Freed, Emory Parnell, Clara Blandick, Zamah Cunningham, Richard Gaines, Roger Moore, Dorothy Ford, Pierre Watkin, Nana Bryant, Victor Sen Yung, Marvin Kaplan, Byron Foulger, Edward Earle, Jack Elam, Frank Ferguson, Alex Gerry, James Harrison, Frank Wilcox, Bill Cartledge, Shirley Lew, Helen Brown, Dick Wessel, Harry Harvey, Sr., James Flavin, Charles Smith. *D:* George Sidney; *P:* Z. Wayne Griffin; *St:* Albert Beich; *Sc:* Robert Riley Crutcher. (1:40) (video) Romantic-comedy of a convention of mayors in San Francisco and two of same (Gable and Young) who find each other.

1407. Khyber Patrol (United Artists/World; 1954). *Cast:* Richard Egan, Dawn Addams, Raymond Burr, Patric Knowles, Donald Randolph, Paul Cavanagh, Philip Tonge, Patrick O'Moore, Laura Mason. *D:* Seymour Friedman; *P:* Edward Small (unc.); *St:* Richard Schayer; *Sc:* Jack DeWitt. (1:11) Action-adventure with the British Army in late 19th century India putting down a rebel insurrection. Color Corporation of America.

The Kid Colossus (G.B. title) *see* **Roogie's Bump**

1408. The Kid from Amarillo (Columbia; 1951). *Cast:* Charles Starrett, Smiley Burnette, Fred F. Sears, Harry Lauter, Don Megowan, George Chesebro, George J. Lewis, Scott Lee, Henry Kulky, Guy Teague, Charles Evans, Jerry Scroggins, The Cass County Boys. *D:* Ray Nazarro; *P:* Colbert Clark; *Sc:* Barry Shipman. (0:56) This western series entry has the "Durango Kid" out to round up silver smugglers. (G.B. title: *Silver Chains*)

1409. The Kid from Broken Gun (Columbia; 1951). *Cast:* Charles Starrett, Smiley Burnette, Jack [Jock] Mahoney, Angela Stevens, Tristram Coffin, Myron Healey, Pat O'Malley, Edgar Dearing, Chris Alcaide, Mauritz Hugo, John Cason, Helen Mowery, Eddie Parker, Edward Hearn, Charles Horvath. *D:* Fred F. Sears; *P:* Colbert Clark; *St: & Sc:* Ed Earl Repp, Barry Shipman. (0:56) The final entry in this long-running series of 64 western films—beginning in 1945—has the "Durango Kid" out to prove his friend innocent of robbery and murder. Much stock footage.

1410. The Kid from Left Field (20th Century–Fox; 1953). *Cast:* Dan Dailey, Anne Bancroft, Billy Chapin, Lloyd Bridges, Ray Collins, Richard Egan, Bob Hopkins, Alex Gerry, Walter Sande, Fess Parker, George Phelps, John Gallaudet, Paul Salata, John Beradino, Gene Thompson, Malcolm Cassell, Ike Jones, Ron Hargrave, John Goddard, John McKee, Claude Olin Wurman, Sammy Ogg, Robert Winans, Jonathan Hole, John Call, Al Green, George Garner, Rush Williams, Leo Cleary, John "Beans" Reardon, James Griffith, James F. Stone, Richard Shackleton, Larry Thor, Robert Kelly, Mark Scott, Ruth Warren, Camillo Guercio, King Donovan, Katherine Givney, Ken Christy, Charles Tannen, Anthony DeMario. *D:* Harmon Jones; *P:* Leonard Goldstein; *Sc:* Jack Sher. (1:20) Baseball comedy of a boy who becomes the manager of a ball team through a misunderstanding. Remade in 1979 as a TV movie. Originally ran on a double bill with *A Blueprint for Murder* (q.v.).

1411. The Kid from Texas (Universal-International; 1950). *Cast:* Audie Murphy (Billy the Kid), Gale Storm, Albert Dekker, Shepperd Strudwick, Will Geer, William Talman, Frank Wilcox (Pat Garrett), Robert Barrat (Gov. Lew Wallace), Paul Ford, Dennis Hoey, Ray Teal, Rosa Turich, Martin Garralaga, Walter Sande, Don Haggerty, Zon Murray, Pilar Del Rey, Harold Goodwin, John Phillips, Dorita Pallais, Tom Trout. *D:* Kurt Neumann; *P:* Paul Short; *St:* Robert Hardy Andrews; *Sc:* Andrews, Karl Kamb. (1:18) Fact-based Technicolor western of Billy the Kid and New Mexico's Lincoln County War. (G.B. title: *Texas Kid—Outlaw*)

1412. Kid Monk Baroni (Realart; 1952). *Cast:* Richard Rober, Bruce Cabot, Allene Roberts (final film), Mona Knox, Leonard Nimoy (title role), Jack Larson, Budd Jaxon, Archer MacDonald, Kathleen Freeman, Joseph Mell, Paul Maxey, Stuart Randall, Chad Mallory, Maurice Cass, Bill Cabanne. *D:* Harold Schuster; *P:* Jack Broder; *Sc:* Aben Kandel. (1:20) Pugilism melodrama of a bowery youth who gets his disfigured face corrected by plastic surgery and becomes a top boxer. His accompanying conceit becomes his downfall. (G.B. title: *Young Paul Baroni*)

1413. Kill or Be Killed (Eagle-Lion; 1950). *Cast:* Lawrence Tierney, George Coulouris, Marisa O'Brien, Rudolph Anders, Lopes da Silva, Veloso Pires, Leonor Maia, Joao Amaro, Licinio Sena, Helga Line, Mira Lobo. *D:* Max Nosseck; *P:* Walter Jurmann; *Sc:* Arnold Phillips, Nosseck, Lawrence Holdman. (1:07) Low budget adventure-melodrama of a man framed for murder who hides out in the South American jungle.

1414. Kill the Umpire (Columbia; 1950). *Cast:* William Bendix, Una Merkel, Ray Collins, Gloria Henry, Richard Taylor [later: Jeff Richards/a former baseball player], Connie Marshall, William Frawley, Tom D'Andrea, Luther Crockett, Glenn Thompson, Jeff York, Bob Wilke, Jim Bannon, Alan Hale, Jr. *D:* Lloyd Bacon; *P:* John Beck; *Sc:* Frank Tashlin. (1:17) Baseball comedy of a man who becomes an umpire, only to become the most hated man in the sport.

1415. Killer Ape (Columbia; 1953). *Cast:* Johnny Weissmuller, Carol Thurston, Nestor Paiva, Ray Corrigan, Paul Marion, Burt Wenland, Nick Stuart, Eddie Foster, Rory Mallinson, Max Palmer, Tamba (chimpanzee). *D:* Spencer G. Bennet; *P:* Sam Katzman; *St:* Carroll Young; *Sc:* Young, Arthur Hoerl. (1:08) A giant apeman and some nefarious scientists are the focus of this low budget "Jungle Jim" adventure series entry, based on the comic strip character created by Alex Raymond.

1416. The Killer Is Loose (United Artists/Crown; 1956). *Cast:* Joseph Cotten, Rhonda Fleming, Wendell Corey, Michael Pate, Alan Hale, Jr., Virginia Christine, John Larch, John Beradino, Paul Bryar, Dee J. Thompson. *D:* Budd Boetticher; *P:* Robert L. Jacks; *St:* John Hawkins, Ward Hawkins; *Sc:* Harold Medford. (1:13) Vengeance is on the mind of a convict who breaks out of jail to do in the wife of the detective who captured him and accidentally killed his wife.

1417. Killer Leopard (Allied Artists; 1954). *Cast:* Johnny Sheffield, Russ Conway, Bill Walker, Milton Wood, Barry Bernard, Donald Murphy, Beverly Garland, Robert "Smoki" Whitfield, Rory Mallinson, Leonard Mudie, Harry Cording, Guy Kingsford, Roy Glenn, Charles Stevens. *D:* Ford Beebe, Edward Morey, Jr.; *P: & Sc:* Beebe. (1:10) "Bomba, the Jungle Boy" comes to the aid of a movie actress in the jungle searching for her husband. The 10th entry in the low budget adventure series begun in 1949. Based on the character created by Roy Rockwood.

1418. Killer Shark (Monogram; 1950). *Cast:* Roddy McDowall, Laurette Luez, Rick Vallin, Edward Norris, Roland Winters, Douglas Fowley, Nacho Galindo, Ralf Harolde, Dick Moore, Ted Hecht, Charles Lang, Robert Espinoza, Julio Sebastian, Julian Rivero, Frank Sully, George Slocum. *D:* Oscar "Budd" Boetticher; *P:* Lindsley Parsons; *Sc:* Charles Lang. (1:16) Melodrama of a youth who goes to Mexico in search of his father.

1419. The Killer Shrews (Hollywood Pictures Corp./McLendon Radio Pictures; 1959). *Cast:* James Best, Ingrid Goude (a former Miss Universe—1957), Baruch Lumet, Ken Curtis, Gordon McLendon (film debut), Alfredo DeSoto, J.H. ["Judge"] DuPree. *D:* Ray Kellogg; *Ex.P:* Gordon McLendon; *P:* Ken Curtis; *Sc:* Jay Simms. (1:09) (video) Science fiction of a scientist's experiments with Blarina shrews that go awry. The shrews grow to the size of large dogs [which they actually are—in costume] and escape the laboratory, proceeding to eat everyone on the isolated island. Filmed at Lake Dallas studios in Texas, it was originally paired with *The Giant Gila Monster* (q.v.) as part of a double feature program.

1420. The Killer That Stalked New York (Columbia; 1950). *Cast:* Evelyn Keyes, Charles Korvin, William Bishop, Dorothy Malone, Lola Albright, Barry Kelley, Carl Benton Reid, Ludwig Donath, Art Smith, Roy Roberts, Whit Bissell, Connie Gilchrist, Dan Riss, Beverly Washburn, Harry Shannon, Celia Lovsky, Richard Egan, Walter Burke, Arthur Space, Jim Backus, Peter Brocco, Tommy Ivo, Angela Clarke, Peter Virgo, Don Kohler. *D:* Earl McEvoy; *P:* Robert Cohn; *Sc:* Harry J. Essex. (1:19) Urban melodrama of a search for diamond smugglers who unknowingly were infected with smallpox when they entered New York City. Based on a magazine article by Milton Lehman. (G.B. title: *Frightened City*)

Killer with a Label (G.B. title) *see* **One Too Many**

1421. Killers from Space (RKO/Planet Filmplays; 1954). *Cast:* Peter Graves, James Seay, Frank Gerstle, Steve Pendleton, John Merrick, Barbara Bestar, Shep Menken, Jack Daly, Ron Kennedy, Ben Welden, Burt Wenland, Lester Dorr, Robert Roark, Ruth Bennett, Mark Scott (narrator). *D: & P:* W. Lee Wilder; *St:* Myles Wilder; *Sc:* Bill Raynor. (1:11—video/1:08) Minimally budgeted science fiction of a scientist killed in a plane crash and brought back to life by alien invaders who brainwash him to do their bidding.

1422. Killer's Kiss (United Artists/Minotaur; 1955). *Cast:* Frank Silvera, Jamie Smith, Irene Kane [aka: Chris Chase], Jerry Jarret, Mike Dana, Felice Orlandi, Ralph Roberts, Phil Stevenson, Julius Adelman, Ruth Sobotka [aka: Mrs. Stanley Kubrick], David Vaughan, Alec Rubin. *D:* Stanley Kubrick; *P:* Morris Bousel, Kubrick; *Sc:* Howard O. Sackler, Kubrick. (1:07) (video/laserdisc) Low budget melodrama of a young man who becomes the target for revenge when he saves a girl from being raped. Originally the co-feature on a double bill with *Fort Yuma* (q.v.). Note: Helmsman Kubrick also originated the story, photographed, and edited this film.

1423. The Killing (United Artists/Harris-Kubrick; 1956). *Cast:* Sterling Hayden, Coleen Gray, Vince Edwards, Jay C. Flippen, Ted de Corsia, Marie Windsor, Elisha Cook, Jr., Timothy Carey, Joe Sawyer, Kola Kwarian, Jay Adler, Joe Turkel, James Edwards, William Benedict, Tito Vuolo. *D:* Stanley Kubrick; *P:* James B. Harris (first film); *Sc:* Kubrick, Jim Thompson. (1:23) (video/laserdisc) A minor classic about the planned robbery of a racetrack for $2,000,000 and the various people directly and indirectly involved in the caper. Based on the novel *Clean Break* by Lionel White, it was in nomination at the British Academy Awards.

1424. Kim (MGM; 1950). *Cast:* Errol Flynn (Mahbub Ali, the Red Beard), Dean Stockwell (Kim), Paul Lukas (Lama), Robert Douglas (Col. Creighton), Thomas Gomez (emissary), Cecil Kellaway (Huree Chunder), Arnold Moss (Lugan Sahib), Reginald Owen (Father Victor), Laurette Luez (Laluli), Richard Hale (Hassan Bey), Hayden Rorke (Maj. Ainsley), Walter Kingsford (Dr. Bronson), Henry Mirelez (Wanna), Frank Lackteen (Shadow), Frank Richards (Abdul), Donna Martell (Haikun), Danny Rees (Biggs), Robin Camp (Thorpe), Betty Daniels (Miss Manners), Wilson Wood (Gerald), Olaf Hytten (Mr. Fairlee), Roman Toporow, Ivan Triesault, Henry Corden, Peter Mamakos, Jeanette Nolan, Rodd Redwing, Michael Ansara, Lal Chand Mehra, Stanley Price, Movita Casteneda, Wallis Clark, Lou Krugman, Adeline de Walt Reynolds, Francis McDonald, Keith McConnell, Bobby Barber, Mitchell Lewis. *D:* Victor Saville; *P:* Leon Gordon; *Sc:* Gordon, Helen Deutsch, Richard Schayer. (1:53) (video) Rudyard Kipling's classic 19th century adventure of rebellion in India came to the screen after much debate at the studio and went on to become one of the 23 top-grossing films of 1950-51. Filmed on location. Remade in 1984 as a TV movie. Technicolor.

1425. Kind Lady (MGM; 1951). *Cast:* Ethel Barrymore (Mary Herries), Maurice Evans (Henry Spring Elcott), Angela Lansbury (Mrs. Edwards), Betsy Blair (Ada Elcott), Keenan Wynn (Edwards), John Williams (Mr. Foster), Doris Lloyd (who also appeared in the '36 Version/Rose), Henri Letondal (Monsieur Malaquaise), Moyna Magill (Mrs. Harkley), Phyllis Morris (Dora), Barry Bernard (Mr. Harkley), Sally Cooper (Lucy Weston), Sherlee Collier (Aggie Edwards), Patrick O'Moore (Constable Orkin), Keith McConnell (Jones), Victor Wood (Doc), John O' Malley (antique dealer), Arthur

Gould-Porter (chauffeur), Leonard Carey (postman). *D:* John Sturges; *P:* Armand Deutsch; *Sc:* Edward Chodorov, Jerry Davis, Charles Bennett; *Costumes:* (AAN-b/w) Walter Plunkett, Gile Steele. (1:18) Successful thriller of a man and his gang of cronies who take over the home of an elderly woman and hold her prisoner. Based on a story of Hugh Walpole that became a play by Edward Chodorov and was filmed by this studio in 1936.

1426. The King and Four Queens (United Artists/Russ–Field–Gabco; 1956). *Cast:* Clark Gable, Eleanor Parker, Jo Van Fleet, Jean Willes, Barbara Nichols, Sara Shane, Jay C. Flippen, Roy Roberts, Arthur Shields. *D:* Raoul Walsh; *P:* David Hempstead; *St:* Margaret Fitts; *Sc:* Fitts, Richard Alan Simmons. (1:26) (video) Searching for money in a western ghost town, a man encounters the wives and the mother of the four brothers who hid the loot. DeLuxe color and CinemaScope.

1427. The King and I (20th Century-Fox; 1956). *Cast:* Yul Brynner (AA + "Best Actor" from the NBR combined with his performance in *Anastasia* and *The Ten Commandments* both q.v./The King), Deborah Kerr (AAN-with the singing voice of Marni Nixon/Anna Leonowens), Rita Moreno (Tuptim), Martin Benson (Kralahome), Terry Saunders (Lady Thiang), Tex Thompson (Louis Leonowens), Carlos Rivas (Lun Tha), Patrick Adiarte (Prince Chulalongkorn), George Toone (Ramsay), Alan Mowbray (British ambassador), Yuriko (Eliza), Marion Jim (Simon Legree), Dusty Worrall (Uncle Thomas), Jocelyn New (Princess Ying Yoowalak), Robert Banas, Gemze de Lappe, Thomas and Dennis Bonilla, Michiko Iseri, Charles Irwin, Leonard Strong, Irene James, Jadin and Jean Wong, Fuji, Weaver Levy, William Yip, Eddie Luke, Josephine Smith. *D:* (AAN) Walter Lang; *P:* (AAN-Best Picture) Charles Brackett; *Sc:* Ernest Lehman; *Music:* (AA) Alfred Newman, Ken Darby; *Cinematographer:* (AAN-color) Leon Shamroy; *ASD:* (AA-color) Lyle Wheeler, John Decuir (art directors), Walter M. Scott, Paul S. Fox (sets); *Costumes:* (AA-color) Irene Sharaff; *Sound:* (AA) Carl Faulkner; *Songs:* "Shall We Dance," "Getting to Know You," "Hello, Young Lovers," "We Kiss in a Shadow," "I Whistle a Happy Tune," "March of the Siamese Children," "I Have Dreamed," "A Puzzlement," "Something Wonderful" and "Song of the King" Richard Rodgers, Oscar Hammerstein II (with original Broadway songs: "My Lord and Master," "Western People Funny" and "Shall I Tell You What I Think of You?" being deleted from the film). (2:13) (video/laserdisc) An English widow and her son travel to 19th century Siam where she is to become teacher of the King's many offspring. Brynner recreates his role in the Rodgers and Hammerstein Broadway smash hit that was adapted from Margaret Landon's *Anna and the King of Siam* and previously filmed by this studio in 1946 under that name. Voted "Best Film of the Year" by *Film Daily*, it was also in nomination with the New York Film Critics for that honor. It placed #2 on the "10 Best" list of the *New York Times* and #3 on the same list of the NBR. One of the 24 top-grossing films of 1955-56, it was photographed in DeLuxe color and CinemaScope 55.

1428. King Creole (Paramount; 1958). *Cast:* Elvis Presley, Carolyn Jones, Dolores Hart, Dean Jagger, Liliane Montevecchi, Walter Matthau, Jan Shepard, Paul Stewart, Vic Morrow, Brian Hutton Jack Grinnage, Dick Winslow, Raymond Bailey. *D:* Michael Curtiz; *P:* Hal B. Wallis; *As.P:* Paul Nathan; *Sc:* Herbert Baker, Michael Vincente Gazzo; *Songs:* "As Long as I Have You," "Crawfish," "Don't Ask Me Why" (Fred Wise–Ben Weisman); "Banana" (sung by Montevecchi); "New Orleans" (Sid Tepper–Roy C. Bennett); "Hard-Headed Woman" (Claude Demetrius); "King Creole," "Steadfast, Loyal and True," "Trouble" (Jerry Leiber–Mike Stoller); "Lover Doll" (Sid Wayne-Abner Silver); "Turtles, Berries and Gumbo" (Al Wood–Kay Twomey/sung by street vendors); "Young Dreams," "Dixie and Rock" (Aaron Schroeder–Martin Kalmanoff). (1:56) (video/laserdisc) Drama of a busboy in a New Orleans gin-joint who rises to singing stardom. Based on Harold Robbins' best-seller *A Stone for Danny Fisher*, this was Presley's fourth film and his final one before entering the U.S. Army. He sings eleven of the thirteen songs on the soundtrack. Partially filmed on location in New Orleans. VistaVision.

1429. King Dinosaur (Lippert/Zimgor; 1955). *Cast:* Bill Bryant, Wanda Curtis, Douglas Henderson, Patricia "Patti" Gallagher, Marvin Miller (Narrator). *D:* Bert I. Gordon; *P: & St:* Gordon, Al Zimbalist; *Sc:* Tom Gries. (0:59) (video) B budget science fiction of an expedition to a newly discovered planet that finds the life forms there are similar to those of earth's prehistory. Another film which utilizes footage from Hal Roach's 1940 production *One Million B.C.* (U.A.).

1430. King of the Bullwhip (Realart/ Western Adventure; 1950–51). *Cast:* Al "Lash" LaRue, Al "Fuzzy" St. John, Jack Holt, Anne Gwynne, Tom Neal, Dennis Moore, George J. Lewis, Michael Whalen, Willis Houck, Cliff Taylor, Frank Jaquet, Jimmie Martin, Roy Butler, Hugh Hooker, Tex Cooper. *D: & P:* Ron Ormond; *St: & Sc:* Jack Lewis, Ira S. Webb. (1:00) (video) A whip-wielding U.S. marshal is called in to eliminate a whip-wielding masked bandit calling himself El Azote, who has been stealing shipments of gold bullion. With all its whip-cracking action, this was one of the more popular of LaRue's series westerns.

1431. King of the Khyber Rifles (20th Century–Fox; 1953). *Cast:* Tyrone Power, Terry Moore, Michael Rennie, John Justin, Guy Rolfe, Richard Stapley, Murray Matheson, Frank DeKova, Argentina Brunetti, Sujata, Frank Lackteen, Gilchrist Stuart, Karam Dhaliwal, Aly Wassil, John Farrow, Richard Peel, Alberto Morin, Alan Lee, Aram Katcher, Gavin Muir, Tom Cound, Patrick Whyte, Ramsey Hill, Maurice Colbourne, David Cota, Naji Cabbay, Mohinder Bedi, Hassan Khayyam, Harry Carter, William [Billy] Wilkerson, George Khoury, George Keymas, Lal Chand Mehra, Eghiche Harout, Joe Sawaya. *D:* Henry King; *P:* Frank P. Rosenberg; *Sc:* Ivan Goff, Ben Roberts. (1:40) Romantic action-adventure of a half-caste British officer who is instrumental in putting down a native uprising. Based on the book by Talbot Mundy, it was previously filmed in 1929 by John Ford as *The Black Watch* (G.B.: *King of the Khyber Rifles*) for Fox Film. Technicolor and CinemaScope.

1432. King of the Wild Stallions (Allied Artists; 1959). *Cast:* George Montgomery, Diane Brewster, Edgar Buchanan, Emile Meyer, Jerry Hartleben, Byron Foulger, Denver Pyle, Dan Sheridan, Rory Mallinson. *D:* R.G. Springsteen; *P:* Ben Schwalb; *Sc:* Ford Beebe. (1:15) Western of a widow and her son in a fight to save their ranch from a crook, who find they are aided by a cowboy and a wild stallion. No relation to the 1942 Monogram production of the same name. DeLuxe color and CinemaScope.

1433. King Richard and the Crusaders (Warner; 1954). *Cast:* Rex Harrison, Virginia Mayo, George Sanders, Laurence Harvey, Robert Douglas, Michael Pate, Paula Raymond, Anthony Eustrel, Henry Corden, Wilton Graff, Lester Matthews, Noel Cravat, Leslie Bradley, Nejla Ates, Larry Chance, Robin Hughes, Leonard Penn, Lumsden Hare, Gavin Moore, Erik Blythe, John Alderson, Harry Cording, Paul Marion, Abdullah Abbas, Mark Hanna, John Epper, Bruce Lester, Mark Dana, Peter Ortiz, Herbert Deans, Otto Reichow, Rudolph Anders. *D:* David Butler; *P:* Henry Blanke; *Sc:* John Twist; *Song:* "Dream, Dream" Twist–Ray Heindorf. (1:54) (video) Purported to be based on Sir Walter Scott's *The Talisman*, this medieval costumer cost a whopping $3,000,000 and spun an epic tale of Richard the Lion-Hearted (Sanders) and Saladin the Saracen (Harrison). WarnerColor and CinemaScope.

1434. King Solomon's Mines (MGM; 1950). *Cast:* Deborah Kerr (Elizabeth Curtis), Stewart Granger (Alan Quartermaine), Richard Carlson (John Goode), Hugo Haas (Van Brun), Lowell Gilmore (Eric Masters), Kimursi (Khiva), Siriaque (Umbopa), Sekaryongo (Chief Gagool), Baziga (King Twala), Corp. Munto Anampio (Chief Bilu), Ivargwema (Blue Star), Benempinga (Black Circle), John Banner (Austin), Henry Rowland (Traum), Gutare (Kafa & double for Umbopa). *D:* Compton Bennett, Andrew Marton; *P:* (AAN-Best Picture) Sam Zimbalist; *Sc:* Helen Deutsch; *Cinematographer:* (AA-color) Robert Surtees; *Editors:* (AA) Ralph E. Winters, Conrad A. Nervig. (1:42) (video/laserdisc) Blockbuster action-adventure of a safari into darkest Africa for the fabled diamond mines of King Solomon. Filmed on location, it was based on the 1885 H. Rider Haggard novel that was previously filmed in Great Britain in 1937. Remade in 1985. One of the 23 top-grossing films of 1950-51, it was a worldwide hit. *Watusi* (q.v.) was a sequel. Technicolor.

1435. Kings Go Forth (United Artists/ Ross-Elton; 1958). *Cast:* Frank Sinatra, Tony Curtis, Natalie Wood, Leora Dana, Karl Swenson, Ann Codee, Jackie Berthe, Marie Isnard; and the jazz combo: Pete Candoli (trumpet), Red Norvo (vibraphone), Mel Lewis (drums), Richie Kamuca (tenor sax), Red Wooten (bass), Jimmy Weible (guitar). *D:* Delmer Daves; *P:* Frank Ross; *As.P:* Richard Ross; *Sc:* Merle Miller. (1:49) (video) Critically panned World War II drama of two G.I.s with antagonistic differences who fall for the same French girl, unaware that her father was a black man. Partially filmed on location near Nice, France, with the villa scenes filmed at the Hollywood estate of Harold Lloyd.

1436. The King's Thief (MGM; 1955). *Cast:* Ann Blyth, Edmund Purdom, David Niven,

George Sanders, Roger Moore, John Dehner, Sean McClory, Alan Mowbray, Melville Cooper, Isobel Elsom, Rhys Williams, Paul Cavanagh, Milton Parsons, Tudor Owen, Joan Elan, Ashley Cowan, Ian Wolfe, Lillian Kemble-Cooper, Lord Layton, Queenie Leonard, Owen McGivney, Bob Pix, Michael Dugan, James Logan, Matt Moore. *D:* Robert Z. Leonard; *P:* Edwin Knopf; *St: & Sc:* Christopher Knopf. (1:18) (video) A lavishly produced hit costumer of intrigues within the court of England's 17th century King Charles II (Sanders). Eastmancolor and CinemaScope.

1437. Kismet (MGM; 1955). *Cast:* Howard Keel, Ann Blyth, Dolores Gray, Monty Woolley (final film—ret.), Susan Cabot, Vic Damone, Jay C. Flippen, Ted de Corsia, Jack Elam, Mike Mazurki, Patricia Dunn, Reiko Sato, Wonci Lui, Julie Robinson. *D:* Vincente Minnelli; *P:* Arthur Freed; *Sc:* Charles Lederer, Luther Davis; *Songs:* "Stranger in Paradise," "And This is My Beloved," "Baubles, Bangles and Beads," "Not Since Nineveh" (Robert Wright–George Forrest, borrowed from themes by Alexander Borodin); "Night of My Nights," "Bored," "Fate," "Gesticulate," "The Olive Tree," "The Sands of Time," "Rahadlakum," "Rhymes Have I" and "Dance of the 3 Princesses of AbaBu" (Wright–Forrest). (1:53) (video/laserdisc) A lavishly produced rendering of the 1911 play by Edward Knoblock and based on the hit Broadway musical adapted from it. Previously filmed in 1920 by Robertson–Cole, 1930 by Warners (both with Otis Skinner), 1931 in Germany and in 1944 by MGM. Eastmancolor and CinemaScope.

1438. A Kiss Before Dying (United Artists/Crown; 1956). *Cast:* Robert Wagner, Virginia Leith, Jeffrey Hunter, Joanne Woodward (her second film), Mary Astor, George Macready, Robert Quarry, Howard Petrie, Bill Walker, Molly McCart, Marlene Felton. *D:* Gerd Oswald (directorial debut); *P:* Robert L. Jacks; *Sc:* Lawrence Roman; *Title song:* Lionel Newman, Carroll Coates (sung by Dolores Hawkins). (1:34) Dramatic thriller of a psychopathic young man who murders his pregnant girlfriend and tries to cover his tracks by making it look like suicide. Based on the novel by Ira Levin, it was remade in 1991. DeLuxe color and CinemaScope.

1439. Kiss Me Deadly (United Artists/Parklane; 1955). *Cast*: Ralph Meeker, Albert Dekker, Paul Stewart, Maxine Cooper, Gaby Rogers, Wesley Addy, Juano Hernandez, Nick Dennis, Cloris Leachman (film debut), Marian Carr, Jack Lambert, Jack Elam, Strother Martin, Fortunio Bonanova, Percy Helton, Nat "King" Cole, Jerry Zimmerman, Silvio Minciotti, Leigh Snowden, Madi Comfort, James Seay, Mara McAfee, Jesslyn Fax, Robert Cornthwaite, James McCallion, Mort Marshall, Marjorie Bennett, Art Loggins, Bob Sherman, Keith McConnell, Paul Richards, Eddie Beal. *D: & P:* Robert Aldrich; *Sc:* A.I. Bezzerides; *Song:* "Rather Have the Blues" Frank DeVol. (1:45) (video/laserdisc) Another of the '50s films which was ahead of its time and has achieved cult status. Detective Mike Hammer (Meeker) goes in search of a mysterious black box. The bizarre characters he meets and the strange situations he finds himself in are the story. Based on Mickey Spillane's novel.

1440. Kiss Me Kate (MGM; 1953). *Cast:* Kathryn Grayson (Lill Vanessi/Katherine), Howard Keel (Fred Graham/Petruchio), Ann Miller (Lois Lane/Bianca), Tommy Rall (Bill Calhoun/Lucentio), Bobby Van (Gremio), Keenan Wynn (Lippy), James Whitmore (Slug), Kurt Kasznar (Baptista), Bob Fosse (film debut/Hortensio), Ron Randell (Cole Porter), Willard Parker (Tex Callaway), Claud Allister (final film—ret.)/Paul), Dave O'Brien (Ralph), Ann Codee (Suzanne), Ted Eckelberry (Nathaniel), Carol Haney, Jeanne Coyne, Hermes Pan (specialty dancers), Mitchell Lewis. *D:* George Sidney; *P:* Jack Cummings; *Adaptation:* Dorothy Kingsley; *Music:* (AAN) Andre Previn, Saul Chaplin; *Songs:* "Too Darn Hot" (a tap dance by Miller), "Why Can't You Behave?," "So in Love," "Wunderbar," "From This Moment On," "Always True to You Darling, in My Fashion," "Brush Up Your Shakespeare," "Out of This World," "I Hate Men," "Were Thine That Special Face," "I've Come to Wive It Wealthily in Padua," "Where is the Life That Late I Led?," "Kiss Me Kate," "Tom, Dick or Harry" and "We Open in Venice" Cole Porter. (1:49) (video/laserdisc) A popular musical-comedy of a married theatrical couple with a relationship akin to that of Shakespeare's Kate and Petruchio in *The Taming of the Shrew*. Based on the hit Broadway musical by Sam and Bella Spewak with songs by Cole Porter. Technicolor and 3-D.

1441. Kiss of Fire (Universal-International; 1955). *Cast:* Barbara Rush, Jack Palance, Rex Reason, Martha Hyer, Leslie Bradley, Alan Reed, Lawrence Dobkin, Joseph Waring, Pat Hogan, Karen Kadler, Steven Geray, Henry Rowland, Bernie Gozier. *D:* Joseph M. Newman; *P:* Samuel Marx; *Sc:* Franklin Coen, Richard

Collins. (1:29) Costumer of a future queen of Spain who resides in New Mexico and must return to Europe, but a new romance changes her mind. Based on the novel *The Rose and the Flame* by Jonreed Lauritzen. Technicolor.

1442. Kiss Them for Me (20th Century-Fox; 1957). *Cast:* Cary Grant, Jayne Mansfield, Suzy Parker, Leif Erickson, Ray Walston (film debut), Larry Blyden, Nathaniel Frey, Werner Klemperer, Jack Mullaney, Ben Wright, Michael Ross, Harry Carey, Jr., Frank Nelson, Ann McCrea, Caprice Yordan, John Doucette, Kip King, Bob St. Angelo, Barbara Gould, Mike Mahoney, Sue Collier, Jan Reeves, Jerry Mathers, Peter Leeds, Jonathan Hale, Hal Baylor, Jane Burgess, William Phipps, Ray Montgomery, Larry Lo Verde, Michael Fox, Robert Sherman, Harry Carter, Richard Shannon, Kathleen Freeman, Nancy Kulp, Richard Deacon, Maudie Prickett, Lincoln Foster, Rachel Stephens, James Stone, Bill Suiter. *D:* Stanley Donen; *P:* Jerry Wald; *Sc:* Julius Epstein; *Title song:* Lionel Newman, Carroll Coates (sung by the McGuire Sisters). (1:43) A comedy-drama detailing the romantic escapades of naval officers on shore leave. Based on the play of the same name by Luther Davis, which was adapted from the novel *Shore Leave* by Frederic Wakeman. DeLuxe color and CinemaScope.

1443. Kiss Tomorrow Goodbye (Warner; 1950). *Cast:* James Cagney, Barbara Payton, Helena Carter, Ward Bond, Luther Adler, Barton MacLane, Steve Brodie, Rhys Williams, Herbert Heyes, John Litel, William Frawley, Robert Karnes, Kenneth Tobey, Dan Riss, Frank Reicher, John Halloran, Neville Brand, George Spaulding, Mark Strong, Jack Gargan, Frank Marlowe, Mack Williams, Ann Tyrrell, Clark Howat, John Day, William Murphy, Dan Ferniel, Matt McHugh, Georgia Caine, Charles Meredith, King Donovan, Dick Rich, Ric Roman, Gordon Richards, Fred Revelala, Frank Wilcox, Thomas Dillon, William Cagney. *D:* Gordon Douglas; *P:* William Cagney; *Sc:* Harry Brown. (1:42) (video/laserdisc) The ruthless accounting of a tough hood who blackmails two crooked cops on the take. Based on the novel by Horace McCoy.

1444. Knights of the Round Table (MGM; 1953). *Cast:* Robert Taylor (Lancelot), Ava Gardner (Guinevere), Mel Ferrer (King Arthur), Stanley Baker (Sir Mordred), Felix Alymer (Merlin), Anne Crawford (Morgan Le Fay), Maureen Swanson (Elaine), Gabriel Woolf (Percival), Anthony Forwood (Gareth), Robert Urquhart (Sir Gawaine), Niall MacGinnis (Green Knight), Ann Hanslip (Nan), Jill Clifford (Bronwyn), Stephen Vercoe (Agravaine), Howard Marion Crawford (Simon), John Brooking (Bedivere), Peter Gawthorne (bishop), Alan Tilvern (steward), John Sherman (Lambert), Dagmar Wunter [later: Dana Wynter/Vivien], Mary Germaine (Brigid), Martin Wyldeck (John), Roy Russell (Leogrance), Gwendoline Evans (Enid), Barry MacKay, Derek Tansley, Michel De Lutry. *D:* Richard Thorpe; *P:* Pandro S. Berman; *Sc:* Noel Langley, Talbot Jennings, Jan Lustig; *ASD:* (AAN-color) Alfred Junge, Hans Peters (art directors), John Jarvis (sets); *Sound:* (AAN) A.W. Watkins. (1:55) (video/laserdisc) Lavishly produced (in England) hit epic rendering of the legendary tale of King Arthur and his Knights of the Round Table. Based on the 15th century prose collection "Le Mort D'Arthur" by Sir Thomas Malory, which was also one of the source materials for *Excalibur* (Warner; 1981), a British epic. One of the 25 top-grossing films of 1953-54 and also MGM's first production in CinemaScope. Technicolor.

1445. Knock on Wood (Paramount; 1954). *Cast:* Danny Kaye (Jerry), Mai Zetterling (U.S. debut/Ilse Nordstrom), Torin Thatcher (Langston), David Burns (Marty Brown), Leon Askin (Gromek), Abner Biberman (Papinek), Otto Waldis (Brodnik), Steven Geray (Dr. Kreuger), Diana Adams (princess), Patricia Denise (Mama Morgan), Virginia Huston (Audrey), Paul England (Chief Inspector Wilton), Johnstone White (Langston's secretary), Lewis Martin (Inspector Cranford), Philip Van Zandt (Brutchik), Gavin Gordon (car salesman), Helen Chapman (Zelda), Christopher Olsen (Danny, Jr.), Rex Evans, Carl Milletaire, Henry Brandon, Winifred Harris, Kenneth Hunter, Noel Drayton, Phil Tully, Donald Lawton, Genevieve Aumont, Tony Christian, John Alderson, Eric Wilton, Alphonse Martell, Larry Arnold, Helen Dickson. *D: & P:* Norman Panama, Melvin Frank; *St: & Sc:* (AAN) Panama, Frank; *Songs:* "The Drastic Livid History of Monahan O'Han," "All About You" and "Knock on Wood" Sylvia Fine; *Choreography:* Michael Kidd. (1:43) Hit comedy of a ventriloquist whose dummy—unbeknownst to him, of course—holds secret papers sought by international spies. It placed #3 on the "10 Best" list of the *New York Times* and became one of the 25 top-grossing films of 1953-54. Technicolor. Note: In 1954 Danny Kaye received a special Oscar for "unique talents, his service to the Academy, the motion picture industry and the American people."

1446. Korea Patrol (Eagle-Lion; 1951). *Cast:* Richard Emory, Al Eben, Benson Fong, Li Sun, Teri Duna, Danny Davenport, Wong Artarne, Harold Fong, John V. Close, Richard Barron. *D:* Max Nosseck; *P:* Walter Shenson; *Sc: & St:* Shenson, Kenneth G. Brown. (0:59) Korean War melodrama of a patrol of six men assigned to destroy a North Korean bridge. Originally the second half of a double bill with *Prehistoric Women* (q.v.).

1447. Kronos (20th Century–Fox/Regal Films; 1957). *Cast:* Jeff Morrow, Barbara Lawrence, John Emery, George O'Hanlon, Morris Ankrum, Kenneth Alton, John Parrish, Jose Gonzales-Gonzales, Richard Harrison, Marjorie Stapp, Robert Shayne, Donald Eitner, Gordon Mills, John Halloran. *D:* Kurt Neumann; *P:* Neumann, Jack Rabin, Irving Block, Louis DeWitt; *St:* Block; *Sc:* Lawrence Louis Goldman. (1:18) (video/laserdisc) Science fiction with an offbeat alien, a huge metallic machine from outer space which propels itself along the ground, absorbing energy from the earth and gaining control of an earth scientist. Originally ran on the top of a double bill with *She Devil* (q.v.). Regalscope.

1448. The Lady and the Bandit (Columbia; 1951). *Cast:* Louis Hayward, Patricia Medina, Suzanne Dalbert, Tom Tully, John Williams, Malu Gatica, Alan Mowbray, Lumsden Hare, Barbara Brown, Malcolm Keen, Stapleton Kent, Sheldon Jett, George Baxter, Ivan Triesault, Norman Leavitt, Frank Reicher (final film—ret.). *D:* Ralph Murphy; *P:* Harry Joe Brown; *St:* Jack DeWitt, Duncan Renaldo [aka: Renault Duncan]; *Sc:* Frank Burt, Robert Libott. (1:19) A costume drama of Britain's famed highwayman, Dick Turpin. Based on the poem "The Highwayman" [aka: "Dick Turpin's Ride"]. In 1925, Tom Mix starred in *Dick Turpin,* a silent by Fox Film on the same subject matter. Originally ran on the top of a double bill with a "Durango Kid" feature, *Cyclone Fury* (q.v.). (G.B. title: *Dick Turpin's Ride*)

1449. Lady and the Tramp (Buena Vista/ Walt Disney Prods.; 1955). *Voices:* Peggy Lee (Darling–Peg–Si and Am), Barbara Luddy (Lady), Larry Roberts (Tramp), Bill Thompson (Jock–Bull–Dachsie), Bill Baucon (Trusty), Stan Freberg (Beaver), Verna Felton (Aunt Sarah), Alan Reed (Boris), George Givot (Tony), Dallas McKennon (Toughy–Professor), Lee Miller (Jim Dear), The Mello Men. *D:* Hamilton Luske, Clyde Geronimi, Wilfred Jackson; *P:* Walt Disney; *As.P:* Erdman Penner; *Songs:* "He's a Tramp," "La La Lu," "Siamese Cat Song," "Peace on Earth," "Bella Notte" Sonny Burke, Peggy Lee. (1:15) (video/laserdisc) Animated canine romance of a cocker spaniel and a dog of the streets. Based on the 1953 story "The Lady and the Tramp" by Ward Greene, it was in production for two years at a cost of $4,000,000 and showed a box office gross of $25,000,000. It was in Technicolor and Disney's first animated feature in CinemaScope.

The Lady from Boston (G.B. title) *see* **Pardon My French**

1450. The Lady from Texas (Universal-International; 1951). *Cast:* Howard Duff, Mona Freeman, Josephine Hull (final film—ret.), Craig Stevens, Gene Lockhart, Barbara Knudson, Jay C. Flippen, Ed Begley, Chris-Pin Martin, Lane Bradford, Kenneth Patterson, Morgan Farley. *D:* Joseph Pevney; *P:* Leonard Goldstein; *St:* Harold Shumate; *Sc:* Gerald Drayson Adams, Connie Lee Bennett. (1:17) Offbeat western drama of a drifter who comes to the aid of a Civil War widow in danger of losing her ranch. Technicolor.

1451. Lady Godiva (Universal-International; 1955). *Cast:* Maureen O'Hara, George Nader, Eduard Franz, Leslie Bradley, Victor McLaglen, Torin Thatcher, Rex Reason, Henry Brandon, Grant Withers, Arthur Shields, Alec Harford, Clint Eastwood, Arthur Gould-Porter, Robert Warwick, Slim Iness, Anthony Eustrel, Kathryn Givney, Thayer Roberts, Rhodes Reason, Olive Sturges, Tom Cloud, Judith Brian, Maya Van Horn, Jack Grinnage, Philo McCullough. *D:* Arthur Lubin; *P:* Robert Arthur; *St:* Oscar Brodney; *Sc:* Brodney, Harry Ruskin. (1:29) 11th century costumer set in Coventry, England, with war waging between the Normans and the Saxons leading to the titled lady's famous horseback ride in the buff. Another historically inaccurate Hollywood production. Technicolor. Preceded by a one reel Vitagraph in 1911.

1452. Lady in the Iron Mask (20th Century–Fox; 1952). *Cast:* Louis Hayward, Patricia Medina (dual role), Alan Hale, Jr., Judd Holdren, Steve Brodie, John Sutton, Hal Gerard, Lester Matthews. *D:* Ralph Murphy; *P:* Walter Wanger, Eugene Frenke; *Sc:* Jack Pollexfen,

Aubrey Wisberg. (1:18) In this low budget costume adventure, D'Artagnan and the Three Musketeers rescue an imprisoned princess. Source material was Alexandre Dumas' *The Three Musketeers*. SuperCinecolor.

1453. The Lady Pays Off (Universal-International; 1951). *Cast:* Linda Darnell, Stephen McNally, Gigi Perreau, Virginia Field, Ann Codee, Nestor Paiva, Lynne Hunter, James Griffith, Billy Wayne, Katherine Warren, Paul McVey, Tristram Coffin, Judd Holdren, Nolan Leary, John Doucette, Billy Newell, Ric Roman. *D:* Douglas Sirk; *P:* Albert J. Cohen; *St: & Sc:* Frank Gill, Jr., Cohen. (1:20) Comedy-drama of a lady schoolteacher who takes on the job of tutor to the daughter of a gambling casino owner to whom she owes a large sum of money.

1454. Lady Possessed (Republic/Portland Pictures; 1952). *Cast:* James Mason, June Havoc, Stephen Dunne, Diana Graves, Fay Compton, Pamela Kellino [aka: Mrs. James Mason], Steven Geray, Odette Myrtil, Eileen Erskine, John P. Monaghan, Enid Mosier, Judy Osborne, Constance Cavendish, Alma Lawton, Anna Grevier, Tonyna Mickey Dolly, Hazel Franklyn. *D:* William Spier, Roy Kellino; *P:* James Mason; *Sc:* Mason, Pamela Kellino [Mrs. Mason]; *Songs:* "My Heart Asks Why" Hans May, Hermione Hannen; "It's You I Love" Allie Wrubel; "More Wonderful Than These" Spier, Kay Thompson. (1:27) Melodramatic thriller of a woman who suffers an identity crisis following a miscarriage. Based on the 1948 novel *Del Palma* [G.B. title: *A Lady Possessed*] by Pamela Kellino [Mrs. Mason]. Note: James Mason sings!

1455. The Lady Says No (United Artists/Ross-Stillman Prods.; 1951). *Cast:* Joan Caulfield, David Niven, James Robertson Justice, Lenore Lonergan, Frances Bavier, Peggy Maley, Henry Jones, Jeff York, George Davis, Robert Williams, Mary Lawrence. *D:* Frank Ross; *P:* Ross, John Stillman, Jr.; *St: & Sc:* Robert Russell. (1:20) (video) Romantic comedy of a woman who writes a best-seller on the superiority of women over men—currently called male bashing—before succumbing to the charms of a male photographer. Note: Caulfield was the wife of director Ross.

1456. The Lady Takes a Flyer (Universal-International; 1958). *Cast:* Jeff Chandler, Lana Turner, Richard Denning, Andra Martin, Chuck Connors, Reta Shaw, Alan Hale, Jr., Nestor Paiva, Dee J. Thompson, Jerry Paris, James Doherty. *D:* Jack Arnold; *P:* William Alland; *St:* Edmund H. North; *Sc:* Danny Arnold. (1:34) Marital drama of a husband and wife flying team, inspired by nonfictional characters. Eastmancolor and CinemaScope.

1457. The Lady Wants Mink (Republic; 1952–53). *Cast:* Dennis O'Keefe, Ruth Hussey, Eve Arden, William Demarest, Gene Lockhart, Hope Emerson, Hillary Brooke, Tommy Rettig, Earl Robie, Mary Field, Isabel Randolph, Thomas Browne Henry, Brad Johnson, Mara Corday, Robert Shayne, Jean Fenwick, Jean Vachon, Vici Raaf, Mary Alan Hokanson, Angela Greene, Barbara Billingsley, Arthur Walsh, Howard J. Negley, Max Wagner, Rodney Bell, Frank Gerstle, Sydney Mason, Joe Mell, Wayne Treadway, Bobby Diamond, Dennis Ross, Gail Bonney, Wade Crosby, Slim Duncan, Michael Barton. *D: & P:* William Seiter; *Ex.P:* Herbert J. Yates; *St:* Leonard Neubauer, Lou Schor; *Sc:* Dane Lussier, Richard Alan Simmons. (1:32) A domestic comedy of the events that transpire when a woman attempts to "grow her own mink coat." Trucolor.

1458. A Lady Without Passport (MGM; 1950). *Cast:* Hedy Lamarr, John Hodiak, James Craig, George Macready, Steve Geray, Bruce Cowling, Trevor Bardette, Nedrick Young, Steven Hill, Robert Osterloh, Charles Wagenheim, Renzo Cesana, Esther Zeitlin, Carlo Tricoli, Marta Mitrovich, Don Garner, Richard Crane, Nita Bieber, Martin Garralaga, Mario Siletti. *D:* Joseph H. Lewis; *P:* Samuel Marx; *St:* Lawrence E. Taylor; *Adaptation:* Cyril Hume; *Sc:* Howard Dimsdale; *Screenplay contribution:* Steve Fisher. (1:12) Programmer melodrama of a woman entering the United States trying to leave Cuba and her past behind.

1459. Lafayette Escadrille (Warner/William A. Wellman; 1958). *Cast:* Tab Hunter, Etchika Choureau, Marcel Dalio, Bill Wellman, Jr. (also narrator), Jody McCrea, Dennis Devine, David Janssen, Paul Fix, Veola Vonn, Clint Eastwood, Will Hutchins (film debut), Bob Hover, Tom Laughlin, Brett Halsey, Henry Nakamura, Maurice Marsac, Raymond Bailey, George Nardelli. *D: & P:* William A. Wellman (final film—ret.); *Sc:* A.S. Fleischman. (1:33) (video) World War I romantic drama of the Lafayette Escadrille, a team of American pilots who flew with the French Air Corps during that war. Based on the story "C'est LaGuerre" by the senior Wellman, the critics were not impressed. (G.B. title: *Hell Bent For Glory*).

1460. Land of the Pharaohs (Warner/ Continental Co., Ltd.; 1954–55). *Cast:* Jack Hawkins, Joan Collins (U.S. debut), James Robertson Justice, Dewey Martin, Alexis Minotis, Luisa Boni, Sydney Chaplin, James Hayter, Piero Giagnoni, Kerima. *D: & P:* Howard Hawks; *Sc:* William Faulkner, Harry Kurnitz, Harold Jack Bloom. (1:43) (video/laserdisc) Lavishly produced epic about the building of Khufu's (Hawkins) Great Pyramid with a cast that exceeded 10,000 extras. In WarnerColor and CinemaScope, it became a $6 million bomb.

1461. The Land Unknown (Universal-International; 1957). *Cast:* Jock Mahoney, Shawn Smith, William Reynolds, Phil Harvey, Henry Brandon, Douglas R. Kennedy. *D:* Virgil Vogel; *P:* William Alland; *Adaptation:* William N. Robson (of an unpublished story by Charles Palmer); *Sc:* Laszlo Gorog; *F/X:* Fred Knoth, Orien Ernest, Jack Kevan. (1:18) (video) Science fiction adventure of four people on a helicopter, forced down into a prehistoric land in Antarctica after colliding with a pterodactyl. In their explorations, they find a survivor of an earlier expedition. CinemaScope.

1462. Laramie Mountains (Columbia; 1952). *Cast:* Charles Starrett, Smiley Burnette, Fred F. Sears, Jack [Jock] Mahoney, Marshall Reed, Rory Mallinson, Zon Murray, John War Eagle, Bob Wilke, Chris Alcaide, Boyd "Red" Morgan. *D:* Ray Nazarro; *P:* Colbert Clark; *St: & Sc:* Barry Shipman. (0:54) In this series entry, Indians are being blamed for a series of wagon train raids until the "Durango Kid" sets the record straight.

1463. Las Vegas Shakedown (Allied Artists; 1955). *Cast:* Dennis O'Keefe, Coleen Gray, Charles Winninger, Thomas Gomez, Dorothy Patrick, Mary Beth Hughes, Elizabeth Patterson, James Millican, Robert Armstrong, Joseph Downing, Lewis Martin, Mara McAfee, Charles Fredericks, Regina Gleason, Murray Alper, James Alexander, Frank Hanley, Allen Mathews. *D:* Sidney Salkow; *P:* William F. Broidy; *St: & Sc:* Steve Fisher. (1:19) Crime melodrama of a gangster's bid to take over a Las Vegas hotel and casino.

1464. The Las Vegas Story (RKO/Howard Hughes; 1952). *Cast:* Jane Russell, Victor Mature, Vincent Price, Hoagy Carmichael, Brad Dexter, Gordon Oliver, Jay C. Flippen, Will Wright, Bill Welsh, Ray Montgomery, Colleen Miller, Robert Wilke, Syd Saylor, George Hoagland, Roger Creed, Jimmy Long, Bert Stevens, Norman Stevens, Ben Harris, Ted Jordan, Philip Ahn, Mary Bayless, Mary Darby, Barbara Freking, Jean Corbett, Hazel Shaw, Evelyn Lovequist, Clarence Muse, Dorothy Abbott, Joan Mallory, Jane Easton, Mavis Russell, Midge Ware, John Merrick, Brooks Benedict, Paul Frees, Carl Sklover, Ralph Alley, Mitchel Rhein, Forrest Lederer, Charles Cross, Connie Castle, Milton Kibbee, Al Murphy, Harry Brooks, Dick Ryan, Howard Darbeen, Wallis Clark, Oliver Hartwell, Roy Darmour, Pat Collins, Sam Finn, Joe Gilbert, Carolyn Block, Betty Onge, Helen Blizard, Mona Knox, Robert Milton, Steve Flagg [aka: Michael St. Angel], Suzanne Ames, Annabelle Applegate, Joyce Niven, Shirley Tegge, Anne Dore, Chili Williams, Sylvia Lewis, Barbara Thatcher, Beverly Thomas, Sue Casey. *D:* Robert Stevenson; *P:* Robert Sparks; *St:* Jay Dratler; *Sc:* Earl Felton, Harry Essex, Paul Jarrico (unc.); *Songs:* "I Get Along Without You Very Well," "The Monkey Song" (Hoagy Carmichael); "My Resistance Is Low" (Carmichael–Harold Adamson). (1:27) (video) Drama of a married couple whose life changes drastically when they visit Las Vegas and the husband starts losing heavily at the dice table.

Lassie's Adventures in the Gold Rush *see* **The Painted Hills**

1465. The Last Angry Man (Columbia/ Fred Kohlmar Prods.; 1959). *Cast:* Paul Muni (AAN/Dr. Sam Abelman, final film—ret.), David Wayne (Woodrow Wilson Thrasher), Betsy Palmer (Anne Thrasher), Luther Adler (Dr. Max Vogel), Joby Baker (Myron Malkin), Joanna Moore (Alice Taggert), Nancy R. Pollock (Sarah Abelman), Billy Dee Williams (film debut/Josh Quincy), Dan Tobin (Ben Loomer), Claudia McNeil (Mrs. Quincy), Robert F. Simon (Lyman Gattling), Godfrey Cambridge (film debut/Nobody Home), Helen Champan (Miss Bannahan), David Winters (Lee Roy), Cicely Tyson (bit). *D:* Daniel Mann; *P:* Fred Kohlmar; *Sc:* Gerald Green (based on his 1956 book); *Adaptation:* Richard Murphy; *ASD:* (AAN-b/w) Carl Anderson (art director), William Kiernan (sets). (1:40) (video) Sentimental drama of a dedicated slum doctor who becomes the subject of a TV documentary. Nominated for "Best Film of the Year" by New York Film Critics. Filmed on location in Brooklyn, N.Y., it became one of the 28 top-grossing films of 1959-60. Remade in 1974 as a TV movie.

1466. The Last Blitzkreig (Columbia; 1958). *Cast:* Van Johnson, Kerwin Mathews, Dick York, Larry Storch, Lise Bourdin, Hans Bentz van den Berg, Leon Askin, Robert Boon, Howard B. Jaffe, Ton Van Duinhoven, Charles Rosenbloom, Gijsbert Tersteeg, Steye Van Brandenberg, Herb Grika, Montgomery Ford, Chris Baay, Fred Oster, Karl Kent, Jan Verkoren, Ronnie Landweer, Adelheid Van Der Most, Yoka Berretty, Sacha Denisent, T. Bolland, Jack Kelling, John T. Greene, Hans Hagemeyer, Pieter Goemans. *D:* Arthur Dreifuss; *P:* Sam Katzman; *Sc:* & *St:* Lou Morheim. (1:24) World War II drama set during the Battle of the Bulge. English-speaking German Nazis infiltrate an American unit. Filmed on location in Amsterdam, Holland.

The Last Bullet *see* **Crooked River**

1467. The Last Command (Republic; 1955). *Cast:* Sterling Hayden (Jim Bowie), Anna Maria Alberghetti, Richard Carlson (William Travis), Arthur Hunnicutt (Davy Crockett), Ernest Borgnine, J. Carrol Naish (General Santa Ana), Ben Cooper, John Russell (Lt. Dickinson), Jim Davis, Virginia Grey (Mrs. Dickinson), Eduard Franz, Otto Kruger (Stephen Austin), Russell Simpson, Roy Roberts, Slim Pickens, Hugh Sanders (Sam Houston). *D:* & *As.P:* Frank Lloyd (final film—ret.); *St:* Sy Bartlett; *Sc:* Warren Duff; *Song:* "Jim Bowie" Max Steiner, Sidney Clare (sung by Gordon MacRae). (1:50) (video) Lavishly produced historical Republic western set in 1834 Texas, detailing the fall of the Alamo and the heroes it produced. Historical accuracy takes a beating by placing many women and children inside the walls during the siege. In reality, Mrs. Dickinson, her daughter and their black servant-boy were the only surviving non-combatants. Trucolor.

1468. The Last Frontier (Columbia; 1955). *Cast:* Victor Mature, Guy Madison, Robert Preston, James Whitmore, Anne Bancroft, Russell Collins, Peter Whitney, Pat Hogan, Mickey Kuhn, Manuel Donde, William Calles, Guy Williams, Jack Pennick, Robert San Angelo, William Traylor. *D:* Anthony Mann; *P:* William Fadiman; *Sc:* Philip Yordan, Russell S. Hughes; *Song:* "The Last Frontier" Lester Lee, Ned Washington (sung by Rusty Draper). (1:37) An army fort commander provokes an Indian uprising. Based on the 1947 novel *The Gilded Rooster* by Richard Emery Roberts. (retitled: *Savage Wilderness*) CinemaScope and Technicolor.

1469. The Last Hunt (MGM; 1956). *Cast:* Robert Taylor, Stewart Granger, Lloyd Nolan, Debra Paget, Russ Tamblyn, Constance Ford, Joe DeSantis, Ainslee Pryor, Terry Wilson, Ralph Moody, Fred Graham, Ed Lonehill, Dan White, Jerry Martin, William "Bill" Phillips, Roy Barcroft, Rosemary Johnston. *D:* & *Sc:* Richard Brooks; *P:* Dore Schary. (1:48) (video) Acclaimed offbeat drama of a maniacally obsessed buffalo hunter, determined to slaughter every one of the ruminants on the western plains. Based on the 1954 novel by Milton Lott, box office returns were disappointing. Location filming at Custer State Park, S.D. Eastmancolor and CinemaScope.

1470. The Last Hurrah (Columbia/John Ford; 1958). *Cast:* Spencer Tracy (voted "Best Actor" by the NBR, combined with his work in *The Old Man and the Sea*, q.v./Frank Skeffington), Jeffrey Hunter (Adam Caulfield), Dianne Foster (Maeve Caulfield), Pat O'Brien (John Gorman), Basil Rathbone (Norman Cass, Sr.), Donald Crisp (the cardinal), James Gleason (final film—d. 1959/Cuke Gillen), Edward Brophy (final film—d. 1960/Ditto Boland), Basil Ruysdael (Bishop Gardner), John Carradine (Amos Force), Willis Bouchey (Roger Sugrue), Ricardo Cortez (Sam Weinberg), Wallace Ford (Hennessey), Frank McHugh (Festus Garvey), Anna Lee (Gert), Jane Darwell (Delia), Frank Albertson (Jack Mangan), Carleton Young (Mr. Winslow), Bob Sweeney (Degnan), Edmund Lowe (cut from final film print), William Leslie (Dan Herlihy), Ken Curtis (Monsignor Kilian), O.Z. Whitehead (Norman Cass, Jr.), Ruth Warren (Ella Davin), Dan Borzage (Pete), Arthur Walsh (Frank Skeffington, Jr.), Charles Fitzsimmons (Kevin McCluskey), Harry Tenbrook (Footsie), Helen Westcott (Mrs. McCluskey), Mimi Doyle (Mamie Burns), Jack Pennick (Riley), Robert Levin (Jules Kowalsky), Julius Tannen (Mr. Kowalsky), James Flavin (police captain), Frank Sully (fire captain), William Forrest (doctor), Richard Deacon, Bill Henry, Harry Lauter, Rand Brooks, Edmund Cobb, Charles Trowbridge, Harry Tyler, Charlie Sullivan, Ruth Clifford, Hal K. Dawson, Clete Roberts, Tommy Earwood, Tommy Jackson. *D:* John Ford (voted "Best Director" by the NBR); *P:* Ford; *Sc:* Frank Nugent. (2:01) (video/laser disc) Critically acclaimed drama of a political boss and his final bid for the mayor's seat. Patterned after former Boston mayor, James Curley, it was based on the 1956 book by Edwin O'Connor and remade in 1977 as a TV movie. It was in nomination for "Best Film of the Year" by the New York Film Critics and placed #3 on the "10 Best" list of the NBR.

1471. The Last Mile (United Artists/Vanguard–R.S. Prods.; 1959). *Cast:* Mickey Rooney, Alan Bunce, Frank Conroy, Leon Janney, Frank Overton, Clifford Davis, Harry Millard, John McCurry, John Seven, Ford Rainey, Michael Constantine, John Vari, Clifton James, Donald Barry, George Marcy, Milton Selzer. *D:* Howard W. Koch; *P:* Milton Subotsky, Max J. Rosenberg; *Sc:* Subotsky, Seton I. Miller. (1:21) "Big House" melodrama of seven death row inmates who instigate a riot and take guards prisoner. Set in the 1930s, it was based on John Wexley's 1930 Broadway play that was first filmed by Sono Art-Worldwide in 1932.

1472. The Last Musketeer (Republic; 1952). *Cast:* Rex Allen, Mary Ellen Kay, Slim Pickens, James Anderson, Boyd "Red" Morgan, Monte Montague, Michael Hall, Alan Bridge, Stan Jones, The Republic Rhythm Riders, Ko-Ko (horse). *D:* William Witney; *As.P:* Edward J. "Eddy" White: *St: & Sc:* Arthur E. Orloff; *Songs:* "I Still Love the West" Foy Willing; "Aura Lee" W.W. Fosdick, George R. Poulton, [aka: "Army Blue"] a U.S. Military Academy song (originally written in 1861); "Down in the Valley" (traditional—ca. 1845). (1:07) (video) A Rex Allen series western of a cowboy who puts the crimps to schemes of greedy land-grabbers.

1473. Last of the Badmen (Allied Artists; 1957). *Cast:* George Montgomery, James Best, Douglas Kennedy, Keith Larsen, Robert Foulk, Tom Greenway, Meg Randall, Willis Bouchey, Michael Ansara, Addison Richards, John Doucette, Harlan Warde, John Damler. *D:* Paul Landres; *P:* Vincent M. Fennelly; *St:* Daniel B. Ullman; *Sc:* Ullman, David Chandler. (1:19) When a Chicago detective is killed by western outlaws, his agency sends two other detectives to find the killer. DeLuxe color and CinemaScope, it was remade in 1964 by this studio as *Gunfight at Comanche Creek.*

1474. Last of the Buccaneers (Columbia; 1950). *Cast:* Paul Henreid, Jack Oakie, Karin Booth, Mary Anderson, John Dehner, Edgar Barrier, Harry Cording, Eugene Borden, Pierre Watkin, Sumner Getchell, Paul Marion, Rusty Wescoatt, Jean Del Val. *D:* Lew Landers; *P:* Sam Katzman; *St: & Sc:* Robert E. Kent. (1:18) Technicolor swashbuckler detailing the exploits of pirate Jean LaFitte (Henreid), following the Battle of New Orleans. Originally ran on a double bill with *The Texan Meets Calamity Jane* (q.v.).

1475. Last of the Comanches (Columbia; 1952). *Cast:* Broderick Crawford, Barbara Hale, Lloyd Bridges, George Mathews, Mickey Shaughnessy, Chubby Johnson, Martin Milner, Carleton Young, Johnny Stewart, Hugh Sanders, Ric Roman, Milton Parsons, John War Eagle, Jack Woody, William Andrews, Bud Osborne, George Chesebro, Rodd Redwing, Jay Silverheels. *D:* Andre De Toth; *P:* Buddy Adler; *St: & Sc:* Kenneth Gamet. (1:25) (video) Technicolor western of U.S. cavalrymen holding off against marauding Comanches in an old mission. A remake of *Sahara* (1943). (G.B. title: *The Sabre and the Arrow*)

1476. Last of the Desperados (Associated Releasing Corp.; 1955). *Cast:* James Craig, Jim Davis, Margia Dean, Barton MacLane, Donna Martell, Myrna Dell, Bob Steele, Stanley Clements, Brad Johnson, Herbert Vigran, Thomas Browne Henry. *D:* Sam Newfield; *P:* Sigmund Neufeld; *St: & Sc:* Orville H. Hampton. (1:10) Offbeat low budget western of the trials and tribulations faced by Pat Garrett (Craig) after gunning down Billy the Kid. Note: Veteran western bad boy Charles King shows up in some stock footage.

1477. Last of the Fast Guns (Universal-International; 1958). *Cast:* Jock Mahoney, Gilbert Roland, Linda Cristal, Eduard Franz, Lorne Greene, Carl Benton Reid, Edward C. Platt, Eduardo Noriega, Jorge Trevino, Lee Morgan, Rafael Alcayde, Milton Bernstein, Stillman Segar, Jose Chavez Trowe, Francisco Reiguera, Richard Cutting. *D:* George Sherman; *P:* Howard Christie; *St: & Sc:* David P. Harmon. (1:22) A gunfighter goes in search of the missing brother of a wealthy industrialist, so the brother can collect a large sum of money due him. The industrialist's partner has other ideas. Eastmancolor and CinemaScope.

1478. Last of the Pony Riders (Columbia/Gene Autry Prods.; 1953). *Cast:* Gene Autry, Kathleen Case, Smiley Burnette, Dick Jones, Howard Wright, Arthur Space, Gregg Barton, Robert "Buzz" Henry, Harry Mackin, Harry Hines, Kermit Maynard, John Downey, Champion (horse). *D:* George Archainbaud (final theatrical film—to TV); *P:* Armand Schaefer; *St: & Sc:* Ruth Woodman; *Songs:* "Song of the Prairie," "Sugar Babe." (0:59) (video) A banker becomes the thorn in the side of Gene when he attempts to acquire a stage line. Notable as Autry's final theatrical film appearance before becoming a TV producer. Originally ran on a double bill with *Paris Model* (q.v.).

1479. The Last Outpost (Paramount/Pine-Thomas; 1951). *Cast:* Ronald Reagan, Rhonda Fleming, Bruce Bennett, Bill Williams, Noah Beery, Jr., Peter Hansen, Hugh Beaumont, John Ridgely, Lloyd Corrigan, Charles Evans, James Burke, Richard Crane, Ewing Mitchell, John War Eagle, Tarbaby (horse). *D:* Lewis Foster; *P:* William H. Pine, William C. Thomas; *St:* David Lang; *Sc:* Geoffrey Homes [Daniel Mainwaring], George Worthing Yates, Winston Miller. (1:28) (video) A box office winner, this Technicolor western spins the tale of two brothers, one a Union officer, the other a Confederate, who unite against hostile Indians. (video title: *Cavalry Charge*)

1480. The Last Posse (Columbia; 1953). *Cast:* Broderick Crawford, Wanda Hendrix, John Derek, Charles Bickford, Warner Anderson, Henry Hull, Tom Powers, Skip Homeier, Monte Blue, Eddy Waller, Will Wright, Raymond Greenleaf, James Kirkwood, James Bell, Guy Wilkerson, Mira McKinney, Helen Wallace, Harry Hayden. *D:* Alfred L. Werker; *P:* Harry Joe Brown; *St:* Connie Lee Bennett, Seymour Bennett; *Sc:* The Bennetts, Kenneth Gamet, John K. Butler (unc.), Harry Essex (unc.). (1:13) Offbeat oater of money stolen (from a cattle baron) and retrieved under unusual circumstances.

1481. Last Stagecoach West (Republic/Ventura; 1957). *Cast:* Jim Davis, Mary Castle, Victor Jory, Lee Van Cleef, Grant Withers, Roy Barcroft, John Alderson, Glenn Strange, Francis McDonald, Tristram Coffin, Willis Bouchey, Lewis Martin. *D:* Joseph Kane; *P:* Rudy Ralston; *St: & Sc:* Barry Shipman (1:07) When the owner of a stageline loses his government mail contract and is put out of business, he exacts revenge on those who sabotaged his livelihood. Naturama.

1482. The Last Time I Saw Paris (MGM; 1954). *Cast:* Elizabeth Taylor, Van Johnson, Donna Reed, Walter Pidgeon, Eva Gabor, Roger Moore, George Dolenz, Kurt Kasznar, Celia Lovsky, Sandy Descher, Peter Leeds, John Doucette, Odette, Luis Urbina & Gilda Fontana (flamenco dancers), Christian Pasques, Ed Hinton, Richard Emory, Steve Wayne, Loulette Sablon, Jean Heremans, Josette Deegan, Mary Ann Hawkins, Matt Moore, Ann Codee, Paul Power, Harry Cody, Gene Coogan. *D:* Richard Brooks; *P:* Jack Cummings; *Sc:* Brooks, Philip Epstein, Julius Epstein. (1:56) (video/laserdisc) Flashback drama of disillusioned expatriate Americans in Paris, following World War II. Based on F. Scott Fitzgerald's 1945 story "Babylon Revisited," it had weak returns. Technicolor.

1483. Last Train from Bombay (Columbia/Esskay Pictures; 1952). *Cast:* Jon Hall, Christine Larson, Lisa Ferraday, Douglas Kennedy, Michael Fox, Donna Martell, Matthew Boulton, James Fairfax, Gregory Gaye, Kenneth Terrell, Frederic Berest, Barry Brooks. *D:* Fred F. Sears; *P:* Sam Katzman; *St: & Sc:* Robert Libott. (1:13) Programmer set in India, detailing an American diplomat's attempts to clear himself of murder charges by saving the life of a prince who has been targeted for assassination.

1484. Last Train from Gun Hill (Paramount/Bryna; 1959). *Cast:* Kirk Douglas, Anthony Quinn, Carolyn Jones, Earl Holliman, Brad Dexter, Brian Hutton, Ziva Rodann, Walter Sande, Bing Russell, Henry Wills, Val Avery, Lars Henderson, John R. Anderson, Len Hendry, William Newell, Sid Tomack, Dabbs Greer, Charles Stevens, Julius Tannen, Ken Becker, Mara Lynn, Courtland Shepard, Ty Hardin, Glenn Strange, Hank Mann, William Benedict, Mike Mahoney, Raymond McWalters, Jack Lomas, Tony Russo, Ricky William Kelman, Walter [Tony] Merrill, Eric Alden, Carl H. Saxe, Frank Hagney, Frank Carter, Bob Scott. *D:* John Sturges; *P:* Hal B. Wallis; *As. P:* Paul Nathan; *Sc:* James Poe, Edward Lewis (unc.). (1:34) (video) Hit adult western drama of a sheriff bent on bringing the son of a friend to justice. The former raped and murdered the sheriff's Indian wife. Based on the story "Showdown" by Les Crutchfield. Filmed on location in Arizona in Technicolor and VistaVision.

1485. The Last Wagon (20th Century-Fox; 1956). *Cast:* Richard Widmark, Felicia Farr, Susan Kohner, Tommy Rettig (final film—to TV's *Lassie*), Stephanie Griffin, Ray Stricklyn, Nick Adams, Carl Benton Reid, Douglas Kennedy, George Mathews, James Drury, Ken Clark, Timothy Carey, Juney Ellis, Abel Fernandez. *D:* Delmer Daves; *P:* William B. Hawks; *St:* Gwen [Bagni] Gielgud; *Sc:* James Edward Grant, Daves, Gielgud. (1:39) Western drama of a man, wanted for murder, who leads the young survivors of a wagon train massacre to safety.

1486. Latin Lovers (MGM; 1953). *Cast:* Lana Turner, Ricardo Montalban (replacing Fernando Lamas), Louis Calhern, John Lund (replacing Michael Wilding), Jean Hagen, Beulah Bondi, Eduard Franz, Joaquin Garay, Robert Burton, Rita Moreno, Archer MacDonald, Dorothy Neumann, Beatrice Gray, Lois Kimbrell, Matt Moore, Gloria Noble, Lynn Sousa, Suzanne Alexander, Tristram Coffin, Melba Meredith, Paul Maxey. *D:* Mervyn LeRoy; *P:* Joe Pasternak; *St: & Sc:* Isobel Lennart; *Songs:* "Night and You," "Carlotta, You Gotta Be Mine," "A Little More of Your Amor," "Come to My Arms" and "I Had to Kiss You" Nicholas Brodzky, Leo Robin. (1:44) (video) Romance of an heiress in search of love in Rio de Janeiro. Technicolor.

1487. The Law and Jake Wade (MGM; 1958). *Cast:* Robert Taylor, Richard Widmark, Patricia Owens, Robert Middleton, Henry Silva, DeForest Kelley, Burt Douglas, Eddie Firestone. *D:* John Sturges; *P:* William Hawks; *Sc:* William Bowers. (1:26) (video) Western drama of an ex-outlaw and his fiancée abducted by his former partner who wants to know the whereabouts of hidden loot. Based on the 1956 novel by Marvin H. Albert, the critics favored it. MetroColor and CinemaScope.

1488. Law and Order (Universal-International; 1953). *Cast:* Ronald Reagan, Dorothy Malone, Preston Foster, Alex Nicol, Ruth Hampton, Russell Johnson, Barry Kelley, Chubby Johnson, Dennis Weaver, Jack Kelly, Valerie Jackson, Don Garner, Thomas Browne Henry, Richard Garrick, Gregg Barton, William O'Neal, Tristram Coffin, Mike Ragan [aka: Holly Bane], John Carpenter, Buddy Roosevelt, Richard Cutting, Britt Wood, Martin Garralaga, Wally Cassell, William Tannen, Jack Daly, James Stone, Harry Harvey, Ken MacDonald, William Gould, Jack Ingram, Ethan Laidlaw, Jimmy Gray, Edwin Parker, Watson Downs, Thor Holmes, Kermit Maynard, Victor Romito. *D:* Nathan Juran; *P:* John W. Rogers; *Adaptation:* Inez Cocke; *Sc:* John Bagni, Gwen Bagni, D. D. Beauchamp. (1:20) An ex-lawman moves to a new town to become a rancher, but finds the town in a state of lawlessness. Based on the 1930 novel *Saint Johnson* by W.R. Burnett, it was filmed three times previously by this studio, in 1932, 1940 and in 1937 as the serial *Wild West Days* with Johnny Mack Brown (who also starred in the '40 version). Technicolor.

1489. The Law and the Lady (MGM; 1951). *Cast:* Greer Garson, Michael Wilding (U.S. debut/dual role), Fernando Lamas, Marjorie Main, Hayden Rorke, Margalo Gillmore, Rhys Williams, Ralph Dumke, Natalie Schafer, Phyllis Stanley, Soledad Jimenez, Lalo Rios, Stanley Logan, Hugh Herbert, John Eldredge, Andre Charlot, Victor Sen Yung, Anna Q. Nilsson, Bess Flowers, Stuart Holmes, Betty Farrington, Nikki Justin, Richard Hale, Spencer Chan, Matt Moore. *D: & P:* Edwin H. Knopf (final film as director); *Sc:* Leonard Spigelgass, Karl Tunberg. (1:44) Caper drama of a duo set on pulling off a series of society jewelry heists. Based on the play by Frederick Lonsdale, it was filmed twice before under his title *The Last of Mrs. Cheyney* in 1929 and again in 1937. Remade in Germany in 1962 as *Frau Cheyney's Ende.*

1490. Law of the Badlands (RKO; 1950). *Cast:* Tim Holt, Richard Martin, Joan Dixon, Robert Livingston, Leonard Penn, Harry Woods, Larry Johns, Robert Bray, Kenneth MacDonald, John Cliff, Sam Lufkin, Danny Sands, Art Felix, Booger McCarthy. *D:* Lesley Selander; *P:* Herman Schlom; *St: & Sc:* Ed Earl Repp. (1:00) Two Texas Rangers pass themselves off as outlaws in an effort to infiltrate a gang of counterfeiters. Another of Holt's series westerns which originally ran on a double bill with *Hunt the Man Down* (q.v.).

1491. Law of the Panhandle (Monogram; 1950). *Cast:* Johnny Mack Brown, Jane Adams, Riley Hill, Marshall Reed, Myron Healey, Ted Adams, Lee Roberts, Carol Henry, Milburn Morante, Kermit Maynard, Bob Duncan, Boyd Stockman, George DeNormand, Tex Palmer, Ray Jones. *D:* Lewis Collins; *P:* Jerry Thomas; *St: & Sc:* Joseph Poland. (0:55) Series western of a cowboy who intervenes in the schemes of landgrabbers with the knowledge of the coming railroad.

1492. The Law vs. Billy the Kid (Columbia; 1954). *Cast:* Scott Brady (Billy the Kid), Betta St. John, James Griffith (Pat Garrett), Alan Hale, Jr., Paul Cavanagh, William "Bill" Phillips, Benny Rubin, Steve Darrell, George Berkeley, William Tannen, Richard H. Cutting, Frank Sully, William Fawcett, Martin Garralaga, Robert Griffin, John Cliff, Otis Garth. *D:* William Castle; *P:* Sam Katzman; *St: & Sc:* John T. Williams. (1:13) Western (which blends fact and fiction) of the legendary outlaw and the lawman who silenced his gun forever. Originally ran on a double bill with *Pushover* (q.v.). Technicolor.

1493. The Lawless (Paramount/Pine-Thomas; 1950). *Cast:* Macdonald Carey, Gail Russell, John(ny) Sands, John Hoyt, Lee Patrick, Lalo Rios, Maurice Jara, Walter Reed, Argentina Brunetti, Guy Anderson, William Edmunds, Gloria Winters, John Davis, Martha Hyer, Frank Fenton, Paul Harvey, Felipe Turich, Noel Reyburn, Ian MacDonald, Tab Hunter (film debut), Russ Conway, James Bush, Julia Faye, Howard Negley, Gordon Nelson, Frank Ferguson, Ray Hyke, Pedro de Cordoba, Robert B. Williams, John Murphy. *D:* Joseph Losey; *P:* William H. Pine, William C. Thomas; *Sc:* Geoffrey Homes [Daniel Mainwaring—based on his book]. (1:23) Melodrama of racial prejudice against Spanish-American fruit pickers in a small California town. (G.B. title: *The Dividing Line*)

1494. The Lawless Breed (Universal-International; 1952). *Cast:* Rock Hudson (starring debut/John Wesley Hardin), Julia [Julie] Adams, John McIntire, Mary Castle, Hugh O'Brian, Forrest Lewis, Lee Van Cleef, Tom Fadden, William Pullen, Glenn Strange, Dennis Weaver, Dick Wessel, Richard Garland, Race Gentry (film debut/Hardin as a young man), Carl Pitti, Ned Davenport, Robert Anderson (Wild Bill Hickok), Stephen Chase, Emory Parnell, George Wallace, Edward Earle, Paul "Tiny" Newlan, Francis Ford, I. Stanford Jolley, Buddy Roosevelt, Ethan Laidlaw, Stanley Blystone, Wheaton Chambers, Tom Jackson, Michael Ansara, Gertrude Graner, Charles B.V. Miller, Bobbie Hoy. *D:* Raoul Walsh; *P: & St:* William Alland; *Sc:* Bernard Gordon. (1:23) Fact and fiction in this acclaimed western which relates events in the life of gunman John Wesley Hardin. Based in part on the 1937 book *They Died With Their Boots On* by Thomas Ripley. Technicolor.

1495. Lawless Cowboys (Monogram/Frontier Pictures; 1951). *Cast:* Whip Wilson, Fuzzy Knight, Jim Bannon, Pamela Duncan, Lee Roberts, Lane Bradford, I. Stanford Jolley, Bruce Edwards, Marshall Reed, Ace Malloy, Stanley Price, Richard Emory. *D:* Lewis Collins; *P:* Vincent M. Fennelly; *St: & Sc:* Maurice Tombragel. (0:58) Whip Wilson series western with a rodeo theme.

1496. The Lawless Eighties (Republic/Ventura; 1957). *Cast:* Buster Crabbe, John Smith, Marilyn Saris, Ted de Corsia, Anthony Caruso, John Doucette, Frank Ferguson, Sheila Bromley, Walter Reed, Robert "Buzz" Henry, Will J. White, Bob Swan. *D:* Joseph Kane; *P:* Rudy Ralston; *Sc:* Kenneth Gamet. (1:10) B budget western of a gunman who aids a circuit rider, beaten by the same outlaws who have also been roughing up local Indians. Based on the 1948 book *Brother Van* by Alson Jesse Smith. Naturama.

1497. The Lawless Rider (United Artists/Royal West; 1954). *Cast:* John Carpenter, Frankie Darro, Douglass Dumbrille, Frank "Red" Carpenter, Noel Neill, Kenne Duncan, Weldon Bascom, Rose Bascom, Bud Osborne, Bill Coontz, Tap Canutt, Roy Canada, Hank Caldwell & His Saddle Kings, Lou Roberson, Bill Chaney. *D:* Yakima Canutt; *P:* John Carpenter, Alex Gordon; *As.P:* Edward D. Wood, Jr.; *St: & Sc:* Carpenter; *Songs:* "Thinking of You" Marguerite McFarlane. (1:12) A U.S. marshal dons the guise of a wanted gunman in order to capture cattle thieves.

1498. A Lawless Street (Columbia/Scott-Brown Prods.; 1955). *Cast:* Randolph Scott, Angela Lansbury, Warner Anderson, Jean Parker, Wallace Ford, John Emery, James Bell, Michael Pate, Don Megowan, Jeanette Nolan, Ruth Donnelly, Frank Hagney, Frank Ferguson, Reed Howes, Jay Lawrence, Harry Tyler, Guy Teague, Peter Ortiz, Harry Antrim, Hal K. Dawson, Stanley Blystone, Edwin Chandler, Barry Brooks, Pat Collins, Don Carlos, Frank Scannell, Charles Williams, Kermit Maynard, Jack Perrin. *D:* Joseph H. Lewis; *P:* Harry Joe Brown, Randolph Scott; *Sc:* Kenneth Gamet. (1:18) (video) Western drama of a marshal's dilemma in cleaning up the town of Medicine Bend. Based on the 1933 novel *Marshal of Medicine Bend* by Brad Ward. Technicolor.

1499. Lay That Rifle Down (Republic; 1955). *Cast:* Judy Canova, Robert Lowery, Jil Jarmyn, Jacqueline de Wit, Richard Deacon, Robert Burton, James Bell, Leon Tyler, Tweeny Canova, Pierre Watkin, Marjorie Bennett, William Fawcett, Paul E. Burns, Edmund Cobb, Donald MacDonald, Mimi Gibson, Rudy Lee. *D:* Charles Lamont; *P:* Sidney Picker; *St: & Sc:* Barry Shipman; *Songs:* "I'm Glad I Was Born on My Birthday," "Sleepy Serenade," "The Continental Correspondence Charm School" Donald Kahn, Jack Elliott. (1:11) (video) Rural comedy of a female hotel worker in a small southern town who dreams of wealth.

1500. Leadville Gunslinger (Republic; 1952). *Cast:* Allan Lane, Eddy Waller, Grant

Withers, Elaine Riley, Roy Barcroft, Richard Crane, I. Stanford Jolley, Kenneth MacDonald, Mickey Simpson, Art Dillard, Ed Hinton, Wesley Hudman, Black Jack (horse). *D: & P:* Harry Keller; *St: & Sc:* M. Coates Webster. (0:54) "Rocky Lane" series entry of a U.S. marshal who comes to town, assigned to put a notorious outlaw gang out of business. Originally ran as a second feature on a double bill with Judy Canova's *Oklahoma Annie* (q.v.).

1501. The Leather Saint (Paramount; 1956). *Cast:* Paul Douglas, John Derek, Jody Lawrence, Cesar Romero, Ernest Truex, Richard Shannon, Ricky Vera, Thomas Browne Henry, Lou Nova, Robert Cornthwaite, Edith Evanson, Baynes Barron, Mary Benoit, Bill Baldwin, Courtland Shepard, Ralph Montgomery, Estelle Etterre, Jan Bradley, Babette Baine, Richard Bender, Cheryl Callaway, Edward G. Pagett, Raymond Winston, Donald Wittenberg, Bill Meader, Lawrence A. Williams. *D:* Alvin Ganzer; *P:* Norman Retchin; *St: & Sc:* Retchin, Ganzer. (1:26) Drama of a clergyman who takes to the boxing ring to raise money for polio victims. VistaVision.

1502. Leave It to the Marines (Lippert/Tom Prods.; 1951). *Cast:* Sid Melton, Mara Lynn, Gregg Martell, Ida Moore, Sam Flint, Douglas Evans, Margia Dean, Richard Monohan, William Haade, Jack George, Paul Bryar, Ezelle Poule, Will Orleans, Richard Farmer, Jimmy Cross. *D:* Sam Newfield; *P:* Sigmund Neufeld; *St: & Sc:* Orville H. Hampton. (1:06) Low budget comedy of what happens when a man goes for a marriage license, but by mistake enlists in the marine corps.

1503. The Left-Handed Gun (Warner/Harroll; 1958). *Cast:* Paul Newman (Billy the Kid), Lita Milan, John Dehner (Pat Garrett), Hurd Hatfield, James Congdon (Charlie Boudre), James Best (Tom Folliard), Colin Keith-Johnston (John Tunstall), John Dierkes, Bob Anderson, Wally Brown, Ainslie Pryor, Martin Garralaga, Denver Pyle, Nestor Paiva, Robert Foulk, Paul Smith, Jo Summers, Anne Barton. *D:* Arthur Penn (directorial debut); *P:* Fred Coe (first film); *Sc:* Leslie Stevens. (1:42) (video) Acclaimed offbeat western with a psychological bent of Billy the Kid out for revenge on the men who killed his friend, John Tunstall. Adapted from the TV play *The Death of Billy the Kid* by Gore Vidal that originally aired on Philco Playhouse in 1955. The film was particularly popular with European audiences.

1504. The Left Hand of God (20th Century–Fox; 1955). *Cast:* Humphrey Bogart, Gene Tierney, Lee J. Cobb, Agnes Moorehead, E.G. Marshall, Jean Porter, Carl Benton Reid, Victor Sen Yung, Phillip Ahn, Benson Fong, Richard Cutting, Peter Chong, Leon Lontoc, Don Forbes, Noel Toy, Marie Tsien, Stephen Wong, Sophie Chin, George Chan, Walter Soo Hoo, Henry S. Quan, Doris Chung, Moy Ming, Georgia Lee, Beal Wong, Stella Lynn, Robert Burton, Soo Yong, May Lee. *D:* Edward Dmytryk; *P:* Buddy Adler; *Sc:* Alfred Hayes. (1:27) (video) Hit adventure-drama of a former American fighter pilot living in China. Donning the robes of a priest, he takes up residence in a small Chinese village and falls for a mission worker. Based on the 1951 novel by William E. Barrett, it was photographed in DeLuxe color and CinemaScope.

1505. Legend of the Lost (United Artists/Batjac–Robert Haggaig–Dear; 1957). *Cast:* John Wayne, Sophia Loren, Rossano Brazzi, Kurt Kasznar, Sonia Moser, Angela Portaluri, Ibrahim El Hadish. *D: & P:* Henry Hathaway; *St: & Sc:* Robert Presnell, Jr., Ben Hecht. (1:49) (video) Drama of three people crossing the Sahara in search of a lost city and hidden treasure. A co-production between the U.S.A., Panama and Italy. Technicolor and technirama. (aka: *Timbuctu*)

1506. The Legend of Tom Dooley (Columbia/Shpetner Prods.; 1959). *Cast:* Michael Landon (title role), Jo Morrow, Jack Hogan, Richard Rust, Dee Pollock, Ken Lynch, Howard Wright, Ralph Moody, John Cliff, Cheerio Meredith, Gary Hunley, Anthony Jochim, Jeff Morris, Jason Johnson, Joe Yrigoyen, Sandy Sanders, Juney Ellis, Maudie Prickett. *D:* Ted Post; *P:-St: & Sc:* Stan Shpetner. (1:19) (video) Western of three Confederates in 1865 who rob a Union stagecoach, kill two soldiers and then find the war has been over for a week. Based on the popular folk ballad of the day, "Tom Dooley" as sung by The Kingston Trio. Originally ran on the top of a double bill with *Woman Eater*, a British horror production.

1507. Legion of the Doomed (Allied Artists/William F. Broidy Pictures; 1959). *Cast:* Bill Williams, Dawn Richard, Anthony Caruso, Kurt Kreuger, Tom Hubbard, John Damler, Rush Williams, George Baxter, Saul Gorss, Joseph Abdullah, Hal Gerard. *D:* Thor Brooks; *P:* William F. Broidy; *As.P:* Erwin Yessin; *St: & Sc:* Tom Hubbard, Fred Eggers. (1:15) Low budget action-adventure of the French foreign legion and an American recruit who discovers his commanding officer is in league with native dissidents to overthrow the French.

1508. The Lemon Drop Kid (Paramount; 1951). *Cast:* Bob Hope (title role), Marilyn Maxwell (Brainy Baxter), Lloyd Nolan (Charley), Jane Darwell (Nellie Thursday), Andrea King (Stella), Fred Clark (Moose Moran), Jay C. Flippen (Straight Flush), William Frawley (Gloomy Willie), Harry Bellaver (Sam the Surgeon), Sid Melton (Little Louie), Ben Welden (Singin' Solly), Ida Moore (Bird Lady), Charles Cooley (Goomba), Society Kid Hogan (himself), Harry Shannon (Policeman John), Bernard Szold (Honest Harry), Richard Karlan (Maxie), Almira Sessions (Mrs. Santoro), Francis Pierlot (Henry Regan), Fred Zendar (Benny Southstreet), Slim Gault (Prof. Murdock), Helen Brown (Ellen), Fred Graff (Pimlico Pete), Jim Hayward (George), Douglas Spencer (thin Santa Claus), Harry O. Tyler (Santa Claus), Ray Cooke (Willie), Roy Gordon, Stanley Andrews, Tor Johnson, Mary Murphy (film debut), Bill Varga, Jean Whitney, Tommy Ivo, Sid Tomack, Jack Kruschen, John Doucette, Bill Sheehan. *D:* Sidney Lanfield, Frank Tashlin (debut/unc.); *P:* Robert L. Welch; *St:* Edmund Beloin, Damon Runyon; *Sc:* Edmund Hartmann, Robert O'Brien, Frank Tashlin; *Additional dialogue:* Irving Elinson; *Songs:* "Silver Bells," "It Doesn't Cost a Dime to Dream," "They Obviously Want Me to Sing" Ray Evans, Jay Livingston. (1:31) (video/laserdisc) Comedy of a racetrack tipster with a penchant for picking losers who owes a bundle to a gangster and must pay up or else. Sort of a remake of the 1934 production by this studio, it became one of the 23 top-grossing films of 1950-51. The song "Silver Bells" became a big hit and a Christmas standard.

1509. Les Girls (MGM/Sol C. Siegel Prods.; 1957). *Cast:* Gene Kelly (Barry Nichols), Mitzi Gaynor (Joy Henderson), Kay Kendall (Lady Wren), Taina Elg (Angele Ducros), Jacques Bergerac (Pierre Ducros), Leslie Phillipe (Sir Gerald Wren), Patrick Macnee (Sir Percy), Stephen Vercoe (Mr. Outward), Luisa Triana (flamenco dancer), Lilyan Chauvin (dancer), Henry Daniell (judge), Philip Tonge, Owen McGiveney, Francis Ravel, Adrienne D'Ambricourt, Maurice Marsac, Gil Stuart, Cyril Delevanti, George Navarro, Marcel de la Brosse, Nestor Paiva, Alberto Morin, Maya van Horn, George Davis, Genevieve Pasques, Dick Alexander. *D:* George Cukor; *P:* Sol C. Siegel; *As.P:* Saul Chaplin; *Sc:* John Patrick; *ASD:* (AAN-color) William A. Horning, Gene Allen (art directors), Edwin B. Willis, Richard Pefferle (sets); *Costumes:* (AA-color) Orry-Kelly; *Sound:* (AAN) Dr. Wesley C. Miller; *Choreography:* Jack Cole; *Songs:* "Ladies in Waiting," "Les Girls," "Flower Song," "Ça, C'est L'Amour," "You're Just Too, Too," "Why Am I So Gone About That Gal?" Cole Porter. (1:54) (video/laserdisc) Via flashbacks, three dancers relay their earlier relationships with their choreographer. A sophisticated romantic musical which marked Cole Porter's final score written for a film. Based on the novel by Vera Caspary, it became one of the 26 top-grossing films of 1957-58. *Film Daily* and the *New York Times* placed it at #6 and #8 respectively on their "10 Best" lists. MetroColor and CinemaScope. Note: Kelly's final film for MGM until 1974.

1510. Les Misérables (20th Century-Fox; 1952). *Cast:* Michael Rennie, Debra Paget, Robert Newton, Edmund Gwenn, Sylvia Sidney, Cameron Mitchell, Elsa Lanchester, James Robertson Justice, Joseph Wiseman, Rhys Williams, Florence Bates, Merry Anders, John Rogers, Charles Keane, John Dierkes, John Costello, Norma Varden, William Cottrell, Queenie Leonard, Bobby Hyatt, Sanders Clark, Patsy Weil, Jean Vachon, Sean McClory, June Hillman, James Craven, Lester Matthews, Jimmy Moss, Ian Wolfe, Alfred Linder, John O'Malley, Leslie Denison, Alex Frazer, Jack Raine, John Sherman, Dayton Lummis, Victor Wood, Robert Adler, Victor Romito, Charlotte Austin, Olaf Hytten, Frank Baker, Michael Granger, Jerry Miley, Jack Baston, Mary Forbes, Moyna Magill, Tudor Owen, Leonard Carey, William Dalzell, Charles Fitzsimmons, Roger Anderson. *D:* Lewis Milestone; *P:* Fred Kohlmar; *Sc:* Richard Murphy. (1:45) Victor Hugo's classic tale of a man's persecution after stealing a loaf of bread. Other filmed versions of the story include: 1909 (U.S.A.), 1913 (France), 1917 (U.S.A.), 1923 (France), 1929 (U.S.A.) as *The Bishop's Candlesticks*, 1934 (France), 1935 (U.S.A.), 1946 (Italy), 1952 (Italy), 1957 (France-Germany), 1978 as a British TV movie, 1982 (France), a 1995 French variation on the story and a 1998 re-do. In 1987 it became a stage musical in Great Britain and later took Broadway by storm.

1511. Let's Dance (Paramount; 1950). *Cast:* Betty Hutton, Fred Astaire, Roland Young, Ruth Warrick, Shepperd Strudwick, Lucile Watson, Barton MacLane, Melville Cooper,

George Zucco, Gregory Moffett, Harold Huber, Peggy Badley, Virginia Toland, Sayre Dearing, Ida Moore, Nana Bryant, Boyd Davis, Bobby Barber, Herbert Vigran, Rolfe Sedan, Ralph Peters, Paul A. Pierce, Eric Alden, Milton Delugg (himself), Harry Woods, Chester Conklin, Major Sam Harris, Bess Flowers, Marion Gray, Peggy O'Neill. *D:* Norman Z. McLeod; *P:* Robert Fellows; *Sc:* Allan Scott, Dane Lussier; *Songs:* "Tunnel of Love," "The Hyacinth," "Piano Dance," "Jack and the Beanstalk," "Can't Stop Talking," "Oh, Them Dudes" and "Why Fight the Feeling?" Frank Loesser. (1:51) (video/laserdisc) Musical of a woman, widowed in the war, involved in a custody fight for her son with her late husband's grandmother. A box office hit, it was suggested by the story "Little Boy Blue" by Maurice Zolotow. Technicolor.

1512. Let's Do It Again (Columbia; 1953). *Cast:* Jane Wyman, Ray Milland, Aldo Ray, Valerie Bettis, Leon Ames, Tom Helmore, Karin Booth, Mary Treen, Dick Wessel, Kathryn Givney, Herbert Heyes, Maurice Stein, Frank Remley, Don Rice, Don Gibson, Bob Hopkins, Anthony DeMario, Herb Vigran, Walter Clinton, Frank Connor, Major Sam Harris, Leoda Richards, Howard Negley, Douglas Evans, Joey Ray. *D:* Alexander Hall; *P:* Oscar Saul; *Sc:* Mary Loos, Richard Sale; *Songs:* "Call of the Wild," "Give Me a Man Who Makes Music," "There Are Things I Remember," "Anyone," "Takin' a Slow Burn" and "Anyone but You" (sung by Dick Haymes) Leonard Lee, Ned Washington. (1:35) A Technicolor musical-comedy remake of *The Awful Truth* (1937) based on the play of that name by Arthur Richman. Concerns a divorced couple and how they go out of their way to mess up each other's current relationships.

1513. Let's Go Navy! (Monogram; 1951). *Cast:* Leo Gorcey, Huntz Hall, Allen Jenkins, Billie Benedict, David Gorcey, Buddy Gorman, Bernard Gorcey, Charlita, Tom Neal, Paul Harvey, Emory Parnell, Richard Benedict, Douglas Evans, Frank Jenks, Tom Kennedy, Dorothy Ford, Harry Lauter, Dave Willock, Peter Mamakos, Jonathan Hale, Ray Walker, George Offerman, Jr., Paul Bryar, Richard Monohan, William Lechner, Mike Lally, Russ Conway, Harry Strang, William Vincent, Lee Graham, Pat Gleason, George Eldredge, William Hudson, Bob Peoples, John Close, Emil Sitka, Ray Dawe, Murray Alper, Jimmy Cross, Bill Chandler, Don Gordon, Neyle Morrow, Joey Ray. *D:* William Beaudine; *P:* Jan Grippo; *Sc:* & *St:* Max Adams; *Additional dialogue:* Bert Lawrence. (1:08) The "Bowery Boys" join the U.S. Navy in this popular entry in the comedy series and round up a gang of crooks passing themselves off as sailors.

1514. Let's Make It Legal (20th Century-Fox; 1951). *Cast:* Claudette Colbert, Macdonald Carey, Zachary Scott, Barbara Bates, Robert Wagner, Marilyn Monroe, Frank Cady, Jim Hayward, Carol Savage, Paul Gerrits, Betty Jane Brown, Vici Raaf, Joan Fisher, Kathleen Freeman, Renny McEvoy, Wilson Wood, Roger Moore, James Magill, Beverly Thompson, Abe Dinovitch, Frank Sully, Jack Mather, Michael Ross, Harry Denny, Harry Harvey, Sr., Ralph Sanford. *D:* Richard Sale; *P:* Robert Bassler; *St:* Mortimer Braus; *Sc:* F. Hugh Herbert, I.A.L. Diamond. (1:17) (video) Comedy about a woman who divorces her husband of twenty years because of his compulsive gambling. Taking up with an old flame who has come back to town does not set well with her ex.

1515. Let's Rock! (Columbia; 1958). *Cast:* Julius LaRosa, Phyllis Newman, Conrad Janis, Joy Harmon, Fred Kareman, Peter Paull, Charles Shelander, Harold Gary, Jerry Hackady, Wink Martindale (himself), Ron McLewdon, Ned Wertimer, Tony Brande, Paul Anka, Della Reese, Roy Hamilton, Danny and the Juniors, The Royal Teens, The Tyrones. *D:* & *P:* Harry Foster; *St:* & *Sc:* Hal Hackady; *Songs:* "I'll Be Waiting There for You" (by Anka), "Lonelyville" Walter Marks, Hal Hackady (by Reese); "Here Comes Love" Jessie Stone; "Secret Path to Love" Charles Singleton, Johnny Woods (both by Hamilton); "At the Hop" (by Danny and the Juniors), "Short Shorts" (by Royal Teens), "Blastoff" Ollie Jones (by Tyrones), "There Are Times," "Casual," "Two Perfect Strangers" Don Gohman, Hackady; "Crazy, Crazy Party" Stone, Paul Winley (all by LaRosa) and "All Love Broke Loose" Singleton, Lee Cathy (by Martindale). (1:19) Drama about a singer of ballads who resists changing his style to the newly emerged rock 'n' roll. (G.B. title: *Keep It Cool*)

Letter from Korea (G.B. title) *see* **A Yank in Korea**

A Letter to Three Husbands *see* **Three Husbands**

1516. The Lieutenant Wore Skirts (20th Century–Fox; 1956). *Cast:* Tom Ewell, Sheree

North, Rita Moreno, Rick Jason, Les Tremayne, Alice Reinheart, Gregory Walcott, Jean Willes, Sylvia Lewis, Edward Platt, Jacqueline Fontaine, Arthur Q. Bryan, Paul Glass, Keith Vincent, Kathy Marlowe, Joe Locke, Bette Arlen, Franklin James, Maury Hill, Janice Carroll, Dorothy Gordon, Ralph Sanford, Pat Marshall, Helene Marshall, Sam Bagley, Marjorie Stapp, Michael Ross, Marianne Candace Kelly, Leslie Parrish, Pat McMahon, Suzanne Ridgeway. *D:* Frank Tashlin; *P:* Buddy Adler; *St:* Albert Beich; *Sc:* Tashlin, Beich; *Song:* "Rock Around the Island" Ken Darby. (1:38) An ex–WAC is called to active duty and her television-writer husband accompanies her. Comic situations abound as he tries to cope with the change.

Life After Dark *see* **Girls of the Night**

1517. Life Begins at 17 (Columbia/Clover Prods.; 1958). *Cast:* Mark Damon, Dorothy Johnson, Edward [Edd] Byrnes, Ann Doran, Hugh Sanders, Luana Anders, Cathy O'Neill, George Eldredge, Tommy Ivo, Bob Dennis, Robert Moechel, Maurice Manson. *D:* Arthur Dreifuss; *P:* Sam Katzman; *St:* & *Sc:* Richard Baer. (1:15) In this low budget teen soaper, a girl feigns pregnancy to get her boyfriend back.

1518. A Life in the Balance (20th Century–Fox/Panoramic; 1955). *Cast:* Ricardo Montalban, Anne Bancroft, Lee Marvin, Jose Perez, Rudolfo Acosta, Carlos Musquiz, Jorge Trevino, Jose Torvay, Eva Calvo, Fanny Schiller, Tamara Garina, Pascual G. Pena, Antonio Carvajal. *D:* Harry Horne; *P:* Leonard Goldstein; *St:* George Simenon; *Sc:* Robert Presnell, Jr., Leo Townsend. (1:14) Thriller (filmed on location in Mexico City) of a psychotic killer who murders people he considers sinners. When a young boy's father is charged with one of the murders, the boy sets out to make sure the police get the real killer, as the youth witnessed the murder his father was charged with.

1519. A Life of Her Own (MGM; 1950). *Cast:* Lana Turner, Ray Milland, Tom Ewell, Louis Calhern, Ann Dvorak, Barry Sullivan, Jean Hagen, Phyllis Kirk, Sara Haden, Margaret Phillips, Hermes Pan, Carol Brannan, Beth Douglas, Roberta Johnson, Alice Wallace, Bunny Waters, Pat Davies, Dorothy Abbott, Bridget Carr, Charlene Hardey, Marlene Hoyt, Tom Seidel, Hilda Plowright, Elizabeth Flournoy, Dorothy Tree, Robert Emmett Keane, Richard Anderson, Wilson Wood, Harry Barris, Beverly Garland, Whit Bissell, Kathleen Freeman, Gertrude Graner, Major Sam Harris, Frankie Darro, Queenie Leonard, Paul Kramer, Kenny Garcia, Arthur Loew, Jr., Peter Thompson, Walter McGrail, Joan Valerie, Kerry O'Day, Carol Brewster, Beverly Thompson, Lee Lynn, Meredith Leeds, Geraldine Wall, Percy Helton, Sarah Padden, Kenne Duncan, Maura Murphy. *D:* George Cukor; *P:* Voldemar Vetluguin; *Sc:* Isobel Lennart. (1:48) (video) Unsuccessful drama of a model with a love vs. career dilemma. Based on the 1935 short story "Abiding Vision" by Rebecca West.

The Light Fantastic (G.B. title) *see* **Love Is Better Than Ever**

1520. The Light in the Forest (Buena Vista/Walt Disney Prods.; 1958). *Cast:* James MacArthur, Carol Lynley (film debut), Fess Parker, Wendell Corey, Joanne Dru, Jessica Tandy, Joseph Calleia, John McIntire, Rafael Campos, Frank Ferguson, Norman Fredric, Marian Seldes, Stephen Bekassy, Sam Buffington. *D:* Herschel Daugherty (a TV director in his feature film debut); *Sc:* Lawrence Edward Watkin; *Songs:* Title song (Paul J. Smith–Gil George); "I Asked My Love a Favor" (Smith-Watkin). (1:33) (video) Disney chose Conrad Richter's 1954 novel for this family oriented drama. Set in 1764, a white youth is returned to his parents after spending most of his life being raised by Delaware Indians. In Technicolor, location filming took place in Tennessee with the Indian camp scenes recreated in California.

1521. The Light Touch (MGM, 1951). *Cast:* Stewart Granger, Pier Angeli, George Sanders, Kurt Kasznar (film debut), Joseph Calleia, Larry Keating, Rhys Williams, Norman Lloyd, Mike Mazurki, Hans Conried, Renzo Cesana, Robert Jefferson, Aram Katcher, Andre Charisse, Gladys Holland, Louise Colombet, George Dee, Paul de Corday, Robert Conte, Louis Velarde, Albert Ben Astar. *D:* & *Sc:* Richard Brooks; *P:* Pandro S. Berman; *St:* Jed Harris, Tom Reed. (1:50) Box office receipts didn't make up for the production costs. This filmed in Europe crime drama is of an art thief and his girl, who unknowingly gets involved in his schemes.

1522. Lightning Guns (Columbia; 1950). *Cast:* Charles Starrett, Smiley Burnette, Gloria Henry, Edgar Dearing, Jock [Mahoney] O'Mahoney, George Chesebro, William Norton Bailey, Chuck Roberson, Joel Friedkin, Raymond

Bond, Ken Houchins, Frank Griffin, Merrill McCormack, Billy Williams. *D:* Fred F. Sears; *P:* Colbert Clark; *St:* Bill Milligan; *Sc:* Victor Arthur. (0:55) In this "Durango Kid" series western with three songs, a future dam site is the object of outlaw raids. (G.B. title: *Taking Sides*) Originally ran on a double bill with *Revenue Agent* (q.v.).

1523. Lightning Strikes Twice (Warner; 1951). *Cast:* Richard Todd, Ruth Roman, Mercedes McCambridge, Zachary Scott, Frank Conroy, Kathryn Givney, Rhys Williams, Darryl Hickman, Nacho Galindo. *D:* King Vidor; *P:* Henry Blanke; *Sc:* Lenore Coffee. (1:31) Melodramatic mystery-thriller of a man who returns to his home town to find out just who did murder his wife, the crime for which he was tried, but freed, because of a hung jury. Based on the 1940 novel *A Man Without Friends* by Margaret Echard.

Lights Out (G.B. title) *see* **Bright Victory**

1524. Li'l Abner (Paramount/Panama-Frank Prods.; 1959). *Cast:* Peter Palmer (title role), Leslie Parrish (Daisy Mae), Stubby Kaye (Marryin' Sam), Howard St. John (Gen. Bullmoose), Julie Newmar (Stupefyin' Jones), Stella Stevens (Appasionata Von Climax), Billie Hayes (Mammy Yokum), Joe E. Marks (Pappy Yokum), Bern Hoffman (Earthquake McGoon), Al Nestor (Evil Eye Fleagle), Robert Strauss (Romeo Scragg), William Lanteau (Available Jones), Ted Thurston (Sen. Jack S. Phogbound), Carmen Alvarez (Moonbeam McSwine), Alan Carney (Mayor Dawgmeat), Stanley Simmons (Rasmussen T. Finsdale), Diki Lerner (Lonesome Polecat), Joe Ploski (Hairless Joe), Valerie Harper & Beth Howland (chorus girls) and Jubilation T. Cornpone (statue). *D:* Melvin Frank; *P:* Norman Panama; *Sc:* Panama, Frank; *Music:* (AAN) Nelson Riddle, Joseph J. Lilley; *Songs:* "A Typical Day," "If I Had My Druthers," "Jubilation T. Cornpone," "Don't That Take the Rag Offen the Bush," "There's Room Enuff for Us," "Namely You," "The Country's in the Very Best of Hands," "Unnecessary Town," "I'm Past My Prime," "Otherwise," "Put 'em Back the Way They Wuz," "The Matrimonial Stomp," "In Society," "Sadie Hawkins' Day Ballet" and "Oh Happy Day" Gene DePaul, Johnny Mercer. (1:53) (video) The residents of Dogpatch learn that the U.S. government wants to wipe out the whole area with an A-bomb test because the latter considers it to be the most expendable area in the U.S. A critically acclaimed adaptation of the hit 1956 stage production with stage actors recreating their roles, with the exception of Parrish who replaced Edie Adams, Stevens who replaced Tina Louise and Hayes who replaced Charlotte Rae. Based on characters created in the comic strip by Al Capp. Technicolor and VistaVision.

1525. Lili (MGM; 1953). *Cast:* Leslie Caron (AAN + a "Best Actress" nomination at the British Academy Awards/Lili Daurier), Mel Ferrer (Paul Berthalet), Jean Pierre Aumont (Marc), Zsa Zsa Gabor (Rosalie), Kurt Kasznar (Jacquot), Amanda Blake (Peach Lips), Ralph Dumke (Monsieur Carvier), Wilton Graff (Monsieur Tonit), George Baxter (Monsieur Erique), Dorothy Jarnac (specialty dancer), Arthur Mendez, Dick Lerner, Frank Radcliffe, Lars Hensen (specialty dancers), Alex Gerry, Eda Reis Merin, George Davis, Reginald Simpson, Mitchell Lewis, Fred Walton, Richard Grayson. *D:* (AAN) Charles Walters; *P:* Edwin H. Knopf; *Sc:* (AAN) Helen Deutsch; *Cin:* (AAN) Robert Planck; *ASD:* (AAN) Cedric Gibbons, Paul Groesse (art directors), Edwin B. Willis, Arthur Krams (sets); *Music:* (AA) Bronislau Kaper; *Choreography:* Charles Walters, Dorothy Jarnac; *Song:* "Hi-Lili, Hi-Lo" Kaper, Deutsch. (1:21) (video) Hit musical of a French orphan, a carnival and a puppeteer who can only express himself through his puppets. Based on the story "The Man Who Hated People" by Paul Gallico which appeared in *Saturday Evening Post*. The *New York Times* placed it at #2 on their "10 Best" list, while on the same lists of the NBR and *Film Daily* it placed #5 and #6 respectively. At the Cannes Film Festival it was voted "Best Entertainment Film." Technicolor.

1526. Limelight (United Artists/Celebrated Pictures; 1952). *Cast:* Charles Chaplin, Claire Bloom, Nigel Bruce, Sydney Chaplin (film debut), Buster Keaton, Norman Lloyd, Marjorie Bennett, Wheeler Dryden, Snub Pollard, Stapleton Kent, Leonard Mudie, Geraldine Chaplin (film debut), Michael Chaplin, Josephine Chaplin, Edna Purviance (final film—ret./bit), Charles Chaplin, Jr. (film debut). *D:-P:-St: & Sc:* Charles Chaplin. (2:25) (video) Drama of a has-been music hall comedian who saves a young ballerina from a suicide attempt, thus through her, regaining his self-confidence. Chaplin's final American film placed #3 on the "10 Best" list of the NBR and on the same list of the *New York Times* it placed #8. It was also in nomination at the British Academy Awards.

Note: This film won an Oscar in 1972 for "Best Original Dramatic Score" (which also includes the hit *Eternally*). The film was first seen in Los Angeles in 1972, sparking the Oscars for Chaplin, Raymond Rasch and Larry Russell.

1527. The Lineup (Columbia/Pajemer Prods.-Frank Cooper; 1957–58). *Cast:* Eli Wallach, Robert Keith, Warner Anderson, Richard Jaeckel, Mary La Roche, William Leslie, Emile Meyer, Marshall Reed, Raymond Bailey, Vaughn Taylor, Cheryl Callaway, Bert Holland, George Eldredge, Robert Bailey, Francis DeSales, Charles Stewart, Jack Carol, Dee Pollock, Chuck Courtney, Junius Matthews, Frank Tang, Clayton Post, Kay English, Al Merin, Billy Snyder, Bill Marsh, John Maxwell, Kathleen O'Malley, Jack Moyles. *D:* Don Siegel; *P:* Jaime Del Valle; *St: & Sc:* Stirling Silliphant. (1:26) Crime melodrama based on characters created by Lawrence Klee in the popular TV show of the same name. A police detective is searching for a kill-crazy hood who is after an illegal shipment of heroin. Fans of director Siegel give this film a minor cult status.

1528. The Lion and the Horse (Warner; 1952). *Cast:* Steve Cochran, Ray Teal, Bob Steele, Harry Antrim, Sherry Jackson, Billy Dix, George O'Hanlon, Ed Hinton, William Fawcett, House Peters, Jr., Lee Roberts, Lane Chandler, Charles Stevens, Jack Williams, Tom Tyler, Steve Peck, Frank Nelson (voice only), Wildfire the Wonder Horse. *D:* Louis King; *P:* Bryan Foy; *St: & Sc:* Crane Wilbur. (1:23) A family-oriented drama of a man and his beloved horse. The second film by this studio to be produced in WarnerColor, which is actually another name for Eastmancolor.

1529. The Lion Hunters (Monogram; 1951). *Cast:* Johnny Sheffield, Morris Ankrum, Ann E. Todd (final film—ret.), Douglas Kennedy, Robert "Smoki" Whitfield, Robert Davis, Woodrow [Woody] Strode. *D: & Sc:* Ford Beebe; *P:* Walter Mirisch. (1:15) (video) "Bomba the Jungle Boy" goes after a band of ruthless lion hunters. The 5th entry in this low budget adventure series, based on the "Bomba" books by Roy Rockwood. (G.B. title: *Bomba and the Lion Hunters*)

1530. A Lion Is in the Streets (Warner/Cagney Prods.; 1953). *Cast:* James Cagney, Barbara Hale, Anne Francis, Warner Anderson, John McIntire, Jeanne Cagney, Lon Chaney, Frank McHugh, Mickey Simpson, Larry Keating, Onslow Stevens, James Millican, Sara Haden, Ellen Corby, Roland Winters, Burt Mustin, Irene Tedrow, James Griffith, Fay Roope, Henry Kulky, Sarah Selby, William "Bill" Phillips, Sam McDaniel. *D:* Raoul Walsh; *P:* William Cagney; *Sc:* Luther Davis. (1:28) (video/laserdisc) Drama of a Louisiana swamp peddler who becomes a politician and sets his sights on the governorship of the state, becoming involved in political corruption. Based on the 1945 best-seller by Adria Locke Langley. Shades of Huey Long! Technicolor.

1531. Lisbon (Republic; 1956). *Cast:* Ray Milland, Maureen O'Hara, Claude Rains, Yvonne Furneaux, Francis Lederer, Percy Marmont (a British actor in his final film—ret.), Jay Novello, Edward Chapman, Harold Jamieson, Humberto Madeira. *D: & P:* Ray Milland; *St:* Martin Rackin; *Sc:* John Tucker Battle. (1:30) (video) Melodrama of a woman who hires another to kill her husband being held behind the Iron Curtain. Trucolor and Naturama.

1532. Little Big Horn (Lippert/Bali Films, Inc.; 1951). *Cast:* Lloyd Bridges, Marie Windsor, John Ireland, Reed Hadley, Jim Davis, Wally Cassell, Hugh O'Brian, Sheb Wooley, King Donovan, Rodd Redwing, Richard Emory, Jack [John] Pickard, Robert Sherwood, Larry Stewart, Richard Baxton, Barbara Woodell, Anne Warren, Ted Avery. *D: & Sc:* Charles Marquis Warren (directorial debut); *P:* Carl K. Hittleman; *St:* Harold Shumate; *Song:* "On the Little Big Horn" Stanley Adams, Maurice Sigler, Larry Stock. (1:26) (video) An offbeat western relating the defeat of General George A. Custer and his men in their last stand against the Cheyenne-Sioux Nation. (G.B. title: *The Fighting 7th*)

1533. Little Boy Lost (Paramount/Perlberg-Seaton; 1953). *Cast:* Bing Crosby (Bill Wainwright), Claude Dauphin (Pierre Verdier), Christian Fourcade (Jean), Gabrielle Dorziat (Mother Superior), Nicole Maurey (Lisa Garret), Colette Dereal (Nelly), Georgette Anys (Madame Quilleboeuf), Peter Baldwin (Lt. Walker), Gladys de Segonzac (Helene), Yola d'Avril (Madame Le Blanc), Bruce Payne, (Ronnie), Jean Del Val (Dr. Biroux), Ninon Straty (Suzanne Pitou), Jacques Gallo (Paul), Tina Glagoi (Sister Therese), Henri Letondal, Michael Moore, Adele St. Maur, Paul Magranville, Christiane Fourcade, Karin Vengay, Arthur Dulac. *D: & Sc:* George Seaton; *P:* William Perlberg. (1:35) (video) Sentimental drama of a reporter who returns to

France after World War II to find the son he has never seen. Notable as Crosby's first all-dramatic role, it was based on the 1949 novel by Marghanita Laski. Filmed on location in Paris, it took a #9 placement on the "10 Best" list of *Film Daily* and went on to become one of the 25 top-grossing films of 1953-54.

1534. Little Egypt (Universal-International; 1951). *Cast:* Mark Stevens, Rhonda Fleming, Nancy Guild, Charles Drake, Tom D'Andrea, Steven Geray, Minor Watson, Verna Felton, John Litel, Kathryn Givney, Dan Riss, Jack George, Ed Clark, John Gallaudet, Freeman Lusk, Fritz Feld, Leon Belasco. *D:* Frederick de Cordova; *P:* Jack Gross; *St:* Oscar Brodney; *Sc:* Brodney, Doris Gilbert; *Additional dialogue:* Lou Breslow. (1:22) Drama of a con job perpetrated on a tobacco tycoon at the 1893 Chicago Exposition. Technicolor. (G.B. title: *Chicago Masquerade*)

1535. The Little Fugitive (Joseph Burstyn, Inc./Little Fugitive Prod. Co.; 1953). *Cast:* Richie Andrusco (Joey), Ricky Brewster (Lennie), Winifred Cushing (the mother), Jay Williams (pony ride man), Will Lee (photographer), Charlie Moss (Harry), Tommy De Canio (Charlie). *D: & Sc:* Ray Ashley, Morris Engel, Ruth Orkin; *P:* Engel, Ashley; *St:* (AAN) Ashley, Engel, Orkin. (1:15) Acclaimed independent drama, with comic touches, of a young boy who flees to Coney Island when he is duped into believing he has killed his brother. The film received the "Silver Lion" at the Venice Film Festival and placed #8 on the "10 Best" list of the NBR.

1536. The Little Hut (MGM; 1957). *Cast:* Ava Gardner, Stewart Granger, David Niven, Finlay Currie, Walter Chiari, Jean Cadell, Henry Oscar, Jack Lambert, Viola Lyel, Jaron Yaltan. *D:* Mark Robson; *P:* Robson, F. Hugh Herbert; *Sc:* Herbert (final film—d. 1958); *Title song:* Eric Maschwitz, Marcell Stellman, Peggy Cochrane. (1:30) Comedy, with sexual innuendos toned down for the screen, of a woman, her husband and another man stranded on a desert island. English stage adaptation by Nancy Mitford from André Roussin's long-running French play. Eastmancolor.

1537. The Little Savage (20th Century-Fox/Associated Producers; 1959). *Cast:* Pedro Armendariz, Rodolfo Hoyos, Terry Rangno, Christiane Martel, Robert Palmer. *D:* Byron Haskin; *P:* Jack Leewood; *As.P:* Clarence Eurist; *Sc:* Eric Norden. (1:13) In this low budget production filmed in Mexico in cooperation with Sotomayor Productions, a pirate is left for dead on an island and nursed back to health by the young survivor of a shipwreck. Based on the 1877 book by Frederick Marryat, it ran on a double bill with *The Sad Horse* (q.v.). Regalscope.

1538. The Littlest Hobo (Allied Artists; 1958). *Cast:* Buddy Hart, Wendy Stuart, Carlyle Mitchell, Howard Hoffman, Robert Kline, Pat Bradley, Bill Coontz, Dorothy Johnson, William Marks, Pauline Moore, Larry Thor, Norman Barthold, London (dog), Fleecie (lamb). *D:* Charles R. Rondeau; *P:* Hugh M. Hooker; *As.P:* Forrest L. Royse; *St: & Sc:* Dorrell McGowan. (1:17) Family drama involving a stray German shepherd dog, a lamb saved from the slaughter, a little boy and the crippled daughter of the state's governor. It originally ran on a double bill with *Snowfire* (q.v.).

1539. The Littlest Outlaw (Buena Vista/Walt Disney Prods.; 1955). *Cast:* Pedro Armendariz, Joseph Calleia, Rudolfo Acosta, Andres Velásquez, Pepe Ortiz (matador/himself), Laila Maley, Gilberto Gonzales, José Torvay, Ferrusquilla, Enriqueta Zazueta, Señor Lee, Carlos Ortigoza, Margarito Luna, Ricardo Gonzales, Maria Eugenia, Pedrito Vargas. *D:* Roberto Galvaldon; *Ex.P:* Walt Disney; *P: & St:* Larry Lansburgh; *Sc:* Bill Walsh. (1:15) (video) A small Mexican boy steals a horse and runs away with it, rather than see it killed by the owner whose daughter was injured while riding the animal. Filmed on location in Mexico. Technicolor.

1540. Live Fast, Die Young (Universal-International/B.R.K., Inc.; 1958). *Cast:* Mary Murphy, Norma Eberhardt, Sheridan Comerate, Michael Connors, Carol Varga, Jay Jostyn, Peggy Maley, Troy Donahue, Joan Marshall, Gordon Jones, Dawn Richard, Jamie O'Hara, Dorothy Provine (film debut). *D:* Paul Henreid; *P:* Harry Rybnick, Richard Kay; *As.P:* Edward B. Barison; *Sc:* Allen Rivkin, Ib Melchior. (1:22) Teen exploitation-melodrama of two sisters, one headed for a life of crime, the other bent on saving her from same. Based on "Seed of Destruction," an unpublished story by Mr. Melchior and Edwin B. Watson. *Girls on the Loose* completed the double bill program.

1541. The Living Desert (Buena Vista/Walt Disney Prods.; 1953). *D:* James Algar; *P:* (AA-Best Documentary) Walt Disney; *As.P:*

Ben Sharpsteen; *Sc:* James Algar, Winston Hibler (who also narrates), Ted Sears; *Cin:* N. Paul Kenworthy, Jr., Robert H. Crandall; *Additional photography:* Stuart V. Jewell, Jack C. Couffer, Don Arlen, Tad Nichols; *Editor:* Norman Palmer. (1:13) (video) Walt Disney's first "True-Life Adventure," dealing with footage of mammals, reptiles, insects and arachnids of the American desert. Critically lambasted in many circles for "Disneyizing" various sequences with music, humor and "trick" photography. Audiences approved of the complete program which included Disney's Oscar-nominated cartoon "Ben and Me" and the live-action short "Stormy (the thoroughbred with an inferiority complex)." It received the "National Recognition Prize" at the 1954 Cannes Film Festival. Note: The first film to be released by Buena Vista, Disney's own distribution company formed after major disagreements with RKO who had been distributing the Disney product since the 1930s. Technicolor.

1542. The Living Idol (MGM; 1957). *Cast:* Steve Forrest, Liliane Montevecchi, James Robertson-Justice, Sara Garcia, Eduardo Noriega. *D:-St: & Sc:* Albert Lewin; *P:* Lewin, Gregorio Walterstein; *Song:* "Tepo" Ismael Diaz. (1:41) Minimally budgeted melodrama—filmed on location in Mexico—of a girl who is haunted by images of ancient Mayan sacrifices to the jaguar gods. Eastmancolor and CinemaScope.

1543. Living It Up (Paramount/York Pictures; 1954). *Cast:* Dean Martin, Jerry Lewis, Janet Leigh, Edward Arnold, Fred Clark, Sheree North, Sammy White, Sid Tomack, Sig Rumann, Richard Loo, Raymond Greenleaf, Walter Baldwin, Marla English, Kathryn [Grant] Grandstaff, Emmett Lynn, Dabbs Greer, Clancy Cooper, John Alderson, Booth Colman, Stanley Blystone, Fritz Feld, Torben Meyer, Art Baker, Grady Sutton, Norman Leavitt, Frankie Darro, Jean Del Val, Lane Chandler, Gino Corrado, Donald Kerr, Al Hill, Hank Mann, Gretchen Houser. *D:* Norman Taurog; *P:* Paul Jones; *Sc:* Jack Rose, Melville Shavelson; *Songs:* "How Do You Speak to An Angel?," "That's What I Like," "Every Street's a Boulevard in Old New York," "Money Burns a Hole in My Pocket," "You're Gonna Dance With Me Baby" and "Champagne and Wedding Cake" Jule Styne, Bob Hilliard. (1:35) Another Martin and Lewis hit, this one a remake of *Nothing Sacred* (U.A./1937). Based on the musical *Hazel Flagg* by Ben Hecht and a story by James Street. Jerry gets the royal publicity treatment when his sinus trouble is diagnosed as radiation poisoning. Technicolor.

1544. Lizzie (MGM/Bryna Prods.; 1957). *Cast:* Eleanor Parker, Richard Boone, Joan Blondell, Hugo Haas, Ric Roman, Dorothy Arnold, John Reach, Marion Ross, Johnny Mathis, Jan Englund, Carol Wells, Karen Green, Gene Walker, Pat Goldin, Dick Paxton, Michael Mark. *D:* Hugo Haas; *P:* Jerry Bresler; *Sc:* Mel Dinelli; *Songs:* "Warm and Tender" Burt Bacharach, Hal David; "It's Not for Me to Say" Robert Allen, Albert Stillman (both sung by Mathis). (1:21) Shirley Jackson's 1954 novel, *The Bird's Nest*, was the source material for this drama of a woman with three distinct and diverse personalities. The release of this film preceded, by several months, *The Three Faces of Eve* (q.v.), a film that also dealt with MPD.

1545. Loan Shark (Lippert/Encore Prods.; 1952). *Cast:* George Raft, Dorothy Hart, Paul Stewart, John Hoyt, Helen Westcott, Henry Slate, Margia Dean, Russell Johnson, Larry Dobkin, Benny Baker, William Phipps, Charles Meredith, Harlan Warde, Spring Mitchell, Robert Bice, Ross Elliott, Robert Williams, Michael Regan, Virginia Carroll, George Eldredge, William Tannen, Jack Daley. *D:* Seymour Friedman; *P:* Bernard Luban; *St:* Martin Rackin; *Sc:* Rackin, Eugene Ling. (1:14) (video) A loan-shark operation is exposed at a factory in this low budget crime-melodrama.

1546. The Lone Gun (United Artists/World Films; 1954). *Cast:* George Montgomery, Dorothy Malone, Neville Brand, Skip Homeier, Douglas Kennedy, Frank Faylen, Fay Roope, Robert Wilke, Douglas Fowley. *D:* Ray Nazarro; *P:* Edward Small; *Sc:* Don Martin, Richard Schayer. (1:18) Western of an ex-marshal who becomes sheriff of a town after eliminating a band of cattle rustlers. Based on the story "Adios My Texas" by L.L. Foreman. Color Corp. of America.

1547. Lone Hand (Universal-International; 1953). *Cast:* Joel McCrea, Barbara Hale, Alex Nicol, Jimmy Hunt, Charles Drake, James Arness, Wesley Morgan, Roy Roberts, Frank Ferguson. *D:* George Sherman; *P:* Howard Christie; *St:* Irving Ravetch; *Sc:* Joseph Hoffman. (1:20) A young boy is shocked to find his widowed father has joined an outlaw gang. Technicolor.

1548. The Lone Ranger (Warner/Lone Ranger Pictures, Inc.–Jack Wrather; 1956). *Cast:* Clayton Moore, Jay Silverheels, Lyle Bettger,

Bonita Granville (final film until 1978), Perry Lopez, Robert Wilke, John Pickard, Beverly Washburn, Michael Ansara, Frank DeKova, Charles Meredith, Mickey Simpson, Zon Murray, Lane Chandler, Silver (horse—received PATSY Award of Excellence-1957). *D:* Stuart Heisler; *P:* Willis Goldbeck; *Sc:* Herb Meadow. (1:26) (video) Another theatrical feature spin-off from a popular TV series (begun originally on radio). The masked man (Moore) and his faithful Indian companion, Tonto (Silverheels), try to put down an Indian uprising instigated by white men's greed. A moneymaker for the studio, it was presented in WarnerColor.

1549. The Lone Ranger and the Lost City of Gold (United Artists/Lone Ranger Pictures, Inc.-Jack Wrather; 1958). *Cast:* Clayton Moore, Jay Silverheels, Douglas Kennedy, Charles Watts, Noreen Nash, Lisa Montell, Ralph Moody, Norman Frederic, John Miljan (final film—d. 1960), Maurice Jara, Bill Henry, Lane Bradford, Belle Mitchell, Silver (horse). *D:* Lesley Selander; *P:* Sherman A. Harris; *St: & Sc:* Robert Schaefer, Eric Freiwald; *Song:* "Hi Ho Silver" Les Baxter, Lenny Adelson. (1:20) (video) The second theatrical feature of the 1950s with the masked man and Tonto. Duo is involved with five medallions, that when put together show a map of a lost city reputed to hold a treasure trove. Eastmancolor.

1550. Lone Star (MGM; 1952). *Cast:* Clark Gable, Ava Gardner, Broderick Crawford, Lionel Barrymore (Andrew Jackson), Beulah Bondi, Ed Begley, James Burke, William Farnum, Lowell Gilmore, Moroni Olsen (Sam Houston), Russell Simpson, William Conrad, Ralph Reed, Ric Roman, Victor Sutherland, Charles Cane, Nacho Galindo, Trevor Bardette, Harry Woods, Emmett Lynn, Jonathan Cott, Dudley Sadler, George Hamilton (not the later star), Roy Gordon, Stanley Andrews, William E. Green, Earle Hodgins, Warren MacGregor, Rex Lease, Davison Clark, Chief Yowlachie, Tony Roux, Rex Bell, Lucius Cook. *D:* Vincent Sherman; *P:* Z. Wayne Griffin; *St: & Sc:* Howard Estabrook, Borden Chase. (1:34) (video) Hit western centered around Texas' fight for independence following the fall of the Alamo and the Battle of San Jacinto. Computer-colored prints have been produced by Turner Entertainment.

Lone Star Lawman *see* **Texas Lawmen**

1551. The Lone Texan (20th Century-Fox/Regal Films; 1959). *Cast:* Willard Parker, Grant Williams, Audrey Dalton, Douglas Kennedy, June Blair, Dabbs Greer, Barbara Heller, Rayford Barnes, Tyler McVey, Lee Farr, Jimmy Murphy, Dick Monohan, Robert Dix, I. Stanford Jolley, Gregg Barton, Sid Melton, Hank Patterson, Tom London, Frank Marlowe, Boyd Stockman, Jerry Summers, Bill Coontz, Shirle Haven, Elena DaVinci, Doe Swain. *D:* Paul Landres; *P:* Jack Leewood; *Sc:* James Landis, Jack Thomas. (1:10) Low budget western-drama of a Union officer returning to his Texas town, only to find things are not the same as when he left. Based on the novel by Mr. Landis, this was Regal Films final production. It originally ran on a double bill with *Alaska Passage* (q.v.). Regalscope.

1552. Lonely Hearts Bandits (Republic; 1950). *Cast:* Dorothy Patrick, John Eldredge, Barbara Fuller, Robert Rockwell, Ann Doran, Richard Travis, Dorothy Granger, Eric Sinclair, Kathleen Freeman, Harry Cheshire, William Schallert, Howard J. Negley, John Crawford, Eddie Dunn, Sammy McKim, Leonard Penn. *D:* George Blair; *As.P:* Stephen Auer; *St: & Sc:* Gene Lewis. (1:00) Crime melodrama of a husband and wife team who scam lonely people for their money and then murder them. Based on a factual criminal case of the late 1940s. (aka: *Lonely Heart Bandits*)

1553. The Lonely Man (Paramount; 1957). *Cast:* Jack Palance, Anthony Perkins, Neville Brand, Robert Middleton, Elaine Aiken, Lee Van Cleef, Elisha Cook, Jr., Claude Akins, Harry Shannon, James Bell, Adam Williams, Denver Pyle, John Doucette, Paul Newlan, Philip Van Zandt, Moody Blanchard, Milton Frome, Tudor Owen, Russell Simpson, Alan Page, Kenneth Hooker, Bill Meader, Taggart Casey, Daniel White, Richard [Dick] Ryan, Billy Dix, Wesley Hudman, Zon Murray, Dirk London. *D:* Henry Levin; *P:* Pat Duggan; *St: & Sc:* Harry Essex, Robert Smith. (1:27) (video) With intent to reform, a gunfighter returns home after seventeen years to the family he deserted. A western adaptation of *Shepherd of the Hills*, a 1941 production from this studio.

1554. Lonelyhearts (United Artists/Schary Prods.; 1958). *Cast:* Montgomery Clift (Adam White), Robert Ryan (William Shrike), Myrna Loy (Florence Shrike), Dolores Hart (Justy Sargent), Maureen Stapleton (AAN-Film debut/Fay Doyle), Frank Maxwell (Pat Doyle), Jackie Coogan (Ned Gates), Mike Kellin (Frank Goldsmith), Frank Overton (Mr. Sargent), Don

Washbrook (Don Sargent), John Washbrook (Johnny Sargent), Onslow Stevens (Mr. Lassiter), Mary Alan Hokanson (Edna), John Gallaudet, Lee Zimmer, J.B. Welch, Charles Wagenheim, Frank Richards, Dorothy Neumann. *D:* Vincent J. Donahue (directorial debut); *P: & Sc:* Dore Schary; *As.P:* Walter Reilly. (1:51) (video) Drama of an advice columnist who gets too involved in his work. Based on Nathanael West's 1933 novel and Howard Teichmann's 1957 Broadway play, both of which were titled *Miss Lonelyhearts*. West's novel was also the source material for *Advice to the Lovelorn* (UA/20th Century; 1933) and *I'll Tell the World* (Univ.; 1945).

1555. The Lonesome Trail (Lippert/ L & B Prods.-International Pictures, Inc.; 1955). *Cast:* John Agar, Wayne Morris, Edgar Buchanan, Adele Jergens, Margia Dean, Earle Lyon, Ian MacDonald, Douglas Fowley, Richard Bartlett, Betty Blythe. *D:* Richard Bartlett; *P:* Earle Lyon; *Sc:* Bartlett, Ian MacDonald. (1:13) Programmer western of landgrabbers and one man's attempt to stop them—with bow and arrows. Based on the story "Silent Reckoning" by Gordon D. Shirreffs, this was the final American feature to be released under the Lippert banner.

1556. The Long Gray Line (Columbia/ Rotha Prods., Ltd.; 1955). *Cast:* Tyrone Power (Marty Maher), Maureen O'Hara (Mary O'Donnell-Maher), Robert Francis (final film—d. 1955 plane crash/James Sundstrom, Jr.), Donald Crisp (old Martin), Ward Bond (Capt. Herman J. Koehler), Betsy Palmer (Kitty Carter), Phil Carey (Charles Dotson), William Leslie ("Red" Sundstrom), Harry Carey, Jr. (Dwight Eisenhower), Patrick Wayne (Cherum Overton), Sean McClory (Dinny Maher), Peter Graves (Rudolph Heinz), Milburn Stone (Capt. John Pershing), Walter D. Ehlers (Mike Shannon), Willis Bouchey (Major Thomas), Don Barclay (McDonald), Martin Milner (Jim O'Carberry), Chuck Courtney (Whitey Larson), Major Philip Kieffer (superintendent), Norman Van Brocklin (Gus Dorais), Elbert Steele (the president), Lisa Davis (Eleanor), Dona Cole (Peggy), Robert Roark (Cadet Pirelli), Robert Hoy (Cadet Kennedy), Robert Ellis (Cadet Short), Mickey Roth (Cadet Curly Stern), Tom Hennesy (Peter Dotson), John Herrin (Cadet Ramsey), James Lilburn (Cadet Thorne), James Sears (Knute Rockne), Erin O'Brien-Moore (Mrs. Koehler), Ken Curtis (specialty singer), Diane DeLaire, Donald Murphy, Jean Moorhead, Pat O'Malley, Harry Denny, Robert Knapp, Jack Pennick, Mickey Simpson. *D:* John Ford; *P:* Robert Arthur; *Sc:* Edward Hope. (2:18) (video) Sentimental Americana of West Point's athletic director of many years, Martin Maher, from his arrival at the Point in 1903 to the 50s. Based on the 1951 book *Bringing Up the Brass* by Maher and Nardi Reeder Campion. One of the 27 top-grossing films of 1954-55. Technicolor and CinemaScope.

1557. The Long Hot Summer (20th Century-Fox/Jerry Wald Prods.; 1958). *Cast:* Paul Newman (voted "Best Actor" at the Cannes Film Festival/Ben Quick), Joanne Woodward (Clara Varner), Anthony Franciosa (Jody Varner), Orson Welles (Will Varner), Lee Remick (Eula Varner), Angela Lansbury (Minnie Littlejohn), Richard Anderson (Alan Stewart), Sarah Marshall (film debut/Agnes Stewart), Mabel Albertson (Mrs. Stewart), J. Pat O'Malley (Ratliff), William Walker (Lucius), George Dunn (Peabody), Jess Kirkpatrick (Armistead), Val Avery (Wilk), I. Stanford Jolley (Houstin), Nicholas King (John Fisher), Lee Rickson (Tom Shortly), Ralph Reed (J.V. Bookright), Terry Rangno (Pete Armistead), Steve Widders (Buddy Peabody), Jim Brandt (Linus Olds), Helen Wallace (Mrs. Houstin), Brian Corcoran (Harry Peabody), Byron Foulger (Harris), Pat Rosemond, Bob Adler, Eugene Jackson, Victor Rodman. *D:* Martin Ritt; *P:* Jerry Wald; *Sc:* Irving Ravetch, Harriet Frank, Jr.; *Title song:* Sammy Cahn, Alex North (sung by Jimmie Rodgers). (1:55) (video) Relationship drama involving a farmer, his son, his unmarried daughter and a newly arrived hired hand suspected of being a barn-burner. Based on "Barn Burning" and "The Spotted Horses"—two short stories—and *The Hamlet*, all by William Faulkner. On the "10 Best" lists of the NBR and *Film Daily* it placed #4 and #8 respectively. One of the 26 top-grossing films of 1957-58, it was remade in 1985 as a TV movie and also had a go at a TV series. Newman and Woodward's first film together, it was filmed on location in Baton Rouge, LA. in DeLuxe color, CinemaScope and stereophonic sound.

1558. The Long, Long Trailer (MGM; 1954). *Cast:* Lucille Ball (Tacy Collini), Desi Arnaz (Nicky Collini), Marjorie Main (Mrs. Hittaway), Howard McNear (Mr. Hittaway), Keenan Wynn (policeman), Gladys Hurlbut (Mrs. Bolton), Emmett Vogan (Mr. Bolton), Moroni Olsen (Mr. Tewitt), Ruth Lee (Mrs. Tewitt), Madge Blake (Aunt Anastacia), Walter Baldwin (Uncle Edgar), Oliver Blake (Mr. Judlow), Herb Vigran (trailer salesman), Dallas

Boyd (minister), Ruth Warren (Mrs. Dudley), Phil Rich (Mr. Dudley), Edna Skinner (Mrs. Barrett), Robert Anderson (Carl Barrett), Alan Lee (Mr. Elliott), John Call (Shorty), Dorothy Neumann (Aunt Ellen), Howard Wright (Uncle Bill), Connie Van (Grace), Dennis Ross (Jody), Christopher Olsen (Tom), Judy Sackett (Bettie), Janet Sackett (Kay), Bert Freed, Perry Sheehan, Charles Herbert, Edgar Dearing, Karl Lukas, Jack Kruschen, Geraldine Carr, Sarah Spencer, Wilson Wood, Ida Moore, Emory Parnell, Fay Roope, Peter Leeds, Frank Gerstle, Dick Alexander, Norman Leavitt, Juney Ellis. *D:* Vincente Minnelli; *P:* Pandro S. Berman; *Sc:* Frances Goodrich, Albert Hackett; *Song:* "Breezin' Along with the Breeze" Haven Gillespie, Seymour Simons, Richard A. Whiting. (1:43) (video/laserdisc) Comedy of newlyweds who embark on their honeymoon with a cumbersome house trailer on the back of their car, setting the stage for many slapstick gags. The popularity of *I Love Lucy* on TV turned this into box office gold for MGM, becoming one of the 25 top-grossing films of 1953-54. Based on the 1951 best-seller by Clinton Twiss. Photographed in Anscocolor with print by Technicolor.

1559. The Long Wait (United Artists/ Parklane Pictures; 1954). *Cast:* Anthony Quinn, Peggie Castle, Mary Ellen Kay, Gene Evans, Charles Coburn, Shawn Smith, Dolores Donlon, Barry Kelley, John Damler, James Millican, Bruno VeSota, Jay Adler, Frank Marlowe. *D:* Victor Saville; *P:* Lesser Samuels; *Sc:* Samuels, Alan Green; *Song:* "Once" Harold Spina, Bob Russell. (1:33) Melodrama of a man with a loss of memory who finds himself charged with several crimes. Based on the 1951 novel by Mickey Spillane.

1560. The Longhorn (Monogram; 1951). *Cast:* William Elliott, Myron Healey, Phyllis Coates, Lane Bradford, John Hart, I. Stanford Jolley, Marshall Reed, William Fawcett, Lee Roberts, Carol Henry, Zon Murray, Steve Clark, Marshall Bradford, Herman Hack, Carl Mathews. *D:* Lewis D. Collins; *P:* Vincent M. Fennelly; *St: & Sc:* Daniel B. Ullman. (1:10) (video) "Wild Bill" Elliott western of a trail drive. The first of eleven westerns by Elliott to be released under the Monogram-Allied Artists banner.

1561. Looking for Danger (Allied Artists; 1957). *Cast:* Huntz Hall, Stanley Clements, Eddie LeRoy, David [Gorcey] Condon, Jimmy Murphy, Richard Avonde, Otto Reichow, Michael Granger, Peter Mamakos, Lili Kardell, Joan Bradshaw, George Khoury, Henry Rowland, Percy Helton, Harry Strang, Paul Bryar, Jane Burgess, John Harmon, Michael Vallon, Dick Elliott. *D:* Austen Jewell; *P:* Ben Schwalb; *St:* Elwood Ullman, Edward Bernds; *Sc:* Ullman. (1:02) In this "Bowery Boys" series entry, Sach (Hall) relates in flashback a tale of their service in World War II, when they posed as Nazis to aid the North African underground and find an agent known as "The Hawk."

1562. Loophole (Allied Artists; 1954). *Cast:* Barry Sullivan, Charles McGraw, Dorothy Malone, Don Haggerty, Mary Beth Hughes, Don Beddoe, Dayton Lummis, Joanne Jordan, John Eldredge, Richard Reeves. *D:* Harold Schuster; *P:* Lindsley Parsons; *As.P: & Sc:* Warren Douglas; *St:* George Bricker, Dwight V. Babcock. (1:19) Crime melodrama of a bank employee suspected of theft who leads police to the guilty parties.

1563. Loose in London (Monogram/ Allied Artists; 1953). *Cast:* Leo Gorcey, Huntz Hall, David Gorcey, Bernard Gorcey, John Dodsworth, Norma Varden, William Cottrell, Angela Greene, Rex Evans, Walter Kingsford, James Logan, Alex Frazer, Joan Shawlee, James Fairfax, Wilbur Mack, Bennie Bartlett, Charles Keane, Clyde Cook (final film—ret.), Teddy Mangean, Gertrude Astor, Matthew Boulton, Charles Wagenheim. *D:* Edward Bernds; *P:* Ben Schwalb; *St: & Sc:* Elwood Ullman, Bernds. (1:02) "Bowery Boys" comedy with Sach (Hall) being erroneously informed that he is related to a British earl, sending the boys on a trip to London where they find the man is being poisoned by relatives.

1564. The Looters (Universal-International; 1955). *Cast:* Rory Calhoun, Julie Adams, Ray Danton, Thomas Gomez, Frank Faylen, Rod Williams, Russ Conway, John Stephenson, James Parnell, Emory Parnell. *D:* Abner Biberman (directorial debut); *P:* Howard Christie; *St:* Paul Schneider; *Sc:* Richard Alan Simmons. (1:27) Melodrama about two men who trek into the Colorado Rockies in search of survivors of a plane crash. They find four survivors and a quarter of a million dollars in cash.

1565. Lord of the Jungle (Allied Artists; 1955). *Cast:* Johnny Sheffield, Wayne Morris, Nancy Hale, Paul Picerni, William Phipps, Robert "Smoki" Whitfield, Leonard Mudie, James Adamson, Harry Lauter, Joel Fluellen, Juanita Moore. *D:-P:-St: & Sc:* Ford Beebe (final film—ret.). (1:09) A herd of elephants, headed by a nasty bull, is creating problems with the local natives and "Bomba the Jungle Boy" (Sheffield) is ordered to slaughter the entire herd. The final entry in this low budget adventure series based on the character created by Roy Rockwood in his books.

1566. Lorna Doone (Columbia; 1951). *Cast:* Richard Green, Barbara Hale (title role), Carl Benton Reid, William Bishop, Ron Randell, Sean McClory, Onslow Stevens, Lester Matthews, John Dehner, Dick Curtis, Anne Howard, Queenie Leonard, Trevor Bardette, Myron Healey, Harry Lauter, Ray Teal, Leonard Mudie, Fred Graham, Sherry Jackson, House Peters, Jr., Gloria Petroff, Orley Lindgren. *D:* Phil Karlson; *P:* Edward Small; *Adaptation:* George Bruce; *Sc:* Jesse L. Lasky, Jr., Richard Schayer. (1:28) Romantic action-drama of old England and simple farmers who are being exploited by oppressive landlords. Based on the 1869 novel by Richard D. Blackmore, it had three previous incarnations: 1920 (Great Britain), 1927 (Associated First National–Thomas Ince) and 1934 (Great Britain). Remade as a British TV movie in 1990. Originally ran on the top of a double bill with *Snake River Desperados* (q.v.). Technicolor.

1567. Lost Continent (Lippert/Tom Prods.; 1951). *Cast:* Cesar Romero, Hillary Brooke, John Hoyt, Hugh Beaumont, Chick Chandler, Sid Melton, Whit Bissell, [Burnu] Acquanetta, Murray Alper, William Green. *D:* Sam Newfield; *P:* Sigmund Neufeld; *St:* Carroll Young; *Sc:* Richard H. Landau. (1:26) (video) Low budget science fiction of a party in search of a lost rocket who discover a plateau where prehistoric animals roam. The film uses footage from *Rocketship X-M* (q.v.).

1568. Lost in Alaska (Universal-International; 1952). *Cast:* Bud Abbott, Lou Costello, Mitzi Green, Tom Ewell, Emory Parnell, Bruce Cabot, Jack Ingram, Iron Eyes Cody, Rex Lease, Joseph Kirk, Minerva Urecal, Howard Negley, Maudie Prickett, Billy Wayne, Julia Montoya, Paul Newlan, Michael Ross, Fred Aldrich, Donald Kerr, George Barton, Bobby Barber. *D:* Jean Yarbrough; *P:* Howard Christie; *St:* Elwood Ullman; *Sc:* Martin A. Ragaway, Leonard Stern. (1:16) (video) Comedy set in the Alaskan gold rush of the 1890s, with Abbott and Costello getting involved with a prospector (Ewell) and his fortune in gold. (aka: *Abbott and Costello Lost in Alaska*)

1569. Lost Lagoon (United Artists/Bermuda Studio Prods.; 1958). *Cast:* Jeffrey Lynn, Peter Donat, Leila Barry, Jane Hartley, Roger Clark, Don Gibson, Celeste Robinson, Stanley Seymour, Isabelle Jones, Hubert Smith and His Coral Islanders. *D: & P:* John Rawlins (final film—ret.); *St: & Sc:* Milton Subotsky; *Adaptation:* Rawlins; *Additional dialogue:* Jeffrey Lynn; *Song:* "To You" Darwin Venneri; *Original calypso songs:* Hubert Smith. (1:19) Romantic drama of a man involved in an unhappy marriage, who is reported drowned, but in reality is living on a Caribbean island with a lonely girl with whom he has fallen in love.

1570. Lost, Lonely and Vicious (Howco-International/Bon Aire; 1959). *Cast:* Ken Clayton, Barbara Wilson, Lilyan Chauvin, Richard Gilden, Carol Nugent, Sandra Giles, Allen Fife, Frank Stallworth, William Quimby, Johnny Erben, Clint Quigley, T. Earl Johnson. *D:* Frank Myers; *P:* Charles M. Casinelli; *St: & Sc:* Norman Graham. (1:13) Melodrama of a disillusioned young Hollywood actor, who lives in the fast lane, on the brink of self destruction. Originally ran on a double bill with *My World Dies Screaming* (q.v.).

1571. The Lost Missile (United Artists/William Berke Prods.; 1958). *Cast:* Robert Loggia, Ellen Parker, Larry Kerr, Phillip Pine, Marilee Earle, Fred Engleberg, Kitty Kelly, Selmer Jackson, Joe Hyams, Bill Bradley. *D: & St:* Lester William Berke (final film—d. 1958); *P:* Lee Gordon; *Sc:* John McPartland, Jerome Bixby. (1:10) Science fiction of a misguided alien missile, circling the earth at 4000 mph, setting cities afire—and it's headed for New York! This U.S.A./Canadian co-production originally ran on a double bill with *Machete* (q.v.).

Lost River (G.B. title) *see* **Trail of the Rustlers**

Lost Stage Valley (G.B. title) *see* **Stage to Tucson**

Lost Treasure of the Amazon (G.B. title) *see* **Jivaro**

1572. The Lost Volcano (Monogram; 1950). *Cast:* Johnny Sheffield, Donald Woods, Marjorie Lord, John Ridgely, Robert Lewis, Elena Verdugo, Tommy Ivo, Don Harvey, Grandon Rhodes. *D:-St: & Sc:* Ford Beebe; *P:* Walter Mirisch. (1:07) "Bomba the Jungle Boy" (Sheffield) leads a group in search of an ancient city inside an active volcano. The third entry in this low budget adventure series begun in 1949 and based on the "Bomba" books by Roy Rockwood.

Lost Women *see* **The Mesa of Lost Women**

Lost Women of Zarpa *see* **The Mesa of Lost Women**

1573. Louisa (Universal-International; 1950). *Cast:* Ronald Reagan (Hal Norton), Charles Coburn (Mr. Burnside), Ruth Hussey (Meg Norton), Spring Byington (Louisa Norton), Edmund Gwenn (Mr. Norton), Piper Laurie (film debut/Cathy Norton), Jimmy Hunt (Chris Norton), Scotty Beckett (Jimmy Blake), Connie Gilchrist (Gladys), Willard Waterman (Dick Stewart), Marjorie Crossland (Lil Stewart), Ann Pearce (Miss Randall), Dave Willock (Joe Collins), Martin Milner (Bob Stewart), Terry Frost (Stacy Walker), Frank Ferguson, Billy Newell, Eddie Parker, George Eldredge, Bill Clauson, Del Henderson, Scotty Groves, Bob Bowman, Robert Miles, Charles [Chuck] Courtney, Howard Keiser, Donna & Diana Norris (twins), Sherry Jackson, John Collum, Richard Michelson, Rev. Neal Dodd. *D:* Alexander Hall; *P:* Robert Arthur; *St: & Sc:* Stanley Roberts; *Sound:* (AAN) Universal-International Sound Dept. (1:30) A successful comedy of romantic pursuits among the "Geritol generation."

1574. Louisiana Territory (RKO; 1953). *Cast:* Val Winter, Leo Zinser, Julian Meister, Phyllis Massicot, Marlene Behrens. *D:* Harry W. Smith; *P:* Jay Bonafield, Douglas Travers; *Sc:* Jerome Brondfield. (1:05) The ghost of Robert Livingston (Winter) returns to marvel at New Orleans in this combination of travelogue and drama. Pathécolor and 3-D. Note: Livingston was involved in the wheeling and dealing of the Louisiana Purchase from France in 1803.

1575. Love in the Afternoon (Allied Artists; 1957). *Cast:* Gary Cooper, Audrey Hepburn, Maurice Chevalier, Van Doude, John McGiver, Lise Bourdin, Bonifas, Audrey Wilder, Gyula Kokas, Michel Kokas, George Cocos, Victor Gazzoli, Olga Valery, Leila Croft, Valerie Croft, Charles Bouillard, Minerva Pious, Filo, Andre Priez, Gaidon, Gregory Gromoff, Janine Dard, Claude Ariel, Francois Moustache, Gloria France, Jean Sylvain, Annie Roudier, Jeanne Charblay, Odette Charblay, Gilbert Constant, Monique Saintey, Jacques Preboist, Anne Laurent, Jacques Ary, Simone Vanlancker, Richard Flagy, Jeanne Guy Delome, Olivia Chevalier, Solon Smith, Eve Marley, Jean Rieubon, Christian Lude, Charles Lemontier, Emile Mylos, Alexander Trauner, Betty Schneider, Georges Perrault, Vera Boccadoro, Marc Aurian, Bernard Musson, Michele Selignac, Diga Valery Gypsies. *D: & P:* Billy Wilder; *Sc:* Wilder, I.A.L. Diamond. (2:10) (video) Acclaimed comedy-drama of an older wealthy American who falls for a young French girl, much to her father's disdain. Based on the 1933 novel *Ariane* by Claude Anet, it was filmed on various French locations and placed #7 on the "10 Best" list of the *New York Times.*

1576. Love Is a Many Splendored Thing (20th Century–Fox; 1955). *Cast:* Jennifer Jones (AAN + *Photoplay* Gold Medal/Han Suyin), William Holden (*Photoplay* Gold Medal/Mark Elliot), Torin Thatcher (Mr. Palmer-Jones), Isobel Elsom (Adeline Palmer-Jones), Murray Matheson (Dr. Tam), Virginia Gregg (Ann Richards), Richard Loo (Robert Hung), Soo Yong (Nora Hung), Jorja Curtwright (Suzanne), Donna Martell (Suchen), Candace Lee (Oh-No), Kam Tong (Dr. Sen), Herbert Heyes (Father Low), Angela Loo (Mei Loo), Marie Tsien (Rosie Wu), Joseph Kim (General Song), Philip Ahn, James Hong, Barbara Jean Wong, Hazel Shon, Jean Wong, Kei Chung, Harry S. Quan, Ashley Cowan, Marc Krah, Salvador Baguez, Edward Colmans, Leonard Strong, Aen Ling Chow, Stella Lynn, Irene Liu, Beulah Kwoh, Hayward Soo Hoo, Walter Soo Hoo, Keye Luke, Lee Tung Foo, John W.T. Chang, Weaver Levy, Eleanor Moore. *D:* Henry King; *P:* (AAN-Best Picture) Buddy Adler; *Sc:* John Patrick; *Title song:* (AA) Sammy Fain, Paul Francis Webster (sung by the Four Aces); *Music:* (AA-drama or comedy) Alfred Newman; *Cin:* (AAN-color) Leon Shamroy; *ASD:* (AAN-color) Lyle Wheeler, George W. Davis (art directors), Walter M. Scott, Jack Stubbs (sets); *Costumes:* (AA-color) Charles LeMaire; *Sound:* (AAN) Carl W. Faulkner. (1:42) (video/laserdisc) Romantic drama of the love affair which develops between a Eurasian doctor and a married war correspondent. Based on the 1952 novel *A Many Splendored Thing* by Han Suyin, the film received the *Photoplay* Gold Medal and placed #10 on the "10 Best" list of *Film Daily*. One of the 27 top-grossing films of 1954-55, it was presented in DeLuxe color and CinemaScope.

Love Is a Weapon *see* **Hell's Island**

1577. Love Is Better Than Ever (MGM; 1952). *Cast:* Larry Parks, Elizabeth Taylor, Josephine Hutchinson, Tom Tully, Ann Doran, Elinor Donahue, Kathleen Freeman, Doreen McCann, Alex Gerry, Gene Kelly (cameo), Dick Wessel, Richard Karlan, Dave Willock, Frank Hyers, Bertil Unger, Nancy Saunders, Margaret Lloyd, George Matkovich, Lucille Curtis, Mae Clarke, William "Bill" Phillips, Ann Tyrrell, Gail Bonney, Tom Hanlon, Jack George, Dan Foster. *D:* Stanley Donen; *P:* William H. Wright; *St: & Sc:* Ruth Brooks Flippen. (1:21) (video) Romantic comedy of a small town dance instructor and a New York talent agent. (G.B. title: *The Light Fantastic*)

1578. Love Island (Astor; 1952). *Cast:* Paul Valentine, Eva Gabor, Malcolm Lee Beggs, Kathryn Chang, Dean Norton, Frank McNeills, Bruno Wick, Richard Shankland, Howard Blain, Vicki Marsden. *D:* Bud Pollard; *P:* Hal Shelton; *Sc:* Daniel Kusell, John E. Gordon. (1:04) Low budget romantic-melodrama of a pilot, forced to land on the island of Bali, where he falls for the chief's daughter who is betrothed to another. Cinecolor.

1579. Love Me or Leave Me (MGM; 1955). *Cast:* Doris Day (Ruth Etting), James Cagney (AAN/Martin "The Gimp" Snyder), Cameron Mitchell (Johnny Alderman), Robert Keith (Bernard V. Loomis), Tom Tully (Frobisher), Harry Bellaver (Georgie), Richard Gaines (Paul Hunter), Peter Leeds (Fred Taylor), Claude Stroud (Eddie Fulton), Audrey Young (jingle girl), John Harding (Greg Trent), Jay Adler (Orry), Claire Carleton (Claire), Robert B. Carson (Mr. Brelston), Dorothy Abbott, Phil Schumacher, Henry Kulky, Otto Reichow, Mauritz Hugo, Veda Ann Borg, Benny Burt, James Drury, Richard Simmons, Michael Kostrick, Roy Engel, John Damler, Genevieve Aumont, Dale Van Sickel, Johnny Day. *D:* Charles Vidor; *P:* Joe Pasternak; *St:* (AA) Daniel Fuchs; *Sc:* (AAN) Fuchs, Isobel Lennart; *Sound:* (AAN) Wesley C. Miller; *Music:* (AAN) Percy Faith, George Stoll; *Songs include:* (AAN-Best Song) "I'll Never Stop Loving You" Nicholas Brodszky, Sammy Cahn. (2:02) (video/laserdisc) Hit musical-biography of singer Ruth Etting's rise to fame, from honky-tonk singer to the stage, in Florenz Ziegfeld's Follies. One of the 27 top-grossing films of 1954-55, it also placed #8 on the "10 Best" list of *Film Daily*. Eastmancolor and CinemaScope.

1580. Love Me Tender (20th Century-Fox; 1956). *Cast:* Richard Egan (Vance Reno), Debra Paget (Cathy Reno), Elvis Presley (film debut/Clint Reno), Robert Middleton (Siringo), William Campbell (Brett Reno), Neville Brand (Mike Gavin), Mildred Dunnock (Mrs. Reno), Bruce Bennett (Major Kincaid), James Drury (Ray Reno), Russ Conway (Ed Galt), Ken Clark (Kelso), Barry Coe (Davis), Paul Burns (Jethro), L.Q. Jones (Fleming), Jerry Sheldon. *D:* Robert D. Webb; *P:* David Weisbart; *St:* Maurice Geraghty; *Sc:* Robert Buckner; *Songs:* Title song (W.W. Fosdick–George R. Fulton—using the melody of "Aura Lee"), "Poor Boy," "We're Gonna Move" and "Let Me" (Elvis Presley-Vera Matson). (1:29) (video) Western, set near the close of the Civil War, of three brothers returning home after robbing a Union payroll. The older brother finds his younger brother (Presley), who did not fight in the war, has married his girl. One of the 24 top-grossing films of 1956-57, it was photographed in CinemaScope. Computer-colored by CSI.

1581. Love Nest (20th Century–Fox; 1951). *Cast:* June Haver, William Lundigan, Frank Fay, Marilyn Monroe, Jack Paar, Leatrice Joy (final film—ret.), Henry Kulky, Marie Blake [aka: Blossom Rock], Patricia Miller, Joe Ploski, Maude Wallace, Martha Wentworth, Faire Binney, Caryl Lincoln, Robert H. [Clifton] Young, Michael Ross, Bob Jellison, John Costello, Leo Cleary, Charles Calvert, Jack Daly, Ray Montgomery, Florence Auer, Edna Holland, Lizz Slifer, Alvin Hammer, Tony DeMario. *D:* Joseph Newman; *P:* Jules Buck; *Sc:* I.A.L. Diamond. (1:24) (video) Comedy of a wannabe writer and his wife who purchase a tenement after World War II and have to deal with an odd assortment of tenants. Based on the 1950 novel *The Reluctant Landlord* by Scott Corbett.

1582. Love Slaves of the Amazon (Universal-International; 1957). *Cast:* Don Taylor, Eduardo Ciannelli, Gianna Segale, Harvey Chalk, John Herbert, Wilson Vianna, Eugenio Carlos, Anna Marie Nabuco, Tom Payne, Gilda Nery, Louis Serrano. *D:-P: & Sc:* Curt Siodmak. (1:21) Adventure programmer of two archaeologists who find a female dominated society in the Amazon jungle. Based on the story "The Amazons" by Mr. Siodmak. The lower half of a double bill with *The Monolith Monsters* (q.v.). Eastmancolor.

1583. Love That Brute (20th Century-Fox; 1950). *Cast:* Paul Douglas, Jean Peters, Cesar Romero, Keenan Wynn, Joan Davis, Arthur Treacher, Peter Price, Jay C. Flippen,

Barry Kelley, Leon Belasco, Edwin Max, Sid Tomack, Phil Tully, Clara Blandick (final film—ret.), Jimmy Hawkins, Judith Ann Vroom, Grayce Hampton, Leif Erickson, Marion Marshall, Dick Wessel, John Doucette, Arthur O'Connell, Eugene Gericke, Lester Allen, Billy Chaney, Dan Riss, Charles Lane, Frank "Billy" Mitchell, Tiny Timbrell, Sid Marion, Charles Evans, Stan Johnson, Mauritz Hugo. *D:* Alexander Hall; *P:* Fred Kohlmar; *St: & Sc:* Karl Tunberg, Darrell Ware, John Lee Mahin; *Song:* "You Took Advantage of Me" Richard Rodgers, Lorenz Hart. (1:25) Comedy of a city crimelord who becomes smitten with the recreation director of a city park, but endeavors to dupe her to hide his criminal activities. A remake of *Tall, Dark and Handsome* (Fox; 1941). Note: Clara Blandick, who plays the landlady in this film and best known for her role as "Auntie Em" in *The Wizard of Oz* (MGM; 1939), committed suicide in 1962, this being her final film.

1584. Lovely to Look At (MGM; 1952). *Cast:* Kathryn Grayson, Red Skelton, Howard Keel, Marge and Gower Champion, Ann Miller, Zsa Zsa Gabor (film debut), Kurt Kaszner, Marcel Dalio, Diane Cassidy. *D:* Mervyn LeRoy; *P:* Jack Cummings; *Sc:* George Wells, Harry Ruby, Andrew Solt; *Songs:* "Opening Night," "Smoke Gets in Your Eyes," "Lovely to Look At," "The Touch of Your Hand," "Yesterdays," "I Won't Dance," "The Most Exciting Night," "I'll Be Hard to Handle" (Jerome Kern, Otto Harbach, Dorothy Fields, Jimmy McHugh, Oscar Hammerstein II); *Choreography:* Hermes Pan; *Fashion Show Director:* Vincente Minnelli. (1:45) (video/laserdisc) Hit musical of an American comic inheriting half interest in a Paris dress salon. A remake of *Roberta* (RKO; 1935) which was based on Alice Duer Miller's novel *Gowns By Roberta* and the 1933 Broadway musical "Roberta" by Kern, Fields and Harbach. Technicolor.

1585. Lovers and Lollipops (Trans-Lux/Spire Production Co.; 1956). *Cast:* Lori March, Gerald S. O'Loughlin, Cathy Dunn, William Ward. *D: & P:* Morris Engel (who also photographed), Ruth Orkin (who also edited); *Sc:* Engel, Orkin, Mary-Madeleine Lanphier. (1:20) Independent comedy-drama of a widow who seeks romance with a businessman, but encounters problems with her daughter.

1586. Loving You (Paramount; 1957). *Cast:* Elvis Presley, Lizabeth Scott (final U.S. film), Wendell Corey, Dolores Hart (film debut), James Gleason, Paul Smith, Ken Becker, Jana Lund, Ralph Dumke, The Jordanaires (themselves), Yvonne Lime, Skip Young, Vernon Rich, David Cameron, Grace Hayle, Dick Ryan, Steve Pendleton, Sydney Chatton, Jack Latham, William Forrest, Irene Tedrow, Hal K. Dawson, Joe Forte, Almira Sessions, Madge Blake, Harry Cheshire, Beach Dickerson, Gail Lund, Gladys Presley (audience extra). *D:* Hal Kanter (directorial debut); *P:* Hal B. Wallis; *Sc:* Kanter, Herbert Baker; *Songs:* "Loving You" (Jerry Leiber–Mike Stoller); "Teddy Bear" (Karl Mann–Bernie Lowe); "Lonesome Cowboy" (Sid Tepper–Roy C. Bennett); "Got a Lot of Livin' to Do" (Aaron Schroder–Ben Weisman); "Party" (Jessie Mae Robinson); "Mean Woman Blues" (Claude Demetrius); "Hot Dog" (Leiber–Stoller). (1:41) (video/laserdisc) Hit romantic-drama of a gas station attendant promoted to singing-stardom. This was Presley's second film and his first of seven for this studio with producer Wallis. Based on the short story "A Call from Mitch Miller" by Mary Agnes Thompson, it was in Technicolor and VistaVision.

1587. Lucky Losers (Monogram; 1950). *Cast:* Leo Gorcey, Huntz Hall, Gabriel Dell, Billy Benedict, David Gorcey, Buddy Gorman, Hillary Brooke, Bernard Gorcey, Joseph Turkel, Harry Tyler, Harry Cheshire, Frank Jenks, Douglas Evans, Wendy Waldron, Glenn Vernon, Chester Clute, Selmer Jackson, Dick Elliott, Mary Treen. *D:* William Beaudine; *P:* Jan Grippo; *Sc:* Charles R. Marion; *Additional dialogue:* Bert Lawrence. (1:09) In this "Bowery Boys" series entry, Slip (L. Gorcey) and Sach (Hall) become stockbrokers and uncover evidence that a purported suicide was actually murder.

1588. Lucky Me (Warner; 1954). *Cast:* Doris Day, Robert Cummings, Phil Silvers, Martha Hyer, Eddie Foy, Jr., Nancy Walker, Bill Goodwin, Marcel Dalio, Hayden Rorke, Herbert Vigran, James Burke, George Sherwood, Percy Helton, James Hayward, Jack Shea, William Bakewell, Cliff Ferre, Charles Cane, Jean DeBriac, Ann Tyrrell, Ray Teal, Tom Powers, Angie Dickinson (film debut), Lucy Marlow, Dolores Dorn, Emmaline Henry, Gladys Hurlbut, Jac George. *D:* Jack Donohue; *P:* Henry Blanke: *St:* James O'Hanlon; *Sc:* O'Hanlon, Robert O'Brien, Irving Elinson, Frank Davis (unc.); *Songs:* Title song, "Superstition Song," "I Speak to the Stars," "Take a Memo to the Moon," "Love You Dearly Parisian Pretties," "Bluebell of Broadway," "Wanna Sing Like An

Angel," "High Hopes" and "Men" Sammy Fain, Paul Francis Webster. (1:40) (video/laserdisc) An old fashioned "puttin-on-a-show" musical of a theatrical troupe stranded in Miami, Florida. WarnerColor.

1589. Lucky Nick Cain (20th Century-Fox/Kaydor-Romulus; 1951). *Cast:* George Raft, Coleen Gray, Enzo Staiola, Charles Goldner, Walter Rilla, Martin Benson, Peter Illing, Hugh French, Peter Bull, Elwyn Brook-Jones, Constance Smith, Greta Gynt, Margot Grahame, Donald Stewart. *D:* Joseph M. Newman; *P:* Joseph Kaufman; *Sc:* George Callahan, William Rose. (1:27) Crime melodrama of an American gambler (Raft) who is duped into becoming a front for a gambling resort. He winds up being charged with the murder of a U.S. Treasury agent who was investigating a counterfeiting operation. Based on the 1947 novel *I'll Get You for This* [aka: *High Stakes*] by James Hadley Chase. Filmed in Italy.

1590. Lucy Gallant (Paramount/Pine-Thomas; 1955). *Cast:* Jane Wyman, Charlton Heston, Thelma Ritter, Claire Trevor, Wallace Ford, William Demarest, Tom Helmore, Roscoe Ates, Gloria Talbott, Edith Head (herself), James Westerfield, Mary Field, Governor Allen Shivers of Texas (himself), Joel Fluellen, Louise Arthur, Jay Adler, Frank Marlowe, Howard Negley, Jack Pepper, Bill Hunter, Barbara Stewart, Edmund Cobb, Gene Roth, Max Wagner, Frank Hagney, Jack Shea, Robert Williams, Joey Ray, Benny Burt, Charles Regan, Beatrice Maude, Fern Barry, Emily Getchell, Mary Boyd, Elizabeth Cloud-Miller. *D:* Robert Parrish; *P:* William H. Pine, William C. Thomas; *Sc:* Winston Miller, John Lee Mahin; *Song:* "How Can I Tell Her" Jay Livingston, Ray Evans. (1:44) Drama of a dressmaker who is determined to create a fashion empire and does so at the expense of her love life with a rich Texas oil man. Based on the novel *The Life of Lucy Gallant* by Margaret Cousins. Technicolor and VistaVision. (aka: *Oil Town*)

1591. Lullaby of Broadway (Warner; 1951). *Cast:* Doris Day, Gene Nelson, S.Z. Sakall, Billy DeWolfe, Gladys George, Florence Bates, Anne Triola, Hanley Stafford, The Page Cavanaugh Trio (themselves), Carlo and Constance DeMattiazzi (specialty), Sheldon Jett, Murray Alper, Edith Leslie, Hans Herbert, Herschel [Daugherty] Dougherty, Elizabeth Flournoy, Donald Kerr, Arlyn Roberts, Philo McCullough, James Aubrey, Bess Flowers, Charles Williams. *D:* David Butler; *P:* William Jacobs; *Sc:* Earl Baldwin; *Songs:* "Lullaby of Broadway," "You're Getting to Be a Habit with Me" Al Dubin, Harry Warren; "Just One of Those Things" Cole Porter; "Somebody Loves Me" George Gershwin, B.G. DeSylva, Ballard MacDonald; "I Love the Way You Say Goodnight" Eddie Pola, George Wyle; "Please Don't Talk About Me When I'm Gone" Sammy Stept, Sidney Clare; "In a Shanty in Old Shanty Town" Jack Little, John Siras, Joe Young; "Zing Went the Strings of My Heart" James F. Hanley; and "Fine and Dandy," "We'd Like to Go on a Trip," "You're Dependable." (1:31) (video/laserdisc) Musical of a singer who returns to New York from London and finds her mother singing in a Greenwich Village bar. Somewhat reminiscent of 1930s musicals, it is filled with old standards and choreography by LeRoy Prinz and Al White. Based on the story "My Irish Molly" by Mr. Baldwin. Technicolor.

1592. Lum and Abner Aboard (Howco; 1956). *Cast:* Chester Lauck, Morris Goff, Jill Alis, Lila Audres, Branko Spoylar, Gene Gary, Vern Mesita, Valdo Stephens, Steven Voyt, Nada Nuchich, Chris Peters, Jim Kiley, Joseph Batistch. *D: & P:* James V. Kern; *St:* Kern, Carl Herzinger; *Sc:* Herzinger. (1:12) Three unrelated TV shows (ca. 1949) were strung together and released theatrically to create this "Lum (Lauck) and Abner (Goff)" movie.

1593. Lure of the Swamp (20th Century-Fox/Regal Films; 1957). *Cast:* Marshall Thompson, Willard Parker, Joan Vohs (final film—ret.), Jack Elam, Joan Lora, James Maloney, Leo Gordon, Skip Homeier. *D:* Hubert Cornfield; *P:* Sam Hersh; *Sc:* William George. (1:14) A swamp guide (Thompson) is hired by a bank robber (Parker) to take him to a cache of hidden cash, the spoils of a robbery. He finds his life in peril when others show up to search for the loot and kill his employer. Based on the novel *Hell's Our Destination* by Gil Brewer.

1594. Lure of the Wilderness (20th Century–Fox; 1952). *Cast:* Jean Peters, Jeffrey Hunter, Walter Brennan, Constance Smith, Tom Tully, Harry Shannon, Will Wright, Jack Elam, Harry Carter, Pat Hogan, Al Thompson, Robert Adler, Sherman Sanders, Robert Karnes, George Spaulding, Walter Taylor, Ted Jordan. *D:* Jean Negulesco; *P:* Robert L. Jacks; *Sc:* Louis Lantz; *St:* Vereen Bell. (1:32) Melodrama of a man accused of a murder he didn't commit, who hides out in a swamp for eight years with his daughter. A remake of *Swamp Water* (1941). Technicolor.

1595. Lust for Life (MGM; 1956). *Cast:* Kirk Douglas (AAN + "Best Actor" by the New York Film Critics/Vincent Van Gogh), Anthony Quinn (AA-BSA/Paul Gauguin), James Donald (Theo Van Gogh), Pamela Brown (Christine), Everett Sloane (Dr. Gachet), Niall MacGinnis (Roulin), Noel Purcell (Anton Mauve), Henry Daniell (Theodorus Van Gogh), Madge Kennedy (Anna Cornelia Van Gogh), Jill Bennett (Willemien), Lionel Jeffries (Dr. Peyron), Laurence Naismith (Dr. Bosman), Eric Pohlmann (Colbert), Jeanette Sterke (Kay), Toni Gerry (Johanna), Wilton Graff (Rev. Stricker), Isobel Elsom (Mrs. Stricker), Davis Horne (Rev. Peters), Noel Howlett (Commissioner Van den Berghe), Ronald Adam (Commissioner De Smet), John Ruddock (Ducrucq), Julie Robinson (Rachel), David Leonard (Camille Pissarro), William Phipps (Emile Bernard), David Bond (Seurat), Frank Perls (Pere Tanguy), Laurence Badie (Adeline Ravous), Rex Evans (Durant-Ruel), Marion Ross (Sister Clothilde), Mitzi Blake (Elizabeth), Anthony Sydes (Cor), Anthony Eustrel (Tersteeg), Ernestine Barrier (Jet), Jerry Bergen (Lautrec), Belle Mitchell (Mme. Tanguy), Alec Mango (Dr. Rey), Fred Johnson (Cordan), Norman MacCowan (Pier), Mickey Maga (Jan), Jay Adler. *D:* Vincente Minnelli; *P:* John Houseman; *As.P:* Jud Kinberg; *Sc:* (AAN) Norman Corwin; *ASD:* (AAN-color) Cedric Gibbons, Hans Peters, Preston Ames (art directors), Edwin B. Willis, F. Keogh Gleason (sets). (2:02) (video/laserdisc) Critically acclaimed biographical-drama on the life of painter Vincent Van Gogh and his relationship with fellow painter Paul Gauguin. On the "10 Best" list of the NBR it placed #4 and on the same list of the *New York Times* it placed #5. One of the 24 top-grossing films of 1956-57, it was also in nomination with the New York Film Critics for "Best Film." Based on the 1934 novel by Irving Stone, it was photographed in MetroColor and CinemaScope.

1596. The Lusty Men (RKO/Wald-Krasna; 1952). *Cast:* Susan Hayward, Robert Mitchum, Arthur Kennedy, Arthur Hunnicutt, Frank Faylen, Walter Coy, Carol Nugent, Maria Hart, Lorna Thayer, Burt Mustin, Karen King, Jimmie Dodd, Eleanor Todd, Riley Hill, Robert Bray, Sheb Wooley, Marshall Reed, Paul E. Burns, Dennis Moore, George Wallace, George Sherwood, Lane Bradford, Glenn Strange, Ralph Volkie, Sally Yarnell, Jean Stratton, Nancy Moore, Louise Saraydar, Mary Jane Carey, Alice Kirby, Chuck Roberson, Chili Williams, Hazel [Sonny] Boyne, Barbara Blaine, Sam Flint, Emmett Lynn, Denver Pyle, Dan White. *D:* Nicholas Ray; *P:* Jerry Wald, Norman Krasna; *As.P:* Tom Gries; *St:* Claude Stanush; *Sc:* Horace McCoy, David Dortort. (1:53) (video/laserdisc) Acclaimed contemporary-western drama of a seasoned rodeo performer training a novice to the business and their romantic rivalry over a tempestuous female.

1597. Lydia Bailey (20th Century–Fox; 1952). *Cast:* Dale Robertson, Anne Francis, Charles Korvin, William Marshall (black actor/film debut), Luis Van Rooten, Adeline de Walt Reynolds, Angos Perez, Bob Evans, Gladys Holland, Will Wright, Roy E. Glenn, Ken Renard, Juanita Moore, Carmen de Lavallade, Martin Wilkins, Albert Morin, William Washington, Clancy Cooper, Muriel Bledsoe, Mildred Boyd, Marjorie Elliott, Suzette Harbin, Roz Hayes, Dolores Mallory, Lena Torrence, Frances Williams, Ken Terrell, Louis Mercier, William Walker, Fred Cavens. *D:* Jean Negulesco; *P:* Jules Schermer; *Sc:* Michael Blankfort, Philip Dunne. (1:29) A lavishly produced costume adventure set in Haiti at the time of the attempted takeover by Napoleon Bonaparte. Based on the epic 1947 novel by Kenneth Roberts. Technicolor.

1598. "M" (Columbia/Superior Pictures; 1951). *Cast:* David Wayne, Howard Da Silva, Luther Adler, Martin Gabel, Steve Brodie, Raymond Burr, Glenn Anders, Karen Morley (final film—blacklisted), Norman Lloyd, John Miljan, Walter Burke, Roy Engel, Jim Backus, Benny Burt, Lennie Bremen, Janine Perreau, Robin Fletcher, Bernard Szold, Jorga Curtwright. *D:* Joseph Losey; *P:* Seymour Nebenzal; *Sc:* Norman Reilly Raine, Leo Katcher; *Additional dialogue:* Waldo Salt. (1:28) Crime drama of a psychotic child-killer hounded by police and the local criminal element who do not want an investigation into underworld activities. A remake of the 1931 German classic starring Peter Lorre and based on the screenplay of that film by Thea von Harbou, Fritz Lang, Paul Falkenberg, Adolf Jansen and Karl Vash, which in turn was based on an article by Egon Jacobson.

1599. Ma and Pa Kettle at Home (Universal-International; 1953-54). *Cast:* Marjorie Main, Percy Kilbride, Alan Mowbray, Ross

Elliott, Alice Kelley, Brett Halsey, Mary Wickes, Emory Parnell, Oliver Blake, Stan Ross, Irving Bacon, Virginia Brissac, Guy Wilkerson, Edmund Cobb, Edgar Dearing, Betty McDonough, Helen Gibson, Judy Nugent, Carol Nugent, Richard Eyer, Donald MacDonald, Coral Hammond, Patrick Miller, Nancy Zane, Gary Pagett, Donna Cregan Moots, Whitey Haupt, Pat Morrow, Tony Epper, James Flavin, Robert Nelson, Rick Vallin, Hank Worden, Ken Terrell. *D:* Charles Lamont; *P:* Richard Wilson; *St:* & *Sc:* Kay Lenard. (1:20) (video) The sixth entry in Universal's box office bonanza series, as the Kettles try to impress a judge and win a scholarship for their son. The Kettles also celebrate Christmas with their brood of fifteen children. Based on characters created by Betty MacDonald in her 1945 book *The Egg and I* which was also the name of the 1947 film that gave the original impetus to this series.

1600. Ma and Pa Kettle at the Fair (Universal-International; 1952). *Cast:* Marjorie Main, Percy Kilbride, Lori Nelson, James Best, Esther Dale, Emory Parnell, Oliver Blake, Russell Simpson, Hallene Hill, Rex Lease, James Griffith, Edmund Cobb, Roy Regnier, Teddy Infuhr, George Arglen, Ronald G. Rondell, Margaret Brown, Jackie Jackson, Billy Clark, Donna Leary, Elana Schreiner, Eugene Persson, Jenny Linder, Sherry Jackson, Gary Lee Jackson, Beverly Mook, Zachary Charles, Frank Ferguson, Syd Saylor, Harry Harvey, Harry Cheshire, Wheaton Chambers, Harry Cording, William Gould, Frank McFarland, Claire Meade, James Guilfoyle, Mel Pogue, Douglas Carter, Bob Donnelly. *D:* Charles Barton; *P:* Leonard Goldstein; *St:* Martin Ridgeway, Leonard Stern, Jack Henley; *Sc:* Richard Morris, John Grant. (1:18) (video) The fourth entry in the hit rural comedy series with the Kettles getting ready for the county fair, planning on winning money to send their daughter to college. Ma (Main) plans on beating Bertie Hicks (Dale) with her jam recipe and Pa (Kilbride) plans on winning the sulky race. Based on characters created by Betty MacDonald.

1601. Ma and Pa Kettle at Waikiki (Universal-International; 1955). *Cast:* Marjorie Main, Percy Kilbride (final film—ret.), Lori Nelson, Byron Palmer, Loring Smith, Mabel Albertson, Lowell Gilmore, Russell Johnson, Hilo Hattie, Fay Roope, Oliver Blake, Teddy Hart, Esther Dale, Ben Welden, Dick Reeves, Myron Healey, Ric Roman, Charles Lung, Byron Kane, Sandra Spence, Harold Goodwin, Norman Field, Elana Schreiner, Beverly Mook, Jenny Linder, Ronnie Rondell, Tim Hawkins, Margaret Brown, Billy Clark, George Arglen, Jon Gardner, Jackie Jackson, Donna Leary, Bonnie Kay Eddy, Luukluluana, Cindy Garner, Claudette Thornton, Ida Moore. *D:* Lee Sholem; *P:* Leonard Goldstein (final film—d. 1955); *St:* Connie Lee Bennett; *Sc:* Jack Henley, Harry Clork, Elwood Ullman. (1:19) (video) The seventh entry in the series finds the Kettles off to Hawaii where Pa is to help a relative run his pineapple processing plant. Based on characters created by Betty MacDonald, this one was followed by *The Kettles in the Ozarks* (q.v.). Originally ran on a double bill with *Cult of the Cobra* (q.v.).

1602. Ma and Pa Kettle Back on the Farm (Universal-International; 1951). *Cast:* Marjorie Main, Percy Kilbride, Richard Long, Meg Randall, Barbara Brown, Ray Collins, Emory Parnell, Teddy Hart, Oliver Blake, Peter Leeds. *D:* Edward Sedgwick (final film—d. 1953); *P:* Leonard Goldstein; *Sc:* Jack Henley. (1:20) (video) Popular rural comedy which has the Kettles returning to their farm in search of uranium. The third entry in the series which was based on characters created by Betty MacDonald in *The Egg and I.*

Ma and Pa Kettle Go to Paris (G.B. title) *see* **Ma and Pa Kettle on Vacation**

1603. Ma and Pa Kettle Go to Town (Universal-International; 1950). *Cast:* Marjorie Main, Percy Kilbride, Richard Long, Meg Randall, Ray Collins, Barbara Brown, Esther Dale, Ellen Corby, Teddy Hart, Oliver Blake, Charles McGraw, Gregg Martell, Jim Backus, Kathryn Givney, Elliott Lewis, Emory Parnell, Bert Freed (film debut), Peter Leeds, Dale Belding, Teddy Infuhr, Rex Lease, Diane Florentine, Paul Dunn, Eugene Persson, Margaret Brown, Donna Leary, Lynn Wood Coloman, Mary Ann Jackson, Jackie Jackson, Sherry Jackson, Beverly Mook, Elana Schreiner, Joyce Holden, Edmund Cobb, Jack Ingram, Gerry Hausner, Verna Kornman, Alice Richey, Steve Wayne, Ann Pearce, Lucille Barkley, Edward Clark, Dee Carroll, Paul McVey, Hal March. *D:* Charles Lamont; *P:* Leonard Goldstein; *Sc:* & *St:* Martin Ragaway, Leonard Stern. (1:19) (video) The second entry in the popular comedy series finds Pa (Kilbride) up to his ears in trouble with gangsters while on a trip to New York City. Based on characters created by Betty MacDonald. (G.B. title: *Goin' to Town*) Originally ran on a double bill with *A Run for Your Money*, a British comedy.

1604. Ma and Pa Kettle on Vacation (Universal-International; 1953). *Cast:* Marjorie Main, Percy Kilbride, Ray Collins, Bodil Miller, Barbara Brown, Sig Rumann, Peter Brocco, Ivan Triesault, Teddy Hart, Oliver Blake, Rita Moreno, Jay Novello, Jean De Briac, Larry Dobkin, Harold Goodwin, Jack Kruschen, Rosario Imperio, Andre D'Arcy, Ken Terrell, Alice Kelley, John Eldredge, Zachary Yaconelli, Sherry Jackson, Gary Lee Jackson, Jackie Jackson, Billy Clark, Elana Schreiner, Ronnie Rondell, Margaret Brown, Jon Gardner, Jenny Linder, Beverly Mook, Donna Leary, Robert Scott, George Arglen, Gloria Pall, Major Sam Harris, Carli Elinor, Eddie LeBaron, Dave Willock. *D:* Charles Lamont; *P:* Leonard Goldstein; *St:* Jack Henley; *Sc:* Henley, Elwood Ullman (unc.). (1:15) (video) The fifth entry in the series based on Betty MacDonald's characters finds the Kettles on vacation in Paris with their son-in-law's parents. And wouldn't you know it, Pa (Kilbride) gets mixed up with a ring of spies. (G.B. title: *Ma and Pa Kettle Go to Paris*)

1605. Macabre (Allied Artists/Susina Assoc.; 1958). *Cast:* William Prince, Jim Backus, Jacqueline Scott, Philip Tonge, Ellen Corby, Susan Morrow, Christine White, Linda Guderman, Jonathan Kidd, Dorothy Morris, Howard Hoffman, Voltaire Perkins. *D: & P:* William Castle; *Sc:* Robb White. (1:13) Thriller of two suspicious deaths, a child's purported kidnapping and the exhumation of a corpse, all leading to a twist-ending. Notable for the gimmick offering a $1,000 life insurance policy to moviegoers in case they died of fright. Based on the 1951 novel *The Marble Forest* by Theo Durrant [a pseudonym for the creative cooperative efforts of Terry Adler, Anthony Boucher, Eunice Mays Boyd, Florence Ostern Faulkner, Allen Hymson, Cary Lucas, Dana Lyon, Lenore Glen Offord, Virginia Rath, Richard Shattuck, Darwin L. Teilhet and William Worley].

1606. Macao (RKO; 1952). *Cast:* Robert Mitchum, Jane Russell, William Bendix, Thomas Gomez, Gloria Grahame, Brad Dexter, Edward Ashley, Philip Ahn, Vladimir Sokoloff, Don Zelaya, Emory Parnell, Nacho Galindo, Philip Van Zandt, George Chan, Sheldon Jett, Genevieve Bell, Tommy Lee, Alex Montoya, James B. Leong, Lee Tung Foo, May Takasugi, Maria Sen Yung, Iris Wong, Alfredo Santos, Marc Krah, Manuel Paris, Art Dupuis, William Yip, Michael Visaroff, W.T. Chang, Weaver Levy, Trevor Bardette, Rico Alaniz, Walter Ng, Abdullah Abbas, Everett Glass, Phil Harmon. *D:* Josef von Sternberg, Nicholas Ray (unc.); *P:* Alex Gottlieb; *St:* Bob Williams; *Sc:* Bernard C. Schoenfeld, Stanley Rubin; *Songs:* "One For My Baby" (Johnny Mercer–Harold Arlen); "Ocean Breeze," "Talk to Me Tomorrow" (Jule Styne-Leo Robin). (1:20) (video/laserdisc) Crime melodrama of efforts to bring to justice a drug kingpin operating on the island of Macao. Originally the top of a double bill with *Whispering Smith vs. Scotland Yard*, a British mystery.

MacDonald of the Canadian Mounties (G.B. title) *see* **Pony Soldier**

1607. Machete (United Artists/J. Howard O'Dell; 1958). *Cast:* Mari Blanchard, Albert Dekker, Juano Hernandez, Carlos Rivas, Lee Van Cleef, Ruth Cains. *D: & P:* Kurt Neumann; *As.P:* Victor Carrady; *St: & Sc:* Neumann, Carroll Young. (1:15) Melodrama of a wealthy plantation owner in Puerto Rico who begins to have suspicions about his new wife and the plantation foreman. Filmed on location, it originally ran on a double bill with *The Lost Missile* (q.v.).

1608. Machine Gun Kelly (American International/El Monte Prods.; 1958). *Cast:* Charles Bronson, Susan Cabot, Morey Amsterdam, Jack Lambert, Wally Campo, Bob Griffin, Barboura Morris, Richard Devon, Ted Thorpe, Mitzi McCall, Frank DeKova, Shirley Falls, Connie Gilchrist, Michael Fox, Larry Thor, George Archambeault, Jay Sayer. *D: & P:* Roger Corman; *Ex.P:* James H. Nicholson, Samuel Z. Arkoff; *St: & Sc:* R. Wright Campbell. (1:24) (video) A fictionalized 1930s gangster flick, detailing the exploits of the titled killer, robber and kidnapper (Bronson) who is finally betrayed by a former associate. Superama.

1609. Mad at the World (Filmakers; 1955). *Cast:* Frank Lovejoy, Keefe Brasselle, Cathy O'Donnell, Karen Sharpe, Stanley Clements, Paul Bryar, Paul Dubov, James Delgado, Joseph Turkel, Senator Estes Kefauver. *D:-St: & Sc:* Harry Essex; *P:* Collier Young. (1:16) Melodrama of a father who goes on a vendetta against a gang of juvenile delinquents after a thrown whiskey bottle seriously injures his infant son.

1610. The Mad Magician (Columbia; 1954). *Cast:* Vincent Price, Mary Murphy, Eva Gabor, John Emery, Donald Randolph, Lenita

Lane, Patrick O'Neal (film debut), Jay Novello. *D:* John Brahm; *P:* Bryan Foy; *St: & Sc:* Crane Wilbur. (1:12) Low budget horror melodrama of a demented magician who snaps when he loses his wife and magic tricks to another magician. This studio's final 3-D film of the 50s, it was in b/w and color.

1611. The Magic Carpet (Columbia/Esskay Pictures; 1951). *Cast:* Lucille Ball, John Agar, Patricia Medina, George Tobias, Raymond Burr, Gregory Gaye, Rick Vallin, Jo Gilbert, William Fawcett, Doretta Johnson, Linda Williams, Perry Sheehan, Eileen Howe, Minka Zorka, Winona Smith. *D:* Lew Landers; *P:* Sam Katzman; *Sc:* David Mathews. (1:24) An Arabian Nights costume-adventure in SuperCinecolor.

1612. The Magic Face (Columbia; 1951). *Cast:* Luther Adler, Patricia Knight, William L. Shirer, Ilka Windish, Heinz Moog, Jasper Von Oertzen, Charles Koenig, Toni Mitterwurzer, Annie Maiers, Herman Ehrhardt. *D:* Frank Tuttle; *P: & Sc:* Mort Briskin, Robert Smith. (1:28) World War II drama of a man who kills Adolph Hitler, impersonates him and sets his sights on the downfall of the Third Reich. Filmed in Austria.

1613. Magic Fire (Republic; 1956). *Cast:* Yvonne De Carlo, Carlos Thompson (Franz Liszt), Rita Gam, Valentina Cortesa, Alan Badel, Peter Cushing, Frederick Valk, Gerhard Riedmann, Eric Schumann, Robert Freytag, Heinz Klinenberg, Charles Regnier, Fritz Rasp, Kurt Grosskurth, Hans Quest, Jan Hendriks. *D: & P:* William Dieterle; *Sc:* Bertita Harding, E.A. Dupont, David Chandler. (1:34) A biography of German composer, Richard Wagner (Badel) which was based on the 1953 book by Bertita Harding. Trucolor.

1614. The Magnetic Monster (United Artists/A-Men; 1953). *Cast:* Richard Carlson (who also narrates), King Donovan, Jean Byron, Leonard Mudie, Harry Ellerbe, Leo Britt, Byron Foulger, Michael Fox, John Zaremba, Frank Gerstle, John Vosper, Michael Granger, Lee Phelps, Bill Benedict, Douglas Evans, Strother Martin, John Dodsworth, Kathleen Freeman, Charlie Williams, Jarma Lewis, Elizabeth Root, Watson Downs. *D:* Curt Siodmak; *P:* Ivan Tors; *St: & Sc:* Siodmak, Tors. (1:16) Science fiction on a low budget of a new radioactive element called serranium which doubles its mass regularly by absorbing energy, creating the potential for future devastation. Footage from *Gold*, a 1934 German production is used in the film's finale.

1615. The Magnificent Matador (20th Century–Fox/National Pictures; 1955). *Cast:* Maureen O'Hara, Anthony Quinn, Richard Denning, Thomas Gomez, William Brooks Ching, Lola Albright, Eduardo Noriega, Lorraine Chanel, Anthony Caruso, Manuel Rojas *and matadors as themselves:* Jesus "Chucho" Solorzano, Rafael Rodriguez, Joaquin "Cagancho" Rodriguez, Antonio Velasquez, Felix Briones, Nacho Trevino, Jorge "Ranchero" Aguilar. *D:* Budd Boetticher; *P:* Edward L. Alperson, Carroll Case; *St:* Boetticher; *Sc:* Charles Lang; *Title song:* E. Alperson, Paul Herrick (sung by Kitty White). (1:34) (video) Drama of a noted matador who is accused of cowardice when he flees the bullring and takes up with a wealthy American woman. Eastmancolor and CinemaScope. (G.B. title: *The Brave and the Beautiful*)

1616. Magnificent Obsession (Universal-International; 1954). *Cast:* Jane Wyman (AAN/Helen Phillips), Rock Hudson (Bob Merrick), Agnes Moorehead (Nancy Ashford), Barbara Rush (Joyce Phillips), Gregg Palmer (Tom Masterson), Otto Kruger (Randolph), Paul Cavanagh (Dr. Giraud), Sara Shane (Valerie), Richard H. Cutting (Dr. Dodge), Judy Nugent (Judy), Helen Kleeb (Mrs. Eden), Robert B. Williams (Sgt. Burnham), Will White (Sgt. Ames), George Lynn (Williams), Alexander Campbell (Dr. Allan), Rudolph Anders (Dr. Fuss), Fred Nurney (Dr. Laradetti), John Mylong (Dr. Hofer), Joe Mell (Dan), Harold Dyrenforth (Dr. Jouvet), Norbert Schiller (Mr. Long), Mae Clarke (Mrs. Miller), Harvey Grant (Chris), Jack Kelly, Lisa Gaye, William Leslie, Lance Fuller, Brad Jackson, Myrna Hansen, Kathleen O'Malley, Joy Hallward, Lee Roberts. *D:* Douglas Sirk; *P:* Ross Hunter; *Sc:* Robert Blees. (1:48) (video) Hit melodrama of a reckless man who blinds a woman and kills her husband via an auto crash, leading him to spend the rest of his life making restitution. A remake of this studio's 1935 hit based on the novel by Lloyd C. Douglas and the 1935 screenplay by Sarah Y. Mason and Victor Heerman with adaptation by Wells Root. The film received the *Photoplay* Gold Medal and became one of the 25 top-grossing films of 1953-54. Technicolor.

1617. Magnificent Roughnecks (Allied Artists; 1956). *Cast:* Jack Carson, Mickey Rooney, Nancy Gates, Jeff Donnell, Myron Healey, Willis Bouchey, Eric Feldary, Alan

Wells, Frank Gerstle, Larry Carr, Matty Fain, Joe Locke. *D:* Sherman A. Rose; *P:* Herman Cohen; *St: & Sc:* Stephen Kandel. (1:13) A programmer romantic melodrama of the South American oil fields.

1618. The Magnificent Yankee (MGM; 1950). *Cast:* Louis Calhern (AAN-repeating his stage role/Oliver Wendell Holmes, Jr.), Ann Harding (Fanny Bowditch Holmes), Eduard Franz (Judge Louis Brandeis), Philip Ober (Mr. Owen Wister), Ian Wolfe (Mr. Adams), Richard Anderson (Reynolds), James Lydon (Clinton), Hayden Rorke (Graham), John Hamilton (Justice White), Edith Evanson (Annie Gough), Guy Anderson (Baxter), Robert Sherwood (Drake), Hugh Sanders (Parker), Harlan Warde (Norton), Charles Evans (Chief Justice Fuller), Dan Tobin (Dixon), Robert Malcolm (Marshall), Everett Glass (Justice Peckham), Hugh Herbert (Justice McKenna), George Spaulding (Justice Hughes), Robert E. Griffin, Stapleton Kent, Marshall Bradford, Selmer Jackson, Todd Karns, Freeman Lusk, David McMahon, Sherry Hall, Jack Gargan, Dick Cogan, Tony Merrill, Robert Board, Wilson Wood, James Horne, Gerald Pierce, Lyle Clark, David Alpert, Tommy Kelly, Bret Hamilton, Jim Drum, Wheaton Chambers, Gayne Whitman, William Johnstone. *D:* John Sturges; *P:* Armand Deutsch; *Sc:* Emmett Lavery; *Costumes:* (AAN-b/w) Walter Plunkett. (1:20) (video) Drama based on the hit 1946 Broadway show by Emmett Lavery. Story of Supreme Court Justice Oliver Wendell Holmes, Jr., and his devoted wife, spanning several decades between the presidential terms of Teddy Roosevelt and F.D.R. Based on the book *Mr. Justice Holmes* by Francis Biddle. (G.B. title: *The Man with Thirty Sons*)

1619. Main Street to Broadway (MGM/ Cinema Prods.; 1953). *Cast:* Tom Morton, Mary Murphy, Agnes Moorehead, Herb Shriner, Rosemary DeCamp, Clinton Sundberg, Florence Bates (final film—d. 1954), Madge Kennedy, Carl Benton Reid, Frank Ferguson, Robert Bray *and as themselves:* Ethel Barrymore, Tallulah Bankhead, Lionel Barrymore (final film—d. 1954), Shirley Booth, Rex Harrison, Mary Martin (final film—ret.), Lilli Palmer, Helen Hayes, Henry Fonda, Louis Calhern, Faye Emerson (final film—ret.), Oscar Hammerstein II, Richard Rodgers, Gertrude Berg, Leo Durocher, Joshua Logan, John Van Druten, Cornel Wilde, Bill Rigney, Chris Durocher, Arthur Shields. *D:* Tay Garnett; *P:* Lester Cowan; *St:* Robert E. Sherwood; *Sc:* Samson Raphaelson; *Song:* "There's Music in You" R. Rogers, O. Hammerstein II. (1:42) (video) A drama of life, love and the pursuit of fame on Broadway's "Great White Way." A film curiosity with many cameos by Broadway personalities.

1620. Make Haste to Live (Republic; 1954). *Cast:* Dorothy McGuire, Stephen McNally, Mary Murphy, Edgar Buchanan, John Howard, Ron Hagerthy, Pepe Hern, Eddy Waller, Carolyn Jones. *D:* William A. Seiter (final film—ret.); *Ex.P:* Herbert J. Yates; *P:* Seiter; *Sc:* Warren Duff. (1:30) (video) Melodrama of a man who is released from prison after serving eighteen years for the murder of his wife, who is still alive and had taken their baby daughter and left him to serve the murder rap. Based on the 1950 novel by Gordon and Mildred Gordon.

1621. Man Afraid (Universal-International; 1957). *Cast:* George Nader, Phyllis Thaxter, Eduard Franz, Tim Hovey, Edward J. Stone, Judson Pratt, Reta Shaw, Mabel Albertson, Martin Milner, Troy Donahue (film debut). *D:* Harry Keller; *P:* Gordon Kay; *St:* Daniel B. Ullman; *Sc:* Herb Meadow. (1:23) Melodrama of a minister who accidentally kills a teenage burglar who is robbing his home, only to become the target of the boy's grief-stricken and vengeful father. CinemaScope.

1622. A Man Alone (Republic; 1955). *Cast:* Ray Milland, Mary Murphy, Ward Bond, Raymond Burr, Arthur Space, Lee Van Cleef, Alan Hale, Jr., Douglas Spencer, Thomas Browne Henry, Martin Garralaga, Grandon Rhodes, Kim Spalding, Howard J. Negley, Julian Rivero, Lee Roberts, Minerva Urecal, Thorpe Whiteman, Dick Rich, Frank Hagney. *D:* Ray Milland (directorial debut); *Ex.P:* Herbert J. Yates; *St:* Mort Briskin; *Sc:* John Tucker Battle. (1:35) (video) Western drama of a gunfighter on the lam from a lynch mob for committing two murders is hidden by the sheriff's daughter. Trucolor.

1623. Man Beast (Associated Producers; 1956). *Cast:* Rock Madison, Virginia Maynor, Tom Maruzzi, Lloyd Nelson, George Wells Lewis, George Skaff, Jack Haffner, Wong Sing. *D: & P:* Jerry Warren; *St: & Sc:* Arthur Cassidy. (1:12) (video) Adventure melodrama of an expedition into the Himalayan mountains to find a girl's brother, that encounters a murderous "abominable snowman" instead.

1624. The Man Behind the Gun (Warner; 1952). *Cast:* Randolph Scott, Patrice Wymore,

Dick Wesson, Philip Carey, Lina Romay, Roy Roberts, Morris Ankrum, Alan Hale, Jr., Katherine Warren, Douglas Fowley, Anthony Caruso, Clancy Cooper, Robert Cabal (Joaquin Murietta), James Brown, Reed Howes, Rory Mallinson, John Logan, Vici Raaf, Lee Morgan, Edward Hearn, Terry Frost, Charles Horvath, Art Millan, Rex Lease, James Bellah, Jack Parker, Billy Vincent, Alberto Morin, Edward Colmans, Ray Spiker, Herbert Deans. *D:* Felix Feist; *P:* Robert Sisk; *St:* Robert Buckner; *Sc:* John Twist. (1:22) Western of a U.S. cavalry officer who poses as a schoolmaster to investigate a secessionist movement in mid-19th century California. Technicolor.

1625. A Man Called Peter (20th Century–Fox; 1955). *Cast:* Richard Todd (Peter Marshall), Jean Peters (final film—ret./Catherine Marshall), Marjorie Rambeau (voted "Best Supporting Actress" by the NBR, combined with her performance in *The View from Pompey's Head* [q.v.]/Miss Fowler), Jill Esmond (Mrs. Findlay), Les Tremayne (Senator Harvey), Robert Burton (Mr. Peyton), Gladys Hurlbut (Mrs. Peyton), Gloria Gordon (Barbara), Billy Chapin (Peter John Marshall), Sally Corner (Mrs. Whiting), Voltaire Perkins (Senator Wiley), Betty Caulfield (Jane Whitney), Marietta Canty (Emma), Edward Earle (Senator Prescott), Peter Votrian (Peter Marshal, ages 7 to 14), Janet Stewart (Nancy), Agnes Bartholomew (grandmother), Ann Davis (Ruby Coleman), Dorothy Neumann (Miss Crilly), Doris Lloyd (Miss Hopkins), Barbara Morrison (Miss Standish), Carlyle Mitchell (Dr. Black), Amanda Randolph (Willie), Rick Kelman (Peter—age 5½), Louis Torres, Jr. (Peter—age 6½), Emmett Lynn (Mr. Briscoe), Roy Glenn, Jr. (Holden), Ben Wright (Mr. Findlay), Florence McAfee (Mrs. Ferguson), Christopher Cook (Bon Hunter), Winston Severn (David Weed), Maudie Prickett (Mrs. Pike), Richard Garrick (Mr. Whiting), Mimi Hutson, Arthur Tovey, Sam McDaniel, Oliver Hartwell, William Forrest, William Walker, Charles Evans, Alexander Campbell, Jonathan Hole, Larry Kent, Ruth Clifford. *D:* Henry Koster; *P:* Samuel G. Engel; *Sc:* Eleanore Griffin; *Cinematographer:* (AAN-color) Harold Lipstein. (1:59) (video) Critically acclaimed biographical drama detailing the life of Peter Marshall, a Scotsman who became chaplain to the U.S. Senate and the various trials and tribulations he encounters in the process, delving much on the messages of his sermons. Based on the biographical book written by his wife Catherine, following his death from tuberculosis. It placed #3 on the "10 Best" list of the *New York Times* and on the same lists of *Film Daily* and the NBR it placed #6 and #7 respectively. One of the 27 top-grossing films of 1954-55. DeLuxe color and CinemaScope.

1626. Man Crazy (20th Century–Fox/ Security Pictures; 1953). *Cast:* Neville Brand, Christine White, Irene Anders, Colleen Miller, John Brown, Joe Turkel, Karen Steele, Jack Larson, Bill Lundmark, John Crawford, Ottola Nesmith, Charles Victor, Frances Osborne. *D:* Irving Lerner; *P:-St: & Sc:* Sidney Harmon, Philip Yordan. (1:19) Programmer melodrama of three teenage girls who steal $28,000 from a drugstore in Minnesota and head for a fun time in California.

1627. The Man from Bitter Ridge (Universal-International; 1955). *Cast:* Lex Barker, Mara Corday, Stephen McNally, John Dehner, Trevor Bardette, Ray Teal, Warren Stevens, Myron Healey, John Harmon, Richard Garland, Jennings Miles, John Cliff. *D:* Jack Arnold; *P:* Howard Pine; *Adaptation:* Teddi Sherman; *Sc:* Lawrence Roman. (1:20) Western of a frontier investigator doing his thing with a series of stagecoach robberies and several killings. Based on the 1952 book *Justice Comes to Tomahawk* by William McLeod Raine, it was in Eastmancolor.

1628. The Man from Cairo (Lippert/ A Michaeldavid Prod.; 1953). *Cast:* George Raft, Gianna Maria Canale, Massimo Serato, Guido Celano, Irene Papas, Alfredo Varelli, Leon Lenoir, Mino Doro, Angelo Dessy, Richard McNamara, Franco Silva. *D:* Ray Enright (final film—ret.); *P:* Bernard Luber; *St:* Ladislas Fodor; *Sc:* Eugene Ling, Philip Stevenson, Janet Stevenson. (1:21) An Italian/U.S. co-production, this melodrama set in Algeria details the efforts of various parties in search of the whereabouts of a huge fortune in gold, hidden in the North African desert during World War II.

1629. Man from Del Rio (United Artists/ Robert L. Jacks; 1956). *Cast:* Anthony Quinn, Katy Jurado, Peter Whitney, John Larch, Douglas Fowley, Whit Bissell, Douglas Spencer, Guinn "Big Boy" Williams, Marc Hamilton, Barry Atwater, Adrienne Marden, Carl Thayer, William Erwin, Otto Waldis, Paul Harber, Jack Hogan, Frank Richards, Katherine DeMille. *D:* Harry Horner; *P:* Robert L. Jacks; *St: & Sc:* Richard Carr. (1:22) A Mexican drifter/gunfighter saves a western town from controlling outlaws.

1630. Man from God's Country (Allied Artists/Scott R. Dunlap Prods.; 1958). *Cast:* George Montgomery, Randy Stuart, Gregg Barton, Kim Charney, Susan Cummings, James Griffith, House Peters, Jr., Philip Terry, Frank Wilcox, Al Wyatt. *D:* Paul Landres; *P:* Scott R. Dunlap; *St:* & *Sc:* George Waggner; *Song:* "New Day at Sundown" Jack Brooks, Gerald Fried. (1:12) A western involving the acquisition of lands in Montana for the coming of the railroad. In DeLuxe color and CinemaScope, it had the pre-release title of "New Day at Sundown."

1631. The Man from Laramie (Columbia/William Goetz Prods.; 1955). *Cast:* James Stewart (Will Lockhart), Cathy O'Donnell (Barbara Waggoman), Arthur Kennedy (Vic Hensbro), Donald Crisp (Alec Waggoman), Aline MacMahon (Kate Canaby), Alex Nicol (Dave Waggoman), Wallace Ford (Charlie O'Leary), Jack Elam (Chris Boldt), Boyd Stockman (Spud Oxton), Gregg Barton (Fritz), Frank DeKova (padre), James Millican (Tom Quigby), John War Eagle (Frank Darrah), Eddy Waller (Dr. Selden), Frosty Royce, Jack Carry, Frank Cordell, William Catching. *D:* Anthony Mann; *P:* William Goetz; *St:* Thomas T. Flynn; *Sc:* Philip Yordan, Frank Burt. (1:44) (video) Western drama of a drifter who winds up in the middle of a range war while searching for his brother's killer. The critics approved and so did the paying public as it became one of the 27 top-grossing films of 1954-55. Technicolor and CinemaScope.

The Man from Nevada (G.B. title) *see* **The Nevadan**

1632. The Man from Planet X (United Artists/Sherill C. Corwin–Mid-Century; 1951). *Cast:* Robert Clarke, Margaret Field, Raymond Bond, William Schallert, Roy Engel, Charles Davis, Gilbert Fallman, David Ormond. *D:* Edgar G. Ulmer; *P:* & *Sc:* Aubrey Wisberg, Jack Pollexfen. (1:10) (video) Low budget science fiction of a peaceful alien visitor who lands in Scotland and his effect on some of the local inhabitants who react with hostility. Note: Filmed on leftover sets from *Joan of Arc* (1948).

1633. Man from Sonora (Monogram; 1951). *Cast:* Johnny Mack Brown, Phyllis Coates, Lyle Talbot, House Peters, Jr., Lee Roberts, John Merton, Stanley Price, Dennis Moore, Ray Jones, Pierce Lyden, Sam Flint, George DeNormand. *D:* Lewis D. Collins; *P:* Vincent M. Fennelly; *St:* & *Sc:* Maurice Tombragel. (0:54) "Man from El Paso" was the pre-release title of this series western involving the apprehension of a gang of stagecoach robbers.

1634. The Man from the Alamo (Universal-International; 1953). *Cast:* Glenn Ford, Julia [Julie] Adams, Chill Wills, Victor Jory, Hugh O'Brian, Mark Cavell, Jeanne Cooper, Myra Marsh, Neville Brand, John Day, Edward Norris, Guy Williams, Dan Poore, George Eldredge, Howard Negley. *D:* Budd Boetticher; *P:* Aaron Rosenberg; *St:* Niven Busch, Oliver Crawford; *Sc:* D.D. Beauchamp, Steve Fisher. (1:19) (video) Western of a man who leaves the Alamo before the final battle to warn families in the area, but is instead branded a coward and accused of desertion. Technicolor.

1635. Man from the Black Hills (Monogram/Silvermine Prods.; 1952). *Cast:* Johnny Mack Brown, James Ellison, Rand Brooks, Lane Bradford, I. Stanford Jolley, Robert Bray, Stanley Price, Ray Bennett, Denver Pyle, Joel Allen, Stanley Andrews, Florence Lake, Bud Osborne, Merrill McCormack, Ralph [Buck?] Bucko, Roy Bucko. *D:* Thomas Carr; *P:* Vincent M. Fennelly; *Sc:* Joseph O'Donnell. (0:51) Another of Brown's series westerns, this one about a crook trying to claim another's gold mine as his own.

The Man He Found *see* **The Whip Hand**

1636. Man in the Attic (20th Century-Fox/Panoramic; 1953). *Cast:* Jack Palance, Constance Smith, Byron Palmer, Frances Bavier, Rhys Williams, Sean McClory, Leslie Bradley, Tita Phillips, Lester Matthews, Harry Cording, Lillian Bond, Lisa Daniels, Isabel Jewell. *D:* Hugo Fregonese; *P:* Robert L. Jacks; *Sc:* Robert Presnell, Jr., Barre Lyndon. (1:22) Melodramatic thriller of a mysterious lodger (Palance), in a London rooming house, who is suspected of being Jack the Ripper. A remake of *The Lodger* (1944) which was also filmed in Great Britain in 1935 as *The Phantom Fiend* (aka: *The Lodger*) and based on the book *The Lodger* by Marie Belloc-Lowndes.

1637. Man in the Dark (Columbia; 1953). *Cast:* Edmond O'Brien, Audrey Totter, Ted de Corsia, Horace McMahon, Nick Dennis, Dayton Lummis, Dan Riss, Shepard Menken, John Harmon, Ruth Warren. *D:* Lew Landers; *P:* Wallace MacDonald; *St:* Tom Van Dycke, Henry Altimus; *Adaptation:* William B. Sackheim; *Sc:* George Bricker, Jack Leonard. (1:10) Crime melodrama of a gangster who tries to escape his past, but his old gang catches up with him. A remake of *The Man Who Lived Twice* (1936) by this studio and also Columbia's first 3-D feature.

1638. The Man in the Gray Flannel Suit (20th Century–Fox; 1956). *Cast:* Gregory Peck (Tom Rath), Jennifer Jones (Betsy Rath), Fredric March (Ralph Hopkins), Marisa Pavan (Maria), Ann Harding (Mrs. Hopkins), Lee J. Cobb (Judge Bernstein), Keenan Wynn (Caesar Gardella), Gene Lockhart (Hawthorne), Gigi Perreau (Susan Hopkins), Portland Mason (Janie), Arthur O'Connell (Walker), Henry Daniell (Bill Ogden), Connie Gilchrist (Mrs. Manter), Joseph Sweeney (Edward Schultz), Sandy Descher (Barbara), Mickey Maga (Pete), Kenneth Tobey (Mahoney), Ruth Clifford (Florence), Geraldine Wall (Miriam), Alex Campbell (Johnson), Jerry Hall (Freddie), Frank Wilcox (Dr. Pearce), Nan Martin (Miss Lawrence), Tristram Coffin (Byron Holgate), William Phillips (Bugala), Leon Alton (Cliff), Phyllis Graffeo (Gina), Dorothy Adams, Jack Mather, Dorothy Phillips, Mary Benoit, John Breen, King Lockwood, Lomax Study, Renata Vanni, Mario Siletti, Lee Graham, Michael Jeffrey, Roy Glenn, Otto Reichow, Jim Brandt, Robert Boon, Harry Lauter, Paul Glass, William Phipps, DeForest Kelley, Alfred Calazza, Raymond Winston, John Crawford. *D: & Sc:* Nunnally Johnson; *P:* Darryl F. Zanuck. (2:33) (video/laserdisc) Critically acclaimed drama of a Madison Avenue executive attempting to get ahead on the job, while dealing with his private home life. Based on the bestseller by Sloan Wilson, it was in nomination at the Cannes Film Festival. One of the 24 top-grossing films of 1955-56, it was photographed in DeLuxe color and CinemaScope.

1639. The Man in the Net (United Artists/Mirisch-Jaguar; 1959). *Cast:* Alan Ladd, Carolyn Jones, Diane Brewster, John Lupton, Charles McGraw, Tom Helmore, Betty Lou Holland, John Alexander, Edward Binns, Kathryn Givney, Susan Gordon, Barbara Beaird, Charles Herbert, Mike McGreevy, Steven Perry, Alvin Childress, Natalie Masterson, Douglas Evans, Pat Miller, Bill Cassidy. *D:* Michael Curtiz; *P:* Walter M. Mirisch; *Sc:* Reginald Rose. (1:37) A man is the prime suspect when his adulterous and alcoholic wife is found murdered beneath the floor of a barn. He flees to the woods and is hidden by five kids, who act as messengers, until he is able to pinpoint the real killer. Based on the 1956 book *Man in the Net: A Novel of Suspense* by Patrick Quentin, it was filmed on locations in Massachusetts and Connecticut.

1640. Man in the Saddle (Columbia/Scott-Brown Prods.; 1951). *Cast:* Randolph Scott, Joan Leslie, Ellen Drew, Alexander Knox, John Russell, Guinn Williams, Alfonso Bedoya, Cameron Mitchell, Richard Crane, Clem Bevans, Richard Rober, Tennessee Ernie Ford (who also sings the title song), George Lloyd, Frank Sully, James Kirkwood, Frank Hagney, Don Beddoe. *D:* Andre De Toth; *P:* Harry Joe Brown; *Sc:* Kenneth Gamet. (1:27) (video) Western drama of conflict on the range amidst a love triangle. Based on the novel by Ernest Haycox. Technicolor. (G.B. title: *The Outcast*)

1641. Man in the Shadow (Universal-International; 1957). *Cast:* Jeff Chandler, Orson Welles, Colleen Miller, Barbara Lawrence (final film—ret.), Ben Alexander (final film—ret.), John Larch, James Gleason, Royal Dano, Paul Fix, Leo Gordon, Martin Garralaga, Mario Siletti, Charles Horvath, William Schallert, Joseph J. Greene, Forrest Lewis, Harry Harvey, Jr., Joe Schneider, Mort Mills. *D:* Jack Arnold; *P:* Albert Zugsmith; *Sc:* Gene L. Coon. (1:20) Acclaimed contemporary western drama of a sheriff investigating the suspicious death of a Mexican laborer on a local ranch. Based on the novel by Harry Whittington. CinemaScope. (G.B. title: *Pay the Devil*)

1642. The Man in the Vault (RKO/Batjac; 1956). *Cast:* William Campbell, Karen Sharpe, Anita Ekberg, Berry Kroeger, Paul Fix, James Seay, Mike Mazurki, Robert Keys, [Pedro] Gonzales-Gonzales, Nancy Duke, Vivian Lloyd. *D:* Andrew V. McLaglen; *P:* Robert E. Morrison; *Sc:* Burt Kennedy; *Song:* "Let the Chips Fall Where They May" Henry Vars, By Dunham. (1:13) Programmer crime melodrama of a locksmith forced to forge keys in an effort to get into a safe deposit box containing $200,000. Based on the 1948 novel *The Lock and the Key* by Frank Gruber.

1643. The Man Is Armed (Republic; 1956). *Cast:* Dane Clark, William Talman, May Wynn, Robert Horton, Barton MacLane, Fredd Wayne, Richard Benedict, Richard Reeves, Harry Lewis, Bob Jordan, Larry J. Blake, Darlene Fields, John Mitchum. *D:* Franklin Adreon (directorial debut); *P:* Edward J. "Eddy" White; *St:* Don Martin; *Sc:* Richard Landau, Robert C. Dennis. (1:10) Melodrama of a man who unknowingly becomes involved with a gang pulling a robbery and proceeds to make things tough for them afterward.

A Man Is Ten Feet Tall (G.B. title) *see* **Edge of the City**

Man-Mad (G.B. title) *see* **No Place to Land**

1644. Man of a Thousand Faces (Universal-International; 1957). *Cast:* James Cagney (Lon Chaney), Dorothy Malone (Cleva Creighton Chaney), Jane Greer (Hazel Bennett), Jim Backus (Clarence Logan), Marjorie Rambeau (final film—ret./Gert), Roger Smith (Creighton Chaney—age 21), Celia Lovsky (Mrs. Chaney), Nolan Leary (Mr. Chaney), Robert Evans (Irving Thalberg), Clarence Kolb (final film—ret./himself), Philip Van Zandt (final film—suicide 1958/George Loane Tucker), Jeanne Cagney (Carrie Chaney), Jack Albertson (Dr. J. Wilson Shields), Robert Lyden (Creighton—age 13), Rickie Sorenson (Creighton—age 8), Dennis Rush (Creighton—age 4), Simon Scott (Carl Hastings), Danny Beck (Max Dill), Hank Mann, Snub Pollard, Marjorie Bennett. *D:* Joseph Pevney; *P:* Robert Arthur; *St:* (AAN) Ralph Wheelwright; *Sc:* (AAN) R. Wright Campbell, Ivan Goff, Ben Roberts. (2:02) (video/laserdisc) A filmed biography of famed silent screen star (at Universal) Lon Chaney, Sr., from his days as a boy born of deaf-mute parents, to his days of stardom on the silver screen. In CinemaScope, it became one of the 24 top-grossing films of 1956-57.

Man of Bronze *see* **Jim Thorpe—All American**

1645. Man of Conflict (Atlas; 1953). *Cast:* Edward Arnold, John Agar, Susan Morrow, Fay Roope, Herbert Heyes, Dorothy Patrick, Bob Carson, Russell Hicks, John Hamilton, Lovyss Bradley, Leslie O'Pace, Frank O'Connor, Lee Phelps, Allan Schute, John Holland. *D: & P:* Hal R. Makelin; *St: & Sc:* Hal Richards. (1:12) Drama of a wealthy industrialist (Arnold), who treats his employees with a lack of compassion and understanding and hopes to get his son to follow in his footsteps to preserve the business, but the son has his own ideas.

1646. Man of the West (United Artists/Ashton Prods.; 1958). *Cast:* Gary Cooper, Julie London, Lee J. Cobb, Arthur O'Connell, Jack Lord, John Dehner, Royal Dano, Robert Wilke, Jack Williams, Guy Wilkerson, Chuck Roberson, Frank Ferguson, Emory Parnell, Tina Menard, Joe Dominguez. *D:* Anthony Mann; *P:* Walter Mirisch; *Sc:* Reginald Rose; *Title song:* Bobby Troup (sung by Julie London). (1:40) (video) Western drama of a reformed bank-robber, who through a set of bizarre circumstances, finds himself in the midst of the gang he was once a member of. Based on the 1955 novel *The Border Jumpers* by Will C. Brown. In DeLuxe color and CinemaScope, with location filming in California's Mojave desert.

1647. Man on a Tightrope (20th Century–Fox; 1953). *Cast:* Fredric March, Terry Moore, Gloria Grahame, Cameron Mitchell, Adolphe Menjou, Robert Beatty, Alex D'Arcy, Richard Boone, Pat Henning, Paul Hartman, John Dehner, Mme. Brumbach, Hansi, Dorothea Wieck, Philip Kenneally, Edelweiss Malchin, William Castello, Margaret Slezak, Peter Beauvais, Robert Charlebois, Gert Frobe, Rolf Naukhoff, Bimbach Circus performers. *D:* Elia Kazan; *P:* Robert L. Jacks; *Sc:* Robert E. Sherwood. (1:45) Factually based drama of a small independently owned circus that seeks to escape Czechoslovakia following the communist takeover. Based on the story "International Incident" by Neil Paterson, it placed #5 on the "10 Best" list of the *New York Times*.

1648. Man on Fire (MGM; 1957). *Cast:* Bing Crosby, Mary Fickett, Inger Stevens (film debut), E.G. Marshall, Malcolm Broderick, Anne Seymour, Richard Eastham, Dan Riss. *D: & Sc:* Ranald MacDougall; *P:* Sol C. Siegel; *Title song:* Sammy Fain, Paul Francis Webster (sung by the Ames Bros.). (1:35) Domestic drama of divorced parents, she who has remarried, who squabble over custody of their son. Based on a TV play by Malvin Wald and Jack Jacobs, it showed poor box office returns.

1649. Man on the Prowl (United Artists/Jana Prods.; 1957). *Cast:* Mala Powers, James Best, Ted de Corsia, Jerry Paris, Vivi Jannis, Josh Freeman, Jeff Freeman, Peggy Maley, Eugenia Paul, Bob Yeakel (himself). *D:* Art Napoleon (directorial debut); *P:-St: & Sc:* Art and Jo Napoleon. (1:26) Melodrama of a psychopath who enters a woman's home and threatens her children, unless she does as he says.

1650. Man or Gun (Republic; 1958). *Cast:* Macdonald Carey, Audrey Totter, James Craig, James Gleason, Warren Stevens, Harry Shannon, Jil Jarmyn, Robert Burton, Ken Lynch, Karl Davis, Julian Burton, Carl York, Harry Klekas, Mel Gaines, Ron McNeil, Larry Grant. *D: & Ex.P:* Albert C. Gannaway; *P:* Vance Skarstedt; *Sc:* Skarstedt, James C. Cassity; *Title* *song:* Gene Garf, Ramez Idriss, Hal Levy. (1:19) Western of a drifter who rids a town of the powerful family which lords over it. Naturama.

1651. The Man Who Cheated Himself (20th Century–Fox; 1950). *Cast:* Lee J. Cobb, John Dall, Jane Wyatt, Lisa Howard, Alan Wells, Harlan Warde, Tito Vuolo, Mimi Aguglia, Charles Arnt, Marjorie Bennett, Bud [Bill] Wolfe, Morgan Farley, Howard Negley, William Gould, Art Millan, Gordon Richards, Terry Frost, Mario Siletti, Charles Victor. *D:* Felix Feist; *P:* Jack M. Warner; *St:* Seton I. Miller; *Sc:* Miller, Phillip MacDonald. (1:26) Film noir involving a woman who shoots her husband while he is robbing his own house, then seeks help from her police lieutenant boy friend in disposing of the body.

1652. The Man Who Died Twice (Republic/Ventura; 1958). *Cast:* Rod Cameron, Vera Ralston (final film—ret.), Mike Mazurki, Gerald Milton, Richard Karlan, Louis Jean Heydt (final film—d. 1960), Don Megowan, John Maxwell, Bob Anderson, Paul Picerni, Don Haggerty, Luana Anders, Jesslyn Fax. *D:* Joe Kane; *P:* Rudy Ralston; *Sc:* Richard C. Sarafian; *Songs:* "There I Was in Love," "One Step From Nowhere" Jerry Gladstone, Al DeLory. (1:10) Melodrama of a woman whose husband is killed in an explosion, and while recovering from that, she also witnesses the murder of two narcotics investigators. Naturama.

1653. The Man Who Knew Too Much (Paramount/Hitchcock Prods.; 1956). *Cast:* James Stewart (Ben McKenna), Doris Day (Jo McKenna), Brenda de Banzie (U.S. debut/Mrs. Drayton), Bernard Miles (Mr. Drayton), Ralph Truman (Buchanan), Daniel Gelin (Louis Bernard), Magens Wieth (ambassador), Alan Mowbray (Val Parnell), Hillary Brooke (Jan Peterson), Christopher Olsen (Hank McKenna), Reggie Nalder (Rien-assassin), Richard Wattis (assistant manager), Noel Willman (Woburn), Alix Talton (Helen Parnell), Cindy Fontaine (Carolyn Jones), Betty Baskcomb (Edna), Bernard Herrman (conductor), Yves Brainville, Alexi Bobrinskoy, Leo Abdelhaq Chraibi, Patrick Aherne, Louis Mercier, Anthony Warde, Lewis Martin, Gladys Holland, Peter Camlin, Ralph Neff, John Marshall, Eric Snowden, Lou Krugman, Milton Frome. *D: & P:* Alfred Hitchcock; *As.P:* Herbert Coleman; *St:* Charles Bennett, D.B. Wyndham-Lewis; *Sc:* John Michael Hayes, Angus MacPhail; *Songs:* (AA-Best Song) "What Ever Will Be Will Be (Que Sera Sera)," "We'll Love Again" Jay Livingston, Ray Evans; "Storm Cloud Cantata" Arthur Benjamin, D.B. Wyndham-Lewis. (2:00) (video/laserdisc) The master of suspense remakes his 1934 British classic of a couple who catch wind of an assassination plot and find their son has been kidnapped to keep their mouths shut, till the deed is completed. In Technicolor and VistaVision, it was in nomination at the Cannes Film Festival. The Oscar-winning song was also a big hit for Doris Day.

1654. The Man Who Turned to Stone (Columbia/Clover Prods.; 1957). *Cast:* Victor Jory, Ann Doran, Charlotte Austin, William Hudson, Paul Cavanagh, Tina Carver, Jean Willes, Victor Varconi, Frederick Ledebur, George Lynn, Barbara Wilson. *D:* Leslie Kardos; *P:* Sam Katzman; *St: & Sc:* Raymond T. Marcus [a pseudonym of blacklisted writer, Bernard Gordon]. (1:20) (video) In this teen-oriented horror film, a doctor and his associates retain their youth by preying on young girls at a female reformatory.

1655. The Man Who Understood Women (20th Century–Fox/Nunnally Johnson; 1959). *Cast:* Leslie Caron, Henry Fonda, Cesare Danova, Myron McCormick, Marcel Dalio, Conrad Nagel, Edwin Jerome, Bern Hoffman, Harry Ellerbe, Frank Cady, Ben Astar. *D:-P: & Sc:* Nunnally Johnson. (2:15) Comedy-drama of a Hollywood director-producer-writer-actor who makes a star out of an unknown, marries her and then due to his busy schedule, neglects her. Based on the 1953 novel *The Colors of the Day* by Romain Gary, it placed #6 on the "10 Best" list of the NBR. DeLuxe color, CinemaScope and stereophonic sound. Note: *Film Facts* and *Motion Picture Guide* list the running time of this film as 2:15, while Leonard Maltin's book lists it as 1:45.

1656. The Man with a Cloak (MGM; 1951). *Cast:* Joseph Cotten, Barbara Stanwyck, Louis Calhern, Leslie Caron, Joe DeSantis, Jim Backus, Margaret Wycherly, Nicholas Joy, Roy Roberts, Richard Hale, Mitchell Lewis, Jean Inness, Hank Worden, Francis Pierlot, Helen Eby-Rock, Charles Watts, Phil Dunham, James Logan, [A.] Cameron Grant, Robin Winans, Rudy Lee, Lynette Bryant, Dan Foster, Duke Johnson, James Gonzales, Melba Snowden, Janet Lewis, Charlotte Hunter, Carmen Clifford, Miriam Hendry, Ernie Flatt, Jonathan Cott. *D:* Fletcher Markle; *P:* Stephen Ames; *Sc:* Frank Fenton. (1:21) Mystery-melodrama, set in 19th century New York City, of a housekeeper with murder on her mind and the mystery man who visits her place of employment. Based on *Gentleman From Paris* by John Dickson Carr. Note: The reason this film bombed at the box office may or may not have had something to do with the fact that Barbara Stanwyck sings!

1657. The Man with My Face (United Artists/Edward F. Gardner; 1951). *Cast:* Barry Nelson (dual role), Lynn Ainley, John Harvey, Carole Mathews, Jim Boles, Jack Warden, Henry Lacoe, Johnny Kane. *D:* Edward J. Montagne; *P:* Edward F. Gardner; *Sc:* Samuel W. Taylor, J.T. McGowan, Vincent Bogert, Montagne. (1:26) Melodramatic thriller, with unexpected results, of a man who returns home to find his life completely taken over by a man who looks exactly like him. Based on the 1948 novel by Mr. Taylor, some location filming took place in Puerto Rico.

1658. The Man with the Golden Arm (United Artists/Carlyle Prods.; 1955). *Cast:* Frank Sinatra (AAN/Frankie), Eleanor Parker (Zosh), Kim Novak (Molly), Arnold Stang (Sparrow), Darren McGavin (Louie), Robert Strauss (Schwiefka), John Conte (Drunky), Doro Merande (Vi), George E. Stone (Markette), George Mathews (Williams), Leonid Kinskey (Dominowski), Emile Meyer (Bednar), Shorty Rogers (himself), Shelly Manne (himself), Frank Richards (Piggy), Will Wright (Lane), Tommy Hart (Kvorka), Frank Marlowe (Antek), Ralph Neff (Chester), Martha Wentworth (Angie). *D: & P:* Otto Preminger; *Sc:* Walter Newman, Lewis Meltzer; *ASD:* (AAN-b/w) Joseph C. Wright (art director), Darrell Silvera (sets); *Music:* (AAN) Elmer Bernstein. (1:59) (video/laserdisc) Drama of a man hooked on narcotics, his crippled wife and the girl who helps him kick the habit, cold turkey. Nothing new for a Preminger film, this one was daring and shocking for audiences of its day. The Motion Picture Association of America would not give its seal of approval, thus causing United Artists to resign from that organization. The accompanying publicity made it one of the 24 top-grossing films of 1955-56. Based on the 1949 novel by Nelson Algren, it was also in nomination at the British Academy Awards.

1659. Man with the Gun (United Artists/Formosa; 1955). *Cast:* Robert Mitchum, Jan Sterling, Karen Sharpe, Henry Hull, Emile Meyer, John Lupton, Barbara Lawrence, Ted de Corsia, Leo Gordon, James Westerfield, Florenz Ames, Robert Osterloh, Jay Adler, Angie Dickinson (in her 2nd film), Amzie Strickland, Stafford Repp, Maudie Prickett, Thom Conroy, Mara McAfee, Norma Calderon, Joe Barry. *D:* Richard Wilson (directorial debut); *P:* Sam Goldwyn, Jr. (first film); *Sc:* N.B. Stone, Jr., Wilson. (1:23) Western drama of a lawman hired by townsmen who later regret their decision when they view his strong-arm methods of keeping the peace. (G.B. title: *The Trouble Shooter*) (aka: *Man Without a Gun*)

The Man with Thirty Sons (G.B. title) *see* **The Magnificent Yankee**

Man Without a Gun *see* **Man with the Gun**

1660. Man Without a Star (Universal-International; 1955). *Cast:* Kirk Douglas, Jeanne Crain, William Campbell, Claire Trevor, Richard Boone, Jay C. Flippen, Mara Corday, Myrna Hansen, Eddy Waller, Sheb Wooley, George Wallace, Roy Barcroft, James Hayward, Paul Birch, Malcolm Atterbury, William Challee, William Phillips, Ewing Mitchell, Mark Hanna, Frank Chase, Gil Patrick, Casey Macgregor, Jack Ingram, Carl Andre, Jack Elam, Myron Healey, Lee Roberts. *D:* King Vidor; *P:* Aaron Rosenberg; *Sc:* Borden Chase, D.D. Beauchamp; *Songs:* Title song—Arnold Hughes, Frederick Herbert (sung by Frankie Laine); "And the Moon Grew Brighter and Brighter" Kimmy Kennedy, Lou Singer (sung by Douglas). (1:29) (video) Acclaimed western drama of a drifter who manages to get himself entangled in a range feud between a woman with a large ranch and several small ranchers. In Technicolor, it was based on the 1952 novel by Dee Linford and was remade by this studio in 1969 as *A Man Called Gannon*.

1661. Manfish (United Artists/W. Lee Wilder; 1956). *Cast:* John Bromfield, Lon Chaney, Victor Jory, Barbara Nichols, Tessa Prendergast, Eric Coverly, Theodore Purcell, Vincent Chang, Vera Johns, Arnold Shanks, Clyde Hoyte, Jack Lewis. *D: & P:* W. Lee Wilder; *St:* Myles Wilder; *Sc:* Joel Murcott; *Songs:* "Big Fish," "Goodbye," "Beware the Caribbean" Rich Koerner, Clyde Hoyte, Albert Elms. (1:16) (video) Low budget adventure melodrama of an expedition to the West Indies in search of sunken treasure. In DeLuxe color, it was based on "The Tell-Tale Heart" and "The Gold Bug," two stories by Edgar Allan Poe. Originally ran on a double bill with *Timetable* (q.v.). (G.B. title: *Calypso*)

Manhunt (G.B. title) *see* **From Hell to Texas**

1662. Manhunt in the Jungle (Warner; 1958). *Cast:* Robin Hughes, Luis Alvarez, James Wilson, Jorge Montoro, John B. Symmes, Natalia Manzuelas, James Ryan, Richard McCloskey, Harry Knapp, Emilio Miners, Enrique Gonzales, M. Torres Acho, Alfonso Santilla. *D:* Tom McGowan; *P:* Cedric Francis; *Sc:* Sam Merwin, Jr., Owen Crump; *Commentary:* Marvin Miller; *Songs:* "Amazon," "Triste Melodia" Howard Jackson (sung by Ricky Torres). (1:19) Commander George M. Dyott's (Hughes) 1928 search for explorer Colonel Percy H. Fawcett (Wilson) who disappeared while investigating reports of a lost white-skinned civilization. Based on Mr. Dyott's 1930 book *Man Hunting in the Jungle*, it was photographed in WarnerColor in the jungle of Brazil. Originally ran on a double bill with *Violent Road* (q.v.).

1663. Many Rivers to Cross (MGM; 1955). *Cast:* Robert Taylor, Eleanor Parker, Victor McLaglen, Jeff Richards, Russ Tamblyn, James Arness, Alan Hale, Jr., John Hudson, Josephine Hutchinson, Rosemary DeCamp, Ralph Moody, Sig Rumann, Rhys Williams, Abel Fernandez, Russell Johnson. *D:* Roy Rowland; *P:* Jack Cummings; *Sc:* Guy Trosper, Harry Brown. (1:32) 19th century romantic comedy of a coarse backwoods gal with the hots for a frontier trapper. Any resemblance to William Shakespeare's *Taming of the Shrew* was probably intended in this money-maker for the studio. Based on a short story by Steve Frazee, it was photographed in Eastmancolor and CinemaScope.

1664. Mara Maru (Warner; 1952). *Cast:* Errol Flynn, Ruth Roman, Raymond Burr, Paul Picerni, Richard Webb, Dan Seymour, Georges Renavent, Robert Cabal, Henry Marco, Nestor Paiva, Howard Chuman, Michael Ross, Paul McGuire, Ben Chavez, Leon Lontoc, Alfredo Santos, Don Harvey, Ralph Sancuyo, Leo Richmond, Ted Laurence. *D:* Gordon Douglas; *P:* David Weisbart (first film); *St:* Philip Yordan, Sidney Harmon, Hollister Noble; *Sc:* N. Richard Nash. (1:38) Treasure-hunting adventure, with the sought-after diamond cross, stolen during World II, aboard a sunken PT boat.

1665. Maracaibo (Paramount/Theodora Prods.; 1958). *Cast:* Cornel Wilde, Jean Wallace, Abbe Lane, Francis Lederer, Michael Landon, Joe E. Ross, Jack Kosslyn, Lillian Buyeff, George Ramsey, Martin Vargas, Lydia Goya, Carmen D'Antonio, Amapola Del Vando, Manuel Lopez, George Navarro, Frank Leyva, Gregory Irvin. *D: & P:* Cornel Wilde; *Sc:* Ted Sherdeman; *Title song:* Jefferson Pascal, Laurindo Almeida (sung by Jean Wallace). (1:28) Romantic actioner of a firefighter sent to battle a blazing oil field in Maracaibo, Venezuela, and two women (one an old flame) he meets and becomes involved with while there. Based on the 1955 novel by Stirling Silliphant. Filmed in and around Caracas, Venezuela, in Technicolor and VistaVision.

1666. The Marauders (MGM; 1955). *Cast:* Dan Duryea, Jeff Richards, Keenan Wynn, Jarma Lewis, John Hudson, Harry Shannon, David Kasday, James Anderson, Richard Lupino, Peter Mamakos, Mort Mills, Michael Dugan, John Damler. *D:* Gerald Mayer; *P:* Arthur M. Loew, Jr.; *Sc:* Earl Felton, Jack Leonard. (1:21) Programmer western of a small rancher who fights back when a wealthy cattle baron targets him for extinction. Based on an unpublished novel by Alan Marcus. Eastmancolor.

Marching Along (G.B. title) *see* **Stars and Stripes Forever**

1667. Mardi Gras (20th Century–Fox/Jerry Wald; 1958). *Cast:* Pat Boone (Paul Newell), Christine Carere (Michelle Marton), Tommy Sands (Barry Denton), Sheree North (Eadie West), Gary Crosby (Tony Runkle), Fred Clark (Mal Curtis), Richard [Dick] Sargent (Dick Saglon), Barrie Chase (Torchy Larue), Jennifer West (Sylvia Simmons), Geraldine Wall (Ann Harris), King Calder (Lt. Col. Vaupell), Robert Burton (Commander Tydings), the Corp of Cadets of V.M.I., Robert Wagner (guest star), Jeffrey Hunter (guest star). *D:* Edmund Goulding (final film—d. 1959); *P:* Jerry Wald; *St:* Curtis Harrington; *Sc:* Winston Miller, Hal Kanter; *Music:* (AAN) Lionel Newman; *Songs:* "The Mardi Gras March," "I'll Remember Tonight," "Loyalty," "Bigger Than Texas," "A Fiddle, a Rifle, an Axe and a Bible," "Bourbon Street Blues," "Stonewall Jackson," "That Man Could Sell Me the Brooklyn Bridge" Sammy Fain, Paul Francis Webster and "Shenandoah." (1:47) Hit musical-comedy of V.M.I. cadets who find romance at the New Orleans Mardi Gras. Location filming at Virginia Military Institute and New Orleans Mardi Gras. DeLuxe color and CinemaScope.

1668. Marjorie Morningstar (Warner/Beachwold; 1958). *Cast:* Gene Kelly (Noel Airman), Natalie Wood (Marjorie Morgenstern), Ed Wynn (Uncle Samson), Claire Trevor (Rose Morgenstern), Everett Sloane (Arnold Morgenstern), Martin Milner (Wally), Carolyn Jones (Marsha Zelenko), George Tobias (Greech), Jesse White (Lou Michaelson), Martin Balsam (Dr. David Harris), Alan Reed (Puddles Podell), Edward [Edd] Byrnes (Sandy Lamm), Howard Bert (Seth), Paul Picerni (Philip Berman), Ruth Lee (Imogene), Patricia Denise (Karen), Carl Sklover (Leon Lamm), Jean Vachon (Mary Lamm), Elizabeth Harrower (Miss Kimble), Guy Raymond (Mr. Klabber), Edward [Eddie] Foster (Carlos), Leslie Bradley (Blair), Maida Severn (Tonia Zelenko), Fay Nuell (Helen Harris), Fred Rapport (Nate), Harry Seymour (Frank), Walter Clinton (Mr. Zelenko), Shelley Fabares (Seth's girl friend), Sandy Livingston (Betsy), Peter Brown (Alec), Gail Ganley (Wally's girl friend), Russell Ash (Harry Morgenstern), Rad Fulton (Romeo), Lester Dorr, Pierre Watkin, Reginald Sheffield. *D:* Irving Rapper; *P:* Milton Sperling; *Sc:* Everett Freeman; *Theme song:* (AAN-Best Song) "A Very Precious Love" Sammy Fain, Paul Francis Webster. (2:03) (video) Romantic drama of a girl from a middle-class Jewish family who has a go at summer stock and falls for her theater director. Based on the 1953 novel by Herman Wouk, it became one of the 26 top-grossing films of 1957-58. WarnerColor.

Mark of the Apache (G.B. title) *see* **Tomahawk Trail**

1669. Mark of the Gorilla (Columbia; 1950). *Cast:* Johnny Weissmuller, Trudy Marshall, Onslow Stevens, Suzanne Dalbert, Robert Purcell, Selmer J(?)ackson, Pierce Lyden, Neyle Morrow. *D:* William Berke; *P:* Sam Katzman; *St: & Sc:* Carroll Young. (1:08) In this entry in the low budget adventure series, "Jungle Jim" (Weissmuller) encounters surviving Nazis disguised as gorillas who are looking for buried loot from the Third Reich. Based on the comic strip character created by Alex Raymond.

1670. Mark of the Renegade (Universal-International; 1951). *Cast:* Ricardo Montalban, Cyd Charisse, J. Carrol Naish, Gilbert Roland, Andrea King, George Tobias, Antonio Moreno, Georgia Backus, Robert Warwick, Armando Silvestre, Bridget Carr, Alberto Morin, Renzo Cesana, Robert Cornthwaite, Edward C. Rios, David Wolfe. *D:* Hugo Fregonese; *P:* Jack Gross; *St:* Johnston McCully; *Sc:* Louis Solomon, Robert Hardy Andrews. (1:21) A costume action-melodrama which unfolds in early 1820s California.

The Mark of the Vampire *see* **The Vampire**

1671. The Marksman (Monogram/Allied Artists-Westwood; 1953). *Cast:* Wayne Morris, Elena Verdugo, Frank Ferguson, Rick Vallin, I. Stanford Jolley, Tom Powers, Robert Bice, Stanley Price, Russ Whiteman, Brad Johnson, William Fawcett, Jack Rice, Tim Ryan. *D:* Lewis D. Collins; *P:* Vincent M. Fennelly; *St: & Sc:* Dan Ullman. (1:02) Low budget western of a man hired as a town marshal, for his ability to use a rifle with a telescopic sight, to hunt down an outlaw gang. One in a series of six done by Morris for Allied Artists.

1672. Marry Me Again (RKO; 1953). *Cast:* Robert Cummings, Marie Wilson, Ray Walker, Mary Costa, Jess Barker, Lloyd Corrigan, June Vincent, Richard Gaines, Moroni Olsen, Frank Cady, Joann Arnold, Bob Thomas (himself). *D: & Sc:* Frank Tashlin; *P: & St:* Alex Gottlieb; *As.P:* Robert Fallon. (1:13) Comedy of a fighter pilot in the Korean conflict who returns home to find his wife to be has just inherited a million dollars, leading him to cancel the marriage plans and wind up under psychiatric examination for his actions.

1673. The Marrying Kind (Columbia; 1952). *Cast:* Judy Holliday, Aldo Ray, Madge Kennedy, Sheila Bond, Rex Williams, John Alexander, Phyllis Povah, Peggy Cass (film debut), Mickey Shaughnessy (film debut), Griff Barnett, Joan Shawlee, Frank Ferguson, Thomas Browne Henry, Susan Hallaran, Barry Curtis, Christine Olsen, Wallace Acton, Elsie Holmes, Larry Blake, Gordon Jones, Joe McGuinn, Charles [Bronson] Buchinski, Nancy Kulp, Robert Hartley, Charles Brewer, Johnny Kaido, Don Mahin, Tom Farrell, John Eliott, Richard Cordon, Patrick Butler, Malan Mills. *D:* George Cukor; *P:* Bert Granet; *St: & Sc:* Garson Kanin, Ruth Gordon. (1:32) Marital comedy-drama of a couple seeking a divorce.

1674. Marshal of Cedar Rock (Republic; 1953). *Cast:* Allan Lane, Eddy Waller, Phyllis Coates, Roy Barcroft, Bill Henry, Robert Shayne, John Crawford, John Hamilton, Kenneth MacDonald, Herbert Lytton, Black Jack (horse). *D:* Harry Keller; *P:* Rudy Ralston; *St:* M. Coates Webster; *Sc:* Albert DeMond. (0:54) (video) "Rocky Lane" series entry of a U.S. marshal who proves a young man, railroaded by a greedy land grabber, innocent of bank robbery.

1675. Marshal of Heldorado (Lippert; 1950). *Cast:* Jimmie Ellison, Russ Hayden, Raymond Hatton, Fuzzy Knight, Betty [Julie] Adams, Tom Tyler, George Lewis, John Cason, Stanley Price, Stephen Carr, George Chesebro, Dennis Moore, Bud Osborne, Jimmie Martin, Ned Roberts, Cliff Taylor, Jack Hendricks, Wally West, James Van Horn, Jack Geddes, Carl Mathews. *D:* Thomas Carr; *P:* Ron Ormond, Murray Lerner; *St: & Sc:* Ormond, Maurice Tombragel; *As.P:* Ira Webb. (0:53) (video) The 2nd of six films in the "Four Star" series with Shamrock (Ellison) and Lucky (Hayden) coming to the aid of a western banker who is being blackmailed. (aka: *Blazing Guns*)

1676. The Marshal's Daughter (United Artists/Sherman A. Harris-Ken Murray; 1953). *Cast:* Laurie Anders, Ken Murray, Hoot Gibson, Harry Lauter, Robert Bray, Bob Duncan, Preston Foster (himself), Jimmy Wakely (himself), Johnny Mack Brown (himself), Buddy Baer (himself), Forrest Taylor, Tom London, Bruce Norman, Cecil Elliott, Bette Lou Walters, Francis Ford, Julian Upton, Bob Gross, Lee Phelps, Ted Jordan, Harry Harvey, Danny Duncan, Tex Ritter (narrator/who also sings). *D:* William Berke; *P:* Ken Murray; *St: & Sc:* Bob Duncan; *Songs:* Marjorie Thrasher, Jimmy Wakely, Jack Rivers, Stan Jones, Ken Murray. (1:11) (video) Western programmer of a U.S. marshal with a singing daughter who helps him clean up their town of its outlaw element.

Marshmallow Moon (G.B. title) *see* **Aaron Slick from Punkin Crick**

1677. Martin Luther (RD-DR Corp./ Louis de Rochemont Assoc.; 1953). *Cast:* Niall MacGinnis (title role), John Ruddock (Vicar von Staupitz), Pierre Lefevre (Spalatin), Guy Verney (Melanchthon), Alastair Hunter (Carlstadt), David Horne (Duke Frederick), Fred Johnson (Prior), Philip Leaver (Pope Leo X), Dr. Egon Strohm (Cardinal Aleander), Alexander Gauge (Tetzel), Irving Pichel (Brueck), Hans Lefebre (Charles V), Annette Carell (Katherine von Bora), Leonard White. *D:* Irving Pichel; *Ex.P:* Louis de Rochemont; *P:* Lothar Wolff; *Sc:* Allen Sloane, Wolff, Jaroslav Pelikan, Theodore G. Tappert; *Cin:* (AAN-b/w) Joseph C. Brun; *ASD:* (AAN-b/w) Fritz Maurischat, Paul Markwitz. (1:45) (video) Acclaimed historical biographical drama on the life of Martin Luther, a monk who protested actions of the Roman Catholic Church, was excommunicated and founded the first Protestant denomination, Lutheranism. Filmed on location in Germany, it was financed by six Lutheran Church groups. It placed #4 on the "10 Best" list of the NBR, while the *New York Times* placed it at #9 on theirs. Luther's life was first documented on film in *Martin Luther: His Life and Time*, a 1924 silent feature commissioned by the Lutheran Church. *Luther* was a 1974 British production of the same subject based on the play by John Osborne.

1678. Marty (United Artists/Hecht-Lancaster–Steven Prods.; 1955). *Cast:* Ernest Borgnine (AA + "Best Actor" by the New York Film Critics and the NBR, with a nomination for the same honor at the British Academy Awards/Marty Pilletti), Betsy Blair (AAN + a "Best Actress" nomination at the British Academy Awards/Clara Snyder), Esther Minciotti (Mrs. Pilletti), Augusta Ciolli (Catherine), Joe Mantell (AAN/Angie), Karen Steele (Virginia), Jerry Paris (Thomas), Frank Sutton (Ralph), Walter Kelley (The Kid), Robin Morse (Joe), Charles Cane (Lou, the bartender), Alan Wells (Herb), Minerva Urecal (Mrs. Rosari), James Bell (Mr. Snyder), Nick Brkich (a bachelor), Ed Sullivan (on TV). *D:* (AA) Delbert Mann (directorial debut); *P:* (AA-Best Picture) Harold Hecht; *Sc:* (AA) Paddy Chayefsky; *Cin:* (AAN-b/w) Joseph LaShelle; *ASD:* (AAN-b/w) Edward S. Haworth, Walter Simonds (art directors), Robert Priestley (sets). (1:31) (video/laserdisc) Critically acclaimed romantic drama of a Bronx butcher with low self-esteem who, though not looking for it, finds love. The New York Film Critics and the NBR voted it "Best Picture," an honor which it also garnered at the Cannes Film Festival when it received the "Golden Palm." *Film Daily* gave it a #2 placement on their "10 Best" list and the British Academy Awards also had it in nomination. *Marty* was presented out of competition at Czechoslovakia's Karlovy Vary Film Festival. One of the 27 top-grossing films of 1954-55, it was based on an original TV play by Mr. Chayefsky which starred Rod Steiger and Nancy Marchand (also available on home video).

1679. Mask of the Avenger (Columbia; 1951). *Cast:* Anthony Quinn, John Derek, Jody Lawrence (film debut), Arnold Moss, Eugene Iglesias, Dickie LeRoy, Harry Cording, Ian

Wolfe, Carlo Tricoli, David Bond, Wilton Graff, Tristram Coffin, Ric Roman, Philip Van Zandt, Chuck Hamilton, Mickey Simpson, Minerva Urecal, Belle Mitchell, Trevor Bardette, Gregory Gay, Lester Sharpe. *D:* Phil Karlson; *P:* Hunt Stromberg; *St:* George Bruce; *Adaptation:* Ralph Bettinson, Philip MacDonald; *Sc:* Jesse L. Lasky, Jr. (1:23) Set in 19th century Italy, this costume swashbuckler is centered around *The Count of Monte Cristo.* Technicolor.

1680. Mask of the Dragon (Lippert; 1951). *Cast:* Richard Travis, Sheila Ryan, Sid Melton, Michael Whalen, Lyle Talbot, Richard Emory, Jack Reitzen, Dee Tatum, Mr. Moto, Karl Davis, John Grant, Carl Barrett's Trailsmen, Eddie Lee, Ray Singer, Carla Martin, Dick Paxton, Barb Atkins. *D:* Sam Newfield; *P:* Sigmund Neufeld; *St: & Sc:* Orville Hampton. (0:55) Programmer comedy-mystery of a murdered Korean War vet.

Mask of the Himalayas *see* **Storm Over Tibet**

1681. Massacre (20th Century–Fox/Associated Film Releasing Prods.; 1956). *Cast:* Dane Clark, James Craig, Marta Roth, Miguel Torruco, Jaime Fernandez, Jose Munoz, Ferrusquilla, Enrique Zambrano, Victor Jordan, Luci Aura Gonzales, Joe Luis Rojas, Jose Palido, Rudolfo Toledo Rivera, Angel Maldonado, Cuauatemoc Ortega, Juan Yanes, Augusto Yanes, Mario Yanes, Sergio Yanes, Ramon Chavez Perez. *D:* Louis King (final film—ret.); *P:* Robert Lippert, Jr., Olallo Rubio, Jr.; *St:* Fred Frieberger, William Tunberg; *Sc:* D.D. Beauchamp. (1:16) Low budget western, filmed in Mexico, of whites selling guns to Yaqui Indians who use them to massacre white settlers. Anscocolor.

1682. Massacre Canyon (Columbia; 1954). *Cast:* Phil Carey, Audrey Totter, Douglas Kennedy, Jeff Donnell, Ross Elliott, Guinn "Big Boy" Williams, Chris Alcaide, John Pickard, Charlita, Ralph Dumke, Mel Welles, Steve Ritch, James Flavin, Bill Hale. *D:* Fred F. Sears; *P:* Wallace MacDonald; *St: & Sc:* David Lang. (1:06) Programmer western of cavalry vs. Indians that are after a wagon train loaded with rifles. Sepiatone.

1683. The Master of Ballantrae (Warner; 1953). *Cast:* Errol Flynn, Roger Livesey, Anthony Steele, Yvonne Furneaux, Beatrice Campbell, Felix Alymer, Mervyn Johns, Jacques Berthier, Charles Goldner, Ralph Truman, Francis De Wolff, Moultrie Kelsall, Charles Carson, Gillian Lynne, Jack Taylor, Stephen Vercoe. *D:* William Keighley (final film—ret.); *P:* Unc.; *Sc:* Herb Meadow, Harold Medford. (1:28) (video/laserdisc) Historical costumer, based on the 1889 book by Robert Louis Stevenson, of efforts to put Bonnie Prince Charles on the throne of England. This U.S.A./British co-production was filmed on locations in England, Scotland and Sicily. Remade in 1984 as a TV movie. Technicolor.

The Master of Terror *see* **4D Man**

1684. Masterson of Kansas (Columbia/Clover Prods.; 1954). *Cast:* George Montgomery (Bat Masterson), Nancy Gates, James Griffith (Doc Holliday), Jean Willes, Benny Rubin, William A. Henry, Gregg Barton, Jay Silverheels, Leonard Geer, Bruce Cowling (Wyatt Earp), David Bruce (final film—ret.), Donald Murphy (Virgil Earp), Sandy Sanders, Gregg Martell, John Maxwell, Wesley Hudman. *D:* William Castle; *P:* Sam Katzman; *St: & Sc:* Douglas Heyes. (1:13) Western of three famed lawmen trying to prevent an Indian uprising. Technicolor.

1685. The Matchmaker (Paramount/Don Hartman Prods., Inc.; 1958). *Cast:* Shirley Booth, Anthony Perkins, Shirley MacLaine, Paul Ford, Robert Morse (repeating his stage role), Wallace Ford, Rex Evans, Russell Collins, Perry Wilson [the director's wife], Gavin Gordon, Torben Meyer. *D:* Joseph Anthony; *P:* Don Hartman (final film—d. 1958); *Sc:* John Michael Hayes. (1:41) (video/laserdisc) Nineteenth century romantic comedy of a wealthy merchant who seeks a marital partner through a busybody matchmaker. Based on Thornton Wilder's 1955 stage hit, which he revised from his unsuccessful 1938 play *The Merchant of Yonkers*, which had its inspiration in a 19th century Viennese comedy of Johann Nestroy, which in turn had its inspiration in an older British farce by John Oxenford titled *A Day Well Spent.* The latest incarnation of the story was the 1964 hit Broadway musical *Hello Dolly!* which was filmed in 1969. VistaVision.

1686. The Mating Game (MGM; 1959). *Cast:* Debbie Reynolds, Tony Randall, Paul Douglas (final film—d. 1959), Fred Clark, Una Merkel, Philip Ober, Charles Lane, Philip Coolidge, Trevor Bardette, Bill Smith, Addison Powell, Rickey Murray, Donald Losby, Cheryl Bailey, Caryl Bailey. *D:* George Marshall; *P:*

Philip Barry, Jr.; *Sc:* William Roberts; *Songs:* "The Mating Game" Charles Strouse; Lee Adams (sung by Reynolds); "I've Got You Under My Skin" Cole Porter. (1:36) (video) "Darling Buds of May" by H.E. Bates was the 1958 source material for this popular comedy romp of a tax agent who falls for the daughter of a local farmer. MetroColor and CinemaScope.

1687. The Mating Season (Paramount; 1951). *Cast:* John Lund (Van McNulty), Gene Tierney (Maggie Carleton), Thelma Ritter (AAN/Ellen McNulty), Miriam Hopkins (Fran Carleton), Cora Witherspoon (Mrs. Williamson), Jan Sterling (Betsy), Larry Keating (Mr. Kellinger, Sr.), Malcolm Keen (Mr. Williamson), James Lorimer (James C. Kellinger, Jr.), Gladys Hurlbut (Mrs. Conger), Ellen Corby (Annie), Billie Bird (Mugsy), Samuel Colt (Colonel Conger), Grayce Hampton (Mrs. Fahnstock), Stapleton Kent (Dr. Chorley), Willa Pearl Curtis (Goldie), William Welsh (Mr. Paget), William Fawcett (Mr. Tuttle), Carol Coombs (Susie), Bob Kortman, Jimmy Hunt, Bess Flowers, Gordon Arnold, John Bryant, Jean Ruth, Laura Elliot, Charles Dayton, Beth Hartman, Mary Young, Martin Doric, Tito Vuolo, Gilda Oliva, Baker Sichol, Franklyn Farnum, Richard Neill, Sam Ash, Jack Richardson, Beulah Christian, Kathryn Wilson, Beulah Parkington, Margaret B. Farrell, Jean Acker, Sally Rawlinson, Tex Brodus, Bob Rich. *D:* Mitchell Leisen; *P:* Charles Brackett; *Sc:* Brackett, Walter Reisch, Richard Breen. (1:41) Marital comedy of a man who moves up the social ladder by marrying an ambassador's daughter—then Mom shows up and is mistaken by others as a new servant, a position she lovingly accepts, setting the stage for many comic situations. Based on "Maggie," an unproduced play by Caesar Dunn, it placed #10 at the Berlin Film Festival.

1688. The Maverick (Allied Artists/Silvermine Prods.; 1952). *Cast:* William Elliott, Phyllis Coates, Myron Healey, Richard Reeves, Terry Frost, Rand Brooks, Russell Hicks, Robert Bray, Florence Lake, Gregg Barton, Denver Pyle, Robert Wilke, Eugene Roth, Joel Allen. *D:* Thomas Carr; *P:* Vincent M. Fennelly; *St: & Sc:* Sidney Theil. (1:11) A series western with the cavalry being called in when settlers are being harassed by gunmen hired by local cattlemen. Sepiatone.

1689. The Maverick Queen (Republic; 1956). *Cast:* Barbara Stanwyck, Barry Sullivan, Scott Brady (Sundance Kid), Mary Murphy, Wallace Ford, Jim Davis (a stranger/Cole Younger), Howard Petrie (Butch Cassidy), Emile Meyer, Walter Sande, George Keymas, John Doucette, Taylor Holmes, Pierre Watkin, Karen Scott, Carol Brewster, William Loftus, Jack Harden, Herbert Jones, Robert Swan, Tristram Coffin, Jack O'Shea. *D:* Joseph Kane; *P:* Herbert J. Yates; *Sc:* Kenneth Gamet, DeVallon Scott. (1:32) (video) Western of a woman, in league with an outlaw gang, who unknowingly falls for a Pinkerton detective working undercover. Based on a novel by Zane Grey that was unfinished at the time of his death in 1939. The book went into publication in 1953 when it was completed by Romer Grey, his son. In Trucolor, it was also Republic's first production in Naturama.

1690. The Maze (Monogram/Allied Artists; 1953). *Cast:* Richard Carlson, Veronica Hurst, Katherine Emery, Michael Pate, John Dodsworth, Hillary Brooke, Stanley Fraser, Lillian Bond, Owen McGiveney, Robin Hughes, Clyde Cook. *D:* William Cameron Menzies; *P:* Richard Heermance; *Sc:* Dan Ullman. (1:21) Offbeat horror film of a man (Carlson) who returns to his ancestral Scottish home shortly before he is to be married. When he doesn't return, his fiancée (Hurst) and her aunt (Emery) make the trip and the lady finds her intended has prematurely aged under a 200-year-old family curse. 3-D. Note: Menzies also did the production design for the gloomy set pieces.

1691. The McConnell Story (Warner; 1955). *Cast:* Alan Ladd, June Allyson, James Whitmore, Frank Faylen, Robert Ellis, Sarah Selby, Willis Bouchey, Gregory Walcott, John Pickard, Frank Ferguson, Perry Lopez, Dabbs Greer, Edward Platt, Vera Marshe. *D:* Gordon Douglas; *P:* Henry Blanke; *St:* Ted Sherdeman; *Sc:* Sherdeman, Sam Rolfe. (1:47) (video/laserdisc) Sentimental biography of ace jet pilot of the Korean War, Captain Joseph McConnell, with a lot of Hollywood fiction thrown in. WarnerColor and CinemaScope. (G.B. title: *Tiger in the Sky*)

1692. Me and the Colonel (Columbia/Court-Goetz Prods.; 1958). *Cast:* Danny Kaye, Curt Jurgens, Nicole Maurey, Francoise Rosay, Akim Tamiroff, Martita Hunt, Alexander Scourby, Liliane Montevecchi, Ludwig Stossel, Gerard Buhr, Celia Lovsky, Eugene Borden, Franz Roehn, Clement Harari, Alain Bouvette, Albert Godderis, Karen Lenay, Maurice Marsac. *D:* Peter Glenville; *P:* William Goetz; *Sc:* Samuel Nathaniel Behrman, George Froeschel (voted "Best Comedy" by the Screenwriters Guild). (1:49) Acclaimed comedy of three people fleeing Paris in 1940 before the Germans arrive. Based on the 1944 play *Jacobowsky and the Colonel* by Frank Werfel, it was partially filmed in France and placed #9 on the "10 Best" list of the NBR.

1693. Meet Danny Wilson (Universal-International; 1952). *Cast:* Frank Sinatra, Shelley Winters, Raymond Burr, Alex Nicol, Tommy Farrell, Vaughn Taylor, Donald MacBride, Barbara Knudson, Carl Sklover, John Day, Jack Kruschen, Tom Dugan, Danny Welton, Pat Flaherty, Carlos Molina, George Eldredge, Bob Donnelly, John Indrisano, Anthony [Tony] Curtis. *D:* Joseph Pevney; *P:* Leonard Goldstein; *St: & Sc:* Don McGuire; *Songs:* "All of Me" Seymour Simons, Gerald Marks; "How Deep Is the Ocean?" Irving Berlin; "She's Funny That Way" Neil Moret, Richard Whiting; "I've Got a Crush on You" George and Ira Gershwin; "That Old Black Magic" Harold Arlen, Johnny Mercer; "A Good Man is Hard to Find" Eddie Green; "When You're Smiling" Mark Fisher, Joe Goodwin, Larry Shay; "You're a Sweetheart" Jimmy McHugh, Harold Adamson; "Lonesome Man Blues" Sy Oliver. (1:25) (video) Comedy-drama of a singer's rise to fame at the hands of a ruthless promoter.

1694. Meet Me After the Show (20th Century–Fox; 1951). *Cast:* Betty Grable, Macdonald Carey, Rory Calhoun, Eddie Albert, Fred Clark, Lois Andrews (final film—ret.), Irene Ryan, Arthur Walge, Edwin Max, Robert Nash, Rodney Bell, Don Kohler, Harry Antrim, Steve Condos, Jerry Brandow, Lovyss Bradley, Jewel Rose, Carol Savage, Michael Darrin, Joe Haworth, Gwen Verdon, Perc Launders, Max Wagner, Al Murphy, Dick Cogan, Billy Newell. *D:* Richard Sale; *P:* George Jessel; *St:* Erna Lazarus, W. Scott Darling; *Sc:* Mary Loos, Sale; *Musical numbers:* "It's a Hot Night in Alaska," "I Feel Like Dancing," "No Talent Joe" and "Bettin' on a Man" Jule Styne, Leo Robin. (1:26) Technicolor musical of a woman, star of her husband-producer's show, who feigns amnesia after finding hubby has been diddling around.

1695. Meet Me at the Fair (Universal-International; 1952). *Cast:* Dan Dailey, Diana Lynn, Chet Allen, Scatman Crothers, Hugh O'Brian, Carole Mathews, Russell Simpson, Rhys Williams, Thomas E. Jackson, George Chandler, Virginia Brissac, Doris Packer, Edna Holland, George L. Spaulding, Paul Gordon, John Maxwell, George Riley, Johnson and Diehl (jugglers), The Black Brothers (comic acrobats), Iron Eyes Cody, Donald Kerr, Franklyn Farnum, Harte Wayne, Roger Moore, Robert Shafto (Prime Minister Disraeli), Dante Dipaolo, George Arglen, Jon Gardner, Sam Pierce, Max Wagner, Jack Gargan, Brick Sullivan, Butch (Spook the dog). *D:* Douglas Sirk; *P:* Albert J. Cohen; *Adaptation:* Martin Berkeley; *Sc:* Irving Wallace; *Songs:* "Meet Me at the Fair" Milton Rosen, Frederick Herbert; "I Was There" Flourney E. Miller, Benjamin "Scatman" Crothers; "Remember the Time" Kenny Williams, Marvin Wright; "Ave Maria" Franz Schubert; "Ezekiel Saw de Wheel" (traditional); "Sweet Genevieve" George Cooper, Henry Tucker; "All God's Chillun Got Wings" (traditional); "I Got the Shiniest Mouth in Town" Stan Freberg; "Oh Susannah!" Stephen Foster; "Bill Bailey Won't You Please Come Home" Hughie Cannon. (1:27) Musical Americana of a traveling medicine man in 1904 who gets into trouble when he befriends a runaway orphan. Based on the novel *The Great Companions* by Gene Markey. Technicolor.

1696. Meet Me in Las Vegas (MGM; 1955). *Cast:* Dan Dailey (Chuck Rodwell), Cyd Charisse (Maria Corvier), Agnes Moorehead (Miss Hattie), Lili Darvas (Sari Hatvani), Jim Backus (Tom Culdane), Oscar Karlweiss (Loisi), Liliane Montevecchi (Lilli), Cara Williams (Kelly Donavan), The Slate Brothers (themselves), George [Chakiris] Kerris, Betty Lynn, Peter Rugolo, John Brascia, John Harding, Benny Rubin, Jack Daly, Henny Backus, Jerry Colonna, Paul Henreid, Frankie Laine, Mitsuko Sawamura, Marc Wilder, Peter Lorre (cameo), Frank Sinatra (cameo), Debbie Reynolds (cameo), Tony Martin (cameo), Vic Damone (cameo), Elaine Stewart (cameo), Sammy Davis, Jr. (voice only). *D:* Roy Rowland; *P:* Joe Pasternak; *St: & Sc:* Isobel Lennart; *Music:* (AAN) Georgie Stoll, Johnny Green; *songs:* "The Girl with the Yaller Shoes" (sung and danced by Dailey and Charisse), "If You Can Dream" (sung over the credits by the Four Aces and reprised by Lena Horne), "Hell Hath No Fury" (by Laine), "Lucky Charm" (by Colonna), "I Refuse to Rock 'n' Roll" (by Williams), "Rehearsal Ballet" and "Sleeping Beauty Ballet" (danced by Charisse) and "Frankie and Johnny" (new lyrics by Sammy Cahn, sung by Sammy Davis, Jr.). (1:52) (video) Hit glitzy musical romance, set in America's showbiz/gambling mecca, of a rancher who finds that holding a girl's hand makes him a sure winner at the roulette table as well as making his hens lay many more eggs back on his ranch. Eastmancolor and CinemaScope. (G.B. title: *Viva Las Vegas*)

Meet the Nelsons *see* **Here Come the Nelsons**

1697. The Member of the Wedding (Columbia/Stanley Kramer Prod.; 1952). *Cast:* Ethel Waters (repeating her stage role/Berenice Sadie Brown), Julie Harris (AAN-film debut, repeating her stage role/Frankie Addams), Brandon de Wilde (film debut, repeating his stage role/John Henry), Arthur Franz (Jarvis), Nancy Gates (Janice), William Hansen (repeating his stage role/Mr. Addams), James Edwards (Honey Camden Brown), Harry Bolden (repeating his stage role/T.T. Williams), Dick Moore (final film—ret./soldier), Danny Mummert (Barney MacKean), June Hedin (Helen), Ann Carter (Doris). *D:* Fred Zinneman; *P:* Stanley Kramer; *Sc:* Edward and Edna Anhalt. (1:31) (video) Drama of a young girl dealing with various life situations as she approaches adolescence. Based on the 1946 novel and hit play by Carson McCullers.

1698. The Men (United Artists/Stanley Kramer Prod.; 1950). *Cast:* Marlon Brando (film debut/Ken), Teresa Wright (Ellen), Everett Sloane (Dr. Brock), Jack Webb (Norm), Richard Erdman (Leo), Arthur Jurado (Angel), Virginia Farmer (Nurse Robbins), Dorothy Tree (final film—ret./Ellen's mother), Howard St. John (Ellen's father), Nita Hunter (Dolores), Patricia Joiner (Laverne), John Miller (Mr. Doolin), Cliff Clark (Dr. Kameran), Ray Mitchell (Thompson), Pete Simon (Mullin), Paul Peltz (Hopkins), Tom Gillick (Fine), Randall Updyke III (Baker), Marshall Ball (Romano), Carlo Lewis (Gunderson), William Lea, Jr. (Walter), Obie Parker, Marguerite Martin, Ray Teal. *D:* Fred Zinneman; *P:* Stanley Kramer; *As. P:* George Glass; *St: & Sc:* (AAN) Carl Foreman. (1:25) (video/laserdisc) Critically acclaimed drama of the psychological rehabilitation of an ex-G.I. who is paralyzed from the waist down. The "10 Best" list of the NBR placed it at #4 while the same listing from the *New York Times* placed it at #6. It was also in nomination at the British Academy Awards. Re-released in 1957 as *Battle Stripe*.

Men Behind Bars (G.B. title) *see* **Duffy of San Quentin**

1699. Men in War (United Artists/Security Pictures; 1957). *Cast:* Robert Ryan, Aldo Ray, Robert Keith, Philip Pine, Vic Morrow, James Edwards, Nehemiah Persoff, L.Q. Jones, Adam Kennedy, Scott Marlowe, Walter Kelley, Robert Normand, Anthony Ray, Michael Miller, Race Gentry (final film—ret.), Victor Sen Yung. *D:* Anthony Mann; *P:* Sidney Harmon; *Sc:* Philip Yordan. (1:44) (video) Acclaimed Korean War drama of a company of soldiers cut off from battalion headquarters and their fight for survival against insurmountable odds. Based on the 1945 novel *Combat* by Van Van Praag.

1700. Men of the Fighting Lady (MGM; 1954). *Cast:* Van Johnson, Walter Pidgeon, Louis Calhern, Dewey Martin, Keenan Wynn, Robert Horton, Frank Lovejoy, Bert Freed, Dick Simmons, Lewis Martin, George Cooper, Chris Warfield, Steve Rowland, Ed Tracy, Paul Smith, John Rosser, Ronald Lisa, Teddy Infuhr, Sarah Selby, Jerry Mather, Ronald Stafford, Joseph "Bucko" Stafford, Ann Baker, Jonathan Hale, Dorothy Patrick. *D:* Andrew Marton; *P:* Henry Berman; *Sc:* Art Cohn. (1:20) (video) The lives of fighter pilots stationed on an aircraft carrier during the Korean War is the focus of this hit drama. Based on two stories, which appeared in *Saturday Evening Post* in 1952, namely: "The Forgotten Heroes of Korea" by James A. Michener and "Case of the Blind Pilot" by Commander Harry A. Burns. Anscocolor.

1701. Merry Andrew (MGM/Sol C. Siegel Prods.; 1958). *Cast:* Danny Kaye, Pier Angeli, [Salvatore] Baccaloni, Robert Coote, Noel Purcell, Tommy Rall, Rex Evans, Patricia Cutts, Walter Kingsford (final film—d. 1958), Peter Mamakos, Rhys Williams. *D:* Michael Kidd (only film as director/also choreographed); *P:* Sol C. Siegel; *As.P:* Saul Chaplin; *Sc:* Isobel Lennart, I.A.L. Diamond; *Songs:* "The Pipes of Pan," "The Square Root of the Hypotenuse," "You Can't Always Have What You Want," "Everything is Tickety-Boo," "Chin Up, Stout Fellow," "Salud" and "Buona Fortuna" Chaplin, Johnny Mercer. (1:43) Comedy of an English schoolmaster who follows his dream to become a circus clown. Based on the book *The Romance of Henry Menafee* by Paul Gallico, it was photographed in MetroColor and CinemaScope.

1702. The Merry Widow (MGM; 1952). *Cast:* Lana Turner (Crystal Radek), Fernando Lamas (Count Danilo), Una Merkel (Kitty Riley), Richard Haydn (Baron Popoff), Thomas Gomez (King of Marshovia), John Abbott (Marshovian ambassador), Marcel Dalio (police sergeant), Robert Coote (Marquis De Crillon),

King Donovan (Nitki), Lisa Ferraday (Marcella), Shepard Menken (Kunjary), Sujata, Ludwig Stossel, Dave Willock, Wanda McKay, Anne Kimbell, Edward Earle, Gwen Verdon, Gregg Sherwood, Joi Lansing. *D:* Curtis Bernhardt; *P:* Joe Pasternak; *Sc:* Sonya Levien, William Ludwig; *ASD:* (AAN-color) Cedric Gibbons, Paul Groesse (art directors), Edwin B. Willis, Arthur Krams (sets); *Costumes:* (AAN-color) Helen Rose, Gile Steele. (1:45) (video) Lavishly produced costume musical, the third time around for Franz Lehar's operetta, with libretto by Victor Leon and Leo Stein. Previously filmed in 1925 (without the music) and 1934. One of the 23 top-grossing films of 1951-52. Technicolor.

1703. The Mesa of Lost Women (Howco/ A.J. Frances White–Joy Houck; 1952–56). *Cast:* Jackie Coogan, Richard Travis, Allan Nixon, Mary Hill, Robert Knapp, Tandra Quinn, Harmon Stevens, Samuel Wu, Chris-Pin Martin, George Barrows, John Martin, Angelo Rossito, Katena Vea, Fred Kelsey, Lyle Talbot (narrator). *D:* Herbert Tevos, Ron Ormond; *P:* Melvin Gale, William Perkins; *St: & Sc:* Tevos. (1:10) Science fiction involving a mad scientist working in the Mexican desert to create a race of superwomen. A low budget item completed in 1952 and not released until 1956. (aka: *Lost Women* and *Lost Women of Zarpa*)

1704. Messenger of Peace (Astor; 1950). *Cast:* John Beal, Peggy Stewart, William Bakewell, Paul Guilfoyle, Fred Essler, Raphael [Ray] Bennett, Maudie Prickett, Alan Bridge, Elizabeth Kerr, William Gould, Edythe Elliott, Brook Shayne, Joe Brown, Jr. *D:* Frank Strayer; *P:* Roland Reed; *St:* Henry Rischel; *Sc:* Glenn Tryon. (1:27) A low budget independent religious drama which follows a man from his days as a seminary student to his twilight years as a man of the cloth.

Meteor Monster *see* **Teenage Monster**

1705. Mexican Manhunt (Monogram/ Allied Artists; 1953). *Cast:* George Brent, Hillary Brooke, Morris Ankrum, Karen Sharpe, Marjorie Lord, Douglas Kennedy, Alberto Morin, Carleton Young, Stuart Randall, Marvin Press. *D:* Rex Bailey; *P:* Lindsley Parsons; *As.P:* Ace Herman; *St: & Sc:* George Bricker. (1:11) Melodrama of a writer in Mexico who sets out to solve a murder which occurred fifteen years before. Brent's final starring role.

1706. Miami Expose (Columbia/Clover Prods.; 1956). *Cast:* Lee J. Cobb, Patricia Medina, Edward Arnold (final film—d. during production), Michael Granger, Eleanore Tanin, Alan Napier, Harry Lauter, Chris Alcaide, Hugh Sanders, Barry L. Connors. *D:* Fred F. Sears; *P:* Sam Katzman; *St: & Sc:* James B. Gordon. (1:13) Crime melodrama of a gambling syndicate in Florida.

1707. The Miami Story (Columbia; 1954). *Cast:* Barry Sullivan, Luther Adler, John Baer, Adele Jergens, Beverly Garland, Dan Riss, Damian O'Flynn, Chris Alcaide, Gene D'Arcy, David Kasday, George E. Stone, Tom Greenway. *D:* Fred F. Sears; *P:* Sam Katzman; *St: & Sc:* Robert E. Kent. (1:15) A melodrama of organized crime in Florida. Introducion by Senator George A. Smathers of that state.

1708. Middle of the Night (Columbia/ Sudan Co.; 1959). *Cast:* Fredric March, Kim Novak, Glenda Farrell, Jan Norris, Lee Grant, Effie Afton (repeating her stage role), Lee Phillips (repeating his stage role), Edith Meiser, Joan Copeland, Martin Balsam (repeating his stage role), David Ford, Audrey Peters, Betty Walker (repeating her stage role), Albert Dekker, Rudy Bond, Lou Gilbert, Doris Weissman, Lee Richardson, Anna Berger, Alfred Leberfeld, Nelson Olmstead. *D:* Delbert Mann; *P:* George Justin; *Sc:* Paddy Chayefsky. (1:58) Romantic drama of an older man and his much younger bride-to-be. Based on the 1954 TV play and the 1956 stage play by Mr. Chayefsky, it placed #5 on the "10 Best" list of the NBR and was in nomination at the Cannes Film Festival.

1709. The Midnight Story (Universal-International; 1957). *Cast:* Tony Curtis, Marisa Pavan, Gilbert Roland, Jay C. Flippen, Argentina Brunetti, Ted de Corsia, Kathleen Freeman, Richard Monda, Herbert Vigran, Peggy June Maley, John Cliff, Russ Conway, Chico Vejar, Tito Vuolo, Helen Wallace, James Hyland. *D:* Joseph Pevney; *P:* Robert Arthur; *St:* Edwin Blum; *Sc:* John Robinson, Blum. (1:27) Crime melodrama, set in San Francisco, of a detective who quits the force to hunt down the murderer of a Roman Catholic priest. CinemaScope. (G.B. title: *Appointment with a Shadow*)

1710. Military Academy with That 10th Avenue Gang (Columbia; 1950). *Cast:* Stanley Clements, Myron Welton, Gene Collins, Leon Tyler, James Millican, William Johnstone, James Seay, John Hamilton, Dick Jones, Buddy

Swan, Conrad Binyon, John Michaels, Buddy Burroughs, John McGuire, Jack Reynolds, Russ Conway, Tim Ryan. *D:* D. Ross Lederman (final film—ret.); *P:* Wallace MacDonald; *St:* & *Sc:* Howard J. Green. (1:04) Programmer drama of four delinquents sent to a military academy instead of reform school. (aka: *Military Academy*) (G.B. title: *Sentence Suspended*)

Military Policeman (G.B. title) *see* **Off Limits**

1711. The Milkman (Universal-International; 1950). *Cast:* Donald O'Connor, Jimmy Durante, Joyce Holden, William Conrad, Piper Laurie, Henry O'Neill, Paul Harvey, Jess Barker, Elisabeth Risdon, Frank Nelson, Charles Flynn, Garry Owen, John Cliff, Bill Nelson, Eddie Acuff, Lucille Barkley, Minerva Urecal, Howard Negley, John "Skins" Miller, Richard Powers [aka: Tom Keene], Norman Field, Ruth Brady, Therese Lyons, Joe Kerr, Edward Clark, Bob Stephenson, Charmienne Harker, Hal Smith, Ralph Montgomery, David Newell, Perc Launders, Vesey O'Davoren, Kippee Valez, Hazel Keener, Jerry Lewis (not the), Marilyn Mercer, Dave Dunbar, Larry McGrath, Charles Hall, Audrey Betz, Marian Dennish, John McKee, Donald Kerr, Frank Malet, Doug Carter, Wally Walker, Pat Combs, Bob Garvin, Jewel Rose, Paul Power, Parke MacGregory, John O'Connor, Chester Conklin, Paul Palmer, Carey Loftin, Dick Crockett, Eddie Parker, Frank McGrath, Frank McMahon, Tom Steele, Gordon Carveth, Jimmy Dundee, Wes Hopper, Wally Rose, Chick Collins, Cliff Lyons. *D:* Charles T. Barton; *P:* Ted Richmond; *St:* Martin Ragaway, Leonard Stern; *Sc:* Ragaway, Stern, Albert Beich, James O'Hanlon; *Songs:* "Girls Don't Want My Money" (Jimmy Durante–Jack Barnett); "That's My Boy" (Durante–Barnett), "It's Bigger Than Both of Us" (Sammy Fain–Barnett); "Early Morning Song" (Fain–Barnett). (1:27) Comedy revolving around the son of a wealthy milk company owner being given a job at a rival milk company.

1712. Million Dollar Mermaid (MGM; 1952). *Cast:* Esther Williams (Annette Kellerman), Victor Mature (James Sullivan), Walter Pidgeon (Frederick Kellerman), David Brian (Alfred Harper), Donna Corcoran (Annette, age 10), Jesse White (Doc Cronnol), Maria Tallchief (Pavlova), Howard Freeman (Aldrich), Adrienne D'Ambricourt (Marie the housekeeper), Queenie Leonard (Mrs. Craves), Gordon Richards (Casey), Rod Rogers (Marcellino the Clown), George Wallace (Bud Williams), Charles Watts, Wilton Graff, Frank Ferguson, James Bell, James Flavin, Willis Bouchey, Clive Morgan, Stuart Torres, James Aubrey, Patrick O'Moore, Elizabeth Slifer, Al Ferguson, Benny Burt, Harry Hines, Clarence Hennecke, Genevieve Pasques, Pat Flaherty, James L. "Tiny" Kelly, Thomas Dillon, Paul Frees, Louise Lorimer, Mack Chandler, Rosemarie Bowe. *D:* Mervyn LeRoy; *P:* Arthur Hornblow, Jr.; *Sc:* Everett Freeman; *Choreography:* Busby Berkeley: *Cin:* (AAN-color) George J. Folsey. (1:55) (video) Biographical Hollywood tale of Australian swimmer Annette Kellerman, a champion in her day known as "The Diving Venus," who made films in Hollywood between 1914 and 1924. Based on her unpublished autobiography, it became one of the 26 top-grossing films of 1952-53. Partial wide-screen and Technicolor. (G.B. title: *The One-Piece Bathing Suit*)

1713. Million Dollar Pursuit (Republic; 1951). *Cast:* Penny Edwards, Grant Withers, Norman Budd, Steve Flagg [aka: Michael St. Angel], Rhys Williams, Mikel Conrad, Paul Hurst, Denver Pyle, Ted Pavalee, John DeSimone, Don Beddoe, Edward Cassidy, Edward Clark, John Hamilton, George Brand, Jack Shea. *D:* R.G. Springsteen; *As.P:* Stephen Auer; *St:* Albert DeMond; *Sc:* DeMond, Bradbury Foote. (0:59) Crime melodrama of a small time hoodlum, prone to run at the mouth, who plans a heist at a department store.

1714. A Millionaire for Christy (20th Century–Fox/Thor; 1951). *Cast:* Fred MacMurray, Eleanor Parker, Richard Carlson, Kay Buckley, Una Merkel, Douglass Dumbrille, Raymond Greenleaf, Nestor Paiva, Chris-Pin Martin, Julian Rivero, Everett Glass, Almira Sessions, Sam Flint, Ralph Peters, Ralph Hodges, Byron Foulger, Walter Baldwin, Lane Chandler, Charles Williams, Emmett Vogan, Robert Bice, Billy Snyder, Al Hill, Emmett Lynn, Gene Geriko, Jo-Carroll Dennison, John Indrisano. *D:* George Marshall; *P:* Bert E. Friedlob; *Sc:* Ken Englund. (1:31) Romantic comedy, reminiscent of the screwball comedies of the late 1930s, of a woman with her sights set on a radio commentator who has just inherited $2,000,000. Based on *The Golden Goose* by Robert Harari.

1715. The Miniver Story (MGM; 1950). *Cast:* Greer Garson, Walter Pidgeon, John Hodiak, Leo Genn, Cathy O'Donnell, Henry Wilcoxon, Reginald Owen, Peter Finch, Anthony

Bushell, William [James] Fox (film debut), Alison Leggatt, Richard Gale, Cicely Paget-Bowman, Ann Wilton, Eliot Makeham, Brian Roper, Paul Demel. *D:* H.C. Potter; *P:* Sidney Franklin; *Sc:* Ronald Miller, George Froeschel. (1:44) (video) Dramatic sequel to 1942's acclaimed hit, *Mrs. Miniver*, tells of the reuniting of the Miniver family following World War II. Filmed on location in England, this G.B./U.S.A. co-production was a box office dud. Based on characters created by Jan Struther in her 1940 book, *Mrs. Miniver*.

1716. The Miracle (Warner; 1959). *Cast:* Carroll Baker, Roger Moore, Walter Slezak, Vittorio Gassman, Katina Paxinou, Isobel Elsom, Dennis King, Gustavo Rojo, Carlos Rivas, Torin Thatcher, Elspeth March, Daria Massey, Lester Matthews. *D:* Irving Rapper; *P:* Henry Blanke; *Sc:* Frank Butler. (2:01) (video) A critically panned drama, set during the Napoleonic Wars of a postulant who questions her position in the convent and leaves for several romantic liaisons, while a statue of the Virgin Mary disappears from its place in the convent and takes her place. Based on Karl Vollmoeller's 1911 play of the same name, which was previously filmed as a 4-reel silent Austrian production in 1912 called *Das Mirakel*. Partially filmed in Spain in Technicolor and Technirama. Note: Max Reinhardt's production of Vollmoeller's play was a heralded theatrical masterpiece first in England in 1911 and in New York in 1924.

1717. Miracle in the Rain (Warner; 1956). *Cast:* Jane Wyman, Van Johnson, Peggie Castle, Eileen Heckart (film debut), Josephine Hutchinson, Barbara Nichols (film debut), William Gargan, Alan King, Paul Picerni, Arte Johnson, Halliwell Hobbes (final film—ret.), Marcel Dalio, George Givot, Irene Seidner, Marian Holmes, Minerva Urecal, Frank Scannell, Walter Kingston, Anna Dewey, Lucita (accordionist), Rose Allen, Jess Kirkpatrick, Allen Ray, Diana Dawson. *D:* Rudolph Maté; *P:* Frank P. Rosenberg; *Sc:* Ben Hecht; *Song:* "I'll Always Believe in You" Ray Heindorf, M.K. Jerome, Ned Washington. (1:47) Tear-jerker of two lonely people who meet on a rainy day in New York City during World War II and have a brief affair, with the G.I. sent overseas shortly after and killed in action. Based on the 1943 novel by Mr. Hecht.

Miracle of Fatima (G.B. title) *see* **The Miracle of Our Lady of Fatima**

1718. The Miracle of Our Lady of Fatima (Warner; 1952). *Cast:* Gilbert Roland (Hugo DaSilva), Angela Clarke (Maria Rosa), Frank Silvera (Arturo Dos Santos), Jay Novello (Antonio), Richard Hale (Father Ferreira), Sherry Jackson (Jacinta Marto), Susan Whitney (Lucia Dos Santos), Sammy Ogg (Francisco Marto), Norman Rice (Manuel Marto), Frances Morris (Olimpia), Carl Millitaire (magistrate). *D:* John Brahm; *P:* Byran Foy; *Sc:* Crane Wilbur, James O'Hanlon; *St:* Wilbur; *Music:* (AAN) Max Steiner. (1:42) (video/laserdisc) Hit religious drama of the three children in 1917 who reported seeing "the lady in the sky" at the Cova of Iria near the Portuguese village of Fatima with the "lady" asking them to return to the spot on the 13th of each month. Based on factual incidents, it became one of the 23 top-grossing films of 1951-52. WarnerColor. (G.B. title: *Miracle of Fatima*)

1719. The Miracle of the Hills (20th Century–Fox/Associated Producers; 1959). *Cast:* Rex Reason, Theona Bryant, Jay North, Gilbert Smith, Van Leslie, Betty Lou Gerson, June Vincent, Tracy Stratford, Gene Roth, I. Stanford Jolley, Gene Collins, Paul Wexler, Kenneth Mayer, Pat O'Hara, Tom Daly, Cecil Elliott, Charles Arnt, Claire Carleton, Kelton Garwood, Vince Townsend, Jr. *D:* Paul Landres; *P:* Richard E. Lyons; *St:* & *Sc:* Charles Hoffman. (1:13) Western drama of a minister seeking to bring salvation to a 19th century mining town, banging heads in the process with the ex-saloon hostess who runs the local mining operation. The titled miracle involves children being trapped in the mine and saved by an earthquake. CinemaScope.

1720. Miss Robin Crusoe (20th Century–Fox; 1953). *Cast:* Amanda Blake, George Nader, Rosalind Hayes. *D:* & *P:* Eugene Frenke; *St:* Al Zimbalist; *Sc:* Harold Nebenzal, Richard Priondo. (1:14) This adventure finds two women and a man stranded on an island. Eastmancolor.

1721. Miss Sadie Thompson (Columbia/Beckwith Corp.; 1953). *Cast:* Rita Hayworth (Sadie Thompson), Jose Ferrer (Alfred Davidson), Aldo Ray (Sgt. Phil O'Hara), Russell Collins (Dr. Robert MacPhail), Diosa Costello (Ameena Horn), Harry Bellaver (Joe Horn), Wilton Graff (governor), Peggy Converse (Mrs. Margaret Davidson), Rudy Bond (Hodges), Henry Slate (Griggs), Charles [Bronson] Buchinski (Edwards), Frances Morris (Mrs. MacPhail), Peter Chong (Chung), Charles Horvath, John Duncan,

Al Kikume, Fred Letuli, Richard G. Anderson, Joe McCabe, Erlynn Botelho, Elizabeth Bartilet, Dennis Medieros, John Grossett, Billy Varga, Teddy Pavelec, Frank Stanlow, Harold Tommy Hart, Ben Harris, Ted Jordan, Eduardo Cansino, Jr. *D:* Curtis Bernhardt; *P:* Jerry Wald; *Sc:* Harry Kleiner; Sadie Thompson's Song "Blue Pacific Blues" (AAN-Best Song) Lester Lee, Ned Washington. (1:31) (video/laserdisc) Drama of a prostitute who is lusted after by a South Seas missionary. Based on Somerset Maugham's *Rain*. Previously filmed in 1928 as *Sadie Thompson* (U.A.), as *Rain* in 1932 (U.A.) and *Dirty Gerty from Harlem, U.S.A.* (Sack Amusement: 1946). Also a play adaptation by John Colton and Clemence Randolph. Technicolor and 3-D.

1722. Missile Monsters (Republic; 1958). *Cast:* Walter Reed, Lois Collier (final film—ret.), Gregory Gay, James Craven, Harry Lauter, Richard Irving, Sandy Sanders, Michael Carr, Dale Van Sickel, Tom Steele, George Sherwood, Jimmy O'Gatty, John DeSimone, Lester Dorr, Dick Cogan. *D:* Fred C. Brannon; *P:* Franklin Adreon; *Sc:* Ronald Davidson. (1:15) Science fiction of an earth scientist in cahoots with a Martian to take over the planet as a Martian satellite. This feature was edited down from Republic's 12-chapter serial of 1951 titled "Flying Disc Man from Mars." Originally ran on a double bill with *Satan's Satellites* (q.v.).

1723. Missile to the Moon (Astor/Marc Frederic-George Foley Prods.; 1958). *Cast:* Richard Travis (final film—ret.), Cathy Downs, K.T. Stevens, Tommy Cook, Nina Bara, Gary Clarke, Michael Whalen, Laurie Mitchell, Marjorie Hellen, Henry Hunter, Lee Roberts + *Beauty contest winners:* Sandra Wirth, Pat Mowry, Tania Velia, Sanita Pelkey, Lisa Simone, Marianne Gaba, Renate Hoy, Mary Ford. *D:* Richard Cunha; *P:* Marc Frederic; *Sc:* H.E. Barrie, Vincent Forte. (1:18) (video) Ultra low budget science fiction of five people on a rocket trip to the moon who encounter an all-female population, walking rock monsters and a giant spider. A remake of *Cat Women of the Moon* [aka: *Rocket to the Moon*] (q.v.). Originally ran on the bottom of a double bill with *Frankenstein's Daughter* (q.v.).

1724. Missing Women (Republic/Stephen Auer Prods.; 1951). *Cast:* Penny Edwards, James Millican, John Gallaudet, John Alvin, Fritz Feld, James Brown, Robert Shayne, Marlo Dwyer, William Forrest, John Hedloe, Mary Alan Hokanson, Patricia Joiner. *D:* Philip Ford; *P:* Stephen Auer; *St: & Sc:* John K. Butler. (1:00) Crime melodrama of a woman who takes drastic steps to bring to justice the car thieves who killed her husband. Originally ran as the second feature on a double bill with *Belle Le Grand* (q.v.).

1725. Mission Over Korea (Columbia; 1953). *Cast:* John Hodiak, John Derek, Audrey Totter, Maureen O'Sullivan, Harvey Lembeck, Richard Erdman, William Chun, Rex Reason, Richard Bowers, Todd Karns, Al Choi. *D:* Fred F. Sears; *P:* Robert Cohn; *St:* Richard Tregaskis; *Sc:* Jesse L. Lasky, Jr., Eugene Ling, Martin M. Goldsmith. (1:25) Korean War drama of the conflicts between two officer pilots. Originally ran on a double bill with *Cruisin' Down the River* (q.v.). (G.B. title: *Eyes in the Skies*)

1726. The Mississippi Gambler (Universal-International; 1953). *Cast:* Tyronne Power (Mark Fallon), Piper Laurie (Angelique Duroux), Julia [Julie] Adams (Ann Conant), John McIntire (Kansas John Polly), William Reynolds (Pierre), Paul Cavanagh (Edmund Duroux), John Baer (Laurent Duroux), Ron Randell (George Elwood), Robert Warwick (Gov. Paul O'Monet), Guy Williams (Andre), Ralph Dumke (Caldwell), Hugh Beaumont (Kennerly), King Donovan (Spud), Dennis Weaver (Julian Conant), Andre Charlot (Keith), Dayton Lummis (Sanford), Maya Van Horn (Mme. Lesanne), Fred Cravens (Emile), Gwen Verdon (voodoo dancer), Alan Dexter, Al Wyatt, Dale Van Sickel, Bert LeBaron, Marcel de la Brosse, Frank Wilcox, Edward Earle, William Vedder, Larry Thor, Bill Walker, Roy Engel, Dorothy Bruce, Angela Stevens, Rolfe Sedan, Saul Martell, Tony Hughes, George Hamilton, David Newell, Paul Bradley, LeRoi Antienne, Anita Ekberg, Renata Hoy, Jackie Loughery, Jeanne Thompson, Eduardo Cansino, Jr., John O'Connor, Paul Kruger, Robert Strong, Jack Del Rio, Buddy Roosevelt, Jon Shepodd. *D:* Rudolph Maté; *P:* Ted Richmond; *St: & Sc:* Seton I. Miller; *Sound:* (AAN) Leslie I. Carey. (1:39) Antebellum New Orleans is the setting for this costumer of an honorable riverboat gambler. A remake of *Mississippi Gambler*, a 1929 production from this studio, it became one of the 26 top-grossing films of 1952-53. Technicolor.

1727. The Missouri Traveler (Buena Vista/Cornelius V. Whitney Pictures; 1958). *Cast:* Brandon de Wilde, Lee Marvin, Gary Merrill, Mary Hosford, Paul Ford, Ken Curtis, Cal Tinney, Frank Cady, Mary Field, Kathleen Freeman, Will Wright, Tom Tiner, Billy Bryant,

Eddie Little, Barry Curtis, Rodney Bell, Helen Brown, Billy Newell, Roy Jensen, Earle Hodgins. *D:* Jerry Hopper; *P:* Patrick Ford; *As.P:* Lowell J. Farrell; *Sc:* Norman Shannon Hall; *Song:* "Brian's Song" Jack Marshall, Johnny Mercer. (1:43) (video) Period drama set in a small Missouri town in 1915 of an orphan boy trying to put down new roots. A film with family appeal, it was based on the 1955 novel by John Burress. Technicolor.

1728. The Missourians (Republic; 1950). *Cast:* Monte Hale, Paul Hurst, Lyn Thomas, Roy Barcroft, Howard Negley, Robert Neil, Lane Bradford, John Hamilton, Sarah Padden, Charles Williams, Percy Ivins. *D:* George Blair; *As.P:* Melville Tucker; *St: & Sc:* Arthur E. Orloff; *Song:* "Roll along Wagon Wheels," (1:00) (video) A Polish refugee seeks to become an American rancher, only to fall victim to prejudice by the locals. Hale's final series western before becoming a comic book cowboy hero.

1729. Mrs. O'Malley and Mr. Malone (MGM; 1950). *Cast:* Marjorie Main, James Whitmore, Ann Dvorak, Phyllis Kirk, Fred Clark, Dorothy Malone, Douglas Fowley, Clinton Sundberg, Willard Waterman, Don Porter, Jack Bailey, Nancy Saunders, Bail Tellou, James Burke, Eddie Walter, Regis Toomey, Herbert Vigran, Fred Brady, Henry Corden, Edward Earle, Elizabeth Flournoy, Noreen Martensen, Mae Clarke, Thelma Rigdon, Stanley Blystone, Bette Arlen, Lisa Lowry, Philo McCullough, Jerry Lacoe, Jr., Pat Williams, Jeffrey Sayre, J. Lewis Smith, Diana Norris, Donna Norris. *D:* Norman Taurog; *P:* William H. Wright; *St:* Craig Rice, Stuart Palmer; *Sc:* William Bowers; *Songs:* Title song and "Possum Up a Gum Stump" (sung by Main). (1:09) Programmer comedy-thriller of various people involved with two murders on a train bound from Chicago to New York City.

1730. Mr. Belvedere Rings the Bell (20th Century–Fox; 1951). *Cast:* Clifton Webb, Joanne Dru, Hugh Marlowe, Zero Mostel, William Lynn, Doro Merande, Frances Brandt, Kathleen Comegys, Jane Marbury, Harry Hines, Warren Stevens, William & Ludwig Provaznik (twins), Cora Shannon, J. Farrell MacDonald, Cecile Weston, Thomas Browne Henry, Hugh Beaumont, Ray Montgomery, Don Kohler, Edward Clark, Norman Leavitt, Dorothy Neumann, Harry Antrim, Harris Brown, Guy Wilkerson, Ferris Taylor, Luther Crockett, Ted Stanhope, Kathryn Sheldon, Ted Pearson, Robert Malcolm. *D:* Henry Koster; *P:* Andre Hakim; *Sc:* Ranald MacDougall. (1:27) Hit comedy of a traveling lecturer who happens upon a home for the elderly, has himself admitted (pretending to be older than he is) and begins to give the tired old residents a new purpose in living. Based on the play *The Silver Whistle* by Robert C. McEnroe and the "Mr. Belvedere" character created by Gwen Davenport. A follow-up to *Mr. Belvedere Goes to College* (1949), which was a follow-up to *Sitting Pretty* (1948).

1731. Mister Cory (Universal-International; 1957). *Cast:* Tony Curtis, Martha Hyer, Charles Bickford, Kathryn Grant, William Reynolds, Russ Morgan, Henry Daniell, Willis Bouchey, Louise Lorimer, Joan Banks, Harry Landers, Dick Crockett, Hylton Socher, Glen Kramer, Paul Bryar, George Eldredge, Charles Horvath, Jack Gargan, Dick Monda, Billy Eagle, Anna Stein. *D: & Sc:* Blake Edwards; *St:* Leo Rosten; *P:* Robert Arthur. (1:32) Drama of a gambler who rises to fame from his humble beginnings as a youth of the slums. Eastmancolor and CinemaScope.

1732. Mister 880 (20th Century–Fox; 1950). *Cast:* Burt Lancaster (Steve Buchanan), Dorothy McGuire (Ann Winslow), Edmund Gwenn (AAN/Skipper Miller), Millard Mitchell (Mac), Minor Watson (Judge O'Neill), Hugh Sanders (Thad Mitchell), James Millican (Ollie Johnson), Howland Chamberlin (Duff), Howard St. John (Chief), Larry Keating (Lee), Geraldine Wall (Miss Gallagher), Helen Hatch (Maggie), Ed Max (Mousie), Fred Wilcox (Mr. Beddington), George Adrian (Carlos), Michael Lally (George), Joe McTurk (Gus), Minerva Urecal (Rosie), Billy Gray (Mickey), Bill McKenzie (Jimmy), John Heistand (narrator), Kathleen Hughes, Mervin Williams, Norman Field, Robert B. Williams, George Gastine, Ray De Ravenne, Paul Bradley, Arthur Dulac, Curt Furberg, Joan Valerie, Jack Daly, Dick Ryan, William J. O'Leary, Billy Nelson, Herb Vigran, Mischa Novy, Erik Neilsen, Michael Little, Patrick Miller, Whitey Haupt, Timmie Hawkins, Tommie Mann Menzies, Gary Pagett, Peter Roman, Ronnie Ralph, Rico Alaniz, Eddie Lee, George Lee, Victor Desny, Sherry Hall, Bessie Wade, Polly Bailey, Robert Boon, Dr. D.W. De Roos. *D:* Edmund Goulding; *P:* Julian Blaustein; *Sc:* Robert Riskin. (1:30) Sentimental comedy-drama with the U.S. Treasury Department coming to the end of their 10-year search for the counterfeiter of $1 bills. The elderly culprit counterfeits the bills solely for meager living expenses and to use his prized printing press. Based on "Old Eight Eighty," an article which appeared in *New Yorker* magazine by St. Clair McKelway—that was based on fact!

Mr. Hobo *see* **The Gunman**

1733. Mr. Imperium (MGM; 1951). *Cast:* Lana Turner (with the dubbed singing voice of Trudy Erwin), Ezio Pinza, Marjorie Main, Barry Sullivan, Cedric Hardwicke, Debbie Reynolds, Ann Codee, Wilton Graff, Giacomo Spadoni, Chick Chandler, Keenan Wynn, Joseph Vitale, Mae Clarke, Don Haggerty, Jimmy Cross, Cliff Clark, Tony Marlo, Matt Moore, Mitchell Lewis, Arthur Walsh, Allan Ray, Wilson Wood, Bobby Troup, Dick Simmons. *D:* Don Hartman; *P:* Edwin H. Knopf; *Sc:* Hartman, Knopf; *Songs:* "My Love and My Mule," "Andiamo," "Let Me Look at You" Harold Arlen, Dorothy Fields; "You Belong to My Heart" (which became a big hit) Ray Gilbert, Augustin Lara. (1:27) (video) The romance of a Hollywood star and an exiled king take up the minutes of this box office fizzle which was based on an unpublished play by Mr. Knopf. (G.B. title: *You Belong to My Heart*) Technicolor.

1734. Mr. Music (Paramount; 1950). *Cast:* Bing Crosby, Nancy Olson, Charles Coburn, Marge and Gower Champion (themselves), Groucho Marx (himself), Robert Stack, Ruth Hussey, Peggy Lee (herself), Dorothy Kirsten (herself), Tom Ewell, Ida Moore, Charles Kemper, Donald Woods, The Merry Macs (themselves), Claude Curdle [aka: Richard Haydn]. *D:* Richard Haydn; *P:* Robert Welch; *Sc:* Arthur Sheekman; *Songs:* "Life Is So Peculiar," "Accidents Will Happen," "High on the List," "Wouldn't It Be Funny," "Wasn't I There," "Mr. Music," "Once More the Blue and White," "Milady" and "Then You'll Be Home" Johnny Burke, Jimmy Van Heusen. (1:53) (video) A musical remake of *Accent on Youth* (1935) of a Broadway songwriter who would rather play golf. Based on the play of that name by Samson Raphaelson. Remade as *But Not for Me* (q.v.).

1735. Mister Roberts (Warner/Orange; 1955). *Cast:* Henry Fonda (repeating his favorite stage role/Lt. [j.g.] Doug Roberts), James Cagney (The Captain), William Powell (final film—ret., ending a 33-year film career/Doc), Jack Lemmon (AA/Ensign Pulver), Betsy Palmer (Lt. Ann Girard), Ward Bond (C.P.O. Dowdy), Phil Carey (Mannion), Nick Adams (Reber), Ken Curtis (Dolan), Harry Carey, Jr. (Stefanowski), Frank Aletter (Gerhart), Fritz Ford (Lindstrom), Buck Kartalian (Mason), William Henry (Lt. Billings), William Hudson (Olson), Stubby Kruger (Schlemmer), Harry Tenbrook (Cookie), Perry Lopez (Rodrigues), Robert Roark (Insigna), Tiger Andrews (Wiley), Patrick Wayne (Bookser), Jim Moloney (Kennedy), Denny Niles (Gilbert), Francis Connor (Cochran), Shug Fisher (Johnson), Danny Borzage (Jonesy), Jim Murphy (Taylor), Duke Kahanamoko (native chief), Martin Milner, Gregory Walcott (shore patrolmen), James Flavin (M.P.), Jack Pennick (marine sergeant), Kathleen O'Malley, Jeanne Murray, Maura Murphy, Lonnie Pierce, Mimi Doyle (nurses). *D:* John Ford; *P:* (AAN-Best Picture) Leland Hayward (first film); *Sc:* Frank Nugent, Joshua Logan; *Sound:* (AAN) William A. Mueller. (2:03) (video) Critically acclaimed World War II comedy-drama of life aboard a cargo ship in the Pacific. Filmed in Hawaii, it was based on the novel by Thomas Heggen and the hit Broadway play adapted from it by Heggen and Joshua Logan. *Film Daily* voted it "Best Film of the Year" while the NBR and the *New York Times* placed it at #3 and #6 respectively on their "10 Best" lists. It was also in nomination for "Best Film" by the New York Film Critics. A take of $8.5 million at the box office made it one of the 27 top-grossing films of 1954-55. In Technicolor, CinemaScope and stereophonic sound. A delayed sequel, *Ensign Pulver*, came to the screen in 1964.

1736. Mr. Rock and Roll (Paramount; 1957). *Cast:* Alan Freed (himself), Rocky Graziano (himself), Teddy Randazzo (himself), Lois O'Brien, Jay Barney, Al Fisher, Lou Marks, Earl George, Ralph Stanley, *and guests:* Little Richard, Clyde McPhatter, Frankie Lymon and the Teenagers, Chuck Berry, Lionel Hampton & Band, Ferlin Husky, The Moonglows, Brook Benton, LaVern Baker, Shaye Cogan. *D:* Charles Dubin; *P:* Ralph Serpe, Howard Kreitsek; *St: & Sc:* James Blumgarten. (1:26) The story of how disc jockey Alan Freed became the #1 promoter of the new music style called "rock 'n' roll." Complete with over thirty songs performed by various vintage singers and groups, the same story was similarly told in *American Hot Wax*, a 1978 production from this studio.

1737. Mister Scoutmaster (20th Century–Fox; 1953). *Cast:* Clifton Webb, Edmund Gwenn, George "Foghorn" Winslow, Frances

Dee, Orley Lindgren, Veda Ann Borg, Jimmy Moss, Sammy Ogg, Jimmy Hawkins, Skip Torgerson, Dee [Lee?] Aaker, Mickey Little, Jon Gardner, Sarah Selby, Amanda Randolph, Otis Garth, Teddy Infuhr, Harry Seymour, Bill McKenzie, Steve Brent, Robert B. Williams, Bob Sweeney, Tina Thompson, Billy Nelson, Stan Malotte, Gordon Nelson, Dabbs Greer, Dee Pollock, Martin Dean, Robert Winans, Dick Fortune, Ralph Gamble, Tom Greenway, Ned Glass, Mary Alan Hokanson, Kay Stewart, Elizabeth Flournoy. *D:* Henry Levin; *P:* Leonard Goldstein; *Sc:* Leonard Praskins, Barney Slater. (1:27) Comedy-drama of a TV star who gets involved with a troop of Boy Scouts to find out what appeals to young boys. Based on the 1952 novel *Be Prepared* by Rice E. Cochran.

1738. Mr. Universe (Eagle-Lion/Laurel Films; 1951). *Cast:* Jack Carson, Janis Paige, Vincent Edwards (film debut), Bert Lahr, Robert Alda, Dennis James, Maxie Rosenbloom, Joyce Matthews, Harry Landers, Donald Novis, Murray Rothenberg. *D: & P:* Joseph Lerner; *Ex.P:* Rex Carlton; *Sc:* Searle Kramer. (1:19) Comedy of two wrestling promoters and their prime discovery.

1739. Mr. Walkie Talkie (Lippert/Rockingham Prods.; 1952). *Cast:* William Tracy, Joe Sawyer, Robert Shayne, Alan Hale, Jr., Russell Hicks, Frank Jenks, Margia Dean, Bill Boyett, James B. Leong, Wong Artarne, John Breed, Peter Ortiz, Ralph Brooke, William Ng. *D:* Fred L. Guiol; *P:* Hal Roach, Jr.; *St: & Sc:* Edward Seabrook, George Carleton Brown; *Song:* "I Love the Men" Leon Klatzkin, Tom Adair. (1:05) A comic sequel to *As You Were* (q.v.) with Sgt. Ames (Sawyer) volunteering for the Korean front to get away from his nemesis, Doubleday (Tracy). Based on characters created by Hal Roach, Sr. in several 1940s streamliners.

1740. The Mob (Columbia; 1951). *Cast:* Broderick Crawford, Betty Buehler, Richard Kiley (film debut), Otto Hulett, Matt Crowley, Neville Brand, Ernest Borgnine, Walter Klavun, Lynne Baggett, Jean Alexander, Ralph Dumke, John Morley, Frank DeKova, Jay Adler, Duke Watson, Emile Meyer, Carleton Young, Fred Coby, Ric Roman, Art Millan, Paul Bryar, Michael McHale, Don Megowan, Kenneth Harvey, Charles [Bronson] Buchinski, Harry Lauter, Paul Dubov, Lawrence "Larry" Dobkin, Jess Kirkpatrick, Richard Irving, Robert Foulk, Tom Greenway, Dick Pinner, Jack Finley, Al Mellon, Don DeLeo, Peter Prouse, Sidney Mason, David McMahon, Ernie Venneri, Robert Anderson, Charles Marsh, Mary Alan Hokanson, Virginia Chapman, William Pullen, Peter Virgo. *D:* Robert Parrish; *P:* Jerry Bresler; *Sc:* William Bowers. (1:27) Crime melodrama of corruption on the waterfront and a cop who goes undercover to expose the mob kingpin. Based on the novel *Waterfront* by Ferguson Findley. (G.B. title: *Remember That Face*)

1741. Mobs, Inc. (Premiere/Onyx Pictures; 1955). *Cast:* Reed Hadley, Douglass Dumbrille, Don Haggerty, Will Geer, Marjorie Reynolds. *D:* William Asher; *P:* Hal Roach, Jr.; *Sc:* Will Gould, Lee Loeb. (1:02) A low budget crime melodrama, inspired by the TV series "Racket Squad," which was hosted by and starred Hadley. Detailed are three separate stories of con artists and the schemes they perpetrate on their unsuspecting and gullible victims. (G.B. title: *Mobs Incorporated*)

1742. Moby Dick (Warner/Moulin; 1956). *Cast:* Gregory Peck (Capt. Ahab), Richard Basehart (voted "Best Supporting Actor" by the New York Film Critics/Ishmael), Leo Genn (Starbuck), Orson Welles (Father Mapple), James Robertson Justice (Capt. Boomer), Harry Andrews (Stubb), Friedrich Ledebur (Queequeg), Edric Connor (Daggoo), Mervyn Johns (Peleg), Noel Purcell (Carpenter), Bernard Miles (Mansman), Joseph Tomelty (Peter Coffin), Francis De Wolff (Capt. Gardiner), Philip Stainton (Bildad), Royal Dano (Elijah), Seamus Kelly (Flask), Tamba Alleney (Pip), Tom Clegg (Tashtego), Ted Howard (blacksmith), Iris Tree (lady with Bibles). *D:* John Huston (voted "Best Director" by both the NBR and the New York Film Critics); *P:* Huston; *As.P:* Lehman Katz; *Adaptation:* Huston, Anthony Veiller; *Sc:* Ray Bradbury. (1:56) (video/laserdisc) Hit retelling of Herman Melville's classic of Captain Ahab and his obsession to kill the great white whale known as Moby Dick. Previously filmed by this studio in 1926 as *The Sea Beast* and again in 1930 as *Moby Dick.* This action-adventure, which used no studio tricks, placed #2, #3 and #6 respectively on the "10 Best" lists of the NBR, the *New York Times* and *Film Daily.* A U.S.A./G.B. co-production, it became one of the 24 top-grossing films of 1955-56. Remade for cable TV in 1998. Technicolor.

1743. The Model and the Marriage Broker (20th Century–Fox; 1951). *Cast:* Jeanne Crain (Kitty Bennett), Scott Brady (Matt Hornbeck), Thelma Ritter (Mae Swazey), Zero Mostel

(Wixted), Michael O'Shea (Doberman), Helen Ford (Emma Swazey), Frank Fontaine (Johannson), Dennie Moore (Miss Gingras), John Alexander (Mr. Perry), Jay C. Flippen (Dan Chancellor), Nancy Kulp (Hazel), Bunny Bishop (Alice), Kathryn Card (Mrs. Kuschner), Maudie Prickett (Delia Seaton), Athalie Daniell (Trudy), Dennis Ross (Joe), Ken Christy (Mr. Kuschner), Shirley Mills (Ina Kuschner), Eve March (Miss Eddy), Tommy Noonan, Jacqueline French, Edna May Wonacott, June Hedin, Frank Ferguson, Harris Brown, Mae Marsh, Joyce MacKenzie. *D:* George Cukor; *P:* Charles Brackett; *Sc:* Brackett, Walter Reisch, Richard Breen; *Costumes:* (AAN-b/w) Charles LeMaire. (1:43) Comedy of a marriage broker who finds her friend is dating a married man and seeks to find her one who isn't already spoken for.

1744. Models, Inc. (Mutual Pictures; 1952). *Cast:* Howard Duff, Coleen Gray, John Howard, Marjorie Reynolds, Louis Jean Heydt, Ed Max, Benny Baker, James Seay, Charles Cane, Sue Carlton, Lou Lubin, Mary Hill, Frank Ferguson. *D:* Reginald LeBorg; *P:* Hal E. Chester; *St: & Adaptation:* Alyce Canfield; *Sc:* Harry Essex, Paul Yawitz. (1:13) Independent crime melodrama of a respectable modeling agency that is targeted by a sleazy ex-con as a front for lascivious shutterbugs to secretly photograph models in skimpy attire. (G.B. title: *That Kind of Girl*)

1745. A Modern Marriage (Monogram; 1950). *Cast:* Reed Hadley, Margaret Field, Robert Clarke, Nana Bryant, Charles Smith, Dick Elliott, Christine McIntyre, Lelah Tyler, Pattee Chapman, Frank Fenton, Edward Keane. *D:* Paul Landres; *P:* David Diamond; *As.P:* William F. Broidy; *St: & Sc:* Sam Roeca, George Wallace Sayre. (1:06) Low budget melodrama of a woman who flees from her husband on their wedding night and attempts suicide. Re-released in 1961 with an added clinical prologue. (aka: *Frigid Wife*)

1746. Mogambo (MGM; 1953). *Cast:* Clark Gable (repeating his role in *Red Dust*/ Victor Marswell), Ava Gardner (AAN/Eloise Kelly), Grace Kelly (AAN-BSA/Linda Nordley), Donald Sinden (Donald Nordley), Philip Stainton (John Brown-Pryce), Eric Pohlman (Leon Boltchak), Laurence Naismith (skipper), Dennis O'Dea (Father Josef), Asa Etula, Wagenia Tribe of Belgian Congo, Samburu Tribe of Kenya Colony, Bahaya Tribe of Tanganyika, M'Beti Tribe of French Equatorial Africa. *D:* John Ford; *P:* Sam Zimbalist; *Sc:* John Lee Mahin (rewriting his 1932 *Red Dust* screenplay). (1:55) (video/laserdisc) Hit remake of *Red Dust* and *Congo Maisie* (1939-40) of a great white hunter and his romantic pursuits in darkest Africa. Based on Wilson Collison's play *Congo Landing*, it took a #9 placement on the "10 Best" list of the NBR as well as being placed in nomination at the British Academy Awards. One of the 25 top-grossing films of 1953-54. Technicolor.

1747. Mohawk (20th Century–Fox; 1956). *Cast:* Scott Brady, Rita Gam, Neville Brand, Lori Nelson, Allison Hayes, John Hoyt, Vera Vague [aka: Barbara Jo Allen], Rhys Williams, Ted de Corsia, Mae Clarke, John Hudson, Tommy Cook, Michael Granger, James Lilburn, Chabon Jadi. *D:* Kurt Neumann; *P:* Edward L. Alperson; *St: & Sc:* Maurice Geraghty, Milton Krims; *Songs:* "Mohawk," "Love Plays the Strings of My Banjo" Edward L. Alperson, Jr., Paul Herrick. (1:19) (video) Colonial costumer, set in New York's Mohawk Valley, of a carefree painter and an Indian girl who thwart an Iroquois uprising instigated by a white man. This film utilizes footage from Fox's 1939 production *Drums Along the Mohawk*. Eastmancolor and Widevision.

1748. The Mole People (Universal-International; 1956). *Cast:* John Agar, Cynthia Patrick, Hugh Beaumont, Alan Napier, Nestor Paiva, Phil Chambers, Rodd Redwing, Robin Hughes, Arthur D. Gilmour, Dr. Frank Baxter (prologue introduction), Yvonne De Lavallade, James Logan, Kay Kuter, John Dodsworth, Marc Hamilton, Pat Whyte, Joseph Abdullah, Billy Miller, Eddie Parker. *D:* Virgil Vogel; *P:* William Alland; *St: & Sc:* Laszlo Gorog; *Makeup:* Bud Westmore. (1:17) (video) Science fiction adventure of explorers who discover an underground civilization of albino Sumerians who use another humanoid species as slaves. Originally ran on a double bill with *Curucu, Beast of the Amazon* (q.v.).

Molly *see* **The Goldbergs**

1749. Money from Home (Paramount; 1953). *Cast:* Dean Martin (Honey Talk Nelson), Jerry Lewis (Virgil Yokum), Marjie Millar (Phyllis Leigh), Pat Crowley (Autumn Claypool), Richard Haydn (Bertie Searles), Robert Strauss (Seldom Seen Kid), Gerald Mohr (Marshall Preston), Sheldon Leonard (Jumbo Schneider), Romo Vincent (the Poojah), Jack Kruschen (Short Boy), Lou Lubin (Sam), Wendell Niles (announcer), Joe McTurk (Hard Top Harry), Frank F. Mitchell (Lead Pipe Louie), Charles Horvath, Richard J. Reeves (henchmen), Sam Logan (Society Kid/himself), Phil Arnold (Crossfire), Louis Nicoletti (Hot Horse Herbie), Edward Clark (Dr. Capulet), Grace Hayle (Mrs. Cheshire), Robin Hughes (Bankfair), Sidney Marion (Grogan the Growler), Carolyn Phillips (Poojah's wife), Maidie Norman (Mattie), Harry Hayden, Henry McLemore, Mortie Dutra, Al Hill, Ben Astar, Mara Corday, Rex Lease. *D:* George Marshall; *P:* Hal B. Wallis; *Adaptation:* James Allardice, Hal Kanter; *Sc:* Kanter; *Songs:* "Moments Like This" Burton Lane, Frank Loesser; "Love is the Same," "Be Careful Song" Jack Brooks, Joseph J. Lilley. (1:40) Hit Martin and Lewis comic hijinks, as they get involved with gangsters, horse racing and an Arab Poojah and his harem. Based on a Damon Runyon story, it became one of the 25 top-grossing films of 1953-54. Technicolor and 3-D.

1750. Money, Women and Guns (Universal-International; 1958). *Cast:* Jock Mahoney, Kim Hunter, Tim Hovey, Gene Evans, William Campbell, Judi Meredith, James Gleason, Lon Chaney, Jr., Jeffrey Stone, Tom Drake, Philip Terry, Richard Devon, Ian MacDonald, Don Megowan, Nolan Leary, Kelly Thorsden. *D:* Richard H. Bartlett; *P:* Howie Horwitz; *St: & Sc:* Montgomery Pittman; *Song:* "Lonely is the Hunter" Jimmy Wakely. (1:20) Western of a detective investigating the murder of a prospector as well as attempting to find the four heirs to his will. Eastmancolor and CinemaScope.

1751. Monkey Business (20th Century-Fox; 1952). *Cast:* Cary Grant, Ginger Rogers, Charles Coburn, Marilyn Monroe, Hugh Marlowe, Henri Letondal, Robert Cornthwaite, Larry Keating, Douglas Spencer, Esther Dale, George "Foghorn" Winslow, Emmett Lynn, Joseph Mell, George Eldredge, Heinie Conklin, Kathleen Freeman, Olan Soule, Harry Carey, Jr., John McKee, Faire Binney, Billy McLean, Paul Maxey, Mack Williams, Forbes Murray, Marjorie Halliday, Harry Seymour, Harry Bartell, Roger Moore, Jerry Paris, Harry Carter, Ruth Warren, Isabel Withers, Olive Carey, Dabbs Greer, Russ Clark, Ray Montgomery, Melinda Plowman, Terry Goodman, Ronnie Clark, Rudy Lee, Mickey Little, Brad Mora, Jimmy Roebuck, Louis Lettieri, Robert Nichols, Mary Field, Jerry Sheldon, Gil Stratton, Jr. *D:* Howard Hawks (whose voice is also heard during the opening credits); *P:* Sol C. Siegel; *St:* Harry Segall; *Sc:* Ben Hecht, Charles Lederer, I.A.L. Diamond. (1:37) (video/laserdisc) Screwball comedy involving a potion, mixed by a chimpanzee, that gets dumped into a water cooler. Everyone who drinks the water temporarily reverts back to a younger period in his or her life. An acclaimed hit for the studio.

1752. Monkey on My Back (United Artists/Imperial; 1957). *Cast:* Cameron Mitchell, Dianne Foster, Paul Richards, Jack Albertson, Barry Kelley, Kathy Garver, Lisa Golm, Dayton Lummis, Lewis Charles, Raymond Greenleaf, Richard Benedict, Brad Harris, Robert Holton. *D:* Andre De Toth; *P:* Edward Small; *Sc:* Crane Wilbur, Anthony Veiller, Paul Dudley. (1:33) Drama detailing aspects in the life of Barney Ross, welterweight boxing champ in the 1930s, who also became a hero at Guadalcanal in World War II, subsequently becoming dependent on drugs after being treated with morphine for wartime wounds. Ivan Bunny supplied the biographical material. Note: A lawsuit filed by Ross (though acting as technical advisor on the production) against U.A. and producer Small for damage to his reputation was lost, but gained publicity for the film.

1753. The Monolith Monsters (Universal-International; 1957). *Cast:* Grant Williams, Lola Albright, Les Tremayne, Trevor Bardette, Phil Harvey, William Flaherty, Harry Jackson, Richard Cutting, Linda Scheley, Dean Cromer, Steve Darrell, William Schallert, Paul Frees (narrator). *D:* John Sherwood; *P:* Howard Christie; *St:* Robert M. Fresco, Jack Arnold; *Sc:* Norman Jolley, Fresco. (1:16) Science fiction of a meteorite, with the ability to petrify human flesh, that lands near a small California town. It is also found to expand its mass when contact is made with H_2O, setting the stage for a destructive finale of rampaging monolithic meteorites during a rainstorm. Originally ran on the top of a double bill with *Love Slaves of the Amazon* (q.v.).

1754. Monsoon (United Artists/C.F.G. (Films) Ltd.-Film Group; 1953). *Cast:* Ursula Thiess (film debut), Diana Douglas, George Nader, Ellen Corby, Philip Stainton, Eric Pohlman, Myron Healey. *D:* Rodney Amateau; *P:* Forrest Judd; *Sc:* Judd, David Robinson, Leonardo Bercovici. (1:19) (video) Romantic drama, set in a remote village in India, of a man who falls for his fiancée's sister. Based on the 1946 play *Romeo et Jeanette* by Jean Anouilh. Technicolor.

1755. The Monster from Green Hell (Distributors Corporation of America/Grosse-Krasne; 1957). *Cast:* Jim Davis, Robert E. Griffin, Barbara Turner, Eduardo Ciannelli, Vladimir Sokoloff, Joel Fluellen, Tim Huntley, Frederic Potler, LaVerne Jones. *D:* Kenneth Crane; *P:* Al Zimbalist; *St: & Sc:* Louis Vittes, Endre Bohem. (1:11) (video) Science fiction of wasps launched into outer space who return to earth in Africa as giant mutants after being exposed to radiation. A safari sets out to discover their whereabouts. The final scene of the exploding volcano is photographed in color. The film also uses footage from *Stanley and Livingston* (Fox; 1939).

1756. The Monster from the Ocean Floor (Lippert/Palo Alto; 1954). *Cast:* Stuart Wade, Anne Kimbell, Dick Pinner, Jack Hayes, Wyott Ordung, Inez Palange, David Garcia. *D:* Wyott Ordung; *P:* Roger Corman; *St: & Sc:* William Danch. (1:04) (video) Programmer science fiction of a woman's encounter with an undersea monster. Only notable for being Roger Corman's premiere feature as a producer, produced in less than a week at a cost of $12,000. (aka: *It Stalked the Ocean Floor*) (Canadian title: *Monster Maker*)

Monster Maker (Canadian title) *see* **The Monster From the Ocean Floor**

1757. The Monster of Piedras Blancas (Film-Service Distributing Corp./Vanwick; 1958). *Cast:* Les Tremayne, Forrest Lewis, John Harmon, Don Sullivan, Jeanne Carmen, Frank Arvidson, Joseph LaCava, Pete Dunn, Wayne Berwick, Jack Kevan (monster). *D:* Irvin Berwick; *P:* Jack Kevan; *St: & Sc:* Haile Chace. (1:11) (video) Ultra low budget horror of a lighthouse keeper who suspects a legendary humanoid monster is lurking in a nearby cave.

1758. Monster on the Campus (Universal-International; 1958). *Cast:* Arthur Franz, Joanna Moore, Judson Pratt, Troy Donahue, Nancy Walters, Phil Harvey, Helen Westcott, Alexander Lockwood, Whit Bissell, Ross Elliott, Hank Patterson, Eddie Parker (monster). *D:* Jack Arnold; *P:* Joseph Gershenson; *St: & Sc:* David Duncan. (1:16) (video) The blood of a dead coelacanth reverts modern living things to their prehistoric forebears in this horror thriller which seems (according to this viewer) to have found its inspiration in *The Neanderthal Man* (q.v.). Originally ran on the bottom of a horror double bill with *Blood of the Vampire*, a British production.

1759. The Monster That Challenged the World (United Artists/Gramercy; 1957). *Cast:* Tim Holt, Audrey Dalton, Hans Conried, Casey Adams [aka: Max Showalter], Harlan Warde, Mimi Gibson, Gordon Jones, Marjorie Stapp, Jody McCrea, Eileen Harley, Barbara Darrow, Dennis McCarthy, Bob Beneveds, Michael Dugan, Mack Williams, William Swan, Charles Tannen, Byron Kane, Hal Taggart, Gil Frye, Don Gachman, Milton Parsons, Ralph Moody. *D:* Arnold Laven; *P:* Jules V. Levey, Arthur Gardner; *St:* David Duncan; *Sc:* Patricia Fielder. (1:23) (video) Science fiction about the discovery of giant mollusks released into California's Salton Sea by an earthquake and the efforts to stop the bloodsuckers before they invade the waterways of the world.

Monsters from the Moon *see* **Robot Monster**

1760. Montana (Warner; 1950). *Cast:* Errol Flynn, Alexis Smith, S.Z. Sakall, Douglas Kennedy, James Brown, Ian MacDonald, Charles Irwin, Monte Blue, Paul E. Burns, Tudor Owen, Lester Matthews, Nacho Galindo, Lane Chandler, Billy Vincent, Warren Jackson, Forrest Taylor, Almira Sessions, Gertrude Astor, Nita Talbot, Philo McCullough, Dorothy Adams, Jack Mower, Creighton Hale, Maudie Prickett, Jessie Adams. *D:* Ray Enright; *P:* William Jacobs; *St:* Ernest Haycox; *Sc:* James R. Webb, Borden Chase, Charles O'Neal. (1:16) Western of an Australian sheepherder who moves into rangeland in Montana's cattle country—with expected results. Technicolor.

1761. Montana Belle (RKO/Fidelity Pictures; 1948–52). Cast: Jane Russell (Belle Starr), George Brent, Scott Brady (Bob Dalton), Forrest Tucker, Andy Devine, Jack Lambert, Ray Teal (Emmett Dalton), Rory Mallinson (Grat Dalton), Roy Barcroft, John Litel, Ned Davenport, Dick Elliott, Glenn Strange, Eugene [Gene] Roth, Stanley Andrews, Holly Bane [aka: Mike Ragan/Ben Dalton], Gregg Barton, Pierce Lyden, George Chesebro, Dennis Moore, Kenneth MacDonald, Rodney Bell, Iron Eyes Cody, Rex Lease, Charles Soldani, Hank Bell, Franklyn Farnum, Frank Ellis, Paul Stader, Terry Wilson, Dave Sharpe, Tom Steele, Joe Yrigoyen. *D:* Allan Dwan; *P:* Howard Welsch; *St:* M. Coates Webster, Welsch; *Sc:* Horace Webster, Norman S. Hall; *Songs:* Portia Nelson, Margaret Martinez. (1:21) (video) In this western Belle Starr joins the Dalton gang on the outlaw trail. Production was completed in 1948 with release held up until 1952. Trucolor.

1762. Montana Desperado (Monogram/ Transwestern Prods.; 1951). *Cast:* Johnny Mack Brown, Virginia Herrick, Myron Healey, Marshall Reed, Steve Clark, Edmund Cobb, Lee Roberts, Carl Mathews, Ben Corbett. *D:* Wallace W. Fox (final film—ret.); *P:* Vincent M. Fennelly; Sc: Daniel B. Ullman. (0:51) Series western about the investigation into the deaths of several ranchers by one of their neighbors.

1763. Montana Incident (Monogram; 1952). *Cast:* Whip Wilson, Noel Neill, Peggy Stewart, Rand Brooks, Hugh Prosser, William Fawcett, Terry Frost, Marshall Reed, Lyle Talbot, Russ Whiteman, Barbara Woodell, Bruce Edwards, Stanley Price. *D:* Lewis Collins; *P:* Vincent M. Fennelly; *St: & Sc:* Daniel B. Ullman. (0:54) In this series western, Whip Wilson rides into a small town run by a powerful family headed by a ruthless woman, (aka: *Gunsmoke Range*)

1764. Montana Territory (Columbia, 1952). *Cast:* Lon McCallister, Wanda Hendrix, Preston Foster, Hugh Sanders, Jack Elam, Clayton Moore, Myron Healey, Eddy Waller, Ethan Laidlaw, Ruth Warren, Trevor Bardette, Robert Griffin, George Chesebro, George Russell, Frank Matts. *D:* Ray Nazarro; *P:* Colbert Clark; *St: & Sc:* Barry Shipman. (1:04) Programmer western of a crooked sheriff idolized by a naïve young man. Technicolor.

1765. The Moon Is Blue (United Artists/Holmby Prods.; Inc.; 1953). *Cast:* William Holden (Donald Gresham), David Niven (David Slater), Maggie McNamara (AAN-film debut/ Patty O'Neill), Tom Tully (Michael O'Neill), Dawn Addams (Cynthia Slater), Fortunio Bonanova (TV announcer), Gregory Ratoff, Hardy Kruger. *D: & P:* Otto Preminger; *Adaptation & Sc:* F. Hugh Herbert (based on his hit 1951 Broadway play); *Editor:* (AAN) Otto Ludwig; *Title song:* (AAN-Best Song) Herschel Burke Gilbert, Sylvia Fine. (1:35) (video/laserdisc) Moral romantic comedy of a girl, picked up by an architect and taken back to his bachelor apartment, with one thing on his mind. He finds his intended conquest has every intention of staying a virgin. At the time of this film's release without the production code's "seal of approval," a furor was raised about the use of the words "virgin" and "seduce" in the screenplay, two words heretofore taboo on the screen. Needless to say, the controversy had patrons lined up at the box office. It also placed #8 on the "10 Best" list of *Film Daily* and was in nomination at the British Academy Awards.

1766. Moonfleet (MGM; 1955). *Cast:* Stewart Granger, George Sanders, Joan Greenwood, Viveca Lindfors, Jon Whiteley, Liliane Montevecchi, Melville Cooper, Alan Napier, Donna Corcoran (final film—ret. at age 12), Jack Elam, Sean McClory, John Hoyt, Ian Wolfe, Dan Seymour, Lester Matthews, Skelton Knaggs, Richard Hale, John Alderson, Ashley Cowan, Booth Colman, Frank Ferguson, Lillian Kemble Cooper, Guy Kingsford, Ben Wright, Wilson Wood, John O'Malley, Peggy Maley. *D:* Fritz Lang; *P:* John Houseman, Jud Kinberg; *Sc:* Jan Lustig, Margaret Fitts. (1:29) (video/laserdisc) A buccaneering adventure which was based on J. Meade Faulkner's novel and filmed on location in England. Eastmancolor and CinemaScope.

1767. The Moonlighter (Warner/J.B. Prods.; 1953). *Cast:* Fred MacMurray, Barbara Stanwyck, Ward Bond, William Ching, John Dierkes, Morris Ankrum, Jack Elam, Charles Halton, Norman Leavitt, Sam Flint, Myra Marsh, Burt Mustin, Byron Foulger, Myron Healey, William Hunter, Robert Bice, Gregg Barton, Ron Kennedy, David Alpert, Steve Rowland, Joel Fluellen. *D:* Roy Rowland; *P: & Ex.P:* Joseph Bernhard; *St: & Sc:* Niven Busch. (1:15) Western of a cattle rustler with intentions of reforming. Originally in 3-D.

1768. The Most Dangerous Man Alive (Columbia/Trans-Global; 1958–61). *Cast:* Ron Randell, Debra Paget, Elaine Stewart, Anthony Caruso, Gregg Palmer, Morris Ankrum, Tudor Owen, Steve Mitchell, Joel Donte. *D:* Allan Dwan (final film—ret.); *P:* Benedict Bogeaus; *Sc:* William Leicester, Philip Rock. (1:22) After being exposed to cobalt rays, a man turns to steel and becomes indestructible. Based on the story "The Steel Monster" by Mr. Rock and Michael Pate, it was filmed in Mexico in 1958 with release held up until 1961.

1769. Mother Didn't Tell Me (20th Century–Fox; 1950). *Cast:* Dorothy McGuire, William Lundigan, June Havoc, Gary Merrill, Jessie Royce Landis, Joyce MacKenzie, Leif Erickson, Reiko Sato, Anthony Cobb, Tracy Cobb, Georgia Backus, Everett Glass, Michael Branden [aka: Archie Twitchell], Mary Bear, Larry Keating, Jean "Babe" London, Wilton Graff,

Ann Tyrrell, Jessie Adams, Louise Lorimer, Frank Jenks, Caryl Lincoln, Ida Moore. *D: & Sc:* Claude Binyon; *P:* Fred Kohlmar. (1:28) Comedy of a doctor's wife and her inability to adjust to his irregular hours, his mother, his female patients, etc. Based on the 1949 book *The Doctor Wears Three Faces* by Mary Bard.

Mother, Sir (G.B. title) *see* **Navy Wife**

1770. Motor Patrol (Lippert; 1950). *Cast:* Don Castle, Jane Nigh, Bill Henry, Gwen O'Connor, Reed Hadley, Onslow Stevens, Dick Travis, Sid Melton, Charles Vidor, Frank Jacquet, Frank Jenks, Lt. Louis Fuller, Charles Wagenheim, Margia Dean, Carla Martin, Joe Greene, Don Avelier, Irene Martin. *D:* Sam Newfield; *P:* Barney A. Sarecky; *As.P:* Murray Lerner; *Sc:* Maurice Tombragel, Orville Hampton (based on an unpublished story by Mr. Tombragel). (1:07) Crime melodrama with the pre-release title of "Highway Patrol" about a gang of car thieves and a motorcycle cop out to break up their operation.

1771. Motorcycle Gang (American International/Golden State Prods.; 1957). *Cast:* Anne Neyland, Steven Terrell, John Ashley, Carl Switzer, Raymond Hatton, Russ Bender, Jean Moorhead, Scott Peters, Eddie Kafafian, Shirley Falls, Aki Aleong, Wayne Taylor, Hal Bogart, Phyllis Cole, Suzanne Sydney, Edmund Cobb, Paul Blaisdell, Zon Murray, Felice Richmond. *D:* Edward L. Cahn; *P:* Alex Gordon; *St: & Sc:* Lou Rusoff. (1:18) (video) Teen exploitation of a youth who realizes too late that he made a big mistake by letting himself be goaded into participating in an illegal drag race. Originally ran on the top half of a drive-in double bill with *Sorority Girl* (q.v.).

1772. Moulin Rouge (United Artists/Romulus; 1952). *Cast:* José Ferrer (AAN/Henri Toulouse-Lautrec & The Comte de Toulouse-Lautrec), Colette Marchand (AAN-BSA/Marie Charlet), Suzanne Flon (Myriamme), Zsa Zsa Gabor (Jane Avril), Katherine Kath (La Goulue), Claude Nollier (Countess de Toulouse-Lautrec), Muriel Smith (Aicha), Tutte Lemkow (Aicha's partner), Georges Lannes (Patou), Rupert John (Chocolat), Walter Crisham (Valentin Dessosse), Eric Pohlman (bar proprietor), Mary Clare (Madame Loubet), Lee Montague (Maurice Joyant), Maureen Swanson (Denise), Jim Gerald (Pere Cotelle), Harold Gasket (Zidler), Jill Bennett (film debut/Sarah), Peter Cushing (racing fan). *D:* (AAN) John Huston; *P:* (AAN-Best Picture) Huston; *As.P:* Jack Clayton; *Sc:* Anthony Veiller, Huston; *Song:* "Theme from Moulin Rouge" Georges Auric; *Costumes* (AA-color) Marcel Vertes; *ASD:* (AA-color) Paul Sheriff (art director), Marcel Vertes (sets); *Editor:* (AAN) Ralph Kemplen. (2:03) (video/laserdisc) The life and times of artist Henri Toulouse-Lautrec of Montmartre, France, whose growth was stunted by a childhood accident. Based on the novel by Pierre LaMure, it was voted "Best Film" by the *New York Times* and placed #5 on the "10 Best" list of *Film Daily*. In nomination at the British Academy Awards, it also became one of the 26 top-grossing films of 1952-53. Technicolor.

1773. The Mountain (Paramount; 1956). *Cast:* Spencer Tracy, Robert Wagner, Claire Trevor, William Demarest, Barbara Darrow, Richard Arlen, E.G. Marshall, Anna Kashfi, Richard Garrick, Harry Townes, Stacy Harris, Yves Brainville, Mary Adams, Jim Hayward, Richard H. Cutting. *D: & P:* Edward Dmytryk; *Sc:* Ranald MacDougall; *Title song:* Mack David, Daniele Amfitheatrof. (1:44) (video) Drama of two brothers ascending the French Alps to the sight of a wrecked passenger plane, each for their own reasons. Based on the 1953 novel by Henri Troyat, some scenes were filmed on location. Technicolor and VistaVision.

Mountain Desperadoes (G.B. title) *see* **Laramie Mountains**

Movie Stunt Men *see* **Hollywood Thrill-Makers**

1774. The Mugger (United Artists/Barbizon/Helprin-Crown; 1958). *Cast:* Kent Smith, Nan Martin, James Franciscus, Stefan Schnable, Connie Vaness, Leonard Stone, Sandra Church, Dick O'Neil, Arthur Storch, Albert Dennable, Boris Aplon, John Alexander. *D: & P:* William Berke; *Sc:* Henry Kane. (1:14) Programmer of a law enforcement psychiatrist trying to find an obsessed mugger with a penchant for slashing the faces of women. Based on the 1956 novel by Ed McBain.

1775. Mule Train (Columbia/Gene Autry Prods.; 1950). *Cast:* Gene Autry, Sheila Ryan, Pat Buttram, Robert Livingston, Vince Barnett, Syd Saylor, Gregg Barton, Stanley Andrews, Kenne Duncan, Pat O'Malley, Bob Wilke, John Miljan, Frank Jaquet, Sandy Sanders, Roy Gordon, Robert Hilton, Robert Carson, Eddie

Parker, George Morrell, John R. McKee, George Slocum, Frank O'Connor, Norman Leavitt, Champion, Jr. (horse). *D:* John English; *P:* Armand Schaefer; *St:* Alan James [nee: Alvin J. Neitz]; *Sc:* Gerald Geraghty; *Songs include:* "Mule Train" (a big hit which was originally introduced in *Singing Guns* [q.v.]) Fred Glickman, Hy Heath, Johnny Lange; "Roomful of Roses," "Cool Water" and "The Old Chisholm Trail." (1:09) (video) Gene Autry helps a friend save his cement claim from the bad guys who want it. Note: This film was selected by New York's Museum of Modern Art as a representative example of Autry's work for its film collection. Sepiatone.

1776. Murder By Contract (Columbia; 1958). *Cast:* Vince Edwards, Philip Pine, Herschel Bernardi, Michael Granger, Caprice Toriel, Frances Osborne, Cathy Browne, Steven Ritch, Joseph Mell, Janet Brandt, Davis Roberts, Don Garrett, Gloria Victor. *D:* Irving Lerner; *P:* Leon Chooluck; *St: & Sc:* Ben Simcoe. (1:21) Drama of a hit man, with a fear of women, who is contracted to kill a woman before she testifies to the federal grand jury.

Murder, Inc. (G.B. title) *see* **The Enforcer**

1777. Murder Is My Beat (Allied Artists; 1955). *Cast:* Paul Langton, Barbara Payton (final film—ret.), Robert Shayne, Selena Royle (final film—ret.), Roy Gordon, Tracey Roberts, Kate MacKenna, Henry A. [Harry] Harvey, Sr., Jay Adler. *D:* Edgar G. Ulmer; *P:* Aubrey Wisberg, Ilse Lahn; *St:* Wisberg, Martin Field; *Sc:* Wisberg. (1:17) Film noir of a woman being taken to prison after being convicted of murder, who sees the supposed victim through the window of a train and convinces her prison escort to pursue the man to prove her innocence. (aka: *Dynamite Anchorage*)

1778. Murder Without Tears (Monogram/Allied Artists; 1953). *Cast:* Craig Stevens, Joyce Holden, Richard Benedict, Eddie Norris, Clair Regis, Tom Hubbard, Murray Alper, Bob Carson, Paul Murray, Edit Angold, Leonard Penn, Hal Gerard, Burt Wenland, Fred Kelsey, Gregg Sanders, Charles Victor, Jack George. *D:* William Beaudine, Sr.; *P:* William F. Broidy; *Sc:* Jo Pagano, Bill Raynor. (1:04) Crime melodrama of a man who plots to kill his wife, commits the crime and gets off by claiming he did it during an alcoholic blackout. A detective suspects there is more to the case. Based on the story "Double Jeopardy" by Mr. Pagano.

1779. Mustang (United Artists/Arnell; 1959). *Cast:* Jack Beutel (final film—ret.), Madalyn Trahey, Steve Keyes, Milton Swift, Robert Gilbert, Paul Spahn, Max M. Gilford, Autumn Moon (horse). *D:* Peter Stephens; *P:* Robert Arnell; *Sc;* Tom Gries. (1:13) Programmer of a rodeo star who saves a wild mustang from destruction. Based on the 1951 novel *Capture of the Golden Stallion* by Rutherford Montgomery.

1780. Mutiny (United Artists/King Bros. Prods.; 1952). *Cast:* Mark Stevens, Angela Lansbury, Patric Knowles, Gene Evans, Rhys Williams, Norman Leavitt, Robert Osterloh, Peter Brocco, Gene Roth, Walter Sande, Clayton Moore, Todd Karns, Morris Ankrum, Louis Jean Heydt, Robin Hughes, Crane Whitley, Emerson Treacy, Harry Antrim. *D:* Edward Dmytryk; *P:* Maurice King; Sc: Philip Yordan, Sidney Harmon (1:17) (video) Fact-based costume swashbuckler of piracy aboard a ship carrying gold bullion from France during the War of 1812. Based on the novel *The Golden Anchor* by Hollister Noble. Technicolor.

Mutiny in Outer Space *see* **Space Master X-7**

1781. My Blue Heaven (20th Century-Fox; 1950). *Cast:* Betty Grable, Dan Dailey, David Wayne, Jane Wyatt, Mitzi Gaynor (film debut), Una Merkel, Louise Beavers, Laura Pierpont, Don Hicks, Beulah Parkington, Ann Burr, Billy Daniels, Larry Keating, Minerva Urecal, Mae Marsh, Noel Reyburn, Phyllis Coates, Barbara Pepper, Myron Healey, Lois Hall, Frank Remley, Melinda Plowman, Vicki Lee Blunt, Gary Pagett, Bill McKenzie, Bobby Stevens, Buddy Pryor, Irving Fulton, Fred Lewis, Conrad Binyon, Alex Gerry, Dorothy Neumann, Isabel Withers, William Baldwin, John Hedloe, Thomas Browne Henry, Eula Guy, Marion Marshall, Harry Carter. *D:* Henry Koster; *P:* Sol C. Siegel; *Sc:* Lamar Trotti, Claude Binyon; *Songs:* "My Blue Heaven" George Whiting, Walter Donaldson; "Live Hard, Work Hard, Love Hard," "What a Man," "It's Deductible," "Don't Rock the Boat, Dear," "Friendly Island," "I Love a New Yorker" and "Halloween" Ralph Blane, Harold Arlen. (1:36) A married radio team who after losing their baby decide to adopt, but through a fluke, wind up with two babies instead of one. Then they discover that she is pregnant again. Based on the story "Storks Don't Bring Babies" by S.K. Lauren. Technicolor.

1782. My Brother, the Outlaw (Eagle-Lion; 1951). *Cast:* Mickey Rooney, Wanda Hendrix, Robert Preston, Robert Stack, Carlos Musquiz, Jose Torvay, Fernando Wagner, Filipe Flores, Hilda Moreno, Guillermo Calles, Margarita Luna, Jose Velasquez, Enrique Cansino, Chel Lopez. *D:* Elliott Nugent; *P:* Benedict Bogeaus; *Sc:* Gene Fowler, Jr.; *Additional dialogue:* Alfred L. Levitt. (1:22) (video) Western of a young man who joins the Texas Rangers when he finds his brother has turned outlaw. Based on Max Brand's 1936 novel *South of the Rio Grande.* (retitled: *My Outlaw Brother*)

1783. My Cousin Rachel (20th Century-Fox; 1952). *Cast:* Olivia de Havilland (Rachel Ashley), Richard Burton (AAN/Philip Ashley), Audrey Dalton (Louise), Ronald Squire (Nick Kendall), George Dolenz (Rainaldi, Rachel's lawyer), John Sutton (Ambrose Ashley), Tudor Owen (Seecombe), J.M. Kerrigan (Rev. Pascoe), Margaret Brewster (Mrs. Pascoe), Alma Lawton (Mary Pascoe), Earl Robie (Philip, age 5), Lumsden Hare (Tamblyn), Trevor Ward (Lewin), Nicolas Koster (Philip, age 10), Robin Camp (Philip, age 15), Ola Lorraine, Kathleen Mason, Mario Siletti, Argentina Brunetti, Victor Wood, George Plues, Bruce Payne, James Fairfax, Oreste Seragnoli. *D:*Henry Koster; *P: & Sc:* Nunnally Johnson; *Cin:* (AAN-b/w) Joseph LaShelle; *ASD:* (AAN-b/w) Lyle Wheeler, John Decuir (art directors), Walter M. Scott (sets); *Costumes:* (AAN-b/w) Charles LeMaire, Dorothy Jeakins. (1:38) Drama, romance and mystery in this adaptation of Daphne du Maurier's best-seller of a man who marries his cousin's widow, with nagging doubts she may have murdered her first husband. Set in early 19th century England.

1784. My Favorite Spy (Paramount; 1951). *Cast:* Bob Hope (dual role), Hedy Lamarr, Francis L. Sullivan, Arnold Moss, John Archer, Luis Van Rooten, Stephen Chase, Morris Ankrum, Angela Clarke, Iris Adrian, Frank Faylen, Mike Mazurki, Marc Lawrence, Ralph Smiley, Joseph Vitale, Nestor Paiva, Tonio Selwart, Suzanne Dalbert, Laura Elliot, Mary Murphy, Torben Meyer, Charles Cooley, Jack Chefe, Rolfe Sedan, Michael A. Cirillo, Dario Piazza, Henry Hope, William C. Quealy, Jerry Lane, Marie Thomas, Michael Ansara, Don Dunning, Roy Roberts, Norbert Schiller, William Johnstone, Jack Pepper, Jimmie Dundee, Jerry James, Lee Bennett, Roger Creed, Peggy Gordon, Suzanne Ridgeway, Charlotte Hunter, Sethma Williams, Patti McKaye, Ivan Triesault, Crane Whitley, Geraldine Knapp, Eugene Borden, Sue Casey, Dorothy Abbott, Monique Chantel, Ralph Byrd, George Lynn, Sayre Dearing, Jean DeBriac, Steven Geray, Nancy Duke, Mimi Berry, Mary Ellen Gleason, Edith Sheets, Leah Waggner, Carolyn Wolfson, Pepe Hern, Alfredo Santos, Vyola [Veola] Vonn, Lillian Molieri, Henry Mirelez, Tony Mirelez, Ed Loredo, Myron Marks, Gay Gayle, Carlos Conte, Felipe Turich, Alphonse Martell, Alberto Morin, Pat Moran, Duke York, Loyal Underwood, Delmar Costello, Rudy Rama, Frank Hagney, Ralph Montgomery, Mike Mahoney, Michael Ross, Paul "Tiny" Newlan, Edward Agresti, Alvina Temple, Fritz Feld, Roy Butler, Jon Tegner, Bobbie Hall, Charles D. Campbell, Helen Chapman, Joan Whitney, Howard Negley, Stanley Blystone, Billy Engle, Chester Conklin, Hank Mann, Ralph Sanford, Lyle L. Moraine, Abdullah Abbas. *D:* Norman Z. McLeod; *P:* Paul Jones; *St: & Adaptation:* Lou Breslow, Edmund Beloin; *Sc:* Edmund L. Hartmann, Jack Sher; *Additional dialogue:* Hal Kanter; *Songs:* "I Wind Up Taking a Fall" Johnny Mercer, Robert Emmett Dolan; "Just a Moment More" Jay Livingston, Ray Evans. (1:33) Hit comedy of a burlesque comic hired by the U.S. Government to replace an agent he resembles and retrieve a valuable microfilm. He bumbles his way through the dangerous mission to Tangier, gets the microfilm, routs out a gang of enemy agents and finds romance.

1785. My Forbidden Past (RKO; 1951). *Cast:* Robert Mitchum, Ava Gardner, Melvyn Douglas, Lucile Watson (final film—ret.), Janis Carter, Gordon Oliver, Basil Ruysdael, Clarence Muse, Walter Kingsford, Jack Briggs, Will Wright, Watson Downs, Cliff Clark, John B. Williams, Louis Payne, Johnny Lee, George Douglas, Ken MacDonald, Everett Glass, Barry Brooks, Daniel DeLaurentis. *D:* Robert Stevenson; *P:* Robert Sparks, Polan Banks; *Sc:* Marion Parsonnet, Leopold Atlas. (1:21) (video) Costume soap opera of a woman who inherits a fortune from her grandmother, who made the cash by selling her favors. The heiress sets her sights on a married man and tries to break up the marriage, only to have the situation drag her into court when the man she hired to seduce her intended's wife is murdered and her intended is blamed. A box office bomb, it was based on the 1947 novel *Carriage Entrance* by Mr. Banks.

1786. My Friend Irma Goes West (Paramount/Wallis-Hazen; 1950). *Cast:* John Lund, Marie Wilson, Diana Lynn, Dean Martin,

Jerry Lewis, Corinne Calvet, Don Porter, Harold Huber, Lloyd Corrigan, Joseph Vitale, Charles Evans, Kenneth Tobey, James Flavin, David Clarke, Wendell Niles, George Humbert, Roy Gordon, Link Clayton, Mike Mahoney, Bob Johnson, Al Ferguson, Napoleon Whiting, Paul Lee, Stan Johnson, Charles Dayton, Jasper D. Weldon, Ivan H. Browning, Julie Montoya, Rose Higgins, Maxie Thrower, Chief Yowlachie, Joe Hecht, Gil Herman, Gregg Palmer, Jimmie Dundee, Pierre (chimpanzee—received #3 PATSY Award in 1951). *D:* Hal Walker; *P:* Hal B. Wallis; *As.P:* Cy Howard; *Sc. & St:* Howard, Parke Levy; *Songs:* "Baby Obey Me," "Querida Mia," "I'll Always Love You," "Fiddle and Gittar Band" and "Love You" Jay Livingston, Ray Evans. (1:30) Popular slapstick comedy of two guys on a trip to Hollywood with friends in search of fame and fortune. A follow-up to the popular 1949 hit *My Friend Irma*, which was based on characters created on the radio show of that name by Mr. Howard. A TV series followed.

1787. My Gun Is Quick (United Artists/ Parklane Pictures–Victor Saville Prods.; 1957). *Cast:* Robert Bray, Whitney Blake, Pat Donahue, Donald Randolph, Pamela Duncan, Booth Colman, Jan Chaney, Gina Core, Richard Garland, Charles Boaz, Peter Mamakos, Claire Carleton, Phil Arnold, John Dennis, Terence de Marnay, Jackie Paul, Leon Askin, Jack Holland. *D: & P:* George A. White, Phil Victor; *Sc:* Richard Collins, Richard Powell. (1:28) Mystery-melodrama which has tough private eye, Mike Hammer (Bray), solving a murder and a jewel robbery. Based on the 1950 novel by Mickey Spillane.

1788. My Man and I (MGM; 1952). *Cast:* Ricardo Montalban, Shelley Winters, Wendell Corey, Claire Trevor, Jack Elam, Robert Burton, Jose Torvay, Pasqual Garcia Pena, George Chandler, Juan Torena, Carlos Conde. *D:* William A. Wellman; *P:* Stephen Ames; *St: & Sc:* John Fante, Jack Leonard. (1:33) Drama of an amiable Mexican handyman infatuated with a suicidal taxi dancer, while the neglected wife of his employer—who hates Mexicans—also has her eye on him.

1789. My Man Godfrey (Universal-International; 1957). *Cast:* June Allyson, David Niven, Jessie Royce Landis, Eva Gabor, Robert Keith, Jeff Donnell, Martha Hyer, Jay Robinson, Herbert Anderson, Eric Sinclair, Dabbs Greer, Jack Mather, Fred Essler, Paul Levitt, Harry Cheshire, Robert Clarke, Robert Brubaker, Fred Coby, Voltaire Perkins, William Hudson, Robert Foulk, Thomas Browne Henry, Richard Deacon. *D:* Henry Koster; *P:* Ross Hunter; *Sc:* Everett Freeman, Peter Berneis, William Bowers; *Title song:* Peggy Lee, Sonny Burke (sung by Sarah Vaughan). (1:32) (video) Comedy of a wealthy, eccentric New York family who happens to acquire a butler, an Austrian refugee in the U.S. illegally. Based on the novel by Eric Hatch and the screenplay of the 1936 version by Hatch and Morrie Ryskind of which this is a remake. Eastmancolor and CinemaScope.

My Outlaw Brother *see* **My Brother, the Outlaw**

1790. My Pal Gus (20th Century–Fox; 1952). *Cast:* Richard Widmark, Joanne Dru, Audrey Totter, George "Foghorn" Winslow, Joan Banks, Regis Toomey, Ludwig Donath, Ann Morrison, Lisa Golm, Christopher Olsen, Robert Foulk, Sandy Descher, Mimi Gibson, Marie M. Brown, Gordon Nelson, William Cottrell, Jay Adler, Frank Marlowe, Franklyn Farnum, William Dyer, Jr., Otto Forrest, James Flavin, Jonathan Hale, Frank Nelson, Mabel Albertson, Jerrilyn Flannery. *D:* Robert Parrish; *P:* Stanley Rubin; *St: & Sc:* Fay Kanin, Michael Kanin. (1:23) Comedy-drama of a father's attempt to keep his son after his ex-wife shows up and says their Mexican divorce is invalid. Originally ran on a double bill with *The Thief of Venice,* an Italian production.

1791. My Sister Eileen (Columbia; 1955). *Cast:* Janet Leigh, Betty Garrett, Jack Lemmon, Bob Fosse (who also choreographed), Kurt Kasznar, Dick York, Lucy Marlow, Tommy Rall, Barbara Brown, Horace McMahon, Henry Slate, Hal March, Alberto Morin, Queenie Smith, Richard Deacon, Ken Christy. *D:* Richard Quine; *P:* Fred Kohlmar; *Sc:* Blake Edwards, Quine; *Songs:* "Give Me a Band and My Baby," "It's Bigger Than You and Me," "There's Nothing Like Love," "As Soon as They See Eileen," "I'm Great," "Conga," "Atmosphere" Jule Styne, Leo Robin. (1:48) (video/laserdisc) Musical comedy of two sisters from Ohio who move into a Greenwich Village apartment in New York City. A remake of the 1942 production by this studio, it was based on the play by Joseph Fields and Jerome Chodorov, which in turn was derived from stories by Ruth McKenney. Also musicalized on Broadway in 1953 as *Wonderful Town* (with a different music score). Technicolor and CinemaScope.

1792. My Six Convicts (Columbia/Stanley Kramer Co.; 1952). *Cast:* Millard Mitchell, Gilbert Roland, John Beal, Marshall Thompson, Alf Kjellin, Henry [Harry] Morgan, Jay Adler, Regis Toomey, Fay Roope, Carleton Young, John Marley, Russ Conway, Charles [Bronson] Buchinski, Byron Foulger, George Eldredge, Peter Virgo, Carol Savage, Fred Kelsey, Barney Phillips, Dick Curtis (final film—d. 1952), John Monoghan, Joe Palma, Edwin Parker, Harry Stanton, Joe McTurk, Frank Mitchell, Vincent Renno, Chester Jones, Joe Haworth, Danny Jackson, Jack Carr, H. George Stern, Dick Cogan, Allen Mathews, Paul Hoffman. *D:* Hugo Fregonese; *P:* Stanley Kramer; *Sc:* Michael Blankfort. (1:44) In this prison drama, six convicts are psychoanalyzed by a prison psychologist. Based on the book by Donald Powell Wilson, it was filmed on location at California's San Quentin prison, utilizing actual prisoner as extras.

1793. My Son John (Paramount/Rainbow Prods.; 1952). *Cast:* Helen Hayes (Lucille Jefferson), Van Heflin (Stedman), Robert Walker (final film—died before production was completed/John Jefferson), Dean Jagger (Dan Jefferson), Minor Watson (Dr. Carver), Frank McHugh (Father McDowd), Richard Jaeckel (Chuck Jefferson), James Young (Ben Jefferson), Todd Karns (Bedford), Irene Winston (Ruth Carlin), Nancy Hale, Frances Morris, William McLean, Fred Sweeney, Russell Conway, Lee Aaker, Vera Stokes, Douglas Evans, Gail Bonney, David Newell, Erskine Sanford, Margaret Wells, David Bond, Eghiche Harout, Jimmie Dundee. *D: & P:* Leo McCarey; *St:* (AAN) McCarey; *Sc:* McCarey, Myles Connolly; *Adaptation:* John Lee Mahin. (2:02) Melodrama of an all-American couple who find their son is a communist. A genuine relic from the McCarthy era of anti-communist hysteria, it placed #10 on the "10 Best" list of the NBR. The film utilizes outtakes from *Strangers On a Train* (q.v.) to fill out Walker's role.

1794. My True Story (Columbia/*True Story* Magazine; 1951). *Cast:* Helen Walker, Willard Parker, Elisabeth Risdon, Emory Parnell, Aldo [Ray] DaRe, Wilton Graff, Ivan Triesault, Ben Welden, Fred F. Sears, Mary Newton, Ann Tyrrell. *D:* Mickey Rooney (directorial debut); *P:* Milton Feldman; *St:* Margit Mantica; *Sc:* Howard J. Green, Brown Holmes. (1:07) Crime melodrama of a female jewel thief who, when paroled, decides to go straight and thwarts criminal plans. Originally ran on a double bill with *Texans Never Cry* (q.v.).

1795. My Wife's Best Friend (20th Century–Fox; 1952). *Cast:* Anne Baxter, Macdonald Carey, Cecil Kellaway, Casey Adams [aka: Max Showalter], Catherine McLeod, Leif Erickson, Frances Bavier, Martin Milner, Billie Bird, Wild Red Berry, Henry Kulky, John Hedloe, John McKee, Phil Hartman, Michael Ross, Junius Matthews, Joe Haworth, Edgar Dearing, Morgan Farley, Ann Staunton, Emmett Vogan, May Winn. *D:* Richard Sale; *P:* Robert Bassler; *St:* John Briard Harding; *Sc:* Isobel Lennart. (1:27) Comedy of the complications that arise when a husband and wife think they are about to die in a plane crash and make confessions to each other, including his of having an affair with her best friend. Then the plane has a safe landing!

1796. My World Dies Screaming (Howco-International/Omecc, Inc.; 1958). *Cast:* Gerald Mohr, Cathy O'Donnell, William Ching, John Qualen, Barry Bernard. *D:* Harold Daniels; *P:* William S. Edwards; *As.P:* Michael Miller; *St: & Sc:* Robert C. Dennis. (1:30) (video) Thriller of a psychologically disturbed Swiss woman, haunted by vivid recurring nightmares of a sinister old house. She marries an American who brings her to the states and his ancestral Florida home—the house in her nightmares! Photographed in PsychoRama (things coming at you), the film was retitled and is better known as *Terror in the Haunted House*, which is also the home video title. Originally ran on a double bill with *Lost, Lonely and Vicious* (q.v.).

The Mysterious Invader (G.B. title) *see* **The Astounding She-Monster**

1797. Mystery Lake (Larry Lansburgh; 1953). *Cast:* George Fenneman, Gloria McGough, Bogue Bell, R.P. Alexander, Edgar Bergen (without "Charlie McCarthy"). *D: & P:* Larry Lansburgh; *St:* Janet Lansburgh; *Sc:* Rosalie Bodrero, John Bodrero. (1:04) Dramatized "documentary" of a naturalist (Fenneman) sent to study wildlife at Reelfoot Lake, Tennessee, where it was filmed on location. Lansburgh was a former Disney employee. Note: Reelfoot Lake was created in 1813 during a series of tremendous earthquakes that rocked central North America in that time period. A large chunk of land sank with the cavity being filled by water from the Mississippi River. Anscocolor.

1798. Mystery Street (MGM; 1950). *Cast:* Ricardo Montalban (Lt. Peter Moralas), Sally Forrest (Grace Shanway), Bruce Bennett (Dr. McAdoo), Elsa Lanchester (Mrs. Smerring), Marshall Thompson (Henry Shanway), Jan Sterling (Vivian Heldon), Edmon Ryan (James Joshua Harkley), Betsy Blair (Jackie Elcott), Wally Maher (Tim Sharkey), James Hayward (Constable Fischer), Eula Guy (Mrs. Fischer), Ned Glass (Dr. Levy), Matt Moore (Dr. Rockton), John Maxwell (Kilrain), Robert Foulk (O'Hara), Louise Lorimer (Mrs. Shanway), Lucille Curtis (Mrs.Harkley), David McMahon (Carrity), Bert Davidson (Dr. Thorpe), Ralph Dumke, Willard Waterman, Walter Burke, Don Shelton, Brad Hatton, Douglas Carter, William F. Leicester, Arthur Lowe, Jr., Sherry Hall, Virginia Mullen, King Donovan, George Cooper, Ralph Brooks, George Sherwood, John Crawford, Fred E. Sherman, Allen O'Locklin, Melvin H. Moore, Maurice Samuels, Jack Shea, Napoleon Whiting, Juanita Quigley, Mary Jane Smith, Charles Wagenheim, Michael Patrick Donovan, Frank Overton, May McAvoy, Mack Chandler, Elsie Baker, Ralph Montgomery, Jim Frasher, Ernesto Morelli, Robert Strong, George Brand, Fred Santley, Perry Ivins, Peter Thompson. *D:* John Sturges; *P:* Frank E. Taylor; *St:* (AAN) Leonard Spigelgass; *Sc:* Sydney Boehm, Richard Brooks. (1:33) Film noir of events in the investigation of a married man who killed his girlfriend, after finding that she was carrying his baby. Set among the bluebloods of Boston, location filming was at Harvard University and various Boston locales.

1799. Mystery Submarine (Universal-International; 1950). *Cast:* Macdonald Carey, Marta Toren, Robert Douglas, Ludwig Donath, Carl Esmond, Jacqueline Dalya Hilliard, Fred Nurney, Katherine Warren, Howard Negley, Bruce Morgan, Ralph Brooke, Paul Hoffman, Peter Michael, Larry Winter, Frank Rawls, Peter Similuk, Lester Sharpe, James Best. *D:* Douglas Sirk; *P: & St:* Ralph Dietrich; *Sc:* George W. George, George F. Slavin. (1:18) Melodrama of an American military officer who attempts to rescue a kidnapped scientist from an enemy submarine. No relation to the 1963 British film of the same name.

1800. Naked Alibi (Universal-International; 1954). *Cast:* Sterling Hayden, Gloria Grahame, Gene Barry, Marcia Henderson, Casey Adams [aka: Max Showalter], Billy Chapin, Chuck Connors, Don Haggerty, Stuart Randall, Don Garrett, Richard Beach, Tol Avery, Paul Leavitt, Fay Roope, Joseph Mell, Bud [Bill] Wolfe, John Day, Frank Wilcox. *D:* Jerry Hopper; *P:* Ross Hunter; Sc: Lawrence Roman (1:25) Chase melodrama of a cop discharged from duty for behavior unbecoming, who goes after the man he believes responsible for a triple cop-killing. Based on the story "Cry Copper" by J. Robert Bren and Gladys Atwater.

1801. The Naked and the Dead (Warner/RKO Teleradio; 1958). *Cast:* Aldo Ray, Cliff Robertson, Raymond Massey, William Campbell, Richard Jaeckel, Lili St. Cyr, Barbara Nichols, James Best, Joey Bishop, L.Q. Jones, Robert Gist, Jerry Paris, Casey Adams [aka: Max Showalter], John Beradino, Edwin Gregson, Edward McNally, Greg Roman, Henry Amargo, Eitoku Oshiro. *D:* Raoul Walsh; *P:* Paul Gregory; *Sc:* Denis Sanders, Terry Sanders. (2:11) (video) Based on Norman Mailer's controversial 1948 novel of World War II and a company of marines on a doomed mission in the Pacific. Popular at the box office, though the raw language of the book had to be toned down or eliminated for 1958 audiences, despite the fact that film censorship was meeting new challenges in the 1950s. A production of RKO studios which was released by Warners, after the former closed its doors. Technicolor and RKOscope.

1802. The Naked Dawn (Universal-International; 1954–55). *Cast:* Arthur Kennedy, Betta St. John, Eugene Iglesias, Charlita, Roy Engel. *D:* Edgar G. Ulmer; *P:* James Q. Radford; *St: & Sc:* Nina and Herman Schneider; *Song:* "Al Hombre" Herschel Burke Gilbert, William Copeland (sung by Charlita). (1:22) Melodrama of a poor Mexican farmer who falls victim to greed when prospects present themselves to acquire ill-gotten loot taken in a robbery.

1803. The Naked Eye (Film Representations, Inc.–Camera Eye Pictures, Inc.; 1956). *D:-P:-St: &* Sc: Louis Clyde Stoumen. (1:11) A feature documentary, which garnered an AAN for Mr. Stoumen for "Best Documentary," on the development of photography as a hobby and as an art form, featuring some of the best in their field.

1804. The Naked Gun (Associated Film Releasing; 1956). *Cast:* Willard Parker, Mara Corday, Barton MacLane, Billy House, Veda Ann Borg, Morris Ankrum, Chick Chandler, Tom Brown, Bill Phillips, Timothy Carey, X Brands, Steve Raines, Rick Vallin, Jim Hayward, Jody McCrea, Tony McCoy, Bill Ward,

Merry Ogden, Helen Jay, Elena DaVinci, Doris Simons. *D:* Edward "Eddie" Dew; *P:* Ron Ormond; *St: & Sc:* Ormond, Jack Lewis. (1:13) Low budget oater of the problems encountered by an insurance agent when he attempts to deliver an Aztec treasure inheritance to its rightful heirs.

1805. The Naked Hills (Allied Artists/LaSalle Prods.; 1956). *Cast:* David Wayne, Keenan Wynn, James Barton, Jim Backus, Marcia Henderson, Denver Pyle, Myrna Dell, Lewis Russell, Frank Fenton, Fuzzy Knight, Jim Hayward, Steve Terrell, Chris Olsen. *D:-P: & Sc:* Josef Shaftel; *St:* Helen S. Bilkie; *Song:* "Four Seasons" Herschel Burke Gilbert, Bob Russell (sung by Barton). (1:12) (video) Western melodrama of an Indiana farmer, smitten with gold fever, who deserts home and family and spends forty years of his life searching for the yellow metal. Pathécolor.

1806. Naked in the Sun (Allied Artists/Empire Studios; 1957) *Cast:* James Craig, Lita Milan, Barton MacLane, Robert Wark, Tony Hunter, Jim Boles, Douglas Wilson, Bill Armstrong, Dennis Cross, Peter Dearing, Tony Morris, Mike Crecco. *D:-P: & Additional dialogue:* John Hugh; *Sc:* Frank G. Slaughter. (1:19) (video) Costume-melodrama of 19th century Florida Indians in conflict with slave traders. Based on the 1956 novel *The Warrior* by Mr. Slaughter.

1807. The Naked Jungle (Paramount; 1953–54). *Cast:* Charlton Heston, Eleanor Parker, Abraham Sofaer, William Conrad, Douglas Fowley, Romo Vincent, John Dierkes, Leonard Strong, Norma Calderon, John Mansfield, Ronald Alan Numkena, Bernie Gozier, Jack Reitzen, Rodd Redwing, Pilar Del Rey, John E. Wood, Jerry Groves, Leon Lontoc, Carlos Rivero. *D:* Byron Haskin; *P:* George Pal; *Sc:* Ranald MacDougall, Philip Yordan. (1:15) (video/laserdisc) South American jungle adventure of a cocoa plantation and its inhabitants threatened by an encroaching army of voracious red ants. Adapted from Carl Stephenson's 1940 short story "Leiningen vs. the Ants" which also appeared on the radio show *Suspense*. A box office hit. Technicolor.

1808. The Naked Maja (United Artists/Titanus; 1959). *Cast:* Ava Gardner, Anthony Franciosa, Amedeo Nazzari, Gino Cervi, Massimo Serato, Lea Padovani, Carlo Rizzo, Renzo Cesana, Audrey MacDonald, Patrick Crean, Tonio Selwart, Peter Meersman, Enzo Fiermonte, Yemiko Fullwood, Carlo Giustini, Erminio Spalla, John Karlson, Paul Muller, Renata Mauro, Pina Bottin, Amru Sani, Carmen Mora, Clayton Hall, Gustavo De Nardo, Andre Eszterhazy, Amina Pirani Maggi, Leonardo Betta, Roberta Primavera, Pamela Sharp, Alberto Plebani, Nadia Balabin, Giuseppe Giardina, Stella Vitelleschi. *D:* Henry Koster, Mario Russo; *P:* Goffredo Lombardo; *St:* Oscar Saul, Talbot Jennings; *Sc:* Georgio Prosperi, Norman Corwin. (1:51) (video) This U.S.A./Italian co-production purports to tell of the affair between 18th century painter Francisco Goya (Franciosa) and his most famous model, The Duchess of Alba (Gardner), who posed for the title painting. Critically panned, it was in Technicolor and Technirama.

1809. Naked Paradise (American International/Sunset Prods.; 1957). *Cast:* Richard Denning, Beverly Garland, Lisa Montell, Leslie Bradley, Richard "Dick" Miller, Jonathan Haze. *D: & P:* Roger Corman; *St: & Sc:* Charles B. Giffith, Mark Hanna. (1:08) Quickie melodrama of a captain who has his schooner chartered by a thief following a robbery. In Pathécolor, it was reworked as *Beast from Haunted Cave* (q.v.). (aka: *Thunder Over Hawaii*)

1810. The Naked Sea (RKO/Theatre Prods.; 1955). *D:-P: & Cin:* Allen H Miner; *As.P: & Narration:* Gerald J. Schnitzer; *Narrator:* William Conrad. (1:10) Color documentary of the *Star-Kist*, a modern 300 ton tuna boat, from the time it sets sail from San Diego, California, on a four-month tuna fishing expedition to the waters of Peru. Includes wildlife footage from the Galapagos Islands.

1811. The Naked Spur (MGM; 1953). *Cast:* James Stewart (Howard Kemp), Janet Leigh (Lina Patch), Robert Ryan (Ben Vandegroat), Ralph Meeker (Roy Anderson), Millard Mitchell (final film—d. 1953/Jesse Tate), Grant Mitchell (final film—d. 1957). *D:* Anthony Mann; *P:* William H. Wright; *St: & Sc:* (AAN) Sam Rolfe, Harold Jack Bloom. (1:31) (video) An acclaimed adult western drama of a bounty hunter on the trail of a wanted man, and the difficulties he encounters in the pursuit and capture. One of the 26 top-grossing films of 1952–53, the book of that title was published in 1953 from the screenplay. Technicolor.

1812. The Naked Street (United Artists/World Films–C-Fame Picts., Inc.; 1955). *Cast:* Farley Granger, Anthony Quinn, Anne Bancroft,

Peter Graves, Else Neft, Jerry Paris, Frank Sully, John Dennis, Angela Stevens, Joy Ferry, G. Pat Collins, Mario Siletti, Whit Bissell, Jeanne Cooper, Sara Berner, James Flavin, Harry Harvey, Judge Stanley, Jackie Loughery, Frank Kreig, Joe Turkel, Harry O. Tyler, Sammie Weiss. *D:* Maxwell Shane; *P:* Edward Small; *St:* Leo Katcher; *Sc:* Katcher, Shane. (1:24) Crime melodrama of a ruthless gangster, running a syndicate that is exposed by a newspaperman who loves the mobster's sister.

1813. Nancy Goes to Rio (MGM; 1950). *Cast:* Jane Powell (title role), Ann Sothern (final film for MGM), Barry Sullivan, Carmen Miranda, Louis Calhern, Scotty Beckett, Fortunio Bonanova, Nella Walker, Hans Conried, Glenn Anders, Frank Fontaine, Leon Belasco, Leonid Kinskey, Danny Scholl, Ransom Sherman, Sig Arno, Pierre Watkin, Forbes Murray, Bess Flowers. *D:* Robert Z. Leonard; *P:* Joe Pasternak; *St:* Jane Hall, Frederick Kohner, Ralph Block; *Sc:* Sidney Sheldon; *Songs:* "Time and Time Again" Earl Brent, Fred Spielman; "Shine on Harvest Moon" Jack Norworth, Nora Bayes; "Cha Bomm Pa Pa," "Yipsee-I-O" Ray Gilbert (both sung by Miranda); "Magic Is the Moonlight" Charles Pasquale, Maria Grever; "Musetta's Waltz" from "La Boheme" Giacomo Puccini; "Love Is Like This" Jay Gilbert; "Nancy Goes to Rio" Georgie Stoll, Brent. (1:39) (video) Hit musical of a mother and daughter both after the same stage role and the same man, each without the knowledge of the other's intentions. A remake of *It's a Date* (Universal; 1940). Technicolor.

1814. The Narcotics Story (Police Science; 1958). *Cast:* Sharon Strand, Darlene Hendricks, Herbert Crisp, Fred Marratto, Allen Pitt, Patricia Lynn, Bob Hopkins. *D: & P:* Robert W Larsen; *St: & Sc:* Roger E. Garris. (1:15) Originally designed as a police training film for drug enforcement, this semi-documentary saw limited theatrical release but via narration depicts the evils involved with taking drugs. It also depict methods of acquiring them! Eastmancolor.

1815. The Narrow Margin (RKO; 1952). *Cast:* Charles McGraw (Walter Brown), Marie Windsor (Mrs. Neil), Jacqueline White (Ann Sinclair), Gordon Gebert (Tommy Sinclair), Queenie Leonard (Mrs. Troll), David Clarke (Kemp), Peter Virgo (Densel), Don Beddoe (Gus Forbes), Paul Maxey (Jennings), Tony Merrill (Officer Allen), Don Haggerty (Detective Wilson), Harry Harvey, Mike Lally, Donald Dillaway, George Sawaya, Howard Mitchell, Milton Kibbee, Johnny Lee, Ivan H. Browning, Clarence Hargrave, Edgar Murray, Napoleon Whiting, Bobby Johnson, Will Lee, Franklin Parker, Jasper Weldon. *D:* Richard Fleischer; *P:* Stanley Rubin; *St:* (AAN) Martin Goldsmith Jack Leonard; *Sc:* Earl Fenton (1:11) (video/laserdisc) A critically acclaimed hit B movie, made for a production cost of less than $250,000, that reaped big bucks at the box office. A detective is assigned to escort the widow of a gangster via train cross-country to testify before the grand jury. The plot thickens and then it begins its twists and turns as three hoods board the train with orders to do in the woman before she testifies. Computer-colored by Turner Entertainment, it was remade in 1990.

1816. Native Son (Classic Pictures/Argentina Sono; 1950–51). *Cast:* Richard Wright (film debut), Jean Wallace, Nicholas Joy, Gloria Madison, Charles Cane, Jean Michael, George Rigaud, George Green, Willa Pearl Curtis, Don Dean, Ruth Roberts, Ned Campbell, Charles Simmonds, Leslie Straughn, Lidia Alves, George Nathanson, George Roos, Lewis McKenzie, Cecile Lezard. *D:* Pierre Chenal; *P:* James Prades; *Sc:* Chenal, Wright. (1:31) (video) Drama of a black man's plight when he accidentally kills the young daughter of the white family that employs him as a chauffeur. Based on Richard Wright's controversial 1940 novel which received literary acclaim. A co-production of the U.S.A. and Argentina, it was filmed on location in Argentina and Chicago, where the story is set. Remade in 1986.

1817. Navajo (Lippert/C.B.F. Prods.; 1951–52). *Cast:* Francis Kee Teller (Son of the Hunter), John Mitchell (Grey Singer), Mrs. Teller (mother), Billy Draper (Ute guide), Hall Bartlett (Indian school counsel), Linda Teller, Eloise Teller. *D:* Norman Foster; *P:* (AAN-Best Documentary) Hall Bartlett (first film); *St: & Sc:* Foster; *Cin:* (AAN) Virgil E. Miller; *Narrator:* Sammy Ogg. (1:10) Acclaimed documentary-style drama of a Navajo Indian youth who doesn't want to go to a "white man's school."

1818. Navy Bound (Monogram; 1951). *Cast:* Tom Neal, Wendy Waldron, Regis Toomey, John Abbott, Murray Alper, Paul Bryar, Harvey Parry, Ric Roman, John Compton, Stephen Harrison, Billy Bletcher, Ray Kemper,Herby Lytton, Riley Hill. *D:* Paul Landres; *P:* William F. Broidy; *Sc:* Sam Roeca. (1:01) Programmer drama of a man who leaves the U.S. Navy to help his debt-ridden father, a tuna fisherman. Based on a *Collier's* magazine story by Talbot Josselyn which ran in the December 14, 1935, issue.

1819. Navy Wife (Allied Artists; 1956). *Cast:* Joan Bennett, Gary Merrill, Judy Nugent, Maurice Manson, Teru Shimada, Tom Komuro, Shizue Nakamura, Robert Nichols, Carol Veazie, John Craven, Shirley Yamaguchi, Arnold Ishii, Ziro Tenkai, Kyoko Kamo, Julia Katayama, Karie Shindo, Micko Shintani, Rollin Moriyama, Tauenko Takahashi, Dona Jean Okubo, Yoshiko Nilya, Dick Tyler, Morgan Jones, Jack Bradford, Michiyo Kamo, Bob Ozazaki, Matsukichi Kamo, John Matautani, Sono Shirai, Mash Kunitomi, Miyoshi Jingu, Kimiko Hiroshigi, Ken Shoji, Karen Yamamoto, Jack Shintani, Kuni Morishima, Tomiji Nagao, Jim Yagi, Maudie Prickett, Phil Arnold, Dorothy Furamura *D:* Edward L. Bernds; *P:* Walter Wanger; Sc: Kay Lenard; *Song:* "Mother, Sir" Hans Salter, Jack Brooks. (1:23) Comedy of Japanese wives, normally obedient to their husbands, who observe the behavior of an American wife to her husband and decide it's time for things to change in how they behave toward their respective spouses. Based on the 1953 book *Mother, Sir* by Tats Blain. (G.B. title: *Mother, Sir*)

1820. The Neanderthal Man (United Artists/Global Prods., Inc.; 1953). *Cast:* Robert Shayne, Joyce Terry, Richard Crane, Doris Merrick, Robert Long, Dick Rich, Jean Quinn, Robert Easton, Beverly Garland. *D:* E.A. Dupont; *P:-St: & Sc:* Aubrey Wisberg, Jack Pollexfen. (1:18) Horror tale of a scientist whose experiments turn his cat into a saber-toothed tiger, and himself into the film's title.

1821. The Nebraskan (Columbia; 1953). *Cast:* Phil Carey, Roberta Haynes, Wallace Ford, Lee Van Cleef, Pat Hogan, Richard Webb, Boyd "Red" Morgan, Regis Toomey, Jay Silverheels, Maurice Jara, Dennis Weaver. *D:* Fred F. Sears; *P:* Wallace MacDonald; *St:* David Lang; *Sc:* Lang, Martin Berkeley. (1:08) A U.S. Army scout tries to prevent an Indian war instigated by the murder of a tribal elder. 3-D and Technicolor.

1822. Nevada Badmen (Monogram/Frontier Pictures; 1951). *Cast:* Whip Wilson, Fuzzy Knight, Jim Bannon, Phyllis Coates, I. Stanford Jolley, Marshall Reed, Riley Hill, Lee Roberts, Pierce Lyden, Bill Kennedy, Bud Osborne, Stanley Price, Artie Ortego, Carl Mathews. *D:* Lewis D. Collins; *P:* Vincent M. Fennelly; *St: & Sc:* Joseph O'Donnell. (0:58) In this series western, Whip Wilson comes to the aid of a lady rancher whose property is about to be foreclosed on by a greedy banker.

1823. The Nevadan (Columbia/Scott-Brown); 1950). *Cast:* Randolph Scott, Dorothy Malone, Forrest Tucker, Frank Faylen, Charles Kemper, Jeff Corey, Tom Powers, Jock [Mahoney] O'Mahoney, James Kirkwood, Stanley Andrews, Kate Drain Lawson, Olin Howlin, Louis Mason. *D:* Gordon Douglas; *P:* Harry Joe Brown; *St: & Sc:* George W. George, George F. Slavin; *Additional dialogue:* Rowland Brown. (1:21) (video) Western drama of an undercover lawman who thwarts attempts to steal a substantial amount of gold. Cinecolor. (G.B. title: *The Man from Nevada*)

1824. Never a Dull Moment (RKO; 1950). *Cast:* Irene Dunne, Fred MacMurray, William Demarest, Andy Devine, Gigi Perreau, Natalie Wood, Philip Ober, Jack Kirkwood, Ann Doran, Margaret Gibson, Lela Bliss, Irving Bacon, Virginia Mullen, Victoria Horne, Connie Van, Edna Holland, Gene Evans, Olin Howlin, Paul "Tiny" Newlan, Anne O'Neal, Chester Conklin, Ralph Peters, Janine Perreau, Jim Hawkins, Jack Jackson, Alan Dinehart III, Carl Sklover, Art Dupuis, Bob Thom, Jacqueline de Wit, George Leigh, Harry Tyler, Jo Ann Marlowe. *D:* George Marshall; *P:* Harriet Parsons; *Sc:* Lou Breslow, Doris Anderson; *Songs:* "Once You Find Your Guy," "Sagebrush Lullaby," "The Man with the Big Felt Hat" Kay Swift. (1:29) (video/laserdisc) Comedy of an urban songwriter who meets a widowed western rancher at a New York rodeo. After love blossoms, she accompanies him back to his ranch, where she finds living is quite a bit different than what she has been accustomed to. Based on the 1943 novel *Who Could Ask for Anything More* by Ms. Swift.

1825. Never Fear (Eagle-Lion/Filmakers; 1949–50). *Cast:* Sally Forrest, Keefe Brasselle, Hugh O'Brian (film debut), Eve Miller, Larry Dobkin, Rita Lupino, Herbert Butterfield, Kevin O'Morrison, Stanley Waxman, Jerry Hausner, John Franco. *D: & P:* Ida Lupino; *As.P:* Norman Cook; *St: & Sc:* Lupino, Collier Young; *Songs:* John Franco, William Earley. (1:22) (video) Modest drama of the various changes she must endure when the female member of a dance team learns she has polio. (aka: *The Young Lovers*) Originally ran on a double bill with *The Sundowners* (q.v.).

1826. Never Let Me Go (MGM; 1953). *Cast:* Clark Gable, Gene Tierney, Richard Haydn, Bernard Miles, Kenneth More, Belita, Theodore Bikel, Karel Stepanek, Anna Valentina, Frederick Valk, Anton Dolin, Peter Illing, Robert Henderson, Stanley Maxted, Meinhart Maur, Alexis Chesnakov, Anton Diffring, The London Festival Ballet. *D:* Delmer Daves; *P:* Clarence Brown; *Sc:* Ronald Millar, George Froeschel. (1:34) (video) Romantic drama of an American reporter attempting to get his ballerina wife out of Russia. A U.S.A./British coproduction, it was based on the 1949 novel *Came the Dawn* by Roger Bax [a pseudonym of Paul Winterton]. Filmed in England.

1827. Never Love a Stranger (Allied Artists/Harold Robbins; 1958). *Cast:* John Drew Barrymore, Lita Milan, Robert Bray, Steven McQueen, Salem Ludwig, Douglas Fletcher Rodgers, R.G. Armstrong, Joseph Leberman, Abe Simon, Augusta Merighi, Dolores Vitina, Dort Clark, Robert O'Connell, Michael O'Dowd, John Dalz, Mike Enserro, Gino Ardito, Joseph Costa, Felice Orlandi, Walter Burke. *D:* Robert Stevens; *P: & Sc:* Harold Robbins, Richard Day; *Songs:* "Never Love a Stranger" (sung by Dorothy Collins and Lita Milan); "Oh, Baby" Raymond Scott, Lawrence Elow (sung by Milan). (1:31) (video) A gangster melodrama which spans the time period from the early part of the 20th century to the Great Depression. Filmed on location in New York City, it was based on the 1948 novel by Harold Robbins [a pseudonym of Harold Rubin].

1828. Never Say Goodbye (Universal-International; 1956). *Cast:* Rock Hudson, Cornell Borchers (U.S. debut), George Sanders, Ray Collins, David Janssen, Shelley Fabares, Helen Wallace, John E. Wengraf, Robert Simon, Raymond Greenleaf, Frank Wilcox, Howard Wendell, Casey Adams [aka: Max Showalter], Jerry Paris, Else Neft, John Banner, Jeane Wood, Ann Loos, Margot Karin, Nancy Matthews, Terry Ann Rossworn, Clint Eastwood, Gia Scala, Kurt Katch, Edward Earle, Ken Alton, June McCall, Otto Reichow. *D:* Jerry Hopper, Douglas Sirk (unc.); *P:* Albert J. Cohen; *Sc:* Charles Hoffman (based on the 1945 screenplay by Bruce Manning, John Klorer and Leonard Lee). (1:36) (video) Romantic melodrama of a California doctor, separated from his wife in Vienna ten years before, who meets her again in Chicago and attempts to reconcile. The film is a remake of *This Love of Ours* (1945) which was based on the 1938 play *Come Prima Meglio di Prima* by Luigi Pirandello. Technicolor.

1829. Never So Few (MGM/Canterbury; 1959). *Cast:* Frank Sinatra (Tom C. Reynolds), Gina Lollobrigida (Carla Vesari), Peter Lawford (Capt. Grey Travis), Steve McQueen (Bill Ringa), Richard Johnson (Capt. Danny de Mortimer), Paul Henreid (Nikko Regas), Brian Donlevy (Gen. Sloane), Dean Jones (Sgt. Jim Norby), Charles Bronson (Sgt. John Danforth), John Hoyt (Col. Reed), Philip Ahn (Nautaung), Whit Bissell (Capt. Alofson), Richard Lupino (Mike Island), Robert Bray (Col. Fred Parkson), Kipp Hamilton (Margaret Fitch), Aki Aleong (Billingsly), Ross Elliott (Dr. Barry), Leon Lontoc (Laurel), Maggie Pierce. *D:* John Sturges; *P:* Edmund Grainger; *Sc:* Millard Kaufman. (2:04) (video/laserdisc) Based on the 1957 best-seller by Tom Chamales, this World War II comedy-drama hit with the movie-going public and it became one of the 28 top-grossing films of 1959-60. In MetroColor and CinemaScope, it was filmed on location in Burma, Thailand and Ceylon.

1830. Never Steal Anything Small (Universal-International; 1959). *Cast:* James Cagney, Shirley Jones, Roger Smith, Cara Williams, Nehemiah Persoff, Royal Dano, Anthony Caruso, Jack Albertson, Horace McMahon, Virginia Vincent, Robert J. Wilke, Herbie Faye, Billy M. Greene, John Duke, Jack Orrison, Roland Winters, Ingrid Goude, Sanford Seeger, Ed "Skipper" McNally, Gregg Barton, Edwin Parker, Jay Jostyn, John Halloran, Harvey Perry, Phyllis Rimedy, Rebecca Sand. *D:* Charles Lederer (final film—ret.); *P:* Aaron Rosenberg; *St: & Sc:* Lederer; *Songs:* Title song, "I Haven't Got a Thing to Wear," "It Takes Love to Build a Home," "Helping Out Friends" and "I'm Sorry—I Want a Ferrari" Alli Wrubel, Maxwell Anderson. (1:34) (video) Offbeat musical comedy-drama of a man who will stop at nothing to become president of a dockworker's union. Based on "The Devil's Hornpipe," an unproduced play by Mr. Anderson and Rouben Mamoulian. Eastmancolor and CinemaScope.

1831. Never Trust a Gambler (Columbia; 1951). *Cast:* Dane Clark, Cathy O'Donnell, Tom Drake, Jeff Corey, Myrna Dell, Rhys Williams, Kathryn Card, Sid Tomack, Ruth Warren, Tom Greenway. *D:* Ralph Murphy; *P:* Louis B. Appleton, Jr., Monty Shaff; *St:* Jerome Odlum; *Sc:* Odlum, Jesse L. Lasky, Jr. (1:19) Crime melodrama of a gambler who takes flight after committing murder. Originally ran on the top of a double bill with *The Big Gusher* (q.v.)

1832. Never Wave at a WAC (RKO/IndependentArtists Pictures; 1952). *Cast:* Rosalind Russell, Paul Douglas, Marie Wilson, William Ching, Arleen Whelan, Leif Erickson, Charles Dingle, Lurene Tuttle, Hillary Brooke, Frieda Inescort, Regis Toomey, Louise Beavers, Frances Zucco, Bernadine Simpson, Jean Dean, Anita Martell, Marya Marco, Frances Morris, Louise Lorimer, Lucia Carroll, Joan Blair, Barbara Woodell, Madelon Mitchel, Vince Townsend, Jr., Virginia Christine, Olan Soule, Barbara Jane Smith, Helen Foster, Howard Smith, Allan Frank, Jo Gilbert, Frances Helm, Jane Seymour, Norma Busse, Omar Bradley (himself). *D:* Norman Z. McLeod; *P:* Frederick Brisson; *As.P:* Gordon Giffith; *St:* Frederick Kohner, Fred Brady; *Sc:* Ken Englund; *Song:* "WAC Song" Jane Douglass, Camilla Mays Frank. (1:27) (video) Hit comedy of a Washington, D.C., socialite who joins the WAC on a lark and finds the going a lot tougher than she expected. Shades of *Private Benjamin* (1980). (G.B. title: *The Private Wore Skirts*)

1833. New Faces (20th Century–Fox/National Pictures Corp; 1953–54). *Cast:* Ronny Graham, Eartha Kitt, Robert Clary, Virginia DeLuce, Alice Ghostley, June Carroll, Paul Lynde (film debut), Bill Mullikin, Rosemary O'Reilly, Allen Conroy, Jimmy Russell, George Smiley, Polly Ward, Carol Lawrence, Johnny Laverty, Elizabeth Logue, Faith Burwell, Clark Ranger. *D:* Harry Horner; *P:* Edward L. Alperson, Berman Schwartz; *Sc:* Ronny Graham, Melvin (Mel) Brooks, Paul Lynde, Luther Davis, John Cleveland, *Songs include:* "C'est si Bon" Henri Betti, Jerry Seelen; "Santa Baby" Joan Javits, Phil Springer, Tony Springer; "Uskadara" Stella Lee; "Monotonous" June Carroll, Ronny Graham, Arthur Siegel (all sung by Kitt); "Bal Petit Bal" Sheldon M. Harnick (sung by Kitt andClary); "Boston Beguine" Harnick (sung by Ghostley); "I'm in Love with Miss Logan" Graham (sung by Clary); "Penny Candy" Carroll, Siegel (sung by Carroll); and "Time for Tea" (sung by Ghostley and Carroll); "Lizzie Borden" (by the entire cast). (1:39) (video) A filmed version of Leonard Sillman's hit Broadway musical-comedy revue, *New Faces of 1952*. Technicolor and CinemaScope.

1834. New Mexico (United Artists/A Joseph Justman Picture–Irving Allen Ent.; 1951). *Cast:* Lew Ayres, Marilyn Maxwell, Robert Hutton, Andy Devine, Raymond Burr, Ted de Corsia, Jeff Corey, Lloyd Corrigan, Verna Felton, John Hoyt, Donald Buka, Robert Osterloh, Ian MacDonald, William Tannen, Arthur Lowe, Jr., Bob Duncan, Jack Kelly, Allen Matthews, Jack Briggs, Peter Price, Walter Greaza, Hans Conried, Ralph Volkie, Bud Rae. *D:* Irving Reis; *P:* Irving Allen; *St: & Sc:* Max Trell; *Songs:* "Soldier, Soldier, Won't You Marry Me?" (sung by Maxwell). (1:16) After the son of a chief is shot, a U.S. Cavalry captain tries to prevent warfare with the Indians, but to no avail as he and his men are trapped on a desert mesa. Anscocolor.

1835. New Orleans After Dark (Allied Artists/M.P.A. Prods.; 1958). *Cast:* Stacy Harris, Louis Sirgo, Ellen Moore, Tommy Pelle, Wilson Bourg, Harry Wood, Johnny Aladdin, Jeanine Thomas, Leo Zinser, Kathryn Copponex, Bob Samuels, Steve Lord, Louis Gurvich, Frank Fiasconaro, Allan Binkley, Claude Evans, Dottie Lee, La Vergne Smith (herself), Bill Matthews. *D:* John Sledge; *P:* Eric Sayers; *St: & Sc:* Frank Phares (based on official records of the New Orleans Police Dept.). (1:09) (video) Programmer melodrama of two New Orleans detectives on the trail of dope smugglers. Filmed on location.

1836. New Orleans, Uncensored (Columbia; 1955). *Cast:* Arthur Franz, Beverly Garland, Helene Stanton, Michael Ansara, Stacy Harris, Bill Henry, Michael Granger, Frankie Ray, Edwin Stafford Nelson, Mike Mazurki, Ralph Dupas (himself), Pete Herman (himself), Al Chittenden (himself), Judge Walter B. Hamlin, Joseph L. Scheuring, Victor Schiro, Howard L. Dey. *D:* William Castle; *P:* Sam Katzman; *Sc:* Orville H. Hampton, Lewis Meltzer. (1:16) Crime melodrama of a U.S. Navy veteran who works with law enforcement to clean up corruption on the docks of New Orleans. Based on the book *Riot on Pier 6* by Mr. Hampton. (G.B. title: *Riot on Pier 6*)

1837. New York Confidential (Warner/Green-Rouse Prods.–Challenge Pictures, Inc.; 1955). *Cast:* Broderick Crawford, Richard Conte, Marilyn Maxwell, Ann Bancroft, J. Carrol Naish, Onslow Stevens, Barry Kelley, Mike Mazurki, Ian Keith, Celia Lovsky, Herbert Hayes, Steven Geray, Bill Phillips, Henry Kulky, Nestor Paiva, Joe Vitale, Carl Milletaire, William Forrest, Charles Evans, Mickey Simpson, Tom Powers, Lee Trent, Lennie Bremen, John Doucette, Frank Ferguson, Hope Landin, Fortunio Bonanova. *D:* Russell Rouse; *P:* Clarence Greene;

Sc: Rouse, Greene. (1:27) Fact-based account of attempts to break up a New York crime syndicate. Based on a 1948 book by Jack Lait and Lee Mortimer.

1838. The Next Voice You Hear (MGM; 1950). *Cast:* James Whitmore, Nancy Davis, Gary Gray, Lillian Bronson, Art Smith, Tom D'Andrea, Jeff Corey, Dore Schary, George Chandler. *D:* William A. Wellman; *P:* Dore Schary; *St:* George Sumner Albee; *Sc:* Charles Schnee. (1:22) (video) An offbeat low budget drama of the reactions of various people in a small American town who turn on the radio and hear the voice of God, not an evangelist proclaiming same, but the real thing! A "message" film of sorts which showed moderate box office returns.

1839. Niagara (20th Century–Fox; 1953). *Cast:* Marilyn Monroe (Rose Loomis), Joseph Cotten (George Loomis), Jean Peters (Polly Cutler), Casey Adams [aka: Max Showalter/Ray Cutler], Dennis O'Dea (Inspector Sharkey), Richard Allan (Patrick), Don Wilson (Mr. Kettering), Lurene Tutte (Mrs. Kettering), Russell Collins (Mr. Qua), Sean McClory (Sam), Norman McKay (Morris), Will Wright, Lester Matthews, Carleton Young, Minerva Urecal, Nina Varela, Tom Reynolds, Winfield Hoeny, Neil Fitzgerald, Gene Wesson, George Ives, Patrick O'Moore, Arch Johnson, Harry Carey, Jr., Henry Beckman, Willard Sage, Robert Ellis, Bill Foster, Gloria Gordon. *D:* Henry Hathaway; *P:* Charles Brackett; *St: & Sc:* Brackett, Walter Reisch, Richard Breen; *Song:* "Kiss" Lionel Newman–Haven Gillespie. (1:29) (video/laserdisc) Monroe stands out in this drama of an adulterous wife who with her young lover plans to murder her older husband, but he finds out and the tables turn. Partially filmed on location at Niagara Falls, it became one of the 26 top-grossing films of 1952-53. Technicolor.

1840. A Nice Little Bank That Should Be Robbed (20th Century–Fox; 1958). *Cast:* Tom Ewell, Mickey Rooney, Mickey Shaughnessy, Dina Merrill, Madge Kennedy, Frances Bavier, Richard Deacon, Stanley Clements, Tom Greenway. *D:* Henry Levin; *P:* Anthony Muto; *Sc:* Sydney Boehm (based on a nonfiction article by Evan Wylie). (1:27) Comedy of two guys who rob a bank and buy a racehorse with part of the money. They bet the rest of the money on the horse after entering him in a race. The horse loses, they rob another bank and get caught. (G.B. title: *How to Rob a Bank*) CinemaScope.

1841. Night and the City (20th Century–Fox; 1950). *Cast:* Richard Widmark, Gene Tierney, Googie Withers, Hugh Marlowe, Francis L. Sullivan, Herbert Lom, Stanislaus [Stanley] Zbyszko, Mike Mazurki, Charles Farrell, Ada Reeve, Ken Richmond, Elliot Makeham, Betty Shale, Russell Westwood, James Hayter, Tony Simpson, Maureen Delaney, Thomas Gallagher, Edward Chapman, Gibb McLaughlin, Aubrey Dexter, Derek Blomfield, Kay Kendall. *D:* Jules Dassin; *P:* Samuel G. Engel; *Sc:* Jo Eisinger. (1:41) (video) Film noir of various lowlifes that cruise the shadowy streets and dark corners of London's underbelly, and one who is the target for extermination of a crime boss. Based on the 1938 novel by Gerald Kersh, it was filmed on location in London and was remade in 1992.

1842. Night Freight (Allied Artists/Wm. F. Broidy Prods.; 1955). *Cast:* Forrest Tucker, Barbara Britton, Keith Larsen, Thomas Gomez, Michael Ross, Myrna Dell, Lewis Martin, G. Pat Collins, Sam Flint, Ralph Sanford, George Sanders, Joe Kirk, Jim Alexander, Charles Fredericks, Guy Rennie, Michael Dale. *D:* Jean Yarbrough; *P:* Ace Herman; *St: & Sc:* Steve Fisher. (1:19) Two railroading brothers set their sights on the same girl, while a vengeful trucker is intent on blowing up their train.

1843. The Night Holds Terror (Columbia; 1955). *Cast:* Jack Kelly, Hildy Parks, Vince Edwards, John Cassavetes, David Cross, Edward Marr, Jack Kruschen, Joyce McCluskey, Jonathan Hale, Barney Phillips, Charles Herbert, Nancy Dee Zane, Joel Marston. *D:-P: & Sc:* Andrew L. Stone; *Song:* "Every Now and Then" Stone. (1:26) Drama of a family of four held captive by three hoodlums. Loosely based on *Blind Alley*, a 1939 production from this studio, and the play *The Desperate Hours* by Joseph Hayes.

Night In Havana (G.B. title) *see* **The Big Boodle**

1844. Night Into Morning (MGM; 1951). *Cast:* Ray Milland, John Hodiak, Nancy Davis, Lewis Stone, Jean Hagen, Rosemary DeCamp, Dawn Addams (film debut), Jonathan Cott, Celia Lovsky, Gordon Gebert, Katherine Warren, Harry Antrim, Mary Lawrence, Herb Vigran, Wheaton Chambers, John Eldredge, Matt Moore, Whit Bissell, Percy Helton, John "Skins" Miller, Otto Waldis, John Maxwell, John Jeffrey. *D:* Fletcher Markle; *P:* Edwin H.

Knopf; *St: & Sc:* Karl Tunberg, Leonard Spigelgass. (1:26) Drama of a university professor who loses his family in a fire and goes on a self-pity trip, which his colleagues have to deal with.

1845. Night of the Blood Beast (American International/Balboa Prods.; 1958). *Cast:* Michael Emmet, Angela Greene, John Baer, Ed Nelson, Tyler McVey, Georgianna Carter, Ross Sturlin. *D:* Bernard L. Kowalski; *Ex. P:* Roger Corman; *P: & St:* Gene Corman; *Sc:* Martin Varno. (1:05) (video) A space explorer returns to earth, only to find he is carrying embryos to start a race of aliens on earth whose own world was destroyed. Originally ran on the top of a double bill with *She Gods of Shark Reef* (q.v.).

1846. Night of the Ghouls (Crown International TV/Atomic; 1959–60). *Cast:* Duke Moore, Paul Marco, Kenne Duncan, Tor Johnson, John Carpenter, Valda Hansen, Criswell, Jeannie Stevens *D:-P:-St: & Sc:* Edward D. Wood, Jr. (1:09) (video/laserdisc) A horror film involving a gang of phony spiritualists headed by one Dr. Acula (Duncan) who bilk unwary customers by performing phony seances, only one night they call forth some real dead spirits. A purported follow-up to *Bride of the Monster* and/or *Plan 9 from Outer Space* (both q.v.) (G.B. title: *Revenge of the Dead*)

1847. The Night of the Hunter (United Artists/Paul Gregory Prods.; 1955). *Cast:* Robert Mitchum, Shelley Winters, Lillian Gish, Evelyn Varden, James Gleason, Billy Chapin, Sally Jane Bruce, Don Beddoe, Peter Graves, Gloria Castillo, Mary Ellen Clemons, Cheryl Callaway, Corey Allen, Paul Bryar. *D:* Charles Laughton (only film as director); *P:* Paul Gregory; *Sc:* James Agee (final film—d. 1955), Laughton (unc.); *Cinematographer:* Stanley Cortez. (1:33) (video/laserdisc) One-of-a-kind film noir thriller of good vs. evil as a self-styled preacher (Mitchum) marries and murders wealthy widows, who wind up pursuing the children (Chapin-Bruce) of his latest victim (Winters) down-river for money hidden in the little girl's doll. The bizarre quality of many of the photographic images in this film caused it to be ignored by Hollywood and the movie-going public on initial release. Based on the 1953 novel by Davis Grubb, the film has gathered a latter day following. A 1991 TV movie was also based on Grubb's novel, but to call it a remake of this film is purely subjective opinion.

1848. Night of the Quarter Moon (MGM/Albert Zugsmith Prods.; 1959). *Cast:* Julie London, John Drew Barrymore, Nat "King" Cole, Anna Kashfi, Dean Jones, Agnes Moorehead, Cathy Crosby (film debut), Ray Anthony, Jackie Coogan, James Edwards, Charles Chaplin, Jr., Billy Daniels, Arthur Shields, Edward Andrews, Robert Warwick, Marguerite Belafonte, Bobi Byrnes, Charlotte Hawkins. *D:* Hugo Haas; *P:* Albert Zugsmith; *St: & Sc:* Frank Davis, Franklin Coen; *Songs:* Title song—James Van Heusen, Sammy Cahn (sung by London and Cole); "To Whom It May Concern" Cole, Charlotte Hawkins (sung by Cole), "Blue Moon" Richard Rodgers, Lorenz Hart (sung by Crosby). (1:36) Melodrama of a San Francisco society couple and the aftershocks that occur, when the wife admits to having a black grandparent. Originally ran on a double bill with *First Man Into Space*, a British science fiction film.

1849. Night Passage (Universal-International; 1957). *Cast:* James Stewart, Audie Murphy, Dan Duryea, Dianne Foster, Brandon de Wilde, Jay C. Flippen, Elaine Stewart, Herbert Anderson, Jack Elam, Robert J. Wilke, Hugh Beaumont, James Flavin, Tommy Cook, Paul Fix, Olive Carey, Donald Curtis, Chuck Roberson, Ellen Corby, Ted Mapes, Patsy Novak. *D:* James Neilson (directorial debut); *P:* Aaron Rosenberg; *Sc:* Borden Chase; *Songs:* Dimitri Tiomkin, Ned Washington. (1:30) Successful western drama of two brothers, one guarding a $10,000 railroad shipment, the other on the opposite side of the law with a gang that robs the train. Filmed on location in Colorado in Technicolor and Technirama.

1850. Night People (20th Century–Fox; 1954). *Cast:* Gregory Peck (Col. Van Dyke), Broderick Crawford (Leatherby), Anita Bjork (U.S. debut/Hoffy), Rita Gam (Miss Cates), Walter Abel (Foster), Buddy Ebsen (Sgt. McColloch), Casey Adams [aka: Max Showalter/Frederick S. Hobart], Jill Esmond (Frau Schindler), Peter Van Eyck (Petrochine), Marianne Koch (Kathy), Paul Carpenter (Col. Whitby), Hugh McDermott (Burns), John Horsley (Stanways), Ted Avery (Johnny), Lionel Murton (Lakeland), Harold Benedict, Tom Boyd, T. Schaank, Sgt. Cleary, E. Haffner, Ruth Garcia, Peter Beauvais, A. Faerber (Mr. Schindler), Otto Reichow. *D:-P: & Sc:* Nunnally Johnson; *St:* (AAN) Jed Harris, Tom Reed. (1:33) Acclaimed Cold War drama set in postwar Berlin. Young American soldier is kidnapped by Russians and held as ransom for an elderly man and his wife who are former Nazis. Technicolor and CinemaScope.

1851. Night Raiders (Monogram/Silvermine Prods.; 1952). *Cast:* Whip Wilson, Fuzzy Knight, Tom Farrell, Lois Hall, Steve Clark, Terry Frost, Lane Bradford, Marshall Reed, Iron Eyes Cody, Boyd Stockman, Edward Cassidy, Carol Henry, Forrest Taylor, Roy Butler, Stanley Price. *D:* Howard Bretherton (final film—ret.); *P:* Vincent M. Fennelly; *Sc:* Maurice Tombragel. (0:52) Series western involving raids on ranchers where nothing is taken.

1852. Night Riders of Montana (Republic; 1951). *Cast:* Allan Lane, Chubby Johnson, Roy Barcroft, Claudia Barrett, Arthur Space, Myron Healey, Mort Thompson, Marshall Bradford, Lester Dorr, Ted Adams, George Chesebro, Don C. Harvey, Zon Murray, Black Jack (horse). *D:* Fred C. Brannon; *P:* Gordon Kay; *St: & Sc:* M. Coates Webster. (1:00) In this series western, ranger "Rocky" Lane comes to the rescue of ranchers besieged by a gang of night riders. Originally ran on a double bill with *Cuban Fireball* (q.v.).

1853. The Night Runner (Universal-International; 1957). *Cast:* Ray Danton, Colleen Miller, Willis Bouchey, Merry Anders, Harry Jackson, Robert Anderson, Jean Innes, Eddy C. Waller, Jan Howard, John Stephenson, Richard Cutting, Alexander Campbell, Steve Pendleton, John Pickard, Paul Weber, Jack Lomas, Natalie Masters, William Erwin, Ethyl May Halls, George Barrows, Sam Flint, Marshall Bradford, Diana Darrin, Lola Kendrick, Dale Van Sickel, Alex Sharpe, Jay Berniker. *D:* Abner Biberman; *P:* Albert J. Cohen; *St:* Owen Cameron; *Sc:* Gene Levitt. (1:19) Melodramatic programmer of a schizophrenic who commits murder after being prematurely released from a mental hospital.

1854. Night Stage to Galveston (Columbia/Gene Autry Prods.; 1952). *Cast:* Gene Autry, Pat Buttram, Virginia Huston, Thurston Hall, Judy Nugent, Robert Livingston, Harry Cording, Clayton Moore, Robert Bice, Steve Clark, Harry Lauter, Dick Alexander, Boyd Stockman, Robert Peyton, Frank Sully, Frank Rawls, Lois Austin, Kathleen O'Malley, Riley Hill, Bob Woodward, Sandy Sanders, Ben Welden, Gary Goodwin, Champion, Jr. (horse). *D:* George Archainbaud; *P:* Armand Schaefer; *St: & Sc:* Norman S. Hall; *Songs:* "Down in Slumberland," "Eyes of Texas," "A Heart as Big as Texas" (all sung by Autry); "Yellow Rose of Texas" (sung by Buttram). (1:01) (video) Gene Autry series western of a crusading newspaperman out to uncover corruption in the Texas Rangers. In Sepiatone, it originally ran on a double bill with *Jungle Jim in the Forbidden Land* (q.v.).

1855. The Night the World Exploded (Columbia/Clover Prods.; 1957). *Cast:* Kathryn Grant, William Leslie, Tristram Coffin, Raymond Greenleaf, Charles Evans, Frank Scannell, Marshall Reed, Fred Coby, Paul Savage, Terry Frost. *D:* Fred F. Sears; *P:* Sam Katzman; *St: & Sc:* Luci Ward, Jack Natteford. (1:04) Science fiction of scientists researching a new element called E-112 found deep within the earth which is causing the planet's core to expand, resulting in earthquakes on the surface. The mineral explodes when exposed to oxygen. Originally ran on a double feature with top-billed *20 Million Miles to Earth* (q.v.).

1856. Night Without Sleep (20th Century–Fox; 1952). *Cast:* Linda Darnell, Gary Merrill, Hildegade Neff, Joyce MacKenzie, June Vincent, Donald Randolph, Hugh Beaumont, Louise Lorimer, William Forrest, Steven Geray, Mauri Lynn, Bill Walker, Mae Marsh, Ben Carter, Sam Pierce, Sylvia Sims, Beverly Tyler, Charles Tannen, Harry Seymour. *D:* Roy Baker; *P:* Robert Bassler; *Sc:* Frank Partos, Elick Moll; *Songs:* "Too Late for Spring" Alfred Newman, Haven Gillespie; "Look at Me" Newman, Ken Darby. (1:17) Suspense melodrama of a psychotic composer who awakens one morning from an alcoholic binge with the feeling that he murdered a woman during the night. Based on the 1950 novel by Mr. Moll.

1857. Nightfall (Columbia/Copa Prods.; 1956). *Cast:* Aldo Ray, Brian Keith, Anne Bancroft, Jocelyn Brando, James Gregory, Frank Albertson Rudy Bond, Eddie McLean, Gene Roth, George Cisar, Lillian Culver, Maya Van Horn, Orlando Beltran, Maria Belmar, Walter Smith, Monty Ash, Art Bucaro, Arline Anderson, Robert Cherry, Jane Lynn, Betty Koch, Lillian Kassan, Joan Fotre, Pat Jones, Annabelle George, Winifred Waring. *D:* Jacques Tourneur; *P:* Ted Richmond; *Sc:* Stirling Silliphant; *Title song:* Sam M. Lewis, Peter DeRose, Charles Harold (sung by Al Hibbler). (1:18) Crime melodrama of a man in flight after being accused of murder, who finds himself pursued by the real killers, intent on getting some stolen money he found at the crime scene. Based on the 1947 book by David Goodis.

1858. Nightmare (United Artists/P-T-S Prods., Inc.; 1956). *Cast:* Edward G. Robinson, Kevin McCarthy, Connie Russell, Virginia Christine, Gage Clarke, Rhys Williams, Marian Carr, Barry Atwater, Meade "Lux" Lewis, Billy May & Orchestra. *D:* Maxwell Shane (final film—ret.); *P:* Howard Pine, William C. Thomas; *Sc:* Shane; *Songs:* "What's Your Sad Story?" Dick Sherman, "The Last I Ever Saw of My Heart" Herschel Burke Gilbert, Doris Houck. (1:29) Melodrama of a jazz musician who kills a man attempting to strangle him and the bizarre circumstances that follow. Based on a story by William Irish [pseudonym of Cornell Woolrich], the film is a remake of *Fear in the Night* (Paramount; 1947) which was also directed and scripted by Shane.

Nights in a Harem *see* **Son of Sinbad**

1859. 99 River Street (United Artists/World Films; 1953). *Cast:* John Payne, Evelyn Keyes, Brad Dexter, Peggie Castle, Jay Adler, Frank Faylen, Jack Lambert, Ian Wolfe, Eddy Waller, Glenn Langan, John Day, Peter Leeds, William Tannen, Gene Reynolds. *D:* Phil Karlson; *P:* Edward Small; *St:* George Zuckerman; *Sc:* Robert Smith. (1:23) Tough little film noir of an ex-fighter turned taxi driver who has to extricate himself from charges that he murdered his cheating wife, when her body is found in the trunk of his cab.

1860. No Down Payment (20th Century-Fox/Jerry Wald Prods.; 1957). *Cast:* Joanne Woodward (voted "Best Actress" by the NBR in conjunction with her performance in *The Three Faces of Eve* [q.v.]), Sheree North, Tony Randall, Jeffrey Hunter, Cameron Mitchell, Patricia Owens, Barbara Rush, Pat Hingle, Robert H. Harris, Aki Aleong, Jim Hayward, Mimi Gibson, Charles Herbert, Donald Towers, Mary Carroll, Nolan Leary. *D:* Martin Ritt; *P:* Jerry Wald; *Sc:* Philip Yordan. (1:45) A drama which deals with the lives of various people living within a suburban housing development. Based on the 1957 novel by John McPartland, it was in nomination at the British Academy Awards. CinemaScope.

1861. No Escape (United Artists/Matthugh Prods.; 1953). *Cast:* Lew Ayres, Marjorie Steele, Sonny Tufts, Lewis Martin, Gertrude Michael, Renny McEvoy, Charles Cane, James Griffith, Jess Kirkpatrick, Robert Watson, Robert Bailey, Leon Burbank, Robert Carson, Barbara Morrison, Carleton Young, Hans Schumm, John Vosper, Joseph Kim, Maudie Prickett, Tim Graham. *D:-St: & Sc:* Charles Bennett. *P:* Hugh Mackenzie, Matt Freed; *Song:* "No Escape" Bert Shefter, Bennett. (1:16) Low budget melodrama, filmed on location in San Francisco, of a songwriter and working girl who think they have committed murder and flee while trying to clear themselves.

No Greater Sin *see* **Eighteen and Anxious**

No Highway (G.B. title) *see* **No Highway in the Sky**

1862. No Highway in the Sky (20th Century–Fox; 1951). James Stewart, Marlene Dietrich, Glynis Johns, Jack Hawkins, Ronald Squire, Janette Scott, Niall MacGinnis, Elizabeth Allan, Kenneth More, David Hutcheson, Hugh Wakefield, Ben Williams, Maurice Denham, Wilfrid Hyde-White, Hector MacGregor, Basil Appleby, Michael Kingsley, Peter Murray, Dora Bryan, Jill Clifford, Felix Alymer, Karel Stepanek, Wilfrid Walter, John Salew, Marcel Poncin, Cyril Smith, Tom Gill, Hugh Gross, Arthur Lucas, Dodd Mehan, Maxwell Foster, Stuart Nichol, Gerald Kent, John Lennox, Douglas Bradley Smith, Philip Vickers, Philip Ray, Roy Russell, Diana Bennett, Michael McCarthy, Robert Lickens, Catherine Leach. *D:* Henry Koster; *P:* Louis D. Lighton; *Sc:* R.C. Sherriff, Oscar Millard, Alec Coppel. (1:38) (video) Drama of an eccentric scientific technician working for an aircraft company, who comes to the conclusion that a newly produced airplane is unsafe and tries to convince someone before disaster strikes. Based on the 1948 novel *No Highway* by Nevil Shute [a pseudonym of Nevil Shute Norway]. A G.B./U.S.A. co-production which was filmed on location in England.

1863. No Holds Barred (Monogram; 1952). *Cast:* Leo Gorcey, Huntz Hall, David [Gorcey] Condon, Bennie Bartlett, Marjorie Reynolds, Leonard Penn, Henry Kulky, Bernard Gorcey, Hombre Montana, Murray Alper, Barbara Grey, Lisa Wilson, Nick Stewart, Sandra Gould, Ray Walker, Tim Ryan, Bob Cudlip, Mort Mills, Bill Page, Meyer Grace, Jimmy Cross, Ted Christy (himself), Pat Fraley, "Brother" Frank Jares, George Eldredge, Leo "Ukie" Sherin, John Indrisano, Mike Ruby, Count John Maximillian Smith (himself). *D:* William Beaudine; *P:* Jerry Thomas; *St: & Sc:* Tim Ryan, Jack Crutcher, Bert Lawrence. (1:05) In this series entry, the "Bowery Boys" become involved with professional wrestling.

1864. No Man of Her Own (Paramount; 1950). *Cast:* Barbara Stanwyck, John Lund, Lyle Bettger (film debut), Jane Cowl, Phyllis Thaxter, Richard Denning, Henry O'Neill, Esther Dale, Carole Mathews, Milburn Stone, Harry Antrim, Catherine Craig, Griff Barnett, Georgia Backus, Ivan Browning, Gaylord [Steve] Pendleton, Stan Johnson, Dooley Wilson, William Haade, Jean Andren, Selmer Jackson, Laura Elliot, Charles Dayton, Dick Keene, Johnny Michaels, Virginia Brissac, Willard Waterman, Thomas Browne Henry, Dave Willock, Kathleen Freeman, Esther Howard, Sumner Getchell, Frank Marlowe, Gordon Nelson, Jean Ruth, Mary Lawrence, Jack Reynolds, Helen Mowery, Emmett Smith, Ashley Cowan, Jimmie Dundee, Philip Tully, Ray Walker, Edna Holland. *D:* Mitchell Leisen; *P:* Richard Maibaum; *Sc:* Catherine Turney, Sally Benson, Leisen (unc.). (1:38) Hit melodrama of an unmarried pregnant woman who pretends to be the widow of a man killed in a train wreck and is later blackmailed by her ex-boyfriend. Based on the 1948 book *I Married A Dead Man* by William Irish [a pseudonym of Cornell Woolrich], it was remade in France in 1982 as *I Married A Shadow.*

1865. No Man's Woman (Republic; 1955). *Cast:* Marie Windsor, John Archer, Patric Knowles, Nancy Gates, Jil Jarmyn, Richard Crane, Fern Hall, Louis Jean Heydt, John Gallaudet, Douglas Wood, Percy Helton, Morris Ankrum. *D:* Franklin Adreon; *P:* Rudy Ralston; *St:* Don Martin; *Sc:* John K. Butler. (1:10) Crime melodrama on the investigation of five suspects in the murder of a ruthless woman.

1866. No Name on the Bullet (Universal-International; 1959). *Cast:* Audie Murphy, Joan Evans, Charles Drake, R.G. Armstrong, Virginia Grey, Warren Stevens, Whit Bissell, Karl Swenson, Willis Bouchey, Edgar Stehli, Charles Watts, Jerry Paris, Simon Scott, John Alderson, Jim Hyland, Russ Bender. *D:* Jack Arnold; *P:* Arnold, Howard Christie; *Sc:* Gene L. Coon. (1:17) Western of a hired gun who drifts into the town of Lordsburg with an intended victim, only no one in the town knows who he is after and paranoia runs rampant. Definitely offbeat, it was based on the story "The Death Rider" by Harold Amacker. Eastmancolor and CinemaScope.

1867. No Place to Hide (Allied Artists/ Shaftel, Inc.–L.V.N. Pictures, Inc.; 1956). *Cast:* David Brian, Marsha Hunt, Hugh Corcoran, Ike Jarelgo, Jr., Celia Flor, Eddie Infante, Manuel Silos, Lou Salvador, Pianing Vidal, Alfonso Carvajal, Vincenta Advincula, Pompom (dog). *D:-P: & St:* Joseph Shaftel; *Sc:* Norman Corwin [who withdrew his on-screen credit]. (1:11) Low budget melodrama of an American doctor working in the Philippines on the cause of a deadly disease which he isolates in small capsules which are found by his son who thinks they are marbles and takes off with them! Filmed on location in DeLuxe color.

1868. No Place to Land (Republic/Albert C. Gannaway; 1958). *Cast:* John Ireland, Mari Blanchard, Gail Russell, Jackie Coogan, Robert Middleton, Douglas Henderson, Bill Ward, Robert E. Griffin, John Carpenter, Bill Coontz, Whitey Hughes, Bill Blatty, James Macklin, Patric Dennis Leigh, Burt Topper. *D:& P:* Albert C. Gannaway; *St: & Sc:* Vance Skarstedt. (1:18) Programmer melodrama of crop dusters and a woman determined to have a man who wants nothing to do with her, as he has his sights set on another. Naturama. (G.B. title: *Man Mad*)

1869. No Questions Asked (MGM; 1951). *Cast:* Barry Sullivan, Arlene Dahl, George Murphy, Jean Hagen, Richard Anderson, Moroni Olsen, Dick Simmons, William Reynolds, Mari Blanchard, Dan Dayton, Howard Petrie, Mauritz Hugo, Robert Sheppard, Michael Dugan, Howland Chamberlain, Richard Bartlett, Robert Osterloh, William Phipps. *D:* Harold F. Kress; *P:* Nicholas Nayfack; *St:* Berne Giler; *Sc:* Sidney Sheldon. (1:21) Low budget crime melodrama of a hood operating an insurance racket.

1870. No Room for the Groom (Universal-International; 1952). *Cast:* Tony Curtis, Piper Laurie, Spring Byington, Don DeFore, Lillian Bronson, Paul McVey, Jack Kelly, Lee Aaker, Stephen Chase, Frank Sully, James Parnell, Lee Turnbull, Dolores Mann, Fess Parker, Helen Noyes, Janet Clark, Fred J. Miller, Lynne Hunter, Harold Lockwood, Catherine Howard, William O'Driscoll, Lucille LaMarr, David Janssen, Richard Mayer, Jack Daly, Alice Richey, Elsie Baker. *D:* Douglas Sirk; *P:* Ted Richmond; *Sc:* Joseph Hoffman. (1:22) Comedy of an ex-G.I. who returns home to find his domicile overrun with his wife's relatives who are unaware of the marriage. Based on the novel *My True Love* by Darwin L. Teilheit.

1871. No Sad Songs for Me (Columbia; 1950). *Cast:* Margaret Sullavan (final film—ret./

Mary Scott), Wendell Corey (Brad Scott), Viveca Lindfors (Chris Radna), Natalie Wood (Polly Scott), JohnMcIntire (Dr. Ralph Frene), Ann Doran (Louise Spears), Richard Quine (Brownie), Jeanette Nolan (Mona Frene), Dorothy Tree (Frieda Miles), Harlan Warde (Lee Corbett), Raymond Greenleaf (Mr. Caswell), Urylee Geonardos (Flora), Margo Woode (Doris Weldon), Harry Cheshire (Mel Fenelly), Sumner Getchell (George Spears), Douglas Evans (Jack Miles), Lucille Browne (Mrs. Hendrickson). *D:* Rudolph Maté; *P:* Buddy Adler; *Sc:* Howard Koch; *Music:* (AAN) George Duning. (1:29) Dramatic tearjerker of a woman who learns she has terminal cancer and attempts to hide the fact from her husband.

No Sleep Till Dawn (G.B. title) *see* **Bombers B-52**

1872. No Time for Flowers (RKO/Morjay Prods.; 1952). *Cast:* Viveca Lindfors, Paul Christian, Ludwig Stossel, Adrienne Gessner, Peter Preses, Manfred Inger, Peter Czeyke, Frederick Berger, Oscar Wegrostek, Helmut Janatsch, Karl Bachmann, Hilde Jaeger, Pepi Glockner-Kramer, Reinhold Seigert, Willi Schumann, Ilka Windisch, Toni Mitterwurzer, Theodore Prokof, Robert Eckertt, Peter Brand, Karl Schweitzer. *D:* Don Siegel; *P:* Mort Briskin; *As. P:* Maurie M. Suess; *St: & Sc:* Laslo Vadnay, Hans Wilhelm. (1:23) Cold War comedy in the vein of *Ninotchka* (MGM; 1939) with a female Czech Communist Party member being tempted by things which dominate in Western capitalistic society, including love.

1873. No Time for Sergeants (Warner; 1958). *Cast:* Andy Griffith (repeating his TV and stage role/Will Stockdale–narrator), Myron McCormick (repeating his stage role/Sgt. King), Nick Adams (Ben Whitledge), Murray Hamilton (Irvin Blanchard), Howard Smith (General Rush), Will Hutchins (Lt. Bridges), Sydney Smith (General Pollard), James Milhollin (psychiatrist), Don Knotts (film debut/Corp. Brown), Henry McCann (Lt. Cover), Jean Willes (W.A.F. captain), William Fawett (Pa Stockdale), Jameel Farah [later: Jamie Farr/Lt. Gardella], Bob Stratton (Lt. Kendall), Peggy Halleck (Rosabelle), Dan Barton (Tiger), Benny Baker (Abel), Verne Smith (announcer's voice), Mary Scott, Bartlett Robinson, Dub Taylor, Raymond Bailey, Jack Mower, Malcolm Atterbury, Sammy Jackson (who starred as Will Stockdale in the 1960s TV series), Rad Fulton, Francis DeSales, Robert Sherman, Dick Wessel, Tom Browne Henry, Tom McKee, George Neise, Fred Coby, John Close. *D: & P:* Mervyn LeRoy; *Sc:* John Lee Mahin. (1:51) (video/laserdisc) Hit comedy of a naive country boy inducted into the U.S. Air Force. Originally a TV show in 1955 on the U.S. Steel Hour, then became a Broadway success. Both were adapted by Ira Levin from the novel by Mac Hyman. One of the 26 top-grossing films of 1957-58, it also emerged in 1964-65 as a TV series.

No Time for Tears (G.B. title) *see* **Purple Heart Diary**

1874. No Time to Be Young (Columbia/Screen Gems, Inc; 1957). *Cast:* Robert Vaughn, Roger Smith (film debut), Tom Pittman, Dorothy Green, Merry Anders, Kathy Nolan, Sarah Selby, Fred Sherman, Ralph Clanton, Don C. Harvey, Bonnie Bolding. *D:* David L. Rich (directorial debut); *P:* Wallace MacDonald; *St:* John McPartland; *Sc:* McPartland, Raphael Hayes. (1:22) Low budget melodrama of three young men out to rob a supermarket, hoping the cash will solve all their problems, only the market manager is killed in the holdup. (G.B. title: *Teenage Delinquents*)

1875. No Way Out (20th Century–Fox; 1950). *Cast:* Richard Widmark (Ray Biddle), Linda Darnell (Edie), Stephen McNally (Dr. Wharton), Sidney Poitier (commercial theatrical debut/Dr. Luther Brooks), Mildred Joanne Smith (Cora), Harry Bellaver (George Biddle), Stanley Ridges (Dr. Moreland), Dotts Johnson (Lefty), Amanda Randolph (Gladys), Bill Walker (Mathew Tompkins), Ruby Dee (Connie), Ken Christy (Kowalski), Ossie Davis (film debut/John), Frank Richards (Mac), George Tyne (Whitey), Bert Freed (Rocky), Will Wright (Dr. Chaney), Frank Jaquet (Reilly), Emmett Smith (Joe), Ralph Hodges (Terry), Wade Dumas (Jonah), Jasper Weldon (Henry), Dick Paxton (Johnnie Biddle), Robert Adler, Jim Toney, Maude Simmons, Ray Teal, Jack Kruschen, Eileen Boyer, Johnnie Jallings, Marie Lampe, Gertrude Tighe, John Whitney, Howard Mitchell, Charles J. Flynn, Kitty O'Neil, Thomas Ingersoll, Fred Graham, William Pullen, Reuben Wendorf, Laiola Wendorf, Stan Johnson, Frank Overton, Harry Lauter, Harry Carter, Don Kohler, Ray Hyke, Ann Tyrrell, Ann Morrison, Eda Reis Merin, Kathryn Sheldon, Ralph Dunn, Ruth Warren, Robert Davis, Ernest Anderson, Victor Kilian, Sr., Mack Williams, Eleanor Audley, Doris Kemper, Phil Tully, J. Louis

Johnson, Ian Wolfe. *D:* Joseph L. Mankiewicz; *P:* Darryl F. Zanuck; *St: & Sc:* (AAN) Mankiewicz, Lesser Samuels. (1:46) Acclaimed drama of racial violence that breaks out when a black doctor attempts to treat a racist wounded in a gun battle. It placed #9 on the "10 Best" list of the NBR.

1876. North by Northwest (MGM; 1959). *Cast:* Cary Grant (Roger Thornhill), Eva Marie Saint (Eva Kendall), James Mason (Phillip Vandamm), Jessie Royce Landis (Clara Thornhill), Leo G. Carroll (Professor), Philip Ober (Townsend), Martin Landau (Leonard), Adam Williams (Valerian), Edward Platt (Victor Larrabee), Robert Ellenstein (Licht), Les Tremayne (auctioneer), Philip Coolidge (Dr. Cross), Edward Binns (Capt. Junket), John Beradino (Sgt. Emile Klinger), Nora Marlowe (Anna the housekeeper), Doreen Lang (Maggie), Alexander Lockwood (Judge Anson B. Flynn), Stanley Adams (Lt. Harding), Frank Wilcox (Weltner), Robert Shayne (Larry Wade), Carleton Young (Fanning Nelson), Paul Genge (Lt. Hagerman), Robert B. Williams (Patrolman Waggoner), Maudie Prickett (Elsie the maid), Alfred Hitchcock (man who misses bus), Josephine Hutchinson, Pat McVey, Ken Lynch, Larry Dobkin, Harvey Stephens, Walter Coy, Madge Kennedy, Tommy Farrell, Harry Seymour James McCallion, Baynes Barron, Doris Singh, Sally Fraser, Susan Whitney, Maura McGiveney, Ned Glass, Howard Negley, Jesslyn Fax, Jack Daly, Malcolm Atterbury, Olan Soule, Helen Spring, Patricia Cutts, Dale Van Sickel, Frank Marlowe, Harry Strang, Sara Berner. *D: & P:* Alfred Hitchcock; *As.P:* Herbert Coleman; *St: & Sc:* (AAN) Ernest Lehman; *ASD:* (AAN) William A. Horning, Robert Boyle, Merrill Pye (art directors), Henry Grace, Frank McKelvy (sets). (2:16) (video/laserdisc) Classic Hitchcock comedy-thriller of an innocent advertising man, who through a set of bizarre circumstances finds himself pursued by spies who think him a double agent and lawmen who believe him to be an assassin. The climactic finale on Mt. Rushmore is memorable and legendary. Location filming took place at the Plaza Hotel Oak Room, New York City; the U.N. building, Grand Central Station, New York City; Long Island, N.Y.; Chicago's Ambassador East; the Indiana Plains and Mt. Rushmore, South Dakota. The "10 Best" lists of *Film Daily*, the *New York Times* and the NBR placed it at #5, #7 and #10 respectively. One of the 26 top-grossing films of 1958-59, it was in Technicolor and VistaVision.

1877. North of the Great Divide (Republic; 1950). *Cast:* Roy Rogers, Penny Edwards, Gordon Jones, Roy Barcroft, Foy Willing and Riders of the Purple Sage, Jack Lambert, Keith Richards, Douglas Evans, Noble Johnson, Iron Eyes Cody, Trigger (horse). *D:* William Witney; *As.P:* Edward J. "Eddy" White; *St: & Sc:* Eric Taylor; *Songs:* "By the Laughing Spring," "Just Keep a-Movin'," Title song (Jack Elliott). (1:07) (video) Western tale of a Canadian Indian agent sent to protect Indian salmon fishing rights from a crook who is damming the river, taking the fish and shipping them to his own Canadian cannery. Trucolor. Originally ran on a double bill with *Rustlers on Horseback* (q.v.).

1878. Northern Patrol (Allied Artists; 1953). *Cast:* Kirby Grant, Marian Carr, Bill Phipps, Claudia Drake, Dale Van Sickel, Gloria Talbott, Richard Walsh, Emmett Lynn, Frank Lackteen, Frank Sully, Chinook (dog). *D:* Rex Bailey; *P:* Lindsley Parsons; *Sc:* Warren Douglas (based on the 1919 book *Nomads of the North: A Story of Romance and Adventure Under the Open Stars* by James Oliver Curwood). (1:02) A Canadian Mountie and his dog investigate the death of a trapper. On the surface it appears to be suicide, but he feels the man was murdered and investigates further to find out "who" and "why." Part of a series begun by Monogram in the 1940s.

1879. Northwest Territory (Monogram; 1951). *Cast:* Kirby Grant, Gloria Saunders, Warren Douglas, Pat Mitchell, Tristram Coffin, John Crawford, Duke York, Don C. Harvey, Sam Flint, Chinook (dog). *D:* Frank McDonald; *P:* Lindsley Parsons; Sc: Bill Raynor. (1:01) Rod Webb (Grant), a Canadian Mountie, and his dog track down the murderer of a prospector. A low budget northwoods adventure, part of a series, that was based on a novel by James Oliver Curwood.

1880. Not as a Stranger (United Artists/ Stanley Kramer Picts. Corp.; 1955). *Cast:* Robert Mitchum (Lucas Marsh), Olivia de Havilland (Kristina Hedvigson), Frank Sinatra (Alfred Boone), Gloria Grahame (Harriet Lang), Broderick Crawford (Dr. Aarons), Charles Bickford (Dr. Runkleman), Myron McCormick (Dr. Snider), Lon Chaney (Job Marsh), Jesse White (Ben Cosgrove), Harry Morgan (Oley), Lee Marvin (Brundage), Virginia Christine (Bruni), Whit Bissell (Dr. Dietrich), Jack Raine (Dr. Lettering), Mae Clarke (Miss O'Dell). *D:* Stanley Kramer (directorial debut); *P:* Kramer; *Sc:*

Edward and Edna Anhalt; *Sound:* (AAN) Watson Jones & Radio Corporation of America. (2:15) (video) Hospital oriented drama of a medical student, his shaky marriage, his wanderings to another and eventual return to his wife. It placed #8 on the "10 Best" list of the NBR, who also voted Charles Bickford "Best Supporting Actor" for his role as Dr. Runkleman. One of the 27 top-grossing films of 1954-55, it was based on the 1954 best-seller by Morton Thompson.

1881. Not of This Earth (Allied Artists/ Los Altos Prods.; 1957). *Cast:* Paul Birch, Beverly Garland, Morgan Jones, William Roerick, Jonathan Haze, Dick Miller, Anne Carroll, Pat Flynn, Roy Engel, Tamar Cooper, Harold Fong, Gail Ganley, Ralph Reed. *D: & P:* Roger Corman; *St: & Sc:* Charles B. Griffith, Mark Hanna. (1:07) A science fiction quickie of a somewhat human-looking outer space alien extracting blood from earthlings to take to the dying inhabitants of Davana, his home planet. Remade in 1988.

1882. The Notorious Mr. Monks (Republic/Ventura Prods.; 1958). *Cast:* Vera Ralston, Don Kelly, Paul Fix, Leo Gordon, Luana Anders, Tom Brown, Lyle Talbot, Emory Parnell, Fuzzy Knight, Hank Worden, Grandon Rhodes. *D:* Joe Kane; *P:* Rudy Ralston; *St:* Peter Paul Fix; *Sc:* Richard C. Sarafian. (1:10) Odd little programmer involving a neglected wife, her drunken husband, a handsome hired man and a teenage runaway, with the hired man eventually being charged with the murder of his drunken boss.

1883. The Nun's Story (Warner; 1959). *Cast:* Audrey Hepburn (AAN + "Best Actress" from the New York Film Critics + "Best British Actress" nomination at the British Academy Awards/Sister Luke), Peter Finch (Dr. Fortunati), Edith Evans ("Best Supporting Actress" from the NBR/Mother Emmanuel), Peggy Ashcroft (Mother Mathilde), Dean Jagger (Dr. Van Der Mal), Mildred Dunnock (Sister Margharita), Beatrice Straight (Mother Christophe), Patricia Collinge (final film—ret./Sister William), Patricia Bosworth (Simone), Ruth White (Mother Marcella), Barbara O'Neil (final film—ret./Mother Katherine), Margaret Phillips (Sister Pauline), Colleen Dewhurst (film debut/ Archangel), Molly Urquhart (Sister Augustine), Dorothy Alison (Sister Aurelie), Niall MacGinnis (Father Vermeuhlen), Rosalie Crutchley (Sister Eleanor), Orlando Martins (Kalulu), Eva Kotthaus (Sister Marie), Errol John (Illunga), Jeannette Sterke (Louise), Richard O'Sullivan (Pierre), Marina Wolkonsky (Marie), Penelope Horner (Jeanette Milonet), Charles Lamb (Pascin), Ave Ninchi (Sister Bernard), Lionel Jeffries (Dr. Coo-Vaerts), Dana Gavin (Sister Ellen), Elfrida Simbar (Sister Timothy), Ludovice Bonhomme (bishop). *D:* (AAN + "Best Director of the Year" from both the New York Film Critics and the NBR) Fred Zinneman; *P:* (AAN-Best Picture) Henry Blanke; *Sc:* (AAN) Robert Anderson; *Cin:* (AAN-color) Franz Planer; *Music:* (AAN-nonmusical) Franz Waxman; *Editor:* (AAN) Walter Thompson; *Sound:* (AAN) George A. Groves-Warner Bros. Sound Dept. (2:29) (video/laserdisc) Critically acclaimed hit drama, based on the novel by Kathryn C. Hulme, of a young girl's decision to serve God by becoming a nun, her work as a nurse in the Belgian Congo, to her final decision to leave her order. It was voted "Best Film of the Year" by the NBR while the *New York Times* and *Film Daily* both placed it at #3 on their "10 Best" lists. One of the 26 top-grossing films of 1958-59, it was also in nomination at the British Academy Awards. Technicolor.

1884. O. Henry's Full House (20th Century–Fox; 1952). A comedy-drama made up of five separate and varying stories authored by O. Henry [William Sidney Porter]. John Steinbeck narrates.

A. "The Cop and the Anthem" with Charles Laughton, Marilyn Monroe, David Wayne, Philip Tonge, Thomas Browne Henry, Richard Karlan, Erno Verebes, William Vedder, Billy Wayne, Nico Lek, Marjorie Holliday, James Flavin. (0:19) A bum tries to get himself arrested as winter rolls in, so he will have a nice warm jail cell to spend the cold blustery months. *D:* Henry Koster.

B. "The Clarion Call" with Dale Robertson, Richard Widmark, Joyce MacKenzie, Richard Rober, Will Wright, House Peters, Sr., Tyler McVey, Phil Tully, Frank Cusack, Stuart Randall, Abe Dinovitch. (0:22) A cop must face the fact that he has to arrest an old friend. *D:* Henry Hathaway.

C. "The Last Leaf" with Anne Baxter, Jean Peters, Gregory Ratoff, Richard Garrick, Steven Geray, Warren Stevens, Martha Wentworth, Ruth Warren, Bert Hicks, Beverly Thompson, Hal J. Smith. (0:23) A woman who lies in her room awaiting death, watches the leaves falling outside her window, believing that when the last one falls, she herself will die. *D:* Jean Negulesco.

D. "The Ransom of Red Chief" with Fred Allen (final film—ret.), Oscar Levant, Lee Aaker, Kathleen Freeman, Alfred Mizner, Irving Bacon, Gloria Gordon, Robert Easton, Robert Cherry, Norman Leavitt. (0:26) Inept kidnappers take a small boy to hold for ransom, but find he is nothing but an uncontrollable brat. They further find that even his parents don't want him back when the kidnappers offer them money to take the boy off their hands. *D:* Howard Hawks.

E. "The Gift of the Magi" with Jeanne Crain, Farley Granger, Sig Rumann, Harry Hayden, Fred Kelsey, Richard Hylton, Richard Allan, Fritz Feld, Frank Jaquet. (0:21) As Christmas approaches, a poor young married couple each part with a prized possession, at the local pawnbroker, to purchase their beloved spouse a meaningful gift. *D:* Henry King.

P: Andre Hakim; *Sc:* Lamar Trotti, Richard Breen, Ben Roberts, Ivan Goff, Walter Bullock, Nunnally Johnson. (1:57) (G.B. title: *Full House*)

1885. Odds Against Tomorrow (United Artists/Harbel; 1959). *Cast:* Harry Belafonte, Robert Ryan, Shelley Winters, Ed Begley, Gloria Grahame, Will Kuluva, Kim Hamilton, Mae Barnes, Richard Bright, Wayne Rogers (film debut), Carmen de Lavallade, Lou Gallo, Fred J. Scollay, Lois Thorne, Zohra Lampert, William Zuckert, Burtt Harris, Ed Preble, Mil Stewart, Marc May, Paul Hoffman, Cicely Tyson (film debut), Robert Jones, William Adams, John Garden, Allen Nourse. *D: & P:* Robert Wise; *As.P:* Phil Stein; *Sc:* John O. Kellens, Nelson Gidding. (1:35) An acclaimed drama of a bank robbery that goes awry because of racial prejudice. Based on the 1957 novel by William P. McGivern, it was filmed on location in New York City and upstate New York.

1886. Off Limits (Paramount; 1953). *Cast:* Bob Hope, Mickey Rooney, Marilyn Maxwell, Eddie Mayehoff, Stanley Clements, Jack Dempsey (himself), Marvin Miller, Tom Harmon (himself), John Ridgely (final film—ret.), Norman Leavitt, Art Aragon (himself), Kim Spalding, Jerry Hausner, Mike Mahoney, Jan Taylor, Carolyn Jones, Mary Murphy. *D:* George Marshall; *P:* Harry Tugend; *St: & Sc:* Hal Kanter, Jack Sher; *Songs:* "All About Love," "Military Policeman" Jay Livingston, Ray Evans. (1:27) (video) Comedy of a fight manager who follows his boxer into military service, only the boxer is 4F, but the manager isn't, leaving him to find a new fighter to train while serving as an M.P. (G.B. title: *Military Policeman*)

Oh! For a Man! *see* **Will Success Spoil Rock Hunter**

1887. Oh! Susanna (Republic; 1951). *Cast:* Rod Cameron, Adrian Booth, Forrest Tucker, Chill Wills, Jim Davis, William Ching, Wally Cassell, Douglas Kennedy, James Lydon, William Haade, John Compton, James Flavin, Charles Stevens, Alan Bridge, Marshall Reed, John Pickard, Ruth Brennan, Louise Kane, Marion Randolph. *D: & P:* Joseph Kane; *St: & Sc:* Charles Marquis Warren; *Songs:* Title song, "Is Someone Lonely?," "The Regular Army, Oh" Ed Harrigan, Jack Elliott. (1:30) Rivalry between cavalry officers, in the midst of an impending Indian uprising, is the substance of this western. Trucolor.

1888. Oh Men! Oh Women! (20th Century–Fox; 1957). *Cast:* Dan Dailey, Ginger Rogers, David Niven, Barbara Rush, Tony Randall (film debut), Natalie Schafer, Rachel Stephens, John Wengraf, Cheryll Clarke, Charles Davis, Clancy Cooper, Joel Fluellen, Renny McEvoy, Franklin Pangborn, Franklyn Farnum, Hal Taggert, Alfred Tonkel, Monty O'Grady, Les Raymaster, Harry Denny. *D:-P: & Sc:* Nunnally Johnson. (1:30) Comedy of a psychiatrist who finds that aspects of his personal life are merging into his medical practice; so much so, that he begins to question his own sanity. Based on the play by Edward Chodorov. DeLuxe color and CinemaScope.

Oil Town *see* **Lucy Gallant**

1889. Okefenokee (Film-Service Distributing Corp.; 1959). *Cast:* Peter Coe, Henry Brandon, Peggy Maley, Serena Sande, Walter Klavun. *D:* Roul Haig; *P:* Aaron A. Danches; *St:* Haig; *Sc:* Jess Abbott. (1:18) (video) Melodrama involving the smuggling of dope and illegal aliens, via a seaplane, to a hidden lake in the titled swampland. (G.B. title: *Indian Killer*)

1890. Okinawa (Columbia; 1952). *Cast:* Pat O'Brien, Cameron Mitchell, Richard Denning, Rhys Williams, James Dobson, Richard Benedict, Rudy Robles, Don Gibson, George Cooper, Alan Dreeban, Norman Budd, Alvy Moore. *D:* Leigh Jason (final film—ret.); *P:* Wallace MacDonald; *St:* Arthur A. Ross; *Sc:*

Jameson Brewer, Ross; *Additional dialogue:* Leonard Stern. (1:07) World War II programmer drama on the effects of the Japanese assault on Okinawa in 1945. Originally ran on a double bill with *The Woman in Question*, a 1950 British production.

1891. Oklahoma! (Magna Theatre Corp./ Rodgers and Hammerstein Prods.; 1955). *Cast:* Gordon MacRae (Curly), Gloria Grahame (Ado Annie), Gene Nelson (Will Parker), Charlotte Greenwood (Aunt Eller), Shirley Jones (film debut/Laurie), Eddie Albert (Ali Hakim), James Whitmore (Carnes), Rod Steiger (Jud Fry), Barbara Lawrence (Gertie), Jay C. Flippen (Skidmore), Roy Barcroft (marshal), James Mitchell, Bambi Linn, Jennie Workman, Kelly Brown, Marc Platt, Lizanne Truex, Virginia Bosler, Evelyn Taylor, Jane Fischer. *D:* Fred Zinneman; *P:* Arthur Hornblow, Jr.; *Sc:* Sonya Levien, William Ludwig; *Cin:* (AAN-color) Robert Surtees; *Music:* (AA) Robert Russell Bennett, Jay Blackton, Adolph Deutsch; *Sound recording:* (AA) Fred Hynes–Todd-AO Sound Dept.; *Editors:* (AAN) Gene Ruggiero, George Boemler; *Songs:* "Oklahoma!," "Oh What a Beautiful Mornin'," "The Surrey with the Fringe on Top," "Everything's Up to Date in Kansas City," "Many a New Day," "People Will Say We're in Love," "The Farmer and the Cowman," "I Can't Say No," "All Er Nuthin'" and "Pore Jud." (2:25) (video/laserdisc) The 1943 Broadway hit musical by Richard Rodgers and Oscar Hammerstein II was based on the play *Green Grow the Lilacs* by Lynn Riggs. Originally produced in two near identical formats, one for CinemaScope, the other in Todd-AO. It placed #9 on the "10 Best" list of the *New York Times* and was in nomination for "Best Picture" with the New York Film Critics. One of the 24 top-grossing films of 1955-56. Eastmancolor. Note: The CinemaScope format was used for the home video release and the Todd-AO format was used for the laserdisc release in 1994.

1892. Oklahoma Annie (Republic; 1952). *Cast:* Judy Canova, John Russell, Grant Withers, Roy Barcroft, Emmett Lynn, Frank Ferguson, Minerva Urecal, Houseley Stevenson, Almira Sessions, Allen Jenkins, Maxine Gates, Emory Parnell, Denver Pyle, House Peters, Jr., Andrew Tombes, Fuzzy Knight, Si Jenks, Marion Martin, Herbert Vigran, Hal Price, Fred Hoose, Lee Phelps, Bobby Taylor, William Fawcett. *D:* R.G. Springsteen; *P:* Sidney Picker; *St:* Jack Townley, Charles E. Roberts; *Sc:* Townley; *Songs:* "Blow the Whistle" S. Sherwin, Harry McClintock; "Have You Ever Been Lonely?" George Brown, Peter DeRose; "Never, Never, Never" Sonny Burke, Jack Elliott. (1:30) (video) Rural comedy of the female owner of a gunshop who takes a shine to the new sheriff and wants him to arrest the local saloon owner. The sheriff makes her his deputy as a form of appeasement. In Trucolor, it originally ran on the top of a double bill with *Leadville Gunslinger* (q.v.).

1893. Oklahoma Justice (Monogram; 1951). *Cast:* Johnny Mack Brown, James Ellison, Phyllis Coates, Barbara Allen, Kenne Duncan, Lane Bradford, Marshall Reed, Zon Murray, I. Stanford Jolley, Stanley Price, Bruce Edwards, Richard Avonde, Carl Mathews, Edward Cassidy, Lyle Talbot, George DeNormand. *D:* Lewis D. Collins; *P:* Vincent M. Fennelly; *Sc:* Joseph O'Donnell. (0:56) Another of Brown's series westerns for Monogram, it had a prerelease title of "Oklahoma Outlaw." A U.S. marshal poses as a wanted outlaw.

1894. The Oklahoma Woman (American Releasing Corp./Sunset Pictures; 1956). *Cast:* Richard Denning, Peggie Castle, Cathy Downs, Tudor Owen, Martin Kingsley, Touch [Michael] Connors, Jonathan Haze, Richard "Dick" Miller, Tom Dillon, Edmund Cobb, Bruno VeSota, Aaron Saxon, Joe Brown. *D: & P:* Roger Corman; *Ex.P:* James H. Nicholson; *St: & Sc:* Lou Rusoff. (1:11) Quickie western of a man who gets out of prison and heads home, only to find his old girl friend now rules the area and tries to frame him. SuperScope.

1895. The Oklahoman (Allied Artists; 1957). *Cast:* Joel McCrea, Barbara Hale, Gloria Talbott, Brad Dexter, Michael Pate, Verna Felton, Douglas Dick, Anthony Caruso, Esther Dale (final film—d. 1961), Adam Williams, Ray Teal, Peter Votrian, John Pickard, Mimi Gibson, I. Stanford Jolley, Jody Williams, Don Marlowe, Diane Brewster, Sheb Wooley, Harry Lauter, Robert Hinkle, Doris Kemper, Dorothy Neumann, Gertrude Astor, Wheaton Chambers, Earle Hodgins, Watson Downs, Tod Farrell, Rankin Mansfield, Laurie Mitchell, Jenny Lea, Scotty Beckett, Lennie Geer, Al Kramer, Kermit Maynard, Bill Foster. *D:* Francis D. Lyon; *P:* Walter Mirisch; *St: & Sc:* Daniel B. Ullman. (1:20) (video) Western of a doctor who intervenes when he learns corrupt whites are trying to cheat an Indian out of his oil rich lands. DeLuxe color and CinemaScope.

1896. The Old Frontier (Republic; 1950). *Cast:* Monte Hale, Paul Hurst, Claudia Barrett,

William Henry, Tristram Coffin, William Haade, Victor Kilian, Lane Bradford, Denver Pyle, Tom London, Almira Sessions. *D:* Philip Ford; *As.P:* Melville Tucker; *St: & Sc:* Bob Williams. (1:00) An outlaw gang, specializing in bank robberies, is secretly headed by a respected attorney. An entry in Monte Hale's series of westerns.

1897. The Old Man and the Sea (Warner; 1958). *Cast:* Spencer Tracy (AAN + "Best Actor" Award from the NBR combined with his work in *The Last Hurrah* [q.v.]/old man-narrator), Filipe Pazos (boy), Harry Bellaver (Martin), Don Diamond, Don Blackman, Joey Ray, Richard Alameda, Tony Rosa, Carlos Rivera, Robert Alderette, Mauritz Hugo, Mary Hemingway. *D:* John Sturges; *P:* Leland Hayward; *Sc:* Peter Viertel; *Cin:* (AAN-color) James Wong Howe; *Music:* (AA) Dimitri Tiompkin. (1:26) Based on the 1952 novella by Ernest Hemingway, this drama details the problems of an elderly fisherman, particularly with the elements, while trying to make a living. Location shooting in the Bahamas, near Cuba, Colombia, near Peru, Ecuador, Panama, the Galapagos Islands and Hawaii. Voted "Best Film of the Year" by the NBR, it did not do well at the box office. In WarnerColor, it was remade in 1990 as a TV movie.

1898. Old Oklahoma Plains (Republic; 1952). *Cast:* Rex Allen, Slim Pickens, Elaine Edwards, Roy Barcroft, John Crawford, Joel Marston, Russell Hicks, Fred Graham, Stephen Chase, The Republic Rhythm Riders, Ko-Ko (horse). *D:* William Witney; *As.P:* Edward J. "Eddy" White; *St:* Albert DeMond; *Sc:* Milton Raison. (1:00) (video) Rex Allen series western with songs and a touch of novelty, as a former cavalry officer decides to use army tanks to curtail lawlessness. Set in the 1920s, the film utilizes stock footage from this studio's *Army Girl* (1938).

1899. Old Overland Trail (Republic; 1953). *Cast:* Rex Allen, Slim Pickens, Virginia Hall, Roy Barcroft, Gil Herman, Wade Crosby, Leonard Nimoy, Zon Murray, Harry Harvey, The Republic Rhythm Riders, Ko-Ko (horse). *D:* William Witney; *As.P:* Edward J. "Eddy" White; *St: & Sc:* Milton Raison; *Songs:* "Cowboys Dream of Heaven" (Jack Elliott), "Just a Wanderin' Buckaroo," "Work, for the Night Is Coming." (1:00) In this entry in Allen's latter-day series, Apache Indians are at odds with immigrant settlers passing through their lands.

1900. The Old West (Columbia/Gene Autry Prods.; 1952). *Cast:* Gene Autry, Gail Davis, Pat Buttram, Lyle Talbot, Dick Jones, House Peters, Jr., House Peters, Sr., Louis Jean Heydt, Tom London, Don C. Harvey, Syd Saylor, Pat O'Malley, John Merton, Frank Ellis, Kathy Johnson, Dee Pollock, Raymond L. Morgan, James Craven, Buddy Roosevelt, Bob Woodward, Frankie Marvin, Tex Terry, Bobby Clark, Robert Hilton, Champion (horse), Champion, Jr. (horse). *D:* George Archainbaud; *P:* Armand Schaefer; *St: & Sc:* Gerald Geraghty; *Songs:* "Somebody Bigger Than You and I," "Music by the Angels." (1:01) Offbeat series western, with Gene helping a minister spread the gospel in a western town and clean up the outlaw element.

1901. Old Yeller (Buena Vista/Walt Disney Prods.; 1957). *Cast:* Dorothy McGuire (Katie Coates), Fess Parker (Jim Coates), Tommy Kirk (film debut/Travis Coates), Kevin Corcoran (Arliss Coates), Jeff York (Bud Searcy), Beverly Washburn (Lisabeth Searcy), Chuck Connors (Burn Sanderson), Spike (dog, #1 PATSY Award, 1958/Old Yeller). *D:* Robert Stevenson; *P:* Walt Disney; *Sc:* Fred Gipson, William Tunberg; *Title song:* Oliver Wallace, Gil George (sung by Jerome Courtland). (1:23) (video/laserdisc) Disney hit the jackpot with this tale of a boy and his dog, set on a rural Texas farm in 1869. Based on a novel by Mr. Gipson, an $8,000,000 gross in the U.S. alone made it one of the 26 top-grossing films of 1957-58. In Technicolor, it was followed in 1963 by the sequel, *Savage Sam.*

1902. Omar Khayyam (Paramount; 1957). *Cast:* Cornel Wilde (title role), Michael Rennie, Debra Paget, Raymond Massey, John Derek, Yma Sumac, Sebastian Cabot, Margaret Hayes, Joan Taylor, Perry Lopez, Morris Ankrum, Abraham Sofaer, Edward Platt, James Griffith, Peter Adams, Henry Brandon, Kem Dibbs, Paul Picerni, Valerie Allen, Charles LaTorre, Dale Van Sickel, John Abbott, Len Hendry, Joyce Meadows, Abdel Salam Moussa. *D:* William Dieterle (final U.S. film); *P:* Frank Freeman, Jr.; *St: & Sc:* Barre Lyndon; *Songs:* "The Loves of Omar Khayyam" Jay Livingston, Ray Evans; "Take My Heart" Victor Young, Mack David; "Lament" Moses Vivanco. (1:41) (video) Romantic costume adventure of the medieval Persian poet-astronomer [notable for writing "The Rubaiyat"]. Technicolor and VistaVision.

1903. On Dangerous Ground (RKO; 1951). *Cast:* Ida Lupino, Robert Ryan, Ward

Bond, Charles Kemper, Anthony Ross, Ed Begley, Ian Wolfe, Sumner Williams, Gus Schilling, Frank Ferguson, Cleo Moore, Olive Carey, Richard Irving, Pat Prest, Bill Hammond, Gene Persson, Tommy Gosser, Ronnie Garner, Dee Garner, Harry Joel Weiss, Ruth Lee, Kate Lawson, Esther Zeitlin, William Challee, Eddie Borden, Steve Roberts, Budd Fine, Mike Lally, Don Dillaway, Al Murphy, Art Dupuis, Frank Arnold, Homer Dickinson, Ken Terrell, William J. O'Brien, Nita Talbot, Joe Devlin, Jim Drum, A.I. Bezzerides, Tracey Roberts, Vera Stokes, Nestor Paiva, Leslie Bennett, Jimmy Conlin, John Taylor. *D:* Nicholas Ray; *P:* John Houseman; *Adaptation:* A.I. Bezzerides; *Sc:* Bezzerides, Ray. (1:22) (video/laserdisc) Film noir of a New York City cop whose job has him living on the edge. He is assigned to investigate a rural murder where he falls for the blind sister of the man suspected of the murder. Based on the 1945 novel *Mad with Much Heart* by Gerald Butler, it became a red-letter entry on the studio's books.

1904. On Moonlight Bay (Warner; 1951). *Cast:* Doris Day (received *Photoplay* Gold Medal/Marjorie Winfield), Gordon MacRae (William Sherman), Jack Smith (film debut/Hubert Wakley), Leon Ames (George Winfield), Rosemary DeCamp (Mrs. Winfield), Mary Wickes (Stella), Ellen Corby (Miss Stevens), Billy Gray (Wesley Winfield), Jeffrey Stevens (Jim Sherman), Esther Dale (Aunt Martha), Suzanne Whitney (Cora), Eddie Marr, Sig Arno, James Dobson, Rolland Morris and *silent movie cast:* Lois Austin, Creighton Hale, Ann Kimbell, Ray Spiker, Hank Mann, Jack Mower, Ralph Montgomery. *D:* Roy Del Ruth; *P:* William Jacobs; *Sc:* Jack Rose, Melville Shavelson; *Songs:* "Love Ya" (Charles Tobias–Peter de Rose); "Christmas Story" (Pauline Walsh); "On Moonlight Bay" (Edward Madden–Percy Wenrich); "Cuddle Up a Little Closer" (Otto Harbach–Karl Hoschna); "Tell Me Why Nights Are Lonely" (W.J. Callahan–Max Kortlander); "I'm Forever Blowing Bubbles" (Jean Kenbrovin–John W. Kellette); "Every Little Movement Has a Meaning All Its Own" (Harbach–Hoschna); "Till We Meet Again" (Ray Evans–Richard Whiting); "Pack Up Your Troubles in Your Old Kit Bag" (Felix Powell–George Asaf) and "Love Your Honey," "Yoo Hoo." (1:35) (video/laserdisc) A nostalgic turn-of-the-century romantic musical which was based on Booth Tarkington's "Penrod" stories and *Alice Adams*. In Technicolor, it was one of the 23 top-grossing films of 1950-51 and was followed by the sequel *By the Light of the Silvery Moon* (q.v.).

1905. On the Beach (United Artists/Lomitas Prods.; 1959). *Cast:* Gregory Peck (Dwight Towers), Ava Gardner (Moira Davidson), Fred Astaire (Julian Osborne), Anthony Perkins (Peter Holmes), Donna Anderson (film debut/Mary Holmes), John Tate (Admiral Bridie), Lola Brooks (Lt. Hosgood), Lou Vernon (Davidson), Guy Doleman (Farrel), Ken Wayne (Benson), John Meillon (Swain), Richard Meikle (Davis), Harp McGuire (Sundstrom), Jim Barrett (Chrysler), Basil Buller Murphy (Sir Douglas Froude), Keith Eden (Dr. Fletcher), Kevin Brennan (Dr. King), C. Harding Brown (Dykers), Grant Taylor (Morgan), Peter Williams (Prof. Jorgenson), Harvey Adams, (Sykes), Stuart Finch (Jones), Joe McCormick (Ackerman), Audine Leith (Betty), Jerry Ian Seals (Fogarty), Katherine Hill (Jennifer Holmes), John Royle, Frank Gatcliff, Paddy Moran, John Casson, Carey Paul Peck. *D: & P:* Stanley Kramer; *Sc:* John Paxton, James Lee Barrett; *Song:* "Waltzing Matilda" A.B. Paterson, Marie Cowan; *Music:* (AAN) Ernest Gold; *Editor:* (AAN) Frederic Knudtson. (2:13) (video/laserdisc) Set in 1964, the world has been devastated by an atomic war and in Australia, a group of people await an approaching cloud of nuclear fallout. A drama with critical acclaim, placing #9 on the "10 Best" list of the NBR and #10 on the same list of the *New York Times*. The New York Film Critics had it in nomination for "Best Film" and at a take of over $5 million it became one of the 28 top-grossing films of 1959-60. Based on the novel by Nevil Shute.

1906. On the Bowery (Film Representations, Inc.–Lionel Rogosin Prods.; 1956). *Cast:* Ray Sayler, Gorman Hendricks, Frank Mathews. *D:* Lionel Rogosin (directorial debut); *P:* (AAN-Best Documentary) Rogosin; *St: & Sc:* Mark Sufrin, Richard Bagley, Rogosin. (1:05) (video) Acclaimed documentary feature of a young alcoholic and his experiences on New York City's "skid row." An award winner at the 1956 Venice Film Festival.

1907. On the Isle of Samoa (Columbia, 1950). *Cast:* Jon Hall, Susan Cabot (film debut), Raymond Greenleaf, Henry Marco, Al Kikume, Rosa Turich, Leon Lontoc, Neyle Morrow, Jacqueline de Wit, Ben Welden. *D:* William Berke; *P:* Wallace MacDonald; *St:* Joseph Santley; *Sc:* Brenda Weisberg, Harold R. Greene. (1:05) Programmer South Seas romantic adventure of a man who crash lands his stolen plane full of stolen loot on an uncharted idyllic island paradise—finds love with a native girl and redemption with a shipwrecked missionary.

1908. On the Loose (RKO/Filmakers; 1951). *Cast:* Joan Evans, Melvyn Douglas, Lynn Bari, Robert Arthur, Hugh O'Brian, Constance Hilton, Michael Kuhn, Susan Morrow, Lillian Hamilton, Elizabeth Flournoy, John Morgan, Larry Dobkin, Tristram Coffin, Edwin Reimers, Mark Tangner, Don Brodie, Jess Kirkpatrick, Don Megowan, Jack Larson, Diane Ware, Leonard Penn, Alan Harris, Jerry Hausner, Lela Bliss, Marc Rohm, Robert Marlowe. *D:* Charles Lederer; *P:* Collier Young; *St:* Young, Malvin Wald; *Sc:* Dale Eunson, Katherine Albert [Eunson]. (1:18) Delinquency drama of a teenage girl who seeks attention from her parents by becoming a "bad girl." Originally ran on a double bill with Tim Holt's *Pistol Harvest* (q.v.). Note: Evans is the real life daughter of screenwriters Dale and Katherine Eunson.

1909. On the Riviera (20th Century-Fox; 1951). *Cast:* Danny Kaye (Henri Duran & Jack Martin), Gene Tierney (Lilli), Corinne Calvet (Colette), Marcel Dalio (Philippe Lebrix), Jean Murat (Periton), Henri Letondal (Louis Forel), Clinton Sundberg (Antoine), Sig Rumann (Gapeaux), Joyce MacKenzie (Mimi), Monique Chantal (Minette), Marina Koshetz (Mme. Cornet), Ann Codee (Mme. Periton), Mari Blanchard (film debut/Eugenie), Ethel Martin, George Martin and Vernal Miller (dance team), Ellen Ray, Gwyneth [Gwen] Verdon (film debut), Rosario Imperio, Antonio Filauri, Charles Andre, Franchesca de Scaffa, Joi Lansing, Eugene Borden, Albert Pollet, Andre Toffel, Albert Morin, George Davis, Tony Laurent, Peter Camlin, Jack Chefe. *D:* Walter Lang; *P:* Sol C. Siegel; *Adaptation:* Jessie Ernst; *Sc:* Valentine Davies, Henry & Phoebe Ephron; *Songs:* "Popo the Puppet," "On the Riviera," "Rhythm of a New Romance," "Happy Ending" Sylvia Fine; "Ballin' the Jack" Jim Burns, Christ Smith; *ASD:* (AAN-color) Lyle Wheeler, Leland Fuller (art directors), Thomas Little, Walter M. Scott (sets), Jon C. Wright (musical settings); *Music:* (AAN) Alfred Newman. (1:29) A Technicolor musical-comedy of mistaken identity. It was a remake of *That Night in Rio* (1941) which was a remake of *Folies Bergère* (1935). Based on a play by Rudolph Lothar and Hans Adler, it became one of the 23 top-grossing films of 1950-51. Technicolor.

1910. On the Threshold of Space (20th Century–Fox; 1956). *Cast:* Guy Madison, Virginia Leith, John Hodiak (final film—d. 1955), Dean Jagger, Warren Stevens, Martin Milner, King Calder, Walter Coy, Ken Clark, Donald Murphy, Barry Coe, Richard Grant, Donald Freed, Ben Wright, Carlyle Mitchell, Robert Cornthwaite, Jo Gilbert, Juanita Close, Helen Bennett, Charles Lind, David Armstrong, Joe Locke. *D:* Robert D. Webb; *P:* William Bloom; *St: & Sc:* Simon Wincelberg, Francis Cockrell. (1:38) Drama of the research and testing by the military for man's eventual ascent into outer space. Location filming at Eglin Air Force Base in Florida and Holloman Air Force Base in New Mexico. DeLuxe color and CinemaScope.

1911. On the Waterfront (Columbia/ Horizon–American Pictures; 1954). *Cast:* Marlon Brando (AA/Terry Malloy), Karl Malden (AAN/Father Barry), Lee J. Cobb (AAN/John Friendly), Rod Steiger (AAN/Charles Malloy), Eva Marie Saint (AA-film debut/Edie Doyle), Pat Henning (film debut/"Kayo" Dugan), Leif Erickson (Glover), James Westerfield (Big Mac), Tony Galento (Truck), Tami Mauriello (Tillio), John Hamilton ("Pop" Doyle), Rudy Bond (Moose), Don Blackman (Luke), John Heldabrand (Mott), Arthur Keegan (Jimmy), Abe Simon (Barney), Barry Macollum (J.P.), Mike O'Dowd (Specs), Marty [Martin] Balsam (film debut/Gillette), Fred Gwynne (film debut/Slim), Thomas Handley (Tommy), Anne Hegira (Mrs. Collins), Nehemiah Persoff (cabbie). *D:* (AA + "Best Director" from the New York Film Critics) Elia Kazan; *P:* (AA-Best Picture) Sam Spiegel; *St: & Sc:* (AA) Budd Schulberg (based on the "Crime on the Waterfront" articles by Malcolm Johnson); *Cinematographer:* (AA-b/w) Boris Kaufman; *Art-Set decoration:* (AA-b/w) Richard Day; *Editor:* (AA) Gene Milford; *Music:* (AAN-non musical) Leonard Bernstein. (1:48) (video/laserdisc) Classic, critically acclaimed, award-winning drama of the New York waterfront and the corruption and violence within the dockworkers' labor unions. In addition to his Oscar, Brando also garnered "Best Actor" honors from the New York Film Critics and the British Academy Awards. The New York Film Critics and the NBR also voted the film "Best of the Year," while it garnered the "Silver Lion" at the Venice Film Festival. On the "10 Best" lists of *Film Daily* and the *New York Times*, it placed #2 and #6 respectively. Filmed on location in New York City and Hoboken, New Jersey, it became one of the 25 top-grossing films of 1953-54.

1912. On Top of Old Smoky (Columbia/ Gene Autry Prods.; 1953). *Cast:* Gene Autry,

Gail Davis, Smiley Burnette, Grandon Rhodes, Sheila Ryan, Kenne Duncan, Zon Murray, Pat O'Malley, Fred S. Martin, Bert Dodson, Robert Bice, Jerry Scroggins, The Cass County Boys, Champ, Jr. (horse). *D:* George Archainbaud; *P:* Armand Schaefer; *St: & Sc:* Gerald Geraghty. (0:59) (video) Gene is a cowboy, mistaken for a wanted Texas Ranger, who helps a girl save her ranch and tollroad from a crook who is after rich mica deposits. The title song was a big hit in the early 1950s. Sepiatone.

1913. Once a Thief (United Artists/ Merit Prods., Inc.; 1950). *Cast:* Cesar Romero, June Havoc, Marie McDonald, Lon Chaney, Jr., Iris Adrian, Jack Daly, Marta Mitrovich, Ann Tyrrell, Kathleen Freeman, Phil Arnold, Dana Wilson, Bill Baldwin, Michael Mark, Joseph Jefferson, Peter Dunne, Fred Kelsey. *D: & P:* W. Lee Wilder; *As.P:* William Stevens; *St:* Mal Colpet, Hans Wilhelm; *Sc:* Richard S. Conway, Wilder. (1:27) Melodrama of a shoplifter and what happens when she gets involved with a no-good.

1914. Once Upon a Horse (Universal-International; 1958). Cast: Dan Rowan (film debut), Dick Martin (film debut), Martha Hyer, Leif Erickson, Nita Talbot, James Gleason, John McGiver, Paul Anderson, David Burns, Max Baer (final film—d. 1959), Buddy Baer, Dick Ryan, Bob Steele, Tom Keene, Bob Livingston, Kermit Maynard, Steve Pendleton, Sydney Chatton, Sam Hearn, Ingrid Goude, Ricky Kelman, Joe Oakie. *D:-P: & Sc:* Hal Kanter; *Title song:* Jay Livingston, Ray Evans. (1:25) Western comedy spoof of two cowboys who can't make it as good guys or as outlaws. Based on the novel *Why Rustlers Never Win* by Henry Gregor Felsen, it was re-released in 1963 under the title *Hot Horse.* CinemaScope.

1915. One Big Affair (United Artists/ Bon-Air Picts., Inc.; 1952). *Cast:* Evelyn Keyes, Dennis O'Keefe, Connie Gilchrist, Mary Anderson, Thurston Hall, Andrew Velasquez, Gus Schilling, Jose Torvay, Charles [Carlos] Musquiz. *D:* Peter Godfrey; *P:* Benedict Bogeaus; *St:* George Bricker; *Adaptation:* Francis Swann; *Sc:* Leo Townsend. (1:20) Romantic comedy of a schoolteacher in Mexico who misses her bus, leading her friends to think she was kidnapped. In reality she was becoming romantically involved with an American lawyer.

1916. One Desire (Universal-International; 1955). *Cast:* Anne Baxter, Rock Hudson, Julie Adams, Carl Benton Reid, Natalie Wood, Betty Garde, William Hopper, William Forrest, Barry Curtis, Adrienne Marden, Fay Morley, Vici Raaf, Lynne Millan, Robert "Smoki" Whitfield, Robert Hoy, John Daheim, Betty Jane Howarth, Howard Wright, Alan DeWitt, Joe Mell, Paul McGuire, Guy Wilkerson, Paul Levitt, Edward Earle, Edmund Cobb, Barbara Knudson, Charles Gray, Joe Golbert, Dennis Moore, Donald Kerr, Terry Frost, Forbes Murray, Paul Keast, Joel Allen. *D:* Jerry Hopper; *P:* Ross Hunter; *Sc:* Lawrence Roman, Robert Blees. (1:34) Romantic melodrama, set in the turn-of-the-century west, of a woman in love with a gambler and another woman who tries to come between them. Based on the 1942 novel *Tacey Cromwell* by Conrad Richter. Technicolor.

1917. One Girl's Confession (Columbia; 1953). *Cast:* Cleo Moore, Hugo Haas, Glenn Langan, Ellen Stansbury, Bert Mustin, Anthony Jochim, Russ Conway, Leonid Snegoff, Jim Nusser, Mara Lea, Gayne Whitman, Leo Mostovoy, Martha Wentworth. *D:-P:-St: & Sc:* Hugo Haas; *As.P:* Robert Erlik. (1:14) Low budget melodrama of a girl sent to prison for stealing money from her guardian. Originally ran on a double bill with *Problem Girls* (q.v.).

One Hour to Doom's Day (G.B. title) *see* **City Beneath the Sea**

One-Man Mutiny (G.B. title) *see* **The Court Martial of Billy Mitchell**

1918. One Minute to Zero (RKO; 1952). *Cast:* Robert Mitchum, Ann Blyth, William Talman, Charles McGraw, Margaret Sheridan, Richard Egan, Eduard Franz, Robert Osterloh, Robert Gist, Roy Roberts, Wally Cassell, Eddie Firestone, Peter Thompson, Steven Flagg [aka: Michael St. Angel], Ted Ryan, Larry Stewart, Lalo Rios, Hal Baylor, Tom Carr, Tom Irish, Alvin Greenman, Maurice Marsac, Dorothy Granger, Karen Hale, Kay Christopher, Wallace Russell, Stuart Whitman, Owen Song, Monya Andre, John Mallory, Buddy Swan, William Forrest, Tyler McVey, Robert Bray, Ray Montgomery, Al Murphy. *D:* Tay Garnett; *P:* Edmund Grainger; *St: & Sc:* Milton Krims, William Wister Haines; *Additional dialogue:* Andrew Solt; *Songs:* "When I Fall in Love" Victor Young; "Tell Me Golden Moon (China Night)" Norman Bennett, Nobuyuki Takeoda. (1:45) (video) A Korean War drama, with romance added, of a hardened army officer trying to outwit the North Koreans. Popular at the box office, it also utilizes actual war footage.

The One-Piece Bathing Suit (G.B. title) *see* **Million Dollar Mermaid**

1000 Years from Now (re-release title) *see* **Captive Women**

1919. 1001 Arabian Nights (Columbia/U.P.A. Picts., Inc.; 1959). *Voices:* Jim Backus, Kathryn Grant, Dwayne Hickman, Hans Conried, Herschel Bernardi, Alan Reed, Dawes Butler, The Clark Sisters. *D:* Jack Kinney; *P:* Stephen Bosustow; *St:* Dick Shaw, Dick Kinney, Leo Salkin, Pete Burness, Lew Keller, Ed Nofziger, Ted Allan, Margaret Schneider, Paul Schneider; *Sc:* Czenzi Ormandi. (1:16) (video) An animated adaptation of *Aladdin* starring near-sighted "Mr. Magoo." The first feature-length cartoon of U.P.A. Technicolor.

1920. One Too Many (Hallmark; 1950). *Cast:* Ruth Warrick (in her final film until 1966), Richard Travis, Ginger Prince, Rhys Williams, William Tracy, Onslow Stevens, Mary Young, Thurston Hall, Larry J. Blake, Victor Kilian, "Buzzy" Bookman, Luther Crockett, Cecil Elliott, Gilbert Fallman, Lester Sharpe, Lelah Tyler, Helen Spring, Harry Stanton, Lyle Talbot, George Eldredge, Roy E. Butler, Harry Hines, Jack Reitzen, Robert Malcolm, William Baldwin, Dan Rense, William Kahn, Sara Perry, Eddie Parker, Tony Layng, Bobo Scharffe, Jane Hampton, Claire James, The Harmonaires, Louis DaPron, Ern Westmore, Carlos Molina & Orchestra. *D:* Erle C. Kenton (final film—ret.); *P: & St:* Kroger Babb; *Adaptation:* Mildred A. Horn; *Sc:* Malcolm Stuart Boylan; *Songs:* various. (1:50) Exploitation melodrama (shown only on roadshow engagements) of a woman alcoholic and how "one too many," too many times, affects her husband and daughter. (G.B. title: *Killer with a Label*)

One Way Out *see* **Convicted**

1921. One Way Street (Universal-International; 1950). *Cast:* James Mason, Marta Toren, Dan Duryea, William Conrad, Jack Elam, King Donovan, Tito Renaldo, Basil Ruysdael, Rudolfo Acosta (U.S. debut), Margarito [Luna?] Lama, George Lewis, Emma Roldan, Robert Espinoza, Jose Dominguez, Julia Montoya, Marguerite Martin, Rock Hudson, Paul Fierro, Freddie Letuli. *D:* Hugo Fregonese; *P:* Leonard Goldstein; *As.P:* Samuel Goldwyn, Jr.; *Sc:* Lawrence Kimble (based on his story "Death on a Side Street"). (1:19) A critically panned box office dud of a doctor, involved with crooks, who absconds to Mexico with a cache of stolen loot.

1922. One Way Ticket to Hell (Eden/Exhibitors Productions; 1952). *Cast:* Barbara Marks, Bamlet L. Price, Jr., Robert A. Sherry, Robert Norman, Elaine Lindenbaum, William Kendall, Anthony Gorsline, Joe Popovich, Joel Climenhaga, Lucile Price, Bamlet L. Price, Sr., Victor Schwartz, Kurt Martell (narrator). *D:-P:-St: & Sc:* Bamlet L. Price, Jr. (1:10) (video) Low budget independent exploitation melodrama of one innocent girl's descent into drugs—using, then pushing. (video title: *Teenage Devil Dolls*)

1923. Onionhead (Warner; 1958). *Cast:* Andy Griffith, Felicia Farr, Walter Matthau, Erin O'Brien, Joe Mantell, Ray Danton, Joey Bishop, James Gregory, Claude Akins, Ainslie Pryor, Roscoe Karns, Peter Brown, Tige Andrews, Sean Garrison, Dan Barton, Mark Roberts, Karl Lukas. *D:* Norman Taurog; *P:* Jules Schermer; *Sc:* Nelson Gidding (1:50) (video) Service comedy-drama, set in 1941, of a man disillusioned with love who joins the U.S. Coast Guard as a cook. Based on a novel by Weldon Hill, it followed hot-on-the-heels of Griffith's hit *No Time for Sergeants* (q.v.).

Only the Best *see* **I Can Get It for You Wholesale**

1924. Only the Valiant (Warner/Cagney Prods.; 1951). *Cast:* Gregory Peck, Barbara Payton, Gig Young, Ward Bond, Lon Chaney, Warner Anderson, Neville Brand, Jeff Corey, Steve Brodie, Terry Kilburn, Herbert Heyes, Art Baker, Hugh Sanders, Michael Ansara, Nana Bryant, Harvey Udell, Claire James, Clark Howat, Harlan Howe, John Halloran, David Clarke, William Newell, John Doucette, William Phillips. *D:* Gordon Douglas; *P:* William Cagney; *Sc:* Edmund H. North, Harry Brown. (1:45) (video/laserdisc) Western drama of a martinet whose disciplinary action incites rebellion from the men in his cavalry command, all of which also have to deal with an Apache uprising. Based on a 1943 novel by Charles Marquis Warren.

Operation Cicero *see* **5 Fingers**

1925. Operation Dames (American International/Camera Eye Picts.–Del Mar Prods.; 1959). *Cast:* Eve Meyer (film debut), Chuck Henderson, Don Devlin, Ed Craig, Cindy Girard, Barbara Skylar, Chuck Van Haren, Andrew Munro, Byron Morrow, Alice Allyn, Ed Lakso, Joe Maierhouser. *D:* Louis Clyde Stoumen; *P:* & St: Stanley Kallis; *Sc:* Edward J. Lakso; *Songs:*

"Girls, Girls, Girls," "Regular Man" Lakso. (1:14) Korean War drama of a troupe of four female U.S.O. entertainers trapped behind enemy lines. They team up with a patrol of G.I.s, cut off from their unit, who are forced to fortify themselves to repel a communist assault. Originally ran on a double bill with *Tank Commandos* (q.v.). (G.B. title: *Girls in Action*) Note: Eve Meyer was the wife of soft-core porn moviemaker, Russ Meyer. She was also a former *Playboy* playmate.

1926. Operation Haylift (Lippert; 1950). *Cast:* Bill Williams, Ann Rutherford (final film appearance until 1972), Tom Brown, Jane Nigh, Joe Sawyer, Richard Travis, Raymond Hatton, James Conlin, Tommy Ivo, M'Liss McClure, Joanna Armstrong, Dink Dean, Frank Jaros, and U.S. Air Force members: Capt. H.G. Fisher, Sgt. Victor Rogers, Sgt. William Dooms, Roger Norton, and other airmen. *D:* William Berke; *P:* Joe Sawyer, Murray Lerner; *St: & Sc:* Sawyer, Dean Reisner. (1:14) Offbeat drama of the disastrous blizzards which hit the U.S. in January of 1949 and how the U.S. Air Force fed starving livestock on grazing land.

1927. Operation Mad Ball (Columbia/Jed Harris Prods.; 1957). *Cast:* Jack Lemmon, Kathryn Grant, Ernie Kovacs (film debut), Arthur O'Connell, Mickey Rooney, Dick York, James Darren, Roger Smith, William Leslie, L.Q. Jones, Sheridan Comerate, Jeanne Manet, Bebe Allen, Mary LaRoche, Dick Crockett, Paul Picerni, David McMahon, Otto Reichow. *D:* Richard Quine; *P:* Jed Harris; *Sc:* Harris, Arthur Carter, Blake Edwards. (1:45) World War II comedy of an army private who plans to throw a wild party unbeknownst to his superiors. Based on the play *The Mad Ball* by Mr. Carter.

1928. Operation Pacific (Warner; 1951). *Cast:* John Wayne (Commander Duke Gifford), Patricia Neal (Mary Stuart), Ward Bond (Capt. "Pop" Perry), Scott Forbes (Larry), Philip Carey (film debut/Bob Perry), Paul Picerni (Jonesy), William Campbell (The Talker), Kathryn Givney (Commander Steele), Martin Milner (Caldwell), Cliff Clark (Comsubpac), Jack Pennick (The Chief), Virginia Brissac (Sister Anna), Sam Edwards (Junior), Gayle Kellogg (Herbie), Steve Wayne (Rafferty), Vincent Forte, Lewis Martin, Louis Mosconi, Bob Nash, William Self, Carl Saxe, James Flavin, Al Kikume, Bob Carson, Ray Hyke, Chris Drake, Harry Lauter, Carleton Young, Harlan Warde, John Baer, Richard Loo. *D:-St: & Sc:* George Waggner; *P:* Louis F. Edelman. (1:51) (video/laserdisc) A romantic wartime drama focused around a submarine titled the "Thunderfish." One of the 23 top-grossing films of 1950-51.

1929. Operation Petticoat (Universal-International/Granarte Co.; 1959). *Cast:* Cary Grant (Admiral Matt Sherman), Tony Curtis (Lt. Nick Holden), Joan O'Brien (Lt. Dolores Crandall), Dina Merrill (Lt. Barbara Duran), Arthur O'Connell (Sam Tostin), Gene Evans (Molumphrey), Richard [Dick] Sargent (Stovall), Virginia Gregg (Major Edna Hayward), Robert F. Simon (Capt. J.B. Henderson), Robert Gist (Watson), Gavin McLeod (Ernest Hunkle), George Dunn (The Prophet), Dick Crockett (Harmon), Madlyn Rhue (Lt. Claire Reid), Marion Ross (Lt. Ruth Colfax), Clarence E. Lung (Ramon), Frankie Darro (Dooley), Tony Pastor, Jr. (Fox), Nicky Blair (Kraus), John Morley (Williams), Robert Hoy (Reiner), Glenn Jacobson, Nino Tempo, Leon Lontoc, James F. Lanphier, Alan Dexter, Nelson Leigh, Francis De Sales, Preston Hanson, Hal Baylor, Bob Stratton, Harry Harvey, Jr., Vi Ingraham, Alan Scott, Francis L. Ward, William R Callinan, Gordon Casell, Tusi Faiivae. *D:* Blake Edwards; *P:* Robert Arthur; *St: & Sc:* (AAN) Paul King, Joseph Stone (story), Stanley Shapiro, Maurice Richlin (screenplay). (2:04) (video/laserdisc) Hit comedy of a World War II submarine commander attempting to make his submersible, the USS *Sea Tiger*, seaworthy, then winds up transporting five nurses from the Philippines to Australia—with his all-male crew. Filmed on location aboard the submarine *Balboa* at Key West, FL. One of the 28 top-grossing films of 1959-60, it was remade in 1977 as a TV movie. Eastmancolor.

1930. Operation Secret (Warner; 1952). *Cast:* Cornel Wilde, Steve Cochran, Phyllis Thaxter, Karl Malden, Paul Picerni, Lester Matthews, Dan O'Herlihy, Jay Novello, Ed Foster, Claude Dunkin, Wilton Graff, Baynes Barron, Philip Rush, Robert Shaw, Henry Rowland, Dan Riss, Gayle Kellogg, John Beattie, George Dee, Rudy Rama, Monte Pittman, Tony Eisley, Joe Espirtallier, Harry Arnie, Paula Sowl, Peter Michael, Gary Kettler, John Logan, Thomas Browne Henry, Ted Lawrence, Don Harvey, Roy Jenson, Craig Morland, Elizabeth Flournoy, Harlan Warde, William Leicester, Kenneth Patterson, John Nelson, William Slack, Frank Jaquet, Larry Winter, Gregg Barton, Frances Zucco, Len Hendry, John Marshall, Charles Flynn, John Pickard, Bob Stevenson, George

Magrill, Jack Lomas, Carlo Tricoli, Wayne Taylor. *D:* Lewis Seiler; *P:* Henry Blanke; *St:* Alvin Josephy, John Twist; *Sc:* James R. Webb, Harold Medford. (1:48) World War II drama of an ex–French foreign legionnaire, accused of murdering an officer, who must uncover the real culprit. Based on "The Life of Peter Ortiz," nonfictional material supplied by Lt. Col. Peter Ortiz.

1931. The Opposite Sex (MGM; 1956). *Cast:* June Allyson, Joan Collins, Dolores Gray, Ann Sheridan (final U.S. film), Ann Miller, Leslie Nielsen, Jeff Richards, Agnes Moorehead, Charlotte Greenwood (final film—ret.), Joan Blondell, Sam Levene, Alice Pearce, Bill Goodwin, Barbara Jo Allen [aka: Vera Vague], Carolyn Jones, Alan Marshal, Sandy Descher, Jerry Antes, Dick Shawn (film debut), Jim Backus, Harry James (himself), Art Mooney (himself), Dean Jones, Jonathan Hale, Celia Lovsky, Harry McKenna, Ann Moriss, Kay English, Gordon Richards, Barrie Chase, Ellen Ray, Gail Bonney, Maxine Semon, Jean Andren, Bob Hopkins, Janet Lake, Jo Gilbert, Donald Dillaway, Joe Karnes, Juanita Moore, Vivian Marshall, Marc Wilder, Marjorie Hellen, Trio Ariston. *D:* David Miller; *P:* Joe Pasternak; *Sc:* Fay and Michael Kanin; *Songs:* Title song, "Dere's Yellow Gold on de Trees (De Bananas)," "A Perfect Love," "Rock and Roll Tumbleweed," "Now! Baby, Now," "Jungle Red" and "Young Man with a Horn" Nicholas Brodszky–Sammy Cahn–George Stoll–Ralph Freed. (1:57) (video/laserdisc) Men and music invade this critically panned reworked remake of Clare Boothe's 1936 play *The Women*, filmed before under that title in 1939 by this studio. MetroColor and CinemaScope.

1932. Oregon Passage (Allied Artists/Lindsley Parsons Prods.; 1957). *Cast:* John Ericson, Lola Albright, Toni Gerry, Edward Platt, Judith Ames, H.M. Wynant, Jon Shepodd, Walter Barnes, Paul Fierro, Harvey Stephens. *D:* Paul Landres; *P:* Lindsley Parsons; *As.P:* John H. Burrows; *Sc:* Jack DeWitt. (1:22) A cavalry officer with a lack of understanding of Indian ways and warfare brings hostilities to the frontier. Adapted from the novel by Gordon D. Shirreffs, it was photographed in DeLuxe color and CinemaScope.

1933. The Oregon Trail (20th Century-Fox/Associated Producers, Inc.; 1959). *Cast:* Fred MacMurray, William Bishop (final film—d. 1959), Nina Shipman, Gloria Talbott, Henry Hull, John Carradine, John Dierkes, Elizabeth Patterson, James Bell, Ralph Sanford, Tex Terry, Arvo Ojala, Roxene Wells, Gene N. Fowler, John Slosser, Sherry Spalding, Ollie O'Toole, Ed Wright, Oscar Beregei, Addison Richards (President Polk), Lumsden Hare. *D:* Gene Fowler, Jr.; *P:* Richard Einfeld; *St:* Louis Vittes; *Sc:* Vittes, Fowler, Jr.; *Songs:* "Ballad of the Oregon Trail" Paul Dunlap, Charles Devlan; "Never Alone" Will Miller. (1:26) Western of a New York newspaperman sent west to investigate whether the U.S. government is sending troops, disguised as settlers, to deal with the English dispute over ownership of the Oregon Territory in 1846. The film finale is an all-out assault by Indians on Fort Laramie. DeLuxe color and CinemaScope. Note: Iron Eyes Cody was the technical advisor.

O'Rourke of the Royal Mounted (G.B. title) *see* **Saskatchewan**

1934. Othello (United Artists/Mercury; 1952). *Cast:* Orson Welles, Michael MacLiammpir, Suzanne Cloutier, Robert Coote, Hilton Edwards, Michael Lawrence, Fay Compton, Nicholas Bruce, Jean Davis, Doris Dowling, Joseph Cotten, Joan Fontaine. *D:-P: & Sc:* Orson Welles (based on William Shakespeare's play). (1:32) (video/laserdisc) Shakespearean drama of the Moor of Venice (Welles) who murders his beloved Desdemona (Cloutier) after believing lies of infidelity from his best friend, Iago (MacLiammpir). Three years in production, it was critically panned on release. A film notable for the fact that Welles took pay from making other movies to finance this production. A co-production of Italy, France and the U.S.A. Other production of this story include: Italy (1914–4 reels), Germany (1922–8 reels), Russia (1960), Great Britain (1965), a 1986 Italian opera and Great Britain (1996). Restored and re-released in 1992.

1935. The Other Woman (20th Century–Fox; 1954). *Cast:* Hugo Haas, Cleo Moore, Lance Fuller, Lucille Barkley, Jack Macy, John Qualen, Jan Arvan, Karolee Kelly, Steve Mitchell, Mark Lowell, Melinda Markey, Sue Casey, Sharon Dexter, Ivan Haas, Jan Englund, Art Marshall. *D:-P: & Sc:* Hugo Haas. (1:21) Melodrama of a producer-director of films who marries a studio boss's daughter and finds himself in a dilemma when another woman, an actress, informs him he is going to be blackmailed.

1936. Our Miss Brooks (Warner/Lute Prods.; 1956). *Cast:* Eve Arden (title role), Gale Gordon, Don Porter, Robert Rockwell, Jane

Morgan, Richard Crenna, Nick Adams, Leonard Smith, Gloria MacMillan, Joe Kearns, William Newell, Philip Van Zandt, Marjorie Bennett, June Blair, Joe Forte, Leo Curley, David Alpert, Herb Vigran, Frank Mitchell. *D:* Al Lewis; *P:* David Weisbart; *Sc:* Joseph Quillan, Lewis (based on an idea by Robert Mann). (1:24) (video) Romantic comedy based on the popular long-running CBS television show of a school teacher's attempts to get the attention of a biology professor, who is tied to his mother's apron strings. Based on characters created by Larry Berns.

1937. Our Very Own (RKO/Samuel Goldwyn; 1950). *Cast:* Ann Blyth (Gail), Farley Granger (Chuck), Joan Evans (Joan), Jane Wyatt (Lois Macaulay), Ann Dvorak (Mrs. Lynch), Donald Cook (final film—ret./Fred Macaulay), Natalie Wood (Penny), Gus Schilling (Frank), Phyllis Kirk (Zaza), Jessie Grayson (Violet), Martin Milner (Bert), Rita Hamilton (Gwendolyn), Ray Teal (Mr. Lynch), Harold Lloyd, Jr. *D:* David Miller; *P:* Samuel Goldwyn; *St: & Sc:* F. Hugh Herbert; *Sound:* (AAN) Goldwyn Sound Dept. (1:33) This melodramatic soaper of how a girl's life is turned upside down when she learns she is adopted went on to become one of the 28 top-grossing films of 1949-50.

Out of the Darkness (G.B. title) *see* **Teenage Caveman**

1937A. Out of This World (Carroll Pictures/Presented by T.R. Kupferman; 1954). *D: & Cin:* Lowell Thomas; *Narrators:* Thomas, Lowell Thomas, Jr. (1:15) Documentary-travelogue of the Thomas's trek over the Himalayan mountains into Tibet in 1949 prior to the communist takeover of China. Photographed with a handheld 16 mm camera, it includes footage of the 15-year-old Dalai Lama, the "Forbidden City" of Lhasa, the great Potala (the lamasery) and Buddhist monks. Color.

Out on Probation *see* **Daddy-O**

The Outcast (1951) (G.B. title) *see* **Man in the Saddle**

1938. The Outcast (Republic; 1954). *Cast:* John Derek, Joan Evans, Jim Davis, Catherine McLeod, Ben Cooper Taylor Holmes, Nana Bryant, Slim Pickens, Frank Ferguson, James Millican, Bob Steele, Nacho Galindo, Harry Carey, Jr., Robert "Buzz" Henry, Nicolas Koster. *D:* William Witney; *P:* William J. O'Sullivan; *Sc:* John K. Butler, Richard Wormser. (1:30) (video) Western drama of a young man who comes up against his uncle when he attempts to gain his father's ranch, his rightful inheritance. Based on the short story "Red Horizon" which appeared in *Esquire* and the novel *Two-Edged Vengeance*, both by Todhunter Ballard [pseudonym of W.T. Ballard]. Trucolor. (G.B. title: *The Fortune Hunter*)

1939. Outcast of Black Mesa (Columbia; 1950). *Cast:* Charles Starrett, Martha Hyer, Smiley Burnette, Richard Bailey, Stanley Andrews, Lane Chandler, Chuck Roberson, William Haade, Robert Wilke, William Gould, Ozie Waters and His Colorado Rangers. *D:* Ray Nazarro; *P:* Colbert Clark; *St:* Elmer Clifton; *Sc:* Barry Shipman. (0:54) A "Durango Kid" series western of crooks out to steal a gold mine. Includes much stock footage. (G.B. title: *The Clue*) Originally paired with *State Penitentiary* (q.v.) on a double feature program.

1940. The Outcasts of Poker Flat (20th Century–Fox; 1952). *Cast:* Anne Baxter, Dale Robertson, Miriam Hopkins, Cameron Mitchell, Craig Hill, Barbara Bates, Billy Lynn, Dick Rich, Russ Conway, Bob Adler, John Ridgely, Harry Shannon, Lee Phelps, Harry Carter, Tom Greenway, Harry Harvey, Jr. *D:* Joseph M. Newman; *P:* Julian Blaustein; *Sc:* Edmund H. North. (1:21) Western drama of undesirables, forced from a western mining town, who take refuge in an isolated mountain cabin during a snowstorm. Based on "The Outcasts of Poker Flat" and "The Luck of Roaring Camp," two stories by Bret Harte. Previously filmed in 1919 by Universal with Harry Carey and again in 1937 by RKO.

1941. Outcasts of the City (Republic/Lorraine Prods.; 1958). *Cast:* Osa Massen (final film—ret.), Robert Hutton, Maria Palmer, Nestor Paiva, John Hamilton, George Neise, Leon Tyler, Larry Blake, Norbert Schiller, Michael Dale, George Sanders (voice only/G.I. announcer), John Close, John Clark, John Harding, James Wilson. *D: & P:* Boris L. Petroff; *Ex.P:* James F. Boccardo; *As.P:* Joe Juliano; *Sc:* Stephen Longstreet; *Song:* "This Is Forever" Victor Young, Stan Freberg (sung by Leda Annest). (1:01) Postwar Germany is the setting for this romantic-melodrama of an American lieutenant who falls for a German fraulein.

The Outlaw and the Lady (G.B. title) *see* **Waco**

Outlaw Fury *see* **Hostile Country**

1942. Outlaw Gold (Monogram; 1950). *Cast:* Johnny Mack Brown, Jane Adams, Myron Healey, Milburn Morante, Marshall Reed, Hugh Prosser, Carol Henry, Bud Osborne, George DeNormand, Frank Jaquet, Carl Mathews, Ray Jones, Steve Clark, Bob Woodward, Merrill McCormack. *D:* Wallace Fox; *P:* Vincent M. Fennelly; *St: & Sc:* Jack Lewis. (0:51) One of Brown's series westerns for this studio, this one dealing with stolen Mexican gold shipments.

1943. Outlaw Queen (Independent; 1957). *Cast:* Andrea King, Harry James, Robert Clarke, Jim Harakas, Ande Lodas, Kenne Duncan. *D:* Herbert Greene; *St: & Sc:* Pete LaRoche. (1:10) An obscure low budget western.

1944. The Outlaw Stallion (Columbia; 1954). *Cast:* Phil Carey, Dorothy Patrick, Billy Gray, Roy Roberts, Gordon Jones, Trevor Bardette, Chris Alcaide, Morris Ankrum, Harry Harvey, Sr., Robert Anderson, Guy Teague, Beauty (horse—received 1955 PATSY Award of Excellence). *D:* Fred F. Sears; *P:* Wallace MacDonald; *St: & Sc:* David Lang. (1:04) Western drama of an outlaw's planned revenge against a family of ranchers. (aka: *The White Stallion*) Technicolor.

Outlaw Territory *see* **Hannah Lee**

1945. Outlaw Treasure (American Releasing Corp./Royal Western Prods.; 1955). *Cast:* John [Carpenter] Forbes (dual role), Adele Jergens, Frank "Red" Carpenter, Glenn Langan, Michael Whalen, Harry Lauter, Frank Jenks, Hal Baylor. *D:* Oliver Drake; *P:-St: & Sc:* John Carpenter. (1:07) Low budget indie oater of an army man sent to recover missing gold shipments.

1946. Outlaw Women (Lippert/Howco; 1952). *Cast:* Marie Windsor, Richard Rober, Allan Nixon, Carla Balenda, Jackie Coogan, Maria Hart, Jacqueline Fontaine, Billy House, Richard Avonde, Leonard Penn, Lyle Talbot, Brad Johnson, Tom Tyler, Angela Stevens, Ted Cooper, Riley Hill. *D:* Sam Newfield, Ron Ormond; *P:* Ormond; *As.P:* June Carr; *St: & Sc:* Orville Hampton; *Songs:* "Frisco Kate" Ben Young; "Crazy Over You" Carr (both sung by Fontaine). (1:15) Western of a gambler elected to the post of U.S. marshal who sets out to rid the town of "Iron" Mae McLeod and her ruthless contingent of female cohorts. Cinecolor.

1947. The Outlaw's Daughter (20th Century-Fox/Alplee Pictures; 1954). *Cast:* Bill Williams, Jim Davis, Kelly Ryan, George Cleveland (final film—to TV as "Gramps" on "Lassie"—d. 1957), Elisha Cook, Jr., Guinn Williams, Sara Haden, Nelson Leigh, George Barrows, Zon Murray, Zabuda, Dick [Richard] Powers [aka: Tom Keene], Regina Gleason, Sam Flint, Paul Stader, Danny Fisher, Eugene Anderson, Jr. *D: & P:* Wesley Barry; *St: & Sc:* Sam Roeca. (1:15) Because of his infamous past as an outlaw, a man's granddaughter becomes suspect in a stagecoach robbery. A low budget western with a questionable title. Eastmancolor.

1948. Outlaws of Texas (Monogram; 1950). *Cast:* Whip Wilson, Andy Clyde, Phyllis Coates, Terry Frost, Tom Farrell, Zon Murray, George DeNormand, Steve Carr, Stanley Price. *D:* Thomas Carr; *P:* Vincent M. Fennelly; *St: & Sc:* Daniel B. Ullman. (0:56) In this series western, two U.S. marshals pose as outlaws to expose a gang of bank robbers headed by a woman.

1949. The Outlaw's Son (United Artists/Bel-Air-Palm Prods.; 1957). *Cast:* Dane Clark (final film appearance until 1970), Ben Cooper, Lori Nelson, Ellen Drew (final film—ret.), Charles Watts, Cecile Rogers, Eddie Foy III, John Pickard, Robert Knapp, Les Mitchell, Joseph "Bucko" Stafford, Guy Prescott, George Pembroke, Jeff Daley, James Parnell, Wendy Stuart, Anna Maria Nanasi, Scott Peters, Buddy Hart, Ernie Dotson, Ken Christy, Audley Anderson, Leslie Kimmell. *D:* Lesley Selander; *P:* Aubrey Schenck; *Sc:* Richard Alan Simmons. (1:29) Western melodrama of a father who returns, after having served a prison term, to save his now grown son from living his life as an outlaw. Based on Clifton Adams' novel *Gambling Man*.

1950. Outrage (RKO/Filmakers; 1950). *Cast:* Mala Powers, Tod Andrews, Robert Clarke, Raymond Bond, Lillian Hamilton, Rita Lupino, Hal March, Kenneth Patterson, Jerry Paris (film debut), Angela Clarke, Roy Engel, Lovyss Bradley, Robin Camp, William Challee, Tristram Coffin, Jerry Hausner, Bernie Marcus, Joyce McCluskey, Albert Mellen, John Morgan, Victor Perrin, John Pelletti, Beatrice Warde. *D:* Ida Lupino; *P:* Collier Young; *St: & Sc:* Lupino, Malvin Wald, Young. (1:15) After a young woman is raped in a small town, she cannot cope with the reactions of her friends and neighbors and moves to another state, where she assumes a new identity. An offbeat melodrama for its day, it originally was paired on a double bill with Tim Holt's *Border Treasure* (q.v.).

1951. The Outriders (MGM; 1950). *Cast:* Joel McCrea, Arlene Dahl, Barry Sullivan, Claude Jarman, Jr., James Whitmore, Ramon Novarro, Jeff Corey, Ted de Corsia, Martin Garralaga. *D:* Roy Rowland; *P:* Richard Goldstone; *St: & Sc:* Irving Ravetch. (1:33) Civil War–era western of rebel soldiers out to rob a gold shipment to further extend the cause of the confederacy. Technicolor. Note: From its beginning in the late 1920s, MGM made few films in the western genre until the 1949 success of *Ambush*, which caused studio heads to change the direction of their thinking. Unfortunately it came just prior to the genre as a whole taking its first decline.

1952. Outside the Law (Universal-International; 1956). *Cast:* Ray Danton, Leigh Snowden, Grant Williams, Onslow Stevens, Raymond Bailey, Judson Pratt, Jack Kruschen, Floyd Simmons, Mel Welles, Alexander Campbell, Karen Verne, Maurice Doner, Jesse B. Kirkpatrick, Arthur Ranson, Richard H. Cutting, George Mather, Amapola Del Vando, Vernon Rich. *D:* Jack Arnold; *P:* Albert J. Cohen; *St:* Peter R. Brooke; *Sc:* Danny Arnold. (1:21) Melodrama of a G.I. brought back from overseas duty to help round up a gang of counterfeiters.

1953. Outside the Wall (Universal-International; 1950). *Cast:* Richard Basehart, Marilyn Maxwell, Signe Hasso, Dorothy Hart, Joseph Pevney, John Hoyt, Henry [Harry] Morgan, Lloyd Gough, Mickey Knox. *D:* Crane Wilbur; *P:* Aaron Rosenberg; *St:* Henry Edward Helseth; *Sc:* Wilbur. (1:20) Melodrama of an ex-con attempting to go straight and the influences he encounters, which tend to lead him back from whence he came.

1954. Over-Exposed (Columbia; 1956). *Cast:* Cleo Moore, Richard Crenna, Isobel Elsom, Raymond Greenleaf, James O'Rear, Shirley Thomas (herself), Donald Randolph, Dayton Lummis, Jeanne Cooper, Jack Albertson, William McLean, Edna M. Holland, Edwin Parker, John Cason, Dick Crockett, Geraldine Hall, Voltaire Perkins, Joan Miller, Helen Eby-Rock, Norma Brooks, Robert B. Williams, Frank Mitchell. *D:* Lewis Seiler; *P:* Lewis J. Rachmil; *St:* Richard Sale, Mary Loos; *Sc:* James Gunn, Gil Orlovitz. (1:20) Melodrama of a female commercial photographer and her rise to fame in her profession. Originally the top of a double bill with *Uranium Boom* (q.v.).

1955. Over the Border (Monogram; 1950). *Cast:* Johnny Mack Brown, Myron Healey, Marshall Reed, Mike Ragan [aka: Holly Bane], House Peters, Jr., Wendy Waldron, Pierre Watkin, Hank Bell, George DeNormand, Milburn Morante, Frank Jaquet, Buck Bailey, George Sowards, Carol Henry, Frank McCarroll, Bud Osborne, Herman Hack, Ray Jones, Artie Ortego, Bob Woodward. *D: & P:* Wallace Fox; *Sc:* J. Benton Cheney. (0:58) Another of Brown's series entries for Monogram, with a Wells Fargo agent investigating the smuggling of silver from Mexico.

1956. Overland Pacific (United Artists/ Reliance Pictures–Superior Pictures; 1954). *Cast:* Jack [Jock] Mahoney, Peggie Castle, William Bishop, Adele Jergens, Chubby Johnson, Walter Sande, Pat Hogan, Chris Alcaide, George Eldredge, Phil Chambers, Dick Rich, House Peters, Jr. *D:* Fred F. Sears; *P:* Edward Small; *St:* Frederic Louis Fox; *Sc:* J. Robert Bren, Gladys Atwater, Martin Goldsmith. (1:13) A railroad investigator is called in to ferret out the reason Comanche Indians are leading attacks on the new railroad being laid through their territory. Color Corp. of America.

1957. Overland Telegraph (RKO; 1951). *Cast:* Tim Holt, Richard Martin, Gail Davis, Hugh Beaumont, Mari Blanchard, George Nader, Robert Wilke, Fred Graham, Cliff Clark, Russell Hicks, Robert Bray. *D:* Lesley Selander; *P:* Herman Schlom; *St:* Carroll Young; *Sc:* Adele Buffington. (1:00) A cowboy is falsely accused in the death of a telegraph lineman. An entry in Holt's RKO series.

1958. The Pace That Thrills (RKO; 1952). *Cast:* Bill Williams, Carla Balenda, Robert Armstrong, Frank McHugh, Steven Flagg [aka: Michael St. Angel], Cleo Moore, John Mallory, Diane Garrett, John Hamilton, Claudia Drake. *D:* Leon Barsha; *P:* Lewis J. Rachmil; *St: & Sc:* DeVallon Scott, Robert Lee Johnson. (1:03) Low budget action-melodrama of two men, one a designer, the other a tester of motorcycles at a factory who both love the same girl. Complete with racing footage filler. Originally ran as a 2nd feature on a double bill with *The Story of Robin Hood* (q.v.). Note: John Mallory is the younger brother of Robert Mitchum.

1959. Pack Train (Columbia/Gene Autry Prods.; 1953). *Cast:* Gene Autry, Gail Davis, Smiley Burnette, Kenne Duncan, Sheila Ryan, Tom London, Harry Lauter, Melinda Plowman, B.G. Norman, Louise Lorimer, Frankie Marvin, Norman E. Westcott, Tex Terry, Wesley Hudman, Kermit Maynard, Frank Ellis, Dick Alexander, Frank O'Connor, Jill Zeller, Herman Hack, Champion (horse). *D:* George Archainbaud; *P:* Armand Schaefer; *St: & Sc:* Norman S. Hall; *Songs:* "God's Little Candles," "Wagon Train" Jimmy Kemecky, Gene Autry; "Hominy Grits" Smiley Burnette. (0:57) Gene deals with crooked merchants who try to sell supplies to gold miners at inflated prices, instead of to settlers who need the goods. Sepiatone.

1960. Pagan Love Song (MGM; 1950). *Cast:* Esther Williams, Howard Keel, Rita Moreno, Minna Gombell, Charles Mauu, Philip Costa, Dione Leilani, Charles Freund, Marcella Corday, Sam Maikai, Helen Rapoza, Birdie DeBolt, Bill Kaliloa, Carlo Cook. *D:* Robert Alton (2nd of 2 films); *P:* Arthur Freed; *Sc:* Robert Nathan, Jerry Davis; *Songs:* "The House of Singing Bamboo," "Singing in the Sun," "Etiquette," "Why Is Love So Crazy?," "Tahiti," "The Sea of the Moon" Harry Warren, Arthur Freed; "Pagan Love Song" (written in 1929) Nacio Herb Brown, Freed; "Coconut Milk" Roger Edens. (1:16) (video) Romance and songs on the Pacific isle of Tahiti. In Technicolor, this box office fizzle was based on William S. Stone's 1946 book *Tahiti Landfall.*

1961. Paid in Full (Paramount; 1950). *Cast:* Robert Cummings, Lizabeth Scott, Diana Lynn, Eve Arden, Ray Collins, Frank McHugh, Stanley Ridges, Louis Jean Heydt, John Bromfield, Kristine Miller, Carol Channing (film debut), Laura Elliot, Ida Moore, James Nolan, Geraldine Wall, Rolland Morris, Lora Lee Michel, Jane Novak, Margaret Field, Carole Mathews, Dorothy Adams, Arlene Jenkins, Christine Cooper, Byron Barr, Marie Blake [aka: Blossom Rock], Jimmie Dundee, Gladys Bale, Douglas Spencer, Dewey Robinson, Charles Bradstreet, Harry Cheshire. *D:* William Dieterle; *P:* Hal B. Wallis; *Sc:* Robert Blees, Charles Schnee. (1:45) Soaper of two sisters who love the same man, one feeling responsible for the death of the child of the other, who gets pregnant to replace the child, knowing full well she will die giving birth. Based on a nonfiction article by Dr. Frederic M. Loomis which appeared in *Reader's Digest* in 1946.

1962. The Painted Hills (MGM; 1951). *Cast:* Lassie, Paul Kelly, Bruce Cowling, Gary Gray, Art Smith, Ann Doran, Chief Yowlachie, Andrea Virginia Lester, Brown Jug [Don Kay] Reynolds. *D:* Harold F. Kress; *P:* Chester M. Franklin; *Sc:* True Boardman. (1:05) (video) Family drama, with a western setting, of a collie named Shep attempting to find his master's killer with the help of a young boy. In Technicolor, it was based on the 1930 novel *Shep of the Painted Hills* by Alexander Hull. (aka: *Lassie's Adventures in the Gold Rush*)

1963. Painting the Clouds with Sunshine (Warner; 1951). *Cast:* Dennis Morgan, Virginia Mayo, Gene Nelson, Virginia Gibson, Tom Conway, Lucille Norman, Wallace Ford, Tom Dugan, Jack Law, S.Z. Sakall, Abe Dinovitch, Harry Mendoza, Dolores Castle, Tristram Coffin, Eddie Acuff, Jack Daley, Brick Sullivan, Paul Gustine, Donald Kerr, Garrett Marks, Joe Recht, Crauford Kent, Frank Dae, William Vedder. *D:* David Butler; *P:* William Jacobs; *Sc:* Harry Clork, Roland Kibbee, Peter Milne; *Songs include:* Title song, "Tip-Toe Through the Tulips" Al Dubin, Joe Burke; "Vienna Dreams" Irving Caesar, Rudolf Sieczy; "With a Song in My Heart" Richard Rodgers, Lorenz Hart; "Birth of the Blues" B.G. DeSylva, Lew Brown, Ray Henderson; "You're My Everything" Harry Warren, Mort Dixon; "Jealousy" Vera Bloom, Jacob Gabe; "Man Is a Necessary Evil" Jack Elliott, Sonny Burke. (1:27) Technicolor musical of three girls in search of wealthy husbands. Based on Avery Hopwood's 1919 play *Gold Diggers,* first filmed by this studio in 1923. A remake of *Gold Diggers of Broadway* (1929) and *Gold Diggers of 1933* (1933), both by this studio.

1964. The Pajama Game (Warner/Abbott–Donen; 1957). *Cast:* Doris Day, John Raitt (only starring film role, repeating his stage role), Carol Haney (repeating stage role), Eddie Foy, Jr. (repeating stage role), Reta Shaw (repeating stage role), Barbara Nichols, Thelma Pelish (repeating stage role), Jack Straw, Ralph Dunn (repeating stage role), Owen Martin, Jackie Kelk, Ralph Chambers (repeating stage role), Mary Stanton, Jack Waldron (repeating stage role), Ralph Volkie, Franklyn Fox, William A. Forester, Buzz Miller (repeating stage role), Kenneth LeRoy (repeating stage role), Peter Gennaro (repeating stage role), Elmore Henderson, Fred Villani, Kathy Marlowe, Otis Griffith. *D: & P:* George Abbott, Stanley Donen; *As.P:* Frederick Brisson, Robert E. Griffith, Harold S. Prince; *Sc:* Abbott, Richard Bissell; *Choreography:* Bob

Fosse; *Songs:* Title song, "I'm Not at All in Love," "Hey There," "Once-A-Year-Day," "Small Talk," "There Once Was a Man," "Steam Heat," "Hernando's Hideaway," "Seven and a Half Cents," "Her Is," "Racing with the Clock" and "I'll Never Be Jealous Again" Richard Adler, Jerry Ross. (1:41) (video/laserdisc) Hit musical, based on the 1954 Broadway hit, of pajama factory workers seeking a 7½ cent raise. Based on Richard Bissell's novel *7½ Cents*, it was in WarnerColor and placed #10 on the "10 Best" list of *Film Daily.*

1965. Pal Joey (Columbia/Essex–George Sidney Prod.; 1957). *Cast:* Frank Sinatra (Joey Evans), Rita Hayworth (Vera Simpson), Kim Novak (Linda English), Barbara Nichols (Gladys), Bobby Sherwood (Ned Galvin), Hank Henry (Mike Miggins), Elizabeth Patterson (Mrs. Casey), Robin Morse (bartender), Frank Wilcox (Col. Langley), Pierre Watkin (Mr. Forsythe), Barry Bernard (Anderson), Ellie Kent (Carol), Mara McAfee (Sabrina), Betty Utey (Patsy), Bek Nelson (Lola), Tol Avery (detective), John Hubbard (Stanley), James Seay (Livingstone), Henry McCann (Shorty), Ernesto Milinari (Chef Tony), Jean Corbett, Robert Anderson, Everett Glass, Frank Sully, George Nardelli, Giselle D'Arc, Bess Flowers, Franklyn Farnum, Hermes Pan (who also choreographed). *D:* George Sidney; *P:* Fred Kohlmar; *Sc:* Dorothy Kingsley; *Songs include:* "The Lady Is a Tramp," "Bewitched, Bothered and Bewildered," "My Funny Valentine," "Small Hotel" Richard Rodgers, Lorenz Hart; *ASD:* (AAN-color) Walter Holscher (art director), William Kiernan, Louis Diage (sets); *Costumes:* (AAN-color) Jean Louis; *Editors:* (AAN) Viola Lawrence, Jerome Thoms; *Sound:* (AAN) John Livadary. (1:51) (video/laserdisc) Musical with a romantic triangle of a singer endeavoring to open his own night club. Based on the 1941 play by John O'Hara, it became one of the 26 top-grossing films of 1957-58. Technicolor.

Pale Arrow (G.B. title) *see* **Pawnee**

1966. The Palomino (Columbia; 1950). *Cast:* Jerome Courtland, Beverly Tyler, Joseph Calleia, Roy Roberts, Tom Trout, Gordon Jones, Trevor Bardette, Robert Osterloh, Harry Garcia, Juan Duval, California (horse, received #2 PATSY Award in 1951). *D:* Ray Nazarro; *P:* Robert Cohn; *St: & Sc:* Tom Kilpatrick. (1:13) Family western of a cattleman helping a girl whose prize palomino horse was stolen. (G.B. title: *Hills of the Brave*) Technicolor.

1967. Pals of the Golden West (Republic; 1951). *Cast:* Roy Rogers, Dale Evans (final film—to TV), Estelita Rodriguez, Pinky Lee, Roy Barcroft, Anthony Caruso, Eduardo Jimenez, Kenneth Terrell, Emmett Vogan, The Roy Rogers Riders, Maurice Jara, Trigger (horse), Bullet (dog). *D:* William Witney; *P:* Edward J. "Eddy" White; *St:* Sloan Nibley; *Sc:* Albert DeMond, Eric Taylor; *Songs:* "Slumber Trail," "Beyond the Great Divide," "You Never Know When Love May Come Along" and Title song, Jack Elliott, Aaron Gonzalez, Jordan Smith. (1:08) Notable as Roy Rogers and Dale Evans' final series western. Cattle infected with hoof-and-mouth disease are being smuggled into the United States from Mexico.

1968. Panama Sal (Republic/Vineland Prods.; 1957). *Cast:* Elena Verdugo, Edward Kemmer, Carlos Rivas, Harry Jackson, Joe Flynn, Christine White, Albert Carrier, Jose Gonzales-Gonzales, Billie Bird, Ukonu and His Afro-Calypsonians. *D:* William Witney; *P:* Edward J. White; *St: & Sc:* Arnold Belgard; *Songs:* Joe and Marilyn Hooven. (1:10) Drama of a playboy who meets a singer in Panama and brings her to the states with the intent of making her a singing sensation. Naturama. Originally paired on a double bill with *Eighteen and Anxious* (q.v.).

1969. Panic in the Streets (20th Century–Fox; 1950). *Cast:* Richard Widmark (Clinton Reed), Paul Douglas (Captain Tom Warren), Barbara Bel Geddes (Nancy Reed), Walter [Jack] Palance (Blackie), Zero Mostel (Raymond Fitch), Dan Riss (Neff), Alexis Minotis (John Mefaris), Guy Thomajan (Poldi), Tommy Cook (Vince Poldi), Edward Kennedy (Jordan), H.T. Tsiang (cook), Lewis Charles (Kochak), Raymond Muller (Dubin), Tommy Rettig (Tommy Reed), Lenka Peterson (Jeanette), Pat Walshe (Pat), Paul Hostetler (Dr. Paul Gafney), George Ehmig (Kleber), John Schilleci (Lee), Waldo Pitkin (Ben), Leo Zinser (Sgt. Phelps), Beverly C. Brown (Dr. Mackey), William Dean (Cortelyou), H. Waller Fowler, Jr. (Murray), Red Moad (Wynant), Irvine Vidacovich (Johnston), Val Winter (Commander Dan Quinn), Wilson Bourg, Jr. (Charlie), Mary Liswood (Angie Fitch), Aline Stevens (Rita Mefaris), Stanley J. Reyes (Redfield), Darwin Greenfield (Violet), Emile Meyer (Capt. Beauclyde), Herman Cottman (Scott), Al Theriot (Al), Henry Mamet (Anson), Juan Villasana, Robert Dorsen, Tiger Joe Marsh, Arthur Tong. *D:* Elia Kazan; *P:* Sol C. Siegel; *Stories:* (AA) "Quarantine" and "Some Like 'em Cold" Edward and Edna Anhalt; *Sc:* Richard Murphy, Daniel Fuchs. (1:33) (video) Acclaimed drama of the state of desperation that ensues when a man murdered on the docks of New Orleans is found to be infected with bubonic plague. It garnered the "International Prize" at the Venice Film Festival and placed #7 on the "10 Best" list of the NBR.

Panther's Moon (G.B. title) *see* **Spy Hunt**

1970. Paratroop Command (American International/Santa Rosa Prods.; 1959). *Cast:* Richard Bakalyan, Ken Lynch, Jack Hogan, Jimmy Murphy, Jeff Morris, Jim Beck, Carolyn Hughes, Patricia Huston, Paul Busch, Sid Lassick, Brad Trumball. *D:* William Witney; *P:-St: & Sc:* Stanley Shpetner. (1:23) (video) World War II drama of paratroopers landing in North Africa during the 1942 invasion and one in the company who appears to be a jinx. Originally released on a double bill with *Submarine Seahawk* (q.v.).

1971. Pardners (Paramount/York Pictures; 1956). *Cast:* Dean Martin, Jerry Lewis, Lori Nelson, Jeff Morrow, Jackie Loughery, Agnes Moorehead, John Baragrey, Lon Chaney, Jr., Lee Van Cleef, Jack Elam, Mickey Finn, Douglas Spencer, Philip Tonge, Bob Steele, Scott Douglas, Stuart Randall, Richard Aherne, Milton Frome, Emory Parnell, Dorothy Ford, Frances Mercer, William Forrest, James Parnell, Mary Newton, Charles Stevens, Len Hendry, Valerie Allen, Johnstone White, Gavin Gordon, Robert Brubaker, Tony Michael, Elaine Riley, Ann McCrea, Don House, Frank Cordell, Robert Garvey, Keith Wilson, Stanley Blystone, Hank Mann, Bobby Barber. *D:* Norman Taurog; *P:* Paul Jones; *St:* Jerry Davis, Jr.; *Sc:* Sidney Sheldon; *Songs:* "Buckskin Beauty," "Pardners," "The Wind! The Wind!" and "Me 'n You 'n the Moon" Jimmy Van Heusen, Sammy Cahn. (1:30) (video) Hit western comedy spoof of an eastern millionaire who goes west and, one way or the other, cleans up the bad guys in town. A remake of this studio's 1936 production *Rhythm on the Range*, which was based on a story by Merwin J. Houser. Technicolor and VistaVision.

1972. Pardon My French (United Artists/Cusick Intl. Films; 1951). *Cast:* Paul Henreid, Merle Oberon, Paul Bonifas, Maximilieene, Jim Gerald, Alexandre Rignault, Marital Rebe, Dora Doll, Lauria Daryl, Lucien Callemand, Victor Merenda, Gilbert Defoucault, Marina, Gerard Rosset, Albert Cullaz, Andre Aversa, Nicole Monnin. *D:* Bernard Vorhaus (final U.S. film—blacklisted); *P:* Peter Cusick, Andre Sarrut; *St: & Sc:* Roland Kibbee. (1:21) Romantic comedy of a prim schoolteacher of Bostonian extraction who inherits a mansion in France and when arriving to claim it, finds it is full of poor French families. A co-production of France and the U.S.A., it was filmed on location in the former. (G.B. title: *The Lady from Boston*)

1973. Paris Follies of 1956 (Allied Artists/Ohio Films, Inc.; 1955). *Cast:* Forrest Tucker, Margaret Whiting, Dick Wesson, Martha Hyer, Barbara Whiting, Lloyd Corrigan, Wally Cassell, Fluff Charlton, James Ferris, William Henry, The Sportsmen (themselves), Frank Parker (himself). *D:* Leslie Goodwins (final film as a solo director); *P:* Bernard Tabakin; *St: & Sc:* Milton Lazarus; *Songs:* "Can This Be Love?," "I Love a Circus," "Have You Ever Been in Paris?," "I'm All Aglow Again," "I'm in the Mood Tonight" Pony Sherrell–Phil Moody, and "The Hum Song" Sid Kuller. (1:13) Musical of a show's producer who finds that his financial backer is a phony. Filmed on location in five days at Hollywood's "Moulin Rouge." (aka: *Fresh From Paris* and *Showtime*)

1974. Paris Holiday (United Artists/Tolda Prods.; 1958). *Cast:* Bob Hope (Robert Leslie Hunter), Fernandel (Fernydel), Anita Ekberg (Zara), Martha Hyer (Ann McCall), Preston Sturges (Serge Vitry), Andre Morell (American ambassador), Alan Gifford, Maurice Teynac, Yves Brainville, Jean Murat. *D:* Gerd Oswald; *P:* Robert Hope; *As.P:* Cecil Foster Kemp; *St:* Hope; *Sc:* Edmund Beloin, Dean Reisner; *Song:* "Everyday's a Holiday in Paris" Jimmy Van Heusen, Sammy Cahn. (1:40) (video) Hit comedy farce, filmed on location in France and Hollywood, of an American comedian who goes to Paris to buy a screenplay and finds himself mixed up with counterfeiters, murder, and is eventually committed to a mental institution. One of the 26 top-grossing films of 1957-58. Technicolor and Technirama.

1975. Paris Model (Columbia/American Pictures Corp.; 1953). *Cast:* Eva Gabor, Tom Conway, Laurette Luez, Aram Katcher, Bibs Borman, Marilyn Maxwell, Cecil Kellaway, Florence Bates, Robert Bice, Byron Foulger, Paulette Goddard, Leif Erickson, Gloria Christian, Barbara Lawrence, Robert Hutton, El Brendel, Prince Michael Romanoff (himself). *D:* Alfred E. Green; *P:* Albert Zugsmith; *As.P:* Larry Gross; *St: & Sc:* Robert Smith. (1:21) Four short stories, each involving the same designer gown from Paris, which serves its purpose for four different women. Originally ran on the top of a double bill with Gene Autry's *Last of the Pony Riders* (q.v.).

1976. Paris Playboys (Allied Artists; 1954). *Cast:* Leo Gorcey, Huntz Hall (dual role), Veola Vonn, Steven Geray, John Wengraf, Bernard Gorcey, Marianne Lynn, David [Gorcey] Condon, Bennie Bartlett, Alphonse Martell, Gordon Clark, Fritz Feld. *D:* William Beaudine; *P:* Ben Schwalb; *St: & Sc:* Elwood Ullman, Edward Bernds. (1:02) "Bowery Boys" series comedy entry with Sach (Hall) being mistaken for a missing French scientist who has developed a new rocket fuel.

1977. Park Row (United Artists/Samuel Fuller Prods.; 1952). *Cast:* Gene Evans, Mary Welch, Tina Rome, Bela Kovacs, Herbert Heyes, Forrest Taylor, J.M. Kerrigan, George O'Hanlon, Don Orlando, Neyle Morrow, Dick Elliott, Stuart Randall, Dee Pollock, Hal K. Dawson, Charles Horvath, Monk Eastman. *D:-P: & Sc:* Samuel Fuller. (1:23) Fact-based drama of rival newspapers in New York City in 1886—*The New York Globe* of Phineas Mitchell vs. *The Star* of Charity Hackett.

1978. The Parson and the Outlaw (Columbia/Charles R. "Buddy" Rogers; 1957). *Cast:* Anthony Dexter (Billy the Kid), Charles "Buddy" Rogers (final film—ret.), Marie Windsor, Sonny Tufts (Jack Slade), Robert Lowery, Jean Parker, Bob Steele, Madalyn Trahey, Bob Duncan, Bob Gilbert, Jack Owell, John Davis, Joe Sodja, Paul Spahn, Richard Reeves, Herman Pulver. *D:* Oliver Drake; *P:* Robert "Bob" Gilbert, Charles R. "Buddy" Rogers; *St: & Sc:* Drake, John Mantley. (1:11) This low budget western has Billy the Kid on a mission of vengeance. Technicolor.

1979. The Party Crashers (Paramount/William Alland Prods.; 1958). *Cast:* Mark Damon, Robert [Bobby] Driscoll (final film), Connie Stevens, Gary Gray, Bob Padget, Skip Torgerson, Frances Farmer (final film), Denver Pyle, Doris Dowling, Walter Brooke, Gene Persson, Joseph Sonessa, Cathy Lewis, Theodore Davitt, Onslow Stevens. *D:* Bernard Girard; *P:* William Alland; *St:* Alland, Dan Lundberg; *Sc:* Girard, Lundberg. (1:18) Drive-in programmer drama of juvenile delinquents who crash parties for kicks and one who snaps when he catches his mother with another man. Notable as Farmer's only film since 1942 after overcoming a bout with alcoholism and mental instability. Similarly, after this film, due to an inability to find work, Driscoll descended into the world of hard drugs until his death in 1968 at the age of 31.

1980. Party Girl (MGM/Euterpe Prod.; 1958). *Cast:* Robert Taylor, Cyd Charisse, Lee J. Cobb, John Ireland, Kent Smith, Claire Kelly, Corey Allen, David Opatashu, Barbara Lang, Lewis Charles, Kem Dibbs, Patrick McVey, Myrna Hansen, Betty Utey, Jack Lambert, Sam McDaniel, Floyd Simmons, Sydney Smith, Rusty Lane, Michael Dugan, Irving Greenberg, Richard Devine, Georges Saurel, Carl Thayler, Mike Pierce, John Franco, Ken Perry, Barrie Chase, Sanita Pelkey, Sandy Warner, Burt Douglas (voice only), Harry Tom McKenna, Erich Von Stroheim, Jr., Herbert Armstrong, Carmen Phillips, Pat Cawley, Marshall Bradford, Tom Hernandez, David McMahon, Andrew Buck, Aaron Saxon, Vaughn Taylor, Peter Bourne, Vito Scotti, Ralph Smiley, Herbert Lytton, Benny Rubin, Paul Keast, Jerry Schumacher, John Damler, Geraldine Wall, Robert B. Williams, Dolores Reed, David Garcia, Harry Hines, Jack Gargan, Margaret Bert, Hy Anzel, Maggie O'Byrne. *D:* Nicholas Ray; *P:* Joe Pasternak; *St:* Leo Katcher; *Sc:* George Wells; *Title song:* Nicholas Brodszky, Sammy Cahn (sung by Tony Martin). (1:39) (video/laserdisc) 1930s tale of a Chicago lawyer and a showgirl tangled up with the city's underworld who try to make a clean break. A film which has gathered a cult following over the years. Metrocolor and CinemaScope.

1981. Passage West (Paramount/Pine-Thomas; 1951). *Cast:* John Payne, Dennis O'Keefe, Arleen Whelan, Frank Faylen, Dooley Wilson (final film—d. 1953), Mary Anderson, Peter Hansen, Richard Rober, Griff Barnet, Mary Field, Richard Travis, Mary Beth Hughes, Arthur Hunnicutt, Lillian Bronson, Susan Whitney, Paul Fierro, Clint Stuart. *D:* Lewis R. Foster; *P:* William H. Pine, William C. Thomas; *St:* Nedrick Young; *Sc:* Foster. (1:20) Western of a wagon train, carrying members of a religious sect, that is joined by six escaped convicts. (G.B. title: *High Venture*) Technicolor.

1982. Passion (RKO/Film Crest Prod.; 1954). *Cast:* Cornel Wilde, Yvonne DeCarlo (dual role), Raymond Burr, Lon Chaney, Jr., John Qualen, Rudolfo Acosta, Anthony Caruso, Frank DeKova, Peter Coe, John Dierkes, Richard Hale, Rosa Turich, Stuart Whitman, James Kirkwood, Robert Warwick, Belle Mitchell, Alex Montoya,

Zon Murray, Rozene Kemper. *D:* Allan Dwan; *P:* Benedict Bogeaus; *St:* Beatrice A. Dresher, Josef Leytes, Miguel Padilla; *Adaptation:* Howard Estabrook; *Sc:* Leytes, Dresher. (1:24) (video) Technicolor western of old California and a man seeking the killer, or killers, of his family.

1983. Pat and Mike (MGM; 1952). *Cast:* Spencer Tracy (Mike Conovan), Katharine Hepburn (Pat Pemberton), Aldo Ray (Davie Hucko), William Ching (Collier Weld), Sammy White (Barney Grau), George Mathews (Spec Cauley), Loring Smith (Mr. Beminger), Phyllis Povah (Mrs. Beminger), Charles [Bronson] Buchinski (Hank Tasling), Frank Richards (Sam Garsell), Jim Backus (Charles Barry), Joseph E. Bernard (Gibby), Chuck Connors (police captain/film debut), Owen McGiveney (Harry MacWade), Hank Weaver (commentator), Tom Harmon (sportscaster), Gussie Moran (herself), Babe Didrickson Zaharias (herself), Don Budge (himself), Alice Marble (herself), Frank Parker (himself), Betty Hicks (herself), Beverly Hanson (herself), Helen Dettweiler (herself), Lou Lubin, Carl Switzer, William Self, Billy McLean, Frankie Darro, Paul Brinegar, "Tiny" Jimmie Kelly, Mae Clarke, Helen Eby-Rock, Elizabeth Holmes. *D:* George Cukor; *P:* Lawrence Weingarten; *St: & Sc:* (AAN) Ruth Gordon, Garson Kanin. (1:35) (video/laserdisc) Hit comedy of a shady sports promoter, his female protégé and a dimwit boxer. One of the 23 top-grossing films of 1951-52. Computer-colored prints have been produced by Turner Entertainment.

1984. The Pathfinder (Columbia; 1952). *Cast:* George Montgomery, Helena Carter, Jay Silverheels, Walter Kingsford, Rodd Redwing, Elena Verdugo, Bruce Lester, Chief Yowlachie, Stephen Bekassy, Russ Conklin, Ed Coch, Jr., Vi Ingraham, Adele St. Maur. *D:* Sidney Salkow; *P:* Sam Katzman; *Sc:* Robert E. Kent. (1:18) The year 1754 on the North American frontier finds conflict between the British, the French and the Indians. Based on the 1840 book by James Fenimore Cooper. Technicolor.

1985. Paths of Glory (United Artists/ Bryna Picts.–Harris–Kubrick Picts. Corp.; 1957). *Cast:* Kirk Douglas, Ralph Meeker, Adolphe Menjou, George Macready, Wayne Morris, Richard Anderson, Timothy Carey, Susanne Christian, Bert Freed, Joseph Turkel, Peter Capell, Kem Dibbs, Emile Meyer, John Stein, Jerry Hausner, Frederic Bell, Harold Benedict. *D:* Stanley Kubrick; *P:* James B. Harris; *Sc:* Kubrick, Calder Willingham, Jim Thompson. (1:26) (video/laserdisc) Critically acclaimed World War I anti-military drama, set in 1916, of three French soldiers executed for cowardice and the top brass trying to keep the situation hushed up. Based on Humphrey Cobb's 1935 novel, which was based on fact. In nomination at the British Academy Awards, the film was banned in some areas of Europe as well as U.S. military theaters.

1986. Patterns (United Artists/Michael Myerberg–Jed Harris; 1956). *Cast:* Van Heflin, Everett Sloane, Ed Begley, Beatrice Straight, Elizabeth Wilson, Joanna Roos, Elene Kiamos, Shirley Standlee, Ronnie Welsh, Jr., Sally Gracie, Adrienne Moore, Michael Dreyfuss, Elaine Kay. *D:* Fielder Cook (feature directorial debut); *P:* Michael Myerberg; *Sc:* Rod Serling. (1:23) (video) Acclaimed drama of a powerful corporation, its ruthless president and the conflicts between executives. Based on the 1956 "Kraft Theatre" TV play by Mr. Serling. (G.B. title: *Patterns of Power*)

1987. Paula (Columbia; 1952). *Cast:* Loretta Young, Kent Smith, Alexander Knox, Tommy Rettig, Otto Hulett, Will Wright, Raymond Greenleaf, Eula Guy, William Vedder, Ann Doran, Kathryn Card, Sydney Mason, Keith Larsen, Ann Tyrrell, Clark Howat, Roy Engel, Jeanne Bates, Sam Harris, Edwin Parker, Gertrude Astor, Lawrence Williams, Helen Dickson, Richard Gordon. *D:* Rudolph Maté; *P:* Buddy Adler; *St:* Larry Marcus; *Sc:* James Poe, William B. Sackheim. (1:20) Drama of a woman who runs down a young boy with her car, eventually helping him regain his speech. (G.B. title: *The Silent Voice*)

1988. Pawnee (Republic/Hilber Corp.; 1957). *Cast:* George Montgomery, Lola Albright, Bill Williams, Francis J. McDonald, Robert E. Griffin, Dabbs Greer, Kathleen Freeman, Charlotte Austin, Ralph Moody, Anne Barton, Raymond Hatton, Charles Horvath, Robert Nash. *D:* George Waggner (final film—ret.); *P:* Jack J. Gross, Philip N. Krasne; *As.P:* Sol Dolgin; *Sc:* Waggner, Louis Vittes, Endre Bohem. (1:20) Western of a white man raised by Indians who must choose sides when whites decide they want Indian lands for themselves. His tribe attacks a wagon train he is leading on the Oregon Trail. Trucolor. (G.B. title: *Pale Arrow*)

The Pay-Off *see* **T-Bird Gang**

Pay the Devil (G.B. title) *see* **Man in the Shadow**

1989. Payment on Demand (RKO; 1951). *Cast:* Bette Davis, Barry Sullivan, Jane Cowl (final film—d. 1950), Kent Taylor, Betty Lynn, John Sutton, Frances Dee, Peggie Castle, Otto Kruger, Walter Sande, Brett King, Richard Anderson, Natalie Schafer, Katherine Emery, Lisa Golm, Kathleen Ellis, Mack Williams, Ilka Grunning, David Leonard, Barbara Davis, Sherry Merrill, Ruth Lee, Jay Brooks, Lela Bliss, Moroni Olsen. *D:* Curtis Bernhardt; *P:* Jack H. Skirball; *St:* Bruce Manning, Bernhardt; *Adaptation:* Walter N. Reilly; *Sc:* Manning, Bernhardt. (1:30) Drama of a woman's reactions and soul-searching when her husband of twenty years informs her he wants a divorce. The film carried the pre-release title of "Story of Divorce."

1990. The Peacemaker (United Artists/ Hal R. Makelim Prods.; 1956). *Cast:* James Mitchell, Rosemarie Bowe, Jan Merlin, Jess Barker, Hugh Sanders, Herbert Patterson, Dorothy Patrick, Taylor Holmes, Robert Armstrong, Philip Tonge, Wheaton Chambers, David McMahon, Harry Shannon, Jack Holland, Nancy Evans. *D:* Ted Post (directorial debut); *P:* Hal R. Makelim; *Sc:* Hal Richards, Jay Ingram. (1:22) Western of a former gunfighter, turned minister, who settles a dispute between ranchers and farmers in his town. Based on the 1954 novel by Richard Poole [pseudonym of Lee E. Wells]. Originally paired on a double bill with *Gun the Man Down* (q.v.).

1991. Pearl of the South Pacific (RKO/ Film Crest Prods.; 1955). *Cast:* Virginia Mayo, Dennis Morgan, David Farrar, Murvyn Vye, Lance Fuller, Basil Ruysdael, Lisa Montell, Carol Thurston. *D:* Allan Dwan; *P:* Benedict Bogeaus; *St:* Anna Hunger; *Sc:* Jesse Lasky, Jr.; *Additional dialogue:* Talbot Jennings. (1:26) (video) South Sea island melodrama of two crooks intent on getting a stash of black pearls hidden in a grotto and guarded by a large octopus. Technicolor and SuperScope.

1992. Pecos River (Columbia; 1951). *Cast:* Charles Starrett, Dolores Sidener, Smiley Burnette, Jack [Jock] Mahoney, Paul Campbell, Steve Darrell, Zon Murray, Edgar Dearing, Maudie Prickett, Eddie Fetherston, Frank Jenks, Harmonica Bill. *D:* Fred F. Sears; *P:* Colbert Clark; *St: & Sc:* Barry Shipman. (0:55) In this series western, "The Durango Kid" investigates some mail robberies. (G.B. title: *Without Risk*)

1993. Peggy (Universal-International; 1950). *Cast:* Diana Lynn, Charles Coburn, Charlotte Greenwood, Barbara Lawrence, Charles Drake, Rock Hudson, Jerome Cowan, Ann Pearce, Connie Gilchrist, Griff Barnett, Charles Trowbridge, James Todd, Ellen Corby, Peter Brocco, Donna Martell, Jack Gargan, Olan Soule, Marjorie Bennett, Sid Marion, Jack Kelly, Wheaton Chambers, David McMahon, Carl Sklover, John Wald, Robert "Smoki" Whitfield, Dudley Dickerson, Floyd Taylor, James Best, Jim Congdon, Tim Graham, Donald Kerr, Jim Hayes, Bill Cassady, Paul Power, Art Howard, Lucille Barkley, David Alison, Joe Recht, John McKee, Felipe Rock, Michael Ross, Robert G. Anderson, Ralph Montgomery, Jim Leighton, David Stollery, Harold De Garro, Felice Richmond, James Stark, Bill Kennedy, Michael Cisney, George Hoagland, Charles J. Conrad, Bill Walker, James "Jim" Davis, Ivan H. Browning, Mickey McCardle, Roger McKee, Bob DeLauer, Bob Porter, Sonny Howe, Larry Carr, Paul Devry. *D:* Frederick de Cordova; *P:* Ralph Dietrich; *Sc:* George F. Slavin, George W. George. (1:17) Romantic comedy set against the Tournament of Roses Parade in Pasadena, California, and two sisters vying for the title of "Queen" of the parade. Suggested by a story by Leon Ware. Technicolor.

1994. Peking Express (Paramount; 1951). *Cast:* Joseph Cotten, Corinne Calvet, Edmund Gwenn, Marvin Miller, Benson Fong, Soo Yong, Gregory Gaye, Robert W. Lee, Victor Sen Yung, Peter Chong, Harold Fong, Eddie E. Lee, Beal Wong, Leon Lontoc, Lane Nakano, George T. Lee, Wing Foo, Alfredo Santos, Wei Fan Hsueh, James B. Leong, Jung Lim, Rollin Moriyama, Walter Ng, Si Lan Chen, Gregory Merims, William Yip, Vanya Dimitrova, Weaver Levy, Hom Wing Gim. *D:* William Dieterle; *P:* Hal B. Wallis; *St:* Harry Hervey; *Adaptation:* Jules Furthman; *Sc:* John Meredyth Lucas. (1:35) Melodrama of various passengers on a train passing through China that is stopped by Chinese rebels. A remake of *Shanghai Express* (1932), which was also filmed in 1943 as *Night Plane From Chungking.*

1995. The People Against O'Hara (MGM; 1951). *Cast:* Spencer Tracy, Pat O'Brien, Diana Lynn, John Hodiak, Eduardo Ciannelli, James Arness, Yvette Dugay, Jay C. Flippen, William Campbell, Richard Anderson, Henry O'Neill, Arthur Shields, Ann Doran, Emile Meyer, Louise Lorimer, Regis Toomey, Katherine Warren, Paul Bryar, Peter Mamakos, Perdita Chandler, Frank Ferguson, C. Anthony Hughes, Donald Dillaway, Lee Phelps, Lawrence Tolan, Tony Barr, Jan Kayne, Virginia Hewitt, Richard Landry,

"Billy" Vincent, Frankie Hyers, Michael Dugan, Lennie Bremen, Jim Toney, Benny Burt, John Maxwell, Mae Clarke, Paul McGuire, Kay Scott, Angi O. Poulis, Julius Tannen, Dan Foster, Harry Cody, Ned Glass, John Butler, Lou Lubin, Michael Mark, Phyllis Graffeo, Maurice Samuels, Celia Lovsky, Charles [Bronson] Buchinsky, Joyce Otis, "Tiny" Jimmie Kelly, Fred Essler, John Albright, John Sheehan, William Self, Jack Kruschen, Jonathan Cott, William Schallert, Sammy Finn, Brooks Benedict, Frank Sully, Ernesto Morelli, Jeff Richards, George Magrill, Budd [Bill] Wolfe, Bill Fletcher, Richard Bartlett. *D:* John Sturges; *P:* William H. Wright; *Sc:* John Monks, Jr. (1:42) (laserdisc) Courtroom drama involving a noted criminal attorney's unethical behavior during an important trial. Based on the 1950 novel by Eleazar Lipsky.

1996. People Will Talk (20th Century-Fox; 1951). *Cast:* Cary Grant, Jeanne Crain, Finlay Currie, Hume Cronyn, Walter Slezak, Sidney Blackmer, Basil Ruysdael, Katherine Locke, Will Wright, Margaret Hamilton, Esther Somers, Carleton Young, Lawrence Dobkin, Jo Gilbert, Ann Morrison, Julia Dean, Gail Bonney, William Klein, George Offerman, Adele Longmire, Billy House, Al Murphy, Parley Baer, Irene Seidner, Joyce MacKenzie, Maude Wallace, Kay Lavelle, Jack Kelly, Paul Lees, William Mauch, Leon Tyler, Stuart Holmes, Ray Montgomery. *D: & Sc:* Joseph L. Mankiewicz; *P:* Darryl F. Zanuck. (1:50) (video) Comedy-drama of a doctor who marries one of his patients. Based on the 1934 play *Dr. Praetorious* by Curt Goetz, it placed #5 on the "10 Best" list of the *New York Times.*

1997. The Perfect Furlough (Universal-International; 1958). *Cast:* Tony Curtis, Janet Leigh, Linda Cristal, Keenan Wynn, Elaine Stritch, Marcel Dalio, Les Tremayne, Jay Novello, King Donovan, Troy Donahue, Alvy Moore, Gordon Jones, Lilyan Chauvin, Dick Crockett, Eugene Borden, James Lanphier, Marcel Rosseau, Roger Etienne, Manuel Paris, Phil Harvey, Hugh Lawrence, Vernon Rich, Carleton Young, Sheila Keddy, Peter Camlin, Albert Carrier, Genevieve Aumont, Karen Scott, Gail Bonney, Frankie Darro, Jack Chefe, Scotty Groves, Vic Romito. *D:* Blake Edwards; *P:* Robert Arthur; *St: & Sc:* Stanley Shapiro. (1:33) (video) Comedy of a soldier, stationed in the Arctic, who wins a trip to Paris, France, with the inevitable romantic complications ensuing. Eastmancolor and CinemaScope. (G.B. title: *Strictly for Pleasure*)

1998. Perfect Strangers (Warner; 1950). *Cast:* Ginger Rogers, Dennis Morgan, Thelma Ritter, Margalo Gillmore, Paul Ford, Alan Reed, Harry Bellaver, Anthony Ross, Howard Freeman, George Chandler, Frank Conlan, Charles Meredith, Frances Charles, Marjorie Bennett, Paul McVey, Edith Evanson, Whit Bissell, Sumner Getchell, Ford Rainey, Sarah Selby, Alan Wood, Ronnie Tyler, Isabel Withers, Max Mellenger, Boyd Davis, Weldon Heyburn, Ezelle Poule, Mike Lally, Charles Lind, Russell De Vorkin, Donald Kerr, Ned Glass, Paul Dubov, Creighton Hale, John Albright, Frank Marlowe, Ed Coke, Lou Marcelle, Frank Pat Henry, Joleen King, Dick Kipling, Sidney Dubin, Art Miles, Joseph Kerr, Richard Bartell, Frank Cady, Hugh Murray, Pat Mitchell. *D:* Bretaigne Windust; *P:* Jerry Wald; *Adaptation:* George Oppenheimer; *Sc:* Edith Sommer. (1:28) Romantic comedy of a married man and an unmarried lady, both serving as jurors on a murder trial, who find themselves attracted to each other. Based on the 1938 Hungarian play *Twelve in a Box* by Ladislaus Bus-Fekete and the 1941 English translation *Ladies and Gentlemen* by Ben Hecht and Charles MacArthur. (G.B. title: *Too Dangerous to Love*)

1999. A Perilous Journey (Republic; 1953). *Cast:* Vera Ralston, David Brian, Scott Brady, Charles Winninger, Hope Emerson, Eileen Christy, Leif Erickson, Veda Ann Borg, Virginia Grey, Dorothy Ford, Ben Cooper, Kathleen Freeman, Barbara Hayden, Paul Fierro, Angela Greene, John Dierkes, Alden Aldrich, Fred Graham, Trevor Bardette, Richard Reeves, Bob Carney, Charles Evans, Philip Van Zandt, Byron Foulger, Denver Pyle, Harry Tyler, Emil Sitka, Jack O'Shea, Brandon Beach, Frank Hagney, Stanley Blystone, Richard Alexander, Gloria Clark, Charles Cane. *D:* R.G. Springsteen; *P:* William J. O'Sullivan; *Sc:* Richard Wormser. (1:30) 19th century drama of the trials and tribulations suffered by a shipload of 49 women bound for California in search of husbands. Based on the 1940 novel *The Golden Tide* by Vingie Roe.

2000. Perils of the Jungle (Lippert/Commodore Prods.–Artists, Inc.; 1953). *Cast:* Clyde Beatty, Stanley Farrar, Phyllis Coates, John Doucette, Joel Fluellen, Leonard Mudie, Roy E. Glenn, Olaf Hytten, Tudor Owen, Shelby Bacon. *D:* George Blair; *P:* Walter White, Jr., *St: & Sc:* Frank Hart Taussig, Robert T. Smith. (1:03) Famed hunter Clyde Beatty searches for lions in this low budget African jungle adventure.

2001. Perri (Buena Vista/Walt Disney Prods.; 1957). *D:* N. Paul Kenworthy, Jr., Ralph Wright; *Ex.P:* Walt Disney; *P:* Winston Hibler (who also narrates); *Sc:* Wright, Hibler; *Cin:* N. Paul Kenworthy, Jr., Joel Colman, Walter Perkins, William Ratcliffe, James R. Simon, John P. Hermann, David Meyer, Warren E. Garst, Roy E. Disney; *Music:* (AAN) Paul J. Smith; *Songs:* "Break of Day" George Bruns, Hibler; "And Now to Sleep (Lullaby of the Wilderness)" Bruns, Hibler, Wright; "Together Time" Smith, Gil George, Wright Hibler; *Editor:* Jack L. Atwood. (1:15) Disney's first "True-Life Fantasy" incorporates documented wildlife footage with fantasy elements to create a story of the cycles of life through seasonal changes, all played out around a female squirrel named Perri. 200,000 feet of Technicolor film were exposed, to be edited down to the 8,000 feet actually used in the film to create the desired effects. Based on Felix Salten's novel translated into English in 1938 by Barrows Mussey, it was a winner at the box office. Technicolor. Note: Salten was also the author of "Bambi."

2002. The Persuader (Allied Artists/World Wide Pictures; 1957). *Cast:* William Talman (dual role), James Craig, Kristine Miller, Darryl Hickman, Georgia Lee, Alvy Moore, Rhoda Williams, Gregory Walcott, Paul Engel, Nolan Leary, Frank Richards, Jason Johnson, John Milford, Joyce Compton, Leilani Sorenson, Wendy Stuart. *D: & P:* Dick Ross; *St: & Sc:* Curtis Kenyon. (1:12) Western of a lawless town, whose law-abiding citizens are given support by a gun-toting minister, in cleaning out the town's riff-raff.

2003. Pete Kelly's Blues (Warner/Mark VII Prod.; 1955). *Cast:* Jack Webb (Pete Kelly—coronet dubbed by Dick Cathcart/narrator), Janet Leigh (Ivy Conrad), Edmond O'Brien (Fran McCarg), Peggy Lee (AAN/Rose Hopkins), Lee Marvin (Al Gannaway), Andy Devine (George Tennell), Ella Fitzgerald (Maggie Jackson), Martin Milner (Joey Firestone), Jayne Mansfield (film debut/cigarette girl), Than Wyenn (Rudy), Herb Ellis (Bedido), John Dennis (Guy Bettenhouser), Mort Marshall (Cootie Jacobs), Nesdon Booth (squat henchman), William Lazerus (Dako), Dick Cathcart (coronetist), Matty Matlock (clarinetist), Moe Schneider (trombonist), Eddie Miller (saxiphonist), George Van Eps (guitarist), Nick Fatool (drummer), Ray Sherman (pianist), Jud de Naut (bass player), Snub Pollard, The Israelite Spiritual Church Choir of New Orleans. *D: & P:* Jack Webb; *St: & Sc:* Richard L. Breen; *Songs:* Title song, Sammy Cahn, Ray Heindorf (sung by Ella Fitzgerald); "Sing a Song," "He Needs Me" Arthur Hamilton; "Somebody Loves Me," "Sugar" Maceo Pinkard, Sidney Mitchell, Edna Alexander (sung by Peggy Lee); "I Never Knew" Gus Kahn, Ted Fiorito, "Hard-Hearted Hannah" Jack Yellen, Milton Ager, Bob Bigelow, Charles Bates (sung by Fitzgerald); "Bye Bye Blackbird" Mort Dixon, Ray Henderson; "What Can I Say After I Say I'm Sorry?" Walter Donaldson, Abe Lyman; "Oh, Didn't He Ramble" Bob Cole, J. Rosamond Johnson [aka: Will Handy]. (1:35) (video/laserdisc) Drama of a jazz cornetist who locks horns with a Kansas City hoodlum. Set in the 1920s, critics approved the production for its feel for the era. WarnerColor and CinemaScope.

2004. Peter Pan (RKO/Walt Disney Prods.; 1953). *Voices:* Bobby Driscoll (Peter Pan), Kathryn Beaumont (Wendy Darling), Hans Conried (Capt. Hook), Bill Thompson (Mr. Smee), Heather Angel (Mrs. Darling), Paul Collins (Mr. Darling), Tommy Luske (John Darling), Candy Candido (Indian chief), Tom Conway (narrator). *D:* Hamilton Luske, Clyde Geronimi, Wilfred Jackson; *P:* Walt Disney; *St:* Ted Sears, Bill Peet, Joe Rinaldi, Erdman Penner, Winston Hibler, Milt Banta, Ralph Wright; *Songs:* "The Elegant Captain Hook," "What Makes the Red Man Red?," "You Can Fly, You Can Fly, You Can Fly," "Your Mother and Mine" Sammy Fain, Sammy Cahn; "A Pirate's Life" Oliver Wallace, Erdman Penner; "Tee-Dum Tee-Dee" Wallace, Ted Sears, Winston Hibler; "Never Smile at a Crocodile" Frank Churchill, Jack Lawrence. (1:16) (video/laserdisc) Hit animated version of James M. Barrie's 1904 play of the boy who didn't want to grow up and his adventures with the three Darling children against Captain Hook and his pirates in Never-Never land. With a production cost of $4,000,000, appreciative audiences made this one of the 26 top-grossing films of 1952-53. Previously filmed in the silent era by Paramount in 1925 with Betty Bronson in live-action. A live-action production also aired on NBC-TV on December 8, 1960, starring Mary Martin in the title role with Cyril Ritchard as "Capt. Hook." In nomination at the Cannes Film Festival, it was filmed in Technicolor.

2005. The Petty Girl (Columbia; 1950). *Cast:* Robert Cummings, Joan Caulfield, Elsa Lanchester, Melville Cooper, Audrey Long, Frank Orth, Mary Wickes, John Ridgely, Raymond Largay, Ian Wolfe, Frank Jenks, Tim

Ryan, Mabel Paige, Kathleen Howard, Sarah Edwards, Everett Glass, Douglas Wood, Edward Clark, Philip Van Zandt, Movita Casteneda, Lyn Thomas, Dorothy Vaughan, Richard Avonde, Ray Teal, Pat Flaherty, Earl Hodgins, Henry Hall, Russell Hicks, Herbert Heywood, Lois Hall, Mona Knox, Shirley Ballard, Jetsy Parker, Barbara Freking, Shirley Whitney, Claire Dennis, Betsy Crofts, Joan Larkin, Lucille LaMarr, Eileen Howe, Carol Rush, Eloise Farmer, Dorothy Abbott, Tippi Hedren (film debut). *D:* Henry Levin; *P:* & *Sc:* Nat Perrin; *St:* Mary E. McCarthy. (1:27). Comedy of a calendar artist and his pursuit of a female college professor. (G.B. title: *Girl of the Year*) Technicolor.

2006. Peyton Place (20th Century–Fox/ Jerry Wald Prods.; 1957). *Cast:* Lana Turner (AAN/Constance MacKenzie), Hope Lange (AAN/Selena Cross), Lee Phillips (Michael Rossi), Diane Varsi (AAN/Allison MacKenzie), Arthur Kennedy (AAN/Lucas Cross), Russ Tamblyn (AAN/Norman Page), Lloyd Nolan (Dr. Matthew Swain), Terry Moore (Betty Anderson), Barry Coe (Rodney Harrington), David Nelson (Ted Carter), Betty Field (Nellie Cross), Mildred Dunnock (Mrs. Thornton), Leon Ames (Harrington), Lorne Greene (prosecutor), Robert H. Harris (Seth Bushwell), Tami Connor (Margie), Staats Cotsworth (Charles Partridge), Peg Hillias (Marion Partridge), Erin O'Brien-Moore (Mrs. Page), Scotty Morrow (Joey Cross), Bill Lundmark (Paul Cross), Alan Reed, Jr. (Matt), Kip King (Pee Wee), Steffi Sidney (Kathy), Tom Greenway (judge), Edith Claire (Miss Colton), Edwin Jerome (Cory Hyde), Ray Montgomery, Jim Brandt, John Doucette, Alfred Tonkel, Bob Adler, Harry Carter, Michael Lally. *D:* (AAN) Mark Robson; *P:* (AAN-Best Picture) Jerry Wald; *Sc:* (AAN) John Michael Hayes; *Cin:* (AAN-color) William Mellor. (originally 2:42/now 2:37) (video) Soap opera par excellence of what goes on behind closed doors in a small New England town. Based on Grace Metalious' best-selling potboiler, it placed #4 on the "10 Best" list of *Film Daily* and became one of the 26 top-grossing films of 1957-58. Followed by the sequel *Return to Peyton Place* (1961) and a later TV series which had a strong following. DeLuxe color and CinemaScope.

2007. Phantom from Space (United Artists/Planet Film Plays; 1953). *Cast:* Ted Cooper, Rudolph Anders, Noreen Nash, James Seay, Harry Landers, Jim Bannon, Jack Daly, Dick Sands, Lela Nelson, Michael Mark. *D:* & *P:* W. Lee Wilder; *St:* Myles H. Wilder; *Sc:* Bill Raynor, Myles H. Wilder. (1:12) (video) Programmer science fiction of an invisible alien that lands near Los Angeles, creating a state of havoc wherever he goes.

2008. The Phantom from 10,000 Leagues (Associated Releasing Corp.; 1956). *Cast:* Kent Taylor, Cathy Downs, Michael Whalen, Helene Stanton, Philip Pine, Rodney Bell, Pierce Lyden, Vivi Janiss, Michael Garth. *D:* Dan Milner; *P:* Jack Milner, Dan Milner; *St:* Dorys Lukather; *Sc:* Lou Rusoff. (1:20) Science fiction of an oceanographer investigating claims that a large sea monster has been gobbling up the locals. Originally paired on a double bill with *The Day the World Ended* (q.v.).

The Phantom Horseman (G.B. title) *see* **Border Outlaws**

2009. Phantom of the Jungle (Lippert/ Arrow Prods.; 1955). *Cast:* Jon Hall, Ray Montgomery, Anne Gwynne, Kenneth MacDonald, Carleton Young, James Griffith, Nick Stewart, Milton Wood, James Fairfax, M'Liss McClure. *D:* Spencer Gordon Bennet; *P:* Rudolph C. Flothow; *Sc:* William Lively, Sherman L. Lowe. (1:15) A feature-length jungle adventure pieced together for theatrical release from episodes of the "Ramar of the Jungle" TV series.

2010. Phantom of the Rue Morgue (Warner; 1954). *Cast:* Karl Malden, Claude Dauphin, Patricia Medina, Steve Forrest, Allyn McLerie, Veola Vonn, Dolores Dorn, Anthony Caruso, Merv Griffin, The Flying Zacchinis, Paul Richards, Rolfe Sedan, Frank Lackteen, Henry Kulky, Erin O'Brien-Moore, Charles Gemora (the gorilla). *D:* Roy Del Ruth; *P:* Henry Blanke; *Sc:* Harold Medford, James R. Webb. (1:23) (video) Mystery-melodrama surrounding the investigation into the grisly murders of several beautiful girls, each case bearing its own set of bizarre circumstances and one common denominator. A remake of Universal's 1932 production *Murders in the Rue Morgue* and based on Edgar Allan Poe's literary creation by that name. Two other versions of the story followed, a variation in 1971 and a TV movie in 1986 which closely followed Poe's original story. WarnerColor and 3-D.

2011. The Phantom Stagecoach (Columbia; 1957). *Cast:* William Bishop, Kathleen

Crowley, Richard Webb, Maudie Prickett, Hugh Sanders, John Doucette, Ray Teal, Frank Ferguson, Percy Helton, Lane Bradford, Eddy Waller, John Lehmann, Robert Anderson. *D:* Ray Nazarro; *P:* Wallace MacDonald; *St: & Sc:* David Lang. (1:09) Programmer western of a war between rival stagecoach lines.

2012. Phantom Stallion (Republic, 1954). *Cast:* Rex Allen, Slim Pickens, Carla Balenda, Harry Shannon, Don Haggerty, Peter Price, Rosa Turich, Zon Murray, Ko-Ko (horse). *D:* Harry Keller; *P:* Rudy Ralston; *St: & Sc:* Gerald Geraghty. (0:54) A cowboy uncovers the truth behind ranchers plagued by disappearing horses. Allen's final series western for Republic.

2013. Pharaoh's Curse (United Artists/ Bel-Air–Sunrise Picts.; 1957). *Cast:* Mark Dana, Ziva Rodann, Diane Brewster, George Neise, Kurt Katch, Terence de Marnay, Alvaro Guillot, Ben Wright, Guy Prescott, Richard Peel, Robert Fortin, Ralph Clanton. *D: & Ex.P:* Lee Sholem; *P:* Howard W. Koch; *St: & Sc:* Richard Landau. (1:06) (video) Supernatural thriller of a 1903 expedition into the Valley of the Kings and what occurs when a sacred tomb is desecrated. Originally paired on the bottom of a double bill with *The Big Boodle* (q.v.).

2014. The Phenix City Story (Allied Artists/Bischoff Enterprises; 1955). *Cast:* John McIntire (Albert Patterson), Richard Kiley (John Patterson), Kathryn Grant (Ellie Rhodes), Edward Andrews (film debut/Rhett Tanner), Lenka Peterson (Mary Jo Patterson), Biff McGuire (Fred Gage), Truman Smith (Ed Gage), Jean Carson (Cassie), Katharine Marlowe (Mamie), John Larch (Clem Wilson), Allen Nourse (Jeb Bassett), James Edwards (Zeke Ward), Helen Martin (Helen Ward), Otto Hulett (Hugh Bentley), George Mitchell (Hugh Britton), Ma Beachie (herself), James E. Seymour (himself). *D:* Phil Karlson; *P:* Samuel Bischoff, David Diamond; *St: & Documentation:* Crane Wilbur; *Sc:* Wilbur, Dan(iel) Mainwaring; *Song:* "Phenix City Blues" Harold Spina (sung by Meg Myles). (1:40—includes 13 min. prologue) A true expose of the vice and corruption which ruled the town of Phenix City, Alabama, for over a hundred years and the lawyer who brings it to an end after his father is gunned down. Filmed on location, it placed #7 on the "10 Best" list of the *New York Times* and became one of the 24 top-grossing films of 1955-56. (G.B. title: *The Phoenix City Story*)

2015. Phffft (Columbia; 1954). *Cast:* Judy Holliday, Jack Lemmon, Kim Novak, Jack Carson, Luella Gear, Donald Randolph, Donald Curtis, Arny Freeman, Merry Anders, Olan Soule, Geraldine Hall, Harry Cheshire, William Newell, Eugene Bordon, Fay Baker, Joyce Jameson, Eddie Searles, Wendy Howard, William Lechner, Sue Carlton, Alphonse Martell, Jerry Hausner, Charlotte Lawrence, Patrick Miller, George Hill, Tom Kingston, Sally Mansfield, Vivian Mason, Maxine Marlowe, Shirlee Allard, Hamil Petroff, Mylee Andreason, Charles Heard, Virgil Johansen, Jimmie Dodd, Frank Arnold, Richard Gordon, Edwana Spence, Joe Karnes, Walter Hastings, Gil Warren, Ted Thorpe. *D:* Mark Robson; *P:* Fred Kohlmar; *Sc:* George Axelrod (based on his unproduced play). (1:31) (video) Comedy of a married couple who divorce, only to discover they need each other and remarry.

The Phoenix City Story (G.B. title) *see* **The Phenix City Story**

2016. Phone Call from a Stranger (20th Century–Fox; 1952). *Cast:* Shelley Winters, Gary Merrill, Michael Rennie, Keenan Wynn, Evelyn Varden, Warren Stevens, Beatrice Straight, Ted Donaldson, Craig Stevens, Helen Westcott, Bette Davis, Sydney Perkins, Hugh Beaumont, Thomas Jackson, Harry Cheshire, Tom Powers, Freeman Lusk, George Eldredge, Nestor Paiva, Perdita Chandler, Genevieve Bell, George Nader, John Doucette, William Neff, Ruth Robinson. *D:* Jean Negulesco; *P:* Nunnally Johnson; *Sc:* Johnson (received a screenplay award at the Venice Film Festival). (1:36) (video) Drama of four people who meet on a plane to the West Coast. When the plane crashes, three are killed and the fourth volunteers to inform the families of the deceased, as he has their phone numbers. Based on a novelette by I.A.R. Wylie, it was in nomination at the Venice Film Festival.

2017. Pickup (Columbia/Forum Prods.; 1951). *Cast:* Hugo Haas, Beverly Michaels, Allan Nixon, Howland Chamberlain, Mark Lowell, Jo Carroll Dennison, Art Lewis, Jack Daly, Bernard Gorcey. *D:* Hugo Haas; *P:* Haas, Edgar E. Walden; *Sc:* Haas, Arnold Phillips. (1:16) Melodrama of a gold digger who marries a man for his money and, with her lover, plots to kill him. Based on the novel *Watchman 47* by Joseph Kopta.

2018. Pickup on South Street (20th Century–Fox; 1953). *Cast:* Richard Widmark

(Skip McCoy), Jean Peters (Candy), Thelma Ritter (AAN/Moe), Murvyn Vye (Capt. Dan Tiger), Richard Kiley (Joey), Willis Bouchey (Zara), Milburn Stone (Wonoki), Henry Slate (MacGregor), Jerry O'Sullivan (Enyart), Harry Carter (Dietrich), George Eldredge (Fenton), Frank Kumagai (Lum), Victor Perry (Lightning Louie), Roger Moore (Mr. Victor), George E. Stone, Stuart Randall, Maurice Samuels, Parley Baer, Jay Loftin, Virginia Carroll, Clancy Cooper, John Gallaudet, Wilson Wood, Ray Montgomery, Ray Stevens, Ralph Moody, George Berkeley, Emmett Lynn. *D: & Sc:* Samuel Fuller; *P:* Jules Schermer; *St:* Dwight Taylor. (1:20) (video) Espionage melodrama of a pickpocket who comes into possession of a top secret microfilm and finds himself the target of communist agents. Another of Fuller's critically acclaimed B masterpieces, it was awarded the "Bronze Medal" at the Venice Film Festival. Remade in 1967 as *The Capetown Affair*.

2019. Picnic (Columbia; 1955). *Cast:* William Holden (Hal Carter), Kim Novak (Madge Owens), Rosalind Russell (Rosemary Sydney), Betty Field (Flo Owens), Susan Strasberg (Millie Owens), Cliff Robertson (film debut/Alan), Arthur O'Connell (AAN/Howard Bevans), Verna Felton (Mrs. Helen Pott), Reta Shaw (Linda Sue Breckenridge), Nick Adams (Bomber), Raymond Bailey (Mr. Benson), Elizabeth W. Wilson (Christine Schoenwalder), Phyllis Newman (Juanita Badger), Henry Pegueo (mayor), Don C. Harvey, Steve Benton, Henry P. Watson, Abraham Weinlood, Wayne R. Sullivan, Warren Frederick Adams, Carle E. Baker, Flomanita Jackson, George E. Bemis. *D:* (AAN) Joshua Logan (solo directorial debut); *P:* (AAN-Best Picture) Fred Kohlmar; *Sc:* Daniel Taradash; *ASD:* (AA) William Flannery, Joe Mielziner (art directors), Robert Priestley (sets); *Music:* (AAN) George Duning; *Editors:* (AA) Charles Nelson, William A. Lyon. (1:55) (video/laserdisc) Drama of the effects a drifter has on various people in a small town. Based on the play by William Inge, it placed #9 on the "10 Best" list of the NBR and on the same list of *Film Daily* in 1956 it placed #7, as well as being in nomination at the British Academy Awards. One of the 24 top-grossing films of 1955-56. Technicolor and CinemaScope. Note: Kim Novak also received the *Photoplay* Gold Medal.

2020. Pier 5 Havana (United Artists/Premium Pictures; 1959). *Cast:* Cameron Mitchell, Allison Hayes, Eduardo Noriega, Michael Granger, Logan Field, Nestor Paiva, Otto Waldis, Paul Fierro, Edward Foster, Ken Terrell, Donna Dale, Vincent Padula, Fred Engelberg, Rick Vallin, Walter Kray, Joe Yrigoyen. *D:* Edward L. Cahn; *P:* Robert E. Kent; *St:* Joseph Hoffman; *Sc:* James B. Gordon. (1:07) Melodrama of a man investigating the disappearance of a friend during the Cuban Revolution.

2021. Pier 23 (Lippert/Spartan Prods.; 1951). *Cast:* Hugh Beaumont, Ann Savage, Edward Brophy, Richard Travis, Mike Mazurki, Margia Dean, David Bruce, Raymond Greenleaf, Eve Miller, Harry Hayden, Joy [Joi] Lansing, Peter Mamakos, Chris Drake, Johnny Indrisano, Bill Varga, Richard Monahan, Charles Wagenheim. *D: & P:* William Berke; *Sc:* Julian Harmon, Victor West. (0:58) Two separate stories make up this programmer mystery-melodrama of amateur detective Denny O'Brien sleuthing two separate cases. The stories are based on a radio play by Louis Morheim and Herbert Margolis.

2022. Pillars of the Sky (Universal-International; 1956). *Cast:* Jeff Chandler, Dorothy Malone, Keith Andes, Ward Bond, Lee Marvin, Michael Ansara, Willis Bouchey, Sydney Chaplin, Olive Carey, Charles Horvath, Orlando Rodriguez, Glen Kramer, Floyd Simmons, Pat Hogan, Felix Noriego, Paul Smith, Martin Milner, Robert Ellis, Ralph Votrian, Walter Coy, Alberto Morin, Richard Hale, Frank DeKova, Terry Wilson, Paul Kieffer, Gilbert Connor. *D:* George Marshall; *P:* Robert Arthur; *Sc:* Sam Rolfe. (1:35) Trouble erupts between Indians and soldiers when the latter begin building a road and fort on land given to the former by treaty. Based on the novel *Frontier Fury* by Will Henry [pseudonym of Henry Allen], it was filmed on location in Oregon in Technicolor and CinemaScope. (G.B. title: *The Tomahawk and the Cross*)

2023. Pillow Talk (Universal-International/Arwin Prods.; 1959). *Cast:* Doris Day (AAN/Jan Morrow), Rock Hudson (Brad Allen), Tony Randall (Jonathan Forbes), Thelma Ritter (AAN/Alma), Nick Adams (Tony Walters), Julia Meade (Marie), Allen Jenkins (Harry), Marcel Dalio (Pierot), Lee Patrick (Mrs. Walters), Mary McCarty (Nurse Resnick), Alex Gerry (Dr. Maxwell), Hayden Rorke (Mr. Conrad), Valerie Allen (Eileen), Jacqueline Beer (Yvette), Arlen Stuart (Tilda), Don Beddoe (Mr. Walters), Robert B. Williams (Mr. Graham), Karen Norris (Miss Dickenson), Muriel Landers, William Schallert, Lois Rayman,

Harry Tyler, Joe Mell, Boyd "Red" Morgan, Dorothy Abbott. *D:* Michael Gordon; *P:* Ross Hunter; *St:* (AA) Russell Rouse, Clarence Greene; *Sc:* (AA) Stanley Shapiro, Maurice Richlin; *ASD:* (AAN-color) Richard H. Riedel, Alexander Golitzen (art directors), Russel A. Gausman, Ruby R. Levitt (sets); *Music:* (AAN) Frank DeVol; *Songs:* Title song—Buddy Pepper, Inez James; "I Need No Atmosphere," "You Lied," "Possess Me," "Inspiration" Joe Lubin, I.J. Roth; "Roly Poly" Elsa Doran, Sol Lake. (1:45) (video/laserdisc) Acclaimed romantic sex comedy of a fashionable interior decorator and a bachelor songwriter who share a partyline. Filmed on locations in New York City, it placed #4 and #8 respectively on the "10 Best" lists of *Film Daily* and the *New York Times*. One of the 28 top-grossing films of 1959-60, it was in Eastmancolor and CinemaScope. Note: Doris Day, Rock Hudson and the film each won a *Photoplay* Gold Medal.

2024. Pirates of Tripoli (Columbia/Clover Prods.; 1955). *Cast:* Paul Henreid, Patricia Medina, Paul Newlan, John Miljan, Lillian Bond (final film—ret.), Jean Del Val, Mel Welles, Louis Mercier, Karl Davis, Peter Mamakos, William Fawcett, Eugene Borden, Frank Richards. *D:* Felix E. Feist (final film—ret.); *P:* Sam Katzman; *St: & Sc:* Allen March. (1:12) A 16th century swashbuckler romance which utilizes footage from *The Golden Hawk* (q.v.). Technicolor.

2025. Pistol Harvest (RKO; 1951). *Cast:* Tim Holt, Richard Martin, Joan Dixon, Mauritz Hugo, Robert Wilke, William Griffith, Guy Edward Hearn, Harper Carter, Lee Phelps, Joan Freeman, Fred Herrick. *D:* Lesley Selander; *P:* Herman Schlom; *St: & Sc:* Norman Houston. (1:00) Two cowboys get on the trail of the rustlers who did in their boss. A Tim Holt series western which was originally paired on a double bill with *On the Loose* (q.v.).

2026. A Place in the Sun (Paramount; 1951). *Cast:* Montgomery Clift (AAN/George Eastman), Elizabeth Taylor (Angela Vickers), Shelley Winters (AAN/Alice Tripp), Anne Revere (Hannah Eastman), Keefe Brasselle (Earl Eastman), Fred Clark (Bellows), Raymond Burr (Marlowe), Herbert Heyes (Charles Eastman), Sheppard Strudwick (Anthony Vickers), Frieda Inescort (Mrs. Vickers), Kathryn Givney (Mrs. Louise Eastman), Walter Sande (Jansen), Lois Chartrand (Marsha), William R. Murphy (Mr. Whiting), Charles Dayton (Kelly), John Ridgely (coroner), Ted de Corsia (judge), Douglas Spencer (boatkeeper), Paul Frees (Morrison), John Reed (Joe Parker), Marilyn Dialon (Frances Morrison), Ian Wolfe (Dr. Wyeland), Mary Kent (Mrs. Roberts), Kathleen Freeman (Martha), James W. Horne (Tom Tipton), Laura Ekkuit (Miss Harper), Pearl Miller (Miss Newton), Josephine Whittell, Frank Yaconelli, Ralph A. Dunn, Bob Anderson, Lisa Golm, Ken Christy, Hans Moebus, Eric Wilson, Mike Mahoney, Al Ferguson, Major Philip Kieffer, Major Sam Harris. *D:* (AA) George Stevens; *P:* (AAN-Best Picture) Stevens; *Sc:* (AA) Michael Wilson, Harry Brown; *Cinematography:* (AA-b/w) William C. Mellor; *Music:* (AA-non musical) Franz Waxman; *Costumes:* (AA-b/w) Edith Head; *Editor:* (AA) William Hornbeck. (2:02) (video/laserdisc) Drama of a young man with amorous designs on a wealthy society girl, who murders the girl friend he impregnated when she threatens to expose him. A remake of *An American Tragedy* (1931), the name of the novel by Theodore Dreiser on which it was based. Critical acclaim ran rampant at the NBR and *Film Daily* who both voted it "Best Film of the Year." The New York Film Critics also had it in nomination for the same honor, while the *New York Times* placed it at #4 on their "10 Best" list. In nomination at the Cannes Film Festival, it also became one of the 23 top-grossing films of 1951-52. Filmed on location at Lake Tahoe in the Sierras.

2027. Plan 9 from Outer Space (Distributors Corp. of America/J. Edward Reynolds Prods.; 1959). *Cast:* Gregory Walcott, Duke Moore, Tom Keene [aka: Richard Powers/final film—d. 1963], Mona McKinnon, Dudley Manlove, Joanna Lee, Tor Johnson, Lyle Talbot, John Breckinridge, Carl Anthony, David DeMering, Norma McCarty, Bill Ash, Reverend Lynn Lemon, Ben Frommer, Conrad Brooks, Gloria Dea, Vampira [aka: Maila Nurmi], Bela Lugosi (final film—d. 1956), Criswell. *D:-P:-St: & Sc:* Edward Davis Wood, Jr. (1:19) (video/laserdisc) Ultra low budget inept science fiction of outer space aliens—in need of acting lessons—who resurrect earth's dead in an effort to destroy the planet before nuclear testing destroys the universe. Much has been said and written about this film and its creator over the years, considered in many circles to be the worst movie ever made and thus a main staple at "bad movie" festivals. Must be seen to be believed, if just for its continuous flow of unintended laughter inducers. On the other hand, it remains a sad testimony to one man's self-delusion as a filmmaker.

(aka: *Grave Robbers from Outer Space*) (see also: *Night of the Ghouls*) (q.v.) Note: Bela Lugosi died shortly after production began, with the remainder of his role being filled out by another [reputed to be Mr. Wood's chiropractor] in a black cape to hide his face and fill out Lugosi's role.

2028. Playgirl (Universal-International; 1954). *Cast:* Shelley Winters, Barry Sullivan, Colleen Miller, Richard Long, Gregg Palmer, Kent Taylor, Jacqueline de Wit, Dave Barry, Philip Van Zandt, James McCallion, Paul Richards, Helen Beverly, Myrna Hansen, Mara Corday, Don Avalier, Carl Sklover. *D:* Joseph Pevney; *P:* Albert J. Cohen; *St:* Ray Buffum; *Sc:* Robert Blees; *Songs:* "There'll Be Some Changes Made" Billy Higgins, W. Benton Overstreet, Herbert Edwards; "Lie to Me" Ray Gilbert. (1:25) Melodrama of life in the big city and one girl's involvement with the criminal element.

2029. Please Believe Me (MGM; 1950). *Cast:* Deborah Kerr, Robert Walker, Peter Lawford, Mark Stevens, James Whitmore, Spring Byington, J. Carrol Naish, George Cleveland, Carol Savage, Drue Mallory, Ian Wolfe, Bridget Carr, Henri Letondal, Gaby Andre, Leon Belasco. *D:* Norman Taurog; *P:* Val Lewton; *St: & Sc:* Nathaniel Curtis. (1:26) Romantic comedy of a woman sailing from England to New York who finds herself being pursued by several eligible bachelors who, unbeknownst to her, are under the assumption that she is an heiress.

2030. Please Murder Me (Distributors Corp. of America; 1956). *Cast:* Angela Lansbury, Raymond Burr, Dick Foran, John Dehner, Lamont Johnson, Robert Griffin, Denver Pyle, Alex Sharpe, Lee Miller, Madge Blake, Russ Thorson. *D:* Peter Godfrey (final film—ret.); *P:* Donald Hyde; *St: & Sc:* Al C. Ward, Hyde. (1:18) Melodrama of an attorney who gets a woman off on the charge of murdering her husband. When he comes to realize she actually committed the murder, he begins to have pangs of guilt and wants her to put him out of his misery.

2031. Plunder of the Sun (Warner/ Wayne-Fellows; 1953). *Cast:* Glen Ford, Diana Lynn, Patricia Medina, Francis L. Sullivan, Sean McClory, Eduardo Noriega, Julio Villareal, Charles Rooner, Douglass Dumbrille, Mona Barrie (final film—ret.). *D:* John Farrow; *P:* Robert Fellows, Farrow; *Sc:* Jonathan Latimer; *Song:* "Sin Ella" E. Fabregat. (1:21) Programmer tale of various people in search of hidden treasure somewhere in the temples of Oaxaca, in Mexico, where it was filmed on location. Based on the 1949 novel by David Dodge.

2032. Plunder Road (20th Century–Fox/ Regal Films; 1957). *Cast:* Gene Raymond, Jeanne Cooper, Wayne Morris (final film—d. 1959), Elisha Cook, Jr., Stafford Repp, Steven Ritch, Nora Hayden, Helene Heigh, Paul Harbor, Don Garrett, Michael Fox, Richard Newton, Charles Conrad, Jim Canino, Robin Riley, Harry Tyler, George Keymas, Stacy Graham (narrator), Douglas Banks (narrator). *D:* Hubert Cornfield; *P:* Leon Chooluck, Laurence Stewart; *St:* Steven Ritch, Jack Charney; *Sc:* Ritch. (1:11) (video) Men rob a train of a shipment of gold bullion and are eventually thwarted by their own devices. A B-series film which received some acclaim. Originally ran on a double bill with *Ride a Violent Mile* (q.v.). Regalscope.

2033. The Plunderers of Painted Flats (Republic; 1959). *Cast:* Corinne Calvet, John Carroll (final film—ret.), Skip Homeier, George Macready, Edmund Lowe, Bea Benaderet, Madge Kennedy, Joe Besser, Allan Lurie, Candy Candido, Ricky Allen, Herb Vigran, Bob Kline, Burt Topper, William Foster, Lee Redman, Roy Gordon, Wade Lane, David Waldor, John Kidd. *D: & P:* Albert C. Gannaway; *As.P:* Phil Shuken; *St: & Sc:* Shuken, John Greene. (1:17) Western of a ruthless cattle baron who is determined to drive out or kill local families of squatters. This was Republic's final theatrical release before closing its doors. Naturama.

2034. Plymouth Adventure (MGM; 1952). *Cast:* Spencer Tracy (Capt. Jones), Gene Tierney (Dorothy Bradford), Van Johnson (John Alden), Leo Genn (Bradford), Dawn Addams (Priscilla Mullins), Lloyd Bridges (Coppin), Barry Jones (William Brewster), John Dehner (Gilbert Winslow), Lowell Gilmore (Edward Winslow), Rhy Williams (Mr. Weston), Kathleen Lockhart (Mary Brewster), John Dierkes (Greene), Paul Cavanagh (John Carver), Tommy Ivo (William Button), Noel Drayton (Miles Standish), Murray Matheson (Christopher Martin), Noreen Corcoran (Ellen Moore), Hugh Pryne (Samuel Fuller), Matt Moore (William Mullins), Elizabeth Flournoy (Elizabeth Standish), Dennis Hoey, William Self, Loren Brown, Damian O'Flynn, Keith McConnell, Elizabeth Harrower, Owen McGiveney, Ivis Goulding, David Sober, Roger Broaddus, Gene

Coogan, Kay English, James Logan. *D:* Clarence Brown (final film as director); *P:* Dore Schary; *Sc:* Helen Deutsch. (1:45) A lavishly produced historical dud about the Pilgrims who set sail on the *Mayflower* for the New World in 1620. Based on the 1950 novel by Ernest Gebler, the film did win the Academy Award for special effects. Technicolor.

2035. Pony Express (Paramount; 1953). *Cast:* Charlton Heston (Buffalo Bill Cody), Forrest Tucker (Wild Bill Hickok), Rhonda Fleming, Jan Sterling, Michael Moore, Porter Hall, Richard Shannon, Henry Brandon, Stuart Randall, Lewis Martin, Pat Hogan, James Davies, Eric Alden, Willard Willingham, Frank Wilcox, Len Hendry, Charles Hamilton, Bob Templeton, Howard Joslin, LeRoy Johnson, Jimmy H. Burke, Robert J. Miles, Bob Scott, John Mansfield, Jerry James, Howard Gardiner, William Hamel. *D:* Jerry Hopper; *P:* Nat Holt; *Sc:* Charles Marquis Warren; *St:* Frank Gruber. (1:41) (video) Western involving the efforts of Buffalo Bill Cody and Wild Bill Hickok to establish the Pony Express in the 1860s and stop the secession of California from the Union. Technicolor.

2036. Pony Soldier (20th Century–Fox; 1951-52). *Cast:* Tyrone Power, Cameron Mitchell, Penny Edwards, Thomas Gomez, Robert Horton, Anthony Earl Numkena [aka: Earl Holliman], Adeline de Walt Reynolds, Howard Petrie, Stuart Randall, Richard Shackleton, James Hayward, Muriel Landers, Frank DeKova, Louis Heminger, John War Eagle, Grady Galloway, Nipo T. Strongheart, Carlow Loya, Anthony Numkena, Sr., Chief Bright Fire, Richard Thunder-Sky. *D:* Joseph M. Newman; *P:* Samuel G. Engel; *Sc:* John C. Higgins. (1:21) (video) A Canadian Mountie is given the assignment of preventing Cree Indians from staging an uprising. Based on the serialized story *Mounted Patrol* by Garnett Weston which appeared in *Saturday Evening Post.* Technicolor. (G.B. title: *MacDonald of the Canadian Mounties*)

Poor White Trash *see* **Bayou**

2037. Porgy and Bess (Columbia/Samuel Goldwyn; 1959). *Cast:* Sidney Poitier (Porgy—with the singing voice of Robert McFerren), Dorothy Dandridge (Bess—with the singing voice of Adele Addison), Sammy Davis, Jr. (Sportin' Life), Pearl Bailey (Maria), Brock Peters (Crown), Leslie Scott (Jake), Diahann Carroll (Clara—with the singing voice of Loulie Jean Norman), Clarence Muse (Peter), Ruth Attaway (Serena—with the singing voice of Inez Matthews), Everdinne Wilson (Annie), Joel Fluellen (Robbins), Earl Jackson (Mingo), Moses LaMarr (Nelson), Margaret Hairston (Lily), Ivan Dixon (Jim), Antoine Durousseau (Scipio), Helen Thigpen (strawberry woman), Vince Townsend, Jr. (elderly man), William Walker (undertaker), Roy Glenn (Frazier), Maurice Manson (coroner), Claude Akins (detective). *D:* Otto Preminger (replacing Rouben Mamoulian who was chosen when the original stage director backed out); *P:* Samuel Goldwyn (his final film); *Cin:* (AAN-color) Leon Shamroy; *Music:* (AA) Andre Previn, Ken Darby; *Costumes:* (AAN-color) Irene Sharaff; *Sound:* (AAN) Gordon E. Sawyer/Goldwyn Studio Sound Dept. and Fred Hynes/Todd-AO Sound Dept; *Songs:* "Summertime," "A Woman Is a Sometime Thing," "Honey Man's Call," "They Pass by Singing," "Oh Little Stars," "Gone, Gone, Gone," "Fill Up de Saucer," "My Man's Gone Now," "The Train Is at the Station," "Oh, I Got Plenty O' Nuttin'," "Bess, You Is My Woman Now," "Oh, I Can't Sit Down," "I Ain't Got No Shame," "It Ain't Necessarily So," "What You Want Wid Bess?," "It Take a Long Pull to Get There," "Strawberry Woman's Call," "Crab Man's Call," "I Loves You, Porgy," "Oh, de Lawd Shake de Heaven," "Dere's Somebody Knockin' at de Do'," "A Red-Headed Woman," "Clara Don't You Be Downhearted," "Dere's a Boat Dat's Leavin' Soon For New York," "Good Mornin', Sistuh," "Bess, Oh Where's My Bess?" and "Oh, Lawd, I'm on My Way" George Gershwin(m), Ira Gershwin, DuBose Heyward(ly). (2:18) The classic musical folk opera of life and love among the poor black residents of Catfish Row. Set in Charleston, S.C., in 1912, it is based on the 1925 book *Porgy* by DuBose Heyward and the 1927 stageplay adapted from it by Heyward and his wife Dorothy. The 1935 musical by George and Ira Gershwin (libretto by Heyward) was a moderate success with 124 performances. Following the death of George Gershwin in 1937, the music became popular and was revived on stage in 1942 and again in 1953, both resounding successes. The film placed #4 on the "10 Best" list of the *New York Times* and became one of the 26 top-grossing films of 1958-59, despite voiced objections by the NAACP. Technicolor and Todd-AO. Note: Production problems and costs abounded on this production, including a fire which broke out on the day shooting was set to begin, destroying the Catfish Row set and many costumes. Total costs: $7,000,000.

2038. Pork Chop Hill (United Artists/ Melville Prods.; 1959). *Cast:* Gregory Peck, Harry Guardino, Rip Torn, George Peppard, James Edwards, Bob Steele, Woody Strode, George Shibita, Norman Fell, Robert Blake, Biff Elliot, Barry Atwater, Michael Garth, Ken Lynch, Paul Comi, Abel Fernandez, Lou Gallo, Cliff Ketchum, Martin Landau, Bert Remson, Kevin Hagen, [Harry] Dean Stanton, Leonard Graves, Syl Lamont, Gavin McLeod, John Alderman, John McKee, Charles Aidman, Chuck Hayward, Barry Maguire, Buzz Martin, Robert Williams, Bill Wellman, Jr., Viraj Amonson. *D:* Lewis Milestone; *P:* Sy Bartlett; *Sc:* James R. Webb. (1:37) (video/laserdisc) Critically acclaimed for its gritty frontline realism, this Korean War drama is based on the writings of Brigadier General S.L.A. Marshall (USA-R). It relates factual events surrounding the taking of Pork Chop Hill (a dubious objective) by a company of 135 men, with only 25 surviving to hold the conquest until reinforcements arrive. Filmed on location in California's San Fernando Valley, this may be considered the quintessential film on that conflict.

2039. Port of Hell (Allied Artists; 1954). *Cast:* Dane Clark, Carole Mathews, Wayne Morris, Marshall Thompson, Harold Peary, Marjorie Lord, Otto Waldis, Tom Hubbard, Charles Fredericks, Jim Alexander, Victor Sen Yung, Gene Roth. *D:* Harold Schuster; *P:* William F. Broidy, Robert Nunes; *St:* Gil Doud, D.D. Beauchamp; *Sc:* Tom Hubbard, Doud, Fred Eggers. (1:20) Cold War communist paranoia shows its face when an atomic bomb set to detonate is found aboard a ship in the harbor of Los Angeles.

2040. Port Sinister (RKO/American Pictures Corp.; 1953). *Cast:* James Warren, Lynn Roberts (final film—ret.), Paul Cavanagh, William Schallert, House Peters, Jr., Marjorie Stapp, Helen Winston, Eric Colmar, Norman Budd, Ann Kimbell, Robert Bice, Merritt Stone, Ken Terrell, Charles Victor, Edward Guy Hearn, Dayton Lummis. *D:* Harold Daniels; *P:-St: & Sc:* Jack Pollexfen, Aubrey Wisberg. (1:05) An adventurer believes that the old pirate stronghold, Port Royal, Jamaica, which sank beneath the waves during an 18th century earthquake, will surface again during another quake with all the pirate goodies easily accessible. Watch out for those giant crabs! (aka: *Beast of Paradise Island/Isle*)

2041. Portland Expose (Allied Artists/ Lindsley Parsons Prod.; 1957). *Cast:* Edward Binns, Carolyn Craig, Virginia Gregg, Russ Conway, Larry Dobkin, Frank Gorshin, Joe Marr, Rusty Lane, Dickie Bellis, Lea Penman, Jeanne Carmen, Stanley Farrar, Larry Thor, Francis DeSales, Kort Falkenberg, Joe Flynn. *D:* Harold Schuster (final film—ret.); *Ex.P:* David E. Rose; *P:* John R. Sloan; *St: & Sc:* Jack DeWitt. (1:12) Based on fact crime-melodrama of an honest man who finds himself intimidated by hoodlums and goes undercover to expose them.

2042. Powder River (20th Century–Fox; 1953). *Cast:* Rory Calhoun, Corinne Calvet, Cameron Mitchell, Penny Edwards, Carl Betz, John Dehner, Raymond Greenleaf, Victor Sutherland, Ethan Laidlaw, Robert Wilke, Harry Carter, Robert Adler, Post Park, Richard Garrick, Frank Ferguson, Henry Kulky, Walter Sande, Zon Murray, Ray Bennett, Archer MacDonald, Val Setz, Harry Hines. *D:* Louis King; *P:* Andre Hakim; *Sc:* Geoffrey Homes [pseudonym of Daniel Mainwaring]. (1:18) Western of a man who becomes sheriff of a town to clear up the murder of his friend, only the man he suspects also winds up dead. Based on the book *Wyatt Earp, Frontier Marshall* by Stuart N. Lake which was also the source material for *Frontier Marshal* (1934), *Frontier Marshal* (1939) and *My Darling Clementine* (1946). Technicolor.

2043. The Power and the Prize (MGM; 1956). *Cast:* Robert Taylor (Cliff Barton), Elisabeth Mueller (Miriam Linka), Charles Coburn (Guy Eliot), Burl Ives (George Salt), Cedric Hardwicke (Mr. Carew), Mary Astor (Mrs. George Salt), Cameron Prud'homme (Rev. John Barton), Nicola Michaels (Joan Salt), Richard Erdman (Lester Everett), Ben Wright (Mr. Chutwell), Jack Raine (Mr. Pitt-Semphill), Thomas Browne Henry (Paul F. Farragut), Richard Deacon (Howard Carruthers). *D:* Henry Koster; *P:* Nicholas Nayfack; *Sc:* Robert Ardrey; *Costumes:* (AAN-b/w) Helen Rose. (1:38) Drama of big business and the private lives of corporate members. Based on the 1954 novel by Harold Swiggett, theater attendance was poor and financial returns, minimal. CinemaScope.

2044. Prairie Roundup (Columbia; 1951). *Cast:* Charles Starrett, Smiley Burnette, Mary Castle, Frank Fenton, Frank Sully, Paul Campbell, Forrest Taylor, Don C. Harvey, George Baxter, Lane Chandler, John Cason, Al Wyatt, Ace Richmond, Alan Sears, Glenn Thompson, The Sunshine Boys. *D:* Fred F. Sears; *P:* Colbert Clark; *St: & Sc:* Joseph O'Donnell. (0:53) "Durango Kid" series entry of mistaken identity and a plot to rustle cattle.

2045. Prehistoric Women (Eagle-Lion/ Alliance Prods., Ltd.; 1950). *Cast:* Allan Nixon, Laurette Luez, Joan Shawlee, Judy Landon, Mara Lynn, Jo Carroll Dennison, Kerry Vaughn, Tony Devlin, James Summers, Dennis Dengate, Jeanne Sorel, Johann Peturrson, John Merrick, Janet Scott. *D:* Gregg Tallas; *P:* Albert J. Cohen, Sam X. Abarbanel; *St: & Sc:* Tallas, Abarbanel. (1:14) (video) Prehistoric "romantic" adventure of a group of scantily clad beauties in search of mates. Originally paired on a double bill with *Korea Patrol* (q.v.). Cinecolor.

Prehistoric World *see* **Teenage Caveman**

2046. The President's Lady (20th Century–Fox; 1953). *Cast:* Susan Hayward (Rachel Donelson Robards), Charlton Heston (Andrew Jackson), John McIntire (Jack Overton), Fay Bainter (Mrs. Donelson), Whitfield Connor (Lewis Robards), Carl Betz (film debut/Charles Dickinson), Gladys Hurlbut (Mrs. Phariss), Ruth Attaway (Moll), Charles Dingle (Capt. Irwin), Nina Varela (Mrs. Stark), Margaret Wycherly (final film—d. 1956/Mrs. Robards), Ralph Dumke (Col. Stark), Jim Davis (Jason), Robert B. Williams (William), Trudy Marshall (Jane), Howard Negley (Cruthers), Dayton Lummis (Dr. May), Harris Brown (Clark), Zon Murray (Jacob), James Best (Samuel), Selmer Jackson (Col. Green), Juanita Evers (Mrs. Green), George Melford (minister), Ann Morrison (Mary), William Walker (Uncle Alfred), Sam McDaniel (Henry), George Spaulding (Chief Justice John Marshall), Willis Bouchey (Judge McNairy), George Hamilton, Vera Francis, Leo Curley, Sherman Sanders, Renee Beard, Mervin Williams, Ronald Numkena. *D:* Henry Levin; *P:* Sol C. Siegel; *Sc:* John Patrick; *ASD:* (AAN-b/w) Lyle Wheeler, Leland Fuller (art directors), Paul S. Fox (sets); *Costumes:* (AAN-b/w) Charles LeMaire, Renie. (1:36) (video) Biographical drama of Andrew Jackson and his wife Rachel, who died before he ascended to the presidency of the United States. Based on the 1951 novel by Irving Stone.

2047. Pretty Baby (Warner; 1950). *Cast:* Dennis Morgan, Betsy Drake, Zachary Scott, Edmund Gwenn, William Frawley, Raymond Roe, Ransom Sherman, Sheila Stephens, Eleanor Audley, George Chandler, Barbara Billingsley. *D:* Bretaigne Windust; *P:* Harry Kurnitz; *Sc:* Everett Freeman, Kurnitz. (1:32) Romantic comedy of a young woman who to—ensure herself a seat on the morning subway—buys a doll, wraps it up and pretends it is a real baby. Based on the story "Gay Deception" by Jules Furthman and John Klorer, it was remade as a 1-hour TV show in the late '50s.

2048. The Price of Fear (Universal-International; 1956). *Cast:* Merle Oberon, Lex Barker, Charles Drake, Warren Stevens, Gia Scala, Phillip Pine, Mary Field, Dan Riss, Konstantin Shayne, Stafford Repp, Tim Sullivan. *D:* Abner Biberman; *P:* Howard Christie; *St:* Dick Irving Hyland; *Sc:* Robert Tallman. (1:19) Crime melodrama of a man accused of two murders of which each crime had he committed them, give an alibi for the other.

2049. The Pride and the Passion (United Artists/Stanley Kramer; 1957). *Cast:* Cary Grant (Capt. Anthony Trumbull), Frank Sinatra (Miguel), Sophia Loren (Juana), Theodore Bikel (General Jouvet), John Wengraf (Sermaine), Jay Novello (Ballinger), Jose Nieto (Carlos), Philip Van Zandt (Vidal), Paco el Laberinto (Manolo), Carlos Larranaga (Jose), Julian Ugarte (Enrique), Felix DePomes (bishop), Carlos Casaravilla (Leonardo), Juan Oliguival (Ramon), Nana De Herrera (Maria), Carlos De Mendoza (Francisco), Luis Guedes + a cast of thousands. *D: & P:* Stanley Kramer; *Sc:* Edna and Edward Anhalt; *Song:* written and sung by Peggy Lee. (2:12) (video) A $5 million epic costume actioner, set in Spain in 1810, of efforts to transport a huge cannon to fight the French. Filmed on location and based on the novel *The Gun* by C.S. Forester, it was given thumbs-down by critics. Nevertheless, all the accompanying publicity hype made it one of the 24 top-grossing films of 1956-57. Technicolor and VistaVision.

2050. Pride of Maryland (Republic; 1950-51). *Cast:* Stanley Clements, Peggy Stewart, Frankie Darro, Joseph Sawyer, Robert H. Barrat, Harry Shannon, Duncan Richardson, Stanley Logan, Joseph Crehan, Emmett Vogan, Clyde Cook, Donald Kerr, Guy Bellis. *D:* Philip Ford; *As.P:* William Lackey; *St: & Sc:* John K. Butler. (1:00) Programmer of a young jockey who runs into trouble when he uses a new riding style, getting him ousted from the track.

2051. The Pride of St. Louis (20th Century–Fox; 1952). *Cast:* Dan Dailey (Dizzy Dean), Joanne Dru (Patricia Nash Dean), Richard Hylton (Johnny Kendall), Richard Crenna (Paul Dean), Hugh Sanders (Horst), James Brown (Moose), Leo T. Cleary (Manager Ed Monroe), Kenny William (Castleman), John

McKee (Delaney), Stuart Randall (Frankie Frisch), William Frambes (Herbie), Damian O'Flynn (Johnnie Bishop), Fred Graham (Alexander), Cliff Clark (Pittsburgh coach), Billy Nelson (Chicago manager), Pattee Chapman (Ella), Richard Reeves (Connelly), Bob Nichols (Eddie), Clyde Trumbull (Mike), Jack Rice (Voorhees), Al Green (Joe), Philip Van Zandt (Louis), Victor Sutherland (Kendall, Sr.), Kathryn Carl (Mrs. Martin), George McDonald (Roscoe), Joan Sudlow (Miss Johnson), Chet Huntley (Tom Weaver), John Doucette (Benny), John Duncan, John Butler, Freeman Lusk, Frank Scannell, Larry Thor, John Wald, Hank Weaver, William Forman, Jack Sherman, Tom Hanlon, Harris Brown. *D:* Harmon Jones; *P:* Jules Schermer; *St:* (AAN) Guy Trosper; *Sc:* Herman J. Mankiewicz (final film—d. 1953). (1:33) (video) A biographical sports drama of baseball great Dizzy Dean. The critics liked it.

2052. Pride of the Blue Grass (Allied Artists; 1954). *Cast:* Lloyd Bridges, Vera Miles, Margaret Sheridan, Arthur Shields, Michael Chapin, Harry Cheshire, Cecile Weston, Emory Parnell, Joan Shawlee, Ray Walker. *D:* William Beaudine; *P:* Hayes Goetz; *St: & Sc:* Harold Shumate. (1:11) Programmer drama of the lady owner of a prize horse, that breaks its leg in a fall, who will not let the animal be destroyed. Color Corp. of America. (G.B. title: *Prince of the Blue Grass*)

2053. Prince of Pirates (Columbia/Esskay Pictures; 1953). *Cast:* John Derek, Barbara Rush, Carla Balenda, Whitfield Connor, Edgar Barrier, Robert Shayne, Harry Lauter, Don C. Harvey, Henry Rowland, Gene Roth, Sandy Sanders, Joe F. McGuinn, Glase Lohman, Bob Peoples, Al Cantor, Edward Colmans. *D:* Sidney Salkow; *P:* Sam Katzman; *St:* William Copeland, Herbert Kline; *Sc:* John O'Dea, Samuel Neuman. (1:18) Low budget swashbuckling adventure of a tyrant overthrown by his brother. Technicolor.

2054. Prince of Players (20th Century-Fox; 1955). *Cast:* Richard Burton (Edwin Booth), Maggie McNamara, John Derek (John Wilkes Booth), Raymond Massey (Junius Brutus Booth), Charles Bickford, Elizabeth Sellars, Eva Le Gallienne (film debut), Christopher Cook, Ian Keith, Paul Stader, Louis Alexander, William Walker, Dayton Lummis, Jack Raine, Charles Cane, Betty Flint, Mae Marsh, Stanley Hall (Abraham Lincoln), Sarah Padden (Mrs. Lincoln), Ruth Clifford, Ivan Hayes, Paul Frees, Ben Wright, Melinda Markey, Eleanor Audley, Percival Vivian, George Dunn, Ruth Warren, Richard Cutting, Lane Chandler, Steve Darrell, George Melford, Tom Fadden, Henry Kulky, Olan Soule. *D: & P:* Philip Dunne; *Sc:* Moss Hart. (1:42) Dramatic historical biography of Edwin Booth, the 19th century stage actor, son of a mad father and brother to a presidential assassin. Based on the 1953 book by Eleanor Ruggles, the film received critical acclaim. DeLuxe color and CinemaScope.

Prince of the Blue Grass (G.B. title) *see* **Pride of the Blue Grass**

2055. Prince Valiant (20th Century-Fox; 1954). *Cast:* James Mason, Janet Leigh, Robert Wagner (title role), Debra Paget, Sterling Hayden, Victor McLaglen, Donald Crisp, Brian Aherne, Barry Jones, Mary Phillips, Howard Wendell, Tom Conway, Sammy Ogg, Neville Brand, Ben Wright, Jarma Lewis, Robert Adler, Ray Spiker, Primo Carnera, Basil Ruysdael, Fortune Gordon, Percival Vivian, Don Megowan, Richard Webb, John Dierkes, Carleton Young, Otto Waldis, John Davidson, Lloyd Aherne, Jr., Lou Nova, Hal Baylor, Mickey Simpson, Gene Roth. *D:* Henry Hathaway; *P:* Robert L. Jacks; *Sc:* Dudley Nichols. (1:40) (video) Popular costume adventure set in the days of King Arthur's Camelot and based on the King Features comic strip by Harold Foster. Technicolor and CinemaScope.

2056. The Prince Who Was a Thief (Universal-International; 1951). *Cast:* Tony Curtis, Piper Laurie, Everett Sloane, Betty Garde, Jeff Corey, Peggie Castle, Nita Bieber, Marvin Miller, Donald Randolph, Hayden Rorke, Fred Graff, Midge Ware, Carol Varga, Susan Cabot, Milada Mladova, King Donovan, Robert Rockwell, James Vincent, Richard Norris, Jack Briggs, Nolan Leary, Frank Lackteen, Buddy Roosevelt, George Magrill. *D:* Rudolph Maté; *P:* Leonard Goldstein; *Sc:* Gerald Drayson Adams, Aeneas Mackenzie. (1:28) Costume actioner with romance, skullduggery and everything else that goes with Arabian Nights–style adventures. Based on a story from the book *Chains* by Theodore Dreiser. Technicolor.

2057. Princess of the Nile (20th Century-Fox/Panoramic Prods.; 1954). *Cast:* Debra Paget, Jeffrey Hunter, Michael Rennie, Dona Drake (final film—ret.), Wally Cassell, Edgar Barrier, Michael Ansara, Jack Elam, Lester Sharpe, Lee Van Cleef, Billy Curtis, Robert Roark, Lisa

Daniels, Merry Anders, Suzanne Alexander, Jeanne Vaughn, Kitty London, Phyllis Winger, Honey Harlow(e), Genice Grayson, Cheryl Clarke, Bobette Bentley. *D:* Harmon Jones; *P:* Robert L. Jacks; *St: & Sc:* Gerald Drayson Adams. (1:11) Costume adventure set in 13th century Egypt as the son of the Caliph of Baghdad falls for a beautiful princess. Filmed on sets left over from *The Robe.* (q.v.). Technicolor.

2058. Prisoner of War (MGM; 1954). *Cast:* Ronald Reagan, Steve Forrest, Dewey Martin, Oscar Homolka, Robert Horton, Paul Stewart, Henry [Harry] Morgan, Stephen Bekassy, Leonard Strong, Darryl Hickman, Jerry Paris, John Lupton, Ralph Ahn, Weaver Levy, Rollin Moriyama, Ike Jones, Clarence Lung, Stuart Whitman, Bob Ellis, Lewis Martin, Otis Greene, Lalo Rios, Lester C. Hoyle, Ron Boyle, Leon Tyler, Edo Mita, Peter Hansen. *D:* Andrew Marton; *P:* Henry Berman; *Sc:* Allen Rivkin. (1:20) Korean War drama of the mistreatment of American POWs at the hands of the North Koreans.

2059. The Prisoner of Zenda (MGM; 1952). *Cast:* Stewart Granger (dual role), Deborah Kerr, James Mason, Jane Greer, Louis Calhern, Lewis Stone (who also appeared in the 1922 version), Robert Douglas, Robert Coote, Francis Pierlot, Peter Brocco, Thomas Browne Henry, Eric Alden, Steven Roberts, Bud [Bill] Wolfe, Peter Mamakos, Joseph Mell, Elizabeth Slifer, Michael Vallon, Kathleen Freeman, Bruce Payne, John Goldsworthy, Stanley Logan, George Lewis, Hugh Prosser, Forbes Murray, Frank Elliott, Gordon Richards, Mary Carroll, Alex Pope, Jay Adler, Peter Votrian, Doris Lloyd, Emilie Cabanne, Paul Marion, William Hazel, Victor Romito, George Slocum, Charles Watts, Alphonse Martell, Manuel Paris, Guy Bellis. *D:* Richard Thorpe; *P:* Pandro S. Berman; *Adaptation:* Wells Root; *Sc:* John L. Balderston (final—d. 1954), Noel Langley. (1:51) (video/laserdisc) Hit costume swashbuckler of Rudolph Rassendyl who is a lookalike for King Rudolph V. Based on the 1894 novel by Anthony J. Hope [pseudonym of Sir Anthony Hope Hawks] as dramatized by Edward Rose, it had three previous filmings; in 1913 by Famous Players, in 1922 by Metro with Ramon Novarro and U.A./ Selznick, Intl. in 1937 with Ronald Colman. Remade as a spoof in 1979. Technicolor.

2060. Prisoners in Petticoats (Republic; 1950). *Cast:* Valentine Perkins, Robert Rockwell, Dani Sue Nolan, Anthony Caruso, Tony Barrett, David Wolfe, Alex Gerry, Michael Carr, Queenie Smith, Bert Conway, Rudy Rama, Marlo Dwyer, Russ Conway, Marta Mitrovich. *D:* Philip Ford; *As.P:* Lou Brock; *St:* Raymond L. Schrock, George Callahan; *Sc:* Bradbury Foote. (1:00) Melodrama of the daughter of a respected professor who gets involved inadvertently in some underworld dealings. Originally paired on a double bill with the Roy Rogers western *Sunset in the West* (q.v.).

2061. Prisoners of the Casbah (Columbia; 1953). *Cast:* Gloria Grahame, Cesar Romero, Turhan Bey (final film—ret.), Nestor Paiva, Paul Newlan, Frank Richards, John Parrish, Lucille Barkley, Philip Van Zandt, Wade Crosby, Gloria Saunders, Nelson Leigh, John Marshall, John Mansfield, Ray Singer. *D:* Richard Bare; *P:* Sam Katzman; *St:* William E. Raynor; *Sc:* DeVallon Scott. (1:18) Low budget costume adventure of a beautiful princess in the clutches of evil. Technicolor.

2062. Private Eyes (Monogram/Allied Artists; 1953). *Cast:* Leo Gorcey, Huntz Hall, David [Gorcey] Condon, Bennie Bartlett, Bernard Gorcey, Rudy Lee, Joyce Holden, Robert Osterloh, William Forrest, William Phillips, Gil Perkins, Peter Mamakos, Lee Van Cleef, Lou Lubin, Emil Sitka, Chick Chandler, Tim Ryan, Edith Leslie, Myron Healey, Carl Saxe. *D:* Edward Bernds; *P:* Ben Schwalb; *St: & Sc:* Bernds, Elwood Ullman. (1:04) Slip (L. Gorcey) opens a detective agency when he finds he can read minds, after getting punched in the nose. Another gimmick to set the "Bowery Boys" up for another entry in their long-running series.

2063. Private Hell 36 (Filmakers; 1954). *Cast:* Ida Lupino, Steve Cochran, Howard Duff, Dean Jagger, Dorothy Malone, Bridget Duff, Jerry Hausner, Dabbs Greer, Chris O'Brien, Kenneth Patterson, George Dockstader, Jimmy Hawkins, King Donovan. *D:* Don Siegel; *P:* Collier Young; *St: & Sc:* Young, Lupino; *Song:* "Didn't You Know?" John Franco (sung by Lupino). (1:21) (video/laserdisc) Crime melodrama of two cops, both dissatisfied with the income from their jobs, who abscond with a stash of cash they find after a suspected felon wrecks his car and is killed.

2064. The Private War of Major Benson (Universal-International; 1955). *Cast:* Charlton Heston (Major Bernard Benson), Julie Adams (Dr. Kay Lambert), William Demarest (John, the handyman), Tim Considine (Cadet Sgt. Hibler), Sal Mineo (Cadet Col. Dusik), Nana Bryant (final film—d. 1955/Mother Redempta), Kay Stewart (Mrs. Flaherty), Mary Field (Sister Mary Theresa), Tim Hovey (Cadet "Tiger" Flaherty), Donald Keeler (Cadet Cpl. Scawalski), Don Haggerty (Mr. Hibler), Yvonne Peattie (Mrs. Hibler), Mary Alan Hokanson (Sister Mary Thomasina), Edward C. Platt (Monsignor Collins), Butch Jones (Cadet Capt. Petri), Milburn Stone (Major General Ramsey), Mickey Little (Cadet Lt. Hanratty), David Janssen, Richard Cutting, Gary Pagett. *D:* Jerry Hopper; *P:* Howard Pine; *St:* (AAN) Joe Connelly, Bob Mosher; *Sc:* William Roberts, Richard Alan Simmons. (1:40) Family oriented comedy-drama of a strict by-the-book military officer who takes over as disciplinary head of a military Catholic school for boys. His outlook on life is changed by the boys and the school's lady doctor. Remade in 1995 as *Major Payne.* Technicolor.

The Private Wore Skirts (G.B. title) *see* **Never Wave at a WAC**

2065. A Private's Affair (20th Century-Fox; 1959). *Cast:* Sal Mineo, Christine Carere, Barry Coe, Barbara Eden, Gary Crosby, Terry Moore, Jim Backus, Jessie Royce Landis, Robert Burton, Alan Hewitt, Robert Denver, Tige Andrews, Ray Montgomery, Rudolph Anders, Debbie Joyce, Robert Montgomery, Jr., Dick Whittinghill, Emerson Treacy, Maida Severn, Carlyle Mitchell. *D:* Raoul Walsh; *P:* David Weisbart; *St:* Ray Livingston Murphy; *Sc:* Winston Miller; *Songs:* "It's the Same Old Army," "36-24-36" and "Warm and Willing" Jimmy McHugh, Jay Livingston. (1:32) Three army inductees find romance and TV exposure by "puttin'-on-a-show." DeLuxe color and CinemaScope.

2066. Problem Girls (Columbia; 1953). *Cast:* Helen Walker, Ross Elliott, Susan Morrow, Anthony Jochim, James Seay, Marjorie Stapp, Ray Regnier, Eileen Stevens, Beverly Garland, Tom Charlesworth, Joyce Jameson, Nan Leslie, Joyce Jarvis, Mara Corday, Tandra Quinn, Norma Eberhardt, Walter Bonn, John Oger, Gladys Kingston, Juney Ellis. *D:* E.A. Dupont; *P:-St: & Sc:* Aubrey Wisberg, Jack Pollexfen. (1:10) Programmer melodrama of skullduggery uncovered at a private school for problem girls. Originally ran on a double bill with *One Girl's Confession* (q.v.).

2067. The Prodigal (MGM; 1955). *Cast:* Lana Turner, Edmund Purdom, Louis Calhern, Audrey Dalton, James Mitchell, Neville Brand, Walter Hampden, Taina Elg (film debut), Francis L. Sullivan (final film—d. 1956), Joseph Wiseman, Sandy Descher, John Dehner, Cecil Kellaway, Philip Tonge, Henry Daniell, Paul Cavanagh, Dayton Lummis, Tracey Roberts, Jarma Lewis, Jay Novello, Dorothy Adams, Peter DeBear, Phyllis Graffeo, Patricia Iannone, Eugene Mazzola, George Sawaya, Richard Devon, Ann Cameron, Gloria Dea, John Rosser, Charles Wagenheim, Gordon Richards, Paul Bryar, Tom Steele, Rex Lease, George Lewis, Almira Sessions, Chuck Roberson, Gloria Stone, Linda Danson, Joanne Dale, Lucille Maracini, Lila Zali, Diane Gump, Patricia Jackson, John Damler, Argentina Brunetti, Jo Gilbert, George Robotham, David Leonard. *D:* Richard Thorpe; *P:* Charles Schnee; *Sc:* Maurice Zimm, Joe Breen, Jr., Samuel James Larsen (based on the biblical story). (1:54) (video/laserdisc) Pooh-poohed by the critics, this lavishly produced costume-drama purports to fill in the gaps of the biblical tale of the Prodigal Son and his adventures with a sexual seductress of Damascus. Eastmancolor and CinemaScope.

2068. Project Moonbase (Lippert/Galaxy Pictures; 1953). *Cast:* Donna Martell, Ross Ford, Larry Johns, Hayden Rorke, Herb Jacobs, Barbara Morrison, Ernestine Barrier, James Craven, John Hedloe, Peter Adams, Robert Karnes, John Straub, Charles Keane, John Tomecko, Robert Paltz. *D:* Richard Talmadge [pseudonym of Ricardo Metzetti]; *P:* Jack Seaman; *As.P:* Karl F. Johnson; *St: & Sc:* Robert A. Heinlein, Seaman. (1:03) (video/0:53) Science fiction set in the year 1970 of an expedition that debarks from a space station on a mission to the moon.

2069. The Proper Time (Lopert/Business Administration Co.; 1959). *Cast:* Tom Laughlin, Nira Monsour, Norma Quine, Richard Shannon, Dennis O'Flaherty, Kip King, Ray Loza, Connie Davis, Al Randall, Roger Rollie. *D:-P:-St: & Sc:* Tom Laughlin. (1:15) Low budget independent drama of a UCLA freshman with a speech impediment and his romantic predicaments after being rejected by a fraternity. Note: The same Tom Laughlin who later created the "Billy Jack" character.

2070. The Proud and the Profane (Paramount/Perlberg-Seaton; 1956). *Cast:* William Holden (Lt. Col. Colin Black), Deborah Kerr

(Lee Ashley), Thelma Ritter (Kate Connors), Dewey Martin (Eddie Woodcik), William Redfield (Chaplain Holmes), Ross Bagdasarian (Louie), Adam Williams (Eustace Press), Marion Ross (Joan), Theodore Newton (Bob Kilpatrick), Richard Shannon (major), Peter Hansen (Lt. [j.g.] Hutchins), Ward Wood (Sgt. Peckinpaugh), Geraldine Hall (Helen), Evelyn Cotton (Beth), Ann Morriss (Pat), Nancy Stevens (Evvie), Larayne Brox (Sissy), Don Roberts (Lt. Fowler), Frank Gorshin (Harry), Genevieve Aumont (Lili Carere), Anthony Moran (Carl), Freeman Morse (Paul), Bob Kenaston, Don House, Taylor Measom, George Brenlin, Robert Morse (film debut), Ray Stricklyn, Claude Akins, Elizabeth Slifer, Joseph Moran, Jack Richardson. *D:* George Seaton; *P:* William Perlberg; *Sc:* Seaton; *ASD:* (AAN-b/w) Hal Pereira, A. Earl Hedrick (art directors), Sam Comer, Frank R. McElvey (sets); *Costumes* (AAN-b/w) Edith Head. (1:51) World War II romantic drama, set on a Pacific island, of a tough marine officer and a war widow working with the Red Cross. A winner at the box office, it was based on the 1954 novel *The Magnificent Bastards* by Lucy Herndon Crockett. VistaVision.

2071. The Proud Ones (20th Century-Fox; 1956). *Cast:* Robert Ryan, Virginia Mayo, Jeffrey Hunter, Robert Middleton, Walter Brennan, Arthur O'Connell, Ken Clark, Rudolfo Acosta, George Mathews, Fay Roope, Edward Platt, Whit Bissell, Paul E. Burns, Richard Deacon, Lois Ray, Jack Low, Kenneth Terrell, Don Brodie, Jackie Coogan, Juanita Close, I. Stanford Jolley, Jack Mather, Steve Darrell, Ed Mundy, Harry Carter, Mary Thomas, Jonni Paris, Frank Gerstle, Charles Tannen, Harrison Lewis, William Fawcett. *D:* Robert D. Webb; *P:* Robert L. Jacks; *Sc:* Edmund H. North, Joseph Petracca. (1:34) Three men ride into a western town, bent on killing the lawman who killed the father of one of the trio. Based on the 1952 novel by Verne Athanas, it was in DeLuxe color and CinemaScope.

2072. The Proud Rebel (Buena Vista/ Formosa Prods.; 1958). *Cast:* Alan Ladd, Olivia de Havilland, Dean Jagger (replacing Adolphe Menjou who was injured during production rehearsals), David Ladd, Cecil Kellaway, [Harry] Dean Stanton, Thomas Pittman, Henry Hull, Eli Mintz, James Westerfield, John Carradine, King (dog, won PATSY "Award of Excellence" in 1959). *D:* Michael Curtiz; *P:* Sam Goldwyn, Jr.; *St:* James Edward Grant; *Sc:* Joseph Petracca, Lillie Hayward. (1:43) (video) Critically acclaimed family drama of a Georgia widower who heads north during the Civil War to find medical help for his mute son. He becomes involved with a woman in danger of losing her lands to wealthy sheepmen. Technicolor.

Prowl Car *see* **Between Midnight and Dawn**

2073. The Prowler (United Artists/Horizon; 1951). *Cast:* Van Heflin, Evelyn Keyes, John Maxwell, Katherine Warren, Madge Blake, Emerson Treacy, Wheaton Chambers, Robert Osterloh, Sherry Hall, Louise Lorimer, George Nader, Benny Burt, Louise Bates, Steve Carruthers, Betty Jane Howarth, Fred Hoose, Alan Harris, Tiny Jones. *D:* Joseph Losey; *P:* S.P. Eagle [Sam Spiegel]; *St:* Robert Thoeren, Hans Wilhelm; *Sc:* Hugo Butler. (1:32) Melodramatic thriller of a cop who has an affair with a married woman, leading eventually to the husband's death. (aka: *The Cost of Living*)

2074. Psychiatric Nursing (Dynamic Films, Inc.; 1958). A documentary feature, which garnered an AAN of "Best Documentary" for producer Nathan Zucker.

2075. Public Pigeon No. One (Universal-International/RKO/Val-Ritchie; 1957). *Cast:* Red Skelton, Vivian Blaine, Janet Blair, Jay C. Flippen, Allyn Joslyn, Benny Baker, Milton Frome, John Abbott, Howard McNear, James Burke, Herb Vigran, The Seven Ashtons. *D:* Norman Z. McLeod; *P:* & *Sc:* Harry Tugend; *St:* Don Quinn, Larry Berns (adapted from a 1956 TV play by Devery Freeman which appeared on *Climax* and also starred Skelton). (1:19) A dimwitted cafeteria worker becomes the victim of swindlers in this comedy produced at RKO and released by Universal, after the former studio closed its doors. Technicolor.

2076. Purple Heart Diary (Columbia; 1951). *Cast:* Judd Holdren, Frances Langford (herself), Ben Lessy (himself), Tony Romano (himself), Aline Towne, Brett King, Warren Mills, Larry Stewart, Joel Marston, Richard Grant, Rory Mallinson, Selmer Jackson, Lyle Talbot, Douglas F. Bank, William R. Klein, Harry Guardino, Marshall Reed, Steve Pendleton, George Offerman, Jr. *D:* Richard Quine; *P:* Sam Katzman; *Sc:* William B. Sackheim; *Songs:* "Hold Me in Your Arms," "Hi, Fellow Tourists," "Where Are You From?" Johnny Bradford-Barbara Hayden–Tony Romano; "Bread and

Butter Woman" Allan Roberts–Lester Lee; "Tattle-Tale Eyes" Bradford–Romano. (1:13) Low budget wartime drama of a USO troupe entertaining the troops. Based on articles written by actress/singer Frances Langford. (G.B. title: *No Time for Tears*).

2077. The Purple Mask (Universal-International; 1955). *Cast:* Tony Curtis, Colleen Miller, Dan O'Herlihy, Gene Barry, Angela Lansbury, George Dolenz, John Hoyt, Paul Cavanagh, Robert Cornthwaite (Napoleon), Donald Randolph, Stephen Bekassy, Myrna Hansen, Allison Hayes, Betty Jane Howarth, Carl Milletaire, Gene D'Arcy, Robert Hunter, Richard Avonde, Glase Lohman, Diane Dubois, Jane Easton, Richard Richonne, Everett Glass, Jean DeBriac, Adrienne D'Ambricourt, George Bruggeman, Albert Godderis. *D:* H. Bruce Humberstone; *P:* Howard Christie; *Adaptation;* Charles Latour (of the French play "Le Chevalier Au Masques" by Paul Armont and Jean Manoussi); *Sc:* Oscar Brodney. (1:22) Costume melodrama of a "Scarlet Pimpernel" wannabe. Technicolor and CinemaScope.

2078. Pushover (Columbia; 1954). *Cast:* Fred MacMurray, Kim Novak (starring debut), Phil Carey, Dorothy Malone, Allen Nourse, E.G. Marshall, Phil Chambers, Alan Dexter, Robert Forrest, Don C. Harvey, Paul Richards, Ann Morriss, Dick Crockett, Marion Ross, Hal Taggart, Ann Loos, Paul Picerni, Mort Mills, Robert Carson, John Tarangelo, James Anderson. *D:* Richard Quine; *P:* Jules Schermer; *Sc:* Roy Huggins. (1:28) (video) Crime melodrama of a gangster's moll who manipulates a cop into doing her bidding. Based on two stories "The Night Watch" by Thomas Walsh and "Rafferty" by William S. Ballinger. Originally ran on a double bill with *The Law vs. Billy the Kid* (q.v.).

2079. Pygmy Island (Columbia; 1950). *Cast:* Johnny Weissmuller, Ann Savage, David Bruce, Steven Geray, William Tannen, Tristram Coffin, Billy Barty, Billy Curtis, Rusty Wescoatt, Pierce Lyden, Tommy Farrell. *D:* William Berke; *P:* Sam Katzman; *St: & Sc:* Carroll Young. (1:09) Based on the comic strip character created by Alex Raymond, this entry in the "Jungle Jim" series finds our hero enlisting the aid of a pygmy chieftain to rescue a downed WAC officer and combat some enemy agents.

2080. Quantez (Universal-International; 1957). *Cast:* Fred MacMurray, Dorothy Malone, James Barton, John Gavin, Sydney Chaplin, John Larch, Michael Ansara. *D:* Harry Keller; *P:* Gordon Kay; *St:* R. Wright Campbell, Ann Edwards; *Sc:* Campbell; *Songs:* "The Lonely One," "The True Love" Frederick Herbert, Arnold Hughes (sung by Malone). (1:20) Western melodrama of an outlaw gang on their way to Mexico after a bank holdup who are forced to hole up in a ghost town saloon when they are surrounded by Apaches. Eastmancolor and CinemaScope.

2081. Quantrill's Raiders (Allied Artists; 1958). *Cast:* Steve Cochran, Diane Brewster, Leo Gordon (Wm. Quantrill), Gale Robbins, Will Wright, Kim Charney, Myron Healey, Robert Foulk, Glenn Strange (final film—to TV and his recurring role as the bartender on "Gunsmoke"), Lane Chandler, Guy Prescott, Thomas Browne Henry, Dan M. White. *D:* Edward Bernds; *P:* Ben Schwalb; *St: & Sc:* Polly James. (1:08) A fictionalized programmer account of the events leading up to and the attack on Lawrence, Kansas, during the Civil War in 1863, by William Quantrill and his followers. DeLuxe color and CinemaScope.

2082. Quebec (Paramount; 1951). *Cast:* John Barrymore, Jr., Corinne Calvet, Barbara Rush, Patric Knowles, John Hoyt, Arnold Moss, Don Haggerty, Patsy Ruth Miller (in her only film appearance since 1931), Howard Joslin, Paul Guevrement, Adrian Belanger, Jacques Champagne, Rene Constantineau, Marcel Sylvian, Rolland Joseph Beaudet, Nikki Duval. *D:* George Templeton; *P:-St: & Sc:* Alan LeMay. (1:25) (video) Romantic actioner set in 1837 Quebec, Canada, of rebellion against the British Crown. Filmed on location. Technicolor.

2083. Queen Bee (Columbia; 1955). *Cast:* Joan Crawford (Eve Phillips), Barry Sullivan (John Avery Phillips), Betsy Palmer (Carol Lee Phillips), John Ireland (Judson Prentiss), Lucy Marlow (Jennifer Stewart), William Leslie (Ty McKinnon), Fay Wray (Sue McKinnon), Katherine Anderson (Miss Breen), Tim Hovey (Ted), Linda Bennett (Trissa), Willa Pearl Curtis (Miss George), Bill Walker (Sam), Olan Soule (Dr. Pearson), Juanita Moore, Bob McCord. *D:* Ranald MacDougall (directorial debut); *P:* Jerry Wald; *Sc:* MacDougall; *Cin:* (AAN-b/w) Charles B. Lang; *Costumes:* (AAN-b/w) Jean Louis. (1:35) Drama of a headstrong woman who manipulates and runs the lives of everyone around her. Crawford seems quite at home in her role, created by Edna Lee [pseudonym of Edna H. Lee Turpin] in her 1949 novel.

2084. Queen for a Day (United Artists/Stillman; 1951). The popular radio show (and later a TV show) is the focal point of three women, in three separate stories, vying for the title "Queen for a Day."

A. Phyllis Avery, Darren McGavin, Rudy Lee, Frances E. Williams, Joan Winfield, Lonny Burr, Tristram Coffin, Jiggs Wood, Casey Folks, George Sherwood. Based on the story "The Gossamer World" by Faith Baldwin.

B. Adam Williams, Kasia Orzazewski, Albert Ben-Astar, Tracey Roberts, Larry Johns, Bernard Szold, Joan Sudlow, Grace Lenard, Leonard [Nimoy] Nemoy (film debut), Danny Davenport, Madge Blake. Based on the story "High Diver" by John Ashworth.

C. Edith Meiser, Dan Tobin, Jessie Davitt, Douglas Evans, Don Shelton, Louise Curry, Sheila Watson, Minna Phillips, Byron Keith. Based on the story "Horsie" by Dorothy Parker.

At the broadcast studio: Jack Bailey (himself), Jim Morgan (himself), Fort Pearson (himself), Melanie York, Cynthia Corley, Kay Wiley, Helen Mowery, Dian Fauntelle. *D:* Arthur Lubin; *P:* Robert Stillman; *Sc:* Seton I. Miller. (1:47) (aka: *Horsie*)

2085. Queen of Outer Space (Allied Artists; 1958). *Cast:* Zsa Zsa Gabor, Eric Fleming, Dave Willock, Laurie Mitchell (title role), Lisa Davis, Paul Birch, Patrick Waltz, Barbara Darrow, Marilyn Buferd, Mary Ford, Marya Stevens, Laura Mason, Lynn Cartwright, Kathy Marlowe, Coleen Drake, Tania Velia, Norma Young, Marjorie Durant, Gerry Gaylor, Joi Lansing. *D:* Edward Bernds; *P:* Ben Schwalb; *St:* Ben Hecht; *Sc:* Charles Beaumont. (1:20) (video) In 1985 a spaceship with three men aboard lands on the planet Venus which is inhabited only by women. Low budget science fiction which utilizes leftover props from *Forbidden Planet, World Without End* and *Flight to Mars* (all q.v.). DeLuxe color and CinemaScope.

Queen of the Gorillas *see* **The Bride and the Beast**

Queen of the West *see* **Cattle Queen**

2086. Quentin Durward (MGM; 1955). *Cast:* Robert Taylor, Kay Kendall, Robert Morley, George Cole, Alec Clunes, Duncan Lamont, Marius Goring, Wilfrid Hyde-White, Ernest Thesiger, Eric Pohlmann, Laya Raki, Harcourt Williams, Michael Goodliffe, John Carson, Nicholas Hannen, Moultrie Kelsall, Frank Tickle, Bill Shine. *D:* Richard Thorpe; *P:* Pandro S. Berman; *Adaptation:* George Froeschel; *Sc:* Robert Ardrey. (1:41) (video) Hit costume action-drama filmed in England of the 15th century hero (Taylor) in the days of France's Louis XI's (Morley) reign. Based on the 1823 novel by Sir Walter Scott. (G.B. title: *The Adventures of Quentin Durward*)

2087. Quicksand (United Artists/Samuel H. Stiefel Prods.; 1950). *Cast:* Mickey Rooney, Jeanne Cagney, Barbara Bates, Peter Lorre, Taylor Holmes, Wally Cassell, John Gallaudet, Minerva Urecal, Art Smith, Patsy O'Connor. *D:* Irving Pichel; *P:* Mort Briskin; *Sc:* Robert Smith. (1:19) (video) Programmer melodrama of a garage mechanic whose infatuation with a tramp leads him into a snowballing life of crime.

2088. The Quiet American (United Artists/Figaro, Inc.; 1958). *Cast:* Audie Murphy, Michael Redgrave, Georgia Moll, Claude Dauphin, Bruce Cabot, Kerima, Fred Sadoff, Richard Loo, Peter Trent, Clinton Andersen, Yoko Tani, Sonia Moser, Phuong Thi Nghiep, Vo Doan Chau, Le Van Le, Le Quynh, Georges Brehat. *D:-P: & Sc:* Joseph L. Mankiewicz. (2:00) Mystery-melodrama set in Indo-China in the year 1952 and based on Grahame Greene's novel (with considerable changes). The anti–American viewpoint of the book becomes an anti-communist one in the film. Locations filmed in Saigon and at Cinecetta studios in Rome.

2089. The Quiet Gun (20th Century-Fox/Regal Films; 1957). *Cast:* Forrest Tucker, Mara Corday, Jim Davis, Kathleen Crowley, Lee Van Cleef, Tom Brown, Lewis Martin, Hank Worden, Everett Glass, Edith Evanson, Gerald Milton, Vince Barnett. *D:* William F. Claxton; *P:* Earle Lyon; *Adaptation:* Eric Norden, Lyon; *Sc:* Norden. (1:19) Programmer western of a rancher forced to commit murder. Based on the 1955 novel *Lawman* by Lauran Paine. Regalscope.

2090. The Quiet Man (Republic/Argosy; 1952). *Cast:* John Wayne (Sean Thornton), Maureen O'Hara (Mary Kate Danaher), Victor McLaglen (AAN/Red Will Danaher), Barry Fitzgerald (Michaeleen Flynn), Ward Bond (Father Peter Lonergan/narrator), Mildred Natwick (Sarah Tillane), Francis Ford (Dan

Tobin), Arthur Shields (Rev. Cyril "Snuffy" Playfair), Eileen Crowe (Elizabeth Playfair), Charles FitzSimons (Forbes), James Lilburn (Father Paul), Sean McClory (Owen Glynn), Jack McGowran (Feeney), Ken Curtis (Dermot Fahy), Pat Cohan (Harry Tyler), Don Hatswell (Guppy), Harry Tenbrook (Sgt. Hanan), May Craig, Joseph O'Dea, Eric Gorman, Kevin Lawless, Paddy O'Donnell, Web Overlander, Mae Marsh, Bob Perry, Major Sam Harris, Melinda Wayne, Patrick Wayne, Mike Wayne, Toni Wayne, Douglas Evans, David H. Hughes, Jack Roper, Al Murphy, Pat O'Malley. *D:* (AA) John Ford; *P:* (AAN-Best Picture) Merian C. Cooper; *St:* Maurice Walsh; *Sc:* (AAN) Frank S. Nugent; *Cinematography:* (AA-color) Winton C. Hoch, Archie Stout; *ASD:* (AAN-color) Frank Hotaling (art director), John McCarthy, Jr., Charles Thompson (sets); *Sound:* (AAN) Daniel J. Bloomberg. (2:09) (video/laserdisc) Comedy and romance abound on Irish locations as an American boxer returns to his native Ireland, falls for a redheaded colleen and when they decide to marry, he runs into all sorts of Irish customs and opposition from her brother. Voted "Best Film of the Year" by the NBR. The Venice Film Festival awarded it the "International Prize" and the New York Film Critics had it in nomination for "Best Picture." On the "10 Best" lists of *Film Daily* and the *New York Times* it placed #2 and #7 respectively. A genuine audience pleaser, it became one of the 23 top-grossing films of 1951-52.

2091. Quincannon, Frontier Scout (United Artists/Bel-Air–Northridge Prod.; 1956). *Cast:* Tony Martin (final U.S. film), Peggie Castle, John Bromfield, John Smith, Ron Randell, Peter Mamakos, Ed Hashim, Morris Ankrum, John Doucette. *D:* Lesley Selander; *P:* Howard W. Koch; *Sc:* John C. Higgins, Don Martin; *Song:* "Frontier Scout" Hal Borne, Sammy Cahn. (1:23) A U.S. army scout is sent on a mission with two soldiers to find out who is selling guns to the Indians. Filmed in the Utah desert in DeLuxe color, it was based on the novel *Frontier Feud* by Will Cook. (G.B. title: *Frontier Scout*) Originally paired on a double bill with *Star of India*, a 1954 British production.

2092. Quo Vadis? (MGM; 1951). *Cast:* Robert Taylor (Marcus Vinicius), Deborah Kerr (Lygia), Leo Genn (AAN/Petronius), Peter Ustinov (AAN/Nero), Patricia Laffan (Poppaea), Finlay Currie (Peter), Abraham Sofaer (Paul), Marina Berti (Eunice), Buddy Baer (Ursus), Felix Alymer (Plautius), Nora Swinburne (Pomponia), Ralph Truman (Tigellinus), Norman Wooland (Nerva), Peter Miles (Nazarius), Geoffrey Dunn (Terpnos), Nicholas Hannen (Seneca), D.A. Clarke-Smith (Phaon), Rosalie Crutchley (Acto), John Ruddock (Chilo), Arthur Walge (Croton), Elspeth March (Miriam), Strelsa Brown (Rufia), Alfredo Varelli (Lucan), Roberto Ottaviano (Flavius), William Tubbs (Anasander), Pietro Tordi (Galba), Lia De Leo (pedicurist), Sophia Loren (extra), Elizabeth Taylor (extra). *D:* Mervyn LeRoy; *P:* (AAN-Best Picture) Sam Zimbalist; *Sc:* John Lee Mahin, S.N. Behrman, Sonya Levien; *Cin:* (AAN-color) Robert Surtees, William V. Skall; *ASD:* (AAN-color) William A. Horning, Cedric Gibbons, Edward Carfagno (art directors), Hugh Hunt (sets); *Music:* (AAN) Miklos Rozsa (based on music of the period); *Costumes:* (AAN) Herschel McCoy; *Editor:* (AAN) Ralph E. Winters. (2:51) (video/laserdisc) A lavishly produced epic costumer of Rome in the days of Emperor Nero, when a Roman soldier must keep his love for a Christian girl a secret. Produced at Cinecetta studios in Rome at a cost of $7,000,000, the film met with worldwide popularity, bringing to MGM the largest gross receipts since *Gone with the Wind* (1939), being one of the 23 such films in 1951-52. On the "10 Best" lists of *Film Daily* and the NBR it placed #8 and #9 respectively. Henryk Sienkiewicz's novel was first filmed in Italy (1912) in 8 reels by director Enrico Guazzoni, an epic production which also gained worldwide fame. Other productions came in 1921 by F.B. Warren and a 1925 Italian production in 9 reels which was released in the U.S. by First National in 1929. Remade for Italian TV in 1985, shown in the U.S. on cable TV. Technicolor.

2093. The Rabbit Trap (United Artists/Canon Prods. for Hecht–Hill–Lancaster; 1959). *Cast:* Ernest Borgnine, David Brian, Bethel Leslie, Kevin Corcoran, June Blair, Jeanette Nolan, Russell Collins, Christopher Dark, Don Rickles. *D:* Philip Leacock; *P:* Harry Kleiner; *Sc:* J.P. Miller (based on his 1955 TV play). (1:12) Drama of a man so obsessed with his work that he neglects his family. Originally ran on a double bill with *Ten Seconds to Hell* (q.v.).

2094. The Race for Space (Wolper, Inc.; 1959). *P:* (AAN-Best Documentary) David L. Wolper. A feature documentary aptly described by the title. Narrated by Mike Wallace.

2095. The Racers (20th Century–Fox; 1954–55). *Cast:* Kirk Douglas, Bella Darvi (final

U.S. film), Gilbert Roland, Cesar Romero, Lee J. Cobb, Katy Jurado, Charles Goldner, John Hudson, George Dolenz, Agnes Laury, John Wengraff, Richard Allan, Franchesca de Scaffa, Norbert Schiller, Mel Welles, Gene D'Arcy, Mike Dengate, Peter Brocco, Stephen Bekassy, June McCall, Frank Yaconelli, Ina Anders, Gladys Holland, Ben Wright, James Barrett, Chris Randall, Anna Cheselka, Joe Vitale, Salvador Baguez, Eddie LeBaron, Peter Norman, George Givot, Carleton Young. *D:* Henry Hathaway; *P:* Julian Blaustein; *Sc:* Charles Kaufman. (1:52) (video) Drama of the European race car circuit and one man, an Italian (Douglas) who rises to fame, takes a dive and later redeems himself. Based on the 1953 novel by Hans Ruesch, it was in DeLuxe color and CinemaScope.

2096. Racing Blood (20th Century–Fox; 1954). *Cast:* Bill Williams, Jean Porter, Jimmy Boyd, George Cleveland, Frankie Darro, John Eldredge, Sam Flint, Fred Kohler, Jr., Fred Kelsey, George Steele, Bobby Johnson. *D:-P: & St:* Wesley Barry; *Sc:* Sam Roeca; *Songs:* "Fa-La-Link-A-Di-Do" and "Pardners." (1:15) Low budget family drama of a stable boy and his uncle who raise a horse, born with a split hoof, that was supposed to be destroyed at birth. SuperCinecolor.

2097. The Rack (MGM; 1956). *Cast:* Paul Newman, Wendell Corey, Walter Pidgeon, Edmond O'Brien, Anne Francis, Lee Marvin, Cloris Leachman, Robert Burton, James Best, Robert Blake, Dean Jones, Rod Taylor, Robert Simon, Trevor Bardette, Adam Williams, Fay Roope, Barry Atwater, Charles Evans, Mary McAdoo, Byron Kane, Willard Sage, David Blair, Ray Stricklyn, Lois Kimbrell, Frank Mills. *D:* Arnold Laven; *P:* Arthur M. Loew, Jr.; *Sc:* Stewart Stern (adapted from a TV play by Rod Serling). (1:40) Drama of a former POW of the Korean War, being court-martialed for treason.

2098. The Racket (RKO/Howard Hughes Presentation; 1951). *Cast:* Robert Mitchum, Lizabeth Scott, Robert Ryan, William Talman, Ray Collins, Joyce MacKenzie, Robert Hutton, Virginia Huston, William Conrad, Walter Sande, Les Tremayne, Don Porter, Walter Baldwin, Brett King, Richard Karlan, Tito Vuolo, Howland Chamberlain, Ralph Peters, Iris Adrian, Jayne Hazard, Claudia Constant, Jack Shea, Eric Alden, Mike Lally, Howard Joslin, Bret Hamilton, Joey Ray, Duke Taylor, Miles Shepard, Curtis Jarrett, Art Dupuis, Harry Lauter, Dulce Daye, Hazel Keener, Steve Roberts, Pat Flaherty, Milburn Stone, Max Wagner, Richard Reeves, Johnny Day, Don Beddoe, Matthew Boulton, Don Dillaway, Barry Brooks, George Sherwood, Jack Gargan, Herbert Vigran, Bud [Bill] Wolfe, Ronald Lee, Dick Gordon, Allen Matthews, Ralph Montgomery, Al Murphy, Robert Bice, Sally Yarnell, Jane Easton, Kate Belmont, Harriet Matthews, Ed Parker. *D:* John Cromwell, Nicholas Ray; *P:* Edmund Grainger; *Sc:* William Wister Haines, W.R. Burnett. (1:28) (video/laserdisc) Film noir of an honest cop battling a powerful crime kingpin, while each fight within their own systems; the cop against corruption, the hood against traitors within. Based on a play of the 1920s by Bartlett Cormack which was first filmed by Howard Hughes in 1928 for Paramount. Computer-colored prints have been produced by Turner Entertainment.

2099. Radar Secret Service (Lippert; 1950). *Cast:* John Howard, Adele Jergens, Tom Neal, Myrna Dell, Sid Melton, Ralph Byrd, Robert Kent, Pierre Watkin, Tristram Coffin, Riley Hill, Robert Carson, Kenne Duncan, Marshall Reed, John McKee, Holly Bane [aka: Mike Ragan], Bob Woodward, Boyd Stockman, Bill Drespinel, Bill Hammond, Jan Kayne. *D:* Sam Newfield; *P:* Barney A. Sarecky; *Sc:* Beryl Sachs. (0:59) Programmer melodrama of the search—via radar—for pilfered atomic materials. The film had the pre-release title of "Radar Patrol."

2100. Rage at Dawn (RKO; 1955). *Cast:* Randolph Scott, Forrest Tucker, Mala Powers, J. Carrol Naish, Edgar Buchanan, Kenneth Tobey, Howard Petrie, Myron Healey, Ralph Moody, Ray Teal, William Forrest, Denver Pyle, Trevor Bardette, Chubby Johnson, Richard Garland, Guy Prescott, Mike Ragan [aka: Holly Bane], Phil Chambers. *D:* Tim Whelan (final film—d. 1957); *P:* Nat Holt; *St:* Frank Gruber; *Sc:* Horace McCoy. (1:27) (video) Technicolor western of undercover agents out to round up the Reno Brothers and their outlaw gang. (aka: *Seven Bad Men*)

2101. The Raging Tide (Universal-International; 1951). *Cast:* Shelley Winters, Richard Conte, Stephen McNally, Charles Bickford, Alex Nicol, John McIntire, Tito Vuolo, Pepito Perez, John "Skins" Miller, Robert O'Neill, Chubby Johnson. *D:* George Sherman; *P:* Aaron Rosenberg; *Sc:* Ernest K. Gann. (1:33) Melodrama of a hood on the run after killing a rival gangster. Based on the 1950 novel *Fiddler's Green* by Mr. Gann.

2102. The Raid (20th Century–Fox/Panoramic; 1954). *Cast:* Van Heflin, Anne Bancroft, Richard Boone, Lee Marvin, Tommy Rettig, Peter Graves, Douglas Spencer, Paul Cavanagh, Will Wright, James Best, John Dierkes, Helen Ford, Harry Hines, Simon Scott, Claude Akins. *D:* Hugo Fregonese; *P:* Robert L. Jacks, Leonard Goldstein; *Sc:* Sydney Boehm. (1:22) A factual Civil War drama in Technicolor of escaped Confederate prisoners in a New England town who plan a raid on the place, and the woman and her son who endeavor to stop it. Based on the story by Francis Cockrell from the article "Affair at St. Albans" by Herbert Ravenal Sass which appeared in *Saturday Evening Post* on 11/1/1947.

2103. The Raiders (Universal-International; 1952). *Cast:* Richard Conte, Viveca Lindfors, Richard Martin, Barbara Britton, Morris Ankrum, William Bishop, Hugh O'Brian, William Reynolds, Lane Bradford, Palmer Lee [aka: Gregg Palmer], Dennis Weaver, Margaret Field, John Kellogg, Riley Hill, Neyle Morrow, Carlos Rivero, George J. Lewis, Francis McDonald. *D:* Lesley Selander; *P:* William Alland; *St:* Lyn Crost Kennedy; *Sc:* Polly James, Lillie Hayward. (1:20) Technicolor western of the 1849 California gold rush. (aka: *Riders of Vengeance*)

2104. Raiders of Old California (Republic; 1957). *Cast:* Jim Davis, Arleen Whelan (final film—ret.), Faron Young, Marty Robbins, Lee Van Cleef, Louis Jean Heydt, Harry Lauter, Douglas Fowley, Larry Dobkin, Bill Coontz, Don Diamond, Rick Vallin, Tom Hubbard. *D: & P:* Albert C. Gannaway; *St: & Sc:* Sam Roeca, Thomas Hubbard. (1:12) Programmer western of U.S. Cavalry officers who try to create their own empire in California following the Mexican War.

2105. Raiders of the Seven Seas (United Artists/Global Prods.; 1953). *Cast:* John Payne, Donna Reed, Gerald Mohr, Lon Chaney, Jr., Anthony Caruso, Henry Brandon, Skip Torgerson, Frank DeKova, William Tannen, Christopher Dark, Howard Freeman (final film until 1965), Claire DuBrey, Anthony Warde. *D: & P:* Sidney Salkow; *St: & Sc:* Salkow, John O'Dea. (1:27) A swashbuckler which has the pirate Barbarossa capturing a Spanish galleon which holds a Spanish countess, thus saving her from marrying a no-account Spanish officer. Technicolor.

2106. Raiders of Tomahawk Creek (Columbia; 1950). *Cast:* Charles Starrett, Kay Buckley, Smiley Burnette, Edgar Dearing, Billy Kimbley, Paul Marion, Paul McGuire, Bill Hale, Lee Morgan, Ted Mapes. *D:* Fred F. Sears; *P:* Colbert Clark; *St:* Robert Schaefer, Eric Freiwald; *Sc:* Barry Shipman. (0:55) A "Durango Kid" series western involving the activities of a corrupt Indian agent. (G.B. title: *Circle of Fear*)

2107. Rails Into Laramie (Universal-International; 1954). *Cast:* John Payne, Mari Blanchard, Dan Duryea, Joyce MacKenzie, Barton MacLane, Ralph Dumke, James Griffith, Harry Shannon, Lee Van Cleef, Myron Healey, Alexander Campbell, George Chandler, Charles Horvath, Stephen Chase, Douglas Kennedy, George Cleveland. *D:* Jesse Hibbs; *P:* Ted Richmond; *St: & Sc:* D.D. Beauchamp, Joseph Hoffman; *Song:* "Laramie" Frederick Herbert, Arnold Hughes (sung by Rex Allen). (1:21) Oater of a saloon owner who is doing his best to prevent the completion of the railroad through Laramie, Wyoming. Originally paired on a western double bill with *Black Horse Canyon* (q.v.). Technicolor.

2108. Rainbow 'Round My Shoulder (Columbia; 1952). *Cast:* Frankie Laine (himself), Billy Daniels, Charlotte Austin, Arthur Franz, Ida Moore, Lloyd Corrigan, Barbara Whiting, Ross Ford, Arthur Space, Frank Wilcox, Diane Garrett, Chester Marshall, Helen Wallace, Eleanore Davis, Eugene Baxter, Ken Garcia, Mira McKinney, Edythe Elliott, Jean Andren. *D:* Richard Quine; *P:* Jonie Taps; *Sc: & St:* Blake Edwards, Quine; *Songs:* "There's A Rainbow 'Round My Shoulder" Dave Dreyer, Billy Rose, Al Jolson; "Bye, Bye, Blackbird" Mort Dickson, Ray Henderson; "She's Funny That Way" Neil Moret, Richard Whiting; "Wrap Your Troubles in Dreams" Harry Barris, Ted Koehler, Billy Moll; "The Last Rose of Summer" Thomas Moore, R.A. Milliken; "Wonderful, Wasn't It?" Hal David, Don Rodney; "Girl in the Wood" Neal Stuart, Terry Gilkyson, and "Pink Champagne" Bob Wright, George Forrest. (1:18) Musical-romance of a girl who heads for Hollywood in hopes of becoming a star. Technicolor.

2109. The Rainmaker (Paramount/Wallis-Hazen; 1956). *Cast:* Burt Lancaster (Starbuck), Katharine Hepburn (AAN/Lizzie Curry), Wendell Corey (File), Lloyd Bridges (Noah Curry), Earl Holliman (Jim Curry), Cameron Prud'homme (H.C. Curry), Wallace Ford (Sheriff Thomas), Yvonne Lime (Snookie), Dottie Lee Baker (Be-linda), Ken Becker (Phil Mackey), Dan White, Stan Jones, John Benson,

James Stone, Tony Merrill, Joe Brown, Michael Bachus. *D:* Joseph Anthony; *P:* Hal B. Wallis, Joseph H. Hazen; *Sc:* N. Richard Nash; *Music:* (AAN) Alex North. (2:01) (video/laserdisc) Comedy of a conman who brings hope to the folks of a drought-ridden area and a spinster who also has romantic hopes for him. Originally a 1955 TV play by Mr. Nash which he expanded into a Broadway play. Later musicalized on Broadway as *110 in the Shade.* Technicolor and VistaVision.

2110. The Rains of Ranchipur (20th Century–Fox; 1955). *Cast:* Lana Turner (Edwina Esketh), Richard Burton (Dr. Safti), Fred MacMurray (Tom Ransome), Joan Caulfield (Fern Simon), Michael Rennie (Lord Esketh), Eugenie Leontovich (Maharani), Gladys Hurlbut (Mrs. Simon), Madge Kennedy (Mrs. Smiley), Carlo Rizzo (Mr. Adoani), Paul H. Frees (Sundar), King Calder (Mr. Smiley), Argentina Brunetti (Mrs. Adoani), John Banner (Ranchid), Ivis Goulding (Louise), Ram Singh (major domo), George Brand (Mr. Simon), Lou Krugman, Rama Bai, Naji Gabbay, Jugat Bhatia, Phyllis Johannes, Trude Wyler, Ram Chandra, Aly Wassil, Elizabeth Prud'homme. *D:* Jean Negulesco; *P:* Frank Ross; *Sc:* Merle Miller; *F/X:* (AAN) Ray Kellogg. (1:44) A talky romantic drama of interracial infidelity as a married English woman seduces an Indian doctor. Then the rains come, followed by an earthquake which shatters the dam and floods everything, setting the stage for the spread of disease. Set in India, this $4,000,000 production highlighted by excellent special effects is a remake of this studio's 1939 production *The Rains Came* and based on the 1937 novel of that name by Louis Bromfield. DeLuxe color and CinemaScope.

2111. Raintree County (MGM; 1957). *Cast:* Montgomery Clift (John Wickliff Shawnessy), Elizabeth Taylor (AAN/Susanna Drake), Eva Marie Saint (Nell Gaither), Nigel Patrick (Prof. Jerusalem Webster Stiles), Lee Marvin (Orville "Flash" Perkins), Rod Taylor (Garwood B. Jones), Agnes Moorehead (Ellen Shawnessy), Walter Abel (T.D. Shawnessy), Jarma Lewis (Barbara Drake), Tom Drake (Bobby Drake), Rhys Williams (Ezra Gray), Russell Collins (Niles Foster), Myrna Hansen (Lydia Gray), John Eldredge (Cousin Sam), Oliver Blake (Jake the bartender), Isabelle Cooley (Soona), Ruth Attaway (Parthenia), Eileene Stevens (Miss Roman), Rosalind Hayes (Bessie), Don Burnett (Tom Conway), Michael Dugan (Nat Franklin), Ralph Vitti [aka: Michael Dante/Jesse Gardner], Bert Mustin (Granpa Peters), Dorothy Granger (Madam Gaubert), Donald Losby (Jim Shawnessy, age 2½), Mickey Maga (Jim Shawnessy, age 4), DeForrest Kelley, Phil Chambers, James Griffith, Owen McGiveney, Charles Watts, Stacy Harris, Robert Foulk, Jack Daly, Bill Walker, Gardner McKay (film debut/better known for his 1960s TV show *Adventures in Paradise*). *D:* Edward Dmytryk; *P:* David Lewis; *Sc:* Millard Kaufman; *ASD:* (AAN-color) William A. Horning, Urie McCleary (art directors), Edwin B. Willis, Hugh Hunt (sets); *Music:* (AAN) Johnny Green; *Costumes:* (AAN-color) Walter Plunkett; *Songs:* "Song of the Raintree" (sung by Nat "King" Cole), "Never Till Now" Green, Paul Francis Webster. (2:48) (video/laserdisc) An opulent production carries this brooding Civil War–era drama of a young woman's disillusionment with her marriage. Location filming for the antebellum South took place in Danville, Kentucky, and in the state of Mississippi, the towns of Natchez and Port Gibson. The swampland scenes were filmed at Reelfoot Lake near Tiptonville, Tennessee. Based on the 1948 novel by Ross Lockridge, Jr., it became one of the 26 top-grossing films of 1957-58. Re-released in 1961. Technicolor, MGM Camera 65 and Perspecta sound.

2112. Rally 'Round the Flag, Boys! (20th Century–Fox; 1958). *Cast:* Paul Newman (Harry Bannerman), Joanne Woodward (Grace Bannerman), Joan Collins (Angela Hoffa), Jack Carson (Capt. Hoxie), Dwayne Hickman (Grady Metcalf), Tuesday Weld (Comfort Goodpasture), Gale Gordon (Capt. Thorwald), Tom Gilson (Opie), O.Z. Whitehead (Isaac Goodpasture, Ralph Osborne III (Danny Bannerman), Stanley Livingston (Peter), Jon Lormer (George Melvin), Joseph Holland (Manning Thaw), Burt Mustin (Milton Evans), Percy Helton (Waldo Pike), Nora O'Mahoney (Betty O'Shiel), Richard Collier (Zack Crummitt), Murvyn Vye (Scar Hoffa). *D: & P:* Leo McCarey; *Sc:* Claude Binyon, McCarey. (1:46) Hit comedy of U.S. Government plans to install a top secret project at Putnam's Landing, Connecticut, and the local citizenry who get up in arms. Based on the 1957 novel by Max Shulman, it became one of the 26 top-grossing films of 1958-59. DeLuxe color and CinemaScope.

Ramar of the Jungle *see* **The White Goddess**

2113. Rancho Notorious (RKO/Fidelity Pictures; 1952). *Cast:* Marlene Dietrich, Arthur

Kennedy, Mel Ferrer, Lloyd Gough, Gloria Henry, William Frawley, Lisa Ferrady, John Raven, Jack Elam, George Reeves, Frank Ferguson, Francis McDonald, Dan Seymour, John Kellogg, Rodd Redwing, Stuart Randall, Roger Anderson, I. Stanford Jolley, Felipe Turich, John Doucette, Joe Dominguez, Charles Gonzalez, Charlita, Ralph Sanford, Lane Chandler, Fuzzy Knight, Fred Graham, Dick Wessel, Dick Elliott, William Haade. *D:* Fritz Lang; *P:* Howard Welsch; *Sc:* Daniel Taradash. (1:29) (video/laserdisc) In this western, Dietrich plays the proprietor of a hideout for wanted men and takes in a man searching for the killer of his girlfriend. Based on the story "Gunsight Whitman" by Silvia Richards. Technicolor.

Rangeland Empire *see* **West of the Brazos**

2114. Ransom (MGM; 1955–56). *Cast:* Glenn Ford, Donna Reed, Leslie Nielsen (film debut), Juano Hernandez, Robert Keith, Richard Gaines, Mabel Albertson, Alexander Scourby, Bobby Clark, Juanita Moore, Robert Burton, Ainslee Pryor, Lori March, Mary Alan Hokanson, Robert Forrest, Dick Rich. *D:* Alex Segal (directorial debut); *P:* Nicholas Nayfack; *Sc:* Cyril Hume, Richard Maibaum (expanded from a TV play titled *Fearful Decision*). (1:49) Successful low budget suspense drama of the marital conflict that is created when a couple's young son is kidnapped. Computer-colored by Turner Entertainment. Remade in 1996 with Mel Gibson.

2115. Raton Pass (Warner; 1951). *Cast:* Dennis Morgan, Patricia Neal, Steve Cochran, Scott Forbes, Dorothy Hart, Basil Ruysdael, Louis Jean Heydt, Roland Winters, James Burke, Elvira Curci, Carlos Conde, John Crawford, Rodolfo Hoyos, Jr. *D:* Edwin L. Marin; *P:* Saul Elkins; *Sc:* Tom W. Blackburn, James R. Webb (based on the 1950 novel by Mr. Blackburn). (1:24) Western of a husband and wife, each of whom own half interest in their cattle ranch, with the wife taking steps to acquire the whole ranch. (G.B. title: *Canyon Pass*)

2116. Raw Edge (Universal-International; 1956). *Cast:* Rory Calhoun, Yvonne De Carlo, Rex Reason, Mara Corday, Herbert Rudley, Neville Brand, Emile Meyer, Robert J. Wilke, John Gilmore, Gregg Barton, Ed Fury, Francis McDonald, Julia Montoya, Paul Fierro, William Schallert, Richard James, Robert Hoy. *D:* John Sherwood; *P:* Albert Zugsmith; *St:* William Kozlenka, James Benson Nablo; *Sc:* Robert Hill, Harry Essex; *Title song:* Terry Gilkyson (sung by Gilkyson). (1:27) Western drama set in a small Oregon town where a man seeks the killer of his younger brother. Technicolor.

2117. Raw Wind in Eden (Universal-International; 1958). *Cast:* Esther Williams, Jeff Chandler, Rossana Podesta, Carlos Thompson, Rik Battaglia, Eduardo di Filippo. *D:* Richard Wilson; *P:* William Alland; *St:* Elizabeth Wilson, Dan Lundberg; *Sc:* Richard and Elizabeth Wilson; *Song:* "The Magic Touch" Jay Livingston, Ray Evans. (1:29) Romantic drama of a fashion model and a playboy whose plane crashes on an isolated island. Filmed in Eastmancolor and CinemaScope on location in Tuscany, Italy.

2118. Rawhide (20th Century–Fox; 1951). *Cast:* Tyrone Power, Susan Hayward, Hugh Marlowe, Dean Jagger, Edgar Buchanan, Jack Elam, George Tobias, Jeff Corey, James Millican, Louis Jean Heydt, William Haade, Milton Corey, Sr., Kenneth Tobey, Dan White, Max Terhune, Judy Ann Dunn, Robert Adler, Vincent Neptune, Walter Sande, Si Jenks, Dick Curtis, Edith Evanson. *D:* Henry Hathaway; *P:* Samuel G. Engel; *St: & Sc:* Dudley Nichols; *Song:* "A Rollin' Stone" Lionel Newman, Bob Russell. (1:26) (video) A gang of desperate men hold a stagecoach relay attendant, a woman and a little girl hostage. A remake of *Show Them No Mercy*, a 1935 crime melodrama by this studio. (TV title: *Desperate Siege*)

2119. The Rawhide Trail (Allied Artists/Terry and Lyon Prods.; 1958). *Cast:* Rex Reason, Nancy Gates, Richard Erdman, Rusty Lane, Frank Chase, Ann Doran, Robert Knapp, Sam Buffington, Jana Davi, Richard Warren, William Murphy, Al Wyatt, John Dierkes, Richard Geary, Chet Sampson. *D:* Robert Gordon; *Ex. P:* J. William Hayes; *P:* Earle Lyon; *As.P:* James Terry; *Sc: & St:* Alexander J. Wells; *Song:* Andre S. Brummer, Jack Lloyd (sung by the Guardsmen). (1:07) Western of two white men who must prove their innocence of collaborating with Comanches in an ambush on a wagon train.

2120. The Rawhide Years (Universal-International; 1956). Cast: Tony Curtis, Colleen Miller, Arthur Kennedy, William Demarest, William Gargan (final film—ret.), Peter Van Eyck, Minor Watson, Donald Randolph, Leigh Snowden, Chubby Johnson, James Anderson, Robert Wilke, Trevor Bardette, Robert Foulk,

Don Beddoe, Malcolm Atterbury, Charles Evans, I. Stanford Jolley, Rex Lease, Chuck Roberson, Marlene Felton, Clarence Lung, Lane Bradford. *D:* Rudolph Maté; *P:* Stanley Rubin; *Adaptation:* Robert Presnell, Jr., D.D. Beauchamp; *Sc:* Earl Felton; *Songs:* "Give Me Your Love," "Happy Go Lucky" Frederick Herbert, Arnold Hughes; "The Gypsy with the Fire in His Shoes" Peggy Lee, Laurindo Almeida (all sung by Miller). (1:25) Western drama of a man who goes into hiding for three years after being accused of murder, then returns to the town of the murder to set the record straight. Based on the 1953 novel by Norman A. Fox. Technicolor.

2121. Rear Window (Paramount/Patron, Inc.; 1954). *Cast:* James Stewart (L.B. "Jeff" Jeffries), Grace Kelly ("Best Actress" by the NBR combined with her work on *Dial M for Murder* and *The Country Girl* [both q.v.]/Lisa Fremont), Thelma Ritter (Stella), Wendell Corey (Thomas J. Doyle), Raymond Burr (Lars Thorwald), Judith Evelyn (Miss Lonelyhearts), Ross Bagdasarian (song writer), Georgine Darcy (Miss Torso), Sara Berner (woman on fire escape), Frank Cady (man on fire escape), Jesslyn Fax (Miss Hearing Aid), Rand Harper (honeymooner), Harris Davenport (newlywed), Irene Winston (Mrs. Thorwald), Marla English (party girl), Kathryn [Grant] Grandstaff (party girl), Alan Lee (landlord), Anthony Warde (detective), Bennie Bartlett (Miss Torso's friend), Iphigenie Castiglioni (bird woman), Ralph Smiley (Carl the waiter), Bess Flowers (woman with poodle), Jerry Antes (dancer), Barbara Bailey (choreographer), Alfred Hitchcock (a butler), Fred Graham, Harry Landers, Dick Simmons, Edwin Parker. *D:* (AAN) Alfred Hitchcock; *P:* Hitchcock; *Sc:* (AAN) John Michael Hayes (based on a 1944 story by Cornell Woolrich); *Cin:* (AAN-color) Robert Burks; *Sound:* (AAN) Loren L. Ryder. (1:52) (video/laserdisc) Classic Hitchcock thriller of a press photographer, confined to his apartment with a broken leg. With a telephoto lens—to pass the time—he spies on his neighbors across the courtyard and suspects one of them has murdered his wife. *Film Daily* placed it at #3 on their "10 Best" list and the British Academy Awards had it in nomination. Box office receipts piled up, making it one of the 25 top-grossing films of 1953-54. Remade in 1998 as a TV movie. Technicolor.

The Rebel (G.B. title) *see* **The Bushwhackers**

2122. Rebel City (Allied Artists/Silvermine Prods.; 1953). *Cast:* Bill Elliott, Marjorie Lord, Robert Kent, Keith Richards, I. Sanford Jolley, Denver Pyle, Henry Rowland, John Crawford, Otto Waldis, Stanley Price, Ray Walker, Michael Vallon, Bill Walker. *D:* Thomas Carr; *P:* Vincent M. Fennelly; *St: & Sc:* Sidney Theil. (1:02) Bill Elliott series western of a man searching for the killer of his father in a Kansas town where a gang of copperheads are aiding the Confederate rebellion. Sepiatone.

2123. Rebel in Town (United Artists/Bel-Air–Prospect Prods.; 1956). *Cast:* John Payne, Ruth Roman, J. Carrol Naish, Ben Cooper, John Smith, James Griffith, Mary Adams, Bobby Clark, Mimi Gibson, Sterling Franck, Joel Ashley, Ben Johnson, Cain Mason. *D:* Alfred Werker; *Ex.P:* Aubrey Schenck; *P:* Howard W. Koch; *St: & Sc:* Danny Arnold; *Title song:* Les Baxter, Lenny Adelson. (1:18) Western drama of a father who vows revenge when his young son is accidentally shot and killed by a member of a family of Confederate bank robbers.

2124. The Rebel Set (Allied Artists/E. & L. Prods.; 1959). *Cast:* Gregg Palmer, Kathleen Crowley, Edward Platt, John Lupton, Ned Glass, Don Sullivan, Vikki Dougan, I. Stanford Jolley, Robert Shayne, Gloria Moreland, Colette Lyons, Joe "Tiger" Marsh. *D:* Gene Fowler, Jr.; *Ex.P:* J. William Hayes; *P:* Earle Lyon; *St: & Sc:* Lou Vittes, Bernard Girard. (1:12) An unscrupulous crook masterminds an armored car robbery and enlists three unsuccessful youths who frequent his beatnik coffee house as accomplices. (aka: *Beatsville*)

2125. Rebel Without a Cause (Warner; 1955). *Cast:* James Dean (Jim), Natalie Wood (AAN/Judy), Sal Mineo (AAN/Plato), Jim Backus (Jim's father), Ann Doran (Jim's mother), Corey Allen (Buzz), William Hopper (Judy's father), Rochelle Hudson (Judy's mother), Virginia Brissac (final film—ret./Jim's grandmother), Nick Adams (Moose), Jack Simmons (Cookie), Dennis Hopper (film debut/Goon), Marietta Canty (Plato's maid), Jack Grinnage (Chick), Beverly Long (Helen), Steffi Sidney (Mil), Frank Mazzola (Crunch), Tom Bernard (Harry), Clifford Morris (Cliff), Ian Wolfe (lecturer), Edward Platt (Ray), Robert Foulk (Gene), Jimmy Baird (Beau), Dick Wessel, Nelson Leigh, Dorothy Abbott, Louise Lane, House Peters, Gus Schilling, Bruce Noonan, Almira Sessions, Peter Miller, Paul Bryar, Paul Birch, Robert B. Williams, David McMahon. *D:* Nicholas Ray;

P: David Weisbart; *St:* (AAN) Ray; *Adaptation:* Irving Shulman; *Sc:* Stewart Stern. (1:51) (video/laserdisc) The quintessential generation gap film of the 1950s of youth at odds with their parents, peer pressure and the need to belong somewhere. A phenomenal success on release, becoming one of the 24 top-grossing films of 1955-56. The film, which was also in nomination at the British Academy Awards, and its star have a cult following to this day, even with those who hadn't been born until after Dean's death. WarnerColor and CinemaScope.

The Reckless Age *see* **Dragstrip Riot**

2126. The Red Badge of Courage (MGM; 1951). *Cast:* Audie Murphy, Bill Mauldin, Douglas Dick, Royal Dano, John Dierkes, Arthur Hunnicutt, Robert Easton Burke, Smith Ballew, Glenn Strange, Dan White, Frank McGraw, Tim Durant, Emmett Lynn, I. Stanford Jolley, William "Bill" Phillips, House Peters, Jr., Frank Sully, George Offerman, Jr., Joel Marston, Robert Nichols, Lou Nova, Fred Kohler, Jr., Dick Curtis, Guy Wilkerson, Buddy Roosevelt, Jim Hayward, Gloria Eaton, Robert Cherry, Whit Bissell, William Phipps, Ed Hinton, Lynn Farr, Andy Devine. *D: & Sc:* John Huston; *P:* Gottfried Reinhardt; *Adaptation:* Albert Band. (1:09) (video) Stephen Crane's classic 1895 Civil War novel of a youth (Murphy) who flees from his first battle, only to return and redeem himself in his own eyes in a later battle. This film (which reportedly originally ran 1:18) was heavily edited after premiering to negative reaction, with narration added by James Whitmore. The NBR placed it at #2 on their "10 Best" list of the year, as well as being in nomination at the British Academy Awards. The film could not recoup its production cost of $1.6 million and it eventually was relegated to the status of double bill showings, probably the most expensive production to attain that distinction. Remade in 1974 as a TV movie.

2127. Red Ball Express (Universal-International; 1952). *Cast:* Jeff Chandler, Alex Nicol, Charles Drake, Judith Braun, Hugh O'Brian, Jacqueline Duval, Jack Kelly, Cindy Garner, Sidney Poitier, Howard Petrie, Buffer Johnson, Robert Davis, John Hudson, Frank Chase, John Pickard, Palmer Lee [aka: Gregg Palmer], Jack Warden, Richard Garland. *D:* Budd Boetticher; *P:* Aaron Rosenberg; *St:* Marcel Klauber, Billy Grady, Jr.; *Sc:* John Michael Hayes (his first). (1:23) Drama of a transport unit during World War II that trucks gasoline and supplies to the frontlines where Patton's troops are pushing toward Paris.

2128. Red Garters (Paramount; 1954). *Cast:* Rosemary Clooney (Calaveras Kate), Jack Carson (Jason Carberry), Guy Mitchell (Reb Randall), Pat Crowley (Susana Martinez De La Cruz), Joanne Gilbert (Sheila Winthrop), Gene Barry (Rafael Moreno), Cass Daley (Minnie Redwing), Frank Faylen (Billy Buckett), Reginald Owen (Judge Winthrop), Buddy Ebsen (Ginger Pete), Richard Hale (Dr. J. Pott Troy). *D:* George Marshall; *P:* Pat Duggan; *St: & Sc:* Michael Fessier; *ASD:* (AAN-color) Hal Pereira, Roland Anderson (art directors), Sam Comer, Ray Mayer (sets); *Songs:* "A Dime and a Dollar," "Meet a Happy Guy," "Vaquero" (all sung by Mitchell); "Lady Killer," "Good Intentions," "Bad News," "Brave Man," "Red Garters" (all sung by Clooney); "Man and Woman" (by Mitchell and Clooney); "This is Greater Than I Thought" (sung by Gilbert); "Big Doins" and specialty dance: Jay Livingston, Ray Evans. (1:31) (video) Offbeat musical-western satire which reminds one of a filmed stage show. A cowboy comes to the town of Paradise Lost in Limbo County, California, seeking the killer of his brother. Audiences were not impressed. Technicolor.

Red Hot Wheels *see* **To Please a Lady**

2129. Red Mountain (Paramount; 1951). *Cast:* Alan Ladd, Lizabeth Scott, John Ireland (William Quantrill), Arthur Kennedy, Neville Brand, Jeff Corey, James Bell, Carleton Young, Walter Sande, Whit Bissell, Bert Freed, Jay Silverheels, Francis McDonald, Iron Eyes Cody, Dan White, Ralph Moody, Crane Whitley, Herbert Belles. *D:* William Dieterle; *P:* Hal B. Wallis; *St:* George F. Slavin, George W. George; *Sc:* John Meredyth Lucas, Slavin, George, Edward Anhalt (unc.), Edna Anhalt (unc.). (1:24) Hit Civil War–era western of a Confederate officer, who goes undercover to bring an end to the nefarious activities of William Quantrill and his raiders throughout Kansas and Missouri. Filmed in Colorado in Technicolor.

2130. Red Planet Mars (United Artists/Melaby Pictures; 1952). *Cast:* Peter Graves, Andrea King, Orley Lindgren, Bayard Veiller, Walter Sande, Marvin Miller, Willis Bouchey, Herbert Berghof, House Peters, Jr., Morris Ankrum, Richard Powers [aka: Tom Kenne], Lewis Martin, Claude Dunkin, Gene Roth, John Topa, Bill Kennedy, Grace Leonard, Vince Barnett.

D: Harry Horner; *P:* Anthony Veiller, Donald Hyde; *Sc:* Veiller, John L. Balderston. (1:27) (video) Low budget anti-communist/pro-religious propaganda in the guise of science fiction as scientists decipher radio signals from Mars which turn out to be from God! Based on the 1933 play *Red Planet* by Balderston and John Hoare, it originally was paired on a double bill with *Outcasts of the Islands*, a British production.

2131. Red River Shore (Republic; 1953). *Cast:* Rex Allen, Slim Pickens, Lyn Thomas, Bill Phipps, Douglas Fowley, Trevor Bardette, William Haade, Emmett Vogan, John Cason, Rayford Barnes, Ko-Ko (horse). *D:* Harry Keller; *As.P:* Rudy Ralston; *St: & Sc:* Arthur Orloff, Gerald Geraghty. (0:54) (video) Series western with Allen as a lawman forced to kill a crooked businessman involved in a phony oil-drilling operation, with complications arising when the man's son arrives in town. Originally paired on the bottom of a double bill with *Jubilee Trail* (q.v.).

2132. Red Rock Outlaw (Friedgen; 1950). *Cast:* Bob Gilbert, Lee "Lasses" White, Ione Nixon, Forrest Matthews, Virginia Jackson, Wanda Cantlon. *D: & Sc:* Elmer [Clifton] Pond; *P:* Unc. (0:56) Ultra low budget oater of an outlaw who concocts a scheme to murder his twin and take his place.

2133. Red Skies of Montana (20th Century-Fox; 1952). *Cast:* Richard Widmark, Constance Smith, Jeffrey Hunter, Richard Boone, Warren Stevens, James Griffith, Joe Sawyer, Gregory Walcott, Richard Crenna (film debut), Bob Nichols, Ralph Reed, William Murphy, Robert Adler, Charles [Bronson] Buchinsky, Mike Mahoney, Larry Dobkin, John Close, Grady Galloway, Henry Kulky, Harry Carter, Charles Tannen, Ron Hargrave, Robert Osterloh, Ted Ryan, John Kennedy, Parley Baer, Barbara Woodell, Ray Hyke, Wilson Wood, Ann Morrison. *D:* Joseph M. Newman; *P:* Samuel G. Engel; *St:* Art Cohn; *Sc:* Harry Kleiner. (1:29) Drama of the men who risk their lives fighting forest fires. (aka: *Smoke Jumpers*) Technicolor.

2134. Red Snow (Columbia/All American Film Corp. Picts.; 1952). *Cast:* Guy Madison, Ray Mala (final film—d. 1952), Carole Mathews, Gloria Saunders, Robert Peyton, John Bryant, Richard Vath, Philip Ahn, Tony Benroy, Gordon Barnes, John Bleifer, Gene Roth, Muriel Maddox, Robert Bice, Richard Emory, Renny McEvoy, Bert Arnold, Richard Pinner, George Pembroke, Robert Carson, William Fletcher, William Shaw (narrator). *D:* Boris L. Petroff, Barry S. Franklin, Ewing Scott (in Alaska); *P:* Petroff; *St:* Robert Peters; *Sc:* Tom Hubbard, Orville H. Hampton. (1:15) Low budget Cold War melodrama of an Eskimo U.S. Air Force unit keeping an eye on nearby Russian activity in Alaska. Includes much stock footage of Eskimos.

2135. Red Sundown (Universal-International; 1955–56). *Cast:* Rory Calhoun, Martha Hyer, Dean Jagger, Robert Middleton, Grant Williams, James Millican (final film—d. 1955), Lita Baron, Trevor Bardette, David Kasday, Leo Gordon, Steve Darrell, Steve Wooten, John Carpenter, Henry Wills, Alex Sharpe, Lee Van Cleef. *D:* Jack Arnold; *P:* Albert Zugsmith; *Sc:* Martin Berkeley; *Title song:* Terry Gilkyson (sung by him). (1:21) Western of an ex-gunfighter who becomes deputy sheriff of the town of Durango and sets out to reconcile problems between local ranchers. Based on the novel *Back Trail* by Lewis B. Patten. Technicolor. Originally ran on a double bill with *The World in My Corner* (q.v.).

2136. The Redhead and the Cowboy (Paramount; 1950). *Cast:* Glenn Ford, Rhonda Fleming, Edmond O'Brien, Alan Reed, Morris Ankrum, Edith Evanson, Perry Ivins, Douglas Spencer, Ray Teal, Janine Perreau, Ralph Byrd, King Donovan, Tom Moore (final film—d. 1955). *D:* Leslie Fenton (final film—ret.); *P:* Irving Asher; *St:* Charles Marquis Warren; *Sc:* Jonathan Latimer, Liam O'Brien. (1:22) The cause for the American Civil War is the background for this western of a female Confederate sympathizer and her plan.

2137. The Redhead from Wyoming (Universal-International; 1952). *Cast:* Maureen O'Hara, Alex Nicol, Robert Strauss, William Bishop, Jeanne Cooper, Alexander Scourby, Jack Kelly, Palmer Lee [aka: Gregg Palmer], Dennis Weaver, Stacy Harris, Claudette Thornton, Ray Bennett, Joe Bailey, Rush Williams, Larry Hudson, David Alpert, Betty Allen, Joe Bassett, Buddy Roosevelt, Edmund Cobb, Philo McCullough, Keith Kerrigan, Bob Merrick, Syd Saylor, George Taylor, Harold Goodwin. Jack Hyde. *D:* Lee Sholem; *P:* Leonard Goldstein; *St:* Polly James; *Sc:* James, Herb Meadow. (1:20) (video) Western of a female saloon keeper who inadvertently finds herself in the middle of a range war and is then charged with murder. Technicolor.

2138. Redwood Forest Trail (Republic; 1950). *Cast:* Rex Allen, Jeff Donnell, Carl Switzer, Jane Darwell, Marten Lamont, Pierre Watkin, Jimmy Ogg, Dick Jones, John Cason, Jack Larson, Robert E. Burns, Joseph Granby, Jimmy Frasher, Bob Larson, Robert W. Wood, Ted Fries, Ko-Ko (horse). *D:* Philip Ford; *As.P:* Franklin Adreon; *St: & Sc:* Bradford Ropes; *Songs:* "Old Smokey," "Sourwood Mountain" and "America the Beautiful." (1:08) Offbeat Rex Allen series western of youths at a rehab ranch for juvenile delinquents who are accused of murder and the cowboy who sets the record straight. "Smokey the Bear" also makes an appearance, giving tips to prevent forest fires.

2139. Reform School Girl (American International/Carmel Prods.; 1957). *Cast:* Gloria Castillo, Ross Ford (final film), Edward Byrnes (film debut), Ralph Reed, Jan Englund, Yvette Vickers, Helen Wallace, Donna Jo Gribble, Luana Anders (film debut), Diana Darrin, Nesdon Booth, Wayne Taylor, Sharon Lee, Jack Kruschen, Linda Rivera, Elaine Sinclair, Dorothy Crehan, Claire Carleton, Lillian Powell, Sally Kellerman (film debut). *D:-St: & Sc:* Edward Bernds; *P:* Robert J. Gurney, Jr., Samuel Z. Arkoff. (1:11) (video) Melodrama of the actions of a reckless and irresponsible young man (Byrnes) that lead two teenage girls to a female reformatory. More or less remade in 1994 as a cable TV movie for Showtime's *Rebel Highway* series. Originally ran on a double bill with *Rock Around the World*, a British production.

2140. The Reformer and the Redhead (MGM; 1950). *Cast:* June Allyson, Dick Powell, David Wayne, Cecil Kellaway, Ray Collins, John Baldwin, Robert Keith, Marvin Kaplan, Kathleen Freeman, Wally Maher, Alex Gerry, Charles Evans, Paul Maxey, Spring Byington (voice only), Herman (lion). *D:-P: & Sc:* Norman Panama, Melvin Frank (their first as a producer-directorial team); *St:* Robert Carson. (1:30) Romantic comedy of a zookeeper's daughter with a pet lion who is wooed by a mayoral candidate.

2141. The Reluctant Debutante (MGM/Avon Prods.; 1958). *Cast:* Rex Harrison, Kay Kendall, John Saxon, Sandra Dee, Angela Lansbury, Peter Myers, Diane Clare, Sheila Raynor, Ambrosine Phillpotts, Charles Cullum. *D:* Vincente Minnelli; *P:* Pandro S. Berman; *Sc:* William Douglas Home (based on his hit 1956 stage play). (1:34) (video) Sophisticated comedy of British parents who must present their daughter to society, with the glitch being that the daughter has been in America and has picked up much American slang, as well as an un-British behavior. In MetroColor and CinemaScope, it was filmed in France instead of England because the Harrisons [Kay Kendall was Mrs. Rex Harrison] owed a large sum of tax money to the British Crown.

2142. Remains to Be Seen (MGM; 1953). *Cast:* June Allyson, Van Johnson, Angela Lansbury, Louis Calhern, Dorothy Dandridge (herself), John Beal, Barry Kelley, Sammy White, Kathryn Card, Helene Millard, Paul Harvey, Morgan Farley, Howard Freeman, Peter Chong, Charles Lane, Larry Blake, Frank Nelson, Robert Foulk, Dabbs Greer, Emmett Smith, Thomas P. Dillon, Dave Willock, Don Anderson, Gregory Gay, Lawrence Dobkin, Frank Scannell, Erno Verebes, Shep Menken, Veronika Pataky, Fernanda Eliscu, Fred Welsh, Dick Simmons, Stuart Holmes. *D:* Don Weis; *P:* Arthur Hornblow, Jr.; *Sc:* Sidney Sheldon. (1:29) A strange blend of comedy and mystery-thriller, with songs, involving an apartment house murder and an heiress in peril. Based on a play by Russell Crouse and Howard Lindsey, the songs include "Too Marvelous for Words," "Toot, Toot, Tootsie" and "Taking a Chance on Love."

2143. The Remarkable Mr. Pennypacker (20th Century–Fox; 1959). *Cast:* Clifton Webb, Dorothy McGuire, Charles Coburn, Jill St. John, Ron Ely, Ray Stricklyn, David Nelson, Dorothy Stickney, Larry Gates, Richard Deacon, Mary Jane Saunders, Mimi Gibson, Donald Losby, Chris Van Scoyk, Jon Van Scoyk, Terry Rangno, Nora O'Mahoney, Doro Merande, Harvey B. Dunne, Ralph Sanford, Joan Freeman, Donald and David Harrison (twins), Pamela Baird, Nancy Ann DeCarl, Anna Marie Nanasi, Diane Mountford, Ray Ferrell. *D:* Henry Levin; *P:* Charles Brackett; *Sc:* Walter Reisch. (1:27) 19th century tale of a Pennsylvania businessman—and former bigamist—who travels between Philadelphia and Harrisburg, as he has a family in each city, totaling seventeen children. Based on a Broadway play which opened in December 1953 by Liam O'Brien.

Remember That Face (G.B. title) *see* **The Mob**

Rendezvous (G.B. title) *see* **Darling, How Could You?**

2144. Reprisal! (Columbia; 1956). *Cast:* Guy Madison, Felicia Farr, Michael Pate, Kathryn Grant, Edward Platt, Frank DeKova, Addison Richards, Otto Hulett, Wayne Mallory, Robert Burton, Ralph Moody, Paul McGuire, Don Rhodes, Philip Breedlove, Malcolm Atterbury, Eve McVeagh, Jack Lomas, John Zaremba, Victor Zamudio, Pete Kellett. *D:* George Sherman; *P:* Lewis J. Rachmil; *Sc:* David P. Harmon, Raphael Hayes, David Dortort. (1:14) Oater of a half-breed's fight for his rights against local prejudice. Based on the 1950 novel by Arthur Gordon, it originally ran on a double bill with *Cha-Cha-Cha Boom!* (q.v.). Technicolor.

2145. The Restless Breed (20th Century-Fox/National Pictures Corp.; 1957). *Cast:* Scott Brady, Anne Bancroft, Jim Davis, Jay C. Flippen, Leo Gordon, Rhys Williams, Myron Healey, Scott Marlowe, Eddy Waller, Harry V. Cheshire, Gerald Milton, Dennis King, Jr., James Flavin, Billy Miller, Evelyn Rudie, Clegg Hoyt, Joe Devlin, Fred Graham, Marty Cariosa, Marilyn Winston. *D:* Allan Dwan; *P:* Edward L. Alperson, Jr.; *As.P:* Ace Herman; *Sc:* Steve Fisher; *Songs:* "Angelita," Never Alone" Edward L. Alperson, Jr., Dick Hughes and Richard Stapley. (1:21) (video/laserdisc) Western melodrama of a man bent on revenge against the party responsible for the death of his father, a secret service agent. Eastmancolor.

2146. The Restless Years (Universal-International; 1958). *Cast:* John Saxon, Sandra Dee, Teresa Wright, James Whitmore, Luana Patten, Margaret Lindsay, Virginia Grey, Alan Baxter, Dorothy Green, Jody McCrea, Hayden Rorke. *D:* Helmut Kautner; *P:* Ross Hunter; *Sc:* Edward Anhalt. (1:26) Melodrama of small town American life and a girl who was told her father died when she was young, when in reality she is illegitimate. Based on the 1955 off-Broadway play *Teach Me How to Cry* by Patricia Joudry. (G.B. title: *The Wonderful Years*) CinemaScope.

2147. Retreat, Hell! (Warner/United States Pictures; 1952). *Cast:* Frank Lovejoy, Richard Carlson, Rusty [Russ] Tamblyn, Ned Young, Anita Louise (final film—ret.), Lamont Johnson, Robert Ellis, Dorothy Patrick, Paul Smith. *D:* Joseph H. Lewis; *P:* Milton Sperling; *Sc:* Sperling, Ted Sherdeman. (1:35) (video) War drama detailing the exploits of the U.S. Marine First Division, during the withdrawal from Korea's Changjin reservoir, after a major Chinese assault.

2148. Return from the Sea (Allied Artists; 1954). *Cast:* Jan Sterling, Neville Brand, John Doucette, Paul Langton, John Pickard, Don Haggerty, Alvy Moore, Robert Arthur, Lloyd Corrigan, Lee Roberts, Robert Wood, Robert Patten, James Best, John Tarangelo, Bill Gentry, Walter Reed. *D:* Lesley Selander; *P:* Scott R. Dunlap; *Sc:* George Waggner. (1:19) Drama of hard-drinking sailor who falls for a lady in San Diego. Their romantic plans are quashed when he is sent to Korea and wounded in action. Based on the short story "No Home of His Own" by Jacland Marmur which appeared in *Saturday Evening Post.*

2149. The Return of Dracula (United Artists/Gramercy Pictures, Inc.; 1958). *Cast:* Francis Lederer, Norma Eberhardt, Ray Stricklyn, Jimmie Baird, Greta Granstedt, Virginia Vincent, John Wengraf, Gage Clark, John McNamara, Harry Harvey, Sr., Mel Allen, Hope Summers, Dan Gachman, Robert Lynn, Norbert Schiller, Charles Tannen. *D:* Paul Landres; *P:* Jules V. Levey, Arthur Gardner; *St: & Sc:* Pat Fielder. (1:17) (video) In this minimally budgeted horror flick, Count Dracula hits the shores of America with stolen papers and resumes his nefarious bloodsucking activities in a small town. Includes a brief color sequence. *The Flame Barrier* (q.v.) was the feature it was paired with on a double bill. (TV title: *The Curse of Dracula*) (G.B. title: *The Fantastic Disappearing Man*)

2150. The Return of Jack Slade (Allied Artists; 1955). *Cast:* John Ericson, Mari Blanchard, Neville Brand, Casey Adams [aka: Max Showalter], Jon Shepodd, Howard Petrie, John Dennis, Angie Dickinson, Donna Drew, Mike Ross, Alan Wells, Raymond Bailey, Lyla Graham. *D:* Harold Schuster; *P:* Lindsley Parsons; *As.P:* John H. Burrows; *St: & Sc:* Warren Douglas; *Song:* "Yellow Rose of Texas" Don George. (1:19) A programmer horse opera which finds the son of outlaw Jack Slade becoming a lawman in an effort to live down his father's reputation. (G.B. title: *Texas Rose*)

2151. The Return of Jesse James (Lippert; 1950). *Cast:* John Ireland, Ann Dvorak, Henry Hull, Reed Hadley (Frank James), Hugh O'Brian, Carleton Young (Bob Ford), Barbara Woodell, Margia Dean, Sid Melton, Victor Kilian, Byron Foulger, Sam Flint, Robin Short, Paul Maxey, Tom Noonan (Charlie Ford). *D:* Arthur Hilton; *P: & St:* Carl K. Hittleman; *Sc:* Jack Natteford. (1:15) (video) In this offbeat low budget western, a ringer for the late Jesse James pulls a robbery and sets folks to wondering if the outlaw is really dead.

Return of the Corsican Brothers (G.B. title) *see* **The Bandits of Corsica**

2152. The Return of the Fly (20th Century–Fox/Associated Producers, Inc.; 1959). *Cast:* Vincent Price, Brett Halsey, David Frankham, John Sutton, Dan Seymour (final film—ret.), Danielle de Metz, Janine Grandel, Richard Flato, Barry Bernard, Francisco Villalobas, Florence Storm, Jack Daly, Michael Mark, Pat O'Hara, Joan Cotton, Gregg Martell. *D: & Sc:* Edward L. Bernds; *P:* Bernard Glasser. (1:20) (video/laserdisc) This sequel to *The Fly* (q.v.—using the source material by George Langelaan) finds the son of the inventor of the matter transference machine following in his father's footsteps, even against the warnings of his uncle. As youth seldom listens to experience, so must this one learn the hard way. Originally ran on the top of a double bill with *The Alligator People* (q.v.).

2153. Return of the Frontiersman (Warner/First National Pictures; 1950). *Cast:* Gordon MacRae, Julie London, Rory Calhoun, Jack Holt, Fred Clark, Edwin Rand, Raymond Bond, Matt McHugh, Britt Wood. *D:* Richard L. Bare; *P:* Saul Elkins; *St: & Sc:* Edna Anhalt; *Songs:* "The Cowboy," "Underneath a Western Sky." (1:14) The son of the sheriff is blamed for a bank robbery and murder. He escapes from his incarceration to find the guilty party. Technicolor.

2154. Return of the Plainsman (Astor; 1952) No information available. Note: Reviewed by *Film Daily* in 1952.

2155. Return of the Texan (20th Century–Fox; 1952). *Cast:* Dale Robertson, Joanne Dru, Walter Brennan, Richard Boone, Tom Tully, Robert Horton, Helen Westcott, Lonnie Thomas, Robert Adler, Kathryn Sheldon, Dennis Ross, Aileen Carlyle, Linda Green, Brad Mora. *D:* Delmer Daves; *P:* Frank P. Rosenberg; *Sc:* Dudley Nichols. (1:28) Western melodrama of a widower who returns to his broken-down ranch, with his father and two sons, to build a new life, but finds a rich rancher is after his property. Based on the 1950 novel *The Home Place* by Fred Gipson.

2156. Return to Paradise (United Artists/Aspen Pictures; 1953). *Cast:* Gary Cooper, Roberta Haynes, Barry Jones, Moira MacDonald, John Hudson, Vala, Hans Cruse, Mamea Mataummua, La'ili, Ezra Williams, Va'a, Herbert Ah Sue, Henrietta Godinet, George Miedeske, Donald Ashford, Terry Dunleavy, Howard Poulson, Malia, Webb Overlander, Frances Gow, Brian McEwen, Kathleen Newick, Kalapu. *D:* Mark Robson; *P:* Theron Warth, Robert Wise, Robson; *Sc:* Charles A. Kaufman; *Title song:* Dimitri Tiomkin (sung by Kitty White). (1:40) (video) In pre–World War II Samoa, a beachcomer has an affair with a native girl, who subsequently dies giving birth to their daughter. He leaves, only to return during the war years to deliver supplies and meet his grown up daughter. Based on the short story "Mr. Morgan" by James Michener which appeared in his 1951 book *Return to Paradise*. Filmed on location in Technicolor.

2157. Return to Treasure Island (United Artists/World Film-Eclipse Films, Inc.; 1954). *Cast:* Tab Hunter, Dawn Addams, Porter Hall, James Seay, Harry Lauter, William Cottrell, Lane Chandler, Henry Rowland, Dayton Lummis, Ken Terrell, Robert Long. *D:* E.A. Dupont (final film—d. 1956); *P:-St: & Sc:* Aubrey Wisberg, Jack Pollexfen. (1:15) This programmer is an updated follow-up (200 years later) sequel to Robert Louis Stevenson's book *Treasure Island*, with a female descendant of Jim Hawkins finding a map to Capt. Flint's buried treasure. Pathécolor.

2158. Return to Warbow (Columbia; 1958). *Cast:* Phil Carey, Catherine McLeod, Andrew Duggan, William Leslie, Robert J. Wilke, James Griffith, Jay Silverheels, Chris Olsen, Harry Lauter, Paul Picerni, Francis De Sales, Joe Forte. *D:* Ray Nazarro; *P:* Wallace MacDonald; *Sc:* Les Savage, Jr. (based on his 1955 book). (1:07) Western of a man's escape from prison and his disappointment when he goes to retrieve his stolen money. Technicolor.

2159. Reunion in Reno (Universal-International; 1951). *Cast:* Mark Stevens, Peggy Dow, Gigi Perreau, Frances Dee, Leif Erickson, Ray Collins, Fay Baker, Myrna Dell, Dick Wessel. *D:* Kurt Neumann; *P:* Leonard Goldstein; *St:* Brenda Weisberg, William Sackheim; *Adaptation:* Lou Breslow; *Sc:* Hans Jacoby, Shirley White. (1:19) Comedy of a little girl who arrives in Reno in search of a divorce from her parents.

2160. Revenge of the Creature (Universal-International; 1955). *Cast:* John Agar, Lori

Nelson, John Bromfield, Robert B. Williams, Nestor Paiva, Grandon Rhodes, Dave Willock, Charles Cane, Clint Eastwood (film debut), Ricou Browning. *D:* Jack Arnold; *P: & St:* William Alland; *Sc:* Martin Berkeley. (1:22) (video/laserdisc) A sequel to *Creature from the Black Lagoon* (q.v.) with the gillman (Browning) being brought from his Amazon river habitat to a Florida aquarium. Followed by *The Creature Walks Among Us* (q.v.). 3-D.

Revenge of the Dead (G.B. title) *see* **Night of the Ghouls**

2161. Revenue Agent (Columbia; 1950). *Cast:* Douglas Kennedy, Jean Willes, Onslow Stevens, Ray Walker, William "Bill" Phillips, David Bruce, Archie Twitchell [aka: Michael Branden], Lyle Talbot, Rick Vallin. *D:* Lew Landers; *P:* Sam Katzman; *St: & Sc:* William B. Sackheim, Arthur A. Ross. (1:12) Low budget crime melodrama, told in a semi-documentary style, of the Internal Revenue Service and its attempts to stop a man from leaving the country with a large amount of gold. Originally ran as part of a double bill with *Lightning Guns* (q.v.).

2162. Revolt at Fort Laramie (United Artists/Bel-Air–Prospect Prods.; 1957). *Cast:* John Dehner, Gregg Palmer, Frances Helm, Don Gordon, Robert Keys, [Harry] Dean Stanton, William "Bill" Phillips, Robert Knapp, Cain Mason, Eddie Little, Bill Barker, Kenne Duncan, Clay Randolph, Frederick Ford. *D:* Lesley Selander; *P:* Howard W. Koch; *St: & Sc:* Robert C. Dennis. (1:13) Western of Union soldiers during the era of the Civil War who rescue a company of Confederate soldiers from the Sioux Indians. DeLuxe color.

2163. Revolt in the Big House (Allied Artists; 1958). *Cast:* Gene Evans, Robert Blake, Timothy Carey, John Qualen, Sam Edwards, John Dennis, Walter Barnes, Frank Richards, Emile Meyer, Arlene Hunter, Francis De Sales, Ed Gelb. *D:* R.G. Springsteen; *P:* David Diamond; *St: & Sc:* Daniel Hyatt, Eugene Lourie. (1:19) Programmer of life in the big house and a planned escape engineered by a self-serving imprisoned hoodlum. Location filming at California's Folsom prison.

2164. The Revolt of Mamie Stover (20th Century–Fox; 1956). *Cast:* Jane Russell (title role), Richard Egan, Joan Leslie (final film—ret.), Agnes Moorehead, Jorja Curtwright, Michael Pate, Richard Coogan, Alan Reed, Eddie Firestone, Jean Willes, Leon Lontoc, Kathy Marlowe, Margia Dean, Jack Mather, John Halloran, Boyd "Red" Morgan, Naidi Lani, Anita Dano, Dorothy Gordon, Irene Bolton, Merry Townsend, Claire James, Sally Jo Todd, Margarita Camacho, Richard Collier, Max Reed, Janan Hart, Johnny Caler, Sherwood Price, Frank Griffin, Charles Keane, Jay Jostyn, Arthur Grady, Kayoka Wakita. *D:* Raoul Walsh; *P:* Buddy Adler; *Sc:* Sydney Boehm; *Songs:* "Keep Your Eyes on the Hands" Tony Todaro, Mary Johnston; "If You Wanna See Mamie Tonight" Sammy Fain, Paul Francis Webster. (1:32) Fact-based drama set in 1940s Hawaii of a Honolulu prostitute—run out of San Francisco—who rises to wealth and notoriety on the islands, at the expense of avoiding the romantic advances of a writer who loves her. Based on the 1951 novel by William Bradley Huie. DeLuxe color and CinemaScope.

2165. Rhapsody (MGM; 1954). *Cast:* Elizabeth Taylor, Vittorio Gassman (violin dubbed by Michael Rabin), John Ericson (piano dubbed by Claudio Arrau), Louis Calhern, Michael Chekhov (final film—d. 1955), Barbara Bates, Richard Hagerman, Celia Lovsky, Richard Lupino, Stuart Whitman, Madge Blake, Jack Raine, Brigit Nielsen, Jacqueline Duval, Norma Nevens. *D:* Charles Vidor; *P:* Lawrence Weingarten; *Sc:* Fay & Michael Kanin; *Adaptation:* Ruth & Augustus Goetz; *Musical interludes:* "Second Piano Concerto in C Minor" Sergei Rachmaninoff, "Violin Concerto in D Major" Peter Ilich Tchaikovsky, and "Hungarian Rhapsody" Franz Liszt. (1:55) (video) Triangular drama of a woman's romantic involvements with both a violinist and a concert pianist. In Technicolor and CinemaScope, it was based on Henry Handel Richardson's 1908 novel *Maurice Guest.*

2166. Rhubarb (Paramount; 1951). *Cast:* Ray Milland, Jan Sterling, Gene Lockhart, William Frawley, Rhubarb (cat—awarded #1 PATSY in 1952), Taylor Holmes, Elsie Holmes, Willard Waterman, Strother Martin, Henry Slate, James Griffith, Jim Hayward, Donald MacBride, Hal K. Dawson, Hilda Plowright, Adda Gleason, Richard Karlan, Edwin Max, Anthony Radecki, Leonard Nimoy, Bill Thorpe, Frank Fiumara, Lee Miller, Roy Gordon, Stuart Holmes, Eric Wilton, Wilbur Mack, Harry Cheshire, John Breen, Tristram Coffin, Donald Kerr, Mack Gray, Oliver Blake, Paul Douglas, Stanley Orr, Robert Richards. *D:* Arthur Lubin;

P: William Perlberg, George Seaton; *Sc:* Dorothy Reid, Francis Cockrell, David Stern; *Song:* "It's a Pleasure to Live in Brooklyn" Jay Livingston, Ray Evans. (1:35) Hit comedy, based on the popular 1946 novel by H.[arry] Allen Smith, of a wealthy man who dies and leaves his estate (as well as his baseball team) to his pet cat, Rhubarb. Much of the comedy comes from the two-leggeds who have to deal with the whole situation.

2167. Rhythm Inn (Monogram; 1951). *Cast:* Kirby Grant, Jane Frazee (final film—ret.), Charles Smith, Lois Collier, Fritz Feld, Ralph Sanford, Armida (final film—ret.), Anson Weeks & His Orchestra, Jean Richey, Amos and Arno, Ramon Ros, Pete Daily, Wingy Manone, Walter Gross, Ralph Peters, Matty Matlock, Joe Yuki, Budd Hatch, Barrett Deems. *D:* Paul Landres; *P:* Lindsley Parsons; *St: & Sc:* Bill Raynor; *Songs:* "It's a Big Wide Wonderful World" John Rox; "Chi Chi" Armida; "Love" Bill Raynor; Edward J. Kay; "B-flat Blues," "Return Trip," "What Does It Matter?" Kay; "With a Twist of the Wrist" Irvin Graham. (1:13) Programmer musical of a Dixieland band forced to pawn their instruments.

2168. Rich, Young and Pretty (MGM; 1951). *Cast:* Jane Powell (Elizabeth Rogers), Danielle Darrieux (Maria Devarones), Wendell Corey (Jim Stauton Rogers), Vic Damone (film debut/Andre Milan), Fernando Lamas (Paul Sarnac), Marcel Dalio (Claude Duval), Una Merkel (Glynnie), Richard Anderson (Bob Lennart), Jean Murat (Mons. Henri Milan), Hans Conried, Duci de Kerekjarto, George & Katrin Tatar, Monique Cantel, The Four Freshmen. *D:* Norman Taurog; *P:* Joe Pasternak; *St:* Dorothy Cooper; *Sc:* Cooper, Sidney Sheldon; *Songs:* "Wonder Why" (AAN-Best Song) Nicholas Brodszky, Sammy Cahn; "Dark Is the Night," "L'Amour Toujour, Tonight for Sure," "I Can See You," "We Never Talk Much," "How Do You Like Your Eggs in the Morning?" Brodszky; "There's Danger in Your Eyes, Cherie" Jack Meskill, Pete Wendling; "The Old Piano Roll Blues" Cy Coben; "Deep in the Heart of Texas" June Hershey, Don Swander; *Choreography:* Nick Castle. (1:35) (video/laserdisc) Popular musical of a young girl, sightseeing in Paris, who finds romance—with a catch. Technicolor.

Richer Than the Earth (G.B. title) *see* **The Whistle at Eaton Falls**

2169. Ricochet Romance (Universal-International; 1954). *Cast:* Marjorie Main, Chill Wills, Rudy Vallee, Pedro Gonzales-Gonzales, Alfonso Bedoya, Ruth Hampton, Benay Venuta, Judith [Rachel] Ames, Irene Ryan, Darryl Hickman, Lee Aaker, Marjorie Bennett, Philip Tonge, Phillip Chambers, Charles Watts. *D:* Charles Lamont; *P:* Robert Arthur, Richard Wilson; *St: & Sc:* Kay Lenard; *Songs:* "Ricochet Romance" Larry Coleman, Jr., Joe Darion (sung by Bedoya); "Las Altenitas," "Para Vigo Me Voy," "Un Tequila" Ernesto Lecuona, Arturo G. Gonzales (all sung by the Guadalajara Trio). (1:20) Comedy with songs of a rowdy speaks-her-mind woman who is hired as a cook on a western ranch.

2170. Ride a Crooked Trail (Universal-International; 1958). *Cast:* Audie Murphy, Gia Scala, Walter Matthau, Henry Silva, Joanna Moore, Eddie Little, Mary Field, Leo Gordon, Mort Mills, Frank Chase, Bill Walker, Ned Wever, Richard Cutting. *D:* Jesse Hibbs (final film—to TV); *P:* Howard Pine; *St:* George Bruce; *Sc:* Borden Chase. (1:28) Western of a bank robber who is mistaken by the town judge for the newly expected marshal, the former playing his newfound mistaken identity for all it's worth. Eastmancolor and CinemaScope.

2171. Ride a Violent Mile (20th Century–Fox/Regal Films; 1957). *Cast:* John Agar, Penny Edwards, John Pickard, Richard Shannon, Charles Gray, Bing Russell, Helen Wallace, Richard Gilden, Sheb Wooley, Patrick O'Moore, Rush Williams, Roberto Contreras, Eva Novak, Merry Townsend, Rocky Shahan, Dorothy Schuyler, Norman Cram, Karl MacDonald. *D:-Ex.P: & St:* Charles Marquis Warren; *P:* Robert Stabler; *Sc:* Eric Norden. (1:20) Civil War–era story of attempts to break the Union blockade of Southern seaports. Originally paired on a double feature program with *Plunder Road* (q.v.). Regalscope.

2172. The Ride Back (United Artists/The Associates and Aldrich Co.; 1957). *Cast:* Anthony Quinn, William Conrad, George Trevino, Lita Milan, Victor Millan, Ellen Hope Monroe, Joe Dominguez, Louis Towers. *D:* Allen H. Miner; *Ex.P:* Robert Aldrich; *P:* William Conrad; *St: & Sc:* Anthony Ellis; *Song:* sung by Eddie Albert. (1:19) Western drama which explores the relationship between a wanted man and the lawman who catches him. As they trek back through Indian country, they also pick up a mute little girl, the sole survivor of an Indian massacre.

2173. Ride Clear of Diablo (Universal-International; 1954). *Cast:* Audie Murphy, Dan

Duryea, Susan Cabot, Abbe Lane, Russell Johnson, Paul Birch, William Pullen, Jack Elam, Denver Pyle, Lane Bradford, Mike Ragan [aka: Holly Bane]. *D:* Jesse Hibbs; *P:* John W. Rogers; *St:* Ellis Marcus; *Sc:* George Zuckerman; *Additional dialogue:* D.D. Beauchamp, *Songs:* "Wanted" Frederick Herbert, Arnold Hughes; "Noche De Ronda" Maria Teresa Lara (sung by Abbe Lane). (1:20) Technicolor western of a cowboy out to get the men responsible for the murders of his father and brother.

2174. Ride Lonesome (Columbia/Ranown; 1959). *Cast:* Randolph Scott, Karen Steele, Pernell Roberts, James Best, Lee Van Cleef, James Coburn (film debut), Boyd Stockman, Roy Jenson, Duke Johnson, Boyd "Red" Morgan, Bennie Dobbins, Lee Marvin, Donna Reed. *D: & P:* Budd Boetticher; *Ex.P:* Harry Joe Brown, Randolph Scott; *St: & Sc:* Burt Kennedy. (1:13) (video) Acclaimed western of a bounty hunter's search for the vicious killer of his wife. In Eastmancolor and CinemaScope, it originally ran on the top of a double bill with *The Two-Headed Spy*, a British production.

2175. Ride Out for Revenge (United Artists/Bryna Prods.; 1957). *Cast:* Rory Calhoun, Gloria Grahame, Lloyd Bridges, Joanne Gilbert, Frank DeKova, Vince Edwards, Michael Winkelman, Richard Shannon, John Merrick, Cyril Delevanti. *D:* Bernard Girard; *P:-St: & Sc:* Norman Retchin; *As.P:* Vic Orsatti. (1:19) Western of whites on U.S. Government orders, trying to remove Cheyenne Indians from their Dakota lands, so they can possess the gold deposits the lands hold. Based on the novel by Burt Arthur.

2176. Ride the High Iron (Columbia/Meridian Prods.; 1956). *Cast:* Don Taylor, Sally Forrest, Raymond Burr, Lisa Golm, Otto Waldis, Nestor Paiva, Mae Clarke, Maurice Marsac, Robert Johnson. *D:* Don Weis; *P:* William Self; *St: & Sc:* Milton Gelman. (1:14) Drama of a Korean War veteran who faces obstacles when he attempts to make it in public relations. Originally intended as a TV production, but released theatrically.

2177. Ride the Man Down (Republic; 1952–53). *Cast:* Brian Donlevy, Rod Cameron, Ella Raines (final U.S. film), Forrest Tucker, Barbara Britton, Chill Wills, J. Carrol Naish, Jim Davis, Taylor Holmes, James Bell, Paul Fix, Roy Barcroft, Douglas Kennedy, Chris-Pin Martin (final film—d. 1953), Jack LaRue, Al Caudebec, Roydon Clark, Claire Carleton. *D: & P:* Joseph Kane; *Sc:* Mary McCall, Jr. (1:30) (video) "Big budget" western from Republic of a girl and a ranch foreman trying to save her late father's ranch from crooks. Trucolor.

2178. Ride, Vaquero! (MGM; 1953). *Cast:* Robert Taylor, Ava Gardner, Howard Keel, Anthony Quinn, Kurt Kasznar, Charlita, Jack Elam, Ted de Corsia, Frank McGrath, Joe Dominguez, Walter Baldwin, Rex Lease, Charles Stevens, Tom Greenway, Paul Fierro, Percy Helton, Norman Leavitt, Movita Casteneda, Almira Sessions, Monte Blue, Philip Van Zandt, Stanley Andrews, Italia De Nublia, Kay English, Joey Ray. *D:* John Farrow; *P:* Stephen Ames; *St: & Sc:* Frank Fenton. (1:30) Hit western drama in widescreen Anscocolor of a young couple attempting to establish a ranch on the Mexican border.

2179. Rider from Tucson (RKO; 1950). *Cast:* Tim Holt, Richard Martin, Elaine Riley, Douglas Fowley, Veda Ann Borg, Robert Shayne, William Phipps, Harry Tyler, Marshall Reed, Stuart Randall, Dorothy Vaughan, Luther Crockett. *D:* Lesley Selander; *P:* Herman Schlom; *St: & Sc:* Ed Earl Repp. (1:00) (video) Series western of a bride-to-be, kidnapped by outlaws, intent on getting her intended's gold claim. Originally half of a double feature program with *Destination Murder* (q.v.).

Riders of Vengeance *see* **The Raiders**

2180. Riders to the Stars (United Artists/A-Men; 1954). *Cast:* William Lundigan, Herbert Marshall, Richard Carlson, Martha Hyer, Dawn Addams, Robert Karnes, Lawrence Dobkin, George Eldredge, Dan Riss, Michael Fox, King Donovan, James K. Best, Kem Dibbs, John Hedloe. *D:* Richard Carlson; *P:* Ivan Tors; *St: & Sc:* Curt Siodmak; *Title song:* Harry Sukman, Leon Pober (sung by Kitty White). (1:20) Early science fiction of rocket travel and the attempts of three travellers on a mission to retrieve a meteor for study. Color Corporation of America.

2181. Ridin' the Outlaw Trail (Columbia; 1951). *Cast:* Charles Starrett, Smiley Burnette, Sunny Vickers, Edgar Dearing, Peter Thompson, Jim Bannon, Lee Morgan, Chuck Roberson, Ethan Laidlaw, Pee Wee King & His Golden West Cowboys, Frank McCarroll. *D:* Fred F. Sears; *P:* Colbert Clark; *St: & Sc:* Victor Arthur. (0:56) A series western which finds the "Durango Kid" on the trail of an outlaw and his stolen gold.

2182. Riding High (Paramount; 1950). *Cast:* Bing Crosby, Coleen Gray, Charles Bickford, Frances Gifford, William Demarest, Raymond Walburn, James Gleason, Ward Bond, Clarence Muse, Percy Kilbride, Harry Davenport (final film—d. 1949), Margaret Hamilton, Paul Harvey, Douglass Dumbrille, Gene Lockhart, Marjorie Hoshelle, Rand Brooks, Willard Waterman, Majorie Lord, Irving Bacon, Joe Frisco (himself), Frankie Darro, Charles Lane, Dub Taylor, Oliver Hardy (final U.S. film), Max Baer, Ish Kabibble. *D: & P:* Frank Capra; *St:* Mark Hellinger; *Sc:* Robert Riskin; *Additional dialogue:* Melville Shavelson, Jack Rose; *Songs:* "Someplace on Anywhere Road," "Sunshine Cake," "We've Got a Sure Thing," "The Horse Told Me" James Van Heusen, Johnny Burke; "The Whiffenpoof Song" Tod B. Galloway, George S. Pomeroy, Meade Minnigerode; "De Camptown Races" Stephen Foster. (1:52) (video/laserdisc) This drama of the racetrack and a horse owner grooming his horse for the big race is a remake of *Broadway Bill* (Columbia; 1934) also directed by Capra. This film utilizes footage from the earlier production. Note: Walburn, Bond, Muse, Harvey and Dumbrille also appeared in the earlier version.

2183. Riding Shotgun (Warner; 1954). *Cast:* Randolph Scott, Wayne Morris, Joan Weldon, Joe Sawyer, James Millican, Charles [Bronson] Buchinsky, James Bell, Fritz Feld, Richard Garrick, Victor Perrin, John Baer, William Johnstone, Kem Dibbs, Alvin Freeman, Edward Coch, Jr., Eva Lewis, Lonnie Pierce, Mary Lou Holloway, Boyd "Red" Morgan, Richard Benjamin, Jay Lawrence, Jack Kenney, Dub Taylor, Jack Woody, Frosty Royce, Ruth Whitney, Phil Chambers, Clem Fuller, Bud Osborne, George Ross, Ray Bennett, Frank Ferguson, Jimmy Mohley, Paul Picerni, Ned Young, Budd Buster, Allegra Varron, Buddy Roosevelt, Joe Brockman, Evan Lowe, Mira McKinney, Holly Brooke, Dick Dickinson, Harry Hines, Opan Evard, Morgan Brown, Bob Stephenson. *D:* Andre De Toth; *P:* Ted Sherdeman; *Sc:* Tom Blackburn. (1:14) Programmer western of a stagecoach shotgun rider who must find the real bad guys and clear his name after he is branded an outlaw. Based on the short story "Riding Solo" by Kenneth Perkins, it was filmed in WarnerColor.

2184. Right Cross (MGM; 1950). *Cast:* June Allyson, Dick Powell, Ricardo Montalban, Lionel Barrymore, Teresa Celli, Barry Kelley, John Gallaudet, Larry Keating, Tom Powers, Mimi Aguglia, Marianne Stewart, David Fresco, Robert "Smoki" Whitfield, Harry Shannon, Frank Ferguson, David Wolfe, Marilyn Monroe, Dewey Robinson, Jim Pierce, Edgar Dearing, Tom Hanlon, King Donovan, Wally Maher, Bert Davison, Ken Tobey. *D:* John Sturges; *P:* Armand Deutsch; *St: & Sc:* Charles Schnee. (1:30) A triangular drama of a sportswriter and a boxer, both romantically inclined toward the same female.

2185. The Ring (United Artists/King Bros. Prods.; 1952). *Cast:* Gerald Mohr, Rita Moreno, Lalo Rios, Robert Arthur, Robert Osterloh, Martin Garralaga, Jack Elam, Peter Brocco, Julia Montoya, Lillian Molieri, Pepe Hern, Victor Millan, Tony Martinez, Ernie Chavez, Edward Sieg, Robert Altuna, Art Aragon (himself). *D:* Kurt Neumann; *P:* Maurice, Frank and Herman King; *Sc:* Irving Shulman (based on his novel). (1:19) (video) Low budget drama of a Mexican-American fighter, encountering prejudice when he takes to the ring to earn money for his poor family.

2186. Ring of Fear (Warner/Wayne-Fellows; 1954). *Cast:* Clyde Beatty (final film/himself), Pat O'Brien, Mickey Spillane (himself), Marian Carr, Sean McClory, John Bromfield, Pedro Gonzales-Gonzales, Jack Strang, Emmett Lynn, Kenneth Tobey, Kathy Cline + 12 circus acts from the Clyde Beatty Circus. *D:* James Edward Grant, William A. Wellman (unc.); *P:* Robert Fellows; *St: & Sc:* Grant, Paul Fix, Philip MacDonald. (1:32) Mystery-melodrama of a series of "accidents" occurring within the confines of the Clyde Beatty Circus. WarnerColor and CinemaScope.

2187. Rio Bravo (Warner/Armada Prods.; 1959). *Cast:* John Wayne (John T. Chance), Dean Martin (Dude), Ricky Nelson (Colorado Ryan), Angie Dickinson (Feathers), Walter Brennan (Stumpy), Ward Bond (final film—d. 1960/Pat Wheeler), John Russell (Nathan Burdette), Pedro Gonzales-Gonzales (Carlos), Claude Akins (Joe Burdette), Malcolm Atterbury (Jake), Harry Carey, Jr. (Harold), Bob Steele (Matt Harris), Estelita Rodriquez (Consuela), Bob Terhune, Nesdon Booth, Ted White, George Bruggeman, Myron Healey, Fred Graham, Riley Hill, Tom Monroe, Bing Russell, Eugene Iglesias. *D: & P:* Howard Hawks; *St:* B.H. Campbell; *Sc:* Jules Furthman (final film—d. 1960), Leigh Brackett;

Songs: "My Rifle, My Pony and Me" Dimitri Tiomkin, Paul Francis Webster (sung by Martin and Nelson); "Cindy" (sung by Nelson) and "Deguello." (2:21) (video/laserdisc) Western drama of a sheriff attempting to hold a prisoner in jail until the U.S. marshal arrives to take custody. Lambasted by critics on release, it became one of the 26 top-grossing films of 1958-59, and has since reached the status of "western classic." Filmed on location in Arizona in Technicolor. *El Dorado* (1967) was a follow-up and *Assault on Precinct 13* (1976) was an urbanized contemporary reworking of the film by John Carpenter.

2188. Rio Grande (Republic/Argosy; 1950). *Cast:* John Wayne, Maureen O'Hara, Ben Johnson, Claude Jarman, Jr., Harry Carey, Jr., Chill Wills, J. Carrol Naish, Victor McLaglen, Grant Withers, Peter Ortiz, Steve Pendleton, Karolyn Grimes, Alberto Morin, Stan Jones, Jack Pennick, Fred Kennedy, Chuck Roberson, Patrick Wayne (film debut), Cliff Lyons and the Sons of the Pioneers: Ken Curtis, Hugh Farr, Karl Farr, Lloyd Perryman, Shug Fisher and Tommy Doss. *D:* John Ford; *P:* Ford, Merian C. Cooper; *Sc:* James Kevin McGuinness (based on the story "Mission with No Record" by James Warner Bellah which appeared in the September 27, 1947, issue of *Saturday Evening Post*); *Songs:* "My Gal Is Purple," "Footsore Cavalry," "Yellow Stripes" Stan Jones, "Aha, San Antone" Dale Evans, "Cattle Call" Tex Owens, "Erie Canal," "I'll Take You Home Again, Kathleen," "Down by the Glen Side" and "You're in the Army Now." (1:45) (video/laserdisc) A big budget western of the U.S. Cavalry dealing with dissident Apaches in the southwest and an officer's relationship with his ex-wife who has just arrived on the post with their son, a new recruit. Critics approved of Ford's third entry in his "U.S. Cavalry trilogy," preceded by *Fort Apache* (1948) and *She Wore A Yellow Ribbon* (1949), both released by RKO. Computer-colored prints have been produced by Turner Entertainment.

2189. Rio Grande Patrol (RKO; 1950). *Cast:* Tim Holt, Richard Martin, Jane Nigh, Douglas Fowley, Cleo Moore, Tom Tyler, Rick Vallin, John Holland, Larry Johns, Harry Harvey, Forrest Burns. *D:* Lesley Selander; *P:* Herman Schlom; *St: & Sc:* Norman Houston. (1:00) Series western involving the border patrol's efforts to curtail gun-smuggling.

2190. Riot in Cell Block 11 (Monogram/Allied Artists; 1954). *Cast:* Neville Brand, Emile Meyer, Frank Faylen, Leo Gordon, Robert Osterloh, Paul Frees, Don Keefer, Alvy Moore, Dabbs Greer, Whit Bissell, James Anderson, Carleton Young, Harold J. Kennedy, William Schallert, Jonathan Hale, Robert Patten, William Phipps, Joel Fluellen, Roy Glenn, Joe Kerr, John Tarangelo, Robert Burton, Frank Hagney. *D:* Don Siegel; *P:* Walter Wanger; *St: & Sc:* Richard Collins. (1:20) (video) A rebellion against prison authority, perpetrated by inmates dissatisfied with prison conditions, brings media attention and reprisal against the rioters. A film that was in nomination at the British Academy Awards.

2191. Riot in Juvenile Prison (United Artists/Vogue Pictures; 1959). *Cast:* Jerome Thor (film debut), Scott Marlowe, Marcia Henderson, John Hoyt, Dick Tyler, Dorothy Provine, Ann Doran, Virginia Aldridge, Jack Grinnage, George Brenlin, Richard Reeves, Al McGrannery, Paul Jasmin. *D:* Edward L. Cahn; *P:* Robert E. Kent; *St: & Sc:* Orville H. Hampton. (1:11) Teen exploitation melodrama of a psychiatrist attempting to turn a reform school into a rehab center.

Riot on Pier 6 (G.B. title) *see* **New Orleans, Uncensored**

2192. River of No Return (20th Century–Fox; 1954). *Cast:* Robert Mitchum, Marilyn Monroe, Rory Calhoun, Tommy Rettig, Murvyn Vye, Will Wright, Douglas Spencer, Ed Hinton, Don Beddoe, Claire Andre, Jack Mather, Edmund Cobb, Jarma Lewis, Hal Baylor, Barbara Nichols, Fay Morley, John Doucette, Arthur Shields, Geneva Gray, Larry Chance, Paul Newlan, Ralph Sanford, Mitchell Lawrence, John Veich, Harry Seymour, Jerome Schaeffer, Ann McCrea, John Cliff, Mitchell Kowal. *D:* Otto Preminger; *P:* Stanley Rubin; *St:* Louis Lantz; *Sc:* Frank Fenton; *Songs:* Title song, "I'm Going to File My Claim," "One Silver Dollar" and "Down in the Meadow" Lionel Newman, Ken Darby. (1:30) (video/laserdisc) Western of a woman (Monroe), abandoned by her husband (Calhoun), who travels down a treacherous river via raft with a widower (Mitchum) and his son (Rettig) after their cabin is burned by Indians. All songs are sung by Marilyn Monroe. Technicolor and CinemaScope.

2193. The River's Edge (20th Century–Fox; 1957). *Cast:* Ray Milland, Anthony Quinn, Debra Paget, Harry Carey, Jr., Chubby Johnson, Byron Foulger, Tom McKee, Frank Gerstle. *D:* Allan Dwan; *P:* Benedict E. Bogeaus; *Sc:*

Harold Jacob Smith, James Leicester. (1:27) Following a robbery, efforts are made to cross the Mexican border with the stolen loot. Filmed on location in Mexico, this western has received latter-day acclaim, though ignored on initial release. Based on the story "The Highest Mountain" by Mr. Smith, the title song was written by Louis Forbes and Bobby Troup and sung by Bob Winn. DeLuxe color and CinemaScope.

2194. Road Agent (RKO; 1952). *Cast:* Tim Holt, Richard Martin, Noreen Nash, Mauritz Hugo, Dorothy Patrick, Robert Wilke, Tom Tyler, Guy Edward Hearn, William Tannen, Sam Flint, Forbes Murray, Stanley Blystone, Tom Kennedy. *D:* Lesley Selander; *P:* Herman Schlom; *St: & Sc:* Norman Houston. (1:00) (video) Series western of a cowboy & his pal who pose as outlaws to retrieve money stolen from the local citizenry by an unscrupulous toll booth operator.

2195. Road to Bali (Paramount/Bing Crosby Enterprises–Hope Enterprises; 1952). *Cast:* Bob Hope (Howard Gridley), Bing Crosby (George Cochran), Dorothy Lamour (Lalah), Murvyn Vye (Ken Arok), Peter Coe (Gung), Ralph Moody (Bhoma Da), Leon Askin (Ramayana), Jack Claus (specialty dancer), Bernie Gozier (Bo Kassar), Bob Crosby (himself), Bunny Lewbel (Lalah, age 7), Harry Cording (Verna's father), Roy Gordon (Eunice's father), Carolyn Jones (film debut/Eunice), Jan Kayne (Verna), Allan Nixon (Eunice's brother), Douglas Yorke (Verna's brother), Dean Martin (cameo), Jerry Lewis (cameo), Jane Russell (cameo), Herman Cantor, Michael Ansara, Donald Lawton, Larry Chance, Richard Keene. *D:* Hal Walker (final film—to TV); *P:* Harry Tugend; *St:* Frank Butler, Tugend; *Sc:* Butler, Hal Kanter, William Morrow; *Songs:* "Chicago Style," "Moonflowers," "Hoots Mon," "To See You," "The Merry Go Runaround" James Van Heusen, Johnny Burke; "Chorale for Brass, Piano and Bongo" Stan Kenton, Pete Rugolo. (1:30) (video) Hit Technicolor comedy (the sixth "road show") of two song and dance men in the South Seas for songs and romance. One of the 26 top-grossing films of 1952-53.

2196. The Road to Denver (Republic; 1955). *Cast:* John Payne, Mona Freeman, Lee J. Cobb, Ray Middleton, Skip Homeier, Andy Clyde (final film—ret.), Lee Van Cleef, Karl Davis, Glenn Strange, Robert "Buzz" Henry, Dan White, Robert Burton, Anne Carroll, Tex Terry. *D:* Joseph Kane; *P:* Herbert J. Yates; *Sc:* Horace McCoy, Allen Rivkin. (1:30) Western melodrama where a conflict of interests between brothers provokes a showdown. Set in Colorado, but filmed on location in Utah. Based on the novel *Man from Texas* by Bill Gulick, which was serialized in *Saturday Evening Post* in 1950. Trucolor.

2197. Roadblock (RKO; 1951). *Cast:* Charles McGraw, Joan Dixon, Lowell Gilmore, Louis Jean Heydt. Milburn Stone, Joseph Crehan, Joe Forte, Barry Brooks, Frank Marlowe, Ben Cameron, Joey Ray, Harold Landon, Martha Mears, John Butler, Peter Brocco, Dewey Robinson, Harry Lauter, Howard Negley, Dave McMahon, Phyllis Planchard, Steve Roberts, Richard Irving, Taylor Reid, Clarence Straight, Jean Dean, Janet Scott, Dave Willock. *D:* Harold Daniels; *P:* Lewis J. Rachmil; *St:* Richard Landau, Geoffrey Homes [aka: Daniel Mainwaring]; *Sc:* Steve Fisher, George Bricker. (1:13) Film noir of an insurance investigator who falls for and marries a money-mad woman, gets involved in a scheme to steal currency due to be destroyed, is framed for murder and eventually pursued by police.

2198. Roadracers (American International/Catalina Prods.; 1959). *Cast:* Joel Lawrence, Marian Collier, Skip Ward, Sally Fraser, Alan Dinehart, Jr., Irene Windust, John Shay, Michael Gibson, Richard G. Pharo, Sumner Williams, Haile Chace, Gloria Marshall. *D:* Arthur Swerdloff; *Ex.P:* James H. Nicholson, Samuel Z. Arkoff; *P: & St:* Stanley Kallis; *Sc:* Ed Lakso, Kallis; *Songs:* "Here You Are" Haru Yanai, Richard Markowitz; "Liz" and "Leadfoot" Lakso. (1:13) Teen market quickie of a race car driver with a penchant for recklessness. Originally paired on a double bill with *Daddy-O* (q.v.). A 1994 production for cable TV utilized the title of this film, but is not a remake.

2199. Roar of the Crowd (Monogram/Allied Artists; 1953). *Cast:* Howard Duff, Helene Stanley, Dave Willock, Louise Arthur, Harry Shannon, Minor Watson, Don Haggerty, Edna Holland, Ray Walker, Paul Bryar, Duke Nalon, Johnnie Parisons, Henry Banks, Manuel Ayulo, Lucien Littlefield. *D:* William Beaudine; *P:* Richard Heermance, William Calihan, Jr.; *St:* Charles R. Marion, Robert Abel; *Sc:* Marion. (1:11) Melodrama of a race car driver obsessed with running in the Indianapolis 500. Of course, he has a wife who wants him to quit racing altogether. Includes intercut racing footage. Cinecolor.

2200. Roaring City (Lippert/Spartan Prods.; 1951). *Cast:* Hugh Beaumont, Edward Brophy, Richard Travis, Joan Valerie, Wanda McKay, Rebel Randall, William Tannen, Greg McClure, Anthony Warde, Abner Biberman, Stanley Price, A.J. Roth, Paul Brooks. *D: & P:* William Berke; *St:* Louis Morheim, Herbert Margolis; *Sc:* Julian Harmon, Victor West. (1:00) Programmer mystery-melodrama which finds amateur sleuth Denny O'Brien (Beaumont) out to solve a series of murders where small time hoods and boxers were the victims. The second and final entry in a short series.

2201. Rob Roy, the Highland Rogue (RKO/Walt Disney British Prods., Ltd.; 1954). *Cast:* Richard Todd, Glynis Johns, James Robertson Justice, Michael Gough, Finlay Currie, Jean Taylor-Smith, Geoffrey Keen, Archie Duncan, Russell Waters, Marjorie Fielding, Eric Pohlmann, Ina De La Hayes, Michael Goodliffe, Martin Boddey, Ewen Solon, James Sutherland, Malcolm Keen. *D:* Harold French; *Ex.P:* Walt Disney; *P:* Perce Pearce; *St: & Sc:* Lawrence E. Watkin. (1:25) (video) Disney's 4th and final British production tells of Scottish Highlander Robert "Rob Roy" MacGregor (Todd), whose opposition to England's King George I (born a German) sets him on a path with fellow clansmen to depose the king. Based on original source material (as opposed to Sir Walter Scott), it is set in the early 18th century, blending historical fact with historical fiction. Robert Frazer portrayed *Rob Roy* in a silent 1913 production, while a U.S.A./Scottish co-production of the same name was released in 1995. (aka: *Rob Roy*) Technicolor.

2202. Robbers' Roost (United Artists/Goldstein-Jacks Prods.; 1955). *Cast:* George Montgomery, Richard Boone, Sylvia Findley, Bruce Bennett, Peter Graves, Warren Stevens, Tony Romano, William Hopper, Leo Gordon, Stanley Clements, Joe Bassett, Leonard Geer, Al Wyatt, Boyd "Red" Morgan. *D:* Sidney Salkow; *P:* Robert Goldstein, Leonard Goldstein; *Sc:* John O'Dea, Maurice Geraghty, Salkow; *Song:* Tony Romano, John Bradford, Barbara Hayden (sung by Romano). (1:22) Western, based on the 1932 novel by Zane Grey, of rival outlaw gangs fighting over a crippled rancher's rangeland. Filmed before in 1933. Eastmancolor.

2203. The Robe (20th Century–Fox; 1953). *Cast:* Richard Burton (AAN/Marcellus Gallio—a role which made him an international star), Jean Simmons ("Best Actress" by the NBR combined with her work in *The Actress* and *Young Bess* [both q.v.]/Diana), Victor Mature (Demetrius), Michael Rennie (Peter), Jay Robinson (Caligula), Dean Jagger (Justus), Torin Thatcher (Senator Gallio), Richard Boone (Pilate), Betta St. John (Miriam), Jeff Morrow (film debut/Paulus), Ernest Thesiger (Emperor Tiberius), Dawn Addams (Julia), Leon Askin (Abidor), Frank Pulaski (Quintus), David Leonard (Marcipor), Michael Ansara (Judas), Nicolas Koster (Jonathan), Francis Pierlot (Dodinius), Thomas Browne Henry (Marius), Anthony Eustrel (Sarpedon), Pamela Robinson (Lucia), Cameron Mitchell (voice of Christ), Helen Beverly (Rebecca), Jay Novello (Tiro), Harry Shearer (David), Emmett Lynn (Nathan), Sally Corner (Cornelia), Rosalind Ivan (Julia), Peter Reynolds (Lucius), Leo Curley (Shalum), Percy Helton (Caleb), George E. Stone (Gracchus), Ben Astar (Cleander), Ford Rainey, Mae Marsh, Virginia Lee, Joan Corbett, Jean Corbett, Gloria Saunders, Roy Gordon, Marc Snow. *D:* Henry Koster; *P:* (AAN-Best Picture) Frank Ross; *Adaptation:* Gina Kaus; *Sc:* Philip Dunne; *Cin:* (AAN-color) Leon Shamroy; *ASD:* (AA-color) Lyle Wheeler, George W. Davis (art directors), Walter M. Scott, Paul S. Fox (sets); *Costumes:* (AA-color) Charles LeMaire, Emile Santiago. (2:15) (video/laserdisc) A fictionalized costume drama of events in the life of the tribune who witnessed the Crucifixion of Jesus Christ and gained possession of his robe. Based on the 1946 novel by Lloyd C. Douglas, it was in nomination for "Best Picture" with the New York Film Critics. *Film Daily* placed it at #3 on their "10 Best" list, while the NBR placed it at #10 on theirs. One of the 25 top-grossing films of 1953-54, it was followed by the sequel *Demetrius and the Gladiators* (q.v.). It was also notable for being the first film released in the widescreen CinemaScope process. Technicolor.

Robin Hood *see* **The Story of Robin Hood**

2204. Robot Monster (Astor/Three Dimensional Pictures; 1953). *Cast:* George Nader, Claudia Barrett, Selena Royle, Gregory Moffett, John Mylong, Pamela Paulson, George Barrows (title role), John Brown (voice only). *D: & P:* Phil Tucker; *St:* Wyott Ordung; *Sc:* Ordung, Guy Reed Ritchie (unc.). (1:03) (video/laserdisc) Another science fiction film which, like *Plan 9 from Outer Space* (q.v.), is a main staple at "bad movie" festivals. The story concerns Ro-Man, an alien (garbed in a gorilla suit and a diver's helmet) ordered to decimate the final six Hu-Mans who survive on earth. Produced on an ultra low budget of $16,000, this film grossed over $1,000,000 from unsuspecting theater patrons, suckered in by publicity hype, who apparently refused to demand their money back! The film also utilizes stock footage from *One Million B.C.* (1940) and *Flight to Mars* (q.v.), neither of which is in 3-D. Tru-Stereo and 3-D. (aka: *Monsters from the Moon*)

2205. Rock-A-Bye Baby (Paramount/York Pictures; 1958). *Cast:* Jerry Lewis, Marilyn Maxwell, Connie Stevens, Baccaloni, Reginald Gardiner, Hans Conried, Ida Moore (final film—ret.), Gary Lewis, Judy Franklin, Isobel Elsom, Alex Gerry, James Gleason, George Sanders, Hope Emerson (final film—d. 1960), Snub Pollard, Hank Mann, Chester Conklin, Franklyn Farnum, Danny Lewis. *D:* Frank Tashlin; *P:* Jerry Lewis; *As.P:* Ernest D. Glucksman; *Sc:* Tashlin; *Songs:* Rock-A-Bye Baby," "Dormi-Dormi-Dormi," "Love is a Lonely Thing," "The White Virgin of the Nile," "Why Can't He Care For Me?," "The Land of La-La-La" Harry Warren, Sammy Cahn. (1:43) Comedy of the bachelor movie fan of a Hollywood sex siren, who cares for the latter's triplets, which she wants to keep a secret from her public. A box office hit, it is a re-working of *The Miracle of Morgan's Creek* (1944). Technicolor and VistaVision.

2206. Rock All Night (American International/Sunset Prods.; 1957). *Cast:* Dick Miller, Abby Dalton, Robin Morse, Richard Cutting, Bruno VeSota, Chris Alcaide, Mel Welles, Barboura Morris, Clegg Hoyt, Russell Johnson, Jonathan Haze, Richard Karlan, Jack DeWitt, Bert Nelson, Beach Dickerson, Ed Nelson, The Platters, The Blockbusters. *D: & P:* Roger Corman (in 5 days); *St:* David P. Harmon; *Sc:* Charles B. Griffith. (1:02) (video) Melodrama of two killers who take refuge in a bar frequented by rock 'n' rollers and hold the patrons and the owner hostage.

2207. Rock Around the Clock (Columbia; 1956). *Cast:* Alan Freed (himself), Johnny Johnston (final film—ret.), Alix Talton, Lisa Gaye, John Archer, Henry Slate, Earl Barton, Bill Haley & His Comets (themselves), The Platters (themselves), Tony Martinez & His Band (themselves), Freddie Bell & the Bellboys (themselves). *D:* Fred F. Sears; *P:* Sam Katzman; *St: & Sc:* Robert E. Kent, James B. Gordon; *Songs:* "Razzle Dazzle," "Happy Baby," "See You Later, Alligator," "Rudy's Rock," "Rock Around the Clock" (performed by Haley & the Comets); "The Great Pretender," "Only You" (performed by the Platters); "Codfish and Potatoes," "Sad and Lonely," "Cuero," "Mambo Capri" (performed by Martinez & Band); "Giddy Up, Ding Dong," "We're Gonna Teach You to Rock" (performed by Bell & the Bellboys). (1:17) (video) A disc jockey (Freed) discovers a band with a new sound and promotes them. Notable as the first musical to feature rock 'n' roll, it was remade in 1961 as *Twist Around the Clock.* Note: This was the film that caused theater riots in England in 1956, leading to the banning of the film, as well as causing the new music phenomenon to get its first bad raps.

2208. Rock Baby, Rock It (Freebar Distributing/Evelyn Rock Prods.; 1957). *Cast:* Johnny Carroll & His Hot Rocks, Johnny Dobbs, Don Coats and the Bon-Aires, Linda Wheeler, Kay Wheeler, Joan Arnold, Cell Block Seven, Bill Brookshire, Five Stars, Gayla Graves, Rosco Gordon and the Red Tops, Mike Biggs, the Belew Twins, Kay Moore, Preacher Smith's Deacons, Lee Young, Dave Miller. *D:* Murray Douglas Sporup; *P:* J.G. Tiger; *St: & Sc:* Herbert Margolis, William Raynor. (1:24) (video) Rock 'n' rollers put on a show and get the best of a bookie operation that is attempting to take away their building. Filmed in Dallas, Texas, with assorted local talent, this low budget indy production is a minor cult item with a following.

2209. Rock Island Trail (Republic; 1950). *Cast:* Forrest Tucker, Adele Mara, Adrian Booth, Bruce Cabot, Chill Wills, Barbara Fuller, Grant Withers, Jeff Corey, Roy Barcroft, Pierre Watkin, Valentine Perkins, Jimmy Hunt, Olin Howlin, Sam Flint, John Holland, Kate Drain Lawson, Dick Elliott, Emory Parnell, Billy Wilkerson, Jack Pennick. *D:* Joseph Kane; *P:* Paul Malvern; *Sc:* James Edward Grant. (1:30) A man overcomes insurmountable odds to extend his railroad in this "big budget" Republic western based on the 1933 novel *A Yankee Dared* by Frank J. Nevins. The offbeat highlight of this film has got to be the fight between Tucker and Cabot with wet mops drenched in hot soup! (G.B. title: *Transcontinental Express*)

Rock 'n' Roll Jamboree *see* **Rock 'n' Roll Revue**

2210. Rock 'n' Roll Revue (Studio Films, Inc.; 1955–56). *Cast:* Duke Ellington, Larry Darnell, Honi Coles & Cholley Atkins, The Clovers, Dinah Washington, Nat "King" Cole,

Lionel Hampton, Conrad "Little Buck" Buckner, Delta Rhythm Boys, Nipsy Russell, Ruth Brown, Mantan Moreland. *D:* Joseph Kohn; *P:* Ben Frye. (1:10 or 1:33) A "Harlem Variety Parade" filmed at various Harlem theaters in 16 mm and tinted. (G.B. title: *Harlem Rock 'n' Roll*) (aka: *Rock' n' Roll Jamboree*) Note: This may be an extended version of *Harlem Jazz Festival*, listed earlier in this work.

2211. Rock Pretty Baby (Universal-International; 1956). *Cast:* Sal Mineo, John Saxon, Luana Patten, Edward C. Platt, Fay Wray, Rod McKuen, John Wilder, Alan Reed, Jr., Douglas Fowley, Shelley Fabares, George Winslow, Bob Courtney, Susan Volkmann, Carol Volkmann, April Kent, Sue George, Walter Reed, Glen Kramer, Johnny Grant (himself), Geri Wilder. *D:* Richard H. Bartlett; *P:* Edmond Chevie; *St: & Sc:* Herbert Margolis, William Raynor; *Songs include:* Title song, "What's It Gonna Be?," "Rockabye Lullabye Blues," "Picnic By the Sea" Bobby Troup + other songs by Sonny Burke, Bill Carey, Rod McKuen, Phil Tuminello and Henry Mancini. (1:29) (video) Teen oriented musical drama, with seventeen rock 'n' roll numbers, of a father's distress over the fact that his son yearns to be a bandleader. Followed by the sequel *Summer Love* (q.v.).

2212. Rock, Rock, Rock (Distributors Corp. of America/Vanguard; 1956). *Cast:* Tuesday Weld (film debut/singing voice dubbed by Connie Francis), Jacqueline Kerr, Ivy Schulman, Fran Manfred, Jack Collins, Carol Moss, Eleanor Swayne, Lester Mack, Bert Conway, David Winters, Alan Freed, Teddy Randazzo, Chuck Berry, The Moonglows, Frankie Lymon and the Teenagers, The Flamingos, Jimmy Cavallo House Rockers, Johnny Burnette Trio, Cirino and the Bowties, the Coney Island Kids, LaVern Baker, Valerie Harper. *D:* Will Price; *P:* Milton Subotsky, Max J. Rosenberg; *St:* Phyllis Coe, Subotsky; *Sc:* Subotsky; *Songs:* Subotsky, Glen Moore, Al Weisman, Ben Weisman, Aaron Schroeder, Buddy Dufault, George Goldner, Johnny Parker, Al Sears, Charles F. Calhoun, Freddie Mitchell, Leroy Kirkland, Chuck Berry. (1:23) (video) Rock 'n' rollers of the era surround a story of a teenage girl who must buy a strapless evening gown for her prom. Songs include "I'm Not a Juvenile Delinquent" by Lymon and the Teenagers; "Tra La La" by Baker and "You Can't Catch Me" by Berry.

2213. Rockabilly Baby (20th Century-Fox/Regal Films; 1957). *Cast:* Virginia Field, Douglas Kennedy, Les Brown (himself), Irene Ryan, Ellen Corby, Lewis Martin, Norman Leavitt, Gene Roth, June Jocelyn, Mary Benoit, Hazel Shermet, Renny McEvoy, Tony Marshall, James Goodwin, Ken Miller, Jimmy Murphy, Barry Truex, Sandy Wirth, Cindy Robbins, Susan Easter, Barbara Gayle, Susan Volkmann, Caryl [Carol] Volkmann, Judy Busch, Marlene Wills, Gary Vinson, Phil Tead, Watson Downs, Frank Marlowe, Frank Sully, Ronald Foster, Fred Darian. *D: & P:* William F. Claxton; *St: & Sc:* Will George, William Driskill; *Songs include:* "We're On Our Way," "Why Can't I?," "Is It Love?," "I'd Rather Be" and "My Calypso Baby" Paul Dunlap, "Teenage Cutie" Dick Kallman (sung by Luis Amando). (1:21) Low budget drama of a woman who takes up residence in a small town with her two offspring and becomes a pillar of the populace. She becomes enamored with the local high school principal, only to have her past catch up with her in the fact that she formerly performed as an exotic fan dancer. Regalscope.

2214. Rocket Attack U.S.A. (Joseph Brenner/Exploit Films; 1959). *Cast:* Monica Davis, John McKay, Daniel Kern, Edward Czerniuk, Arthur Metrano, Philip St. George. *D: & P:* Barry Mahon; *Sc:* uncredited (?). (1:11) (video) Ultra low budget melodrama, padded with much stock footage, of a Russian nuclear attack on New York City. Another product of the communist paranoia which permeated the U.S. in the 1950s.

2215. The Rocket Man (20th Century-Fox/Panoramic Prods.; 1954). *Cast:* Charles Coburn, Spring Byington, Anne Francis, John Agar, George "Foghorn" Winslow, Emory Parnell, Stanley Clements, Beverly Garland, June Clayworth, Don Haggerty, Lawrence Ryle. *D:* Oscar Rudolph (directorial debut); *Ex.P:* Leonard Goldstein; *P:* Robert L. Jacks; *St:* George W. George, George F. Slavin; *Sc:* Lenny Bruce (see note), Jack Henley. (1:19) A family oriented fantasy of a young boy (Winslow) who comes into possession of a special ray gun, which when turned on people forces them to tell the truth. Note: The same Lenny Bruce whose 1974 film biography *Lenny*—based on his play and starring Dustin Hoffman—relayed Bruce's days of persecution as a foul-mouthed night club comic.

Rocket to the Moon *see* **Cat-Women of the Moon**

2216. Rocketship X-M (Lippert; 1950). *Cast:* Lloyd Bridges, Osa Massen, John Emery, Noah Beery, Jr., Hugh O'Brian, Morris Ankrum, Patrick Aherne, John Dutra, Katherine Marlowe, Sherry Moreland, Judd Holdren. *D:-P:-St: & Sc:* Kurt Neumann. (1:17) (video/laserdisc) Early science fiction film of an expedition to the moon which is forced to land on Mars. A film which had the pre-release title of "Rocketship Expedition Moon," it was filmed at Red Rock Canyon, California, with scenes for Mars tinted red. Additional footage filmed in 1976 by producer Wade Williams was included in the home video cassette release of this film. (aka: *Expedition Moon*)

2217. Rockin' the Blues (Fritz Pollard Associates/Austin Prods.; 1956). *Cast:* Mantan Moreland, Flourney E. Miller, Connie Carroll, The Wanderers, The Harptones, The Hurricanes, The Five Miller Sisters, Pearl Woods, Linda Hopkins, Hal Jackson, Reese LaRue, Marilyn Bennett, Elyce Roberts, Lee Lynn, The Cuban Dancers. *D:* Arthur Rosenblum; *P:* Fritz Pollard. (1:06) (video) A "rhythm 'n' blues revue" featuring all-black entertainers.

2218. Rocky Mountain (Warner/First National Pictures; 1950). *Cast:* Errol Flynn, Patrice Wymore, Scott Forbes, Guinn "Big Boy" Williams, Slim Pickens (film debut), Dick Jones, Peter Coe, Howard Petrie, Chubby Johnson, Robert "Buzz" Henry, Sheb Wooley, Rush Williams, Steve Dunhill, Alex Sharpe, Nakai Snez, Yakima Canutt. *D:* William Keighley; *P:* William Jacobs; *Sc:* Alan LeMay, Winston Miller. (1:23) Civil War–era western of troops from both Union and Confederate forces banding together during an Indian attack. Based on the story "Ghost Mountain" by Mr. LeMay.

2219. Rodeo (Monogram; 1952). *Cast:* Jane Nigh, John Archer, Wallace Ford, Gary Gray, Frances Rafferty, Sara Haden, Frank Ferguson, Myron Healey, Fuzzy Knight, Robert Karnes, Jim Bannon, I. Stanford Jolley, Dave Willock, Ann Doran, Milton Kibbee. *D:* William Beaudine; *P:* Walter Mirisch; *As.P:* Richard Heermance; *St: & Sc:* Charles R. Marion. (1:10) A contemporary family oriented western drama of a girl who takes over a rodeo to get her father out of debt. Cinecolor.

2220. Rodeo King and the Senorita (Republic; 1951). *Cast:* Rex Allen, Mary Ellen Kay, Buddy Ebsen, Roy Barcroft, Tristram Coffin, Bonnie DeSimone, Don Beddoe, Jonathan Hale, Harry Harvey, Rory Mallinson, Joe Forte, Buff Brady, Ko-Ko (horse). *D:* Philip Ford; *As.P:* Melville Tucker; *St: & Sc:* John K. Butler; *Songs:* "Strawberry Roan" Curley Fletcher, Caroline Norton, "Juanita" Fred Howard, Nat Vincent. (1:07) (video) Series western of a rodeo star (Allen) who suffers a setback when he gets involved with feuding ranchers. A remake of the 1946 Roy Rogers feature *My Pal Trigger* by this studio.

2221. Rogue Cop (MGM; 1954). *Cast:* Robert Taylor (Christopher Kelvaney), Janet Leigh (Karen Stephenson), George Raft (Dan Beaumonte), Steve Forrest (Eddie Kelvaney), Anne Francis (Nancy Karlane), Alan Hale, Jr. (Johnny Stark), Robert F. Simon (Ackerman), Robert Ellenstein (Sidney Y. Myers), Anthony Ross (Father Aherne), Vince Edwards (Langley), Peter Brocco ("Wrinkles" Fallon), Olive Carey (Selma), Roy Barcroft (Lt. Vince D. Bardeman), Dale Van Sickel (Manny), Dick Simmons (Ralston), Guy Prescott (Ferrari), Ray Teal (Mullins), Phil Chambers (Dirksen), Herb Ellis (barkeep), Lillian Buyeff (Gertrude), Joe Waring (Rivers), Nesdon Booth (Garrett), Connie Marshall (Frances), Nicky Blair (Marsh), Richard Deacon (Stacy), Dallas Boyd (Higgins), George Taylor (Dr. Leonard), Paul Bryar (Marx), Russell Johnson (Carland), Michael Fox (Rudy), Milton Parsons (Tucker), Robert Burton (Cassidy), Carleton Young (D.A. Powell), George Selk [aka: Budd Buster/Parker], Jimmy Ames, Paul Brinegar, Paul Hoffman, Gilda Oliva, Dick Ryan, Benny Burt, Gene Coogan, Mitchell Kowal, Jari Victor. *D:* Roy Rowland; *P:* Nicholas Nayfack; *Sc:* Sydney Boehm; *Cin:* (AAN-b/w) John Seitz. (1:32) Hit low budget drama of a cop on the take, in search of his brother's killer. Based on the 1954 novel by William P. McGivern, computer-colored prints have been produced by Turner Entertainment.

2222. Rogue River (Eagle-Lion/Ventura Pictures; 1950). *Cast:* Rory Calhoun, Peter Graves (film debut), Ellye Marshall, Frank Fenton, Ralph Sanford, George Stern, Roy Engel, Jane Liddell, Robert Rose, Steven Roberts, Duke York. *D:* John Rawlins; *P:* Frank Melford; *As.P:* Irving D. Koppel; *Sc:* Louis Lantz. (1:21) A contemporary western melodrama of a law enforcement officer's efforts to extricate an old prospector from his believed involvement in a robbery. Cinecolor.

2223. Rogue's March (MGM; 1952). *Cast:* Peter Lawford, Richard Greene, Janice

Rule, Leo G. Carroll, John Abbott, Patrick Aherne, John Dodsworth, Herbert Deans, Hayden Rorke, John Lupton, Michael Pate, Lester Matthews, Barry Bernard, Charles Davis, Jack Raine, Richard Hale, Skelton Knaggs, Sean McClory, Otto Waldis, Leslie Denison, Hugh French, Ramsey Hill, Arthur Gould-Porter, Robin Hughes, Francis Bethancourt, Bruce Lester, Elaine Stewart. *D:* Allan Davis; *P:-St: & Sc:* Leon Gordon. (1:24) Lots of stock footage pads this action-adventure of one of the Queen's military men, trying to redeem himself in the eyes of his father, in 19th century India.

2224. Rogues of Sherwood Forest (Columbia; 1950). *Cast:* John Derek, Diana Lynn, George Macready, Alan Hale (final film—d. 1950), Paul Cavanagh, Lowell Gilmore, Billy House, Billy Bevan, Lester Matthews, Wilton Graff, John Dehner, Donald Randolph, Gavin Muir, Tim Huntley, Paul Collins, Olaf Hytten, Symona Boniface, Nelson Leigh, Campbell Copelan, James Logan, Valentine Perkins, Gilliam Blake, Patrick Aherne, Paul Bradley, Matthew Boulton, Colin Keith-Johnston, Byron Poindexter. *D:* Gordon Douglas; *P:* Fred M. Packard; *St:* Ralph Bettinson; *Sc:* George Bruce. (1:20) Action-adventure with the son of Robin Hood returning to Sherwood Forest and regrouping the Merry Men to force King John to sign the Magna Carta. Technicolor.

2225. Roman Holiday (Paramount; 1953). *Cast:* Gregory Peck (Joe Bradley), Audrey Hepburn (U.S. film debut—AA + "Best Actress" from the New York Film Critics and a nomination for "Best British Actress" from the British Academy Awards/Princess Anne), Eddie Albert (AAN/Irving Radovitch), Hartley Power (Mr. Hennessy), Margaret Rawlings (Countess Vereberg), Tullio Carminati (General Provno), Paolo Carlini (Mario Delani), Harcourt Williams (ambassador), Claudio Ermelli (Giovanni), Heinz Hindrich (Dr. Bonnachoven), Laura Solari (Hennessy's secretary), Paola Borboni (charwoman), Gorella Gori (shoe seller), Alfredo Rizzo (taxi driver), John Horne (master of ceremonies); Count Andre Eszterhazy, Col. Ugo Ballerini, Ugo De Pascale, Bruno Baschiera (embassy aides); Princess Alma Cattaneo, Diane Lanti (ladies-in-waiting); Giacomo Penza (H.E. the Papal Nuncio, Monsignor Altomonto), Eric Oulton (Sir Hugo Macy de Farmington); Rapindranath Mitter, Princess Lilamani (H.R.R. The Maharajah and the Raikuuari of Khanipur); Cesare Viori (Prince Istvan Barossy Nagyavaros); Col. Nichola Kopleff, Baroness Teresa Gauthier (Ihre Hoheit der Furst und die Furstin von un zu Luchtenstichenholz); Hari Singh, Kmark Singh (themselves); Luigi Bocchi, Helen Fondra (Count and Countess Von Marstrand); Mario Lucinni, Gherdo Fehrer (Senor & Senora Joaquin de Capoes); Luis Marino (Hasaan El Din Pasha), Armando Annuale (admiral dancing with Princess Anne), Luigi Moneta (old man dancing with Princess Anne), Marco Tulli (pallid young man dancing with Princess Anne), Maurizio Arena (young boy with motorcar); John Fostini, George Higgins, Alfred Browne, John Cortay, Richard McNamara, Sidney Gordon (correspondents at poker game); Richard Neuhaus (embassy guard reporting), Alcide Tico (sculptor), Tania Weber (Irving's model), Armando Ambrogi (man at telephone), Patricia Varner (schoolmarm), Gildo Bocci (flower seller), Giustino Olivieri (cafe waiter), Dianora Veita, Dominique Rika (girls at cafe), Gianna Segale (girl with Irving), Carlo Rizzo (police official), Mimmo Poli (workman), Octave Senoret, Pietro Pastore (faceless men on barge), Giuliano Raffaelli (faceless man on gangplank), Hank Werbe, Adam Jennette, Jan Dijkgraaf, Piero Scanziani, Kurt Klinger, Maurice Montabre, Sytske Galema, Jacques Ferrier, Otto Gross, J. Cortes Cavanillas, Friedrich Lampe, Julio Moriones, Stephen House, Ferdinando De Aldisio, Edward Hitchcock, Desiderio Nobile. *D:* (AAN) William Wyler; *P:* (AAN-Best Picture) Wyler; *St:* (AA) Ian McLellan Hunter (fronting for blacklisted writer Dalton Trumbo); *Sc:* (AAN) Hunter (Trumbo), John Dighton; *Cin:* (AAN-b/w) Frank Planer, Henry Alekan; *ASD:* (AAN-b/w) Hal Pereira, Walter Tyler; *Costumes:* (AA-b/w) Edith Head; *Editor:* (AAN) Robert Swink. (1:59) (video/laserdisc) Hit romantic comedy of a princess who flees from her royal restrictions and has a fling with a reporter. It placed #4, #6 and #8 respectively on the "10 Best" lists of *Film Daily*, the NBR and the *New York Times*. It was also in nomination for "Best Film" with the New York Film Critics, with nominations also in evidence from the British Academy Awards. Hepburn's captivating charm took America by storm, making this a real audience pleaser and one of the 26 top-grossing films of 1952-53. Remade as a TV movie in 1987.

Rommel—Desert Fox (G.B. title) *see* **The Desert Fox**

2226. Roogie's Bump (Republic/John Bash Prods.; 1954). *Cast:* Robert Marriot, Ruth Warrick, Olive Blakeney, Robert F. Simon,

William Harrigan, David Winters, Michael Mann, Archie Robbins, Louise Troy, Guy Rennie, Ted Lawrence (narrator), Michael Keene, The Brooklyn Dodgers, Roy Campanella (himself), Billy Loes (himself), Carl Erskine (himself), Russ Meyer (himself), Robbie (dog). *D:* Harold Young (final film—ret.); *P:* John Bash, Elizabeth Dickinson; *St:* Frank Warren, Joyce Selznick; *Sc:* Jack Henley, Dan Totheroh. (1:11) Fantasy of a young man who with the help of the ghost of a former Brooklyn Dodger becomes a star player for the team. (G.B. title: *The Kid Colossus*)

2227. The Rookie (20th Century–Fox; 1959). Tommy Noonan (himself), Pete Marshall, Julie Newmar, Jerry Lester, Joe Besser, Vince Barnett, Claude Stroud, Dick Reeves, Herbert Armstrong, Norman Leavitt, Peter Leeds, Patrick O'Moore, Rodney Bell, Don Corey, George Eldredge. *D:* George O'Hanlon; *P:* Tommy Noonan; *St: & Sc:* O'Hanlon, Noonan; *Songs:* "I'm Going Home" (O'Hanlon, Paul Dunlap); "You Broke My Saccaphone" (Noonan, Dunlap). (1:26) Stereotypical service comedy, set in the 1940s, of a threesome marooned on a deserted island. Originally paired on a double bill with *Blood and Steel* (q.v.). CinemaScope.

2228. Rookie Fireman (Columbia; 1950). *Cast:* Bill Williams, Barton MacLane, Marjorie Reynolds, Gloria Henry, Richard Quine, John Ridgely, Richard Benedict, Cliff Clark, Barry Brooks, George Eldredge, Gaylord [Steve] Pendleton, Ted Jordan, Frank Sully. *D:* Seymour Friedman; *P:* Milton Feldman; *St:* Harry Fried; *Sc:* Jerry Sackheim. (1:03) While on strike from his regular job as a dock worker, a man takes another job as a fireman and finds it more rewarding. Originally ran on a double bill program with *Indian Territory* (q.v.), a Gene Autry production.

2229. Room for One More (Warner; 1952). *Cast:* Cary Grant, Betsy Drake [the real life Mrs. Grant at the time], Lurene Tuttle, Randy Stuart, John Ridgely, Iris Mann, Gay Gordon, Clifford Tatum, Jr., George Winslow (film debut), Malcolm Cassell, Irving Bacon, Mary Lou Treen, Hayden Rorke, Larry Olsen, Mary Newton, Ezelle Poule, Dorothy Kennedy, Marcorita Hellman, Karen Hale, Doris Kemper, Mary Alan Hokanson, Felice Richmond, Ray Page, Charles Meredith, Oliver Blake, Frank Ferguson, Don Beddoe, Lillian Bronson, William Bakewell, Douglas Fowley, John McGovern, Gretchen Hartman, Tony Taylor, Dabbs Greer, Stevie Wooten, Tramp Jr. (dog—received 1953 PATSY Award of Excellence). *D:* Norman Taurog; *P:* Henry Blanke; *Sc:* Jack Rose, Melville Shavelson. (1:38) Fact-based family oriented domestic comedy of a married couple with three children of their own and two adopted children. Based on the 1950 novel by Anna Perrott Rose, this film inspired the later TV series of the same name. (retitled: *The Easy Way*). Note: Received special mention at the Childrens' Film Fete at the Venice Film Festival.

2230. The Roots of Heaven (20th Century–Fox; 1958). *Cast:* Errol Flynn, Juliette Greco, Trevor Howard, Eddie Albert, Orson Welles, Paul Lukas, Herbert Lom, Gregoire Aslan, Andre Luguet, Friedrich Ledebur, Edric Connor, Oliver Hussenot, Pierre Dudan, Marc Doelnitz, Dan Jackson, Maurice Cannon, Habib Benglia, Jacques Martin, Bachir Toure, Alain Saury, Roscoe Stallworth, Assane Fall, Francis DeWolff. *D:* John Huston; *P:* Darryl F. Zanuck; *As.P:* Robert L. Jacks; *Sc:* Romain Gary, Patrick Leigh-Fermor. (2:11) Philosophical drama of a diverse group of people in Africa attempting to prevent the slaughter of pachyderms. Based on Mr. Gary's 1956 novel, the interiors were filmed in France and the exteriors in French Equatorial Africa. DeLuxe color and CinemaScope.

2231. The Rose Bowl Story (Monogram; 1952). *Cast:* Marshall Thompson, Vera Miles, Keith Larsen, Natalie Wood, Jim Backus, Richard Rober, Tom Harmon, Ann Doran, James Dobson, Clarence Kolb, Barbara Woodell, Bill Walsh, Nancy Thorne (Queen of the 1952 Tournament of Roses Parade) *and her court:* Ann Cottingham, Diana Dial, Carolyn Graves, Barbara Fisher, Sharon Ann Kelley, Marcia Long. *D:* William Beaudine; *Ex.P:* Walter Mirisch; *P:* Richard Heermance; *St: & Sc:* Charles R. Marion. (1:13) Low budget gridiron drama of a quarterback with a swelled head. Includes football footage and footage from the 1952 Rose Bowl Parade in Pasadena, California. Cinecolor.

2232. Rose Marie (MGM; 1954). *Cast:* Ann Blyth, Howard Keel, Fernando Lamas, Bert Lahr, Marjorie Main, Joan Taylor, Ray Collins, Chief Yowlachie, James Logan, Thurl Ravenscroft, Abel Fernandez, Billy Dix, Al Ferguson, Frank Hagney, Marshall Reed, Sheb Wooley, Dabbs Greer, John Pickard, John Damler, Sally Yarnell, Gordon Richards, Lumsden Hare, Mickey Simpson, Pepi Lanzi. *D: & P:* Mervyn LeRoy; *Sc:* Ronald Millar, George Froeschel; *Songs:* "Rose Marie" (sung by Keel), "Indian

Love Call" (sung by Keel and Blyth) Rudolph Friml, Otto Harbach, Oscar Hammerstein II; "Totem Tom Tom" (by chorus), "The Mounties" (sung by Keel and chorus) Friml, Harbach, Hammerstein II & Herbert Stothart; *and written for the film:* "I'm the Mountie Who Never Got His Man" (sung by Lahr) Georgie Stoll, Herbert Baker; "I Have the Love," "The Right Place for a Girl" and "Free to Be Free" Friml, Paul Francis Webster. (1:55) (video/laserdisc) A Mountie falls for a rough girl of the northwoods in this third go-round for the 1924 operetta by Rudolph Friml, Otto A. Harbach, Oscar Hammerstein II and Herbert Stothart; with added DeLuxe color and wide-screen CinemaScope. Closer to the authors' original than the 1936 favorite with Jeanette MacDonald and Nelson Eddy, it was also made as a silent for 1928 release. The Choreography for the lavish "Totem Tom Tom" number, with Joan Taylor, was by none other than Busby Berkeley. Note: "Indian Love Call" was reported to be the favorite song of Dwight D. Eisenhower.

2233. Rose of Cimarron (20th Century-Fox/Alco Pictures; 1952). *Cast:* Jack Beutel, Mala Powers (title role), Bill Williams, Jim Davis, Dick Curtis, Tom Monroe, William Phipps, Bob Steele, Alex Gerry, Lillian Bronson, Irving Bacon. Art Smith, Lane Bradford, Monte Blue, Argentina Brunetti, John Doucette. *D:* Harry Keller; *P:* Edward L. Alperson; *St: & Sc:* Maurice Geraghty. (1:12) Offbeat western of a woman raised by Indians who seeks revenge against those whites who killed her adoptive family. Natural-color.

2234. The Rose Tattoo (Paramount/Wallis-Hazen; 1955). *Cast:* Anna Magnani (U.S. debut, AA + "Best Actress" by the New York Film Critics and the NBR with a nomination for "Best Actress by the British Academy Awards/ Serafina Delle Rose), Burt Lancaster (Alvaro Mangiacavallo), Marisa Pavan (AAN/Rosa Delle Rose), Ben Cooper (Jack Hunter), Virginia Grey (Estelle Hohnegarten), Jo Van Fleet (Bessie), Mimi Aguglia (Assunta), Florence Sundstrom (Flora), Rossana San Marco (Peppina), Augueta Merighi (Guiseppina), Rosa Rey (Mariella), Georgia Simmons (the strega), Zolya Talma (Miss Mangiacavallo), George Humbert (Mr. Mangiacavallo), Margherita Pasquero (Grandma Mangiacavallo), May Lee (Mama Shigura, tattoo artist), Larry Chance (Rosario Delle Rose), Jean Hart (Violetta), Roland Vildo (Salvatore), Albert Atkins (Mario), Dorrit Kelton (school teacher), Lewis Charles, Roger Gunderson, Virgil Osborne. *D:* Daniel Mann (who also directed on stage); *P:* (AAN-Best Picture) Hal B. Wallis, Joseph H. Hazen; *Adaptation:* Hal Kanter; *Sc:* Tennessee Williams; *Cinematography:* (AA-b/w) James Wong Howe; *ASD:* (AA-b/w) Hal Pereira, Tambi Larsen (art directors), Sam Comer, Arthur Krams (sets); *Music:* (AAN) Alex North; *Costumes:* (AAN-b/w) Edith Head; *Editor:* (AAN) Warren Low. (1:57) (video/laserdisc) Acclaimed drama of the romance between a widowed Italian dressmaker and a truck driver in an American Gulf Coast town. Based on the Broadway play by Tennessee Williams (who had Magnani in mind for the role of Serafina when he wrote it). The NBR placed it at #6 on their "10 Best" list of the year, while *Film Daily* placed it at #10 on their "10 Best" list of 1956. One of the 24 top-grossing films of 1955-56, it was also in nomination for "Best Picture" with the New York Film Critics. VistaVision.

Rough Company (G.B. title) *see* **The Violent Men**

2235. Rough Riders of Durango (Republic; 1950). *Cast:* Allan Lane, Walter Baldwin, Aline Towne, Steve Darrell, Ross Ford, Denver Pyle, Stuart Randall, Tom London, Hal Price, Russ Whiteman, Dale Van Sickel, Bob Burns, Black Jack (horse). *D:* Fred C. Brannon; *As.P:* Gordon Kay; *St: & Sc:* M. Coates Webster. (1:00) "Rocky" Lane series western of farmers plagued by grain shipment hijackers. A low budget effort with much stock footage.

2236. The Rough, Tough West (Columbia; 1952). *Cast:* Charles Starrett, Smiley Burnette, Jack [Jock] Mahoney, Carolina Cotton, Pee Wee King and His Golden West Cowboys, Marshall Reed, Fred F. Sears, Bert Arnold, Tommy Ivo, Boyd "Red" Morgan, Valeria Fisher, Tommy Kingston. *D:* Ray Nazarro; *P:* Colbert Clark; *St: & Sc:* Barry Shipman; *Song:* "Cause I'm in Love" Stan Jones (sung by Cotton). (0:54) Latter-day "Durango Kid" series western of a scheme to rob local miners of the fruits of their labors. *Barbed Wire* (q.v.), a Gene Autry western, filled out the double bill matinee program.

2237. The Royal African Rifles (Monogram/Allied Artists; 1953). *Cast:* Louis Hayward, Veronica Hurst, Michael Pate, Angela Greene, Steven Geray, Roy Glenn, Bruce Lester, Barry Bernard, Robert Osterloh, John Warburton, Pat Aherne. *D:* Lesley Selander; *P:* Richard Heermance; *St: & Sc:* Dan Ullman. (1:15) A

British officer (Hayward) is assigned the task of delivering machine guns to the Royal African Rifles in East Africa. An action programmer set in 1910. (G.B. title: *Storm Over Africa*)

2238. Royal Wedding (MGM; 1951). *Cast:* Fred Astaire (Tom Brown), Jane Powell (replacing Judy Garland/Ellen Bowen), Peter Lawford (Lord John Brindale), Sarah Churchill (U.S. debut, replacing Jane Powell, who replaced Judy Garland/Anne Ashmond), Keenan Wynn (Irving Klinger/Edgar Klinger), Albert Sharpe (James Ashmond), Viola Roache (Sarah Ashmond), Alex Frazer (Chester), Jack Reilly (Pete Cumberly), William Cabanne (Dick), John Hedloe (Billy), Francis Bethancourt (Charles Gordon), Jack Daley (Pop), Kerry O'Day (Linda), Pat Williams (Barbara), Jimmy Fairfax (Harry), David Thursby, Henri Letondal, James Finlayson (final film—d. 1953), James Horne, Jack Gargan, Mae Clarke, Wendy Howard, Eric Wilton, Helen Winston, Wilson Benge, Margaret Bert, Leonard Mudie, Phyllis Morris, Bess Flowers, Oliver Cross, Wilson Wood. *D:* Stanley Donen (solo directorial debut); *P:* Arthur Freed; *St: & Sc:* Alan Jay Lerner; *Choreography:* Nick Castle; *Songs:* "You're All the World to Me," "How Could You Believe Me When I Said I Love You When You Know I've Been a Liar All My Life?," "Sunday Jumps," "Every Night at Seven," "Open Your Eyes," "The Happiest Day of My Life," "I Left My Hat in Haiti," "Too Late Now" (AAN-Best Song), "What a Lovely Day For a Wedding," "I Got Me a Baby" Lerner, Burton Lane. (1:33) (video/laserdisc) Hit musical set in London at the time of the marriage between Elizabeth II and Prince Philip. Notable for Astaire's dance on the ceiling, it became one of the 23 top-grossing films of 1950-51. (G.B. title: *Wedding Bells*) Technicolor.

2239. Ruby Gentry (20th Century–Fox/ Bernhard-Vidor Prods.; 1952). *Cast:* Jennifer Jones (title role), Charlton Heston, Karl Malden, Tom Tully, Bernard Phillips, James Anderson, Josephine Hutchinson, Phyllis Avery, Herbert Heyes, Myra Marsh, Charles Cane, Sam Flint, Frank Wilcox. *D:* King Vidor; *P:* Joseph Bernhard; *As.P:* Vidor; *St:* Arthur Fitz-Richard; *Sc:* Silvia Richards; *Song:* "Ruby" Heinz Roemheld, Mitchell Parish (which became a big hit on the harmonica by Larry Adler). (1:22) (video) Melodrama of wealth, poverty, love, hate and a spite marriage, all of which contribute to murder. A box office hit, set in the back country of North Carolina.

2240. Rumble on the Docks (Columbia/ Clover Prods.; 1956). *Cast:* James Darren (film debut), Laurie Carroll, Michael Granger, Jerry Janger, Robert Blake, Edgar Barrier, Celia Lovsky, David Bond, Timothy Carey, Barry Froner, Dan Terranova, Don Devlin, Stephen H. Sears, Robert C. Ross, Salvatore Anthony, Joseph Vitale, David Orrick, Larry Blake, Steve Warren, Don Garrett, Joel Ashley, Freddie Bell & the Bellboys. *D:* Fred F. Sears; *P:* Sam Katzman; *Sc:* Lou Morheim, Jack DeWitt. (1:22) The leader of a street gang gets involved with hoodlums and corruption on the docks. Based on the 1953 book by Frank Paley [pseudonym of Frank Palescandolo]. Originally ran on the bottom of a double bill with *Don't Knock the Rock* (q.v.).

2241. Run for Cover (Paramount/Pine-Thomas; 1955). *Cast:* James Cagney, Viveca Lindfors, John Derek, Jean Hersholt (final film—d. 1956), Grant Withers, Jack Lambert, Ernest Borgnine, Ray Teal, Irving Bacon, Trevor Bardette, John Miljan, Gus Schilling, Emerson Treacy, Denver Pyle, Henry Wills, Phil Chambers, Harold Kennedy, Joe Haworth, Rocky Shahan, Bob Folkerson, Jack Montgomery, Frank Cordell, Frank Bailes, Howard Joslin. *D:* Nicholas Ray; *P:* William H. Pine, William C. Thomas; *St:* Irving Ravetch, Harriet Frank, Jr.; *Sc:* Winston Miller. (1:33) Offbeat western of an ex-con who becomes sheriff, only to find himself drawn into a train robbery by his troublesome sidekick. One of Cagney's rare excursions into the western genre. Technicolor and VistaVision.

2242. Run for the Hills (Realart/Kinego-Rand; 1953). *Cast:* Sonny Tufts, Barbara Payton, John Harmon, Mauritz Hugo, Harry Lewis, Vici Raaf, Jack Wrightson, Paul Maxey, John Hamilton, Byron Foulger, Sid Slate, Deeann Johnson, George Sanders, Rosemary Colligan, Jack McElroy, Charles Victor, William Fawcett, Ray Parsons, Jean Willes, Richard Benedict, Michael Fox. *D:* Lew Landers; *P:* Mark O. Rice, R.D. Ervin; *St:* Leonard Neubauer; *Sc:* Richard Straubb. (1:12) A low budget effort of a family in fear of nuclear attack who hide in a cave. Note: Screenwriter Straubb had his on-screen credit withdrawn from this film!

2243. Run for the Sun (United Artists/ Russ-Field Corp.; 1956). *Cast:* Richard Widmark, Trevor Howard, Jane Greer, Peter Van Eyck, Carlos Henning, Juan Garcia, Jose Antonio Gerbajal, Jose Chavez Trowe, Guillermo

Talles, Margarito Luna, Guillermo Bravo Sosa, Enedina Diaz de Leon. *D:* Roy Boulting; *P:* Harry Tatelman; *Sc:* Dudley Nichols, Boulting; *Songs:* "Taco," "Triste Ranchero" Frederick Steiner, Nestor Amaral. (1:39) (video) An author and a magazine reporter are on a plane downed in the jungle, who come across a plantation owned by a British traitor and a Nazi fugitive. Filmed in Mexico, it was based on Richard Connell's short story "The Most Dangerous Game." Filmed under that title by RKO in 1932 and remade by that same studio in 1946 as *Game of Death*. Eastmancolor and SuperScope 235.

2244. Run of the Arrow (Universal-International/RKO-Globe Enterprises; 1957). *Cast:* Rod Steiger, Sarita Montiel, Brian Keith, Ralph Meeker, Jay C. Flippen, Charles Bronson, Colonel Tim McCoy, Olive Carey, H.M. Wynant, Neyle Morrow, Frank DeKova, Stuart Randall, Frank Warner, Billy Miller, Chuck Hayward, Chuck Roberson, Carleton Young, Don Orlando, Bill White, Jr., Frank Baker (General Robert E. Lee), Emile Avery (General U.S. Grant), Angie Dickinson (voice over for Sarita Montiel). *D:-P:-St: & Sc:* Samuel Fuller. (1:26) (video) Offbeat western of a Confederate soldier who cannot accept the defeat brought about by the Civil War and aligns himself with Sioux Indians against whites. Produced for RKO, with release by Universal after the former studio closed up shop. Paired on a double bill with *Joe Dakota* (q.v.). (video title: *Hot Lead*) Technicolor and RKO-Scope.

2245. Run Silent, Run Deep (United Artists/Jeffrey Prods., Inc. *for* Hecht–Hill-Lancaster; 1958). *Cast:* Clark Gable, Burt Lancaster, Jack Warden, Brad Dexter, Don Rickles (film debut), Nick Cravat, Joe Maross, Eddie Foy III, Mary LaRoche, Rudy Bond, H.M. Wynant, John Bryant, Ken Lynch, Joel Fluellen, Jimmie Bates, John Gibson. (1:33) (video) World War II drama set on a submarine of the sub's commander on an obsessive vendetta against the Japanese ship that once sank him while his second-in-command thinks his superior is ready for a "section 8." Based on the 1955 novel by Commander Edward L. Beach.

2246. Runaway Daughters (American International; 1956). *Cast:* Marla English, Anna Sten, John Litel, Lance Fuller, Adele Jergens, Mary Ellen Kay, Gloria Castillo, Jay Adler, Steve Terrell, Nicky Blair, Frank J. Gorshin, Maureen Cassidy, Reed Howes, Anne O'Neal, Edmund Cobb. *D:* Edward L. Cahn; *P:* Alex Gordon; *Sc: & St:* Lou Rusoff. (1:32) Melodrama of three teenage girls who head for Hollywood to escape their problematic domestic situations with their parents, but find life in tinseltown creates its own set of problems. Remade in 1994 by "Showtime" for their *Rebel Highway* cable series. Originally paired on a double bill with *Shake, Rattle and Rock* (q.v.).

2247. Running Target (United Artists/Canyon Pictures; 1956). *Cast:* Arthur Franz, Doris Dowling, Richard Reeves, Myron Healey, James Parnell, Charles Delaney, Gene Roth, James Anderson, Frank Richards, Nicholas Rutgers. *D:* Marvin R. Weinstein; *P:* Jack C. Couffer; *As.P:* Nicholas Rutgers; *Sc:* Weinstein, Couffer, Conrad Hall. (1:23) The story "My Brother Down There" by Steve Frazee was the source material for this melodrama of a manhunt for four escaped convicts in the Colorado Rockies. In DeLuxe color, it was originally paired on a double bill with *The Wild Party* (q.v.).

2248. Running Wild (Universal-International; 1955). *Cast:* William Campbell, Mamie Van Doren, Keenan Wynn, Kathleen Case, Jan Merlin, John Saxon, Walter Coy, Grace Mills, Chris Randall, Michael Fox, Will J. White, Richard Castle, Otto Waldis, Sumner Williams. *D:* Abner Biberman; *P:* Howard Pine; *Sc:* Leo Townsend. (1:21) (video) Programmer crime melodrama of a young rookie cop, posing as a teen, to get the goods on a gang of car thieves. Based on the 1954 novel *Girl in the Cage* by Ben Benson.

2249. Rustlers on Horseback (Republic; 1950). *Cast:* Allan Lane, Eddy Waller, Roy Barcroft, Claudia Barrett, John Eldredge, George Nader, Forrest Taylor, John Cason, Stuart Randall, Douglas Evans, Tom Monroe, Black Jack (horse). *D:* Fred C. Brannon; *As.P:* Gordon Kay; *St: & Sc:* Richard Wormser. (1:00) "Rocky" Lane series oater of two cowpokes who intervene on an outlaw gang's intent to steal a ranch for resale. Originally ran on a double bill with *North of the Great Divide* (q.v.).

2250. Saadia (MGM; 1953). *Cast:* Cornel Wilde, Rita Gam, Mel Ferrer, Michel Simon, Cyril Cusack, Wanda Rotha, Richard Johnson, Marcel Poncin, Anthony Marlowe, Helene Vallier, Mahjoub Ben Brahim, Jacques Dufilho, Bernard Farrell, Peter Copley, Marne Maitland, Edward Leslie, Harold Kasket, Peter Bull,

Abdullah Menneghi. *D:-P: & Sc:* Albert Lewin. (1:21) Romantic actioner set in the deserts of Morocco of two men in love with a superstitious dancing girl. A box office bomb, it was based on the 1950 novel *Echee au Destin* by Francis D'Autheville. Technicolor.

2251. Sabaka (United Artists/Frank Ferrin Prods.; 1953–55). *Cast:* Nino Marcel, Boris Karloff, June Foray, Lou Krugman, Reginald Denny, Victor Jory, Jay Novello, Lisa Howard, Peter Coe, Paul Marion, Vito Scotti, Lou Merrill, Larry Dobkin, Jeanne Bates. *D:-P:-St: & Sc:* Frank Ferrin. (1:21) (video) Adventure tale of a youth who finds a religious cult headed by a ruthless woman is responsible for the deaths of his parents. In Eastmancolor, it was first released in 1953 under its original title *The Hindu.*

The Sabre and the Arrow (G.B. title) *see* **Last of the Comanches**

2252. Sabre Jet (United Artists/Carl Krueger Prods.; 1953). *Cast:* Robert Stack, Coleen Gray, Julie Bishop, Richard Arlen, Leon Ames, Amanda Blake, Reed Sherman, Michael Moore, Lucille Knoch, Tom Irish, Kathleen Crowley, Jerry Paris, Jan Shepard, Ray Montgomery, Johnny Sands, Frank Kumagai. *D:* Louis King; *P: & St:* Carl Krueger; *Sc:* Dale Eunson, Katherine Albert, Donald E. Baruch (unc.), Krueger (unc.), Hugh King (unc.). (1:36) Drama, set during the Korean "police action" of fighter pilots and their waiting wives, wondering if their husbands will return from their missions. Cinecolor.

2253. Sabrina (Paramount; 1954). *Cast:* Humphrey Bogart (Linus Larrabee), Audrey Hepburn (AAN/Sabrina Fairchild), William Holden (*Photoplay* Gold Medal/David Larrabee), Walter Hampden (Oliver Larrabee), John Williams (voted "Best Supporting Actor" by the NBR, combined with his work on *Dial M for Murder* [q.v.]/Thomas Fairchild), Martha Hyer (Elizabeth Tyson), Joan Vohs (Gretchen Van Horn), Marcel Dalio (Baron), Marcel Hillaire (The Professor), Nella Walker (final film—ret./Maude Larrabee), Francis X. Bushman (Mr. Tyson), Kay Riehl (Mrs. Tyson), Ellen Corby (Miss McCardle), Marjorie Bennett (Marjorie the cook), Emory Parnell (Charles the butler), Nancy Kulp (Jenny the maid), Kay Kuter, Paul Harvey, Emmett Vogan, Colin Campbell, Harvey Dunne, Marion Ross, Charles Harvey. *D:* (AAN) Billy Wilder; *P:* Wilder; *Sc:* (AAN) Wilder, Ernest Lehman, Samuel Taylor; *Cin:* (AAN-b/w) Charles B. Lang, Jr.; *ASD:* (AAN-b/w) Hal Pereira, Walter Tyler (art directors), Sam Comer, Ray Moyer (sets); *Costumes:* (AA-b/w) Edith Head. (1:53) (video/laserdisc) Critically acclaimed romantic comedy of two wealthy brothers vying for the affections of the newly arrived daughter of their chauffeur. *Film Daily* and the NBR placed it at #7 on their "10 Best" lists, while the *New York Times* placed it at #8. Based on Samuel Taylor's play *Sabrina Fair*, it became one of the 27 top-grossing films of 1954-55. Remade in 1995. (G.B. title: *Sabrina Fair*)

Sabrina Fair (G.B. title) *see* **Sabrina**

2254. Sabu and the Magic Ring (Allied Artists; 1957). *Cast:* Sabu, Daria Massey, Robert Shafto, Peter Mamakos, John Doucette, William Marshall, George Khoury, Vladimir Sokoloff, Robin Morse, Bernie Rich, Kenneth Terrell, John Lomma. *D:* George Blair; *P:* Maurice Duke; *Sc:* Benedict Freeman, John Fenton Murray, Sam Roeca (based on stories from *Arabian Nights*). (1:01) Low budget adventure, with the hero being aided by a genie in saving the beautiful princess from the bad guys. Photographed in color and originally destined as a TV pilot; it failed in that medium and was released theatrically instead.

2255. The Sad Horse (20th Century-Fox/Associated Producers; 1959). *Cast:* David Ladd, Chill Wills, Rex Reason, Patrice Wymore, Gregg Palmer, Leslie Bradley, Eve Brent, William Yip, David DePaul, North Wind (horse, received #3 PATSY in 1960). *D:* James B. Clark; *P:* Richard E. Lyons; *Sc:* Charles Hoffman; *Title song:* Tom Walton, Walter Kent. (1:18) Family oriented programmer of a crippled boy, his mongrel dog and a dejected racehorse. Based on an unpublished novel by Zoe Akins, it originally ran on a double bill with *The Little Savage* (q.v.). DeLuxe color & CinemaScope.

2256. The Sad Sack (Paramount; 1957). *Cast:* Jerry Lewis (Bixby), David Wayne (Dolan), Phyllis Kirk (final film—to TV/Major Shelton), Peter Lorre (Abdul), Joe Mantell (Pvt. Stan Wenaslawsky), Gene Evans (Sgt. Pulley), George Dolenz (Ali Mustapha), Liliane Montevecchi (Zita), Shepperd Strudwick (George Vanderslip), Abraham Sofaer (Hassim), Mary Treen (Sgt. Hansen), Drew Cahill (Lt. Wilson), Michael G. Ansara (Moki), Don Haggerty (Capt. Ward), Yvette Vickers (Hazel), Danny Davenport (Capt. Schultz), Anitra Stevens (Gloria), Jacqueline Park (Lorraine), Barbara Knudson

(Donnelly), Jean Del Val (French general), Dan Seymour (Arab chieftain), Jacques Gallo, Leon Tyler, Marilyn Hanold, Isabella Rye, Tony Merrill. *D:* George Marshall; *P:* Hal B. Wallis; *As.P:* Paul Nathan; *Sc:* Edmund Beloin, Nate Monaster; *Title song:* Hal David, Burt Bacharach. (1:38) (video) Based on the comic strip character created by George Baker, this comedy of an army misfit became one of the 26 top-grossing films of 1957-58.

2257. Saddle Legion (RKO; 1951). *Cast:* Tim Holt, Richard Martin, Dorothy Malone, Robert Livingston, James Bush, Mauritz Hugo, Movita Casteneda, Cliff Clark, George J. Lewis, Robert Wilke, Stanley Andrews, Dick Foote. *D:* Lesley Selander; *P:* Herman Schlom; *St: & Sc:* Ed Earl Repp. (1:01) Series western involving a lawless group perpetrating a scheme to steal cattle by running a "diseased cattle" scam.

2258. Saddle the Wind (MGM; 1958). *Cast:* Robert Taylor, Julie London, John Cassavetes, Donald Crisp, Charles McGraw, Royal Dano, Richard Erdman, Douglas Spencer, Ray Teal, Jay Adler, Stanley Adams, Nacho Galindo, Irene Tedrow. *D:* Robert Parrish; *P:* Armand Deutsch; *Screen story:* Thomas Thompson; *Sc:* Rod Serling; *Title song:* Jay Livingston, Ray Evans (sung by London). (1:24) Western drama of a gunman who forces a showdown with his brother, a former gunman now turned respectable rancher. A box office hit, it was filmed in Metrocolor and CinemaScope.

2259. Saddle Tramp (Universal-International; 1950). *Cast:* Joel McCrea, Wanda Hendrix, John Russell, John McIntire, Jeanette Nolan [the real-life wife of John McIntire], Russell Simpson, Ed Begley, Jimmy Hunt, Gordon Gebert, Orley Lindgren, Gregory Moffett, Antonio Moreno, John Ridgely, Walter Coy, Joaquin Garay, Peter Leeds, Michael Steele, Paul Picerni. *D:* Hugo Fregonese; *P:* Leonard Goldstein; *St: & Sc:* Harold Shumate. (1:17) Family oriented western of a carefree cowpoke who suddenly finds himself the guardian of four kids. Technicolor.

2260. Safari Drums (Allied Artists/ 1953). *Cast:* Johnny Sheffield, Barbara Bestar, Emory Parnell, Paul Marion, Douglas Kennedy, Robert "Smoki" Whitfield, Leonard Mudie, James Adamson, Carleton Young, Rory Mallinson, Jack Williams, Russ Conway. *D:-P:-St: & Sc:* Ford Beebe. (1:11) An entry in the "Bomba, the Jungle Boy" series with the young hero seeking the killer of a geologist within a group of filmmakers working on a wildlife documentary. Based on the literary character created by Roy Rockwood. (G.B. title: *Bomba and the Safari Drums*)

2261. The Saga of Hemp Brown (Universal-International; 1958). *Cast:* Rory Calhoun, Beverly Garland, John Larch, Russell Johnson, Fortunio Bonanova, Allan Lane, Trevor Bardette, Morris Ankrum, Yvette Vickers, Addison Richards, Victor Sen Yung, Theodore Newton, Frances McDonald, Charles Boaz, Marjorie Stapp. *D:* Richard Carlson; *P:* Gordon Kay; *St:* Bernard Girard; *Sc:* Bob Williams. (1:20) Western of a disgraced U.S. Cavalry officer attempting to right the wrong, after being falsely accused of an ambush where several people died, including his commander's wife. Eastmancolor & CinemaScope.

The Saga of the Viking Women and Their Voyage to the Waters of the Great Sea Serpent *see* **Viking Women and the Sea Serpent**

2262. Saginaw Trail (Columbia/Gene Autry Productions; 1953). *Cast:* Gene Autry, Smiley Burnette, Connie Marshall, Eugene Borden, Ralph Reed, Henry Blair, Myron Healey, Mickey Simpson, John War Eagle, Rodd Redwing, Gregg Barton, John Merton, Bill Wilkerson, John Parrish, Charlie Hayes, Champion, Jr. (horse). *D:* George Archainbaud; *P:* Armand Schaefer; *St: & Sc:* Dorothy Yost, Dwight Cummings; *Songs:* "Beautiful Dreamer" (Stephen Foster, sung by Autry); "Learn I Love You" (Smiley Burnette, sung by him). (0:56) (video) Indian trouble is being stirred up by a fur trapper against settlers on the early 19th century Michigan frontier. Sepiatone.

2263. Sailor Beware (Paramount/Wallis-Hazen; 1951). *Cast:* Dean Martin (Al Crowthers), Jerry Lewis (Melvin Jones), Corinne Calvet (guest star), Marion Marshall (Hilda Jones), Robert Strauss (Lardoski), Leif Erickson (Commander Lane), Don Wilson (Mr. Chubby), Vincent Edwards (Blayden), Skip Homeier (Mac), Dan Barton (Bama), Mike Mahoney (Tiger), Mary Treen (Ginger), Danny Arnold (Turk), Louis Jean Heydt (navy doctor), Elaine Stewart (film debut/Lt. Saunders), Drew Cahill (Bull), Don Haggerty (Lt. Connors), Darr Smith (Jeff Spenser), Bobby and Eddie Mayo (Mayo Brothers), Eddie Simms (Killer Jackson), Stephen Gregory (McDurk), Elaine Riley (female commentator), Larry McGrath (referee), Betty Hutton (Betty), The Marimba Merry Makers (themselves), James Flavin, Mary Murphy, Jerry Hausner, Richard Karlan, Robert Carson, Richard Emory, Marshall Reed, John V. Close, Duke Mitchell, James Dean (film debut/bit as sailor at boxing match), Donald MacBride, Dick Stabile. *D:* Hal Walker; *P:* Hal B. Wallis; *Adaptation:* Elwood Ullman; *Sc:* James Allardice, Martin Rackin; *Additional dialogue:* John Grant; *Songs:* "Sailors' Polka," "Never Before," "Merci Beaucoup," "The Old Calliope," "Today, Tomorrow, Forever" Mack David–Jerry Livingston (sung by Martin). (1:48) The comic adventures of two sailors in service to their country with the U.S. Navy. Based on the play of the same name by Kenyon Nicholson and Charles Robinson, the film is a remake of *Lady Be Careful* (1936) and *The Fleet's In* (1942), both by this studio. One of the 23 top-grossing films of 1951-52.

2264. St. Benny the Dip (United Artists/Danziger Bros.; 1951). *Cast:* Dick Haymes, Nina Foch, Roland Young, Lionel Stander, Freddie Bartholomew (final film—ret.), Oscar Karlweis, Dort Clark, Will Lee, Verne Colette, Richard Gordon. *D:* Edgar G. Ulmer; *P:* Edward J. Danziger, Harry Lee Danziger; *St: & Sc:* George Auerbach, Joe Roeburt; *Song:* "I Believe" (sung by Haymes). (1:20) (video) A tale of three conmen posing as priests who open a mission in New York's Bowery leading to their eventual reform. Filmed on location. (G.B. title: *Escape Me If You Can*) Originally paired on a double bill with *Two Gals and a Guy* (q.v.).

2265. Saint Joan (United Artists/Wheel; 1957). *Cast:* Jean Seberg (film debut/title role), Richard Todd, Richard Widmark, Anton Walbrook, John Gielgud, Felix Alymer, Harry Andrews, Barry Jones, Finlay Currie, Bernard Miles, Patrick Barr, Kenneth Haigh, Archie Duncan, Margot Grahame (final film—ret.), Francis De Wolff, Victor Maddern, David Oxley, Sydney Bromley, David Langton, David Hemmings. *D: & P:* Otto Preminger; *Sc:* Graham Greene. (1:50) (video/laserdisc) Dramatic multi-million dollar epic of France's "Maid of Orleans" from her humble beginnings to her death at the stake for heresy. A major box office bomb that was critically lambasted mainly due to its neophyte star. Based on the 1923 play by George Bernard Shaw, computer-colored prints have been produced.

2266. St. Louis Blues (Paramount; 1958). *Cast:* Nat "King" Cole, Eartha Kitt, Ruby Dee, Pearl Bailey, Cab Calloway, Juano Hernandez, Ella Fitzgerald (herself), Mahalia Jackson, Teddy Buckner, Barney Bigard, George "Red" Callender, Lee Young, George Washington, Billy Preston. *D:* Allen Reisner (final film); *P:* Robert Smith; *Sc:* Ted Sherdeman, Smith (based on the life and music of W.C. Handy); *Songs:* "St. Louis Blues," "Beale Street Blues," "Careless Love" (added lyrics by Martha Koenig and Spencer Williams), "Way Down South Where the Blues Began," "Memphis Blues," "Goin' to See My Sarah," "Harlem Blues," "John Henry Blues," "Morning Star" (new lyrics by Mack David), "Friendless Blues" (lyrics by Mercedes Gilbert), "Got No Mo' Home Dan a Dog," "Hist De Window, Noah," "Yellow Dog Blues," "Chantez Les Bas," "Steal Away to Jesus," "They That Sow in Tears" and "Sheriff Honest John Baile" (new lyrics by Mack David). (1:33) Hollywood's purported biography of blues legend W.C. Handy (Cole) [aka: "The Father of the Blues"]. A film more notable for its cast and its musical numbers, which are the whole show. VistaVision. Note: W.C. Handy died March 28, 1958, in New York city at the age of 84 years, shortly before this film was released.

2267. Sally and Saint Anne (Universal-International; 1952). *Cast:* Ann Blyth, Edmund Gwenn, John McIntire, Hugh O'Brian, Jack Kelly, Palmer Lee [aka: Gregg Palmer], King Donovan, Frances Bavier, Lamont Johnson, Otto Hulett, Kathleen Hughes, George Mathews, Robert Nichols, Alix Talton. *D:* Rudolph Maté; *P:* Leonard Goldstein; *St:* James O'Hanlon; *Sc:* O'Hanlon, Herb Meadow. (1:30) Comedy of a screwball Irish family that receives celestial assistance from St. Anne, the patron saint of young girls. Originally ran on a double bill with *Francis Goes to West Point* (q.v.).

2268. Salome (Columbia/Beckworth Corp.; 1953). *Cast:* Rita Hayworth (Princess Salome), Stewart Granger (Commander Claudius), Charles Laughton (King Herod), Judith Anderson (Queen Herodias), Sir Cedric Hardwicke (Caesar Tiberius), Alan Badel (John the Baptist), Basil Sydney (Pontius Pilate), Maurice Schwartz (Ezra), Rex Reason (Marcellus Fabius), Arnold Moss (Micha), Charles Wagenheim (Simon), Michael Granger (Capt. Quintus), Sujata & Asoka (specialty dancers), Robert Warwick (courier), Carmen D'Antonio (Salome's servant), Karl "Killer" Davis (slave master), Tristram Coffin (guard), Mickey Simpson (Herod's Captain of the Guards), Eduardo Cansino (Roman guard), Lou Nova (executioner), Fred

Letuli (sword dancer), John Wood (sword dancer), William Spaeth (fire eater), Duke Johnson (juggler), Earl Brown and Bud Cokes (Galilean soldiers), Joe Schilling, David Wold, Ray Beltran, Joe Sawaya, Anton Northpole, Carlo Tricoli, Franz Roehn, William McCormick (advisors), Abel Pina, Jerry Pina, Henry Pina, Henry Escalante, Gilbert Marques, Richard Rivas, Ramiro Rivas, Ruben T. Rivas, Miguel Gutierrez, Hector Urtiaga (acrobats), George Khoury, Leonard George (assassins), Eva Hyde (Herodias' servant), Italia De Nublia, David Ahdar, Charles Soldani, Dimas Sotello, William [Billy] Wilkerson, Mario Lamm, Tina Menard (converts), Leslie Denison (court attendant), Henry Dar Boggia, Michael Couzzi, Bobker Ben Ali, Don De Leo, John Parrish, Eddy Fields, Robert Garabedion, Sam Scar (politicians), Bruce Cameron, John Crawford (guards), Michael Mark (old farmer), David Leonard, Ralph Moody, Maurice Samuels (old scholars), Saul Martell (dissenting scholar), Paul Hoffman (sailmaster), Stanley Waxman (patrician), Rick Vallin, George Keymas, Carleton Young, Guy Kingsford, Jack Low, Bert Rose, Tom Hernandez, Trevor Ward, Barry Brooks, Roque Barry, Fred Berest. *D:* William Dieterle; *P:* Buddy Adler; *St:* Jesse Lasky, Jr., Harry Kleiner; *Sc:* Kleiner. (1:43) (video) Biblical drama of the lady whose main claim to fame was her involvement in the fate of John the Baptist and her "dance of the seven veils" for King Herod. Promotional publicity made this one of the 26 top-grossing films of 1952-53. Previously filmed in 1918 with Theda Bara and again in 1923 with Nazimova. Technicolor.

2269. Salt Lake Raiders (Republic; 1950). *Cast:* Allan Lane, Eddy Waller, Roy Barcroft, Martha Hyer, Byron Fougler, Myron Healey, Clifton Young, Stanley Andrews, Rory Mallinson, Kenneth MacDonald, George Chesebro, Black Jack (horse). *D:* Fred C. Brannon; *As.P:* Gordon Kay; *St: & Sc:* M. Coates Webster. (1:00) In this series entry, U.S. marshal "Rocky" Lane is given the assignment of tracking down an escaped convict who was falsely accused of murder and imprisoned.

2270. Salt of the Earth (International Union of Mine, Mill and Smelter Workers/Independent Prods. Corp.; 1954). *Cast:* Rosaura Revueltas (voted "Best Actress" at Czechoslovakia's Karlovy Vary Film Festival), Will Geer, David Wolfe, Melvin Williams, David Sarvis, Juan Chacon, Henrietta Williams, Ernest Velasquez, Angela Sanchez, Joe T. Morales, Clorinda Alderette, Charles Coleman, Virginia Jencks, Clinton Jencks. E.A. Rockwell, William Rockwell, Frank Talavera, Mary Lou Castillo, Floyd Bostick, Victor Torres, E.S. Conerly, Elvira Molano, Adolfo Barela, Albert Munoz and the Brothers and Sisters of Local 890, International Union of Mine, Mill and Smelter Workers, Bayard, New Mexico. *D:* Herbert J. Biberman (blacklisted); *P:* Paul Jarrico (blacklisted), Sonja Dahl Biberman, Adolfo Barela; *Sc:* Michael Wilson (blacklisted), Herbert Biberman. (1:34) (video/laserdisc) A drama of striking Chicano mine workers and their families in New Mexico. Efforts to limit distribution of this film in the United States were successful until it made general release in 1965. In the 1950s, the film found a waiting audience in communist-ruled countries and France. It was voted "Best Picture" by the French Motion Picture Academy and at the Karlovy Vary Film Festival in Czechoslovakia, it garnered the same award by winning the "Grand Prix" prize. Note: Actor Will Geer (second-billed in the cast) was also on Hollywood's blacklist at the time of the film's release.

2271. San Antone (Republic; 1953). *Cast:* Rod Cameron, Arleen Whelan, Forrest Tucker, Katy Jurado, Rudolfo Acosta, Roy Roberts, Bob Steele, Harry Carey, Jr., James Lilburn, Andrew Brennan, Richard Hale (Abraham Lincoln), Martin Garralaga, Argentina Brunetti, Douglas Kennedy, Paul Fierro, George Cleveland. *D: & P:* Joseph Kane; *Sc:* Steve Fisher; *Songs:* "South of San Antone," "Ten Thousand Cattle" and "The Cowboy's Lament" (sung by Steele, Carey, Jr., and Lilburn). (1:30) "Big Budget" Republic western, set during the era of the Civil War, of a rancher who is conned into leading a cattle drive through enemy territory. Based on the 1950 novel *The Golden Herd* by Curt Carroll.

2272. The San Francisco Story (Warner/Fidelity-Vogue Picts.; 1952). *Cast:* Joel McCrea, Yvonne De Carlo, Sidney Blackmer, Richard Erdman, Florence Bates, Onslow Stevens, Ralph E. Dumke, O.Z. Whitehead, John Raven, Robert Foulk, Lane Chandler, Trevor Bardette, John Doucette, Peter Virgo, Tor Johnson, Frank Hagney, Fred Graham. *D:* Robert Parrish; *P:* Howard Welsch; *Sc:* D.D. Beauchamp. (1:20) Western drama of the wild and woolly gold rush days of 1856 San Francisco, when corruption and vigilantes ruled the town. Based on the 1949 novel *Vigilante* by Richard Aldrich Summers.

2273. Sangaree (Paramount/Pine-Thomas; 1953). *Cast:* Fernando Lamas, Arlene Dahl, Patricia Medina, Francis L. Sullivan, Charles Korvin, Tom Drake, John Sutton, Willard Parker, Charles Evans, Lester Matthews, Roy Gordon, Lewis L. Russell, Russell Gaige, William Walker, Felix Nelson, Voltaire Perkins. *D:* Edward Ludwig; *P:* William H. Pine, William C. Thomas; *Adaptation:* Frank Moss; *Sc:* David Duncan. (1:34) Historical costume-melodrama of the 1780s, detailing the story of a slave who inherits his master's estate. Based on the 1948 novel by Frank G. Slaughter, it was filmed in wide-screen 3-D. Technicolor.

2274. Santa Fe (Columbia/Producers Actors; 1951). *Cast:* Randolph Scott, Janis Carter, Jerome Courtland, John Archer, Warner Anderson, Jock Mahoney, Harry Cording, Irving Pichel, Paul E. Burns, Chief Thundercloud, Blackie Whiteford, Lane Chandler, Charles Hamilton, Roy Roberts, Edgar Dearing, Peter Thompson, Billy House, Olin Howlin, Arlene Roberts, Sven-Hugo Borg, Frank Ferguson, Harry Tyler, Reed Howes, Charles Meredith, Paul Stanton, Richard Cramer, William Haade, Francis McDonald, Frank O'Connor, Harry Tenbrook, James [Jim] Mason, Guy Wilkerson, Frank Hagney, James Kirkwood, William Tannen, Al Kunde, Stanley Blystone, Art Loeb, Budd Fine, Richard [Dick] Fortune, Charles Evans, George Sherwood, Louis Mason, Roy Butler, Ralph Sanford, William McCormack. *D:* Irving Pichel; *P:* Harry Joe Brown; *St:* Louis Stevens; *Sc:* Kenneth Gamet. (1:29) (video) Post–Civil War western story of the Santa Fe Railroad. Based on the 1945 book *Santa Fe, the Railroad That Built an Empire* by James Leslie Marshall. Technicolor.

2275. Santa Fe Passage (Republic; 1955). *Cast:* John Wayne, Faith Domergue, Rod Cameron, Slim Pickens, Irene Tedrow, George Keymas, Leo Gordon, Anthony Caruso. *D:* William Witney; *Ex.P:* Herbert J. Yates; *P:* Sidney Picker; *Sc:* Lillie Hayward. (1:10) Western saga of perils faced by members of a wagon train heading to New Mexico. Based on a short story by Clay Fisher which appeared in *Esquire*. Trucolor.

2276. Santiago (Warner; 1956). *Cast:* Alan Ladd, Rossana Podesta, Lloyd Nolan, Chill Wills, L.Q. Jones, Frank DeKova, Paul Fix, George J. Lewis, Royal Dano, Don Blackman, Francisco Ruiz, Clegg Hoyt, Ernest Sarracino, Natalie Masters, Willard Willingham, Russ M. Saunders, Edward Colmans, Rico Alaniz. *D:* Gordon Douglas; *P: & St:* Martin Rackin; *Sc:* Rackin, John Twist. (1:32) Action-adventure set in the days of the Spanish-American War, with rival gunrunners shipping their wares to Cuba via a paddle wheeler. (G.B. title: *The Gun Runner*) WarnerColor/WarnerScope.

2277. The Saracen Blade (Columbia; 1954). *Cast:* Ricardo Montalban, Betta St. John, Rick Jason, Carolyn Jones, Michael Ansara, Whitfield Connor, Edgar Barrier, Nelson Leigh, Pamela Duncan, Frank Pulaski, Leonard Penn, Ed Coch, Nira Monsour, Gene D'Arcy, Poppy del Vando. *D:* William Castle; *P:* Sam Katzman; *Sc:* DeVallon Scott, George Worthing Yates. (1:17) 13th century costume swashbuckler of a man out to avenge the death of his father. Based on the 1952 book by Frank Yerby. Technicolor and b/w-tinted.

2278. Sarumba (Eagle-Lion; 1950). *Cast:* Michael Whalen, Doris Dowling, Tommy Wonder, Dolores Tatum, Rodriguez Molina, Sheila Garret, Manuel Folgoso, Red Davis, Collins Hay, John D. Bonin, Ira Wolfert, Laurette Campeau. *D:* Marion Gering; *P:* Gering, George P. Quigley, Julian Roffman; *Sc:* Jay Victor. (1:05) Low budget drama with Latin American music of an AWOL sailor who falls for a girl in Cuba. Filmed on location.

2279. Saskatchewan (Universal-International; 1954). *Cast:* Alan Ladd (Sgt. Thomas O'Rourke), Shelley Winters (Grace Markey), J. Carrol Naish (Batoche), Hugh O'Brian (Marshal Smith), Robert Douglas (Inspector Benton), George J. Lewis (Lawton), Richard Long (Scanlon), Jay Silverheels (Cajou), Antonio Moreno (Chief Dark Cloud), Lowell Gilmore (Banks), Frank Chase (Keller), Anthony Caruso (Spotted Eagle), John Cason (Cook), Henry Wills (Merrill), Robert D. Herron (Brill). *D:* Raoul Walsh; *P:* Aaron Rosenberg; *St: & Sc:* Gil Doud. (1:27) 19th century action-adventure of a Canadian Mountie who takes it upon himself to stop the American Sioux Indian tribe from stirring up the Canadian Cree Indian tribe to an uprising. Filmed in the Canadian Rockies on a lavish budget, it became one of the 25 top-grossing films of 1953-54. (G.B. title: *O'Rourke of the Royal Mounted*) Technicolor.

2280. Satan's Satellites (Republic; 1958). *Cast:* Judd Holdren, Aline Towne, Wilson Wood, Lane Bradford, Stanley Waxman, John Crawford, Craig Kelly, Ray Boyle, Leonard Nimoy,

Tom Steele, Dale Van Sickel, Roy Engel, Jack Harden, Paul Stader, Gayle Kellogg, Jack Shea, Robert Garabedian. *D:* Fred C. Brannon; *P:* Franklin Adreon; *Sc:* Ronald Davidson. (1:10) (video) Science fiction of outer space aliens attempting to blow up the earth so another planet can take its place and benefit from earth's superior climate. Originally ran on a double bill with *Missile Monsters* (q.v.). Note: This feature film was edited down from the 1952 twelve-chapter serial *Zombies of the Stratosphere*, which was a sequel to the serial *Radar Men from the Moon*, also a 1952 release in 12 chapters. Both starred "Commando Cody."

2281. Satchmo the Great (United Artists/CBS; 1957). *Cast:* Louis "Satchmo" Armstrong, Edward R. Murrow, Leonard Bernstein, W.C. Handy, Edmund Hall (clarinet), Trummy Young (trombone), Barrett Deems (drums), Billy Kyle (piano), Arvell Shaw & Jack Lesberg (bass). *P:* Edward R. Murrow, Fred W. Friendly; *As.P:* Palmer Williams; *Narrator:* Murrow; *Cin:* Charles Mack; *Editor:* Mili Lerner. (1:03) A documentary account of Louis Armstrong's world tour.

2282. Saturday's Hero (Columbia; 1951). *Cast:* John Derek, Donna Reed, Sidney Blackmer, Alexander Knox, Elliott Lewis, Otto Hulett, Howard St. John, Aldo [Ray] DaRe, Alvin Baldock, Wilbur Robertson, Charles Mercer Barnes, Bill Martin, Mickey Knox, Don Gibson, Peter Virgo, Robert C. Foulk, John W. Bauer, Mervin Williams, Peter Thompson, Noel Reyburn, Steve Clark, Sandro Giglio, Tito Vuolo, Don Garner. *D:* David Miller; *P:* Buddy Adler; *Sc:* Millard Lampell, Sidney Buchman. (1:49) Drama of a youth who wins a college football scholarship, but an injury changes his life drastically. Based on the 1949 book *The Hero* by Mr. Lampell. (G.B. title: *Idols in the Dust*).

2283. The Savage (Paramount; 1952). *Cast:* Charlton Heston, Susan Morrow, Peter Hanson, Joan Taylor, Richard Rober, Donald Porter, Ted de Corsia, Ian MacDonald, Milburn Stone, Angela Clarke, Orley Lindgren, Larry Tolan, Howard Negley, Frank Richards, John Miljan. *D:* George Marshall; *P:* Mel Epstein; *Sc:* Sydney Boehm. (1:35) Western drama of a white man raised by Indians who is forced to choose sides during white/Indian hostilities. Based on the 1942 novel *The Renegade* by L.L. Foreman. Technicolor.

2284. Savage Drums (Lippert/Tom Prods.; 1951). *Cast:* Sabu, Lita Baron, H.B. Warner, Sid Melton, Steven Geray, Bob Easton, Margia Dean, Francis Pierlot, Paul Marion, Ray Kinney, John Mansfield, Edward Clark, Hugh Beaumont, Harold Fong, Nick Thompson. *D: & P:* William Berke; *St: & Sc:* Fenton Earnshaw. (1:13) Low budget adventure melodrama of a man who returns to his island home to battle communists.

2285. The Savage Eye (Trans-Lux Films & Kingsley International/City Films; 1959). *Cast:* Barbara Baxley, Gary Merrill, Herschel Bernardi, Jean Hidey, Elizabeth Zemach. *D:-P:-St: & Sc:* Ben Maddow, Sidney Meyers, Joseph Strick. (1:08) Drama of a divorcée who after a 9-year marriage, arrives in Los Angeles in an attempt to make a new life for herself, but various disappointments almost lead to self-destruction. Filmed on location in L.A. over a period of four years at a cost of $65,000, it took 1st Prize at the 1959 Edinburgh Festival, was in nomination at the Mannheim Film Festival and won a special "Award of Merit" that same year at the Venice Film Festival, although it was shown out of competition. Not released in the U.S. until 1960.

2286. Savage Frontier (Republic; 1953). *Cast:* Allan Lane, Eddy Waller, Bob Steele, Dorothy Patrick, Roy Barcroft, Richard Avonde, William Phipps, Jimmy Hawkins, Lane Bradford, John Cason, Kenneth MacDonald, Bill Henry, John Hamilton, Gerry Flash, Lee Shumway, Black Jack (horse). *D:* Harry Keller; *As.P:* Rudy Ralston; *St: & Sc:* Dwight Babcock, Gerald Geraghty. (0:54) An ex-con, now a farmer, finds his parole in jeopardy when he is implicated in the deeds of a gang of local outlaws. A latter-day entry in the "Rocky" Lane series of westerns.

2287. The Savage Horde (Republic; 1950). *Cast:* William Elliott, Adrian Booth, Grant Withers, Jim Davis, Barbara Fuller, Noah Beery, Jr., Douglass Dumbrille, Bob Steele, Will Wright, Roy Barcroft, Earle Hodgins, Stuart Hamblen, Hal Taliaferro, Lloyd Ingraham (final film—ret.), Marshall Reed, Crane Whitley, Charles Stevens, James Flavin, Ed Cassidy, Kermit Maynard, George Chesebro, Jack O'Shea, Monte Montague, Bud Osborne, Reed Howes. *D: & As.P:* Joseph Kane; *St:* Thames Williamson, Gerald Geraghty; *Sc:* Kenneth Gamet. (1:30) Western drama of a gunman who reforms and aids local ranchers against landgrabbers, while former gang members side with the lawless element. Elliott's final big budget western for this studio, it was originally paired on a double bill with Roy Rogers' *Trigger, Jr.* (q.v.).

2288. Savage Mutiny (Columbia/Esskay Pictures; 1953). *Cast:* Johnny Weissmuller, Angela Stevens, Lester Matthews, Nelson Leigh, Charles Stevens, Paul Marion, Gregory Gaye, Leonard Penn, Ted Thorpe, George Robotham, Tamba (chimp). *D:* Spencer Gordon Bennet; *P:* Sam Katzman; *St: & Sc:* Sol Shor. (1:13) "Jungle Jim" series entry, with our hero having to combat foreign agents while trying to remove natives from a proposed atom bomb site. Based on the comic strip creation of Alex Raymond.

Savage Wilderness *see* **The Last Frontier**

2289. Say One for Me (20th Century-Fox/Bing Crosby Prods.; 1959). *Cast:* Bing Crosby (Father Conroy), Debbie Reynolds (Holly LaMaise), Robert Wagner (Tony Vincent), Ray Walston (Phil Stanley), Les Tremayne (Harry LaMaise), Connie Gilchrist (Mary Manning), Frank McHugh (Jim Dugan), Joe Besser (Joe Greb), Alena Murray (Sunny), Stella Stevens (film debut/chorine), Nina Shipman (Fay Flagg), Sebastian Cabot (Monsignor Stratford), Judy Harriet (June January), Dick Whittinghill (Lou Christy), Murray Alper (Otto), Richard Collier (Capt. Bradford), David Leonard (Rabbi Berman), Thomas Browne Henry (Dr. Leventhal), Wilkie DeMartel (Rev. Kendall), Alexander Campbell (Pastor Johnson), Bruce McFarlane (Detective Minelli), The Steiner Brothers (themselves), Robert Montgomery, Jr. (hotel clerk). *D: & P:* Frank Tashlin; *St: & Sc:* Robert O'Brien; *Music:* (AAN) Lionel Newman; *Songs:* Title song, "The Secret of Christmas," "The Night Rock 'n' Roll Died," "The Girl Most Likely to Succeed," "He's Starting to Get to Me," "I Couldn't Care Less" and "You Can't Love 'Em All" James Van Heusen, Sammy Fain. (1:59) Comedy of a Catholic priest, his Broadway parish and his involvement with various residents of the Great White Way, including a showgirl and her disreputable boss. One of the 26 top-grossing films of 1958-59. DeLuxe color/CinemaScope.

2290. Sayonara (Warner/Goetz Pictures-Pennebaker, Inc.; 1957). *Cast:* Marlon Brando (AAN/Major Lloyd Gruver), Red Buttons (AA-BSA/Joe Kelly), Ricardo Montalban (Nakamura), Miiko Taka (film debut/Hana-ogi), Miyoshi Umeki (AA-BSA/film debut/Katsumi), Patricia Owens (Eileen Webster), James Garner (Capt. Mike Bailey), Martha Scott (Mrs. Webster), Kent Smith (General Webster), Douglas Watson (Colonel Craford), Reiko Kuba (Fumiko-san), Soo Yong (Teruko-san), Harlan Warde (consul), The Shochuku Kagekidan Girls Revue. *D:* (AAN) Joshua Logan; *P:* (AAN-Best Picture) William Goetz; *Sc:* (AAN) Paul Osborn; *Cin:* (AAN-color) Ellsworth Fredericks; *ASD:* (AA-color) Ted Haworth (art director), Robert Priestley (sets); *Editors:* (AAN) Arthur P. Schmidt, Phillip W. Anderson; *Sound recording:* (AA) George R. Groves/Warner Bros. Sound Dept.; *Title song:* Irving Berlin. (2:27) (video/laserdisc) Critically acclaimed box office smash hit of ill-fated interracial love. Based on the 1954 novel by James A. Michener, it was primarily filmed on location in Kobe, Japan. On the "10 Best" list of *Film Daily* it placed #2 and on the same list of the *New York Times*, it took a #9 placement. The New York Film Critics had it in nomination for "Best Picture." A gross take of $10.5 million made it one of the 26 top-grossing films of 1957-58. Technicolor/Technirama.

2291. Scandal at Scourie (MGM; 1953). *Cast:* Greer Garson, Walter Pidgeon, Agnes Moorehead, Donna Corcoran, Arthur Shields, Philip Ober, Rhys Williams, Margalo Gillmore, John Lupton, Ian Wolfe, Philip Tonge, Wilton Graff, Michael Pate, Tony Taylor, Patricia Tiernan, Victor Wood, Perdita Chandler, Walter Baldwin, Ida Moore, Maudie Prickett, Ivis Goulding, Alex Frazer, Matt Moore, Charles Watts, Roger Moore, Al Ferguson, Jack Bonigul, Eugene Borden, Rudy Lee, Max Willenz, Ivan Triesault, Wayne Farlow, Joann Arnold, Peter Roman, George Davis, Vicki Joy Kreutzer, Gary Lee Jackson, Jill Martin, Coral Hammond, Nolan Leary, Owen McGiveney, Archer MacDonald, Earl Lee, Howard Negley, Robert Ross, John Sherman. *D:* Jean Negulesco; *P:* Edwin H. Knopf; *Sc:* Norman Corwin, Leonard Spigelgass, Karl Tunberg; *Songs:* "Greensleeves," "Frere Jacques." (1:30) Based on the short story "Good Boy" by Mary McSherry, this domestic drama set in Canada relates the story of a Protestant couple who make tongues wag when they plan to adopt a Catholic child. Technicolor.

2292. Scandal Incorporated (Republic; 1956). *Cast:* Robert Hutton, Paul Richards, Claire Kelly, Patricia Wright, Robert Knapp, Harris Davenport, Reid Hammond, Nestor Paiva, Gordon Wynne, Guy Prescott, Donald Kirke,

Marjorie Stapp. Enid Blaine, Mauritz Hugo, Joe Breen, Allen O'Locklin, George Cisar, Tracey Morgan, Mimi Simpson. *D:* Edward Mann (directorial debut and only film until 1966); *P:-St: & Sc:* Milton Mann; *Songs:* Sid Shrager, Al Chorney, Hal Shrager. (1:19) Programmer melodrama of an actor who is suspected when a ruthless reporter for a Hollywood scandal magazine is murdered.

2293. Scandal Sheet (Columbia; 1952). *Cast:* John Derek, Donna Reed, Broderick Crawford, Rosemary DeCamp, Henry O'Neill, Henry [Harry] Morgan, James Millican, Griff Barnett, Jonathan Hale, Pierre Watkin, Ida Moore, Ralph Reed, Luther Crockett, Charles Cane, Jay Adler, Don Beddoe, Kathryn Card, Victoria Horne, Peter Virgo, Matt Willis, Ric Roman, Eugene Baxter, Katherine Warren, Helen Brown, Mike Mahoney, Tom Kingston, Charles Coleman, Harry Hines, Harry Wilson, Ralph Volkie, John "Skins" Miller, Garry Owen, Guy Wilkerson, Duke Watson. *D:* Phil Karlson; *P:* Edward Small; *Sc:* Ted Sherdeman, Eugene Ling, James Poe. (1:22) Low budget crime melodrama of a tabloid newspaper reporter who uncovers a dark secret held by his editor. Based on the 1944 novel *The Dark Page* by Samuel Fuller, it was originally paired on a double bill with *Indian Uprising* (q.v.). (G.B. title: *The Dark Page*)

2294. Scaramouche (MGM; 1952). *Cast:* Stewart Granger, Eleanor Parker, Janet Leigh, Mel Ferrer, Henry Wilcoxon, Nina Foch, Richard Anderson, Robert Coote, Lewis Stone [who also appeared in the 1923 version], Elisabeth Ridson (final film—d. 1952), Howard Freeman, John Dehner, John Litel, Curtis Cooksey, Jonathan Cott, Dan Foster, Owen McGiveney, Hope Landin, Frank Mitchell, Carol Hughes, Richard Hale, Henry Corden, John Eldredge, Mitchell Lewis, Ottola Nesmith, Dorothy Patrick, John Sheffield, Douglass Dumbrille, Frank Wilcox, Anthony Marsh, John Crawford, Bert LeBaron. *D:* George Sidney; *P:* Carey Wilson; *Sc:* Ronald Millar, George Froeschel. (1:58) (video/laserdisc) Lavishly produced costume swashbuckler, set in 18th century France, of a man out to avenge the death of his friend. Based on Rafael Sabatini's 1921 novel, it was previously filmed in 1923 by Merit with Ramon Novarro. Remade as *Adventures of Scaramouche* a French/Italian/Spanish co-production of 1964. Technicolor.

2295. Scared Stiff (Paramount; 1953). *Cast:* Dean Martin (Larry Todd), Jerry Lewis (Myron Myron Mertz), Lizabeth Scott (Mary Carroll), Carmen Miranda (final film—d. 1955/ Carmelita Castina), George Dolenz (Mr. Cortega), Dorothy Malone (Rosie), Tom Powers (police lieutenant), William Ching (Tony Warren), Leonard Strong (Shorty), Henry Brandon (Pierre), Hugh Sanders (cop), Frank Fontaine (drunk), Jack Lambert (zombie), Paul Marion (dual role/The Carriso Twins), Tony Barr (Trigger), Bob Hope (unbilled cameo), Bing Crosby (unbilled cameo), Earl Holliman. *D:* George Marshall; *P:* Hal B. Wallis; *Sc:* Herbert Baker, Walter De Leon; *Additional dialogue:* Ed Simmons, Norman Lear; *Songs:* "San Domingo," "Song of the Enchilada Man" Jerry Livingston, Mack David; "Mama Yo Quiero" Al Stillman, Jarca Paiva, Vincente Paiva; "You Hit the Spot" Mack Gordon, Harry Revel; "I Don't Care If the Sun Don't Shine" David; "I'm Your Pal" Livingston, David; "When Somebody Thinks You're Wonderful" Harry Woods. (1:48) (video) Hit comedy, with some thrills, of a girl who inherits a gloomy mansion in the Caribbean and must go there to claim it. Previously filmed in 1914 in 4 reels as *Ghost Breaker* with H.B. Warner, in 1922 as *The Ghost Breaker* with Wallace Reid and in 1940 as *The Ghost Breakers* with Bob Hope. Based on an old stageplay by Paul Dickey and Charles W. Goddard, it became one of the 26 top-grossing films of 1952-53. A comic highlight of this film is Lewis in drag, as Miranda, pantomiming "Mama Yo Quiero."

2296. The Scarf (United Artists/Gloria; 1951). *Cast:* John Ireland, Mercedes McCambridge, Emlyn Williams, James Barton, Lloyd Gough, Basil Ruysdael, David Wolfe, Harry Shannon, David McMahon, Chubby Johnson, Frank Jenks, Frank Jaquet, Emmett Lynn, John Merrick, Lyle Talbot, King Donovan, O.Z. Whitehead, Frank Richards, Sue Casey, Celia Lovsky, Dick Wessel. *D: & Sc:* E.A. Dupont; *P:* I.G. Goldsmith; *St:* Goldsmith, Edwin A. Rolfe. (1:33) Melodrama of a man who escapes from an asylum for the criminally insane to prove he didn't strangle his fiancée, the crime for which he was incarcerated.

2297. The Scarlet Angel (Universal-International; 1952). *Cast:* Yvonne DeCarlo, Rock Hudson, Richard Denning, Whitfield Connor, Amanda Blake, Bodil Miller, Henry O'Neill, Henry Brandon, Maude Wallace, Dan Riss, Tol Avery, Arthur Page, George Hamilton, Dale Van Sickel, Mickey Pfleger, Harry Harvey, George Spaulding, Thomas Browne Henry, Fred Graham, Fred Coby, Eddie Dew, Nolan

Leary, Elizabeth Root, Wilma Francis, Betty Allen, Leo Curley, Dabbs Greer, John Roy, Martin Cichy, Jack Perry, Buddy Sullivan, Sally Corner, Ada Adams, Joe Forte, Vera Marshe, Fred Berest, Coleman Francis, Jack Daley, Jean Andren, George Ramsey, Charles Horvath, Bud [Bill] Wolfe, Frankie Van, Carl Saxe, Edwin Parker, Gil Patrick, Creighton Hale, Ed Hinkle, Bert LeBaron, Lila Finn, Louis G. Hart. *D:* Sidney Salkow; *P:* Leonard Goldstein; *St: & Sc:* Oscar Brodney. (1:20) Costume drama of a New Orleans saloon girl who assumes the identity of a wealthy deceased woman and heads for San Francisco society, until her past catches up with her. Originally ran on a double bill with *Just Across the Street* (q.v.). Technicolor.

2298. The Scarlet Coat (MGM; 1955). *Cast:* Cornel Wilde, Michael Wilding, George Sanders, Anne Francis, Bobby Driscoll, Robert Douglas (Benedict Arnold), John McIntire (General Robert Howe), Rhys Williams, Paul Cavanagh, John Dehner, James Westerfield, Ashley Cowan, John Alderson, John O'Malley, Robin Hughes, Anthony Dearden, Vernon Rich, Dabbs Greer, Olaf Hytten, Gordon Richards, Leslie Denison, Harlan Warde, John Blackburn, Tristram Coffin, Byron Foulger, Wilson Benge, Dennis King, Jr., Robert Dix, Charles Watts, Peter Adams, Wesley Hudman, Robert Forrest, Tom Cound, Keith McConnell, Phyllis Coghlan, Gil Stuart, Owen McGiveney, Charles R. Keane, Richard Simmons, Jim Hayward, Rush Williams, Ivan Hayes, Michael Fox, Don C. Harvey, Barry Reagan, Rick Vallin, Ronald Green, Joe Locke, Jennifer Raine, Guy Kingsford, Richard Peel, Vesey O'Davoren, Anne Kunde, George Peters, Ethan Laidlaw. *D:* John Sturges; *P:* Nicholas Nayfack; *St:* Hollister Noble, Sidney Harmon; *Sc:* Karl Tunberg. (1:41) A lavishly produced costumer of colonial America which relates the story of Benedict Arnold, a man whose name is synonymous with "traitor" in American history. Filmed in the area of Hudson Bay in Eastmancolor and CinemaScope, this curiously enough was a moneymaker for MGM.

2299. The Scarlet Hour (Paramount; 1956). *Cast:* Tom Tryon (film debut), Carol Ohmart, James Gregory, Jody Lawrence, Elaine Stritch (film debut), E.G. Marshall, Edward Binns, Scott Marlowe, Billy Gray, Jacques Aubuchon, David Lewis, Johnstone White, James F. Stone, Maureen Hurley, James Todd, Benson Fong, Joe Conley, Barry Atwater, Richard Collier, Almira Sessions, Richard Deacon, Harry Hickox, Peter Gray, Bill Tischer, Autumn Russell, Theron Jackson, Enid Baine, Bill Anders, Gilmore Bush, Max Power, Nat "King" Cole. *D: & P:* Michael Curtiz; *Sc:* Rip Von Ronkel, Frank Tashlin, John Meredyth Lucas (based on the story "The Kiss Off" by Von Ronkel and Tashlin); *Song:* "Never Let Me Go" Jay Livingston, Ray Evans (sung by Cole). (1:35) Drama of a self-serving woman in an adulterous affair who brings about the death of her husband. VistaVision.

2300. The Scavengers (Hal Roach/ Valiant–Lynn–Romero; 1959). *Cast:* Vince Edwards, Carol Ohmart, Tamar Benamy, Efren Reyes, John Wallace, Ric Diaz. *D:* John Cromwell; *P:-St: & Sc:* Edhar Romero. (1:19) A former smuggler in Hong Kong runs into his missing wife, finds she is hopelessly enmeshed in a web of criminal activities. A U.S.A./Philippine co-production that originally ran on a double bill with *Terror Is a Man* (q.v.). (aka: *City of Sin*)

School for Violence *see* **High School Hellcats**

2301. Scorching Fury (Independent; 1952). *Cast:* Richard Devon, William Leslie, Peggy Nelson, Sherman Price, Audrey Dineen. *D:* Rick Freers. (1:08) Western of a man who leads a double life, that of a respectable citizen and that of a notorious gunfighter.

2302. Screaming Eagles (Allied Artists; 1956). *Cast:* Tom Tryon, Jan Merlin, Alvy Moore, Martin Milner, Jacqueline Beer, Joe Di Reda, Mark Damon, Paul Burke, Pat Conway, Edward G. Robinson, Jr., Ralph Votrian, Paul Smith, Bobby Blake, Bob Roark, Bob Dix, Wayne Taylor, Robert Boon, Peter Michaels. *D:* Charles Haas; *P:* Samuel Bischoff, David Diamond; *St:* Virginia Kellogg; *Sc:* David Lang, Robert Presnell, Jr. (1:20) World War II drama of the obstacles encountered by a group of young paratroopers who parachute into France prior to the D-Day Normandy invasion.

2303. Screaming Mimi (Columbia/Sage Prods.; 1958). *Cast:* Anita Ekberg, Phil Carey, Gypsy Rose Lee, Harry Townes, Linda Cherney, Romney Brent (final film—ret.), Alan Gifford, Oliver McGowan, The Red Norvo Trio, Vaughn Taylor, Stephen Ellsworth, Frank Scannell. *D:* Gerd Oswald; *P:* Harry Joe Brown, Robert Fellows; *Sc:* Robert Blees; *Song:* "Put the Blame on Mame" Doris Fisher, Allan Roberts—originally written for *Gilda* in 1946 (sung by

Gypsy Rose Lee). (1:19) Offbeat melodrama of efforts to prove an attack on a stripper was linked with a series of unsolved murders. Based on the 1949 book by Frederic Brown.

2304. The Screaming Skull (American International; 1958). *Cast:* John Hudson, Peggy Webber, Toni Johnson, Russ Conway, Alex Nicol. *D:* Alex Nicol; *Ex.P:* T. Frank Woods; *P:-St: & Sc:* John Kneubuhl. (1:10) (video) Low budget horror film of a man who returns with his new wife to the home he shared with his first wife. Weird sounds and manifestations commence.

2305. The Sea Around Us (RKO; 1953). *D:* Irwin Allen (directorial debut); *P:* (AA-Best Documentary) Allen; *Narrator:* Don Forbes. (1:01) (video) A documentary feature in color based on Rachel Carson's 1951 book of the same name, detailing her studies of the oceans and the various forms of life they support.

2306. The Sea Chase (Warner; 1955). *Cast:* John Wayne, Lana Turner, Lyle Bettger, David Farrar, Tab Hunter, James Arness, Wilton Graff, Richard Davalos, John Qualen, Paul Fix, Luis Van Rooten, Peter Whitney, Alan Hale, Jr., Lowell Gilmore, Claude Akins, John Doucette, Alan Lee, Adam Williams, Fred Stromsoe, James Lilburn, Tony Travers, John Indrisano, Joey Ray, [A.] Cameron Grant, Gavin Muir, Gloria Dea, Josephine Para, Lucita, Isabel Dwan, Theresa Tudor, Renata Hoy, John Sheffield, Anthony Eustrel, Tudor Owen, Jean DeBriac, Patrick O'Moore, Gail Robinson, Gilbert Perkins. *D: & P:* John Farrow; *Sc:* John Twist, James Warner Bellah. (1:57) (video/laserdisc) Adventure drama, based on the 1948 novel by Andrew Geer, of a freighter during World War II making its way from Sydney, Australia, to the North Sea with a Hitler-hating German captain at the helm. WarnerColor/CinemaScope.

2307. The Sea Hornet (Republic; 1951). *Cast:* Rod Cameron, Adele Mara, Adrian Booth (final film—ret.), Chill Wills, Jim Davis, Richard Jaeckel, Ellen Corby, James Brown, Grant Withers, William Ching, William Haade, Hal Taliaferro, Emil Sitka, Byron Foulger, Monte Blue, Jack Pennick. *D. & As.P:* Joseph Kane; *St: & Sc:* Gerald Drayson Adams; *Songs:* Jack Elliott, Nathan Scott. (1:24) Adventure melodrama of the search for a ship that sank with a load of gold on board. When the ship is finally found, the gold is missing. This feature originally ran on the top of a double bill with *Arizona Manhunt* (q.v.).

2308. Sea of Lost Ships (Republic; 1953). *Cast:* John Derek, Wanda Hendrix, Walter Brennan, Richard Jaeckel, Tom Tully, Barton MacLane, Erin O'Brien-Moore, Ben Cooper, Darryl Hickman, Roy Roberts, Tom Powers, Richard Hale, James Brown, Douglas Kennedy, Steve Brodie, John Hudson. *D: & P:* Joseph Kane; *Ex.P:* Herbert J. Yates; *St:* Norman Reilly Raine; *Sc:* Steve Fisher; *Song:* "Just One Kiss" Victor Young, Ned Washington. (1:25) Drama of two young men who join the Coast Guard Academy, have a falling out over a girl, then reconcile when they realize their friendship is more important.

2309. Sea Tiger (Monogram; 1952). *Cast:* John Archer, Marguerite Chapman, Harry Lauter, Ralph Sanford, Marvin Press, John Mylong, Mara Corday (film debut), Paul McGuire, Lyle Talbot, Sam Flint, Chad Mallory, John Reese. *D:* Frank McDonald; *P:* William F. Broidy, Wesley E. Barry; *Sc:* Sam Roeca. (1:11) Low budget mystery-melodrama of thieves and a crooked insurance agent, all after a shipboard stash of jewels. Based on the short story "Island Freighter" by Charles Yerkow.

The Sea Wall *see* **This Angry Age**

2310. Sealed Cargo (RKO; 1951). *Cast:* Dana Andrews, Carla Balenda, Claude Rains, Philip Dorn, Onslow Stevens, Skip Homeier, Eric Feldary, J.M. Kerrigan, Arthur Shields, Morgan Farley, Dave Thursby, Henry Rowland, Charles A. Browne, Don Dillaway, Al Hill, Lee MacGregor, William Andrews, Richard Norris, Kathleen Ellis, Karen Norris, Harry Mancke, Whit Bissell, Kay Morley, Bert Kennedy, Larry Johns, George Ovey, Carl Sklover, Bessie Wade, Bruce Cameron, Ned Roberts, Dick Crockett, Bob Morgan, Wes Hopper, Art Dupuis, Zachary Berger, Bob Smitts, John Royce, Peter Bourne, William Yetter, Geza De Rosner, Robert Boon. *D:* Alfred Werker; *P:* William Duff; *Sc:* Dale Van Every, Oliver H.P. Garrett, Roy Huggins. (1:30) After coming across a damaged ship in the North Atlantic off Newfoundland, a fisherman begins to suspect the ship is actually a supply ship for Nazi U-boats and sets about on a plan to sink the ship and its potentially deadly cargo. Based on the 1943 novel *The Gaunt Woman* by Edmund Gilligan, it was originally paired on a double bill with *Tokyo File 212* (q.v.).

2311. The Search for Bridey Murphy (Paramount; 1956). *Cast:* Teresa Wright, Louis Hayward, Nancy Gates, Kenneth Tobey, Richard Anderson, Walter Kingsford, James Kirkwood (final film—ret.), Tom McKee, Janet Riley, Charles Boaz, Lawrence Fletcher, Charles Maxwell, Noel Leslie (Edgar Cayce), William J. Barker (himself), Eilene Janssen, Bradford Jackson, Hallene Hill, Denise Freeborn, Ruth Robinson, James Bell (Hugh Lynn Cayce), Flora Jean Engstrom, Marion Gray, Jeane Wood, Hugh Corcoran, Thomas P. Dillon, Dick Ryan. *D: & Sc:* Noel Langley; *P:* Pat Duggan. (1:24) (video) Based on the popular and controversial book of the time by Morey Bernstein [which has since been discredited] purporting to tell of the factual case of an American housewife taken back via hypnosis to a former lifetime as Irish peasant girl, Bridey Murphy. VistaVision.

2312. Search for Paradise (Stanley Warner Cinerama Corp.; 1957). *D:* Otto Lang; *P:* Lowell Thomas; *Sc: & Narration:* Prosper Buranelli, Thomas, Lang (based on an idea by Thomas who also photographed); *Songs:* Title song (sung by Robert Merrill on the soundtrack), "Happy Land of the Hunza" Dimitri Tiomkin, Ned Washington, Thomas. (2:00) The 4th Cinerama feature is a Technicolor travelogue highlighted by the lavish splendor of the coronation of the King of Nepal in 1956. Also included is the Temple of Lankatilaka in Ceylon with its priests and giant Buddha, a wild jeep ride to the Mir of Hunza for polo and sword-dancing, a rubber raft ride down the Indus river, scenes of Kashmir and Katmandu, concluding with shots of jets flying over Eglin Air Force Base in Florida.

2313. The Searchers (Warner/C.V. Whitney Pictures, Inc.; 1956). *Cast:* John Wayne (Ethan Edwards), Jeffrey Hunter (Martin Pawley), Vera Miles (Laurie Jorgenson), Ward Bond (Capt. Rev. Clayton), Natalie Wood (Debbie Edwards), John Qualen (Lars Jorgenson), Olive Carey (Mrs. Jorgenson), Henry Brandon (Chief Scar), Ken Curtis (Charlie McCorry), Harry Carey, Jr. (Brad Jorgenson), Antonio Moreno (final film—ret./Emilio Figueroa), Patrick Wayne (Lt. Greenhill), Hank Worden (Mose Harper), Lana Wood (Debbie as a child), Walter Coy (Aaron Edwards), Dorothy Jordan (Martha Edwards), Pippa Scott (Lucy Edwards), Beulah Archuletta (Look), Bill Steele (Ranger Nesbitt), Cliff Lyons (Col. Greenhill), Chuck Roberson, Billy Cartledge, Chuck Hayward, Slim Hightower, Fred Kennedy, Frank McGrath, Dale Van Sickel, Henry Wills, Terry Wilson, Away Luna, Billy Yellow, Bob Many Mules, Exactly Sonnie Betsuie, Feather Hat, Jr., Harry Black Horse, Jack Tin Horn, Many Mules Son, Percy Shooting Star, Pete Gray Eyes, Pipe Line Begishe, Smile White Sheep. *D:* John Ford; *Ex.P:* Merian C. Cooper; *P:* C.V. Whitney; *As.P:* Patrick Ford; *Sc:* Frank S. Nugent; *Title song:* Stan Jones. (1:59) (video/laserdisc) Acclaimed hit western of a relentless five year search by an Indian-hating Civil War veteran and a half-breed for a girl taken by Comanche Indians. Location filming at Monument Valley in Utah and Arizona; Gunnison, Colorado, and Alberta, Canada. Based on the 1954 novel by Alan LeMay, it became one of the 24 top-grossing films of 1955-56 and has achieved "classic" status. Comanche Indians are portrayed by members of the Navajo tribe. Technicolor/VistaVision.

2314. Second Chance (Protestant Film Commission; 1950). *Cast:* Ruth Warrick, John Hubbard, Hugh Beaumont, David Holt, Pat Combs, Ellye Marshall. *D:* William Beaudine; *Sc:* Robert Presnell, Jr. (1:12) A low budget independent religious drama based on a short story by Faith Baldwin. Note: Details were lacking on five other productions that Beaudine directed for the Protestant Film Commission. They are: *Again-Pioneers!* (1950), *For Every Child* (1953), *The Hidden Heart* (1953), *More for Peace* (1954) and *Each According to His Faith* (1955).

2315. Second Chance (RKO/Edmund Grainger; 1953). *Cast:* Robert Mitchum, Linda Darnell, Jack Palance, Sandro Giglio, Rodolfo Hoyos, Jr., Reginald Sheffield, Margaret Brewster, Roy Roberts, Salvador Baguez, Maurice Jara, Jody Walsh, Dan Seymour, Fortunio Bonanova, Milburn Stone, Abel Fernandez, Michael Tolan, Richard Vera, Virginia Linden, Manuel Paris, Eddie Gomez, Martin Garralaga, Jose [Joe] Dominguez, Luis Alvarez, Oresta Seragnoli, Tony Martinez, Tina Menard, Orlando Beltran, Judy Landon, Marc Wilder, Pere Rand, Max Wagner, Ricardo Alba, Dan Bernaducci, Bob Castro, John Cliff, Henry Escalante, Joe Herrera, Eddie Kerrant, Eddie LeBaron, David Morales, George Navarro, Shirley Patterson, Tony Roux. *D:* Rudolph Maté; *P:* Sam Weisenthal; *Ex.P:* Edmund Grainger; *St: & Adaptation:* D.M. Marshman; *Sc:* Oscar Millard, Sydney Boehm (1:22) (video/laserdisc) In Mexico, a boxer becomes enamoured of a lady, the former companion of an American crime figure, who has a price on her head to keep her mouth shut from testifying before a Senate crime committee. Filmed on location, taut suspense prevails at the finale aboard a disabled cable car. Technicolor, Stereophonic sound and 3-D.

2316. The Second Face (Eagle-Lion/E.J. Leven Prods.; 1950). *Cast:* Ella Raines, Bruce Bennett, Rita Johnson, John Sutton, Patricia Knight, Roy Roberts, Jane Darwell, Pierre Watkin. *D:* Jack Bernhard; *P:* Edward J. Leven; *St: & Sc:* Eugene Vale. (1:17) (video) Melodrama of a dress designer who has plastic surgery to correct her horribly disfigured facial features, opening the door to true love.

2317. The Second Greatest Sex (Universal-International; 1955). *Cast:* Jeanne Crain, George Nader, Kitty Kallen, Bert Lahr, Mamie Van Doren, Keith Andes, Kathleen Case, Paul Gilbert, Tommy Rall, Edna Skinner, Jimmy Boyd, Cynthia May Carver, Ward Ellis, Mary Marlo, Sheb Wooley, George Wallace, Sharon Bell, The Midwesterners (themselves). *D:* George Marshall; *P:* Albert J. Cohen; *St: & Sc:* Charles Hoffman; *Choreography:* Lee Scott; *Songs:* "Lysistrata," "Send Us a Miracle," "Travellin' Man," "My Love is Yours," "What Good is a Woman Without a Man?," "There's Gonna Be a Wedding" Pony Sherrell, Phil Moody; "The Second Greatest Sex" Jay Livingston, Ray Evans (sung by Lahr) and "How Lonely Can I Get?" Joan Whitney, Alex Kramer (sung by Kallen). (1:27) A 19th century musical set in Kansas of townswomen who go on a sex strike to stop their feuding menfolk. A variation on Aristophanes' "Lysistrata," filmed in Technicolor and CinemaScope.

2318. The Second Woman (United Artists/Cardinal Pictures; 1951). *Cast:* Robert Young, Betsy Drake, John Sutton, Henry O'Neill, Florence Bates, Morris Carnovsky (final film until 1961), Jean Rogers, Steven Geray, Jason Robards, Raymond Largay, Shirley Ballard, Vici Raaf, John Gallaudet, Jimmie Dodd, Robert "Smoki" Whitfield, Cliff Clark. *D:* James V. Kern; *P:* Mort Briskin; *As.P:-St: & Sc:* Robert Smith. (1:31) (video) Melodrama of a man who believes himself responsible for the accidental death of his fiancée, and the woman in his life who believes otherwise. (G.B. title: *Ellen*) (aka: *Here Lies Love* and *Twelve Miles Out*)

The Secret Four (G.B. title) *see* **Kansas City Confidential**

2319. The Secret Fury (RKO/Loring Theatre Corp.; 1950). *Cast:* Claudette Colbert, Robert Ryan, Jane Cowl, Paul Kelly, Philip Ober (film debut), Elisabeth Risdon, Doris Dudley, David Barbour, Vivian Vance, Percy Helton, Dick Ryan, Ann Codee, Joseph Forte, Edit Angold, Adele Rowland, Howard Quinn, John Mantley, Marjorie "Babe" Kane, Ralph Dunn, Ruth Robinson, Pat Barton, Charmienne Harker, Eddie Dunn, Willard Parker, Vivian Oakland, Abe Dinovitch, Paul Picerni, Wheaton Chambers, Bert Moorhouse, Vangie Beilby, June Benbow, Sonny Boyne, Connie Van, Gail Bonney, Frank Scannell, Margaret Wells, Burk Symon, Gene Brown. *D:* Mel Ferrer; *P:* Jack H. Skirball, Bruce Manning; *St:* Jack R. Leonard, James O'Hanlon; *Sc:* Lionel Houser. (1:26) Mystery-melodrama of a woman who is about to be married and facing the accusation that she is already wed, though she has no such recollection. The plot thickens when her husband is tracked down and soon thereafter winds up the victim of murder, leaving her as the chief suspect.

Secret Interlude (G.B. title) *see* **The View From Pompey's Head**

2320. The Secret of Convict Lake (20th Century–Fox; 1951). *Cast:* Glenn Ford, Gene Tierney, Ethel Barrymore, Zachary Scott, Ann Dvorak (final film—ret.), Barbara Bates, Cyril Cusack, Richard Hylton, Helen Westcott, Jeanette Nolan, Ruth Donnelly, Harry Carter, Jack Lambert, Mary Carroll, Houseley Stevenson, Charles Flynn, David Post, Max Wagner, Tom London, Ray Teal, Raymond Greenleaf, William Leicester, Frances Endfield, Bernard Szold. *D:* Michael Gordon; *P:* Frank P. Rosenberg; *St:* Anna Hunger, Jack Pollexfen; *Adaptation:* Victor Trivas; *Sc:* Oscar Saul. (1:23) In this offbeat western melodrama, a settlement occupied solely by women is invaded by a gang of escaped convicts, one of which is in search of hidden money.

2321. Secret of the Incas (Paramount; 1954). *Cast:* Charlton Heston, Robert Young (final film—to TV's *Father Knows Best*), Nicole Maurey, Yma Sumac [aka: Amy Camus], Thomas Mitchell, Glenda Farrell, Michael Pate, Leon Askin, William Henry, Kurt Katch, Edward Colmans, Grandon Rhodes, Geraldine Hall, Harry Stanton, Booth Colman, Rosa Rey, Robert Tafur, Martin Garralaga, Alvy Moore, Rodolfo Hoyos, Zacharias Yaconelli, Marion Ross, John Marshall, Carlos Rivero, Delmar

Costello, Dimas Sotello, Miguel Contreras, Anthony Numkena. *D:* Jerry Hopper; *P:* Mel Epstein; *Sc:* Ranald MacDougall, Sydney Boehm. (1:40) Adventure of a man following a map in search of a fabled hidden treasure, but finds the site has already been reached by archeologists. Based on the story "Legend of the Incas" by Mr. Boehm. Technicolor.

2322. Secret of Treasure Mountain (Columbia; 1956). *Cast:* Valerie French, Raymond Burr, William Prince, Lance Fuller, Susan Cummings, Rodolfo Hoyos, Pat Hogan, Reginald Sheffield, Paul McGuire, Tom Hubbard, Boyd Stockman. *D:* Seymour Friedman (final film as director); *P:* Wallace MacDonald; *St: & Sc:* David Lang. (1:08) (video) Programmer western of a search for long hidden Indian gold that has a curse attached to it.

2323. Secrets of Life (Buena Vista/Walt Disney; 1956). *D:-St: & Sc:* James Algar; *Ex.P:* Walt Disney; *P:* Ben Sharpsteen; *Animation:* Joshua Meador, Art Riley; *Cinematography:* Stuart V. Jewell, Robert H. Crandall, Murl Deusing, George and Nettie MacGinitie, Tilden W. Roberts, William A. Anderson, Claude Jendrusch, Arthur Carter, Frank William Hall, Jack C. Couffer, Roman Vishniac, Donald L. Sykes, John Nash Ott, Jr., William H. Harlow, Rex R. Elliott, Vincent J. Schaefer; *Editor:* Anthony Gerard; *Narrator:* Winston Hibler. (1:15) (video) Disney's 4th "True-Life Adventure" feature which details various life forces instrumental in forming the earth. It includes cycles of plant life from seed to flower, done in time lapse photography, to Ravel's "Bolero," and blossoms to ripening fruit. Bees, ant wars and protozoa lead into a segment on sea life, including the life cycle of the grunion, and closing with transformation of the earth's crust by volcanos. A time consuming production with contributions from eighteen photographers. A winner at the box office which received critical praise as well. Technicolor.

2324. Secrets of Monte Carlo (Republic; 1951). *Cast:* Warren Douglas, Lois Hall, June Vincent, Stephen Bekassy, Robin Hughes, Otto Waldis, Charles LaTorre, Philip Ahn, Isabel Randolph, Charles Lung, Sue Casey, Georges Renavent, Bruce Lester, George Davis, Howard Chuman. *D:* George Blair; *As.P:* William Lackey; *St: & Sc:* John K. Butler. (1:00) Programmer crime melodrama of an American businessman in Monte Carlo who gets in the middle of a big jewel heist; the victim, a wealthy rajah.

2325. Security Risk (Allied Artists; 1954). *Cast:* John Ireland, Dorothy Malone, Keith Larsen, Dolores Donlon Peggy, John Craven, Suzanne Ta Fel, Joe Bassett, Burt Wenland, Steven Clark, Murray Alper, Harold Kennedy. *D:* Harold Schuster; *P:* William F. Broidy; *St:* John Rich; *Sc:* Jo Pagano, Rich. (1:09) Espionage melodrama set at Big Bear resort of an FBI agent who uncovers a communist plot involving the murder of a scientist and the theft of his important papers.

2326. Seeds of Destruction (Astor; 1952). *Cast:* Kent Taylor, Gene Lockhart, Gloria Holden, David Bruce. *D:* Frank Strayer. (1:24) Pure unabashed Cold War propaganda, this independent melodrama spins the tale of a Russian spy on the shore of America, attempting to spread communist thought throughout the nation until a taste of democracy leads him to dump his former ideology.

2327. The Sellout (MGM; 1952). *Cast:* Walter Pidgeon, John Hodiak, Audrey Totter, Paula Raymond, Thomas Gomez, Cameron Mitchell, Karl Malden, Everett Sloane, Frank Cady, Jonathan Cott, Hugh Sanders, Griff Barnett, Burt Mustin, Whit Bissell, Roy Engel, Jeff Richards, Vernon Rich, Bob Stevenson, Cy Stephens, Frankie Darro, Ann Tyrrell, Benny Rubin, Jack Sherman, Robert Williams, John Dierkes, Roy Butler, Cliff Clark, Mabel Smaney. *D:* Gerald Mayer; *P:* Matthew Rapf; *As.P:* Nicholas Nayfack; *St:* Rapf; *Sc:* Charles Palmer. (1:23) Small town crime melodrama of a local newspaper editor who sets out to tackle corruption involving the local sheriff's department.

2328. Seminole (Universal-International; 1953). *Cast:* Rock Hudson, Barbara Hale, Anthony Quinn (Osceola), Richard Carlson, Hugh O'Brian, Russell Johnson, Lee Marvin, James Best, Ralph Moody, Frank Chase, Earl Spainard, Scott Lee, Fay Roope, Don Gibson, John Day, Howard Erskine, Duane Thorsen, Walter Reed, Robert Karnes, Robert Dane, John Phillips, Soledad Jimenez, Don Garrett, Robert Bray, Alex Sharpe, William Janssen, Dan Poore. *D:* Budd Boetticher; *P:* Howard Christie; *St: & Sc:* Charles K. Peck, Jr. (1:27) Set in Florida in 1837, this fact-based fictional action-drama tells of attempts to rid the Everglades of the Seminole Indian tribe and a newly graduated West Point officer who opposes the action. Technicolor.

2329. Seminole Uprising (Columbia/Eros Films, Ltd.; 1955). *Cast:* George Montgomery,

Karin Booth, William Fawcett, Kenneth MacDonald, Steven Ritch, John Pickard, Ed Hinton, Jim Maloney, Rory Mallinson, Howard Wright, Russ Conklin, Jonni Paris, Joanne Rio, Richard H. Cutting, Paul McGuire, Rube Schaffer, Edward Coch. *D:* Earl Bellamy (directorial debut); *P:* Sam Katzman; *Sc:* Robert E. Kent. (1:14) A U.S. Army officer is sent to Texas to return a band of Seminole Indians to their Florida reservation. Based on the 1952 novel *Bugle's Wake* by Curt Brandon [pseudonym of Curtis Bishop]. Technicolor.

2330. Senior Prom (Columbia; 1958). *Cast:* Jill Corey, Paul Hampton, Jimmie Komack, Barbara Bostock, Tom Laughlin, Frieda Inescort, Selene Walters, Francis DeSales, Peggy Moffitt, Louis Prima, Keely Smith, Sam Butera and the Witnesses, Ed Sullivan, Mitch Miller, Connee Boswell (final film appearance), Bob Crosby, Toni Arden, Freddy Martin & Orchestra, Jose Melis, Les Elgart, Howard Miller (disc jockey-himself), Marvin Miller (narrator). *D:* David Lowell Rich; *P:* Harry Romm; *Sc:* Hal Hackady; *Songs:* "Big Daddy" Lee Pockriss, Peter Udell; "The Longer I Love You," "My Heart Will Play the Music," "The Best Way to Keep a Man," "Ivy Wall," "You Know When It's Him," "Never Before," "One Year Older," "Senior Prom," "Love," "Let's Fall in Love," "Now is the Time," "Rockabye in Beardland," "Do You Care?," "El Cumbanchero" Don Gohman, Hal Hackady + "That Old Black Magic" (sung by Prima and Smith); "Put the Blame on Mame" Allan Roberts, Doris Fisher (sung by Laughlin); "Sorrento" (sung by Arden); "When the Saints Come Marching In" (sung by Boswell); and "Pennies From Heaven" Arthur Johnston, Johnny Burke (by Martin and Orchestra). (1:22) A programmer musical with twenty songs and many guest stars.

Sentence Suspended (G.B. title) *see* **Military Academy with That 10th Avenue Gang**

2331. Separate Tables (United Artists/ Clifton Prods. for Hecht–Hill–Lancaster; 1958). *Cast:* Rita Hayworth (Ann Shankland), Deborah Kerr (AAN/Sybil Railton-Bell), David Niven (AA + "Best Actor" by the New York Film Critics/Major Pollock), Wendy Hiller (AA/Pat Cooper), Burt Lancaster (John Malcolm), Gladys Cooper (Mrs. Railton-Bell), Cathleen Nesbitt (Lady Matheson), Felix Alymer (Mr. Fowler), Rod Taylor (Charles), Audrey Dalton (Jean), May Hallatt (repeating her stage role/Miss Meacham), Priscilla Morgan (Doreen), Hilda Plowright (Mabel). *D:* Delbert Mann; *P:* (AAN-Best Picture) Harold Hecht; *Sc:* (AAN) Terence Rattigan, John Gay; *Cin:* (AAN) Charles B. Lang, Jr.; *Music:* (AAN) David Raksin; *Song:* Harold Adamson, Harry Warren (sung by Vic Damone) (1:38) (video) A critically acclaimed drama of various people and their problems, all of which are currently guests at a British seaside resort. Based on two one-act 1956 Broadway playlets, combined here as one, by Terence Rattigan. It placed #2 on the "10 Best" list of the NBR, while on the same list of *Film Daily* it placed #7. In nomination for "Best Picture" by the New York Film Critics, it also became one of the 26 top-grossing films of 1958-59.

2332. September Affair (Paramount; 1950). *Cast:* Joan Fontaine, Joseph Cotten, Francoise Rosay, Jessica Tandy, Robert Arthur, Fortunio Bonanova, Anna Demetrio, Jimmy Lawrence, Grazia Narciso, Jimmy Lydon, Lou Steele, Frank Yaconelli, Charles Evans, Jimmy Frasco, Michael Frasco, Charles LaTorre, Gilda Oliva, Saverio Lomedico, George Nardelli, Nick Borgani, Jeanne Lafayette, Dino Bolognese, Georgia Clancy, Dick Elliott, Rudy Rama, Franz G. Roehn, George Humbert, Harry Cheshire, Iphigenie Castiglioni, Inez Palange, Zacharias Yaconelli, Victor Desny, James R. Scott, Stan Johnson, Douglas Grange, Larry Arnold, Walter Merrill, Christopher Dark (film debut). *D:* William Dieterle; *P:* Hal B. Wallis; *St:* Fritz Rotter; *Sc:* Robert Thoeren, Andrew Solt (unc.); *Additional dialogue:* Solt (unc.); *Song:* Kurt Weill, Maxwell Anderson. (1:44) (video/laserdisc) Hit romantic drama of a married man and a concert pianist in Naples who miss their flight and are listed among the dead when the plane crashes. Walter Huston's rendering of "September Song" permeated the soundtrack and went on to become a hit for the second time!

2333. Serenade (Warner; 1956). *Cast:* Mario Lanza, Joan Fontaine, Sarita Montiel, Vincent Price, Joseph Calleia, Harry Bellaver, Vince Edwards, Silvio Minciotti, Frank Puglia, Edward Platt, Frank Yaconelli, Mario Siletti, Maria Serrano, Eduardo Noriega, Jean Fenn, Joseph Vitale, Victor Romito, Norma Zimmer, Licia Albanese, Francis Barnes, Lillian Molieri, Laura Mason, Richard Cable, Richard Lert, Jose Goves, Antonio Triana, Nick Mora, Joe DeAngelo, William Fox, Jack Santoro, Mickey Golden, Elizabeth Flournoy, Creighton Hale, Martha Acker, Joe [Jose] Torvay, Don Turner, Johnstone White, Ralph Volkie, Vincent Paula, Stephen Bekassy, Leo Mostovoy, Martin Garralaga, Perk Lazelle, April Stride, Diane Gump.

D: Anthony Mann; *P:* Henry Blanke; *Sc:* Ivan Goff, Ben Roberts, John Twist; *Songs:* "Serenade," "My Destiny" Nicholas Brodszky, Sammy Cahn; "Torna A Sorrento" Ernesto de Curtis, Claude Aveling; "Nessun Dorma" (from Giacomo Puccini's *Turandot*); "Ave Maria" Franz Schubert; "Italian Tenor Aria" (from Richard Strauss' *Der Rosenkavalier*), "LaMento di Federico" (from Francesco Cilea's *L'Arlesiana*), "Amor Ti Vieta" (from Umberto Giordano's *Fedora*), "Il Mio Tesoro" (from Wolfgang Amadeus Mozart's *Don Giovanni*), "La Danza" Gioacchino Antonio Rossini, "Di Quella Pira" (from Giuseppe Verdi's *Il Trovatore*), "O Paradis," "Sorti de L'Onde" (from Giacomo Meyerbeer's *L'Africaine*), "O Soave Fanciulla" (from Puccini's *La Bohème* sung with Jean Fenn) and "Dio Ti Giocondi" (from Verdi's *Otello* sung with Licia Albanese). (2:01) (video) The rise of a California vineyard worker to famous operatic tenor is told, taken from the 1937 novel by James M. Cain. A box office hit. WarnerColor/CinemaScope.

2334. Serpent Island (Medallion-TV; 1954). *Cast:* Sonny Tufts, Rosalind Hayes, Mary Munday. *D:-P:-St: & Sc:* Bert I. Gordon. (1:03) (video) Low budget adventure of a Caribbean expedition that becomes witness to voodoo rituals.

2335. Serpent of the Nile (Columbia; 1953). *Cast:* Rhonda Fleming, William Lundigan, Raymond Burr, Jean Byron, Michael Ansara, Michael Fox, Conrad Wolfe, John Crawford, Jane Easton, Robert Griffin (Brutus), Frederic Berest, Julie [Newmar] Newmeyer. *D:* William Castle; *P:* Sam Katzman; *Sc:* Robert E. Kent. (1:21) Another Katzman quickie, is this low budget costumer of Cleopatra (Fleming) and Marc Antony (Burr); utilizes the leftover sets of *Salome* (q.v.). Technicolor.

2336. Seven Angry Men (Allied Artists; 1955). *Cast:* Raymond Massey, Debra Paget, Jeffrey Hunter, Larry Pennell, Leo Gordon, John Smith, James Best, Dennis Weaver, Guy Williams, Tom Irish, James Anderson, James Edwards, John Pickard, Robert "Smoki" Whitfield, Jack Lomas, Robert Simon, Dabbs Greer, Ann Tyrrell, Robert Osterloh (Col. Robert E. Lee). *D:* Charles Marquis Warren; *P:* Vincent M. Fennelly; *St: & Sc:* Daniel B. Ullman. (1:30) A historical mid–19th century drama which received critical acclaim of abolitionist John Brown (Massey), his six sons and their involvement with freeing slaves and killing slave owners which makes them fugitives.

Seven Bad Men *see* **Rage at Dawn**

2337. Seven Brides for Seven Brothers (MGM; 1954). *Cast:* Jane Powell (Milly), Howard Keel (Adam), Jeff Richards (Benjamin), Matt Mattox (Caleb), Marc Platt (Daniel), Jacques D'Amboise (Ephraim), Tommy Rall (Frank), Russ Tamblyn (Gideon), Howard Petrie (Pete Perkins), Virginia Gibson (Liza), Ian Wolfe (Rev. Elcott), Julie [Newmar] Newmeyer (Dorcas), Nancy Kilgas (Alice), Betty Carr (Sarah), Ruta [Lee] Kilmonis (Ruth), Norma Doggett (Martha), Earl Barton (Harry), Dante DiPaolo (Matt), Kelly Brown (Carl), Matt Moore (Ruth's uncle), Dick Rich (Dorcas' father), Marjorie Wood (Mrs. Bixby), Russell Simpson (Mr. Bixby), Anna Q. Nilsson (Mrs. Elcott), Larry Blake (drunk), Phil Rich (prospector), Walter Beaver (Lem), Jarma Lewis (Lem's girlfriend), Sheila James (Dorcas' sister), Lois Hall, Russ Sanders, Terry Wilson, George Robotham, I. Stanford Jolley, Tim Graham. *D:* Stanley Donen; *P:* (AAN-Best Picture) Jack Cummings; *Sc:* (AAN) Albert Hackett, Frances Goodrich, Dorothy Kingsley; *Cin:* (AAN-color) George Folsey; *Music:* (AA) Adolph Deutsch, Saul Chaplin; *Editor:* (AAN) Ralph E. Winters; *Choreography:* (special award from the NBR) Michael Kidd; *Songs:* "Bless Your Beautiful Hide," "Wonderful, Wonderful Day," "When You're in Love," "Sobbin' Women," "Goin' Courtin'," "Lament (Lonesome Polecat)," "June Bride" and "Spring, Spring, Spring" Johnny Mercer, Gene DePaul. (1:43) (video/laserdisc) This musical of seven rowdy brothers from the backwoods of Oregon in search of wives became the studio's most phenomenal success of the year, receiving accolades and dollar bills from all over the world. Set in 1850, it was based on Stephen Vincent Benet's 1937 work *The Sobbin' Women*. The NBR placed it at #2 on their "10 Best" list, while the *New York Times* and *Film Daily* placed it at #5 and #6 respectively. In nomination at the British Academy Awards, it became one of the 25 top-grossing films of 1953-54. Later a Broadway musical and a TV series. Anscocolor and CinemaScope.

2338. Seven Cities of Gold (20th Century–Fox; 1955). *Cast:* Richard Egan, Anthony Quinn, Michael Rennie, Jeffrey Hunter, Rita Moreno, Eduardo Noriega, Leslie Bradley, John Doucette, Kathleen Crowley, Miguel Inclan, Carlos Musquiz, Pedro Galvan, Angelo DeStiffney, Ricardo Adalid Black, Fernando Wagner, Guillermo Calles, Eduardo Gonzales Pliego, Anna Marie Gomez, Jaime Gonzalez Quinones,

Luciel Nieto, Olga Gutierrez, Juan Jose Hutado, Victor Junco, Julio Villareal, Yerye Beirute, Jack Mower. *D:* Robert D. Webb; *P:* Webb, Barbara McLean [Mr. & Mrs.]; *Sc:* Richard L. Breen, John C. Higgins; *Additional dialogue:* Joseph Petracca. (1:43) (video) Fact-based costume-adventure of an 18th century Spanish expedition to the "American" Southwest in search of the fabled seven cities of gold. Based on the 1951 novel *The Nine Days of Father Sierra* by Isabelle Gibson Zeigler. DeLuxe color/CinemaScope.

2339. 711 Ocean Drive (Columbia/Essaness Pictures Corp.; 1950). *Cast:* Edmond O'Brien, Joanne Dru, Don Porter, Sammy White, Dorothy Patrick, Barry Kelley, Otto Kruger, Howard St. John, Robert Osterloh, Bert Freed, Carl Milletaire, Charles LaTorre, Fred Aldrich, Charles Jordan, Sidney Dubin. *D:* Joseph M. Newman; *P:* Frank N. Seltzer; *St: & Sc:* Richard English, Francis Swann. (1:42) A crime melodrama of the bookmaking racket that became a box office hit in that it mirrored the newspaper headlines of the day.

2340. Seven Guns to Mesa (Allied Artists/Wm. F. Broidy Pictures Corp.; 1958). *Cast:* Charles Quinlivan, Lola Albright, James Griffith, Jay Adler, Burt Nelson, John Merrick, Charles Keane, Jack Carr, Don Sullivan, Rush Williams, Reed [Howes] Hawes, Mauritz Hugo, Dan Sheridan, Gerald Frank, John Cliff, Neil Grant, Harvey Russell. *D:* Edward Dein; *P:* William F. Broidy; *St:* Myles Wilder; *Sc:* Wilder, E. Dein, Mildred Dein. (1:09) Stagecoach passengers are being held captive by outlaws bent on robbing a gold-carrying wagon train that is guarded by U.S. Cavalry.

2341. The Seven Hills of Rome (MGM/LeCloud Prods.–Titanus; 1958). *Cast:* Mario Lanza, Peggie Castle (final film—ret.), Marisa Allasio, Renato Rascel, Rossella Como, Clelia Matania, Amos Davoli, Guido Celano, Carlo Rizzo, Marco Tulli, Giorgio Gandos, Carlo Guiffre, Adriana Hart, Patrick Crean, Pennachi, April Hannessy, Luisa DiMoo, Stuart Hart. *D:* Roy Rowland; *P:* Lester Welch; *St:* Giuseppe Amato; *Sc:* Art Cohn, Giorgio Prosperi, Rowland (unc.); *Songs:* "Arrivederci Roma" Renato Rascel, Carl Sigman; "The Seven Hills of Rome" Victor Young, Harold Adamson; "Never Till Now" Johnny Green, Paul Francis Webster; "Earthbound" Jack Taylor, Clive Richardson, Bob Musett; "Calypso Italian" George Stoll; "Questa O Quella" (G. Verdi from *Rigoletto*), "Temptation" Arthur Freed, Nacio Herb Brown; "Memories Are Made of This" Terry Gilkyson, Richard Dehr, Frank Miller; "Jezebel" Wayne Shanklin + "M'Appari," "All the Things You Are," "Come Dance With Me," "Lolita," "Imitation Routine," "When the Saints Come Marching In," "Ay, Ay, Ay," "The Loveliest Night of the Year," "Ti Voglio Benne Tanto Tanto," "Na Canzone Pe Fa Ammore," "Venticello de Roma," "E'Arrivato La Bufera," "Ostricaro Innamorato," "Vogliamaci Tanto Bene" and "There's Gonna Be a Party Tonight." (1:44) (video) Hit musical-drama of a temperamental Italian-American singer who loses his job in the states and makes a comeback in Rome. A curiosity, in that it paralleled exactly what happened to its star, Mario Lanza. Filmed on location in Rome. Technicolor and Technirama.

2342. The Seven Little Foys (Paramount/Hope Enterprises-Scribe Prods.; 1955). *Cast:* Bob Hope (Eddie Foy), Milly Vitale (singing voice dubbed by Veola Vonn/Madeleine Morando), George Tobias (Barney Green), Angela Clarke (Clara), Billy Gray (Brynie), Lee Erickson (Charley), Paul De Rolf (Richard Foy), Lydia Reed (Mary Foy), Linda Bennett (Madeleine Foy), Jimmy Baird (Eddie Foy, Jr.), Tommy Duran (Irving Foy), James Cagney (George M. Cohan), Lester Matthews (Father O'Casey), Joe Evans & George Boyce (elephant act), Oliver Blake (Santa Claus), Milton Frome (Driscoll), King Donovan (Harrison), Jerry Mathers (Brynie, age 5), Eddie Foy, Jr. (narrator), Herbert Heyes, Richard Shannon, Jimmy Conlin, Marian Carr, Harry Cheshire, Renata Vanni, Betty Uitti, Noel Drayton, Jack Pepper, Dabbs Greer, Billy Nelson, Joe Flynn, Lewis Martin. *D:* Melville Shavelson (directorial debut); *P:* Jack Rose; *Sc:* (AAN) Shavelson, Rose; *Songs:* "Mary's a Grand Old Name," "I'm a Yankee Doodle Dandy" (George M. Cohan), "I'm the Greatest Father of Them All" (William Jerome, Joseph J. Lilley, Eddie Foy, Sr.), "Row, Row, Row" (Jerome, James V. Monaco), "Nobody" (Bert Williams, Alex Rogers), "Comedy Ballet" (Lilley), "I'm Tired," "Chinatown, My Chinatown" (Jean Schwartz, Jerome). (1:35) (video) Hit biopic of entertainer Eddie Foy and how following the death of his wife, he formed his family of seven children into a top vaudeville act. Technicolor/VistaVision. Note: The Iroquois theater fire of December 30, 1903, in Chicago which is touched on and played down here, was a fire of disastrous proportions, killing 639 people, mostly women and children attending a matinee performance.

2343. Seven Men from Now (Warner/Batjac; 1956). *Cast:* Randolph Scott, Gail Russell, Lee Marvin, Walter Reed, John Larch, Donald Barry, Fred Graham, John [Beradino] Barradino, John Phillips, Chuck Roberson, Steve Mitchell, Pamela Duncan, Stuart Whitman. *D:* Budd Boetticher; *P:* Andrew V. McLaglen, Robert E. Morrison; *St: & Sc:* Burt Kennedy. (1:17) Western of an ex-sheriff who tracks down the seven men who held up a stagecoach relay station and killed his wife. WarnerColor.

2344. Seven Wonders of the World (Stanley Warner Cinerama Corp.; 1956). *D:* Tay Garnett, Paul Mantz, Andrew Marton, Ted Tetzlaff, Walter Thompson; *P: & Narrator:* Lowell Thomas; *Scenario & Narration:* Prosper Buranelli, William Lipscomb (based on an idea by Mr. Thomas). (2:00) The 3rd travelogue in wide-screen Cinerama opens with scenes of the only remaining example of the seven wonders of the ancient world, the pyramid of Cheops and the Sphinx at Gizeh. From there the camera scans to various wonders of the modern world, including Iguazu Falls of Brazil, cherry trees in bloom at the Buddha temple in Japan, Angkor Wat of Cambodia, Benares and the Taj Mahal of India, a monkey temple and a runaway train ride down the mountain of Darjeeling. Additional sequences cover the Holy Land, Central Africa, Arabia, Greece and Rome with a procession of cardinals and the blessing of the crowd by the Pope at the Vatican. Closing scenes include the American West. Technicolor/Cinerama.

2345. The Seven Year Itch (20th Century–Fox/Charles K. Feldman Group; 1955). *Cast:* Marilyn Monroe (the girl), Tom Ewell (Richard Sherman), Evelyn Keyes (Helen Sherman), Sonny Tufts (Tom McKenzie), Robert Strauss (Kruhulik), Oscar Homolka (Dr. Brubaker), Marguerite Chapman (Miss Morris), Victor Moore (final film—ret./plumber), Roxanne (Elaine), Donald MacBride (Mr. Brady), Carolyn Jones (Miss Finch), Butch Bernard (Ricky), Doro Merande (waitress), Dorothy Ford, Mary Young, Ralph Sanford. *D:* Billy Wilder; *P:* Charles K. Feldman, Wilder; *Sc:* Wilder, George Axelrod. (1:45) (video/laserdisc) Comedy of a married man who indulges in some wild sexual fantasies about the beautiful blonde who just moved into the apartment upstairs, following the departure of his wife and son for their vacation. Based on Mr. Axelrod's 1952 play, it was filmed on location in New York City. One of the 27 top-grossing films of 1954-55. DeLuxe color/CinemaScope. Note: This is the film which shows Monroe's dress blowing upward as she stands over a subway grate, one of many sequences within the film which project her naive sexiness to the max.

2346. 7th Cavalry (Columbia/Producers Actors Corp.; 1956) *Cast:* Randolph Scott, Barbara Hale, Jay C. Flippen, Jeanette Nolan, Frank Faylen, Leo Gordon, Denver Pyle, Harry Carey, Jr., Michael Pate, Donald Curtis, Pat Hogan, Frank Wilcox, Russell Hicks (final film—d. 1957), Peter Ortiz, William Leslie, Jack Parker, Edward F. Stidder, Al Wyatt. *D:* Joseph H. Lewis; *P:* Harry Joe Brown; *As.P:* Randolph Scott; *Sc:* Peter Packer. (1:15) (video) A western of events following the Battle of the Little Big Horn. Based on *A Horse for Mrs. Custer* by Glendon F. Swarthout. Technicolor.

2347. The Seventh Sin (MGM; 1957). *Cast:* Eleanor Parker, Bill Travers, George Sanders, Jean Pierre Aumont, Francoise Rosay, Ellen Corby. *D:* Ronald Neame; *P:* David Lewis; *Sc:* Karl Tunberg. (1:34) Flop remake of W. Somerset Maugham's *The Painted Veil* (MGM; 1934) of a doctor's wife and her adulterous affair. Location filming in Hong Kong. CinemaScope.

2348. The 7th Voyage of Sinbad (Columbia/Morningside Prods.; 1958). *Cast:* Kerwin Mathews (Captain Sinbad), Kathryn Grant (Princess Parisa), Richard Eyer (Baronni the genie), Torin Thatcher (Sokurah), Alec Mango (caliph), Danny Green (Karim), Harold Kasket (sultan), Alfred Brown (Harufa), Nana de Herrera (Sadi), Nino Falanga, Luis Guedes, Virgilio Texeira. *D:* Nathan Juran; *P:* Charles H. Schneer; *Sc: & St:* Kenneth Kolb; *F/X:* Ray Harryhausen (his first in color). (1:27) (video/laserdisc) Costume adventure-fantasy dealing with Sinbad's efforts to get a princess returned to normal size after being shrunk by an evil magician. Harryhausen's special effects include a giant roc, a cyclops, a sword-wielding skeleton and a fire-breathing dragon. One of the 26 top-grossing films of 1958-59, it was filmed in Technicolor and Dynamation.

2349. Shack Out on 101 (Allied Artists/Wm. F. Broidy Pictures; 1955). *Cast:* Terry Moore, Frank Lovejoy, Keenan Wynn, Lee Marvin, Whit Bissell, Jess Barker, Donald Murphy, Frank DeKova, Len Lesser, Fred Gabourie. *D:* Edward Dein; *P:* Mort Millman; *St: & Sc:* Mildred and Edward Dein; *Song:* "A Sunday Kind of Love" Barbara Belle, Louis Prima, Anita

Leonard, Stan Rhodes. (1:20) (video) Melodrama, set at a roadside greasy spoon, of a scientist making plans to sell U.S. government secrets to a foreign agent. A film with a following.

2350. Shadow in the Sky (MGM; 1951). *Cast:* Ralph Meeker, Nancy Davis, James Whitmore, Jean Hagen, Gladys Hurlbut, Eduard Franz, John Lupton, Jonathan Cott, Dennis Ross, Nadene Ashdown. *D:* Fred M. Wilcox; *P:* William H. Wright; *Sc:* Ben Maddow, Margaret Fitts (unc.), Evelyn Frohman (unc.). (1:18) Drama, on a modest budget, of a shell-shocked war veteran whose fear of rainstorms adversely affects everyone around him. Based on the story "Come Another Day" by Edward Newhouse.

2351. Shadow on the Wall (MGM; 1950). *Cast:* Zachary Scott, Ann Sothern, Gigi Perreau, Nancy Davis, Kristine Miller, Tom Helmore, John McIntire, Barbara Billingsley, Marcia Van Dyke, Helen Brown, Anthony Sydes, Jimmy Hunt. *D:* Patrick Jackson (U.S. debut); *P:* Robert Sisk; *Sc:* William Ludwig. (1:24) Suspense drama of a young child who goes into shock after witnessing the murder of her wicked stepmother. She is unable to tell the truth when her father becomes the chief suspect, but snaps out of it when the killer zeroes in on her as his next victim. Based on the 1943 story "Death in the Doll's House" by Hannah Lees [pseudonym of Elizabeth Head Fetters] and Lawrence P. Bachmann.

2352. The Shadow on the Window (Columbia; 1957). *Cast:* Phil Carey, Betty Garrett (final film—ret.), John Barrymore, Jr., Corey Allen, Gerold Sarracini, Jerry Mathers, Sam Gilman, Rusty Lane, Ainslie Pryor, Paul Picerni, William Leslie, Doreen Woodbury, Angela Stevens, Mort Mills, Carl Milletaire, Julian Upton, Nesdon Booth, Jack Lomas. *D:* William Asher; *P:* Jonie Taps; *Sc:* Leo Townsend, David P. Harmon. (1:13) Programmer crime melodrama of a young boy who becomes mute after witnessing a murder and the kidnapping of his mother. Based on the short story "The Missing Witness" by John and Ward Hawkins.

2353. Shadows of Tombstone (Republic; 1953). *Cast:* Rex Allen, Slim Pickens, Jeanne Cooper, Roy Barcroft, Emory Parnell, Ric Roman, Richard Avonde, Julian Rivero, Ko-Ko (horse). *D:* William Witney; *As.P:* Rudy Ralston; *St: & Sc:* Gerald Geraghty. (0:54) Latter-day Rex Allen western of a cowboy who runs for sheriff with the help of a local female newspaper editor.

2354. The Shaggy Dog (Buena Vista/ Walt Disney Prods.; 1959). *Cast:* Fred MacMurray (Wilson Daniels), Jean Hagen (Frieda Daniels), Tommy Kirk (Wilby Daniels), Annette Funicello (Allison D'Allessio), Tim Considine (Buzz Miller), Kevin Corcoran (Moochie Daniels), Cecil Kellaway (Prof. Plumcutt), Alexander Scourby (Dr. Mikhail Andrassy), Roberta Shore (film debut/Franceska Andrassy), James Westerfield (Officer Hanson), Jacques Aubuchon (Stefano), Strother Martin (Thurm), Forrest Lewis (Officer Kelly), Ned Wever (E.P. Hackett), Gordon Jones (Capt. Scanlon), Mack Williams (Betz), Paul Frees (psychiatrist & opening narrator), John Hart (police broadcaster), Jack Albertson (reporter), Sam (dog/ Shaggy—1st Place PATSY in 1960). *D:* Charles Barton; *P:* Walt Disney; *As.P:* Bill Walsh; *Sc:* Walsh, Lillie Hayward. (1:44) (video/laserdisc) Disney's first live-action comedy with a touch of fantasy as a teenager comes into possession of a ring that shapeshifts him into a big shaggy dog like the one belonging to a neighbor, back to a boy, back to a dog, etc.—always at the most inopportune moments. A whopping $8,000,000 passed through the box office on Disney's investment of less than $1,000,000 to make this one of the 26 top-grossing films of 1958-59 and setting the stage for the many popular comedies that followed in the 1960s. Based on the 1923 novel *The Hound of Florence* by Felix Salten, it was followed in 1976 by the sequel *The Shaggy D.A.* and was remade for TV in 1994. Computer-colored prints have been produced.

2355. Shake, Rattle and Rock! (American International/Sunset Prods.; 1957). *Cast:* Fats Domino (himself), Joe Turner (himself), Lisa Gaye, Touch [Mike] Connors, Sterling Holloway, Raymond Hatton, Douglass Dumbrille, Margaret Dumont, Tommy Charles (himself), Annita Ray (herself), Paul Dubov, Eddie Kafafian, Clarence Kolb, Percy Helton, Choker Campbell (himself), Charles Evans, Frank Jenks, Pierre Watkin, Joe Devlin, Jimmy Pickford, Nancy Kilgas, Giovanna Fiorino, Leon Tyler, Patricia Gregory. *D:* Edward L. Cahn; *Ex.P:* Samuel Z. Arkoff; *P:* James H. Nicholson; *St: & Sc:* Lou Rusoff; *Songs:* "I'm in Love Again," "Ain't That a Shame?," "Honey Chile" (performed by Domino), "Feelin' Happy,"

"Lipstick, Powder and Paint" (performed by Turner), "Sweet Love on My Mind" and "Rockin' on Saturday Night" (performed by Charles and Ray). (1:14) (video) Comedy of conservative parents who attempt to put a stop to a "rock 'n' roll" club due to open in their town. Partially remade in 1994 for Showtime cable, it was originally paired on a double bill with *Runaway Daughters* (q.v.).

2356. Shakedown (Universal-International; 1950). *Cast:* Howard Duff, Brian Donlevy, Peggy Dow, Lawrence Tierney, Bruce Bennett, Anne Vernon, Stapleton Kent, Peter Virgo, Charles Sherlock, Will Lee, Carl Sklover, Josephine Whittell, Steve Roberts, John Miller, Ken Patterson, Leota Lorraine, Charles Flynn, Jack Reitzen, Roy Engel, Jack Rice, Bert Davidson, Ralph Brooks, Doug Carter, Kay Riehl, Wendy Waldron, Donald Kerr, Elsie Baker, Doretta Johnson, Jack Chefe, Forbes Murray, William Marks, Steve Wayne, Joe Dougherty, Bill O'Brien, James Garwood, Chester Conklin, Rock Hudson, Peggie Castle. *D:* Joseph Pevney (directorial debut); *P:* Ted Richmond; *St:* Nat Dallinger, Don Martin; *Sc:* Alfred Lewis Levitt, Martin Goldsmith. (1:20) Melodrama of a ruthless news photographer (Duff) who will stop at nothing, including blackmail, to make it to the top of his profession.

2357. Shane (Paramount; 1953). *Cast:* Alan Ladd (*Photoplay* Gold Medal/Shane), Jean Arthur (final film—ret./Mrs. Starrett), Van Heflin (Mr. Starrett), Brandon de Wilde (AAN/Joey Starrett), Walter [Jack] Palance (AAN/Wilson), Ben Johnson (Chris), Edgar Buchanan (Lewis), Emile Meyer (Ryker), Elisha Cook, Jr. (Torrey), Douglas Spencer (Mr. Shipstead), John Dierkes (Morgan), Ellen Corby (Mrs. Torrey), Paul McVey (Grafton), John Miller (Atkey), Edith Evanson (Mrs. Shipstead), Leonard Strong (Wright), Ray Spiker (Johnson), Janice Carroll (Susan Lewis), Martin Mason (Howells), Helen Brown (Mrs. Lewis), Nancy Kulp (Mrs. Howells), Howard J. Negley (Pete), Beverly Washburn (Ruth Lewis), George J. White, Charles Quirk, Jack Sterling, Henry Wills, Rex Moore, Ewing Brown. *D:* (AAN + "Best Director" by the NBR) George Stevens; *P:* (AAN-Best Picture) Stevens; *As.P:* Ivan Moffat; *Associate director:* Fred Guiol; *Sc:* (AAN) A.B. Guthrie, Jr.; *Additional dialogue:* Jack Sher; *Cin:* (AA-color) Loyal Griggs. (1:58) (video/laserdisc) All-time classic western of a drifter who comes to the aid of a family of homesteaders under fire from a ruthless cattle baron, becoming idolized by the young son. Based on the novel by Jack Schaefer, it was part of Paramount's backlog of Ladd films, produced earlier with delayed release. It placed #2 on the "10 Best" lists of both the NBR and *Film Daily* and #3 on the same list of the *New York Times*. One of the 26 top-grossing films of 1952-53, taking in over $9,000,000 in the U.S.A. alone. The British Academy Awards also had it in nomination. Technicolor.

2358. The Shanghai Story (Republic/A Herbert J. Yates Presentation; 1954). *Cast:* Ruth Roman, Edmond O'Brien, Richard Jaeckel, Barry Kelley, Whit Bissell, Basil Ruysdael, Marvin Miller, Yvette Dugay, Paul Picerni, Isabel Randolph, Philip Ahn, Frances Rafferty, Frank Ferguson, James Griffith, John Alvin, Frank Puglia, Victor Sen Yung, Janine Perreau, Richard Loo. *D: & P:* Frank Lloyd; *St:* Lester Yard; *Sc:* Seton I. Miller, Steve Fisher. (1:39) Melodrama set in the titled Chinese city following the communist takeover, involving the rounding up of Americans and Europeans suspected of being spies.

Shark Reef (G.B. title) *see* **She-Gods of Shark Reef**

2359. Shark River (United Artists/John Rawlins Prods.; 1953). *Cast:* Steve Cochran, Carole Mathews, Warren Stevens, Robert Cunningham, Spencer Fox, Ruth Foreman, Bill Piper. *D:-P: & St:* John Rawlins; *Sc:* Joseph Carpenter, Lewis Meltzer; *Song:* Meltzer. (1:20) 19th century action-melodrama of three men escaping through the Florida swamps who come upon a woman, her young son and her mother-in-law, followed by a Seminole Indian attack. Vivid [Cinecolor].

2360. The Sharkfighters (United Artists/Formosa Prods.; 1956). *Cast:* Victor Mature, Karen Steele, James Olson, Philip Coolidge, Claude Akins, Rafael Campos, George Neise, Nathan Yates, Jesus Hernandez, Lorin Johns, David Westlein, Charles Collingwood (narrator). *D:* Jerry Hopper; *P:* Sam Goldwyn, Jr.; *St:* Jo & Art Napoleon; *Sc:* Lawrence Roman, John Robinson; *Song:* Mercy Ferrer, Cesar Portillo (sung by the Aida Quartette). (1:13) Adventure story of U.S. Navy scientists researching a shark repellent for flyers downed at sea. Filmed on location in Cuba. Technicolor and CinemaScope.

2361. She Couldn't Say No (RKO; 1954). *Cast:* Robert Mitchum, Jean Simmons, Arthur

Hunnicutt, Edgar Buchanan, Wallace Ford, Raymond Walburn, Jimmy Hunt, Ralph Dumke, Hope Landin, Gus Schilling, Eleanor Todd, Pinky Tomlin, Bert Mustin, Edith Leslie, Martha Wentworth, Gloria Winters, Barry Brooks, Wallis Clark, Florence Lake, Jonathan Hale, Keith Harrington, John Craven, Tol Avery, Mary Bayless, Joy Hallward, Morgan Brown, Clyde Courtwright, Coleman Francis, Mike Lally, Leo Sulky, Clarence Muse, Maxie Thrower, Dabbs Greer, Dan White, Bob Hopkins, Charles Watts, Ruth Packard, Teddy Mangean, Sammy Shack, Carl Sklover, Charles Cane, Tony Terrill, Marjorie Holliday, Marilyn Gladstone. *D:* Lloyd Bacon (final film—d. 1955); *P:* Robert Sparks; *Sc:* D.D. Beauchamp, William Bowers, Richard Flournoy. (1:28) (video) Comedy-drama based on the story "Enough for Happiness" by Mr. Beauchamp of a woman who upsets the lives of various people in her small town when she makes monetary gifts to them in repayment for a kindness they did for her when she was younger. Produced in 1952 with release held up until 1954. (G.B. title: *Beautiful But Dangerous*)

2362. The She-Creature (American International/Golden State Prods.; 1956). *Cast:* Chester Morris, Marla English, Tom Conway, Cathy Downs, Lance Fuller, Ron Randell, Frieda Inescort, Frank Jenks, El Brendel (final film—ret.), Paul Dubov, Bill Hudson, Flo Bert, Jeanne Evans, Kenneth MacDonald, Paul Blaisdell (creature). *D:* Edward L. Cahn; *P:* Samuel Z. Arkoff, Alex Gordon; *St:* Jerry Zigmond; *Sc:* Lou Rusoff. (1:17) (video) Horror thriller of a girl who, when put under hypnosis, brings forth her former self, a monstrous creature from the local lake which goes on a killing spree. Remade in 1968 as *Creature of Destruction*. Note: Paul Blaisdell's monster creation was recycled twice, once for an appearance in *Voodoo Woman* (q.v.) as were English, Conway and Fuller, and again in *Ghost of Dragstrip Hollow* (q.v.).

2363. She Demons (Astor/Screencraft Enterprises; 1958). *Cast:* Irish McCalla, Tod Griffin, Victor Sen Yung, Charlie Opuni, Gene Roth, Rudolph Anders, Leni Tana, Billy Dix, Bill Coontz, The Diana Nellis Dancers. *D:* Richard E. Cunha; *P:* Arthur A. Jacobs; *As.P:* Marc Frederic; *St: & Sc:* Cunha, H.E. Barrie. (1:20) (video) Low budget horror film of people stranded on a volcanic island where an escaped Third Reich Nazi doctor is experimenting on females in order to restore his wife's beauty. It originally ran on a double bill as a second feature with *Giant from the Unknown* (q.v.).

2364. She Devil (20th Century-Fox/Regal Films; 1957). *Cast:* Albert Dekker, Jack Kelly, Mari Blanchard, Blossom Rock [aka: Marie Blake], John Archer, Fay Baker, Paul Cavanagh, George Baxter, Helen Jay, Joan Bradshaw, Tod Griffin. *D: & P:* Kurt Neumann; *Sc:* Neumann, Carroll Young. (1:17) Low budget horror tale of a woman dying of TB who is given an experimental serum, which is found to carry a side effect of homicidal tendencies. Based on the 1941 short story "The Adaptive Ultimate" by John Jessel, it originally ran on the bottom of a double bill with *Kronos* (q.v.). Regalscope.

2365. She-Gods of Shark Reef (American International/Radford Films Corp.; 1958). *Cast:* Don Durant, Bill Cord, Lisa Montell, Jeanne Gerson, Carol Lindsay. *D:* Roger Corman; *P:* Ludwig H. Gerber; *St: & Sc:* Robert Hill, Victor Stoloff; *Song:* "Nearer My Love to You" Jack Lawrence, Frances Hall (sung by Sylvia Sims). (1:03) (video) B budget adventure of two brothers, washed ashore on an island inhabited only by women pearl divers, who are forbidden to love or marry. Filmed on location in Hawaii, it originally ran on the bottom of a double bill with *Night of the Blood Beast* (q.v.). Pathécolor. (G.B. title: *Shark Reef*)

She Monster of the Night *see* **Frankenstein's Daughter**

2366. The Sheepman (MGM; 1958). *Cast:* Glenn Ford (Jason Sweet), Shirley MacLaine (Dell Payton), Leslie Nielsen (John Bledsoe—aka: Col. Stephen Bedford), Mickey Shaughnessy (Jumbo McCall), Edgar Buchanan (Milt Masters), Willis Bouchey (Mr. Payton), Pernell Roberts (Choctaw), Robert "Buzz" Henry (Red), Slim Pickens (Marshall), Pedro Gonzales-Gonzales (Angelo). *D:* George Marshall; *P:* Edmund Grainger; *St: & Sc:* (AAN) James Edward Grant (story), William Bowers (adaptation). (1:25) Popular western with a light touch on the old cattleman vs. sheepman theme. The film was popular with critics, was in nomination at the British Academy Awards and became a good moneymaker for MGM. Metrocolor & CinemaScope.

The Sheriff's Daughter *see* **A Ticket to Tomahawk**

2367. She's Back on Broadway (Warner; 1953). *Cast:* Virginia Mayo, Gene Nelson, Frank Lovejoy, Steve Cochran, Patrice Wymore, Virginia Gibson, Larry Keating, Paul Picerni, Ned

Young, Condos and Brandow (specialty dancers), Douglas Spencer, Jacqueline de Wit, Mabel Albertson, Lenny Sherman, Cliff Ferre, Ray Kyle, Sy Melano, Taylor Holmes, Paul Bryar, Harry Tyler, Phyllis Coates, Caleen Calder, Howard Price, Ray Walker, Minerva Urecal, Harland Hoagland, Jack Kennedy, Kathleen Freeman, Percy Helton. *D:* Gordon Douglas; *P:* Henry Blanke; *St: & Sc:* Orin Jannings; *Songs:* "I'll Take You as You Are," "One Step Ahead of Everybody," "The Ties That Bind," "Breakfast in Bed," "Behind the Mask" Bob Hilliard, Carl Sigman + "I Think You're Wonderful." (1:35) Romantic musical-drama of a Hollywood star who attempts to make a comeback on Broadway. A sequel to *She's Working Her Way Through College* (q.v.). WarnerColor.

2368. She's Working Her Way Through College (Warner; 1952). *Cast:* Virginia Mayo, Ronald Reagan, Gene Nelson, Don DeFore, Phyllis Thaxter, Patrice Wymore, Roland Winters, Raymond Greenleaf, The Blackburn Twins (themselves), Norman Barthold, Amanda Randolph, Henrietta Taylor, Hope Sansberry, George Meader, Eve Miller, Dick Reeves, Donald Kerr, Patricia Hawks, Donna Ring, Frances Zucco, Frank Scannell, Jimmy Ames, Paul Maxey, Charles Watts, John Perri, Glenn Turnbull, Bette Arlen, Valerie Vernon, Hazel Shaw, Barbara Ritchie, Mark Lowell, Jimmy Ogg, Charles Marsh, Jack Gargan, Ray Linn, Jr., Jessie Arnold, Rolland Morris, Malcolm Mealey, Louis Cutelli, Ginger Crowley, Larry Craig. *D:* H. Bruce Humberstone; *P:* William Jacobs; *Sc:* Peter Milne; *Songs:* "I'll Be Loving You," "The Stuff That Dreams Are Made Of," "Give 'Em What They Want," "Am I in Love?," "Love is Still for Free," "She's Working Her Way Through College" Sammy Cahn, Vernon Duke; and "With Plenty of Money and You" Al Dubin, Harry Warren (originally introduced in *The Gold Diggers of 1937*). (1:41) A musical re-working of *The Male Animal* (1942) and based on the play of that name by James Thurber and Elliott Nugent. A stripper attempts to put her past behind and get a college education. In Technicolor, it was followed by the sequel *She's Back on Broadway* (q.v.).

2369. Shield for Murder (United Artists/Camden Prods.–Koch Prods.; 1954). *Cast:* Edmond O'Brien, Marla English, John Agar, Emile Meyer, Carolyn Jones, Claude Akins, Larry Ryle, Herbert Butterfield, Hugh Sanders, William Schallert, David Hughes, Richard Cutting. *D:* Edmond O'Brien (directorial debut), Howard W. Koch; *P:* Aubrey Schenck; *Adaptation:* Richard Alan Simmons; *Sc:* Simmons, John C. Higgins, Don Martin (unc.). (1:20) Crime melodrama of a crooked cop who steals $25,000 from a gangster he murders and becomes the target suspect of an investigating colleague. Based on the 1951 novel by William P. McGivern.

2370. Shoot-Out at Medicine Bend (Warner; 1957). *Cast:* Randolph Scott, James Craig, Angie Dickinson, Dani Crayne, James Garner, Gordon Jones, Trevor Bardette, Don Beddoe, Myron Healey, John Alderson, Harry Harvey, Sr., Robert Warwick, Howard Negley, Marshall Bradford, Ann Doran, Daryn Hinton, Dickie Bellis, Edward Hinton, Lane Bradford, Frances Morris, Robert Lynn, Sam Flint, Philip Van Zandt, Guy Wilkerson, Syd Saylor, Harry Rowland, Marjorie Bennett, Jesslyn Fax, Marjorie Stapp, Nancy Kulp, George Meader, Rory Mallinson, Dee Carroll, Dale Van Sickel, Gil Perkins, Harry Lauter, Carol Henry, George Pembroke, Tom Monroe, Buddy Roosevelt, George Bell. *D:* Richard L. Bare; *P:* Richard Whorf; *St: & Sc:* John Tucker Battle, D.D. Beauchamp; *Song:* "Kiss Me Quick" Ray Heindorf, Wayne Shanklin (sung by Crayne). (1:27) Sioux Indians slaughter several families after they find a crooked trader sold them defective ammunition, setting several men on the vengeance trail.

2371. Short Cut to Hell (Paramount; 1957). *Cast:* Robert Ivers, Georgann Johnson, William Bishop, Murvyn Vye, Yvette Vickers, James Cagney (appears in prologue), Jacques Aubuchon, Peter Baldwin, Milton Frome, Jacqueline Beer, Gail Land, Dennis McMullen, William [Billy] Newell, Sarah Selby, Mike Ross, Douglas Spencer, Danny Lewis, Richard Hale, Douglas Evans, Hugh Lawrence, Joe Bassett, William Pullen, Russell Trent, Joe Forte, John Halloran, Roscoe Ates. *D:* James Cagney (only film as director); *P:* A.C. Lyles; *Sc:* Ted Berkman, Raphael Blau. (1:27) Melodrama of a psychotic killer who takes on the mob when he finds he's been double-crossed. A remake of *This Gun for Hire* and based on the screenplay of that 1942 film by W.R. Burnett and the book by Graham Greene. Remade for cable TV in 1991 under that title. VistaVision.

2372. Short Grass (Allied Artists/Monogram; 1950). *Cast:* Rod Cameron, Cathy Downs, Johnny Mack Brown, Alan Hale, Jr., Morris Ankrum, Jeff York, Raymond Walburn, Jonathan Hale, Riley Hill, Harry Woods, Stanley

Andrews, Tristram Coffin, Myron Healey, Jack Ingram, Rory Mallinson, Marlo Dwyer, Felipe Turich, George J. Lewis, Lee Tung Foo, Lee Roberts, Frank Ellis, Tom Monroe, Kermit Maynard. *D:* Lesley Selander; *P:* Scott R. Dunlap; *Sc:* Tom W. Blackburn. (1:22) (video) Oater of a sheriff and a rancher who band together to put the crimps to a crooked land scheme after the rancher is forced from his land. Based on Mr. Blackburn's 1949 novel *Range War.*

2373. Shotgun (Allied Artists; 1955). *Cast:* Sterling Hayden, Yvonne DeCarlo, Zachary Scott, Robert J. Wilke, Guy Prescott, Ralph Sanford, John Pickard, Ward Wood, Rory Mallinson, Paul Marion, Harry Harvey, Jr., Lane Chandler, Angela Greene, Robert E. Griffin, Al Wyatt, Bob Morgan, Peter Coe, Charles Morton, James Parnell, Richard Cutting, Fiona Hale, Francis McDonald. *D:* Lesley Selander; *P:* John Champion; *Sc:* Clark E. Reynolds, Rory Calhoun; *Additional dialogue:* Champion. (1:21) (video) Western of a sheriff and a bounty hunter who vie for the affections of a half-breed showgirl while all three search for a killer—at the same time eluding Apaches. Technicolor.

2374. Show Boat (MGM; 1951). *Cast:* Kathryn Grayson (Magnolia Hawks), Ava Gardner (Julie Laverne/singing voice dubbed by Annette Warren), Howard Keel (Gaylord Ravenal), Joe E. Brown (Capt. Andy Hawks), Marge Champion (Ellie May Shipley), Gower Champion (Frank Schultz), Robert Sterling (Stephen Baker), Agnes Moorehead (Parthy Hawks), Adele Jergens (Cameo McQueen), William Warfield (Joe), Leif Erickson (Pete), Owen McGiveney (Windy McClain), Frances Williams (Queenie), Regis Toomey (Sheriff Ike Vallon), Frank Wilcox (Mark Hallson), Chick Chandler (Herman), Emory Parnell (Jake Green), Sheila Clark (Kim), Louis Mercier (Dabney), Lisa Ferraday (Renee), Ian MacDonald, Fuzzy Knight, Norman Leavitt, Lyn Wilde, Joyce Jameson, Edward Keane, Tom Irish, Jim Pierce, Marjorie Wood, William Tannen, Anna Q. Nilsson, Bert Roach, Frank Dae, Harry Seymour, William Hall, Earle Hodgins, Ida Moore, Alphonse Martell. *D:* George Sidney; *P:* Arthur Freed; *Sc:* John Lee Mahin; *Cin:* (AAN-color) Charles Rosher; *Music:* (AAN) Adolph Deutsch, Conrad Salinger; *Choreography:* Robert Alton, *Songs:* "Why Do I Love You?," "Make Believe," "Old Man River," "Can't Help Lovin' That Man," "Bill" (Jerome Kern, Oscar Hammerstein II); "You Are Love," "Ballyhoo," "Gambler's Song," "I Fall Back on You," "Life Upon the Wicked Stage" (Kern, Hammerstein II, P.G. Wodehouse) + "After the Ball." (1:47) (video/laserdisc) Super hit Technicolor musical-drama of life on a 19th century show boat, based on the best-selling novel by Edna Ferber which became a Broadway smash in 1927, with subsequent revivals over the years. First filmed by Universal in 1929 as a part singing/talkie with a subsequent remake in 1936 with added songs. It was at this point MGM bought the 1936 production and all rights to the Jerome Kern-Oscar Hammerstein II musical with intent for this "future" remake. The added songs of the 1936 production were eliminated and the non-Kern/Hammerstein II number "After the Ball" was returned to the plethora of musical numbers. Critically panned by virtually every reviewer except the people who paid to see it; they won out making this one of the 23 top-grossing films of 1950-51, as well as the top-grossing film of 1951 worldwide. Its popularity also gained it *Photoplay's* "Gold Medal"—so much for movie critics. A "what if?" sidenote: Jerome Kern, who wrote the music for this legendary piece of musical Americana, had booked passage to sail on the *Lusitania* on May 1, 1915, with intent of talking to renowned producer Charles Frohman. On that day, Kern's alarm clock failed and he missed the boat by minutes. On May 8th off the coast of Ireland, the *Lusitania* was torpedoed by a German U-Boat. Frohman perished along with 1,197 of the 2,000+ passengers and crew.

2375. The Showdown (Republic; 1950). *Cast:* William Elliott, Walter Brennan, Marie Windsor, Henry [Harry] Morgan, Rhys Williams, Jim Davis, William Ching, Nacho Galindo, Leif Erickson, Henry Rowland, Charles Stevens, Victor Kilian, Yakima Canutt, Guy Teague, William Steele, Jack Sparks. *D: & Sc:* Dorrell and Stuart McGowan; *P:* William Elliott, William J. O'Sullivan. (1:26) (video) Western of a former lawman, now trail herding, who hunts down the man who murdered his brother. Based on the story "Sleep All Winter" by Richard Wormser and Dan Gordon which appeared in *Esquire.*

2376. Showdown at Abilene (Universal-International; 1956). *Cast:* Jock Mahoney, Martha Hyer, Lyle Bettger, David Janssen, Grant Williams, Ted de Corsia, Harry Harvey, Sr., Dayton Lummis, Richard Cutting, Robert G. Anderson, John Maxwell, Lane Bradford. *D:* Charles Haas, *P:* Howard Christie; *Sc:* Berne Giler. (1:20) Western of a Civil War vet and former sheriff who returns to his town and finds his girl linked up with the town troublemaker.

Based on the novel *Gun Shy* by Clarence Upson Young, it was remade by this studio in 1967 as *Gunfight in Abilene*. Technicolor.

2377. Showdown at Boot Hill (20th Century–Fox/Regal Films; 1958). *Cast:* Charles Bronson, Robert Hutton, John Carradine, Carole Mathews, Paul Maxey, Thomas Browne Henry, Fintan Meyler, William Stevens, Martin Smith, Joseph McGuinn, George Douglas, Michael Mason, George Pembroke, Argentina Brunetti, Ed Wright, Dan Simmons, Barbara Woodell, Norman Leavitt. *D:* Gene Fowler, Jr.; *P:* Harold E. Knox; *St: & Sc:* Louis Vittes. (1:12) (video) Offbeat western of bounty hunter Luke Welsh who trails a wanted man to a town and kills him, only to find the man was liked in the town and no one will identify him making it difficult to collect the bounty money. Regalscope.

Showtime *see* **Paris Follies of 1956**

2378. The Shrike (Universal-International; 1955). *Cast:* Jose Ferrer, June Allyson, Joy Page, Kendall Clark, Isabel Bonner [the real "shrike" of the title on whom the play was based], Jay Barney, Somer Alberg, Edward Platt (film debut), Dick Benedict, Herbie Faye, Will Kuluva, Martin Newman, Billy Greene, Joe Comadore, Leigh Whipper, Mary Bell, Adrienne Marden. *D:* Jose Ferrer (directorial debut); *P:* Aaron Rosenberg; *Sc:* Ketti Frings. (1:28) Drama of a Broadway stage director who is driven to a nervous breakdown by his psychotic wife. Based on the Pultizer Prize–winning Broadway play by Joseph Kramm.

2379. The Sickle or the Cross (Astor 1949–51). *Cast:* Gloria Holden, Gayne Whitman, Arthur Stone, Charles Halton. *D:* Frank Strayer; *St:* T.G. Eggers; *Sc:* Jesse Lasky, Jr. A low budget drama of religion vs. communism. Produced in 1949 with release held up until 1951.

2380. Sideshow (Monogram; 1950). *Cast:* Don McGuire, Tracey Roberts, John Abbott, Eddie Quillan, Ray Walker, Richard Foote, Jimmy Conlin, Iris Adrian, Ted Hecht, Stephen Chase, Donald Kerr, Frank Fenton, Kathy Johnson, Jack Ingram, Dale Van Sickel. *D:* Jean Yarbrough; *P: & St:* William F. Broidy; *As.P:* Wesley Brown; *Sc:* Sam Roeca. (1:07) Jewel smugglers are operating out of a traveling carnival in this programmer melodrama.

2381. The Siege at Red River (20th Century–Fox/Panoramic Prods.; 1954). *Cast:* Van Johnson, Joanne Dru, Richard Boone, Milburn Stone, Jeff Morrow, Craig Hill, Rico Alaniz, Robert Burton, Pilar Del Ray, Ferris Taylor, John Cliff. *D:* Rudolph Maté; *P:* Leonard Goldstein; *St:* J. Robert Bren, Gladys Atwater; *Sc:* Sydney Boehm. (1:21) Civil War–era western of a Confederate spy on orders to steal a Gatling gun who falls for a Yankee nurse. The titled siege by Indians occurs before the fadeout.

2382. Sierra (Universal-International; 1950). *Cast:* Wanda Hendrix, Audie Murphy, Burl Ives, Dean Jagger, Richard Rober, Anthony [Tony] Curtis, Houseley Stevenson, Elisabeth Risdon, Sara Allgood, Elliott Reid, Griff Barnett, Roy Roberts, Gregg Martell, James Arness, Ted Jordan. I. Stanford Jolley, Jack Ingram, Erskine Sanford, John Doucette. *D:* Alfred E. Green; *P:* Michel Kraike; *Sc:* Edna Anhalt; *Additional dialogue:* Milton Gunzburg; *Songs:* Frederick Herbert, Arnold Hughes, Burl Ives. (1:23) Technicolor western of a man and his son on the lam from the law. A remake of Universal's 1938 production *Forbidden Valley* and based on the novel of that name by Stuart Hardy [pseudonym of Oscar Schisgall]. Includes six songs vocalized by Ives.

2383. Sierra Baron (20th Century–Fox; 1958). *Cast:* Brian Keith, Rick Jason, Rita Gam, Mala Powers, Steve Brodie, Carlos Musquiz, Lee Morgan, Allan Lewis, Pedro Galvan, Fernando Wagner, "Ferrusquilla" [Jose Espinoza], Enrique Lucero, Alberto Mariscal, Lynn Ehrlich, Michael Schmidt, Tommy Riste, Reed Howes, Robin Glattley, Enrique Inigo, Faith Perry, Doris Contreras, Marc Lambert, Stillman Segar, Alicia del Lago, Jose Trowe, Armando Saenz, Lolla Davila, Roy Fletcher, Ricardo Adalid, John Courier, Mark Zachary, Paul Arnett, Bob Janis. *D:* James B. Clark; *P:* Plato A. Skouras; *Sc:* Houston Branch. (1:20) In 1848 California, a brother and sister inherit a vast Spanish land grant from their late father. On attempting to claim it, they find parcels of the land have been sold by a landgrabber to settlers who have built a town. Based on the 1955 novel by Thomas W. Blackburn, it was filmed in Mexico. DeLuxe color/CinemaScope.

2384. Sierra Passage (Monogram; 1951). *Cast:* Wayne Morris, Lola Albright, Lloyd Corrigan, Alan Hale, Jr., Roland Winters, Jim Bannon, Billy Gray, Paul McGuire, Richard Karlan, George Eldredge. *D:* Frank McDonald; *P:* Lindsley Parsons; *As.P:* Wayne Morris, Ace Herman; *Sc: & St:* Warren D. Wandberg, Sam

Roeca, Thomas W. Blackburn; *Songs:* "Down the Lane" Buddy Burns, George Howe; "Love is Magic" Charles Dixon, Max Goodwin and "Let's Break the Ice" Hugo Peretti, Herb Pine (all sung by Albright). (1:21) Western of a sharpshooter with a traveling minstrel show, in search of his father's killer.

2385. Sierra Stranger (Columbia/Nacirema Prods.; 1957). *Cast:* Howard Duff, Gloria McGhee, Dick Foran, John Hoyt, Barton MacLane, George E. Stone, Ed Kemmer, Henry "Bomber" Kulky, Byron Foulger, Robert C. Foulk, Eve McVeagh. *D:* Lee Sholem; *Ex.P:* David T. Yokozeki; *P:* Norman T. Herman; *As.P:* Byron Roberts; *St: & Sc:* Richard J. Dorso. (1:14) Western programmer of a man saved from a beating by a man who later realizes the one he saved was getting what was coming to him.

2386. Sign of the Pagan (Universal-International; 1954). *Cast:* Jeff Chandler, Jack Palance, Ludmilla Tcherina, Rita Gam, Jeff Morrow, Allison Hayes, Eduard Franz, George Dolenz, Alexander Scourby, Moroni Olsen (final film—d. 1954/Pope Leo), Sara Shane, Walter Coy, Pat Hogan, Howard Petrie, Michael Ansara, Leo Gordon, Rusty Wescoatt, Chuck Roberson, Charles Horvath, Robo Bechi, Sam Iness. *D:* Douglas Sirk; *P:* Albert J. Cohen; *St:* Oscar Brodney; *Sc:* Brodney, Barre Lyndon. (1:32) Epic costumer of a centurion's attempts to convince the emperor of Rome that Attila the Hun (Palance) and his horde are planning to sack the city. In Technicolor and CinemaScope, it was a box office flop.

Silent Death *see* **Voodoo Island**

2387. Silent Raiders (Lippert/Enterprise Cinema; 1954). *Cast:* Richard Bartlett, Earle Lyon, Jeannette Bordeaux, Earle Hansen, Robert Knapp, Fred Foote, Frank Stanlow, Carl Swanstrom. *D:-St: & Sc:* Richard Bartlett; *P:* Earle Lyon; *Song:* Elmer Bernstein, Bartlett, J.A. Wenzel. (1:08) Programmer World War II drama of a seven man recon unit out to destroy a German communications center.

The Silent Stranger (G.B. title) *see* **Step Down to Terror**

The Silent Voice (G.B. title) *see* **Paula**

2388. Silk Stockings (MGM; 1957). *Cast:* Fred Astaire, Cyd Charisse (singing voice dubbed by Carole Richards), Janis Paige, Peter Lorre, George Tobias, Jules Munshin, Joseph Buloff, Barrie Chase, William Sonneveld, Belita, Ivan Triesault, Da Utti, Tybee Afra. *D:* Rouben Mamoulian (final film—ret.); *P:* Arthur Freed; *St:* Melchior Lengyel; *Sc:* Leonard Spigelgass, Leonard Gershe [Harry Kurnitz-unc.]; *Songs:* "All of You," "Stereophonic Sound," "Too Bad," "Paris Loves Lovers," "Fated to be Mated" (film only), "The Ritz Rock 'n Roll" (film only), "Silk Stockings" (dance only), "Red Blues," "Josephine," "Satin and Silk," "Without Love," "Chemical Reaction" and "Siberia" Cole Porter. (1:57) (video/laserdisc) Based on the Broadway success, this film is a musical remake of *Ninotchka* (MGM; 1939). Romance and comedy in a tale of a hard-nosed Russian female army officer who learns how to live it up in Paris. Based on the musical play by George S. Kaufman, Leueen McGrath and Abe Burrows, and the 1939 screenplay by Billy Wilder, Charles Brackett and Walter Reisch, it took a #6 placement on the "10 Best" list of the *New York Times*. Metrocolor/CinemaScope.

2389. The Silver Bandit (Friedgen; 1949–50). *Cast:* Spade Cooley, Bob Gilbert, Virginia Jackson, Richard [Dick] Elliott, Billy Dix, Jene Gray. *D:* Elmer Clifton; *P:* J.R. Camomile; *Sc:* Elmer [Clifton] S. Pond. (0:54) (video) Cooley warbles the songs in this minimally budgeted western with a plot revolving around thefts from a silver mine.

2390. Silver Canyon (Columbia/Gene Autry Prods.; 1951). *Cast:* Gene Autry, Gail Davis, Pat Buttram, Jim Davis, Bob Steele, Edgar Dearing, Dick Alexander, Terry Frost, Steve Clark, Stanley Andrews, John R. McKee, Peter Mamakos, Duke York, Eugene Borden, Bobby Clark, Frankie Marvin, Sandy Sanders, William Haade, Jack O'Shea, Jack Pepper, Frank Matts, James Magill, Martin Wilkins, Boyd Stockman, Kenne Duncan, Bill Hale, Stanley Blystone, John Merton, Pat O'Malley, John Daheim, Eddie Parker, Champion, Jr. (horse). *D:* John English; *P:* Armand Schaeffer; *St:* Alan James; *Sc:* Gerald Geraghty. (1:10) A scout for the Union army attempts to apprehend a guerrilla leader in Utah. An Autry series western which includes four songs. Sepiatone. Originally paired on a double bill with *Two of a Kind* (q.v.).

Silver Chains (G.B. title) *see* **The Kid from Amarillo**

2391. The Silver Chalice (Warner/Victor Saville Prods.; 1954). *Cast:* Virginia Mayo

(Helena), Pier Angeli (Deborra), Jack Palance (Simon), Paul Newman (film debut/Basil), Walter Hampden (Joseph), Joseph Wiseman (Mijamin), Alexander Scourby (Luke), Lorne Greene (film debut/Peter), Natalie Wood (Helena as a girl), E.G. Marshall (Ignatius), Jacques Aubuchon (Nero), Herbert Rudley (Linus), Albert Dekker (Kester), Michael Pate (Aaron), Terence DeMarnay (Sosthene), Don Randolph (Selech), David Stewart (Adam), Philip Tonge (Ohad), Ian Wolfe (Theron), Robert Middleton (Idbash), Mort Marshall (Benjie), Larry Dobkin (Ephraim), Peter Reynolds (Basil as a boy), Mel Welles (Marcos), Beryl Machin (Eulalia), Jack Raine, John Sheffield, John Marlowe, Paul Power, Frank Hagney, Harry Wilson, Charles Bewley, David Bond, Allen Michaelson, Lester Sharpe, Anthony Eustrel, The Laguna Festival of Art Players. *D:* & *P:* Victor Saville; *Sc:* Lesser Samuels; *Cin:* (AAN-color) William V. Skall; *Music:* (AAN) Franz Waxman. (2:23) (video) A fictional biblical-style epic based on the 1952 novel by Thomas B. Costain of a Greek slave (Newman) given his freedom to design a stand for the cup used by Jesus at the Last Supper. A critically panned $4.5 million financial fiasco. Despite it being the beginning of his film career, in later years Paul Newman even apologized for making the film! WarnerColor/CinemaScope.

2392. Silver City (Paramount; 1951). *Cast:* Edmond O'Brien, Yvonne DeCarlo, Barry Fitzgerald, Richard Arlen, Gladys George, Laura Elliot, Edgar Buchanan, Michael Moore, John Dierkes, Don Dunning, Warren Earl Fisk, James Van Horn, John Mansfield, Harvey Parry, Boyd "Red" Morgan, Frank Cordell, Leo J. McMahon, Howard Joslin, Robert G. Anderson, Frank Fenton, Myron Healey, James R. Scott, Paul E. Burns, Cliff Clark, Billy House, Howard Negley, Ray Hyke, Slim Gault. *D:* Byron Haskin; *P:* Nat Holt; *As.P:* Harry Templeton; *Sc:* Frank Gruber. (1:30) Western of a mining engineer who after being caught with his hands in the till, assumes another identity and sets up shop in another mining camp. A minor hit for the studio, it was based on the 1948 novel *High Vermilion* by Luke Short. (G.B. title: *High Vermilion*) Technicolor.

2393. Silver City Bonanza (Republic; 1951). *Cast:* Rex Allen, Buddy Ebsen, Mary Ellen Kay, Billy Kimbley, Bill Kennedy, Alix Ebsen, Gregg Barton, Clem Bevans, Frank Jenks, Hank Patterson, Harry Lauter, Harry Harvey, Ko-Ko (horse). *D:* George Blair; *As.P:* Melville Tucker; *Sc:* Bob Williams; *Songs:* "Lollipop Lane," "Sweet Evalina," "I Ride an Old Paint." (1:07) Rex Allen series western of a cowboy who gets to the bottom of some mysterious goings on when a blind man is murdered at a ranch reputed to be haunted. Originally ran on a double bill with *Insurance Investigator* (q.v.).

2394. Silver Lode (RKO/Pinecrest Prods.; 1954). *Cast:* John Payne, Lizabeth Scott, Dan Duryea, Dolores Moran, Emile Meyer, Harry Carey, Jr., Morris Ankrum, John Hudson, Robert Warwick, Stuart Whitman, Alan Hale, Jr., Frank Sully, Paul Birch, John Dierkes, Myron Healey, Hugh Sanders, Roy Gordan, Hal Hill, Gene Roth, Al Haskell, William Haade, Frank Ellis, I. Stanford Jolley, Barbara Woodell, Sheila Bromley, Lane Chandler, Joe Devlin, Burt Mustin, Byron Foulger, Ralph Sanford. *D:* Allan Dwan; *P:* Benedict Bogeaus; *St:* & *Sc:* Karen DeWolfe. (1:20) (video) When a man is accused of murder on his wedding day, he takes it on the lam as the only way to prove his innocence. Technicolor.

2395. Silver Raiders (Monogram; 1950). *Cast:* Whip Wilson, Andy Clyde, Virginia Herrick, Leonard Penn, Patricia Rios, Dennis Moore, Reed Howes, Riley Hill, Marshall Reed, George DeNormand, Kermit Maynard, Ed Cassidy, Frank Hagney, Frank Ellis. *D:* Wallace W. Fox; *P:* Vincent M. Fennelly; *St:* & *Sc:* Daniel B. Ullman. (0:55) Whip Wilson series western focused around Mexican silver thefts.

2396. The Silver Star (Lippert/B & L Prods.; 1955). *Cast:* Edgar Buchanan, Marie Windsor, Lon Chaney, Jr., Earle Lyon, Richard Bartlett, Barton MacLane, Morris Ankrum, Edith Evanson, Michael Whalen, Steve Rowland, Bob Karnes, Tim Graham, Earl Hansen, Bill Anders, Chris O'Brien, Jill Richards, Charles Knapp. *D:* Richard Bartlett; *P:* Earle Lyon; *As.P:* Ian MacDonald; *St:* & *Sc:* Bartlett, MacDonald; *Title song:* Jimmy Wakely, Bartlett (sung by Wakely). (1:13) Western of a sheriff whose pacifist ideals are challenged when he is targeted by gunmen.

2397. The Silver Whip (20th Century-Fox; 1953). *Cast:* Dale Robertson, Rory Calhoun, Robert Wagner, Kathleen Crowley (film debut), James Millican, Lola Albright, J.M. Kerrigan, John Kellogg, Harry Carter, Ian MacDonald, Robert Adler, Clancy Cooper, Burt Mustin, Dan White, Paul Wexler, Bobby Diamond, Jack Rice, Charles Watts, [A.] Cameron Grant. *D:* Harmon Jones; *P:* Robert Bassler, Michael Abel;

Sc: Jesse Lasky, Jr. (1:13) Western of a young man (Wagner) who takes a job as a stagecoach driver and fails his responsibility when the stage is held up by outlaws. Based on the novel *Big Range* by Jack Schaefer.

2398. Sincerely Yours (Warner/International Artists, Ltd.; 1955). *Cast:* Liberace, Joanne Dru, Dorothy Malone, Alex Nicol, William Demarest, Lori Nelson, Lurene Tuttle, Richard Eyer, James Bell, Herbert Heyes, Edward Platt, Guy Williams, Ian Wolfe, Otto Waldis, Barbara Brown. *D:* Gordon Douglas; *P:* Henry Blanke; *Sc:* Irving Wallace; *Piano interludes:* "Minuet in G" (Ignacy Paderewski); "Sonata No. 9" (Wolfgang Amadeus Mozart); "Traumerei," "Liebestraum" (Franz Liszt); "Rhapsody in Blue," "The Man I Love," "Embraceable You," "I Got Rhythm," "Liza" (George Gershwin); "Cornish Rhapsody" (Hubert Bath); "Tea for Two" (Vincent Youmans–Irving Caesar); "Sincerely Yours" (Liberace, Paul Francis Webster) + "The Notre Dame Fight Song," "Chopsticks," "The Beer Barrel Polka" and "When Irish Eyes Are Smiling." (1:55) (video/laserdisc) A critically panned box office bomb about a concert pianist who loses his hearing. A remake of *The Man Who Played God* (1932) with George Arliss, it was taken from the play by Jules Eckert Goodman. A latter-day camp classic in WarnerColor.

2399. Sing Boy Sing (20th Century–Fox; 1958). *Cast:* Tommy Sands (film debut), Lili Gentle, Edmond O'Brien, John McIntire, Nick Adams, Diane Jergens, Josephine Hutchinson, Jerry Paris, Tami Connor, Regis Toomey, Marie Brown, Madge Cleveland, Tom Greenway, Lloyd Harter, Patrick Miller, Art Ford, Bill Randle, Biff Collie. *D: & P:* Henry Ephron; *Sc:* Claude Binyon; *Songs:* "Gonna Walk and Talk with My Lord," "Crazy 'Cause I Love You," "Your Daddy Wants to Do Right," "Soda-Pop Pop," "Sing, Boy, Sing," "Rock of Ages," "People in Love," "Bundle of Dreams," "Just a Little Bit More," "How About You?," "Who, Baby, Who?," "That's All I Want from You" and "Would I Love You?" (1:30) Musical drama of the grandson of a country preacher who rises to the top of the music charts via a manipulating manager. He suffers guilt when his grandfather dies and takes to the pulpit with unsatisfactory results. Based on *The Singing Idol* by Paul Monash, which was originally presented as a TV drama on Kraft Playhouse. CinemaScope/stereophonic sound.

2400. Singin' in the Rain (MGM; 1952). *Cast:* Gene Kelly (Don Lockwood), Donald O'Connor (Cosmo Brown), Debbie Reynolds (singing voice of Betty Royce/Kathy Selden), Jean Hagen (AAN/Lina Lamont), Millard Mitchell (R.F. Simpson), Rita Moreno (Zelda Zanders), Douglas Fowley (Roscoe Dexter), Cyd Charisse (dancer in "Broadway Rhythm" ballet), Madge Blake (Dora Bailey), King Donovan (Rod), Kathleen Freeman (Phoebe Dinsmore, diction coach), Tommy Farrell (Sid Phillips, assistant director), Jimmie Thompson (male lead in "Beautiful Girl" number), Judy Landon (Olga Mara), John Dodsworth (Baron de la May de la Toulon), Stuart Holmes (J.C. Spendrill III), Mae Clarke (hairdresser), Dan Foster (assistant director), Margaret Bert (wardrobe woman), Dennis Ross (Don Lockwood as a boy), Bill Lewis (Bert, the western villain), Richard Emory (Phil, the cowboy hero), Carl Milletaire (villain in "Dueling Cavalier" and "Broadway Rhythm"), Wilson Wood (Rudy Vallee impersonator), Julius Tannen, Dawn Addams, Elaine Stewart, Jac George, Dorothy Patrick, William Lester, Charles Evans, Joi Lansing, David Sharpe, Russ Saunders. *D:* Gene Kelly, Stanley Donen; *P:* Arthur Freed; *St: & Sc:* Adolph Green, Betty Comden; *Music:* (AAN) Lennie Hayton; *Songs:* "Would You?" Nacio Herb Brown, Arthur Freed (from *San Francisco*, 1936); "Singin' in the Rain" Brown, Freed (from *Hollywood Revue of 1929*); "All I Do is Dream of You" Brown, Freed (from *Sadie McKee*, 1934); " I've Got a Feeling You're Fooling" Brown, Freed (from *The Broadway Melody of 1936*, 1935); "Wedding of the Painted Doll" Brown, Freed (from *The Broadway Melody*, 1929); "Should I?" Brown, Freed (from *Lord Byron of Broadway*, 1930); "Make 'em Laugh" Brown, Freed; "You Were Meant for Me" (from *The Broadway Melody*), "You Are My Lucky Star" Brown, Freed (from *The Broadway Melody of 1936*); "Fit as a Fiddle and Ready for Love" Freed, Al Hoffman, Al Goodhart (from *College Coach*, Warner/1933); "Good Morning" Brown, Freed (from *Babes in Arms*, 1939); "Moses Supposes" Betty Comden, Adolph Green, Roger Edens; "Beautiful Girl" Brown, Freed (from *Going Hollywood*, 1933); "Broadway Rhythm" Brown, Freed (from *The Broadway Melody of 1936*) and "Broadway Melody" Brown, Freed (from *The Broadway Melody*). (1:43) (video/laserdisc) A musical tribute to the days when Hollywood was making the transition from silents to talkies and is considered in many circles as one of the all-time great musicals. Reynolds received recognition as a "Hollywood star" for her zesty performance and the film which placed #8 on the "10 Best" lists of both the NBR and *Film Daily* went on to become one of the 23 top-grossing films of 1951-52. The British Academy Awards had it in nomination and the New York Film Critics had it in nomination for "Best Picture." Later a Broadway musical. Technicolor.

2401. Singing Guns (Republic/Palomar Pictures; 1950). *Cast:* Vaughn Monroe (starring debut/Rhiannon), Ella Raines (Nan Morgan), Walter Brennan (Dr. Mark), Ward Bond (Cardac), Jeff Corey (Richards), Barry Kelley (Mike), Harry Shannon (Judge Waller), George Chandler (Smitty), Billy Gray (Albert), Rex Lease (stage driver), Tom Fadden, Ralph Dunn, Mary Bear, Jimmie Dodd. *D:* R.G. Springsteen; *P:* Abe Lyman, Melville Tucker; *Sc:* Dorrell & Stuart McGowan (based on the 1938 novel by Max Brand); *Songs:* "Mule Train" (AAN) Fred Glickman, Hy Heath, Johnny Lange + "Singing My Way Back Home" and "Mexican Trail." (1:31) Singer/band leader Monroe plays a notorious outlaw who saves the life of the lawman tracking him, takes a new identity and becomes sheriff of a western town. The Oscar nominated song "Mule Train" went on to become an enormous hit for Mr. Monroe. Trucolor.

2402. Singing in the Dark (Budsam/A.N.O.; 1956). *Cast:* Moishe Oysher, Joey Adams, Phyllis Hill, Lawrence Tierney, Kay Medford, Mickey Knox, Dave Starr, Cindy Heller, Al Kelly, Henry Sharp, Stan Hoffman, Paul Andor, Abe Simon. *D:* Max Nosseck; *P:* Joey Adams; *St:* Aben Kandel [from an idea by Oysher and Nosseck]; *Sc:* A. Kandel, Ann Hood, Stephen Kandel. (1:24) Drama of a Nazi concentration camp survivor who comes to America following World War II and has a go at show business, but eventually quits to become a cantor.

The Sinner *see* **Desert Desperadoes**

2403. Sins of Jezebel (Lippert/Jezebel Prods.; 1953). *Cast:* Paulette Goddard (title role), George Nader (Jehu), Eduard Franz (Ahab), John Hoyt (Elijah the prophet), Ludwig Donath, John Shelton (final film—ret.), Joe Besser, Margia Dean, Carmen D'Antonio. *D:* Reginald LeBorg; *P:* Sigmund Neufeld; *Ex.P:* Robert L. Lippert, Jr.; *Sc:* Richard Landau [based on the Biblical story]. (1:14) Low budget Biblical drama of the evil Baal-worshipping Phoenician princess who marries Ahab, the King of Israel. Anscocolor.

2404. Siren of Bagdad (Columbia; 1953). *Cast:* Paul Henreid, Hans Conried, Patricia Medina, Charlie Lung, Laurette Luez, Anne Dore, George Keymas, Vivian Mason, Michael Fox, "Killer" Karl Davis, Carl Milletaire. *D:* Richard Quine; *P:* Sam Katzman; *St:* & *Sc:* Robert E. Kent; *Additional dialogue:* Larry Rhine (unc.). (1:17) A costume comedy in the Arabian Nights vein of attempts to rescue a princess. Technicolor.

2405. Sirocco (Columbia/Santana Pictures; 1951). *Cast:* Humphrey Bogart, Marta Toren, Lee J. Cobb, Everett Sloane, Gerald Mohr, Zero Mostel, Nick Dennis, Onslow Stevens, Ludwig Donath, David Bond, Vincent Renno, Martin Wilkins, Peter Ortiz, Peter Brocco, Jay Novello, Leonard Penn, Harry Guardino, Edward Colmans, Al Eben. *D:* Curtis Bernhardt; *P:* Robert Lord; *Sc:* A.I. Bezzerides, Hans Jacoby. (1:38) (video/laserdisc) Dramatic actioner of an arms dealer in 1920s Syria. Based on the 1931 novel *Coup De Grace* by Joseph Kessel. Originally paired on the top of a double bill with *China Corsair* (q.v.).

2406. Sitting Bull (United Artists/W.R. Frank; 1954). *Cast:* Dale Robertson, Mary Murphy, J. Carrol Naish, John Litel, Iron Eyes Cody, Douglas Kennedy, Joel Fluellen, William Hopper, William Tannen, John Hamilton (Pres. U.S. Grant), Tom Browne Henry, Felix Gonzales, Al Wyatt. *D:* Sidney Salkow; *P:* W.R. Frank, Alfred Strauss; *Sc:* & *St:* Jack De Witt, Salkow. (1:45) (video) Hollywood once again rewrites American history in this filmed in Mexico western dealing with Sitting Bull (Naish), Crash Horse (Cody), Custer (Kennedy), etc. Eastmancolor/CinemaScope.

2407. Six Bridges to Cross (Universal-International; 1955). *Cast:* Tony Curtis, Julia [Julie] Adams, George Nader, Jay C. Flippen, Kendall Clark, Sal Mineo (film debut), Jan Merlin, Richard Castle, William Murphy, Kenny Roberts, Peter Avramo, Hal Conklin, Don Keefer, Harry Bartell, Tito Vuolo, Ken Patterson, Paul Dubov, Peter Leeds, James F. Stone, Howard Wright, Elizabeth Kerr, Charles Victor, Carl Frank, Grant Gordon, Di Di Roberts, Doris Meade, Harold W. Miller, John J. Muldoon, Claudia Hall, Anabel Shaw, Carey Loftin. *D:* Joseph Pevney; *P:* Aaron Rosenberg; *Sc:* Sydney Boehm; *Song:* Henry Mancini, Jeff Chandler (sung by Sammy Davis, Jr.). (1:36) Fictionalized crime drama of a delinquent who grows up to mastermind the famous Brinks armored car robbery in Boston in 1950. Includes location filming in Boston. It was based on "They

Stole $2,500,000—And Got Away With It" by Joseph F. Dinneen.

2408. Six-Gun Mesa (Monogram; 1950). *Cast:* Johnny Mack Brown, Gail Davis, Riley Hill, Marshall Reed, Leonard Penn, Steve Clark, Milburn Morante, Carl Mathews, Bud Osborne, George DeNormand, Stanley Blystone, Frank Jaquet, Artie Ortego, Merrill McCormack, Holly Bane [aka: Mike Ragan]. *D:* Wallace W. Fox; *P:* Eddie Davis; *St: & Sc:* Adele Buffington. (0:57) In this Johnny Mack Brown series western, a man is wrongfully accused of starting a stampede which killed several men.

The Sixth of June *see* **D-Day, The Sixth of June**

2409. Skabenga (Allied Artists; 1956). A feature documentary based on the book *African Fury* by George Michael with narration written by Edward Bernds.

2410. Ski Champs (Wm. H. Brown; 1951). *D:* Dick Durrance (who also photographed); *P:* William H. Brown; *Narrators:* Lowell Thomas, Tor Toland. A color documentary/travelogue with a focus on Dagmar Rom of Austria and Zeno Cole of Italy as they train in the Swiss Alps for the international ski meet at Aspen, Colorado in 1950 as well as the meet itself.

2411. Skipalong Rosenbloom (United Artists; 1951). *Cast:* Maxie Rosenbloom, Max Baer, Jackie Coogan, Hillary Brooke, Fuzzy Knight, Jacqueline Fontaine, Raymond Hatton, Ray Walker, Sam Lee, Al Shaw, Joseph Greene, Dewey Robinson, Whitey Haupt, Carl Mathews, Artie Ortego. *D:* Sam Newfield; *P:* Wally Kline; *St:* Eddie Forman; *Sc:* Dean Reisner, Forman; *Song:* Jack Kenney. (1:12) A slapstick comedy/satire which opens with a family squabbling about which TV show to watch—settling on "Skipalong Rosenbloom"—which tells the comedy tale of an Eastern gangster who heads west to combat a notorious gunfighter. (aka: *The Square Shooter*). Originally paired on the top of a double bill with *Badman's Gold* (q.v.).

2412. The Skipper Surprised His Wife (MGM; 1950). *Cast:* Robert Walker, Joan Leslie, Edward Arnold, Jan Sterling, Spring Byington, Leon Ames, Paul Harvey, Kathryn Card, Anthony Ross, Tommy Myers, Rudy Lee, Finnegan Weatherwax, Muscles (dog). *D:* Elliott Nugent; *P:* William H. Wright; *St: & Sc:* Dorothy Kingsley. (1:25) Comedy of an ex-ship's captain who runs his home in the same manner that he did his ocean going vessel. Based on "The Skipper Surprised His Wife" and "I Taught My Wife to Keep House the Navy Way," two articles by Commander W.J. Lederer, U.S.N. which appeared in *Reader's Digest* in March/1949).

2413. Skirts Ahoy! (MGM; 1952). *Cast:* Esther Williams, Vivian Blaine, Joan Evans, Barry Sullivan, Keefe Brasselle, Billy Eckstine (himself), Dean Miller, Margalo Gillmore, The DeMarco Sisters, Jeff Donnell, Thurston Hall, Debbie Reynolds (herself), Bobby Van (himself), Russell "Bubba" Tongay, Kathy Tongay, Roy Roberts, Emmett Lynn, Hayden Rorke, Paul Harvey, Ruth Lee, Whit Bissell, Rudy Lee, Madge Blake, Mae Clarke, Byron Foulger, Henny Backus, Juanita Moore, Millie Bruce, Suzette Harbin, Robert Board, Mary Foran, William Haade, The Marimba Merrymakers (themselves). *D:* Sidney Lanfield (final film—ret.); *P:* Joe Pasternak; *St: & Sc:* Isobel Lennart; *Songs:* "Oh By Jingo" Lew Brown, Albert Von Tilzer; "Hold Me Close to You," "What Makes a WAVE?," "What Good Is a Gal Without a Guy?," "Skirts Ahoy!," "Glad to Have You Aboard," "The Navy Waltz," "I Get a Funny Feeling," "We Will Fight" and "Hilda Matilda" Harry Warren, Ralph Blane. (1:49) (video) Romance and musical numbers in a story of three WAVES and their pursuit of love. Technicolor.

2414. Sky Commando (Columbia; 1953). *Cast:* Dan Duryea, Frances Gifford (final film—ret.), Touch [Mike] Connors, Michael Fox, Freeman Morse, William R. Klein, Dick Paxton, Selmer Jackson, Dick Lerner, Morris Ankrum, Paul McGuire. *D:* Fred F. Sears, *P:* Sam Katzman; *St:* William B. Sackheim, Arthur E. Orloff, Samuel Newman; *Sc:* Newman. (1:09) Low budget World War II drama of dissent among a squadron of flyers and the squadron leader who is despised by his men.

2415. Sky Full of Moon (MGM; 1952). *Cast:* Carleton Carpenter, Jan Sterling, Keenan Wynn, Elaine Stewart, Robert Burton, Douglass Dumbrille, Emmett Lynn, Sheb Wooley, Jonathan Cott. *D: & Sc:* Norman Foster; *P:* Sidney Franklin, Jr.; *Song:* Charles Wolcott, Harry Hamilton, Paul Campbell. (1:13) Programmer romantic comedy of a naive young rodeo cowboy infatuated with a Las Vegas gal who's been around the block a few times.

2416. Sky High (Lippert/Spartan-Tom Prods.; 1951). *Cast:* Sid Melton, Mara Lynn, Sam

Flint, Douglas Evans, Fritz Feld, Marc Krah, Margia Dean, Paul Bryar, Thayer Roberts, Don Frost, John Peletti, Ernie Venneri, John Phillips, Will Orleans, Peter Damon. *D:* Sam Newfield; *P:* Sigmund Neufeld; *St: & Sc:* Orville H. Hampton. (1:00) Programmer service comedy of a doofus G.I. who just happens to be a lookalike for a spy.

Slade (G.B. title) *see* **Jack Slade**

2417. Slander (MGM; 1956). *Cast:* Van Johnson, Ann Blyth, Steve Cochran, Marjorie Rambeau, Richard Eyer, Harold J. Stone, Lurene Tuttle, Philip Coolidge, Lewis Martin. *D:* Roy Rowland; *P:* Armand Deutsch; *Sc:* Jerome Weidman. (1:21) Drama of a TV personality (Johnson) who is targeted by a scandal magazine and its ruthless publisher (Cochran). Based on a TV play titled *A Public Figure* by Harry W. Junkin.

2418. Slaughter on Tenth Avenue (Universal-International; 1957). *Cast:* Richard Egan, Jan Sterling, Dan Duryea, Julie Adams, Walter Matthau, Charles McGraw, Mickey Shaughnessy, Harry Bellaver, Nick Dennis, Sam Levene, Ned Wever, Billy M. Green, John McNamara, Amzie Strickland, Mickey Hargitay, George Beewar. *D:* Arnold Laven; *P:* Albert Zugsmith; *Sc:* Lawrence Roman; *Title theme music:* Richard Rodgers. (1:43) Acclaimed melodrama of corruption on the New York waterfront and how the "code of silence" permitted crime to flourish and criminals to go unpunished. Taken from the fact-based 1956 novel *The Man Who Rocked the Boat* by William J. Keating and Richard Carter.

2419. The Slaughter Trail (RKO; 1951). *Cast:* Brian Donlevy, Gig Young, Virginia Grey, Andy Devine, Robert Hutton, Terry Gilkyson (who also narrates), Lew Bedell, Myron Healey, Ken Koutnik, Eddie Parks, Ralph Peters, Ric Roman, Lois Hall, Robin Fletcher, Ralph Volkie, Fenton Jones. *D: & P:* Irving Allen; *St: & Sc:* Sid Kuller. (1:18) (video) The U.S. Cavalry is called in to bring an end to an outlaw gang operating on the Slaughter Trail. Cinecolor.

The Slave Girl *see* **Captain Kidd and the Slave Girl**

2420. Slaves of Babylon (Columbia; 1953). *Cast:* Richard Conte, Linda Christian, Maurice Schwartz (final film—ret.), Terence [Terry] Kilburn, Michael Ansara, Leslie Bradley, Ruth Storey, John Crawford, Ric Roman, Robert Griffin, Beatrice Maude, Wheaton Chambers, Paul Purcell, Julie [Newmar] Newmeyer, Ernestine Barrier. *D:* William Castle; *P:* Sam Katzman; *St: & Sc:* DeVallon Scott. (1:22) Old Testament Biblical drama of Daniel (Schwartz), Nebuchadnezzar (Bradley) and the rescue of the Israelites from the Babylonians. Technicolor.

2421. Sleeping Beauty (Buena Vista/Walt Disney Prods.; 1959). *Voices:* Mary Costa (Princess Aurora), Bill Shirley (Prince Phillip), Eleanor Audley (Maleficent), Verna Felton (Flora), Barbara Jo Allen [aka: Vera Vague/Fauna], Barbara Luddy (Merryweather), Taylor Holmes (King Stefan), Bill Thompson (King Hubert), Candy Candido (goon). *D:* Clyde Geronimi; *P:* Walt Disney; *Production supervisor:* Ken Peterson; *Additional story:* Joe Rinaldi, Winston Hibler, Bill Peet, Ted Sears, Ralph Wright, Milt Banta, *Music:* (AAN) George Bruns; *Songs:* "Once Upon a Dream" Sammy Fain, Jack Lawrence; "Hail the Princess Aurora" Tom Adair, Bruns; "I Wonder" Hibler, Sears, Bruns; "The Skump Song" Adair, Erdman Penner, Bruns and "The Sleeping Beauty Song" Adair, Bruns. (1:15) (video/laserdisc) This was Disney's final attempt at an animated fairy tale (in his lifetime), coming in at a cost of $6,000,000 and grossing only $5,300,000 on initial release (at inflated admissions). The basic story of the princess put into a deep sleep and later awakened by a kiss from a prince came to life with soundtrack music by Peter Ilich Tchaikovsky from his *Sleeping Beauty Ballet* and many Disneyesque embellishments which so characterize his animated features. Based on the Charles Perrault version of the fairy tale, adapted by Erdman Penner. Technicolor, Technirama 70 and stereophonic sound.

2422. The Sleeping City (Universal-International; 1950). *Cast:* Richard Conte, Coleen Gray, Alex Nicol (film debut), John Alexander, Richard Taber, Peggy Dow, James J. Van Dyk, Hugh Reilly, Michael Strong, Frank M. Thomas, Richard Kendrick, Henry Hart, Robert Strauss, Herbert Ratner, Mickey Cochran, Ernest Sarracino, Russell Collins, Mrs. Priestley Morrison, James O'Neill, Frank Tweddell, Victor Sutherland, Jack Lescoulie, Carroll Ashburn, Tom Hoirer, William Martell, James Little, Terry Denim, Harold Bayne, Frank Baxter, James Daly (film debut), Dort Clark, Mimi Strongin, Rod McLennan, Ralph Hertz. *D:* George Sherman; *P:* Leonard Goldstein; *St: & Sc:*

Jo Eisinger. (1:25) Crime melodrama of a New York cop who goes undercover at Bellevue Hospital to unravel the mystery surrounding a murder, a suicide and narcotics theft.

2423. A Slight Case of Larceny (MGM; 1953). *Cast:* Mickey Rooney, Eddie Bracken, Elaine Stewart, Marilyn Erskine, Douglas Fowley, Robert Burton, Charles Halton, Henry Slate, Rudy Lee, Mimi Gibson, Joe Turkel, Al Jackson, Russ Saunders, Bob Meinhart, Walter Ridge. *D:* Don Weis; *P:* Henry Berman; *St:* James Poe; *Sc:* Jerry Davis. (1:11) Programmer comedy of two buddies who open a gas station, with intent of increasing their profits by siphoning gasoline from a local oil refinery.

2424. Slightly Scarlet (RKO/Filmcrest Prods.; 1956). *Cast:* John Payne, Arlene Dahl, Rhonda Fleming, Kent Taylor, Ted de Corsia, Lance Fuller, Frank Gerstle, Buddy Baer, George E. Stone, Ellen Corby, Roy Gordon. *D:* Allan Dwan; *P:* Benedict Bogeaus; *Sc:* Robert Blees. (1:30) (video) *Film noir* (in Technicolor!) of a gangland figure who is forced to flee when the heat is put on him by a rival hood, with the deposed kingpin vowing revenge on his replacement. Loosely based on James W. Cain's 1942 novel *Love's Lovely Counterfeit*. Technicolor/ SuperScope.

2425. Slim Carter (Universal-International; 1957). *Cast:* Jock Mahoney, Julie Adams, Tim Hovey, William Hopper (final film before becoming a regular on TV's *Perry Mason*), Ben Johnson, Joanna Moore, Walter Reed, Maggie Mahoney, Bill Williams, Barbara Hale, Roxanne Arlen, Jean Moorhead, Donald Kerr, Jim Healey. *D:* Richard H. Bartlett; *P:* Howie Horwitz; *St:* David Bramson, Mary C. McCall, Jr.; *Sc:* Montgomery Pittman. (1:22) Comedy of a cowboy star who acquired a swelled head along with his stardom, who has his views changed by a young orphan boy who enters his life. Eastmancolor.

2426. Small Town Girl (MGM; 1953). *Cast:* Jane Powell (Cindy Kimbell), Farley Granger (Rick Livingston), Ann Miller (Lisa Bellmount), S.Z. Sakall (Eric Schlemmer), Billie Burke (Mrs. Livingston), Bobby Van (Ludwig Schlemmer), Robert Keith (Judge Gordon Kimbell), Fay Wray (Mrs. Gordon Kimbell), Nat "King" Cole (himself), Dean Miller (Mac), William Campbell (Ted), Chill Wills (Happy, the jailer), Philip Tonge (Hemmingway), Jonathan Cott (Jim, the cop), Bobby Hyatt (Dennis), Rudy Lee (Jimmy), Beverly Wills (Diedre), Gloria Noble (Patsy), Jane Liddell (Betty), Janet Stewart (Sandra), Nancy Valentine (Mary), Peggie McIntire (Susie), Virginia Hall, Marie Blake [aka: Blossom Rock]. *D:* Leslie Kardos; *P:* Joe Pasternak; *St:* Dorothy Cooper; *Sc:* Dorothy Kingsley, Cooper; *Choreography:* Busby Berkeley; *Songs:* "I've Gotta Hear That Beat," "Fine, Fine, Fine," "The Fellow I'd Follow," "My Flaming Heart" (AAN-Best Song/sung by Cole), "Lullaby of the Lord," "Small Towns are Smile Towns" and "My Gaucho" Nicholas Brodszky, Leo Robin. (1:33) (video/laserdisc) The romance of a playboy and a small town sheriff's daughter is the stuff of this lesser MGM Technicolor musical reworking of the 1936 production of the same name, based on a novel by Ben Ames Williams.

Smoke Jumpers *see* **Red Skies of Montana**

2427. Smoke Signal (Universal-International; 1955). *Cast:* Dana Andrews, Rex Reason, Piper Laurie, William Talman, Milburn Stone, Douglas Spencer, Gordon Jones, William Schallert, Bill Phipps, Robert Wilke, Pat Hogan, Peter Coe. *D:* Jerry Hopper; *P:* Howard Christie; *St: & Sc:* George F. Slavin, George W. George. (1:28) Western of a surviving cavalry detachment escaping down the Colorado River from warring Indians. Technicolor.

2428. Smoky Canyon (Columbia; 1952). *Cast:* Charles Starrett, Dani Sue Nolan, Smiley Burnette, Jack [Jock] Mahoney, Tristram Coffin, Forrest Taylor, Larry Hudson, LeRoy Johnson, Chris Alcaide, Charles Stevens, Sandy Sanders, Boyd "Red" Morgan. *D:* Fred F. Sears; *P:* Colbert Clark; *St: & Sc:* Barry Shipman. (0:55) A "Durango Kid" series western of an impending range war between cattlemen and sheepmen.

2429. Smuggler's Gold (Columbia; 1951). *Cast:* Cameron Mitchell, Amanda Blake, Carl Benton Reid, Peter Thompson, William "Bill" Phillips, William Forrest, Robert Williams, Harlan Warde, Al Hill, Paul Campbell. *D:* William Berke; *P:* Milton Feldman; *St:* Al Martin; *Sc:* Daniel B. Ullman. (1:04) Programmer crime melodrama of efforts to retrieve sunken gold and smuggle it out of the U.S.

2430. Smuggler's Island (Universal-International; 1951). *Cast:* Jeff Chandler, Evelyn Keyes, Philip Friend, Marvin Miller, Ducky

Louie, David Wolfe, Jay Novello, H.T. Tsiang. *D:* Edward Ludwig; *P:* Ted Richmond; *St: & Adaptation:* Herbert Margolis, Louis Morheim; *Sc:* Leonard Lee. (1:15) Technicolor adventure-melodrama involving the search for sunken gold.

2431. Snake River Desperadoes (Columbia; 1951). *Cast:* Charles Starrett, Don Kay Reynolds, Smiley Burnette, Tommy Ivo, Monte Blue, Boyd "Red" Morgan, George Chesebro, John Pickard, Sam Flint, Duke York, Charles Horvath. *D:* Fred F. Sears; *P:* Colbert Clark; *Sc: & St:* Barry Shipman; *Song:* "Brass Band Polka." (0:54) "Durango Kid" series western of impending hostilities between whites and Indians, triggered by whites dressed as Indians. Originally ran on the lower part of a double bill with *Lorna Doone* (q.v.).

2432. The Sniper (Columbia/Stanley Kramer Prods.; 1952). *Cast:* Adolphe Menjou (Lt. Kafka), Arthur Franz (Eddie Miller), Gerald Mohr (Sgt. Ferris), Marie Windsor (Jean Darr), Frank Faylen (Insp. Anderson), Richard Kiley (Dr. James G. Kent), Marlo Dwyer (May Nelson), Jay Novello (Pete), Max Palmer (Cadwick), Mabel Paige (landlady), Dani Sue Nolan (Sandy), Hurb Latimer (Sam), George Dockstader (Mapes), Les Sketchley (Flaherty), Carl Benton Reid (Liddell), Byron Foulger (Pete Eureka), Paul Marion (Al), Grandon Rhodes (Mr. Fitzpatrick), Lillian Bond (Mrs. Fitzpatrick), Kay Sharpe (Millie), Harlan Warde (Harper), John Brown (Wise), John Eldredge (Stonecroft), Ralph Smiley (Tony Debiaci, suspect), John Pickard (Allen Martin, suspect), Ralph O. Clark (man who falls from smokestack), Geraldine Carr (checker), Ralph Peters, Sidney Miller, Harry Cheshire (mayor), Cliff Clark, Robert Foulk, Vern Martell, Fred Hartman, Don Michaelian, Renaldo Viri, Kernan Cripps, Rory Mallinson, J. Anthony Hughes, John Bradley, Danny Mummert, Ray Maypole, Patricia Toun, Helen Lindstrom, Wanda Wirth, Luanna Scott, Kathleen O'Reilly, Elsa Weber, Helen Eliot, Mary Holly, Aline Watson, Alice Bartlett, Betty Shute, Gail Bonney, Sarah Selby, Robin Raymond, Marlene Lyden, Jean Willes, Kathleen O'Malley, Adrienne Marden, Jessie Arnold, Elizabeth Whitney, John H. Algate, Thomas Heidt, Richard Freye, Harry Bechtel, Willis West, Norman Nazarr, Nolan Leary, Robert Day, Billy Wayne, Paul Dubov, Charles Lane, Harry Harvey, John A. Butler, Frank Sully, Donald Kerr. Ralph Volkie, Joe Miksak, Richard Glyer, Howard Negley, David McMahon, Robert Malcolm, Charles Watts, Steve Darrell, Frank Shaw, Frank Kreig, Victor Sen Yung, Gaylord [Steve] Pendleton, Clark Howat, Dudley Dickerson, Edgar Novak, Mike Lally, George Chesebro, Charles Marsh, Joe Palma, Barry Brooks, Bruce Cameron, Tommy Hawkins, Lucas Fararc, Al Hill. *D:* Edward Dmytryk (first U.S. film since being blacklisted); *P:* Stanley Kramer; *St:* (AAN) Edward Anhalt, Edna Anhalt; *Sc:* Harry Brown. (1:27) Acclaimed crime melodrama of police efforts to stop a deranged sniper, picking off women with a high-powered rifle.

2433. The Snow Creature (United Artists/Planet Filmways; 1954). *Cast:* Paul Langton, Leslie Denison, Teru Shimada, Rollin Moriyama, Robert Kino, Robert Hinton, Darlene Fields, George Douglas, Robert Bice, Rudolph Anders, Bill Phipps, Jack Daly, Rusty Wescoatt, Dick Sands (creature), Keith Richards. *D: & P:* W. Lee Wilder; *St: & Sc:* Myles Wilder. (1:10) (video) Horror melodrama of a hairy humanoid creature brought to the U.S. from the Himalayas by a botanist, only to have it escape and run amuck in Los Angeles. Originally the 2nd half of a double bill with *The Steel Cage* (q.v.).

2434. Snow Dog (Monogram; 1950). *Cast:* Kirby Grant, Chinook the Wonder Dog, Elena Verdugo, Rick Vallin, Milburn Stone, Richard Karlan, Jane Adrian, Hal Gerard, Richard Avonde, Duke York, Guy Zanette. *D:* Frank McDonald; *P:* Lindsley Parsons; *Sc:* William Raynor. (1:03) A Mountie and his dog investigate when several trappers are reported to have been killed by a wolf. Based on the James Oliver Curwood story "Tentacles of the North."

2435. Snowfire (Allied Artists/Snowfire Prods.; 1958). *Cast:* Don Megowan, Molly McGowan, Claire Kelly, John Cason, Michael Vallon, Melody McGowan, Rusty Wescoatt, Bill Hale, Paul Keast, Snowfire (horse). *D:-P:-St: & Sc:* The Brothers McGowan (Dorrell and Stuart). (1:13) The object of this family western is a white wild stallion whose capture is the goal of rival ranchers. Filmed in Bryce Canyon, Utah, and Southern California, it originally ran on the top of a double bill with *The Littlest Hobo* (q.v.). Eastmancolor. Note: Molly and Melody McGowan are the daughters of Dorrell McGowan.

2436. The Snows of Kilimanjaro (20th Century–Fox; 1952). *Cast:* Gregory Peck (Harry), Susan Hayward (Helen), Ava Gardner (Cynthia),

Hildegarde Neff (Countess Liz), Leo G. Carroll (Uncle Bill), Torin Thatcher (Johnson), Ava Norring (Beatrice), Richard Allan (Spanish dancer), Helene Stanley (Connie), Marcel Dalio (Emile), Vincente Gomez (guitarist), Leonard Carey (Dr. Simmons), Paul Thompson (witch doctor), Emmett Smith (Molo), Victor Wood (Charles), Agnes Laury (Margot), Monique Chantal (Georgette), Janine Grandel (Annette), John Dodsworth (Compton), Bert Freed (American soldier), Charles Bates (Harry, age 17), Lisa Ferraday (Vendeuse), Maya Van Horn, Ivan Lebedeff (final film—d. 1953), Martin Garralaga, Salvador Baguez, George Navarro, George Davis, Julian Rivero, Edward Colmans, Ernest Brunner, Arthur Brunner. *D:* Henry King: *P:* Darryl F. Zanuck; *Sc:* Casey Robinson; *Cin:* (AAN-color) Leon Shamroy; *ASD:* (AAN-color) Lyle Wheeler, John Decuir (art directors), Thomas Little, Paul S. Fox (sets); *Song:* "Love Is Cynthia" Alfred Newman. (1:57) (video) Drama, based on the short story of Ernest Hemingway of a man recuperating from injuries in Africa who reviews his life to see if it has had any meaning to the present day. It placed #5 on the "10 Best" list of the NBR and became one of the 26 top-grossing films of 1952-53. Technicolor.

2437. So Big (Warner; 1953). *Cast:* Jane Wyman, Sterling Hayden, Nancy Olson, Steve Forrest, Martha Hyer, Tommy Rettig, Elisabeth Fraser, Richard Beymer, Walter Coy, Jacques Aubuchon, Roland Winters, Ruth Swanson, Dorothy Christy (final film—ret.), Oliver Blake, Lillian Kemble-Cooper, Noralee Norman, Jill Janssen, Kerry Donnelly, Kenneth Osmond, Lotte Stein, Vera Miles, Evan Loew, Frances Osborne, Jean Garvin, Carol Grel, Grandon Rhodes, Bud Osborne, Dorothy Granger, Elizabeth Russell, Dick Alexander, David McMahon, Kenner G. Kemp, Paul Brinegar, Marjorie Bennett, Frank Ferguson, Douglas Evans. *D:* Robert Wise; *P:* Henry Blanke; *Sc:* John Twist. (1:41) Rural drama of a woman who must raise her young son, following the death of her husband. Based on Edna Ferber's 1924 Pulitzer Prize winning novel, previously filmed by First National in 1925 and again in 1932 by Warner Brothers (both in feature format).

So Bright the Flame (G.B. title) *see* **The Girl in White**

2438. So This Is Love (Warner; 1953). *Cast:* Kathryn Grayson, Merv Griffin (film debut), Walter Abel, Rosemary DeCamp, Jeff Donnell, Douglas Dick, Joan Weldon, Ann Doran, Margaret Field. *D:* Gordon Douglas; *P:* Henry Blanke; *Sc:* John Monks, Jr.; *Songs:* "The Kiss Waltz," "Time on My Hands" Harold Adamson, Mack Gordon, Vincent Youmans; "Remember" Irving Berlin; "I Wish I Could Shimmy Like My Sister Kate" Armand J. Piron, Peter Bocage; "Ciribiribin" Harry James, Jack Lawrence, A. Pestalozza + extracts from *The Marriage of Figaro* Wolfgang Amadeus Mozart; *Faust* Charles Francis Gounod and *La Bohème* Giacomo Puccini. (1:41) Musical drama, a biopic of singer Grace Moore, from her childhood in Tennessee, to her debut at the Metropolitan Opera. Based on Moore's 1944 autobiography "You're Only Human Once." (G.B. title: *The Grace Moore Story*) Technicolor.

2439. So This Is Paris (Universal-International; 1954). *Cast:* Tony Curtis, Gloria DeHaven, Gene Nelson, Corinne Calvet, Mara Corday, Paul Gilbert, Allison Hayes, Sandy Descher, Christiane Martel, Myrna Hansen, Ann Codee, Arthur Gould-Porter, Roger Etienne, Lizette Guy, Michelle Ducasse, Maithe Iragui, Lucien Plauzoles, Numa Lapeyre, Pat Horn, Regina Dombek, Jean DeBriac, Rolfe Sedan, Andre Villon, Marcel de la Brosse, Carlos Albert. *D:* Richard Quine; *P:* Albert J. Cohen; *St:* Ray Buffum; *Sc:* Charles Hoffman; *Songs:* Title song, "Two of Us," "Looking For Someone to Love," "A Dame's a Dame," "Three Bon Vivants," "Wait Till Paris Sees Us," "If You Want to Be Famous," "If You Were There" Pony Sherrell, Phil Moody; "I Can't Give You Anything But Love" Dorothy Fields, Jimmy McHugh (sung by DeHaven in French). (1:36) Musical romance of three sailors on leave in Paris who meet three girls. Technicolor.

2440. So Young, So Bad (United Artists/Individual Pictures; 1950). *Cast:* Paul Henreid, Catherine McLeod, Grace Coppin, Cecil Clovelly, Anne Jackson (film debut), Enid Pulver, Anne Francis, Rosita [Rita] Moreno. *D:* Bernard Vorhaus; *P:* Edward J. Danziger, Harry Lee Danziger; *St: & Sc:* Vorhaus, Jean Rouverol (1:31) Hit melodrama of delinquent girls behind the bars of a correctional institution run by a cold director and a sadistic matron with an understanding compassionate psychiatrist standing by to balance things out. Filmed in New York City, the film had a pre-release title of "Escape If You Can."

2441. Soldier of Fortune (20th Century-Fox; 1955). *Cast:* Clark Gable, Susan Hayward, Michael Rennie, Gene Barry, Tom Tully, Alex

D'Arcy, Anna Sten, Russell Collins, Leo Gordon, Richard Loo, Soo Yong, Frank Tang, Jack Kruschen, Mel Welles, Jack Raine, George Wallace, Alex Finlayson, Noel Toy, Beal Wong, Robert Burton, Robert Quarry, Charles Davis, Victor Sen Yung, Frances Fong, Ivis Goulding, Barry Bernard, Kam Tong, George Chan, William Yip, Danny Chang. *D:* Edward Dmytryk; *P:* Buddy Adler; *Sc:* Ernest K. Gann (based on his 1954 novel). (1:36) (video) A woman hires an adventurer to help her locate her missing photographer husband in Hong Kong. Location filming in that city. DeLuxe color/CinemaScope.

2442. Soldiers Three (MGM; 1951). *Cast:* Stewart Granger, Walter Pidgeon, David Niven, Robert Newton, Cyril Cusack, Greta Gynt, Dan O'Herlihy, Robert Coote, Frank Allenby, Michael Ansara, Richard Hale, Walter Kingsford, Charles Cane, Patrick Whyte, Movita Castaneda, Charles Lang, Cyril McLaglen, Harry Martin, Pat O'Moore, Dave Dunbar, Stuart Hall, John Sheehan, Clive Morgan, Pat Aherne, Wilson Wood. *D:* Tay Garnett; *P:* Pandro S. Berman; *Sc:* Marguerite Roberts, Tom Reed, Malcolm Stuart Boylan. (1:27) The comic adventures of three soldier buddies stationed in 19th century India who are constantly in and out of trouble. Shades of *Gunga Din* (RKO; 1939): it was based on a book of short stories by Rudyard Kipling.

2443. The Solid Gold Cadillac (Columbia; 1956). *Cast:* Judy Holliday (Laura Partridge), Paul Douglas (Edward L. McKeever), Fred Clark (Clifford Snell), John Williams (John T. Blessington), Hiram Sherman (Harry Harkness), Neva Patterson (Amelia Shotgraven), Ralph Dumke (Warren Gillie), Ray Collins (Alfred Metcalfe), Arthur O'Connell (Jenkins), Richard Deacon (Williams), Marilyn Hanold (Miss L'Arriere), Jack Latham (Bill Parker), Harry Antrim (Senator Simpkins), Ann Loos, Audrey Swanson, Larry Hudson, Sandra White, Paul Weber, Emily Getchell, Maurice Manson, Suzanne Alexander, Oliver Cliff, Voltaire Perkins, Joe Hamilton, Jean G. Harvey, Bud Osborne, Lulu Mae Bohrman, Madge Blake, George Burns (narrator). *D:* Richard Quine; *P:* Fred Kohlmar; *Sc:* Abe Burrows; *ASD:* (AAN-b/w) Ross Bellah (art director), William R. Kiernan, Louis Diage (sets); *Costumes:* (AA) Jean Louis. (1:39) Hit comedy, based on the 1954 play by George S. Kaufman and Howard Teichmann, of a small corporate stockholder who crusades against a crooked board of directors in her company. The final scene (with the titled Cadillac) is in color. One of the 24 top-grossing films of 1956-57.

2444. Solomon and Sheba (United Artists/Edward Small; 1959). *Cast:* Yul Brynner (replacing Tyrone Power who died during production/Solomon), Gina Lollobrigida (Sheba), George Sanders (Adonijah), David Farrar (Pharaoh), Marisa Pavan (Abishag), John Crawford (Joab), Laurence Naismith (Hezrai), Jose Nieto (Ahab), Alejandro Rey (Sittar), Harry Andrews (Baltor), Julio Pena (Zadok), Maruchi Fresno (Bathsheba), William Devlin (Nathan), Felix De Pomes (Egyptian general), Jean Anderson (Takyan), Jack Gwillim (Josiah), Finlay Currie (King David), Tyrone Power (still can be seen in some battlefield longshots). *D:* King Vidor (final film—ret.); *P:* Ted Richmond; *St:* Crane Wilbur; *Sc:* Anthony Veiller, Paul Dudley, George Bruce. (2:19) (video/laserdisc) Epic Biblical drama of the seduction of King Solomon by the Queen of Sheba, to aid the armies of Pharaoh in overthrowing the Israelites. Filmed on locations in Spain, production costs soared to $5,000,000 due to the reshooting of major scenes following the death of Tyrone Power. One of the 28 top-grossing films of 1959-60. Technicolor/Super Technirama 70. Note: TV and video prints run 2:00, while the laserdisc has been restored to 2:19.

2445. Sombrero (MGM; 1953). *Cast:* Ricardo Montalban, Pier Angeli, Vittorio Gassman, Cyd Charisse, Yvonne DeCarlo, Rick Jason, Nina Foch, Kurt Kasznar, Walter Hampden, Jose Greco, Thomas Gomez, John Abbott, Andres Soler, Fanny Schiller, Luz Alba, Rosaura Revueltas, Alfonso Bedoya, Jorge Trevino, Tito Novaro, Manuel Arvide, Felipe De Flores, Beatriz Ramos, Florencio Castello, Arturo Rangel, Salvador Baguez, Juan Duval, Rita Conde, Pascual Pena, Louise De Carlo, Gabrielle Roussellon, Tom Hernandez, Orlando Beltran, George Derrick, Carlos Barbee, Eduardo Cansino, Miguel Contreras, Alms Beltram, Amapola Del Vando, Pilar Del Rey, Dorita Pallais, Delmar Costello. *D:* Norman Foster; *P:* Jack Cummings; *Sc:* Foster, Josefina Niggli. (1:43) Melodrama of three separate romantic affairs in a small Mexican village. Song and dance included. Based on the 1945 novel *A Mexican Village* by Ms. Niggli, the film was a box office loser in the U.S., but popular in other countries. Technicolor.

2446. Some Came Running (MGM/Sol C. Siegel Prods.; 1958). *Cast:* Frank Sinatra (Dave Hirsh), Dean Martin (Bama Dillert), Shirley

MacLaine (AAN/Ginny Moorhead), Martha Hyer (AAN-BSA/Gwen French), Arthur Kennedy (AAN-BSA/Frank Hirsh), Nancy Gates (Edith Barclay), Leora Dana (Agnes Hirsh), Betty Lou Keim (Dawn Hirsh), Larry Gates (Prof. Robert Haven French), Steven Peck (Raymond Lanchak), Connie Gilchrist (Jane Barclay), Ned Wever (Smitty), Carmen Phillips (Rosalie), John Brennan (Wally Dennis), William Schallert (Al), Roy Engel (sheriff), Marion Ross (Sister Mary Joseph), Denny Miller (Dewey Cole), Paul Jones (George Huff), Geraldine Wall (Mrs. Stevens), Janelle Richards (Virginia Stevens), George Brengel (Ned Deacon), George Cisar (Hubie Nelson), Donald Kerr (Doc Henderson), Don Haggerty (Ted Harperspoon), Ric Roman (Joe), George E. Stone (Slim), Anthony Jochim (Judge Baskin), Chuck Courtney, Jan Arvan, Frank Mitchell, Dave White, Len Lesser. *D:* Vincente Minnelli; *P:* Sol C. Siegel; *Sc:* John Patrick, Arthur Sheekman; *Song:* (AAN) "To Love and Be Loved" James Van Heusen, Sammy Cahn; *Costumes:* (AAN-color) Walter Plunkett. (2:16) (video/laserdisc) A character study of various residents in a post-World War II midwestern American town. Based on the 1957 best-seller by James Jones, it became one of the 26 top-grossing films of 1958-59 and took a #10 placement on the "10 Best" list of *Film Daily* in 1959. MetroColor/CinemaScope.

2447. Some Like It Hot (United Artists/Mirisch-Ashton; 1959). *Cast:* Marilyn Monroe (SugarKane Kumulchek), Tony Curtis (Joe/Josephine), Jack Lemmon (AAN + "Best Actor" nomination by the British Academy Awards, Jerry/Daphne), George Raft (Spats Columbo), Pat O'Brien (Mulligan), Joe E. Brown (Osgood Fielding III), Nehemiah Persoff (Bonaparte), Joan Shawlee (Sweet Sue), Billy Gray (Sig Poliakoff), George E. Stone (Toothpick Charlie), Dave Barry (Beinstock), Beverly Wills (Dolores), Barbara Drew (Nellie), Edward G. Robinson, Jr. (Paradise), Mike Mazurki (henchman), Harry Wilson (henchman), Tom Kennedy (bouncer), John Indrisano (waiter). *D:* (AAN) Billy Wilder; *P:* Wilder; *As.P:* Doane Harrison, I.A.L. Diamond; *Sc:* (AAN) Wilder, Diamond (based on the screenplay of the German film *Fanfares of Love* by Robert Thoeren and M. Logan); *Cin:* (AAN-b/w) Charles Lang, Jr.; *ASD:* (AAN-b/w) Ted Haworth (art director), Edward G. Boyle (sets); *Costumes:* (AA-b/w) Orry-Kelly; *Songs:* "Runnin' Wild" A.H. Gibbs, Leo Wood; "I Wanna Be Loved By You" Herbert Stothart, Bert Kalmar, "I'm Through With Love" Matty Malneck, Gus Kahn. (1:59) (video/laserdisc) Classic gender-bender slapstick sex comedy of two out-of-work musicians, witnesses to Chicago's 1929 St. Valentine's Day Massacre, who don female garb, join an all-girl band and head to Florida. This laugh-riot grossed $7,000,000 the first year, making it one of the 26 top-grossing films of 1958-59. On the "10 Best" lists of both the NBR and *Film Daily* it placed #7.

2448. Somebody Loves Me (Paramount; 1952). *Cast:* Betty Hutton, Ralph Meeker, Adele Jergens, Robert Keith, Henry Slate, Sid Tomack, Billie Bird, Jack Benny (unbilled bit), Ludwig Stossel, Sydney Mason, Nick Adams (film debut), Virginia Hall, Bea Allen, Les Clark, Howard Joslin, Jimmie Dundee, George Chandler, Lester Dorr, Franklyn Farnum, Herbert Vigran, Kenneth R. MacDonald, Milton Parsons, Charles O'Curran, James Cross, Richard N. Gordon, Charles Quirk, The Chez Paree Adorables. *D:-St: & Sc:* Irving Brecher; *P:* George Seaton, William Perlberg; *St: & Sc:* Brecher; *Songs:* Title song, George Gershwin, B.G. "Buddy" DeSylva; "Way Down Yonder in New Orleans" Henry Creamer, J. Turner Layton; "I Cried For You" Gus Arnheim, Arthur Freed, Abe Lyman; "Smiles" J. Will Callahan, Lee S. Roberts; "Teasing Rag" Joe Jordan; "Rose Room" Harry Williams, Art Hickman; "Jealous" Jack Little, Tommy Malie, Dick Finch; "Dixie Dreams" Arthur Johnston, George W. Meyer, Grant Clarke, Roy Turk; "On San Francisco Bay" Vincent Bryan, Gertrude Hoffman; "June Night" Cliff Friend, Abel Baer; "I'm Sorry I Made You Cry" N.J. Clesi, Theodore Morse; "Toddling the Todalo" E. Ray Goetz, A. Baldwin Sloane; "Wang Wang Blues" Gus Mueller, Buster Johnson, Henry Busse; "I Can't Tell You Why I Love You" Will J. Cobb, Gus Edwards; "Love Him," "Thanks to You" and "Honey, Oh My Honey" Jay Livingston, Ray Evans. (1:37) Fictionalized Technicolor Hollywood biopic on vaudevillian performers Blossom Seeley (Hutton) and Benny Fields (Meeker).

2449. Somebody Up There Likes Me (MGM; 1956). *Cast:* Paul Newman (Rocky Graziano), Pier Angeli (Norma), Everett Sloane (Irving Cohen), Eileen Heckart (Ma Barbella), Joseph Buloff (Benny), Sammy White (Whitey Bimstein), Arch Johnson (Heldon), Theodore Newton (Commissioner Eagan), Steve McQueen (film debut/Fidel), Robert Loggia (film debut/Frankie Peppo), Matt Crowley (Lou Stillman), Judson Pratt (Johnny Hyland), Donna Jo

Gribble (Yolanda Barbella), Jack Kelk (George), Russ Conway (Capt. Grifton), Harry Wisman (himself), Courtland Shepard (Tony Zale), Tony Rangno (Rocky at 8), Jan Gillum (Yolanda at 12), Ralph Vitti [aka: Michael Dante] (Shorty), Walter Cartier (Polack), John Eldredge (Warden Niles), Clancy Cooper (Capt. Lancheck), Ray Stricklyn (Bryce), Caswell Adams (Sam), Charles Green (Curtis Hightower), Angela Cartwright (Audrey), David Leonard (Mr. Mueller), Ray Walker (ring announcer), Robert Easton, Billy Nelson, James Todd, Sam Taub, Dean Jones. *D:* Robert Wise; *P:* Charles Schnee; *As.P:* James E. Newcom; *Sc:* Ernest Lehman; *Cin:* (AA-b/w) Joseph Ruttenberg; *ASD:* (AA-b/w) Cedric Gibbons, Malcolm F. Brown (art directors), Edwin B. Willis, F. Keogh Gleason (sets); *Editor:* (AAN) Albert Akst. (1:53) (video) Critically acclaimed film biography of middleweight boxer Rocky Graziano, from New York City street punk to ring stardom. Based on Graziano's 1955 autobiography (ghosted by Rowland Barber), it placed #6 on the "10 Best" list of the NBR. Computer-colored prints produced by Turner Entertainment.

2450. Something for the Birds (20th Century–Fox; 1952). *Cast:* Victor Mature, Patricia Neal, Edmund Gwenn, Larry Keating, Gladys Hurlbut, Hugh Sanders, Christian Rub (final film—d. 1956), Wilton Graff, Archer MacDonald, Richard Garrick, Ian Wolfe, Russell Gaige, John Brown, Camillo Guercio, Joan Miller, Madge Blake, Norman Field, Gordon Nelson, Emmett Vogan, John Ayres, Charles Watts, Rodney Bell, Norma Varden, Elizabeth Flournoy, Herbert Lytton, Fred Datig, Jr., Paul Power, Robert Livingston, Edmund Cobb, Joan Shawlee, Walter Baldwin, Louise Lorimer, Leo Curley, John Maxwell, Sam McDaniel. *D:* Robert Wise; *P:* Samuel G. Engel; *Sc:* I.A.L. Diamond, Boris Ingster (based on stories by Alvin M. Josephy, Joseph Petracca and Ingster). (1:21) Romantic comedy of a woman lobbying in Washington, D.C., to save the California condors from extinction.

2451. Something of Value (MGM; 1957). *Cast:* Rock Hudson, Dana Wynter, Sidney Poitier, Wendy Hiller, Frederick O'Neal, Juano Hernandez, William Marshall, Robert Beatty, Walter Fitzgerald, Michael Pate, Ken Renard, Ivan Dixon, Samadu Jackson, Paul Thompson, Lester Matthews, Garry Stafford, Duncan Richardson, Mme. Sul-te-wan, Leslie Denison, Barbara Foley, Carl Christian, Bob Anderson, Bruce Lester, Wesley Bly, Pauline Myers, Kim Hamilton, Barry Bernard, Morgan Roberts, Ottola Nesmith, Naaman Brown, Ike Jones. *D:* Richard Brooks; *P:* Pandro S. Berman; *Sc:* Brooks. (1:53) (video) Hit drama based on Robert C. Ruark's 1955 best-seller of the newsmaking Mau Mau revolt in Kenya, Africa, in 1953 when the ritualistic cult declared war on white African settlers, leading to slaughter. A forward is included by British Prime Minister Sir Winston Churchill. The Venice Film Festival had it in nomination.

2452. Something to Live For (Paramount; 1952). *Cast:* Joan Fontaine, Ray Milland, Teresa Wright, Richard Derr, Douglas Dick, Herbert Heyes, Frank Orth, Robert Cornthwaite, Helen Spring, Rudy Lee, Patric Mitchell, Paul Valentine, Richard Barron, Harry Bellaver, John Indrisano, Ruby Dee, Jessie Proctor, Lillian Clayes, Genevieve Bell, Patsy O'Byrne, Helen Dickson, Cora Shannon, Mari Blanchard, Ida Moore, Mary Field, Judith Allen, Kerry Vaughn, Jean Acker Valentino, Sue Carlton, Alex Akimoff, Eric Alden, Jody Gilbert, Norman Field, Maurice Cass, Erville Alderson, Paul Maxey, Douglas Spencer, Donald Dillaway, Al Kunde, George M. Lynn, Arthur Tovey, James E. Moss, Lee Aaker, Slim Gault, Anne M. Kunde, Raymond Bond, Peter Hanson, Laura Elliot, Charles Dayton, Sherry Jackson, Susan Freeman, Gerald Courtemarch, Helen Brown, Rolfe Sedan, Marcel de la Brosse, Charles Andre, Jeanne Lafayette, Harold Miller, Dulce Daye, Korla Pandit, King Donovan, Gloria Dea, Josette Deegan, Lavonne Battle. *D:* & *P:* George Stevens; *As.P:* Ivan Moffatt; *St:* & *Sc:* Dwight Taylor. (1:29) A melodrama of alcoholism and infidelity which did not do well at the box office.

2453. Son of Ali Baba (Universal-International; 1952). *Cast:* Tony Curtis, Piper Laurie, Susan Cabot, William Reynolds, Hugh O-Brian, Victor Jory, Morris Ankrum, Philip Van Zandt, Leon Belasco, Palmer Lee [aka: Gregg Palmer], Barbara Knudson, Alice Kelley, Gerald Mohr, Milada Mladova, Katherine Warren, Robert Barrat. *D:* Kurt Neumann; *P:* Leonard Goldstein; *As.P:* Ross Hunter; *St:* & *Sc:* Gerald Drayson Adams. (1:15) (video) Technicolor Arabian Nights style romantic epic with the son of Ali Baba out to do in the evil caliph who is out to get his father's treasure.

2454. Son of Belle Starr (Allied Artists; 1953). *Cast:* Keith Larsen, Dona Drake, Peggie

Castle, Regis Toomey, James Seay, Myron Healey, Frank Puglia, Robert Keys, I. Stanford Jolley, Paul McGuire, Lane Bradford, Mike Ragan [aka: Holly Bane], Joe Dominguez, Alex Montoya. *D:* Frank McDonald; *P:* Peter Sully; *St:* Jack DeWitt; *Sc:* D.D. Beauchamp, William Raynor. (1:10) Fictional programmer western of the famous female outlaw's son trying to live down his mother's notoriety. Cinecolor.

2455. The Son of Dr. Jekyll (Columbia; 1951). *Cast:* Louis Hayward, Jody Lawrence, Alexander Knox, Lester Matthews, Gavin Muir, Paul Cavanagh, Rhys Williams, Doris Lloyd, Claire Carleton, Patrick O'Moore, Robin Camp, Holmes Herbert, Wheaton Chambers, Olaf Hytten, Joyce Jameson, Robin Hughes, Frank Hagney, Guy Kingsford, Leonard Mudie, James Logan, Leslie Denison, Bruce Lester, Matthew Boulton, Pat Aherne, Vesey O'Davoren, Harry Martin, Stapleton Kent, Betty Fairfax, Keith Hitchcock, Ottola Nesmith, Carol Savage, Dave Dunbar, Benita Booth, Ida McGill, Ola Lorraine, Phyllis Morris, Alec Harford, David Cole, Jimmie Long, Robert Reeves. *D:* Seymour Friedman; *P:* Unc.; *St:* Mortimer Braus, Jack Pollexfen; *Sc:* Edward Huebsch. (1:17) A minor horror spinoff of the old Robert Louis Stevenson story *The Strange Case of Dr. Jekyll and Mr. Hyde.*

2456. Son of Paleface (Paramount/Hope Enterprises; 1952). *Cast:* Bob Hope (Junior), Jane Russell (Mike), Roy Rogers (himself), Trigger (horse/himself—whose "bedroom scene" with Hope won the 3rd place PATSY in 1953), Bill Williams (Kirk), Lloyd Corrigan (Doc Lovejoy), Paul E. Burns (Ebeneezer Hawkins), Douglass Dumbrille (Sheriff McIntyre), Harry Von Zell (Stoner), Iron Eyes Cody (Indian chief), "Wee" Willie Davis (blacksmith), Charlie Cooley (Charley), Charles Norton (Ned), Don Dunning (Wally), Leo J. McMahon (Crag), Felice Richmond (Genevieve), Charmienne Harker (Bessie), Isabel Cushin (Isabel/"Becky"), Jane Easton (Clara), Lyle Moraine (Weaverly), Hank Mann (1st bartender), Michael A. Cirillo (2nd bartender/"Mickey"), Chester Conklin ("Chester"), Flo Stanton ("Flo"), John George ("Johnny"), Charles Quirk (Zeke), Frank Cordell (Dade), Willard Willingham (Jeb), Warren Fiske (Trav), Jean Willes (Penelope), Jonathan Hale (governor), Homer Dickinson (townsman), Cecil B. DeMille (cameo), Bing Crosby (cameo), Robert L. Welch (cameo). *D:* Frank Tashlin; *P:* Robert L. Welch; *Sc:* Tashlin, Welch, Joseph Quillan; *Songs:* "Buttons and Bows" (revised), "Wing Ding Tonight," "California Rose," "What a Dirty Shame" Jay Livingston, Ray Evans; "Am I in Love?" (AAN-Best Song), "Four-legged Friend" Jack Brooks; "There's a Cloud in My Valley of Sunshine" Jack Hope, Lyle Moraine. (1:35) (video/laserdisc) One of the 23 top-grossing films of 1951-52 was this sequel to *The Paleface* (1948) which has the son of Painless Peter Potter returning to collect the gold left to him by his father. Many hilarious moments in this western comedy-spoof with songs. Technicolor.

2457. Son of Sinbad (RKO; 1955). *Cast:* Dale Robertson, Sally Forrest, Lili St. Cyr, Vincent Price, Mari Blanchard, Leon Askin, Jay Novello, Raymond Greenleaf, Nejla Ates, Kalantan, Ian MacDonald, Donald Randolph, Larry Blake, Edwin Hazard, Fred Aldrich, John Merton, George Sherwood, M.U. Smith, Woody Strode, George Barrows, Marilyn Bonney, Janet Comerford, Alyce Cronin, Mary Ann Edwards, Dawn Oney, Marvleen Prentice, Joan Pastin, Judy Ulian, Suzanne Alexander, Randy Allen, Jane Easton, Jeanne Evans, Helen Hayden, Joanne Jordan, Wayne Berk, James Griffith, Bette Arlen, Joann Arnold, Gwen Caldwell, Anne Carroll, Carolea Cole, Claire DeWitt, Nancy Dunn, Marjorie Holliday, Judy Jorell, Joi Lansing, Diane Mumby, Jonni Paris, Jeanne Shores, Maureen Stephenson, Libby Vernon, Doreen Woodbury, Betty Onge, Dee Gee Sparks, De-De Moore, Sue Casey, Carol Brewster, Chris Fortune, Helen Chapman, Barbara Drake, Bobette Bentley, Joan Whitney, Dolores Michaels, Barbara Lohrman, Zanne Shaw, Gloria Watson, Ann Ford, Donna Hall, Pat D'Arcy, Charlotte Alpert, Roxanne Arlen, Eleanor Bender, Evelyn Bernard, Shirley Buchanan, Roxanne Delman, Mary Ellen Gleason, Diane James, Keith Kerrigan, Mary Langan, Gloria Laughlin, Vonne Lester, Nancy Neal, Gloria Pall, Lynne Forrester, Audrey Allen, Nancy Moore, Phyllis St. Pierre, Evelyn Lovequist, Gerri Patterson, Kim Novak, Rosemary Webster, Laura Carroll, Penny Sweeney, Trudy Wroe, Joyce Johnson, Bob Wilke, Tom Monroe, Peter Ortiz, Virginia Bates, Katherine Cassidy, Honey King, Sally Musik, Leonteen Danies, Elaine Dupont, Gilda Fontana, Joy Lee, La Rue Malouf, Anna Navarro, Paula Vernay, Michael Ross, Michael Mark, Bob Hopkins, Gus Schilling, Max Wagner, Nancy Westbrook, Elizabeth Smith, Wanda Barbour, Irene Bolton, Joy Langstaff, Betty Sabor, Eileen Maxwell, Louisa Von Kories, Annabelle Thiele, Arlene Hunter, Naji Gabby. *D:* Ted Tetzlaff; *P:* Robert Sparks; *St:* Aubrey

Wisberg, Jack Pollexfen; *Sc:* Wisberg, Pollexfen, Jeff Bailey (unc.). (1:28) (video) Arabian Nights style adventure which was produced and completed in 1953 but held up for release until 1955 by Howard Hughes. If lots of scantily clad beautiful women (in Technicolor) are your thing, then this is the movie you've been waiting for. (aka: *Nights in a Harem* or *A Night in a Harem*) SuperScope/Technicolor.

2458. Son of the Renegade (United Artists/Royal West Prods.; 1953). *Cast:* John Carpenter, Lori Irving, John McKellen, Valley Keene, Jack Ingram, Verne Teters, Bill Coontz, Ted Smile, Bill Ward, Roy Canada, Whitey Hughes, Ewing Brown, Lennie Smith, Freddie Carson, Percy Lennon, Jack Wilson, Pat McGeehan (narrator). *D:* Reg Browne; *P: & Sc:* John Carpenter. (0:57) B budget western of a cowboy framed for a series of robberies.

2459. Song of the Land (United Artists/Kesler; 1953). *D:* Ed N. Harrison, Frances Roberts, Henry S. Kesler; *P: & St:* Kesler; *Narration:* Joseph Henry Steele. (1:11) A feature-length documentary on the wonders of nature. Based on an idea by F. Herrick Herrick. Color Corp. of America. Originally the lower half of a double bill with *Captain John Smith and Pocahontas* (q.v.).

The Song Parade *see* **Hit Parade of 1951**

2460. Sons of New Mexico (Columbia/Gene Autry Prods.; 1950). *Cast:* Gene Autry, Gail Davis (her first Autry film), Robert Armstrong, Dick Jones, Frankie Darro, Clayton Moore, Russell Arms, Irving Bacon, Kenne Duncan, Pierce Lyden, Marie Blake [aka: Blossom Rock], Sandy Sanders, Roy Gordon, Frankie Marvin, Paul Raymond, Harry Mackin, Bobby Clark, Gaylord [Steve] Pendleton, Billy Lechner, Champion, Jr. (horse). *D:* John English; *P:* Armand Schaefer; *St: & Sc:* Paul Gangelin. (1:11) Gene sets out to keep a youth out of trouble in this series entry. (G.B. title: *The Brat*)

Sons of the Musketeers (G.B. title) *see* **At Sword's Point**

2461. The Sorcerer's Village (Continental Distributing/Grand Prize Films; 1958) *D:* Capt. Hassoldt Davis; *P:* Sidney Kaufman; *Sc:* Kaufman; *Cin:* Ruth Staudinger Davis. (1:10) A documentary feature dealing with various forms of native African witchcraft, including sixteen ritual dances complete with authentic music. Based on the 1956 novel by Mr. Davis, it was narrated by Burgess Meredith. Pathécolor.

2462. Sorority Girl (American International/Sunset Prods.; 1957). *Cast:* Susan Cabot, Dick Miller, Barbara O'Neill, June Kenney, Barbara Crane, Fay Baker, Jeane Wood. *D: & P:* Roger Corman; *Ex.P:* James H. Nicholson; *St:* Leo Lieberman; *Sc:* Ed Waters. (1:00) (video) Melodrama of a college girl rejected by a sorority who makes things tough for the "Greek club." Remade for Showtime cable in 1994 as *Confessions of a Sorority Girl*. (G.B. title: *The Bad One*) Originally paired on a double bill with *Motorcycle Gang* (q.v.).

2463. The Sound and the Fury (20th Century–Fox/Jerry Wald; 1959). *Cast:* Yul Brynner, Joanne Woodward, Margaret Leighton, Stuart Whitman, Ethel Waters (final film—ret.), Jack Warden, Francoise Rosay, John Beal, Albert Dekker, Stephen Perry, William Gunn, Roy Glenn, Esther Dale, Adrian Martin. *D:* Martin Ritt; *P:* Jerry Wald; *Sc:* Irving Ravetch, Harriet Frank, Jr. (1:55) Drama which opened to some critical acclaim of a dysfunctional southern family. Based on the 1929 novel by William Faulkner. DeLuxe color/CinemaScope.

2464. The Sound of Fury (United Artists/Robt. Stillman; 1950). *Cast:* Frank Lovejoy, Lloyd Bridges, Richard Carlson, Katherine Locke, Kathleen Ryan, Irene Vernon, Adele Jergens, Cliff Clark, Art Smith, Carl Kent, Renzo Cesana, Donald Smelick, Dabbs Greer, Mack Williams, Jane Easton, John Pelletti, Mary Lawrence, Lynn Gray. *D:* Cyril Endfield; *P:* Robert Stillman; *Sc:* Jo Pagano. (1:31) (video) Melodrama of a reporter who stirs up a town's wrath against two men after one kidnaps a boy and then brutally kills him. Based on the novel *The Condemned* by Mr. Pagano, it was in nomination at the British Academy Awards. (video title: *Try and Get Me*)

2465. Sound Off (Columbia; 1952). *Cast:* Mickey Rooney, Anne James, Sammy White, John Archer, Gordon Jones, Wally Cassell, Arthur Space, Pat Williams, Marshall Reed, Helen Ford, Mary Lou Geer, Boyd "Red" Morgan. *D:* Richard Quine; *P:* Jonie Taps; *St: & Sc:* Quine, Blake Edwards; *Songs:* "My Lady Love" Lester Lee, Bob Russell; "Blow Your Horn" Rooney, Freddy Karger, Paul Mertz, George Duning. (1:23) Comedy of a feisty singer who is inducted into the U.S. Army. SuperCinecolor.

2466. South of Caliente (Republic; 1951). *Cast:* Roy Rogers, Douglas Evans, Pinky Lee (himself), Douglas Fowley, Pat Brady, Charlita, Ric Roman, Leonard Penn, Willie Best (final film—to TV), Frank Richards, George J. Lewis, The Roy Rogers Riders, Lillian Molieri, Marguerite McGill, Trigger (horse). *D:* William Witney; *P:* Edward J. "Eddy" White; *St: & Sc:* Eric Taylor. (1:07) Roy sets out to retrieve the racehorse that was stolen while he was responsible for delivering it to Mexico.

2467. South Pacific (Magna Theatre Corp./ South Pacific Enterprises; 1958). *Cast:* Rossano Brazzi (Emile de Becque/singing voice dubbed by Giorgio Tozzi), Mitzi Gaynor (Nellie Forbush), John Kerr (Lt. Cable/singing voice dubbed by Bill Lee), Ray Walston (Luther Billis), Juanita Hall (Bloody Mary/repeating her stage role, singing voice dubbed by Muriel Smith), France Nuyen (Liat/film debut), Russ Morgan (Capt. Brackett), Jack Mullaney (Professor), Ken Clark (Stewpot), Floyd Simmons (Harbison), Candace Lee (Ngana, Emile's daughter), Warren Hsieh (Jerome, Emile's son), Tom Laughlin (Buzz Adams), Galvan DeLeon (sub-chief), Ronald Ely (co-pilot), Robert Jacobs (communications man), Archie Savage (native chief), Darleen Engle (nurse/dancer), Richard Cutting (Admiral Kester), John Gabriel, Doug McClure, James Stacy. *D:* Joshua Logan; *P:* Buddy Adler; *Sc:* Paul Osborn; *Cin:* (AAN-color) Leon Shamroy; *Music:* (AAN) Alfred Newman, Ken Darby; *Sound:* (AA) Fred Hynes–Todd-AO Sound Dept.; *Songs:* "Dites-moi," "A Cockeyed Optimist," "Twin Soliloquies," "Some Enchanted Evening," "There Is Nothing Like a Dame," "Bali Ha'i," "I'm Gonna Wash That Man Right Outa My Hair," "I'm in Love With a Wonderful Guy," "Younger Than Springtime," "Happy Talk," "Honey Bun," "My Girl Back Home," "You've Got to Be Taught" and "This Nearly Was Mine." (2:51) (video/laserdisc) The hit Broadway musical brought to the screen is a romantic tale set on a South Pacific island during World War II. Based on *Tales of the South Pacific* by James A. Michener and the stage success by Richard Rodgers, Oscar Hammerstein II and Joshua Logan which ran on Broadway between 1949–54 with Ezio Pinza and Mary Martin in the leads. One of the 26 top-grossing films of 1957-58.

2468. South Pacific Trail (Republic; 1952). *Cast:* Rex Allen, Slim Pickens, Estelita Rodriguez, Roy Barcroft, Nestor Paiva, Douglas Evans, Forrest Taylor, Joe McGuinn, The Republic Rhythm Riders: Michael Barton, Darol Rice, George Bamby, Slim Duncan and Ko-Ko (horse). *D:* William Witney; *P:* Edward J. "Eddy" White; *St: & Sc:* Arthur Orloff; *Songs:* Jack Elliott, Aaron Gonzales, Allen. (1:00) Rex Allen series western with songs of a rancher who finds his foreman is involved with others to pull off a gold heist.

2469. South Sea Sinner (Universal-International; 1950). *Cast:* Macdonald Carey, Shelley Winters, Frank Lovejoy, Luther Adler, Helena Carter, Art Smith, John Ridgely, James Flavin, Liberace (film debut), Molly Lamont, Silan Chan, Henry Kulky, Fred Nurney, Phil Nazir. *D:* H. Bruce Humberstone; *P:* Michel Kraike; *St:* Ladislas Foder, Laslo Vadnay; *Sc:* Joel Malone, Oscar Brodney; *Adaptation:* Malone; *Songs:* "It Had to Be You" Gus Kahn, Isham Jones; "I'm the Lonesomest Gal in Town" Lew Brown, Albert Von Tilzer; "Blue Lagoon" Frederick Herbert. Arnold Hughes; "One Man Woman" Jack Brooks, Milton Schwarzwald and "Piano Concerto No. 1" Franz Liszt. (1:28) Melodrama of a man on a South Sea island whose past catches up with him. A remake of *Seven Sinners* (1940).

2470. South Sea Woman (Warner; 1953). *Cast:* Burt Lancaster, Virginia Mayo, Chuck Connors, Arthur Shields, Hayden Rorke, Barry Kelley, Leon Askin, Veola Vonn, Robert Sweeney, Cliff Clark, John Alderson, Paul Burke, Raymond Greenleaf, Rudolph Anders, Henri Letondal, Georges Saurel, William O'Leary, John Damler, Alena Awes, Jacqueline Duval, Violet Daniels, Paul Bryar, Anthony Radecki, Keye Luke, Frank Kumagai, Edo Mita, Robert Kino, Rollin Moriyama, Tony Garsen, Guy de Vestal, Gregory Gay, Strother Martin, Jim Hayward, Peter Chong, Grace Lem, Danny Chang, Paul Liu, Noel Cravat, Gisele Vertaine, Al Hill, Jack Kenney, Sam Harris, Joe Connor. *D:* Arthur Lubin; *P:* Sam Bischoff; *Adaptation:* Earl Baldwin, Stanley Shapiro; *Sc:* Edwin Blum. (1:39) Romantic World War II action-drama of two A.W.O.L. marines who do their own thing against the Axis powers. Based on the play *General Court-Martial* by William M. Rankin.

2471. South Seas Adventure (Stanley Warner Cinerama Corp.; 1958). *Cast:* Diane Beardmore, Marlene Lizzio, Tommy Zahn, Igor Allan, Ed Olsen, Walter Gibbons-Fly, Fred Bosch, Eddie Titiki, Ramine, Jay Ashworth, Maxine Stone, Don Middleton, Hans Farkash, Janice Dinnen, Eric Reiman, Sean Scully, and *as themselves:* Commodore Harold Gillespie, Don the Beachcomber, Marcel, Singing Chorus of Queen's College, Tonga Free Wesleyan Church choir, Mrs. Gibbs (schoolteacher of the air), Frank Basden, Dr. Huxley and Vic, The Norman Luboff Choir (soundtrack vocals). *D:* Francis D. Lyon, Walter Thompson, Basil Wrangell, Richard Goldstone, Carl Dudley; *P:* Dudley; *Co-P:* Goldstone; *Sc:* Charles A. Kaufman, Joseph Anson, Harold Medford; *Narrators:* Orson Welles, Shepard Menken, Walter Coy, Ted de Corsia. (2:00) Basically a Technicolor travelogue with a minimal story and wide-screen Cinerama photography, covering Hawaii, Tahiti, Tonga, Fiji, New Hebrides, Pentecost, New Zealand and Australia. The fifth Cinerama offering and it did not particularly please the film critics.

South Seas Fury *see* **Hell's Island**

2472. Southside 1-1000 (Monogram/Allied Artists; 1950). *Cast:* Don DeFore, Andrea King, George Tobias, Barry Kelley, Morris Ankrum, Robert Osterloh, Charles Cane, Kippee Valez. *D:* Boris Ingster; *P:* Frank King, Maurice King; *St:* Milton M. Raison, Bert C. Brown; *Sc:* Leo Townsend, Ingster; *Song:* "Je T'aime" Fritz Rotter, Harold Stern (sung by Valez). (1:13) *Film noir* of a U.S. Treasury agent on the trail of a counterfeiting operation in Los Angeles. (G.B. title: *Forgery*)

2473. Southwest Passage (United Artists/ Eclipse Films; 1954). *Cast:* Joanne Dru, Rod Cameron, John Ireland, Guinn "Big Boy" Williams, Mark Hanna, Darryl Hickman, Stuart Randall, Morris Ankrum, Kenneth MacDonald, Stanley Andrews, John Dehner. *D:* Ray Nazarro; *P:* Edward Small; *St:* Harry Essex; *Sc:* Essex, Geoffrey Homes [Daniel Mainwaring]. (1:22) Offbeat western involving experiments with camels in the American desert. (G.B. title: *Camels West*) 3-D and Pathécolor.

2474. The Space Children (Paramount/ Wm. Alland Prods.; 1958). *Cast:* Adam Williams, Peggy Webber, Michel Ray, John Crawford, Jackie Coogan, Sandy Descher, Richard Shannon, Johnny Washbrook, Russell Johnson, Raymond Bailey. *D:* Jack Arnold; *P:* William Alland; *St:* Tom Filer; *Sc:* Bernard C. Schoenfeld. (1:09) B budget sci-fi of children of rocket scientists who come under control of a space alien that has taken up residence in a local cave. Originally ran as the second feature on a double bill with *The Colossus of New York* (q.v.). VistaVision.

2475. Space Master X-7 (20th Century-Fox/Regal Films; 1958). *Cast:* Bill Williams, Lyn Thomas, Robert Ellis, Paul Frees, Joan Barry, Thomas Browne Henry, Fred Sherman, Jesse Kirkpatrick, Moe Howard, Rhoda Williams, Carol Varga, Thomas Wilde, Gregg Martell, Court Shepard, Al Baffert, Robert Bice, Don Lamond, Judd Holdren, Ellen Shaw, Nesdon Booth, John Ward, Helen Jay, Lane Chandler, Edward McNally, Joe Becker. *D:* Edward Bernds; *P:* Bernard Glasser; *St: & Sc:* George Worthing Yates, Daniel Mainwaring. (1:11) (video) Blood rust is an alien fungus that has hitched a ride to earth aboard a returning satellite, with a capacity to rapidly spread and destroy the human race. (aka: *Mutiny in Outer Space*) Regalscope.

Spacemen Saturday Night *see* **Invasion of the Saucer Men**

2476. Spanish Affair (Paramount/Nomad-CEA-Benito Perojo; 1958). *Cast:* Richard Kiley, Carmen Sevilla, Jose Guardiola, Jesus Tordesillas, Jose Marco Davo, Jose Manuel Martin, Francisco Bernal, Punta Vargas, Antonio S. Amaya, Rafael Farina. *D:* Don Siegel; *P:* Bruce Odlum; *St: & Sc:* Richard Collins; *Song:* "The Flaming Rose" Mack David, Daniele Amfitheatrof (sung by Sevilla). (1:35) Triangular romantic melodrama scenically filmed on location in Spain of an American architect, his Spanish interpreter and her jealous boyfriend. A U.S.A./Spanish co-production. Technicolor/VistaVision.

2477. Speed Crazy (Allied Artists/Viscount Films; 1959). *Cast:* Brett Halsey, Yvonne Lime, Charles Willcox, Slick Slavin, Jacqueline Ravell, Baynes Barron, Regina Gleason, Keith Byron, Mark Sheeler, Lucita, Charlotte Fletcher, Vic Marlo, Robert Swan, Jackie Joseph, Troy Patterson, Eddie Durkin. *D:* William Hole, Jr.; *P:* Richard Bernstein; *Ex.P:* Richard B. Duckett; *St: & Sc:* Bernstein, George Waters; *Song:* Slick Slavin. (1:15) (video) A racecar enthusiast accidentally kills a garage mechanic in a holdup. He heads for a racing event in a nearby town and gets involved with some locals, until the police finally catch up with him. The racing sequences were filmed at Griffith Park in Hollywood.

2478. The Spell of the Hypnotist (Exploitation Films; 1956). *Cast:* Nancy Malone, Eric Fleming, Frank Marth, Humphrey Davis, Dean L. Almquist, Elizabeth Watts, Amelia Conley, Walter Kalven, Ned Glass, Norman

Burton, Tom Reynolds, Robert Gardett, Norman MacKay, Don Douglas, Philip Kenneally, Sid Raymond, Chris Bohn, Alney Alba. *D: & P:* W. Lee Wilder; *St: & Sc:* Myles H. Wilder. (1:08) Melodrama of a woman under hypnosis who believes she was the lover of Crown Prince Rudolph of Austria and committed suicide with him in 1889. (aka: *Fright*)

2479. The Spider (American International/James H. Nicholson and Samuel Z. Arkoff Present; 1958). *Cast:* Ed Kemmer, June [Kenney] Kenny, Gene Persson, Gene Roth, Hal Torey, June Jocelyn, Mickey Finn, Sally Fraser, Troy Patterson, Skip Young, Howard Wright, Bill Giorgio, Hank Patterson, Jack Kosslyn, Bob Garnet, Shirley Falls, Bob Tetrick, Nancy Kilgas, George Stanley, David Tomack, Merritt Stone. *D:-P: & St:* Bert I. Gordon; *Sc:* Laszlo Gorog, George Worthing Yates. (1:12) (video) Teen exploitation sci-fi of a giant arachnid found in a cave outside a small town. The spider is thought to be killed, but is revived by rock 'n' roll music and wreaks havoc on the town. (aka: *Earth vs. the Spider*) Originally ran on the top of a double bill with *The Brain Eaters* (q.v.).

2480. The Spirit of St. Louis (Warner/Leland Hayward Prods.-Billy Wilder Prods.; 1957). *Cast:* James Stewart (Charles Lindbergh), Murray Hamilton (Bud Gurney), Patricia Smith (mirror girl), Bartlett Robinson (B.F. Mahoney), Robert Cornthwaite (Knight), Sheila Bond (model-dancer), Marc Connelly (Father Hussman), Arthur Space (Donald Hall), Harlan Warde (Boedecker), Dabbs Greer (Goldsborough), Paul Birch (Blythe), David Orrick (Harold Bixby), Robert Burton (Major Lambert), James L. Robertson, Jr. (William Robertson), Maurice Manson (E. Lansing Ray), James O'Rear (Earl Thompson), David McMahon (Lane), Griff Barnett (Dad, the farmer), John Lee (Jess, the cook), Herb Lytton (Casey Jones), Jack Daly (Louie), Erville Alderson (Burt), Aaron Spelling (Mr. Fearless), Ann Morrison (Mrs. Fearless), Charles Watts (O.W. Schultz), Richard Deacon (Levine), Nelson Leigh (director), Roy Gordon (associate producer), Carleton Young, Eugene Borden, Olin Howlin, Virginia Christine, Syd Saylor, Ray Walker, Lee Roberts, Robert B. Williams, Percival Vivian, George Selk [aka: Budd Buster], Paul Brinegar, Chief Yowlachie. *D:* Billy Wilder; *P:* Leland Hayward; *Adaptation:* Charles Lederer; *Sc:* Wilder, Wendell Mayes; *Music:* (AAN) Franz Waxman; *F/X:* (AAN) Louis Lichtenfield. (2:18) (video) A multi-million dollar production detailing Charles Lindbergh's 3,600 mile, 33½ hour nonstop flight from New York to Paris in 1927. Despite a #3 placement on the "10 Best" list of the NBR as well as being one of the 24 top-grossing films of 1956-57, the studio considered this one of their biggest financial flops. Based on Lindbergh's 1953 Pulitzer Prize winning book. WarnerColor/CinemaScope.

2481. Split Second (RKO; 1953). *Cast:* Stephen McNally, Alexis Smith, Jan Sterling, Keith Andes, Arthur Hunnicutt, Paul Kelly, Robert Paige, Richard Egan, Frank DeKova. *D:* Dick Powell (directorial debut); *P:* Edmund Grainger; *St:* Chester Erskine, Irving Wallace; *Sc:* Wallace, William Bowers. (1:25) (video) Drama of three escaped convicts holding six hostages in a western ghost town, eventually learning that a nuclear bomb is to be detonated on the site.

2482. The Spoilers (Universal-International; 1955). *Cast:* Anne Baxter, Jeff Chandler, Rory Calhoun, Ray Danton, Barbara Britton (final film—ret.), John McIntire, Wallace Ford, Carl Benton Reid, Raymond Walburn (final film—ret.), Ruth Donnelly, Willis Bouchey, Forrest Lewis, Roy Barcroft, Dayton Lummis, John Harmon, Paul McGuire, Frank Sully, Bob Steele, Byron Foulger, Arthur Space, Lane Bradford, Terry Frost. *D:* Jesse Hibbs; *P:* Ross Hunter; *Sc:* Oscar Brodney, Charles Hoffman. (1:24) The fifth go-round for Rex Beach's 1906 novel of gold miners, greed and claim jumpers in the frontier gold fields of Alaska. Previous versions: Selig (1914), Samuel Goldwyn (1923), Paramount (1930) and Universal (1942). Technicolor.

2483. Spoilers of the Forest (Republic; 1957). *Cast:* Rod Cameron, Vera Ralston, Ray Collins, Hillary Brooke (final film—ret.), Edgar Buchanan, Carl Benton Reid, Sheila Bromley, Hank Worden, John Compton, Angela Greene, Paul Stader, Mary Alan Hokanson, Raymond Greenleaf, Eleanor Audley, Don Haggerty, William Haade, Jo Ann Lilliquist, Bucko Stafford, Robert Karnes, Kem Dibbs, Rory Mallinson, Virginia Carroll, John Patrick, Bob Swan, Mack Williams, Theresa Harris, Helen Wallace, Pauline Moore, Judd Holdren. *D: & P:* Joseph Kane; *Ex.P:* Herbert J. Yates; *St: & Sc:* Bruce Manning. (1:08) Programmer melodrama of a timber baron who uses deceit to acquire choice trees from a girl's 64,000 acre property. Trucolor/Naturama.

2484. Spoilers of the Plains (Republic; 1951). *Cast:* Roy Rogers, Penny Edwards, Gordon Jones, Foy Willing and Riders of the Purple Sage, Grant Withers, Fred Kohler, Jr., William Forrest, Don Haggerty, House Peters, Jr., George Meeker, Keith Richards, Trigger (horse), Bullet (dog). *D:* William Witney; *P:* Edward J. White; *St: & Sc:* Sloan Nibley; *Songs:* Jack Elliott, Aaron Gonzales, Foy Willing. (1:08) Contemporary Roy Rogers series western with an oil field foreman suspecting a rival has planted saboteurs within his operation.

2485. Spook Chasers (Allied Artists; 1957). *Cast:* Huntz Hall, Stanley Clements, David Gorcey, Jimmy Murphy, Percy Helton, Darlene Fields, Eddie LeRoy, Bill Henry, Peter Mamakos, Ben Welden, Robert Shayne, Robert Christopher, Pierre Watkin, Audrey Conti, Anne Fleming, Bill Cassady. *D:* George Blair; *P:* Ben Schwalb; *St: & Sc:* Elwood Ullman. (1:02) "Bowery Boys" comedy series entry with the gang getting involved when a friend purchases a dilapidated farm house that appears to be "haunted."

Spread Eagle *see* **The Eagle and the Hawk**

2486. Spring Reunion (United Artists/Bryna Prods.; 1957). *Cast:* Dana Andrews, Betty Hutton (final film—ret.), Jean Hagen, Sara Berner, Robert Simon, Laura La Plante (a silent screen star in her final film), Gordon Jones, James Gleason, Irene Ryan, Richard Shannon, Ken Curtis, Herbert Anderson, George Chandler, Richard Benedict, Vivi Janiss, Florence Sundstrom, Mimi Doyle, Sid Tomack, Shirley Mitchell, Dorothy Neumann, Barbara Drew, Richard Deacon, Don Haggerty, Leon Tyler. *D:* Robert Pirosh; *P:* Jerry Bresler; *Sc:* Pirosh, Elick Moll (based on the TV drama by Robert Alan Aurthur); *Song:* Johnny Mercer, Harry Warren (sung by the Mary Kaye Trio). (1:19) Romance blossoms at the 15th reunion of Carson High's class of 1941. Originally ran on a double bill with *Hit and Run* (q.v.).

2487. Springfield Rifle (Warner; 1952). *Cast:* Gary Cooper, Phyllis Thaxter, David Brian, Paul Kelly, Philip Carey, Lon Chaney, Martin Milner, Guinn "Big Boy" Williams, James Brown, James Millican, Alan Hale, Jr., Jack Woody, Vince Barnett, Fess Parker, Richard Lightner, Ewing Mitchell, Poodles Hanneford, George Ross, Eric Hoeg, Wilton Graff, Ned Young, William Fawcett, Richard Hale, Ben Corbett, Guy Edward Hearn, George Eldredge, Ralph Sanford, Rory Mallinson, Ric Roman, Jack Mower, Michael Chapin. *D:* Andre DeToth; *P:* Louis F. Edelman; *St:* Sloan Nibley; *Sc:* Charles Marquis Warren, Frank Davis. (1:33) (video) Tried and true western plot of a Union officer who infiltrates a gang to find out who is stealing government guns. WarnerColor.

2488. Spy Chasers (Allied Artists, 1956). *Cast:* Leo Gorcey, Huntz Hall, Bernard Gorcey, David [Gorcey] Condon, Bennie Bartlett, Leon Askin, Sig Rumann, Veola Vonn, Lisa Davis, Linda Bennett, Frank Richards, Paul Burke, Richard Benedict, Mel Welles, John Bleifer. *D:* Edward Bernds; *P:* Ben Schwalb; *St: & Sc:* Bert Lawrence, Jerome S. Gottler. (1:01) Another comedy in the "Bowery Boys" series as they get involved in a Ruritanian kingdom and its political intrigues to overthrow the rightful ruler.

2489. Spy Hunt (Universal-International; 1950). *Cast:* Howard Duff, Marta Toren, Philip Friend, Robert Douglas, Philip Dorn, Walter Slezak, Kurt Kreuger, Aram Katcher, Otto Waldis, Ivan Triesault, Jay Barney, Carl Milletaire, Antonio Filauri, Peter Ortiz, Peter Applequist, Carlo Tricoli, Betty Greco, Carmela Restivo, Jack Chefe, Rudy Silva. *D:* George Sherman; *P:* Ralph Dietrich; *Sc:* George Zuckerman, Leonard Lee. (1:15) Melodrama involving a panther with a much sought after microfilm hidden in its collar. Based on the 1948 novel *Panther's Moon* by Victor Canning. (G.B. title: *Panther's Moon*)

2490. Spy in the Sky (Allied Artists; 1958). *Cast:* Steve Brodie, Andrea Domburg, George Coulouris, Sandra Francis, Bob de Lange, Hans Tiemeyer, Herbert Curiel, Dity Oorthuis, Leon Dorian, A.E. Gollin, E.F. Beavis, Alex Zweers, Harold Horsten, Rob Milton. *D: & P:* W. Lee Wilder; *Sc:* Myles H. Wilder. (1:15) Ultra low budget espionage melodrama of a German scientist who escapes after being forced to work on the Sputnik satellite project. Based on the 1954 novel *Counterspy Express* by A.S. Fleischman.

2491. Square Dance Katy (Monogram; 1950). *Cast:* Vera Vague [aka: Barbara Jo Allen], Phil Brito, Virginia Welles, Warren Douglas, Sheila Ryan, Dorothy Vaughan, Fenton "Jonesy" Jones, Harry Cheshire, Jon Riffel, Warren Jackson, Donald Kerr, Paul Bryar, Earle Hodgins, Frank Sully, Russell Hicks, Stanley Blystone, Lee Phelps, Tristram Coffin, Edward Gargan, Joseph Crehan, Ray Walker, William Forrest, Jimmie Davis & His Sunshine Band. *D:* Jean

Yarbrough; *P:* Lindsley Parsons; *St:* & *Sc:* Warren Wilson. (1:16) Low budget musical romance of a country girl brought to New York City to become a TV singer.

2492. The Square Jungle (Universal-International; 1956). *Cast:* Tony Curtis, Pat Crowley, Ernest Borgnine, Paul Kelly, Jim Backus, Leigh Snowden, John Day, David Janssen, Carmen McRae, John Marley, Joe Louis (himself), Barney Phillips, Joseph Vitale, Wendell Niles, Kay Stewart, Frank Marlowe, Frankie Van, Walter J. Ekwert, Clancy Cooper, Jesse Kirkpatrick, Frank Moran, Dennis Moore, Barry Reagan, Jimmy Cross. *D:* Jerry Hopper; *P:* Albert Zugsmith; *St:* & *Sc:* George Zuckerman. (1:26) Pugilism drama centered around the training of a young boxer.

The Square Shooter *see* **Skipalong Rosenbloom**

The Squared Circle (G.B. title) *see* **Joe Palooka in the Squared Circle**

2493. Stage Fright (Warner; 1950). *Cast:* Jane Wyman, Marlene Dietrich, Michael Wilding, Richard Todd, Alastair Sim, Kay Walsh, Dame Sybil Thorndike, Miles Malleson, Hector MacGregor, Joyce Grenfell, Andre Morell, Patricia Hitchcock, Ballard Berkeley, Irene Handl, Arthur Howard, Everly Gregg, Cyril Chamberlain, Helen Goss, Alfred Hitchcock (man on street). *D:* & *P:* Alfred Hitchcock; *Adapt:* Alma Reville; *Sc:* Whitfield Cook, Ranald MacDougall (unc.); *Additional dialogue:* James Bridie; *Song:* "The Laziest Gal in Town" Cole Porter. (1:50) (video/laserdisc) A drama student is suspect in the murder of a wealthy man. Based on "Man Running" and "Outrun the Constable," two stories by Selwyn Jepson. Filmed in England, the film took a #10 placement on the "10 Best" of the NBR.

Stage from Blue River *see* **Stage to Blue River**

2494. Stage Struck (Buena Vista/RKO; 1958). *Cast:* Henry Fonda, Susan Strasberg, Joan Greenwood, Herbert Marshall, Christopher Plummer (film debut), Daniel Ocko, Pat Harrington, Frank Campanella, John Fielder, Patricia Englund, Jack Weston, Sally Gracie, Nina Hansen, Harold Grau, Leon Bibb, Estelle Richie, Clint Young, Hilda Haynes, Roger C. Carmel. *D:* Sidney Lumet; *P:* Stuart Miller; *Sc:* Ruth and Augustus Goetz. (1:35) (video/laserdisc) Drama of a young actress who aspires to stardom on Broadway. A remake of *Morning Glory* (RKO; 1933) with Katharine Hepburn, it was based on the play of that name by Zoe Akins. Produced by RKO and released by Buena Vista after the former studio closed down. Technicolor.

2495. Stage to Blue River (Monogram/ Frontier Pictures; 1951). *Cast:* Whip Wilson, Fuzzy Knight, Phyllis Coates, Lee Roberts, John Hart, Pierce Lyden, Lane Bradford, Terry Frost, I. Stanford Jolley, William Fawcett, Steve Clark, Stanley Price, Bud Osborne. *D:* Lewis Collins; *P:* Vincent M. Fennelly; *St:* & *Sc:* Joseph Poland. (0:55) Series western of a woman who seeks help when her stagecoach line is being disrupted by a gang of outlaws led by the local sheriff. (aka: *Stage from Blue River*).

2496. Stage to Tucson (Columbia; 1950). *Cast:* Rod Cameron, Wayne Morris, Kay Buckley, Carl Benton Reid, Roy Roberts, Sally Eilers (final film—ret.), Harry Bellaver, Douglas Fowley, John Pickard, Olin Howlin, Charles Evans, Boyd Stockman, Reed Howes, John Sheehan, James Kirkwood. *D:* Ralph Murphy; *P:* Harry Joe Brown; *Sc:* Bob Williams, Frank Burt, Robert Libott. (1:21) (video) Based on the 1948 book *Lost Stage Valley* by Frank Bonham, this Technicolor Civil War western relates the efforts of Southern sympathizers to hijack Union stagecoaches. (G.B. title: *Lost Stage Valley*)

2497. Stagecoach Driver (Monogram/ Frontier Pictures; 1951). *Cast:* Whip Wilson, Fuzzy Knight, Jim Bannon, Gloria Winters, Lane Bradford, Barbara Allen, John Hart, Leonard Penn, Stanley Price, Marshall Reed, George DeNormand. *D:* Lewis D. Collins; *P:* Vincent M. Fennelly; *St:* & *Sc:* Joseph O'Donnell. (0:52) Series western of the newly arrived telegraph.

2498. Stagecoach to Fury (20th Century-Fox/Regal Films; 1956). *Cast:* Forrest Tucker (Frank Townsend), Mari Blanchard (Barbara Deval), Wallace Ford (Lester Farrell), Rodolfo Hoyos (Lorenzo Garcia), Paul Fix (Tim O'Connors), Rico Alaniz (Miquel Torres), Wright King (Ralph Slader), Margia Dean (Ruth), Ian MacDonald (Sheriff Ross), Ellen Corby (Sarah), Alex Montoya (Oro), Rayford Barnes (Zick), Leslye Banning (Ann Stewart), Steven Geray (Nichols), Paul Fierro (Pedro), Robert Karnes (Talbot), William Phillips, Norman Leavitt. *D:*

William F. Claxton; *P:* Earl Lyon; *St:* Eric Norden, Lyon; *Sc:* Norden; *Cin:* (AAN-b/w) Walter Strenge. (1:16) Low budget oater of stagecoach passengers being held prisoner by Mexican bandits who seek the gold shipment on the next stage through. Curious for a low budget western in that it received an Oscar nomination for photography. Regalscope.

2499. Stakeout on Dope Street (Warner; 1958). *Cast:* Yale Wexler, Jonathan Haze, Morris Miller, Abby Dalton, Allen Kramer, Herman Rudin, Phillip Monsour, Frank Harding, Herschel Bernardi, Bill Shaw, Andrew J. Fenady, Slate Harlow, Carol Nelson, Ed Schaff, Matt Resnick, Charles Gaustl, Ida Morgan, Wendy Wilde, John Savage, Barbara O'Bannon, Larry Raimond, Byrd Holland, Hal Saunders, Miles Stephens, Geri Willis, Jim Giles, Coleman Francis, Ginny Roberts, Mike Stoycoff, Ernie Kaufman, Lillian Kay, Lester Miller, Larry Frost and The Hollywood Chamber Jazz Group: Bob Drasnin, Ollie Mitchell, Dick Houlgate, Phil Gray, Gene Estes, Mel Pollan, Ritchie Frost, Rubin Leon. *D:* Irvin Kershner; *P:* Andrew J. Fenady; *St: & Sc:* Fenady, Kershner, Irwin Schwartz. (1:23) Low budget melodrama of three teens who find a two-pound tin of uncut heroin and go into business for themselves.

2500. Stalag 17 (Paramount; 1953). *Cast:* William Holden (AA/Sefton), Don Taylor (Lt. Dunbar), Otto Preminger (Oberst Von Scherbach), Robert Strauss (AAN/repeating his stage role/Stosh), Harvey Lembeck (repeating his stage role/Harry), Richard Erdman (Hoffy), Peter Graves (Price), Neville Brand (Duke), Sig Rumann (Schulz), Michael Moore (Manfredi), Peter Baldwin (Johnson), Robinson Stone (Joey), Robert Shawley (Blondie), William Pierson (Marko), Gil Stratton, Jr. (Cookie), Jay Lawrence (Bagradian), Edmund Trzcinski (Triz, and a co-author of the original play), Erwin Kalser (Geneva man), Jerry Singer (The Crutch), Ross Bagdasarian, Robin Morse, Tommy Cook, Peter Leeds, Harold D. Maresh, Carl Forcht, Alex J. Wells, Bob Templeton, Paul T. Salata, Max Willenz. *D:* (AAN) Billy Wilder; *P:* Wilder; *Sc:* (AAN) Wilder, Edwin Blum. (2:00) (video/laserdisc) Critically acclaimed drama of Americans in a World War II German P.O.W. camp and one of their number they suspect as a traitor, giving away their escape plans. Based on the hit Broadway play by Donald Bevan and Edmund Trzcinski (who also acts in the film), it placed #6 and #7 respectively on the "10 Best" lists of the *New York Times* and the NBR. One of the 26 top-grossing films of 1952-53.

Stampeded (G.B. title) *see* **The Big Land**

2501. The Stand at Apache River (Universal-International; 1953). *Cast:* Stephen McNally, Julia [Julie] Adams, Hugh Marlowe, Jaclynne Greene, Hugh O'Brian, Russell Johnson, Jack Kelly, Edgar Barrier, Forrest Lewis. *D:* Lee Sholem; *P:* William Alland; *Sc:* Arthur Ross. (1:17) Western of eight people under siege by Indians at a stagecoach relay station. Based on the 1951 novel *Apache Landing* by Robert J. Hogan. Technicolor.

2502. The Star (20th Century–Fox; 1952). *Cast:* Bette Davis (AAN/Margaret Elliot), Sterling Hayden (Jim Johannson), Natalie Wood (Gretchen), Warner Anderson (Harry Stone), Minor Watson (Joe Morrison), June Travis (final film & her only film appearance since 1939/Phyllis Stone), Katherine Warren (Mrs. Morrison), Kay Riehl (Mrs. Adams), Barbara Woodell (Peggy Morgan), Fay Baker (Faith), Barbara Lawrence (herself), David Alpert (Keith Barkley), Paul Frees (Richard Stanley). *D:* Stuart Heisler; *P:* Bert E. Friedlob; *St: & Sc:* Katherine Albert, Dale Eunson. (1:29) (video) Margaret Elliot (Davis) is a faded star of Hollywood, bankrupt and alone, living in the illusion that she will soon make her big "comeback."

2503. Star in the Dust (Universal-International; 1956). *Cast:* John Agar, Mamie Van Doren, Richard Boone, Leif Erickson, Coleen Gray, James Gleason, Randy Stuart, Terry Gilkyson, Paul Fix, Henry [Harry] Morgan, Stuart Randall, Robert Osterloh, John Day, Stanley Andrews, Stafford Repp, Lewis Martin, Renny McEvoy, Jesse Kirkpatrick, James Parnell, Anthony Jochim, Clint Eastwoood. *D:* Charles Haas; *P:* Albert Zugsmith; *Sc:* Oscar Brodney. (1:20) Western of a sheriff (Agar) who is forced to hold townsmen at bay who want to hang the gunman (Boone) that he is holding in his jail. Based on the novel *Lawman* by Lee Leighton [pseudonym of Wayne D. Overholser]. Technicolor.

2504. A Star Is Born (Warner/Transcona Enterprises; 1954). *Cast:* Judy Garland (AAN/Esther Blodget/Vicki Lester), James Mason (AAN/Norman Maine), Charles Bickford (Oliver Niles), Jack Carson (Libby), Tommy Noonan (Danny McGuire), Lucy Marlow (Lola Lavery), Amanda Blake (Susan Ettinger), Irving Bacon

(Graves), Hazel Shermet (Libby's secretary), James Brown (Glenn Williams), Lotus Robb (Miss Markham), Joan Shawlee (announcer), Bob Jellison (Eddie), Blythe Daly (Miss Fusselow), Olin [Howlin] Howland (Charley), Willis Bouchey (McBride), Grady Sutton (Carver), Richard Webb (Wallace), Steve Wyman (Nigel Peters), Henry Kulky (Cuddle), Percy Helton (Gregory), Nadene Ashdown (Esther at age 6), Heidi Meadows (Esther at age 3), Dub Taylor, Louis Jean Heydt, Chick Chandler, Kathryn Card, Leonard Penn, Eddie Dew, Emerson Treacy, Mae Marsh, Rex Evans, Tristram Coffin, Frank Ferguson, Dale Van Sickel. *D:* George Cukor; *P:* Sid Luft; *St:* William A. Wellman, Robert Carson; *Sc:* Moss Hart; *ASD:* (AAN-color) Malcolm Bert, Gene Allen, Irene Sharaff, George James Hopkins; *Music:* (AAN) Ray Heindorf; *Costumes:* (AAN-color) Jean Louis, Mary Ann Nyberg, Irene Sharaff; *Songs:* "Born in a Trunk" Roger Edens, Leonard Gershe (with choreography by Richard Barstow); "The Man That Got Away" (AAN-Best Song), "Gotta Have Me Go With You," "It's a New World," "Here's What I'm Here For," "Someone at Last" and "Lose That Long Face" (which was edited from the final release print) Harold Arlen, Ira Gershwin. (2:34) (video/laserdisc) Drama with songs of a married couple, she a singer on the way up, he an alcoholic actor on the way down. A remake of the 1937 U.A./Selznick production which was inspired by *What Price Hollywood?* (RKO; 1932) by Adela Rogers St. John. This film placed #4 on the "10 Best" list of the NBR and went on to become one of the 27 top-grossing films of 1954-55. Remade in 1976. Technicolor/CinemaScope. Note: This film originally premiered at a running time of 3:01 and shortly thereafter was edited to a 2:34 running time for general release. The edited footage was apparently destroyed, as in 1983 a 2:50 restoration was made with existing soundtrack and Sepiatone stills.

2505. Star of Texas (Allied Artists/Westwood Prods.; 1953). *Cast:* Wayne Morris, Paul Fix, Frank Ferguson, Rick Vallin, Jack Larson, James Flavin, William Fawcett, Robert Bice, Mickey Simpson, George Wallace, John Crawford, Stanley Price, Lyle Talbot. *D:* Thomas Carr; *P:* Vincent M. Fennelly; *St: & Sc:* Dan Ullman. (1:08) Programmer western of a Texas Ranger passing himself off as an escaped convict in order to get the goods on an outlaw gang recruiting ex-prison inmates. Told in sort of a semi-documentary style. One of a series of six films by Morris for Allied Artists.

The Star Said No (G.B. title) *see* **Callaway Went Thataway**

2506. Starlift (Warner; 1951). *Cast:* Janice Rule, Dick Wesson, Ron Hagerthy, Richard Webb, Hayden Rorke, Howard St. John, Ann Doran, Tommy Farrell, John Maxwell, Don Beddoe, Mary Adams, Bigelow Sayre, Eleanor Audley, Pat Henry, Gordon Polk, Robert Hammack, Ray Montgomery, Bill Neff, Stan Holbrook, Jill Richards, Joe Turkel, Rush Williams, Brian McKay, Jack Larson, Lyle Clark, Dorothy Kennedy, Jean Dean, Dolores Castle, William Hunt, Elizabeth Flournoy, Walter Brennan, Jr., Dick Ryan, James Brown, Steve Gregory, Bill Hudson, Sarah Spencer, Eddie Coonz, Robert Karnes, John Hedloe, Richard Monohan, Joe Recht, Herb Latimer, Ezelle Poule + *Cameos:* Doris Day, Gordon MacRae, Virginia Mayo, Gene Nelson, Ruth Roman, Gary Cooper, James Cagney, Virginia Gibson, Phil Harris, Frank Lovejoy, Lucille Norman, Louella Parsons, Randolph Scott, Jane Wyman, Patrice Wymore. *D:* Roy Del Ruth; *P:* Robert Arthur; *St:* John Klorer; *Sc:* Klorer, Karl Kamb; *Songs:* "Liza" (lyrics by Ira Gershwin and Gus Kahn, music by George Gershwin); " 'S Wonderful" (George and Ira Gershwin); "You Ought to Be in Pictures" (Edward Heyman, Dana Seusse); "You Do Something to Me," "What Is This Thing Called Love?" (Cole Porter); "It's Magic" (Sammy Cahn, Jule Styne); "I May Be Wrong But I Think You're Wonderful" (Harry Ruskin, Henry Sullivan); "Look Out Stranger, I'm a Texas Ranger" (Ruby Ralesin, Phil Harris); "You're Gonna Lose Your Gal" (Joe Young, James V. Monaco); "Good Green Acres of Home" (Irving Kahal, Sammy Fain) and "Noche Carib" (Percy Faith). (1:43) Musical of the romance between an actress and an Air Force Corporal during "Operation Starlift," when Hollywood sent big name stars to San Francisco to entertain troops bound for Korea.

2507. Stars and Stripes Forever (20th Century–Fox; 1952). *Cast:* Clifton Webb, Debra Paget, Robert Wagner, Ruth Hussey, Finlay Currie, Benay Venuta, Roy Roberts, Tom Browne Henry, Lester Matthews, Maudie Prickett, Erno Verebes, Richard Garrick, Romo Vincent, Roy Gordon (President Harrison), Florence Shirley, Delos Jewkes, Norman Leavitt, Hellen Van Tuyl, Walter Woolf King, Roger Moore, Thomas E. Jackson, Maude Wallace, Lenee Martin, Sharon Jan Altman, Nicolas Koster, William Vedder, Olan Soule, Aileen Carlyle, Paul Maxey, Frank

Ferguson, Jack Rice, The Atlanta Stone Mountain Choir. *D:* Henry Koster; *P:* Lamar Trotti; *Sc:* Trotti, Ernest Vajda; *Songs:* "Stars and Stripes Forever," "El Capitan," "Washington Post March," "King Cotton March," John Philip Sousa; "The Battle Hymn of the Republic" Julia Ward Howe, William Steffe; "Dixie" Daniel Decatur Emmett; "Light Cavalry" Franz Von Suppe; "Turkey in the Straw" traditional; "Hail to the Chief" John Sanderson; "The Bowery" Percy Gaunt, Charles Hoyt. (1:29) (video) A fictionalized Hollywood biography of "March King" John Philip Sousa, based on his 1928 autobiography *Marching Along*. (G.B. title: *Marching Along*) Technicolor.

2508. The Stars Are Singing (Paramount; 1953). *Cast:* Rosemary Clooney (film debut), Anna Maria Alberghetti, Lauritz Melchior (final film—ret.), Bob Williams, Fred Clark, Tom Morton, John Archer, Mikhail Rasumny, Lloyd Corrigan, Don Wilson (himself), Red Dust (dog). *D:* Norman Taurog; *P:* Irving Asher; *St:* "Goddess" by Paul Hervey Fox; *Sc:* Liam O'Brien; *Songs:* "Come-On-A-My-House" (a big hit for Clooney in 1951) Ross Bagdasarian, William Saroyan; "I Do, I Do, I Do," "Haven't Got a Worry to My Name," "My Heart Is Home," "My Kind of Day," "Feed Fido Some Rruff," "New Father," "Lovely Weather for Ducks" Jay Livingston, Ray Evans; "Voices of Spring" Johann Strauss; "Una Voce Poco Fa" Gioacchino (Antonio) Rossini (from *The Barber of Seville*); "Because" Edward Teschemacher, Guy d'Hardelot; "Ah Fors e Lui che l'Anima" Giuseppe Verdi (from *La Traviata*), and "Vesti la Giubba" Ruggiero Leoncavallo (from *Pagliacci*). (1:39) Musical of a singer who befriends an illegal Polish immigrant to the United States. Technicolor.

2509. Stars in My Crown (MGM; 1950). *Cast:* Joel McCrea, Ellen Drew, Dean Stockwell, Lewis Stone, James Mitchell, Alan Hale, Juano Hernandez, Amanda Blake, Connie Gilchrist, Arthur Hunnicutt, Charles Kemper, Jack Lambert, James Arness, Marshall Thompson (narrator). *D:* Jacques Tourneur; *P:* William H. Wright; *Adaptation:* Joe David Brown (of his 1947 novel); *Sc:* Margaret Fitts [Scott]. (1:29) (video) Americana of a 19th century southern rural minister and his family. Brown's novel was originally serialized in *Saturday Evening Post*. The title refers to the clergyman's favorite hymn.

2510. State Penitentiary (Columbia/Kay Pictures; 1950). *Cast:* Warner Baxter (final film—d. 1951), Onslow Stevens, Karin Booth, Robert Shayne, Richard Benedict, Brett King, John Bleifer, Leo T. Cleary, Rick Vallin, William Fawcett, Rusty Wescoatt, John Hart. *D:* Lew Landers; *P:* Sam Katzman; *St:* Henry E. Helseth; *Sc:* Howard J. Green, Robert Libott, Frank Burt. (1:06) Low budget melodrama of a wrongly imprisoned man who escaped to find the guilty party. Filmed on location at the Nevada State Penitentiary. Originally paired on a double bill with *Outcast of Black Mesa* (q.v.).

Stazione Termini (Italian title) *see* **Indiscretion of an American Wife**

2511. The Steel Cage (United Artists/Phoenix Films; 1954). *Cast:* Paul Kelly, Maureen O'Sullivan, Walter Slezak, John Ireland, Lawrence Tierney, Alan Mowbray, Lyle Talbot, George E. Stone, Arthur Franz, Kenneth Tobey, George Cooper, Elizabeth Fraser, Stanley Andrews, Morris Ankrum, Don Beddoe, Robert Bice, George Chandler, Henry Kulky, Herb Jacobs, Ned Glass, Charles Nolte, Gene Roth, James Seay, Charles Tannen, Ben Welden. *D:* Walter Doniger; *P:* Berman Schwartz, Doniger; *St:* "The Hostages" Doniger, Schwartz/"The Face" Scott Littleton; *Sc:* "The Hostages" Oliver Crawford, "The Chef" Doniger, Schwartz and "The Face" Guy Trosper. (1:20) Prison melodrama relating three different stories of three different men incarcerated in California's San Quentin Prison. A sequel to *Duffy of San Quentin* (q.v.) and based on the 1950 book *The San Quentin Story* by Clinton T. Duffy and Dean Jennings. Originally ran on a double bill with *The Snow Creature* (q.v.).

2512. The Steel Fist (Monogram/Wm. F. Broidy; 1952). *Cast:* Roddy McDowall, Kristine Miller, Harry Lauter, Rand Brooks, Byron Foulger, Kate Lawson, Murray Alper, Bob Peoples, Gil Perkins, Fred Krone. *D: & P:* Wesley Barry; *Sc:* C.K. Kivari. (1:13) Cold War melodrama of a dissident youth who flees from a communist labor program in the Soviet Union. Based on the story "Flight Into Freedom" by Phyllis Parker.

2513. The Steel Helmet (Lippert/Deputy Corp.; 1951). *Cast:* Gene Evans, Robert Hutton, Richard Loo, Steve Brodie, James Edwards, Sid Melton, Richard Monahan, William Chun, Harold Fong, Neyle Morrow, Lynn Stalmaster. *D:-P: & Sc:* Samuel Fuller. (1:24) (video) Korean War drama which received moderate acclaim. Released just six months after the beginning of the "police action," the film is a staple of the followers of Fuller, a production which he completed in just ten days.

2514. The Steel Jungle (Warner; 1956). *Cast:* Perry Lopez, Beverly Garland, Walter Abel, Ted de Corsia, Kenneth Tobey, Allison Hayes, Gregory Walcott, Leo Gordon, Kay Kuter, Bob Steele, Ralph Moody, Stafford Repp, Billy Vincent, Charles Crane, Fred Graham, Carey Loftin, Jack Kruschen, Edward Platt, Lyle Latell, Richard Karlan, Frank Gerstle, Tom McKee, Eddie Baker, Joe Smith, Lane Bradford, Malcolm Atterbury, Mack Williams, Robert Bray, Peter Gray. *D:-St: & Sc:* Walter Doniger; *P:* David Weisbart. (1:26) Melodrama of an incarcerated hood who keeps his outside operation going from behind bars. Originally half of a double bill program with *The River Changes*, a German production.

2515. The Steel Lady (United Artists/World Films-Edward Small; 1953). *Cast:* Rod Cameron, Tab Hunter, John Dehner, Richard Erdman, John Abbott, Frank Puglia, Anthony Caruso, Christopher Dark, Dick Rich, Charles Victor, Carmen d'Antonio. *D:* E.A. Dupont; *P:* Grant Whytock; *St:* Aubrey Wisberg; *Sc:* Richard Schayer. (1:24) Low budget action drama of a plane crew of oil scouts downed in the Sahara desert who find an old tank from the German Afrika Korps, uncovered in a sandstorm which happens to hold a cache of valuable jewels. (G.B. title: *Treasure of Kalifa*). Originally paired on a double bill with *The Village*, a British/Swiss coproduction.

2516. Steel Town (Universal-International; 1952). *Cast:* Ann Sheridan, Howard Duff, John Lund, Eileen Crowe, William Harrigan, Chick Chandler, James Best, Nancy Kulp, Elaine Riley, Tudor Owen, Frank Marlowe, Robert Karnes, Herbert Lytton, Lorin Raker, Lois Wilde, James McLaughlin. *D:* George Sherman; *P:* Leonard Goldstein; *St:* Leonard Freeman; *Sc:* Gerald Drayson Adams, Lou Breslow. (1:25) Melodrama of steel workers who are rivals for the same girl. Technicolor.

2517. The Steel Trap (20th Century-Fox/Thor Prods.; 1952). *Cast:* Joseph Cotten, Teresa Wright, Eddie Marr, Aline Towne, Bill Hudson, Benny Burt, Joey Ray, Sam Flint, Charlie Collins, Kurt Martell, Jonathan Hale, Stephanie King, Carleton Young, Katherine Warren, Walter Sande, Tom Powers. *D:-St: & Sc:* Andrew L. Stone; *P:* Bert E. Friedlob; *Song:* "So Much to Me" Dimitri Tiomkin, Stan Jones (sung by Helen Humes). (1:25) Comedy of the assistant manager of an L.A. bank whose criminal tendencies get the best of him. He absconds with a million dollars and the intention of fleeing to Brazil with his family.

2518. Stella (20th Century-Fox; 1950). *Cast:* Ann Sheridan, Victor Mature, David Wayne, Randy Stuart, Marion Marshall, Frank Fontaine, Leif Erickson, Evelyn Varden, Lea Penman, Joyce MacKenzie, Hobart Cavanaugh (final film—d. 1950), Charles Halton, Walter Baldwin, Larry Keating, Mary Bear, Paul Harvey, Chill Wills, Lorelie Witek. *D: & Sc:* Claude Binyon; *P:* Sol C. Siegel. (1:23) (video) Screwball "black" comedy of a family who has one of their own die an accidental death and fearing they will be implicated as murderers, bury the body in a remote place—eventually forgetting where! Based on the 1949 novel *Family Skeleton* by Doris Miles Disney.

2519. Step Down to Terror (Universal-International; 1958). *Cast:* Colleen Miller, Charles Drake, Rod Taylor, Josephine Hutchinson, Jocelyn Brando, Alan Dexter, Ricky Kelman, Ann Doran. *D:* Harry Keller; *P:* Joseph Gershenson; *Sc:* Mel Dinelli, Chris Cooper, Czenzi Ormondi. (1:15) Melodramatic programmer of a man who returns home after a six year absence. It soon becomes apparent to everyone, the man is a psychopath. A remake of *Shadow of a Doubt* (1943), it was remade under that title in 1991 as a TV movie. Based on "Uncle Charlie," an unpublished story by Gordon McDonell. (G.B. title: *The Silent Stranger*)

2520. Stolen Identity (Helen Ainsworth; 1953). *Cast:* Francis Lederer, Donald Buka, Joan Camden, Adrienne Gessner, Inge Konrads, Gisele Wilke, Herman Erhard, Egon Von Jordan, Manfred Inger. *D:* Gunther Fritsch; *P:* Turhan Bey; *Adaptation & Sc:* Robert Hill. (1:21) Melodrama of a cab driver in Vienna who assumes the identity of a murdered American businessman in his effort to make entry into the United States. An independent production based on the novel *I Was Jack Mortimer* by Alexander Lernet-Holenia.

2521. The Stooge (Paramount/Wallis-Hazen; 1951–52). *Cast:* Dean Martin, Jerry Lewis, Polly Bergen, Eddie Mayehoff, Marion Marshall, Richard Erdman, Frances Bavier. *D:* Norman Taurog; *P:* Hal B. Wallis; *St:* Fred Finklehoffe, Sid Silvers; *Sc:* Finklehoffe, Martin

Rackin; *Additional dialogue:* Elwood Ullman; *Songs:* "A Girl Named Mary, A Boy Named Bill" Mack David, Jerry Livingston; "Who's Your Little Whozis?" Al Goering, Ben Bernie, Walter Hirsch; "Just One More Chance" Arthur Johnston, Sam Coslow; "With My Eyes Wide Open I'm Dreaming" Mack Gordon, Harry Revell; "Louise" Leo Robin, Richard Whiting and "I'm Yours" E.Y. Harburg, Johnny Green. (1:40) (video) A vaudevillian song-and-dance man, a swellhead, reacts when his stooge begins garnering all of the attention with his comic routines. Apparently the studio was unsure how audiences would take this Martin and Lewis vehicle, completing it in 1951 and holding up release until 1952.

Stooges Go West (G.B. title) *see* **The Gold Raiders**

2522. Stop That Cab (Lippert/Spartan Prods.–Magna Film Prods.; 1951). *Cast:* Sid Melton, Iris Adrian, Marjorie Lord, Tom Neal, Greg McClure, Chester Clute, Minerva Urecal, Glenn Denning, Diane Garrett, Mario Siletti, Renata Vanni, Jack Roper, Ed East, Jesse B. Kirkpatrick, Vito Scotti, Michael McHale, Joe Devlin. *D:* Eugenio de Liguoro; *P:* Abrasha Haimson; *St: & Sc:* Louella McFarlane, Walter Abbott. (0:58) Comedy programmer of a cabbie with much to deal with in life when crooks leave stolen jewels in his cab.

2523. Stop, You're Killing Me (Warner; 1952). *Cast:* Broderick Crawford, Claire Trevor, Virginia Gibson, Bill Hayes, Margaret Dumont, Howard St. John, Charles Cantor, Sheldon Leonard, Joe Vitale, Louis Lettieri, Henry [Harry] Morgan, Stephen Chase, Don Beddoe, Henry Slate, Ned Glass, Jack Pepper, Joe McTurk, Ralph Sanford, John Crawford, Phil Arnold, Frank Richards, Mushy Callahan, Phyllis Kirk, Sherry Moreland, Joann Arnold, Dolly Jarvis. *D:* Roy Del Ruth; *P:* Louis F. Edelman; *Sc:* James O'Hanlon; *Songs:* Title song, "You're My Everloving" Bob Hilliard, Carl Sigman + "Baby Face" and "Someone Like You." (1:26) Black comedy of a racketeer battling the odds when he decides to go straight. A remake of *A Slight Case of Murder* (1938), it was based on an unsuccessful play by Damon Runyon and Howard Lindsey. WarnerColor.

2524. Stopover Tokyo (20th Century–Fox; 1957). *Cast:* Robert Wagner, Joan Collins, Edmond O'Brien, Ken Scott, Reiko Oyama, Larry Keating, Sarah Selby, Solly Nakamura, H. Okhawa, K.J. Seijto, Demmei Susuki, Yuki Kaneko, Michei Miura. *D:* Richard L. Breen; *P:* Walter Reisch; *Sc:* Reisch, Breen. (1:40) (video) Melodrama of a U.S. Intelligence agent, hired to protect an American ambassador in Japan, the latter not believing his life is in danger—until the agent discovers a planted bomb. Based on the 1957 novel by John P. Marquand. DeLuxe color/ CinemaScope.

2525. Storm Center (Columbia/Phoenix Prods.; 1956). *Cast:* Bette Davis, Brian Keith, Kim Hunter, Paul Kelly, Kevin Coughlin, Joe Mantell, Sallie Brophy, Howard Wierum, Curtis Cooksey, Michael Raffetto, Edward Platt, Kathryn Grant, Howard Wendell, Burt Mustin, Edith Evanson, Joseph Kearns, Dora Dee and Lora Lee Stansauk (twins), Bucko Stafford, Malcolm Atterbury, Edwin Parker, Paul Ryan, George Selk [aka: Budd Buster], Mildred Hayes, Emlen Davies, Alex Campbell, Ted Marc, Rudy Lee, Phillip Crampton. *D:* Daniel Taradash; *P:* Julian Blaustein; *St: & Sc:* Taradash, Elick Moll. (1:25) Drama of the controversy surrounding a librarian and her refusal to remove a subversive book from the library shelves.

2526. Storm Fear (United Artists/Theodora Prods.; 1956). *Cast:* Cornel Wilde, Jean Wallace, Dan Duryea, Lee Grant, David Stollery, Dennis Weaver, Keith Britton, Steven Hill. *D: & P:* Wilde; *Sc:* Horton Foote. (1:28) Film noir of three fugitives from justice who hide out at the home of one of the fugitive's ex-girlfriends and her family in a secluded mountainous area.

Storm Over Africa (G.B. title) *see* **Royal African Rifles**

2527. Storm Over Tibet (Columbia/Summit; 1952). *Cast:* Rex Reason (film debut), Diana Douglas, Myron Healey, Robert Karnes, Strother Martin, Harold Fong, Harald Dyrenforth, Jarmila Marton, William Schallert, John Dodsworth, M. Concepcion. *D:* Andrew Marton; *P:* Ivan Tors, Laslo Benedek; *St: & Sc:* Tors, Sam Meyer. (1:27) Action melodrama of the events that follow the theft of a sacred mask from a Tibetan temple. (aka: *Mask of the Himalayas*) Originally part of a double bill program with *Harem Girl* (q.v.).

2528. Storm Over Wyoming (RKO; 1950). *Cast:* Tim Holt, Richard Martin, Noreen Nash, Richard Powers [aka: Tom Keene], Betty Underwood, Kenneth MacDonald, Leo McMahon, Bill Kennedy, Holly Bane [aka: Rike

Ragan], Don Haggerty, Richard Kean. *D:* Lesley Selander; *P:* Herman Schlom; *St: & Sc:* Ed Earl Repp. (1:00) Rangeland trouble between cattlemen and sheepmen are instigated by a foreman on a sheep ranch in this western series entry. Originally the bottom of a double bill with *The Tattooed Stranger* (q.v.).

2529. The Storm Rider (20th Century-Fox/Regal Films; 1957). *Cast:* Scott Brady, Mala Powers, Bill Williams, Olin Howlin, William Fawcett, John Goddard, Hank Patterson, James Dobson, John Close, Jim Hayward, Cortland Shepard, Ricky Shahan, Frank Richards, Ronald Foster, Rick Vallin, Tom London, Britt Wood, Al Baffert, Roy Engel, George Keymas, Rock Lundy, John Cason, Bud Osborne, Jean Ann Lewis, Wayne Mallory. *D:* Edward Bernds; *P:* Bernard Glasser; *Sc:* Bernds, Don Martin. (1:10) (video) Western of a wealthy rancher and his conflict of interests with local cattlemen. Based on the novel by L.L. [Leonard London] Foreman, it was originally half of a double bill program with *China Gate* (q.v.). Regalscope.

2530. Storm Warning (Warner; 1950). *Cast:* Ginger Rogers [replacing Lauren Bacall], Ronald Reagan, Doris Day, Steve Cochran, Hugh Sanders. Lloyd Gough, Raymond Greenleaf, Ned Glass, Walter Baldwin, Lynne Whitney, Sean McClory, Stuart Randall, Paul E. Burns, Dave McMahon, Robert Williams, Charles Watts, Charles Phillips, Dale Van Sickel, Anthony Warde, Paul Brinegar, Tom Wells, King Donovan, Len Hendry, Ned Davenport, Frank Marlowe, Charles Marsh, Lillian Albertson, Eddie Hearn, Harry Harvey, Janet Barrett, Walter Bacon, Norman Field, Donald Dillaway, Michael McHale, Dewey Robinson, Gene Evans, Dick Anderson, Lloyd Jenkins, Mary Alan Hokanson, Fern Barry, Dabbs Greer, Grandon Rhodes, Charles Conrad, Alex Gerry, Leo Cleary, Tommy Walker. *D:* Stuart Heisler; *P:* Jerry Wald; *Sc:* Daniel Fuchs, Richard Brooks [based on their story "Stormcenter"]. (1:33) Melodrama of a woman who arrives on a family visit to a southern town just in time to witness a murder by the Ku Klux Klan then finds her sister is married to the man she saw commit the murder. Filmed on location in Corona, California, it was remade in 1995 as the TV movie *Deadly Family Secrets* (minus the Ku Klux Klan). Note: This film often carries a release date of 1951 though it was reviewed by *Film Daily* on December 7, 1950.

The Story of a Divorce *see* **Payment on Demand**

2531. The Story of Mankind (Warner/Cambridge Prods.; 1957). *Cast:* Ronald Colman (final film—d. 1958/The Spirit of Man), Vincent Price (The Devil), Cedric Hardwicke (High Judge), Hedy Lamarr (Joan of Arc), Harpo Marx (final film—ret./Isaac Newton), Virginia Mayo (Cleopatra), Agnes Moorehead (Queen Elizabeth I), Peter Lorre (Nero), John Carradine (Khufu), Dennis Hopper (Napoleon), Marie Wilson (Marie Antoinette), Edward Everett Horton (Sir Walter Raleigh), Reginald Gardiner (William Shakespeare), Francis X. Bushman (Moses), Groucho Marx (Peter Minuit), Marie Windsor (Josephine), Charles Coburn (Hippocrates), Frankllin Pangborn (final film—d. 1958/Marquis de Varennes), Bobby Watson (final film—ret./Adolph Hitler), Helmut Dantine (Anthony), Henry Daniell (Bishop of Beauvais), Jim Ameche (Alexander Graham Bell), Dani Crayne (Helen of Troy), Anthony Dexter (Christopher Columbus), Austin Green (Abraham Lincoln), Reginald Sheffield (Caesar), George E. Stone, Chico Marx (final film—ret.), Cesar Romero, Cathy O'Donnell, Melville Cooper, Nick Cravat, Alexander Lockwood, Melinda Marx, Bart Mattson, Don Megowan, Marvin Miller, Nancy Miller, Leonard Mudie, Major Sam Harris, Abraham Sofaer, Tudor Owen, Toni Gerry, Richard Cutting, William Schallert, Ziva Rodann, David Bond, Eden Hartford, Harry Ruby, Angelo Rossito. *D: & P:* Irwin Allen; *Sc:* Allen, Charles Bennett. (1:40) A critically panned one-of-a-kind oddball film which has the Devil and the Spirit of Man debating the pros and cons of the human race throughout history. Adapted from the 1921 book by Henrik Willem van Loon. Technicolor.

2532. The Story of Robin Hood (RKO/Walt Disney British Prods., Ltd.; 1952). *Cast:* Richard Todd (Robin Hood), Joan Rice (Maid Marian), Peter Finch (Sheriff of Nottingham), James Hayter (Friar Tuck), James Robertson Justice (Little John), Martita Hunt (Queen Eleanor), Hubert Gregg (Prince John), Bill Owen (Stutely), Reginald Tate (Hugh Fitzooth), Elton Hayes (Allan-a-Dale), Anthony Eustrel (Archbishop of Canterbury), Patrick Barr (King Richard), Anthony Forwood (Will Scarlet), Hal Osmond (Midge the miller), Michael Hordern (Scathelock), Clement McCallin (Earl of Huntingdon), Louise Hampton (Tyb), Archie Duncan (Red Gill), Julian Somers (posse leader), Bill Travers (posse man), David Davies (forester) and the Merrie Men: Ivan Craig, Ewen Solon, John Stamp, John Brooking, John Martin, Geoffrey Lumsden, Larry Mooney, John French, Nigel

Neilson, Charles Perry, Richard Graydon, Jack Taylor. *D:* Ken Annakin; *Ex.P:* Walt Disney; *P:* Perce Pearce; *Sc:* Lawrence E. Watkin. (1:23) (video/laserdisc) Lavish hit rendering of the famous story of a man and his efforts to fight oppression in his land. A Technicolor co-production of Great Britain and the U.S.A., it became one of the 23 top-grossing films of 1951-52. (G.B. title: *The Story of Robin Hood and His Merrie Men*). Originally paired on a double bill with the co-feature *The Pace That Thrills* (q.v.). Note: Produced in England with Disney profits held in that country.

The Story of Robin Hood and His Merrie Men (G.B. title) *see* **The Story of Robin Hood**

2533. The Story of Three Loves (MGM; 1953). A lavishly produced drama of three separate love affairs, related in flashback by passengers on an ocean cruise. A dud at the box office.

A. "The Jealous Lover" *Cast:* Moira Shearer (Paula Woodward), James Mason (Charles Coudray), Agnes Moorehead (Aunt Lydia), Jacob Gimpel, Miklos Rozsa, John Lupton, Jack Raine, Lysa Baughter, Flo Wix, Towyna Dally, Colin Kenny, Major Sam Harris, Ottola Nesmith, Bruce Lasbury, Bruce Edwards, Ivan Hayes, Anne Howard, Paula Allen, Reginald Sheffield. *D:* Gottfried Reinhardt; *Sc:* John Collier. The tale of a ballet impresario and the reason he only staged his ballet *Astarte* one time.

B. "Mademoiselle" *Cast:* Ethel Barrymore (Mrs. Pennicott), Leslie Caron (Mademoiselle), Farley Granger (Thomas Campbell, Jr.), Ricky Nelson (Tommy, age 12), Paula Raymond (Mrs. Campbell), Hayden Rorke (Mr. Rorke), Larry Olsen (Terry), Manuel Paris (Mr. Carlos), Alberto Morin (Mr. Sandes), Zsa Zsa Gabor, Andre Simeon, Zach Yaconelli, Peter Brocco, Phyllis Garffeo, Argentina Brunetti, Nick Thompson, Tom Quinn, Rudy Lee, Noreen Corcoran, Ernesto Morelli, Ed Agresti, Victor Desney. *D:* Vincente Minnelli; *St:* Arnold Phillips; *Sc:* Jan Lustig, George Froeschel. When the governess of a young preteen becomes bored with her charge, a witch changes him into an adult for four hours.

C. "Equilibrium" *Cast:* Pier Angeli (Nina), Kirk Douglas (Pierre Narval), Robert Anderson (Marcel), Steven Geray (Legay), Alix Talton (Rose), Karen Verne (Madame Legay), Ken Anderson (Jacques), Peter Norman (Rudolph Kramer), Torben Meyer, Jack Tesler, Joan Miller, Paul Bryar, Kay English, Elizabeth Slifer, Christofer Appel, Bertha Feducha, Frank Scannell, Paul Maxey, Leo Mostovoy, Frank Wilcox, John Pickard. *D:* Gottfried Reinhardt; *St:* Ladislas Vajda, Jacques Maret; *Sc:* John Collier, Jan Lustig, George Froeschel. A former circus trapeze artist reflects back on how he met and married his wife. *P:* Sidney Franklin; *ASD:* (AAN) Cedric Gibbons, Preston Ames, Edward Carfagno, Gabriel Scognamillo (art directors), Edwin B. Willis, Keogh Gleason, Arthur Krams, Jack D. Moore (sets). (2:02) Technicolor.

2534. The Story of Will Rogers (Warner; 1952). *Cast:* Will Rogers, Jr., Jane Wyman, Carl Benton Reid, Eve Miller, James Gleason, Slim Pickens, Noah Beery, Jr., Mary Wickes, Steve Brodie, Margaret Field, Eddie Cantor (final film—ret./himself), Pinky Tomlin, Virgil S. Taylor, Richard Kean, Jay Silverheels, William Forrest (Florenz Ziegfeld), Earl Lee (President Woodrow Wilson), Brian Daly, Robert Scott Correll, Carol Ann Gainey, Michael Gainey, Carol Nugent, Jack Burnette, Paul McWilliam, Dub Taylor, Olan Soule, Madge Journeay, Denver Dixon, Bob Rose, Monte Blue. *D:* Michael Curtiz; *P:* Robert Arthur; *Adaptation:* John C. Moffett; *Sc:* Frank Davis, Stanley Roberts. (1:49) A biographical depiction of the life of the rodeo star turned humorist from the time he met his wife until his fateful 1935 flight with Wiley Post (Beery). Based on *Uncle Clem's Boy*, the 1941 biographical reminiscences of Betty Blake Rogers. Technicolor.

2535. The Story on Page One (20th Century–Fox/Company of Artists; 1959). *Cast:* Rita Hayworth, Anthony Franciosa, Gig Young, Mildred Dunnock, Hugh Griffith, Sanford Meisner, Robert Burton, Alfred Ryder, Katherine Squire, Raymond Greenleaf, Myrna Fahey, Leon[ard] Penn, Sheridan Comerate, Bill Elliott, Tom Greenway, Jay Adler, Carol Seflinger, Theodore Newton, James O'Rear, Richard LePore, Dan Riss, William Challee, Joe Besser, Joseph McGuinn, Leonard George, Miranda Jones, George Turley, Jerry Sheldon, Bru Danger, Art Salter, Valerie French, Virginia Carroll. *D:* Clifford Odets (final as director); *P:* Jerry Wald; *Sc: & St:* Odets. (2:03) Drama of a woman and her boyfriend who go on trial for killing her abusive husband. CinemaScope.

The Story Without a Name *see* **Without Warning**

2536. A Strange Adventure (Republic; 1956). *Cast:* Joan Evans, Ben Cooper, Marla

English, Jan Merlin, Nick Adams, Peter Miller, Paul Smith, Emlen Davies, Frank Wilcox, Thomas Browne Henry, John Maxwell, Steve Wayne. *D:* William Witney; *As.P:* William J. O'Sullivan; *St: & Sc:* Houston Branch. (1:10) Melodrama of a hot-rodder with a penchant for recklessness who gets mixed up with a female who leads him into a life of crime.

2537. **The Strange Door** (Universal-International; 1951). *Cast:* Charles Laughton, Boris Karloff, Sally Forrest, Richard Stapley, Michael Pate (U.S. film debut), Paul Cavanagh, Alan Napier, William Cottrell, Morgan Farley, Charles Horvath, Edwin Parker. *D:* Joseph Pevney; *P:* Ted Richmond; *Sc:* Jerry Sackheim. (1:21) Melodrama with horror overtones of an evil French nobleman with a taste for vengeance. Based on the 1900 story "The Sire de Maletroit's Door" by Robert Louis Stevenson.

2538. **Strange Fascination** (Columbia; 1952). *Cast:* Hugo Haas, Cleo Moore, Mona Barrie, Rick Vallin, Karen Sharpe, Marc Krah, Genevieve Aumont, Patrick Holmes, Maura Murphy, Brian O'Hara, Anthony Jochim, Gayne Whitman, Roy Engel, Robert Knapp. *D:-P:-St: & Sc:* Hugo Haas. (1:20) Low budget melodrama of a concert pianist (Haas) and how his fascination for a young woman (Moore) leads to his ruin.

2539. **Strange Intruder** (Allied Artists; 1956). *Cast:* Edmund Purdom, Ida Lupino, Ann Harding (final film—ret.), Jacques Bergerac, Gloria Talbott, Carl Benton Reid, Douglas Kennedy, Donald Murphy, Ruby Goodwin, Mimi Gibson, Eric Anderson, Marjorie Bennett. *D:* Irving Rapper; *P:* Lindsley Parsons; *Sc:* David Evans, Warren Douglas. (1:22) Off-the-wall melodrama of a man who agrees to fulfill his war buddy's last request that he kill the latter's two children so that the children's mother will be deprived of their offspring, due to the husband's vindictiveness toward her. Based on the 1952 novel *The Intruder* by Helen Fowler.

2540. **Strange Lady in Town** (Warner/Mervyn LeRoy; 1955). *Cast:* Greer Garson, Dana Andrews, Cameron Mitchell, Lois Smith, Walter Hampden, Pedro Gonzales-Gonzales, Joan Camden, Anthony Numkena [aka: Earl Holliman], Jose Torvay, Adele Jergens, Robert Wilke, Frank DeKova, Russell Johnson, Gregory Walcott, Douglas Kennedy, Ralph Moody (Governor Lew Wallace), Nick Adams (Billy the Kid), Jack Williams, Antonio and Luisa Triana, Joey Costarello, Robert Foulk, Jose Lopez, Louise Lorimer, Helen Spring, Joe Hamilton, George Wallace, Marshall Bradford. *D: & P:* Mervyn LeRoy; *St: & Sc:* Frank Butler. (1:52) Western drama of the romance and the difficulties encountered by a lady medico in Santa Fe, New Mexico, in the 1880s. The title song is sung by Frankie Laine. WarnerColor/CinemaScope.

2541. **The Strange One** (Columbia/Horizon; 1957). *Cast:* Ben Gazzara, Pat Hingle, Peter Mark Richman, Arthur Storch, Paul Richards, Larry Gates, Clifton James, Geoffrey Horne, James Olson, Julie Wilson, George Peppard (film debut). *D:* Jack Garfein; *P:* Sam Spiegel; *Sc:* Calder Willingham (based on his book and play *End as a Man*). (1:40) Drama of a Southern military academy and a cadet who doesn't hesitate to throw his weight around against underclassmen. (G.B. title: *End As a Man*)

2542. **Stranger at My Door** (Republic; 1956). *Cast:* Macdonald Carey, Patricia Medina, Skip Homeier, Stephen Wooten, Louis Jean Heydt, Howard Wright, Slim Pickens, Fred Sherman, Malcolm Atterbury. *D:* William Witney; *As.P:* Sidney Picker; *St: & Sc:* Barry Shipman. (1:25) Offbeat western drama of a minister who puts his family in jeopardy when he attempts to reform a young outlaw.

2543. **Stranger in My Arms** (Universal-International; 1959). *Cast:* June Allyson, Jeff Chandler, Sandra Dee, Mary Astor, Conrad Nagel, Charles Coburn, Peter Graves, Hayden Rorke, Reita Green, Bartlett Robinson, Howard Wendell. *D:* Helmut Kautner; *P:* Ross Hunter; *Sc:* Peter Berneis. (1:28) Drama of attempts by a mother to get the Medal of Honor for her son, believing him to be a hero who was killed in Korea, when in fact the opposite was true. Based on Robert Wilder's 1951 novel *And Ride a Tiger*. CinemaScope.

2544. **Stranger on Horseback** (United Artists/Leonard Goldstein; 1955). *Cast:* Joel McCrea, Kevin McCarthy, Nancy Gates, Miroslava, Jaclynne Greene, John Carradine, John McIntire, Emile Meyer, Robert Cornthwaite, Walter Baldwin, James Bell. *D:* Jacques Tourneur; *P:* Robert Goldstein; *St:* Louis L'Amour; *Sc:* Herb Meadow, Don Martin. (1:06) Western drama of a judge who rides into a town lorded over by a wealthy family, with intent of arresting one of their number for murder. Anscocolor.

2545. **The Stranger Wore A Gun** (Columbia/Scott-Brown; 1953). *Cast:* Randolph

Scott, Claire Trevor, Joan Weldon, George Macready, Alfonso Bedoya, Lee Marvin, Ernest Borgnine, Pierre Watkin, Clem Bevans, Roscoe Ates, Franklyn Farnum, Frank Ellis, Francis McDonald, Terry Frost, Richard Benjamin, Harry Seymour, Joseph Vitale, Paul Maxey, Reed Howes, Frank Scannell, Guy Wilkerson, Edward Earle (final film—ret.), Mary Newton, Mary Lou Holloway, Barry Brooks, Tap Canutt, Al Haskell, Frank Hagney, Phil Tulley, Al Hill, Harry Mendoza, Diana Dawson, Herbert Rawlinson, Britt Wood, James Millican, Jack Woody, Rudy Germaine, Rayford Barnes, Edith Evanson, Guy Teague. *D:* Andre De Toth; *P:* Harry Joe Brown; *As.P:* Randolph Scott; *Sc:* Kenneth Gamet. (1:23) (video) Offbeat western of a former Civil War spy and his dilemma following the war. Based on the novel *Yankee Gold* by John M. Cunningham. Technicolor/3-D.

2546. Strangers on a Train (Warner; 1951). *Cast:* Farley Granger (Guy Haines), Robert Walker (Bruno Antony), Ruth Roman (Anne Morton), Leo G. Carroll (Senator Morton), Patricia Hitchcock (Barbara Morton), Laura Elliot (Miriam Joyce Haines), Marion Lorne (Mrs. Antony), Jonathan Hale (Mr. Antony), Howard St. John (Capt. Turley), John Brown (Prof. Collins), Norma Varden (Mrs. Cunningham), Robert Gist (Det. Leslie Hennessy), John Doucette (Detective Hammond), Jack Cushingham (Fred Reynolds), Dick Wessel (Bill), Ed Clark (Miller), Charles Meredith (Judge Donahue), Edna Holland (Mrs. Joyce), Eddie Hearn (Lt. Campbell), George[s] Renavent (M. Darville), Odette Myrtil (Mme. Darville), Laura Treadwell (Mrs. Anderson), Alfred Hitchcock (man with bass fiddle), Al Hill, Dick Ryan, Sam Flint, Leonard Carey, Tommy Farrell, Rolland Morris, Louis Lettieri, Murray Alper, John Butler, Mary Alan Hokanson, Moyna Andre, J. Louis Johnson, Minna Phillips, Joe Warfield, Ralph Moody, Harry Hines. *D: & P:* Alfred Hitchcock; *Adapt:* Whitfield Cook; *Sc:* Raymond Chandler, Czenzi Ormonde; *Cin:* (AAN-b/w) Robert Burks. (1:41) (video/laserdisc) Critically acclaimed suspense drama of two men who meet on a train and plot "exchange" murders. The Hitchcock film with the memorable climax involving a runaway merry-go-round. The NBR placed it at #8 on their "10 Best" list. Based on the 1950 novel by Patricia Highsmith, it was remade in 1969 as *Once You Kiss a Stranger* and again for TV in 1996 as *Once You Meet a Stranger*. This film was also the inspiration for 1987s *Throw Mama From the Train*.

2547. Strategic Air Command (Paramount; 1955). *Cast:* James Stewart (Lt. Col. Robert "Dutch" Holland), June Allyson (Sally Holland), Frank Lovejoy (Gen. Ennis C. Hawkes), Barry Sullivan (Lt. Col. Rocky Samford), Alex Nicol (Ike Knowland), Bruce Bennett (Gen. Espy), Jay C. Flippen (Doyle), James Millican (Gen. Castle), James Bell (Rev. Thorne), Rosemary DeCamp (Mrs. Thorne), John R. McKee (Capt. Symington), Henry [Harry] Morgan (Sgt. Bible), David Vaile (Capt. Brown), Vernon Rich (Capt. Johnson), Richard Shannon, Don Haggerty, Glenn Denning, Anthony Warde, Strother Martin, Helen Brown, William Hudson, Harlan Warde, [Robert] House Peters, Jr. *D:* Anthony Mann; *P:* Samuel J. Briskin; *St:* (AAN) Beirne Lay, Jr.; *Sc:* Valentine Davies, Lay, Jr. (1:54) (video/laserdisc) Drama of a man who gives up his baseball career to fly jets for the U.S. Air Force. One of the 27 top-grossing films of 1954-55, as well as the studio's biggest grosser of the year. Technicolor/VistaVision. Note: A special award was given by the NBR for the special air photography which was a major highlight of the film.

2548. Street Bandits (Republic; 1951). *Cast:* Penny Edwards, Robert Clarke, Ross Ford, Roy Barcroft, John Eldredge, Helen Wallace, Arthur Walsh, Harry Hayden, Emmett Vogan, Jane Adams, Charles Wagenheim, Richard Bartlett, Norman Field, Robert Long, Dick Cogan. *D:* R.G. Springsteen; *As.P:* William Lackey; *St: & Sc:* Milton Raison. (0:54) Programmer crime melodrama of a pair of young lawyers who go against their principles when they take on a mobster as their client.

2549. Street Fighter (Joseph Brenner-States Rights/North Star; 1959). *Cast:* Vic Savage [aka: A.N. White], Ann Atmar, Marlene Robbins, Ahmed Bey. *D: & Sc:* A.N. White; *P:* Bradley N. Nichols, Karl G. Kappel. (1:11) Indy melodrama of a streetwise tough whose thinking toward the world around him changes when a girl he cares for is senselessly killed.

2550. Street of Darkness (Republic/Robert Keys; 1958). *Cast:* Robert Keys, John Close, James Seay, Julie Gibson, Sheila Ryan (final film—ret.), Dub Taylor, Henry Rowland, Richard Crockett, Val Winter, Edwin Nelson, Walter Hamlin, Steve Raines, Pork Chops & Kidney Stew (themselves). *D:* Robert Walker; *P:* Robert Keys; *As.P:* Nathan Barragar, Joseph H. Plunkett; *St: & Sc:* Malvin Wald, Maurice Tombragel; *Song:* "Born for Love" Frank Worth,

Irving Bibo (sung by Gibson). (1:00) Programmer of two adventurers who get mixed up with a Cuban narcotics smuggling ring. Filmed on location in New Orleans.

2551. Street of Sinners (United Artists/ Security Pictures; 1957). *Cast:* George Montgomery, Geraldine Brooks, Nehemiah Persoff, Marilee Earle, William Harrigan, Stephen Joyce, Clifford David, Diana Milay, Sandra Rehn, Danny Dennis, Ted Irwin, Melvin Decker, Lou Gilbert, Barry McGuire, Elia Clark, Jack Hartley, Billy James, Liza Balesca, Eva Gerson, John Holland, Bob Duffy, Joey Faye, Fred Herrick, Charlie Jordan, John Barry, Wolfe Barzell, Stephen Elliott. *D: & P:* William Berke; *St:* Philip Yordan; *Sc:* John McPartland. (1:16) Melodrama of a rookie cop in New York and the various things he has to deal with while on duty, including a woman's suicide.

2552. A Streetcar Named Desire (Warner/Chas. K. Feldman Group; 1951). *Cast:* Vivien Leigh (AA + "Best Actress" by the New York Film Critics and the Venice Film Festival along with a nomination for same at the 1952 British Academy Awards/Blanche Dubois), Marlon Brando (AAN/Stanley Kowalski), Kim Hunter (AA-BSA/Stella Kowalski), Karl Malden (AA-BSA/Mitch), Rudy Bond (Steve), Peg Hillias (Eunice), Nick Dennis (Pablo), Wright King, Edna Thomas, Ann Dere, Richard Garrick, Mickey Kuhn, Chester Jones, Marietta Canty, Charles Wagenheim, Maxie Thrower, Lyle Latell, Mel Archer. *D:* (AAN + "Best Director" by the New York Film Critics) Elia Kazan; *P:* (AAN-Best Picture + "Best Film of the Year" by the New York Film Critics), Charles K. Feldman; *Adaptation:* Oscar Saul; *Sc:* (AAN) Tennessee Williams [based on his own play]; *Cin:* (AAN-b/w) Harry Stradling; *ASD:* (AA-b/w) Richard Day (art director), George James Hopkins (sets); *Music:* (AAN) Alex North; *Costumes:* (AAN-b/w) Lucinda Ballard; *Sound:* (AAN) Nathan Levinson. (2:02) (video/laserdisc) Acclaimed drama based on Tennessee Williams play of the tense relationships between a husband and wife and her sister when the latter moves in with them. A #2 placement was given it on the "10 Best" list of *Film Daily*, while the same lists of the NBR and the *New York Times* gave it a #6 placement. A box office gross of $4,250,000 made it one of the 23 top-grossing films of 1951-52. In 1993 this film was re-released with several minutes of footage restored that was censored in 1951 due to "sexual content." Remade twice for TV, one of which was in 1984 with Ann-Margret in her acclaimed portrayal of "Blanche Dubois." Note: At the Venice Film Festival, the film received a Special Award "for having reproduced a stage play on the screen, poetically interpreting the lost humanity of the characters, thanks to masterful direction."

2553. Streets of Ghost Town (Columbia; 1950). *Cast:* Charles Starrett, Mary Ellen Kay, Smiley Burnette, Stanley Andrews, John Cason, Don Kay Reynolds, Frank Fenton, George Chesebro, Jack Ingram, Ozie Waters and His Colorado Rangers. *D:* Ray Nazarro; *P:* Colbert Clark; *St: & Sc:* Barry Shipman; *Songs:* "Streets of Laredo" (sung by Burnette) and "Oh, Susanna" (sung by Waters). (0:54) The search for hidden ghost town gold is the plot of this "Durango Kid" series western.

2554. Strictly Dishonorable (MGM; 1951). *Cast:* Ezio Pinza, Janet Leigh, Millard Mitchell, Gale Robbins, Arthur Franz, Maria Palmer, Esther Minciotti, Silvio Minciotti, Sandro Giglio, Hugh Sanders, Mario Siletti. *D:-P:-St: & Sc:* Norman Panama, Melvin Frank. (1:26) An opera singer marries an infatuated fan to save her reputation. Based on the play by Preston Sturges, it was previously filmed by Universal in 1931.

Strictly for Pleasure (G.B. title) *see* **The Perfect Furlough**

2555. The Strip (MGM; 1951). *Cast:* Mickey Rooney (Stanley Maxton), Sally Forrest (Jane Tafford), William Demarest (Fluff), James Craig (Delwyn "Sonny" Johnson), Kay Brown (Edna), Tommy Rettig (Artie), Vic Damone (singer), Louis Armstrong and Band (band), Monica Lewis (singer), Jack Teagarden (singer), Tom Powers (Det. Bonnabel), Jonathan Cott (Behr), Tommy Farrell (Boynton), Myrna Dell (Paulette Ardrey), Jacquline Fontaine (Frieda), Earl "Fatha" Hines, Barney Bigard, Robert Foulk, John McGuire, Russell Trent, Fred Grahame, Don Haggerty, William Tannen, Frank Hyers, John Maxwell, Sherry Hall, Tom Quinn, Fred Datig, Jr., Dan Foster, John Richards, Dolores Castle, Joyce Jameson, Art Lewis, Samuel London, Larry Hudson, Roger Moore, Sam Finn, Tay Dunne, Bert Davidson, Donald Kerr, Sid Frolich, Helen Spring, Alex Frazer, Lester Dorr, Robert Malcolm, Earle Hodgins, Bette Arlen, Betty Jane Howarth, Carl Saxe, Joel Allen, Wilson Wood, Dee Turnell, Carmen Clifford, Ward Ellis, Jack Regas, Leo Scott, Bert May. *D:* Leslie Kardos; *P:* Joe Pasternak; *St: & Sc:*

Allen Rivkin; *Song:* "A Kiss to Build a Dream On" (AAN-Best Song) Bert Kalmar, Harry Ruby, Oscar Hammerstein II; *Musical numbers:* "Ain't Misbehavin'" Fats Waller, Andy Razaf (by Rooney and Armstrong), "Basin Street Blues" Spencer Williams (by Armstrong and Teagarden), "Shadrack" Robert MacGimsey (by Armstrong), "Rose Room" Art Hickman, Harry Williams (by Armstrong), "La Bota" Charles Wolcott, Haven Gillespie II (by Lewis) and "Don't Blame Me" Jimmy McHugh, Dorothy Fields (by Damone). (1:25) Musical drama of a former drummer involved with Hollywood's criminal element who helps a girl get started in a movie career.

Stronger Than Fear (G.B. title) *see* **Edge of Doom**

2556. The Student Prince (MGM; 1954). *Cast:* Edmund Purdom [singing voice dubbed by Mario Lanza], Ann Blyth, John Ericson, Louis Calhern, Edmund Gwenn, S.Z. "Cuddles" Sakall (final film—d. 1955), Betta St. John, John Williams, Richard Anderson, Evelyn Varden, John Hoyt, Steve Rowland, John Qualen, Roger Allen, Chris Warfield, Gilbert Legay, Archer MacDonald, Charles Davis. *D:* Richard Thorpe; *P:* Joe Pasternak; *Sc:* William Ludwig, Sonya Levien; *Songs:* Golden Days," "Serenade," "Deep in My Heart," "To the Inn We're Marching," "The Drinking Song," "Come Boys, Let's All Be Gay, Boys" Sigmund Romberg, Dorothy Donnelly [revised lyrics by Paul Francis Webster], "I'll Walk With God," "Beloved" and "Summertime in Heidelberg" Nicholas Brodszky, Webster [written for the film] and "Gaudeamus Igitur" (traditional); *Choreography:* Hermes Pan. (1:47) (video/laserdisc) The only filmed musical version of Sigmund Romberg's 1924 operetta which he adapted from the 1902 play *Old Heidelberg* by Rudolph Bleichman and the 1904 book *Karl Heinrich* by Wilhelm Meyer-Foerster. Heir to the throne, Prince Karl Heinrich, before assuming his royal responsibilities, falls in love with a Heidelberg barmaid during his last days of freedom. First filmed as *Old Heidelberg* (Triangle/Fine Arts; 1915) by D.W. Griffith (in 5 reels) with Wallace Reid. Remade by MGM in 1927 as *The Student Prince* (aka: *The Student Prince in Old Heidelberg*) with Ramon Novarro. Germany also released two versions of the story *The Student Prince*, a 1923 silent and *Alt-Heidelberg* in 1959. Technicolor/CinemaScope.

2557. Submarine Command (Paramount; 1951). *Cast:* William Holden, Nancy Olson, William Bendix, Don Taylor, Darryl Hickman, Arthur Franz, Jack Kelly, Moroni Olsen, Peggy Webber, Jack Gregson, Don Dunning, Jerry Paris, Charles Meredith, Philip Van Zandt, Gordon Polk, Walter Reed, Noel Neill, Fred Zendar, John V. Close, George Wallace, Richard Gerggren, Harold Fong, Jerry James. *D:* John Farrow; *P:* Joseph Sistrom; *St: & Sc:* Jonathan Latimer. (1:27) A submarine commander proves his mettle off the coast of Korea, during that conflict.

2558. Submarine Seahawk (American International/Golden State Prods.; 1959). *Cast:* John Bentley, Brett Halsey, Wayne Heffley, Steve Mitchell, Henry McCann, Frank Gerstle, Paul Maxwell, Jan Brooks, Mabel Rea, Leon Tyler, Nicky Blair, Hal Bogart, Don Fenwick, Frank Watkins, Marilyn Hanold, Dolores Domasin, Robin Priest, Frank Ray, Brian Wood, Scott Peters, Ted Fish, Vince Williams, Alan Aric, Howard Hampton. *D:* Spencer G. Bennet; *P:* Alex Gordon; *Ex.P:* Lou Rusoff; *St: & Sc:* Rusoff, Owen Harris. (1:23) Stock World War II footage is included in this drama of a submarine on a secret reconnaissance patrol against the Japanese in the Pacific. Originally paired on a double bill with *Paratroop Command* (q.v.).

Such Men Are Dangerous (G.B. title) *see* **The Racers**

2559. Sudden Danger (Allied Artists; 1955). *Cast:* Bill Elliott, Tom Drake, Beverly Garland, Dayton Lummis, Helene Stanton, Lucien Littlefield, Minerva Urecal, Lyle Talbot, Frank Jenks, Pierre Watkin, John Close, Ralph Gamble. *D:* Hubert Cornfield (directorial debut); *P:* Ben Schwalb; *St:* Daniel Ullman; *Sc:* D. Ullman, Elwood Ullman. (1:25) Crime melodrama of a woman's murder, with the blind son as a chief suspect.

Sudden Death (TV title) *see* **Fast on the Draw**

2560. Sudden Fear (RKO/Joseph Kaufman Prods.; 1952). *Cast:* Joan Crawford (AAN/Myra Hudson), Jack Palance (AAN-BSA/ Lester Blaine), Gloria Grahame (Irene Neves), Bruce Bennett (Steve Kearney), Virginia Huston (Ann Taylor), Touch [Mike] Connors (film debut/ Junior Kearney). *D:* David Miller; *P:* Joseph Kaufman; *Sc:* Lenore Coffee, Robert Smith; *Cin:* (AAN-b/w) Charles B. Lang, Jr.; *Costumes:* (AAN-b/w) Sheila O'Brien; *Song:* "Afraid" Elmer Bernstein, Jack Brooks. (1:50) (video) Suspense thriller of a wealthy female mystery writer who begins some specialized scheming of her own when she learns her new husband is plotting to do away with her. Based on a 1948 novel by Edna Sherry, this audience pleaser became one of the 23 top-grossing films of 1951-52, as well as receiving critical acclaim.

2561. Suddenly (United Artists/Libra Prods.; 1954). *Cast:* Frank Sinatra, Sterling Hayden, James Gleason, Nancy Gates, Kim Charney, Paul Frees, Christopher Dark, Willis Bouchey, Paul Wexler, Jim Lilburn, Charles Smith, Kem Dibbs, Clark Howat, Dan White, Richard Collier, Roy Engel, Ted Stanhope, Charles Wagenheim, John Beradino. *D:* Lewis Allen; *P:* Robert Bassler; *St: & Sc:* Richard Sale. (1:17) (video/laserdisc) Taut drama of three assassins who after selecting a home near the train station, hold the resident family hostage while waiting to kill the president of the United States when he arrives via train and makes a stop at Suddenly, California. Computer-colored prints have been produced of this minor classic after it became scarce following the assassination of John F. Kennedy in 1963.

2562. Suddenly Last Summer (Columbia/Horizon Ltd.–Academy Picts.–Camp Films; 1959). *Cast:* Elizabeth Taylor (AAN/Catherine Holly), Montgomery Clift (Dr. John Cukrowicz), Katharine Hepburn (AAN/Mrs. Violet Venable), Albert Dekker (Dr. Hockstader), Mercedes McCambridge (Mrs. Holly), Gary Raymond (George Holly), Mavis Villiers (Mrs. Foxhill), Patricia Marmont (Nurse Benson), Joan Young (Sister Felicity), Maria Britneva (Lucy), Sheila Robbins, David Cameron, Roberta Woolley. *D:* Joseph L. Mankiewicz; *P:* Sam Spiegel; *Sc:* Gore Vidal, Tennessee Williams; *ASD:* (AAN-b/w) Oliver Messel, William Kellner (art directors), Scott Slimon (sets). (1:54) (video/laserdisc) Drama of a wealthy woman (Hepburn) and the relating of events of the preceding summer when her son met his death. Based on "Garden District" and "Suddenly," two one-act plays by Tennessee Williams. The censors lightened up when the film was remade for British TV in 1992. It placed #8 on the "10 Best" list of the NBR, and on the same list of *Film Daily* in 1960, it placed #7. One of the 28 top-grossing films of 1959-60. Computer-colored prints have been produced.

2563. Sugarfoot (Warner; 1951). *Cast:* Randolph Scott, Adele Jergens, Raymond Massey, S.Z. Sakall, Robert Warwick, Gene Evans, Arthur Hunnicutt, Hugh Sanders, Hope Landin, Hank Worden, Edward Hearn, John Hamilton, Cliff Clark, Kenneth MacDonald, Dan White, Paul Newlan, Philo McCullough. *D:* Edwin L. Marin; *P:* Saul Elkins; *Adaptation:* Russell Hughes [of the 1942 novel by Clarence Buddington Kelland]; *Song:* "Oh, He Looked Like He Might Buy Wine" Ray Heindorf, Sammy Cahn (sung by Jergens). (1:20) Technicolor western of two men, a rancher who wants to settle down and a rival, who have a showdown in Prescott, Arizona. (Retitled: *A Swirl of Glory*)

2564. Suicide Battalion (American International/Zuma Prods.; 1958). *Cast:* Michael Connors, John Ashley, Jewell Lain, Russ Bender, Bing Russell, Scott Peters, Walter Maslow, John McNamara, Clifford Kawada, Bob Tetrick, Marjorie Stapp, Jan England, Isabelle Cooley, Hilo Hattie, Sammy Tong, Gordon Barnes, Art Gilmore, Jackie Joseph. *D:* Edward L. Cahn; *Ex. P:* Samuel Z. Arkoff; *P:-St: & Sc:* Lou Rusoff. (1:19) (video) Low budget World War II melodrama of a five-man demolition team sent into the Philippines to destroy American papers left behind during the evacuation of those islands prior to the Japanese invasion. Originally half of a double bill program with *Jet Attack* (q.v.).

2565. Summer Love (Universal-International; 1958). *Cast:* John Saxon, Judi Meredith, John Wilder, Rod McKuen, Jill St. John, Molly Bee, George Winslow, Fay Wray, Edward C. Platt, Shelley Fabares, Gordon Gebert, Beverly Washburn, Bob Courtney, Troy Donahue, Hylton Socher, Marjorie Durant, Walter Reed, *and as the Ding-A-Lings:* Rock Murphy (guitar), Robert Bain (bass guitar), Plas Johnson, Jr. (tenor sax), David Pell (baritone sax), Alvin Stoller (drums), Ray Sherman (piano), Mike Pacheco (bongos). *D:* Charles Haas; *P:* William Grady, Jr.; *St: & Sc:* William Raynor, Herbert Margolis; *Songs:* "To Know You Is To Love You," "Summer Love," "Beatin' on the Bongos," "Ding-A-Ling" Henry Mancini, Bill Carey, "Calypso Rock" Rod McKuen, "Magic Penny" Malvina Reynolds and "So Good Night" Milton Rosen, Everett Carter. (1:25) Romance and seven rock 'n' roll numbers pretty much account for this teen oriented sequel to *Rock Pretty Baby* (q.v.). Paired on a double bill program with equally teen oriented *The Big Beat* (q.v.).

Summer Madness (G.B. title) *see* **Summertime**

2566. A Summer Place (Warner; 1959). *Cast:* Richard Egan (Ken Jorgenson), Dorothy

McGuire (Sylvia Hunter), Sandra Dee (Molly Jorgenson), Arthur Kennedy (Bart Hunter), Troy Donahue (received *Photoplay* "Gold Medal" for "Best Newcomer"/John Hunter), Constance Ford (Helen Jorgenson), Beulah Bondi (Mrs. Hamilton Hamble), Jack Richardson (Claude Andrews), Martin Eric (Todd Hasper), Junius Matthews (Mr. Hamble), Peter Constanti (Captain), Gertrude Flynn (Mrs. Carter), Marshall Bradford (Dr. Matthias), Phil Chambers (sheriff), Robert Griffin (Englehardt), Roberta Shore (Anne Talbert), Ann Doran (Mrs. Talbert), Eleanor Audley (Mrs. Harrington), Howard Hoffman (Alvin Frost), Arthur Space, George Taylor, Dale J. Nicholson, Lewis Martin, Helen Wallace, Everett Glass, Richard Deacon, Nancy Matthews, Susan Odin, Cheryl Holdridge, Bonnie Franklin. *D:-P: & Sc:* Delmer Daves. (2:10) (video/laserdisc) Hit Technicolor "sex" drama of love and lust at a Maine resort house [which incidentally was built by architect Frank Lloyd Wright]. The hit theme song was part of the soundtrack by Max Steiner, and the popularity of the film made it one of the 28 top-grossing films of 1959-60. Based on the 1958 novel by Sloan Wilson.

2567. Summer Stock (MGM; 1950). *Cast:* Judy Garland (Jane Falbury), Gene Kelly (Joe D. Ross), Eddie Bracken (Orville Wingait), Gloria DeHaven (Abigail Falbury), Marjorie Main (Esme), Phil Silvers (Herb Blake), Ray Collins (Jasper G. Wingait), Carleton Carpenter (Artie), Nita Bieber (Sarah Higgins), Hans Conried (Harrison I. Keath), Paul E. Burns (Frank), Erville Alderson (Zeb), Almira Sessions (Constance Fliggerton), Kathryn Sheldon (Amy Fliggerton), Carol Haney, Arthur Loew, Jr., Jimmy Thompson, Bette Arlen, Bunny Waters, Jack Gargan, Michael Chapin, Teddy Infuhr, [A.] Cameron Grant, Jack Daley, Reginald Simpson, Eddie Dunn. *D:* Charles Walters; *P:* Joe Pasternak; *St:* Sy Gomberg; *Sc:* George Wells, Gomberg; *Songs:* "Friendly Star," "Mem'ry Island," "Dig-Dig-Dig for Your Dinner," "If You Feel Like Singing, Sing," "Happy Harvest," "Blue Jean Polka" Mack Gordon, Harry Warren; "Howdy Neighbor," "All for You," "Portland Fancy," "Get Happy" Ted Koehler, Harold Arlen; "Heavenly Music" Saul Chaplin; "You Wonderful You" Gordon, Warren, Jack Brooks, Chaplin. (1:49) (video/laserdisc) Hit musical of a girl who acquires a taste for show business when a theater troupe takes over her farm. One of the 28 top-grossing films of 1949-50. Technicolor.

2568. Summertime (United Artists/LFP-Lopert; 1955). *Cast:* Katharine Hepburn (AAN/Jane Hudson), Rossano Brazzi (Renato Di Rossi), Isa Miranda (Signora Fiorini), Darren McGavin (Eddie Yaeger), Mari Aldon (Phyl Yaeger/final film—ret.), Jane Rose (Mrs. McIlhenny), MacDonald Barke (Mr. McIlhenny), Gaitano Audiero (Mauro), Jeremy Spenser (Vito Di Rossi), Virginia Simeon (Giovann), Andre Morell. *D:* (AAN + "Best Director" by the New York Film Critics) David Lean; *Ex.P:* Alexander Korda; *P:* Ilya Lopert; *Sc:* Lean, H.E. Bates. (1:39) (video/laserdisc) Acclaimed romantic drama of the brief affair between an American spinster and a married antique dealer in Venice, Italy. A co-production between Great Britain and the U.S.A., it was filmed on location in Italy and based on the stage play "The Time of the Cuckoo" by Arthur Laurents. It placed #9 on the "10 Best" list of *Film Daily* as well as being in nomination at the British Academy Awards. The New York Film Critics had it in nomination for "Best Picture." (G.B. title: *Summer Madness*) Eastmancolor.

2569. The Sun Also Rises (20th Century-Fox; 1957). *Cast:* Tyrone Power, Ava Gardner, Mel Ferrer, Errol Flynn, Eddie Albert, Gregory Ratoff, Juliet Greco (U.S. debut), Marcel Dalio, Henry Daniell, Bob Cunningham, Danik Patisson, Robert J. Evans, Rebecca Iturbi, Eduardo Noriega, Jacqueline Evans, Carlos Musquiz, Carlos David Ortigos, Lilia Guizar, Lee Morgan, Ninos Cantoros De Morelia (choir). *D:* Henry King; *P:* Darryl F. Zanuck; *Sc:* Peter Viertel. (2:09) A romantic drama set among American expatriates living in Spain following World War I. The film came in at $5,000,000 and became a moneymaker for Fox. Filmed in Mexico and Pamplona, Spain, utilizing the running of the bulls in a sequence which gained fame for the film. Based on the 1926 novel by Ernest Hemingway, it was remade as a TV movie in 1984. DeLuxe color/CinemaScope.

The Sun Demon *see* **The Hideous Sun Demon**

2570. The Sun Sets at Dawn (Eagle-Lion/Holiday; 1950). *Cast:* Sally Parr, Philip Shawn, Walter Reed, Lee Frederick [aka: Robert Peyton], Houseley Stevenson, Howard St. John, Louise Lorimer, Raymond Bramley, Charles Meredith, Jack Reynolds, King Donovan, Charles Arnt, Sam Edwards, Percy Helton, Perry Ivins. *D: & Sc:* Paul H. Sloane (final film—ret.); *P:* Sloane, Helen H. Rathvon. (1:11) Melodrama of a young man sentenced to die in the electric chair for a crime he didn't commit.

Originally ran on a double bill with *Paper Gallows*, a British production.

2571. The Sun Shines Bright (Republic/Argosy; 1953). *Cast:* Charles Winninger, Arleen Whelan, John Russell, Stepin Fetchit (repeating his role from the 1934 version), Russell Simpson, Ludwig Stossel, Francis Ford (final film—d. 1953), Paul Hurst, Mitchell Lewis, Grant Withers, Milburn Stone, Dorothy Jordan, Elzie Emanuel, Henry O'Neill, Slim Pickens, James Kirkwood, Ernest Whitman, Trevor Bardette, Eve March, Hal Baylor, Jane Darwell, Ken Williams, Clarence Muse, Mae Marsh, Jack Pennick, Patrick Wayne. *D:* John Ford; *P:* Ford, Merian C. Cooper; *Sc:* Laurence Stallings; *Songs:* "Tenting on the Old Camp Ground," "My Old Kentucky Home" Stephen Foster. (1:30) (video) 19th century Americana of an honest judge in a small southern town who finds consistent challenges for his job. Based on "The Sun Shines Bright," "The Mob from Massac" and "The Lord Provides," three stories by Irvin S. Cobb. A remake of Ford's 1934 production *Judge Priest* (Fox Film) which starred Will Rogers. In nomination at the British Academy Awards. Video prints (a director's print) have a longer running time than the original theatrical prints. Note: John Ford's personal favorite of all his films.

2572. The Sundowners (Eagle-Lion/Nuys Theatre Corp.; 1950). *Cast:* Robert Preston, Robert Sterling, Chill Wills, John Litel, Cathy Downs, Jack Elam, Don Haggerty, John Barrymore, Jr. [aka: John Drew Barrymore/film debut], Stanley Price, Clem Fuller, Frank Cordell, Dave Kashner. *D:* George Templeton; *P: & Sc:* Alan LeMay. (1:23) (video) Range war western drama of two law-abiding brothers who are opposed by a third brother, who is anything but law-abiding. Based on Mr. LeMay's 1934 novel *Thunder in the Dust*, it originally ran with *Never Fear* (q.v.) on a double bill program. (G.B. title: *Thunder in the Dust*) Technicolor.

2573. Sunny Side of the Street (Columbia; 1951). *Cast:* Frankie Laine (himself), Billy Daniels (himself), Terry Moore, Jerome Courtland, Tony Arden, Audrey Long, Dick Wesson, Lynn Bari, William Tracy, Willard Waterman, Jonathan Hale, Amanda Blake, Paul Dubov, Peter Price, Benny Payne. *D:* Richard Quine; *P:* Jonie Taps; *St:* Harold Conrad; *Sc:* Lee Loeb; *Songs:* "I Get a Kick Out of You" Cole Porter, "On the Sunny Side of the Street" Dorothy Fields, Jimmy McHugh, "Let's Fall in Love" Ted Koehler, Harold Arlen, "I'm Gonna Live Till I Die" Al Hoffman, Mann Curtis and "I May Be Wrong But I Think You're Wonderful" Harry Ruskin, Henry Sullivan. (1:11) Low budget musical of a singer trying to make it on television. SuperCinecolor.

2574. Sunset Blvd. (Paramount; 1950). *Cast:* William Holden (AAN/Joe Gillis), Gloria Swanson (AAN + "Best Actress" by the NBR/ Norma Desmond), Erich Von Stroheim (AAN-BSA/Max Von Mayerling), Nancy Olson (AAN-BSA/Betty Schaefer), Fred Clark (Sheldrake), Jack Webb (Artie Green), Lloyd Gough (Morino), Cecil B. DeMille (himself), Hedda Hopper (herself), Buster Keaton (himself), Anna Q. Nilsson (herself), H.B. Warner (himself), Ray Evans (himself), Jay Livingston (himself), Sidney Skolsky (himself), Fanklyn Farnum (undertaker), Bert Moorhouse (Gordon Cole), Julia Faye (Hisham), Bernice Mosk (herself), Robert Emmett O'Connor (Jonesy), Gerry Ganzer (Connie), Larry Blake, Charles Dayton, Eddie Dew, Michael Branden [aka: Archie Twitchell], Ruth Clifford, E. Mason Hopper, Virginia Randolph, Stanley Johnson, William Sheehan, Gertrude Astor, Frank O'Connor, Eva Novak, Gertie [Gertrude] Messinger, John "Skins" Miller, Tommy Ivo, Emmett Smith, Ottola Nesmith, Howard Negley, Ken Christy, Len Hendry. *D:* (AAN) Billy Wilder; *P:* (AAN-Best Picture) Charles Brackett; *St: & Sc:* (AA) Brackett, Wilder, D.M. Marshman, Jr.; *Cin:* (AAN-b/w) John F. Seitz; *ASD:* (AA-b/w) Hans Dreier, John Meehan (art directors), Sam Comer, Ray Moyer (sets); *Music:* (AA-non musical) Franz Waxman; *Editors:* (AAN) Arthur Schmidt, Doane Harrison. (1:50) (video/laserdisc) Critically acclaimed hit bittersweet black comedy of a faded Hollywood actress from the silent screen, a Hollywood screenwriter she takes into her home and her butler, formerly one of her directors. This classic bit of "Hollywood on Hollywood" was voted "Best Film of the Year" by the NBR and placed #7 on the "10 Best" list of the *New York Times*. It was also in nomination for "Best Picture" 'with the New York Film Critics. Based on the story "A Can of Beans" by Brackett and Wilder, it also became a Broadway musical in the 1990s. One of the 28 top-grossing films of 1949-50.

2575. Sunset in the West (Republic; 1950) *Cast:* Roy Rogers, Estelita Rodriguez, Penny Edwards, Gordon Jones, Foy Willing and Riders of the Purple Sage, Will Wright, Pierre Watkin, Charles LaTorre, William Tannen, Gaylord [Steve] Pendleton, Paul E. Burns, Dorothy Ann White, Trigger (horse). *D:* William Witney; *P:*

Edward J. "Eddy" White; *St: & Sc:* Gerald Geraghty; *Songs:* "Rollin' Wheels," "Sunset in the West" Foy Willing and "When a Pretty Girl Passes By" Jack Elliott, Aaron Gonzales (sung by Rodriguez). (1:07) Gun smugglers are also causing train wrecks in this Roy Rogers series western. Trucolor. Originally ran on a double bill program with *Prisoners in Petticoats* (q.v.).

2576. Superman and the Mole Men (Lippert; 1951). *Cast:* George Reeves (Clark Kent/Superman), Phyllis Coates (Lois Lane), Jeff Corey, Walter Reed, J. Farrell MacDonald, Beverly Washburn, Stanley Andrews, Ray Walker, Hal K. Dawson, Frank Reicher, Stephen Carr, Margia Dean, Paul Burns, Irene Martin, Byron Foulger, John Phillips, John Baer, Adrienne Marden and as the mole men: Jack Banbury, Billy Curtis, Jerry Marvin, Tony Baris. *D:* Lee Sholem; *P:* Robert Maxwell, Barney A. Sarecky; *St: & Sc:* Richard Fielding [a pseudonym of Robert Maxwell]. (1:07) (video) Feature film debut of "Superman," a character created by Jerry Siegel and Joe Schuster, previously depicted only in cartoons and serials. The story concerns four mole men which emerge from their home at the center of the earth after being disturbed by the drilling of oil men. They become the targets of fearful townspeople. A prelude to the popular TV series of the 1950s, this film was edited and shown in two parts on the TV series as "The Unknown People." (G.B. title: *Superman and the Strange People*)

2577. Surrender (Republic; 1950). *Cast:* Vera Ralston, John Carroll, Walter Brennan, Francis Lederer, William Ching, Maria Palmer, Jane Darwell, Roy Barcroft, Paul Fix, Esther Dale, Edward Norris, Howland Chamberlain, Norman Budd, Nacho Galindo, Jeff York, Mickey Simpson, Dick Elliott, Ralph Dunn, Virginia Farmer, J. Louis Johnson, Elizabeth Dunne, Cecil Elliott, Kenne Duncan, Glenn Strange, Paul Stader, Wesley Hopper, Tex Terry, Charles Morton, Doris Cole, Al Rhein, Al Murphy, Tina Menard, Frank Dae, Petra Silva, Tony Roux, Shelby Bacon, Fred Hoose. *D:* Allan Dwan; *P:* Herbert J. Yates; *St:* James Edward Grant; *Sc:* Grant, Sloan Nibley; *Title song:* Jack Elliott, John Carroll. (1:30) Offbeat western of a married woman who resorts to bigamy to beat the law. When her first husband shows up she kills him and tries to flee across the border with her 2nd husband's friend.

2578. Surrender—Hell! (Allied Artists/ Cory Film Corp.; 1959). *Cast:* Keith Andes, Susan Cabot, Paraluman, Nestor de Villa. *D:* John Barnwell; *Ex.P:* Paul Schreibman, Newton P. Jacobs; *P:* Edmund Goldman; *Sc:* Barnwell; *Narration:* Charles Martin. (1:25) Fact based World War II drama of Colonel Donald D. Blackburn of the U.S. Army who organized Philippine villagers and over a thousand headhunters in an all out attempt to stop the Japanese takeover of the Philippine Islands. Officially his force was known as the 11th Infantry of the United States and fought under orders from General Douglas MacArthur. Based on the 1955 book *Blackburn's Headhunters* by Philip Harkins. The real Donald Blackburn served as technical advisor on the film.

2579. Susan Slept Here (RKO; 1954). *Cast:* Dick Powell (final film as actor/Mark), Debbie Reynolds (Susan), Anne Francis (Isabelle), Alvy Moore (Virgil), Glenda Farrell (Maude), Horace McMahon (Maizel the cop), Herb Vigran (Hanlon the cop), Les Tremayne (Harvey), Mara Lane (Marilyn), Maidie Norman (Georgette), Rita Johnson (Dr. Rawley), Ellen Corby, Benny Rubin, Barbara Darrow, Sue Carlton, Oliver Blake, Louella O. Parsons (voice only). *D:* Frank Tashlin; *P:* Harriet Parsons; *Sc:* Alex Gottlieb; *Songs:* "Hold My Hand" (AAN-Best Song) Jack Lawrence, Richard Myers (sung by Don Cornell), "Susan Slept Here" Lawrence; *Sound:* (AAN) John O. Aalberg. (1:38) (video/laserdisc) "Sex" comedy of a writer (Powell) researching juvenile delinquency who finds himself strapped with an 18-year-old female delinquent (Reynolds), causing assorted problems. Based on the 1952 play *Susan* by Alex Gottlieb and Steve Fisher, it went on to become one of the 25 top-grossing films of 1953-54. Technicolor.

Suspected (G.B. title) *see* **Texas Dynamo**

Swamp Diamonds *see* **Swamp Women**

2580. Swamp Women (Favorite Films of California/Woolner Bros.; 1956). *Cast:* Carole Mathews, Marie Windsor, Beverly Garland, Jil Jarmyn, Touch [Mike] Connors, Susan Cummings, Lou Place, Jonathan Haze, Ed Nelson. *D:* Roger Corman; *P:* Bernard Woolner; *St: & Sc:* David Stern. (1:13) (video) Melodrama of a policewoman who goes undercover to hook up with three tough babes incarcerated for diamond theft, with the intent they all escape and head for the hiding place of the diamonds. Color. (aka: *Cruel Swamp*) (video & alternate title: *Swamp Diamonds*) A small cult following.

2581. The Swan (MGM; 1956). *Cast:* Grace Kelly (final film—released before *High Society*, q.v.), Alec Guinness, Louis Jourdan, Agnes Moorehead, Jessie Royce Landis, Brian Aherne, Estelle Winwood, Leo G. Carroll, Robert Coote, Edith Barrett (final film—ret.), Doris Lloyd. *D:* Charles Vidor; *P:* Dore Schary; *Sc:* John Dighton. (1:52) (video/laserdisc) Ferenc Molnar's play of romance amidst royalty is lavishly brought to the screen for the third time, precisely timed for its star's marriage into the royal house of Monaco. This ruritanian romance was first filmed by Paramount in 1925 with Frances Howard and remade in 1930 (U.A./Art Cinema) with Lillian Gish as *One Romantic Night*. Location filming at the "Biltmore Estate" in North Carolina. Eastmancolor/CinemaScope.

2582. Sweet Smell of Success (United Artists/Norma-Curtleigh Prods.; 1957). *Cast:* Burt Lancaster, Tony Curtis, Susan Harrison, Martin Milner, Sam Levene, Barbara Nichols, Jeff Donnell, Joseph Leon, Edith Atwater, Emile Meyer, Joe Frisco, David White, Lawrence Dobkin, Lurene Tuttle, Queenie Smith, Autumn Russell, Jay Adler, Lewis Charles, Chico Hamilton Quintet. *D:* Alexander MacKendrick (U.S. directorial debut); *P:* James Hill; *Sc:* Ernest Lehman, Clifford Odets. (1:36) (video/laserdisc) Drama of a ruthless New York gossip columnist and his association with a lowlife press agent, set against the night life of New York City where it was filmed. Too intense for the 1957 audience, the film has gathered a latter-day following. Based on "Tell Me About It Tomorrow," a novelette by Mr. Lehman which appeared in *Cosmopolitan*.

2583. Sweethearts on Parade (Republic; 1953). *Cast:* Ray Middleton, Lucille Norman, Eileen Christy, Bill Shirley, Estelita [Rodriguez], Clinton Sundberg, Harry Carey, Jr., Irving Bacon, Leon Tyler, Marjorie Wood, Mara Corday, Ann McCrea, Tex Terry, Emory Parnell. *D:* Allan Dwan; *Ex.P:* Herbert J. Yates; *St: & Sc:* Houston Branch; *Songs:* "You Naughty, Naughty Man," "Young Love," "If," "Romance," "Ah, So Pure," "Blue Juniata," "Mating Time," "In the Evening By the Moonlight," "Flow Gently, Sweet Afton," "Molly Darling," "Regnava Nil Silencio," "Sweet Genevieve," "Nelly Bly," "Extension for Romance," "Then You'll Remember Me," "Ah Non Guin Ge," "I Wish I Was Single Again," "Ah, Rovin'," "Wanderin'," "Cindy" and "Love Is a Pain" by various writers. (1:30) Period musical with its background, a traveling medicine show. Trucolor.

A Swirl of Glory *see* **Sugarfoot**

2584. The Sword and the Rose (RKO/Walt Disney British Prods., Ltd.; 1953). *Cast:* Richard Todd, Glynis Johns (Mary Tudor), James Robertson Justice (Henry VIII), Michael Gough, Jane Barrett, Peter Copley, Rosalie Crutchley (Queen Catherine of Aragon), D.A. Clarke-Smith (Cardinal Wolsey), Ernest Jay, Bryan Coleman, Jean Mercure (Louis XII of France), Gerard Oury, Fernand Fabre, Gaston Richer, Helen Goss, John Vere, Phillip Lennard, Philip Glasier, Robert LeBeal. *D:* Ken Annakin; *Ex.P:* Walt Disney; *P:* Perce Pearce; *Sc:* Lawrence E. Watkin. (1:33) (video/laserdisc) Historical characters and historical fiction blend into this lavish costume drama produced in England and based on Charles Major's 1899 novel *When Knighthood Was in Flower*, the title of the story's previous cinematic incarnation by Paramount in 1927 with Marion Davies. Technicolor (G.B. title: *When Knighthood Was In Flower*) Note: First filmed by Biograph in 1908 (1 reel) as *When Knights Were Bold*, starring Mr. & Mrs. D. W. Griffith.

2585. The Sword of Monte Cristo (20th Century–Fox; 1951). *Cast:* George Montgomery, Paula Corday, Berry Kroeger, William Conrad, Rhys Williams, Steve Brodie, Robert Warwick, David Bond, Lillian Bronson, [Burnu] Acquanetta, Trevor Bardette, Crane Whitley, Leonard Mudie, John Davidson, George Baxter, Steve Darrell, Ken MacDonald, Henry Corden, Michael Vallon, Stuart Holmes. *D: & Sc:* Maurice Geraghty; *P:* Edward L. Alperson. (1:20) (video) Costume swashbuckler of a female masked avenger (Corday) who sets out to topple the evil French government, using a sword which formerly belonged to the Count of Monte Cristo. Based on a novel by Alexandre Dumas. Super-Cinecolor.

2586. Sword of Venus (RKO; 1953). *Cast:* Robert Clarke, Catherine McLeod, Dan O'Herlihy, William Schallert, Marjorie Stapp, Merritt Stone, Renee de Marco, Eric Colmar, Stuart Randall. *D:* Harold Daniels; *P:-St: & Sc:* Aubrey Wisberg, Jack Pollexfen. (1:13) Swashbuckling adventure of a nefarious scoundrel who schemes against the son of the Count of Monte Cristo with the intent of acquiring his father's wealth. (G.B. title: *Island of Monte Cristo*)

2587. The System (Warner; 1953). *Cast:* Frank Lovejoy, Joan Weldon, Robert Arthur, Paul Picerni, Don Beddoe, Jerome Cowan, Dan

Seymour, Sarah Selby, Fay Roope, Frank Richards, Victor Perrin, Henry Corden, Howard Negley, Al Gordon, Bruno VeSota, Richard Garrick. *D:* Lewis Seiler; *P:* Sam Bischoff; *Sc:* Jo Eisinger. (1:30) Crime melodrama of a bookmaker and a gambling syndicate. Based on the story "Investigation" by Edith and Samuel Grafton.

2588. T-Bird Gang (Filmgroup/Sparta Prods.; 1959). *Cast:* Ed Nelson, John Brinkley, Pat George, Beach Dickerson, Tony Miller. *D:* Richard Harbinger; *P:* Stan Bickman; *St: & Sc:* Brinkley, Miller. (1:15) Crime melodrama of a young man who co-operates with police and goes undercover to expose a crime syndicate responsible for the death of his father. (aka: *The Pay-Off*) Originally paired on the top of a double bill with *High School Big Shot* (q.v.).

2589. The Tahitian (Crane–Knott–Long; 1956). *Cast:* Ana, Vahio, Taia Tepava, Tehapaitua Salmon, Dr. George Thooris, Dr. Henry K. Beye, Ben Brambridge, William A. Robinson, Tetoa Mauu, Denise Pottier, Miri Rei (narrator). *D:* James Knott; *P:* Cornelius Crane, Knott, Lotus Long; *St: & Sc:* Knott, Long; *Narration:* Annabel Ross. (1:19) Low budget independent drama of medical doctors trying to overcome native superstition to properly treat a deadly disease being spread through the Tahitian population by mosquitoes. Filmed on location in Eastmancolor.

2590. Take a Giant Step (United Artists/Sheila Prods.; 1959). *Cast:* Johnny Nash, Estelle Hemsley, Ruby Dee, Frederick O'Neal, Ellen Holly, Pauline Meyers, Beah Richards, Boyce Wallace, Frances Foster, Del Erickson, Dee Pollock, Frank Killmond, Joseph Sonessa, Sherman Raskin. *D:* Philip Leacock; *P:* Julius J. Epstein; *Sc:* Louis S. Peterson (based on his play); *Title song:* Jay Livingston, Ray Evans (sung by Nash). (1:40) Drama of a black teenager and the problems he faces while growing up in a white world. Aspects from the play were toned down for the screen treatment.

2591. Take Care of My Little Girl (20th Century–Fox; 1951). *Cast:* Jeanne Crain, Dale Robertson, Mitzi Gaynor, Jean Peters, Jeffrey Hunter, Betty Lynn, Helen Westcott, Lenka Peterson, Carol Brannon, Natalie Schafer, Beverly Dennis, Kathleen Hughes, Peggy O'Connor, Charlene Hardey, Janet Stewart, Gail Davis, Judy Walsh, John Litel, Irene Martin, Penny McGuiggan, Pattee Chapman, Mary Thomas, Palma Shard, Jean Romaine, Margia Dean, William A. Mahan, Marjorie Crossland, June Alden, Billy Lechner, Jill Kraft, George Nader, Grandon Rhodes, Dusty Anderson, Harry Harvey, Garnet Marks, Virginia Hunt, Eleanor Lawson, Shirley Tegge, King Donovan. *D:* Jean Negulesco; *P:* Julian Blaustein; *Sc:* Julius J. & Philip G. Epstein. (1:33) Based on the 1950 novel by Peggy Goodin, this drama details a young girl's attempts to join the college sorority that her mother belonged to, but obstacles she encounters convince her that she doesn't need to "belong" to make it in college. Technicolor.

2592. Take Me to Town (Universal-International; 1953). *Cast:* Ann Sheridan, Sterling Hayden, Philip Reed, Lee Patrick, Phyllis Stanley, Lee Aaker, Harvey Grant, Larry Gates, Dusty Henley, Forrest Lewis, Dorothy Neumann, Ann Tyrrell, Robert Anderson, Frank Sully, Lane Chandler, Guy Williams, Alice Kelley, Ruth Hampton, Jackie Loughery [Miss U.S.A. in 1952), Valerie Jackson, Anita Ekberg, Fess Parker, Dusty Walker, Mickey Little, Jimmy Karath, Jerry Wayne, The Pickett Sisters. *D:* Douglas Sirk; *P:* Ross Hunter, Leonard Goldstein; *Sc:* Richard Morris [based on his story "Flame of the Timberline"]. *Songs:* "The Tale of Vermilion O'Toole" Frederick Herbert, "Holy, Holy, Holy" (a traditional hymn), "Oh, You Red-Head" Herbert, Milton Rosen, "Take Me to Town" Lester Lee, Dan Shapiro. (1:20) Family comedy with songs of a woman on the lam from the law who hides out in a lumber town where she eventually finds acceptance with the locals and romance with a widowed lumberjack preacher with three kids. Technicolor.

2593. Take the High Ground (MGM; 1953). *Cast:* Richard Widmark (Sgt. Thorne Ryan), Karl Malden (Sgt. Laverne Holt), Elaine Stewart (Julie Mollison), Steve Forrest (Lobo Naglaski), Russ Tamblyn (Paul Jamison), Carleton Carpenter (Merton Tolliver), Jerome Courtland (Elvin Carey), Robert Arthur (Donald Q. Dover IV), William Hairston (Daniel Hazard), Maurice Jara (Franklin D. No Bear), Bert Freed (Sgt. Vince Opperman), Regis Toomey (chaplain), Chris Warfield, Ft. Bliss Personnel. *D:* Richard Brooks; *P:* Dore Schary; *St: & Sc:* (AAN) Millard Kaufman; *Songs:* Dimitri Tiomkin, Ned Washington. (1:41) Hit drama of U.S. Army Infantry training at Fort Bliss, Texas. Filmed on location, it also carried a tale of romantic rivalry. Anscocolor.

Take the Stage (G.B. title) *see* **Curtain Call at Cactus Creek**

Taking Sides (G.B. title) *see* **Lightning Guns**

2594. Tales of Robin Hood (Lippert; 1951). *Cast:* Robert Clarke (title role), Mary Hatcher, Paul Cavanagh, Wade Crosby, Whit Bissell, Ben Welden, Robert Bice, Keith Richards, Bruce Lester, Tiny Stowe, Lester Matthews, John Vosper, Norman Bishop, Margia Dean, Lorin Raker, George Slocum, John Doucette, John Harmon, Matt McHugh, David Stollery. *D:* James Tinling (final film—to TV); *P:* Hal Roach, Jr.; *St: & Sc:* Leroy H. Zehren. (0:59) Low budget actioner with the hero of Sherwood Forest out to conquer the Normans. A theatrical release which was originally an unsold pilot for a TV series.

2595. Talk About a Stranger (MGM; 1952). *Cast:* George Murphy (final film—ret.), Nancy Davis, Billy Gray, Kurt Kasznar, Lewis Stone, Anna Glomb, Katherine Warren, Teddy Infuhr, Stanley Andrews, Maude Wallace, Cosmo Sardo, Jon Gardner, Donald Gordon, Warren Farlow, Wayne Farlow, Gary Stewart, Margaret Bert (voice only), Tudor Owen, Harry Lauter, Dan Riss, Charles LaTorre, Kathleen Freeman, Burt Mustin, Ralph Moody, Jack Williams, Jack Moore, William Tannen, Leslie K. O'Pace, Harry Hines, Ed Cassidy, Virginia Farmer. *D:* David Bradley (professional directorial debut); *P:* Richard Goldstone; *Sc:* Margaret Fitts. (1:05) Programmer about a family with a mysterious neighbor and the young son who sets out to investigate when his dog is poisoned. Based on the short story "The Enemy" by Charlotte Armstrong.

The Tall Lie *see* **For Men Only**

2596. Tall Man Riding (Warner; 1955). *Cast:* Randolph Scott, Dorothy Malone, Peggie Castle, John Dehner, Robert Barrat (final film—ret.), William Ching, Lane Chandler, Paul Richards, Russ Conway, John Baragrey, Mickey Simpson, Joe Bassett, Charles Watts, Mike Ragan [aka: Holly Bane], Carl Andre, John Logan, Guy [Edward] Hearn, William Fawcett, Nolan Leary, Phil Rich, Eva Novak, Buddy Roosevelt, Jack Henderson, Bob Peoples, Dub Taylor, William Bailey, Bob Stephenson, Roger Creed, Vernon Rich. *D:* Lesley Selander; *P:* David Weisbart; *Sc:* Joseph Hoffman. (1:23) Western of a cowpoke who tangles with a hated Montana cattle baron and other ranchers. Based on the 1951 novel by Norman A. Fox. WarnerColor.

2597. The Tall Men (20th Century–Fox; 1955). *Cast:* Clark Gable, Jane Russell, Robert Ryan, Cameron Mitchell, Juan Garcia, Harry Shannon, Emile Meyer, Steve Darrell, Will Wright, Robert Adler, Russell Simpson, Tom Wilson, Tom Fadden, Dan White, Argentina Brunetti, Doris Kemper, Carl Harbaugh, Post Park, Jack Mather, Gabrile Del Valle, Meyito Pulito, Frank Leyva. *D:* Raoul Walsh; *P:* William A. Bacher, William B. Hawks; *Sc:* Sydney Boehm, Frank Nugent; *Songs:* "The Tall Men" Ken Darby, "Cancion Mixteca" Jose Lopez Alaves. (2:02) (video) Post–Civil War era tale of two brothers who head west and seek their fortune, find love and adventure. Based on the 1954 novel by Clay Fisher. DeLuxe color/CinemaScope.

2598. The Tall Stranger (Allied Artists; 1957). *Cast:* Joel McCrea, Virginia Mayo, Barry Kelley, Michael Ansara, Whit Bissell, James Dobson, George Neise, Adam Kennedy, Michael Pate, Leo Gordon, Ray Teal, George J. Lewis, Robert Foulk, Guy Prescott, Philip Phillips, Jennifer Lea, Ralph Reed, M. Huga, Ann Morrison, Tom London, Lennie Geer, Don McGuire, Danny Sands. *D:* Thomas Carr; *P:* Walter Mirisch; *Sc:* Christopher Knopf. (1:21) Western tale of a man saved by members of a wagon train who receive help from him when they encounter problems on their new land. Based on the story "Plunder" [aka: "Showdown Trail"] by Louis L'Amour. DeLuxe color/CinemaScope.

2599. The Tall T (Columbia/Producers Actors Corp.; 1957). *Cast:* Randolph Scott, Maureen O'Sullivan, Richard Boone, Arthur Hunnicutt, Skip Homeier, Henry Silva, John Hubbard, Chris Olsen, Robert Anderson, Robert Burton, Fred E. Sherman. *D:* Budd Boetticher; *P:* Harry Joe Brown; *Sc:* Burt Kennedy. (1:18) (video) Offbeat western drama of captives held by a trio of outlaws. Based on "The Captives" by Elmore Leonard, the film has a latter-day following. Technicolor.

2600. The Tall Target (MGM; 1951). *Cast:* Dick Powell, Paula Raymond, Adolphe Menjou, Marshall Thompson, Leif Erickson, Ruby Dee, Will Geer, Richard Rober, Florence Bates, Victor Kilian (final film—ret.), Regis Toomey, Tom Powers, Jeff Richards, Katherine Warren, Peter Brocco, Barbara Billingsley, Will Wright, Leslie Kimmell (Abraham Lincoln), James Harrison (Allan Pinkerton), Dan Foster. *D:* Anthony Mann; *P:* Richard Goldstone; *St:* George Worthing Yates, Geoffrey Homes [Daniel Mainwaring]; *Sc:* Yates, Homes [Mainwaring],

Art Cohn, Joseph Losey (unc.). (1:18) Pinkerton detective, John Kennedy (Powell) is following a tip that Abraham Lincoln is going to be assassinated during a train trip in 1861.

2601. The Tall Texan (Lippert/T.F. Woods Prods.; 1953). *Cast:* Lloyd Bridges, Lee J. Cobb, Marie Windsor, Luther Adler, Samuel R. Herrick, Syd Saylor, Dean Train, George Steele. *D:* Elmo Williams (directorial debut); *P:* T. Frank Woods; *St: & Sc:* Samuel Roeca; *Additional dialogue:* Elizabeth Reinhardt. (1:22) Western of prospectors who run into trouble while panning for gold on sacred Indian lands.

Tall Timber *see* **Big Timber**

The Tall Trouble *see* **Hell Canyon Outlaws**

2602. Taming Sutton's Gal (Republic/Variety; 1957). *Cast:* John Lupton, Gloria Talbott, Jack Kelly, May Wynn, Verna Felton. *D:* Lesley Selander; *P:* William J. O'Sullivan; *St:* Thames Williamson; *Sc:* Williamson, Frederic Louis Fox. (1:11) A man's trip to the backwoods of California leads him into the clutches of a moonshiner's lusty wife. Naturama.

Tammy (G.B. title) *see* **Tammy and the Bachelor**

2603. Tammy and the Bachelor (Universal-International; 1957). *Cast:* Debbie Reynolds (Tammy Tyree), Leslie Nielsen (Peter Brent), Walter Brennan (Grandpa), Mala Powers (Barbara), Fay Wray (Mrs. Brent), Sidney Blackmer (Prof. Brent), Mildred Natwick (Aunt Renie), Louise Beavers (Osia), Philip Ober (Alfred Bissle), Craig Hill (Ernie), April Kent (Tina). *D:* Joseph Pevney; *P:* Ross Hunter; *Sc:* Oscar Brodney; *Song:* "Tammy" (AAN-Best Song) Jay Livingston, Ray Evans (sung by the Ames Brothers—reprised by Reynolds). (1:29) (video) Hit romantic comedy of a backwoods girl who saves a man's life in a plane crash and gets invited to spend time at his Southern plantation with his wealthy family. Based on the 1948 novel *Tammy Out of Time* by Cid Ricketts Sumner. Followed in 1961 by the sequel *Tammy Tell Me True*. Technicolor/CinemaScope. (G.B. title: *Tammy*) Note: Debbie Reynolds received a *Photoplay* "Gold Medal" in 1958.

2604. Tanganyika (Universal-International; 1954). *Cast:* Van Heflin, Ruth Roman, Howard Duff, Jeff Morrow, Noreen Corcoran, Gregory Marshall, Joe Comadore, Naaman Brown, Edward C. Short, Murray Alper. *D:* Andre De Toth; *P:* Albert J. Cohen; *St:* William R. Cox; *Sc:* Richard Alan Simmons, William Sackheim. (1:20) Much stock footage fills in this turn-of-the-century East African adventure of a man bent on stopping a white renegade from inciting an uprising among a native tribe. Technicolor.

2605. Tanga-Tika (Norton-Condon; 1953). *Cast:* Adeline Tatahaimuai, Paul Meoe, Alice Swenson, Tumaatura, Roger Soui, Governor Anzani (himself), Mayor Poeui (himself), Capt. Darr (himself), Ah Fu (himself). *D:* Dwight Long; *P:* Arch Monson, Long; *St:* Lela Rogers; *Narration:* Charles Tedford; *Song:* "Tahiti, My Island" Victor Young. (1:15) Semi-documentary focusing on the idyllic life of residents of the island of Tahiti, including a young couple who plan to marry. Filmed on location in 16 mm with stock transferred to 35 mm. Narrated by George Fenneman. Eastmancolor.

2606. Tangier Incident (Monogram/Allied Artists; 1953). *Cast:* George Brent, Mari Aldon, Dorothy Patrick, Bert Freed, Dan Seymour, Dayton Lummis, Alix Talton, John Harmon, Richard Karlan, Shepard Menken, Benny Rubin, Mike Ross. *D:* Lew Landers; *P:* Lindsley Parsons; *St: & Sc:* George Bricker. (1:17) Espionage melodrama of efforts to stop three scientists working toward a deal to sell atomic secrets to the Russians and an American agent out to thwart their plans.

2607. Tank Battalion (American International/James H. Nicholson and Samuel Z. Arkoff Prod.; 1958). *Cast:* Don Kelly, Marjorie Hellen, Edward G. Robinson, Jr., Frank Gorshin, Regina Gleason, Barbara Luna (film debut), Bob Padget, Mark Sheeler, Baynes Barron, Tetsu Komai, John Trigonis, Don Devlin, Warren Crosby, Troy Patterson. *D:* Sherman A. Rose (final film); *P:* Richard Bernstein; *Ex.P:* Richard B. Duckett; *As.P:* George W. Waters; *St:* Waters; *Sc:* Bernstein, Waters. (1:20) War melodrama set in the Korean conflict of four G.I.s and their problems with their tank when trapped between a sheer cliff and a communist machine gun nest. (G.B. title: *The Valley of Death*). Originally paired on a double bill program with *Hell Squad* (q.v.).

Tank Commando (G.B. title) *see* **Tank Commandos**

2608. Tank Commandos (American International/El Monte Prods.; 1959). *Cast:* Robert Barron, Maggie Lawrence, Wally Campo, Donato Farretta, Leo V. Metranga, Jack Sowards, Anthony Rich, Larry Hudson, Maria Monay, Carmen D'Antonio, David Addis, Russ Prescott, Freddy Roberto, Jerry Lear, Fred Gavlin, Joan Connors, Larry Shuttleworth, Lee Redman, Norberto Kermer. *D:-P:-St: & Sc:* Burt Topper. (1:21) World War II drama of a U.S. demolition team in Italy to destroy an underwater bridge used by the Germans to transport their fighting equipment. Originally ran on a double bill with *Operation Dames* (q.v.).

2609. The Tanks Are Coming (Warner; 1951). *Cast:* Steve Cochran, Philip Carey, Mari Aldon, Paul Picerni, Harry Bellaver, James Dobson, Robert Boon, George O'Hanlon, John McGuire, Michael Steele. *D:* Lewis Seiler, D. Ross Lederman; *P:* Bryan Foy; *St:* Samuel Fuller; *Sc:* Robert Hardy Andrews. (1:30) (video) World War II saga of the Third Armored Division moving into Germany in 1944, padded with lots and lots of authentic war footage to preserve the budget. Not a big deal on original release, but the film has gathered a latter-day cult following.

2610. Tarantula (Universal-International; 1955). *Cast:* John Agar, Mara Corday, Leo G. Carroll, Nestor Paiva, Ross Elliott, Hank Patterson, Ed Rand, Raymond Bailey, Jane Howard, Billy Wayne, Dee Carroll, Bert Holland, Steve Darrell, Tom London, Edgar Dearing, James J. Hyland, Stuart Wade, Vernon Rich, Bob Nelson, Eddie Parker, Clint Eastwood, Bing Russell, Ray Quinn, Robert R. Stephenson, Don Dillaway, Bud [Bill] Wolfe, Jack Stoney, Rusty Wescoatt. *D:* Jack Arnold; *P:* William Alland; *St:* Arnold, Robert Fresco; *Sc:* Fresco, Martin Berkeley. (1:20) (video/laserdisc) Acclaimed science fiction of a scientist and his unstable experimental serum that turns the titled average arachnid into a mammoth crawling terror.

2611. Tarawa Beachhead (Columbia/ Morningside Prods.; 1958). *Cast:* Kerwin Mathews, Julie Adams, Ray Danton, Karen Sharpe, Onslow Stevens, Russell Thorsen, Eddie Ryder, John Baer, Michael Garth, Larry Thor, Buddy Lewis, Lee Farr, Bill Boyett, Don Reardon. *D:* Paul Wendkos; *P:* Charles H. Schneer; *St: & Sc:* Richard Alan Simmons. (1:17) World War II drama involving the murder of an officer by his superior in combat and a sergeant who witnesses the act and keeps quiet.

2612. Target (RKO; 1952). *Cast:* Tim Holt, Richard Martin, Linda Douglas, Walter Reed, Harry Harvey, John Hamilton, Lane Bradford, Riley Hill, Mike Ragan [aka: Holly Bane]. *D:* Stuart Gilmore; *P:* Herman Schlom; *St: & Sc:* Norman Houston. (1:00) A latter-day entry in the Tim Holt series of westerns of two cowpokes aided by a female marshal who tangle with an outlaw gang headed by a crooked land agent. This one originally ran on the bottom of a double bill with *Tarzan's Savage Fury* (q.v.).

2613. Target Earth (Allied Artists/Abtcom Pictures; 1954). *Cast:* Richard Denning, Kathleen Crowley, Virginia Grey, Richard Reeves, Robert Roark, Mort Marshall, Arthur Space, Whit Bissell, Jim Drake, Steve Pendleton, House Peters, Jr. *D:* Sherman A. Rose (directorial debut); *P:* Herman Cohen (first film); *Sc:* William Raynor. (1:14) (video) Science fiction of an alien attack force made up of an army of robots who decimate most of the populace of Chicago, with the few survivors doing what they have to in an effort to remain alive. Based on the story "The Deadly City" by Paul W. Fairman.

Target for Scandal (G.B. title) *see* **Washington Story**

2614. Target Hong Kong (Columbia; 1953). *Cast:* Richard Denning, Nancy Gates, Richard Loo, Soo Yong, Ben Astar, Michael Pate, Philip Ahn, Henry Kulky, Victor Sen Yung, Weaver Levy, Kam Tong, Robert W. Lee. *D:* Fred F. Sears; *P:* Wallace MacDonald; *St: & Sc:* Herbert Purdum. (1:06) Low budget actioner of mercenaries in Hong Kong, hired to stop a communist takeover of that British city.

2615. Target Unknown (Universal-International; 1951). *Cast:* Mark Stevens, Alex Nicol, Robert Douglas, Don Taylor, Gig Young, Joyce Holden, Suzanne Dalbert, Malu Gatica, James Best, Richard Carlyle, John[ny] Sands, James Young, Steven Geray, Tony Christian. *D:* George Sherman; *P:* Aubrey Schenck; *Sc:* Harold Medford [based on his story "Target Unknown"]. (1:30) World War II drama of airmen downed in Nazi occupied France who are being interrogated by the Germans regarding an Allied bombing mission.

2616. Target Zero (Warner; 1955). *Cast:* Richard Conte, Peggie Castle, Charles Bronson, Richard Stapley, L.Q. Jones, Chuck Connors, John Alderson, Terence De Marney,

Strother Martin, John Dennis, Abel Fernandez, Angela Loo, Richard Park, Don Dreck, Aaron Spelling, George Chan, Joby Baker, Leo K. Kuter, Hal Sheiner. *D:* Harmon Jones; *P:* David Weisbart; *Sc:* Sam Rolfe. (1:32) Korean conflict melodrama of an American infantry platoon, three members of a British tank crew and a female correspondent who are cut off from their main companies. Based on the story "Bug Out" by James Warner Bellah.

2617. Tarnished (Republic; 1950). *Cast:* Dorothy Patrick, Arthur Franz, Barbara Fuller, James Lydon, Harry Shannon, Don Beddoe, Byron Barr, Alex Gerry, Hal Price, Stephen Chase, Esther Somers, Paul E. Burns, Ethel Wales, Michael Vallon. *D:* Harry Keller; *P:* Sidney Picker; *Sc:* John K. Butler. (1:00) Based on the 1945 novel *Turn Home* by Eleanor R. Mayo, this drama details the story of a man who returns to his small town following a stint in the U.S. Marines, but finds the townsfolk only remember his earlier tainted past.

2618. The Tarnished Angels (Universal-International; 1958). *Cast:* Rock Hudson, Robert Stack, Dorothy Malone, Jack Carson, Robert Middleton, Alan Reed, Alexander Lockwood, Chris Olsen, Robert J. Wilke, William Schallert, Troy Donahue, Betty Utey, Phil Harvey, Steve Drexel, Eugene Borden, Stephen Ellis. *D:* Douglas Sirk; *P:* Albert Zugsmith; *Sc:* George Zuckerman. (1:31) Acclaimed aviation drama of a New Orleans reporter who gets mixed up with a barnstorming pilot, but more so with the latter's wife. Based on the 1935 novel *Pylon* by William Faulkner. Set in the early 1930s, the story was based on the exploits of William Faulkner's deceased brother. CinemaScope.

Tarzan and the Jungle Queen (G.B. title) *see* **Tarzan's Peril**

2619. Tarzan and the She-Devil (RKO/Sol Lesser Prods.; 1953). *Cast:* Lex Barker, Joyce MacKenzie, Monique Van Vooren, Raymond Burr, Tom Conway, Robert Bice, Mike Ross, Henry Brandon, Michael Granger, Cheta (chimp). *D:* Kurt Neumann; *P:* Sol Lesser; *St: & Sc:* Karl Kamb, Carroll Young. (1:16) Edgar Rice Burrough's jungle hero is taken captive by a vicious band of ivory hunters headed by an equally vicious female. This film which utilizes footage from 1934's *Wild Cargo* was Barker's last for the series.

2620. Tarzan and the Slave Girl (RKO/Sol Lesser Prods.; 1950). *Cast:* Lex Barker, Vanessa Brown, Robert Alda, Hurd Hatfield, Arthur Shields, Robert Warwick, Anthony Caruso, Denise Darcel, Tito Renaldo, Mary Ellen Kay, Shirley Ballard, Rosemary Bertrand, Gwen Caldwell, Martha Clemmons, Mona Knox, Josephine Parra, Jackee Waldron, Cheta (chimp). *D:* Lee Sholem; *P:* Sol Lesser; *St: & Sc:* Hans Jacoby, Arnold Belgard. (1:14) Adventure melodrama with Edgar Rice Burroughs' jungle hero tangling with a tribe of lion-worshippers who have kidnapped Jane and other women from local tribes.

2621. Tarzan, the Ape Man (MGM; 1959). *Cast:* Dennis [Denny] Milller, Joanna Barnes, Cesare Danova, Robert Douglas, Thomas Yangha. *D:* Joseph Newman; *P:* Al Zimbalist; *St: & Sc:* Robert Hill [based on characters created by Edgar Rice Burroughs]. (1:22) Little can be said of this cheap-jack bargain basement remake of the Weissmuller-O'Sullivan classic of 1932 which utilizes tinted footage from that feature as well as stock footage from *King Solomon's Mines* (q.v.). Less can be said of the 1981 remake with Bo Derek and Miles O'Keefe. Technicolor. Note: Miller was a former U.C.L.A. basketball star.

2622. Tarzan's Fight for Life (MGM/Sol Lesser Prods.; 1958). *Cast:* Gordon Scott, Eve Brent, Rickie Sorenson, Jil Jarmyn, Carl Benton Reid, James Edwards, Henry [Harry] Lauter, Nick Stewart, Woody Strode, Darrell Harris, Pauline Myers, Roy Glenn, Cheta (chimp). *D:* H. Bruce Humberstone; *P:* Sol Lesser; *Sc:* Thomas Hal Phillips [based on the character created by Edgar Rice Burroughs]. (1:26) Tarzan aids a doctor in overcoming native superstitions. A low budget studio-bound entry in the series which was partially filmed in Africa. Eastmancolor.

2623. Tarzan's Hidden Jungle (RKO/Sol Lesser Prods.; 1955). *Cast:* Gordon Scott (debut as Tarzan), Vera Miles, Peter Van Eyck, Don Beddoe, Jester Hairston, Rex Ingram, Jack Elam, Charles Fredericks, Richard Reeves, Ike Jones, Maidie Norman, Cheta (chimp), Lucky (chimp). *D:* Harold Schuster; *P:* Sol Lesser; *St: & Sc:* William Lively. (1:13) A jungle hunter is doing away with a large portion of the animal inhabitants of the jungle in an effort to acquire skins, tallow and ivory. The final entry in the series to be released by RKO. Based on the character created by Edgar Rice Burroughs.

2624. Tarzan's Peril (RKO/Sol Lesser Prods.; 1951). *Cast:* Lex Barker, Virginia Huston, George Macready, Douglas Fowley, Glenn Anders, Frederick O'Neal, Dorothy Dandridge, Alan Napier, Edward Ashley, James Moultrie, Walter Kingsford, Cheta (chimp, received the #3 PATSY Award in 1952). *D:* Byron Haskin, Phil Brandon; *P:* Sol Lesser; *St: & Sc:* Samuel Newman, Francis Swann; *Additional dialogue:* John Cousins. (1:19) Gunrunners are stirring up trouble between two tribes in British East Africa (where some location filming took place). Tarzan becomes a target for assassination when he tries to smooth out the difficulties. Based on the character created by Edgar Rice Burroughs. (G.B. title: *Tarzan and the Jungle Queen*)

2625. Tarzan's Savage Fury (RKO/Sol Lesser Prods.; 1952). *Cast:* Lex Barker, Dorothy Hart, Patric Knowles, Charles Korvin, Tommy Carlton, Cheta (chimp, received a PATSY Award of Excellence, 1953). *D:* Cy[ril] Endfield; *P:* Sol Lesser; *St:* Cyril Hume, Hans Jacoby; *Sc:* Hume, Jacoby, Shirley White. (1:20) Diamond thieves passing themselves off as British agents give Tarzan a royal jungle pain in this adventure based on the character created by Edgar Rice Burroughs. Originally ran on the top of a double bill with Tim Holt's *Target* (q.v.).

A Taste of Hot Lead *see* **Hot Lead**

2626. The Tattered Dress (Universal-International; 1957). *Cast:* Jeff Chandler, Jeanne Crain, Jack Carson, Gail Russell, Elaine Stewart, George Tobias, Edward Andrews, Philip Reed, Edward C. Platt, Paul Birch, Alexander Lockwood, Edwin Jerome, William Schallert, Joseph Granby, Frank Scannell, Floyd Simmons, Ziva Shapir, Marina Orschel, Ingrid Goude, Billy Snyder, Helene Marshall, Charles J. Conrad, John Phillips, Forrest Stanley, Vincent G. Perry, Gordon Morehouse, Jack Shutta, Dick Wilson, Clarence Straight, June McCall, Robert Malcolm, Todd Ferrell, Charles Herbert, Napoleon Whiting, Freda Jones, King Lockwood, Joseph Gilbert, Arthur Tovey, Danny Dowling, Murray Pollack, Maurice Marks, Mary Bayless, Jack Del Rio, Jeffrey Sayre, Jerry Elliott, Charles E. Perry, Donald Chaffin, Beau Anderson, Richard Dale Clark, Lillian Ten Eyck. *D:* Jack Arnold; *P:* Albert Zugsmith; *St: & Sc:* George Zuckerman. (1:33) Melodrama of a lawyer who becomes the target of the local sheriff. With the help of a woman, they get the former charged with jury tampering. CinemaScope.

2627. The Tattooed Stranger (RKO; 1950). *Cast:* John Miles, Patricia [Barry] White, Walter Kinsella, Frank Tweddell, Rod McLennan, Henry Lasko, Arthur Jarrett, Jim Boles, William Gibberson. *D:* Edward J. Montagne; *P:* Jay Bonafield; *St: & Sc:* Philip Reisman, Jr. (1:04) New York City police search for the killer of a woman whose body was found in Central Park. Filmed on location, it originally ran as part of a double bill with *Storm Over Wyoming* (q.v.).

2628. Taxi (20th Century-Fox; 1953). *Cast:* Dan Dailey, Constance Smith, Neva Patterson, Blanche Yurka, Kyle MacDonnell, Walter Woolf King, Anthony Ross, Mark Roberts, Harry Clark, Jack Diamond, Stubby Kaye, B.S. Pulley, Bert Thorn, Curtis Cooksey, Bill Neil, Frank McNellis, Elliott Sullivan, Hilda Haynes, James Little, Ann Dere, Geraldine Page (professional film debut), Rex O'Malley, Bruno Wick, Art Hannes, DeForest Kelley, Melville Ruick, Henry Jones, Ralph Dunn, Betty Buehler, Virginia Vincent, Mario Siletti, John Kullers, Glenn Hardy, Jonathan Hale, Al Eben, John Cassavetes. *D:* Gregory Ratoff (final U.S. film); *P:* Samuel G. Engel; *Sc:* D.M. Marshman, Jr., Daniel Fuchs (based on the French screenplay *Sans Laisser d'Adresse* by Hans Jacoby, Fred Brady, Alex Joffe and Jean Paul LeChanois). (1:17) Romantic comedy-drama of a New York City cabbie who helps a young and pregnant Irish lass find the father of her baby so she will not be deported, but when he is found, he rejects his responsibility.

2629. Taza, Son of Cochise (Universal-International; 1954). *Cast:* Rock Hudson, Barbara Rush, Gregg Palmer, Bart Roberts [aka: Rex Reason], Morris Ankrum, Robert Burton (General Crook), Eugene Iglesias, Richarad Cutting, Ian MacDonald, Joseph Sawyer, Lance Fuller, Brad Jackson, James Van Horn, Charles Horvath, Robert Hoy, William Leslie, Dan White, Edna Parrish, Seth Bigman, John Kay Hawks, Barbara Burck, Jeff Chandler (Cochise—unbilled). *D:* Douglas Sirk; *P:* Ross Hunter; *St: & Adaptation:* Gerald Drayson Adams; *Sc:* George Zuckerman. (1:19) The two sons of Apache chief Cochise hold opposing views in dealing with the white man, Taza (Hudson) seeking the path of peace and Maiche (Roberts), the path of war with Geronimo. A sequel to *Battle of Apache Pass* (q.v.), it was filmed on location in Moab, Utah. Technicolor/3-D.

2630. Tea and Sympathy (MGM; 1956). *Cast:* Deborah Kerr (repeating her stage role),

John Kerr (repeating his stage role), Leif Erickson (repeating his stage role), Edward Andrews, Darryl Hickman, Norma Crane, Dean Jones (film debut), Jacqueline de Wit, Tom Laughlin (film debut), Ralph Votrian, Steven Terrell, Kip King, Jimmy Hayes, Richard Tyler, Don Burnett, Mary Alan Hokanson, Ron Kennedy, Peter Miller, Bob Alexander, Michael Monroe, Paul Bryar, Del Erickson, Byron Kane, Harry Harvey, Jr., Bobby Ellis, Saul Gorss, Dale Van Sickel, Peter Leeds. *D:* Vincente Minnelli; *P:* Pandro S. Berman; *Sc:* Robert Anderson [based on his long running Broadway play which opened in 1953]. (2:02) (video/laserdisc) Hit drama of a prep school student's affair with his headmaster's wife. Unacceptable references to homosexuality in the play were toned down in Anderson's adapted screenplay. *Film Daily* placed it at #9 on their "10 Best" list of the year. MetroColor/CinemaScope.

2631. Tea for Two (Warner; 1950). *Cast:* Doris Day (Nanette Carter), Gordon MacRae (Jimmy Smith), Gene Nelson (Tommy Trainor), Patrice Wymore (film debut/Beatrice Darcy), Eve Arden (Pauline Hastings), Billy DeWolfe (Larry Blair), S.Z. Sakall (J. Maxwell Bloomhaus), Bill Goodwin (William Early), Virginia Gibson (Mabel Wiley), Crauford Kent (final film/Stevens), Mary Eleanor Donahue (Lynne), Johnny McGovern (Richard), Harry Harvey, George Baxter, Herschel Daugherty, Abe Dinovitch, Elizabeth Flournoy, Buddy Shaw, John Hedloe, Jack Daley, Art Gilmore. *D:* David Butler; *P:* William Jacobs; *Sc:* Harry Clork; *Songs:* "I Know That You Know" Anne Caldwell, Vincent Youmans; "Crazy Rhythm" Irving Caesar, Roger Wolfe Kahn, Joseph Meyer; "I Only Have Eyes For You" Al Dubin, Harry Warren; "Tea for Two," "I Want to Be Happy" Caesar, Youmans; "Do Do Do" George and Ira Gershwin; "Oh Me, Oh My" Arthur Francis, Youmans. (1:38) (video/laserdisc) Hit musical fluff, loosely based on the 1924 Broadway musical *No, No Nanette* by Frank Mandel, Otto Harbach, Vincent Youmans and Emil Nyitray. A girl must answer "No" to every question put to her for one week to win a bet which will give her money to finance a show and also be its star. Filmed twice previously as *No, No Nanette*, in 1930 by this studio and in 1940 by RKO. One of the 28 top-grossing films of 1949-50. Technicolor.

2632. Teacher's Pet (Paramount/Perlsea Co.; 1958). *Cast:* Clark Gable (James Gannon), Doris Day (Erica Stone), Gig Young (AAN-BSA/Dr. Hugo Pine), Mamie Van Doren (Peggy DeFore), Nick Adams (Barney Kovac), Peter Baldwin (Harold Miller), Marion Ross (Katy Fuller), Charles Lane (Roy), Florenz Ames (J.L. Ballentine), Jack Albertson (guide), Harry Antrim (Lloyd Crowley), Vivian Nathan (Mrs. Kovac), Terry Becker (Mr. Appino), Elizabeth Harrower (Clara Dibney), Margaret Muse (Miss Gross), Merritt Smith (Mr. Cory), Steffi Sidney, Cyril Delevanti, Norton Mockridge, Sandra Gould, Frank Richards, Army Acherd, Sidney Skolsky, Vernon Scott, Joe Hyams, Paine Knickerbocher, Erskine Johnson, Frank P. Quinn. *D:* George Seaton; *P:* William Perlberg; *St:* & *Sc:* (AAN) Fay and Michael Kanin; *Songs:* Title song, "The Girl Who Invented Rock and Roll" Joe Lubin; "Teacher's Pet Mambo" Luis Alvarez, Lubin. (2:00) (video/laserdisc) Hit romantic comedy of a hard-boiled journalist/newspaper editor who bangs heads with a young journalism teacher. Voted "Best Film of the Year" by the *New York Times*, it was also one of the 26 top-grossing films of 1957-58. VistaVision.

2633. The Teahouse of the August Moon (MGM; 1956). *Cast:* Marlon Brando (Sakini), Glenn Ford (Capt. Fisby), Machiko Kyo (Lotus Blossom), Eddie Albert (Capt. McLean), Paul Ford (reprising his Broadway role—replacing Louis Calhern who succumbed to a heart attack during production/Colonel Purdy), Jun Negami (Mr. Seiko), Nijiko Kiyokawa (Miss Higa Jiga), Mitsuko Sawamura (little girl), Henry [Harry] Morgan (Sgt. Gregovich), Scichizo Takeda (ancient man), Kichizaemon Saramaru (Mr. Hokaida), Frank Takunaga (Mr. Omura), Raynum K. Tsukamoto (Mr. Oshira), Nishida (Mr. Sumata), Dansho Miyazaki, Miyoshi Jingu, Aya Oyama, Tsuruta Yozan, John Grayson, Roger McGee, Harry Harvey, Jr., Carlo Fiore, Philip Ahn. *D:* Daniel Mann; *P:* Jack Cummings; *Sc:* John Patrick. (2:03) (video/laserdisc) Hit comedy of U.S. Army officers involved in the Americanization of Okinawa following the end of World War II. Based on the book by Vern J. Sneider and the hit Broadway play adapted from it by Mr. Patrick. One of the 24 top-grossing films of 1956-57, it was also in nomination at the Berlin Film Festival. MetroColor/CinemaScope.

2634. Teenage Caveman (American International/James H. Nicholson and Samuel Z. Arkoff; 1958). *Cast:* Robert Vaughn, Leslie Bradley, Darrah Marshall, Frank DeKova, Joseph Hamilton, Marshall Bradford, Robert Shayne, Beach Dickerson, June Jocelyn, Charles P. Thompson, Jonathan Haze. *D:* & *P:* Roger

Corman; *St: & Sc:* R. Wright Campbell. (1:05) (video) Ultra low budget exploitation item of a primitive tribe that lives across the river from "the forbidden land." (G.B. title: *Out of the Darkness*) (aka: *Prehistoric World*). Originally ran on the bottom of a double bill with *How to Make a Monster* (q.v.). Superama.

2635. Teen-Age Crime Wave (Columbia/Clover Prods.; 1955). *Cast:* Tommy Cook, Mollie McCart, Sue England, Frank Griffin, James Bell, Kay Riehl, Guy Kingsford, Larry Blake, James Ogg, Robert Bice, Helen Brown, Sydney Mason, George Cisar. *D:* Fred F. Sears; *P:* Sam Katzman; *St:* Ray Buffum; *Sc:* Harry J. Essex, Buffum (1:17) (video) Exploitation delinquency melodrama of teens on the run from the law who hold a farm family hostage.

Teenage Delinquents (G.B title) *see* **No Time to Be Young**

Teenage Devil Dolls (video title) *see* **One-Way Ticket to Hell**

2636. Teenage Doll (Allied Artists/Woolner Bros.; 1957). *Cast:* June Kenney, Fay Spain, John Brinkley, Collette Jackson, Barbara Wilson, Ziva Rodann, Sandy Smith, Barboura Morris, Richard Devon, Jay Sayer, Richard Cutting, Dorothy Neumann, Ed Nelson, Bruno VeSota. *D: & P:* Roger Corman; *St: & Sc:* Charles B. Griffith. (1:08) A female member of a teenage gang stabs a female member of a rival gang and goes into hiding. A teen exploitation melodrama, climaxing with a gang rumble, which clearly shows that Corman had his eye on the drive-in movie crowd of the day.

Teenage Frankenstein (G.B. title) *see* **I Was a Teenage Frankenstein**

2637. Teenage Monster (Howco International/Marquette-Favorite Films; 1957). *Cast:* Anne Gwynne, Stuart Wade, Gloria Castillo, Charles Courtney, Gilbert Perkins (title role), Frank Davis, Stephen Parker, Norman Leavitt, Jim McCullough, Gabye Moordian, Arthur Berkeley. *D: & P:* James Marquette; *St: & Sc:* Ray Buffum. (1:05) (video) When a meteor crashes to earth in the 19th century, a young boy is horribly disfigured, a condition which terrifies the locals. His mother protects him and a posse hunts him. (TV and video title: *Meteor Monster*) Originally ran on the bottom of a double bill with *Teenage Thunder* (q.v.).

2638. Teenage Rebel (20th Century–Fox; 1956). *Cast:* Ginger Rogers (Nancy Fallon), Michael Rennie (Jay Fallon), Mildred Natwick (Grace Hewitt), Rusty Swope (Larry Fallon), Lili Gentle (Gloria), Louise Beavers (Willamay), Irene Hervey (Helen McGowan), John Stephenson (Eric McGowan), Betty Lou Keim (Dodie), Warren Berlinger (film debut/Dick Hewitt), Diane Jergens (Jane Hewitt), Suzanne Luckey (Madeleine Johnson), James O'Rear (Mr. Heffernan), Gary Gray (Freddie), Pattee Chapman (Erna), James Stone (Pappy Smith), Wade Dumas, Richard Collier, Sheila James, Joan Freeman, Gene Foley. *D:* Edmund Goulding; *P:* Charles Brackett; *Sc:* Walter Reisch, Brackett; *Songs:* "Cool It, Baby" Leigh Harline, Carroll Coates, "Dodie" Ralph Freed, Goulding; *ASD:* (AAN-b/w) Lyle R. Wheeler, Jack Martin Smith (art directors), Walter M. Scott, Stuart A. Reiss (sets); *Costumes:* (AAN-b/w) Charles LeMaire, Mary Wills. (1:34) Comedy-drama of a remarried divorcee who must adapt to the fact that her teenage daughter has just moved in with her and her new family after having lived with her father for years. Based on the play *A Roomful of Roses* by Edith Sommer. CinemaScope.

2639. Teenage Thunder (Howco International/Marquette Prods.; 1957). *Cast:* Charles Courtney, Melinda Byron, Robert Fuller, Tyler McVey, Paul Bryar, Helene Heigh, Gilbert Perkins, Bing Russell, Gregory Marshall, Marshall Kent, Mona McKinnon. *D:* Paul Helmick; *P:* Jacques Marquette; *St: & Sc:* Rudy Makoul; *Song:* "Teenage Kisses" Walter Greene (sung by David Houston). (1:18) Teen melodrama of an adolescent garage mechanic who readies a hot rod and wins a big race, creating a better relationship between he and his father. Originally ran on a double bill with *Teenage Monster* (q.v.).

2640. Teenage Zombies (Governor Films/G.B.M. Prods.; 1958). *Cast:* Don Sullivan, Katherine Victor, Steve Conte, Paul Pepper, Bri Murphy, Mitzi Albertson, Jay Hawk, Nan Green, J.L.D. Morrison, Mike Concannon, Chuck Miles, Don Neely. *D:-P:-St: & Sc:* Jerry Warren, Jacques Lecotier. (1:13) (video) Low budget sci-fi/horror of teen waterskiers captured by a female doctor who wants to use them in her experiments. Re-worked in 1981 as *Frankenstein Island*, it was originally paired on the bottom of a double bill with *The Incredible Petrified World* (q.v.).

2641. Teenagers from Outer Space (Warner/Topaz; 1959). *Cast:* David Love, Dawn Anderson, Harvey B. Dunne, Bryan Grant, Tom

Lockyear [aka: Tom Graeff], Ursula Hensen, Robert King Moody, Helen Sage, Frederic Welch, Sonia Torgenson. *D:-P:-St: & Sc:* Tom Graeff [who also wore caps for cinematography, editing, special effects, sound and music editing]; *Production Associates:* C.R. Kaltenthaler, Gene Sterling, Bryan G. Pearson. (1:26) (video) Cheapie sci-fi thriller of alien teens sent to earth to destroy it with a monster called a gargon, but the leader of the group finds love with an earth girl and has second thoughts. (G.B. title: *The Gargon Terror*). Note: The gargon monster which looks to be the shadow of a lobster behind a screen rivals any special effects that Edward D. Wood, Jr. ever came up with.

Tell It to the Marines (G.B. title) *see* **Here Come the Marines**

2642. The Ten Commandments (Paramount/Motion Pictures Associates, Inc.; 1956). *Cast:* Charlton Heston (Moses the man), Yul Brynner ("Best Actor of the Year" by the NBR combined with his work in *The King and I* and *Anastasia*—both q.v./Rameses), Anne Baxter (Nefretiri), Edward G. Robinson (Dathan), Yvonne De Carlo (Sephora), Debra Paget (Lilia), John Derek (Joshua), Sir Cedric Hardwicke (Sethi), Nina Foch (Bithia), Martha Scott (Yochabel), Judith Anderson (Memnet), Vincent Price (Baka), John Carradine (Aaron), Eduard Franz (Jethro), Olive Deering (Miriam), Donald Curtis (Mered), Douglass Dumbrille (Jannes), Lawrence Dobkin (Hur Ben Caleb), Frank DeKova (Abiram), H. B. Warner (Amminadab/final film—d. 1958), Henry Wilcoxon (Pentaur), Julia Faye (Elisheba); Lisa Mitchell, Noelle Williams, Joanna Merlin, Pat Richard, Joyce Vanderveen, Diane Hall (Jethro's 6 daughters); Fraser Heston (Moses the infant), Abbas El Boughdadly (Rameses' charioteer), John Miljan (the Blind One), Tommy Duran (Gershom), Francis J. McDonald (Simon), Eugene Mazzola (Rameses' son), Ian Keith (final film—ret./Rameses I), Ramsey Hill (Korah), Paul De Rolf (Eleazar), Joan Woodbury (Korah's wife), Woodrow "Woody" Strode (King of Ethiopia), Esther Brown & Rushti Abaza (Princess Tharbis), Touch [Michael] Connors (Amalekite herder), Clint Walker (Sardinian captain), Luis Alberni (old Hebrew), Michael Ansara (taskmaster), Frankie Darro (slave), Walter Woolf King (Herald), Robert Vaughn (Hebrew spearman), Harry Woods (final film—ret.). *D:* Cecil B. DeMille; *P:* (AAN-Best Picture) DeMille; *As.P:* Henry Wilcoxon; *Sc:* Aeneas Mackenzie, Jesse L. Lasky, Jr., Jack Garliss, Fredric M. Frank; *Cinematography:* (AAN-color) Loyal Griggs; *Additional photography:* J. Peverell Marley, John Warren, Wallace Kelley; *ASD:* (AAN-color) Hal Pereira, Walter M. Tyler, Albert Nozaki (art directors), Sam M. Comer, Ray Moyer (sets); *Sound:* (AAN) Loren L. Ryder & Paramount Sound Dept.; *Editor:* (AAN) Anne Bauchens; *Costumes:* (AAN) Edith Head, Ralph Jester, John Jensen, Dorothy Jeakins, Arnold Friberg; *F/X:* (AA) John Fulton. (3:39) (video/laserdisc) Epic rendering of the Biblical story of Moses from being cast adrift on the Nile by his mother to escape a slaughter of infants to his leading his people out of slavery in Egypt, across the Red Sea and finally his ascent to Mt. Sinai where he received the Ten Commandments. This monumental production came in at an unheard cost of $13,000,000, utilizing on location filming at Mt. Sinai with 12,000 extras (for the Exodus) as well as 12 soundstages in Paris, France, and 18 soundstages at Paramount and RKO studios. Based on Holy Scriptures and other ancient writings, as well as *Prince of Egypt* by Dorothy Clarke Wilson, *Pillar of Fire* by Rev. J.H. Ingraham and *On Eagle's Wings* by Rev. A.E. Southon. One of the 24 top-grossing films of 1956-57, it grossed over $80,000,000 worldwide, coming in second only to *Gone with the Wind* (MGM/Selznick; 1939) in total receipts at the time. Still a favorite with audiences, receiving regular network TV showings. Considered a remake of DeMille's 1923 silent of the same name, when in reality it is only an expanded version of the first part of that film, of which the latter part told a contemporary parallel story. *Film Daily* placed it at #8 on their "10 Best" list for the year. Technicolor/VistaVision.

2643. Ten Days to Tulara (United Artists/Producciones George Sherman; 1958). *Cast:* Sterling Hayden, Grace Raynor, Rodolfo Hoyos, Carlos Musquiz, Tony Carvajal, Juan Garcia, Rafael Alcayde, Felix Gonzales, Jose Pulido, Major M. Badager, Milton Bernstein, Barry Grail, Paco Arenas. *D:* George Sherman; *P:* Clarence Eurist, Sherman; *As.P:-St: & Sc:* Laurence Mascott. (1:17) Programmer adventure melodrama of an American pilot in Central America who gets involved with latin banditos who have kidnapped his son. Filmed in Mexico.

2644. Ten North Frederick (20th Century–Fox; 1958). *Cast:* Gary Cooper (Joe Chapin), Diane Varsi (Ann Chapin), Suzy Parker (Kate Drummond), Geraldine Fitzgerald (Edith Chapin), Ray Stricklyn (Joby Chapin), Philip Ober (Lloyd Williams), John Emery (Paul Donaldson), Stuart Whitman (Charley Bongiorno),

Linda Watkins (Peg Slattery), Barbara Nichols (Stella), Joe McGuinn (Dr. English), Jess Kirkpatrick (Arthur McHenry), Nolan Leary (Harry Jackson), Helen Wallace (Marian Jackson), Jack Harding (Robert Hooker), Mack Williams (Lt. General Coates), Beverly Jo Morrow, Buck Class, Rachel Stephens, Bob Adler, Lincoln Foster, Dudley Manlove, Vernon Rich, Mary Carroll, George Davis, Joey Faye, Fred Essler, Irene Seidner, Melinda Byron, Sean Meaney, John Indrisano, Michael Potaki, Michael Morelli, Charles Bronson. *D: & Sc:* Philip Dunne; *P:* Charles Brackett. (1:42) (video) Drama of an ambitious wife with aspirations to be First Lady of the U.S. who goads her husband into politics. In failing at that he turns to the affections of a much younger woman and drink. Set in the 1940s, it is based on the 1955 novel by John O'Hara and became one of the 26 top-grossing films of 1957-58. CinemaScope.

2645. Ten Seconds to Hell (United Artists/Hammer-Seven Arts; 1959). *Cast:* Jeff Chandler, Jack Palance, Martine Carol, Robert Cornthwaite, Dave Willock, Wesley Addy, Jimmy Goodwin, Virginia Baker, Richard Wattis, Nancy Lee, Charles Nolte, Jim Hutton. *D:* Robert Aldrich; *P:* Michael Carreras; *Sc:* Aldrich, Teddi Sherman. (1:33) Drama of a six-man bomb disposal unit operating in Berlin following World War II. A G.B./U.S.A. co-production filmed on location, it was based on the 1955 novel *The Phoenix* by Lawrence P. Bachmann. Originally ran on a double bill with *The Rabbit Trap* (q.v.).

2646. Ten Tall Men (Columbia/Norma Prods.; 1951). *Cast:* Burt Lancaster, Jody Lawrence, Gilbert Roland, Kieron Moore, George Tobias, John Dehner, Nick Dennis, Mike Mazurki, Gerald Mohr, Ian MacDonald, Mari Blanchard, Donald Randolph, Robert Clary, Henry Rowland, Michael Pate, Stephen Bekassy, Raymond Greenleaf, Paul Marion, Philip Van Zandt, Shimen Ruskin, Mickey Simpson, Henri Letondal, Joy Windsor, JoAnn Arnold, Edith Sheets, Diana Dawson, Gwen Caldwell, Helen Reichman, George Khoury, Nick Cravat, Carlo Tricoli, Tom Conroy, Alan Ray, Frank Arnold, Ralph Volkie, Charlita, Rita Conde, Benny Burt. *D:* Willis Goldbeck; *P:* Harold Hecht; *St:* Goldbeck, James Warner Bellah; *Sc:* Frank Davis, Roland Kibbee. (1:37) Action and comedy highlight this Technicolor tale of the French Foreign Legion. A box office winner.

2647. Ten Thousand Bedrooms (MGM; 1957). *Cast:* Dean Martin, Anna Maria Alberghetti, Eva Bartok, Dewey Martin, Walter Slezak, Paul Henreid, Jules Munshin, Marcel Dalio, Dean Jones, Joyce Taylor, Evelyn Varden, Lisa Montell, Lisa Gaye, John Archer, Steve Dunne, Monique Van Vooren. *D:* Richard Thorpe; *P:* Joe Pasternak; *Sc:* William Ludwig, Laslo Vadnay, Art Cohn, Leonard Spigelgass; *Songs:* Title song, "Money Is a Problem," "You I Love," "Only Trust Your Heart" Nicholas Brodszky, Sammy Cahn; "The Man Who Plays the Mandolin" George Fancuilli; "Nisa" Marilyn Keith, Alan Bergman, "We're Gonna Rock Around the Clock" Max C. Freedman, Jimmy DeKnight, "No One But You" Jack Lawrence, Brodszky. (1:54) Musical-comedy of the playboy manager of a hotel in Rome. Martin's first solo effort without Jerry Lewis. MetroColor/CinemaScope.

2648. Ten Wanted Men (Columbia/Ranown Prods.-Producers Actors Corp.; 1955). *Cast:* Randolph Scott, Jocelyn Brando, Richard Boone, Alfonso Bedoya, Skip Homeier, Leo Gordon, Tom Powers, Dennis Weaver, Denver Pyle, Lee Van Cleef, Francis McDonald, Jack Perrin, Terry Frost, Franklyn Farnum, Minor Watson, Kathleen Crowley, Donna Martell, Clem Bevans, Lester Matthews, Louis Jean Heydt, Boyd "Red" Morgan, Pat Collins, Paul Maxey, Julian Rivero, Carlos Vera, Edna Holland, Reed Howes, George Boyce. *D:* H. Bruce Humberstone; *P:* Harry Joe Brown; *St:* Irving Ravetch, Harriet Frank, Jr.; *Sc:* Kenneth Gamet. (1:20) (video/laserdisc) Technicolor western drama involving opposing views by two ranchers, one lawful, the other unlawful.

Tender Hearts *see* **Edge of Hell**

2649. The Tender Trap (MGM; 1955). *Cast:* Frank Sinatra (Charlie Y. Reader), Debbie Reynolds (Julie Gillis), David Wayne (Joe McCall), Celeste Holm (Sylvia Crewes), Jarma Lewis (Jessica Collins), Carolyn Jones (Helen), Lola Albright (Poppy Matson), James Drury (Eddie), Tom Helmore (Mr. Loughran), Howard St. John (Sam Sayers), Joey Faye (Sol Z. Steiner), Benny Rubin (Mr. Wilson), Willard Sage, Marc Wilder, Jack Boyle, Reginald Simpson, Gil Harmon, Madge Blake, Wilson Wood, Frank Sully, Gordon Richards, Lennie Bremen, Dave White. *D:* Charles Walters; *P:* Lawrence Weingarten; *Sc:* Julius J. Epstein; *Song:* "(Love Is) The Tender Trap" (AAN-Best Song) James Van Heusen, Sammy Cahn (sung by Frank Sinatra). (1:50) (video/laserdisc) Hit romantic comedy of a swinging N.Y. bachelor lured into marriage by an irresistable bachelorette. Based on the Broadway success by Max Shulman and Robert Paul Smith. The title song became a big hit. Eastmancolor/CinemaScope.

2650. Tennessee Champ (MGM; 1954). *Cast:* Shelley Winters, Keenan Wynn, Dewey Martin, Earl Holliman, Dave O'Brien, Yvette Dugay, Charles [Bronson] Buchinsky, Frank Richards, Jack Kruschen, John Indrisano, Alvin J. Gordon, Paul Hoffman, Bruno VeSota, John Damler, William "Billy" Newell. *D:* Fred M. Wilcox; *P:* Sol Baer Fielding; *Sc:* Art Cohn; *Song:* "Weary Blues" Harry Warren, Ralph Blane. (1:12) Programmer pugilism drama of a young boxer (Martin) who reforms his shady owner (Wynn) with religion. Based on "The World in His Corner" and other stories by Eustace Cockrell. Anscocolor.

2651. Tennessee's Partner (RKO/Filmcrest; 1955). *Cast:* John Payne, Rhonda Fleming, Ronald Reagan, Coleen Gray, Anthony Caruso, Leo Gordon, Myron Healey, Morris Ankrum, Chubby Johnson, Joe Devlin, John Mansfield, Angie Dickinson. *D:* Allan Dwan; *P:* Benedict Bogeaus; *Sc:* Milton Krims, D.D. Beauchamp, Teddi Sherman, Graham Baker; *Song:* "Heart of Gold" Louis Forbes, Dave Franklin. (1:27) (video) Offbeat western tale of a man who saves another from bushwhackers, only to have his new friend make a play for his girlfriend. Based on a 1907 Bret Harte story that was previously filmed by Paramount in 1918 as *Tennessee's Pardner* and again in 1924 by PRC as *The Flaming Forties*. Technicolor/SuperScope.

2652. Tension at Table Rock (RKO; 1956). *Cast:* Richard Egan, Dorothy Malone, Cameron Mitchell, Billy Chapin, Royal Dano, Edward Andrews, John Dehner, DeForest Kelley, Angie Dickinson, Joe DeSantis, Paul Richards. *D:* Charles Marquis Warren; *P:* Sam Weisenthal; *Sc:* Winston Miller; *Song:* "The Ballad of Wes Tancred" Josef Myrow, Robert Wells (sung by Eddy Arnold). (1:33) Western of an outlaw who takes it on the lam after being forced to kill his partner in self defense. Based on Frank Gruber's 1954 novel *Bitter Sage*. Technicolor.

2653. Teresa (MGM; 1951). *Cast:* Pier Angeli (U.S. debut/Teresa), John Ericson (film debut/Philip Quas), Patricia Collinge (Philip's mother), Richard Bishop (Philip's father), Peggy Ann Garner (Susan), Ralph Meeker (film debut/Sgt. Dobbs), Bill Mauldin (Grissom), Ave Ninchi (Teresa's mother), Edward Binns (Sgt. Brown), Rod Steiger (film debut/Frank), Tommy Lewis (Walter), Aldo Silvani (Prof. Crocce), Franco Interlenghi (Mario), Edith Atwater (Mrs. Lawrence), Lewis Ciannelli (Cheyenne), William King (Boone), Richard McNamara (G.I. cook). *D:* Fred Zinneman; *P:* Arthur M. Loew, Jr.; *St:* (AAN) Stewart Stern, Alfred Hayes; *Sc:* Stern. (1:42) Hit drama of a G.I. who brings his Italian war bride to his hometown and meets with prejudice from local townsfolk. Filmed on location in Italy and New York, it was in nomination at the Venice Film Festival.

Terminal Station *see* **Indiscretion of an American Wife**

2654. Terror at Midnight (Republic; 1956). *Cast:* Scott Brady, Joan Vohs, Frank Faylen, John Dehner, Virginia Gregg, Ric Roman, John Gallaudet, Kem Dibbs, Percy Helton, Francis DeSales, John Maxwell. *D:* Franklin Adreon; *As.P:* Rudy Ralston; *St:* John K. Butler, Irving Shulman; *Sc:* Butler. (1:10) Crime melodrama of a police sergeant who suspects his girlfriend of being involved with a stolen car operation—but on investigating, finds she is being blackmailed.

Terror from 5,000 A.D. *see* **Terror from the Year 5,000**

Terror from the Sun *see* **The Hideous Sun Demon**

2655. Terror from the Year 5,000 (American International/James H. Nicholson and Samuel Z. Arkoff; 1958). *Cast:* Ward Costello, Joyce Holden, John Stratton, Frederic Downs, Fred Herrick, Beatrice Furdeaux, Jack Diamond, Fred Taylor, Salome Jens (film debut/title role). *D:-P:-St: & Sc:* Robert J. Gurney, Jr.; *Assistant Producer:* Gene Searchinger. (1:14) (video) Low budget sci-fi of a scientist who invents a "time" machine that will materialize objects from the future. The terror begins when he brings forth a female from the year 5,000 who is contaminated with radioactivity. (G.B. title: *Cage of Doom*) (aka: *Terror from 5,000 A.D.* and *The Girl from 5,000 A.D.*)

2656. Terror in a Texas Town (United Artists/Seltzer Films; 1958). *Cast:* Sterling Hayden, Sebastian Cabot, Carol Kelly, Eugene Martin, Marilee Earle, Gil Lamb, Ned Young, Victor Millan, Ann Varela, Sheb Wooley, Fred Kohler, Jr., Steve Mitchell, Jamie Russell, Tyler McVey, Ted Stanhope, Frank Ferguson, Hank

Patterson. *D:* Joseph H. Lewis (final film—to TV); *P:* Frank N. Seltzer; *St: & Sc:* Ben L. Perry. (1:20) Offbeat western of a town overrun with corruption and the Scandinavian whaler who cleans up the town with his harpoon!

Terror in the Haunted House *see* **My World Dies Screaming**

2657. Terror Is a Man (Valiant/Lynn-Romero Prods.; 1959). *Cast:* Francis Lederer, Greta Thyssen, Richard Derr, Oscar Keesee, Lilia Duran, Peyton Keesee, Flory Carlos. *D:* Gerry DeLeon; *P:* Kane Lynn, Eddie Romero; *Sc: & St:* Harry Paul Harber. (1:29) (video) Sci-fi/horror of a shipwrecked American seaman washed ashore on an island inhabited by a doctor experimenting with turning a panther into a man. A U.S.A.-Philippine co-production filmed on location in the Philippines. (aka: *Blood Creature*) Originally ran on a double bill program with *The Scavengers* (q.v.).

The Terror Strikes *see* **War of the Colossal Beast**

2658. The Texan Meets Calamity Jane (Columbia; 1950). *Cast:* James Ellison, Evelyn Ankers (Calamity Jane), Ruth Whitney, Lee "Lasses" White, Jack Ingram, Frank Pharr, Hugh Hooker, Walter Strand, Sally Weidman, Rudy De Saxe, Paul Barney, Ferrell Lester, Ronald Marriott, Bill Orisman, Lou W. Pierce, Elmer Herzberg, Ray Jones. *D:-P:-St: & Sc:* Ande Lamb. (1:11) A woman is in danger of losing her saloon business in this appropriately titled low budget western which was photographed in Cinecolor. Originally paired on a double bill with *Last of the Buccaneers* (q.v.).

2659. Texans Never Cry (Columbia/Gene Autry Prods.; 1951). *Cast:* Gene Autry, Gail Davis, Pat Buttram, Mary Castle, Russell Hayden, Don C. Harvey, I. Stanford Jolley, Richard Powers [aka: Tom Keene], Minerva Urecal, Frank Fenton, John R. McKee, Harry McKim, Sandy Sanders, Michael "Mike" Ragan [aka: Holly Bane], Roy Gordon, Duke York, Richard Flato, Roy Cutler, Champion (horse). *D:* Frank McDonald; *P:* Armand Schaefer; *St: & Sc:* Norman S. Hall. (1:10) In this series western, Gene goes after an outfit that is counterfeiting Mexican lottery tickets. Sepiatone. *My True Story* (q.v.) completed the original double bill program.

2660. Texas Bad Man (Monogram/Allied Artists; 1953). *Cast:* Wayne Morris, Elaine Riley, Frank Ferguson, Sheb Wooley, Denver Pyle, Myron Healey, Mort Mills, Nelson Leigh. *D:* Lewis D. Collins; *P:* Vincent M. Fennelly; *St: & Sc:* Joseph Poland. (1:02) Programmer western of a lawman forced to confront his father and the latter's activities with an outlaw gang. One in a series of six westerns that Morris did for Allied Artists.

2661. Texas Carnival (MGM; 1951). *Cast:* Esther Williams, Red Skelton, Howard Keel, Ann Miller, Paula Raymond, Keenan Wynn, Tom Tully, Glenn Strange, Dick Wessel, Donald MacBride, The Red Norvo Trio, Foy Willing and Riders of the Purple Sage, Hans Conried, Thurston Hall, Marjorie Wood, Duke Johnson, Wilson Wood, Michael Dugan, Doug Carter, Earle Hodgins, Gil Patrick, Rhea Mitchell, Emmett Lynn, Bess Flowers, Jack Daley, Fred Santley, Joe Roach, Manuel Petroff, Robert Fortier, William Lundy, Alex Goudovitch. *D:* Charles Walter; *P:* Jack Cummings; *St:* George Wells, Dorothy Kingsley; *Sc:* Kingsley; *Songs:* "It's Dynamite," "Whoa! Emma," "Young Folks Should Get Married," "Carnie's Pitch" Dorothy Fields, Harry Warren; "Clap Your Hands," "Deep in the Heart of Texas" June Hershey, Don Swander and "Schnaps" Maurice Vandair. (1:17) (video/laserdisc) Popular Technicolor musical-comedy romance of a pauperish sideshow carny who is mistaken for a Texas millionaire.

2662. Texas City (Monogram/Silvermine Prods.; 1952). *Cast:* Johnny Mack Brown, James Ellison, Lois Hall, Lorna Thayer, Lane Bradford, Marshall J. Reed, Terry L. Frost, Lyle Talbot, Pierce Lyden, John Hart, Lennie [Bud] Osborne, Stanley Price. *D:* Lewis D. Collins; *P:* Vincent M. Fennelly; *St: & Sc:* Joseph Poland. (0:55) A U.S. marshal investigates the theft of gold shipments in this series western which had the pre-release title of "Ghost Town."

2663. Texas Dynamo (Columbia; 1950). *Cast:* Charles Starrett, Smiley Burnette, Lois Hall, Jock [Mahoney] O'Mahoney, John Dehner, Gregg Barton, George Chesebro, Emil Sitka, Fred F. Sears, Marshall Reed, Lane Bradford, Slim Duncan. *D:* Ray Nazarro; *P:* Colbert Clark; *St: & Sc:* Barry Shipman. (0:54) "Durango Kid" series western with the kid taking on the guise of a hired killer known as "Texas Dynamo." (G.B. title. *Suspected*)

Texas Kid—Outlaw (G.B. title) *see* **The Kid from Texas**

2664. Texas Lady (RKO; 1955). *Cast:* Claudette Colbert, Barry Sullivan, Gregory

Walcott, James Bell, Horace McMahon, Ray Collins, Walter Sande, Don Haggerty, Douglas Fowley, Celia Lovsky, John Litel, Harry Tyler, Alexander Campbell, LeRoy Johnson, Florenz Ames, Kathleen Mulqueen, Robert Lynn, Grandon Rhodes, Bruce Payne, George Brand, Raymond Greenleaf. *D:* Tim Whelan (final film—d. 1957); *P:* Nat Holt; *St: & Sc:* Horace McCoy; *Song:* "Texas Lady" Paul Sawtell, Johnnie Mann (sung by Les Paul and Mary Ford). (1:26) (video) Offbeat western drama of a woman who wins a large sum of money gambling and with it buys a newspaper and goes up against the local crime boss. Technicolor/SuperScope.

2665. Texas Lawmen (Monogram/Frontier Pictures; 1951). *Cast:* Johnny Mack Brown, James Ellison, I. Stanford Jolley, Lee Roberts, Lane Bradford, Marshall Reed, John Hart, Lyle Talbot, Pierce Lyden, Stanley Price, Terry Frost. *D:* Lewis D. Collins; *P:* Vincent M. Fennelly; *St:* Myron Healey; *Sc:* Joseph Poland. (0:54) Johnny Mack Brown series western of the attempts to capture a lawman's lawless father and brother. (aka: *Lone Star Lawman*)

2666. The Texas Rangers (Columbia/Edward Small Prods.; 1951). *Cast:* George Montgomery, Gale Storm, Jerome Courtland, Noah Beery, Jr., William Bishop (Sam Bass), John Litel, Douglas Kennedy (Dave Rudabaugh), John Dehner (John Wesley Hardin), Ian MacDonald (The Sundance Kid), John Doucette (Butch Cassidy), Jock [Mahoney] O'Mahoney, Joseph Fallon, Myron Healey, Julian Rivero, Trevor Bardette, Stanley Andrews, Edward Earle. *D:* Phil Karlson; *P:* Bernard Small; *St:* Frank Gruber; *Sc:* Richard Schayer. (1:14) (video) Western of the early days of the Texas Rangers as they set out to round up the notorious "Hole-in-the-Wall" gang. SuperCinecolor.

Texas Rose (G.B. title) *see* **The Return of Jack Slade**

2667. That Certain Feeling (Paramount/P & F Prods.–Hope Enterprises; 1956). *Cast:* Bob Hope, Eva Marie Saint, George Sanders, Pearl Bailey, Al Capp (himself), Jerry Mathers, David Lewis, Herbert Rudley, Florenz Ames, Richard Shannon, Valerie Allen, Jacqueline Beer, Jeanette Miller, Herbert Vigran, Paul Dubov, Jeff Hayden, Emory Parnell, Douglas Wood, Lawrence Dobkin, Sid Tomack, Eric Alden, Jan Bradley, Jack Pepper, Jack Lomas, Richard Keene, Joseph Kerr. *D: & P:* Norman Panama, Melvin Frank; *Sc:* Panama, Frank, I.A.L. Diamond, William Altman; *Songs:* "That Certain Feeling" George and Ira Gershwin (sung by Pearl Bailey); "Hit the Road to Dreamland" Johnny Mercer, Harold Arlen; "Zing Went the Strings of My Heart" James F. Hanley. (1:43) Critically panned romantic comedy with songs of a cartoonist with creative burnout who hires an artist to ghost for him, only the artist's ex-wife is the cartoonist's girlfriend. Based on the play *The King of Hearts* by Jean Kerr and Eleanor Brooke. Technicolor/VistaVision.

That Kind of Girl (G.B. title) *see* **Models, Inc.**

2668. That Kind of Woman (Paramount/Ponti-Girosi; 1959). *Cast:* Sophia Loren, Tab Hunter, George Sanders, Jack Warden, Keenan Wynn, Barbara Nichols, John Fielder, Bea Arthur. *D:* Sidney Lumet; *P:* Carlo Ponti, Marcello Girosi; *St:* Robert Lowry; *Sc:* Walter Bernstein. (1:32) Comedy-drama of a soldier who falls for a woman and she him, only she has a millionaire waiting in the wings. Based on the play *Private Pettigrew's Girl* by Dana Burnet, its previous incarnations were *Pettigrew's Girl* (Paramount; 1919), *The Shopworn Angel* (Paramount; 1929) a part-talkie and *Shopworn Angel* (MGM; 1938). Filmed in New York City, it was in nomination at the Berlin Film Festival. VistaVision.

2669. That Man from Tangier (United Artists/Elemsee Overseas Prods.; 1953). *Cast:* Nils Asther (final film—ret.), Roland Young (final film—d. 1953), Nancy Coleman, Margaret Wycherly, Sarita Montiel, Jose Saurez. *D:* Robert Elwyn; *P:* Elwyn, Larry Corcoran; *St: & Sc:* John Meehan, Jr. (1:28) The romance of a spoiled rich American woman who has a poor Spanish nobleman pose as her husband.

2670. That Night (Universal-International/RKO-Galahad; 1957). *Cast:* John Beal, Augusta Dabney, Malcolm Broderick, Dennis Kohler, Beverly Lunsford, Shepperd Strudwick, Rosemary Murphy, Bill Darrid, Joe Julian. *D:* John Newland; *P:* Himan Brown; *Sc:* Robert Wallace, Burton J. Rowles [based on their TV drama "The Long Way Home"]. (1:28) Drama of a Madison Avenue ad executive and the events that transpire when he suffers a heart attack, including the effects it has on his family members. Another production of RKO that was released by Universal. This film was also in nomination at the British Academy Awards.

2671. That's My Boy (Paramount/Wallis-Hazen; 1951). *Cast:* Dean Martin (Bill Baker),

Jerry Lewis ("Junior" Jackson), Ruth Hussey (Ann Jackson), Marion Marshall (Terry Howard), Eddie Mayehoff ("Jarring Jack" Jackson), Polly Bergen (Betty Hunter), John McIntire (Benjamin Green—psychiatrist), Hugh Sanders (Coach Wheeler), Francis Pierlot (Henry Baker), Lillian Randolph (May), Selmer Jackson (Doc Hunter), Tom Harmon (sports announcer). *D:* Hal Walker; *P:* Hal B. Wallis; *St: & Sc:* Cy Howard; *Songs:* "I'm in the Mood For Love" Jimmy McHugh, Dorothy Fields; "Ridgeville Fight Song" Jay Livingston, Ray Evans; "Ballin' the Jack" Chris Smith, Jim Burris. (1:38) A hypochondriac, at the insistence of his father, joins his college football team and gets through the ordeal with the help of his roommate. A comedy that became one of the 23 top-grossing films of 1950-51, it was also the inspiration for a later TV series.

Their Secret Affair (G.B. title) *see* **Top Secret Affair**

2672. Them! (Warner; 1954). *Cast:* James Whitmore (Sgt. Ben Peterson), Edmund Gwenn (Dr. Harold Medford), Joan Weldon (Dr. Patricia Medford), James Arness (Robert Graham), Onslow Stevens (Brig. Gen. O'Brien), Sean McClory (Major Kibbee), Chris Drake (Officer Ed Blackburn), Sandy Descher (little girl in desert), Mary Alan Hokanson (Mrs. Lodge), Fess Parker (Crotty), Olin Howlin (Jensen), Frederick J. Foote (Dixon), Robert Scott Correll (Jerry), Richard Bellis (Mike), Matthew McCue (Gramps), John Maxwell (Dr. Grant), Joe Forte (Putnam the coroner), Robert Berger (Sutton), John Beradino (Ryan), Don Shelton, Leonard Nimoy, Dub Taylor, Ann Doran, Joel Smith, Cliff Ferre, Wally Duffy, Fred Shellac, Norman Field, Otis Garth, Janet Stewart, Dick Wessel, Russell Gaige, Dorothy Green, Dean Cromer, Lawrence Dobkin, Chad Mallory, Gayle Kellogg, Victor Sutherland, Charles Perry, Warren Mace, Jack Perrin, Marshall Bradford, John Close (voice only), Waldron Boyle, Willis Bouchey, Alexander Campbell, Harry Tyler, Oscar Blanke, Eddie Dew, James Cardwell, Walter Coy, Booth Colman, Hubert Kerns, Royden Clark, Charles Meredith, Richard Deacon. *D:* Gordon Douglas; *P:* David Weisbart; *St:* George Worthing Yates; *Adapatation:* Russell Hughes; *Sc:* Ted Sherdeman; *F/X:* (AAN) Ralph Ayres, William Mueller, Francis J. Scheid. (1:33) (video/laserdisc) Science fiction of giant mutated ants discovered in the desert of the southwest U.S., eventually making their way to the sewers of Los Angeles. This acclaimed entry in the genre was the studio's highest grossing film of the year.

2673. There's Always Tomorrow (Universal International; 1956). *Cast:* Barbara Stanwyck, Fred MacMurray, Joan Bennett, Pat Crowley, William Reynolds, Gigi Perreau, Judy Nugent, Race Gentry, Myrna Hansen, Jane Darwell, Paul Smith, Jane Howard, Helen Kleeb, Frances Mercer, Sheila Bromley, Louise Lorimer, Dorothy Bruce, Hermione Sterler, Fred Nurney, Hal Smith, James Rawley, Jack Lomas, Jean Byron, Bert Holland, Carlyle Mitchell, Mack Williams, Richard Mayer, Pat Meller, Vonne Lester, Lorelei Vitek, June Clayworth, Ross Hunter (bit). *D:* Douglas Sirk; *P:* Ross Hunter; *St:* Ursula Parrott; *Sc:* Bernard C. Schoenfeld. (1:24) Soapish melodrama of a man who meets an old flame and has thoughts of leaving his wife and children. A remake of the 1934 production by this studio.

2674. There's No Business Like Show Business (20th Century–Fox; 1954). *Cast:* Ethel Merman (Molly Donahue), Donald O'Connor (Tim Donahue), Marilyn Monroe (Vicky), Dan Dailey (Terrance Donahue), Johnnie Ray (Steve Donahue), Mitzi Gaynor (Katy Donahue), Richard Eastham (Lew Harris), Hugh O'Brian (Charles Gibbs), Frank McHugh (Eddie Duggan), Rhys Williams (Father Dineen), Lee Patrick (Marge), Chick Chandler (Harry), Robin Raymond (Lillian Sawyer), Gavin Gordon (Geoffrey), Mimi Gibson (Katy, age 4), Linda Lowell (Katy, age 8), John Potter (Steve, age 2), Jimmy Baird (Steve, age 6), Billy Chapin (Steve, age 10), Neal McCaskill (Tim, age 2), Donald Gamble (Tim, age 6), Charlotte Austin (Lorna), Isabel Dawn (Sophie Tucker), Donald Kerr (Bobby Clark), Eve Miller, Lyle Talbot, George Melford, Alvy Moore, Henry Slate, Nolan Leary, John Doucette, George Chakiris (unbilled dancer). *D:* Walter Lang; *P:* Sol C. Siegel; *St:* (AAN) Lamar Trotti; *Sc:* Phoebe Ephron, Henry Ephron; *Music:* (AAN) Alfred Newman, Lionel Newman; *Costumes:* (AAN-color) Charles LeMaire, Travilla, Miles White; *Songs:* "Heat Wave," "Alexander's Ragtime Band," "When the Midnight Choo Choo Leaves for Alabam'," "Let's Have Another Cup of Coffee," "Play a Simple Melody," "After You Get What You Want, You Don't Want It," "You'd Be Surprised," "A Sailor's Not a Sailor," "A Pretty Girl Is Like a Melody," "Lazy," "If You Believe Me," "A Man Chases a Girl Until She Catches Him," "Marie" and "There's No Business Like Show Business" Irving Berlin. (1:57) (video/laserdisc) Hit musical-comedy-drama of the ups and downs of a prominent show-biz family during the days of vaudeville. The musical highlight of this production has got to be Monroe's song and dance rendition of Berlin's "Heat Wave." DeLuxe color/CinemaScope.

2675. These Thousand Hills (20th Century–Fox; 1959). *Cast:* Don Murray, Richard Egan, Lee Remick, Patricia Owens, Stuart Whitman, Albert Dekker, Milburn J. Stone, Royal Dano, Jean Willes, Douglas Fowley, Fuzzy Knight, Robert Adler, Ned Wever, Barbara Morrison, Ken Renard, Steve Darrell, Tom Greenway, Frank Lavier, Nelson Leigh, Ben Wright, Jesse Kirkpatrick, John Epper. *D:* Richard Fleischer; *P:* David Weisbart; *Sc:* Alfred Hayes; *Title song:* Harry Warren, Ned Washington (sung by Randy Sparks). (1:36) Acclaimed western drama of two cowhands, one who wants to settle down, the other who chooses to be a law-breaker. Set in Montana, but filmed in Colorado, it is based on A.B. Guthrie, Jr.'s 1956 novel of loyalty to friends. DeLuxe color/CinemaScope.

2676. These Wilder Years (MGM; 1956). *Cast:* James Cagney, Barbara Stanwyck, Walter Pidgeon, Betty Lou Keim, Don Dubbins, Edward Andrews, Basil Ruysdael, Grandon Rhodes, Will Wright, Lewis Martin, Dorothy Adams, Dean Jones, Herb Vigran, Ruth Lee, Matt Moore, Jack Kenney, Harry Tyler, Luana Lee, William Forrest, John Maxwell, Emmett Vogan, Charles Evans, Michael Landon, Leon Tyler, Sid Tomack, Russ Whitney, Tom Laughlin, Audrey Swanson, Jimmy Hayes, Bob Alden, Jimmy Ogg, Nesdon Booth, Ricky McGough, Louis Towers, Mary Alan Hokanson, Marc Platt, Mary Lawrence, Elizabeth Flournoy, Charles Herbert, Kathleen Mulqueen, Burt Mustin, Russell Simpson, Bruce Irwin, Charles Tannen, Billy Wayne, Lillian Powell, Edna Holland, Ralph Neff, Lois Kimbrell, Frank Connor, Eleanor Grumer, Byron Amidon, Janet Lake, Don Burnett. *D:* Roy Rowland; *P:* Jules Schermer; *St:* Ralph Wheelwright; *Sc:* Frank Fenton. (1:31) Melodramatic soaper of a middle-aged multimillionaire's (Cagney) search for his born-out-of-wedlock son (Dubbins), born 20 years previous.

2677. They Came to Cordura (Columbia/Goetz Pictures-Baroda Prods.; 1959). *Cast:* Gary Cooper, Rita Hayworth, Van Heflin, Tab Hunter, Richard Conte, Michael Callan (film debut), Dick York, Robert Keith, Carlos Romero, Jim Bannon, Edward Platt, Maurice Jara, Sam Buffington, Arthur Hanson, Wendell Hoyt. *D:* Robert Rossen; *P:* William Goetz; *Sc:* Ivan Moffat, Rossen. (2:03) (video/laserdisc) Drama set in 1916 Mexico of an "Awards officer" and his trek through the desert with five candidates for the Medal of Honor, though each of their personalities are less than honorable. Based on the 1958 book by Glendon F. Swarthout, it was filmed in Nevada and Utah. Eastmancolor/CinemaScope.

2678. They Rode West (Columbia; 1954). *Cast:* Robert Francis, Donna Reed, May Wynn, Phil Carey, Onslow Stevens, Roy Roberts, Jack Kelly, Stuart Randall, Eugene Iglesias, James Best, Peggy Converse, Frank DeKova, John War Eagle, Ralph Dumke, Julia Montoya, George Keymas, Maurice Jara. *D:* Phil Karlson; *P:* Lewis J. Rachmil; *St:* Leo Katcher; *Sc:* DeVallon Scott, Frank Nugent. (1:24) Western drama of an army doctor who gets into trouble when he aids a tribe of Indians during a malaria outbreak. Technicolor.

2679. The Thief (United Artists/Fran Prods.; 1952). *Cast:* Ray Milland (Allan Fields), Rita Gam (film debut/the girl), Martin Gabel (Mr. Bleck), Harry Bronson (Harris), Rita Vale (Miss Philips), Rex O'Malley (Beal), John McKutcheon (Dr. Linstrum), Joe Conlin (Walters). *D:* Russell Rouse; *P:* Clarence Greene; *St:* Rouse, Greene; *Music:* (AAN) Herschel Burke Gilbert. (1:25) (video) Melodrama (with no dialogue) of a nuclear physicist who passes top secret information to enemy agents. Filmed on location in New York City and Washington, D.C., it placed #6 on the "10 Best" list of the NBR.

2680. The Thief of Damascus (Columbia; 1952). *Cast:* Paul Henreid, John Sutton, Jeff Donnell, Lon Chaney, Elena Verdugo, Robert Clary, Edward Colmans, Nelson Leigh, Philip Van Zandt, Leonard Penn, Larry Stewart, Robert Conte. *D:* Will Jason (final film—ret.); *P:* Sam Katzman; *St: & Sc:* Robert E. Kent. (1:18) "Arabian Nights" type adventure with the city of Damascus threatened by invaders and Sinbad (Chaney), Aladdin (Clary) and Ali Baba (Van Zandt) out to rescue Princess Scheherazade (Donnell). The film which utilizes footage from *Joan of Arc* (RKO; 1948) originally ran on the top of a double bill with *A Yank in Indo-China* (q.v.). Technicolor.

2681. The Thing (RKO/Winchester Pictures; 1951). *Cast:* Kenneth Tobey, Margaret Sheridan, James Arness (title role), Robert Cornthwaite, Douglas Spencer, James Young, Dewey Martin, Robert Nichols, William Self, Eduard Franz, John Dierkes, Sally Creighton, Paul Frees, George Fenneman, David McMann,

Billy Curtis (the shrinking "Thing"), Everett Glass, Tom Steele, Norbert Schiller, Edmund Breon, William Neff, Lee Tung Foo, Walter Ng, Robert Stevenson, Robert Gutknecht, Robert Bray, Ted Cooper, Allan Ray, Nicholas Byron. *D:* Christian Nyby (debut/credited), Howard Hawks (unc.); *P:* Hawks; *Sc:* Charles Lederer. (1:27) (video/laserdisc) Critically acclaimed science fiction-horror of a group of scientists at the North Pole who uncover a spaceship and a humanoid alien frozen in the ice. The alien is accidentally thawed out and goes on a murderous rampage. A major box office hit, it was remade in 1982. Based on the story "Who Goes There?" by Don A Stuart (pseudonym of John W. Campbell, Jr.), computer-colored prints have been produced by Turner Entertainment. (aka: *The Thing from Another World*)

2682. The Thing That Couldn't Die (Universal-International; 1958). *Cast:* Andra Martin, William Reynolds, Carolyn Kearney, Jeffrey Stone, Charles Horvath, James Anderson, Peggy Converse, Robin Hughes (title role), Forrest Lewis. *D: & P:* Will Cowan; *Sc:* David Duncan [based on his story idea "The Water Witch"]. (1:09) On a western ranch, the living head of a member of Sir Francis Drake's crew named Gideon Drew is discovered and it directs one of the residents where to find the rest of his body that was buried in 1579. This low budget horror thriller originally ran on the bottom of a double bill with *Horror of Dracula*, a British production.

2683. Third Man on the Mountain (Buena Vista/Walt Disney Prods.; 1959). *Cast:* Michael Rennie, James MacArthur, Janet Munro, James Donald, Herbert Lom, Laurence Naismith, Lee Patterson, Walter Fitzgerald, Nora Swinburne, Ferdy Mayne, James Ramsey Ullman (bit), Helen Hayes (cameo). *D:* Ken Annakin; *Ex.P:* Walt Disney; *P:* William H. Anderson; *Sc:* Eleanore Griffin; *Songs:* "Climb the Mountain" Franklyn Marks, By Dunham; "Good Night Valais" G. Haenni, Tom Adair. (1:45) (video) Technicolor adventure drama of a youth determined to climb a mountain which took the life of his father in a similar attempt. Based on the book *Banner in the Sky* by James Ramsey Ullman, it was filmed on location in Switzerland. Another box office disappointment for Disney. (aka: *Banner in the Sky*)

Third Party Risk *see* **The Deadly Mantis**

2684. The Thirteenth Letter (20th Century–Fox; 1951). *Cast:* Linda Darnell, Charles Boyer, Michael Rennie, Constance Smith, Francoise Rossay, Judith Evelyn, Guy Sorel, June Hedin, Camille Ducharme, Paul Guevremont, George Alexander, J. Leo Cagnon, Ovila Legare, Wilford Davidson, Arthur Grouix, Sheila Coonan, L.P. Herbert, Odie Lemire, Gilles Pelletier, C. Bosvier, J.L. Roux, Blanche Gauthier, Jerry Rowan, Louis Roux, Eleanor Stuart, Lucie Boitres, Jacques Auger, Patrick O'Moore, Robin Hughes, Stanley Mann, Vernon Steele. *D: & P:* Otto Preminger; *Sc:* Howard Koch. (1:25) Drama, set in a French Canadian town of a series of poison pen letters delivered to various people, creating various reactions to the letters, with all determined to find the author. Based on the story and screenplay of *Le Corbeau* by Louis Chavance, a 1943 French production of Westport International released in the U.S. in 1948 as *The Raven*.

2685. -30- (Warner/Mark VII Ltd.; 1959). *Cast:* Jack Webb, William Conrad, David Nelson, Whitney Blake, Louise Lorimer, John Nolan, James Bell, Nancy Valentine, Richard Bakalyan, Dick Whittinghill, Joe Flynn, Donna Sue Needham. *D: & P:* Jack Webb; *St: & Sc:* William Bowers; *Song:* "Boy" Don Ralke, Bowers (sung by David Nelson). (1:36) (video) Melodrama of one eight-hour night in a big city newspaper, with the main focus, getting out the next day's edition. (G.B. title: *Deadline Midnight*)

2686. The 30-Foot Bride of Candy Rock (Columbia/D.R.B. Prods.; 1959). *Cast:* Lou Costello (final film—d. 1959), Dorothy Provine, Gale Gordon, Jimmy Conlin, Charles Lane, Robert Burton, Will Wright, Lenny Kent, Ruth Perrott, Peter Leeds, Robert Nichols, Bobby Barber, Jack Straw, Russell Trent, Joe Greene, Joey Faye, Doodles Weaver, Jack Rice, Veola Vonn. *D:* Sidney Miller; *P:* Lewis J. Rachmil; *Ex.P:* Edward Sherman; *St:* Lawrence L. Goldman [based on an idea by Jack Rabin and Irving Block]; *Sc:* Rowland Barber, Arthur A. Ross. (1:15) (video) Science fiction comedy of garbage collector and inventor who accidentally turns his girlfriend into a giantess and is forced by her father to marry her when he misunderstands the fact that she is getting "bigger." Amazoscope.

2687. This Angry Age (Columbia/Dino De Laurentiis; 1958). *Cast:* Anthony Perkins, Silvana Mangano, Richard Conte, Jo Van Fleet, Nehemiah Persoff, Alida Valli, Yvonne Sanson, Chu Shao Chuan, Guido Celano. *D:* Rene Clement; *P:* Dino De Laurentiis; *As.P:* Ralph B.

Serpe; *Sc:* Irwin Shaw, Clement; *Songs:* "Uh-Huh!" (The Crawl) LeRoy Kirkland, Billy Dawn (performed by Perkins and Mangano); "Ya Ya Ya" Alvy West (performed by Little Band with the Rosalyn Teen Agers), "One Kiss Away From Heaven" A. Romeo, Sam Coslow (by Perkins); "Only You" Ram and Rand (performed by the Four Riders with orchestra). (1:51) Drama of a French widow and her two grown children who work their rice farm behind a wall, built to keep the sea out. An Italian–French–U.S.A. co-production based on the novel *Sea Wall* by Marguerite Duras, it was filmed on location in Thailand. Critics were divided. (Original title: *The Sea Wall*) Technicolor/Technirama.

2688. This Could Be the Night (MGM; 1957). *Cast:* Jean Simmons, Paul Douglas, Anthony Franciosa (film debut), Julie Wilson, Neile Adams, Joan Blondell, J. Carrol Naish, Rafael Campos, ZaSu Pitts, Tom Helmore, Murvyn Vye, Ray Anthony & Band (themselves), Vaughn Taylor, Frank Ferguson, William Ogden Joyce, James Todd, John Harding, Percy Helton, Richard Collier, Edna Holland, Betty Uitti, Lew Smith, June Blair, Nita Talbot, Harry Hines, Gregg Martell, Matty Fain and the Archie Savage Trio [A. Savage, Andrew Robinson and Walter Davis]. *D:* Robert Wise; *P:* Joe Pasternak; *Sc:* Isobel Lennart; *Songs:* Title song, "Hustlin' News Gal," "I Got It Bad" Duke Ellington, Paul Francis Webster; "I'm Gonna Live Till I Die" Al Hoffman, Walter Kent, Mann Curtis; "Taking a Chance on Love" John Latouche, Ted Fetter, Vernon Duke; "Trumpet Boogie," "Mamba Combo," "Blue Moon" Richard Rodgers, Lorenz Hart; "Dream Dancing" Cole Porter; "The Tender Trap" Jimmy Van Heusen, Sammy Cahn. (1:43) (video/laserdisc) Musical-comedy of a teacher who also works as a secretary for a criminally involved New York nightclub owner and the lothario who sets his sights on her. Based on "Protection for a Tough Racket" and "It's Hard to Find Mecca in Flushing," two stories by Cordelia Baird Gross. CinemaScope.

2689. This Earth Is Mine (Universal-International/Vintage Prods.; 1959). *Cast:* Rock Hudson (John Rambeau), Jean Simmons (Elizabeth), Dorothy McGuire (Martha Fairon), Claude Rains (Philippe Rambeau), Kent Smith (Francis Fairon), Cindy Robbins (Buz Dietrick), Anna Lee (Charlotte Rambeau), Ken Scott (Luigi Griffanti), Peter Cong (Chu), Francis Bethencourt (Andre Swann), Augusta Merighi (Mrs. Griffanti), Geraldine Wall (Maria), Alberto Morin (Petucci), Penny Santon (Mrs. Petucci), Jack Mather (Dietrick), Ben Astar (Yakowitz), Daniel White (Judge Gruber), Lawrence Ung (David), Ford Dunhill (Tim Rambeau). *D:* Henry King; *P:* Casey Robinson, Claude Heilman; *Sc:* Robinson; *Title song:* James Van Heusen, Sammy Cahn (sung by Don Cornell). (2:05) Generation gap drama of differing opinions among members of a wine producing family in the Napa Valley of California. Based on the novel *The Cup and the Sword* by Alice Tisdale Hobart, it was filmed on location. One of the 26 top-grossing films of 1958-59. Technicolor/CinemaScope.

2690. This Happy Feeling (Universal-International; 1958). *Cast:* Debbie Reynolds, Curt Jurgens, John Saxon, Alexis Smith, Estelle Winwood, Mary Astor, Troy Donahue, Hayden Rorke, Gloria Holden (final film–ret.), Alex Gerry, Joe Flynn, Alexander Campbell, Clem Fuller and the unnamed seagull. *D:* Blake Edwards; *P:* Ross Hunter; *Sc:* Edwards; *Title song:* Jay Livingston, Ray Evans (sung by Reynolds). (1:32) (video) Romantic comedy of a young girl's infatuation with a retired bachelor matinee idol of old films. Based on the 1947 play *For Love or Money* by F. Hugh Herbert. Eastmancolor/CinemaScope.

2691. This Is Cinerama (Cinerama Prods.; 1952). *P:* Merian C. Cooper, Robert L. Bendick; *Prologue Director:* Ernest B. Schoedsack; *Prologue Screenplay:* Ruth Rose, Cooper; *Music:* (AAN) Louis Forbes; *Introduction:* Lowell Thomas; *Narrators:* Thomas, Prosper Buranelli. (2:00) The premiere Cinerama feature travelogue, a theatrical innovation which enabled the viewer to utilize his or her peripheral vision while viewing the production on a 146° screen in stereophonic sound. The projection equipment consisted of three projectors, each casting a separate image to form the total on screen image, creating a "you are there" type of effect, experiencing whatever is being shown on the screen. The program which included an intermission consisted of a performance of the Long Island Choral Society doing Handel's *Messiah*, gondola boating in the "streets" of Venice, Italy, a parade by a Scottish Highlander band at Edinburgh Castle, a garden performance by the Vienna Boys Choir, a bullfight crowd in Madrid, a roller-coaster ride (with a front seat view), a ballet at the La Scala in Milan, Italy, a helicopter trip over Niagara Falls, a performance of the finale of Act II of *Aida*, motorboats and waterskiing at Cypress Gardens, Florida, sightseeing over the U.S. by airplane taking in New York City, Washington,

D.C., Chicago, Illinois farmlands, the Grand Tetons and more. Technicolor.

2692. This Is Korea! (Republic; 1951). *D: & P:* John Ford; *Narrators:* uncredited. (1:20) A feature documentary of the U.S. Navy utilizing combat footage by combat photographers of the First Marine Division and the Seventh Fleet (with a bow to the U.S. Army). Trucolor. Note: Also available in a 40 min.+ format.

2693. This Is My Love (RKO/Allan Dowling Pictures; 1954). *Cast:* Linda Darnell, Rick Jason, Dan Duryea, Faith Domergue, Hal Baylor, Connie Russell (herself), Jerry Mathers, Susie Mathers, Mary Young, William Hopper, Stuart Randall, Kam Tong, Judd Holdren, Carl Switzer. *D:* Stuart Heisler; *P:* Hugh Brooke; *Sc:* Hagar Wilde, Brooke; *Title song:* Franz Waxman, Brooke. (1:31) Melodrama of romantic rivalry for a young man between sisters, which evolves into the murder of the married sister's husband. Based on *Fear Has Black Wings* by Mr. Brooke. Pathécolor.

2694. This Is Russia (Universal-International; 1957). *D: & P:* Sid Feder (who also photographed). A feature length documentary-travelogue of the cities of the Soviet Union, delivered with a dialogue that conveyed suspicion and alarmism in those days of the Cold War.

2695. This Is Your Army (United Artists/ Fox Movietone News–U.S. Army; 1954). *D:* John J. Gordon; *P:* Edmund Reek; *Sc:* Joseph Kenas, Capt. James Altieri; *Cinematography:* Jack Painter, Bill Storz (supervised by the Army Signal Corps); *Narrators:* Joe King, Phil Tonken. (0:55) A feature documentary of life in the "New U.S. Army" which includes footage of training in Korea, Greece, Turkey, Italy, France, Germany and Formosa, footage of the 55-ton 280 mm "atomic cannon" in action at Frenchman's Flat, Nevada, and a Nike missile destroying a B-17 bomber. Two years in production. Technicolor.

2696. This Island Earth (Universal-International; 1955). *Cast:* Jeff Morrow, Faith Domergue, Rex Reason, Russell Johnson, Lance Fuller, Douglas Spencer, Robert Nichols, Karl Lindt, Eddie Parker, Regis Parton, Olan Soule, Richard Deacon, Robert B. Williams, Marc Hamilton, Coleman Francis, Spencer Chan, Lizalotta Valesca, Edward Ingram, Jack Byron, Guy Edward Hearn, Les Spears. *D:* Joseph Newman, Jack Arnold (unc.); *P:* William Alland; *Sc:* Franklin Coen, Edward G. O'Callaghan. (1:26) (video/laserdisc) Critically acclaimed science fiction tale of earth scientists drawn to the planet Metaluna under false pretenses. When there, they find they are to help save the planet from alien invaders. Based on the 1952 novel by Raymond F. Jones. Technicolor.

This Rebel Age *see* **The Beat Generation**

2697. This Side of the Law (Warner; 1950). *Cast:* Viveca Lindfors, Kent Smith, Janis Paige, Robert Douglas, John Alvin, Monte Blue, Frances Morris, Nita Talbot. *D:* Richard L. Bare; *P:* Saul Elkins; *Sc:* Russell Hughes. (1:14) Low budget tale of a crooked lawyer who uses a man to pose as a millionaire in order to perpetrate a financial scam concerning a will. Based on the short story "The Doctor Doubles in Death" by Richard Sale.

2698. This Woman Is Dangerous (Warner; 1952). *Cast:* Joan Crawford, Dennis Morgan, David Brian, Richard Webb, Mari Aldon, Philip Carey, Ian MacDonald, Katherine Warren, Sherry Jackson, William Challee, George Chandler, Douglas Fowley, Harry Lauter, Karen Hale, Charles Sullivan, Jean Carry, Dick Bartell, Mary Alan Hokanson, Eileen Stevens, Dee Carroll, Kenneth Patterson, Harry Tyler, Gladys Blake, Cecile Weston. *D:* Felix Feist; *P:* Robert Sisk; *Sc:* Geoffrey Homes [Daniel Mainwaring], George Worthing Yates. (1:40) Melodrama of a cold-blooded killer and his ruthless female friend who seeks true love with her eye surgeon. Based on the story "Stab of Pain" by Bernard Girard.

2699. Those Redheads from Seattle (Paramount; 1953). *Cast:* Rhonda Fleming, Gene Barry, Agnes Moorehead, Teresa Brewer, Guy Mitchell, The Bell Sisters [Kay and Cynthia], Bill Pullen, Jean Parker, Roscoe Ates, John Kellogg, Frank Wilcox, Walter Reed, William Fuller, Michael Ross, Ed Rand. *D:* Lewis R. Foster; *P:* William H. Pine, William C. Thomas; *St: & Sc:* Foster, Geoffrey Homes [Daniel Mainwaring], George Worthing Yates; *Songs:* "Baby, Baby, Baby" Jerry Livingston, Mack David (sung by Brewer); "Chick-a-Boom" Bob Merrill (sung by Mitchell); "I Guess It Was You All the Time" Hoagy Carmichael, Johnny Mercer (by Brewer); "Mr. Banjo Man" Jay Livingston, Ray Evans (by Brewer) and "Take Back Your Gold" Louis W. Pritzkow, M.H. Rosenfeld (sung by the Bell Sisters). (1:30) Musical of a woman who heads for the Klondike with her four daughters fearing her husband is in financial trouble, but finds he was murdered. Technicolor/3-D.

2700. Three Bad Sisters (United Artists/ Bel-Air–Northridge Prods.; 1956). *Cast:* Marla English, Kathleen Hughes, Sara Shane, John Bromfield, Jess Barker, Madge Kennedy, Tony George, Patsy Nayfack, Eric Wilton, Brett Halsey, Marlene Felton. *D:* Gilbert L. Kay; *P:* Howard W. Koch; *St:* Devery Freeman; *Sc:* Gerald Drayson Adams. (1:16) Melodramatic potboiler of the title siblings feuding over their late father's estate and the man who gets in the middle of the whole mess.

2701. Three Brave Men (20th Century–Fox; 1957). *Cast:* Ray Milland, Ernest Borgnine, Frank Lovejoy, Nina Foch, Dean Jagger, Virginia Christine, Edward Andrews, Frank Faylen, Diane Jergens, Warren Berlinger, Andrew Duggan, Joseph Wiseman, James Westerfield, Richard Anderson, Olive Blakeney, Robert Burton, Jason Wingreen, Ray Montgomery, Sandy Descher, Patty Ann Gerrity, Jonathan Hole, Barbara Gould, Fern Barry, Lee Roberts, Sherry Jackson, John Close, Keith Vincent, Tom Daly, Juanita Close, Edith Claire, Walter Woolf King, Gene O'Donnell, Carleton Young, Joseph McGuinn, Samuel Colt, Bill Hughes, Leonard Graves, Helen Mayon. *D:* Philip Dunne; *P:* Herbert B. Swope, Jr.; *Sc:* Dunne [based on Pulitzer Prize winning articles by Anthony Lewis]. (1:28) Based on the actual case of Abraham Chasanow, this drama relates the story of a man relieved of his long-held security job with the U.S. Navy when suspected of communist leanings, who hires a lawyer and fights the military's decision. CinemaScope.

2702. Three Came Home (20th Century–Fox; 1950). *Cast:* Claudette Colbert, Patric Knowles, Florence Desmond, Sessue Hayakawa, Sylvia Andrew, Mark Keuning, Phyllis Morris, Howard Chuman, Drue Mallory, Virginia Kelley, Mimi Heyworth, Helen Westcott, Taka Iwashaiki, Devi Dja, Leslie Thomas, John Burton, James Yanari, George Leigh, Li Sun, Duncan Richardson, Melinda Plowman, Lee MacGregor, Masaji "Butch" Yamamota, Pat Whyte, David Matsushama, Alex Frazer, Frank Kobata, Al Saijo, Jim Hagimori, Patricia O'Callaghan, Ken Kurosa, Giro Murashami, Leonard Willey, Harry Martin, Pat O'Moore, Clarke Gordon, Douglas Walton, Robin Hughes, John Santley, James Logan, Campbell Copelin (voice only), Leslie Denison (voice only). *D:* Jean Negulesco; *P:-Adaptation & Sc:* Nunnally Johnson. (1:46) (video) World War II drama of non-combatant prisoners, the brutality and starvation they endured over a three-year period after being taken from the island of Borneo by the Japanese and interred in concentration camps. Based on the 1947 autobiography of Agnes Newton Keith relating her experiences after being taken, along with her British husband.

2703. Three Coins in the Fountain (20th Century–Fox; 1954). *Cast:* Clifton Webb (Shadwell), Dorothy McGuire (Miss Francis), Jean Peters (Anita), Louis Jourdan (Prince Dino Di Cessi), Maggie McNamara (Maria), Rossano Brazzi (Georgio), Howard St. John (Burgoyne), Kathryn Givney (Mrs. Burgoyne), Cathleen Nesbitt (Principessa), Vincent Padula (Dr. Martinelli), Willard Waterman (Mr. Hoyt), Renata Vanni (Anna), Mario Siletti, Alberto Morin, Tony De Mario, Dino Bolognese, Jack Mattis, Zachary Yaconelli, Celia Lovsky, Larry Arnold, Grazia Narciso, Gino Corrado, Iphigenie Castiglioni, Norma Varden, Merry Anders, Charles LaTorre, Maurice Brierre, Luciana Paluzzi (film debut). *D:* Jean Negulesco; *P:* (AAN-Best Picture) Sol C. Siegel; *Sc:* John Patrick; *Cinematography:* (AA-color) Milton Krasner; *Title Song:* (AA) Jule Styne, Sammy Cahn (sung by Frank Sinatra). (1:42) (video/ laserdisc) The romantic pursuits of three American women in Rome is about all there is to the plot of this Fox moneymaker which placed #10 on the "10 Best" list of *Film Daily*. The first film to be filmed on location in CinemaScope and DeLuxe color. Based on the 1952 novel *Coins in the Fountain* by John H. Secondari, it became one of the 25 top-grossing films of 1953-54. Remade in 1964 as *The Pleasure Seekers*.

2704. Three Desperate Men (Lippert/ Mayflower Prods.; 1951). *Cast:* Preston Foster, Jim Davis, Virginia Grey, Ross Latimer, Monte Blue, William Haade, Sid Melton, Rory Mallinson, John Brown, Margaret Seddon, Anthony Jochim, House Peters, Jr., Joel Newfield, Lee Bennett, Steve Belmont, Carol Henry, Kermit Maynard, Bert Dillard, Gene Randall, Milton Kibbee, William Norton Bailey. *D:* Sam Newfield; *P:* Sigmund Neufeld; *St: & Sc:* Orville Hampton. (1:11) Programmer western of three brothers who go on a crime spree after being forced on the lam after one of the trio is accused of a crime he didn't commit. (re-issue title: *Three Outlaws*)

2705. The Three Faces of Eve (20th Century–Fox; 1957). *Cast:* Joanne Woodward (AA + "Best Actress" by the NBR combined with her work in *No Down Payment*, q.v./title roles), David Wayne (Ralph White), Lee J. Cobb (Dr. Luther), Edwin Jerome (Dr. Day), Nancy Kulp (Mrs. Black), Douglas Spencer (Mr. Black), Terry Ann Ross (Bonnie), Ken Scott (Earl), Mimi Gibson (Eve, age 8), Alena Murray, Alistair Cooke (narrator). *D:-P: & Sc:* Nunnally Johnson. (1:31) (video/laserdisc) Fact-based drama of a married woman with emotional problems who is found to have three distinct personalities. A hit for the studio, it was based on the book *A Case of Multiple Personality* by Corbett H. Thigpen, M.D., and Hervey M. Cleckley, M.D., the two doctors who treated the real "Eve White." CinemaScope.

2706. Three for Bedroom C (Warner/ Brenco Pictures; 1952). *Cast:* Gloria Swanson (in her final starring role in an American film), James Warren, Fred Clark, Hans Conried, Steve Brodie, Janine Perreau, Ernest Anderson, Richard "Skeets" Gallagher (final film—d. 1955), Margaret Dumont. *D: & Sc:* Milton H. Bren; *P:* Edward L. Alperson, Jr., Bren. (1:14) (video) A critically panned flop comedy of romance between an actress and a scientist aboard a transcontinental train. Based on the 1947 novel by Goddard Lieberson. Natural color.

2707. Three for Jamie Dawn (Allied Artists/Hayes Goetz; 1956). *Cast:* Laraine Day, Ricardo Montalban, Richard Carlson, June Havoc, Maria Palmer, Eduard Franz, Regis Toomey, Herbert Vigran, Marilyn Simms (title role), Dorothy Adams, Scotty Beckett (final film—ret.). *D:* Thomas Carr; *P:* Hayes Goetz; *St: & Sc:* John Klempner. (1:21) Crime melodrama of a wealthy socialite on trial for murder whose shady lawyer tries to buy off three jury members to gain a not guilty verdict.

2708. Three for the Show (Columbia; 1955). *Cast:* Betty Grable, Marge Champion, Gower Champion, Jack Lemmon, Myron McCormick, Paul Harvey, Robert Bice, Hal K. Dawson, Charlotte Lawrence, Willard Waterman, Gene Wesson, Aileen Carlyle, Rudy Lee, Eugene Borden. *D:* H.C. Potter; *P:* Jonie Taps; *Sc:* Leonard Stern, Edward Hope; *Songs:* "Someone to Watch Over Me" George & Ira Gershwin; "Which One?" Lester Lee, Ned Washington; "Down Boy" Hoagy Carmichael, Harold Adamson; "I've Been Kissed Before" Lee, Bob Russell; "I've Got a Crush On You" The Gershwins; "How Come You Like Me Like You Do?" Gene Austin, Roy Gergere; "Swan Lake" excerpt by Tchaikovsky + "The Homecoming" and "Three for the Show." (1:33) (laserdisc) Musical-comedy remake of *Too Many Husbands* (1940) of a woman's dilemma when she remarries. Based on the play *Too Many Husbands* by W. Somerset Maugham. An original condemnation by the Catholic Legion of Decency prompted the studio to re-edit. Technicolor and CinemaScope.

2709. Three Guys Named Mike (MGM; 1951). *Cast:* Jane Wyman, Van Johnson, Barry Sullivan, Howard Keel, Phyllis Kirk, Jeff Donnell, Hugh Sanders, Barbara Billingsley, Ann Sargent, Herbert Heyes, Robert Sherwood, Don McGuire, John Maxwell, Lewis Martin, Ethel "Pug" Wells (herself), Sydney Mason, Percy Helton, Dan Foster, Jack Shea, King Mojave, Arthur Space, Matt Moore, Mae Clarke, Jack Gargan. *D:* Charles Walters; *P:* Armand Deutsch; *Sc:* Sidney Sheldon. (1:30) (video) Romantic story by Ruth Brooks Flippen, from suggestions made by Ethel "Pug" Wells of an air hostess with her choice of three guys named Mike.

2710. Three Hours to Kill (Columbia; 1954). *Cast:* Dana Andrews, Donna Reed, Dianne Foster, Stephen Elliott, Laurence Hugo, Richard Webb, Carolyn Jones, Whit Bissell, Francis McDonald, Richard Coogan, James Westerfield, Charlotte Fletcher, Felipe Turich, Arthur Fox, Syd Saylor, Frank Hagney, Paul E. Burns, Hank Mann, Buddy Roosevelt, Edward Earle, Ada Adams, Reed Howes, Julian Rivero, Robert A. Paquin, Elsie Baker. *D:* Alfred L. Werker; *P:* Harry Joe Brown; *St:* Alex Gottlieb; *Sc:* Richard Alan Simmons, Roy Huggins; *Additional dialogue:* Maxwell Shane. (1:17) Western of a man freed by a lynch mob who seeks the guilty party in the murder of the brother of his former fiancée, the crime for which he was originally blamed. Technicolor.

2711. Three Husbands (United Artists/ Gloria Film Prods.; 1950). *Cast:* Eve Arden, Ruth Warrick, Vanessa Brown, Howard DaSilva, Shepperd Strudwick, Robert Karnes, Emlyn Williams (U.S. debut), Billie Burke, Louise Erickson, Jonathan Hale, Jane Darwell, Benson Fong, Frank Cady, Dorothy Wolbert, Ralph Peters, Marta Mitrovich, Jill Kraft, Jerry Hausner, Dorothy Vaughan, John Dierkes, Alvin Hammer, Richard Flato, William Simpson, Maurice Marsac, Gay Gayle, Stanley Prager. *D:* Irving Reis;

P: I.G. Goldsmith: *St:* Vera Caspary; *Sc:* Caspary, Edward Eliscu; *Song:* "Poor Chap" Herschel Burke Gilbert, Eliscu. (1:18) (video) A comic takeoff on *A Letter to Three Wives* (Fox; 1948) as three husbands get letters from a deceased playboy claiming he dallied with their wives. (aka: *A Letter to Three Husbands*)

2712. Three Little Words (MGM; 1950). *Cast:* Fred Astaire (Bert Kalmar), Red Skelton (Harry Ruby), Vera-Ellen (Jessie Brown Kalmar/singing voice dubbed by Anita Ellis), Arlene Dahl (Eileen Percy), Keenan Wynn (Charlie Kope), Gale Robbins (Terry Lordel), Gloria DeHaven (Mrs. Carter DeHaven), Phil Regan (himself), Harry Shannon (Clannahan), Debbie Reynolds (Helen Kane/singing voice dubbed by Kane), Paul Harvey (Al Masters), Carleton Carpenter (Dan Healy), George Melkovich (Al Schacht), Harry Mendoza (Mendoza the Great), Pierre Watkin (Philip Goodman), Beverly Michaels (Francesca Ladovan), Alex Gerry (Marty Collister), Billy Gray, Pat Flaherty, Syd Saylor, Elzie Emanuel, Sherry Hall, Pat Williams, Charles Wagenheim, Tony Taylor, Phyllis Kennedy, Donald Kerr, Bert Davidson, William Tannen, George Sherwood, Harry Barris. *D:* Richard Thorpe; *P:* Jack Cummings; *Sc:* George Wells; *Choreography:* Hermes Pan; *Music:* (AAN) Andre Previn; *Songs:* "Thinking of You," "She's Mine, All Mine," "Three Little Words," "So Long Oo-Long," "All Alone Monday," "Hooray for Captain Spaulding," "I Love You So Much," "Up in the Clouds," "Mr. and Mrs. Hoofer at Home" Bert Kalmar, Harry Ruby; "Where Did You Get That Girl?" Kalmar, Ruby, Harry Puck; "Come on Papa" Ruby, Edgar Leslie; "My Sunny Tennessee" Kalmar, Ruby & Herman Ruby; "Who's Sorry Now?" Kalmar, Ruby, Ted Snyder; "I Wanna Be Loved By You" Kalmar, Ruby, Herbert Stothart and "You Are My Lucky Star" Arthur Freed, Nacio Herb Brown. (1:42) (video/laserdisc) Hit Technicolor musical biography of song writers Bert Kalmar and Harry Ruby, a showcase for many of their well known songs. One of the 28 top-grossing films of 1949-50.

Three Outlaws (1951) *see* **Three Desperate Men**

2713. The Three Outlaws (Associated Film Releasing; 1956). *Cast:* Neville Brand, Bruce Bennett, Alan Hale, Jeanne Carmen, Jose Gonzales-Gonzales, Rodolfo Hoyos, Robert Tafur, Bill Henry, Robert Christopher, Lillian Molieri, Vincent Padula, Henry Escalante, Jonathan Hale, Stanley Andrews. *D:* Sam Newfield; *P:* Sigmund Neufeld; *St: & Sc:* Orville H. Hampton. (1:14) Low budget oater of U.S. lawmen crossing the Mexican border to round up the Butch Cassidy gang.

2714. Three-Ring Circus (Paramount; 1954). *Cast:* Dean Martin, Jerry Lewis, Joanne Dru, Zsa Zsa Gabor, Wallace Ford, Sig Rumann, Gene Sheldon, Elsa Lanchester, Nick Cravat, Douglas Fowley, Sue Casey, Mary L. Orozco, Frederick E. Wolfe, Philip Van Zandt, Ralph Peters, Chick Chandler, Kathleen Freeman, Robert McKibbon, Neil Levitt, Al Hill, Robert LeRoy Diamond, George E. Stone, Lester Dorr, Donald Kerr, James Davies, Louis Michael Lettieri, Sandy Descher, Billy Curtis, Harry Monty, Milton A. Dickonson, Bobby Kay, Sonny Vallie, Robert Locke Lorraine, John Minshull, Joe Evans, George Boyce. *D:* Joseph Pevney; *P:* Hal B. Wallis; *St: & Sc:* Don McGuire; *Songs:* "It's a Big Wide Wonderful World" John Rox, "Hey Punchinello" Jay Livingston, Ray Evans. (1:43) Comedy of two ex-servicemen who take it upon themselves to join a circus. Recut and re-released as *Jerrico, the Wonder Clown.* Technicolor/VistaVision.

2715. Three Sailors and a Girl (Warner; 1953). *Cast:* Jane Powell, Gordon MacRae, Gene Nelson, Sam Levene, George Givot, Veda Ann Borg, Archer MacDonald, Raymond Greenleaf, Henry Slate, Jack E. Leonard, Burt Lancaster, Mickey Simpson, Elizabeth Flournoy, Philip Van Zandt, Wayne Taylor, Al Hill, Guy Edward Hearn, Grandon Rhodes (George Abbott), David Bond (Moss Hart), Alex Gerry (Ira Gershwin), Frank Scannell, Roy Engel, Claire Meade, Dick Simmons, John Parrish, Everett Glass, Bob Carson, King Donovan, Harold Miller, Cliff Ferre, Paul Burke, Murray Alper, Ed Hinton, John Crawford, Dennis Dengate, Merv Griffin, Arthur Walsh, Jack Larson, Bess Flowers, Michael Pierce. *D:* Roy Del Ruth; *P:* Sammy Cahn; *Sc:* Roland Kibbee, Devery Freeman; *Songs:* "Home Is Where the Heart Is," "Kiss Me or I'll Scream," "Face to Face," "There Must Be a Reason," "When It's Love," "My Heart Is a Singing Heart," "The Lately Song," "Show Me a Happy Woman and I'll Show You a Miserable Man," "You're But Oh So Right," "I Got Butterflies," "The Five Senses" and "I Made Myself a Promise" Sammy Fain, Sammy Cahn. (1:35) Musical romance of three sailors who invest their ship's surplus finances into a Broadway show with dubious chances of it becoming a hit. The film had five previous incarnations, including: *The Butter and Egg Man* (1928) by

First National, *the Tenderfoot* (1932), *Hello, Sweetheart* (Great Britain; 1935), *Dance, Charlie Dance* (1937) and *An Angel From Texas* (1940). Based on George S. Kaufman's play *The Butter and Egg Man*. Technicolor.

2716. Three Secrets (Warner/United States Pictures; 1950). *Cast:* Eleanor Parker, Patricia Neal, Ruth Roman, Frank Lovejoy, Leif Erickson, Ted de Corsia, Edmon Ryan, Larry Keating, Katherine Warren, Arthur Franz, Duncan Richardson. *D:* Robert Wise; *P:* Milton Sperling; *Sc:* Martin Rackin, Gina Kaus [based on their story "Rock Bottom"]. (1:38) (video) Drama of three women each with a secret who await the identity of a 5-year-old boy, the lone survivor of a plane crash, each believing the child is theirs.

2717. Three Steps North (United Artists/W. Lee Wilder; 1951). *Cast:* Lloyd Bridges, Lea Padovani, Aldo Fabrizi, William C. Tubbs, Dino Galvani, Adriano Ambrogi, Gianna Rizzo, John Fostini, Peggy Doro, Adam Genett. *D: & P:* W. Lee Wilder; *St:* Robert Harari; *Sc:* Lester Fuller. (1:25) A U.S.A./Italian co-production which tells of an American ex-con who returns to Italy in search of a stash of cash placed there during World War II. Originally ran on a double bill with *Four in a Jeep*. A Swiss production.

2718. Three Stripes in the Sun (Columbia; 1955). *Cast:* Aldo Ray, Phil Carey, Dick York, Mitsuko Kimura, Chuck Connors, Henry Okawa, Tatsuo Saito, Camille Janclaire, Chiyaki (himself), Sgt. Demetrios (himself), Sgt. Romaniello (himself), L. Tamaki, Lt. Col. Mike Davis, Lt. Thomas Brazil (himself), Takeshi Kamikubo, Tamao Nakamura, Teruko Omi, Kamiko Tachibana. *D: & Sc:* Richard Murphy; *P:* Fred Kohlmar; *Adapt:* Albert Duffy. (1:33) Drama of post-war Japan and a U.S. Army sergeant who takes on the cause of Japanese orphans. Based on "The Gentle Wolfhound" by E.J. Kahn, Jr., which appeared in *The New Yorker* magazine. Fact-based on experiences of Hugh O'Reilly, a master sergeant. (G.B. title: *The Gentle Sergeant*).

2719. 3:10 to Yuma (Columbia; 1957). *Cast:* Van Heflin, Glenn Ford, Felicia Farr, Leora Dana, Henry Jones, Richard Jaeckel, Robert Emhardt, Sheridan Comerate, Robert Ellenstein, George Mitchell, Ford Rainey, Barry Curtis, Jerry Hartleben. *D:* Delmer Daves; *P:* David Heilweil; *St:* Elmore Leonard; *Sc:* Halsted Welles; *Title song:* George Duning, Ned Washington (sung by Frankie Laine). (1:32) (video/laserdisc) Psychological western style drama of a simple farmer who agrees to escort a wanted outlaw to the train that will take him to Yuma prison, while the outlaw's gang has other ideas. Critically acclaimed, it was in nomination at the British Academy Awards.

3,000 A.D. *see* **Captive Women**

2720. Three Violent People (Paramount; 1956). *Cast:* Charlton Heston, Anne Baxter, Gilbert Roland, Tom Tryon, Forrest Tucker, Bruce Bennett, Elaine Stritch, Barton MacLane, Bobby Blake, Peter Hansen, Robert Arthur, John Harmon, Ross Bagdasarian, Raymond Greenleaf, Don Devlin, Roy Engel, Argentina Brunetti, Leo Castillo, Don Dunning, Jameel Farah [later: Jamie Farr], Ernestine Wade, Paul Levitt, Kenneth MacDonald. *D:* Rudolph Maté; *P:* Hugh Brown; *St:* Leonard Praskins, Barney Slater; *Sc:* James Edward Grant; *Song:* "Un Momento" Mack David, Martita. (1:40) (video) Western of a rancher who returns to his spread after the Civil War with his new bride, only to have to deal with carpetbaggers after his land and his new wife's shady past. Technicolor/VistaVision.

2721. Three Young Texans (20th Century–Fox/Panoramic; 1954). *Cast:* Mitzi Gaynor, Keefe Brasselle, Jeffrey Hunter, Harvey Stephens, Dan Riss, Michael Ansara, Aaron Spelling, Morris Ankrum, Frank Wilcox, Helen Wallace, John Harmon, Alex Montoya, Vivian Marshall. *D:* Henry Levin; *P:* Leonard Goldstein; *Sc:* Gerald Drayson Adams; *Song:* "Just Let Me Love You" Lionel Newman, Eliot Daniel. (1:18) When ruthless blackmailers intimidate a man's father into pulling a train robbery, his son commits the act instead so his father won't be forced to. A western drama based on the novel by William MacLeod Raine. Technicolor.

Through Hell to Glory *see* **Jet Attack**

Thunder Across the Pacific (G.B. title) *see* **Wild Blue Yonder**

2722. Thunder Bay (Universal-International; 1953). *Cast:* James Stewart, Joanne Dru, Gilbert Roland, Dan Duryea, Marcia Henderson (film debut), Robert Monet, Jay C. Flippen, Antonio Moreno, Henry [Harry] Morgan, Fortunio Bonanova, Mario Siletti, Antonio Filauri,

Frank Chase, Allen Pinson, Dale Van Sickel, Ted Mapes, Ben Welden, Jean Hartelle, Jack Tesler, Adrine Champagne, Donald Green, Laurie Fining, Emanuel Russo. *D:* Anthony Mann; *P:* Aaron Rosenberg; *St:* John Michael Hayes [based on an idea by George W. George and George F. Slavin]; *Sc:* Gil Doud, Hayes. (1:43) (video) Action drama with romance of oil drillers at loggerheads with Louisiana shrimp fishermen. Originally filmed in wide screen process and stereophonic sound. Technicolor.

2723. Thunder in God's Country (Republic; 1951). *Cast:* Rex Allen, Buddy Ebsen, Mary Ellen Kay, Ian MacDonald, Paul Harvey, Harry Lauter, John Doucette, Harry V. Cheshire, John Ridgely, Frank Ferguson, Wilson Wood, Ko-Ko (horse). *D:* George Blair; *P:* Melville Tucker; *St: & Sc:* Arthur E. Orloff; *Songs:* "Melody of the Plains" Irving Beriau, Leonard M. Sive; "Molly Darling" and "John Henry" (sung by Allen). (1:07) In this series western, an escaped convict causes trouble in a western town until a cowboy artist steps in.

Thunder in the Dust (G.B. title) *see* **The Sundowners**

2724. Thunder in the East (Paramount; 1951–53). *Cast:* Alan Ladd, Deborah Kerr, Charles Boyer, Cecil Kellaway, Corinne Calvet, John Williams, Mark Cavell, John Abbott, Philip Bourneuf, Charlie Lung, Leonard Carey, Nelson Welch, Queenie Leonard, George J. Lewis, Aram Katcher, John Davidson, Trevor Ward, Bruce Payne, Maeve MacMurrough, Margaret Brewster, Arthur Gould-Porter, Robert Ben Ali, Jill St. John (film debut). *D:* Charles Vidor; *P:* Everett Riskin; *Adapt:* George Tabori, Frederick Hazlitt Brennen; *Sc:* Jo Swerling; *Additional dialogue:* Lewis Meltzer (unc.). (1:37) Romantic adventure of a gunrunner selling arms to a pacifist Indian prince in the newly independent country in 1947. Completed in 1951 with release delayed on request of the U.S. State Department. Never shown in India or Pakistan. A box office bomb, it was based on the 1948 novel *Rage of the Vulture* by Alan Moorehead.

2725. Thunder in the Sun (Paramount/ Seven Arts–Carrollton; 1959). *Cast:* Susan Hayward, Jeff Chandler, Jacques Bergerac, Blanche Yurka (final film—ret.), Carl Esmond, Fortunio Bonanova, Felix Locher, Bertrand Castelli, Veda Ann Borg, Pedro de Cordoba. *D: & Sc:* Russell Rouse; *P:* Clarence Greene; *Original St:* Guy Trosper, James Hill; *Adapt:* Stewart Stern; *Song:* "Mon Petit" Cyril Mockridge, Ned Washington (sung by Bergerac). (1:21) Slightly offbeat "wagon train attacked by Indians" western as Basque immigrants head west to plant vineyards in California. Eastmancolor.

2726. Thunder on the Hill (Universal-International; 1951). *Cast:* Claudette Colbert, Ann Blyth, Robert Douglas, Anne Crawford (U.S. debut), Gladys Cooper, Michael Pate, Philip Friend, John Abbott, Connie Gilchrist, Gavin Muir, Phyllis Stanley, Norma Varden, Valerie Cardew, Queenie Leonard, Patrick O'-Moore. *D:* Douglas Sirk; *P:* Michel Kraike; *Sc:* Oscar Saul, Andrew Solt. (1:24) Drama of an English nun who sets out to prove a girl innocent of murdering her brother. Based on the 1950 play *Bonaventure* by Charlotte Hastings. (G.B. title: *Bonaventure*)

Thunder on the Trail (G.B. title) *see* **The Thundering Trail**

2727. Thunder Over Arizona (Republic; 1956). *Cast:* Skip Homeier, Kristine Miller, George Macready, Wallace Ford, Jack Elam, Gregory Walcott, Nacho Galindo, George Keymas, John Doucette, John Compton, Bob Swan, Julian Rivero, Francis McDonald. *D: & As.P:* Joseph Kane; *St: & Sc:* Sloan Nibley. (1:15) (video) A tale of greed and corruption sparked by a silver strike in a small western town. Trucolor/ Naturama.

Thunder Over Hawaii *see* **Naked Paradise**

2728. Thunder Over Sangoland (Lippert/Arrow Prods.; 1955). *Cast:* Jon Hall, Ray Montgomery, Marjorie Lord, House Peters, Jr., Myron Healey, Nick Stewart, Frank Richards, James Edwards, Louise Franklin, James Fairfax, M'Liss McClure. *D:* Sam Newfield; *P:* Rudolph C. Flothow; *Sc:* Sherman L. Lowe. (1:13) An American doctor helps a missionary and his sister in Africa, trying to prevent a native uprising. A feature length jungle adventure pieced together for theatrical release from episodes of the "Ramar of the Jungle" TV series.

2729. Thunder Over the Plains (Warner; 1953). *Cast:* Randolph Scott, Lex Barker, Phyllis Kirk, Henry Hull, Charles McGraw, Elisha Cook, Jr., Fess Parker, Hugh Sanders, Richard Benjamin (film debut), Lane Chandler, James Brown, Trevor Bardette, Mark Dana,

Frank Matts, Steve Darrell, Earle Hodgins, Jack Woody, John Cason, Monte Montague, Carl Andre, Charles Horvath, John McKee, Gail Robinson, Boyd "Red" Morgan, Gayle Kellogg. *D:* Andre De Toth; *P:* David Weisbart; *St:* & *Sc:* Russell Hughes. (1:22) Western programmer of a U.S. Cavalry detachment in post–Civil War Texas, dealing with carpetbaggers and renegades. Warnercolor.

2730. Thunder Pass (Lippert/Wm. F. Broidy Pictures; 1954). *Cast:* Dane Clark, Dorothy Patrick, Andy Devine, Raymond Burr, John Carradine, Mary Ellen Kay, Raymond Hatton, Nestor Paiva, Charles Fredericks, Tom Hubbard, Rick Vallin, Tommy Cook, Paul McGuire, Elizabeth Harrower, Gordon Wynne. *D:* Frank McDonald; *P:* A. Robert Nunes; *St:* George Van Marter; *Sc:* Tom Hubbard, Fred Eggers. (1:16) (video) Western of the U.S. Cavalry trying to quell an Indian uprising.

2731. Thunder Road (United Artists/DRM Prods.; 1958). *Cast:* Robert Mitchum, Gene Barry, Jacques Aubuchon, Keely Smith, Trevor Bardette, Sandra Knight, James Mitchum (film debut), Betsy Holt, Frances Koon, Randy Sparks, Mitchell Ryan (film debut), Peter Breck, Peter Hornsby, Jerry Hardin, Robert Porterfield. *D:* Arthur Ripley (final film—d. 1961); *P:* Robert Mitchum (unc.); *St:* R. Mitchum; *Sc:* Walter Wise, James Atlee Phillips; *Theme song:* "Whippoorwill" R. Mitchum, Don Raye (sung by Keely Smith and later recorded by Mitchum as a hit record). (1:32) (video) Action-drama of moonshiners operating out of Harlan County, Kentucky, who run up against big city gangsters and U.S. Treasury agents. A film with a present day cult following.

2732. Thunderbirds (Republic; 1952). *Cast:* John Derek, John Barrymore, Jr., Mona Freeman, Gene Evans, Eileen Christy, Ward Bond, Barton MacLane, Wally Cassell, Ben Cooper (film debut), Robert Neil, Slim Pickens, Armando Silvestre, Benny Baker, Norman Budd, Mae Clarke, Sam McKim, Allene Roberts, Richard Simmons, Walter Reed, Suzanne Dalbert, Barbara Pepper, Pepe Hern, Victor Millan. *D:* & *P:* John H. Auer; *Ex.P:* Herbert J. Yates; *St:* Kenneth Gamet; *Sc:* Mary C. McCall, Jr. (1:38) Two young members of the Oklahoma National Guard are called to active duty and trained as flyers for service in various World War II battlefronts from Italy to France.

Thundercloud *see* **Colt .45**

2733. Thundering Caravans (Republic; 1952). *Cast:* Allan Lane, Eddy Waller, Mona Knox, Roy Barcroft, Isabel Randolph, Richard Crane, Billy Henry, Edward Clark, Pierre Watkin, Stanley Andrews, Boyd "Red" Morgan, Black Jack (horse). *D:* Harry Keller; *P:* Rudy Ralston; *St:* & *Sc:* M. Coates Webster. (0:54) A series western which finds U.S. marshal "Rocky" Lane called in by his friend, a local sheriff, to investigate the theft of ore shipments.

2734. Thundering Jets (20th Century–Fox/Regal Films; 1958). *Cast:* Rex Reason, Dick Foran, Audrey Dalton, Robert Dix, Lee Farr, Barry Coe, Buck Class, John Douglas, Robert Conrad (film debut), Sid Melton, Gregg Palmer, Lionel Ames, Dick Monahan, Maudie Prickett, Jimmie Smith, Bill Bradley, Robert Rothwell, Kevin Enright, Walter Kent. Tom Walton, Ronald Foster, Kenneth Edwards & the men of the U.S. Air Force. *D:* Helmut Dantine (only film as director); *P:* Jack Leewood; *As.P:* Dantine; *St:* & *Sc:* James Landis; *Song:* "Blast Off!—The Song of the Jet Command" Walter Kent, Tom Walton. (1:13) At Edwards Air Force Base in California, a former World War II flying ace, now an instructor, deals with a new batch of jet pilots in training. Regalscope.

2735. The Thundering Trail (Favorite Films/Western Adventure; 1951). *Cast:* Al "Lash" LaRue, Al St. John, Sally Anglim, Archie Twitchell [aka: Michael Branden], Ray Bennett, Reed Howes, Bud Osborne, John Cason, George Chesebro, Clarke Stevens, Jimmie Martin, Mary Lou Webb, Sue Hussey, Ray Broome, Cliff Taylor. *D:* & *P:* Ron Ormond; *St:* & *Sc:* Alexander White. (0:55) (video) Series western which finds LaRue and St. John as U.S. marshals called in to protect the new territorial governor whose life has been threatened several times by a gang of outlaws. (G.B. title: *Thunder on the Trail*)

2736. Thy Neighbor's Wife (20th Century–Fox/Hugo Haas Prods.; 1953). *Cast:* Cleo Moore, Hugo Haas, Ken Carlton, Kathleen Hughes, Tony Jochim, Tom Fadden, Darr Smith, Oscar O'Shea, Tom Wilson, Roy Engel, Robert Knapp, Joe Duval, Henry Corden. *D:* *P:* & *Sc:* Hugo Haas. (1:17) Melodrama set in a 19th century Moravian village of an elderly judge who goes off the deep end when his young wife begins keeping company with a former old flame. Based on the 1933 novelette "The Peasant Judge" by Oskar Jellinek.

2737. A Ticket to Tomahawk (20th Century–Fox; 1950). *Cast:* Dan Dailey, Anne Baxter, Rory Calhoun, Walter Brennan, Charles Kemper, Connie Gilchrist, Arthur Hunnicutt, Will Wright, Chief Yowlachie, Victor Sen Yung, Mauritz Hugo, Raymond Greenleaf, Harry Carter, Harry Seymour, Robert Adler, Chief Thundercloud, Marion Marshall, Marilyn Monroe, Joyce MacKenzie, Barbara Smith, Jack Elam, Paul Harvey, Lee MacGregor, Raymond Bond, Charles Stevens, John War Eagle, Shooting Star, Herbert Heywood, William Self, Guy Wilkerson, Edward Clark, Olin Howlin. *D:* Richard Sale; *P:* Robert Bassler; *St: & Sc:* Mary Loos, Sale; *Songs:* "Oh, What a Forward Young Man You Are" Ken Darby, John Read, + "A Ticket to Tomahawk." (1:30) (video) The railroad and a stagecoach company are rivals in this popular western comedy. Technicolor. (aka: *The Sheriff's Daughter*)

Tiger in the Sky (G.B. title) *see* **The McConnell Story**

2738. Tight Spot (Columbia; 1955). *Cast:* Ginger Rogers, Edward G. Robinson, Brian Keith, Lucy Marlow, Lorne Greene, Katherine Anderson, Allen Nourse, Peter Leeds, Doye O'Dell, Eve McVeagh, Helen Wallace, Frank Gerstle, Gloria Ann Simpson, Robert Shield, Norman Keats, Kathryn Grant, Ed "Skipper" McNally, Erik Paige, Tom Greenway, Kevin Enright, John Marshall, Will J. White, Patrick Miller, Tom de Graffenried, Joseph Hamilton, Alan Reynolds, Alfred Linder, Ed Hinton, John Larch, Bob Hopkins, Robert Nichols, Kenneth N. Mayer, Dean Cromer. *D:* Phil Karlson; *P:* Lewis J. Rachmil; *Sc:* William Bowers. (1:37) Acclaimed crime drama of a woman (Rogers) used as a witness to convict a crime boss, her former boy friend. Based on the play *Dead Pigeon* by Leonard Kantor.

2739. The Tijuana Story (Columbia/Clover Prod.; 1957). *Cast:* Rudolfo Acosta, James Darren, Robert McQueeney, Jean Willes, Joy Stoner, Paul Coates (a newsman on whom the story is based/narrator), Paul Newlan, George E. Stone, Robert Blake, Michael Fox, William Fawcett, Rick Vallin, Ralph Valencia, Susan Seaforth, William Tannen, Suzanne Ridgeway. *D:* Leslie Kardos; *P:* Sam Katzman; *St: & Sc:* Lou Morheim. (1:12) Fact-based crime melodrama of a newspaperman rubbed out by a Mexican crime syndicate and his son who takes up the cause.

2740. Timber Fury (Eagle-Lion/Jack Schwarz–Outdoor Action Prods.; 1950). *Cast:* David Bruce, Laura Lee, Nicia Di Bruno, Sam Flint, George Slocum, Lee Phelps, Gilbert Frye, Paul Hoffman, Spencer Chan, Zoro (dog). *D: & P:* Bernard B. Ray; *Sc:* Michael Hansen; *Adaptation:* Sam Neuman, Nat Tanchuck; *Songs:* "Blue in Love Again," "My Baby and Me" Nicia Di Bruno (who also sings). Programmer northwoods adventure of a man and his daughter attempting to protect their property from timber thieves. Based on "Retribution," a short story by James Oliver Curwood.

2741. Timberjack (Republic; 1955). *Cast:* Sterling Hayden, Vera Ralston, David Brian, Adolphe Menjou, Hoagy Carmichael, Chill Wills, Jim Davis, Howard Petrie, Ian MacDonald, Wally Cassell, Elisha Cook, Jr., Karl Davis, Tex Terry, George Marshall. *D:* Joe Kane; *Ex.P:* Herbert J. Yates; *Sc:* Allen Rivkin; *Songs:* "He's Dead But He Won't Lie Down" Johnny Mercer, Hoagy Carmichael; "Timberjack" Victor Young, Ned Washington. (1:34) Western of a man whose inherited timberland is threatened by a greedy land owner. Based on the novel by Dan Cushman. Trucolor.

Timbuctu *see* **Legend of the Lost**

2742. Timbuktu (United Artists/Imperial Pictures; 1959). *Cast:* Victor Mature, Yvonne De Carlo, George Dolenz, John Dehner, Marcia Henderson, James Fox, Leonard Mudie, Paul Wexler, Robert Clarke, Willard Sage, Mark Dana, Larry Perron, Steve Darrell, Larry Chance, Allen Pinson. *D:* Jacques Tourneur; *P:* Edward Small (unc.); *St: & Sc:* Anthony Veiller, Paul Dudley. (1:31) Action-adventure of an American smuggling guns to the Arabs in 1942, working toward an Arab overthrow of the French colonials.

Time for Action (G.B. title) *see* **Tip on a Dead Jockey**

2743. Time Limit (United Artists/Heath Prods.; 1957). *Cast:* Richard Widmark, Richard Basehart, Dolores Michaels, June Lockhart, Martin Balsam, Rip Torn, Carl Benton Reid, James Douglas, Alan Dexter, Yale Wexler, Manning Ross, Kaie Deei, Skip McNally, Joe Di Reda, Kenneth Alton, Jack Webster. *D:* Karl Malden (only film as director); *P:* Richard Widmark, William Reynolds; *Adaptation & Sc:* Henry Denker. (1:36) Drama set against the court-martial of an army major accused of collaboration with the enemy while a P.O.W. of the North Koreans. Based on the play by Mr. Denker and Ralph Berkey.

A Time to Love *see* **A Time to Love and a Time to Die**

2744. A Time to Love and a Time to Die (Universal-International; 1958). *Cast:* John Gavin (Ernst Graeber), Lilo Pulver (Elizabeth Kruse), Jock Mahoney (Immerman), Don DeFore (Boettcher), Keenan Wynn (Reuter), Thayer David (Oscar Binding), Dieter Borsche (Capt. Rahe), Charles Regnier (Joseph), Erich Maria Remarque (Prof. Pohlmann), Dana [Jim] Hutton (film debut/Hirschland), Dorothea Weick (Frau Lieser), Klaus Kinski (Gestapo lieutenant), Agnes Windeck (Frau Witte), Clancy Cooper (Sauer), Bengt Lindstrom (Steinbrenner), Lisa Helwig (Frau Kleiner), Kurt Meisel (Heini), Alice Treff (Frau Langer), Karl-Ludwig Lindt (Dr. Karl Fresenburg), Alexander Engel, Barbara Rutting, John Van Dreelen. *D:* Douglas Sirk; *P:* Robert Arthur; *Sc:* Orin Jannings; *Sound:* (AAN) Leslie I. Carey. (2:13) (video) World War II drama of a German soldier home on leave who marries a girl and then must return to the Russian front. Based on Erich Maria Remarque's 1954 novel; one cannot help making parallels to his earlier *All Quiet on the Western Front* (Universal; 1930). Filmed on location in West Germany, it was in nomination at the Berlin Film Festival. (aka: *A Time to Love*) Eastmancolor/CinemaScope.

2745. Timetable (United Artists/Mark Stevens; 1956). *Cast:* Mark Stevens, King Calder, Felicia Farr (film debut), Marianne Stewart, Wesley Addy, Alan Reed, Rudolfo Hoyos, Jr., John Marley, Jack Klugman (film debut). *D: & P:* Mark Stevens; *St:* Robert Angus; *Sc:* Aben Kandel; *Song:* "Salud Felicidad y Amor" Walter Scharf, Jack Brooks. (1:19) Crime melodrama of an insurance investigator who engineers a half-million dollar train heist, only to have it backfire. Originally ran on a double bill with *Manfish* (q.v.).

2746. The Tin Star (Paramount/Perlsea Co.; 1957). *Cast:* Henry Fonda (Morg Hickman), Anthony Perkins (Sheriff Ben Owens), Betsy Palmer (Nona Mayfield), Michel Ray (Kip Mayfield), Neville Brand (Bart Bogardus), John McIntire (Dr. McCord), Mary Webster (Millie Parker), Peter Baldwin (Zeke McGaffey), Richard Shannon (Buck Henderson), Lee Van Cleef (Ed McGaffey), James Bell (Judge Thatcher), Howard Petrie (Harvey King), Russell Simpson (Clem Hall), Hal K. Dawson (Andy Miller), Jack Kenney (Sam Hodges), Mickey Finn (McCall), Frank Cady (Abe Pickett), Bob Kenaston (Hardman), Allen Gettel (Sloan), Tim Sullivan (Virgil Hough), Frank McGrath (Jim Clark), Frank Cordell. *D:* Anthony Mann; *P:* William Perlberg, George Seaton; *St:* "The Tin Badge" (AAN) Barney Slater, Joel Kane; *Sc:* (AAN) Dudley Nichols; *Title song:* Elmer Bernstein. (1:33) (video) Acclaimed western drama of a young inexperienced sheriff (Perkins) who with the help of a seasoned bounty hunter and ex-sheriff (Fonda), eventually overcomes the lawlessness of the town. The British Academy Awards had it in nomination.

2747. The Tingler (Columbia/Wm. Castle; 1959). *Cast:* Vincent Price, Judith Evelyn, Darryl Hickman, Patricia Cutts, Pamela Lincoln, Philip Coolidge. *D: & P:* William Castle; *As.P:* Dona Holloway; *St: & Sc:* Robb White. (1:22) (video/laserdisc) Popular horror film with a gimmick (theatrically) of vibrating seats (termed Percepto) of a creature which grows on the spinal cords of people who experience fear. A sequence involving a bathtub full of blood is tinted red. Note: An additional gimmick was used in some theatrical showings of this film in the form of a shill, a woman who purportedly faints in the audience and is carried out in full view of other audience members as the house lights go on briefly and Price calms the paying patrons.

2748. Tip on a Dead Jockey (MGM; 1957). *Cast:* Robert Taylor, Dorothy Malone, Gia Scala, Martin Gabel, Jack Lord, Marcel Dalio, Joyce Jameson. *D:* Richard Thorpe; *P:* Edwin H. Knopf; *Sc:* Charles Lederer; *Song:* "You Found Me and I Found You" P.G. Wodehouse, Jerome Kern. (1:38) Drama of various people involved in a smuggling racket in Madrid, Spain. Based on a story by Irwin Shaw which appeared in *The New Yorker* magazine in March 1954. CinemaScope. (G.B. title: *Time for Action*)

2749. The Titan—Story of Michelangelo (Michelangelo Co.–Classics Picture, Inc./Pandora Films; 1950). *D:* Richard Lyford; *P:* (AA-Best Documentary) Robert Snyder; *Sc:* Norman Borisoff. (1:08) (video) A documentary feature of the great artist, telling the story of the man through his works. Originally a 1938 Swiss production, it was re-edited by Robert Snyder for American release. Narrated by Fredric March, it was also voted "Best Film of the Year" by the *New York Times*.

2750. Titanic (20th Century–Fox; 1953). *Cast:* Clifton Webb (Richard Sturges), Barbara Stanwyck (Julia Sturges), Robert Wagner (Giff Rogers), Audrey Dalton (Annette Sturges), Thelma Ritter (Mrs. Maude Young/a fictitious character name for the real-life Mrs. J.J. Brown—aka: "The Unsinkable Molly Brown"), Brian Aherne (Capt. E.J. Smith), Richard Basehart (George Healey), Allyn Joslyn (Earl Meeker), James Todd (Sandy Comstock), William Johnstone (John Jacob Astor), Charles Fitzsimmon (Chief Officer Wilde), Barry Bernard (1st Officer Murdock), Harper Carter (Norman Sturges), Edmund Purdom (film debut/2nd Officer Lightoller), Camillo Guercio (Mr. Benjamin Guggenheim), Anthony Eustrel (Sanderson), Alan Marston (quartermaster), James Lilburn (Devlin), Frances Bergen (Mrs. John Jacob Astor), Guy Standing, Jr. (George D. Widener), Roy Gordon (Mr. Isidor Straus), Hellen Van Tuyl (Mrs. Isidor Straus), Marta Mitrovich (Mrs. Uzcadam), Ivis Goulding (Emma), Dennis Fraser (Bride), Ashley Cowan (Phillips), Lehmer "Lee" Graham (Symons), Elizabeth Flournoy (woman with baby), Merry Anders, Gloria Gordon, Melinda Markey, Ronald F. Hagerthy, Conrad Feia, Richard West, Mae Marsh, William Cottrell, Owen McGiveney, Donald Chaffin, Ralph Grosh, Michael Ferris, John Fraser, David Hoffman, Gordon Richards, Robin Hughes, Robin Camp, Pat Aherne, David Thursby, Pat O'Moore, John Costello, Nicolas Koster, Christopher Severn, Michael Hadlow, Ivan Hayes, Robin Sanders Clark, Herbert Deans, John Dodsworth, Charles Keane, Salvador Baguez, Eugene Borden, Alberto Morin, Richard Peel, Harry Cording, Joan Hayes, Bert Stevens, Duke Seba, Joyce Newhard, George Boyce. *D:* Jean Negulesco; *P:* Charles Brackett; *St: & Sc:* (AA) Brackett, Walter Reisch, Richard Breen; *ASD:* (AAN-b/w) Lyle Wheeler, Maurice Ransford (art directors), Stuart Reiss (sets). (1:38) (video/laserdisc) A melodramatic rendering of the most famous maritime disaster of the 20th century, blending fact and fiction of the fateful night of April 15, 1912, when the passenger liner *Titanic* on her maiden voyage, struck an iceberg and sank beneath the icy waters of the North Atlantic, taking with her 1,503 passengers and crew members. Other filmed versions of the famed disaster: *Night and Ice* (German; 1912) in 3 reels; *Atlantic* (Elstree; 1929), a British production; *Titanic,* a 1943 production from Nazi Germany by directors Herbert Selpin and Werner Klinger; *A Night to Remember* (J. Arthur Rank; 1958), an acclaimed British production based on Walter Lord's 1955 best-seller; *S.O.S. Titanic,* a 1979 TV movie; *Titanic,* a 1996 TV movie (the latter two both originally presented in two parts); and *Titanic,* a 1997 theatrical release that received many awards. One of the 26 top-grossing films of 1952-53.

2751. To Catch a Thief (Paramount; 1955). *Cast:* Cary Grant (John Robie), Grace Kelly (Frances Stevens), Jessie Royce Landis (Mrs. Stevens), John Williams (H.H. Hughson), Charles Vanel (Bertani), Brigitte Auber (Danielle), Jean Martinelli (Foussard), Georgette Anys (Germaine), Roland Lesaffre (Claude), Jean Hebey (Mercier), Rene Blanchard (Lepic), Dominique Davray (Antoinette), Russell Gaige (Mr. Sanford), Marie Stoddard (Mrs. Sanford), Frank Chelland (chef), Otto F. Schulze (chef), Wee Willie Davis, Edward Manouk, Paul "Tiny" Newlan, Lewis Charles, Aimee Torriani, Don Megowan, John Alderson, Leonard Penn, Michael Hadlow, Philip Van Zandt, Steven Geray, Gladys Holland, Louis Mercier. *D: & P:* Alfred Hitchcock; *Sc:* John Michael Hayes; *Cin:* (AA-color) Robert Burks; *ASD:* (AAN-color) Hal Pereira, Joseph McMillan Johnson (art directors), Sam Comer, Arthur Krams (sets); *Costumes:* (AA-color) Edith Head. (1:43) (video/laserdisc) Change of pace Hitchcock with the emphasis on romantic comedy as a reformed cat burglar (Grant) becomes suspect when a new rash of jewel robberies occur, sets out to find the real culprit. Based on the 1952 novel by David Dodge, it was filmed on location on the French Riviera. One of the 24 top-grossing films of 1955-56. Technicolor/VistaVision. Note 1: It was during the production of this film that Grace Kelly met Prince Rainier III of Monaco, who became her husband in 1956, giving her the title Princess Grace Grimaldi. Note 2: An ironic sidenote to this film (not surprising, it being a Hitchcock picture) is that Grace Kelly and Cary Grant can be seen driving in a sportscar on the same road from which Princess Grace's sportscar plunged in 1982 resulting in her death.

2752. To Hell and Back (Universal-International; 1955). *Cast:* Audie Murphy (himself), Marshall Thompson (Johnson), Jack Kelly (Kerrigan), Charles Drake (Brandon), Paul Picerni (Valentino), Gregg Palmer (Lt. Manning), David Janssen (Lee), Richard Castle (Kovak), Paul Langton (Colonel Howe), Bruce Cowling (Capt. Marks), Julian Upton (Steiner), Denver Pyle (Thompson), Felix Noriego (Swope), Art Aragon (Sanchez), Brett Halsey (Saunders), Tommy Hart (Klasky), Anthony Garden (Lt. Burns), Gordon Gebert (Audie Murphy as a boy),

Mary Field (Mrs. Murphy), Howard Wright (Mr. Huston), Edna Holland (Mrs. Huston), Anabel Shaw (Helen), Susan Kohner (film debut/Maria), Maria Costi (Julia), Didi Ramati (Carla), Barbara James (Cleopatra), Joey Costarella (Vincenti), Rand Brooks (Lt. Harris), Nan Boardman (Maria's mother), Henry Kulky (Stack), John Pickard (M.P.), Rankin Mansfield (Dr. Snyder), Madge Meredith (Corinne), John Bryant (Jim), Ashley Cowan (Scottish soldier), Don Kennedy, Ralph Sanford, Howard Price, Alexander Campbell, Mort Mills. *D:* Jesse Hibbs; *P:* Aaron Rosenberg; *Sc:* Gil Doud. (1:46) (video) Drama based on the autobiography of Audie Murphy and how during World War II while with Company B, 15th Infantry Regiment, Third Division, 7th Army, seeing action in North Africa, Tunisia, Italy, France, Germany and Austria, he became the most decorated (24 medals including the Congressional Medal of Honor) soldier in the history of his country. Needless to say, a big box office hit, becoming one of the 27 top-grossing films of 1954-55. Technicolor/ CinemaScope.

2753. To Please a Lady (MGM; 1950). *Cast:* Clark Gable, Barbara Stanwyck, Adolphe Menjou, Will Geer, Roland Winters, Frank Jenks, Emory Parnell, William C. McGaw, Lela Bliss, Helen Spring, Bill Hickman, Lew Smith, Ted Husing, Richard W. Joy (voice only), William Welsh, John McGuire, Lee Phelps, Dominic "Pee Wee" Distarce, Henry Banks, Johnny Parsons, Johnny Tolan, Al Hill, Raymond H. Brown, Joe Garson, John Gallaudet, Hal K. Dawson, Billy Newell, Byron Foulger, Arthur Loew, Jr., Marilyn Rich, Frank Hyers, Tom Hanlon, Dick Simmons, Marcel de la Brosse, Carlotta Monti, Ernest Ohman, Jean Ransome, Holmes Herbert, Anne O'Neal, Jerry Hausner, Tim Ryan, Cecil Green, Jack McGrath, Cay Forrester. *D: & P:* Clarence Brown, *St: & Sc:* Barre Lyndon, Marge Decker. (1:31) (video) The romance of a tough lady journalist and a less than honorable race car driver. A box office disappointment, it was later re-issued under the title *Red Hot Wheels.*

2754. The Toast of New Orleans (MGM; 1950). *Cast:* Mario Lanza (Pepe Abellard Duvalle), Kathryn Grayson (Suzette Micheline), David Niven (Jacques Riboudeaux), J. Carrol Naish (Nicky Duvalle), Rita Moreno (Tina), James Mitchell (Pierre), Clinton Sundberg (Oscar), Sig Arno (mayor), Richard Hagerman (Maestro P. Trellini), Romo Vincent (Manuelo), Marietta Canty (Angelique), Wallis Clark (Mr. O'Neill), Paul Frees (narrator), Fred Essler (Emile), George Davis, Alex Gerry, Henry Corden, Nick Thompson, Mary Benoit, Betty Daniels, Louise Bates, Leon Belasco, Nino Pipitone, Eduard Moreno, Dino Bolognese, Guy DeVestal. *D:* Norman Taurog; *P:* Joe Pasternak; *St: & Sc:* Sy Gomberg, George Wells; *Songs:* "Be My Love" (AAN-Best Song), "Tina Lina," "I'll Never Love You," Title song, "Song of the Bayou," "Boom Biddy Boom Boom" Nicholas Brodszky, Sammy Cahn; "Je Suis Titania" from *Mignon* by Ambroise Thomas; "M'Appari" from *Martha* by Fredrich von Flotow; "Flower Song" from Georges Bizet's *Carmen*; "Brindisi" from Giuseppe Verdi's *La Traviata*; "O Paradiso" from Amilcare Ponchielli's *La Giaconda*; and the love duet from Giacomo Puccini's *Madama Butterfly*. (1:37) (video/laserdisc) Hit Technicolor musical of a New Orleans fisherman propelled to fame as an operatic tenor. The Oscar nominated "Be My Love" became a big hit.

2755. Tobor the Great (Republic/Dudley Pictures Corp.; 1954). *Cast:* Charles Drake, Karin Booth, Billy Chapin, Taylor Holmes, Steven Geray, Henry Kulky, Franz Roehn, Hal Baylor, Alan Reynolds, Peter Brocco, Norman Field, Robert Shayne, Lyle Talbot, Emmett Vogan, William Schallert, Helen Winston, Jack Daly, Maury Hill. *D:* Lee Sholem; *P:* Richard Goldstone; *St:* Carl Dudley; *Sc:* Goldstone, Philip MacDonald. (1:17) (video/laserdisc) Science fiction-fantasy of a little boy and his attachment to his grandfather's robot, Tobor, giving room for the latter to rescue his creator and his young friend when they are kidnapped by communists.

2756. Tokyo After Dark (Paramount/ Nacirema Prods.; 1959). *Cast:* Michi Kobi, Richard Long, Lawrence Dobkin, Paul Dubov, Teru Shimada, Robert Okazaki, Carlyle Mitchell, Frank Kumagai, John Brinkley, Edo Mita, Butch Yamaoto, Nobu McCarthy, Don Keigo Takeuchi, Jerry Adler, Lowell Brown. *D:* Norman T. Herman; *P:-St: & Sc:* Herman, Marvin Segal. (1:20) Low budget based-on-fact melodrama of an American M.P. who goes on the lam in Japan, after accidentally killing a young boy. Filmed in "Little Tokyo," an ethnic section of Los Angeles, California.

2757. Tokyo File 212 (RKO; 1951). *Cast:* Florence Marley, Robert Peyton [aka: Lee Frederick], Katsu Kaika Haida, Reiko Otani, Tatsuo Saito, Satoshi Nakamura, Suisei Matsui,

Byron Michie, Hoirachiro Okawa, Jun Tazaki, Dekao Yokoo, Hideto Hayabusa, Gen Shimizu, Major Richard W.N. Childs (USA-R), Cpl. Stuart Zimmerly, USA, Pvt. James Lyons, USA, Lt. Richard Finiels, USA. *D: & Sc:* Dorrell McGowan, Stuart McGowan; *P:* George Breakston, D. McGowan; *St:* Breakston; *Song:* "Oyedo Boogie" Yasuo Shimizu, Shizuo Yoshikawa (performed by Ichimaru and the Tainosuke Mochizuki Band). (1:24) A post-war crime melodrama that was originally paired on a double bill with *Sealed Cargo* (q.v.).

2758. tom thumb (MGM/Galaxy Pictures, Ltd.; 1958). *Cast:* Russ Tamblyn (starring debut/tom thumb), Alan Young (Woody the Piper), Terry-Thomas (Ivan), Peter Sellers (Tony), Jessie Matthews (a British actress in her final film—ret., singing voice dubbed by Norma Zimmer/Anna), June Thorburn (Forest Queen), Bernard Miles (Bernard Miles), Ian Wallace (the cobbler), Peter Butterworth (the bandmaster), Peter Bull (town crier), Barbara Ferris (voice of puppetoon "Thumbelina"), Stan Freberg (voice of puppetoon "The Yawning Man"), Dal McKennon (voice of "Con-fu-shon"). *D: & P:* George Pal (feature debut as director); *Sc:* Ladislas Fodor; *F/X:* (AA) Tom Howard; *Songs:* "tom thumb's tune," "Are You a Dream?" Peggy Lee; "The Talented Shoes," "After All These Years" Fred Spielman, Janice Torre; "The Yawning Song" Spielman, Kermit Goell. (1:38) (video/laserdisc) A tiny boy is taken in by a kindly couple and later exploited by a villainous duo. Based on Grimm's fairy tale, this British/American co-production was filmed on location in England with miniature work filmed in Hollywood, CA. Eastmancolor.

2759. Tomahawk (Universal-International; 1951). *Cast:* Van Heflin (Jim Bridger), Yvonne De Carlo, Alex Nicol, Preston Foster, Jack Oakie, Tom Tully, Ann Doran, John War Eagle, Rock Hudson, Susan Cabot, Arthur Space (Capt. Fetterman), Stuart Randall, John Peters, Russell Conway, Ray Montgomery, David Sharpe, David H. Miller, Regis Toomey, Sheila Darcy, Chief American Horse, Chief Bad Bear. *D:* George Sherman; *P:* Leonard Goldstein; *St:* Daniel Jarrett; *Sc:* Silvia Richards, Maurice Geraghty. (1:22) U.S. Cavalry vs. Indians is the plot of this western centered around the historic Fetterman massacre, sparked by a fort commandant with the attitude that "the only good Indian is a dead one." Technicolor. (G.B. title: *The Battle of Powder River*)

The Tomahawk and the Cross (G.B. title) *see* **Pillars of the Sky**

The Tomahawk Trail (1950) (G.B. title) *see* **The Iroquois Trail**

2760. Tomahawk Trail (United Artists/Bel-Air–Sunrise Pictures; 1957). *Cast:* Chuck Connors, John Smith, Susan Cummings, Lisa Montell, George Neise, Robert Knapp, Eddie Little, Frederick Ford, [Harry] Dean Stanton. *D:* Robert Parry [aka: Lesley Selander]; *P:* Howard W. Koch; *St:* Gerald Drayson Adams; *Sc:* David Chandler. (1:00) Programmer western of the clash between a by-the-book West Point graduate officer and a hands-on-experienced Indian fighter at a western fort after a column of troopers return to their fort and find that all have been massacred. (G.B. title: *Mark of the Apache*)

2761. Tomorrow Is Another Day (Warner; 1951). *Cast:* Steve Cochran, Ruth Roman, Lurene Tuttle, Ray Teal, Morris Ankrum, Bobby Hyatt, John Kellogg, Lee Patrick, Hugh Sanders, Stuart Randall, Harry Antrim, Walter Sande. *D:* Felix Feist; *P:* Henry Blanke; *Sc:* Art Cohn, Guy Endore [based on the story "Spring Kill" by Mr. Endore]. (1:30) Drama of an ex-con who takes it on the lam to California when his female friend leads him to think he has committed murder.

2762. Tonight We Sing (20th Century–Fox; 1953). *Cast:* David Wayne (Sol Hurok), Ezio Pinza (final film—d. 1957/Feodor Chaliapin), Roberta Peters (Elsa Valdine), Tamara Toumanova (Anna Pavlova), Anne Bancroft (Emma Hurok), Isaac Stern (Eugene Ysaye), Byron Palmer (singing voice dubbed by Jan Peerce), Oscar Karlweiss, Mikhail Rasumny, Steven Geray, Walter Woolf King, Serge Perrault, John Meek (Hurok at age 10), Eda Reis Merin, Russell Cantor, Alex Zakin, Alex Steinert, Oscar Beregei, Leo Mostovoy, Raymond Largay, Wolfgang Fraenkel. *D:* Mitchell Leisen; *P:* George Jessel; *Sc:* Harry Kurnitz, George Oppenheimer; *Musical Interludes:* "Madam Butterfly" love duet by Giacomo Puccini; "Le Cygne" by Camille Saint Saens (danced by Toumanova); "Vous Qui Faites L'Endormie" from Charles Francois Gounod's *Faust*; "Sempre Libera" from Giuseppe Verdi's *La Traviata*; "Qu Attendez-Vous Encore" (also from *Faust*); "Andante Le Triste Vero" (also from *Madama Butterfly*); "Addio Fiorito Asil" (also from *Faust*), "Mattinata" by Ruggiero Leoncavallo; "Valse Caprice in E Flat" by

Anton Rubenstein (played by Stern); "Valse Caprice," "Dragonfly," "Pas De Deux" and "The Swan" (danced by Toumanova); Felix Mendelssohn's Violin Concerto (first and final movements—played by Stern) and Modest Mussorgsky's "Processional" from *Boris Goudonov.* (1:49) A Technicolor cinematic biography of musical impressario Sol Hurok, relating his ability to recognize musical talent, though he had none of his own. Based on the book *Impressario* by Mr. Hurok and Ruth Goode.

2763. Tonka (Buena Vista/Walt Disney Prods.; 1958). *Cast:* Sal Mineo, Philip Carey, Jerome Courtland, Rafael Campos, H.M. Wynant, Joy Page, Britt Lomond (General Custer), Herbert Rudley (Capt. Benteen), Sydney Smith (General Terry), John War Eagle (Chief Sitting Bull), Gregg Martell, Slim Pickens, Robert "Buzz" Henry, Tonka (horse—#2 PATSY Award in 1959). *D:* Lewis R. Foster; *Ex.P:* Walt Disney; *P:* James Pratt; *Sc:* Foster, Lillie Hayward. (1:37) (video) Low budget Disney western, based on the 1951 novel *Comanche* by David Appel of a wild horse trained by an Indian youth and named Tonka. He sets the horse free, only to have the horse become a cavalry mount renamed Comanche, who subsequently becomes the sole cavalry survivor of General George Armstrong Custer's defeat at the Little Big Horn. Technicolor family fare which became a box office hit. (retitled: *A Horse Named Comanche*).

Too Dangerous to Love (G.B. title) *see* **Perfect Strangers**

2764. Too Much, Too Soon (Warner; 1958). *Cast:* Dorothy Malone (Diana Barrymore), Errol Flynn (John Barrymore), Efrem Zimbalist, Jr., Ray Danton, Neva Patterson, Murray Hamilton, Martin Milner, John Dennis, Edward Kemmer, Robert Ellenstein, Kathleen Freeman, John Doucette, Michael Mark, Francis DeSales, Jay Jostyn, Herb Ellis, Louis Quinn, Robert S. Carson, Paul Bryar, Sid Tomack, Jack Lomas, Larry Blake, Don Hayden, James Elsegood, Bess Flowers, Charles Evans, Lyn Osborn, Nesdon Booth, Jack Rice, Gail Bonney. *D:* Art Napoleon; *P:* Henry Blanke; *Sc:* Art and Jo Napoleon. (2:01) The rise and fall (through alcohol) of actress Diana Barrymore (Malone), daughter of John Barrymore (Flynn). Based on her 1957 autobiography of the same name co-written with Gerold Frank.

2765. Too Young to Kiss (MGM; 1951). *Cast:* June Allyson (Cynthia Potter), Van Johnson (Eric Wainwright), Gig Young (John Tirsen), Paula Corday (Denise Dorcet), Kathryn Givney (Miss Benson), Larry Keating (Danny Butler), Hans Conried (Mr. Sparrow), Esther Dale (Mrs. Boykin), Antonio Filauri (Veloti), Jo Gilbert (Gloria), Lisa Ferraday (Nina Marescu), Teddy Infuhr (Jeffrey), Josephine Whittell (Mrs. Fullerton), Matt Moore (Charles), Jonathan Cott, Alexander Steinert, Bob Jellison, Ruthelma Stevens, Albert Morin, Ludwig Stossel, Betty Farrington, Elizabeth Flournoy, Grace Hayle, George McDonald, Erno Verebes, Peter Brocco, Everett Glass, Jack Gargan, Jimmy Ames, Robert Strong, Roger Moore, Ray Walker, Bob Stephenson, John McKee, John Maxwell, Larry Harmon. *D:* Robert Z. Leonard; *P:* Sam Zimbalist; *St:* Everett Freeman; *Sc:* Francis Goodrich, Albert Hackett; *ASD:* (AAN-b/w) Cedric Gibbons, Paul Groesse (art directors), Thomas Little, Claude Carpenter (sets). (1:31) Romantic comedy of a 34-year-old woman posing as a 14-year-old child prodigy on the piano who is finally exposed when she falls for her instructor. Audiences put out their money to see it.

2766. Top Banana (United Artists/Road Show Prods., Inc.; 1954). *Cast:* Phil Silvers, Rose Marie, Danny Scholl, Judy Lynn, Jack Albertson, Johnny Coy, Joey & Herbie Faye, Walter Dare Wahl, Bradford Hatton, Dick Dana, Johnny Trama, Gloria Smith, George Marci, Carolyn Anderson, Marcia Mann, Kaye Gordon, Iris Burton, Mickey Barton, Mara Lynn, Vito Durante, Bill Joyce, Walter Koremin, Nikki Cellini, Charles Zuleski, Sammy Steen, Lee Whitney, Dee Harless, Kathy Collins, Gloria Wallace, Arlen Stuart, Patti Shafter, Joyce Stansell, Emmaline Henry, Candy Montgomery, Dave Gard, Pat Welch, Ed Whitman, Dell Hanley, Wayne MacIntyre, Hank Roberts, Tommy Ryan, Dean Campbell. *D:* Alfred E. Green (final film—ret.); *P:* Albert Zugsmith, Ben Peskay; *Book:* Hy Kraft; *Adaptation & Sc:* Gene Towne; *Songs:* "If You Want to Be a Top Banana," "My Home Is in My Shoes," "I Fought Every Step of the Way," "A Word a Day," "Sans Souci," "Only If You're in Love" and "The Man of the Year This Week" Johnny Mercer. (1:40) (video) A bevy of burlesque routines highlight this filmed version of the 1951 Broadway hit (with screen adaptation by Gene Towne), utilizing the same cast. Purported to be based on Milton Berle, it was filmed at the Winter Garden Theatre in New York. Color Corporation of America. 3-D.

2767. Top Gun (United Artists/Fame Pictures; 1955). *Cast:* Sterling Hayden, Karin Booth, William Bishop, James Millican, Regis Toomey, Hugh Sanders, John Dehner, Rod Taylor, Denver Pyle, Bill Phillips, Richard "Dick" Reeves. *D:* Ray Nazarro; *P:* Edward Small (unc.); *St:* Steve Fisher; *Sc:* Fisher, Richard Schayer. (1:13) Western melodrama of a gunman who rides into his old hometown in search of his mother's killer, eventually becoming town marshal and cleaning up the town—as well as fulfilling his original purpose.

2768. Top of the World (United Artists/ Landmark Prods.; 1955). *Cast:* Dale Robertson, Frank Lovejoy, Evelyn Keyes, Nancy Gates, Paul Fix, Robert Arthur, Peter Hansen, Nick Dennis, Russell Conway, William Schallert, Peter Bourne, David McMahon, Marya Marco. *D:* Lewis R. Foster; *P:* Michael Baird, Foster; *St: & Sc:* John D. Klorer, N. Richard Nash. (1:30) Relationship drama set at a weather observation unit in North Alaska.

2769. Top Secret Affair (Warner/Carrollton, Inc.; 1957). *Cast:* Kirk Douglas, Susan Hayward, Paul Stewart, Jim Backus, John Cromwell, Roland Winters, Michael Fox, Frank Gerstle, Arthur Gould-Porter, Charles Lane, Edna Holland, Ivan Triesault, Lee Choon Wha, Franco Corsaro, Lyn Osborn, Patti Gallagher, Sydney Chatton, Jonathan Hale, Charles Meredith, James Flavin, Hal K. Dawson, Hugh Lawrence, Richard Cutting. *D:* H.C. Potter (final film—ret.); *P:* Martin Rackin; *Supervising Producer:* Milton Sperling; *St: & Sc:* Roland Kibbee, Allan Scott. (1:40) Based on characters created in John P. Marquand's 1951 *Melville Goodwin, U.S.A.*, this comedy tells of a lady publisher who knows Senator Goodwin's past and seeks to expose him—but romance takes its course. (G.B. title: *Their Secret Affair*)

2770. Topeka (Monogram/Allied Artists–Westwood; 1953). *Cast:* Bill Elliott, Phyllis Coates, Rick Vallin, John James, Denver Pyle, Dick Crockett, Harry Lauter, Dale Van Sickel, Ted Mapes, Henry Rowland, Fuzzy Knight, Edward Clark, I. Stanford Jolley, Michael Colgan, Michael Vallon. *D:* Thomas Carr; *P:* Vincent M. Fennelly; *St: & Sc:* Milton Raison. (1:09) A bit novel in approach, this Bill Elliott series western relates the tale of an outlaw and members of his former gang who clean up a lawless town. Sepiatone.

2771. The Torch (Eagle-Lion/Kaladore Corp.; 1950). *Cast:* Paulette Goddard, Pedro Armendariz, Gilbert Roland, Walter Reed, Julio Villareal, Carlos Musquiz, Margarito Luna, Jose Torvay, Garcia Pena, Antonio Kaneem. *D:* Emilio Fernandez; *P:* Bert Granet; *Sc:* Inigo de Martino Noriega, Fernandez. (1:30) (video) In Mexico, a band of rebels take over a small town and the leader falls for the daughter of a wealthy land owner. A U.S. remake of Fernandez's 1946 Mexican film *Enamorada*. (G.B. title: *Bandit General*) Originally paired on a double bill with *The Jackie Robinson Story* (q.v.).

2772. Torch Song (MGM; 1953). *Cast:* Joan Crawford (singing voice dubbed by India Adams/Jenny Stewart), Michael Wilding (piano dubbed by Walter Gross/Tye Graham), Marjorie Rambeau (AAN-BSA/Mrs. Stewart), Gig Young (Cliff Willard), Henry [Harry] Morgan (Joe Denner), Dorothy Patrick (Martha), Benny Rubin (Charlie Maylor), Nancy Gates (Celia Stewart), Charles Walters (dancer), James Todd (Philip Norton), Eugene Loring (Gene, dance director), Paul Guilfoyle (Monty Rolfe), Peter Chong (Peter), Maidie Norman (Anne), Chris Warfield (Chuck Peters), Norma Jean Salina (Margaret), Mimi Gibson (Susie), Mitchell Lewis (Bill, doorman), Peggy King (Cora), Ralph Ellis, Rudy Render, John Rosser, Reginald Simpson, Adolph Deutsch. *D:* Charles Walters; *P:* Henry Berman, Sidney Franklin, Jr.; *Sc:* John Michael Hayes, Jan Lustig; *Songs:* "Two-Faced Woman" Howard Dietz, Arthur Schwartz; "Tenderly" Jack Lawrence, Walter Gross; "You Won't Forget Me" Fred Spielman, Kermit Goell; "Blue Moon" Richard Rodgers, Lorenz Hart, "Follow Me" Adolph Deutsch. (1:30) (video/laserdisc) Technicolor drama of a bitchy Broadway musical star who meets her match in a blind piano player who won't take her guff. Based on "Why Should I Cry?" a story by I.A.R. Wylie, the film showed poor box office returns.

2773. Torpedo Alley (Allied Artists; 1953). *Cast:* Mark Stevens, Dorothy Malone, Charles Winninger, Bill Williams, Douglas Kennedy, James Millican, Bill Henry, James Seay, Robert Rose, John Alvin, Carleton Young, Ralph Sanford, Ralph Reed, Carl Christian, John Close, Keith Larsen, William Schallert, Ross Thompson, Richard Garland. *D:* Lew Landers; *P:* Lindsley Parsons; *St: & Sc:* Sam Roeca, Warren Douglas. (1:24) (video) War drama of a former U.S. Navy pilot feeling guilt for the deaths of fellow crew members during the war, who continues his military service after the war on a submarine.

2774. Torpedo Run (MGM; 1958). *Cast:* Glenn Ford (Lt. Comdr. Barney Doyle), Ernest Borgnine (Lt. Archer Sloan), Diane Brewster (Jane Doyle), Dean Jones (Lt. Jake "Fuzz" Foley), L.Q. Jones ("Hash" Benson), Philip Ober (Adm. Samuel Setton), Richard Carlyle (Comdr. Don Adams), Fredd Wayne (Orville Goldstein), Don Keefer (Ensign Ron Milligan), Robert Hardy (Lt. Redley), Paul Picerni (Lt. Burl Fisher). *D:* Joseph Pevney; *P:* Edmund Grainger; *Sc:* Richard Sale, William Wister Haines; *F/X:* (AAN) A. Arnold Gillespie, Harold Humbrock. (1:38) (video) World War II drama of a submarine commander on a personal vendetta against a Japanese aircraft carrier. A box office winner, it was based on stories by Mr. Sale. Filmed off the coast of San Diego and Long Beach, California. MetroColor/CinemaScope.

2775. Touch of Evil (Universal-International; 1958). *Cast:* Charlton Heston, Orson Welles (voted "Best Actor" at the Brussels Film Festival), Janet Leigh, Joseph Calleia, Akim Tamiroff, Joanna Moore, Ray Collins, Dennis Weaver, Valentin de Vargas, Mort Mills, Zsa Zsa Gabor (unbilled cameo), Joseph Cotten (unbilled cameo), Mercedes McCambridge (unbilled cameo), Keenan Wynn (unbilled cameo), Marlene Dietrich (unbilled cameo), Victor Millan, Lalo Rios, Michael Sargent, Phil Harvey, Harry Shannon, Rusty Wescoatt, Arlene McQuade, Jennie Dias, Yolanda Bojorquez, Eleanor Dorado, Joi Lansing, Wayne Taylor, Ken Miller, Raymond Rodriguez, Domenick Delgarde, Joe Basulto. *D:* Harry Keller, Orson Welles (unc.); *P:* Albert Zugsmith; *Sc:* Welles. (1:48 and 1:35) (video/laserdisc) Critically acclaimed *film noir* set in a Mexican border town as a Mexican narcotics agent clashes with a corrupt sheriff who has framed a young man for murder. Based on Whit Masterson's 1955 novel *Badge of Evil.*

2776. The Tougher They Come (Columbia; 1950). *Cast:* Wayne Morris, Preston Foster, Kay Buckley, William Bishop, Frank McHugh, Gloria Henry, Mary Castle (film debut), Joseph Crehan, Frank O'Connor, Alan Bridge, Al Thompson. *D:* Ray Nazarro; *P:* Wallace MacDonald; *St: & Sc:* George Bricker. (1:09) Action-melodrama of the logging business and one man's fight to keep his inherited business against ruthless corporate sabotage. Sepiatone.

2777. The Toughest Gun in Tombstone (United Artists/Peerless Prods.; 1958). *Cast:* George Montgomery, Beverly Tyler, Don Beddoe, Jim Davis, Scotty Morrow, Harry Lauter, Charles Wagenheim, Jack Kenney, John Merrick, Al Wyatt, Joey Ray, Gerald Milton, Lane Bradford, Gregg Barton, Hank Worden, Tex Terry, Charles Hayes, Kathleen Mulqueen, Rudolfo Hoyos, Alex Montoya, Rico Alaniz, Jack Carr, William Forrest, Harry Strang, Mary Newton, Gloria Rhodes. *D:* Earl Bellamy; *P:* Robert E. Kent; *St: & Sc:* Orville H. Hampton. (1:12) Tried and true "B" western plotline of a lawman posing as an outlaw to get the gang responsible for the death of his wife.

2778. The Toughest Man Alive (Allied Artists; 1955). *Cast:* Dane Clark, Lita Milan, Anthony Caruso, Ross Elliott, Myrna Dell, Thomas Browne Henry, Paul Levitt, John Eldredge, Dehl Berti, Richard Karlan, Syd Saylor, Jonathan Seymour, Don Mathers. *D:* Sidney Salkow; *P:* William F. Broidy; *St: & Sc:* Steve Fisher; *Songs:* "I Hear a Rhapsody" George Fragos, Jack Baker, Dick Gasparre; "You Walk By" Ben Raleigh, Bernie Wayne (sung by Milan). (1:12) Programmer action-melodrama of a U.S. agent posing as a gun smuggler to put an end to an operation that is selling guns to South American revolutionaries.

2779. The Toughest Man in Arizona (Republic; 1952). *Cast:* Vaughn Monroe, Joan Leslie, Edgar Buchanan, Victor Jory, Jean Parker, Henry [Harry] Morgan, Ian MacDonald, Diana Christian, Lee MacGregor, Bobby Hyatt, Charlita, Nadene Ashdown, Francis Ford, Paul Hurst, John Doucette. *D:* R.G. Springsteen; *As.P:* Sidney Picker; *St: & Sc:* John K. Butler. (1:30) Western of a widowed sheriff who falls for a beautiful girl while in pursuit of a wanted outlaw responsible for supplying guns to Indians that resulted in a massacre with few survivors. Includes three songs sung by Monroe. Trucolor.

2780. Toward the Unknown (Warner/Toluca Prods.; 1956). *Cast:* William Holden, Lloyd Nolan, Virginia Leith, Charles McGraw, Murray Hamilton, James Garner (film debut), Paul Fix, L.Q. Jones, Karen Steele, Bartlett Robinson, Malcolm Atterbury, Ralph Moody, Maura Murphy, Carol Kelly, Robert Hover, Les Johnson, Rad Fulton, Jean Willes, Nelson Leigh, Will White, William Henry, Don Harvey, Cathy Ferrara, Jon Provost, Autumn Russell, Bob Stratton, Major James Wilson, John Day. *D: & P:* Mervyn LeRoy; *As.P:-St: & Sc:* Bierne Lay, Jr.; *Song:* Robert Crawford. (1:55) Drama which involves the testing of the Bell X-2 rocket plane with a maximum speed of 1,900 mph and a test pilot who must regain the confidence of the men under him. WarnerColor/WarnerScope. (G.B. title: *Brink of Hell*)

2781. Toy Tiger (Universal-International/Christie; 1956). *Cast:* Jeff Chandler, Laraine Day, Tim Hovey, Cecil Kellaway, David Janssen, Richard Haydn, Judson Pratt, Butch Bernard, Jacqueline de Wit, Brad Morrow, Mary Field, Robert Anderson. *D:* Jerry Hopper; *P:* Howard Christie; *Screenstory & Sc:* Ted Sherdeman (suggested by a story by Frederick Kohner and Marcella Murke). (1:28) Family comedy of a fatherless boy in a boarding school who talks a man into pretending to be his father. A loose re-working of *Mad About Music* (Universal; 1938). Technicolor.

2782. Track of the Cat (Warner/Wayne-Fellows Prods.; 1954). *Cast:* Robert Mitchum, Teresa Wright, Tab Hunter, Diana Lynn, Beulah Bondi, Philip Tonge, William Hopper, Carl Switzer. *D:* William A. Wellman; *P:* John Wayne, Robert Fellows; *Sc:* A.I. Bezzerides. (1:42) Drama set at an isolated farmhouse in the backwoods of California in the 1880s of family conflicts inside and a hunt for a killer cougar outside. Based on the 1949 novel by Walter Van Tilburg Clark, the color photography by William Clothier utilizing many shades of black and white is unique. WarnerColor/CinemaScope.

2783. Trail Blazers (Monogram/Allied Artists-Newhall Prods.; 1953). *Cast:* Alan Hale, Jr., Richard Tyler, Barney McCormack, Jim Flowers, Henry Blair. *D:* Wesley Barry. (1:09) An obscure programmer western.

2784. Trail Guide (RKO; 1952). *Cast:* Tim Holt, Richard Martin, Linda Douglas, Frank Wilcox, Robert Sherwood, John Pickard, Wendy Waldron, Patricia Knight, Kenneth MacDonald, Tom London, Mauritz Hugo, John Merton. *D:* Lesley Selander; *P:* Herman Schlom; *St:* William Lively; *Sc:* Arthur E. Orloff. (1:00) Series western with Holt as a wagon train scout leading homesteaders to land that he finds is controlled by ruthless cattlemen.

2785. Trail of Robin Hood (Republic; 1950). *Cast:* Roy Rogers (himself), Penny Edwards, Gordon Jones, Jack Holt (himself), Foy Willing and Riders of the Purple Sage (themselves), Rex Allen (himself), George Chesebro (himself), Ray "Crash" Corrigan (himself), Monte Hale (himself), William Farnum (himself), Allan "Rocky" Lane (himself), Tom Keene (himself), Kermit Maynard (himself), Tom Tyler (himself), Emory Parnell, Clifton Young, James Magill, Carol Nugent, Ed Cassidy, Trigger (horse), Ko-Ko (horse), Black Jack (horse). *D:* William Witney; *As.P:* Edward J. "Eddy" White; *St: & Sc:* Gerald Geraghty; *Songs:* Jack Elliott, Foy Willing. (1:07) (video) Various Republic cowboy stars come to the aid of a former famous cowboy star (Holt) who is now growing Christmas trees for the needy, only thieves are also after the harvest. Trucolor.

2786. Trail of the Rustlers (Columbia; 1950). *Cast:* Charles Starrett, Gail Davis, Smiley Burnette, Tommy Ivo, Myron Healey, Don C. Harvey, Mira McKinney, Gene Roth, Chuck Roberson, Blackie Whiteford, Eddie Cletro and His Roundup Boys. *D:* Ray Nazarro; *P:* Colbert Clark; *St: & Sc:* Victor Arthur. (0:55) In this "Durango Kid" series western, the cowboy with the secret identity is out to stop landgrabbers. (G.B. title: *Lost River*)

2787. Train to Tombstone (Lippert/Donald Barry Prods.; 1950). *Cast:* Don Barry, Robert Lowery, Wally Vernon, Tom Neal, Judith Allen, Barbara Stanley, Minna Phillips, Nan Leslie, Claude Stroud, Edward Cassidy, Bill Kennedy. *D: & P:* William Berke; *St:* Don Barry; *Sc:* Victor West, Orville Hampton. (0:56) Programmer western of train passengers in peril by Indians and outlaws.

Transcontinent Express (G.B. title) *see* **Rock Island Trail**

The Transvestite *see* **Glen or Glenda**

2788. The Trap (Paramount/Parkwood Ent.-Heath Prods.; 1959). *Cast:* Richard Widmark, Lee J. Cobb, Tina Louise, Earl Holliman, Carl Benton Reid, Lorne Greene, Peter Baldwin, Charles Wassil, Richard Shannon, Carl Milletaire. *D:* Norman Panama; *P:* Panama, Melvin Frank; *St: & Sc:* Panama, Richard Alan Simmons. (1:24) (video) Hit crime melodrama of hoodlums holed up in a southwestern desert community who harass, intimidate and terrorize the residents. Technicolor. (G.B. title: *The Baited Trap*).

2789. Trapeze (United Artists/Susan Prods.-Joanna Prods.; 1956). *Cast:* Burt Lancaster (Mike Ribble), Tony Curtis (Tino Orsini), Gina Lollobrigida (Lola), Katy Jurado (Rosa),

Thomas Gomez (Bouglione), Johnny Puleo (Mex, the dwarf), Minor Watson (John Ringling North), Gerard Landry (Chikki), J.P. Kerrien (Otto), Sidney James (snake man), Pierre Tabard (Paul), Gamil Ratab (Stefan), Michel Thomas (ringmaster), Gabrielle Fontan. *D:* Carol Reed; *P:* James Hill; *Adaptation:* Liam O'Brien; *Sc:* James R. Webb. (1:45) (video/laserdisc) Romantic drama set in the Cirque D'Hiver in Paris as two trapeze artists vie for the affections of a fellow female high-flyer. Based on *The Killing Frost* by Max Catto [pseudonym of Max Finkell], it became one of the 24 top-grossing films of 1955-56. The Berlin Film Festival gave it a #3 vote and awarded Burt Lancaster "Best Actor" honors. DeLuxe color/CinemaScope.

2790. The Traveling Saleswoman (Columbia/Joan Davis Prods.; 1950). *Cast:* Joan Davis, Andy Devine, Joe Sawyer, Adele Jergens, Dean Reisner, John Cason, Chief Thundercloud, Harry Hayden, Charles Halton, Minerva Urecal, Eddy Waller, Teddy Infuhr, Robert Cherry, William Newell, Harry Woods, Ethan Laidlaw, Harry Tyler, Stanley Andrews, Emmett Lynn, Al Bridge, George Chesebro, Heinie Conklin, Chief Yowlachie, Bill Wilkerson, Nick Thompson, Jessie Arnold, Robert Wilke. *D:* Charles F. Riesner (final film—to TV); *P:* Tony Owen; *St: & Sc:* Howard Dimsdale; *Songs:* "Every Baby Needs a Daddy," "He Died With His Boots On" Allan Roberts, Lester Lee. (1:15) The comic misadventures of a traveling female soap peddler and her fiancé in the old west.

2791. Treasure Island (RKO/Walt Disney Prods.; 1950). *Cast:* Bobby Driscoll, Robert Newton, Basil Sydney, Walter Fitzgerald, Denis O'Dea, Ralph Truman, Finlay Currie, John Laurie, Francis DeWolff, Geoffrey Wilkinson, David Davies, Andrew Blackett, Paddy Brannigan, Ken Tuckle, John Gregson, Howard Douglas, Geoffrey Keen, William Devlin, Diarmuid Kelly, Sam Kydd, Eddie Moran, Harry Locke, Harold Jamieson, Stephen Jack, Jack Arrow, Jim O'Brady, Chris Adcock, Reginald Drummond, Gordon Mulholland, Patrick Troughton, Leo Phillips, Fred Clark (a British actor), Tom Lucas, Bob Head. *D:* Byron Haskin; *Ex.P:* Walt Disney; *P:* Perce Pearce; *Sc:* Lawrence E. Watkin. (1:36) (video/laserdisc) Robert Louis Stevenson's 1886 classic tale of pirate Long John Silver (Newton) and his efforts to get a treasure map from cabinboy Jim Hawkins (Driscoll). Filmed in England, it was a disappointment at the box office. Previous versions include: Fox Film, 1918; Paramount, 1920; MGM, 1934; and Brandon, 1941, a noncommercial feature by David Bradley. Remade in Great Britain in 1972 and most recently a 1990 TV adaptation by Turner Entertainment. Technicolor. Note: The home video has some violence deleted which was restored on the laserdisc.

Treasure of Kalifa (G.B. title) *see* **The Steel Lady**

2792. The Treasure of Lost Canyon (Universal-International; 1952). *Cast:* William Powell, Julia [Julie] Adams, Charles Drake, Henry Hull, Rosemary DeCamp, Tommy Ivo, Chubby Johnson, John Doucette, Marvin Press, Frank Wilcox, Griff Barnett, Jack Perrin, Virginia Mullen, Philo McCullough, Paul "Tiny" Newlan, George Taylor, Jimmy Ogg, Ed Hinkle, Hugh Prosser, Edward Rickard. *D:* Ted Tetzlaff; *P:* Leonard Goldstein; *Sc:* Brainard Duffield, Emerson Crocker. (1:22) Drama of what happens to various people after a treasure is discovered. Loosely based on the Robert Louis Stevenson story "The Treasure of Franchard." Technicolor.

2793. The Treasure of Pancho Villa (RKO/Edmund Grainger Prods.; 1955). *Cast:* Rory Calhoun, Shelley Winters, Gilbert Roland, Joseph Calleia, Fanny Schiller, Tony Carvajal, Pasqual Pena, Carlos [Musquiz] Mosquiz. *D:* George Sherman; *P:* Edmund Grainger; *St:* J. Robert Bren, Gladys Atwater; *Sc:* Niven Busch. (1:36) (video) A government train with a shipment of gold is sought by an American mercenary working with Pancho Villa, only the gold is stolen before the theft can occur. Technicolor/SuperScope.

2794. Treasure of Ruby Hills (Allied Artists; 1955). *Cast:* Zachary Scott, Carole Mathews, Barton MacLane, Dick Foran, Lola Albright, Gordon Jones, Raymond Hatton, Lee Van Cleef, Steve Darrell, Rick Vallin, Charles Fredericks, Stanley Andrews, James Alexander. *D:* Frank McDonald; *P:* William F. Broidy; *St:* Louis L'Amour; *Sc:* Tom Hubbard, Fred Eggers. (1:11) Programmer western of greedy cattlemen vs. a rancher over rangeland and water rights.

2795. Treasure of the Golden Condor (20th Century–Fox; 1953). *Cast:* Cornel Wilde, Constance Smith, Finlay Currie, Walter Hampden, Anne Bancroft, George Macready, Fay Wray, Leo G. Carroll, Konstantin Shayne, Louis

Heminger, Tudor Owen, Gil Donaldson, Ken Herman, Bobby Blake, Jerry Hunter, Wende Weil, Ray Beltram, Edna Holland, Harry Cording, Crane Whitley, Donald Lawton, Robert Filmer, Camillo Guercio, House Peters, Sr., John Parrish, Alphonse Martell, May Wynn, Paul Bryar, Margaret Brayton. *D: & Sc:* Delmer Daves; *P:* Jules Buck. (1:33) (video) Costume swashbuckler of a man in search of a treasure in the jungle of Guatemala which will allow him to reclaim his stolen estate. A remake of Fox's *Son of Fury* (1942), it was based on the novel by Edison Marshall. Technicolor.

2796. **Trial** (MGM; 1955). *Cast:* Glenn Ford (David Blake), Dorothy McGuire (Abbe Nyle), Arthur Kennedy (AAN-BSA/Barney Castle), John Hodiak (John J. Armstrong), Katy Jurado (Consuela Chavez), Rafael Campos (Angel Chavez), Juano Hernandez (Judge Theodore Motley), Robert Middleton (A.S. "Pete" Sanders), John Hoyt (Ralph Castillo), Paul Guilfoyle (Cap Grant), Elisha Cook, Jr. (Finn), Anna Lee (Gail Wiltse), Whit Bissell (Sam Wiltse), Richard Gaines (Dr. Schacter), Barry Kelley (Jim Backett), Frank Cady (Canford), Sheb Wooley (Butteridge), Charlotte Lawrence (Mrs. Webson), Percy Helton (Youval), Dorothy Green (Mrs. Ackerman), Everett Glass (Dean), Grandon Rhodes (Terry Bliss), Robert Bice (Abbott), John Maxwell (Benedict), Michael Dugan (Pine), Vince Townsend (Dr. Tenfold), Frank Ferguson (Kiley), Rodney Bell (Lew Bardman), Richard Tyler (Johnson), Charles Tannen, David Leonard, John Rosser, James Todd, Charles Evans, Frank Wilcox, Wilson Wood, Robert Forrest, Mort Mills, Mitchell Lewis. *D:* Mark Robson; *P:* Charles Schnee; *As.P:* James E. Newcom; *Sc:* Don M. Mankiewicz (based on his 1955 novel). (1:45) Courtroom drama of a Spanish-American youth accused of murder with 1950s communism threat a main ingredient. *Film Daily* placed it at #7 on their "10 Best" list.

2797. **Trial Without Jury** (Republic; 1950). *Cast:* Robert Rockwell, Barbara Fuller, Kent Taylor, Audrey Long, K. Elmo Lowe, Stanley Waxman, John Whitney, Barbara Billingsley, Ruthelma Stevens, William Gruenberg, Christine Larson, Theodore von Eltz (final film as actor), James Craven, William Haade, Bill Baldwin, Sid Marion. *D:* Philip Ford; *As.P:* Stephen Auer; *St:* Rose Simon Kohn; *Adaptation:* Lawrence Goldman; *Sc:* Albert DeMond. (1:00) Programmer mystery-melodrama of a man researching a murder case to write a play, who finds he is under suspicion.

Triangle on Safari (G.B. title) *see* **The Woman and the Hunter**

2798. **Tribute to a Badman** (MGM; 1956). *Cast:* James Cagney (his final western role, replacing Spencer Tracy who walked out over differences with director Wise), Don Dubbins, Stephen McNally, Irene Papas, Vic Morrow, James Griffith, Onslow Stevens, James Bell, Jeanette Nolan, Chubby Johnson, Royal Dano, Lee Van Cleef, Peter Chong, James McCallion, Tony Hughes, Roy Engel, Bud Osborne, Tom London, John Halloran, Dennis Moore, Buddy Roosevelt, Clint Sharp, Carl Pitti, Billy Dix. *D:* Robert Wise; *P:* Sam Zimbalist; *Sc:* Michael Blankfort. (1:35) (video) Successful western drama of a rancher determined to retain what is his. Based on the short story "Jeremy Rodock" [aka: "Hanging's for the Lucky"] by Jack Schaefer. Eastmancolor/CinemaScope.

2799. **Trigger, Jr.** (Republic; 1950). *Cast:* Roy Rogers, Dale Evans, Pat Brady, Gordon Jones, Foy Willing and Riders of the Purple Sage, Grant Withers, Peter Miles, George Cleveland, Frank Fenton, I. Stanford Jolley, Stanley Andrews, The Raynor Lehr Circus, Trigger (horse). *D:* William Witney; *As.P:* Edward J. "Eddy" White; *St: & Sc:* Gerald Geraghty; *Songs:* Foy Willing, Peter Tinturin, Carol Rice. (1:08) (video) Roy is the owner of a rodeo show who finds local ranchers are being victimized by a range protection service, utilizing a killer horse. Originally ran as a co-feature on a twin bill with *The Savage Horde* (q.v.). Trucolor.

2800. **Triple Cross** (Monogram; 1951). *Cast:* Joe Kirkwood, Jr., Cathy Downs, James Gleason (replacing Leon Errol), John Emery, Steve Brodie, Don Harvey, Rufe Davis, Jimmy Wallington, Mary Young, Eddie Gribbon, Sid Tomack, Dickie LeRoy, Jimmy Lloyd, Cliff Clark, Hank Worden. *D:* Reginald LeBorg; *P:* Hal E. Chester; *St:* Harold Bancroft; *Sc:* Jan Jeffries [based on the comic strip characters created by Ham Fisher]. (1:00) Joe Palooka (Kirkwood), his wife Anne (Downs) and Knobby Walsh (Gleason) are kidnapped by escaped convicts while returning from a fishing trip. The 11th and final entry in the pugilism series which later became a TV series with Kirkwood and Downs. (aka: *Joe Palooka in Triple Cross*)

2801. **Triple Trouble** (Monogram; 1950). *Cast:* Leo Gorcey, Huntz Hall, Gabriel Dell, Richard Benedict, Pat Collins, Lyn Thomas, Bernard Gorcey, Billy Benedict, David Gorcey,

Paul Dubov, Joseph Turkel, George Chandler, Eddie Gribbon, Jonathan Hale, Joseph Crehan, Effie Laird, Edward Gargan, Eddie Foster, Frank Marlowe, Tom Kennedy, Lyle Talbot. *D:* Jean Yarbrough; *P:* Jan Grippo; *Sc:* Charles R. Marion; *Additional dialogue:* Bert Lawrence. (1:06) A "Bowery Boys" series entry with Slip (L. Gorcey) and Sach (Hall) going to prison after being convicted of a warehouse robbery.

2802. Tripoli (Paramount/Pine-Thomas; 1950). *Cast:* Maureen O'Hara, John Payne, Howard Da Silva, Philip Reed, Grant Withers, Lowell Gilmore, Connie Gilchrist, Alan Napier, Herbert Heyes, Alberto Morin, Emil Hanna, Grandon Rhodes, Frank Fenton, Rosa Turich, Ray Hyke, Walter Reed, Paul Livermore, Gregg Barton, Don Sumners, Jack Pennick, Ewing Mitchell. *D:* Will Price; *P:* William H. Pine, William C. Thomas; *Sc:* Winston Miller. (1:35) Action-adventure of American marines attempting to clear out Barbary pirates from the coast of the U.S. in 1805. Based on *The Barbarians* by Mr. Price and Mr. Miller. (aka: *First Marines*) Technicolor.

2803. Trooper Hook (United Artists/ Fielding Prods., Inc. 1957). *Cast:* Joel McCrea, Barbara Stanwyck, Earl Holliman, Edward Andrews, John Dehner, Susan Kohner, Celia Lovsky, Terry Lawrence, Rudolfo Acosta, Royal Dano, Stanley Adams, Pat O'Moore, Jeanne Bates, Rush Williams, Dick Shannon, Sheb Wooley, Cyril Delevanti, Charles Gray, Mary Gregory, Alfred Linder, Jody McCrea, Dee J. Thompson, Paul "Tiny" Newlan. *D:* Charles Marquis Warren; *P:* Sol Baer Fielding; *Sc:* David Victor, Herbert Little, Martin Berkeley, Jr.; *Title song:* Gerald Fried, Mitzi Cummings (sung by Tex Ritter). (1:21) Western drama of a woman taken by Indians who bore a son to a chief. When she is returned to her husband, the man rejects the halfbreed boy.

2804. Tropic Zone (Paramount/Pine-Thomas; 1953). *Cast:* Ronald Reagan, Rhonda Fleming, Estelita [Rodriguez], Noah Beery, Jr., Grant Withers, John Wengraf, Argentina Brunetti, Rico Alaniz, Maurice Jara, Pilar Del Rey. *D: & Sc:* Lewis R. Foster; *P:* William H. Pine, William C. Thomas. (1:34) Melodramatic action-adventure of troubles on a South American banana plantation. Based on the 1940 novel *Gentleman of the Jungle* by Tom Gill. Technicolor.

2805. Tropical Heat Wave (Republic; 1952). *Cast:* Estelita [Rodriguez], Robert Hutton, Grant Withers, Kristine Miller, Edwin Max, Lou Lubin, Martin Garralaga, Earl Lee, Lennie Bremen, Jack Kruschen. *D:* R.G. Springsteen; *Ex.P:* Herbert J. Yates; *As.P:* Sidney Picker; *St: & Sc:* Arthur T. Horman; *Songs:* "My Lonely Heart and I" Sammy Wilson, Horman; "I Want to Be Kissed" Wilson, Nestor Amaral; "What Should Happen to You" Wilson. (1:14) Crime melodrama of a woman who goes to her uncle's nightclub in Cuba to become a singer, finds hoods trying to muscle in on the operation. Originally ran on a double bill with *Desperadoes' Outpost* (q.v.).

2806. Trouble Along the Way (Warner; 1953). *Cast:* John Wayne, Donna Reed, Charles Coburn, Tom Tully, Sherry Jackson, Marie Windsor, Tom Helmore, Douglas Spencer, Leif Erickson, Dabbs Greer, Lester Matthews, Chuck Connors, Bill Radovich, Richard Garrick, Murray Alper, James Flavin, Ned Glass, Phil Chambers, Frank Ferguson, Howard Petrie, Renata Vanni, Tim Graham, Robert Keys, James Dean. *D:* Michael Curtiz; *P:* Melville Shavelson; *St:* "It Figures" Douglas Morrow, Robert Hardy Andrews; *Sc:* Jack Rose, Shavelson. (1:50) (video/ laserdisc) Comedy-drama with a touch of the sentimental of what a football coach at a Catholic college has to do to retain custody of his daughter.

The Trouble Shooter (G.B. title) *see* **Man With the Gun**

2807. The Trouble with Harry (Paramount/Alfred Hitchcock Prods.; 1955). *Cast:* Edmund Gwenn, John Forsythe, Shirley MacLaine (film debut), Mildred Natwick, Mildred Dunnock, Jerry Mathers, Royal Dano, Parker Fennelly, Barry Macollum, Dwight Marfield, Leslie Woolf, Philip Truex, Ernest Curt Bach. *D: & P:* Alfred Hitchcock; *Sc:* John Michael Hayes; *Song:* "Flaggin' the Train to Tuscaloosa" Mack David, Raymond Scott. (1:39) (video/laserdisc) The "Harry" of the title is a corpse found deep in the woods of autumnal Vermont by various people and what they do with or about the body. A black comedy from Hitchcock which was one of his personal favorites despite low audience attendance. Based on the 1950 novel by Jack Trevor Story. Technicolor/VistaVision

2808. The True Story of Jesse James (20th Century–Fox; 1957). *Cast:* Robert Wagner (Jesse James), Jeffrey Hunter (Frank James), Hope Lange (Zerelda "Zee" Mims-James), Agnes Moorehead (Mrs. Samuel), Alan Hale, Jr. (Cole

Younger), Alan Baxter, John Carradine, Rachel Stephens, Barney Phillips, Biff Elliot (Jim Younger), Frank Overton, Chubby Johnson, Frank Gorshin (Charley Ford), Carl Thayler (Bob "Robby" Ford), John Doucette, Robert Adler, Clancy Cooper, Sumner Williams, Tom Greenway, Mike Steen, Jason Wingreen, Aaron Saxon, Anthony Ray (Bob Younger), Clegg Hoyt, Tom Pittman, Louis Zito, Mark Hickman, Adam Marshall, Joseph Di Reda, J. Frederick Albeck, Kellogg Junge, Jr., Barry Atwater, Marian Seldes. *D:* Nicholas Ray; *P:* Herbert B. Swope, Jr.; *Sc:* Walter Newman [based on the 1939 screenplay by Nunnally Johnson]. (1:32) The story of Jesse and Frank James, told in flashback, following the disastrous bank robbery attempt at Northfield, Minnesota. A remake of *Jesse James* (1939), utilizing footage from that film. (G.B. title: *The James Brothers*) DeLuxe color/CinemaScope.

2809. The True Story of Lynn Stuart (Columbia; 1958). *Cast:* Betsy Palmer, Jack Lord, Barry Atwater, Kim Spalding, Karl Lukas, Casey Walters, Harry Jackson, John Anderson, Claudia Bryar, Rita Duncan, Lee Farr, Louis Towers. *D:* Lewis Seiler (final film—ret.); *P:* Bryan Foy; *Sc:* John Kneubuhl. (1:18) Fact-based crime melodrama of a California housewife (Palmer) who works undercover to nail some drug dealers. Based on news articles by Pat Michaels.

Try and Get Me *see* **The Sound of Fury**

2810. Tumbleweed (Universal-International; 1953). *Cast:* Audie Murphy, Lori Nelson, Chill Wills, Roy Roberts, K.T. Stevens, Russell Johnson, Madge Meredith, Lee Van Cleef, I. Stanford Jolley, Eugene Iglesias, Ralph Moody, Ross Elliott, Phil Chambers, Lyle Talbot, King Donovan, Harry Harvey, Tumbleweed (horse). *D:* Nathan Juran; *P:* Ross Hunter; *Sc:* John Meredyth Lucas. (1:19) Western of a man accused of desertion during an Indian raid on a wagon train. Based on the novel *Three Were Renegades* by Kenneth Parker, it was originally paired on a double bill with *Project M-7* (G.B. title: *The Net*), a British espionage melodrama. Technicolor.

2811. The Tunnel of Love (MGM/Joseph Fields Prods.-Arwin Prods.; 1958). *Cast:* Doris Day, Richard Widmark, Gig Young, Gia Scala, Elisabeth Fraser (repeating her stage role), Elizabeth Wilson (repeating her stage role), Vicki Dougan, Doodles Weaver, Charles Wagenheim, Robert Williams, The Esquire Trio. *D:* Gene Kelly; *P:* Joseph Fields, Martin Melcher; *Sc:* Fields [based on his hit 1957 Broadway play, written with Peter de Vries on whose 1954 novel the play was based]; *Songs:* "Have Lips Will Kiss in the Tunnel of Love" Patty Fisher, Bob Roberts; "Run Away Skidaddle Skidoo" Ruth Roberts, Bill Katz (both sung by Day). (1:38) (video/laserdisc) Hit domestic comedy of a married couple wishing to adopt. CinemaScope.

2812. The Turning Point (Paramount; 1952). *Cast:* William Holden, Edmond O'Brien, Alexis Smith, Tom Tully, Ed Begley, Dan Dayton, Adele Longmire, Ray Teal, Ted de Corsia, Don Porter, Howard Freeman, Neville Brand, Peter Baldwin, Judith Ames, Mary Murphy, Leonard George, Ben Cameron, Russell Johnson, Leonard "Lennie" Bremen, Eugene White, Buddy Sullivan, Robert Rockwell, Joel Marston, Russell Conway, George Ford, Charles Sherlock, Lee Phelps, Chalky Williams, George Dempsey, Charles Campbell, Albin Robeling, Jean Ransome, Gretchen Hale, Grace Hayle, Ruth Packard, Hazel Boyne, Carolyn Jones, Whit Bissell, Harry Hines, Franz Roehn, Tony Barr, Tom Moore, Jamesson Shade, Jerry James, John Maxwell, Soledad Jimenez, Diane Garrett, Ralph Sanford, Ralph Montgomery, Jay Adler. *D:* William Dieterle; *P:* Irving Asher; *Sc:* Warren Duff. (1:25) Hit crime melodrama inspired by the (Estes) Kefauver Committee hearings into organized crime in 1951 and an unpublished story by Horace McCoy titled "Storm in the City."

2813. 12 Angry Men (United Artists/Orion Prods.-Nova Prods.; 1957). *Cast:* Henry Fonda (juror #8), Martin Balsam (juror #1), John Fielder (juror #2), Lee J. Cobb (juror #3), E.G. Marshall (juror #4), Jack Klugman (juror #5), Edward Binns (juror #6), Jack Warden (juror #7), Joseph Sweeney (juror #9), Ed Begley (juror #10), George Voskovec (juror #11), Robert Webber (juror #12), Rudy Bond (judge), James A. Kelly (guard), Bill Nelson (court clerk), John Savoca (defendant). *D:* (AAN) Sidney Lumet (feature directorial debut); *P:* (AAN-Best Picture) Henry Fonda, Reginald Rose; *As.P:* George Justin; *Sc:* (AAN) Rose [based on his 1955 TV play]. (1:35) (video/laserdisc) Critically acclaimed drama of a jury of twelve men, one of which has a reasonable doubt and must convince the other eleven in a case where a youth is charged with stabbing his father to death. This sleeper which was filmed in 20 days became one of the 24 top-grossing films of 1956-57. The NBR placed it at #2 on their "10 Best" list while *Film Daily* and the *New York Times* both placed it at #3 on their's. The New York Film Critics had it in nomination for "Best Picture" of the year, the Berlin Film Festival awarded it the "Golden Bear" and Fonda was in nomination for "Best Actor" at the British Academy Awards. Remade in 1997 as a cable TV movie.

Twelve Miles Out *see* **The Second Woman**

2814. 20 Million Miles to Earth (Columbia/Morningside Prods.; 1957). *Cast:* William Hopper, Joan Taylor, Frank Puglia, John Zaremba, Tito Vuolo, Thomas Browne Henry, Jay Arvan, Arthur Space, Bart Bradley, George Peeling, George Khoury, Don Orlando, Rollin Moriyama, Ray Harryhausen (man feeding elephants), Dale Van Sickel. *D:* Nathan Juran; *P:* Charles H. Schneer; *St:* Charlotte Knight; *Sc:* Bob Williams, Christopher Knopf; *F/X:* Ray Harryhausen. (1:22) Acclaimed science fiction of a rocketship which returns to earth, crashing into the sea off Italy, carrying one human survivor and an egg from a Venusian life form which hatches and rapidly begins to grow in earth's atmosphere. One of the better genre entries from the decade highlighted by Mr. Harryhausen's stop-motion special effects, it was originally paired on the top of a twin bill with *The Night the World Exploded* (q.v.).

2815. The 27th Day (Columbia/Romson Prods.; 1957). *Cast:* Gene Barry, Valerie French, George Voskovec, Arnold Moss, Stefan Schnabel, Ralph Clanton, Frederick Ledebur, Paul Birch, Azemat Janti, Marie Tsien, Ed Hinton, Grandon Rhodes, David Bond, Emil Sitka, Philip Van Zandt, Paul Frees, Tom Daly, Doreen Woodbury, Jerry Janger, Mark Warren, Don Spark, Eric Feldary, Weaver Levy, Monty Ash, Irvin Ash Kenszy, Hank Clemin, Theodore Marcuse, Peter Norman, John Bleifer, Mel Welles, Sigfrid Tor, Don Rhodes, Ralph Montgomery, John Dodsworth, Jacques Gallo, Charles Bennett, Welda Winchell, Michael Harris, Arthur Lovejoy, John Bryant, John Mooney, Paul Power. *D:* William Asher; *P:* Helen Ainsworth; *Ex.P:* Lewis J. Rachmil; *Sc:* John Mantley [based on his book]. (1:15) Science fiction in which an alien gives a capsule to each of five diversified earthlings, each capable of destroying all life on earth. 1950s Cold War propaganda and anti-communist sentiment are in evidence in the story.

2816. 20,000 Leagues Under the Sea (Buena Vista/Walt Disney Prods.; 1954). *Cast:* Kirk Douglas (Ned Land), James Mason (Captain Nemo), Paul Lukas (Prof. Aronnax), Peter Lorre (Conseil), Robert J. Wilke (first mate of the *Nautilus*), Carleton Young (John Howard), Ted de Corsia (Capt. Farragut), Percy Helton (diver), Ted Cooper (mate of the *Abraham Lincoln*), Fred Braham (Casey Moore), J.M. Kerrigan (Billy), Edward Marr, Harry Harvey, Herb Vigran, Esmeralda (seal—received #3 PATSY in 1955). *D:* Richard Fleischer; *P:* Walt Disney; *Sc:* Earl Felton; *ASD:* (AA-color) John Meehan (art director), Emile Kuri (sets); *F/X:* (AA) John Hench, Joshua Meador, Ralph Hammeras; *Editor:* (AAN) Elmo Williams. (2:07) (video/laserdisc) 19th century science fiction-fantasy based on the 1870 novel by Jules Verne of demented Captain Nemo, whose hatred of all mankind has him on a mission to destroy it, until he rescues three survivors from a ship he has sunk with his submarine, the *Nautilus*. This piece of Disney magic placed #8 on the "10 Best" list of the NBR and became one of the 27 top-grossing films of 1954-55. Previously filmed in 1916 as *Twenty Thousand Leagues Under the Sea* by Universal, with copies of that early production still surviving the nitrate decay that has destroyed many a silent film. Technicolor/CinemaScope. Remade in 1997 as a TV movie. First filmed in France in 1907 as 1 reel by Georges Méliès.

2817. 23 Paces to Baker Street (20th Century–Fox; 1956). *Cast:* Van Johnson, Vera Miles, Cecil Parker, Patricia Laffan, Maurice Denham, Estelle Winwood, Liam Redmond, Isobel Elsom, Martin Benson, Natalie Norwick, Terence de Marney, Queenie Leonard, Charles Keane, Lucie Lancaster, A. Cameron Grant, Ashley Cowan, Les Sketchley, Ben Wright, Reginald Sheffield, Phyllis Montifiere, Arthur Gomez, Janice Kane, Robert Raglan, Howard Lang, Margaret McGrath, Walter Horsborough, Fred Griffith, Charles Stanley, Robin Alalouf, Yorke Sherwood, Michael Trubeshawe. *D:* Henry Hathaway; *P:* Henry Ephron; *Sc:* Nigel Balchin. (1:43) (video) Suspense drama of a blind writer who overhears a plot for a kidnapping, but no one will believe him. Based on the 1938 novel *Warrant for X* by Philip MacDonald. DeLuxe color/CinemaScope.

2818. Twilight for the Gods (Universal-International; 1958). *Cast:* Rock Hudson, Cyd Charisse, Arthur Kennedy, Leif Erickson, Charles McGraw, Judith Evelyn, Wallace Ford, Richard Haydn, Ernest Truex, Vladimir

Sokoloff, Celia Lovsky, Robert Hoy, Charles Horvath, Maurice Marsac, Virginia Gregg, William Challee, Morris Ankrum, Arthur Space, William Yip, Kimo Mahi. *D:* Joseph Pevney; *P:* Gordon Kay; *Sc:* Ernest K. Gann (based on his 1956 novel); *Title theme:* David Raksin. (2:00) Mini disaster melodrama of various passengers and crew aboard a two-masted schooner that has sprung a leak and is beginning to sink. Filmed in Hawaii. Eastmancolor.

2819. Twilight in the Sierras (Republic; 1950). *Cast:* Roy Rogers, Dale Evans, Estelita Rodriguez, Pat Brady, Russ Vincent, George Meeker, Fred Kohler, Jr., Edward Keane, House Peters, Jr., Pierce Lyden, Foy Willing and Riders of the Purple Sage, Joseph A. Garro, William Lester, Bob Burns, Don Frost, Robert Wilke, Trigger (horse). *D:* William Witney; *As.P:* Edward J. "Eddy" White; *St: & Sc:* Sloan Nibley: *Songs:* "It's One Wonderful Day," "Rootin' Tootin' Cowboy" and "Pancho's Rancho" Sid Robin, Foy Willing. (1:07) (video) In this series entry, Roy breaks up a counterfeiting operation. Trucolor.

Twinkle and Shine *see* **It Happened to Jane**

2820. The Twinkle in God's Eye (Republic; 1955). *Cast:* Mickey Rooney, Coleen Gray, Hugh O'Brian, Joey Forman, Don Barry, Touch [Mike] Connors, Jil Jarmyn, Kem Dibbs, Tony Garsen, Raymond Hatton, Ruta Lee, Clem Bevans. *D:* George Blair; *Ex.P:* Herbert J. Yates; *P:* Mickey Rooney (unc.); *St: & Sc:* P.J. Wolfson; *Title song:* Rooney (sung by Eddie Howard). (1:13) Offbeat western of a minister in a western town trying to make converts to the Lord with his sense of humor.

2821. Two Dollar Bettor (Realart; 1951). *Cast:* John Litel, Marie Windsor, Steve Brodie, Barbara Logan, Robert Sherwood, Barbara Bestar, Walter Kingsford, Don Shelton, Kay La Velle, Carl Switzer, Isabel Randolph, Ralph Reed, Barbara Billingsley, Ralph Hodges, Madelon Mitchel, Philip Van Zandt. *D: & P:* Edward L. Cahn; *Sc:* Howard Emmett Rogers (based on his novel *The Far Turn*); *Additional dialogue:* Bill Raynor; *Song:* "Querido" Jean Logan. (1:12) (video) A man begins gambling on a lark, but finds it turning into a compulsive obsession which leads him to steal money from the bank at which he is employed to pay his gambling debts. (G.B. title: *Beginner's Luck*)

Two-Fisted Agent (G.B. title) *see* **Bonanza Town**

2822. Two Flags Meet (20th Century-Fox; 1950). *Cast:* Joseph Cotten, Linda Darnell, Jeff Chandler, Cornel Wilde, Dale Robertson, Jay C. Flippen, Noah Beery, Jr., Harry Von Zell, John[ny] Sands, Arthur Hunnicutt, Jack Lee, Robert Adler, Harry Carter, Ferris Taylor, Sally Corner, Everett Glass, Marjorie Bennett, Lee MacGregor, Roy Gordon, Aurora Castillo, Stanley Andrews, Don Garner. *D:* Robert Wise; *P:* Casey Robinson; *St:* Frank S. Nugent, Curtis Kenyon; *Sc:* Casey Robinson. (1:32) Civil War-era western of Confederate P.O.W.s who get out of prison and agree to fight Indians at a western fort, although the commandant of the fort has no sympathy for anyone fighting for the Southern cause.

2823. Two Gals and a Guy (United Artists/Weisner Bros.; 1951). *Cast:* Robert Alda, Janis Page (dual role), James Gleason, Lionel Stander, Arnold Stang, Linda Preston, Patty McCormack (film debut, age 6), The Three Suns (themselves), Rock Rogers, Morris Lieb, Cecil Clovelly, Myrtle Ferguson, Rhea Scott, Ray Morgan, Lupe Garnica, Patti Crowe. *D:* Alfred E. Green; *P:* John W. Arent; *St: & Sc:* Searle Kramer; *Songs:* "Laugh and Be Happy," "So Long For Now," "Sunshowers" Morty Nevins, Hal David. (1:10) Drama of the problems that arise in a marriage when the wife who is one half of a singing duo wants to leave the act and raise an adopted family. Originally paired on a double bill with *St. Benny the Dip* (q.v.).

2824. Two-Gun Lady (Associated Releasing Corp.; 1956). *Cast:* Peggie Castle, William Talman, Marie Windsor, Earle Lyon, Robert Lowery, Joe Besser, Ian MacDonald, Barbara Turner, Norman Jolley, Susan Lang, Kit Carson, Arvo Ojala, Karl Hansen, Dave Tomack, Sid Lopez, Gregory Moffet, Ben Cameron. *D: & P:* Richard Bartlett; *Ex.P:* Earle Lyon; *As.P:* Ian MacDonald; *St:* Norman Jolley; *Sc:* Jolley, Bartlett. (1:15) Western of a girl adept at handling a pair of six-shooters and a lawman who track down those responsible for killing the former's father.

2825. Two Guns and a Badge (Allied Artists/Silvermine Prods.; 1954). *Cast:* Wayne Morris, Morris Ankrum, Beverly Garland, Roy Barcroft, William Phipps, Damian O'Flynn, I. Stanford Jolley, Robert Wilke, Chuck Courtney, Henry Rowland, John Pickard, Gregg Barton. *D:* Lewis D. Collins (final film—d. 1954);

P: Vincent M. Fennelly; *St:* & *Sc:* Dan Ullman. (1:09) When an ex-convict is mistaken for a deputy sheriff, he proceeds to clean up a corrupt western town, while romancing a local girl. The final entry in Morris' series of six westerns for Allied Artists and the swan song of "B" series westerns produced in Hollywood. Note: The "series western," a Hollywood staple since the silent era was for the most part produced in a series of six features (sometimes eight), each with the same star attraction. They were primarily the product of "poverty row" studios and independent producers, though several did emerge from major studios over the years. Often a series was begun and proved unpopular—such as the "Rough Ridin' Kids" for Republic—and the series was terminated, leaving that series with less than its planned number. The "Kids" ceased production after four features (see index).

2826. Two Lost Worlds (Eagle-Lion/ Sterling Prods.; 1950). *Cast:* Laura Elliot, Jim Arness, Bill Kennedy, Gloria Petroff, Tom Hubbard, Jane Harlan, Pierre Watkin, Bob Carson, Guy Bellis, John Guilfoyle, Fred Kohler, Jr., Tom Monroe, Tim Graham, Richard Bartell. *D:* Norman Dawn; *P:* & *Story idea:* Boris Petroff; *Adaptation:* Tom Hubbard, Phyllis Parker; *Sc:* Hubbard. (1:01) (video) Programmer adventure tale of people shipwrecked on an island who are terrorized by dinosaur footage from *One Million B.C.* (U.A./Hal Roach; 1940).

2827. Two of a Kind (Columbia; 1951). *Cast:* Edmond O'Brien, Lizabeth Scott, Terry Moore, Alexander Knox, Griff Barnett, Robert Anderson, Virginia Brissac, J.M. Kerrigan, Claire Carleton, Louis Jean Heydt. *D:* Henry Levin; *P:* William Dozier; *Sc:* Lawrence Kimble, James Gunn. (1:15) Suspense drama of con-artists attempting to dupe an elderly couple of their finances. Based on the novelette "Lefty Farrell" by James Edward Grant, it was originally paired on a double bill program with *Silver Canyon* (q.v.).

2828. Two Tickets to Broadway (RKO/ Howard Hughes Presents; 1951). *Cast:* Tony Martin (Dan Carter), Janet Leigh (Nancy Peterson), Gloria DeHaven (Hannah Holbrook), Eddie Bracken (Lew Conway), Ann Miller (Joyce Campbell), Barbara Lawrence ("Foxy" Rogers), Bob Crosby (himself), The Charlivels (acrobats), Joe Smith (Harry), Charles Dale (Leo), Taylor Holmes (Willard Glendon), Norval Mitchell (Mr. Peterson), Helen Spring (Mrs. Peterson), Buddy Baer, Frieda Stoll, Fred Gillett, John Gallaudet, Isabel Randolph, Donald MacBride, John Sheehan, Don Blackman, Vera Miles (film debut), Jean Corbett, Helene Hayden, Claudette Thornton, Hazel Shaw, Barbara Logan, Charlotte Alpert, Victoria Lynn, Jeane Dyer, Pat Hall, Maura Donatt, Joi Lansing, Mara Corday, Joan Evans, June McCall, Joan Alander, Noreen Mortensen, Joel Robinson, Georgia Clancy, Elizabeth Burgess, Barbara Thatcher, Shirley Buchanan, Carol Brewster, Mildred Carroll, Carmelita Eskew, Joanne Frank, Mary Ellen Gleason, Joan Jordan, Lola Kendrick, Shirley Kimball, Evelyn Lovequist, Kathleen O'Malley, June Paul, Marylin Symons, Beverly Thomas, Joan Whitney, Barbara Worthington, George Nader, Lester Dorr, Garry Owen, Linda Williams, Ann Zika, Libby Taylor, Herman Cantor, Jimmy Dundee, Millicent Deming, Jerry Hausner, Jack Gargan, Jane Easton, Shirley Tegge, Martha O'Brian, Lucy Knoch, Rosalee Calbert, Joan Shawlee, Joan Barton, Shirley Whitney, Marilyn Johnson, Gwen Caldwell, Barbara Freking, Mona Knox, Rosemary Knighton, Kathy Case, Eileen Coghlan, Marie Thomas, Billy Curtis, Mike Lally, Bennett Green, Larry Barton, Gene Banks, Vincent Graeff, Maxine Willis, Joann Arnold, Ann Melton, Ann Kramer, Marg Pemberton, Anne Kimbell, Anne O'Neal, Charlete Hardy, Lillian West, Sid Tomack, Tony Felice, Marty Rhiel, Buris DeJong, Gene Marshall, Marie Allison, Miles Shepard, Bob Thom, Ralph Hodges, Michael Pierce, Suzanne Ames. *D:* James V. Kern (final film—ret.); *P:* Jerry Wald, Norman Krasna, Howard Hughes (unc.); *St:* Sammy Cahn; *Sc:* Sid Silvers, Hal Kanter; *Choreography:* Busby Berkeley; *Sound:* (AAN) John O. Aalberg; *Songs:* "Are You a Beautiful Dream?," "The Closer You Are," "Baby, You'll Never Be Sorry," "Let the Worry Bird Worry for You," "Big Chief Hole-in-the-Ground," "Pelican Falls High," "It Began in Yucatan" Jule Styne, Leo Robin; "Manhattan" Richard Rodgers, Lorenz Hart; "There's No Tomorrow" Al Hoffman, Leo Corday, Leon Carr; "Prologue" from *Pagliacci* Ruggiero Leoncavallo and "Let's Make Comparisons" Cahn, Bob Crosby. (1:46) (video) Music, comedy and romance as four girls attempt to get a singing spot on Bob Crosby's TV show. Another venture from Howard Hughes that bombed at the box office due to production excesses. Technicolor.

2829. Two Weeks with Love (MGM; 1950). *Cast:* Jane Powell, Ricardo Montalban, Louis Calhern, Ann Harding, Carleton Carpenter, Debbie Reynolds, Clinton Sundberg,

Tommy Rettig, Gary Gray, Charles Smith. *D:* Roy Rowland; *P:* Jack Cummings; *Sc:* John Larkin, Dorothy Kingsley; *St:* Larkin; *Choreography:* Busby Berkeley; *Songs:* "Aba Daba Honeymoon" Arthur Fields, Walter Donaldson; "The Oceana Roll" Roger Lewis, Lucien Denni; "A Heart That's Free" Thomas T. Railey, Alfred G. Robyn; "By the Light of the Silvery Moon" Gus Edwards, Edward Madden; "My Hero" Stanislaus Stange, Oscar Straus; "Row, Row, Row" William Jerome, James V. Monaco; "That's How I Need You" Joe McCarthy, Joe Goodwin and "Beautiful Lady" Ivan Caryll, C.H.S. McClellan. (1:32) (video) Hit domestic musical-comedy with romance and period flavor of a family vacationing in the Catskills. Most notable for Reynolds and Carpenter's duet of "Aba Daba Honeymoon," a hit from 1914 which topped the charts for a second time in 1950. Technicolor.

2830. The Twonkey (United Artists/Arch Oboler Prods., Ltd.; 1953). *Cast:* Hans Conried, Billy Lynn, Gloria Blondell, Janet Warren, Ed Max, Al Jarvis, Norman Field, William Phipps, Steve Roberts, Florence Ravenel, Trilby Conried (infant). *D:-P: & Sc:* Arch Oboler; *St:* Lewis Padget [pseudonym of Henry Kuttner]. (1:12) Satirical fantasy of a college professor's television set which takes on a life of its own, subsequently interfering in every aspect of his own life, the set being possessed by a spirit from the future.

2831. Tyrant of the Sea (Columbia; 1950). *Cast:* Rhys Williams, Ron Randell, Valentine Perkins, Doris Lloyd, Lester Matthews, Harry Cording, Terry Kilburn, Maurice Marsac, William Fawcett, Ross Elliott, Don C. Harvey, James Fairfax. *D:* Lew Landers; *P:* Sam Katzman; *St: & Sc:* Robert Libott, Frank Burt. (1:10) A swashbuckling costume adventure of a tyrannical sea captain during the Napoleonic Wars and his efforts to prevent Napoleon's invasion of England.

UFO *see* **Unidentified Flying Objects**

U.S.S. Teakettle *see* **You're in the Navy Now**

2832. Unchained (Warner/Hall Bartlett Prods.; 1955). *Cast:* Elroy "Crazylegs" Hirsch (Steve Davitt), Barbara Hale (Mary Davitt), Chester Morris (Kenyon J. Scudder), Todd Duncan (Bill Howard), Johnnie Johnston (Eddie Garrity), Peggy Knudsen (Elaine), Jerry Paris (Joe Ravens), John Qualen (Leonard Haskins), Bill Kennedy (Sanders), Henry Nakamura (Jerry Hakara), Kathryn Grant (Sally Haskins), Bob Patten (Swanson), Don Kennedy (Gladstone), Mack Williams (Mr. Johnson), Tim Considine (Win Davitt), Dexter Gordon (saxaphone dubbed by George Auld), Saul Gorss. *D:-P:-Screenstory: & Sc:* Hall Bartlett; Theme song: (AAN) "Unchained Melody" Alex North, Hy Zarek (which became a big hit). (1:15) *Prisoners are People,* a 1952 book by Kenyon J. Scudder, was the source material for this fact-based drama of life at California's Chino prison, a prison farm where men are incarcerated to do their time without walls, armed guards, uniforms or prison cells. Mr. Scudder had been the supervisor at that institution.

2833. Uncle Vanya (Continental Distributing/The "Uncle Vanya" Company; 1958). *Cast:* Franchot Tone, Dolores Dorn-Heft, George Voscovec, Peggy McCay, Clarence Derwent, Gerald Hiken, Mary Perry, Shirley Gale. *D:* John Goetz, Franchot Tone; *P:* Marion Parsonnet, Tone; *Sc:* Stark Young (unc.). (1:38) Drama of interrelationships between various people at a Russian country estate in the late 19th century. Based on the play by Anton Chekov, as translated by Stark Young, it was filmed at Parsonnet Studios in Long Island, N.Y. The cast is the same as the off–Broadway production which opened in 1956 with the exception of Signe Hasso who was replaced by Ms. Dorn-Heft who went on to win "Best Actress" honors at the San Francisco International Film Festival in December 1957. Chekov's drama was remade in Russia in 1972 and again in Great Britain in 1977 and 1996.

The Unconquered *see* **Helen Keller in Her Story**

2834. The Undead (American International/Balboa Prods.; 1957). *Cast:* Pamela Duncan (dual role), Richard Garland, Allison Hayes, Val DuFour, Mel Welles, Dorothy Neuman, Billy Barty, Bruno VeSota, Aaron Saxon, Richard Devon, Dick Miller. *D: & P:* Roger Corman; *St: & Sc:* Charles Griffith, Mark Hanna. (1:15) (video) Off-the-wall horror flick from Roger Corman involving a prostitute who through an experiment is returned to one of her previous lifetimes as a witch in the Middle Ages who has been condemned to death. Mr. Corman obviously sought to cash in on the late 1950s interest in reincarnation.

2835. Under Fire (20th Century–Fox/Regal Films; 1957). *Cast:* Rex Reason, Henry [Harry] Morgan, Steve Brodie, Peter Walker,

Robert Levin, Jon Locke, Gregory Lafayette, Karl Lukas, Frank Gerstle, Tom McKee, John Murphy, Edmund Penney, Seymour Green, Dave Tomack, Walter Maslow, David Carlisle, William Allyn, Rita Paul, Kay Kuter, Keith Byron, Neyle Morrow, K.L. Smith, Robert Hinkle, Robert Colbert, Al Shelley, Troy Patterson, Dehl Berti, Ronald Foster, Sid Melton, George Chakiris (a former chorus boy in his acting debut), Ed Hinton, Nico Minardos, Calvin Booth, Lorraine Martin, Merry Townsend. *D:* James B. Clark (a former film editor in his directorial debut); *P:* Plato Skouras; *St: & Sc:* James Landis. (1:18) Drama of four American soldiers accused of desertion and killing a fellow soldier. When they are court-martialed, a defense attorney proves that the real culprits were four Germans disguised as Americans. Note: Gregory Lafayette who plays "Corporal Quinn," one of the accused four in this drama, was killed in a car crash on July 4, 1957, with his wife Judy Tyler, a young actress who had only made two film appearances (see index).

2836. Under Mexicali Stars (Republic; 1950). *Cast:* Rex Allen, Dorothy Patrick, Roy Barcroft, Buddy Ebsen, Percy Helton, Walter Coy, Steve Darrell, Alberto Morin, Ray Walker, Frank Ferguson, Stanley Andrews, Robert Bice, Ko-Ko (horse). *D:* George Blair; *As.P:* Melville Tucker; *St: & Sc:* Bob Williams. (1:07) (video) Contemporary series western of a U.S. Treasury agent (Allen) assigned to track down a counterfeiting operation which is turning smuggled gold into counterfeit coins. Includes three songs: "Old Black Mountain Trail," "Born in the Saddle" and "The Railroad Corral."

2837. Under My Skin (20th Century-Fox; 1950). *Cast:* John Garfield, Micheline [Prelle] Presle (U.S. debut), Luther Adler, Orley Lindgren, Ann Codee, Steven Geray, Noel Drayton, A.A. Merola, Otto George, Paul Bryar, Joseph Warfield, Eugene Borden, Loulette Sablon, Alphonse Martell, Ernesto Morelli, Jean Del Val, Hans Herbert, Esther Zeitlin, Maurice Brierre, Gordon Clark, Frank Arnold, Elizabeth Flournoy, Mario Siletti, Guy Zanette, Andre Charisse, Harry Martin. *D:* Jean Negulesco; *P: & Sc:* Casey Robinson. (1:26) Sentimental low budget melodrama of a disreputable jockey and his attempts to reform for his son. Based on the 1931 short story "My Old Man" by Ernest Hemingway, it was remade in 1979 as the TV movie *My Old Man.*

2838. Under the Gun (Universal-International; 1950). *Cast:* Richard Conte, Audrey Totter, Sam Jaffe, John McIntire, Shepherd Strudwick, Royal Dano, Richard Taber, Gregg Martell, Phillip Pine, Don Randolph. *D:* Ted Tetzlaff; *P:* Ralph Dietrich; *St:* Daniel B. Ullman; *Sc:* George Zuckerman; *Song:* "I Cried For You" Arthur Freed, Gus Arnheim, Abe Lyman. (1:23) Prison melodrama of a convicted killer's plot to gain his freedom by causing the death of another prisoner.

2839. Undercover Girl (Universal-International; 1950). *Cast:* Alexis Smith, Scott Brady, Richard Egan, Gladys George, Edmon Ryan, Gerald Mohr, Royal Dano (film debut), Harry Landers, Connie Gilchrist, Regis Toomey, Angela Clarke, Lynn Ainley, Tristram Coffin, Lawrence Cregar, Harold Gary, Ed Rand, Mel Archer, Betty Lou Gerson. *D:* Joseph Pevney; *P:* Aubrey Schenck; *St:* Francis Rosenwald; *Sc:* Harry Essex. (1:23) Melodrama of a trainee lady cop (Smith) and a seasoned cop (Brady) who go undercover as drug buyers to investigate the gang doing the dealing as well as the death of the lady's father.

2840. Undersea Girl (Allied Artists/Nacirema Prods.; 1957). *Cast:* Mara Corday, Florence Marley, Dan Seymour, Ralph Clanton, Myron Healey, Lewis Charles, Jerry Eskow, Dehl Berti, Sue George, Mickey Simpson, Mike Mason, Brick Sullivan, Don Warren, Jess Kirkpatrick, Russ Thorsen, Corrine Laine, William Dendis, Mack Chandler. *D:* John Peyser; *P:* Norman T. Herman; *St: & Sc:* Arthur V. Jones; *Song:* "Daydreams" Alexander Courage, Hal Levy. (1:14) Adventure-melodrama of a female skindiver who uncovers the body of a man with $1,800 on his person, part of a larger cache of money stolen from the U.S. Navy.

2841. Underwater! (RKO/Howard Hughes; 1955). *Cast:* Jane Russell, Gilbert Roland, Richard Egan, Lori Nelson, Robert Keith, Joseph Calleia, Eugene Iglesias, Ric Roman, Max Wagner, Robert Polo, Dan Bernaducci, Jamie Russell. *D:* John Sturges; *P:* Harry Tatelman; *Sc:* Walter Newman (based on the story "The Big Rainbow" by Hugh King and Robert B. Bailey). (1:39) (video/laserdisc) Adventure melodrama of various people out to secure a treasure from a sunken Spanish galleon. Due to excessive promotional hoopla, this opus made money at the box office. The critics weren't impressed and neither were the people who paid their money to see it. Technicolor/SuperScope.

2842. Underwater Warrior (MGM/Ivan Tors Pictures, Inc.–Hunterhaven, Inc.; 1958). *Cast:* Dan Dailey, Claire Kelly, James Gregory, Ross Martin, Raymond Bailey, Genie Coree, Charles Keane, Jon Lindberg [the son of Charles Lindbergh], Zale Parry, Alex Fane. *D:* Andrew Marton; *P:* Ivan Tors; *As.P:* John Florea; *St: & Sc:* Gene Levitt. (1:31) Independently produced fact-based drama about frogmen operating in the Pacific from the days before World War II to the Korean conflict. Filmed on location at San Clemente and Coronado, CA, and in the Hawaiian and Marshall Islands, it was based on the life of Comdr. Francis D. Fane USNR, who also served as technical advisor. CinemaScope.

The Underworld Story *see* **The Whipped**

2843. The Unearthly (Republic/AB-PT Pictures; 1957). *Cast:* John Carradine, Allison Hayes, Myron Healey, Sally Todd, Marilyn Buferd, Arthur Batanides, Tor Johnson, Harry Fleer, Roy Gordon, Guy Prescott, Paul MacWilliams. *D: & P:* Brooke L. Peters; *St:* Jane Mann; *Sc:* Geoffrey Dennis, Mann. (1:13) (video) Science fiction/horror of a mad scientist (Carradine—who else?) experimenting with human immortality, the results creating nothing more than hideous creatures which he stores in his basement! Originally paired for drive-in double bills with *Beginning of the End* (q.v.). Note: AB-PT=American Broadcast-Paramount Theatres.

2844. The Unguarded Moment (Universal-International; 1956). *Cast:* Esther Williams, George Nader, John Saxon, Edward Andrews, Les Tremayne, Jack Albertson, Dani Crayne, John Wilder, Edward C. Platt, Eleanor Audley, Robert B. Williams. *D:* Harry Keller; *P:* Gordon Kay; *Sc:* Herb Meadow, Larry Marcus [based on the story "The Gentle Web" by Rosalind Russell and Mr. Marcus]. (1:35) Drama of a high school teacher who becomes involved in the problems of one of her male students, a sexual psychopath. Technicolor.

2845. The Unholy Wife (Universal-International/RKO–Treasure Prods.; 1957). *Cast:* Diana Dors (U.S. debut), Rod Steiger, Tom Tryon, Beulah Bondi, Marie Windsor, Arthur Franz, Luis Van Rooten, Argentina Brunetti, Tol Avery, James Burke, Steve Pendleton, Gary Hunley, Douglas Spencer, Joe De Santis. *D: & P:* John Farrow; *St:* William Durkee; *Sc:* Jonathan Latimer. (1:34) (video) Melodrama of a woman whose nefarious deeds eventually catch up with her—exemplifying the term "blind justice." A remake of *They Knew What They Wanted* (1940). Technicolor.

2846. Unidentified Flying Objects (United Artists/Ivar Prods.; 1956). *D:* Winston Jones; *P:* Clarence Greene; *St: & Sc:* Francis Martin. (1:32) (video) A documentary which follows the investigation of unidentified flying objects over the United States (prior to 1956). B/W & Color. (aka: *UFO*)

2847. Union Station (Paramount; 1950). *Cast:* William Holden, Nancy Olson, Lyle Bettger, Barry Fitzgerald, Jan Sterling, Allene Roberts, Ralph Sanford, Herbert Heyes, Don Dunning, Fred Graff, James Seay, Parley Baer, Richard Karlan, Bigelow Sayre, Charles Dayton, Jean Ruth, Paul Lees, Harry Hayden, Ralph Byrd, Edith Evanson, Queenie Smith, George M. Lynn, Richard Barron, Joe Warfield, Trevor Bardette, Robert Wood, Mike Mahoney, Robert Cornthwaite, Clifton Young, Freddie Zendar, Howard J. Negley, Dick Elliott, Douglas Spencer, Byron Foulger, Edgar Dearing, Thomas E. Jackson, Al Ferguson, Howard Mitchell, Sumner Getchell, Bob Easton, Bob Hoffman, Ralph Montgomery, Jerry James, Bernard Szold, Joe Recht, John Crawford, Gil Warren, Eric Alden, Charles Sherlock, Jack Gargan, Bill Meader, Hans Moebus, Jack Roberts, Mike P. Donovan, Laura Elliot, Barbara Knudsen, Gerry Ganzer, Charmienne Harker, Isabel Cushin, June Earle, Betty Corner. *D:* Rudolph Maté; *P:* Jules Schermer; *Sc:* Sydney Boehm. (1:20) (video) This thriller tells of the manhunt for the kidnapper of a blind girl with the climax taking place amid the hustle and bustle of the titled railway station. Based on Thomas Walsh's novel *Nightmare in Manhattan*, it was a box office winner.

2848. The Unknown Man (MGM; 1951). *Cast:* Walter Pidgeon, Ann Harding, Barry Sullivan, Keefe Brasselle, Lewis Stone, Eduard Franz, Richard Anderson, Dawn Addams, Mari Blanchard, Philip Ober, Konstantin Shayne, Don Beddoe, Holmes Herbert, Jean Andren, Richard Hale, Jeff York, John Maxwell, Margaret Brayton, Rush Williams, John Butler, Harry Hines, Ronald Brogan, Robert Scott, Robert Griffin, Frank Gerstle, Jimmie Dodd, Larry Carr, Eric Sinclair, Frank Scannell, King Donovan, Katherine Meskill, Phil Tead, Dabbs Greer, Mira McKinney, Rhea Mitchell, Wheaton Chambers, Richard Karlan, Bradford Hatton, Robert Foulk, Emmett Vogan, Paul Kruger, Jack

Gargan, Fred Rapport, Monya Andre, Anna Q. Nilsson, Bess Flowers, Mae Clarke Langdon, Estelle Etterre, Fred Aldrich, Harte Wayne, Tay Dunne, Harry Cody, Frank Pershing, John Alvin, Jack Shea. *D:* Richard Thorpe; *P:* Robert Thomsen; *St: & Sc:* Ronald Millar, George Froeschel. (1:26) Melodrama of a trial lawyer who finds his client was guilty after being found innocent and the plot he sets in motion to set justice right.

2849. **The Unknown Terror** (20th Century–Fox/Regal Films; 1957). *Cast:* John Howard, Mala Powers, Paul Richards, May Wynn, Gerald Milton, Duane Grey, Charles Gray, Charles Postal, Patrick O'Moore, William Hamel, Richard Gilden, Martin Garralaga, Sir Lancelot (himself). *D:* Charles Marquis Warren; *P:* Robert Stabler; *St: & Sc:* Kenneth Higgins. (1:16) Science fiction/horror of a couple who take off for the jungles of South America in search of the woman's brother, find his mind has slipped a few gears and he is now creating fungus-men. Regalscope. Originally paired on a double bill with *Back From the Dead* (q.v.).

2850. **Unknown World** (Lippert; 1951). *Cast:* Victor Kilian, Bruce Kellogg, Otto Waldis, Jim Bannon, Tom Handley, Dick Cogan, Marilyn Nash, George Baxter. *D:* Terrell [Terry] O. Morse; *P:* Jack Rabin, Irving A. Block; *St: & Sc:* Milllard Kaufman. (1:13) (video) Science fiction of a scientist who invents a device called a cyclotram to bore into the earth in search of areas to escape from atomic fallout.

2851. **Unmasked** (Republic; 1950). *Cast:* Robert Rockwell, Barbara Fuller, Raymond Burr, Hillary Brooke, Paul Harvey, Norman Budd, John Eldredge, Emory Parnell, Russell Hicks, Grace Gillern, Lester Sharpe, Charles Quigley, Barbara Pepper, Charles Trowbridge, Harry Harvey. *D:* George Blair; *As.P:* Stephen Auer; *St:* Manuel Seff, Paul Yawitz; *Sc:* Albert DeMond, Norman S. Hall. (1:00) Programmer melodrama of the police search for a killer (Burr) who thinks he has covered his tracks.

2852. **Untamed** (20th Century–Fox; 1955). *Cast:* Tyrone Power, Susan Hayward, Richard Egan, John Justin, Agnes Moorehead, Rita Moreno, Hope Emerson, Brad Dexter, Henry O'-Neill, Paul Thompson, Alexander D. Havemann, Louis Mercier, Emmett Smith, Jack Macy, Trude Wyler, Louis Polliman Brown, Edward Mundy, Catherin Pasques, Christian Pasques, John Dodsworth, Robert Adler, Alberto Morin, Philip Van Zandt, Kevin Corcoran (film debut), Eleanor Audley, John Carlyle, Cecile Weston, Anne Cornwall, Myna Cunard, Forrest Burns, Leonard Casey, Alan Maraton, Maya Van Horn, Robin Hughes, Linda Lowell, Tina Thompson, Gary Diamond, Bobby Diamond, Brian Corcoran (film debut), Kem Dibbs, Michael Ross, Charles Evans. *D:* Henry King; *P:* Bert E. Friedlob, William A Bacher; *Sc:* Talbot Jennings, Frank Fenton, Michael Blankfort. (1:51) The trials and tribulations of families of Boer settlers as they trek via wagon train through the hostile territory of South Africa in search of new homes. The drama focuses on Katie O'Neill and her husband who leave Ireland during the potato famine and join the Dutch Boers. The Zulu attack on the wagon train is impressive and on location filming in South Africa adds to the spectacle. Based on the 1950 novel by Helga Moray, as adapted by Mr. Bacher and Mr. Jennings. DeLuxe color/CinemaScope.

2853. **Untamed Frontier** (Universal-International; 1952). *Cast:* Joseph Cotten, Shelley Winters, Scott Brady, Suzan Ball (film debut), Minor Watson, Katherine Emery, Antonio Moreno, Douglas Spencer, John Alexander, Lee Van Cleef, Richard Garland, Robert Anderson, Fess Parker (film debut), Ray Bennett. *D:* Hugo Fregonese; *P:* Leonard Goldstein; *St:* Houston Branch, Eugenia Night; *Sc:* Gerald Drayson Adams, John Bagni, Gwen Bagni; *Additional dialogue:* Polly James. (1:15) Western melodrama of a crippled Texas cattle tycoon who takes steps to prevent homesteaders from settling on his grazing lands. Technicolor.

2854. **Untamed Heiress** (Republic; 1954). *Cast:* Judy Canova, Donald Barry, George Cleveland, Taylor Holmes, Chick Chandler, Jack Kruschen, Hugh Sanders, Douglas Fowley, William Haade, Ellen Corby, Dick Wessel, James Flavin, Tweeny Canova. *D:* Charles Lamont; *P:* Sidney Picker, Herbert J. Yates; *St:* Jack Townley; *Sc:* Barry Shipman; *Songs:* "A Dream for Sale" Jack Elliott, Donald Kahn; "Sugar Daddy" Elliott, "Welcome" (all sung by Canova). (1:10) Geared to Canova's following is this tale of a millionaire's search for a woman who once loaned him money, only to find she has died and her only daughter is living in an orphanage.

The Untamed West *see* **The Far Horizons**

2855. **Untamed Women** (United Artists/ Jewell Enterprises; 1952). *Cast:* Mikel Conrad,

Doris Merrick, Richard Monahan, Mark Lowell, Morgan Jones, Midge Ware, Carol Brewster, Judy Brubaker, Autumn Rice, Lyle Talbot, Montgomery Pittman, Miriam Kaylor. *D:* W. Merle Connell; *P:* Richard Kay; *St:* & *Sc:* George W. Sayre. (1:10) Programmer high camp melodrama of a bomber crew downed at sea who find themselves on an island inhabited by all female residents, descendants of the Druids. Another cheapie which utilizes footage from *One Million B.C.* (U.A./Hal Roach; 1940).

2856. Untamed Youth (Warner; 1957). *Cast:* Mamie Van Doren, Lori Nelson (final film—ret.), John Russell, Don Burnett, Eddie Cochran, Lurene Tuttle, Yvonne Lime, Jeanne Carmen, Robert Foulk, Wayne Taylor, The Hollywood Rock 'n' Rollers, Jerry Barclay, Keith Richards, Valerie Reynolds, Lucita, Glenn Dixon, Wally Brown. *D:* Howard W. Koch; *P:* Aubrey Schenck; *St:* Stephen Longstreet; *Sc:* John C. Higgins; *Songs:* "Cottonpicker" Les Baxter (sung by Cochran); "Salamander," "Go, Go Calypso," Baxter; "Rolling Stone" Baxter, Lenny Adelson and "Oobala Baby" Baxter, Adelson, Cochran, Jerry Capehart (all sung by Van Doren). (1:20) Melodrama with unintentionally humorous dialogue and rock 'n' roll songs of two teenage sisters (Van Doren and Nelson) sentenced to pick cotton on a work farm run by a scumbag (Russell).

2857. Until They Sail (MGM; 1957). *Cast:* Jean Simmons, Joan Fontaine, Paul Newman, Piper Laurie, Charles Drake, Sandra Dee (film debut), Wally Cassell, Alan Napier, Ralph Votrian, John Wilder, Adam Kennedy, Patrick Macnee, Ben Wright, Kendrick Husham, James Todd, David Thursby, Hilda Plowright, Dean Jones, Robert Keys, Ann Wakefield, Vesey O'Davoren, Pat O'Hara, Stanley Fraser, James Douglas, Tige Andrews, Mickey Shaughnessy, Nicky Blair, Morgan Jones, Pat Waltz, William Boyett, Jimmy Hayes, Pat Colby, Dan Eitner, Tom Mayton, Roger McGee, John Rosser, Jim Cox, Alma Lauton, Dee Humphrey, Dorris Ritter, Pamela Light, Phyllis Douglas. *D:* Robert Wise; *P:* Charles Schnee; *Sc:* Robert Anderson; *Title song:* David Raksin, Sammy Cahn (sung by Eydie Gorme). (1:35) (video) Romantic melodrama in a soap opera vein of four sisters in World War II New Zealand. Based on the short story in James Michener's "Return to Paradise" collection. CinemaScope.

2858. Unwed Mother (Allied Artists; 1958). *Cast:* Norma Moore, Robert Vaughn, Claire Carleton, Ken Lynch, Billie Bird, Sam Buffington, Diana Darrin, Dorothy Adams, Ralph Gamble, Timothy Carey, Jeanne Cooper, Ron Hargrave, Kathleen Hughes, Collette Jackson. *D:* Walter A. Doniger; *P:* Joseph Justman; *As.P:* Maurice Horn; *St:* Anson Bond; *Sc:* Bond, Alden Nash; *Song:* "Young Romance" Ron Hargrave, Hal Brandle (sung by Hargrave). (1:14) Programmer melodrama of a young girl who falls for a no-good liar who gets her involved in a robbery and pregnant to boot.

Up from the Depths *see* **From Hell It Came**

2859. Up Front (Universal-International; 1951). *Cast:* David Wayne, Tom Ewell, Marina Berti, Jeffrey Lynn, Richard Egan, Maurice Cavell, Vaughn Taylor, Silvio Minciotti, Paul Harvey, Roger DeKoven, Grazia Narciso, Tito Vuolo, Mickey Knox. *D:* Alexander Hall; *P:* Leonard Goldstein; *Sc:* Stanley Roberts, Oscar Brodney (unc.). (1:32) World War II comedy set during the Italian campaign. Based on Bill Mauldin's characters "Willie and Joe" (Ewell and Wayne respectively) of World War II cartoon fame and his 1945 book of the same name. Followed by a sequel *Back at the Front* (q.v.).

2860. Up in Smoke (Allied Artists; 1957). *Cast:* Huntz Hall, Stanley Clements, Judy Bamber, Eddie LeRoy, David Gorcey, Ric Roman, Byron Foulger, Dick Elliott, Ralph Sanford, Joe Devlin, James Flavin, Earle Hodgins, John Mitchum, Jack Mulhall, Fritz Feld, Wilbur Mack, Benny Rubin. *D:* William Beaudine; *P:* Richard Heermance; *St:* Elwood Ullman, Bert Lawrence; *Sc:* Jack Townley. (1:04) Comedy which finds Sach (Hall) selling his soul to the devil (Foulger) after getting involved with the mob and playing the ponies. The next to last entry in the "Bowery Boys" series.

2861. Up Periscope (Warner/Lakeside; 1959). *Cast:* James Garner, Edmond O'Brien, Andra Martin, Alan Hale, Carleton Carpenter (final film), Frank Gifford, William Leslie, Richard Bakalyan, Edward Byrnes, Sean Garrison, Henry Kulky, George Crise, Warren Oates (film debut). *D:* Gordon Douglas; *P:* Aubrey Schenck; *Sc:* Richard Landau. (1:51) (video/laserdisc) Popular World War II submarine drama of conflict between a by-the-book commander and a demolitions specialist with a vital Japanese code he must acquire. Based on the 1956 novel by Robb White. Technicolor/WarnerScope.

2862. Uranium Boom (Columbia/Clover Prods.; 1956). Cast: Dennis Morgan (final film—ret.), Patricia Medina, William Talman, Tina Carver, Philip Van Zandt, Mel Curtis, Bill Henry, Henry Rowland, Ralph Sanford, S. John Launer, Frank Wilcox, Nick Tell, Michael Bryant, Carlyle Mitchell. *D:* William Castle; *P:* Sam Katzman; *St:* George F. Slavin, George W. George; *Sc:* Slavin, George, Norman Retchin. (1:06) Low budget melodrama of two uranium prospectors who yearn for the affections of the same female. Originally paired as a 2nd feature on a double bill with *Over-Exposed* (q.v.).

2863. Utah Blaine (Columbia/Clover Prods.; 1957). *Cast:* Rory Calhoun, Susan Cummings, Max Baer, Angela Stevens, Paul Langton, Ray Teal, Gene Roth, Terry Frost, Steve Darrell, Dennis Moore, Jack Ingram, George Keymas, Norman Frederic, Ken Christy. *D:* Fred F. Sears; *P:* Sam Katzman; *Sc:* Robert E. Kent, James B. Gordon. (1:15) Based on the novel by Louis L'Amour, this western involves a saddle tramp who gets involved with a rancher who has become the target of landgrabbers.

2864. Utah Wagon Train (Republic; 1951). *Cast:* Rex Allen, Penny Edwards, Buddy Ebsen, Roy Barcroft, Sarah Padden, Grant Withers, Arthur Space, Edwin Rand, Robert Karnes, William Holmes, Stanley Andrews, Frank Jenks. *D:* Philip Ford; *As.P:* Melville Tucker; *St: & Sc:* John K. Butler; *Songs:* "Toolie Rollum," "The Colorado Trail" (written and sung by Allen). (1:07) (video) Offbeat series western tale of a contemporary wagon train trek, following the same trail as another wagon train did a century before.

2865. The Vagabond King (Paramount; 1956). *Cast:* Kathryn Grayson (final film—ret.), Oreste [Kirkop], Rita Moreno, Sir Cedric Hardwicke, Walter Hampden (final film—d. 1955/King Louis XI), Leslie Nielsen, William Prince, Jack Lord, Billy Vine, Harry McNaughton, Florence Sundstrom, Lucie Lancaster, Raymond Bramley, Gregory Morton, Richard Tone, Ralph Sumpter, G. Thomas Duggan, Gavin Gordon, Vincent Price (narrator), Joel Ashley, Ralph Clanton, Gordon Mills, Sam Schwartz, Phyllis Newman, Slim Gault, Albie Gaye, Laura Raynair, Frances Lansing, Jeanette Miller, Richard Shannon, Larry Pennell, Nancy Bajer, Rita Marie Tanno, Dolores Starr and David Nillo (specialty dancers). *D:* Michael Curtiz; *P:* Pat Duggan; *Sc:* Noel Langley, Ken Englund; *Songs* (written for the film): "This Same Heart," "Bon Jour," "Vive Le You," "Comparisons," "Watch Out for the Devil," "Lord I'm Glad I Know Thee" Rudolf Friml (his final work before his death), Johnny Burke; *Original songs:* "Only A Rose," "Song of the Vagabonds," "Some Day," "Huguette's Waltz." (1:26) Operetta of Francois Villon (Oreste), the poet-scoundrel, based on the 1925 smash Broadway musical by Rudolf Friml with book and lyrics by William H. Post and Brian Hooker. The original source material was R.H. Russell's novel *If I Were King*, which was dramatized in 1901 by Justin Huntley McCarthy. Earlier film incarnations based on the original source material include: *If I Were King* (Fox Film; 1920); *The Beloved Rogue* (U.A./Art Cinema; 1927) with John Barrymore; *The Vagabond King* (Paramount; 1930) with music and this studio's first all-talkie; and *If I Were King* (Paramount; 1938) with Ronald Colman. Paramount's current and last incarnation was a box office bomb. Technicolor/Vista Vision.

2866. Valentino (Columbia; 1951). *Cast:* Anthony Dexter (film debut/title role), Eleanor Parker, Richard Carlson, Patricia Medina, Joseph Calleia, Dona Drake, Lloyd Gough, Otto Kruger, Marietta Canty, Paul Bryar, Eric Wilton. *D:* Lewis Allen; *P:* Edward Small; *St: & Sc:* George Bruce. (1:42) Critically lambasted fictionalized biography of silent screen romantic idol Rudolph Valentino. Another "biography" of the silent screen hearthrob, whose funeral following his death in 1926 nearly caused a riot in New York City, was made by Ken Russell in 1977. Technicolor.

2867. Valerie (United Artists/Hal R. Makelim; 1957). *Cast:* Sterling Hayden, Anita Ekberg (title role), Anthony Steele (real-life husband of Ekberg), Malcolm Atterbury, Jerry Barclay, Peter Walker, John Wengraf, Iphigenie Castiglioni, Robert Adler, Tom McKee, Gage Clarke, Sydney Smith, Juney Ellis, Stanley Adams, Brian O'Hara, John Dierkes. *D:* Gerd Oswald; *P:* Hal R. Makelim; *St: & Sc:* Leonard Heideman, Emmett Murphy. (1:24) A 19th century courtroom melodrama told in flashbacks of a Civil War veteran on trial for injuring his wife and killing her parents.

The Valley of Death (G.B. title) *see* **Tank Battalion**

2868. Valley of Fire (Columbia/Gene Autry Prods.; 1951). *Cast:* Gene Autry, Gail Davis, Pat Buttram, Russell Hayden (final film—ret.), Christine Larson, Harry Lauter, Terry Frost, Barbara Stanley, Teddy Infuhr, Marjorie Liszt,

Riley Hill, Victor Sen Yung, Gregg Barton, William Fawcett, Bud Osborne, Syd Saylor, Pat O'Malley, Duke York, Sandy Sanders, Fred Sherman, James Magill, Frankie Marvin, Wade Crosby, John Miller, Champion, Jr. (horse). *D:* John English (final film—ret.); *P:* Armand Schaefer; *St:* Earle Snell; *Sc:* Gerald Geraghty. (1:10) (video) After cleaning out the trouble-makers, the all-male residents of a western frontier town attempt to get themselves some womenfolk. An offbeat series western which includes the song "On Top of Old Smoky." Sepiatone.

Valley of Fury (G.B. title) *see* **Chief Crazy Horse**

2869. Valley of Head-Hunters (Columbia/Esskay Prods.; 1953). *Cast:* Johnny Weissmuller, Christine Larson, Nelson Leigh, Robert C. Foulk, Steven Ritch, Joseph Allen, Jr., George Eldredge, Neyle Morrow, Vince M. Townsend, Jr., Don Blackman, Paul Thompson, Peggy (chimp, PATSY "Award of Excellence" in 1954). *D:* William Berke; *P:* Sam Katzman; *St: & Sc:* Samuel Newman. (1:07) "Jungle Jim" comes to the aid of a native tribe whose mineral deposits are in danger of being purloined. Part of a series based on the newspaper comic strip creation of Alex Raymond.

2870. Valley of the Kings (MGM; 1954). *Cast:* Robert Taylor, Eleanor Parker, Carlos Thompson, Kurt Kasznar, Victor Jory, Leon Askin, Aldo Silvani, Samia Gamal. *D:* Robert Pirosh; *P:* uncredited; *Screenstory & Sc:* Pirosh, Karl Tunberg. (1:26) On location photography is the only notable asset in this dud adventure of Egyptian tomb excavations at the turn-of-the-century. Based on "Gods, Graves and Scholars," a 1951 writing by C.W. Ceram [pseudonym of Kurt W. Marek]. Eastmancolor.

2871. The Vampire (United Artists/Gramercy Pictures; 1957). *Cast:* John Beal, Coleen Gray, Kenneth Tobey, Lydia Reed, Dabbs Greer, Raymond Greenleaf, Herb Vigran, Ann Staunton, James Griffith, Paul Brinegar, Natalie Masters, Mauritz Hugo, Louise Lewis, Wood Romoff, Brad Morrow, Hallene Hill, Anne O'Neal, George Selk [aka: Budd Buster], Walter A. Merrill, Christine Rees, Arthur Gardner. *D:* Paul Landres; *P:* Arthur Gardner, Jules V. Levey; *St: & Sc:* Pat Fielder. (1:14) Horror thriller of a scientist (Beal) working with a serum that turns him into a blood-sucking fiend. (aka: *The Mark of the Vampire*) Note: *El Vampiro*, a Mexican production (U.S. title: *The Vampire*), was also released in 1957.

2872. The Vanishing American (Republic; 1955). *Cast:* Scott Brady, Audrey Totter, Forrest Tucker, Gene Lockhart, Jim Davis, John Dierkes, Gloria Castillo, Julian Rivero, Lee Van Cleef, George Keymas, Charles Stevens, Jay Silverheels, James Millican, Glenn Strange. *D:* Joseph Kane; *P:* Herbert J. Yates; *Sc:* Alan LeMay. (1:30) A Navajo Indian fights those who are trying to take his tribe's land. Based on the 1925 novel by Zane Grey, this is a low budget account of the work which was filmed more successfully in 1925 by Paramount.

2873. Vanishing Outpost (Realart/Western Adventures; 1951). *Cast:* Al "Lash" LaRue, Al St. John, Riley Hill, Clarke Stevens, Bud Osborne, Lee Morgan, Ted Adams, Ray Broome, Archie Twitchell [aka: Michael Branden], Cliff Taylor, Sharon Hall, Sue Hussey, Johnny Paul. *D: & P:* Ron Ormond; *St: & Sc:* Alexander White. (0:56) Saddle pals are recruited by the Pinkerton detective agency to bring an outlaw gang to justice. An entry in LaRue's series with much stock footage.

2874. The Vanishing Prairie (Buena Vista/Walt Disney Prods.; 1954). *D:* James Algar; *P:* (AA-Best Documentary) Walt Disney; *As.P:* Ben Sharpsteen; *St: & Sc:* Algar, Ted Sears, Winston Hibler (who also narrates); *Cin:* Tom McHugh, James R. Simon, N. Paul Kenworthy, Jr., Cleveland P. Grant, Lloyd Beebe, Herb Crisler, Dick Borden, Warren Garst, Murl Deusing, Olin Sewall Peggingill, Jr., Stuart V. Jewell; *Editor:* Lloyd Richardson. (1:15) (video) Walt Disney's 2nd True-Life Adventure detailing footage of denizens of the American prairie including bison, coyotes, prairie dogs, pronghorn antelopes, bighorn sheep and assorted birdlife. The film culminates in a prairie fire which is eventually doused by a cloudburst. Well received by the critics (for the most part) and the paying public, it placed #6 on the "10 Best" list of the NBR. Technicolor. Sidenote: Disney and his film came into conflict with the New York State censorship board because it shows the live birth of a bison calf. Disney won and New York lost in its efforts to ban the film.

2875. The Vanishing Westerner (Republic; 1950). *Cast:* Monte Hale, Paul Hurst, Aline Towne, Roy Barcroft, Arthur Space, Richard Anderson, William Phipps, Don Haggerty, Dick Curtis, Rand Brooks, Edmund Cobb,

Harold Goodwin. *D:* Philip Ford; *As.P:* Melville Tucker; *St: & Sc:* Bob Williams. (1:00) (video) Two cowboys are used as a front for the illegal activities of a rancher who later plans to kill them to cover his tracks. Some offbeat plotting in this entry in Hale's series.

2876. The Vanquished (Paramount/Pine-Thomas; 1953). *Cast:* John Payne, Coleen Gray, Jan Sterling, Lyle Bettger, Willard Parker, Roy Gordon, Russell Gaige, Leslie Kimmell, Voltaire Perkins, Sam Flint, Ellen Corby, John Dierkes, Charles Evans, Ernestine Barrier, Louis Jean Heydt, Freeman Morse, Richard Shannon, Karen Sharpe, Howard Joslin, Llewellyn Johnson, John Halloran, Harry Cody, William Berry, Major Sam Harris, Jack Hill, Richard Beedle, Richard Bartell, Brad Mora. *D:* Edward Ludwig; *P:* William H. Pine, William C. Thomas; *Screenstory: & Sc:* Winston Miller, Frank Moss, Lewis R. Foster. (1:24) Following the Civil War, a Confederate officer returns to his home to find the town government full of corruption. Based on the novel *Decision to Kill* by Karl Brown. Technicolor.

2877. Varieties on Parade (Lippert/Spartan Prods.; 1951). *Cast:* Jackie Coogan, Tom Neal, Eddie Dean, Iris Adrian, Lyle Talbot, The Bobby Harrison Trio, Jimmie and Mildred Mulcay, Duke and Harry Johnson, Paul Gordon, The Diacoffs, The Russ Saunders Troupe, Al Mardo, Ormond McGill & His East Indian Miracle Show, Armando and Lita, Boyce Evans and Betty Jane, The Lee Sisters, Jean Carroll, The Darling Sisters, Harry Rose. *D: & P:* Ron Ormond. (1:00) Programmer musical-comedy with many specialty acts, hosted by Eddie Garr.

2878. The Veils of Bagdad (Universal-International; 1953). *Cast:* Victor Mature, Mari Blanchard, Virginia Field, James Arness, Guy Rolfe, Leon Askin, Palmer Lee [aka: Gregg Palmer], Nick Cravat, Ludwig Donath (final film appearance until 1966), Dave Sharpe, Jackie Loughery, Howard Petrie, Charles Arnt, Glenn Strange, Sammy Stein, Robby [Robert] Blake, Charles Wagenheim, Bob St. Angelo, Stuart Whitman, Ben Welden, George J. Lewis, Dale Van Sickel, Thomas Browne Henry, Chester Hayes, Hans Schnabel, Tom Renesto, Vic Holbrook, Russ Saunders Troupe (acrobats). *D:* George Sherman; *P:* Albert J. Cohen; *St: & Sc:* William R. Cox. (1:22) Technicolor Arabian Nights–style costumer with the hero disposing of evil rulers.

2879. Vendetta (RKO/Hughes Prods.; 1950). *Cast:* Faith Domergue, George Dolenz, Hillary Brooke, Nigel Bruce, Joseph Calleia, Hugo Haas, Robert Warwick, Donald Buka. *D:* Mel Ferrer (replacing Howard Hughes who replaced Max Ophuls who replaced original director Preston Sturges with Stuart Heisler also listed in there somewhere—uncredited); *P:* Howard Hughes, Preston Sturges (unc.); *Adaptation:* Peter O'Crotty, Sturges (unc.); *Sc:* W.R. Burnett. (1:24) Another expensive Howard Hughes bomb, this costume melodrama of old Corsica was based on the 1897 novel *Columba* by Prosper Mérimée.

2880. Vengeance Valley (MGM; 1951). *Cast:* Burt Lancaster, Robert Walker, Joanne Dru, Sally Forrest, Ray Collins, John Ireland, Hugh O'Brian, Carleton Carpenter, Ted de Corsia, Will Wright, Grace Mills, James Hayward, James Harrison, Stanley Andrews, Glenn Strange, Paul E. Burns, Robert E. Griffin, Harvey B. Dunne, John McKee, Tom Fadden, Monte Montague, Al Ferguson, Roy Butler, Margaret Bert, Norman Leavitt, Dan White, Robert Wilke, Louis Nicoletti. *D:* Richard Thorpe; *P:* Nicholas Nayfack; *Sc:* Irving Ravetch. (1:23) (video) Hit western drama of a ranch foreman dealing with his boss' unruly son. Based on the 1950 novel by Luke Short [pseudonym of Frederick D. Glidden]. Technicolor.

2881. Vera Cruz (United Artists/Flora Prods.; 1954). *Cast:* Gary Cooper (Benjamin Trane), Burt Lancaster (Joe Erin), Denise Darcel (Countess Marie Duvarre), Cesar Romero (Marquis De Labordere), Sarita Montiel (Nina), George Macready (Emperor Maximilian), Ernest Borgnine (Donnegan), Morris Ankrum (General Aguilar), James McCallion (Little-Bit), Jack Lambert (Charles), Henry Brandon (Danette), Charles [Bronson] Buchinsky (Pittsburgh), Jack Elam (Tex), James Seay (Abilene), Archie Savage (Ballard), Charles Horvath (Reno), Juan Garcia (Pedro). *D:* Robert Aldrich; *P:* James Hill; *St:* Borden Chase; *Sc:* Roland Kibbee, James R. Webb; *Title song:* Hugo Friedhofer, Sammy Cahn. (1:34) (video/laserdisc) Western of an American Confederate colonel and an American horse thief who get involved with the Emperor Maximilian of Mexico and a rebel plot to overthrow him in 1866. One of the 27 top-grossing films of 1954-55, grossing $11,000,000 worldwide. Technicolor/SuperScope.

2882. Verboten! (Columbia/RKO–Globe Enterprises; 1959). *Cast:* James Best, Susan

Cummings, Tom Pittman, Paul Dubov, Harold Daye, Dick Kallman, Stuart Randall, Steven Geray, Anna Hope, Robert Boon, Sasha Harden, Paul Busch, Neyle Morrow, Joseph Turkel, Charles Horvath. *D:-P:-St: & Sc:* Samuel Fuller; *Title song:* Harry Sukman, Mack David (sung by Paul Anka). (1:33) (video/laserdisc) Post-war drama set in Germany of an American soldier who marries a German girl whose neo–Nazi brother is a member of a renegade Hitler youth group called "werewolves." The film which incorporates graphic footage of Nazi atrocities was originally produced by RKO and released by Columbia after RKO closed down in 1957.

2883. Vertigo (Paramount/Alfred Hitchcock Prods.; 1958). *Cast:* James Stewart (John "Scottie" Ferguson), Kim Novak (Madeleine Elster & Judy Barton), Barbara Bel Geddes (Midge), Tom Helmore (Gavin Elster), Lee Patrick (mistaken identity), Raymond Bailey (doctor), Konstantin Shayne (Pop Leibel/final film—ret.), Ellen Corby (manageress), Henry Jones (coroner). *D: & P:* Alfred Hitchcock; *As.P:* Herbert Coleman; *Sc:* Samuel Taylor, Alec Coppel; *ASD:* (AAN-color) Hal Pereira, Henry Bumstead (art directors), Sam Comer, Frank McElvey (sets); *Sound:* (AAN) George Dutton & Paramount Sound Dept. (with Harold Lewis and Winston Leverett receiving on-screen credit). (2:07) (video/laserdisc) Controversial Hitchcock creation of an acrophobic San Francisco detective hired to shadow the wife of a friend and the unpredictable turn of events that occur. A much discussed cult classic among Hitchcock buffs, it was based on the 1954 French novel *D'entre les Morts* [*Death Enters*] by Pierre Boileau and Thomas Narcejac. Technicolor/VistaVision.

2884. Vice Raid (United Artists/Imperial Pictures; 1959). *Cast:* Mamie Van Doren, Richard Coogan, Brad Dexter, Barry Atwater, Frank Gerstle, Carol Nugent, Joseph Sullivan, Chris Alcaide, Jeanne Bates, Julie Reding, George Cisar, Shep Sanders, Nestor Paiva, Jack Kenney, Russ Bender, Tom McKee, George Eldredge, John Zaremba, Alex Goda, John Hart, Lester Dorr, Evans Davis. *D:* Edward L. Cahn; *P:* Robert E. Kent; *St: & Sc:* Charles Ellis. (1:11) In this crime programmer, New York police set up a sting to break up a callgirl operation.

2885. Vice Squad (United Artists/Sequoia Pictures; 1953). *Cast:* Edward G. Robinson, K.T. Stevens, Porter Hall (final film—d. 1953), Paulette Goddard, Edward Binns, Lee Van Cleef, Adam Williams, Joan Vohs, Barry Kelley, Jay Adler, Dan Riss, Mary Ellen Kay. *D:* Arnold Laven; *P:* Jules V. Levey, Arthur Gardner; *Sc:* Lawrence Roman; *Additional dialogue:* Andrew Solt (unc.), Leo Townsend (unc.), Charles O'Neal (unc.). (1:27) Drama of a day in the life of police detective Captain Barnaby, his cases and the various people who pass in and out. Based on the 1937 novel *Harness Bull* by Leslie T. White. (G.B. title: *The Girl in Room 17*).

2886. The Vicious Years (Film Classics/ Emerald Prods.; 1950). *Cast:* Tommy Cook, Sybil Merritt, Eduard Franz, Gar Moore, Anthony Ross, Marjorie Eaton, Rusty [Russ] Tamblyn, Eve Miller, Lester Sharpe, John Doucette, Crane Whitley, Paul Gardini, Carlo Tricoli, James Lombardo, Ida Smeraldo, Nick Thompson, Myron Welton, Fred Gavlin, Charles Hall (final film—ret.). *D:* Robert Florey; *P:* Anson Bond; *St: & Sc:* N. Richard Nash. (1:21) Crime melodrama of a youth who witnessed a murder and uses that act to gain entrance into the home of a wealthy family whose offspring committed the crime. Set in post–World War II Italy. (G.B. title: *The Gangster We Made*)

2887. Vicki (20th Century–Fox; 1953). *Cast:* Jeanne Crain, Jean Peters (title role), Elliott Reid, Richard Boone, Casey Adams [aka: Max Showalter], Alex D'Arcy, Carl Betz, Aaron Spelling, Billy Nelson, John Dehner, Richard Garland, Ramsay Ames, Frank Fenton, Izetta Jewel, Helene Hayden, Harry Seymour, Irene Seidner, Richard West, Chet Brandenberg, Bonnie Paul, Ron Hargrave, Kathryn Sheldon, Burt Mustin, June Glory, Ethel Bryant, Charles Wagenheim, Al Hill, Kenneth Gibson, Herschel Graham, R.C. McCracken, Brandon Beach, Heinie Conklin, Robert Adler, Harry Carter, Paul Kruger, Roy Engel, Frank Gerstle, Stuart Randall, Russ Conway, Parley Baer, Jack Gargan, Norman Stevens, Jack Mather, Jerome Sheldon, Mike Stark. *D:* Harry Horner; *P:* Leonard Goldstein; *Sc:* Dwight Taylor; *Additional dialogue:* Harold Greene, Leo Townsend; *Title song:* Ken Darby. (1:25) Crime melodrama of a police detective who harbors a secret as he investigates the murder of a beautiful model. A remake of *I Wake Up Screaming* (1942), it was based on the 1941 novel of that name by Steve Fisher.

2888. Victory at Sea (United Artists/ National Broadcasting Co.; 1954). *D: & P:* Henry Salomon; *Sc:* Salomon, Richard Hanser; *Music:* Richard Rodgers. (1:48) (video) Feature documentary of the Allied victory at sea during

World War II. Edited down from the NBC TV series, it is narrated by Alexander Scourby.

2889. The View from Pompey's Head (20th Century–Fox; 1955). *Cast:* Richard Egan, Dana Wynter, Cameron Mitchell, Sidney Blackmer, Marjorie Rambeau (voted "Best Supporting Actress" by the NBR combined with her work in *A Man Called Peter*, q.v.), Dorothy Patrick Davis, Rosemarie Bowe, Jerry Paris, Ruby Goodwin, Pamela Stufflegeam, Evelyn Rudie, Howard Wendell, Bess Flowers, Dayton Lummis, Cheryl Callaway, Charles Herbert, Florence Mitchell, DeForest Kelley, Robert Johnson, Anna Mabry, Wilma Jacobs, Bill Walker, Frances Driver, Jack Mather, Charles Watts, Wade Dumas, Tom Wilson. *D:-P: & Sc:* Philip Dunne. (1:35) Drama of a New York lawyer, hired to return to his Southern hometown to investigate some missing royalty checks from a known writer whose past holds a secret for which he is being blackmailed. Based on the 1954 novel by Hamilton Basso. DeLuxe color/CinemaScope. (G.B. title: *Secret Interlude*)

2890. Vigilante Hideout (Republic; 1950). *Cast:* Allan Lane, Eddy Waller, Virginia Herrick, Roy Barcroft, Cliff Clark, Don Haggerty, Paul Campbell, Guy Teague, Chick Hannon, Art Dillard, Bob Woodward, Black Jack (horse). *D:* Fred C. Brannon; *As.P:* Gordon Kay; *St: & Sc:* Richard Wormser. (1:00) A series western of ranchers who need help against the depredations of individuals who connive to deprive them of much needed water.

2891. Vigilante Terror (Monogram/Allied Artists–Westwood; 1953). *Cast:* Bill Elliott, Mary Ellen Kay, Myron Healey, Fuzzy Knight, I. Stanford Jolley, Henry Rowland, George Wallace, Zon Murray, Richard Avonde, Michael Colgan, Denver Pyle, Robert Bray, Al Haskell, John James. *D:* Lewis D. Collins; *P:* Vincent M. Fennelly; *St: & Sc:* Sid Theil. (1:10) A gang of masked men hijack some gold and lay the blame on the local storekeeper. A latter-day Bill Elliott series western.

2892. Viking Women and the Sea Serpent (American International/Malibu Prods.; 1957). *Cast:* Abby Dalton, Susan Cabot, Betsy Jones-Moreland, Brad Jackson, Richard Devon, Jonathan Haze, Gary Conway, June Kenney, Jay Sayer, Michael Forest. *D: & P:* Roger Corman (on a 10-day schedule and a budget of $110,000); *Ex.P:* James H. Nicholson; *St:* Irving Block; *Sc:* [Lawrence] Louis Goldman. (1:06) (video) In 9th century Scandinavia, a group of Viking women set sail in search of their men who have not returned from a hunting expedition. Note: Two other (or alternate) titles are associated with this Corman curiosity: *The Saga of the Viking Women and Their Voyage to the Waters of the Great Sea Serpent* and *The Voyage of the Viking Women to the Waters of the Great Sea Serpent.* One of these titles was apparently an early release title for a double bill program, neither title of which would fit on a marquee (much less with another film title).

2893. The Vikings (United Artists/Bryna Prods.; 1958). *Cast:* Kirk Douglas (Einar), Tony Curtis (Eric), Ernest Borgnine (Ragnar), Janet Leigh (Morgana), James Donald (Egbert), Alexander Knox (Father Godwin), Frank Thring (film debut/Aella), Maxine Audley (Enid), Eileen Way (Kitala), Edric Connor (Sandpiper), Dandy Nichols (Bridget), Per Buckhoj (Bjorm), Almut Berg (Pigtails). *D:* Richard Fleischer; *P:* Jerry Bresler; *Adaptation:* Dale Wasserman; *Sc:* Calder Willingham. (1:54) (video) Epic 9th century action-adventure of Vikings returning to Scandinavia with booty and captives taken in English pillage. The producers of this film pillaged the box office to the tune of $7,000,000 making this one of the 26 top-grossing films of 1957-58. Based on *The Viking*, a 1951 best-seller by Edison Marshall. Technicolor/Technirama.

2894. Villa! (20th Century–Fox; 1958). *Cast:* Brian Keith, Cesar Romero, Margia Dean, Rodolfo Hoyos (title role), Carlos Musquiz, Mario Navarro, Ben Wright, Elisa Loti, Enrique Lucero, Rosenda Monteros, Felix Gonzales, Jose Espinosa, Rafael Alcayde, Alberto Gutierrez, Jorge Trevino, Jose Trowe, Jorge Russek, Guillermo Bianchi, Gisela Martinez, Lamberto Gayou, Lee Morgan, Raphael Sevilia, Jr., Eduardo Pliego, Alberto Pedret, Jose Lopez, Angelina Regis, Carlos Guarneros. *D:* James B. Clark; *P:* Plato A. Skouras; *As.P:* Harold E. Knox; *St: & Sc:* Louis Vittes; *Songs:* "Men, Men, Men" Lionel Newman, Ken Darby (with additional lyrics by Margia Dean); "Just Between Friends" Tom Walton, Walter Kent and "A Lonely Kind of Love" Margia Dean (based on an old Mexican folk song). (1:12) Low budget "historical western" filmed on location in Mexico of events in the life of Mexican revolutionary Pancho Villa in the days preceding his national notoriety. DeLuxe color/CinemaScope.

2895. The Vintage (MGM; 1957). *Cast:* Pier Angeli, Mel Ferrer, John Kerr, Michelle

Morgan, Theodore Bikel, Leif Erickson, Jack Mullaney, Joe Verdi. *D:* Jeffrey Hayden; *P:* Edwin H. Knopf; *Sc:* Michael Blankfort. (1:32) Drama of two sisters who find their humdrum lives turned upside down when their vineyard is invaded by two brothers, fugitives from the law. Taken from a 1953 novel by Ursula Keir, it was filmed on location in France. MetroColor/CinemaScope.

2896. Violated (Palace/Panther; 1953). *Cast:* Wim Holland, Lili Dawn, Mitchell Kowal, Vicki Carlson, William Martell, Jason Niles, Michael Keene, Fred Lambert, William Paul Mishkin, Sally Peters, Mary Noble, Charles Uday, Juana, Pete Caudreaux, Wambly Bald. *D:* Walter Strate; *P:* William [Wim] Holland; *Sc:* William Paul Mishkin. (1:18) Low budget indy crime melodrama of New York police on the trail of a murderous sex fiend.

2897. The Violators (Universal-International/RKO-Galahad; 1957). *Cast:* Arthur O'Connell, Nancy Malone, Fred Beir, Clarice Blackburn, Henry Sharp, Mary Michael, Joe Julian, Bill Darrid, Sheila Coplan, Bernie Lenrow, Martin Freed, Mercer McLeod, Eva Stern, Norman Rose, Maxine Stewart, Margaret Draper, Frank Maxwell, John McGovern, Norman Field, Tom Middleton. *D:* John Newland; *P:* Himan Brown; *Sc:* Ernest Pendrell. (1:16) Melodrama of a New York City probation officer who is the sole support of his daughter and his old maid sister. Based on the 1954 novel by Israel Beckhardt and Wenzell Brown.

The Violent Hour (G.B. title) *see* **Dial 1119**

2898. The Violent Men (Columbia; 1955). *Cast:* Glenn Ford, Barbara Stanwyck, Edward G. Robinson, Dianne Foster, Brian Keith, May Wynn, Warner Anderson, Basil Ruysdael, Richard Jaeckel, Lita Milan, Willis Bouchey, Jack Kelly, James Westerfield, Harry Shannon, Peter Hanson, Don C. Harvey, Carl Andre, James Anderson, Katherine Warren, Thomas B. Henry, William Phipps, Edmund Cobb, Frank Ferguson, Raymond Greenleaf, Ethan Laidlaw, Kenneth Patterson, John Halloran, Robert Bice, Walter Beaver. *D:* Randolph Maté; *P:* Lewis J. Rachmil; *Sc:* Harry Kleiner. (1:36) (video/laserdisc) Western drama of an aging landbaron (Robinson) who attempts to drive other ranchers out of a nearby valley. Based on the novel *Smoky Valley* by Donald Hamilton. (G.B. title: *Rough Company*) Technicolor. Note: Columbia's first production in CinemaScope.

2899. Violent Road (Warner/Lakeside Pictures; 1958). *Cast:* Brian Keith, Dick Foran, Efrem Zimbalist, Jr., Merry Anders, Sean Garrison, Joanna Barnes (film debut), Perry Lopez, Arthur Batanides, Ed Prentiss, Ann Doran, Bob Alderette, John Dennis, Venetia Stevenson. *D:* Howard W. Koch; *P:* Aubrey Schenck; *Sc:* Richard Landau. (1:26) Melodrama of men carrying high explosives over bumpy terrain, each reviewing his own life. Based on the story "Hell's Highway" by Don Martin. (aka: *Hell's Highway*) Originally ran on a double bill with *Manhunt in the Jungle* (q.v.).

2900. Violent Saturday (20th Century-Fox; 1955). *Cast:* Victor Mature, Richard Egan, Stephen McNally, Virginia Leith, Tommy Noonan, Lee Marvin, Margaret Hayes, J. Carrol Naish, Sylvia Sidney, Ernest Borgnine, Dorothy Patrick, Billy Chapin, Brad Dexter, Donald Gamble, Raymond Greenleaf, Richey Murray, Robert Adler, Ann Morrison, Donna Corcoran, Kevin Corcoran, Noreen Corcoran, Boyd "Red" Morgan, Harry Seymour, Jeri Weil, Pat Weil, Sammy Ogg, John Alderson, Esther Somers, Harry Carter, Florence Ravenel, Dorothy Phillips, Virginia Carroll, Ralph Dumke, Robert Osterloh, Helen Mayon, Fred Shellac, Ellen Bowers, Joyce Newhard, Mack Williams, Richard Garrick. *D:* Richard Fleischer; *P:* Buddy Adler; *Sc:* Sydney Boehm. (1:31) Crime drama of events that transpire when three men rob a bank in a small Arizona town and how various townspeople react to the criminals and their violence. Based on the 1955 novel by William L. Heath. DeLuxe color/CinemaScope.

2901. Violent Women (Joseph Brenner Assoc./Exploit Films; 1959). *Cast:* Jennifer Statler, Jo Ann Kelly, Sandy Lyn, Eleanor Blair, Pati Magee, Paula Scott, Pamela Perry. *D: & P:* Barry Mahon; *Sc:* uncredited. (1:03) Ultra low budget independent melodrama of five women who plan a prison escape but are thwarted in making good the escape after a sixth threatens to inform on them and they kill her. Originally paired on a double bill with *Cuban Rebel Girls* (q.v.).

2902. The Violent Years (Headliner Prods.; 1956). *Cast:* Jean [Moorhead] Moorehead, Barbara Weeks, Theresa Hancock, Joanne Cangi, Glenn Corbett, Gloria Farr, Lee Constant, Art Millan, I. Stanford Jolley. *D:* Franz

Eichorn [using the pseudonym of William M. Morgan]; *P:* O'Camp, A.O. Bayer; *St: & Sc:* Edward D. Wood, Jr. (?:??) (video) Low budget indy exploitation crime melodrama involving the various criminal activities of a gang of vicious teen females, including robbery, rape and murder. (aka: *Female*). Note: Four of the sources used for running times for films show a major contradiction with the film, indicative of what anyone who has worked with films has found. Does this film exist in various versions? Leonard Maltin's *Movie and Video Guide* for 1996 lists a running time of (0:57) with a reference to (video). Mick Martin and Marsha Porter in the 1997 *Video Movie Guide* list a running time of (1:05), while the *Motion Picture Guide* and *Bowker's 1992 Video Guide* both list running times of (1:25). Help!

2903. The Virgin Queen (20th Century-Fox; 1955). *Cast:* Bette Davis (Queen Elizabeth I), Richard Todd (Sir Walter Raleigh), Joan Collins (Beth Throgmorton), Jay Robinson (Chadwick), Herbert Marshall (Lord Leicester), Dan O'Herlihy (Lord Derry), Robert Douglas (Sir Christopher Hatton), Marjorie Hellen [Later: Leslie Parish/Anne], Lisa Daniels (Mary), Lisa Davis (Jane), Barry Bernard (Patch Eye), Margery Weston (Dame Bragg), Rod Taylor (Cpl. Gwilym), Romney Brent (French ambassador), Robert Adler, Noel Drayton, Ian Murray, David Thursby, Arthur Gould-Porter, John Costello, Nelson Leigh, Frank Baker, Ashley Cowan. *D:* Henry Koster; *P:* Charles Brackett; *Sc:* Harry Brown, Mindret Lord; *Story idea:* Lord; *Costumes:* (AAN-color) Charles LeMaire, Mary Wills. (1:32) (video) Costume drama of 16th century England, the relationship between Queen Elizabeth and Sir Walter Raleigh and its effects on other members of the Queen's court. DeLuxe color/CinemaScope.

2904. Virgin Sacrifice (Releasing Corp. of Independent Producers/Pan American; 1959). *Cast:* David Da Lie, Antonio Gutierrez, Angelica Morales, Fernando Wagner, Linda Cordova, Philip Pearl, Hamdy Sayed + Vicuni Indian dancers: Clarence Landry, Nina Peron, Bob Larca, Lydia Goya and Joe Lanza. *D:* Fernando Wagner; *P:* Joseph F. Horn; *Ex:P:* Jonathan Daniels, Victor Purcell; *St: & Sc:* V.J. Rheims (based on an idea by David Da Lie). (1:03) Adventure on a low budget of a jungle hunter in Guatemala in search of jaguars who meets and falls for a girl, only she is kidnapped by a Vicuni warrior who wants her for a virgin sacrifice to his Tiger God. Filmed in San Jose, Guatemala.

Viva Las Vegas (G.B. title) *see* **Meet Me in Las Vegas**

2905. Viva Zapata! (20th Century–Fox; 1952). *Cast:* Marlon Brando (AAN + "Best Actor" at the Cannes Film Festival + a nomination for "Best Actor" at the British Academy Awards/ Emiliano Zapata), Anthony Quinn (AA/Eufemio Zapata), Jean Peters (Josefa Espejo), Joseph Wiseman (Fernando Aguirre), Arnold Moss (Don Nacio), Alan Reed (Pancho Villa), Margo (La Soldadera), Harold Gordon (Don Francisco Madero), Lou Gilbert (Pablo), Mildred Dunnock (Senora Espejo), Frank Silvera (film debut/Huerta), Nina Varela (Aunt), Florenz Ames (Senor Espejo), Bernie Gozier (Zapatista), Frank DeKova (Col. Guajarado), Joseph Granby (Gen. Fuentes), Pedro Regas (Innocente), Fay Roope (Diaz), Will Kuluva (Lazaro), Harry Kingston (Don Garcia), Henry Silva (film debut/Hernandez), Guy Thomajan (Eduardo), George J. Lewis (Rurale), Richard Garrick, Ross Bagdasarian, Leonard George, Fernanda Eliscu, Abner Biberman, Philip Van Zandt, Lisa Fusaro, Belle Mitchell, Ric Roman, Henry Corden, Nestor Paiva, Robert Filmer, Salvador Baguez, Peter Mamakos, Julia Montoya. *D:* Elia Kazan; *P:* Darryl F. Zanuck; *Screenstory & Sc:* (AAN) John Steinbeck; *ASD:* (AAN-b/w) Lyle Wheeler, Leland Fuller (art directors), Thomas Little, Claude Carpenter (sets); *Music:* (AAN) Alex North. (1:53) (video/laserdisc) Critically acclaimed biographical drama of Mexican peasant Emiliano Zapata and his rise to the presidency of Mexico. The *New York Times* placed it at #3 on their "10 Best" list and it was in nomination at the British Academy Awards.

2906. Voice in the Mirror (Universal-International; 1958). *Cast:* Richard Egan, Julie London, Walter Matthau, Arthur O'Connell, Ann Doran, Bart Bradley, Hugh Sanders, Doris Singleton, Harry Bartell, Casey Adams [aka: Max Showalter], Phil Harvey, Mae Clarke, Troy Donahue, Peggy Converse, Ken Lynch, Dave Barry, Richard Hale. *D:* Harry Keller; *P:* Gordon Kay; *St: & Sc:* Larry Marcus; *Title song:* Bobby Troup, Julie London (sung by London). (1:45) Drama of a man who turns to alcohol following the death of his young daughter, subsequently forming a self-help group of other alcoholics. CinemaScope.

2907. Voodoo Island (United Artists/Bel-Air–Oak Pictures, Inc.; 1957). *Cast:* Boris Karloff, Beverly Tyler, Murvyn Vye, Elisha Cook, Jr., Rhodes Reason, Jean Engstrom, Frederick

Ledebur, Glenn Dixon, Owen Cunningham, Herb Patterson, Jerome Frank. *D:* Reginald LeBorg; *P:* Howard W. Koch; *St: & Sc:* Richard Landau. (1:16) Horror thriller of a group of people who make a trip to an island destined to become a resort and find strange goings-on. (aka: *Silent Death*)

2908. Voodoo Tiger (Columbia; 1952). *Cast:* Johnny Weissmuller, Jean Byron, James Seay, Jean Dean, Charles Horvath, Robert Bray, Michael Fox, Paul Hoffman, Richard Kipling, Frederic Berest, William R. Klein, Alex Montoya, Rick Vallin, John Cason, Tamba (chimp). *D:* Spencer G. Bennet; *P:* Sam Katzman; *St: & Sc:* Samuel Newman. (1:07) Low budget "Jungle Jim" series entry involving the search for a hidden treasure stolen from France during World War II. Based on the character created in the comic strip by Alex Raymond.

2909. Voodoo Woman (American International/Carmel Prods.; 1957). *Cast:* Marla English, Tom Conway, Touch [Mike] Connors, Lance Fuller (dual role), Mary Ellen Kay, Paul Dubov, Martin Wilkins, Norman Willis, Otis Greene, Emmett E. Smith, Paul Blaisdell (monster), Giselle D'Arc, Jean Davis. *D:* Edward L. Cahn; *P:* Alex Gordon; *St: & Sc:* Russell Bender, V.I. Voss; *Song:* "Black Voodoo" Darrell Calker, John Blackburn (sung by D'Arc). (1:17) (video) Low budget horror of a mad doctor who turns a beautiful woman into a loathsome monster that obeys his telepathic biddings of murder. Note: The film utilizes the same monster created by Paul Blaisdell for *The She Creature* (q.v.).

The Voyage of the Viking Women to the Waters of the Great Sea Serpent *see* **Viking Women and the Sea Serpent**

2910. Wabash Avenue (20th Century-Fox; 1950). *Cast:* Betty Grable (Ruby Summers), Victor Mature (Andy Clark), Phil Harris (Uncle Mike), Reginald Gardiner (English Eddie), James Barton (Hogan), Barry Kelley (Bouncer), Margaret Hamilton (Tillie Hutch), Jacqueline Dalya (Cleo), Robin Raymond (Jennie), Hal K. Dawson (Healy), Irving Bacon (Harlan), Marie Bryant (Elsa), Colette Lyons (Beulah), Charles Arnt (Carter), Alexander Pope (Charlie), Henry Kulky (Joe), Claire Carleton (Tessie), Walter Long, Billy Daniels, Marion Marshall, Percy Helton, Dorothy Neumann, Dick Crockett, John "Skins" Miller, Harold Cornsweet, George Beranger, David Clarke, Paul "Tiny" Newlan, Ruby Dale Hearn, Barbara A. Pellegrino, Michael Ross, Mickey Simpson, Douglas Carter, Bill Phillips, Peggy Leon, Dick Wessel. *D:* Henry Koster; *P:* William Perlberg; *St: & Sc:* Harry Tugend, Charles Lederer; *Songs:* "Walking Along with Billy," "Baby Won't You Say You Love Me," "Wilhelmina" (AAN-Best Song), "May I Tempt You With a Big Rosy Apple?," "Clean Up Chicago," "Down on Wabash Avenue" Josef Myrow, Mack Gordon; "I Wish I Could Shimmy Like My Sister Kate" Armand J. Piron, Peter Bocage; "I've Been Floating Down the Old Green River" Bert Kalmar, Joe Cooper; "I Remember You" Victor Schertzinger, Johnny Mercer + many old standards. (1:32) (video) Set during Chicago's 1893 Columbian Exposition, this musical of romantic rivalry is a remake of Grable's 1943 musical *Coney Island.* Technicolor.

2911. The WAC from Walla Walla (Republic; 1952). *Cast:* Judy Canova, Stephen Dunne, George Cleveland, June Vincent, Irene Ryan, Roy Barcroft, Allen Jenkins, George Chandler, Elizabeth Slifer, Thurston Hall, Sarah Spencer, Dick Wessel, Pattee Chapman, The Republic Rhythm Riders (themselves), Dick Elliott, Carl Switzer, Tom Powers, Jarma Lewis, Emlen Davies, Virginia Carroll, Evelynne Smith, Phyllis Kennedy. *D:* William Witney; *P:* Sidney Picker; *Ex.P:* Herbert J. Yates; *Sc:* Arthur T. Horman; *Songs include:* "Lovey," "If Only Dreams Came True," "Boy, Oh Boy," "Song of the Women's Army Corps" Jack Elliott, Harold Spina. (1:23) Low budget comedy with songs of a female hillbilly who accidentally enlists in the army. (G.B. title: *Army Capers*)

2912. Waco (Monogram/Silvermine Prods.; 1952). *Cast:* William Elliott, Pamela Blake, I. Stanford Jolley, Paul Fierro, Rand Brooks, Richard Avonde, Pierce Lyden, Lane Bradford, Terry Frost, Stanley Price, Stanley Andrews, Michael Whalen, Ray Bennett, Rory Mallinson, Richard Paxton, Russ Whiteman, Ray Jones, House Peters, Jr., Ed Cassidy. *D:* Lewis D. Collins; *P:* Vincent M. Fennelly; *St: & Sc:* Daniel B. Ullman. (1:08) A man on the lam from the law for killing a gambler and being denied due process is given the job of sheriff of Waco, Texas. Another of Elliott's series westerns. (G.B. title: *The Outlaw and the Lady*) Sepiatone.

2913. Wagon Team (Columbia/Gene Autry Prods.; 1952). *Cast:* Gene Autry, Pat Buttram, Gail Davis, Dick Jones, Gordon Jones, Harry Harvey, Henry Rowland, George J. Lewis,

John Cason, Gregg Barton, Pierce Lyden, Syd Saylor, Carlo Tricoli, Sandy Sanders, The Cass County Boys, Fred S. Martin, Bert Dotson, Jerry Scroggins, Champion, Jr. (horse). *D:* George Archainbaud; *P:* Armand Schaefer; *St: & Sc:* Gerald Geraghty. (1:01) An agent posing as a singer with a medicine show attempts to recover a stolen payroll in this series western which includes the Autry standard "Back in the Saddle Again." Sepiatone.

2914. Wagonmaster (RKO/Argosy Pictures; 1950). *Cast:* Ward Bond, Ben Johnson, Harry Carey, Jr., Joanne Dru, Charles Kemper, Jane Darwell, Alan Mowbray, Ruth Clifford, Russell Simpson, Kathleen O'Malley, James Arness, Fred Libby, Hank Worden, Mickey Simpson, Francis Ford, Cliff Lyons, Don Summers, Movita Castenada, Jim Thorpe (final film—d. 1953), Chuck Hayward, The Sons of the Pioneers. *D:* John Ford; *P:* Ford, Merian C. Cooper; *St:* Ford, Frank S. Nugent; *Sc:* Nugent, Patrick Ford. (1:26) (video/laserdisc) Acclaimed hit western of two young cowboys (Johnson & Carey) who lead a wagon train of Mormons on their way to Utah, bearing trials and tribulations along the way. Computer-colored prints have been produced by Turner Entertainment. Note: This film was the inspiration for the popular *Wagon Train* TV series which ran from 1957 into the 1960s, starring Bond, Robert Horton, Terry Wilson and Frank McGrath (original cast).

2915. Wagons West (Monogram; 1952). *Cast:* Rod Cameron, Noah Beery, Jr., Peggie Castle, Michael Chapin, Henry Brandon, Sara Haden, Frank Ferguson, Anne Kimbell, Wheaton Chambers, Riley Hill, I. Stanford Jolley, Effie Laird, Almira Sessions, Harry Tyler, Glenn Strange, Harry Strang, John Parrish, Charles Stevens. *D:* Ford Beebe; *P:* Vincent M. Fennelly; *St: & Sc:* Daniel B. Ullman. (1:10) Members of a wagon train are found to be selling guns to the Indians in this programmer western which utilizes footage from *Fort Osage* (q.v.). Cinecolor.

2916. Wait 'til the Sun Shines, Nellie (20th Century–Fox; 1952). *Cast:* David Wayne, Jean Peters, Hugh Marlowe, Albert Dekker, Helene Stanley, Tommy Morton, Joyce MacKenzie, Alan Hale, Jr., Richard Karlan, Merry Anders, Jim Maloney, Warren Stevens, Charles Watts, David Wolfe, Dan White, Erik Neilsen, Jerrilyn Flannery, Noreen Corcoran, William Walker, James Griffith, Kermit Echols, Eugene Mazzola, Tony Barr, Maudie Prickett, Mary Hain. *D:* Henry King; *P:* George Jessel; *Adaptation:* Allan Scott, Maxwell Shane; *Sc:* Scott. (1:48) Small town Americana of the trials and tribulations of a barber told in a time span of 50 years. Based on the 1946 novel *I Heard Them Sing* by Ferdinand Reyher. Technicolor.

2917. Wakamba! (RKO/American Museum of Natural History; 1955). *D: & P:* Edgar M. Queeny; *Sc:* Charles L. Telford; *Narrator:* Paul E. Prentiss. (1:05) Adventure documentary, apparently sanctioned by the American Museum of Natural History, of the E.M. Queeny expedition into Central E. Africa, intercutting scenes of tribal life and wild animal footage from the dark continent. Technicolor.

2918. Walk East on Beacon (Columbia/RD-DR Corp.; 1952). *Cast:* George Murphy, Finlay Currie, Virginia Gilmore (final film—ret.), Karel Stepanek, Louisa Horton, Peter Capell, Bruno Wick, Karl Weber, Jack Manning, Rev. Robert Dunn, Vilma Kurer, Michael Garrett, Robert Carroll, Ernest Graves, Rosemary Pettit, George Roy Hill, Bradford Hatton, Eva Condon, Paul Andor, Lotte Palfi, Ann Thomas, Nancy Heyl, Suzanne Moulton, John Farrell, Stephen Mitchell. *D:* Alfred L. Werker; *P:* Louis de Rochemont; *Screenstory & Sc:* Leo Rosten; *Additional writing:* Virginia Shaler, Emmett Murphy, Leonard Heideman. (1:38) Espionage melodrama related in a documentary style of FBI attempts to corner a communist spy ring. Produced with the cooperation of that organization, it was based on a magazine story "The Crime of the Century" by J. Edgar Hoover which appeared in *Reader's Digest* in May 1951. (G.B. title: *The Crime of the Century*)

2919. Walk Softly, Stranger (RKO/Vanguard-RKO; 1950). *Cast:* Joseph Cotten, [Alida] Valli, Spring Byington, Paul Stewart, Jack Paar, Jeff Donnell, John McIntire, Howard Petrie, Frank Puglia [replacing Moroni Olsen], Esther Dale, Marlo Dwyer, Robert Ellis. *D:* Robert Stevenson; *P:* Robert Sparks; *St:* Manuel Seff, Paul Yawitz; *Sc:* Frank Fenton. (1:21) (video) Melodrama of a crooked small-time gambler who moves to a small Ohio town to escape his past and is reformed by the love of a crippled girl. Another delayed release from RKO, being completed in 1948 with release held up until 1950. The studio's biggest bomb of the year was A Dore Schary Presentation.

2920. Walk the Dark Streets (Associated Artists–Dominant Pictures–Valor; 1956). *Cast:* Chuck Connors, Don Ross, Regina Gleason,

Eddie Kafafian, Vonne Godfrey, Ewing Brown, Don Orlando, Fred Darian, LaRue Malouf, Ernest Dominy, Jay Lawrence. *D:-P:-St: & Sc:* Wyott Ordung. (1:14) Offbeat urban melodrama of a big-game hunter who blames an army officer for his brother's death and challenges him to a cat-and-mouse manhunt with special rifles through the streets of Los Angeles.

2921. Walk the Proud Land (Universal-International; 1956). *Cast:* Audie Murphy, Anne Bancroft, Pat Crowley, Charles Drake, Tommy Rall, Robert Warwick, Jay Silverheels, Eugene Mazzola, Anthony Caruso, Victor Millan, Morris Ankrum, Addison Richards, Ainslie Pryor, Eugene Iglesias, Maurice Jara, Frank Chase, Ed Hinton, Marty Carrizosa. *D:* Jesse Hibbs; *P:* Aaron Rosenberg; *Sc:* Jack Sher, Gil Doud. (1:28) Fact-based western of attempts by John Philip Clum (Murphy) to bring self government to the Apache Indians and forcing a surrender of the Apache chief Geronimo and his followers. Based on the 1936 biography *Apache Agent* by Woodworth Clum. Technicolor/CinemaScope.

2922. Walking My Baby Back Home (Universal-International; 1953). *Cast:* Donald O'-Connor, Janet Leigh, Buddy Hackett (film debut), Scatman Crothers, Lori Nelson, Kathleen Lockhart, George Cleveland, John Hubbard, Paula Kelly (who was also Janet Leigh's singing voice), The Sportsmen, The Modernaires, Norman Abbott, Phil Garris, Walter Kingsford, Sidney Miller. *D:* Lloyd Bacon; *P:* Ted Richmond; *St:* Don McGuire; *Sc:* McGuire, Oscar Brodney; *Songs include:* "Man's Gotta Eat" Flourney E. Miller, Scatman Crothers; "Walking My Baby Back Home" Roy Turk, Fred Ahlert; "Glow Worm" Paul Lincke, Johnny Mercer; "Honeysuckle Rose" Fats Waller, Andy Razaf; "South Rampart Street Parade" Ray Baudec, Bob Haggart, Steve Allen; "De Campton Races" Stephen Foster; "Muskrat Ramble" Kid Ory, Ray Gilbert + "Liebestraum," "Hi Lee, Hi Low" and "Largo Al Factotum Della Citta." (1:35) Musical-comedy of an ex-G.I. who tries to make a go of it in the music world. Technicolor.

2923. Wanted—Dead or Alive (Monogram/Frontier Pictures; 1951). *Cast:* Whip Wilson, Fuzzy Knight, Jim Bannon, Christine McIntyre, Leonard Penn, Lane Bradford, Zon Murray, Stanley Price, Marshall Reed, Ray Jones, Jack O'Shea. *D:* Thomas Carr; *P:* Vincent M. Fennelly; *St: & Sc:* Clint Johnson. (0:59) Series western of a gang that murders wanted men for reward money.

2924. War and Peace (Paramount/Ponti-De Laurentiis; 1956). *Cast:* Audrey Hepburn (Natasha Rostov), Henry Fonda (Pierre Bezukhov), Mel Ferrer (Prince Andrei Bolkonsky), Vittorio Gassman (Anatole Kuragin), John Mills (Platon Karatsev), Herbert Lom (Napoleon), Oscar Homolka (Gen. Mikhail Kutuzov), Anita Ekberg (Helene, later Pierre's first wife), Helmut Dantine (Dolokhov), Barry Jones (Count Ilya Rostov), Anna Maria Ferrero (Mary Bolkonsky), Milly Vitale (Lise, Prince Andrei's wife), Jeremy Brett (Nicholas Rostov), Lea Seidl (Countess Rostov), Wilfred Lawson (Prince Nicholas Bolkonsky), Sean Barrett (Petya Rostov), Tullio Carminati (Prince Vasili Kuragin), May Britt (U.S. debut/Sonya Rostov), Patrick Crean (Vasili Denisov), Gertrude Flynn (Peronskaya), Teresa Pellati (Masa), Maria Zanoli (Mayra), Alberto Carlo Lolli (Rostov's majordomo), Clelia Matania (Mlle. Georges), Mario Addobati, Gualtiero Tumiati, Gianni Luda, Eschilo Tarquini, Alex D'Alessio, Alfredo Rizzo, Mauro Lanciani, Ina Alexeiva, Don Little, John Horne, Sdenka Kirchen, Nando Gallai, Michael Tor, Piero Pastore, Vincent Barbi, John Douglas, Robert Stephens, Luciano Angelini, Charles Fawcett, Piero Palermini, Angelo Galassi, David Crowley, Patrick Barrett, Michael Billingsley, Aldo Saporetti, Dimitri Konstantinov, Robin White Cross, Lucio de Santis, Robert Cunningham, Andre Eszterhazy, Marianne Leibl, Marisa Allasio, Stephen Garrett, Micaela Biustiniani, Cesare Barbetti, Francis Foucaud, Savo Raskovitch, Georges Brehat, Gilberto Tofano, Umberto Sacripante, Paole Quagliero, Christopher Hofer, Carlo Delmi, Enrico Olivieri, Eric Oulton, Archibald Lyall, John Stacey, Mino Doro, Alan Furlan, Joop Van Hulsen, Giovanni Rossi-Loti, Giacomo Rossi-Stuart, Guido Celano, Jerry Riggio, Geoffrey Copplestone, Mimmo Palmara, Giorgio Constantini, Richard McNamara, Andrea Fantasia, Stephen Lang, Carlo Dale, Paul Davis. *D:* (AAN) King Vidor; *P:* Dino De Laurentiis, Carlo Ponti; *Sc:* Bridget Boland, Robert Westerby, Vidor, Mario Camerini, Ennio De Concini, Ivo Perilli; *Cin:* (AAN-color) Jack Cardiff; *Costumes:* (AAN-color) Marie De Matteis. (3:28) (video/laserdisc) Leo Tolstoy's sprawling 1869 novel of the Napoleonic wars is brought to the screen in epic proportions. An Italian/U.S.A. co-production, filmed in Italy at a cost of $6,000,000, critics were divided, with the NBR voting it "Best Foreign Film." *Film Daily* placed it at #3 on their "10 Best" list and it went on to become one of the 24 top-grossing films of 1956-57. First filmed as a Russian silent in 1915 in 10 reels, the remake (released in the U.S. in 1968) is eye/mind boggling in its scope and detail (and a running time which exceeds 6 hours). Technicolor/VistaVision.

2925. War Arrow (Universal-International; 1953). *Cast:* Maureen O'Hara, Jeff Chandler, John McIntire, Suzan Ball, Noah Beery, Jr., Charles Drake, Henry Brandon, Dennis Weaver, Jay Silverheels, Steve Wyman, Jim Bannon, Brad Jackson, Lance Fuller, Bill Ward, Dee Carroll, Roy Whatley, Darla Ridgeway. *D:* George Sherman; *P:* John W. Rogers; *St: & Sc:* John Michael Hayes. (1:18) (video) Purportedly based on fact western actioner of the U.S. Cavalry recruiting Seminole Indians to quell a Kiowa uprising. Technicolor.

2926. War Drums (United Artists/Bel-Air–Palm Prods.; 1957). *Cast:* Lex Barker, Joan Taylor, Ben Johnson, Larry Chance, Richard Cutting, James Parnell, John Pickard, John Colicos, Tom Monroe, Jil Jarmyn, Jeanne Carmen, Mauritz Hugo, Ward Ellis, Fred Sherman, Paul Fierro, Alex Montoya, Stuart Whitman, Barbara Perry, Boyd "Red" Morgan, Monie [Ellis] Freeman. *D:* Reginald LeBorg; *P:* Howard W. Koch; *St. & Sc:* Gerald Drayson Adams. (1:15) Pro-Indian (and somewhat feminist) western of an Apache chief making war ca. 1860s against encroaching white gold miners. DeLuxe color.

2927. War of the Colossal Beast (American International/Carmel Prods.; 1958). *Cast:* Sally Fraser, Dean Parkin, Roger Pace, Russ Bender, Charles Stewart, George Becwar, Robert Hernandez, Rico Alaniz, George Alexander, George Navarro, John McNamara, Bob Garnet, Howard Wright, Roy Gordon, George Milan, Warren Frost, Bill Giorgio, Loretta Nicholson, June Jocelyn, Jack Kosslyn, Stan Chambers. *D:-P: & St:* Bert I. Gordon; *Ex.P:* James H. Nicholson, Samuel Z. Arkoff; *Assistant P:* Henry Schrage; *Sc:* George Worthing Yates. (1:08) (video) Sequel to *The Amazing Colossal Man* (q.v.) with giant Glen Manning (this time played by Parkin) surviving his fall from the dam, emerging in Mexico with a disfigured face and demented brain. The final scene is in color. Originally ran on the top of a double bill with *Attack of the Puppet People* (q.v.). (aka: *The Terror Strikes*)

2928. War of the Satellites (Allied Artists; 1958). *Cast:* Dick Miller, Susan Cabot, Richard Devon, Robert Shayne, Jerry Barclay, Eric Sinclair, Michael Fox, Jay Sayer, Mitzi McCall, Beach Dickerson, John Brinkley. *D: & P:* Roger Corman; *Co-Producers: & St:* Irving Block, Jack Rabin; *Sc:* Lawrence Louis Goldman. (1:06) An alien life force threatens to destroy earth unless experimental U.N. rocket launches are curtailed. Another Corman quickie inspired by the launching of the U.S. satellite *Explorer* in 1958. Originally paired on a double bill with *Attack of the 50-Ft. Woman* (q.v.).

2929. The War of the Worlds (Paramount; 1953). *Cast:* Gene Barry (Clayton Forrester), Ann Robinson (Sylvia Van Buren), Les Tremayne (Gen. Mann), Bob Cornthwaite (Dr. Pryor), Sandro Giglio (Dr. Bilderbeck), Lewis Martin (Rev. Matthew Collins), Paul Frees (radio announcer), Bill Phipps (Wash Perry), Vernon Rich (Col. Ralph Heffner), Jack Kruschen (Salvatore), Edgar Barrier (Prof. McPherson), Ralph Dumke (Buck Monahan), Alex Frazer (Dr. James), Ann Codee (Dr. DuPrey), Ivan Lebedeff (Dr. Cratzman), Alvy Moore (Zippy), Robert Rockwell (ranger), Paul Birch (Alonzo Hogue), Frank Kreig (Fiddler Hawkins), Charles Gemora (Martian), Russ Bender (Dr. Carmichael), George Pal (bum), Houseley Stevenson, Jr., Henry Brandon, Carolyn Jones, Pierre Cressoy, Walter Sande, Ned Glass, Anthony Warde, Gertrude Hoffman, Freeman Lusk, Sydney Mason, Peter Adams, Ted Hecht, Teru Shimada, Herbert Lytton, Wally Richard, Morton C. Thompson, Jerry James, Ralph Montgomery, Douglas Henderson, Bud [Bill] Wolfe, Jimmie Dundee, Joel Marston, Bill Meader, Al Ferguson, Rudy Lee, Waldon Williams, Gus Taillon, Ruth Barnell, Dorothy Vernon, Frank Freeman, Hugh Allen, Stanley W. Orr, Charles J. Stewart, Freddie Zendar, Jim Davies, Dick Fortune, Edward Wahrman, Martin Coulter, Hazel Boyne, Cora Shannon, Mike Mahoney, David Sharpe, Dale Van Sickel, Fred Graham. *D:* Byron Haskin; *P:* George Pal; *Sc:* Barre Lyndon; *F/X:* (AA) Gordon Jennings (died before the film was complete), Paul Lerpae, Wallace Kelly, Ivyl Burks, Jan Domela, Irmin Roberts, Walter Hoffman, Chesley Bonestell; *Editors:* (AAN) Everett Douglas; *Sound:* (AAN) Loren L. Ryder; *Introductory Narrator:* Paul Frees; *Commentary:* Cedric Hardwicke. (1:25) (video/laserdisc) Based on H.G. Wells' 1898 novel of an invasion of earth by Martians, this Paramount moneymaker had been gathering dust at the studio since Jesse Lasky purchased it from the author in 1924! Later a TV series. Technicolor. Note: This was the final film of cinematographer George Barnes who died in 1953.

2930. War Paint (United Artists/K-B Prods.; 1953). *Cast:* Robert Stack, Joan Taylor,

Charles McGraw, Peter Graves, Keith Larsen, Robert Wilke, William Pullen, Richard Cutting, Douglas Kennedy, Walter Reed, Charles Nolte, James Parnell, Paul Richards, John Doucette. *D:* Lesley Selander; *P:* Howard W. Koch; *St:* Fred Frieberger, William Tunberg; *Sc:* Richard Alan Simmons, Martin Berkeley; *Song:* "Elaine" Emil Newman, Johnny Lehrnann. (1:29) Action-filled western of the trials and tribulations of a cavalry detachment sent to deliver a peace treaty and prevent an Indian uprising. Pathécolor.

War Shock (G.B. title) *see* **A Woman's Devotion**

2931. Warlock (20th Century–Fox; 1959). *Cast:* Richard Widmark, Henry Fonda, Anthony Quinn, Dorothy Malone, Dolores Michaels, Wallace Ford, Tom Drake, Richard Arlen, De-Forest Kelley, Regis Toomey, Vaughn Taylor, Don Beddoe, Whit Bissell, J. Anthony Hughes, Donald Barry, Frank Gorshin, Ian MacDonald, Stan Kamber, Paul Comi, L.Q. Jones, Mickey Simpson, Robert Osterloh, James Philbrook, David Garcia, Robert Adler, Joel Ashley, Joe Turkel, Saul Gorss, Bartlett Robinson, Ann Doran, Henry Worth, June Blair, Walter Coy, Wally Campo, Hugh Sanders. *D: & P:* Edward Dmytryk; *St: & Sc:* Robert Alan Aurthur. (2:01) (video/laserdisc) Critically acclaimed adult western with character study of various individuals involved in cleaning up a lawless town. Based on the 1958 novel by Oakley Hall, it was filmed on location in Utah in DeLuxe color and CinemaScope.

2932. Warpath (Paramount; 1951). *Cast:* Edmond O'Brien, Dean Jagger, Forrest Tucker, Polly Bergen, Harry Carey, Jr., Wallace Ford, James Millican (Gen. George Armstrong Custer), Paul Fix, Louis Jean Heydt, Paul Lees, Walter Sande, Charles Dayton, Robert Bray, Douglas Spencer, James Burke, Chief Yowlachie, Monte Blue, Frank Ferguson, Cliff Clark, Charles Stevens, Paul Burns, John Hart, John Mansfield. *D:* Byron Haskin; *P:* Nat Holt; *Sc:* Frank Gruber. (1:35) Western action of a lawyer in the days following the Civil War out to get the three men who killed his fiancée. Based on the 1949 novel *Broken Lance* by Mr. Gruber. Technicolor.

2933. Washington Story (MGM; 1952). *Cast:* Van Johnson, Patricia Neal, Louis Calhern, Sidney Blackmer, Elizabeth Patterson, Philip Ober, Patricia Collinge, Reinhold Schunzel (final U.S. film), Moroni Olsen, Fay Roope, Dan Riss, Joan Banks, Raymond Greenleaf, Gregory Marshall, Perry Sheehan, Jimmie Fox, Katherine Warren, Don Beddoe, Hugh Beaumont, Willis Bouchey, Carleton Young, Lawrence Dobkin, Emory Parnell. *D:-St: & Sc:* Robert Pirosh; *P:* Dore Schary. (1:21) Romance blossoms between a reporter and the U.S. congressman she has targeted for investigation. Location filming in Washington, D.C.

2934. The Wasp Woman (Filmgroup; 1959). *Cast:* Susan Cabot (final film—ret.), Fred [Anthony] Eisley, Barboura Morris, Michael Mark, William Roerick, Frank Gerstle, Bruno VeSota, Frank Wolff. *D: & P:* Roger Corman; *St: & Sc:* Leo Gordon (1:06) (video) A Corman horror quickie with a cult following of the head of a cosmetics firm, concerned about her aging skin who undergoes experimental serum from wasps. When the treatments are unable to be continued, she turns into a waspish monster.

2935. Watch the Birdie (MGM; 1950). *Cast:* Red Skelton (triple role), Ann Miller, Arlene Dahl, Leon Ames, Pamela Britton, Richard Rober, Mike Mazurki, Dick Wessel, Jacqueline Duval, Paula Drew, Georgia Pelham. *D:* Jack Donohue; *P:* Harry Ruskin; *St:* Marshall Neilan, Jr.; *Sc:* Ruskin, Ivan Tors, Devery Freeman. (1:10) (video) Slapstick comedy of a cameraman who can't seem to avoid getting into one difficulty after another. In this reworking of *The Cameraman* (1928), Skelton plays his own character as well as his father and grandfather. Includes clips from *Boom Town* (1940) and *Johnny Eager* (1941).

2936. Watusi (MGM; 1959). *Cast:* George Montgomery, Taina Elg, David Farrar, Rex Ingram, Dan Seymour, Robert Goodwin, Anthony B. Davis, Paul Thompson, Harold Dyrenforth. *D:* Kurt Neumann; *P:* Al Zimbalist; *As.P:* Donald Zimbalist; *Sc:* James Clavell. (1:25) A follow-up to this studio's 1950 production of *King Solomon's Mines* (q.v.) based on the 1886 novel by H. Rider Haggard. The son of Allan Quartermaine arrives in Africa to retrace his father's footsteps in search of precious gems. The film utilizes leftover footage from the original as well as other stock shots. Technicolor.

2937. Way of a Gaucho (20th Century–Fox; 1952). *Cast:* Rory Calhoun, Gene Tierney, Richard Boone, Hugh Marlowe, Everett Sloane, Enrique Chaico, Roland Dumas, Lidia Campos, John Henchley, Douglas Poole, Mario Abdah, John Paris, Jorge Villoldo, Hugh Mancini, Nestor Yoan, Raoul Astor, Alex Peters, Kim Dillon,

Lia Centano, Claudio Torres, Teresa Acosta, Oscar Lucero, Anthony Ugrin. *D:* Jacques Tourneur; *P: & Sc:* Philip Dunne. (1:31) South American "western" melodrama of a young couple who try to make a life for themselves in 1875 on the Argentine pampas. Based on the 1948 novel by Herbert Childs. Technicolor.

2938. The Way to the Gold (20th Century–Fox; 1957). *Cast:* Jeffrey Hunter, Sheree North, Barry Sullivan, Walter Brennan, Neville Brand, Jacques Aubuchon, Ruth Donnelly (final film—ret.), Tom Pittman, Philip Ahn, Geraldo A. Mandia, Alan Jeffrey, Ted Edwards, Ken Scott, Jonathan Hale, Frank Mazzola. *D:* Robert D. Webb; *P:* David Weisbart; *Sc:* Wendell Mayes; *Songs:* "Strange Weather," "Drive-In Rock" Lionel Newman, Carroll Coates. (1:34) Melodrama of various people in search of a cache of gold, buried by a convict (now deceased) thirty years previous. Based on the 1955 novel by Wilbur Daniel Steele. CinemaScope.

2939. The Wayward Bus (20th Century-Fox; 1957). *Cast:* Joan Collins, Jayne Mansfield, Dan Dailey, Rick Jason, Betty Lou Keim, Dolores Michaels, Larry Keating, Robert Bray, Kathryn Givney, Dee Pollock, Will Wright. *D:* Victor Vicas; *P:* Charles Brackett; *Sc:* Ivan Moffat. (1:29) Melodrama of various character types aboard a bus, coming into conflict with each other while enduring inclement weather conditions. Based on the 1947 novel by John Steinbeck. CinemaScope.

2940. The Wayward Girl (Republic; 1957). *Cast:* Marcia Henderson, Peter Walker, Katherine Barrett, Whit Bissell, Rita Lynn, Peg Hillias, Tracey Roberts, Ray Teal, Ric Roman, Barbara Eden, Grandon Rhodes, Francis DeSales, John Maxwell. *D:* Lesley Selander; *P:* William J. O'Sullivan; *St: & Sc:* Houston Branch, Frederic Louis Fox. (1:11) Melodrama of a teenage girl (Henderson) who believes she murdered her boyfriend and is incarcerated. It is revealed that her stepmother (Barrett) actually killed the boy. Widescreen Naturama.

Wedding Bells (G.B. title) *see* **Royal Wedding**

Wedding Breakfast (G.B. title) *see* **The Catered Affair**

2941. Weddings and Babies (20th Century–Fox/Morris Engel; 1958–60). *Cast:* Viveca Lindfors, John Myhers, Chiarina Barile, Leonard Elliott, Joanna Merlin, Chris (son of Ms. Lindfors), Gabriel Kohn, Mary Faranda. *D:-P:-St: & Cin:* Morris Engel (final film—ret.); *As.P:* Joel Glickman; *Sc:* Mary Madeleine Lanphier, Blanche Hanalis, Irving Sunasky. (1:22) Low budget indie drama of a New York photographer caring for a senile mother and avoiding marriage to his long-time girlfriend. Completed and exhibited at the Venice Film Festival (winning the "Critic's Prize") in 1958, it was not shown in the U.S. until 1960 as distributors and exhibitors were leery of the "uncommercial" product.

2942. Weekend with Father (Universal-International; 1951). *Cast:* Van Heflin, Patricia Neal, Gigi Perreau, Virginia Field, Richard Denning, Jimmy Hunt, Janine Perreau, Tommy Rettig, Gary Pagett, Frances Williams, Forrest Lewis, Elvia Allman, Maudie Prickett, Robert Rockwell, Martha Mears. *D:* Douglas Sirk; *P:* Ted Richmond; *St:* George F. Slavin, George W. George; *Sc:* Joseph Hoffman. (1:23) Comedy of a widow with two boys and a widower with two girls who fall for each other, much to the disdain of their offspring.

2943. The Well (United Artists/Cardinal Pictures; 1951). *Cast:* Gwendolyn Laster (Carolyn Crawford), Richard Rober (Sheriff Ben Kellogg), Maidie Norman (Mrs. Crawford), George Hamilton (Grandfather/black actor), Ernest Anderson (Mr. Crawford), Dick Simmons (Mickey), Lane Chandler (Stan), Pat Mitchell (Peter), Margaret Wells (schoolteacher), Wheaton Chambers (Woody), Michael Ross (Frank), Russell Trent (Chet), Allen Matthews (Hal), John Phillips (Fred), Walter Morrison (Art), Christine Larson (Casey), Jess Kirkpatrick (Quigley), Roy Engel (Gleason), Alfred Grant (Gaines), Robert Osterloh (Wylie), Henry [Harry] Morgan (Claude Packard), Barry Kelley (Sam Packard), Walter Kelly (Chip), Mary Ellen Kay (Lois), Beverly Jons (Sally), Tom Powers (mayor), Bill Walker (Dr. Billings), Douglas Evans (Lobel), Sherry Hall (Manners), Ed Max, Guy Beach, Elzie Emanuel. *D:* Leo C. Popkin, Russell Rouse (directorial debut); *P:* Popkin, Clarence Green; *Sc:* (AAN) Rouse, Green; *Editor:* (AAN) Chester Schaeffer. (1:25) (video) A five-year-old black girl disappears and it is rumored she was last seen with a white man. The various reactions of the people in the town form a social comment. It is later found that the girl has fallen down a well and the townspeople rally together to rescue her. Based on fact, it placed #6 at the Berlin Film Festival.

2944. Wells Fargo Gunmaster (Republic; 1951). *Cast:* Allan Lane, Mary Ellen Kay, Chubby Johnson, Michael Chapin, Roy Barcroft, Walter Reed, Stuart Randall, William Bakewell, George Meeker, Anne O'Neal, James Craven, Forrest Taylor, Lee Roberts, Black Jack (horse). *D:* Philip Ford; *As.P:* Gordon Kay; *St: & Sc:* M. Coates Webster. (1:00) In this series oater, "Rocky" Lane investigates a series of Wells Fargo robberies. The 2nd half of a matinee double bill with Roy Rogers' *In Old Amarillo* (q.v.).

2945. We're No Angels (Paramount; 1955). *Cast:* Humphrey Bogart, Aldo Ray, Peter Ustinov, Joan Bennett, Basil Rathbone, Leo G. Carroll, John Smith, Gloria Talbott, John Baer, Lea Penman, Louis Mercier, George Dee, Torben Meyer, Paul Newlan, Ross Gould, Victor Romito, Jack Del Rio, Joe Ploski. *D:* Michael Curtiz; *P:* Pat Duggan; *Sc:* Ranald MacDougall; *Songs:* "Sentimental Moments" Frederick Hollander, Ralph Freed, "Ma France Bien-Aimee" G. Martini, Roger Wagner. (1:46) (video/laserdisc) Oddball comedy of three Devil's Island escapees who find refuge with a French family and proceed to help them out of their difficulties, including eviction, by bringing about the death of their landlord. Based on the play *Le Cuisine De Anges* by Albert Husson, which was also the source material for the 1989 production of the same name which could hardly be called a remake. Technicolor/VistaVision.

2946. We're Not Married (20th Century-Fox; 1952). *Cast:* Ginger Rogers, Fred Allen, Victor Moore, Marilyn Monroe, David Wayne, Eve Arden, Paul Douglas, Eddie Bracken, Mitzi Gaynor, Louis Calhern, Zsa Zsa Gabor, James Gleason, Paul Stewart, Jane Darwell, Tom Powers, Victor Sutherland, Alan Bridge, Harry Golder, Kay English, Lee Marvin, O.Z. Whitehead, Marjorie Weaver (final film—ret.), Forbes Murray, Maurice Cass (final film—d. 1954), Margie Liszt (voice only), Maude Wallace, Richard Buckley, Alvin Greenman, Eddie Firestone, Phyllis Brunner, Steve Pritko, Robert Dane, James Burke, Robert Forrest, Bill Hale, Ed Max, Richard Reeves, Ralph Dumke, Harry Antrim, Byron Foulger, Harry Harvey, Selmer Jackson, Harry Carter, Dabbs Greer, Emile Meyer, Henry Faber, Larry Stamps. *D:* Edmund Goulding; *P: & Sc:* Nunnally Johnson; *St:* Gina Kaus, Jay Dratler; *Adaptation:* Dwight Taylor. (1:25) (video) Domestic comedy of the varied problems created for five couples when they receive a letter from the judge who married them, informing them that his license had been expired when he performed their ceremonies—hence!

2947. The Werewolf (Columbia/Clover Prods.; 1956). *Cast:* Steven Ritch, Don Megowan, Joyce Holden, Eleanore Tanin, Kim Charney, Larry Blake, Harry Lauter, Ken Christy, James Gavin, Don C. Harvey, Ford Stevens, Marjorie Stapp, S. John Launer, George M. Lynn, George Cisar, Jean Harvey, Jean Charney. *D:* Fred F. Sears; *P:* Sam Katzman; *St: & Sc:* Robert E. Kent, James B. Gordon. (1:23) A family man turns into a lycanthrope after taking a serum. Originally the bottom of a double bill program with *Earth vs. the Flying Saucers* (q.v.).

2948. West of the Brazos (Lippert; 1950). *Cast:* Jimmie Ellison, Russ Hayden, Raymond Hatton, Fuzzy Knight, Betty [Julie] Adams, Tom Tyler, George J. Lewis, John Cason, Stanley Price, Stephen Carr, Dennis Moore, Bud Osborne, George Chesebro, Jimmie Martin, Judith Webster, Gene Roth. *D:* Thomas Carr; *P:* Ron Ormond, Murray Lerner; *St: & Sc:* Ormond, Maurice Tombragel. (0:58) Crooks are out to attain oil lands in this programmer horse opera, #5 of six in the "Shamrock (Ellison) & Lucky (Hayden)" series. (aka: *Rangeland Empire*)

2949. West of Wyoming (Monogram; 1950). *Cast:* Johnny Mack Brown, Gail Davis, Myron Healey, Dennis Moore, Stanley Andrews, Milburn Morante, Mary Gordon (final film—ret.), Carl Mathews, Paul Cramer, John Merton, Mike Ragan [aka: Holly Bane], Steve Clark, Frank McCarroll, Bud Osborne. *D:* Wallace W. Fox; *P:* Eddie Davis; *St: & Sc:* Adele Buffington. (0:57) There's a feud brewing between cattlemen and homesteaders in this series shoot-em-up.

2950. West Point Story (Warner; 1950). *Cast:* James Cagney (Elwin Bixby), Gordon MacRae (Tom Fletcher), Virginia Mayo (Eve Dillon), Doris Day (Jan Wilson), Gene Nelson (Hal Courtland), Alan Hale, Jr. (Bull Gilbert), Roland Winters (Harry Eberhart), Raymond Roe (Bixby's "wife"), Wilton Graff (Lt. Col. Martin), Jerome Cowan (Jocelyn), Frank Ferguson, Russ Saunders, Jack Kelly, Glen Turnbull, Walter Ruick, Lute Crockett, Victor Desney, Wheaton Chambers, James Dobson, Joel Marston, Boby Hayden, DeWitt Bishop, John Hedloe, Don Shartel, James Young. *D:* Roy Del Ruth; *P:* Louis F. Edelman; *Sc:* John Monks, Jr., Charles Hoffman, Irving Wallace (based on the story "Classmates" by Wallace); *Music:* (AAN) Ray

Heindorf; *Songs:* "It Could Only Happen in Brooklyn," "Military Polka," "You Love Me and Ten Thousand Sheep," "By the Kissing Rock," "Long Before I Knew You" and "Brooklyn" Jule Styne, Sammy Cahn. (1:47) Musical of a has-been Broadway producer who agrees to put on a show at the famed military academy. (G.B. title: *Fine and Dandy*)

2951. Westbound (Warner; 1959). *Cast:* Randolph Scott, Virginia Mayo, Karen Steele, Michael Dante, Andrew Duggan, Michael Pate, Wally Brown, John Day, Walter Barnes, Fred Sherman, Mack Williams, Ed Prentiss, Rory Mallinson, Rudi Dana, Tom Monroe, Jack Perrin, Buddy Roosevelt, Charles Morton, John Epper, Gary Epper, Kermit Maynard, William A. Green, Jack E. Henderson, Felice Richmond, Creighton Hale, Gertrude Keeler, Walter Reed, Jack C. Williams, Gerald Roberts, John Hudkins, May Boss, Don Happy, Bobby Heron, Fred Stromscoe. *D:* Budd Boetticher; *P:* Henry Blanke; *Sc:* Berne Giler [based on his story "The Great Divide No. 2," written with Albert Shelby LeVino]. (1:12) Western of a Union Cavalry officer assigned to the task of re-establishing a stagecoach line to ship gold from California to the east, during the era of the Civil War. WarnerColor.

2952. Western Pacific Agent (Lippert; 1950). *Cast:* Kent Taylor, Sheila Ryan, Mickey Knox, Morris Carnovsky, Robert Lowery, Sid Melton, Frank Richards, Ted Jacques, Dick Elliott, Anthony Jochim, Lee Phelps, Carla Martin, Margia Dean, Gloria Grey, Vera Marshe, Jack Geddes, Jason Robards. *D:* Sam Newfield; *P:* Sigmund Neufeld; *St:* Milton Raison; *Sc:* Fred Myton. (1:04) The law vs. the lawless in this programmer melodrama as an agent sets out to capture a murderous robbery suspect.

2953. Westward Ho, the Wagons (Buena Vista/Walt Disney Prods.; 1956). *Cast:* Fess Parker, Kathleen Crowley, Jeff York, David Stollery, Sebastian Cabot, George Reeves (final film—d. 1959), Doreen Tracey, Barbara Woodell, John War Eagle, Cubby O'Brien, Tommy Cole, Leslie Bradley, Morgan Woodward, Iron Eyes Cody, Anthony Numkena [aka: Earl Holliman], Karen Pendleton, Jane Liddell, Jon Locke, Brand Stirling. *D:* William Beaudine; *Ex.P:* Walt Disney; *P:* Bill Walsh; *Sc:* Tom Blackburn; *Songs:* "John Colter," "Westward Ho, the Wagons" George Bruns, Blackburn; "Pioneer's Prayer" Paul J. Smith, Gil George; "Wringle Wrangle" Stan Jones and "I'm Lonely, My Darlin'" Bruns, Fess Parker. (1:30) (video) Episodic western tale of a wagon trek through Wyoming (actually filmed on location in California) and various incidents which occur. Based on the 1934 novel *Children of the Covered Wagon* by Mary Jane Carr, the film was moderately successful at the box office, largely due to the appearances of Tracey, O'Brien, Cole and Pendleton, four "Mouseketeers" on the Mickey Mouse Club and Stollery who appeared in the "Spin and Marty" episodes on that same show. Technicolor/CinemaScope.

2954. Westward the Women (MGM; 1951). *Cast:* Robert Taylor, Denise Darcel, Hope Emerson, Marilyn Erskine (film debut), Julie Bishop, John McIntire, Beverly Dennis, Lenore Lonergan, Henry Nakamura, Renata Vanni, Guido Martufi, Bruce Cowling, Frankie Darro, George Chandler. *D:* William A. Wellman; *P:* Dore Schary; *St:* Frank Capra; *Sc:* Charles Schnee. (1:58) (video) Offbeat western tale of a misogynistic scout, hired to escort a wagon train of women to their western destination, a town populated by only men who are to become their husbands. Along the way they contend with outlaws, Indians, the elements, petty bickering, catfights and the birth of a baby. Computer-colored prints have been produced by Turner Entertainment.

2955. Wetbacks (Banner Prods.; 1956). *Cast:* Lloyd Bridges, Nancy Gates, Barton MacLane, John Hoyt, Harold Peary, Nacho Galindo, Robert Keys, David Colmans, Jose Gonzales-Gonzales, Louis Jean Heydt, Scott Douglas, Wally Cassell, Richard Powers [aka: Tom Keene], Salvador Baguez. *D: & P:* Hank McCune; *St: & Sc:* Peter LaRoche. (1:29) Melodrama of Mexican illegals being smuggled into the U.S. as cheap labor.

What Lola Wants (G.B. title) *see* **Damn Yankees**

2956. What Price Glory? (20th Century-Fox; 1952). *Cast:* James Cagney, Corinne Calvet, Dan Dailey, William Demarest, Craig Hill, Robert Wagner, Marisa Pavan (film debut), Casey Adams [aka: Max Showalter], James Gleason, Wally Vernon, Henri Letondal, Fred Libby, Ray Hyke, Paul Fix, James Lilburn, Henry [Harry] Morgan, Dan Borzage, Bill Henry, Henry Kulky, Jack Pennick, Ann Codee, Stanley Johnson, Luis Alberni (final film—ret.), Barry Norton, Torben Meyer, Alfred Zeisler, George Bruggeman,

Sean McClory, Scott Forbes, Charles Fitzsimmons, Louis Mercier, Mickey Simpson, Olga Andre, Tom Tyler. *D:* John Ford; *P:* S.C. Siegel; *Sc:* Phoebe Ephron, Henry Ephron; *Songs:* "My Love, My Life" and "Oui, Oui, Marie" Jay Livingston, Ray Evans. (1:51) (video) World War I comedy of an army captain and his top sergeant who have a serious rivalry over the affections of the daughter of a French tavern keeper. The film which is a remake of the famed 1926 silent of the same name didn't set well with the critics of the day, though the film has found a following in recent years. Based on the play by Maxwell Anderson and Laurence Stallings. Technicolor. Note: Barry Norton also appeared in the silent version.

2957. When Gangland Strikes (Republic; 1956). *Cast:* Raymond Greenleaf, Marjie Miller, John Hudson, Anthony Caruso, Marian Carr, Slim Pickens, Mary Treen, Ralph Dumke, Morris Ankrum, Robert Emmett Keane, Addison Richards, John Gallaudet, Paul Birch, Richard Deacon, James Best, Jim Hayward, Peter Mamakos, Fred Siterman, Dick Elliott, Norman Leavitt, Jack Perrin. *D:* R.G. Springsteen; *P:* William J. O'Sullivan; *Sc:* John K. Butler, Frederic Louis Fox. (1:10) (video) Crime melodrama of a prosecutor who reacts when he finds his daughter is being blackmailed by a hoodlum. A remake of *Main Street Lawyer*, a 1939 production from this studio.

2958. When Hell Broke Loose (Paramount/Dolworth Prods.; 1958). *Cast:* Charles Bronson, Violet Rensing, Richard Jaeckel, Arvid Nelson, Robert Easton, Dennis McCarthy, Kathy Carlyle, Ann Wakefield, Eddie Foy III, Bob Stevenson, John Morley, Ed Penney. *D:* Kenneth G. Crane; *P:* Oscar Brodney, Sol Dolgin; *Sc:* Brodney. (1:18) (video) World War II drama of a conman who joins the U.S. Army to avoid prison and through a female acquaintance uncovers a Nazi plot to assassinate General Eisenhower. Based on articles by Ib Melchior.

2959. When I Grow Up (Eagle-Lion/Horizon Prods.; 1951). *Cast: 1890:* Bobby Driscoll, Robert Preston, Martha Scott, Sherry Jackson, Johnny McGovern, Frances Cheney, Poodles Hanneford, Ralph Dumke, Paul Guilfoyle, Paul Levitt, Griff Barnett, Margaret Lloyd. *Modern:* Driscoll, Charley Grapewin, Henry [Harry] Morgan, Elisabeth Fraser, Bobby Hyatt, Robin Camp, Ruth Lee, Donald Gordon (harmonica dubbed by George Fields). *D:-St: & Sc:* Michael Kanin; *P:* S.P. Eagle (Sam Spiegel). (1:20) Drama of a young boy feeling unloved by his parents who confides in his grandfather who relates a personal story which he experienced when he was a boy, when he had similar feelings toward his own father.

2960. When in Rome (MGM; 1952). *Cast:* Van Johnson, Paul Douglas, Joseph Calleia, Carlo Rizzo, Tudor Owen, Dino Nardi, Aldo Silvani, Mario Siletti, Argentina Brunetti, Emory Parnell, Sarah Churchill (2nd and final U.S. film), Carlo Borrelli, Giuseppe Pierozzi, Guido Martufi, Joe Faletta, Charles Fawcett, Mimi Aguglia, Alberto Lolli, Adriano Ambrogi, Amina Pirani Maggi, Angela Clarke. *D: & P:* Clarence Brown; *St:* Robert Buckner; *Sc:* Charles Schnee, Dorothy Kingsley. (1:18) Comedy-drama of a Catholic priest and a prison escapee posing as a priest who make a pilgrimage to Rome in the Holy Year 1950, which eventually leads the latter to find faith. Location filming in Rome.

When Knighthood Was in Flower (G.B. title) *see* **The Sword and the Rose**

2961. When the Redskins Rode (Columbia; 1951). *Cast:* Jon Hall, Mary Castle, James Seay (George Washington), Sherry Moreland, John Dehner, Lewis L. Russell, Pedro de Cordoba, William Bakewell, Milton Kibbee, Gregory Gaye, Rusty Wescoatt, Rick Vallin, John Ridgely (Christopher Gist). *D:* Lew Landers; *P:* Sam Katzman; *St: & Sc:* Robert E. Kent. (1:18) Costume actioner set during the mid–18th century French and Indian War, with the English seeking an alliance with the Delaware Indians against the French. SuperCinecolor.

2962. When Willie Comes Marching Home (20th Century–Fox; 1950). *Cast:* Dan Dailey (Bill Kluggs), Corinne Calvet (Yvonne), Colleen Townsend (Marge Fettles), William Demarest (Herman Kluggs), James Lydon (Charles Fettles), Lloyd Corrigan (Mayor Adams), Evelyn Varden (Gertrude Kluggs), Charles Halton (Mr. Fettles), Mae Marsh (Mrs. Fettles), Mickey Simpson (M.P.-Kerrigan), Frank Pershing (Major Bickford), Don Summers (M.P.-Sherve), Gil Herman (Lt. Comdr. Crown), Peter Ortiz (Pierre), Cecile Weston (Mrs. Barnes), Harry Tenbrook (Joe), Russ Clark (Sgt. Wilson), George Spaulding (Judge Tate), Larry Keating (Gen. G. Reeding), Dan Riss (Gen. Adams), Robert Einer (Lt. Bagley), Russ Conway (Major J.A. White), Whit Bissell (Lt. Handley), Ray Hyke (Major Crawford), Gene Collins (Andy), James Flavin (Gen. Brevort), David McMahon

(Col. Ainsley), Charles Trowbridge (Gen. Merrill), Kenneth Tobey (Lt. K. Geiger), Kenny Williams, Lee Clark, Jack Pennick, Luis Alberni, John Shulick, John McKee, Clarke Gordon, Robin Hughes, James Eagle, Harry Strang, George Magrill, Hank Worden, Ann Codee, Major Sam Harris, Alberto Morin, Louis Mercier, Paul Harvey, James Waters, Ken Lynch, Frank Baker, J. Farrell MacDonald, Vera Miles. *D:* John Ford; *P:* Fred Kohlmar; *St:* (AAN) Sy Gomberg; *Sc:* Mary Loos, Richard Sale. (1:22) Comedy of a Virginia training instructor in a small town who suddenly finds himself a hero for action in World War II. Based on the story "When Leo Comes Marching Home" by Mr. Gomberg.

2963. When Worlds Collide (Paramount; 1951). *Cast:* Richard Derr (Dave Randall), Barbara Rush (Joyce Hendron), Peter Hanson (Dr. Tony Drake), John Hoyt (Sydney Stanton), Larry Keating (Dr. Cole Hendron), Stephen Chase (Dr. Dean George Frey), Judith Ames (Julie Cummings), Frank Cady (Harold Ferris), Hayden Rorke (Dr. Emory Bronson), Sandro Giglio (Ottinger), Jim Congdon (Eddie Carson), Frances Sanford (Alice), Laura Elliot (stewardess), Freeman Lusk (Rudolph Marston), Joseph Mell (Glen Spiro), Art Gilmore (Paul), Keith Richards (Stanley), Gay Nelson (Leda), Rudy Lee (Mike), Harry Stanton (Dr. Zenta), Marcel de la Brosse, Queenie Smith, Leonard Mudie, John Ridgely, James Seay Donovan, Hassan Khayyam, Bill Meader, Ramsey Hill, Gene Collins, Sam Finn, Gertrude Astor, Estelle Etterre, Mary Murphy, Stuart Whitman (film debut), Kirk Alyn, Robert Chapman, Charmienne Harker, Walter Kelley, Chad Madison, Dolores Mann, Robert Sully, Richard Vath, Paul Frees (Narrator). *D:* Rudolph Maté; *P:* George Pal; *Sc:* Sydney Boehm; *Cin:* (AAN-color) John F. Seitz, W. Howard Greene; *F/X:* (AA) George Pal, Gordon Jennings, Harry Barndollar. (1:21) (video/laserdisc) Science fiction of a planet on a collision course with earth and various people planning to escape the cataclysm by rocketship. Based on the 1950 novel *When Worlds Collide and After Worlds Collide* by Edwin Balmer and Philip Wylie. Technicolor.

2964. When You're Smiling (Columbia; 1950). *Cast:* Jerome Courtland, Frankie Laine (film debut/himself), Lola Albright, Jerome Cowan, Margo Woode, Collette Lyons, Robert Shayne, Ray Teal, Don Otis (himself), Jimmy Lloyd, Donna Hamilton, Edward Earle, Frank Nelson, Neyle Morrow, Bob Crosby and His Bobcats, Kay Starr, Billy Daniels, The Modernaires, The Mills Brothers. *D:* Joseph Santley (final film—ret.); *P:* Jonie Taps; *St: & Sc:* Karen DeWolf, John R. Roberts; *Songs:* "When You're Smiling" Mark Fisher, Joe Goodwin, Larry Shay (by Laine, Courtland and the Modernaires); "That Old Black Magic" Harold Arlen, Johnny Mercer (sung by Daniels); "When the Wind Was Green" Don Hunt (by Courtland); "Georgia on My Mind" Stuart Garrell, Hoagy Carmichael (by Laine); "Up a Lazy River" Sidney Arodin, Carmichael (by the Mills Bros.); "Deed I Do" Walter Hirsch, Fred Rose (by Daniels); "Juke Box Saturday Night" Al Stillman, Paul McGrane (by the Modernaires); "Mama Goes Where Papa Goes" (by Starr) and "If You Can't Get a Drum with a Boom, Boom, Boom" (by Crosby and the Bobcats). (1:15) Musical of a cowboy (Courtland) who heads to Hollywood and becomes a record star. A thin plot to parade many popular musical guests of the day.

2965. Where Danger Lives (RKO; 1950). *Cast:* Robert Mitchum, Faith Domergue, Claude Rains, Maureen O'Sullivan, Charles Kemper, Ralph Dumke, Billy House, Harry Shannon, Philip Van Zandt, Jack Kelly, Lillian West, Ruth Lewis, Joey Faye, Dorothy Abbott, Gaylord "Steve" Pendleton, Joey Ray, Don House, Jerry James, Len Hendry, Carl Saxe, Marvin Jones, Lester Dorr, Art Dupuis, Stanley Andrews, Jack Kruschen, Elaine Riley, Gordon Clark, Geraldine Wall, David Stollery, Sherry Jackson, Clifford Brooke, Jim Dundee, Tol Avery, Robert R. Stevenson, Ethan Laidlaw, William N. Bailey, Stuart Holmes, Earle Hodgins, Ray Teal, Carl Sklover, Gene Barnes, Duke York, Marie Allison, Grace McNaughton, Betty Hannon, Julian Rivero, George Sheehan, James Brick Sullivan, Carlos Albert, Mike Lally, Philip Ahn, Tina Menard, Jeraldine Jordan, Hazel Boyne, Ann Zika, Erno Verebes, Allen Matthews, Florence Hamblin, Amilda Cuddy, Maxine Gates, Herschel Daugherty, Phil Boutelje, Linda Johnson, Marie Thomas, Gerry Ganzer, Bob Coleman, Helen Brown, William E. Green, Frank Leyva. *D:* John Farrow; *P:* Irving Cummings, Jr.; *St:* Leo Rosten; *Sc:* Charles Bennett. (1:24) Film noir of a doctor (Mitchum) who unwittingly finds himself involved with a neurotic murderess (Domergue) who killed her husband and led him to believe he was the one who committed the act.

Where the River Bends (G.B. title) *see* **Bend of the River**

2966. Where the Sidewalk Ends (20th Century–Fox; 1950). *Cast:* Dana Andrews, Gene Tierney, Gary Merrill, Bert Freed, Tom Tully, Karl Malden, Ruth Donnelly, Craig Stevens, Harry Von Zell, Robert F. Simon, Don Appell, Neville Brand, Grace Mills, Lou Krugman, David McMahon, David Wolfe, Steve Roberts, Phil Tully, Ian MacDonald, John Close, John McGuire, Lou Nova, Oleg Cassini (himself), Louise Lorimer, Lester Sharpe, Chili Williams, Robert Foulk, Eda Reis Merin, Mack Williams, Duke Watson, Clancy Cooper, Bob Evans, Joseph Granby, Harry Brooks, Anthony George, Wanda Smith, Shirley Tegge, Peggy O'Connor, Milton Gowman, Lee MacGregor, Charles J. Flynn, Larry Thompson, Ralph Peters, Robert B. Williams, John Marshall, Clarence Straight, Bob Patten, Louise Lane, Kathleen Hughes, John Trebach, Herbert Lytton, John Daheim, Tony Barr, Fred Graham. *D: & P:* Otto Preminger; *As.P:* Frank P. Rosenberg; *Adaptation:* Victor Trivas, Rosenberg, Robert E. Kent; *Sc:* Ben Hecht. (1:35) Acclaimed film noir of a ruthless police detective who tries to conceal a murder he committed while searching for another murderer, attempting to pin the murder on a mobster, but finds an innocent cab driver is accused instead. His days are numbered when he falls for his victim's widow. Based on the 1948 novel *Night Cry* by William L. Stuart.

2967. Where's Charley? (Warner; 1952). *Cast:* Ray Bolger (repeating his stage role), Allyn McLerie (repeating her stage role), Robert Shackleton, Mary Germaine, Horace Cooper (film debut at age 70), Margaretta Scott, Howard Marion Crawford, Henry Hewitt, H.G. Stoker, Martin Miller, Jean Marshe. *D:* David Butler; *P:* Ernest Martin, Cy Feuer; *Sc:* John Monks, Jr.; *Choreography:* Michael Kidd; *Songs include:* "Make a Miracle," "The New Ashmolean Marching Society and Students Conservatory Band," "My Darling, My Darling," "Once in Love With Amy," "At the Red Rose Cotillion" and "Better Get Out of Here" Frank Loesser. (1:37) Based on the Broadway success, this musical-comedy version of Brandon Thomas' Victorian play *Charley's Aunt* was by George Abbott and Frank Loesser. Comic complications abound when an Oxford student poses as his own maiden aunt to chaperone a pair of young lovers. Filmed in England at Warner's studio and locations at Oxford University, this is technically a U.S.A. production, shot in England, using local talent and U.S. funds held in England at the time. Technicolor.

2968. While the City Sleeps (RKO/Thor; 1956). *Cast:* Dana Andrews, Rhonda Fleming, Sally Forrest (final film—ret.), Thomas Mitchell, Vincent Price, Howard Duff, Ida Lupino, George Sanders, James Craig, John Barrymore, Jr., Vladimir Sokoloff, Robert Warwick, Ralph Peters, Larry Blake, Edward Hinton, Mae Marsh, Sandy White, Celia Lovsky, Pitt Herbert, David Andrews, Andrew Lupino, Carleton Young. *D:* Fritz Lang; *P:* Bert E. Friedlob; *Sc:* Casey Robinson; *Title song:* Herschel Burke Gilbert, Joseph Mullendore. (1:40) (video/laserdisc) Crime drama of tabloid journalists and police scouring the city of New York for a demented rapist-murderer, each of the newsmen with his own motive for scooping the story and using unethical methods to achieve same. Based on the 1953 novel *The Bloody Spur* by Charles Einstein. SuperScope.

2969. The Whip Hand (RKO/Howard Hughes; 1951). *Cast:* Carla Balenda, Elliott Reid, Edgar Barrier, Raymond Burr, Lurene Tuttle, Otto Waldis, Michael Steele, Peter Brocco, Lewis Martin, Frank Darien, Olive Carey, Jamesson Shade, Art Dupuis, Robert Foulk, William Challee, Brick Sullivan, Robert Thom. *D:* William Cameron Menzies; *Ex.P:* Howard Hughes; *P:* Lewis J. Rachmil; *St:* Roy Hamilton; *Sc:* George Bricker, Frank L. Moss. (1:22) Melodrama of communist agents lurking in a deserted resort town with intention of unleasing germ warfare on the U.S. Another box office bomb for Hughes, it had the pre-release title of "The Man He Found."

2970. Whip Law (Monogram; 1950). This film shows up as a "Whip Wilson" series western, and is also listed under the credits of director Howard Bretherton, one of two he directed in the series. Other information is elusive, indicating the film may never have been released.

2971. The Whipped (United Artists/ Film Craft Trading Corp.; 1950). *Cast:* Dan Duryea, Herbert Marshall, Gale Storm, Howard Da Silva, Michael O'Shea, Mary Anderson, Gar Moore, Melville Cooper, Frieda Inescort, Art Baker, Harry Shannon, Alan Hale, Jr., Stephen Dunne, Roland Winters, Sue England, Lew L. Russell, Frances Chaney. *D:* Cyril Endfield; *P:* Hal E. Chester; *Adaptation:* Endfield; *Sc:* Henry Blankfort. (1:29) (video) Melodrama of a reporter who gets a job on a small town newspaper and finds the town wreaking with corruption, violence and injustice when a maid is accused of the murder of her employer. Based on the novel *The Big Story* by Craig Rice. (aka: *The Underworld Story*)

2972. Whirlwind (Columbia/Gene Autry Prods.; 1951). *Cast:* Gene Autry, Smiley Burnette, Gail Davis, Thurston Hall, Harry Lauter, Dick Curtis, Harry Harvey, Tommy Ivo, Gregg Barton, Kenne Duncan, Al Wyatt, Gary Goodwin, Pat O'Malley, Boyd Stockman, Bud Osborne, Frankie Marvin, Stan Jones, Leon DeVoe, Champion, Jr. (horse). *D:* John English; *P:* Armand Schaefer; *St: & Sc:* Norman S. Hall. (1:10) A series western of a postal inspector out to break up a crime ring. Originally ran as a co-feature on a double bill with *Five* (q.v.). Sepiatone.

2973. The Whistle at Eaton Falls (Columbia; 1951). *Cast:* Lloyd Bridges, Dorothy Gish (final film until 1963), Carleton Carpenter, Murray Hamilton, James Westerfield, Lenore Lonergan, Russell Hardie, Helen Shields, Ernest Borgnine, Parker Fennelly, Doro Merande, Diana Douglas, Anne Francis, Anne Seymour, Arthur O'Connell, Donald McKee, Joe Foley, Rev. Robert A. Dunn, Victor Sutherland, Herbert J. Moss, Lawrence Paquin, Andrew W. Donaldson, Seth Arnold, Joe Sullivan, Verne Davenport, John Farrell, James Nolan, William Kent, Bob Maher. *D:* Robert Siodmak; *P:* Louis de Rochemont; *Sc:* Lemist Esler, Virginia Shaler; *Song:* "Ev'ry Other Day" Carleton Carpenter; *Additional dialogue:* Leo Rosten, Lawrence J. Dugan, Leonard Heideman (all uncredited). (1:36) Drama in a documentary style of labor unrest at a New Hampshire plastics factory. Based on the research of J. Sterling Livingston. (G.B. title: *Richer Than the Earth*)

2974. Whistling Hills (Monogram/Frontier Picts.; 1951). *Cast:* Johnny Mack Brown, James Ellison, Noel Neill, Lee Roberts, I. Stanford Jolley, Marshall Reed, Lane Bradford, Pamela Duncan, Bud Osborne, Pierce Lyden, Frank Ellis, Ray Jones, Merrill McCormack. *D:* Derwin Abrahams; *P:* Vincent M. Fennelly; *St: & Sc:* Jack Lewis. (0:58) A series of stagecoach robberies are the focus of this entry in Brown's series of westerns for Monogram.

2975. White Christmas (Paramount; 1954). *Cast:* Bing Crosby (Bob Wallace), Danny Kaye (replacing Donald O'Connor/Phil Davis), Rosemary Clooney (Betty), Vera-Ellen (final U.S. film/Judy), Dean Jagger (General Waverly), Mary Wickes (Emma), John Brascia (Joe), Anne Whitfield (Susan), Richard Shannon (adjutant), Grady Sutton (general's guest), Sig Rumann (landlord), Robert Crosson (Albert), Herb Vigran (Novello), Dick Keene (assistant stage manager), Johnny Grant (Ed Harrison), Gavin Gordon (General Carlton), Marcel de la Brosse (maitre d'), James Parnell (sheriff), Percy Helton (conductor), Elizabeth Holmes (fat lady), Barrie Chase (Doris), I. Stanford Jolley (station master), George Chakiris (Specialty dancer), Mike P. Donovan, Glen Cargyle, Lorraine Crawford, Joan Bayley, Lester Clark, Ernest Flatt, Bea Allen. *D:* Michael Curtiz; *P:* Robert Emmett Dolan; *St: & Sc:* Norman Krasna, Norman Panama, Melvin Frank; *Songs:* "Count Your Blessings Instead of Sheep" (AAN-Best Song) by Crosby—reprised by Clooney; "Love, You Didn't Do Right By Me" by Clooney; "Choreography" by Kaye, Brascia and Vera-Ellen; "The Old Man," "Blue Skies," "Heat Wave" by Crosby, Kaye; "Minstrel Show and Mandy" by all, "Abraham" by Brascia, Vera-Ellen; "Sisters" by Clooney, Vera-Ellen and mimed by Crosby and Kaye; "Gee, I Wish I Was Back in the Army" by Crosby, Kaye, Clooney and Vera-Ellen; "What Can You Do With a General?" by Crosby; "The Best Things Happen While You're Dancing" by Kaye, Vera-Ellen; "Snow" by Crosby, Kaye, Clooney and Vera-Ellen; "Let Me Sing" by Crosby, Kaye and "White Christmas" by Crosby, Kaye, Clooney and Vera-Ellen. (2:00) (video/laserdisc) Romance and songs (15 new and old by Irving Berlin) highlight a tale of two army buddies attempting to help make their former commanding officer's winter resort a success. Indifferent critical reviews didn't affect the public's desire to see this holiday classic as it became one of the 27 top-grossing films of 1954-55, grossing almost $24,000,000 worldwide. To this day, the film still has a loyal following of fans. More or less a reworking of *Holiday Inn*, an acclaimed 1942 production from Paramount which originally introduced the song "White Christmas" and garnered the Oscar for "Best Song" that year. Paramount's first presentation in VistaVision. Technicolor.

2976. White Feather (20th Century–Fox/Panoramic Prods.; 1955). *Cast:* Robert Wagner, John Lund, Debra Paget, Jeffrey Hunter, Eduard Franz, Noah Beery, Jr., Virginia Leith, Emile Meyer, Hugh O'Brian, Milburn Stone, Iron Eyes Cody. *D:* Robert D. Webb; *P:* Robert L. Jacks; *Sc:* Delmer Daves, Leo Townsend.(1:42) Lavishly produced western of efforts to get the Cheyenne Indian tribe to move from Wyoming to a reservation to make way for encroaching white settlers. Based on the story "My Great-Aunt Appearing Day" by John Prebble which appeared in *Lilliput* magazine. Technicolor/ CinemaScope.

2977. The White Goddess (Lippert/Arrow Prods.; 1953). *Cast:* Jon Hall, Ray Montgomery, M'Liss McClure, Ludwig Stossel, Joel Fluellen, James Fairfax, Darby Jones, Lucian Prival, Robert Williams, Millicent Patrick. *D:* Wallace Fox; *P:* Rudolph Flothow; *St: & Sc:* Sherman L. Lowe, Eric Taylor. (1:13) A white doctor searches for jungle herbs in this cheapjack feature jungle adventure pieced together from TV episodes of *Ramar of the Jungle.* (G.B. title: *Ramar of the Jungle*)

2978. White Lightning (Monogram/Allied Artists; 1953). *Cast:* Stanley Clements, Steve Brodie, Gloria Blondell, Barbara Bestar, Lyle Talbot, Frank Jenks, Paul Bryar, Lee Van Cleef, Myron Healey, Riley Hill, Tom Hanlon, Jane Easton, John Bleifer, Duncan Richardson, Joel Marston. *D:* Edward Bernds; *P:* Ben Schwalb; *St: & Sc:* Charles R. Marion. (1:01) Sports melodrama of a hockey team with a hot shot player and mobsters interfering with bribes to make the team lose.

2979. The White Orchid (United Artists/Cosmos Prods.; 1954). *Cast:* William Lundigan, Peggie Castle, Armando Silvestre, Jorge Trevino, Rosenda Monteros, Alejandro de Montenegro, Miguel A. Gallardo. *D: & P:* Reginald LeBorg; *St: & Sc:* LeBorg, David Duncan; *Song:* "Femme Fatale" Chuy Hernandez (sung by de Montenegro and Gallardo in Spanish and by Don Durant in English). (1:21) Adventure melodrama of two explorers searching for a lost Toltec civilization in the jungles of Mexico who rescue a woman about to be sacrificed by a superstitious tribe of natives. Filmed on location in Eastmancolor.

2980. The White Squaw (Columbia/ Screen Gems, Inc.; 1956). *Cast:* David Brian, May Wynn, William Bishop, Nancy Hale, William Leslie, Myron Healey, Robert C. Ross, Frank DeKova, George Keymas, Roy Roberts, Grant Withers, Wally Vernon, Paul Birch, Neyle Morrow, Guy Teague. *D:* Ray Nazarro; *P:* Wallace MacDonald; *Sc:* Les Savage, Jr. (1:15) Western of a half-breed woman, raised by Sioux Indians who helps them save their land. Based on the story "The Gun Witch of Wyoming" by Larabie Sutter [aka: Les Savage, Jr.]. Originally ran on a double bill program with *Spin a Dark Web*, a British production.

The White Stallion *see* **The Outlaw Stallion**

2981. The White Tower (RKO; 1950). *Cast:* Glenn Ford, [Alida] Valli, Claude Rains, Oscar Homolka, Sir Cedric Hardwicke, Lloyd Bridges, June Clayworth, Lotte Stein, Fred Essler, Edit Angold. *D:* Ted Tetzlaff; *P:* Sid Rogell; *Sc:* Paul Jarrico. (1:38) (video) Drama of a group of people of varied nationalities and diverse backgrounds, all of who for different reasons attempt to ascend the titled obstacle in the French Alps where it was filmed on location. Based on the 1945 best-seller by James Ramsey Ullman. Technicolor.

2982. White Wilderness (Buena Vista/ Walt Disney Prods.; 1958). *D:-St: & Sc:* James Algar; *Ex.P:* Walt Disney; *P:* (AA-Best Documentary) Ben Sharpsteen; *Music:* (AAN) Oliver Wallace; *Cinematography:* James R. Simon, Hugh A. Wilmar, Lloyd Beebe, Herb and Lois Crisler, William Carrick, Tom McHugh, Carl Thomsen, Cecil Rhode, Dick Bird, Richard Tegstrom; *Editor:* Norman Palmer. (1:13) (video) Disney's final "True-Life" feature of the 1950s deals with the Arctic and the various forms of wildlife that abound there, including the walrus, polar bear, caribou, musk ox, wolverine, snowshoe rabbit, various types of birdlife and the ever-puzzling ritual mass suicide of a small rodent called the lemming, all photographed through seasonal changes. The combined efforts of eleven photographers over a three-year period. A box office winner, which Disney already knew despite his carping critics.

2983. White Witch Doctor (20th Century-Fox; 1953). *Cast:* Susan Hayward, Robert Mitchum, Walter Slezak, Mashood Ajala, Joseph C. Narcisse, Elzie Emanuel, Timothy Carey, Otis Greene, Charles Gemora (gorilla), Paul Thompson, Naaman Brown, Myrtle Anderson, Everett Brown, Dorothy Harris, Michael Ansara, Michael Granger, Leo C. Aldridge-Milas, Louis Polliman Brown, Floyd Shackleford, Henry Hastings, John Iboko, Gabriel Ukaegbu, Anyaogu, Elechukwu N. Njakar, Nnaemeka Akosa, Chukemeka Okeke, Jackie (lion, PATSY "Award of Excellence" in 1954). *D:* Henry Hathaway; *P:* Otto Lang; *Sc:* Ivan Goff, Ben Roberts. (1:36) Melodramatic jungle adventure of a white lady doctor ca. 1907 who heads into the African interior to treat the Bakuba tribe, while the men leading the expedition are only interested in stealing the fabled gold of the tribe. Based on the 1950 novel by Louise A. Stinetorf. Technicolor.

2984. Wichita (Allied Artists; 1955). *Cast:* Joel McCrea (Wyatt Earp), Vera Miles, Lloyd Bridges, Wallace Ford, Edgar Buchanan, Peter Graves (Morgan Earp), Keith Larsen (Bat Masterson), Carl Benton Reid, John Smith (James Earp), Walter McCoy, Walter Sande, Robert Wilke (Ben Thompson), Jack Elam, Mae Clarke, Gene Wesson, Rayford Barnes. *D:* Jacques Tourneur; *P:* Walter Mirisch; *As.P:* Richard Heermance; *St: & Sc:* Daniel Ullman; *Title song:* Hans Salter, Ned Washington (sung by Tex Ritter). (1:21) (video) In 1874, the town of Wichita, Kansas, is suffering from a major bout of lawlessness, especially from rowdy trail herders who like to shoot up the town when they get drunk. After a young boy is accidentally shot and killed, Wyatt Earp agrees to bring it all to an end. A hit for the studio. Technicolor/CinemaScope.

2985. Wicked Woman (United Artists/ World Films; 1953). *Cast:* Beverly Michaels, Richard Egan, Percy Helton, Evelyn Scott, Robert Osterloh, William Phillips, Frank Ferguson, Bernadene Hayes, Herb Jeffries. *D:* Russell Rouse; *P:* Clarence Greene; *Sc:* Greene, Rouse; *Songs:* "Wicked Woman" (sung by Jeffries), "One Night in Acapulco" Buddy Baker, Joe Mullendore. (1:17) Melodrama of a sultry woman and her various male conquests. Note: Considered "adult" entertainment in 1953.

2986. The Wild and the Innocent (Universal-International; 1959). *Cast:* Audie Murphy, Joanne Dru, Gilbert Roland, Sandra Dee, Jim Backus, Peter Breck, Wesley Marie Tackett, George Mitchell, Strother Martin, Betty Harford, Mel Leonard, Lillian Adams, Val Benedict, Steven Roberts, Tammy Windsor, Jim Sheppard, John Qualls, Ed Stroll, Frank Wolff, Rosemary Eliot, Louise Glenn, Barbara [Barboura] Morris. *D:* Jack Sher; *P: & St:* Sy Gomberg; *Sc:* Sher, Gomberg; *Song:* "A Touch of Pink" Diane Lampert, Richard Loring (sung by Murphy). (1:24) Offbeat western of the romance which blossoms between a trapper and a crude country girl in a wild and woolly town during a 4th of July celebration. The film had two prerelease titles: "The Wild Innocents" and "The Buckskin Kid and the Calico Gal." Eastmancolor/CinemaScope.

2987. The Wild Blue Yonder (Republic; 1951). *Cast:* Wendell Corey, Vera Ralston, Forrest Tucker, Phil Harris, Walter Brennan, William Ching, Ruth Donnelly, Harry Carey, Jr., Penny Edwards, Wally Cassell, James Brown, Richard Erdman, Philip Pine, Martin Kilburn, Hal Baylor, Joe Brown, Jr., Jack Kelly, Bob Beban, Peter Coe, Hall Bartlett, William Witney, David Sharpe, Paul Livermore, Jay Silverheels, Glenn Vernon, Joel Allen, Don Garner, Gayle Kellogg, Gil Herman, Freeman Lusk, Reed Hadley, Richard Avonde, Robert Karnes, Kathleen Freeman, Jim Leighton, Ray Hyke, John Hart, Paul McGuire, Robert Kent, Amy Iwanabe (VO), Andy Brennan, Bob Morgan, Steve Wayne, Stan Holbrook, Jack Sherman (VO), Myron Healey (VO). *D:* Allan Dwan; *P:* Herbert J. Yates; *St:* Andrew Geer, Charles Grayson; *Sc:* Richard Tregaskis; *Songs:* "The Thing" (sung by Harris), "The Man Behind the Armor-Plated Desk," "The U.S. Air Force" and "The Heavy Bomber Song" Robert Crawford, Victor Young, Ned Washington, Allan Dwan, Charles R. Green. (1:38) World War II drama of the men who fly the B-29 Superfortress, with two Army Air Corps officers doing their duty while a rivalry builds between them over an army nurse. A lack of returns at the box office. (G.B. title: *Thunder Across the Pacific*)

2988. The Wild Dakotas (Associated Film Distributors; 1956). *Cast:* Bill Williams, Coleen Gray, Jim Davis, John Litel, Dick Jones, Lisa Montell, John Miljan, I. Stanford Jolley, Wally Brown, Iron Eyes Cody, Billy Dix. *D:* Sam Newfield; *P:* Sigmund Neufeld; *Sc:* Thomas W. Blackburn. (1:13) Knowing there will be trouble from local Indians, a wagon scout opposes the leader of a wagon train who wants to settle his people on Indian land.

2989. Wild Heritage (Universal-International; 1958). *Cast:* Will Rogers, Jr., Maureen O'Sullivan, Rod McKuen, Casey Tibbs, Troy Donahue, Judi Meredith, Gigi Perreau, George Winslow (final film—ret. at age 12), Gary Gray, Jeanette Nolan, Paul Birch, John Beradino, Phil Harvey, Lawrence Dobkin, Stephen Ellsworth, Ingrid Goude, Christopher Dark, Guy Wilkerson. *D:* Charles Haas; *P:* John E. Horton; *Sc:* Paul King, Joseph Stone. (1:18) Family oriented western drama of the trials and tribulations of two families heading cross-country in covered wagons. Based on the short story "Death Rides the Trail" by Steve Frazee. Eastmancolor/CinemaScope.

2990. Wild Horse Ambush (Republic/ Valley Vista Prods.; 1952). *Cast:* Michael Chapin, Eilene Janssen, James Bell, Richard Avonde, Roy Barcroft, Julian Rivero, Movita (Castaneda), Drake Smith, Scott Lee, Alex Montoya, John

Daheim, Ted Cooper, Wayne Burson. *D:* Fred C. Brannon; *As.P:* Rudy Ralston; *St: & Sc:* William Lively. (0:54) A young boy and girl get involved in bringing a counterfeiting operation to an end. The 4th and final entry in the "Rough Ridin' Kids" western series, it ran on the bottom of a double bill with *Gobs and Gals* (q.v.).

2991. Wild Is the Wind (Paramount; 1957). *Cast:* Anna Magnani (AAN + "Best Actress" at the Berlin Film Festival/Gioia), Anthony Quinn (AAN/Gino), Anthony Franciosa (Bene), Dolores Hart (Angie), Joseph Calleia (Alberto), Lili Valenti (Teresa), James Flavin (wool buyer), Dick Ryan (priest), Joseph Vitale, Iphigenie Castiglioni, Ruth Lee, Frances Morris, Beauty (horse, #2 PATSY in 1958). *D:* George Cukor; *P:* Hal B. Wallis; *As.P:* Paul Nathan; *Sc:* Arnold Schulman; *Songs:* "Wild Is the Wind" (AAN-Best Song) Dimitri Tiomkin, Ned Washington (sung by Johnny Mathis), "Scapricciatiello" Pacifico Vento, Fernando Albano (sung by Magnani). (1:54) Drama of a widower who marries his sister-in-law. Set in the American West, the film is a remake of the 1946 Italian film *Furia*, based on the novel of that name by Vittorio Nino Novarese. VistaVision.

2992. The Wild North (MGM; 1952). *Cast:* Stewart Granger, Wendell Corey, Cyd Charisse, Morgan Farley, J.M. Kerrigan, Howard Petrie, Ray Teal, Houseley Stevenson, Lewis Martin, John War Eagle, Clancy Cooper, Henry Corden, Robert Stephenson, G. Pat Collins, Holmes Herbert, Cliff Taylor, Rex Lease. *D:* Andrew Marton; *P:* Stephen Ames; *Screenplay & Sc:* Frank Fenton [based on "When Terror Stalked Behind," a chapter in the 1930 book *Pioneers of Justice* by Walter W. Liggett]. (1:37) Popular outdoor adventure of a fur trapper, thought to be a murderer who is hunted by a Canadian Mountie. (aka: *The Big North*). Anscocolor.

2993. The Wild One (Columbia; 1954). *Cast:* Marlon Brando, Mary Murphy, Robert Keith, Lee Marvin, Jay C. Flippen, Peggy Maley, Hugh Sanders, Ray Teal, John Brown, Will Wright, Robert Osterloh, Robert Bice, William Vedder, Yvonne Doughty, Keith Clarke, Gil Stratton, Jr., Darren Dublin, Johnny Tarangelo, Jerry Paris, Gene Peterson, Alvy Moore, Harry Landers, Jim Connell, Don Anderson, Angela Stevens, Bruno VeSota, Pat O'Malley, Eve March, Wally Albright, Timothy Carey, John Doucette. *D:* Laslo Benedek; *P:* Stanley Kramer; *Sc:* John Paxton. (1:19) (video/laserdisc). Drama of events that transpire when a rowdy gang of forty motorcyclists ride into a small town. Inspired by *The Cyclists' Raid* by Frank Mooney, relating actual events that occurred on the 4th of July weekend of 1947 when thousands of bikers took over the small town of Hollister, California, and destroyed it.

2994. The Wild Party (United Artists/ Security Picts.; 1956). *Cast:* Anthony Quinn, Carol Ohmart, Arthur Franz, Nehemiah Persoff, Kathryn Grant, Jay Robinson, Paul Stewart, Barbara Nichols, Jana Mason, William Phipps, Maureen Stephenson, Nestor Paiva, Michael Ross, Carl Milletaire, James Bronte, Joe Greene, The Buddy DeFranco Quartet Combo (DeFranco, Buddy Bregman, Teddy Buckner, Pete Jolly). *D:* Harry Horner; *P:* Sidney Harmon; *St: & Sc:* John McPartland. (1:21) Crime melodrama with a jazz score by Buddy Bregman of various misfits who kidnap a man and his girl and hold them at a sleazy roadhouse. Originally paired on a double bill with *Running Target* (q.v.).

2995. Wild Stallion (Monogram; 1952). *Cast:* Ben Johnson, Edgar Buchanan, Martha Hyer, Hayden Rorke, Hugh Beaumont, Orley Lindgren, Don Haggerty, Susan Odin, I. Stanford Jolley, Barbara Woodell, John Halloran, Don Garner. *D:* Lewis D. Collins; *P:* Walter Mirisch; *As.P:* Richard Heermance; *St: & Sc:* Daniel B. Ullman. (1:10) After graduating from West Point, a young cavalry officer returns to the army post where he was raised after being orphaned in an Indian attack. Cinecolor.

2996. Wild Women of Wongo (Tropical Pictures; 1958). *Cast:* Jean Hawkshaw, Johnny Walsh, Mary Ann Webb, Cande Gerrard, Ed Fury, Adrienne [Barbeau] Bourbeau, Val Phillips, Roy Murray, Rex Richards, Pat Crowley, Steve Klisanin. *D:* James L. Wolcott; *P:* George R. Black; *St: & Sc:* Cedric Rutherford. (1:12) (video) The beautiful women of the isle of Wongo have ugly mates, while south of them the ugly women of the isle of Goona have handsome mates. This unintentionally humorous sexploitation item tells how the beautiful women of Wongo wound up with the handsome men of Goona and the ugly men of Wongo mated up with the ugly women of Goona. Filmed in Florida. Pathécolor. Note: The author has never viewed this film, but the plotline description alone sounds as though it has all the ingredients of a "so bad it's good" camp classic.

2997. Will Success Spoil Rock Hunter? (20th Century–Fox; 1957). *Cast:* Jayne Mansfield, Tony Randall, Betsy Drake, Joan Blondell, John Williams, Henry Jones, Lili Gentle, Mickey Hargitay, Georgia Carr, Groucho Marx (cameo), Dick Whittinghill, Ann McCrea, Lida Piazza, Bob Adler, Phil Chambers, Larry Kerr, Sherrill Terry, Mack Williams, Patrick Powell, Carmen Nisbit, Richard Deems, Don Corey (VO), Benny Rubin, Minta Durfee, Edith Russell, Alberto Morin, Louis Mercier. *D:-P:-St: & Sc:* Frank Tashlin (based on the 1956 play by George Axelrod); *Song:* "You Got It Made" Bobby Troup. (1:34) (video) Critically acclaimed biting (and hilarious) satire of 1950s' TV advertising and one man's rise to the top of the advertising profession when he gets a big star (Mansfield—reprising her Broadway role) to endorse a brand of lipstick. DeLuxe color/CinemaScope. (G.B. title: *Oh! For A Man!*)

Willie and Joe Back at the Front *see* **Back at the Front**

Win, Place and Show (G.B. title) *see* **Crazy Over Horses**

2998. Winchester '73 (Universal-International; 1950). *Cast:* James Stewart (Lin McAdam), Shelley Winters (Lola Manners), Dan Duryea (Waco Johnny Dean), Stephen McNally (Dutch Henry Brown), Millard Mitchell (High Spade), Charles Drake (Steve Miller), John McIntire (Joe Lamont), Will Geer (Wyatt Earp), Jay C. Flippen (Sgt. Wilkes), Rock Hudson (Young Bull), John Alexander (Jack Riker), Steve Brodie (Wesley), James Millican (Wheeler), Abner Biberman (Latigo Means), Anthony [Tony] Curtis (Doan), James Best (Crater), Gregg Martell (Mossman), Chuck Roberson (Long Tom), Carol Henry (Dudeen), Ray Teal (Marshal Noonan), Virginia Mullen (Mrs. Jameson), John Doucette (Roan Daley), Steve Darrell (Masterson), Ray Bennett (Charles Bender), Guy Wilkerson (Virgil), Bob Anderson (Bassett), Gary Jackson (Bunny Jameson), Bonnie Kay Eddy (Bonnie Jameson), Frank Chase, Chief Yowlachie, Frank Conlan, Larry Olsen, Edmund Cobb, Forrest Taylor, Ethan Laidlaw, Bud Osborne, Jennings Miles, John War Eagle, Duke York, Ted Mapes, Norman Kent, Norman Olestad, Tony Taylor, Tim Hawkins, Mel Archer, Bill McKenzie. *D:* Anthony Mann; *P:* Aaron Rosenberg; *St:* Stuart N. Lake; *Sc:* Robert L. Richards, Borden Chase. (1:32) (video/laserdisc) Acclaimed western drama of a man's attempts to retrieve his prized Winchester rifle, stolen by his brother. Remade for TV in 1967. One of the 28 top-grossing films of 1949-50.

2999. Wind Across the Everglades (Warner/Schulberg; 1958). *Cast:* Burl Ives, Christopher Plummer, Gypsy Rose Lee, George Voskovec, Tony Galento, Howard I. Smith, Emmett Kelly, Pat Henning, Chana Eden, Curt Conway, Peter Falk (film debut), Fred Grossinger, Sammy Renick, Toch Brown, MacKinlay Kantor, Frank Rothe, Mary Pennington, Cory Osceola, Mary Osceola, Hugh Parker, Brad Bradford, Dorothy Rogers, Sumner Williams, Tony Bruce. *D:* Nicholas Ray; *P:* Stuart Schulberg; *Sc:* Budd Schulberg [based on his story "Across the Everglades"]. (1:33) A drunken conservationist battles land developers and poachers in search of bird plummage for ladies' hats in the Florida Everglades at the turn-of-the-century. Filmed on location in Technicolor.

3000. Windjammer (National Theatres/Cinemiracle; 1958). *Cast:* Yngvar Kjelstrup, Lasse Kolstad (A.B.), Harald Tusberg (cadet), Sven Erik Libaek (cadet), Kaare Terland (cadet) + other officers and cadets of the *S.S. Christian Radich* and guest artists: Pablo Casals, Arthur Fiedler conducting the Boston "Pops" orchestra and Wilbur de Paris and His New Orleans Jazz Band. *D:* Louis de Rochemont III, Bill Colleran; *P:* Louis de Rochemont; *As.P:* Borden Mace, Thomas Orchard, Lothar Wolff; *Sc:* Capt. Alan Villiers [based on his story "The School of a Sea and Sailing a Square Rigger"], James L. Shute; *Cin:* Joseph Brun, Gayne Rescher, Colman T. Conroy, Jr., Finn Bergan, Asmund Revold and "Weegee" (the New York photography); *songs:* "Karl Waits for Me," "The Sea Is Green," "Everybody Loves Saturday Night," "The Village of New York," "Sweet Sugar Cane," "Don't Hurry-Worry Me," "Marianne" and "Life on the Ocean Wave" Terry Gilkyson, Richard Dehr, Frank Miller; "Song of the Birds" played by Casals, and "Piano Concerto in A Minor" Edvard Grieg. (2:07) Documentary/travelogue style adventure aboard the *Christian Radich*, a three-masted square-rigger, as it sails from Oslo, Norway, with a crew of 61 officers and cadets, following Columbus' route to the New World. The film placed #5 on the "10 Best" list of the NBR and received generally good critical reviews. Cinemiracle was a process similar to, but an improvement of, the Cinerama process, using a wide screen and three camera photography. Eastmancolor/Cinemiracle.

3001. The Wings of Eagles (MGM; 1957). *Cast:* John Wayne, Maureen O'Hara, Dan Dailey, Ward Bond, Ken Curtis, Edmund Lowe, Kenneth Tobey, James Todd, Barry Kelley, Sig Rumann, Henry O'Neill (final film—ret.), Willis Bouchey, Dorothy Jordan (final film—ret.), Peter Ortiz, Louis Jean Heydt, Tige Andrews, Dan Borzage, William Tracy (final film—ret.), Harlan Warde, Jack Pennick, Bill Henry, Alberto Morin, Mimi Gibson, Evelyn Rudie, Charles Trowbridge, Mae Marsh, Janet Lake, Fred Graham, Stuart Holmes, Olive Carey, Major Sam Harris, May McEvoy, William Paul Lowery, Chuck Roberson, James Flavin, Cliff Lyons, Veda Ann Borg, Christopher James. *D:* John Ford; *P:* Charles Schnee; *Sc:* Frank Fenton, William Wister Haines. (1:50) (video) Frank "Spig" Wead, a World War I flying pioneer who became a Hollywood screenwriter following a crippling accident is the focus of this cinema biography based on the life and writings of Commander Frank W. Wead, U.S.N. and his autobiography *Wings of Men.* MetroColor. Note: Ward Bond's character "John Dodge" is none other than a portrayal of the film's director John Ford, whose film *Airmail* (1932) had a story by Wead and the acclaimed *They Were Expendable* (1945) for which Wead wrote the screenplay.

3002. Wings of the Hawk (Universal-International; 1953). *Cast:* Van Heflin, Julia [Julie] Adams, George Dolenz, Abbe Lane, Antonio Moreno, Pedro Gonzales-Gonzales, Noah Beery, Jr., Rudolfo Acosta, Paul Fierro, Mario Siletti, Rico Alaniz, John Daheim, Ricardo Alba, Nancy Westbrook. *D:* Budd Boetticher; *P:* Aaron Rosenberg; *Sc:* James E. Moser [based on the adaptation by Kay Lenard of Gerald Drayson Adams' novel]. (1:20) Action-adventure of an American mining engineer who gets involved in the Mexican revolution of Pancho Villa. Technicolor and 3-D.

3003. Wink of an Eye (United Artists/ Ivar Prods.; 1958). *Cast:* Jonathan Kidd, Doris Dowling, Barbara Turner, Irene Seidner, Jaclynne Green, Wally Brown, Taylor Holmes, Max Rich, Paul Smith, Jack Grinnage, Lucien Littlefield (final film—d. 1960), Rodney Bell, Dick Nelson, Sam Levin, Howard Roberts, Henry Slate, Tom Browne Henry. *D:* Winston Jones; *P:* Fernando Carrerre; *St:* Chester Davis Jones; *Sc:* Robert Radnitz, Robert Presnell, Jr., James Edmiston. (1:12) Mystery melodrama with comic touches of a henpecked chemist who with the help of his secretary plans to do away with his annoying "better" half.

3004. Winning of the West (Columbia/ Gene Autry Prods.; 1953). *Cast:* Gene Autry, Gail Davis, Smiley Burnette (final film—ret.), Richard Crane, Robert Livingston, House Peters, Jr., Gregg Barton, William Fawcett, Ewing Mitchell, Rodd Redwing, Eddie Parker, Terry Frost, George Chesebro (final film—ret.), Boyd "Red" Morgan, Bob Woodward, Frank Jacquet, James Kirkwood, Charles Delaney, Charles Soldani, Champion, Jr. (horse). *D:* George Archainbaud; *P:* Armand Schaefer; *St: & Sc:* Norman S. Hall. (0:57) (video) Series western of a ranger out to put the crimps to a protection racket of which his kid brother is a member. Includes the songs: "Cowboy Blues," "Give Me My .45" and "Cowpoke Poking Along." Sepiatone.

3005. The Winning Team (Warner; 1952). *Cast:* Doris Day, Ronald Reagan (Grover Cleveland Alexander), Frank Lovejoy (Roger Hornsby), Eve Miller, Rusty [Russ] Tamblyn, James Millican, Gordon Jones, Hugh Sanders, Frank Ferguson, Walter Baldwin, Dorothy Adams, Bonnie Kay Eddy, James [Jimmie] Dodd, Fred Millican, Pat Flaherty, Tom Greenway, Frank McFarland, Arthur Page, Thomas Browne Henry, Larry Blake, Frank Marlowe, Kenneth Patterson, Glenn Turnbull, John Hedloe, Henry Blair, Gordon Clark, John Kennedy, Allan Wood, Alan Forster, Alex Sharpe, William Kalvino, Robert Orrell, Russ Clark, Bob Lemon (cameo), Peanuts Lowrey (cameo), Hank Sauer (cameo), Gene Mauch (cameo), Jerry Priddy (cameo), George Netkovich (cameo), Irving Noven (cameo), Al Zarilla (cameo). *D:* Lewis Seiler; *P:* Bryan Foy; *St:* Seeleg Lester, Merwin Gerard; *Sc:* Ted Sherdeman, Lester, Gerard; *Songs:* "Take Me Out to the Ball Game" Albert Von Tilzer, Jack Norworth, "I'll String Along with You" Al Dubin, Harry Warren, "Lucky Day" B.G. DeSylva, Lew Brown, Ray Henderson, "Ain't We Got Fun" Gus Kahn, Richard Whiting + "Jolly Old St. Nicholas." (1:38) (video/ laserdisc) Biographical drama of Hall of Fame baseball pitcher Grover Cleveland Alexander, his relationship with his wife and how both dealt with his alcoholism. The film recreates the day when Alexander led his team, the St. Louis Cardinals, on to win the 1926 World Series against the New York Yankees. Note: Alexander also suffered with epilepsy, a situation the studio chose to avoid mentioning in the film.

The Winning Way (G.B. title) *see* **The All-American**

3006. Wiretappers (EM–Continental Distributing/Great Commission; 1956). *Cast:* Bill Williams, Georgia Lee, Douglas Kennedy, Phil Tead, Stanley Clements, Ric Roman, Richard Benedict, Paul Picerni, Steve Conte, Melinda Plowman, Art Gilmore, Howard Wendell, Dorothy Kennedy, Barbara Hudson, Evangeline Carmichael. *D:* Dick Ross; *P:* Jim Vaus; *Sc:* John O'Dea. (1:20) Fact-based melodrama of a small time Mafia hood who turns his life around following a Christian conversion through evangelist Billy Graham. Based on the 1956 book *Why I Quit Syndicated Crime* by Jim Vaus [Jr.]. (aka: *The Jim Vaus Story*)

3007. With a Song in My Heart (20th Century–Fox; 1952). *Cast:* Susan Hayward (AAN + *Photoplay* "Gold Medal"/Jane Froman, voice dubbed by Jane Froman), Rory Calhoun (John Burns), David Wayne (Don Ross), Thelma Ritter (AAN-BSA/Clancy), Robert Wagner (G.I. paratrooper), Helen Westcott (Jennifer March), Una Merkel (Sister Maria), Richard Allan (dancer), Max Showalter [aka: Casey Adams/Guild], Lyle Talbot (radio director), Leif Erickson (general), Stanley Logan (diplomat), Frank Sully (Texas), George Offerman (Muleface), Ernest Newton (specialty), William Baldwin (announcer), Maude Wallace (Sister Margaret), Dick Ryan (officer), Douglas Evans (colonel), Beverly Thompson (USO girl), Eddie Firestone (USO man), Carlos Molina, Nestor Paiva, Emmett Vogan (doctors). *D:* Walter Lang; *P:-St: & Sc:* Lamar Trotti; *Music:* (AA) Alfred Newman; *Costumes:* (AAN-color) Charles LeMaire; *Sound:* (AAN) Thomas T. Moulton; *Songs:* "California, Here I Come" B.G. DeSylva, Al Jolson, Joseph Meyer; "Alabamy Bound" DeSylva, Jolson, Meyer, Bud Green; "Blue Moon," "With a Song in My Heart" Richard Rodgers, Lorenz Hart; "Dixie" Daniel D. Emmett; "Tea for Two" Irving Caesar, Vincent Youmans; "That Old Feeling" Sammy Fain, Lew Brown; "I've Got a Feelin' You're Foolin'" Nacio Herb Brown, Arthur Freed; "It's a Good Day" Dave Barbour, Peggy Lee; "I'll Walk Alone" Jule Styne, Sammy Cahn; "They're Either Too Young or Too Old" Frank Loesser, Arthur Schwartz; "Chicago" Fred Fisher; "America the Beautiful" Samuel Ward, Katherine Lee Bates; "I'm Through With Love" Gus Kahn, Matty Malneck, Fud Livingston; "On the Gay White Way" Ralph Rainger, Leo Robin; "Embraceable You" George and Ira Gershwin; "Jim's Toasted Peanuts," "Wonderful Home, Sweet Home" Ken Darby; "Get Happy" Ted Koehler, Harold Arlen; "Carry Me Back to Old Virginny" James Bland; "Give My Regards to Broadway" George M. Cohan; "Deep in the Heart of Texas" Don Swander, June Hershey; "The Right Kind of Love" Charles Henderson, Don George; "Maine Stein Song" Lincoln Colcord, E.A. Fenstad; "Montparnasse" Eliot Daniel, Alfred Newman; "Hoe That Corn" Jack Woodford, Max Showalter and "Back Home Again in Indiana" James F. Hanley, Ballard MacDonald; *Soundtrack "Background Groups":* The Skylarks, The Modernaires, The Melody Men, The King's Men, The Starlighters and The Four Girlfriends (all uncredited). (1:57) Musical biography of famed singer Jane Froman from the beginning of her career in 1936 to the plane crash that crippled her, followed by her determination to carry on despite her disability. The film was the recipient of *Photoplay's* "Gold Medal" and placed #9 on the "10 Best" list of *Film Daily*. The bevy of old standards made this a genuine audience pleaser and one of the 23 top-grossing films of 1951-52. Technicolor.

3008. With These Hands (Classic Pictures/Promotional Films Co., Inc.; 1950). *Cast:* Sam Levene, Arlene Francis, Alexander Scourby (film debut), Joseph Wiseman (film debut). *D:* Jack Arnold (directorial debut); *P:* (AAN-Best Documentary) Arnold, Lee Goodman; *Story idea:* Arnold; *Sc:* Morton Wishengrad. (0:50) A semi-documentary feature produced for the I.L.G.W.U. (International Ladies Garment Workers Union.)

Without Risk (G.B. title) *see* **Pecos River**

3009. Without Warning (United Artists/Allart Picts.; 1952). *Cast:* Adam Williams, Meg Randall, Edward Binns, Harlan Warde, John Maxwell, Angela Stevens, Byron Kane, Charles Tannen, Marilee Phelps, Robert Foulk, Connie Vera, Robert Shayne. *D:* Arnold Laven (directorial debut); *P:* Arthur Gardner, Jules Levey; *Sc:* Bill Raynor [based on material supplied by the Los Angeles Sheriff's Homicide Dept.]. (1:15) Melodrama of a spurned husband whose blonde wife ran off with another man. His solution—kill all lookalike blonde females with garden shears! (aka: *The Story Without a Name*). Originally paired on a double bill with *The Captive City* (q.v.).

3010. Witness for the Prosecution (United Artists/Edward Small–Arthur Hornblow Pictures; 1957). *Cast:* Tyrone Power (final film—d. 1958/Leonard Vole), Marlene Dietrich (Christina Vole), Charles Laughton (AAN/Sir

Wilfrid Robarts), Elsa Lanchester (AAN-BSA/Miss Plimsoll), John Williams (Brogan-Moore), Henry Daniell (Mayhew), Ian Wolfe (Carter), Una O'Connor (final film—d. 1959/ Janet McKenzie), Torin Thatcher (Mr. Myers), Francis Compton (judge), Norma Varden (Mrs. French), Philip Tonge (Inspector Hearne), Ruta Lee (Diana), Molly Roden (Miss McHugh), Ottola Nesmith (Miss Johnson), Marjorie Eaton (Miss O'Brien), J. Pat O'Malley (salesman). *D:* (AAN) Billy Wilder; *P:* (AAN-Best Picture) Arthur Hornblow, Jr.; *Adaptation:* Larry Marcus; *Sc:* Wilder, Harry Kurnitz; *Song:* "I May Never Go Home Anymore" Ralph Arthur Roberts, Jack Brooks; *Editor:* (AAN) Daniel Mandell; *Sound:* (AAN) Gordon Sawyer/Goldwyn Studio Sound Dept. (1:54) (video/laserdisc) Acclaimed drama with comic overtones of a crippled London barrister defending a man accused of the murder of a wealthy woman. Based on the story and play by Agatha Christie, it was placed #6 on the "10 Best" list of *Film Daily.* One of the 26 top-grossing films of 1957-58. Remade as a TV movie in 1982. Note: This was Tyrone Power's final completed film, as he died during production of *Solomon and Sheba*, with his footage reshot with Yul Brynner. Long shots of Power remain in that film.

3011. Witness to Murder (United Artists/Chester Erskine Pictures; 1954). *Cast:* Barbara Stanwyck, George Sanders, Gary Merrill, Jesse White, Harry Shannon, Claire Carleton, Lewis Martin, Dick Elliott, Harry Tyler, Juanita Moore, Joy Hallward, Gertrude Graner, Brad Trumbull, Hugh Sheraton, Fred Graham, Sam Edwards, Jean Fenwick, Adeline de Walt Reynolds (final film—ret.), Helen Kleeb, Ted Thorpe, Lyn Thomas. *D:* Roy Rowland; *P:-St: & Sc:* Chester Erskine; *Song:* Herschel Burke Gilbert, Sylvia Fine. (1:22) Suspense thriller of a woman who witnesses a murder, but finds the police don't believe her story as the killer has covered his tracks. When she finally finds evidence to back up her story, she becomes the killer's next target. Taut climax.

3012. Wolf Larsen (Allied Artists/Lindsley Parsons; 1958). *Cast:* Barry Sullivan, Peter Graves, Gita Hall, Thayer David, John Alderson, Rico Alaniz, Robert Gist, Jack Grinnage, Jack Orrison, Henry Rowland. *D:* Harmon Jones; *P:* Lindsley Parsons; *Sc:* Jack DeWitt, Turnley Walker. (1:23) (video) Low budget adaptation of Jack London's 1904 novel *The Sea Wolf*, of a tyrannical sea captain (Sullivan) who finally gets his come-uppance. First filmed in 1910 by the New York Motion Picture Co. as *The Sea Wolves*; six times as *The Sea Wolf*; Bosworth, 1913; Paramount, 1920; Ince-Triangle, 1925; Fox Film, 1930; Warner, 1941; and a 1993 made for cable TV feature. 1950 saw the story adapted to a western format in *Barricade* (q.v.), followed by a 1975 Italian production *Wolf of the Seven Seas* (U.S. title: *Wolf Larsen*) (aka: *Legend of the Sea Wolf*). Note: Filmed off the coast of California aboard a ship owned by actor Sterling Hayden.

3013. The Woman and the Hunter (Gross–Krasne–Phoenix/N.T.A. Pictures; 1957). *Cast:* Ann Sheridan, David Farrar, John Loder, Jan Merlin. *D:* George Breakston; *P: & Sc:* uncredited. (1:19) Melodrama of a romantic triangle which developed in the jungle of Kenya. (G.B. title: *Triangle on Safari*)

3014. Woman from Headquarters (Republic; 1950). *Cast:* Virginia Huston, Robert Rockwell, Barbara Fuller, Norman Budd, Frances Charles, K. Elmo Lowe, Otto Waldis, Grandon Rhodes, Jack Kruschen, Bert Conway, Marlo Dwyer, Sid Marion, John DeSimone, Gil Herman, Leonard Penn. *D:* George Blair; *P:* Stephen Auer; *St: & Sc:* Gene Lewis. (1:00) Crime melodrama of a female police officer and the situations she has to deal with on a day to day basis while on duty. Originally paired on a double bill program with *Destination Big House* (q.v.).

3015. Woman in the Dark (Republic; 1952). *Cast:* Penny Edwards, Ross Elliott, Rick Vallin, Richard Benedict, Argentina Brunetti, Martin Garralaga, Edit Angold, Peter Brocco, Barbara Billingsley, John Doucette, Richard Irving, Lute Crockett, Carl Thompson, Charles Sullivan. *D:* George Blair; *P:* Stephen Auer; *Sc:* Albert DeMond. (1:00) Programmer melodrama of a family of three brothers, one a priest, one a lawyer and the third who can't keep out of trouble. Based on the play by Nicholas Cosentino.

3016. Woman Obsessed (20th Century–Fox; 1959). *Cast:* Susan Hayward, Stephen Boyd, Barbara Nichols, Dennis Holmes, Theodore Bikel, Ken Scott, Arthur Franz, James Philbrook, Florence MacMichael, Jack Raine, Mary Carroll, Fred Graham, Mike Lally, Richard Monahan, Dainty Doris, Harry "Duke" Johnson, Lou Manley, Tommy Farrell, Freeman Morse, Jimmy Ames, Al Hustin. *D:* Henry Hathaway; *P: & Sc:* Sydney Boehm. (1:42) Melodrama of a widow who marries a widower who shows contempt for her son, leading to marital discord. Based on the 1958 novel *The Snow Birch* by John Mantley, the film is set in the backwoods of Canada, but is filmed in the Sierra Madre mountains of California. DeLuxe color/CinemaScope.

3017. A Woman of Distinction (Columbia; 1950). *Cast:* Ray Milland, Rosalind Russell, Edmund Gwenn, Janis Carter, Mary Jane Saunders, Jerome Courtland, Francis Lederer, Alex Gerry, Charles Evans, Charlotte Wynters, Clifton Young, Jean Willes, Gale Gordon, Lucille Ball (cameo), Myron Healey, Charles Trowbridge, Harry Strang, Wanda McKay, Elizabeth Flournoy, Harry Tyler, Robert Malcolm, William E. Green, Harry Cheshire, Dudley Dickerson, Gail Bonney, John Smith, Billy Newell, Richard Bartell, Charles Jordan, Larry Barton, Donald Kerr, Ted Jordan, Harry Harvey, Jr., Maxine Gates, Lucille Brown, Walter Sande, Marie Blake [aka: Blossom Rock], Ed Keane, Lois Hall, Mira McKinney, Lelah Tyler, Napoleon Whiting, Wilda Biber, Kathryn Moore, Patricia Reynolds, Ethel Sway, Elaine Towne. *D:* Edward Buzzell; *P:* Buddy Adler; *St:* Hugo Butler, Ian McClellan Hunter; *Sc:* Charles Hoffman, Ray Singer (unc.), Dick Chevillat (unc.); *Additional dialogue:* Frank Tashlin. (1:25) (video/laserdisc) Romantic comedy of a scandalous affair at a woman's college.

3018. Woman of the North Country (Republic; 1952). *Cast:* Rod Cameron, Ruth Hussey, John Agar, Gale Storm (final film—to TV), J. Carrol Naish, Jim Davis, Jay C. Flippen, Taylor Holmes, Barry Kelley, Grant Withers, Howard Petrie, Hank Worden, Virginia Brissac, Stephen Bekassy. *D: & P:* Joseph Kane; *St:* Charles Marquis Warren, Prescott Chaplin; *Sc:* Norman Reilly Raine; *Songs:* "Jimmy Crack Corn" [aka: "Blue Tail Fly"] credited (1846) Daniel Decatur Emmett; "Erie Canal" traditional, ca. 1825. (1:30) Melodrama of a mining camp owner and his dilemma with a ruthless female rival who is determined to put him out of business. Trucolor.

3019. Woman on the Run (Universal-International/Fidelity Pictures; 1950). *Cast:* Ann Sheridan, Dennis O'Keefe, Robert Keith, Frank Jenks, John Qualen, Ross Elliott, J. Farrell MacDonald, Thomas P. Dillon, Joan Shawlee, Steven Geray, Reiko Sato, Victor Sen Yung. *D:* Norman Foster: *P:* Howard Welsch; *Sc:* Foster, Alan Campbell. (1:17) (video) Acclaimed low budget melodrama of a woman in search of her husband, the sole witness to a gangland rubout. Based on a story by Sylvia Tate which appeared in *American Magazine* in April 1948, it was filmed on location in San Francisco, CA.

3020. The Woman They Almost Lynched (Republic; 1953). *Cast:* John Lund, Brian Donlevy (Wm. Quantrill), Audrey Totter, Joan Leslie, Ben Cooper (Jesse James), Nina Varela, James Brown (Frank James), Ellen Corby, Fern Hall, Minerva Urecal, Jim Davis (Cole Younger), Reed Hadley, Ann Savage (final film—ret.), Virginia Christine, Marilyn Lindsey, Nacho Galindo, Richard Simmons, Gordon Jones, Post Park, Frank Ferguson, Richard Crane, Ted Ryan, James Kirkwood, Tom McDonough, Carl Pitti, Joe Yrigoyen, Jimmie Hawkins, Paul Livermore, Hal Baylor. *D: & P:* Allan Dwan; *Ex.P:* Herbert J. Yates; *Sc:* Steve Fisher; *Songs:* Victor Young, Peggy Lee, Sam Stept, Sidney Mitchell. (1:30) A woman inherits a saloon in a western town, but when she goes to claim it, she is framed by local crooks and is suspected of being a Confederate spy. Based on the story of the same name by Michael Fessier which appeared in *Saturday Evening Post* June 1, 1951.

Woman with a Whip *see* **Forty Guns**

3021. A Woman's Devotion (Republic; 1956). *Cast:* Ralph Meeker, Janice Rule, Paul Henreid, Rosenda Monteros, Fanny Schiller, Jose Torvay, Yerye Beirute, Tony Carvajal, Jaime Gonzalez, Carlos Requelme. *D:* Paul Henreid; *P:* John Bash; *St: & Sc:* Robert Hill; *Song:* Les Baxter, Gwen Davis. (1:28) (video) A man suffering from the aftereffects of his World War II experience, is honeymooning with his wife in Acapulco, Mexico, when he is suspected in the murders of two women. Trucolor. (G.B. title: *War Shock*) (video title: *Battle Shock*)

3022. A Woman's World (20th Century-Fox; 1954). *Cast:* Clifton Webb, June Allyson, Van Heflin, Lauren Bacall, Fred MacMurray, Arlene Dahl, Cornel Wilde, Elliott Reid, Margalo Gillmore, Alan Reed, David Hoffman, George Melford, Eric Wilton, Conrad Feia, George E. Stone, George Eldredge, Paul Power, William Tannen, Jonathan Hole, Rodney Bell, Carleton Young, Beverly Thompson, Eileen Maxwell, Mclinda Markey, Maudie Prickett, Kathryn Card, Anne Kunde, Jean Walters, Janet Stewart, Billie Bird, Jarma Lewis, George Spaulding, Edward Astran, Marc Snow, Bert Stevens. *D:* Jean Negulesco; *P:* Charles Brackett; *Sc:* Claude Binyon, Mary Loos, Richard Sale; *Additional* *dialogue:* Howard Lindsey, Russell Crouse; *Song:* "It's a Woman's World" Cyril J. Mockridge, Sammy Cahn (sung by the Four Aces and a big hit). (1:34) (video) Drama of the head of an auto manufacturing company who must pick a new sales manager for his company and determines which of three vice presidents would be suitable for the job by judging the men's wives as opposed to the men themselves. Based on the story "May the Best Wife Win" by Mona Williams. Technicolor/CinemaScope.

3023. The Women of Pitcairn Island (20th Century–Fox/Regal Films; 1956). *Cast:* James Craig, Lynn Bari, John Smith, Arleen Whelan, Sue England, Rico Alaniz, John Stevens, Carol Thurston, Sonia Sorel, Charlita, Lorna Thayer, Roxanne Reed, Millicent Patrick, Harry Lauter, Pierce Lyden, Henry Rowland, Paul Sorenson, House Peters, Jr., Richard Devon, Rad Fulton, Michael Miller, Robert Cabal, Robert Kendall, Joel Collins, Tim Johnson. *D:* Jean Yarbrough; *P:* Yarbrough, Aubrey Wisberg; *St:* & *Sc:* Wisberg. (1:12) Melodrama which purports to tell what happened after *The Mutiny on the Bounty* (1935) with the women and children of the mutineers arriving on Pitcairn island where they are harassed by a band of ruthless pirates who have survived a shipwreck. Regalscope.

3024. Women's Prison (Columbia; 1955). *Cast:* Ida Lupino, Jan Sterling, Cleo Moore, Audrey Totter, Phyllis Thaxter, Howard Duff, Warren Stevens, Barry Kelley, Gertrude Michael, Vivian Marshall, Mae Clarke, Ross Elliott, Adele August, Don C. Harvey, Juanita Moore, Edna Holland, Mira McKinney, Lynne Millan, Mary Newton, Diane DeLaire, Frances Morris, Jana Mason, Lorna Thayer, Murray Alper, Ruth Vann, Mary Lou Devore, Eddie Foy III. *D:* Lewis Seiler; *P:* Bryan Foy; *St:* Jack DeWitt; *Sc:* DeWitt, Crane Wilbur. (1:20) Melodrama of a riot in a women's prison incited by the actions of the prison's psychotic warden (Lupino).

3025. The Wonderful Country (United Artists/D.R.M. Prods.; 1959). *Cast:* Robert Mitchum, Julie London, Gary Merrill, Pedro Armendariz, Jack Oakie, Albert Dekker, Charles McGraw, John Banner, Jay Novello, Mike Kellin, Tom Lea, Victor Mendoza, Satchel Paige, Max Slaten, Joe Haworth, Chester Hayes, Chuck Roberson, Anthony Caruso, Claudio Brook. Judy Marsh, Mike Luna. *D:* Robert Parrish; *P:* Chester Erskine; *Sc:* Robert Ardrey. (1:36) Western actioner (filmed on location in Mexico) of a gunrunner between the U.S. and Mexico who also has the hots for the wife of the head of the Texas Rangers. Based on the 1952 novel by Tom Lea. Technicolor.

The Wonderful Years (G.B. title) *see* **The Restless Years**

3026. World for Ransom (Allied Artists/Plaza; 1954). *Cast:* Dan Duryea, Gene Lockhart, Patric Knowles, Reginald Denny, Nigel Bruce (final film—d. 1953), Marian Carr, Douglass Dumbrille, Keye Luke, Charlie Lung, Lou Nova, Arthur Shields, Carmen D'Antonio. *D:* Robert Aldrich; *P:* Aldrich, Bernard Tabakin; *St:* Lindsay Hardy; *Sc:* Hardy, Hugo Butler (unc.); *Song:* "Too Soon" Walter Samuels. (1:22) Film noir of a private detective who gets involved in the kidnapping of a nuclear physicist in Singapore. A feature length film adapted from the old TV series *China Smith* (starring Duryea), it was originally shown on a double bill program with *Dragonfly Squadron* (q.v.).

3027. The World in His Arms (Universal-International; 1952). *Cast:* Gregory Peck, Ann Blyth, Anthony Quinn, John McIntire, Eugenie Leontovich, Carl Esmond, Andrea King, Hans Conried, Rhys Williams, Bill Radovich, Sig Rumann, Gregory Gay, Henry Kulky, Gregg Barton, Bryan Forbes, Gregg Martell, Carl Andre, George Scanlon, Carl Harbaugh, Frank Chase, Eve Whitney, Millicent Patrick, Syl Lamont, Leo Mostovoy, Wee Willie Davis. *D:* Raoul Walsh; *P:* Aaron Rosenberg; *Sc:* Borden Chase; *Additional dialogue:* Horace McCoy. (1:44) Lavish romantic action drama of an American seal poacher and a Russian countess seeking to escape an arranged marriage. Critically acclaimed, it was set in mid–19th century San Francisco and was based on the novel of 1946 by Rex Beach. Technicolor. Note: The source material for this film was Mr. Beach's final completed novel prior to his death in 1949.

3028. World in My Corner (Universal-International; 1956). *Cast:* Audie Murphy, Barbara Rush, Jeff Morrow, John McIntire, Tommy Rall, Howard St. John, Chico Vejar, Steve Ellis, Cisco Andrade, Baby Ike, Sheila Bromley, Dani Crayne, H. Tommy Hart, James F. Lennon, Art Aragon, Freddie Herman, Sammy Shack, Pat Miller. *D:* Jesse Hibbs; *P:* Aaron Rosenberg; *St:* Jack Sher, Joseph Stone; *Sc:* Sher. (1:22) Melodrama of a promising welterweight boxer who finds himself involved in the seamier side of the sport. Originally paired on a double bill with *Red Sundown* (q.v.).

3029. The World, the Flesh and the Devil (MGM/Sol C. Siegel–Harbel; 1959). *Cast:* Harry Belafonte, Inger Stevens, Mel Ferrer. *D: & Sc:* Ranald MacDougall; *P:* George Englund. (1:35) (video) Fantasy-drama of a black man trapped in a mine cave-in in Pennsylvania for five days who emerges to find there are no other people, gets a car, heads to Manhattan and finds things the same there and learns atomic war was responsible. He then finds two others alive in the city. Partially filmed in New York City, the critics were impressed for the most part. Based on the story "The End of the World" by Ferdinand Reyher which was suggested by the 1902 novel *The Purple Cloud* by Matthew Phipps Shiel. CinemaScope.

3030. The World Was His Jury (Columbia/Clover Prods.; 1958). *Cast:* Edmond O'-Brien, Mona Freeman (final film—ret.), Karin Booth, Robert McQueeney, Paul Birch, John Beradino, Richard H. Cutting, Harvey Stephens, Carlos Romero, Gay Goodwin, Hortense Petra, Kelly Junge, Jr. *D:* Fred F. Sears; *P:* Sam Katzman; *St: & Sc:* Herbert Abbott Spiro. (1:22) Programmer melodrama of an attorney defending a sea captain charged with negligence in a ship disaster which claimed 162 lives. Utilizes footage from the sea disaster climax from *Dante's Inferno* (Fox Film; 1935).

3031. World Without End (Allied Artists; 1956). *Cast:* Hugh Marlowe, Nancy Gates, Nelson Leigh, Rod Taylor, Shawn Smith, Lisa Montell, Christopher Dark, Booth Colman, Everett Glass, Stanley Fraser, William Vedder, Rankin Mansfield, Paul Brinegar, Mickey Simpson. *D:* Edward Bernds; *P:* Richard Heermance; *St: & Sc:* Bernds. (1:20) Science fiction of four astronauts on a test flight who find themselves on the earth in the year 2508 after it has been ravaged by nuclear war and encounter the various life forms, including cyclopean mutants, giant spiders and a subterranean society. Technicolor/CinemaScope.

3032. The Wreck of the Mary Deare (MGM/Julian Blaustein Prods.–Baroda Prods.; 1959). *Cast:* Gary Cooper (final U.S. film—d. 1961), Charlton Heston, Michael Redgrave, Emlyn Williams, Cecil Parker, Alexander Knox, Virginia McKenna, Richard Harris, Ben Wright, Peter Illing, Terence De Marnay, Ashley Cowan, Charles Davis, Alexander Archdale, John Le Mesurier, Louis Mercier, Albert Carrier, Lilyan Chauvin, Paul Bryar, Lomax Study, Jean Del Val, Kalu K. Sonkur, Noel Drayton, Charles Lamb, John Dearth, George Dee. *D:* Michael Anderson (replacing Alfred Hitchcock); *P:* Julian Blaustein; *Sc:* Eric Ambler. (1:45) (video/laserdisc) A U.S.A./British co-production, this drama based on the 1956 novel by Hammond Innes details conflict in the efforts to salvage a wrecked ship. MetroColor/CinemaScope.

3033. Written on the Wind (Universal-International; 1956). *Cast:* Rock Hudson (Mitch Wayne), Lauren Bacall (Lucy Moore Hadley), Robert Stack (AAN-BSA/Kyle Hadley), Dorothy Malone (AA-BSA/Marylee Hadley), Robert Keith (Jasper Hadley), Grant Williams (Biff Miley), Robert J. Wilke (Dan Willis), Edward C. Platt (Dr. Paul Cochrane), Harry Shannon (Hoak Wayne), John Larch (Roy Carter), Roy Glenn (Sam), Maidie Norman (Bertha), Joseph Granby (R.J. Courtney), Susan Odin (Marylee as a girl), Robert Lyden (Kyle as a boy), Robert Winans (Mitch as a boy), Dani Crayne, Jane Howard, Floyd Simmons, Cynthia Patrick, Joanne Jordan, William Schallert, Robert Brubaker, Bert Holland, Don C. Harvey, Carl Christian, Gail Bonney, Paul Bradley, Dorothy Porter, Robert Malcolm, Glen Kramer, Phil Harvey, Coleen McClatchey, Carlene King Johnson, Kevin Corcoran, June Valentine, Hedi Duval, George DeNormand. *D:* Douglas Sirk; *P:* Albert Zugsmith; *Sc:* George Zuckerman (based on the 1946 novel by Robert Wilder); *Title song:* (AAN-Best Song) Victor Young, Sammy Cahn (sung by the Four Aces). (1:39) (video) Acclaimed melodrama of various members of a self-destructive wealthy Texas oil family. One of the 24 top-grossing films of 1956-57. Technicolor.

The Wrong Kind of Girl *see* **Bus Stop**

3034. The Wrong Man (Warner; 1956). *Cast:* Henry Fonda, Vera Miles, Anthony Quayle, Harold J. Stone, Esther Minciotti, Charles Cooper, Nehemiah Persoff, Laurinda Barrett, Norma Connolly, Doreen Lang, Frances Reid, Lola D'Annunzio, Robert Essen, Kippy Campbell, Dayton Lummis, John Heldabrand, Richard Robbins, John Vivyan, Will Hare, Werner Klemperer, Mel Dowd, Peggy Webber, Anna Karen, Michael Ann Barrett, Alexander Lockwood, Emerson Treacy, Bill Hudson, Marc May, William Le Massena, William Crane, Josef Draper, Leonard Capone, Charles J. Guiotta, Thomas J. Murphy, Harold Berman, John Caler, Silvio Minciotti, Barry Atwater, Dino

Terranova, Rossana San Marco, Daniel Ocko, Olga Fabian, Otto Simanek, Dave Kelly, Maurice Manson, John McKee, Gordon Clark, Paul Bryar, Sammy Armaro, Allan Ray, John Truax, Richard Bennett, Clarence Straight, Don Turner, Penny Santon, Bonnie Franklin, Pat Morrow, Charles Aidman, Richard Durham, [Harry] Dean Stanton (film debut), Mike Keene, Frank Schofield, Chris Gampel, Maurice Wells, Helen Shields, Don McGovern, Cherry Hardy, Elizabeth Scott, Walter Kohler, Spencer Davis, Ed Bryce, Harry Beckman, Maria Reid, Paul Carr, Tuesday Weld, Barbara Karen, Dallas Midgette, Donald May, John C. Becher, Earl George, Mary Boylan, Natalie Priest, Rhodelle Heller, Olive Stacey, John Stephen. *D: & P:* Alfred Hitchcock; *Sc:* Maxwell Anderson, Angus MacPhail. (1:45) (video/laserdisc) Circumstances and evidence pile up against a bass player at New York's Stork Club, as being responsible for the robbery of an insurance office, though he was not. The stress of the whole situation sends his wife's mental state over the edge. Based on *The True Story of Christopher Emmanuel Balestrero* by Mr. Anderson, a nonfiction work. Filmed on location in New York where the real incidents occurred, including the Stork Club, Mr. Balestrero's apartment, etc. Note: For those who look for the traditional Hitchcock "cameo" in his films, they need not look in this one.

3035. Wyoming Mail (Universal-International; 1950). *Cast:* Stephen McNally, Alexis Smith, Roy Roberts, Howard De Silva, Ed Begley, Dan Riss, Whit Bissell, James Arness, Armando Silvestre, Richard Jaeckel, Frankie Darro, Felipe Turich, Richard Egan, Gene Evans, Frank Fenton, Emerson Treacy. *D:* Reginald LeBorg; *P:* Aubrey Schenck; *St:* Robert Hardy Andrews; *Sc:* Harry Essex, Leonard Lee; *Songs:* "Endlessly" and "Take Me to Town" Dan Shapiro, Lester Lee. (1:27) Western of a postal inspector who poses as an escaped bank robber to get the goods on a gang of postal thieves. Technicolor.

3036. Wyoming Renegades (Columbia; 1955). *Cast:* Phil Carey, Gene Evans (Butch Cassidy), Martha Hyer, William Bishop (Sundance Kid), Roy Roberts, Douglas Kennedy, Don Beddoe, Aaron Spelling, John Cason, Harry Harvey, Don C. Harvey, Boyd Stockman, George Keymas, Mel Welles, Henry Rowland, Don Carlos, Guy Teague (Black Jack Ketchum), Bob Woodward. *D:* Fred F. Sears; *P:* Wallace MacDonald; *St: & Sc:* David Lang. (1:13) Programmer western (with a twist ending) of a former outlaw's attempts to go straight with the help of a girl. Technicolor.

3037. Wyoming Roundup (Monogram; 1952). *Cast:* Whip Wilson, Tommy Farrell, Phyllis Coates, Henry Rowland, House Peters, Jr., I. Stanford Jolley, Richard Emory, Bob Wilke, Stanley Price. *D:* Thomas Carr; *P:* Vincent M. Fennelly; *St: & Sc:* Daniel B. Ullman. (0:53) Ranchers are being harassed by "Hired Guns," which was the pre-release title of this entry in Wilson's series.

3038. A Yank in Indo-China (Columbia/Esskay Prods.; 1952). *Cast:* John Archer, Douglas Dick, Jean Willes, Maura Murphy, Hayward Soo Hoo, Don C. Harvey, Harold Fong, Rory Mallison, Leonard Penn, Pierre Watkin, Kam Tong, Peter Chong. *D:* Wallace A. Grissell; *P:* Sam Katzman; *St: & Sc:* Samuel Newman. (1:07) Two air freight flyers decide to take on the communists in this low budget war/action drama. (G.B. title: *Hidden Secret*) Originally ran on a double bill with *The Thief of Damascus* (q.v.).

3039. A Yank in Korea (Columbia; 1951). Cast: Lon McCallister, William "Bill" Phillips, Brett King, Larry Stewart, William Tannen, Tommy Farrell, Norman Wayne, Rusty Wescoatt, William Haade, Sunny Vickers, Richard Paxton, Ralph Hodges, Richard Gould. *D:* Lew Landers; *P:* Sam Katzman; *St:* Leo Lieberman; *Sc:* William B. Sackheim. (1:13) Low budget war drama of the Korean "police action" and one soldier's carelessness that endangers the rest of the company. (G.B. title: *Letter from Korea*)

3040. Yankee Buccaneer (Universal-International; 1952). *Cast:* Jeff Chandler, Scott Brady, Suzan Ball, Joseph Calleia, George Mathews, Rudolfo Acosta, James Parnell, David Janssen, Jay Silverheels, Michael Ansara, Joseph Vitale. *D:* Frederick de Cordova; *P:* Howard Christie; *St: & Sc:* Charles K. Peck, Jr. (1:26) Technicolor swashbuckler of a U.S. frigate in search of pirates in the Caribbean.

3041. Yankee Pasha (Universal-International; 1954). *Cast:* Jeff Chandler, Rhonda Fleming, Mamie Van Doren, Bart Roberts [aka: Rex Reason], Lee J. Cobb, Christiane Martel ["Miss Universe"], Tudor Owen, Arthur Space, Benny Rubin, Philip Van Zandt, Harry Lauter, Forbes Murray, John Day, Myrna Hansen ["Miss United States"], Kinuko Ito ["Miss Japan"], Emita Arosemena ["Miss Panama"], Synove Gulbrandsen

["Miss Norway"], Alicia Ibanez ["Miss Uruguay"], Ingrid Mills ["Miss South Africa"], Maxine Morgan ["Miss Australia"]. *D:* Joseph Pevney; *P:* Howard Christie; *Adaptation: & Sc:* Joseph Hoffman. (1:24) Swords, sand and a bevy of beautiful women (contestants from the "Miss Universe" pageant) are some of the ingredients in this swashbuckler of a girl taken from New England by pirates and sold into a Moroccan harem and the adventurer who sets out to rescue her. Based on *Yankee Pasha: The Adventures of Jason Starbuck*, a 1941 novel by Edison Marshall. Technicolor.

3042. Yaqui Drums (Allied Artists/Wm. F. Broidy Prods.; 1956). *Cast:* Rod Cameron, Mary Castle, J. Carrol Naish, Robert Hutton, Roy Roberts, Keith Richards, Denver Pyle, Ray Walker, Donald Kerr, John Merrick, Paul Fierro, G. Pat Collins, Fred Gabourie, Saul Gorss. *D:* Jean Yarbrough; *P:* William F. Broidy; *St:* Paul L. Peil; *Sc:* Jo Pagano, D.D. Beauchamp. (1:11) Programmer western of a corrupt saloon owner who is opposed by a rancher and a gang of Mexican outlaws who muffed a stagecoach robbery.

3043. The Yellow Cab Man (MGM; 1950). *Cast:* Red Skelton, Gloria DeHaven, Walter Slezak, Edward Arnold, James Gleason, Jay C. Flippen, Paul Harvey, Polly Moran (final film—d. 1952), Guy [Herbert] Anderson, John Butler, John Indrisano. *D:* Jack Donohue; *P:* Richard Goldstone; *St:* Devery Freeman; *Sc:* Freemen, Albert Beich; *Additional dialogue:* Edward Sedgewick (unc.). (1:25) (video) Hit comedy of the accident prone inventor of a new unbreakable glass that gets involved with gangsters and murder.

3044. Yellow Fin (Monogram; 1951). *Cast:* Wayne Morris, Adrian Booth, Gloria Henry, Damian O'Flynn, Gordon Jones, Paul Fierro, Nacho Galindo, Warren Douglas, Guy Zanette. *D:* Frank McDonald; *P:* Lindsley Parsons; *St: & Sc:* Warren D. Wandberg, Clint Johnson. (1:14) Low budget action-drama of a tuna fishing family with a run of bad luck.

3045. The Yellow Mountain (Universal-International; 1954). *Cast:* Lex Barker, Mala Powers, Howard Duff, William Demarest, John McIntire, Leo Gordon, Dayton Lummis, Hal K. Dawson, William Fawcett, James Parnell. *D:* Jesse Hibbs; *P:* Ross Hunter; *Adaptation:* Robert Blees; *Sc:* George Zuckerman, Russell Hughes. (1:18) Western of two men who squabble over a girl and a gold mine. Based on the story "Nevada Gold" by Harold Channing Wire which appeared in *Blue Book*. Technicolor.

3046. The Yellow Tomahawk (United Artists/Bel-Air–K.B. Prods.; 1954). *Cast:* Rory Calhoun, Peggie Castle, Noah Beery, Jr., Warner Anderson, Peter Graves, Lee Van Cleef, Rita Moreno, Walter Reed, Dan Riss, Adam Williams, Ned Glass. *D:* Lesley Selander; *P:* Howard W. Koch; *St:* Harold Jack Bloom; *Sc:* Richard Alan Simmons. (1:22) The friendship between an army scout and an Indian is tested when cavalry troops attack an Indian village and the Indians retaliate. Color Corp. of America. Originally paired on a double bill with *Captain Kidd and the Slave Girl* (q.v.).

3047. Yellowneck (Republic/Empire Studios; 1955). *Cast:* Lin McCarthy, Stephen Courtleigh, Berry Kroeger, Harold Gordon, Bill Mason. *D: & St:* R. John Hugh; *P:* Harlow G. Frederick; *Sc:* Nat C. Linden. (1:23) Low budget independent melodrama set in the 1860s of five deserting Confederate soldiers who attempt to make their way through the perilous Everglades of Florida to safety in Cuba. Trucolor.

3048. Yellowstone Kelly (Warner; 1959). *Cast:* Clint Walker (title role), Edward [Edd] Byrnes, John Russell, Ray Danton, Claude Akins, Rhodes Reason, Andra Martin, Gary Vinson, Warren Oates, Harry Shannon. *D:* Gordon Douglas; *P:* Unc.; *Sc:* Burt Kennedy. (1:31) Hit western drama (largely due to the star's popularity on Warner's *Cheyenne* TV series) of a fur-trapper caught in the middle of U.S. Cavalry–Indian hostilities. Based on the 1957 novel by Clay Fisher, it was filmed on location in the San Francisco Peaks area. Technicolor.

3049. Yes Sir, Mr. Bones (Lippert/Spartan Prods.; 1951). *Cast:* Cotton & Chick Watts, Ches Davis, Flourney E. Miller, Billy Green, Elliott Carpenter, The Hobnobbers, Ellen Sutton, Sally Anglim, Gary Jackson, Phil Arnold, Slim Williams, Emmett Miller, Ned Haverly, Brother Bones, Scatman Crothers, Monette Moore, Jimmy O'Brien, Archie Twitchell [aka: Michael Branden], Cliff Taylor, Boyce and Evans, Pete Daily & His Chicagoans, Jester Hairston Singers. *D:-P:-St: & Sc:* Ron Ormond; *Songs:* "I Want to Be a Minstrel Man," "Stay Out of the Kitchen," "Is Your Rent Paid Up in Heaven?," "Flying Saucers," "Memphis Bill," "Southland." (1:00) Programmer musical of various performers reminiscing back to the by-gone days of minstrel shows.

3050. Yesterday and Today (United Artists/Abner J. Greshler Prods.; 1953). *D: & P:* Abner J. Greshler; *St: & Sc:* George Jessel. (0:57) A documentary which highlights clips from the early days of the silent motion picture.

You Belong to My Heart (G.B. title) *see* **Mr. Imperium**

3051. You Can't Run Away from It (Columbia; 1956). *Cast:* June Allyson, Jack Lemmon, Charles Bickford, Paul Gilbert, Jim Backus, Stubby Kaye, Henny Youngman, Allyn Joslyn, Byron Foulger, Howard McNear, Frank Sully, Jack Albertson, Dub Taylor, Larry Blake, Walter Baldwin (final film—ret.), Jacques Scott, Richard Cutting, Elvia Allman, Louise Beavers, Raymond Greenleaf, Edwin Chandler, Queenie Smith, William Forrest, Steve Benton, Bill Walker, Herb Vigran. *D: & P:* Dick Powell; *Sc:* Claude Binyon, Robert Riskin; *Songs:* Title song (sung by the Four Aces), "Howdy, Friends and Neighbors!," "Temporarily," "Thumbin' a Ride," "Scarecrow Ballet," "Old Reporters Never Die" and "Finale" Gene DePaul, Johnny Mercer. (1:35) Musical-comedy-romance of an heiress who runs away from an arranged marriage and meets up with a newspaper reporter. A remake of this studio's 1934 hit *It Happened One Night*, it was based on the screenplay of that movie by Mr. Riskin and the story "Night Bus" by Samuel Hopkins Adams. Technicolor/CinemaScope.

3052. You for Me (MGM; 1952). *Cast:* Peter Lawford, Jane Greer, Gig Young, Paula Corday, Howard Wendell, Otto Hulett, Barbara Brown, Barbara Ruick, Elaine Stewart, Kathryn Card, Tommy Farrell, Paul Smith, Helen Winston, Perry Sheehan, Stephen Chase, Ned Glass, Nikki Justin, Martha Wentworth, Jerry Hausner, John Rosser, John Close, Robert Smiley, Ivan Browning, Hal Smith, Alvy Moore, Ralph Grosh, Joann Arnold, Diann James, Marjorie Jackson, Kathy Qualen, Tommy Walker, Alan Harris, Julia Dean. *D:* Don Weis; *P:* Henry Berman; *St: & Sc:* William Roberts. (1:11) Programmer romantic comedy of a nurse and her various suitors, one of which is a carefree millionaire.

3053. You Never Can Tell (Universal-International; 1951). *Cast:* Dick Powell, Peggy Dow, Charles Drake, Joyce Holden, Albert Sharpe, Frank Nelson, Sarah Taft, Will Vedder, Watson Downs, Lou Polan, Anthony George, Henry Kulky, Olan Soule, King (dog), Tillie (dog), Boots (cat). *D: & St:* Lou Breslow; *P:* Leonard Goldstein; *Sc:* Breslow, David Chandler. (1:18) Successful fantasy-comedy of a wealthy German shepherd dog who is murdered and returns to Earth as a man (with a female friend who was formerly a horse) to solve his murder. A novel story idea that was reversed in 1980s *Oh, Heavenly Dog!* as a murdered man comes back as a dog to find his killer. (G.B. title: *You Never Know*)

You Never Know (G.B. title) *see* **You Never Can Tell**

3054. Young and Dangerous (20th Century-Fox/Regal Films; 1957). *Cast:* Mark Damon, Lili Gentle, Edward Binns, Frances Mercer, Dabbs Greer, Ann Doran, George Brenlin, Jerry Barclay, William Stevens, Connie Stevens (film debut), Danny Welton, Shirley Falls, Ronald Foster, Bill Shannon, Marilyn Carrol, Joan Bradshaw, Marion Collier, June Burt, James Canino, X Brands, William Boyett, Don Devlin, Paul Bryar, Buddy Mason, Judy Bamber, Kim Scala, Doris Kemper, Brandy Bryan, Roy Darmour, Ron Barbanell, Clancy Herne. *D: & P:* William F. Claxton; *St: & Sc:* James Landis. (1:18) A reckless young man with shallow interests in life undergoes a transformation when he meets a nice girl. Originally ran on a double bill program with *Rockabilly Baby* (q.v.). Regalscope.

3055. Young and Wild (Republic/Esla Pictures; 1958). *Cast:* Gene Evans, Scott Marlowe, Carolyn Kearney (film debut), Robert Arthur (final film—ret.), James Kevin, Tom Gilson, Ken Lynch, Emlen Davies, Morris Ankrum, Wendell Holmes, John Zaremba. *D:* William Witney; *P:* Sidney Picker; *St: & Sc:* Arthur T. Horman. (1:09) Low budget teen melodrama of three wayward youths who steal a car, attempt to rape a girl, but thwarted in that, they leave the scene and run down a woman pedestrian. Naturama. Originally paired on a double bill with *Juvenile Jungle* (q.v.).

3056. Young at Heart (Warner/Arwin Prods.; 1954). *Cast:* Doris Day, Frank Sinatra, Gig Young, Ethel Barrymore, Dorothy Malone, Robert Keith, Elisabeth Fraser, Alan Hale, Jr., Lonny Chapman, Frank Ferguson, Marjorie Bennett, John Maxwell, William McLean, Barbara Pepper, Robin Raymond, Tito Vuolo, Grazia Narciso, Ivan Browning, Joe Forte, Cliff Ferre, Harte Wayne, Celeste Bryant. *D:* Gordon Douglas; *P:* Henry Blanke; *Adaptation:* Liam O'-Brien [of the Oscar nominated 1938 screenplay of *Four Daughters* by Leonore Coffee and Julius J. Epstein]; *Songs:* "Young at Heart" Johnny Richards, Carolyn Leigh (sung by Sinatra); "Hold Me in Your Arms" Ray Heindorf, Charles Henderson, Don Pippin (sung by Day); "Ready, Willing and Able" Floyd Huddleston, Al Rinker (by Day); "Till My Love Comes Back to Me" (to Felix Mendelssohn's "On Wings of Song" lyrics by Paul Francis Webster (sung by Day); "There's a Rising Moon for Every Falling Star" Sammy Fain, Webster (by Day); "Someone to Watch Over Me" George and Ira Gershwin (by Sinatra); "Just One of Those Things" Cole Porter (by Sinatra); "One For My Baby (and One More for the Road)" Harold Arlen, Johnny Mercer (by Sinatra) and "You, My Love" Mack Gordon, Jimmy Van Heusen (a duet by Sinatra and Day). (1:57) (video) A sentimental musical remake of this studio's 1938 production of *Four Daughters*, based on the *Cosmopolitan* story "Sister Act" by Fannie Hurst of a New England girl from a respectable family who marries a no-account loser. WarnerColor (print by Technicolor).

3057. Young Bess (MGM; 1953). *Cast:* Jean Simmons ("Best Actress" from the NBR combined with her work in *The Robe* and *The Actress*—both q.v./Elizabeth I, "Young Bess"), Stewart Granger (Thomas Seymour), Deborah Kerr (Catherine Parr), Charles Laughton (King Henry VIII), Kay Walsh (Mrs. Ashley), Guy Rolfe (Ned Seymour), Kathleen Byron (Anne Seymour), Cecil Kellaway (Mr. Parry), Leo G. Carroll (Mr. Mums), Rex Thompson (Edward), Robert Arthur (Barnaby), Norma Varden (Lady Tyrwhitt), Alan Napier (Robert Tyrwhitt), Noreen Corcoran (Young Bess, age 6), Ivan Triesault (Danish envoy), Elaine Stewart (Anne Boleyn), Dawn Addams (Catherine Howard), Doris Lloyd (Mother Jack), Lumsden Hare (Archbishop Thomas Cranmer), Lester Matthews (Sir William Paget), Ann Tyrrell (Mary), Fay Wall, Patrick Whyte, Frank Eldridge, John Sheffield, Carl Saxe, Major Sam Harris, Raymond Lawrence, David Cavendish, Clive Morgan, Charles Keane, Ian Wolfe, Reginald Sheffield, John Trueman. *D:* George Sidney; *P:* Sidney Franklin; *Sc:* Arthur Wimperis, Jan Lustig; *ASD:* (AAN-color) Cedric Gibbons, Urie McCleary (art directors), Edwin B. Willis, Jack D. Moore (sets); *Costumes:* (AAN-color) Walter Plunkett. (1:52) (video) Fact and fiction blend in this lavishly produced historical costume epic of Elizabeth, heiress to the throne of Henry VIII. A box office hit. Technicolor.

3058. The Young Captives (Paramount; 1959). *Cast:* Steven Marlo [aka: Morris Miller], Tom Selden, Luana Patten, Ed Nelson, Dan Sheridan, James Chadler, Joan Granville, Marjorie Stapp, Miles Stephens, Edward Schaaf, William C. Shaw, Carlo Fiore, Lawrence J. Gelbmann, Dan Blocker, Allen Kramer, Phillip A. Mansour, Lenore Kingston, Raymond Guth, Carol Nelson, Herb Armstrong. *D:* Irvin Kershner; *P:* Andrew Fenady; *St:* Gordon Hunt, Al Burton; *Sc:* Fenady. (1:01) Programmer melodrama of a young couple eloping to Mexico who run afoul of a psychopathic killer who holds them captive.

3059. Young Daniel Boone (Monogram; 1950). *Cast:* David Bruce, Kristine Miller, Damian O'Flynn, Don Beddoe, Mary Treen, John Mylong, William Roy, Stanley Logan, Herbert Baish, Nipo T. Strongheart, Richard Foote, Stephen S. Harrison. *D:* Reginald LeBorg; *P:* James S. Burkett; *St:* Clint Johnson; *Sc:* LeBorg, Johnson. (1:11) Frontier adventure with the young frontiersman (Bruce) trekking into the wilderness in search of two sisters, survivors of an Indian massacre. Cinecolor.

3060. The Young Don't Cry (Columbia/ Philip A. Waxman Pictures; 1957). *Cast:* Sal Mineo, James Whitmore, J. Carrol Naish, Gene Lyons, Paul Carr, Leigh Whipper, Thomas Carlin, James Reese, Ruth Attaway, Leland Mayforth, Dick Wigginton, Stanley Martin, Josephine Smith, Joseph Killorin, Phillips Hamilton, Victor Johnson. *D:* Alfred L. Werker (final film—ret.); *P:* Philip A. Waxman; *Sc:* Richard Jessup [based on his 1954 book *The Cunning and the Haunted*]. (1:29) Low budget drama of an escaped convict (Whitmore) who seeks the help of an amiable orphaned teen. Filmed on locations in Savannah, GA.

3061. The Young Guns (Allied Artists; 1956). *Cast:* Russ Tamblyn, Gloria Talbott, Perry Lopez, Walter Coy, Chubby Johnson, Scott Marlowe, Wright King, Myron Healey, James Goodwin, Rayford Barnes, [I.] Stanford Jolley. *D:* Albert Band (directorial debut); *P:* Richard Heermance; *St:* & *Sc:* Louis Garfinkle; *Song:* "Song of the Young Guns" Imogen Carpenter, Lenny Adelson (sung by Guy Mitchell). (1:24) Based on fact western of a young man who has difficulty living with the fact that his father was a notorious gunslinger. Set in 1897.

Young Hellions *see* **High School Confidential!**

The Young Invaders (G.B. title) *see* **Darby's Rangers**

3062. The Young Land (Columbia/C.V. Whitney Pictures, Inc.; 1959). *Cast:* Patrick Wayne (Jim Ellison), Yvonne Craig (Elenade la Madrid), Dennis Hopper (Hatfield Carnes), Dan O'Herlihy (Judge Isham), Ken Curtis (Lee Hearn), Roberto de la Madrid (Don Roberto de la Madrid), Cliff Ketchum (Ben Stroud), Pedro Gonzales-Gonzales (Santiago), Edward Sweeney (Sully), Miguel Camacho (Miguel), Cliff Lyons (jury foreman), Mario Arteaga (Mario), Charles Heard (Tolliver), Carlos Romero (Quiroga), John Quijada (Carlos), Tom Tiner. *D:* Ted Tetzlaff; *P:* Patrick Ford; *As.P:* Lowell Farrell; *Sc:* Norman S. Hall; *Song:* (AAN-Best Song) "Strange Are the Ways of Love" Dimitri Tiomkin, Ned Washington (sung by Randy Sparks). (1:29) (video) Western drama of an Anglo who goes on trial for killing a Mexican in 1848 California. Filmed on locations at Thousand Oaks, CA. Based on *Frontier Frenzy* a serialized novel by John Reese which appeared in *Saturday Evening Post.* Technicolor.

3063. The Young Lions (20th Century-Fox; 1958). *Cast:* Marlon Brando (Lt. Christian Diestl), Montgomery Clift (Noah Ackerman), Dean Martin (Michael Whiteacre), Hope Lange (Hope Plowman), Barbara Rush (Margaret Freemantle), May Britt (Gretchen Hardenberg), Maximilian Schell (Capt. Hardenberg), Dora Doll (Simone), Lee Van Cleef (Sgt. Rickett), Liliane Montevecchi (Francoise), Parley Baer (Brant), Arthur Franz (Lt. Green), Hal Baylor (Pvt. Burnecker), Richard Gardner (Pvt. Cowley), Herbert Rudley (Capt. Colclough), John Alderson (Corp. Kraus), Sam Gilman (Pvt. Faber), L.Q. Jones (Pvt. Donnelly), Julian Burton (Pvt. Brailsford), Ashley Cowan (Maier), Paul Comi (Pvt. Abbott), Michael Pataki (Pvt. Hagstrom), Vaughn Taylor (Mr. Plowman), John Gabriel (Burn), Kendall Scott (Emerson), Stan Kamber (Acaro), Robert Ellenstein (rabbi), Robert Burton (Col. Mead), Harvey Stephens (Gen. Rockland), Kurt Katch (final film—d. 1958), Gene Roth, Stephen Bekassy, Ivan Triesault, Clive Morgan, Jeffrey Sayre, Milton Frome, Otto Reichow, Anne Stebbins, Mary Pierce, Ann Codee, Christian Pasques, Doris Wiss, Alfred Tonkel, John Banner, Norbert Schiller, Henry Rowland, Art Reichle, David Dabov, Wade Cagle, Lee Winter, Nicholas King, Harry Ellerbe, Craig Karr, Michael Smith, Voltaire Perkins, Ann Daniels, Alberto Morin, George Meader, Joan Douglas, Ed Rickard, Joe Brooks, Hubert Kerns, Ann Paige. *D:* Edward Dmytryk; *P:* Al Lichtman; *Sc:* Edward Anhalt; *Cin:* (AAN-b/w) Joe MacDonald; *Sound:* (AAN) Carl Faulkner; *Music:* (AAN) Hugo Friedhofer. (2:47) (video/laserdisc) Acclaimed hit World War II character study of three soldiers, two American and one idealistic Nazi officer who gradually begins to question his ideals. Based on the Irwin Shaw novel, it became one of the 26 top-grossing films of 1957-58. *Film Daily* placed it at #9 on their "10 Best" list while the British Academy Awards had it in nomination. CinemaScope.

The Young Lovers *see* **Never Fear**

Young Man of Music (G.B. title) *see* **Young Man with a Horn**

3064. Young Man with a Horn (Warner; 1950). *Cast:* Kirk Douglas (trumpet dubbed by Harry James), Lauren Bacall, Doris Day, Hoagy Carmichael (narrator/some piano dubbed by Buddy Cole), Juano Hernandez (trumpet dubbed by Jimmy Zito), Jerome Cowan, Mary Beth Hughes, Nestor Paiva, Orley Lindgren, Walter Reed, Jack Kruschen, Alex Gerry, Jack Shea, James Griffith, Dean Reisner, Everett Glass, Dave Dunbar, Robert O'Neill, Paul E. Burns, Julius Wechter, Ivor James, Larry Rio, Hugh Charles, Sid Kane, Vivian Mallah, Lorna Jordan, Lewell Enge, Bridget Brown, Dan Seymour, Paul Dubov, Keye Luke, Frank Cady, Murray Leonard, Hugh Murray, Dick Cogan, Katharine Kurasch, Burk Symon, Bill Walker, Helene Heigh, Ted Eckelberry. *D:* Michael Curtiz; *P:* Jerry Wald; *Sc:* Carl Foreman, Edmund H. North; *Songs include:* "The Very Thought of You" Ray Noble; "I May Be Wrong" Henry Sullivan, Harry Ruskin; "The Man I Love" George and Ira Gershwin; "Too Marvelous for Words" Johnny Mercer, Richard A. Whiting; "Get Happy" Harold Arlen, Ted Koehler; "I Only Have Eyes for You," "Lullaby of Broadway" Al Dubin, Harry Warren; "With a Song in My Heart" Richard Rodgers, Lorenz Hart; "Pretty Baby" Egbert Van Alstyne, Tony Jackson; "Limehouse Blues" Philip Braham, Douglas Furber; "Melancholy Rhapsody" Sammy Cahn, Ray Heindorf. (1:52) (video/laserdisc) Musical drama of the rise and fall of a jazz musician who eventually makes his way back. Based on Dorothy Baker's 1938 novel which was inspired by the life of late jazz great, Bix Beiderbecke. (G.B. title: *Young Man of Music*)

3065. Young Man with Ideas (MGM; 1952). *Cast:* Glenn Ford, Ruth Roman, Denise

Darcel, Nina Foch, Donna Corcoran, Ray Collins, Mary Wickes, Sheldon Leonard, Bobby Diamond, Dick Wessel, Carl Milletaire, Curtis Cooksey, Karl Davis, Fay Roope, John Call, Nadene Ashdown, Barry Rado, Norman Rado (twins), Wilton Graff, Martha Wentworth, Selmer Jackson. *D:* Mitchell Leisen; *P:* William H. Wright, Gottfried Reinhardt; *St:* Ben Barzman; *Sc:* Arthur Sheekman. (1:24) Comedy-drama of a lawyer attempting to deal with various problems after moving his family to California.

Young Paul Baroni (G.B. title) *see* **Kid Monk Baroni**

3066. The Young Philadelphians (Warner; 1959). *Cast:* Paul Newman (Tony Lawrence), Barbara Rush (Joan Dickinson), Alexis Smith (Carol Wharton), Brian Keith (Mike Flanagan), Diane Brewster (Kate Judson), Billie Burke (Mrs. J.A. Allen), John Williams (Gil Dickinson), Robert Vaughn (AAN-BSA/Chet Gwynn), Otto Kruger (John M. Wharton), Adam West (film debut/William Lawrence), Paul Picerni (Louis Donetti), Robert Douglas (Morton Stearnes), Fred "Anthony" Eisley (Carter Henry), Frank Conroy (Dr. S. Stearnes), Richard Deacon (George Archibald), Isobel Elsom (Mrs. Lawrence), Lennie Bremen (Carson), Helen Jay (Honey), J. Anthony Hughes, Al McGrannery. *D:* Vincent Sherman; *P:* Unc.; *Sc:* James Gunn; *Cin:* (AAN-b/w) Harry Stradling, Jr.; *Costumes:* (AAN-b/w) Howard Shoup. (2:16) (video) Critics were divided on this popular melodrama of a Philadelphia lawyer who makes his way up the societal ladder, despite the fact he was illegitimately conceived. Based on the 1956 novel *The Philadelphians* by Richard Powell. (G.B. title: *The City Jungle*)

The Young Rebels *see* **Teenage Doll**

3067. The Young Stranger (Universal-International/RKO; 1957). *Cast:* James MacArthur (film debut, repeating his TV role), Kim Hunter, James Daly, James Gregory, Whit Bissell, Jeff Silver, Jack Mullaney, Eddie Ryder, Jean Corbett, Gary Vinson, Charles Davis, Marian Seldes, Terry Kelman, Edith Evanson, Tom Pittman, Howard Price. *D:* John Frankenheimer (theatrical feature directorial debut, repeating his role as director of the TV production); *P:* Stuart Miller; *Sc:* Robert Dozier (based on his 1955 TV play "Deal a Blow" which appeared on *Climax*). (1:24) (laserdisc) Drama of a 16-year-old boy feeling alienated from his father's affections who assaults a theatre manager and gets arrested, without the truth of the assault coming out. An RKO production that was distributed by Universal following the demise of the former studio.

3068. You're in the Navy Now (20th Century–Fox; 1951). *Cast:* Gary Cooper, Jane Greer, Millard Mitchell, Eddie Albert, John McIntire, Ray Collins, Harry Von Zell, Jack Webb, Richard Erdman, Harvey Lembeck, Henry Slate, Ed Begley, Fay Roope, Charles Tannen, Charles [Bronson] Buchinsky (film debut), Jack Warden, Ken Harvey, Lee Marvin (film debut), Jerry Hausner, Charles Smith, James Cornell, Glenn Gordon, Laurence Hugo, Damian O'Flynn, Biff McGuire, Norman McKay, John McGuire, Elsa Peterson, Herman Cantor, Joel Fluellen, William Leicester, Ted Stanhope, Rory Mallinson, Bernard Kates. *D:* Henry Hathaway; *P:* Frederick Kohlmar; *Sc:* Richard Murphy. (1:33) World War II comedy of a "green" lieutenant in charge of an equally "green" crew aboard a test naval vessel powered by steam, a situation which creates almost insurmountable problems for everyone. Based on the nonfiction article "Flying Teakettle" which appeared in *The New Yorker* magazine on January 21, 1950, by John W. Hazard. (aka: *U.S.S. Teakettle*)

3069. You're Never Too Young (Paramount/York Pictures; 1955). *Cast:* Dean Martin, Jerry Lewis, Diana Lynn, Nina Foch, Raymond Burr, Mitzi McCall, Veda Ann Borg, Margery Maude, Romo Vincent, Nancy Kulp, Milton Frome, Donna Percy, Emory Parnell, James Burke, Tommy Ivo, Whitey Haupt, Mickey Finn, Peggy Moffitt, Johnstone White, Richard Simmons, Louise Lorimer, Isabel Randolph, Robert Carson, Hans Conried, Stanley Blystone, Bobby Barber, Donna Jo Gribble, Irene Walpole, Gloria Penny Moore, Bob Morgan, Marty Newton, Richard Cutting. *D:* Norman Taurog; *P:* Paul Jones; *Sc:* Sidney Sheldon. (1:42) Comedy of a barber, fleeing a murderous thief who passes himself off as a preteen boy and hides out at a girls school. A remake of *The Major and the Minor* (1942) that was suggested by the play *Connie Goes Home* by Edward Childs Carpenter and the story "Sunny Goes Home" by Fannie Kilbourne which appeared in *Saturday Evening Post.* Technicolor/VistaVision.

3070. Yukon Gold (Monogram; 1952). *Cast:* Kirby Grant, Chinook the Wonder Dog (received PATSY "Award of Excellence," 1953),

Martha Hyer, Harry Lauter, Phil Van Zandt, Frances Charles, Mauritz Hugo, James Parnell, Sam Flint, I. Stanford Jolley. *D:* Frank McDonald; *P:* William F. Broidy; *Sc:* William Raynor. (1:02) Northwoods adventure of a Mountie and his dog on the trail of a killer in a mining camp. Based on James Oliver Curwood's 1909 book *The Gold Hunters.* Part of a series begun by Monogram in 1949.

3071. Yukon Manhunt (Monogram; 1951) *Cast:* Kirby Grant, Chinook the Wonder Dog (received PATSY "Award of Excellence," 1952), Gail Davis, Margaret Field, Ran Brooks, Nelson Leigh, John Doucette, Paul McGuire, Dick Barron. *D:* Frank McDonald; *P:* Lindsley Parsons; *Sc:* William Raynor. (1:03) A Mountie and his dog are on the trail of payroll robbers. Based on a short story by James Oliver Curwood, the film was part of a low budget series begun in 1949.

3072. Yukon Vengeance (Allied Artists; 1954). *Cast:* Kirby Grant, Chinook the Wonder Dog, Monte Hale, Mary Ellen Kay, Henry Kulky, Carol Thurston, Marshall Bradford, Park MacGregor, Fred Gabourie, Billy Wilkerson. *D:* William Beaudine; *P:* William F. Broidy; *Sc:* William Raynor. (1:08) A Mountie and his dog investigate the deaths of three mail carriers in a remote area. A low budget northwoods adventure based on writings of James Oliver Curwood and an entry in the series begun in 1949 under the Monogram banner.

3073. Zanzabuku (Republic; 1956). *P:* Lewis Cotlow; *Narration:* Ronald Davidson. (1:04) A feature length documentary in Trucolor.

3074. Zero Hour! (Paramount/Carmel Enterprises–Delta Enterprises; 1957). *Cast:* Dana Andrews, Linda Darnell, Sterling Hayden, Elroy "Crazylegs" Hirsch, Geoffrey Toone, Jerry Paris, Peggy King, Carole Eden, Charles Quinlivan, Raymond Ferrell, David Thursby, Russell Thorsen, Joanne Wade, Richard Keith, Steve London, John Ashley, Willis Bouchey, Maxine Cooper, Noel Drayton, Fintan Meyler, Larry Thor, Robert Stevenson, Mary Newton, Willard Sage, Will White, Hope Summers, Arthur Hanson, Roy Gordon. *D:* Hall Bartlett; *P:* John Champion; *Sc:* Arthur Hailey, Bartlett, Champion. (1:21) Drama of a passenger plane in trouble when the pilots and some passengers are felled by ptomaine poisoning and a traumatized war pilot must take the controls. Based on an acclaimed TV play "Flight Into Danger" by Arthur Hailey, it was remade in 1971 as the TV movie *Terror in the Sky* and was the inspiration for the 1980 disaster spoof *Airplane!.*

3075. Zombies of Mora Tau (Columbia/Clover Prods.; 1957). *Cast:* Gregg Palmer, Allison Hayes, Autumn Russell, Joel Ashley, Morris Ankrum, Marjorie Eaton, Gene Roth, Leonard Geer, Lewis Webb, Ray "Crash" Corrigan, Mel Curtis, Frank Hagney, Karl Davis, William Baskin. *D:* Edward L. Cahn; *P:* Sam Katzman; *St:* George H. Plympton; *Sc:* Raymond T. Marcus. (1:10) (video) Programmer horror involving a sunken ship that holds a cache of diamonds that are guarded by zombies. (G.B. title: *The Dead That Walk*)

Award-Winning and Nominated Films

Following is a list of films which received recognition and critical acclaim from various institutions, namely: The Academy of Motion Pictures Arts and Science, Academy Awards (AA) Academy Award Nominations (AAN), Berlin Film Festival (B), British Academy Awards (BA), Brussells Film Festival (BR), Cannes Film Festival (C), Edinburgh Film Festival (E), *Film Daily's* "10 Best" list (F), French Motion Pictures Academy (FM), Karlovy Vary Film Festival (K), Mannheim Film Festival (M), the National Board of Review's "10 Best" list as well as Acting Awards and others (NBR), the New York Film Critics (NYFC), the *New York Times* newspaper's "10 Best" list (NYT), the PATSY (animal) Awards (PAT), *Photoplay* magazine (P), the San Francisco International Film Festival (SF), and the Venice Film Festival (V).

Above and Beyond (1952) AAN, NBR
Ace in the Hole (1951) AAN, NBR, V
The Actress (1953) AAN, NBR
Affair in Trinidad (1952) AAN
An Affair to Remember (1957) AAN, P
The African Lion (1956) NBR
The African Queen (1951) AA, AAN, BA, F, NYFC
Albert Schweitzer (1957) AA, NBR
Alice in Wonderland (1951) AAN, V
All About Eve (1950) AA, AAN, BA, C, NBR, NYFC, NYT
All the Brothers Were Valiant (1953) AAN
An American in Paris (1951) AA, AAN, BA, F, NBR, NYFC, NYT
Anastasia (1956) AA, AAN, F, NBR, NYFC, NYT
Anatomy of a Murder (1959) AAN, BA, F, NBR, NYFC, NYT, V
Androcles and the Lion (1952) PAT
Annie Get Your Gun (1950) AA, AAN, P
April Love (1957) AAN
Around the World in 80 Days (1956) AA, AAN, F, NBR, NYFC, NYT
Ask Any Girl (1959) BA
The Asphalt Jungle (1950) AAN, BA, NBR, NYFC, NYT, V
The Atomic City (1952) AAN
Attack! (1956) V
Auntie Mame (1958) AAN, F
Autumn Leaves (1956) B
Baby Doll (1956) AAN, BA
The Bachelor Party (1957) AAN, BA, C, NBR
Back to God's Country (1953) PAT
The Bad and the Beautiful (1952) AA, AAN, BA, NBR
Bad Day at Black Rock (1955) AAN, BA, C, F, NBR, NYT
The Bad Seed (1956) AAN
The Band Wagon (1953) AAN
The Barefoot Contessa (1954) AA
Battle Cry (1955) AAN
Beat the Devil (1954) NBR
Because You're Mine (1952) AAN
Behave Yourself (1951) PAT
Bell, Book and Candle (1958) AAN, PAT
Ben-Hur (1959) AA, AAN, BA, F, NBR, NYFC, NYT
Beneath the 12-Mile Reef (1953) AAN
The Best of Everything (1959) AAN
The Best Things in Life Are Free (1956) AAN
Between Heaven and Hell (1956) AAN
The Big Country (1958) AA, AAN, BA NYFC
The Big Fisherman (1959) AAN
The Big Knife (1955) V
The Big Sky (1952) AAN
Bigger Than Life (1956) V
Black Horse Canyon (1954) PAT
The Black Orchid (1959) V
The Black Rose (1950) AAN
Blackboard Jungle (1955) AAN, F
The Blue Veil (1951) AAN
The Bold and the Brave (1956) AAN
Bonzo Goes to College (1952) PAT
Born Yesterday (1950) AA, AAN, F, NYT, V
Boy on a Dolphin (1957) AAN

The Bravados (1958) NBR
The Brave Bulls (1951) NYT
The Brave One (1956) AA, AAN
The Bridges at Toko-Ri (1954) AA, AAN, NYT
Brigadoon (1954) AAN
Bright Victory (1951) AAN, B, C, F, NYFC
Broken Arrow (1950) AAN
Broken Lance (1954) AA, AAN
The Brothers Karamozov (1958) AAN, C, NBR
The Buccaneer (1958) AAN
A Bullet Is Waiting (1954) PAT
The Bullfighter and the Lady (1951) AAN
Bus Stop (1956) AAN, NBR, NYT
The Caddy (1953) AAN
Caged (1950) AAN, V
The Caine Mutiny (1954) AAN, BA, F
Calamity Jane (1953) AA, AAN
Call Me Madam (1953) AA, AAN
Captain Carey, U.S.A. (1950) AA
Career (1959) AAN, NYFC
Carmen Jones (1954) AAN, B, BA, NYFC
Carrie (1952) BA, V
Cat on a Hot Tin Roof (1958) AAN, BA, F, NBR, NYT
The Catered Affair (1956) NBR
A Certain Smile (1958) AAN
Cinderella (1950) AAN, B, V
Come Back Little Sheba (1952) AA, AAN, BA, C, F, NBR, NYFC, NYT
Compulsion (1959) BA, C, F
The Country Girl (1954) AA, AAN, C, F, NBR, NYFC, NYT
The Court-Martial of Billy Mitchell (1955) AAN
Cowboy (1958) AAN
Crazylegs, All-American (1953) AAN
Cyrano de Bergerac (1950) AA, F, NBR
Daddy Long Legs (1955) AAN
Damn Yankees (1958) AAN, NYT
David and Bathsheba (1951) AAN
Death of a Salesman (1951) AAN, B, BA, F, NBR, NYFC, NYT
Decision Before Dawn (1951) AAN, NBR, NYT
The Defiant Ones (1958) AA, AAN, B, BA, F, NYFC, NYT, P
Demetrius and the Gladiators (1954) PAT
The Desert Rats (1953) AAN, NBR
Designing Woman (1957) AA
Desire Under the Elms (1958) AAN, C
Desiree (1954) AAN
The Desperate Hours (1954) NBR
Destination Moon (1950) AA, AAN, NYT
The Detective Story (1951) AAN, BA, C, F, NBR, NYT
The Devil's Doorway (1950) NYFC
Dial M for Murder (1954) NBR, NYFC
The Diary of Anne Frank (1959) AA, AAN, F, NBR, NYFC, NYT, P
A Dog of Flanders (1959) PAT
Don't Go Near the Water (1957) F
Dream Wife (1953) AAN
East of Eden (1955) AA, AAN, BA, C, F, NBR
The Eddy Duchin Story (1956) AAN
Edge of Doom (1950) NBR
Edge of the City (1957) BA
The Egyptian (1954) AAN
The Enemy Below (1957) AA, NBR
Executive Suite (1954) AAN, BA, F, NBR, V
A Face in the Crowd (1957) F
Face to Face (1952) NBR
A Farewell to Arms (1957) AAN, NBR, P
Father of the Bride (1950) AAN, NYT
Fearless Fagan (1952) PAT
Five Fingers (1952) AAN, F, NBR, NYT
The Five Pennies (1959) AAN
The 5,000 Fingers of Dr. T (1953) AAN
The Flame and the Arrow (1950) AAN
Flame of Araby (1951) PAT
Flat Top (1952) AAN
Forbidden Planet (1956) AAN
The Four-Poster (1952) AAN, V
Fourteen Hours (1951) AAN, BA, NBR, NYT, V
Francis Covers the Big Town (1953) PAT
Francis Goes to the Races (1951) PAT
Francis Goes to West Point (1952) PAT
Francis in the Haunted House (1956) PAT
Francis in the Navy (1955) PAT
Francis Joins the WACs (1954) PAT
Friendly Persuasion (1956) AAN, C, F, NBR, NYT, PAT
The Frogmen (1951) AAN
From Here to Eternity (1953) AA, AAN, BA, C, F, NBR, NYFC, NYT, P
Funny Face (1957) AAN, C, NBR, NYT
The Furies (1950) AAN
The Gazebo (1959) AAN, PAT
The Geisha Boy (1958) PAT
Gentlemen Prefer Blondes (1953) P
Giant (1956) AAN, F, NYFC, NYT, P, PAT
Gigi (1958) AA, BA, F, NBR, NYFC, NYT, P
The Glenn Miller Story (1954) AA, AAN, F, NYT, P
Go for Broke! (1951) AAN
The Goddess (1958) AAN, BR, NBR, NYT
God's Little Acre (1958) NYT, V
Golden Girl (1951) AAN
Goodbye My Lady (1956) PAT
The Great Caruso (1951) AA, AAN, F, P
The Great Man (1956) NYT
The Greatest Show on Earth (1952) AA, AAN, F, NYFC, NYT
Gunfight at the O.K. Corral (1957) AAN
The Gunfighter (1950) AAN
Guys and Dolls (1955) AAN, BA

Gypsy Colt (1954) PAT
The Hanging Tree (1959) AAN
Hans Christian Andersen (1952) AAN, NYFC
Hansel and Gretel (1954) NBR
The Harder They Fall (1956) AAN, C
Harvey (1950) AA, AAN
A Hatful of Rain (1957) AAN, F, NBR, NYFC, NYT, V
Heaven Knows Mr. Allison (1957) AAN, BA, F, NYFC
Helen Keller in Her Story (1955) AA, NBR
Hell and High Water (1954) AAN
Here Comes the Groom (1951) AA, AAN
The Hidden World (1958) AAN
The High and the Mighty (1954) AA, AAN, F
High Noon (1950) AA, AAN, F, NBR, NYFC, NYT, P
High Society (1956) AAN
A Hole in the Head (1959) AA, NYT
Hollywood or Bust (1956) PAT
Hondo (1953) AAN, PAT
Hot Spell (1958) NYFC
The House on Telegraph Hill (1951) AAN
Houseboat (1958) AAN
How to Marry a Millionaire (1953) AAN, BA
I Confess (1953) C
I Want to Live (1958) AA, AAN, F, NYFC, NYT
I Want You (1951) AAN
I Was a Communist for the F.B.I. (1951) AAN
I'll Cry Tomorrow (1955) AA, AAN, C
I'll Get By (1950) AAN
Imitation of Life (1959) AAN
Indiscreet (1958) BA
Indiscretion of an American Wife (1953) AAN
The Inn of the Sixth Happiness (1958) AAN, NBR
Interrupted Melody (1955) AA, AAN
Invitation to the Dance (1956) B
It Should Happen to You (1954) AAN
It's a Dog's Life (1955) PAT
It's Always Fair Weather (1955) AAN, NYT
Ivanhoe (1952) AAN, F, NYT
The Jazz Singer (1953) AAN
The Joker Is Wild (1957) AA
Journey to the Center of the Earth (1959) AAN
Julie (1956) AAN
Julius Caesar (1952) AA, AAN, BA, NBR, NYT
Just for You (1952) AAN
Kelly and Me (1957) PAT
The Kentuckian (1955) PAT
The Killing (1956) BA
Kind Lady (1951) AAN
The King and I (1956) AA, AAN, F, NBR, NYFC, NYT
King Solomon's Mines (1950) AA, AAN
Kiss Me Kate (1953) AAN
Knights of the Round Table (1953) AAN
Knock on Wood (1954) AAN, NYT
The Last Angry Man (1959) AAN, NYFC
The Last Hurrah (1958) NBR, NYFC
Les Girls (1957) AA, AAN, F, NYT
Li'l Abner (1959) AAN
Lili (1953) AA, AAN, BA, C, F, NBR, NYT
Limelight (1952) BA, NBR, NYT, AA-1972
Little Boy Lost (1953) F
The Little Fugitive (1953) AAN, V, NBR
The Living Desert (1953) AA, C
The Lone Ranger (1956) PAT
Lonelyhearts (1958) AAN
The Long Hot Summer (1958) C, F, NBR
Louisa (1950) AAN
Love in the Afternoon (1957) NYT
Love Is a Many Splendored Thing (1955) AA, AAN, F, P
Love Me or Leave Me (1955) AA, AAN, F
Lust for Life (1956) AA, AAN, NBR, NYFC, NYT
Magnificent Obsession (1954) AAN, P
The Magnificent Yankee (1950) AAN
A Man Called Peter (1956) AAN, F, NBR, NYT
The Man in the Gray Flannel Suit (1956) C
Man of a Thousand Faces (1957) AAN
Man on a Tightrope (1953) NYT
The Man Who Knew Too Much (1956) AA, C
The Man Who Understood Women (1959) NBR
The Man with the Golden Arm (1955) AAN, BA
Mardi Gras (1958) AAN
Marjorie Morningstar (1958) AAN
Martin Luther (1953) AAN, NBR, NYT
Marty (1955) AA, AAN, BA, C, F, NBR, NYFC
The Mating Season (1951) AAN, B
Me and the Colonel (1958) NBR
Meet Me in Las Vegas (1955) AAN
The Member of the Wedding (1952) AAN
The Men (1950) AAN, BA, NBR, NYT
The Merry Widow (1952) AAN
Middle of the Night (1959) C, NBR
Million Dollar Mermaid (1952) AAN
The Miracle of Our Lady of Fatima (1952) AAN
Miss Sadie Thompson (1953) AAN
The Mississippi Gambler (1953) AAN
Mister 880 (1950) AAN
Mister Roberts (1955) AA, AAN, F, NBR, NYFC, NYT
Moby Dick (1956) F, NBR, NYFC, NYT
The Model and the Marriage Broker (1951) AAN
Mogambo (1953) AAN, BA, NBR
The Moon Is Blue (1953) AAN, BA, FD
Moulin Rouge (1952) AA, AAN, BA, F, NYT
My Cousin Rachel (1952) AAN
My Friend Irma Goes West (1950) PAT
My Son John (1952) AAN, NBR

Mystery Street (1950) AAN
The Naked Eye (1956) AAN
The Naked Spur (1953) AAN
The Narrow Margin (1952) AAN
Navajo (1952) AAN
Night People (1954) AAN
No Down Payment (1957) BA, NBR
No Sad Songs for Me (1950) AAN
No Way Out (1950) AAN, NBR
North by Northwest (1959) AAN, F, NBR, NYT
Not as a Stranger (1955) AAN, NBR
The Nun's Story (1959) AAN, BA, F, NBR, NYFC
Oklahoma! (1955) AA, AAN, NYT, NYFC
The Old Man and the Sea (1958) AA, AAN, NBR
Old Yeller (1957) PAT
On Moonlight Bay (1951) P
On the Beach (1959) AAN, NBR, NYFC, NYT
On the Bowery (1956) AAN, V
On the Riviera (1951) AAN
On the Waterfront (1954) AA, AAN, BA, F, NBR, NYFC, NYT, V
Operation Petticoat (1959) AAN
Our Very Own (1950) AAN
The Outlaw Stallion (1954) PAT
Pal Joey (1957) AAN
The Palomino (1950) PAT
Panic in the Streets (1950) AA, NBR, V
Pat and Mike (1952) AAN
Paths of Glory (1957) BA
People Will Talk (1951) NYT
Perri (1957) AAN
Pete Kelly's Blues (1955) AAN
Peter Pan (1953) C
Peyton Place (1957) AAN, F
The Phenix City Story (1955) NYT
Phone Call from a Stranger (1952) V
Pickup on South Street (1953) AAN, V
Picnic (1955) AA, AAN, BA, F, NBR, P
Pillow Talk (1959) AA, AAN, F, NYT, P
A Place in the Sun (1951) AA, AAN, C, F, NBR, NYFC, NYT
Porgy and Bess (1959) AA, AAN, NYT
The Power and the Prize (1956) AAN
The President's Lady (1953) AAN
The Pride of St. Louis (1952) AAN
The Private War of Major Benson (1955) AAN
The Proud and the Profane (1956) AAN
The Proud Rebel (1958) PAT
Psychiatric Nursing (1958) AAN
Queen Bee (1955) AAN
The Quiet Man (1952) AA, AAN, F, NBR, NYFC, NYT, V
Quo Vadis? (1951) AAN, F, NBR
The Race for Space (1959) AAN
The Rainmaker (1956) AAN
The Rains of Ranchipur (1955) AAN
Raintree County (1957) AAN
Rear Window (1954) AAN, BA, F, NBR
Rebel Without a Cause (1955) AAN, BA
The Red Badge of Courage (1951) BA, NBR
Red Garters (1954) AAN
Rhubarb (1951) PAT
Rich, Young and Pretty (1951) AAN
Riot in Cell Block 11 (1954) BA
The Robe (1953) AA, AAN, F, NBR, NYFC
Rogue Cop (1954) AAN
Roman Holiday (1953) AA, AAN, BA, F, NBR, NYFC, NYT
Room for One More (1952) PAT, V
The Rose Tattoo (1955) AA, AAN, BA, F, NBR, NYFC
Royal Wedding (1951) AAN
Sabrina (1954) AA, AAN, F, NBR, NYT, P
The Sad Horse (1959) PAT
Salt of the Earth (1954) FM, K
The Savage Eye (1959) E, M, V
Say One for Me (1959) AAN
Sayonara (1957) AA, AAN, F, NYT, NYFC
The Sea Around Us (1953) AA
Separate Tables (1958) AA, AAN, F, NBR, NYFC
Seven Brides for Seven Brothers (1954) AA, AAN, BA, F, NBR, NYT
The Seven Little Foys (1955) AAN
The Shaggy Dog (1959) PAT
Shane (1953) AA, AAN, BA, F, NBR, NYT, P
The Sheepman (1958) AAN, BA
Show Boat (1951) AAN, P
Silk Stockings (1957) NYT
The Silver Chalice (1954) AAN
Singin' in the Rain (1952) AAN, BA, F, NBR, NYFC
Singing Guns (1950) AAN
Sleeping Beauty (1959) AAN
Small Town Girl (1958) AAN
The Sniper (1952) AAN
The Snows of Kilimanjaro (1952) AAN, NBR
The Solid Gold Cadillac (1956) AA, AAN
Some Came Running (1958) AAN, F
Some Like It Hot (1959) AA, AAN, BA, F, NBR
Somebody Up There Likes Me (1956) AA, AAN, NBR
Something of Value (1957) V
Son of Paleface (1952) AAN, PAT
South Pacific (1958) AA, AAN
The Spirit of St. Louis (1957) AAN, NBR
Stage Fright (1950) NBR
Stagecoach to Fury (1956) AAN
Stalag 17 (1953) AA, AAN, NBR, NYT
The Star (1952) AAN
A Star Is Born (1954) AAN, NBR
The Story of Three Loves (1953) AAN

Strangers on a Train (1951) AAN, NBR
Strategic Air Command (1955) AAN, NBR
A Streetcar Named Desire (1951), AA, AAN, BA, F, NBR, NYFC, NYT, V
The Strip (1951) AAN
Sudden Fear (1952) AAN
Suddenly Last Summer (1959) AAN, F, NBR
A Summer Place (1959) P
Summertime (1955) AAN, BA, F, NYFC
The Sun Shines Bright (1953) BA
Sunset Blvd. (1950) AA, AAN, NBR, NYFC, NYT
Susan Slept Here (1954) AAN
Take the High Ground (1954) AAN
Tammy and the Bachelor (1957) AAN, P
Tarzan's Peril (1951) PAT
Tarzan's Savage Fury (1952) PAT
Tea and Sympathy (1956) F
Teacher's Pet (1958) AAN, NYT
The Teahouse of the August Moon (1956) B
Teenage Rebel (1956) AAN
The Ten Commandments (1956) AA, AAN, F, NBR
The Tender Trap (1955) AAN
Teresa (1951) AAN, V
That Kind of Woman (1959) B
That Night (1957) BA
Them! (1954) AAN
There's No Business Like Show Business (1954) AAN
The Thief (1952) AAN, NBR
This Is Cinerama (1952) AAN
Three Coins in the Fountain (1954) AA, AAN, F
The Three Faces of Eve (1957) AA, NBR
Three Little Words (1950) AAN
3:10 to Yuma (1957) BA
A Time to Love and a Time to Die (1958) AAN, B
The Tin Star (1957) AAN, BA
The Titan—Story of Michelangelo (1950) AA, NYT
Titanic (1953) AA, AAN
To Catch a Thief (1955) AA, AAN
The Toast of New Orleans (1950) AAN
tom thumb (1958) AA
Tonka (1958) PAT
Too Young to Kiss (1951) AAN
Torch Song (1953) AAN
Torpedo Run (1958) AAN
Touch of Evil (1958) BR
Trapeze (1956) B
Trial (1955) AAN, F
12 Angry Men (1957) AAN, B, BA, F, NBR, NYFC, NYT
20,000 Leagues Under the Sea (1954) AA, AAN, NBR, PAT
Two Tickets to Broadway (1951) AAN
Unchained (1955) AAN
Uncle Vanya (1958) SF
Valley of Head-Hunters (1953) PAT
The Vanishing Prairie (1954) AA, NBR
Vertigo (1958) AAN
The View from Pompey's Head (1955) NBR
The Virgin Queen (1955) AAN
Viva Zapata! (1952) AA, AAN, BA, C, NYT
Wabash Avenue (1950) AAN
War and Peace (1956) AAN, F, NBR
War of the Worlds (1953) AA, AAN
Weddings and Babies (1958) V
The Well (1951) AAN, B
West Point Story (1950) AAN
When Willie Comes Marching Home (1950) AAN
When Worlds Collide (1951) AA, AAN
White Christmas (1954) AAN
White Wilderness (1958) AA, AAN
White Witch Doctor (1953) PAT
Wild Is the Wind (1957) AAN, B, PAT
Windjammer (1958) NBR
With a Song in My Heart (1952) AA, AAN, F, P
With These Hands (1950) AAN
Witness for the Prosecution (1958) AAN, F
Written on the Wind (1956) AA, AAN
Young Bess (1953) AAN, NBR
The Young Land (1959) AAN
The Young Lions (1958) AAN, BA, F
The Young Philadelphians (1959) AAN
Yukon Gold (1952) PAT
Yukon Manhunt (1951) PAT

Bibliography

Academy of Motion Picture Arts and Sciences—The Writer's Guild of America, West, Inc. *Who Wrote the Movie (and What Else Did He Write?) (1936–1969).* Los Angeles: Academy of Motion Picture Arts & Sciences, 1970.

Autry, Gene, and Mickey Herskowitz. *Back in the Saddle Again.* Garden City, NY: Doubleday, 1978.

Bergen, Ronald. *The United Artists Story.* New York: Crown, 1986. Also by Octopus Books, Ltd.

Bowker, R.R. *Bowker's Complete Video Guide.* 2 volumes. New Providence, NJ: Reed Publishing, 1992.

Dimmet, Richard Bertrand. *A Title Guide to the Talkies.* Metuchen, NJ: Scarecrow Press, 1965.

Eames, John Douglas. *The M-G-M Story.* New York: Crown, 1985.

_____. *The Paramount Story.* New York: Crown, 1985.

Film and Television Daily. *The 1969 Film Daily Year Book of Motion Pictures—Fifty-First Annual Edition.* New York: National Screen Service, 1969.

Hirschhorn, Clive. *The Universal Story.* New York: Crown, 1983. (1987 edition).

_____. *The Warner Brothers Story.* New York: Crown, 1979.

Katz, Ephraim. *The Film Encyclopedia.* New York: Putnam, 1979.

Klotman, Phyllis Rauch. *Frame by Frame—A Black Filmography.* Bloomington: Indiana University Press, 1979.

Maltin, Leonard. *The Disney Films.* New York: Bonanza Books, 1973.

_____, ed.; Luke Sader, assoc. ed.; Ben Herndon, managing ed.; Mike Clark, Rob Edelman, Alvin H. Marill, Bill Warren, contributing eds.; Casey St. Charnez, video ed.; Cathleen Anderson, Spencer Green, Pete Hammond, Kevin Maynard, Michael Scheinfeld, Marsha Treiber, contributors. *Leonard Maltin's Movie and Video Guide—1996 edition.* New York: Signet, 1995.

Martin, Len D. *The Columbia Checklist.* Jefferson, NC: McFarland, 1991.

Martin, Mick, Marsha Porter, Derrick Bang, contributing ed. *Video Movie Guide 1997.* New York: Random House, 1996. A Ballantine book.

Michael, Paul. *The American Movies Reference Book—The Sound Era.* Englewood Cliffs, NJ: Prentice-Hall, 1969.

Nash, Jay Robert, and Stanley Ralph Ross. *The Motion Picture Guide.* Chicago: Cinebooks, 1985. (12 volumes).

The New York Times Directory of the Film. Salem, NH: Arno Press, 1974.

Nye, Douglas E. *Those Six-Gun Heroes.* Spartanburg, SC: ETV Endowment of South Carolina, 1982.

Okuda, Ted. *Grand National, Producers Releasing Corporation, and Screen Guild/Lippert.* Jefferson, NC: McFarland, 1989.

____. *The Monogram Checklist: 1931–1952,* Jefferson, NC: McFarland, 1987.

Parmentier, ____, ed. *Film Facts.* New York: (Jan/1958–Mar/1960)

Pitts, Michael R. *Western Movies.* Jefferson, NC.: McFarland, 1986.

Quinlan, David. *The Illustrated Encyclopedia of Movie Character Actors.* New York: Harmony Books, 1985.

Shale, Richard. *Academy Awards.* New York: Ungar, 1978.

Name Index

Feature Films, 1950–1959

Also by Alan G. Fetrow:

Feature Films, 1940–1949:
A United States Filmography
(McFarland, 1994)

Sound Films, 1927–1939:
A United States Filmography
(McFarland, 1992)